These maps of the World, United States and Europe indicate locations of the regional maps found on pages 27-160. The colored outlines show the scale of each map (per the accompanying legend) and the extent of each map's coverage. Page numbers of the same color are found in the center of each outline. Large scale map insets are noted by outline, name and page number. Small scale maps are indicated by name and page number only. A map of the world appears on pages 22-23.

HAMMOND

CONCISE

WORLD

ATLAS

Mapmakers for the 21st Century

HAMMOND

CONCISE
WORLD
ATLAS

Mapmakers for the 21st Century

Contents

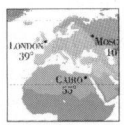

Australia, New Zealand and Pacific

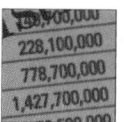

North America

South America and Polar Regions

The section on World Statistics includes the planets of the solar system, dimensions of the earth, oceans and major seas, major mountain peaks, longest rivers, largest lakes and major islands. The computer-generated Time Zones of the World is completely new and reflects the world's most recent time zone changes. A Master Index lists 60,000 places and other features appearing in this atlas, complete with page numbers and easy-to-use alpha-numeric references.

Concise World Atlas

ENTIRE CONTENTS
© COPYRIGHT 2000 BY
HAMMOND WORLD ATLAS CORPORATION
All rights reserved. No part of this book may be reproduced or utilized in any form or by any means, electronic or mechanical, including photocopying, recording or by any information storage and retrieval system, without permission in writing from the Publisher. Printed in Italy.

PHOTO CREDITS: NASA - National Aeronautics and Space Administration Earth from Space images: Greece-Peloponnisos Peninsula-p.26; Pakistan-Indus River Delta-p.66; Egypt-Sinai Peninsula-p.92; Australia-Lake Eyre-p.108; United States-Grand Canyon-p.118; Argentina/Chile-Andes Mountains-p.146.

LIBRARY OF CONGRESS
CATALOGING-IN-PUBLICATION DATA

Hammond World Atlas Corporation.
    Hammond concise world atlas.
       p. cm.
    Includes index.
    ISBN 0-8437-1386-0 (hc: alk. paper).
    ISBN 0-8437-1387-9 (sc: alk. paper).
    1. Atlases. I. Title.
    II. Title: Concise world atlas.
    G1021. H2668   2000 <G&M>

    912--DC21   00-038861
                               CIP
                            MAPS

Map Projections

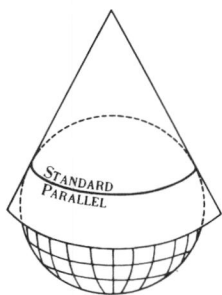

Simply stated, the map-maker's challenge is to project the earth's curved surface onto a flat plane. To achieve this elusive goal, cartographers have developed map projections — equations which govern this conversion of geographic data.

This section explores some of the most widely used projections. It also introduces a new projection, the Hammond Optimal Conformal.

GENERAL PRINCIPLES AND TERMS

The earth rotates around its axis once a day. Its end points are the North and South poles; the line circling the earth midway between the poles is the equator. The arc from the equator to either pole is divided into 90 degrees of latitude. The equator represents 0° latitude. Circles of equal latitude, called parallels, are traditionally shown at every fifth or tenth degree.

The equator is divided into 360 degrees. Lines circling the globe from pole to pole through the degree points on the equator are called meridians, or great circles. All meridians are equal in length, but by international agreement the meridian passing through the Greenwich Observatory near London has been chosen as the prime meridian or 0° longitude. The distance in degrees from the prime meridian to any point east or west is its longitude.

While meridians are all equal in length, parallels become shorter as they approach the poles. Whereas one degree of latitude represents approximately 69 miles (112 km.) anywhere on the globe, a degree of longitude varies from 69 miles (112 km.) at the equator to zero at the poles. Each degree of latitude and longitude is divided into 60 minutes. One minute of latitude equals one nautical mile (1.15 land miles or 1.85 km.).

HOW TO FLATTEN A SPHERE: THE ART OF CONTROLLING DISTORTION

There is only one way to represent a sphere with absolute precision: on a globe. All attempts to project our planet's surface onto a plane unevenly stretch or tear the sphere as it flattens, inevitably distorting shapes, distances, area (sizes appear larger or smaller than actual size), angles or direction.

Since representing a sphere on a flat plane always creates distortion, only the parallels or the meridians (or some other set of lines) can maintain the same length as on a globe of corresponding scale. All other lines must be either too long or too short. Accordingly, the scale on a flat map cannot be true everywhere; there will always be different scales in different parts of a map. On world maps or very large areas, variations in scale may be extreme. Most maps seek to preserve either true area relationships (equal area projections) or true angles and shapes (conformal projections); some attempt to achieve overall balance.

PROJECTIONS: SELECTED EXAMPLES

Mercator (Fig. 1): This projection is especially useful because all compass directions appear as straight lines, making it a valuable navigational tool. Moreover, every small region conforms to its shape on a globe — hence the name conformal. But because its meridians are evenly-spaced vertical lines which never converge (unlike the globe), the horizontal parallels must be drawn farther and farther apart at higher latitudes to maintain a correct relationship.

FIGURE 1 **Mercator Projection**

FIGURE 2 **Robinson Projection**

Only the equator is true to scale, and the size of areas in the higher latitudes is dramatically distorted.

Robinson (Fig. 2): To create the World-Physical and World-Political maps on pages 22-25, the Robinson projection was used. It combines elements of both conformal and equal area projections to show the whole earth with relatively true shapes and reasonably equal areas.

Conic (Fig. 3): This projection has been used frequently for air navigation charts and to create most of the national and regional maps in this atlas. (See text in margin at right).

HAMMOND OPTIMAL CONFORMAL

As its name implies, this new conformal projection (Fig. 4) presents the optimal view of an area by reducing shifts in scale over an entire region to the minimum degree possible. While conformal maps generally preserve all small shapes, large shapes can become very distorted because of varying scales, causing considerable inaccuracy in distance measurements. The concept underlying the Optimal Conformal is that for any region on the globe, there is an ideal projection for which scale variation can be made as small as possible. Consequently, unlike other projections, the Optimal Conformal does not use one standard formula to construct a map. Each map is a unique projection — the optimal projection for that particular area.

After a cartographer defines the subject area, a sophisticated computer program evaluates the size and shape of the region, and projects the most distortion-free conformal map possible.

Using This Atlas

SYMBOLS USED ON MAPS OF THE WORLD

FIRST ORDER (NATIONAL) BOUNDARY

- Demarcated Land Boundary
- Demarcated Water Boundary
- Disputed Boundary
- Armistice Boundary
- De Facto Boundary
- Undefined

SECOND ORDER (INTERNAL) BOUNDARY

- Land Boundary
- Water Boundary

THIRD ORDER (INTERNAL) BOUNDARY

- Land Boundary
- Water Boundary

CITIES AND TOWNS

- Stockholm — First Order (National) Capital
- Salt Lake City — Second Order (Internal) Capital
- Manchester — Third Order (Internal) Capital
- Towns
- Neighborhood
- City and Urban Area Limits

TRANSPORTATION

- International Airport
- Other Airport
- Highways/Roads
- Railroads
- Ferries
- Tunnels (Road, Railroad)

DRAINAGE FEATURES

- Shoreline, River
- Intermittent River
- Canal
- Lake, Reservoir
- Intermittent Lake
- Dry Lake
- Salt Pan
- Swamp/Marsh

OTHER PHYSICAL FEATURES

- ▲ Elevation
- ⤞ Pass
- ● Falls
- ✳ Rapids
- Desert/Sand Area
- Lava Flow
- Glacier/Ice Shelf

CULTURAL FEATURES

- Ruins
- ● Dam
- ♣ Park
- Wildlife Area
- ■ Point of Interest
- ⤳ Well
- ⊗ Air Base
- ⊘ Naval Base
- International Date Line

OTHER SYMBOLS

- Ancient Walls
- Native Reservation/Reserve
- Military/Government Reservation
- State Park/Recreation Area
- National Park/Forest/Recreation/Wildlife Area

ELEVATION LEGEND

HEIGHT
m./ft.

| 60 / 197 |
| 40 / 130 |
| 20 / 65 |
| 15 / 50 |
| 10 / 33 |
| 5 / 16 |
| 2 / 7 |
| 0 |
| 2 / 7 |
| 5 / 16 |
| 10 / 33 |
| 20 / 65 |
| 30 / 98 |
| 40 / 130 |
| 50 / 164 |
| 60 / 197 |
| m./ft. |

DEPTH
(Figures in Hundreds)

The color tints in this bar represent both elevation of land areas and depth of the oceans. The changes between colors are labeled in feet and meters, and are given in hundreds. Selective shading for the land areas highlights those regions with significant relief variations.

PRINCIPAL MAP ABBREVIATIONS

Abor. Rsv.	ABORIGINAL RESERVE	Ft.	FORT	NCA	NATIONAL	Plat.	PLATEAU
Admin.	ADMINISTRATION	G.	GULF		CONSERVATION AREA	PN	PARK NATIONAL
AFB	AIR FORCE BASE	Govt.	GOVERNMENT	NHP	NATIONAL HISTORICAL	Prom.	PROMONTORY
Amm. Dep.	AMMUNITION DEPOT	Gd.	GRAND		PARK	Prsv.	PRESERVE
Arch.	ARCHIPELAGO	Gt.	GREAT	NHS	NATIONAL HISTORIC	Pt.	POINT
Aut.	AUTONOMOUS	Har.	HARBOR		SITE	R.	RIVER
B.	BAY	Hist.	HISTORIC(AL)	NL	NATIONAL LAKESHORE	Rec.	RECREATION(AL)
Bfld.	BATTLEFIELD	Hts.	HEIGHTS	NM	NATIONAL MONUMENT	Ref.	REFUGE
Bk.	BROOK	I., Is.	ISLAND(S)	NMEM	NATIONAL MEMORIAL	Reg.	REGION
Br.	BRANCH	Ind. Res.	INDIAN RESERVATION	NMILP	NATIONAL MILITARY	Rep.	REPUBLIC
C.	CAPE	Int'l	INTERNATIONAL		PARK	Res.	RESERVOIR,
Can.	CANAL	IR	INDIAN RESERVATION	No.	NORTHERN		RESERVATION
Cap.	CAPITAL	Isth.	ISTHMUS	NP	NATIONAL PARK	Sa.	SIERRA
C.G.	COAST GUARD	Jct.	JUNCTION	NPP	NATIONAL PARK AND	Sd.	SOUND
Chan.	CHANNEL	L.	LAKE		PRESERVE	So.	SOUTHERN
Co.	COUNTY	Lag.	LAGOON	NPRSV	NATIONAL PRESERVE	SP	STATE PARK
Consv.	CONSERVATION	Mem.	MEMORIAL	NRA	NATIONAL	Spr., Sprs.	SPRING, SPRINGS
Cord.	CORDILLERA	Mil.	MILITARY		RECREATION AREA	St.	STATE
Cr.	CREEK	Mon.	MONUMENT	NRIV	NATIONAL RIVER	Sta.	STATION
Ctr.	CENTER	Mt.	MOUNT	NRSV	NATIONAL RESERVE	Stm.	STREAM
Dep.	DEPOT	Mtn.	MOUNTAIN	NS	NATIONAL SEASHORE	Str.	STRAIT
Depr.	DEPRESSION	Mts.	MOUNTAINS	NWR	NATIONAL WILDLIFE	Terr.	TERRITORY
Des.	DESERT	Nat.	NATURAL		RESERVE	Tun.	TUNNEL
Dist.	DISTRICT	Nat'l	NATIONAL	Obl.	OBLAST	Twp.	TOWNSHIP
DMZ	DEMILITARIZED ZONE	Nav.	NAVAL	Occ.	OCCUPIED	UNDOF	UNITED NATIONS
Est.	ESTUARY	NB	NATIONAL	Okr.	OKRUG		DISENGAGEMENT
Fed.	FEDERAL		BATTLEFIELD	Passg.	PASSAGE		OBSERVER FORCE
Fk.	FORK	NBP	NATIONAL	Pen.	PENINSULA	Val.	VALLEY
For.	FOREST		BATTLEFIELD PARK	Pk.	PEAK	Vill.	VILLAGE

The *Concise World Atlas* has been designed to be easy and enjoyable to use. Only a short time is neeeded to familiarize yourself with its organization.

MAP SYMBOLS, COLORS AND LABELS

The cartographer selects the natural and cultural features most valuable to the map user. Map legibility requires that small features be represented by symbols that are actually larger than true scale size. Due to the larger symbol sizes and the resulting loss of map space, it is necessary to omit less important features in congested areas.

Most map features are represented by the use of conventional symbols, lines, and patterns printed in appropriate colors. The chart to the left shows the standard symbols used in this atlas. Water features are shown in blue. Lines of various weights, styles, and colors represent the many different linear features in this atlas. Individual point features are represented by a pictorial and/or generic symbol.

Notes may also be added to explain features that cannot be depicted clearly.

MAP SCALES

A map's scale is the relationship of any length on the map to an identical length on the earth's surface. A scale of 1:3M means that one inch on the map represents 3,000,000 inches (47 miles, 76 km.) on the earth's surface. Thus, a 1:1M scale is larger than 1:3M, just as 1/1 is larger than 1/3.

The most densely populated areas are shown at a scale of 1:1M, while selected metropolitan areas are covered at either 1:500,000 or 1:1M. Other populous areas are presented at 1:3M and 1:6M, allowing you to accurately compare areas and distances of similar regions. Remaining regions, including the continent maps, are presented at 1:9M and smaller scales.

BOUNDARY POLICIES

This atlas observes the boundary policies of the U.S. Department of State. Disputed, armistice and de facto boundaries are handled with a special symbol treatment. The portrayal of independent nations follows their recognition by the United Nations and/or United States government.

Map Type Styles

Cartographers use a variety of type styles to differentiate between map features. The following styles are used in this Atlas.

Major Political Areas
LUXEMBOURG

Internal Political Divisions
SAXONY-ANHALT

Regions
Polabská Nižina

Cities and Towns
Norfolk Sumter Smyrna

Neighborhoods
BIGGIN HILL

Points of Interest
MISSION SAN BUENAVENTURA

Water Features
L. Elsinore

Capes, Points, Peaks, Passes
Pt. La Jolla   Pacifico Mtn.

Islands, Peninsulas
Cape Breton I.

Mountains, Uplands
Serra do Norte

Deserts, Plains, Valleys
San Fernando Valley

A Word About Names

Our source for all foreign names is the decision lists of the U.S. Board of Geographic Names and/or official foreign government maps and official gazetteers. This atlas also uses accepted conventional names for certain major foreign place names. The U.S. Board of Geographic Names defines a conventional name as "a name approved for use in addition to, or in lieu of, an approved local official name or names."

In order to make the maps more readily understandable to English-speaking readers, many foreign physical features are translated into more recognizable English forms.

The rendering of city, town and village names for the United States follows the.forms and spelling of the U.S. Postal Service.

Population

WORLD'S LARGEST URBAN AREAS

MILLIONS OF INHABITANTS

TOKYO, Japan 26.5

NEW YORK, U.S. 18.0

SÃO PAULO, Brazil 16.9

OSAKA, Japan 16.9

SEOUL, Korea, 15.8

MEXICO, Mexico 15.5

SHANGHAI, China 14.7

MUMBAI, India 14.5

LOS ANGELES, U.S. 14.5

MOSCOW, Russia 13.1

BEIJING, China 12.0

CALCUTTA, India 11.4

LONDON, U.K. 11.1

RIO DE JANEIRO, Brazil 11.0

JAKARTA, Indonesia 11.0

URBAN & RURAL POPULATION COMPONENTS

SELECTED COUNTRIES

☐ URBAN   ☐ RURAL

Uruguay 87% / 13%

Australia 85% / 15%

Japan 77% / 23%

United States 74% / 26%

Russia 73% / 27%

Hungary 62% / 38%

Iran 54% / 46%

Egypt 44% / 56%

Philippines 37% / 63%

Portugal 30% / 70%

China 26% / 74%

Maldives 20% / 80%

Bangladesh 15% / 85%

Nepal 6% / 94%

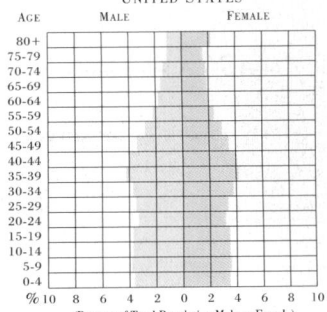

UNITED STATES

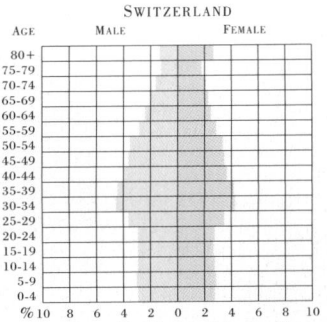

SWITZERLAND

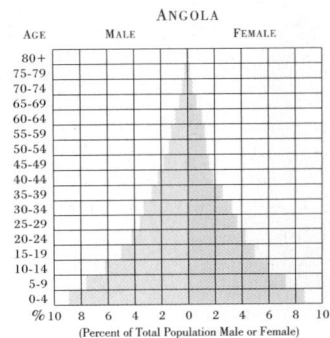

ANGOLA

Source: U.S. Bureau of the Census, International Database

POPULATION DENSITY PER SQUARE MILE (SQ. KM.)

1,000 - 5,000 (390 - 2,000)	500 - 1,000 (195 - 390)	100 - 500 (39 - 195)	30 - 100 (12 - 39)	UNDER 30 (UNDER 12)

Source: U.S. Bureau of the Census, International Database

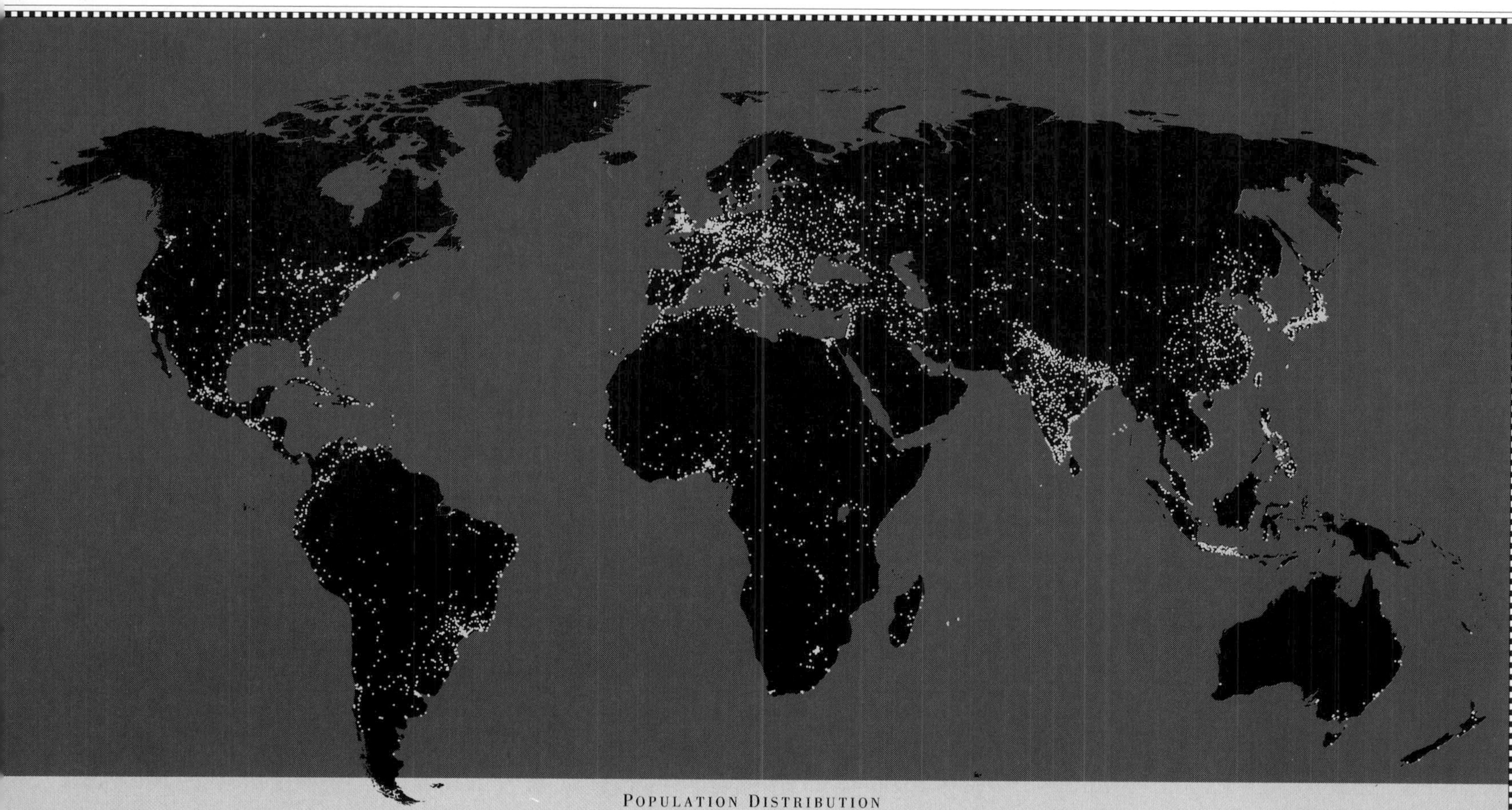

POPULATION DISTRIBUTION

This map provides a dramatic perspective by illuminating populated areas with one point of light for each city over 50,000 residents. Over 675 million people live in cities with populations in excess of 500,000. According to the latest census data, there are 10,000 people per square mile (3,860 per sq km) in London. In New York, there are 11,000 (4,250). Hong Kong has over 16,000 people per square mile (6,200 per sq km), and the Tokyo-Yokohama agglomeration includes over 25,000 (9,650). During the last decade, the movement to the cities has accelerated dramatically, particulary in developing nations. In Lagos, Nigeria, where there are over 24,000 people per square mile (9,290 per sq km), most live in shantytowns. In São Paulo, Brazil, 2,000 buses arrive each day, bringing field hands, farm workers and their families in search of a better life. Tokyo, Mexico and Mumbai are the world's largest urban agglomerations. According to the United Nations, 15 of the 20 largest urban agglomerations are located in less-industrialized nations.

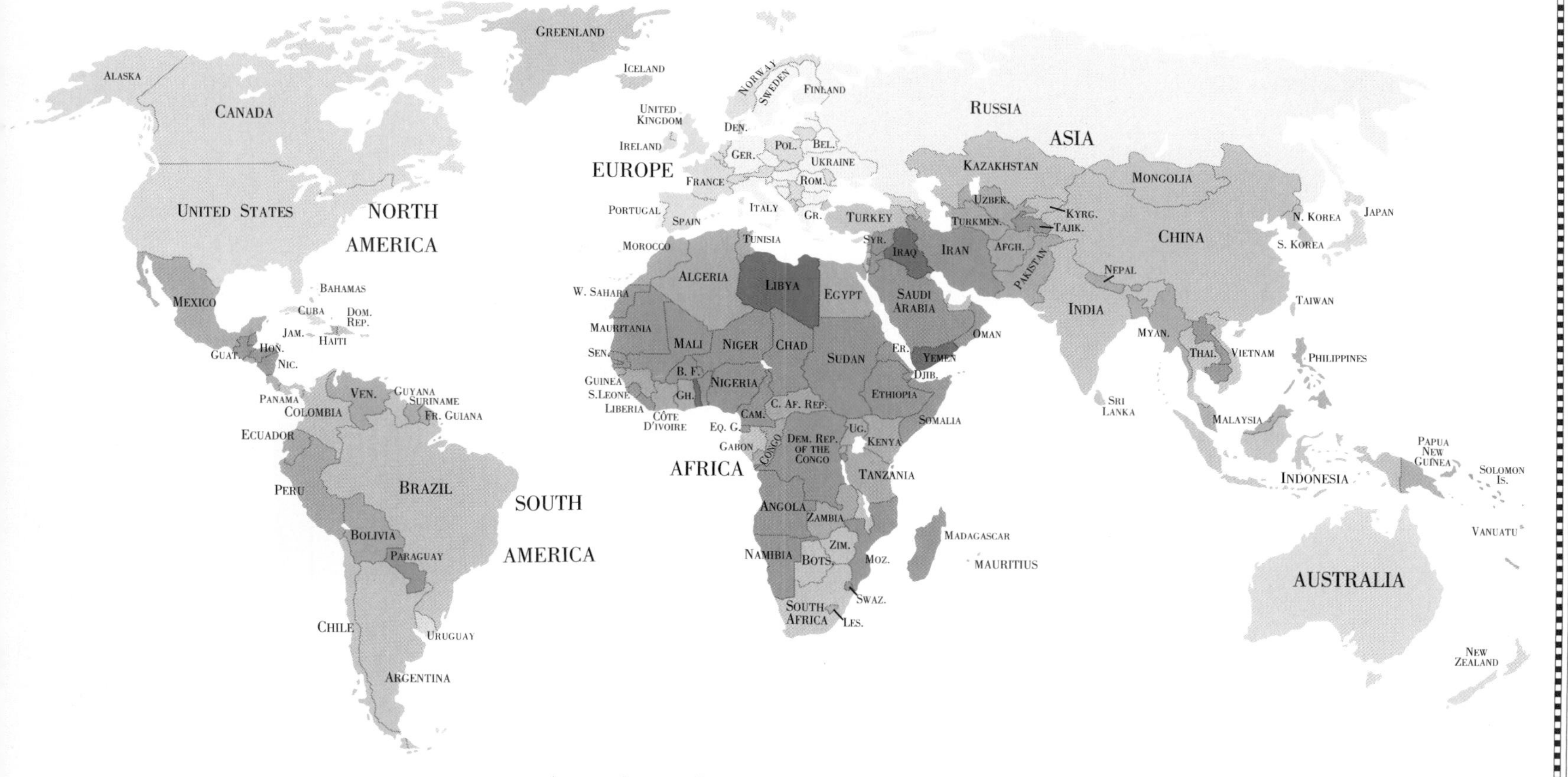

ANNUAL RATE OF POPULATION (NATURAL) INCREASE

- 3.5 PERCENT OR MORE
- 2.6 TO 3.4 PERCENT
- 1.8 TO 2.5 PERCENT
- .09 TO 1.7 PERCENT
- .01 TO .08 PERCENT
- 0.0 OR DECREASE

Source: U.S. Bureau of the Census, International Database

Standards of Living

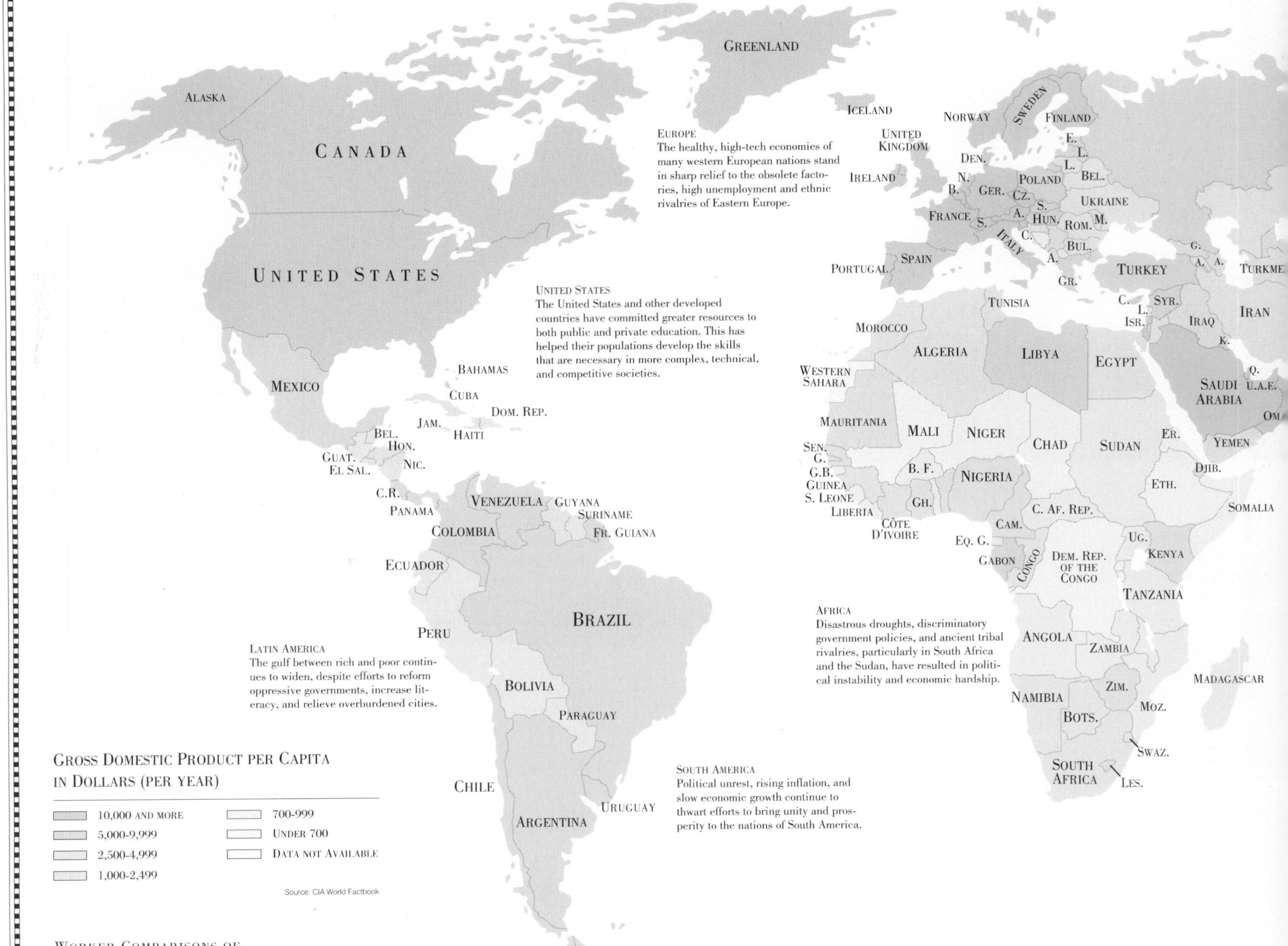

GREENLAND
ALASKA
CANADA
ICELAND
NORWAY
SWEDEN
FINLAND
UNITED KINGDOM
DEN.
E.
L.
L.
IRELAND
N.
B.
GER.
POLAND
BEL.
CZ.
S.
UKRAINE
FRANCE
S.
A.
HUN.
ROM.
M.
C.
ITALY
BUL.
PORTUGAL
SPAIN
A.
GR.
G.
A.
A.
TURKEY
TURKME
UNITED STATES
TUNISIA
C.
L.
ISR.
SYR.
IRAQ
IRAN
K.
MOROCCO
ALGERIA
LIBYA
EGYPT
Q.
U.A.E.
SAUDI ARABIA
OM
BAHAMAS
MEXICO
CUBA
DOM. REP.
JAM.
HAITI
BEL.
HON.
GUAT.
EL SAL.
NIC.
C.R.
PANAMA
WESTERN SAHARA
MAURITANIA
MALI
NIGER
CHAD
SUDAN
ER.
YEMEN
SEN.
G.
G.B.
GUINEA
S. LEONE
LIBERIA
B. F.
GH.
NIGERIA
DJIB.
ETH.
SOMALIA
CÔTE D'IVOIRE
CAM.
C. AF. REP.
EQ. G.
GABON
CONGO
DEM. REP. OF THE CONGO
UG.
KENYA
TANZANIA
VENEZUELA
GUYANA
SURINAME
FR. GUIANA
COLOMBIA
ECUADOR
PERU
BRAZIL
BOLIVIA
PARAGUAY
CHILE
ARGENTINA
URUGUAY
ANGOLA
ZAMBIA
ZIM.
MOZ.
MADAGASCAR
NAMIBIA
BOTS.
SWAZ.
SOUTH AFRICA
LES.
EUROPE
The healthy, high-tech economies of many western European nations stand in sharp relief to the obsolete factories, high unemployment and ethnic rivalries of Eastern Europe.
UNITED STATES
The United States and other developed countries have committed greater resources to both public and private education. This has helped their populations develop the skills that are necessary in more complex, technical, and competitive societies.
LATIN AMERICA
The gulf between rich and poor continues to widen, despite efforts to reform oppressive governments, increase literacy, and relieve overburdened cities.
AFRICA
Disastrous droughts, discriminatory government policies, and ancient tribal rivalries, particularly in South Africa and the Sudan, have resulted in political instability and economic hardship.
SOUTH AMERICA
Political unrest, rising inflation, and slow economic growth continue to thwart efforts to bring unity and prosperity to the nations of South America.

Gross Domestic Product per Capita in Dollars (per year)

- 10,000 and more
- 5,000-9,999
- 2,500-4,999
- 1,000-2,499
- 700-999
- Under 700
- Data not available

Source: CIA World Factbook

Worker Comparisons of Selected Countries

Country	Avg. Actual Hours Worked per Week	Years of Formal Schooling	Percent Women of Labor Force
Australia	39	13.6	38
Austria	34	14.6	39
Belgium	33	14.4	33
Canada	38	17.6	40
France	39	14.6	41
Germany	38	14.6	39
Greece	41	13.2	27
Hungary	37	12.0	44
Ireland	41	13.1	29
Israel	42	NA	34
Japan	38	13.5	40
Luxembourg	41	NA	32
Netherlands	40	15.5	31
New Zealand	42	15.4	36
Norway	37	15.5	41
Romania	38	10.8	45
South Africa	46	12.0	36
South Korea	49	13.7	34
Spain	37	14.7	25
United Kingdom	43	14.9	39
United States	42	16.0	41

NA=DATA NOT AVAILABLE

SOURCE: UNITED NATIONS

Gross Domestic Product Growth Rates

Best Growth Rates		Worst Growth Rates	
Lesotho	13.5	Azerbaijan	-17
China	10.3	Tajikistan	-12.4
Equatorial Guinea	10	Georgia	-11
Eritrea	10	Belarus	-10
Malawi	9.9	Turkmenistan	-10
Malaysia	9.5	Kazakhstan	-8.9
Vietnam	9.5	Congo, Dem. Rep. of the	-7.4
South Korea	9	Mexico	-6.9
Singapore	8.9	Morocco	-6.5
Thailand	8.6	Kyrgyzstan	-6
Chile	8.5	North Korea	-5
Laos	8	Argentina	-4.4
Solomon Islands	8	Russia	-4
Indonesia	7.5	Sierra Leone	-4
Israel	7.1	Ukraine	-4
Uganda	7.1	Djibouti	-3
Ireland	7	Moldova	-3
Myanmar	6.8	Papua New Guinea	-3
Peru	6.8	Rwanda	-2.7
Turkey	6.8	Mozambique	-2.5

Source: CIA World Factbook

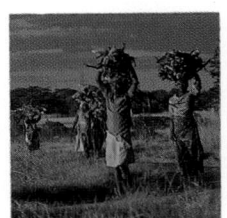

In the United States, the average person earns about $27,500 - the highest per capita Gross Domestic Product in the world. In Rwanda, the same person would earn about $400 in a year.

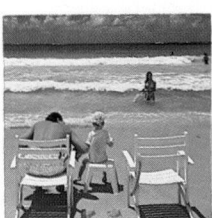

American workers typically get only 2 or 3 weeks of annual paid vacation, while western Europeans enjoy 4 to 6 weeks off.

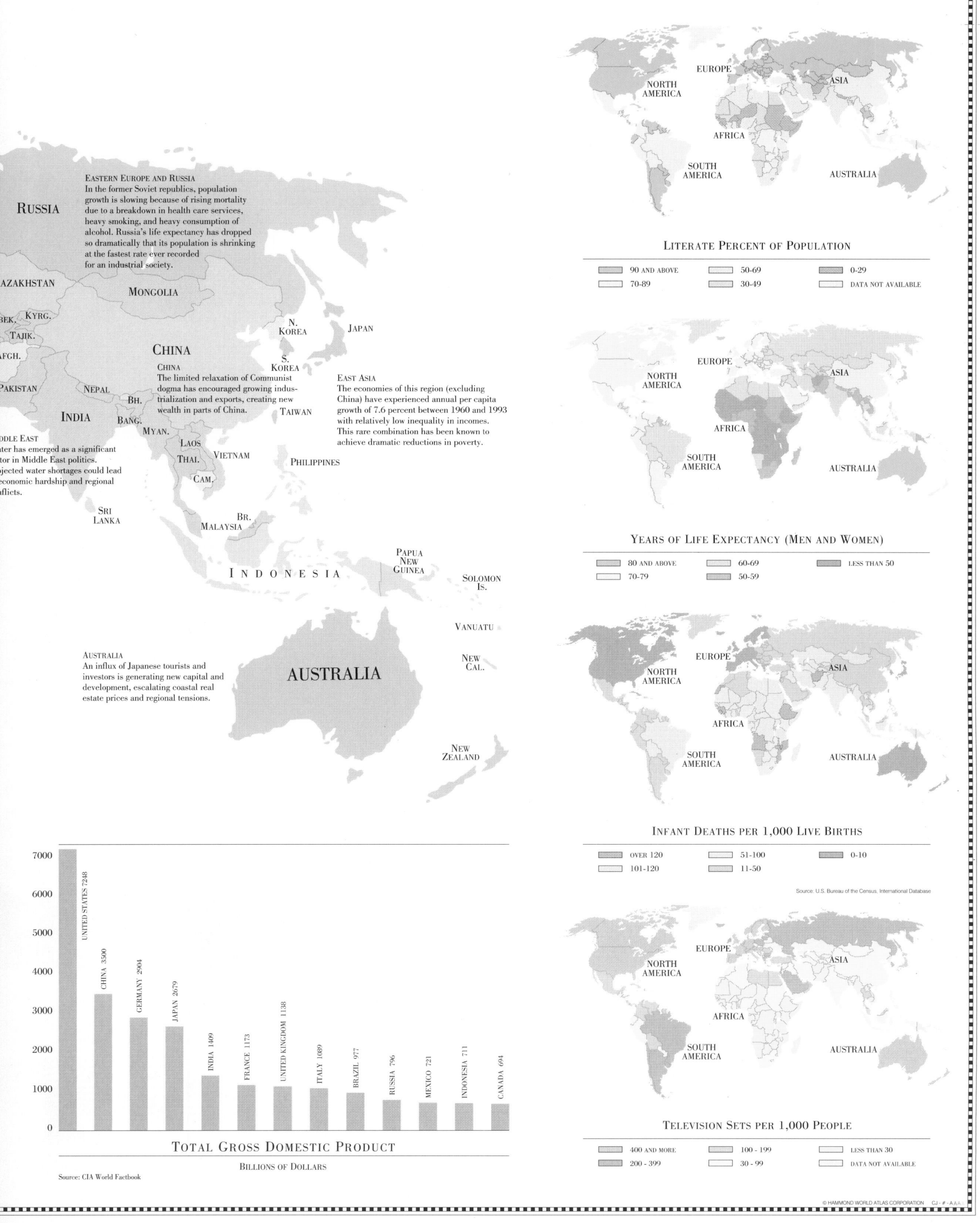

EASTERN EUROPE AND RUSSIA
In the former Soviet republics, population growth is slowing because of rising mortality due to a breakdown in health care services, heavy smoking, and heavy consumption of alcohol. Russia's life expectancy has dropped so dramatically that its population is shrinking at the fastest rate ever recorded for an industrial society.

RUSSIA

KAZAKHSTAN

MONGOLIA

ZBEK. KYRG.

TAJIK.

AFGH.

PAKISTAN

NEPAL

INDIA

BH.

BANG.

MYAN.

CHINA

CHINA
The limited relaxation of Communist dogma has encouraged growing industrialization and exports, creating new wealth in parts of China.

N. KOREA

JAPAN

S. KOREA

TAIWAN

EAST ASIA
The economies of this region (excluding China) have experienced annual per capita growth of 7.6 percent between 1960 and 1993 with relatively low inequality in incomes. This rare combination has been known to achieve dramatic reductions in poverty.

MIDDLE EAST
Water has emerged as a significant factor in Middle East politics. Projected water shortages could lead to economic hardship and regional conflicts.

LAOS

THAI.

VIETNAM

CAM.

PHILIPPINES

SRI LANKA

BR. MALAYSIA

I N D O N E S I A

PAPUA NEW GUINEA

SOLOMON IS.

VANUATU

NEW CAL.

AUSTRALIA
An influx of Japanese tourists and investors is generating new capital and development, escalating coastal real estate prices and regional tensions.

AUSTRALIA

NEW ZEALAND

LITERATE PERCENT OF POPULATION

90 AND ABOVE	50-69	0-29
70-89	30-49	DATA NOT AVAILABLE

YEARS OF LIFE EXPECTANCY (MEN AND WOMEN)

80 AND ABOVE	60-69	LESS THAN 50
70-79	50-59	

INFANT DEATHS PER 1,000 LIVE BIRTHS

OVER 120	51-100	0-10
101-120	11-50	

Source: U.S. Bureau of the Census, International Database

TELEVISION SETS PER 1,000 PEOPLE

400 AND MORE	100 - 199	LESS THAN 30
200 - 399	30 - 99	DATA NOT AVAILABLE

TOTAL GROSS DOMESTIC PRODUCT
BILLIONS OF DOLLARS

UNITED STATES 7248
CHINA 3500
GERMANY 2904
JAPAN 2679
INDIA 1409
FRANCE 1173
UNITED KINGDOM 1138
ITALY 1089
BRAZIL 977
RUSSIA 796
MEXICO 721
INDONESIA 711
CANADA 694

Source: CIA World Factbook

Climate

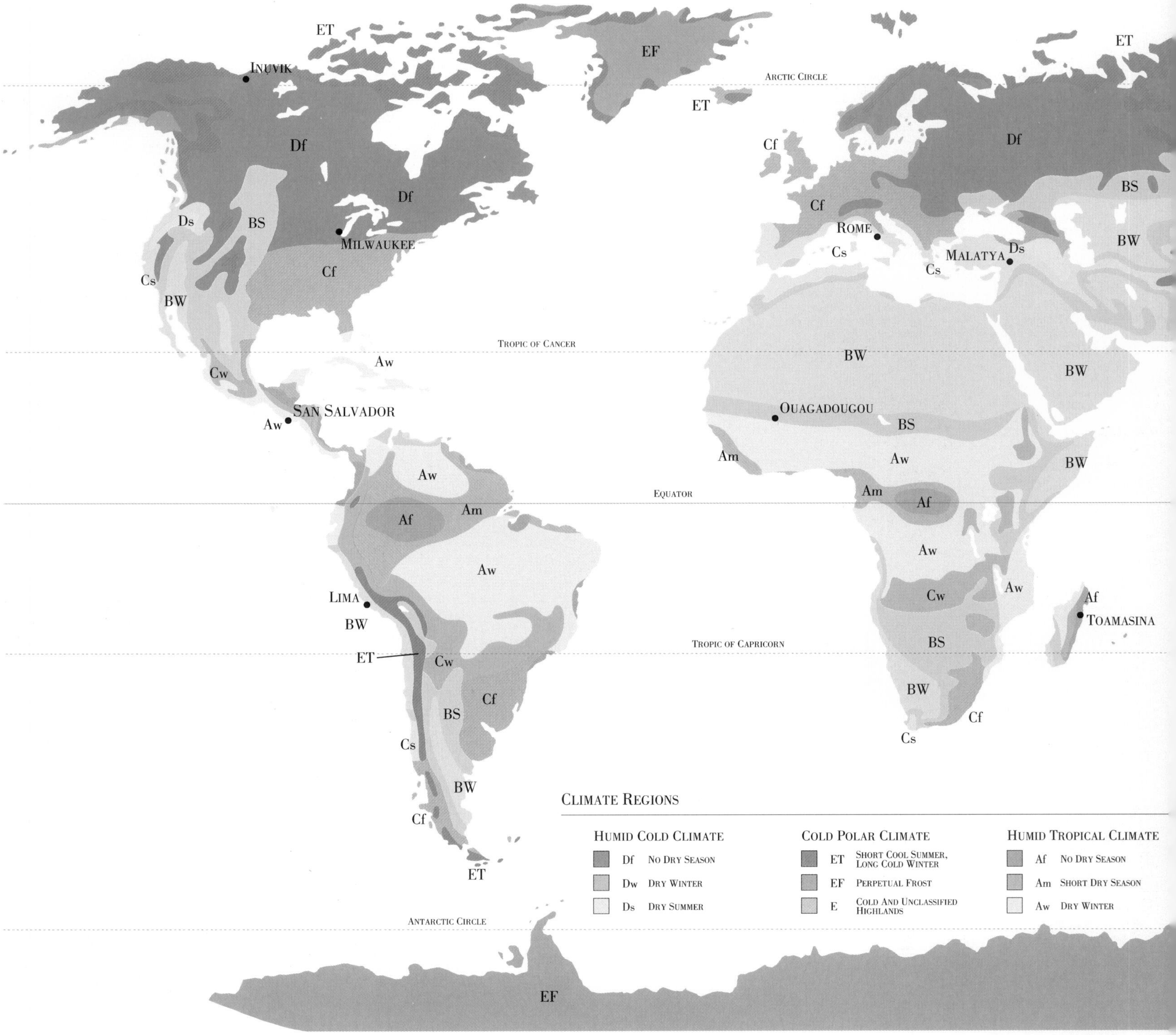

ET

EF

Arctic Circle

ET

INUVIK

Df

Cf

Df

Df

Ds

BS

Cf

Df

Cf

BS

Ds

Cf

MILWAUKEE

ROME

MALATYA

BW

Cs

Cf

Cs

Cs

Cw

BW

Tropic of Cancer

BW

BW

Aw

San Salvador

Aw

Ouagadougou

BS

BW

Aw

Am

Aw

Am

Aw

Equator

Af

Am

Af

Af

Lima

Aw

Aw

Cw

Aw

Toamasina

BW

BS

ET

Cw

Tropic of Capricorn

BW

BS

Cs

Cf

Cf

Cs

Cs

BW

Cf

ET

ANTARCTIC CIRCLE

EF

Climate Regions

Humid Cold Climate
- Df — No Dry Season
- Dw — Dry Winter
- Ds — Dry Summer

Cold Polar Climate
- ET — Short Cool Summer, Long Cold Winter
- EF — Perpetual Frost
- E — Cold And Unclassified Highlands

Humid Tropical Climate
- Af — No Dry Season
- Am — Short Dry Season
- Aw — Dry Winter

Selected Climate Stations

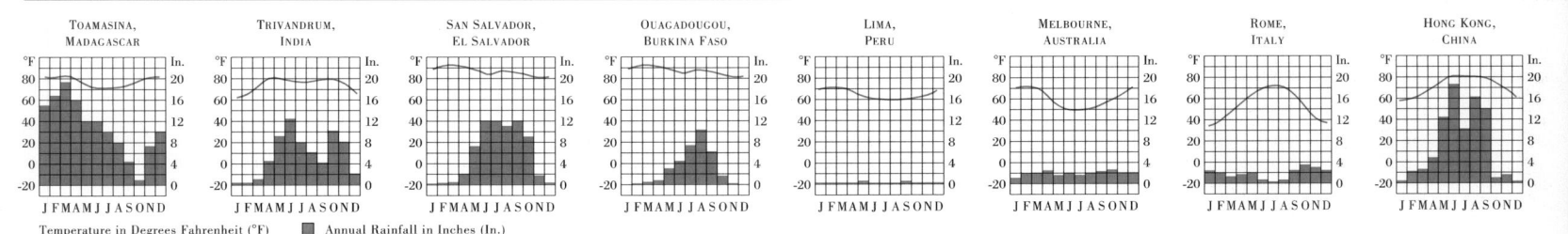

Temperature in Degrees Fahrenheit (°F) ▪ Annual Rainfall in Inches (In.)

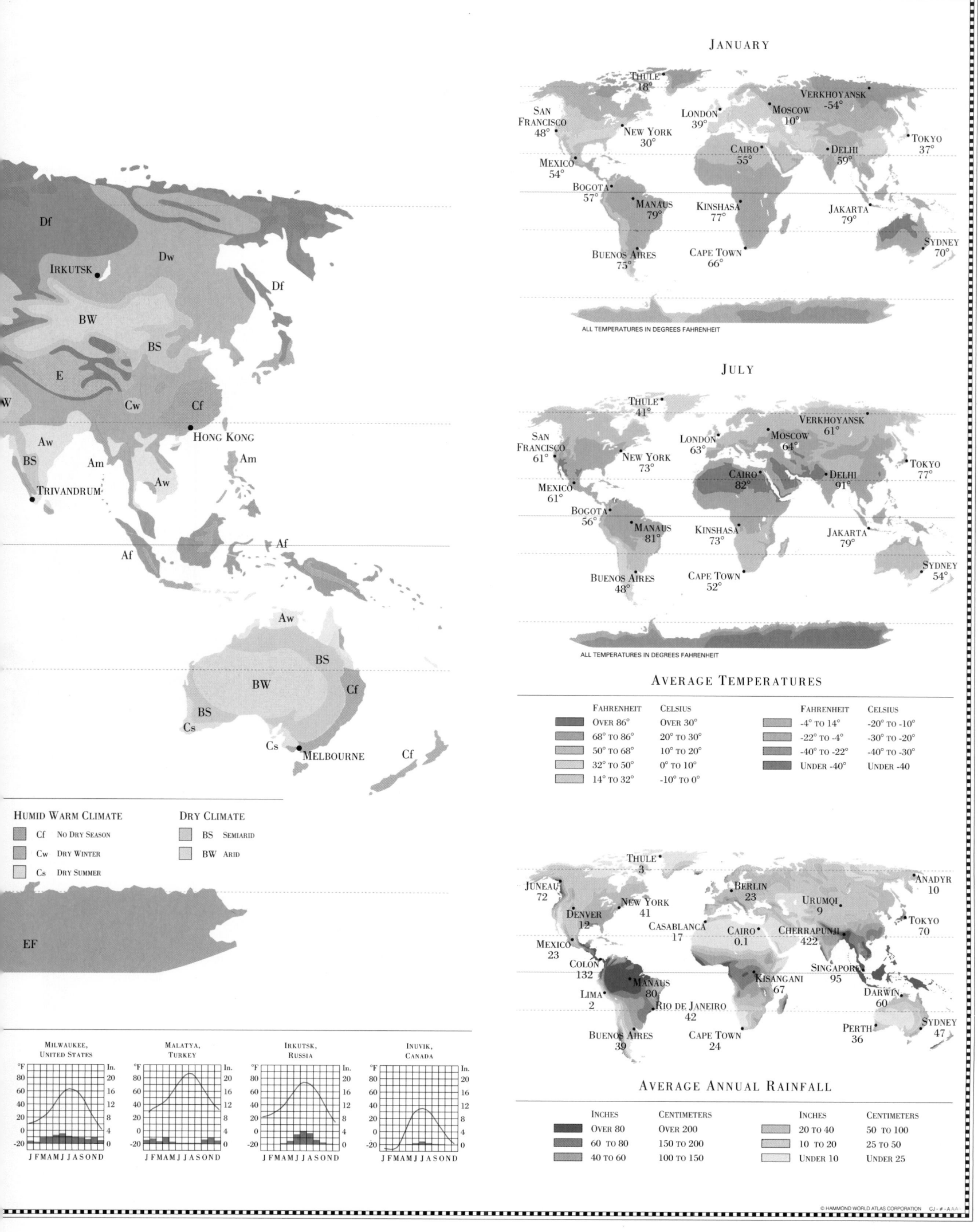

JANUARY

THULE 18°
VERKHOYANSK -54°
SAN FRANCISCO 48°
LONDON 39°
MOSCOW 10°
NEW YORK 30°
TOKYO 37°
CAIRO 55°
DELHI 59°
MEXICO 54°
BOGOTA 57°
MANAUS 79°
KINSHASA 77°
JAKARTA 79°
BUENOS AIRES 75°
CAPE TOWN 66°
SYDNEY 70°

ALL TEMPERATURES IN DEGREES FAHRENHEIT

JULY

THULE 41°
VERKHOYANSK 61°
SAN FRANCISCO 61°
LONDON 63°
MOSCOW 64°
NEW YORK 73°
TOKYO 77°
CAIRO 82°
DELHI 91°
MEXICO 61°
BOGOTA 56°
MANAUS 81°
KINSHASA 73°
JAKARTA 79°
BUENOS AIRES 48°
CAPE TOWN 52°
SYDNEY 54°

ALL TEMPERATURES IN DEGREES FAHRENHEIT

AVERAGE TEMPERATURES

	FAHRENHEIT	CELSIUS		FAHRENHEIT	CELSIUS
	OVER 86°	OVER 30°		-4° TO 14°	-20° TO -10°
	68° TO 86°	20° TO 30°		-22° TO -4°	-30° TO -20°
	50° TO 68°	10° TO 20°		-40° TO -22°	-40° TO -30°
	32° TO 50°	0° TO 10°		UNDER -40°	UNDER -40
	14° TO 32°	-10° TO 0°			

Climate map (left)

Df

IRKUTSK

Dw

Df

BW

BS

E

Cw

Cf

HONG KONG

Aw

BS

Am

Am

TRIVANDRUM

Aw

Af

Af

Aw

BS

BW

Cf

BS

Cs

Cs

MELBOURNE

Cf

EF

HUMID WARM CLIMATE
- Cf NO DRY SEASON
- Cw DRY WINTER
- Cs DRY SUMMER

DRY CLIMATE
- BS SEMIARID
- BW ARID

AVERAGE ANNUAL RAINFALL

THULE 3
ANADYR 10
JUNEAU 72
BERLIN 23
URUMQI 9
NEW YORK 41
TOKYO 70
DENVER 12
CASABLANCA 17
CAIRO 0.1
CHERRAPUNJI 422
MEXICO 23
COLON 132
KISANGANI 67
SINGAPORE 95
LIMA 2
MANAUS 80
DARWIN 60
RIO DE JANEIRO 42
PERTH 36
BUENOS AIRES 39
CAPE TOWN 24
SYDNEY 47

	INCHES	CENTIMETERS		INCHES	CENTIMETERS
	OVER 80	OVER 200		20 TO 40	50 TO 100
	60 TO 80	150 TO 200		10 TO 20	25 TO 50
	40 TO 60	100 TO 150		UNDER 10	UNDER 25

Climate graphs (bottom left)

MILWAUKEE, UNITED STATES
MALATYA, TURKEY
IRKUTSK, RUSSIA
INUVIK, CANADA

J F M A M J J A S O N D

Environmental Concerns

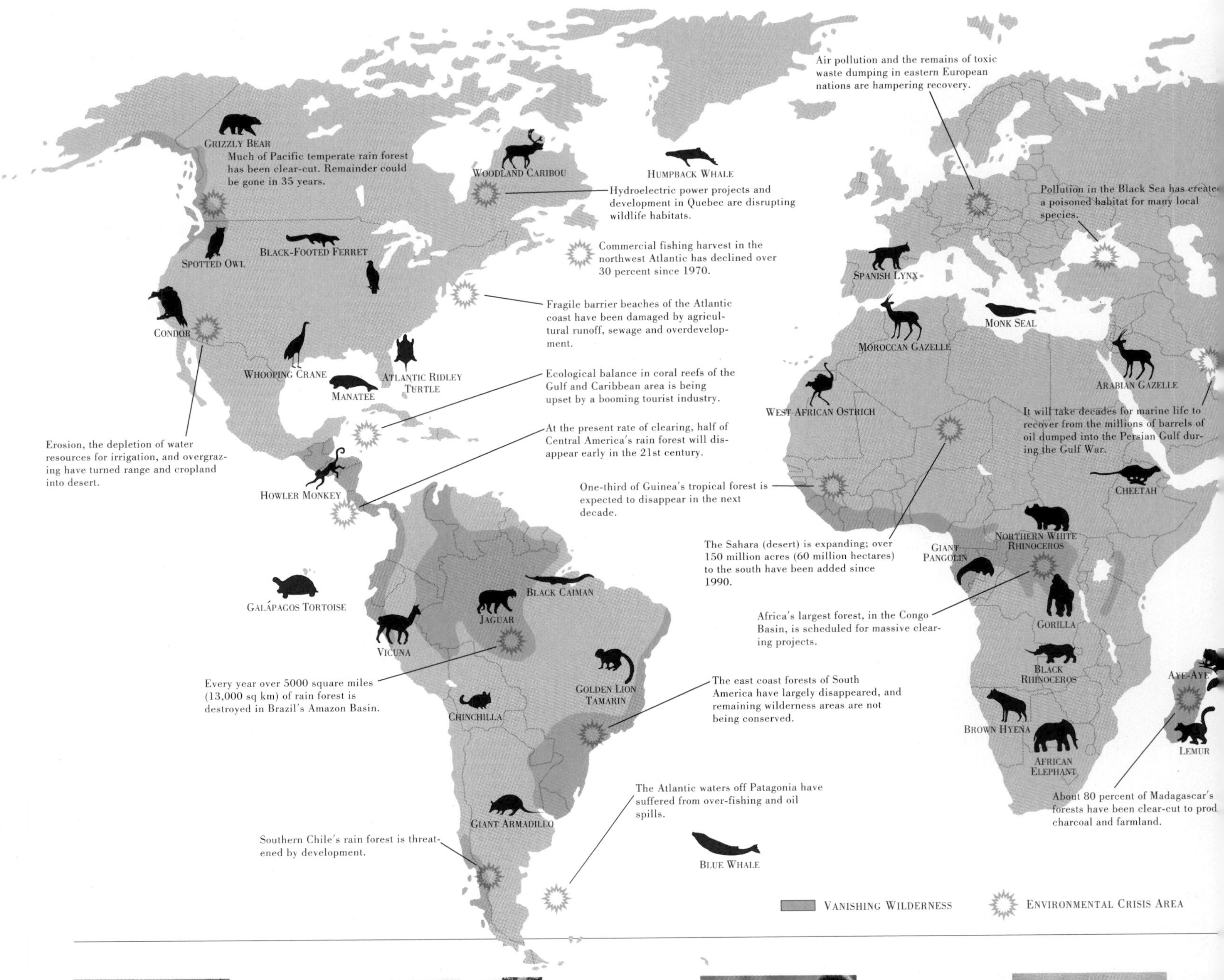

Air pollution and the remains of toxic waste dumping in eastern European nations are hampering recovery.

Pollution in the Black Sea has created a poisoned habitat for many local species.

GRIZZLY BEAR
Much of Pacific temperate rain forest has been clear-cut. Remainder could be gone in 35 years.

WOODLAND CARIBOU

HUMPBACK WHALE
Hydroelectric power projects and development in Quebec are disrupting wildlife habitats.

Commercial fishing harvest in the northwest Atlantic has declined over 30 percent since 1970.

SPANISH LYNX

MONK SEAL

SPOTTED OWL

BLACK-FOOTED FERRET

Fragile barrier beaches of the Atlantic coast have been damaged by agricultural runoff, sewage and overdevelopment.

MOROCCAN GAZELLE

ARABIAN GAZELLE

CONDOR

Ecological balance in coral reefs of the Gulf and Caribbean area is being upset by a booming tourist industry.

WHOOPING CRANE

MANATEE

ATLANTIC RIDLEY TURTLE

At the present rate of clearing, half of Central America's rain forest will disappear early in the 21st century.

WEST AFRICAN OSTRICH

It will take decades for marine life to recover from the millions of barrels of oil dumped into the Persian Gulf during the Gulf War.

Erosion, the depletion of water resources for irrigation, and overgrazing have turned range and cropland into desert.

One-third of Guinea's tropical forest is expected to disappear in the next decade.

HOWLER MONKEY

CHEETAH

The Sahara (desert) is expanding; over 150 million acres (60 million hectares) to the south have been added since 1990.

GIANT PANGOLIN

NORTHERN WHITE RHINOCEROS

GALÁPAGOS TORTOISE

BLACK CAIMAN

Africa's largest forest, in the Congo Basin, is scheduled for massive clearing projects.

GORILLA

JAGUAR

VICUNA

Every year over 5000 square miles (13,000 sq km) of rain forest is destroyed in Brazil's Amazon Basin.

GOLDEN LION TAMARIN

The east coast forests of South America have largely disappeared, and remaining wilderness areas are not being conserved.

BLACK RHINOCEROS

AYE-AYE

CHINCHILLA

BROWN HYENA

LEMUR

AFRICAN ELEPHANT

The Atlantic waters off Patagonia have suffered from over-fishing and oil spills.

About 80 percent of Madagascar's forests have been clear-cut to produce charcoal and farmland.

GIANT ARMADILLO

Southern Chile's rain forest is threatened by development.

BLUE WHALE

VANISHING WILDERNESS   ENVIRONMENTAL CRISIS AREA

Acid Rain

Acid rain of nitric and sulfuric acids has killed all life in thousands of lakes, and over 15 million acres (6 million hectares) of virgin forest in Europe and North America are dead or dying.

Deforestation

Each year, 50 million acres (20 million hectares) of tropical rainforests are being felled by loggers. Trees remove carbon dioxide from the atmosphere and are vital to the prevention of soil erosion.

Extinction

Biologists estimate that over 50,000 plant and animal species inhabiting the world's rain forests are disappearing each year due to pollution, unchecked hunting, and the destruction of natural habitats.

Air Pollution

Billions of tons of industrial emissions and toxic pollutants are released into the air each year, depleting our ozone layer, killing our forests and lakes with acid rain, and threatening our health.

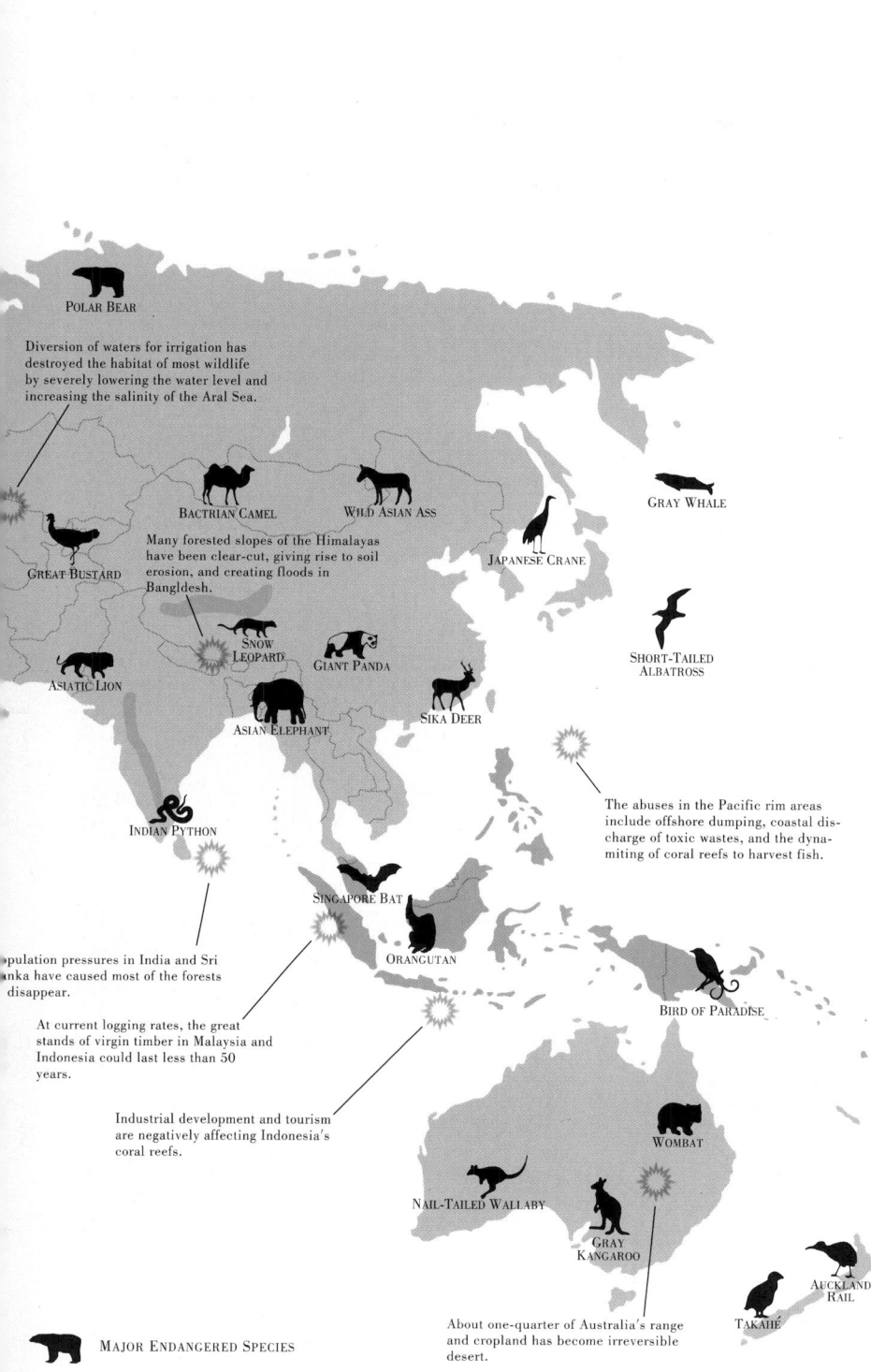

POLAR BEAR

Diversion of waters for irrigation has destroyed the habitat of most wildlife by severely lowering the water level and increasing the salinity of the Aral Sea.

GRAY WHALE

BACTRIAN CAMEL WILD ASIAN ASS

Many forested slopes of the Himalayas have been clear-cut, giving rise to soil erosion, and creating floods in Bangldesh.

JAPANESE CRANE

GREAT BUSTARD

SNOW LEOPARD GIANT PANDA

SHORT-TAILED ALBATROSS

ASIATIC LION

ASIAN ELEPHANT SIKA DEER

INDIAN PYTHON

The abuses in the Pacific rim areas include offshore dumping, coastal discharge of toxic wastes, and the dynamiting of coral reefs to harvest fish.

SINGAPORE BAT

ORANGUTAN

BIRD OF PARADISE

pulation pressures in India and Sri anka have caused most of the forests disappear.

At current logging rates, the great stands of virgin timber in Malaysia and Indonesia could last less than 50 years.

Industrial development and tourism are negatively affecting Indonesia's coral reefs.

WOMBAT

NAIL-TAILED WALLABY

GRAY KANGAROO

AUCKLAND RAIL

TAKAHE

About one-quarter of Australia's range and cropland has become irreversible desert.

MAJOR ENDANGERED SPECIES

Water Pollution

Only 3 percent of the earth's water is fresh. Pollution from cities, farms, and factories has made much of it unfit to drink. In the developing world, most sewage flows untreated into lakes and rivers.

Ozone Depletion

The layer of ozone in the stratosphere shields earth from harmful ultraviolet radiation. But man-made gases are deystroying this vital barrier, increasing the risk of skin cancer and eye disease.

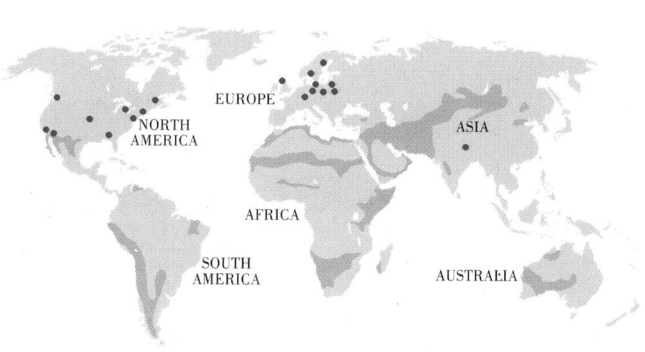

EUROPE

NORTH AMERICA

ASIA

AFRICA

SOUTH AMERICA

AUSTRALIA

DESERTIFICATION AND ACID RAIN DAMAGE

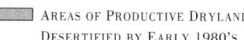

AREAS OF PRODUCTIVE DRYLANDS DESERTIFIED BY EARLY 1980'S

AREAS OF DAMAGE FROM ACID RAIN AND OTHER AIRBORNE POLLUTANTS

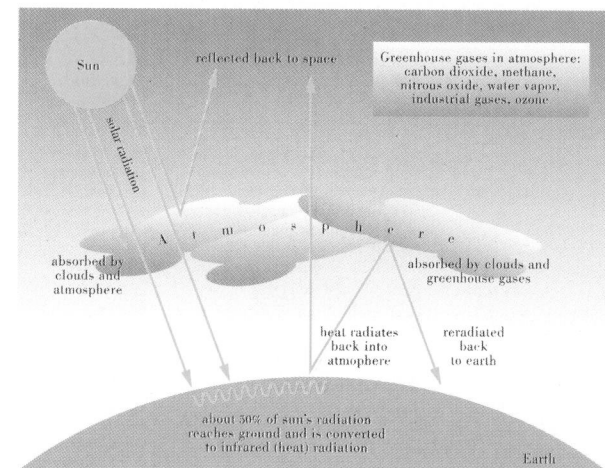

Sun

reflected back to space

Greenhouse gases in atmosphere: carbon dioxide, methane, nitrous oxide, water vapor, industrial gases, ozone

solar radiation

Atmosphere

absorbed by clouds and atmosphere

absorbed by clouds and greenhouse gases

heat radiates back into atmosphere

reradiated back to earth

about 50% of sun's radiation reaches ground and is converted to infrared (heat) radiation

Earth

GREENHOUSE EFFECT

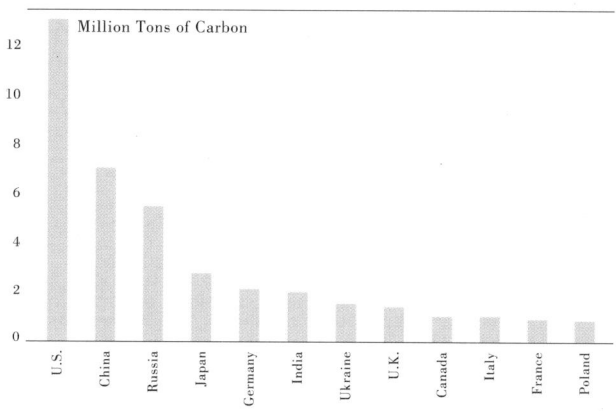

Million Tons of Carbon

12

10

8

6

4

2

0

U.S. | China | Russia | Japan | Germany | India | Ukraine | U.K. | Canada | Italy | France | Poland

GREENHOUSE EMISSIONS

CARBON DIOXIDE EQUIVALENTS

Source: Handbook of International Economic Statistics

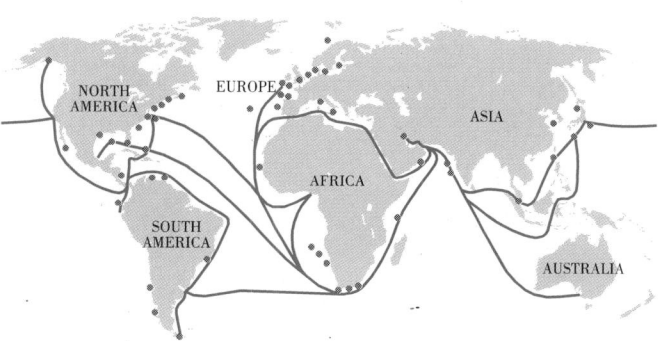

NORTH AMERICA

EUROPE

ASIA

AFRICA

SOUTH AMERICA

AUSTRALIA

MAIN TANKER ROUTES AND MAJOR OIL SPILLS

ROUTES OF VERY LARGE CRUDE OIL CARRIERS MAJOR OIL SPILLS

World Flags and Reference Guide

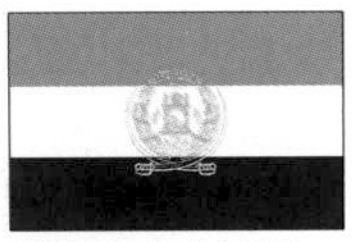

Afghanistan* 89/H2
Capital: Kabul
Area: 250,000 sq. mi.
647,500 sq. km.
Pop.: 26,668,251; growth rate: 2.497%
Govt.: transitional government
Independence: August 19, 1919
U.N. Admission: November 19, 1946
GDP: $18.1 billion; per capita: $800
Currency: afghani

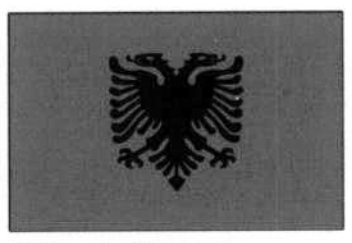

Albania* 75/F2
Capital: Tiranë
Area: 11,100 sq. mi.
28,749 sq. km.
Pop.: 3,401,126; growth rate: 1.115%
Govt.: emerging democracy
Independence: November 28, 1912
U.N. Admission: December 14, 1955
GDP: $4.4 billion; per capita: $1,290
Currency: lek

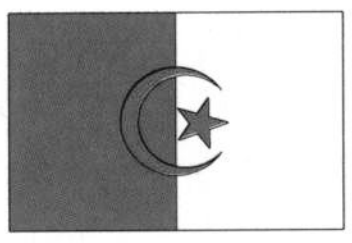

Algeria* 96/F2
Capital: Algiers
Area: 919,591 sq. mi.
2,381,740 sq. km.
Pop.: 31,787,647; growth rate: 2.060%
Govt.: republic
Independence: July 5, 1962
U.N. Admission: October 8, 1962
GDP: $115.9 billion; per capita: $4,000
Currency: Algerian dinar

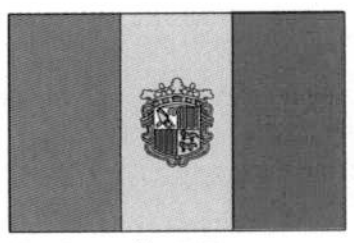

Andorra* 73/F1
Capital: Andorra la Vella
Area: 174 sq. mi.
450 sq. km.
Pop.: 67,673; growth rate: 2.941%
Govt.: parliamentary democracy
Independence: 1278
U.N. Admission: July 28, 1993
GDP: $1.2 billion; per capita: $18,000
Currency: French franc

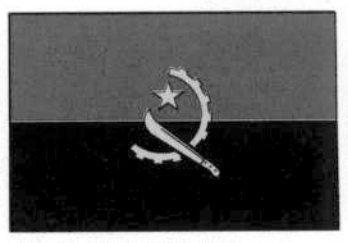

Angola* 105/C3
Capital: Luanda
Area: 481,351 sq. mi.
1,246,700 sq. km.
Pop.: 11,486,729; growth rate: 2.623%
Govt.: transitional government
Independence: November 11, 1975
U.N. Admission: December 1, 1976
GDP: $8.3 billion; per capita: $800
Currency: new kwanza

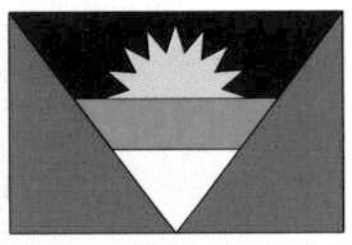

Antigua & Barbuda* 141/N8
Capital: St. John's
Area: 170 sq. mi.
440 sq. km.
Pop.: 64,461; growth rate: .313%
Govt.: parliamentary democracy
Independence: November 1, 1981
U.N. Admission: November 11, 1981
GDP: $446 million; per capita: $6,800
Currency: EC dollar

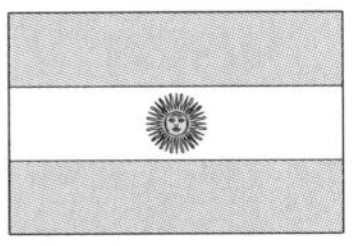

Argentina* 157/C4
Capital: Buenos Aires
Area: 1,068,296 sq. mi.
2,766,890 sq. km.
Pop.: 37,214,757; growth rate: 1.289%
Govt.: republic
Independence: July 9, 1816
U.N. Admission: October 24, 1945
GDP: $296.9 billion; per capita: $8,600
Currency: nuevo peso argentino

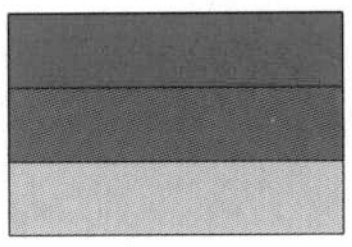

Armenia* 63/H5
Capital: Yerevan
Area: 11,506 sq. mi.
29,800 sq. km.
Pop.: 3,396,184; growth rate: -.391%
Govt.: republic
Independence: September 23, 1991
U.N. Admission: March 2, 1992
GDP: $9.7 billion; per capita: $2,800
Currency: dram

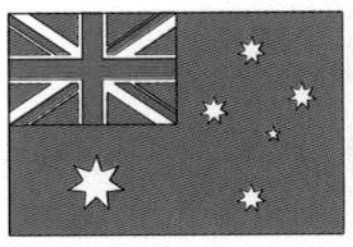

Australia* 109
Capital: Canberra
Area: 2,967,893 sq. mi.
7,686,850 sq. km.
Pop.: 18,950,108; growth rate: .868%
Govt.: federal parliamentary state
Independence: January 1, 1901
U.N. Admission: November 1, 1945
GDP: $430.5 billion; per capita: $23,600
Currency: Australian dollar

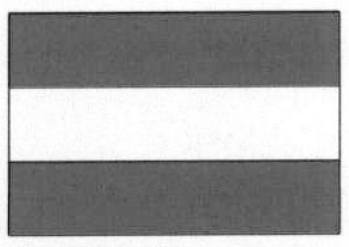

Austria* 43/L3
Capital: Vienna
Area: 32,375 sq. mi.
83,851 sq. km.
Pop.: 8,148,007; growth rate: .124%
Govt.: federal republic
Independence: 1156
U.N. Admission: December 14, 1955
GDP: $157.6 billion; per capita: $19,700
Currency: Austrian schilling

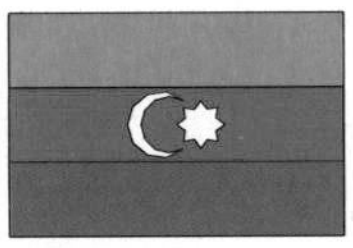

Azerbaijan* 63/H4
Capital: Baku
Area: 33,436 sq. mi.
86,600 sq. km.
Pop.: 7,955,772; growth rate: .566%
Govt.: republic
Independence: August 30, 1991
U.N. Admission: March 9, 1992
GDP: $11.9 billion; per capita: $1,550
Currency: manat

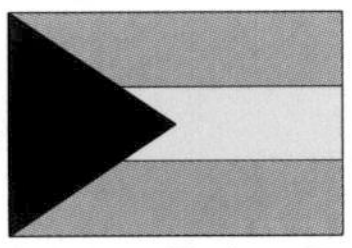

Bahamas, The* 141/F2
Capital: Nassau
Area: 5,382 sq. mi.
13,939 sq. km.
Pop.: 287,548; growth rate: 1.331%
Govt.: commonwealth
Independence: July 10, 1973
U.N. Admission: September 18,1973
GDP: $4.8 billion; per capita: $18,700
Currency: Bahamian dollar

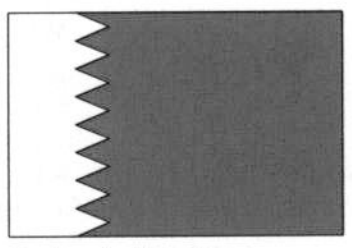

Bahrain* 88/F3
Capital: Manama
Area: 240 sq. mi.
622 sq. km.
Pop.: 641,539; growth rate: 1.917%
Govt.: traditional monarchy
Independence: August 15, 1971
U.N. Admission: September 21, 1971
GDP: $7.7 billion; per capita: $13,000
Currency: Bahraini danar

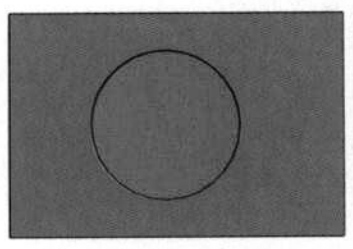

Bangladesh* 82/E3
Capital: Dhaka
Area: 55,598 sq. mi.
144,000 sq. km.
Pop.: 129,146,695; growth rate: 1.576%
Govt.: republic
Independence: December 16, 1971
U.N. Admission: September 17, 1974
GDP: $155.1 billion; per capita: $1,260
Currency: taka

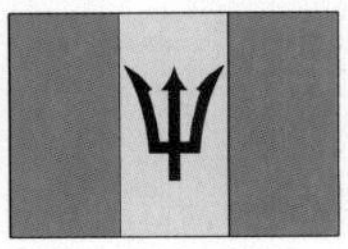

Barbados* 141/P9
Capital: Bridgetown
Area: 166 sq. mi.
430 sq. km.
Pop.: 259,248; growth rate: .001%
Govt.: parliamentary democracy
Independence: November 30, 1966
U.N. Admission: December 9, 1966
GDP: $2.65 billion; per capita: $10,300
Currency: Barbadian dollar

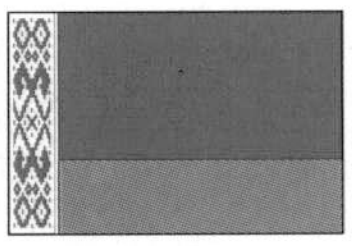

Belarus* 27/G3
Capital: Minsk
Area: 80,154 sq. mi.
207,600 sq. km.
Pop.: 10,390,697; growth rate: -.125%
Govt.: republic
Independence: August 25, 1991
U.N. Admission: October 24, 1945
GDP: $51.9 billion; per capita: $5,000
Currency: Belarusian ruble

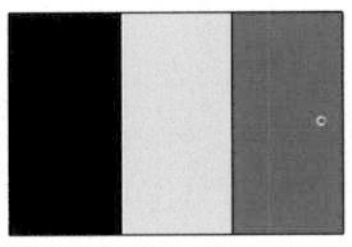

Belgium* 40/C3
Capital: Brussels
Area: 11,780 sq. mi.
30,510 sq. km.
Pop.: 10,185,894; growth rate: .021%
Govt.: constitutional monarchy
Independence: October 4, 1830
U.N. Admission: December 27, 1945
GDP: $204.8 billion; per capita: $20,300
Currency: Belgian franc

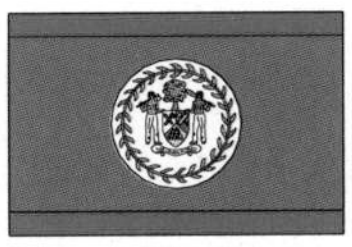

Belize* 144/D2
Capital: Belmopan
Area: 8,865 sq. mi.
22,960 sq. km.
Pop.: 241,546; growth rate: 2.409%
Govt.: parliamentary democracy
Independence: September 21, 1981
U.N. Admission: September 25, 1981
GDP: $649 million; per capita: $2,960
Currency: Belizean dollar

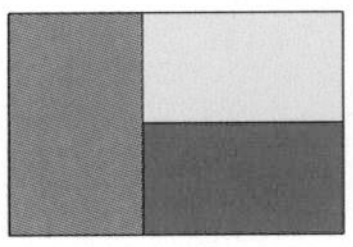

Benin* 103/F4
Capital: Porto-Novo
Area: 43,483 sq. mi.
112,620 sq. km.
Pop.: 6,516,630; growth rate: 3.288%
Govt.: republic
Independence: August 1, 1960
U.N. Admission: September 20, 1960
GDP: $8.2 billion; per capita: $1,440
Currency: CFA franc

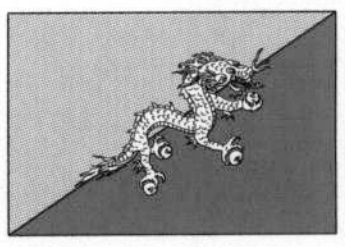

Bhutan* 82/E2
Capital: Thimphu
Area: 18,147 sq. mi.
47,000 sq. km.
Pop.: 1,996,221; growth rate: 2.233%
Govt.: monarchy
Independence: August 8, 1949
U.N. Admission: September 21, 1971
GDP: $1.3 billion; per capita: $730
Currency: ngultrum

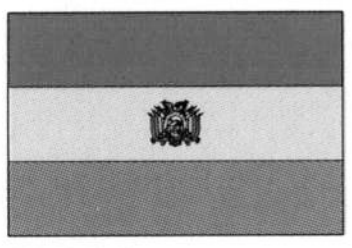

Bolivia* 150/F7
Capital: La Paz; Sucre
Area: 424,163 sq. mi.
1,098,582 sq. km.
Pop.: 8,139,180; growth rate: 1.919%
Govt.: republic
Independence: August 6, 1825
U.N. Admission: November 14, 1945
GDP: $21.5 billion; per capita: $3,000
Currency: boliviano

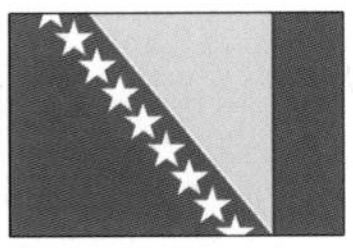

Bosnia & Herzegovina* 48/C3
Capital: Sarajevo
Area: 19,781 sq. mi.
51,233 sq. km.
Pop.: 3,591,618; growth rate: 2.977%
Govt.: emerging democracy
Independence: April 1992
U.N. Admission: May 22, 1992
GDP: $1.9 billion; per capita: $600
Currency: dinar

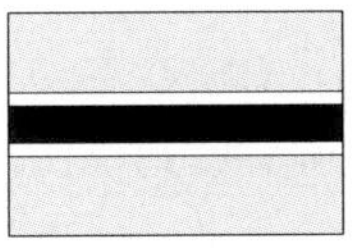

Botswana* 105/D5
Capital: Gaborone
Area: 231,803 sq. mi.
600,370 sq. km.
Pop.: 1,479,039; growth rate: .976%
Govt.: parliamentary republic
Independence: September 30, 1966
U.N. Admission: October 17, 1966
GDP: $4.6 billion; per capita: $3,100
Currency: pula

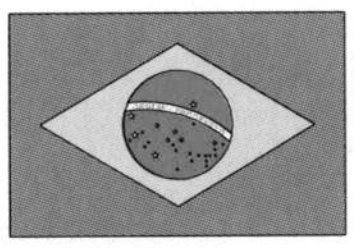

Brazil* 150/F5
Capital: Brasília
Area: 3,286,470 sq. mi.
8,511,965 sq. km.
Pop.: 173,790,810; growth rate: 1.083%
Govt.: federal republic
Independence: September 7, 1822
U.N. Admission: October 24, 1945
GDP: $1.022 trillion; per capita: $6,300
Currency: real

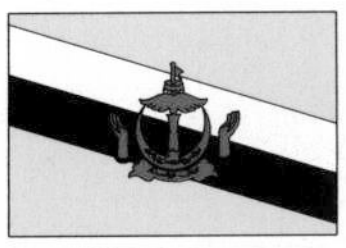

Brunei* 80/D2
Capital: Bandar Seri Begawan
Area: 2,228 sq. mi.
5,770 sq. km.
Pop.: 330,689; growth rate: 2.334%
Govt.: constitutional sultanate
Independence: January 1, 1984
U.N. Admission: September 21, 1984
GDP: $4.6 billion; per capita: $15,800
Currency: Bruneian dollar

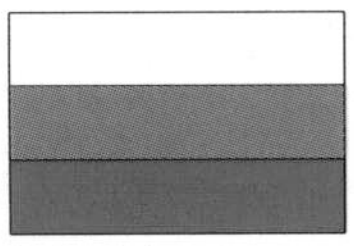

Bulgaria* 62/C4
Capital: Sofia
Area: 42,823 sq. mi.
110,912 sq. km.
Pop.: 8,155,828; growth rate: -.438%
Govt.: emerging democracy
Independence: September 22, 1908
U.N. Admission: December 14, 1955
GDP: $39.9 billion; per capita: $4,630
Currency: lev

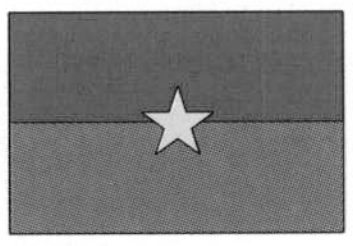

Burkina Faso* 141/E3
Capital: Ouagadougou
Area: 105,869 sq. mi.
274,200 sq. km.
Pop.: 11,892,029; growth rate: 2.687%
Govt.: parliamentary
Independence: August 5, 1960
U.N. Admission: September 20, 1960
GDP: $8 billion; per capita: $740
Currency: CFA franc

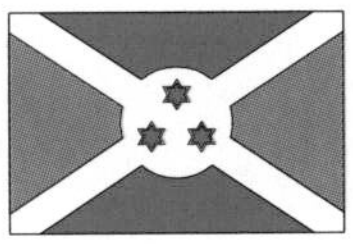

Burundi* 104/A3
Capital: Bujumbura
Area: 10,745 sq. mi.
27,830 sq. km.
Pop.: 5,930,805; growth rate: 3.150%
Govt.: republic
Independence: July 1, 1962
U.N. Admission: September 18, 1962
GDP: $4 billion; per capita: $600
Currency: Burundi franc

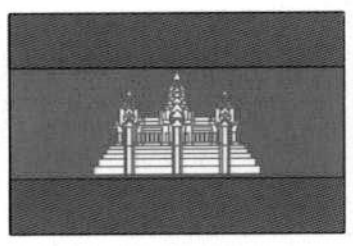

Cambodia* 83/H5
Capital: Phnom Penh
Area: 69,900 sq. mi.
181,040 sq. km.
Pop.: 11,918,865; growth rate: 2.482%
Govt.: constitutional monarchy
Independence: November 9, 1949
U.N. Admission: December 14, 1955
GDP: $7.7 billion; per capita: $710
Currency: new riel

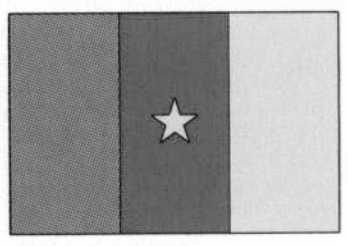

Cameroon* 96/H7
Capital: Yaoundé
Area: 183,568 sq. mi.
475,441 sq. km.
Pop.: 15,891,531; growth rate: 2.768%
Govt.: unitary republic
Independence: January 1, 1960
U.N. Admission: September 20, 1960
GDP: $17.5 billion; per capita: $1,230
Currency: CFA franc

* United Nations member (Yugoslavia suspended)
Note – Page and letter-number references in blue type follow the country names. For example: **Bulgaria** 62/C4 refers to page 62, index grid square C4.

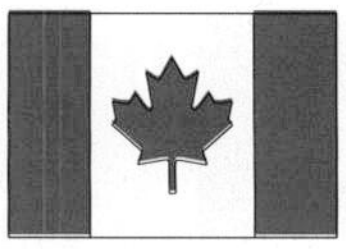

Canada* 122
Capital: Ottawa
Area: 3,851,787 sq. mi.
9,976,139 sq. km.
Pop.: 31,330,255; growth rate: 1.023%
Govt.: parliamentary democracy
Independence: July 1, 1867
U.N. Admission: November 9, 1945
GDP: $721 billion; per capita: $25,000
Currency: Canadian dollar

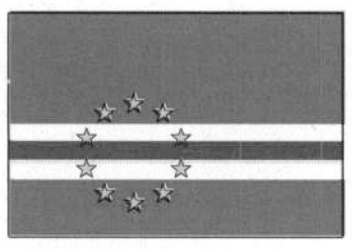

Cape Verde* 93/J9
Capital: Praia
Area: 1,556 sq. mi.
4,030 sq. km.
Pop.: 411,487; growth rate: 1.374%
Govt.: republic
Independence: July 5, 1975
U.N. Admission: September 16, 1975
GDP: $472 million; per capita: $1,000
Currency: Cape Verdean escudo

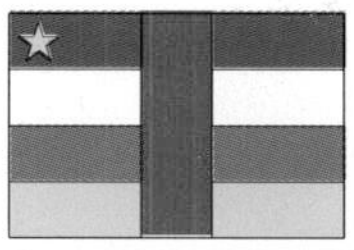

Central African Republic* 97/J6
Capital: Bangui
Area: 240,533 sq. mi.
622,980 sq. km.
Pop.: 3,515,657; growth rate: 2.026%
Govt.: republic
Independence: August 13, 1960
U.N. Admission: September 20, 1960
GDP: $2.5 billion; per capita: $800
Currency: CFA franc

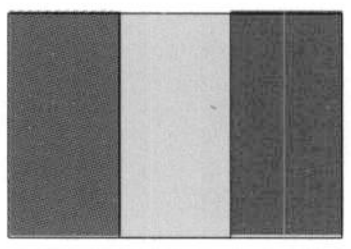

Chad* 97/J4
Capital: N'Djamena
Area: 495,752 sq. mi.
1,283,998 sq. km.
Pop.: 7,760,252; growth rate: 2.647
Govt.: republic
Independence: August 11, 1960
U.N. Admission: September 20, 1960
GDP: $3.3 billion; per capita: $600
Currency: CFA franc

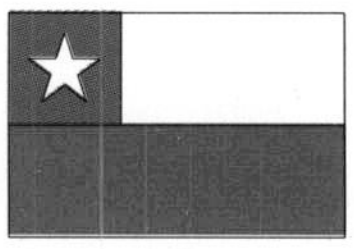

Chile* 157/B3
Capital: Santiago
Area: 292,258 sq. mi.
756,950 sq. km.
Pop.: 15,155,495; growth rate: 1.184%
Govt.: republic
Independence: September 18, 1810
U.N. Admission: October 24, 1945
GDP: $120.6 billion; per capita: $8,400
Currency: Chilean peso

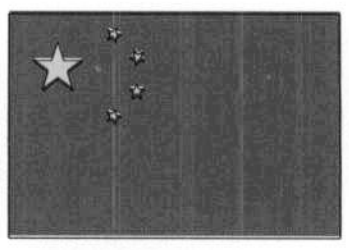

China* 70/G4
Capital: Beijing
Area: 3,705,386 sq. mi.
9,596,960 sq. km.
Pop.: 1,256,167,701; growth rate: .715%
Govt.: Communist state
Independence: October 1, 1949
U.N. Admission: October 24, 1945
GDP: $3.39 trillion; per capita: $2,800
Currency: yuan

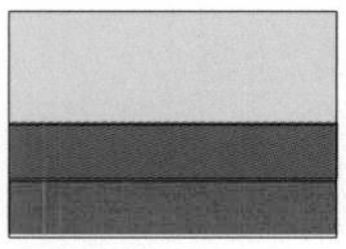

Colombia* 150/D3
Capital: Bogotá
Area: 439,733 sq. mi.
1,138,910 sq. km.
Pop.: 40,036,927; growth rate: 1.816%
Govt.: republic
Independence: July 20, 1810
U.N. Admission: November 5, 1945
GDP: $201.4 billion; per capita: $5,400
Currency: Colombian peso

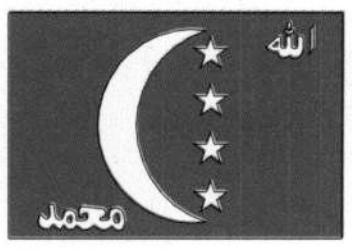

Comoros* 107/G5
Capital: Moroni
Area: 838 sq. mi.
2,170 sq. km.
Pop.: 580,509; growth rate: 3.116%
Govt.: independent republic
Independence: July 6, 1975
U.N. Admission: November 12, 1975
GDP: $370 million; per capita: $650
Currency: Comoran franc

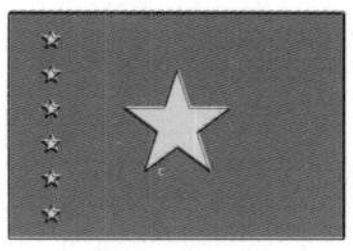

Congo, Dem. Rep. of the* 93/E5
Capital: Kinshasa
Area: 905,563 sq. mi.
2,345,410 sq. km.
Pop.: 51,987,773; growth rate: 2.921%
Govt.: republic
Independence: June 30, 1960
U.N. Admission: September 20, 1960
GDP: $16.5 billion; per capita: $400
Currency: zaire

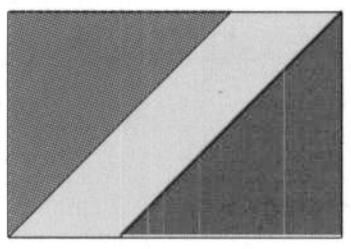

Congo, Rep. of the* 93/D4
Capital: Brazzaville
Area: 132,046 sq. mi.
342,000 sq. km.
Pop.: 2,775,659; growth rate: 2.123%
Govt.: republic
Independence: August 15, 1960
U.N. Admission: September 20, 1960
GDP: $4.9 billion; per capita: $1,960
Currency: CFA franc

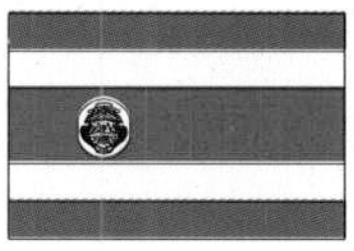

Costa Rica* 145/F4
Capital: San José
Area: 19,730 sq. mi.
51,100 sq. km.
Pop.: 3,743,677; growth rate: 1.839%
Govt.: democratic republic
Independence: September 15, 1821
U.N. Admission: November 2, 1945
GDP: $19 billion; per capita: $5,500
Currency: Costa Rican colon

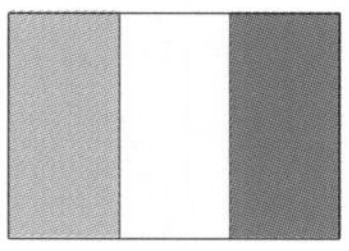

Côte d'Ivoire* 102/D5
Capital: Yamoussoukro
Area: 124,502 sq. mi.
322,460 sq. km.
Pop.: 16,190,105; growth rate: 2.298%
Govt.: republic
Independence: August 7, 1960
U.N. Admission: September 20, 1960
GDP: $23.9 billion; per capita: $1,620
Currency: CFA franc

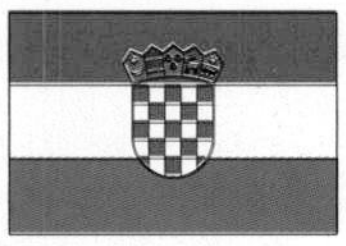

Croatia* 48/B3
Capital: Zagreb
Area: 22,050 sq. mi.
57,110 sq. km.
Pop.: 4,681,015; growth rate: .076%
Govt.: parliamentary democracy
Independence: June 25, 1991
U.N. Admission: May 22, 1992
GDP: $21.4 billion; per capita: $4,300
Currency: Croatian kuna

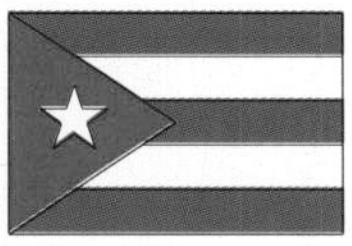

Cuba* 145/F1
Capital: Havana
Area: 42,803 sq. mi.
110,860 sq. km.
Pop.: 11,139,412; growth rate: .374%
Govt.: Communist state
Independence: May 20, 1902
U.N. Admission: October 24, 1945
GDP: $16.2 billion; per capita: $1,480
Currency: Cuban peso

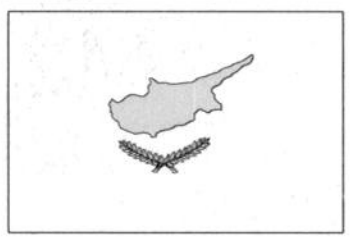

Cyprus* 91/C2
Capital: Nicosia
Area: 3,571 sq. mi.
9,250 sq. km.
Pop.: 759,048; growth rate: .651%
Govt.: republic
Independence: August 16, 1960
U.N. Admission: September 20, 1960
GDP: $8.8 billion; per capita: $11,800
Currency: Cypriot pound

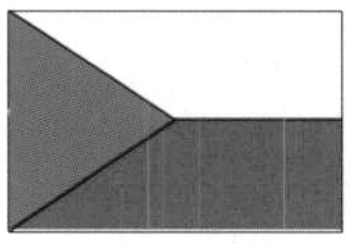

Czech Republic* 41/H4
Capital: Prague
Area: 30,387 sq. mi.
78,703 sq. km.
Pop.: 10,283,762; growth rate: .074%
Govt.: parliamentary democracy
Independence: January 1, 1993
U.N. Admission: January 19, 1993
GDP: $114.3 billion; per capita: $11,100
Currency: koruna

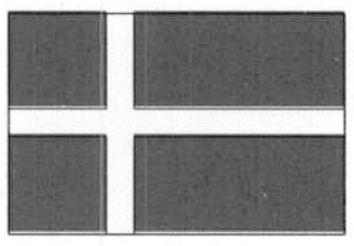

Denmark* 38/C4
Capital: Copenhagen
Area: 16,629 sq. mi.
43,069 sq. km.
Pop.: 5,374,554; growth rate: .277%
Govt.: constitutional monarchy
Independence: 1849
U.N. Admission: October 24, 1945
GDP: $118.2 billion; per capita: $22,700
Currency: Danish krone

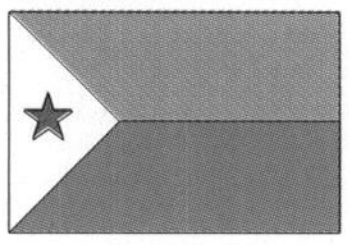

Djibouti* 97/P5
Capital: Djibouti
Area: 8,494 sq. mi.
22,000 sq. km.
Pop.: 454,294; growth rate: 1.532%
Govt.: republic
Independence: June 27, 1977
U.N. Admission: September 20, 1977
GDP: $500 million; per capita: $1,200
Currency: Djiboutian franc

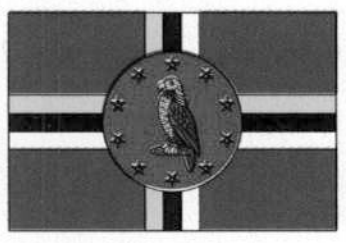

Dominica* 141/N9
Capital: Roseau
Area: 290 sq. mi.
751 sq. km.
Pop.: 63,944; growth rate: -1.497%
Govt.: parliamentary democracy
Independence: November 3, 1978
U.N. Admission: December 18, 1978
GDP: $208 million; per capita: $2,500
Currency: EC dollar

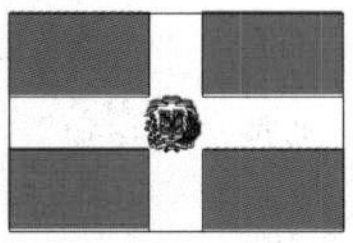

Dominican Republic* 141/H4
Capital: Santo Domingo
Area: 18,815 sq. mi.
48,730 sq. km.
Pop.: 8,261,536; growth rate: 1.600%
Govt.: republic
Independence: February 27, 1844
U.N. Admission: October 24, 1945
GDP: $29.8 billion; per capita: $3,670
Currency: Dominican peso

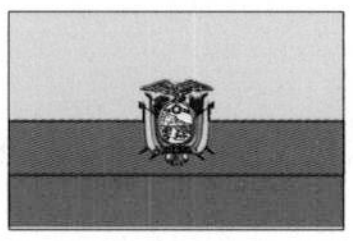

Ecuador* 150/C4
Capital: Quito
Area: 109,483 sq. mi.
283,561 sq. km.
Pop.: 12,782,161; growth rate: 1.693%
Govt.: republic
Independence: May 24, 1822
U.N. Admission: December 21, 1945
GDP: $47 billion; per capita: $4,100
Currency: sucre

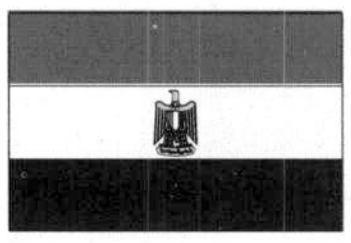

Egypt* 97/L2
Capital: Cairo
Area: 386,659 sq. mi.
1,001,447 sq. km.
Pop.: 68,494,584; growth rate: 1.779%
Govt.: republic
Independence: February 28, 1922
U.N. Admission: October 24, 1945
GDP: $183.9 billion; per capita: $2,900
Currency: Egyptian pound

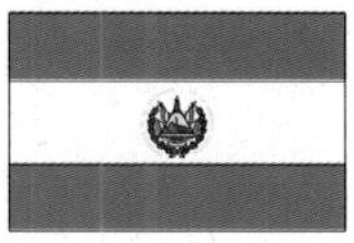

El Salvador* 144/D3
Capital: San Salvador
Area: 8,124 sq. mi.
21,040 sq. km.
Pop.: 5,925,374; growth rate: 1.496%
Govt.: republic
Independence: September 15, 1821
U.N. Admission: October 24, 1945
GDP: $12.2 billion; per capita: $2,080
Currency: Salvadoran colon

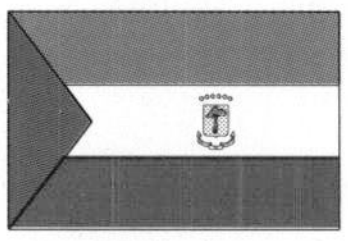

Equatorial Guinea* 96/G7
Capital: Malabo
Area: 10,831 sq. mi.
28,052 sq. km.
Pop.: 477,763; growth rate: 2.545%
Govt.: republic in transition
Independence: October 12, 1968
U.N. Admission: November 12, 1968
GDP: $328 million; per capita: $800
Currency: CFA franc

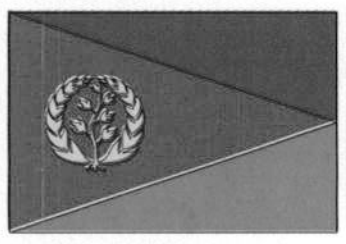

Eritrea* 97/N5
Capital: Asmara
Area: 46,842 sq. mi.
121,320 sq. km.
Pop.: 4,142,481; growth rate: 3.887%
Govt.: transitional government
Independence: May 27, 1993
U.N. Admission: May 28, 1993
GDP: $2 billion; per capita: $570
Currency: nafka

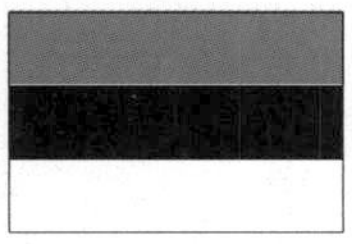

Estonia* 39/L2
Capital: Tallinn
Area: 17,413 sq. mi.
45,100 sq. km.
Pop.: 1,398,140; growth rate: -.655%
Govt.: republic
Independence: September 6, 1991
U.N. Admission: September 17, 1991
GDP: $8.1 billion; per capita: $5,560
Currency: Estonian kroon

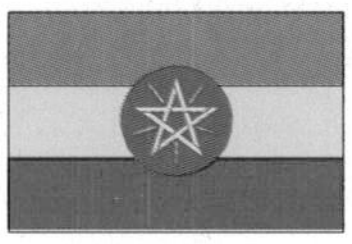

Ethiopia* 97/N5
Capital: Addis Ababa
Area: 435,184 sq. mi.
1,127,127 sq. km.
Pop.: 60,967,436; growth rate: 2.107%
Govt.: federal republic
Independence: c. 2nd cent. A.D.
U.N. Admission: November 13, 1945
GDP: $24.8 billion; per capita: $430
Currency: birr

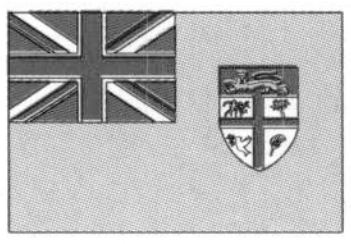

Fiji* 116/G6
Capital: Suva
Area: 7,055 sq. mi.
18,272 sq. km.
Pop.: 823,376; growth rate: 1.280%
Govt.: republic
Independence: October 10, 1970
U.N. Admission: October 13, 1970
GDP: $5.1 billion; per capita: $6,500
Currency: Fijian dollar

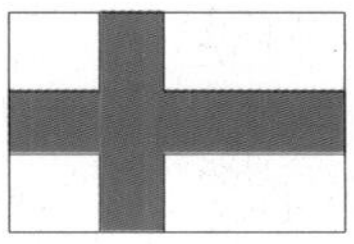

Finland* 37/H2
Capital: Helsinki
Area: 130,128 sq. mi.
337,032 sq. km.
Pop.: 5,164,825; growth rate: .100%
Govt.: republic
Independence: December 16, 1917
U.N. Admission: December 14, 1955
GDP: $97.1 billion; per capita: $19,000
Currency: markka

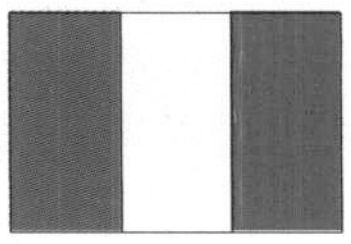

France* 42/D3
Capital: Paris
Area: 211,208 sq. mi.
547,030 sq. km.
Pop.: 59,128,187; growth rate: .234%
Govt.: republic
Independence: 486
U.N. Admission: October 24, 1945
GDP: $1.22 trillion; per capita: $20,900
Currency: French franc

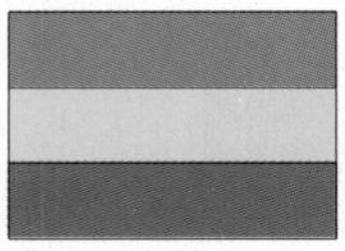

Gabon* 96/H7
Capital: Libreville
Area: 103,347 sq. mi.
267,670 sq. km.
Pop.: 1,244,192; growth rate: 1.488%
Govt.: republic
Independence: August 17, 1960
U.N. Admission: September 20, 1960
GDP: $6.3 billion; per capita: $5,400
Currency: CFA franc

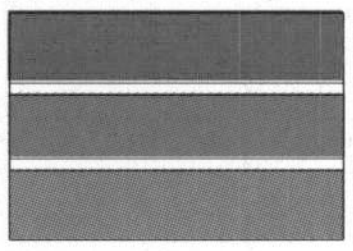

Gambia, The* 102/B3
Capital: Banjul
Area: 4,363 sq. mi.
11,300 sq. km.
Pop.: 1,381,496; growth rate: 3.296%
Govt.: republic
Independence: February 18, 1965
U.N. Admission: September 21, 1965
GDP: $1.1 billion; per capita: $1,100
Currency: dalasi

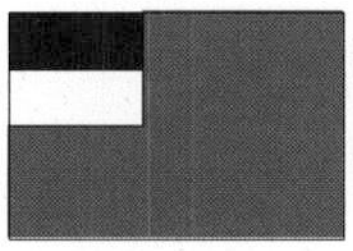

Georgia* 63/G4
Capital: T'bilisi
Area: 26,911 sq. mi.
69,700 sq. km.
Pop.: 5,034,051; growth rate: -.549%
Govt.: republic
Independence: April 9, 1991
U.N. Admission: July 31, 1992
GDP: $7.1 billion; per capita: $1,350
Currency: lari

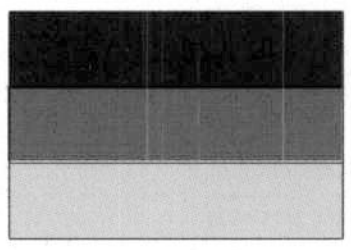

Germany* 40/E3
Capital: Berlin
Area: 137,803 sq. mi.
356,910 sq. km.
Pop.: 82,081,365; growth rate: -.019%
Govt.: federal republic
Independence: January 18, 1871
U.N. Admission: September 18, 1973
GDP: $1.7 trillion; per capita: $23,100
Currency: deutsche mark

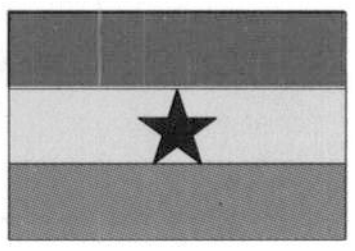

Ghana* 103/E4
Capital: Accra
Area: 92,100 sq. mi.
238,540 sq. km.
Pop.: 19,271,744; growth rate: 1.976%
Govt.: constitutional democracy
Independence: March 6, 1957
U.N. Admission: March 8, 1957
GDP: $27 billion; per capita: $1,530
Currency: new cedi

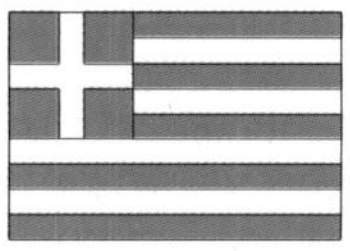

Greece* 47/G3
Capital: Athens
Area: 50,942 sq. mi.
131,940 sq. km.
Pop.: 10,750,705; growth rate: .398%
Govt.: parliamentary republic
Independence: 1829
U.N. Admission: October 25, 1945
GDP: $106.9 billion; per capita: $10,000
Currency: drachma

Sources: The Flag Research Center; U.S. Bureau of the Census, International Data Base; CIA World Factbook

World Flags and Reference Guide

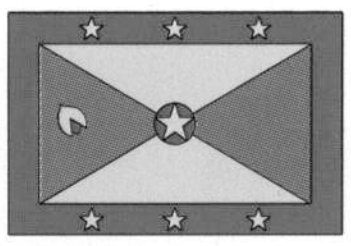

Grenada* 141/N10
Capital: St. George's
Area: 131 sq. mi.
340 sq. km.
Pop.: 97,913; growth rate: .984%
Govt.: parliamentary democracy
Independence: February 7, 1974
U.N. Admission: September 17, 1974
GDP: $300 million; per capita: $3,160
Currency: EC dollar

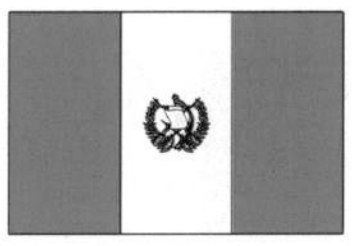

Guatemala* 144/D3
Capital: Guatemala
Area: 42,042 sq. mi.
108,889 sq. km.
Pop.: 12,669,576; growth rate: 2.660%
Govt.: republic
Independence: September 15, 1821
U.N. Admission: November 21, 1945
GDP: $39 billion; per capita: $3,460
Currency: quetzal

Guinea* 102/C4
Capital: Conakry
Area: 94,927 sq. mi.
245,860 sq. km.
Pop.: 7,610,869; growth rate: 1.077%
Govt.: republic
Independence: October 2, 1958
U.N. Admission: December 12, 1958
GDP: $7.1 billion; per capita: $950
Currency: Guinean franc

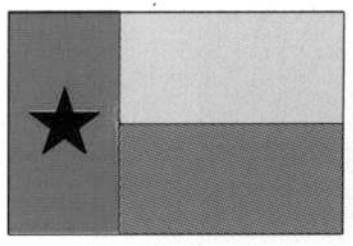

Guinea-Bissau* 102/B3
Capital: Bissau
Area: 13,946 sq. mi.
36,120 sq. km.
Pop.: 1,263,341; growth rate: 2.300%
Govt.: republic
Independence: September 10, 1974
U.N. Admission: September 17, 1974
GDP: $1.1 billion; per capita: $950
Currency: Guinea-Bissauan peso

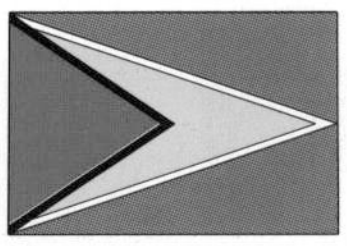

Guyana* 153/G3
Capital: Georgetown
Area: 83,000 sq. mi.
214,970 sq. km.
Pop.: 703,399; growth rate: -.174%
Govt.: republic
Independence: May 26, 1966
U.N. Admission: September 20, 1966
GDP: $1.8 billion; per capita: $2,490
Currency: Guyanese dollar

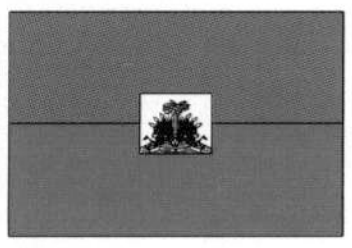

Haiti* 145/H2
Capital: Port-au-Prince
Area: 10,714 sq. mi.
27,750 sq. km.
Pop.: 6,991,589; growth rate: 1.562%
Govt.: republic
Independence: January 1, 1804
U.N. Admission: October 24, 1945
GDP: $68 billion; per capita: $1,000
Currency: gourde

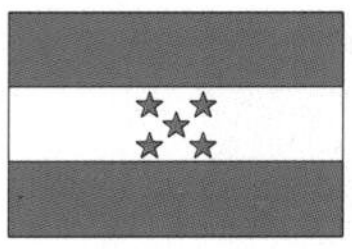

Honduras* 144/E3
Capital: Tegucigalpa
Area: 43,277 sq. mi.
112,087 sq. km.
Pop.: 6,130,135; growth rate: 2.143%
Govt.: republic
Independence: September 15, 1821
U.N. Admission: December 17, 1945
GDP: $11.5 billion; per capita: $2,000
Currency: lempira

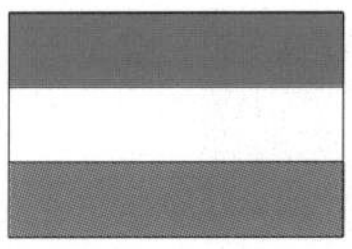

Hungary* 48/D2
Capital: Budapest
Area: 35,919 sq. mi.
93,030 sq. km.
Pop.: 10,167,182; growth rate: -.178%
Govt.: republic
Independence: 1001
U.N. Admission: December 14, 1955
GDP: $74.7 billion; per capita: $7,500
Currency: forint

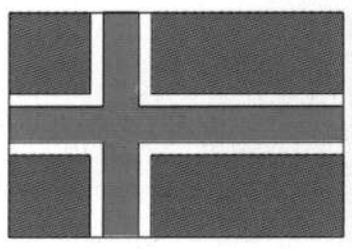

Iceland* 37/N7
Capital: Reykjavík
Area: 39,768 sq. mi.
103,000 sq. km.
Pop.: 274,141; growth rate: .622%
Govt.: constitutional republic
Independence: June 17, 1944
U.N. Admission: November 19, 1946
GDP: $5.3 billion; per capita: $19,800
Currency: krona

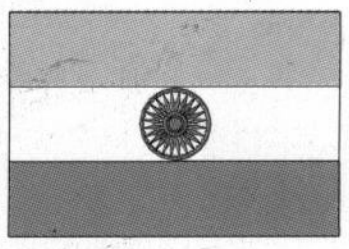

India* 67/G7
Capital: New Delhi
Area: 1,269,339 sq. mi.
3,287,588 sq. km.
Pop.: 1,017,645,163; growth rate: 1.648%
Govt.: federal republic
Independence: August 15, 1947
U.N. Admission: October 30, 1945
GDP: $1.538 trillion; per capita: $1,600
Currency: Indian rupee

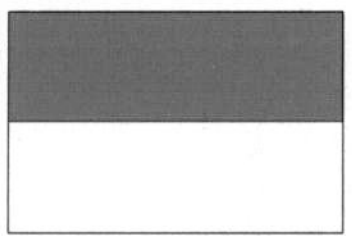

Indonesia* 81/E4
Capital: Jakarta
Area: 741,096 sq. mi.
1,919,440 sq. km.
Pop.: 219,266,557; growth rate: 1.438%
Govt.: republic
Independence: August 17, 1945
U.N. Admission: September 28, 1950
GDP: $779.7 billion; per capita: $3,770
Currency: Indonesian rupiah

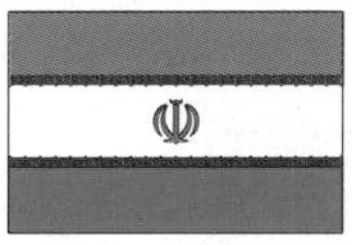

Iran* 67/E6
Capital: Tehran
Area: 636,293 sq. mi.
1,648,000 sq. km.
Pop.: 65,865,302; growth rate: 1.022%
Govt.: theocratic republic
Independence: April 1, 1979
U.N. Admission: October 24, 1945
GDP: $343.5 billion; per capita: $5,200
Currency: Iranian rial

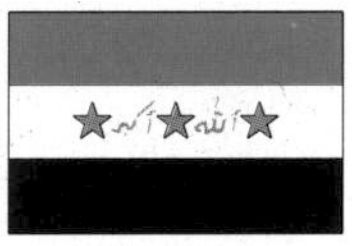

Iraq* 88/D2
Capital: Baghdad
Area: 168,753 sq. mi.
437,072 sq. km.
Pop: 23,150,926; growth rate: 3.167%
Govt.: republic
Independence: October 3, 1932
U.N. Admission: December 21, 1945
GDP: $42 billion; per capita: $2,000
Currency: Iraqi dinar

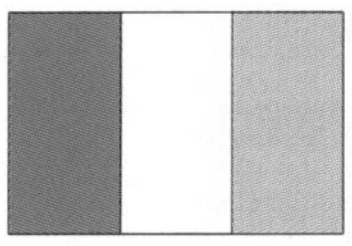

Ireland* 31/P10
Capital: Dublin
Area: 27,136 sq. mi.
70,282 sq. km.
Pop.: 3,647,348; growth rate: .408%
Govt.: republic
Independence: December 6, 1921
U.N. Admission: December 14, 1955
GDP: $59.9 billion; per capita: $16,800
Currency: Irish pound

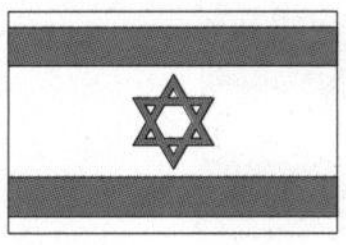

Israel* 91/C3
Capital: Jerusalem
Area: 8,019 sq. mi.
20,770 sq. km.
Pop.: 5,851,913; growth rate: 1.714%
Govt.: republic
Independence: May 14, 1948
U.N. Admission: May 11, 1949
GDP: $585.7 billion; per capita: $16,400
Currency: new Israeli shekel

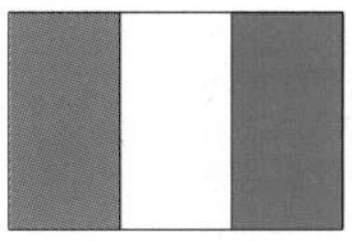

Italy* 27/F4
Capital: Rome
Area: 116,305 sq. mi.
301,230 sq. km.
Pop.: 56,686,568; growth rate: -.087%
Govt.: republic
Independence: March 12, 1861
U.N. Admission: December 14, 1955
GDP: $1.12 trillion; per capita: $19,600
Currency: Italian lira

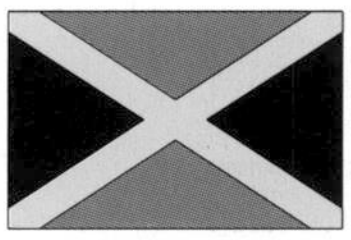

Jamaica* 145/G2
Capital: Kingston
Area: 4,243 sq. mi.
10,990 sq. km.
Pop.: 2,668,740; growth rate: .582%
Govt.: parliamentary democracy
Independence: August 6, 1962
U.N. Admission: September 18, 1962
GDP: $8.4 billion; per capita: $3,260
Currency: Jamaican dollar

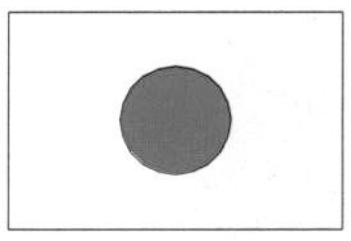

Japan* 71/Q4
Capital: Tōkyō
Area: 145,882 sq. mi.
377,835 sq. km.
Pop.: 126,434,470; growth rate: .198%
Govt.: constitutional monarchy
Independence: 660 B.C.
U.N. Admission: December 18, 1956
GDP: $2.85 trillion; per capita: $22,700
Currency: yen

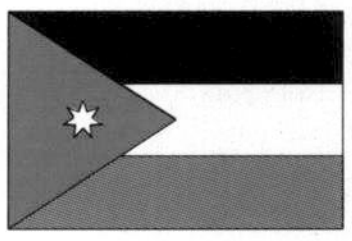

Jordan* 88/C2
Capital: Amman
Area: 34,445 sq. mi.
89,213 sq. km.
Pop.: 4,700,843; growth rate: 2.967%
Govt.: constitutional monarchy
Independence: May 25, 1946
U.N. Admission: December 14, 1955
GDP: $20.9 billion; per capita: $5,000
Currency: Jordanian dinar

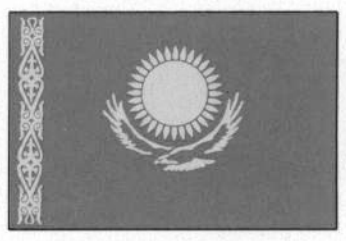

Kazakhstan* 64/G5
Capital: Astana
Area: 1,049,150 sq. mi.
2,717,300 sq. km.
Pop.: 16,816,150; growth rate: -.012%
Govt.: republic
Independence: December 16, 1991
U.N. Admission: March 2, 1992
GDP: $48.6 billion; per capita: $2,880
Currency: Kazakstani tenge

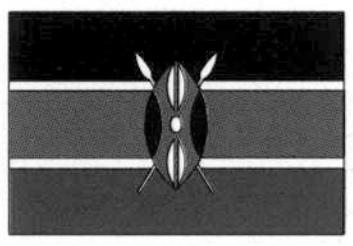

Kenya* 104/C2
Capital: Nairobi
Area: 224,960 sq. mi.
582,646 sq. km.
Pop.: 29,250,541; growth rate: 1.458%
Govt.: republic
Independence: December 12, 1963
U.N. Admission: December 16, 1963
GDP: $39.2 billion; per capita: $1,400
Currency: Kenyan shilling

Kiribati* 116/H5
Capital: Tarawa
Area: 277 sq. mi.
717 sq. km.
Pop.: 87,025; growth rate: 1.489%
Govt.: republic
Independence: July 12, 1979
U.N. Admission: September 14, 1999
GDP: $62 million; per capita: $800
Currency: Australian dollar

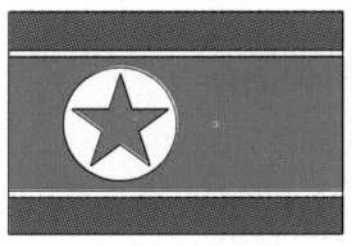

Korea, North* 73/D2
Capital: P'yŏngyang
Area: 46,540 sq. mi.
120,539 sq. km.
Pop.: 21,687,550; growth rate: 1.354%
Govt.: Communist state
Independence: September 9, 1948
U.N. Admission: September 17, 1991
GDP: $20.9 billion; per capita: $900
Currency: North Korean won

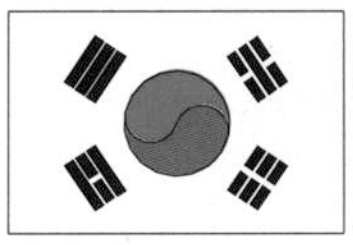

Korea, South* 73/D4
Capital: Seoul
Area: 38,023 sq. mi.
98,480 sq. km.
Pop.: 47,350,529; growth rate: .980%
Govt.: republic
Independence: August 15, 1948
U.N. Admission: September 17, 1991
GDP: $647.2 billion; per capita: $14,200
Currency: South Korean won

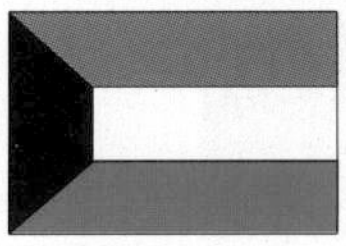

Kuwait* 88/E3
Capital: Kuwait
Area: 6,880 sq. mi.
17,820 sq. km.
Pop.: 2,067,728; growth rate: 3.675%
Govt.: constitutional monarchy
Independence: June 19, 1961
U.N. Admission: May 14, 1963
GDP: $32.5 billion; per capita: $16,700
Currency: Kuwaiti dinar

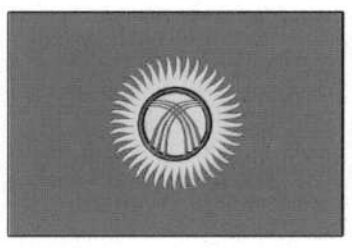

Kyrgyzstan* 87/F4
Capital: Bishkek
Area: 76,641 sq. mi.
198,500 sq. km.
Pop.: 4,584,341; growth rate: .995%
Govt.: republic
Independence: August 31, 1991
U.N. Admission: March 2, 1992
GDP: $5.8 billion; per capita: $1,290
Currency: Kyrgyzstani som

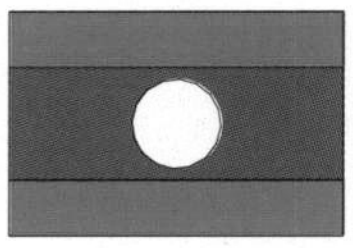

Laos* 78/C2
Capital: Vientiane
Area: 91,428 sq. mi.
236,800 sq. km.
Pop.: 5,556,821; growth rate: 2.713%
Govt.: Communist state
Independence: July 19, 1949
U.N. Admission: December 14, 1955
GDP: $5.7 billion; per capita: $1,150
Currency: new kip

Latvia* 39/L3
Capital: Riga
Area: 24,749 sq. mi.
64,100 sq. km.
Pop.: 2,326,689; growth rate: -1.074%
Govt.: republic
Independence: September 6, 1991
U.N. Admission: September 17, 1991
GDP: $9.4 billion; per capita: $3,800
Currency: Latvian let

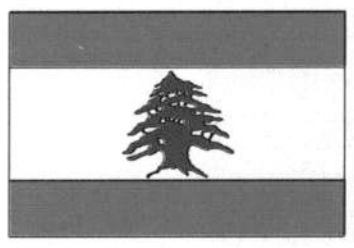

Lebanon* 91/D3
Capital: Beirut
Area: 4,015 sq. mi.
10,399 sq. km.
Pop.: 3,619,971; growth rate: 1.585%
Govt.: republic
Independence: November 22, 1943
U.N. Admission: October 24, 1945
GDP: $13 billion; per capita: $3,400
Currency: Lebanese pound

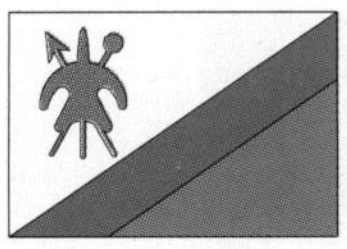

Lesotho* 106/E6
Capital: Maseru
Area: 11,718 sq. mi.
30,350 sq. km.
Pop.: 2,166,520; growth rate: 1.697%
Govt.: constitutional monarchy
Independence: October 4, 1966
U.N. Admission: October 17, 1966
GDP: $27 billion; per capita: $1,860
Currency: leti

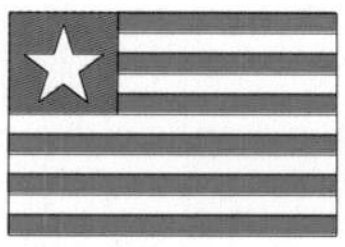

Liberia* 102/C5
Capital: Monrovia
Area: 43,000 sq. mi.
111,370 sq. km.
Pop.: 3,089,980; growth rate: 6.103%
Govt.: republic
Independence: July 26, 1847
U.N. Admission: November 2, 1945
GDP: $2.4 billion; per capita: $1,100
Currency: Liberian dollar

Libya* 97/J2
Capital: Tripoli
Area: 679,358 sq. mi.
1,759,537 sq. km.
Pop.: 5,114,032; growth rate: 2.399%
Govt.: military dictatorship
Independence: December 24, 1951
U.N. Admission: December 14, 1955
GDP: $34.5 billion; per capita: $6,570
Currency: Libyan dinar

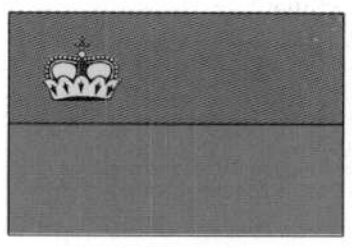

Liechtenstein* 57/F3
Capital: Vaduz
Area: 62 sq. mi.
160 sq. km.
Pop.: 32,410; growth rate: 1.108%
Govt.: constitutional monarchy
Independence: January 23, 1719
U.N. Admission: September 18, 1990
GDP: $713 million; per capita: $23,000
Currency: Swiss franc

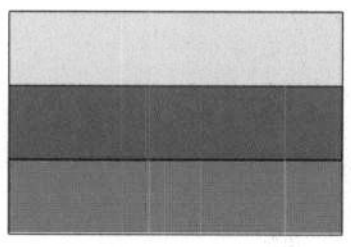

Lithuania* 39/K4
Capital: Vilnius
Area: 25,174 sq. mi.
65,200 sq. km.
Pop.: 3,571,552; growth rate: -.351%
Govt.: democratic republic
Independence: September 6, 1991
U.N. Admission: September 17, 1991
GDP: $14.1 billion; per capita: $3,870
Currency: Lithuanian litas

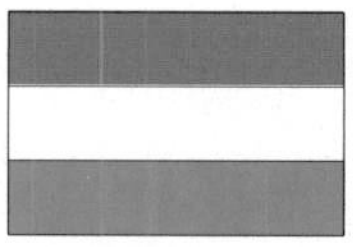

Luxembourg* 53/E4
Capital: Luxembourg
Area: 999 sq. mi.
2,587 sq. km.
Pop.: 432,577; growth rate: .74%
Govt.: constitutional monarchy
Independence: 1839
U.N. Admission: October 24, 1945
GDP: $10 billion; per capita: $24,500
Currency: Luxembourg franc

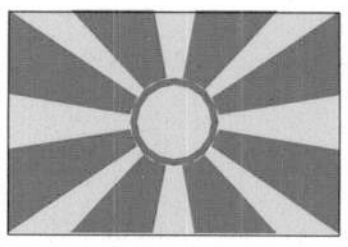

Macedonia (F.Y.R.O.M.)* 47/G2
Capital: Skopje
Area: 9,781 sq. mi.
25,333 sq. km.
Pop.: 2,035,044; growth rate: .591%
Govt.: emerging democracy
Independence: September 17, 1991
U.N. Admission: April 8, 1993
GDP: $2 billion; per capita: $960
Currency: Macedonian denar

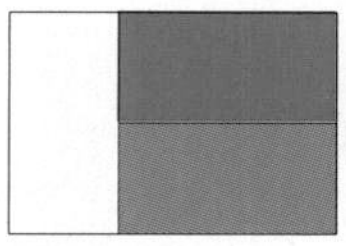

Madagascar* 107/H8
Capital: Antananarivo
Area: 226,657 sq. mi.
587,041 sq. km.
Pop.: 15,294,535; growth rate: 2.788%
Govt.: republic
Independence: June 26, 1960
U.N. Admission: September 20, 1960
GDP: $12.1 billion; per capita: $880
Currency: Malagasy franc

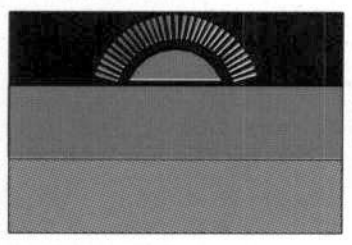

Malawi* 105/F3
Capital: Lilongwe
Area: 45,745 sq. mi.
118,480 sq. km.
Pop.: 10,154,299; growth rate: 1.484%
Govt.: multiparty democracy
Independence: July 6, 1964
U.N. Admission: December 1, 1964
GDP: $7.5 billion; per capita: $800
Currency: Malawian kwacha

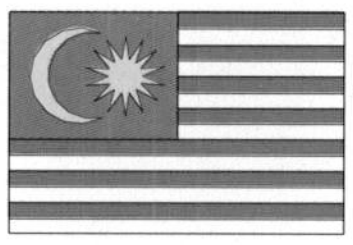

Malaysia* 80/C2
Capital: Kuala Lumpur
Area: 127,316 sq. mi.
329,750 sq. km.
Pop.: 21,820,143; growth rate: 2.037%
Govt.: constitutional monarchy
Independence: August 31, 1957
U.N. Admission: September 17, 1957
GDP: $214.7 billion; per capita: $10,750
Currency: ringgit

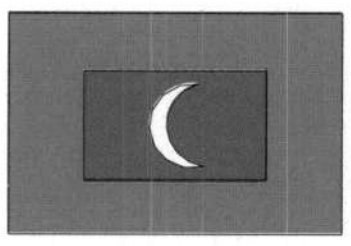

Maldives* 67/G9
Capital: Male
Area: 116 sq. mi.
300 sq. km.
Pop.: 310,425; growth rate: 3.319%
Government: republic
Independence: July 26, 1965
U.N. Admission: September 21, 1965
GDP: $423 million; per capita: $1,620
Currency: rufiyaa

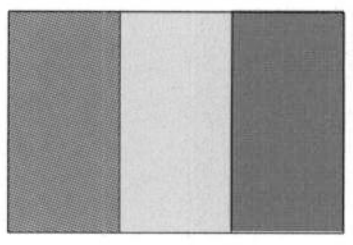

Mali* 96/E4
Capital: Bamako
Area: 478,764 sq. mi.
1,240,000 sq. km.
Pop.: 10,750,686; growth rate: 3.066%
Government: republic
Independence: September 22, 1960
U.N. Admission: September 28, 1960
GDP: $5.8 billion; per capita: $600
Currency: CFA franc

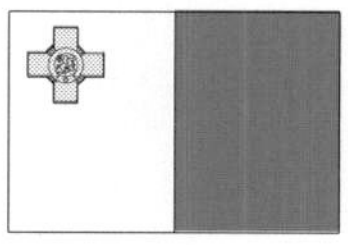

Malta* 46/L7
Capital: Valletta
Area: 124 sq. mi.
320 sq. km.
Pop.: 383,285; growth rate: .391%
Govt.: parliamentary democracy
Independence: September 21, 1964
U.N. Admission: December 1, 1964
GDP: $4.7 billion; per capita: $12,600
Currency: Maltese lira

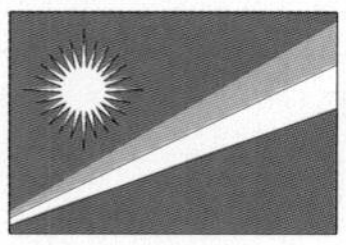

Marshall Islands* 116/G3
Capital: Majuro
Area: 70 sq. mi.
181 sq. km.
Pop.: 68,088; growth rate: 3.870%
Govt.: constitutional government
Independence: October 21, 1986
U.N. Admission: September 17, 1991
GDP: $94 million; per capita: $1,680
Currency: United States dollar

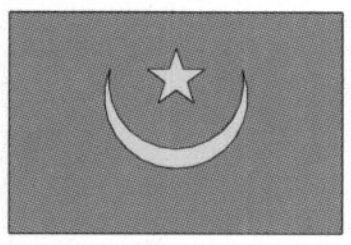

Mauritania* 96/C4
Capital: Nouakchott
Area: 397,953 sq. mi.
1,030,700 sq. km.
Pop.: 2,660,155; growth rate: 2.994%
Govt.: republic
Independence: November 28, 1960
U.N. Admission: October 7, 1961
GDP: $12.8 billion; per capita: $1,200
Currency: ouguiya

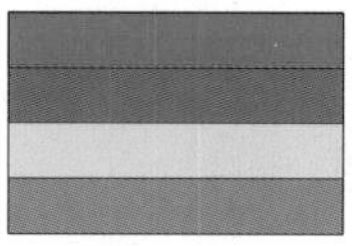

Mauritius* 107/T15
Capital: Port Louis
Area: 718 sq. mi.
1,860 sq. km.
Pop.: 1,196,172; growth rate: 1.168%
Govt.: parliamentary democracy
Independence: March 12, 1968
U.N. Admission: April 24, 1968
GDP: $11.7 billion; per capita: $10,350
Currency: Mauritian rupee

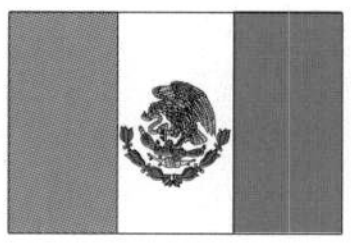

Mexico* 119/G7
Capital: Mexico
Area: 761,601 sq. mi.
1,972,546 sq. km.
Pop.: 102,026,691; growth rate: 1.693%
Govt.: federal republic
Independence: September 16, 1810
U.N. Admission: November 7, 1945
GDP: $777.3 billion; per capita: $8,100
Currency: new Mexican peso

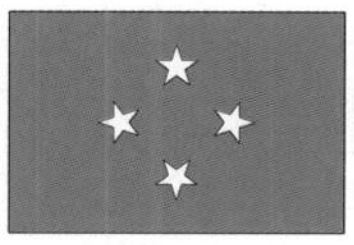

Micronesia* 116/D4
Capital: Palikir
Area: 271 sq. mi.
702 sq. km.
Pop.: 133,144; growth rate: 3.279%
Govt.: constitutional government
Independence: November 3, 1986
U.N. Admission: September 17, 1991
GDP: $205 million; per capita: $1,700
Currency: United States dollar

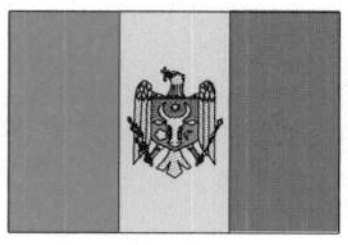

Moldova* 49/H2
Capital: Chişinău
Area: 13,012 sq. mi.
33,700 sq. km.
Pop.: 4,466,758; growth rate: .165%
Govt.: republic
Independence: August 27, 1991
U.N. Admission: March 2, 1992
GDP: $10.8 billion; per capita: $2,400
Currency: Moldovan leu

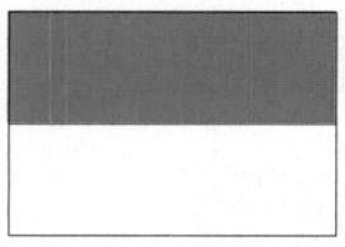

Monaco* 58/J8
Capital: Monaco
Area: 0.7 sq. mi.
1.9 sq. km.
Pop.: 32,231; growth rate: .205%
Govt.: constitutional monarchy
Independence: 1419
U.N. Admission: May 28, 1993
GDP: $800 million; per capita: $25,000
Currency: French franc

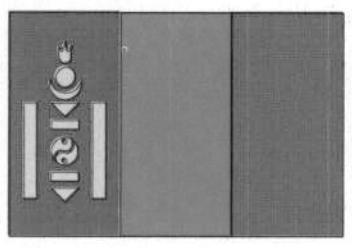

Mongolia* 70/G2
Capital: Ulaanbaatar
Area: 606,163 sq. mi.
1,569,962 sq. km.
Pop.: 2,654,572; growth rate: 1.368%
Govt.: republic
Independence: March 13, 1921
U.N. Admission: October 27, 1961
GDP: $5.1 billion; per capita: $2,060
Currency: tughrik

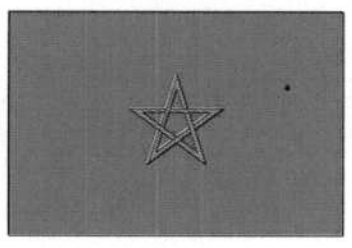

Morocco* 98/D2
Capital: Rabat
Area: 172,414 sq. mi.
446,550 sq. km.
Pop.: 30,205,387; growth rate: 1.795%
Govt.: constitutional monarchy
Independence: March 2, 1956
U.N. Admission: November 12, 1956
GDP: $897.6 billion; per capita: $3,260
Currency: Moroccan dirham

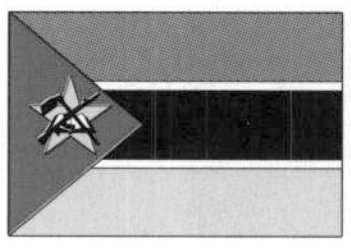

Mozambique* 105/G4
Capital: Maputo
Area: 309,494 sq. mi.
801,590 sq. km.
Pop.: 19,614,345; growth rate: 2.517%
Govt.: republic
Independence: June 25, 1975
U.N. Admission: September 16, 1975
GDP: $12.2 billion; per capita: $670
Currency: metical

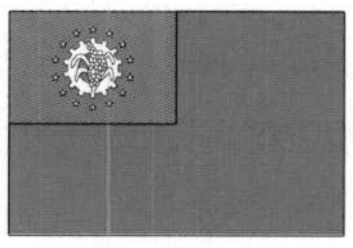

Myanmar (Burma)* 83/G3
Capital: Yangon (Rangoon)
Area: 261,969 sq. mi.
678,500 sq. km.
Pop.: 48,852,098; growth rate: 1.572%
Govt.: military regime
Independence: January 4, 1948
U.N. Admission: April 19, 1948
GDP: $51.5 billion; per capita: $1,120
Currency: kyat

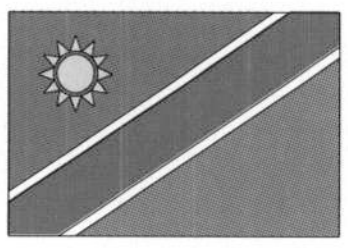

Namibia* 105/C5
Capital: Windhoek
Area: 318,694 sq. mi.
825,418 sq. km.
Pop.: 1,674,116; growth rate: 1.541%
Govt.: republic
Independence: March 21, 1990
U.N. Admission: April 23, 1990
GDP: $6.2 billion; per capita: $3,700
Currency: Namibian dollar

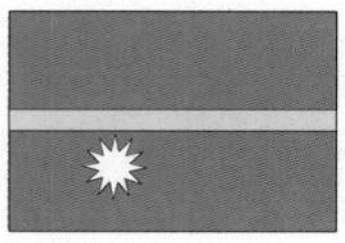

Nauru* 116/F5
Capital: Yaren (district)
Area: 8 sq. mi.
21 sq. km.
Pop.: 10,704; growth rate: 1.333
Govt.: republic
Independence: January 31, 1968
U.N. Admission: September 14, 1999
GDP: $100 million; per capita: $10,000
Currency: Australian dollar

Nepal* 84/D1
Capital: Kāthmāndu
Area: 54,363 sq. mi.
140,800 sq. km.
Pop.: 24,920,211; growth rate: 2.505%
Govt.: parliamentary democracy
Independence: 1768
U.N. Admission: December 14, 1955
GDP: $26.5 billion; per capita: $1,200
Currency: Nepalese rupee

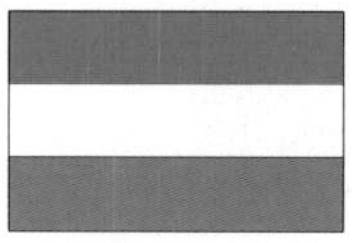

Netherlands* 40/C3
Capital: The Hague; Amsterdam
Area: 14,413 sq. mi.
37,330 sq. km.
Pop.: 15,878,304; growth rate: .426%
Govt.: constitutional monarchy
Independence:1579
U.N. Admission: December 10, 1945
GDP: $317.8 billion; per capita: $20,500
Currency: Netherlands guilder

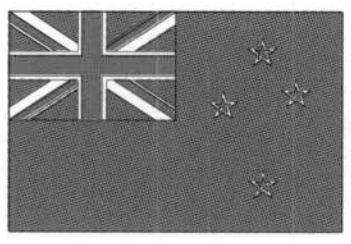

New Zealand* 117/R10
Capital: Wellington
Area: 103,736 sq. mi.
268,676 sq. km.
Pop.: 3,697,850; growth rate: .945%
Govt.: parliamentary democracy
Independence: September 26, 1907
U.N. Admission: October 24, 1945
GDP: $65.6 billion; per capita: $18,500
Currency: New Zealand dollar

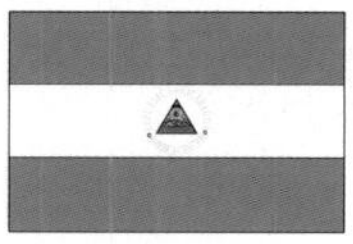

Nicaragua* 145/E3
Capital: Managua
Area: 49,998 sq. mi.
129,494 sq. km.
Pop.: 4,850,976; growth rate: 2.759%
Govt.: republic
Independence: September 15, 1821
U.N. Admission: October 24, 1945
GDP: $7.7 billion; per capita: $1,800
Currency: gold cordoba

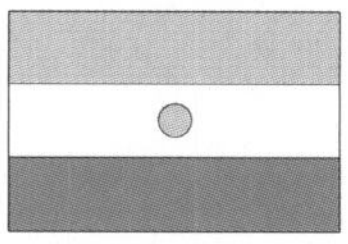

Niger* 96/G4
Capital: Niamey
Area: 489,189 sq. mi.
1,267,000 sq. km.
Pop.: 10,260,316; growth rate: 2.943%
Govt.: republic
Independence: August 3, 1960
U.N. Admission: September 20, 1960
GDP: $5.9 billion; per capita: $640
Currency: CFA franc

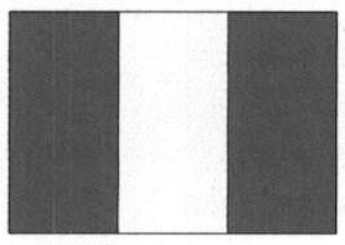

Nigeria* 96/G6
Capital: Abuja
Area: 356,668 sq. mi.
923,770 sq. km.
Pop.: 117,170,948; growth rate: 2.872%
Govt.: military government
Independence: October 1, 1960
U.N. Admission: October 7, 1960
GDP: $143.5 billion; per capita: $1,380
Currency: naira

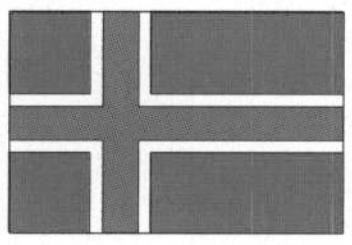

Norway* 37/C3
Capital: Oslo
Area: 125,181 sq. mi.
324,220 sq. km.
Pop.: 4,455,707; growth rate: .368%
Govt.: constitutional monarchy
Independence: October 26, 1905
U.N. Admission: November 27, 1945
GDP: $114.1 billion; per capita: $26,200
Currency: Norwegian kroner

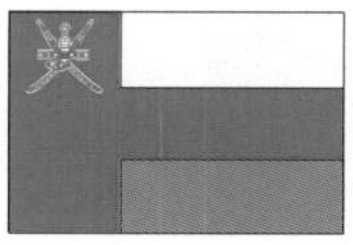

Oman* 89/G4
Capital: Muscat
Area: 82,031 sq. mi.
212,460 sq. km.
Pop: 2,532,556; growth rate: 3.449%
Govt.: monarchy
Independence: 1650
U.N. Admission: October 7, 1971
GDP: $20.8 billion; per capita: $9,500
Currency: Omani rial

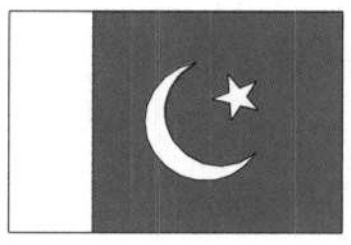

Pakistan* 89/H3
Capital: Islamabad
Area: 310,403 sq. mi.
803,944 sq. km.
Pop.: 141,145,344; growth rate: 2.152%
Govt.: federal republic
Independence: August 14, 1947
U.N. Admission: September 30, 1947
GDP: $296.5 billion; per capita: $2,300
Currency: Pakistani rupee

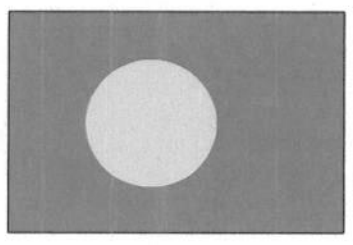

Palau* 116/C4
Capital: Koror
Area: 177 sq. mi.
458 sq. km.
Pop.: 18,827; growth rate: 1.912%
Govt.: constitutional government
Independence: October 1, 1994
U.N. Admission: December 15, 1994
GDP: $81.8 million; per capita: $5,000
Currency: United States dollar

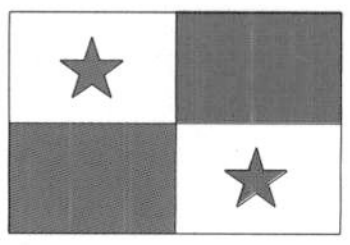

Panama* 145/F4
Capital: Panamá
Area: 30,193 sq. mi.
78,200 sq. km.
Pop.: 2,821,085; growth rate: 1.507%
Govt.: constitutional republic
Independence: November 3, 1903
U.N. Admission: November 13, 1945
GDP: $14 billion; per capita: $5,300
Currency: balboa

World Flags and Reference Guide

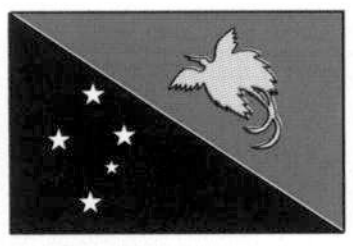

Papua New Guinea* 116/D5
Capital: Port Moresby
Area: 178,259 sq. mi.
461,690 sq. km.
Pop.: 4,811,939; growth rate: 2.233%
Govt.: parliamentary democracy
Independence: September 16, 1975
U.N. Admission: October 10, 1975
GDP: $10.7 billion; per capita: $2,400
Currency: kina

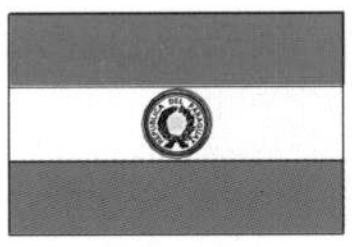

Paraguay* 147/C5
Capital: Asunción
Area: 157,047 sq. mi.
406,752 sq. km.
Pop.: 5,579,503; growth rate: 2.627%
Govt.: republic
Independence: May 14, 1811
U.N. Admission: October 24, 1945
GDP: $17.7 billion; per capita: $3,200
Currency: guarani

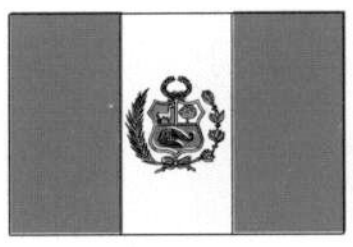

Peru* 156/C3
Capital: Lima
Area: 496,223 sq. mi.
1,285,220 sq. km.
Pop.: 27,135,689; growth rate: 1.877%
Govt.: republic
Independence: July 28, 1821
U.N. Admission: October 31, 1945
GDP: $92 billion; per capita: $3,800
Currency: nuevo sol

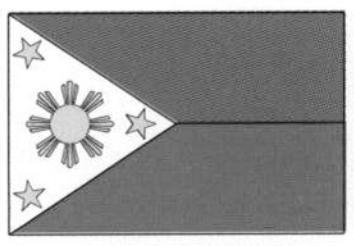

Philippines* 79/D5
Capital: Manila
Area: 115,830 sq. mi.
300,000 sq. km.
Pop.: 80,961,430; growth rate: 1.992%
Govt.: republic
Independence: July 4, 1946
U.N. Admission: October 24, 1945
GDP: $194.2 billion; per capita: $2,600
Currency: Philippine peso

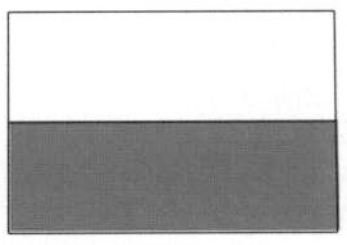

Poland* 41/K2
Capital: Warsaw
Area: 120,725 sq. mi.
312,678 sq. km.
Pop.: 38,644,184; growth rate: .134%
Govt.: democratic state
Independence: November 11, 1918
U.N. Admission: October 24, 1945
GDP: $246.3 billion; per capita: $6,400
Currency: zloty

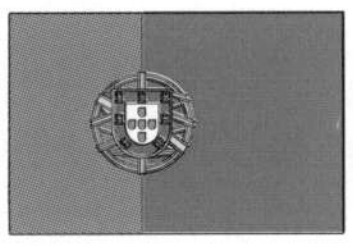

Portugal* 44/A3
Capital: Lisbon
Area: 35,552 sq. mi.
92,080 sq. km.
Pop.: 9,902,147; growth rate: -.194%
Govt.: parliamentary democracy
Independence: October 5, 1910
U.N. Admission: December 14, 1955
GDP: $122.1 billion; per capita: $12,400
Currency: Portuguese escudo

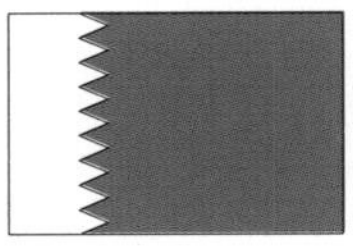

Qatar* 88/F3
Capital: Doha
Area: 4,247 sq. mi.
11,000 sq. km.
Pop.: 749,542; growth rate: 3.442%
Govt.: traditional monarchy
Independence: September 3, 1971
U.N. Admission: September 21, 1971
GDP: $11.7 billion; per capita: $21,300
Currency: Qatari riyal

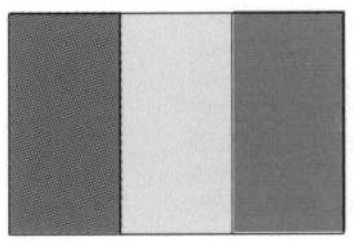

Romania* 49/F3
Capital: Bucharest
Area: 91,699 sq. mi.
237,500 sq. km.
Pop.: 22,291,200; growth rate: -.153%
Govt.: republic
Independence:1881
U.N. Admission: December 14, 1955
GDP: $113.2 billion; per capita: $5,200
Currency: leu

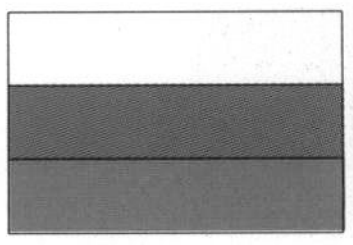

Russia* 64/H3
Capital: Moscow
Area: 6,592,735 sq. mi.
17,075,200 sq. km.
Pop.: 145,904,542; growth rate: -.342%
Govt.: federation
Independence: August 24, 1991
U.N. Admission: October 24, 1945
GDP: $767 billion; per capita: $5,200
Currency: ruble

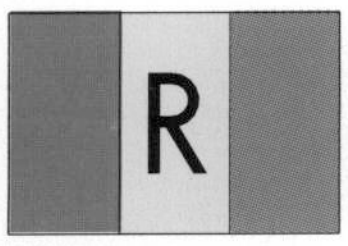

Rwanda* 104/A3
Capital: Kigali
Area: 10,169 sq. mi.
26,337 sq. km.
Pop.: 8,336,995; growth rate: 1.987%
Govt.: republic
Independence: July 1, 1962
U.N. Admission: September 18, 1962
GDP: $3.8 billion; per capita: $400
Currency: Rwandan franc

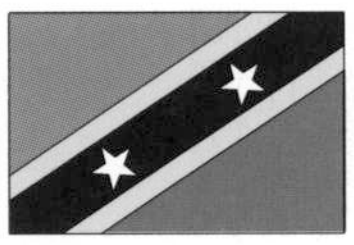

Saint Kitts & Nevis* 141/N8
Capital: Basseterre
Area: 104 sq. mi.
269 sq. km.
Pop.: 43,441; growth rate: 1.455%
Govt.: constitutional monarchy
Independence: September 19, 1983
U.N. Admission: September 23, 1983
GDP: $235 million; per capita: $5,700
Currency: EC dollar

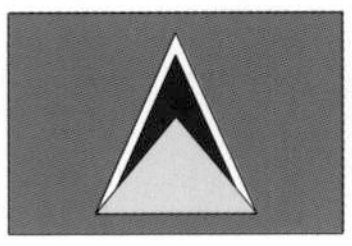

Saint Lucia* 141/N9
Capital: Castries
Area: 239 sq. mi.
620 sq. km.
Pop.: 155,678; growth rate: 1.055%
Govt.: parliamentary democracy
Independence: February 22, 1979
U.N. Admission: September 18, 1979
GDP: $695 million; per capita: $4,400
Currency: EC dollar

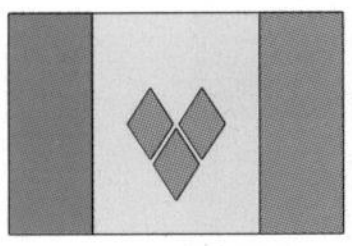

St. Vinc. & Grenadines* 141/N9
Capital: Kingstown
Area: 131 sq. mi.
340 sq. km.
Pop.: 121,188; growth rate: .539%
Govt.: parliamentary democracy
Independence: October 27, 1979
U.N. Admission: September 16, 1980
GDP: $259 million; per capita: $2,190
Currency: EC dollar

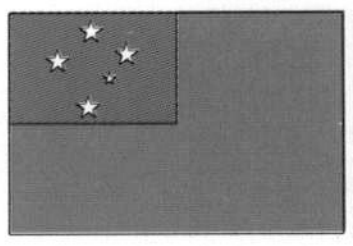

Samoa* 117/H6
Capital: Apia
Area: 1,104 sq. mi.
2,860 sq. km.
Pop.: 235,302; growth rate: 2.274%
Govt.: parliamentary democracy
Independence: January 1, 1962
U.N. Admission: December 15, 1976
GDP: $415 million; per capita: $1,900
Currency: tala

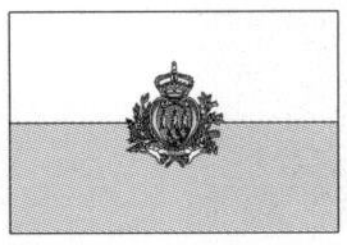

San Marino* 59/F5
Capital: San Marino
Area: 23.4 sq. mi.
60.6 sq. km.
Pop.: 25,215; growth rate: .583%
Govt.: republic
Independence: 301 A.D.
U.N. Admission: March 2, 1992
GDP: $408 million; per capita: $16,900
Currency: Italian lira

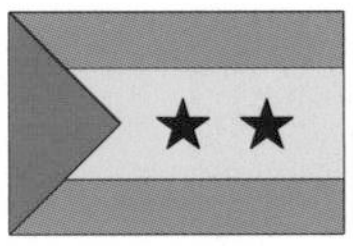

São Tomé & Príncipe* 96/F7
Capital: São Tomé
Area: 371 sq. mi.
960 sq. km.
Pop.: 159,832; growth rate: 3.161%
Govt.: republic
Independence: July 12, 1975
U.N. Admission: September 16, 1975
GDP: $149 million; per capita: $1,000
Currency: dobra

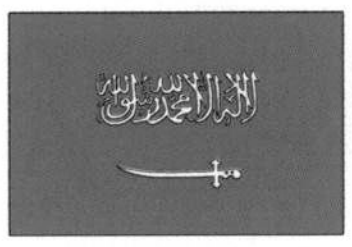

Saudi Arabia* 88/D4
Capital: Riyadh
Area: 756,981 sq. mi.
1,960,582 sq. km.
Pop.: 22,245,751; growth rate: 3.384%
Govt.: monarchy
Independence: September 23, 1932
U.N. Admission: October 24, 1945
GDP: $205.6 billion; per capita: $10,600
Currency: Saudi riyal

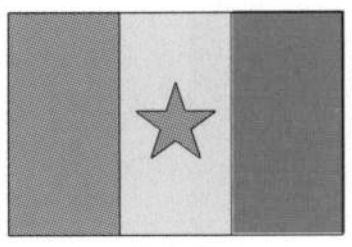

Senegal* 102/B3
Capital: Dakar
Area: 75,749 sq. mi.
196,190 sq. km.
Pop.: 10,390,296; growth rate: 3.304%
Govt.: multiparty democracy
Independence: April 4, 1960
U.N. Admission: September 28, 1960
GDP: $15.6 billion; per capita: $1,700
Currency: CFA franc

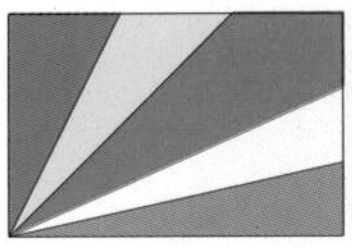

Seychelles* 23/M6
Capital: Victoria
Area: 176 sq. mi.
455 sq. km.
Pop.: 79,672; growth rate: .628%
Govt.: republic
Independence: June 29, 1976
U.N. Admission: September 1, 1976
GDP: $450 million; per capita: $6,000
Currency: Seychelles rupee

Sierra Leone* 102/B4
Capital: Freetown
Area: 27,699 sq. mi.
71,740 sq. km.
Pop.: 5,509,263; growth rate: 3.550%
Govt.: constitutional democracy
Independence: April 27, 1961
U.N. Admission: September 27, 1961
GDP: $4.7 billion; per capita: $980
Currency: leone

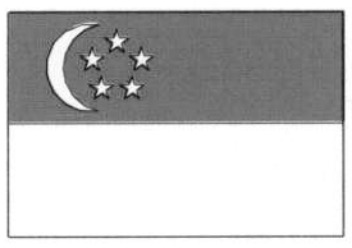

Singapore* 80/B3
Capital: Singapore
Area: 244 sq. mi.
632.6 sq. km.
Pop.: 3,571,710; growth rate: 1.107%
Govt.: republic
Independence: August 6, 1965
U.N. Admission: September 21, 1965
GDP: $72.2 billion; per capita: $21,200
Currency: Singapore dollar

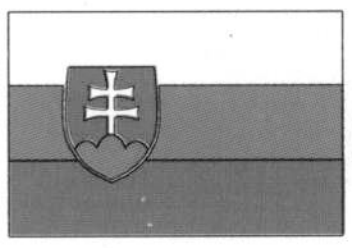

Slovakia* 41/K4
Capital: Bratislava
Area: 18,859 sq. mi.
48,845 sq. km.
Pop.: 5,401,134; growth rate: .145%
Govt.: parliamentary democracy
Independence: January 1, 1993
U.N. Admission: January 19, 1993
GDP: $42.8 billion; per capita: $8,000
Currency: koruna

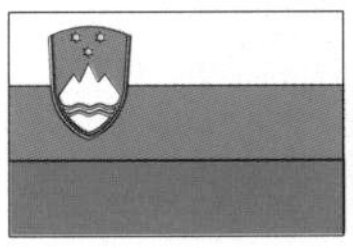

Slovenia* 48/B3
Capital: Ljubljana
Area: 7,836 sq. mi.
20,296 sq. km.
Pop.: 1,970,056; growth rate: -.011%
Govt.: emerging democracy
Independence: June 25, 1991
U.N. Admission: May 22, 1992
GDP: $24 billion; per capita: $12,300
Currency: tolar

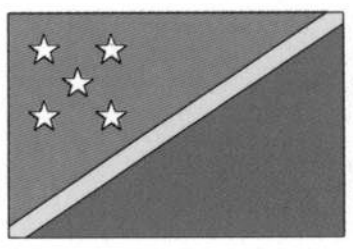

Solomon Islands* 116/E6
Capital: Honiara
Area: 10,985 sq. mi.
28,450 sq. km.
Pop.: 470,000; growth rate: 3.118%
Govt.: parliamentary democracy
Independence: July 7, 1978
U.N. Admission: September 19, 1978
GDP: $1.2 billion; per capita: $3,000
Currency: Solomon Islands dollar

Somalia* 97/Q6
Capital: Mogadishu
Area: 246,200 sq. mi.
637,658 sq. km.
Pop.: 7,433,922; growth rate: 3.927%
Govt.: none
Independence: July 1, 1960
U.N. Admission: September 20, 1960
GDP: $3.6 billion; per capita: $500
Currency: Somali shilling

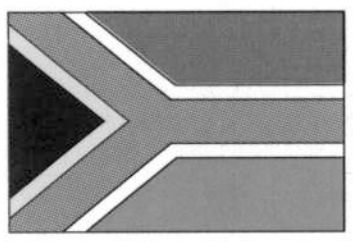

South Africa* 105/D6
Capital: Cape Town; Pretoria
Area: 471,008 sq. mi.
1,219,912 sq. km.
Pop.: 43,981,758; growth rate: 1.220%
Govt.: republic
Independence: May 31, 1910
U.N. Admission: November 7, 1945
GDP: $227 billion; per capita: $5,400
Currency: rand

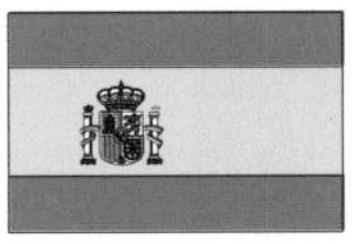

Spain* 44/C2
Capital: Madrid
Area: 194,884 sq. mi.
504,750 sq. km.
Pop.: 39,208,236; growth rate: .111%
Govt.: parliamentary monarchy
Independence: 1492
U.N. Admission: December 14, 1955
GDP: $593 billion; per capita: $15,300
Currency: peseta

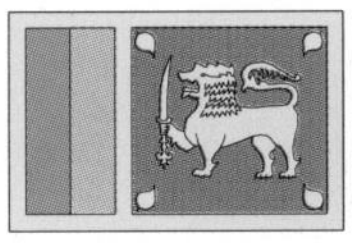

Sri Lanka* 82/D6
Capital: Colombo
Area: 25,332 sq. mi.
65,610 sq. km.
Pop.: 19,355,053; growth rate: 1.083%
Govt.: republic
Independence: February 4, 1948
U.N. Admission: December 14, 1955
GDP: $69.7 billion; per capita: $3,760
Currency: Sri Lankan rupee

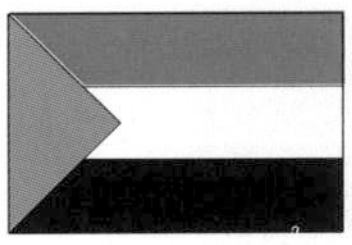

Sudan* 97/L5
Capital: Khartoum
Area: 967,494 sq. mi.
2,505,809 sq. km.
Pop.: 35,530,371; growth rate: 3.310%
Govt.: transitional
Independence: January 1, 1956
U.N. Admission: November 12, 1956
GDP: $26.6 billion; per capita: $860
Currency: Sudanese pound

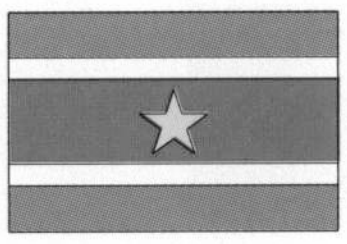

Suriname* 153/G3
Capital: Paramaribo
Area: 63,039 sq. mi.
163,270 sq. km.
Pop.: 434,093; growth rate: .650%
Govt.: republic
Independence: November 25, 1975
U.N. Admission: December 4, 1975
GDP: $1.4 billion; per capita: $3,150
Currency: Surinamese guilder

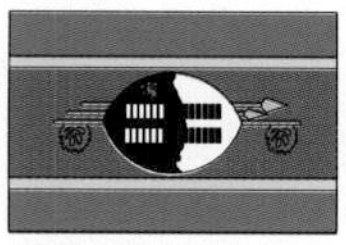

Swaziland* 107/E2
Capital: Mbabane; Lobamba
Area: 6,703 sq. mi.
17,360 sq. km.
Pop.: 1,004,072; growth rate: 1.859%
Govt.: monarchy
Independence: September 6, 1968
U.N. Admission: September 24, 1968
GDP: $3.8 billion; per capita: $3,800
Currency: lilangeni

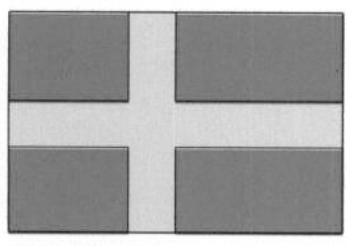

Sweden* 37/E3
Capital: Stockholm
Area: 173,731 sq. mi.
449,964 sq. km.
Pop.: 8,938,559; growth rate: .320%
Govt.: constitutional monarchy
Independence: June 6, 1523
U.N. Admission: November 19, 1946
GDP: $184.3 billion; per capita: $20,800
Currency: Swedish krona

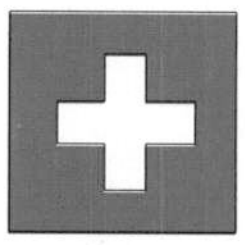

Switzerland 59/D4
Capital: Bern
Area: 15,943 sq. mi.
41,292 sq. km.
Pop.: 7,288,715; growth rate: .168%
Govt.: federal republic
Independence: August 1, 1291
U.N. Admission: observer status
GDP: $161.3 billion; per capita: $22,600
Currency: Swiss franc

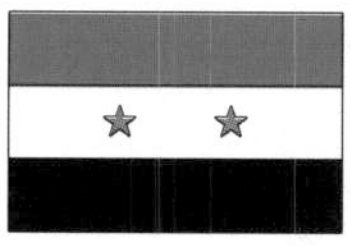

Syria* 90/D3
Capital: Damascus
Area: 71,498 sq. mi.
185,180 sq. km.
Pop.: 17,758,925; growth rate: 3.081%
Govt.: military regime
Independence: April 17, 1946
U.N. Admission: October 24, 1945
GDP: $98.3 billion; per capita: $6,300
Currency: Syrian pound

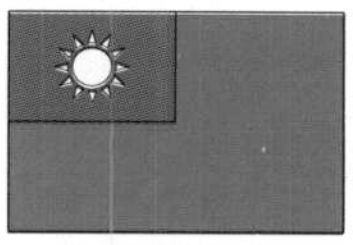

Taiwan 79/D3
Capital: T'aipei
Area: 13,892 sq. mi.
35,980 sq. km.
Pop.: 22,319,222; growth rate: .925%
Govt.: multiparty democracy
Independence: 1949 (Nationalist govt.)
U.N. Admission: non-member
GDP: $315 billion; per capita: $14,700
Currency: New Taiwan dollar

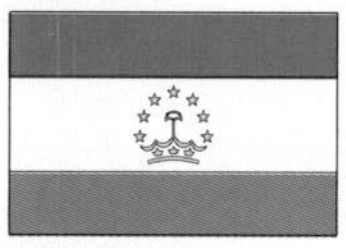

Tajikistan* 87/E5
Capital: Dushanbe
Area: 55,251 sq. mi.
143,100 sq. km.
Pop.: 6,194,373; growth rate: 1.549%
Govt.: republic
Independence: September 9, 1991
U.N. Admission: March 2, 1992
GDP: $5.4 billion; per capita: $920
Currency: Tajikistani ruble

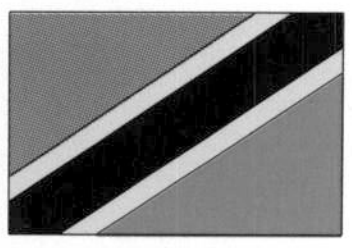

Tanzania* 104/B4
Capital: Dar es Salaam
Area: 364,699 sq. mi.
945,090 sq. km.
Pop.: 31,962,769; growth rate: 2.239%
Govt.: republic
Independence: April 26, 1964
U.N. Admission: December 14, 1961
GDP: $18.9 billion; per capita: $650
Currency: Tanzanian shilling

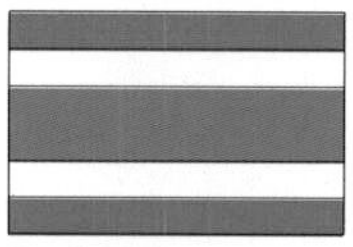

Thailand* 78/C3
Capital: Bangkok
Area: 198,455 sq. mi.
513,998 sq. km.
Pop. 61,163,833; growth rate: .892%
Govt.: constitutional monarchy
Independence: 1238 (traditional date)
U.N. Admission: December 16, 1946
GDP: $455.7 billion; per capita: $7,700
Currency: baht

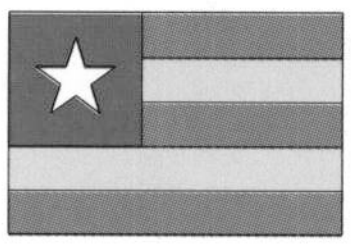

Togo* 103/F4
Capital: Lomé
Area: 21,927 sq. mi.
56,790 sq. km.
Pop.: 5,262,611; growth rate: 3.498%
Govt.: transitional government
Independence: April 27, 1960
U.N. Admission: September 20, 1960
GDP: $4.45 billion; per capita: $970
Currency: CFA franc

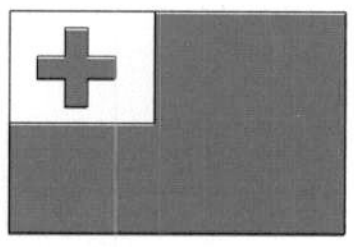

Tonga* 117/H7
Capital: Nuku'alofa
Area: 289 sq. mi.
748 sq. km.
Pop.: 109,959; growth rate: .799%
Govt.: constitutional monarchy
Independence: June 4, 1970
U.N. Admission: September 14, 1999
GDP: $228 million; per capita: $2,140
Currency: pa'anga

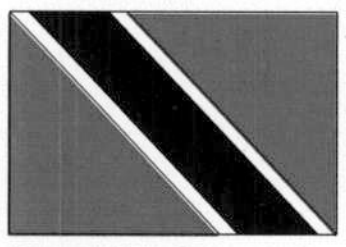

Trinidad & Tobago* 141/N10
Capital: Port-of-Spain
Area: 1,980 sq. mi.
5,128 sq. km.
Pop.: 1,086,908; growth rate: -1.427%
Govt.: parliamentary democracy
Independence: August 31, 1962
U.N. Admission: September 18, 1962
GDP: $17.1 billion; per capita: $13,500
Currency: Trinidad and Tobago dollar

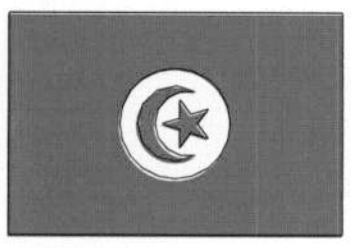

Tunisia* 99/H2
Capital: Tunis
Area: 63,170 sq. mi.
163,610 sq. km.
Pop.: 9,645,499; growth rate: 1.361%
Govt.: republic
Independence: March 20, 1956
U.N. Admission: November 12, 1956
GDP: $43.3 billion; per capita: $4,800
Currency: Tunisian dollar

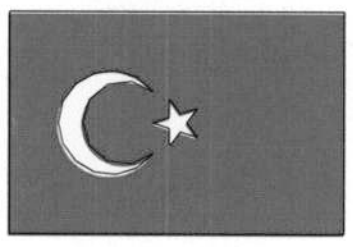

Turkey* 90/C2
Capital: Ankara
Area: 301,382 sq. mi.
780,580 sq. km.
Pop.: 66,620,120; growth rate: 1.524%
Govt.: parliamentary democracy
Independence: October 29, 1923
U.N. Admission: December 24, 1945
GDP: $379.1 billion; per capita: $6,100
Currency: Turkish lira

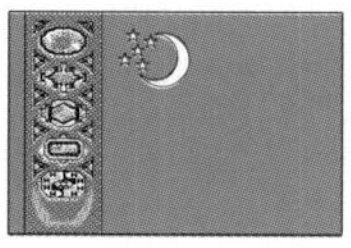

Turkmenistan* 87/C5
Capital: Ashgabat
Area: 188,455 sq. mi.
488,100 sq. km.
Pop.: 4,435,507; growth rate: 1.562%
Govt.: republic
Independence: October 27, 1971
U.N. Admission: March 2, 1992
GDP: $11.8 billion; per capita: $2,840
Currency: Turkmen manat

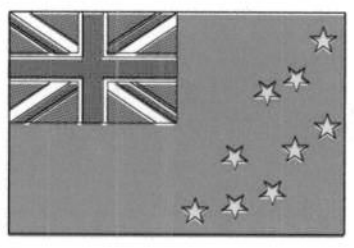

Tuvalu 116/G5
Capital: Funafuti
Area: 10 sq. mi.
26 sq. km.
Pop.: 10,730; growth rate: 1.333%
Govt.: democracy
Independence: October 1, 1978
U.N. Admission: non-member
GDP: $57.8 million; per capita: $800
Currency: Tuvaluan or Australian dollar

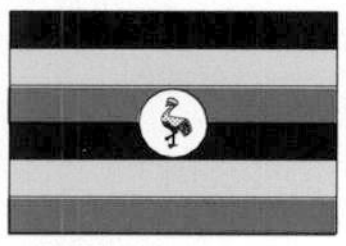

Uganda* 104/B2
Capital: Kampala
Area: 91,135 sq. mi.
236,040 sq. km.
Pop.: 23,451,687; growth rate: 2.766%
Govt.: republic
Independence: October 9, 1962
U.N. Admission: October 25, 1962
GDP: $16.8 billion; per capita: $900
Currency: Ugandan shilling

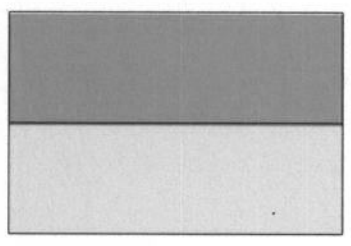

Ukraine* 62/D2
Capital: Kiev
Area: 233,089 sq. mi.
603,700 sq. km.
Pop.: 49,506,779; growth rate: -.605%
Govt.: republic
Independence: December 1, 1991
U.N. Admission: October 24, 1945
GDP: $161.1 billion; per capita: $3,170
Currency: hryvnia

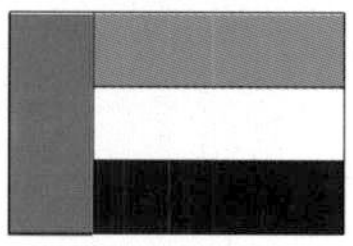

United Arab Emirates* 88/F4
Capital: Abu Dhabi
Area: 29,182 sq. mi.
75,581 sq. km.
Pop.: 2,386,472; growth rate: 1.781%
Govt.: federation
Independence: December 2, 1971
U.N. Admission: December 9, 1971
GDP: $72.9 billion; per capita: $23,800
Currency: Emirian dirham

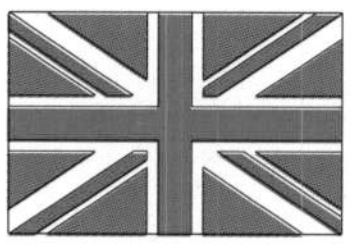

United Kingdom* 31/R9
Capital: London
Area: 94,525 sq. mi.
244,820 sq. km.
Pop.: 59,247,439; growth rate: .217%
Govt.: constitutional monarchy
Independence: January 1, 1801
U.N. Admission: October 24, 1945
GDP: $1.19 trillion; per capita: $20,400
Currency: British pound

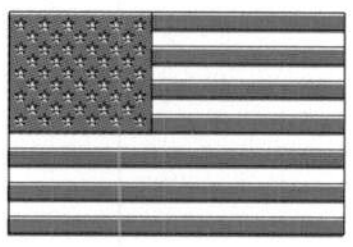

United States* 124
Capital: Washington, D.C.
Area: 3,618,765 sq. mi.
9,372,610 sq. km.
Pop.: 274,943,496; growth rate: .840%
Govt.: federal republic
Independence: July 4, 1776
U.N. Admission: October 24, 1945
GDP: $7.61 trillion; per capita: $28,600
Currency: United States dollar

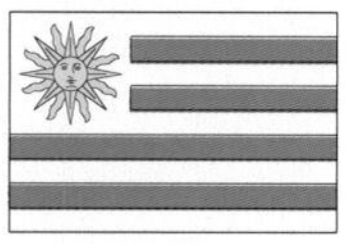

Uruguay* 157/E3
Capital: Montevideo
Area: 68,039 sq. mi.
176,220 sq. km.
Pop.: 3,332,782; growth rate: .736%
Govt.: republic
Independence: August 25, 1828
U.N. Admission: December 18, 1945
GDP: $26 billion; per capita: $8,000
Currency: Uruguayan pesos

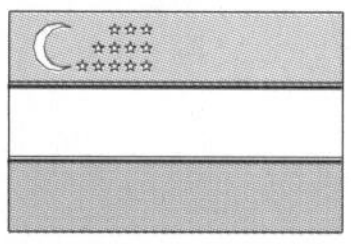

Uzbekistan* 87/D4
Capital: Tashkent
Area: 172,741 sq. mi.
447,400 sq. km.
Pop.: 24,422,518; growth rate: 1.314%
Govt.: republic
Independence: August 31, 1991
U.N. Admission: March 2, 1992
GDP: $57 billion; per capita: $2,430
Currency: som

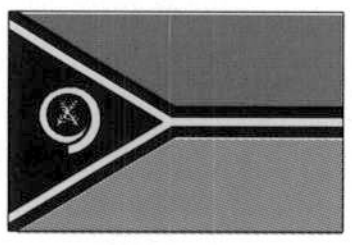

Vanuatu* 116/F6
Capital: Port-Vila
Area: 5,699 sq. mi.
14,760 sq. km.
Pop.: 192,848; growth rate: 1.970%
Govt.: republic
Independence: July 30, 1980
U.N. Admission: September 15, 1981
GDP: $219 million; per capita: $1,230
Currency: vatu

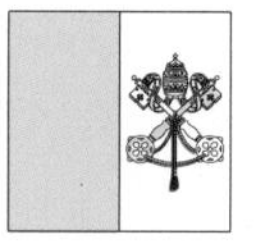

Vatican City 46/C2
Capital: —
Area: 0.17 sq. mi.
0.44 sq. km.
Pop.: 860; growth rate: 1.15%
Govt.: monarchial-sacredotal state
Independence: February 11, 1929
U.N. Admission: observer status
GDP: N/A
Currency: Vatican lira

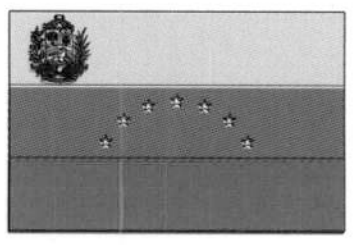

Venezuela* 153/E3
Capital: Caracas
Area: 352,143 sq. mi.
912,050 sq. km.
Pop.: 23,595,822; growth rate: 1.646%
Govt.: republic
Independence: July 5, 1811
U.N. Admission: November 15, 1945
GDP: $197 billion; per capita: $9,000
Currency: bolivar

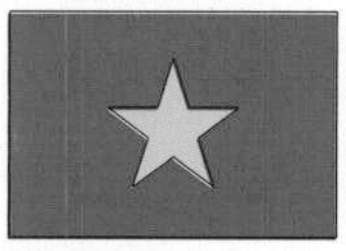

Vietnam* 78/D2
Capital: Hanoi
Area: 127,243 sq. mi.
329,560 sq. km.
Pop.: 78,349,503; growth rate: 1.300%
Govt.: Communist state
Independence: September 2, 1945
U.N. Admission: September 20, 1977
GDP: $108.7 billion; per capita: $1,470
Currency: new dong

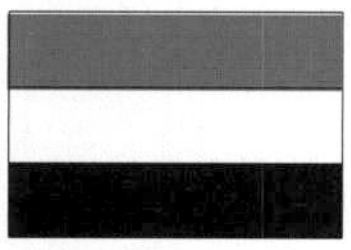

Yemen* 88/E5
Capital: Sanaa
Area: 203,849 sq. mi.
527,970 sq. km.
Pop.: 17,521,085; growth rate: 3.376%
Govt.: republic
Independence: May 22, 1990
U.N. Admission: September 30, 1947
GDP: $39.1 billion; per capita: $2,900
Currency: Yemeni rial

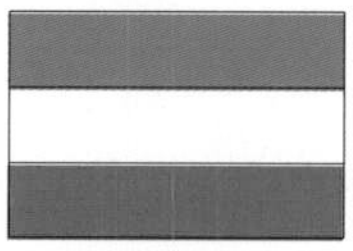

Yugoslavia* 48/D3
Capital: Belgrade
Area: 39,517 sq. mi.
102,350 sq. km.
Pop.: 11,210,243; growth rate: .039%
Govt.: republic
Independence: April 11, 1992
U.N. Admission: October 24, 1945
GDP: $21 billion; per capita: $1,900
Currency: Yugoslav new dinar

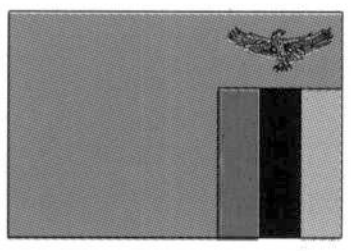

Zambia* 105/E3
Capital: Lusaka
Area: 290,583 sq. mi.
752,610 sq. km.
Pop.: 9,872,007; growth rate: 2.152%
Govt.: republic
Independence: October 24, 1964
U.N. Admission: December 1, 1964
GDP: $9.7 billion; per capita: $1,060
Currency: Zambian kwacha

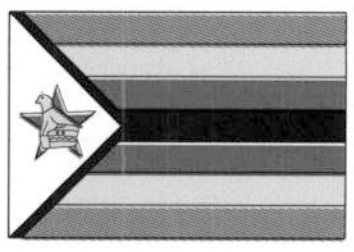

Zimbabwe* 105/E4
Capital: Harare
Area: 150,803 sq. mi.
390,580 sq. km.
Pop.: 11,272,013; growth rate: .920%
Govt.: parliamentary democracy
Independence: April 18, 1980
U.N. Admission: August 25, 1980
GDP: $26.4 billion; per capita: $2,340
Currency: Zimbabwean dollar

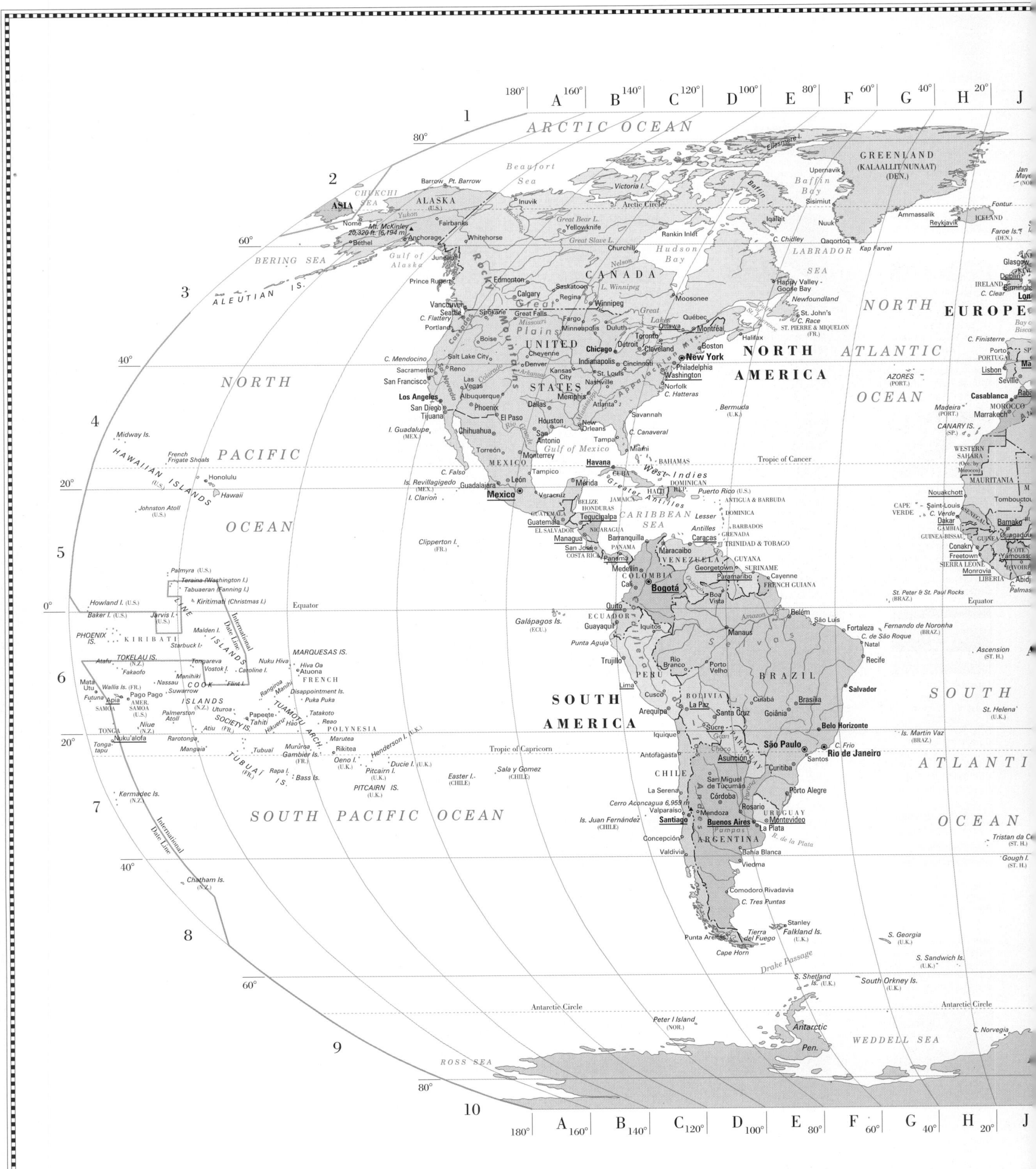

World

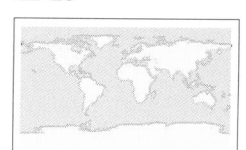

K 20° L 40° M 60° N 80° P 100° Q 120° R 140° S 160° T 180°

ARCTIC OCEAN

FRANZ JOSEF LAND (RUS.)

SVALBARD (NOR.)

Severnaya Zemlya

New Siberian Is.

80°

BARENTS SEA

Kara Sea

Hammerfest Tromsø North Cape Murmansk

Novaya Zemlya

Khatanga

Noril'sk

Norden

Kiruna Oulu

Nar'yan-Mar Vorkuta Salekhard

FINLAND Helsinki

St. Petersburg Nizhniy Novgorod Perm' Nizhnivartovsk Tomsk

Verkhoyansk

Arctic Circle

60°

BERING SEA

SEA OF OKHOTSK

Anadyr

RUSSIA

Siberia

Tura

Yakutsk

Magadan

Kamchatka

Petropavlovsk-Kamchatskiy

Mys Lopatka

Int'l Date Line

3

Moscow Yaroslavl' Izhevsk Yekaterinburg

Minsk Smolensk Tula Ryazan' Ufa Chelyabinsk Omsk Novosibirsk Krasnoyarsk Bratsk L. Baykal Chita

Blagoveshchensk Okhotsk Khabarovsk Sakhalin

KAZAKHSTAN Astana Barnaul Novokuznetsk Irkutsk Ulan-Ude Choybalsan Qiqihar Harbin Vladivostok N. KOREA Hokkaido Sapporo

40°

Berlin Warsaw POLAND BELARUS KIEV UKRAINE Kharkov Volgograd Astrakhan' Aral Sea Balkhash Almaty Yining Ürümqi MONGOLIA Gobi Ulaanbaatar Baotou Shenyang Changchun Jilin Pyongyang Seoul JAPAN Sendai Tōkyō Yokohama

NORTH PACIFIC OCEAN

Budapest Bucharest Istanbul Ankara Tashkent UZBEKISTAN KYRGYZSTAN Dushanbe TAJIKISTAN Takla Makan Tibet Lanzhou Beijing Tianjin Dalian Pusan S. KOREA Kyōto Ōsaka Kōbe Fukuoka Kyūshū

Rome Athens Izmir TURKEY Adana TURKMEN. Ashgabat Mashhad Kabul Islāmābād Lhasa Xi'an Taiyuan Jinan Nanjing Shanghai Huang CHINA SEA Okinawa RYUKYU IS. (JAP.) 4

Tehrān Tabriz Esfahān AFGHANISTAN Lahore Delhi NEPAL Mt. Everest 8,848 m BHUTAN Chengdu Chongqing Wuhan Changsha Fuzhou T'aipei TAIWAN BONIN IS. (JAP.)

Baghdad IRAQ IRAN Shīrāz PAKISTAN New Delhi Kānpur BANGLA- DESH Dhaka MYANMAR Guiyang Guangzhou HONG KONG VOLCANO IS. (JAP.) Iwo Jima Minami-Tori-Shima (JAP.) Tropic of Cancer

Alexandria Cairo Amman Damascus Riyadh Karāchi Ahmadābād Hyderābād Calcutta Mandalay Nanning Hainan PHILIPPINE SEA Farallon de Pajaros Maug Is. Wake I. (U.S.) 20°

SAUDI ARABIA Mecca Medina BAHRAIN QATAR U.A.E. Muscat OMAN Mumbai INDIA Pune Hyderabad Bangalore Chennai Yangon THAI- LAND VIETNAM Manila C. Engaño Luzon NORTHERN MARIANAS (U.S.) Pagan Alamagan Anathan Saipan Guam (U.S.)

LIBYA EGYPT Aswān Port Sudan Sabhā Asyūt RED SEA YEMEN Sanaa Gulf of Aden Socotra (YEMEN) Caseyr ARABIAN SEA Lakshadweep Is. (INDIA) Coimbatore Bangkok Phnom Penh Ho Chi Minh City CAMBODIA SOUTH CHINA SEA Palawan PHILIPPINES Samar Davao Mindanao Yap Is. Ulithi Ngulu Hall Is. Namonuito Truk Is. Hagåtña CAROLINE IS. 5

CHAD SUDAN Khartoum Omdurman ERITREA Asmara DJIBOUTI SRI LANKA Colombo Dondra Head MALDIVES Male ANDAMAN AND NICOBAR IS. (INDIA) C. Comorin BRUNEI MALAYSIA SINGA- PORE Kuala Lumpur Medan Sulu Sea Celebes Sea Koror Babelthuap PALAU Elato Lamotrek Satawan Sonsorol Is. FED. STATES OF MICRONESIA

NIGER NIGERIA N'Djamena Abuja CENTRAL AFRICAN REP. ETHIOPIA SOMALIA Mogadishu Malakāl Juba Sumatra Borneo Celebes Halmahera Equator 0°

Bangui Yaoundé CAMEROON GABON DEM. REP. OF THE CONGO UGANDA KENYA Nairobi Kampala Lake Victoria Jakarta Palembang INDONESIA Banjarmasin Ujung Pandang Banda Sea New Guinea PAPUA NEW GUINEA New Ireland Bismarck Arch. Admiralty Is. Ontong Java Nukumanu Butaritari GILBERT Tarawa NAURU KIRIBATI Banaba Tabiteuea Arorae

Brazzaville Kinshasa RWANDA BURUNDI L. Tanganyika TANZANIA Dar es Salaam Bandung Java Bali Surabaya Ujung Pandang Sumba Timor Arafura Sea New Britain Bougainville SOLOMON IS. Honiara Guadalcanal Sta. Isabel Malaita Nanumea TUVALU Funafuti 6

ANGOLA Luanda Benguela Huambo ZAMBIA MALAWI Lilongwe L. Nyasa Mbeya L. Tanganyika Mombasa SEYCHELLES Mahé Amirante Is. (SEY.) Aldabra Is. (SEY.) Farquhar Group COMOROS Mayotte (FR.) INDIAN OCEAN BRITISH INDIAN OCEAN TERR. Chagos Arch. Diego Garcia Christmas I. (AUSTL.) Cocos Is. (AUSTL.) Timor Sea Darwin Gulf of Carpentaria Cape York Pen. Port Moresby Torres Str. CORAL SEA Rennell I. San Cristobal Sta. Cruz Is. (S.I.) Espiritu Santo VANUATU Port-Vila Rotuma I. (FIJI) Suva FIJI

NAMIBIA BOTSWANA ZIMBABWE Harare MOZAMBIQUE MADAGASCAR Antananarivo Toamasina Tanjona Vohimena Réunion (FR.) MAURITIUS Port Louis Rodrigues (MRTS.) Tromelin I. (FR.) Agalega Is. (MRTS.) Amsterdam I. (FR.) Tropic of Capricorn North West C. Port Hedland Great Sandy Desert Alice Springs Rockhampton New Caledonia (FR.) Nouméa Loyalty Is. 20°

Windhoek Gaborone Pretoria Johannesburg Bloemfontein Maputo SWAZILAND LESOTHO Durban Kalahari Orange SOUTH AFRICA Cape Town Cape of Good Hope C. Agulhas Port Elizabeth Toliara **AUSTRALIA** Geraldton Perth Kalgoorlie Great Victoria Desert Whyalla Broken Hill Darling Newcastle Lord Howe I. (AUSTL.) Norfolk I. (AUSTL.) North C. 7

Prince Edward Is. (S. AFR.) Crozet Is. (FR.) Kerguélen (FR.) St. Paul I. (FR.) C. Leeuwin Albany Great Australian Bight Adelaide Murray Canberra Sydney Mt. Kosciusko 2,228 m Melbourne TASMAN SEA North I. Auckland NEW ZEALAND Wellington 40°

McDonald Is. (AUSTL.) South East C. Hobart Tasmania Macquarie I. (AUSTL.) Campbell I. (N.Z.) Bounty Is. (N.Z.) Antipodes Is. (N.Z.) Auckland Is. (N.Z.) Christchurch South C. Dunedin South I. 8

Bouvet I. (NOR.) 60°

Antarctic Circle

C. Batterbee

ANTARCTICA

C. Adare

ROSS SEA 9

80° 10

K 20° L 40° M 60° N 80° P 100° Q 120° R 140° S 160° T 180°

© HAMMOND WORLD ATLAS CORPORATION CJ-1-AAA

POPULATION OF CITIES AND TOWNS
⊛ OVER 5,000,000   ⊕ 500,000 - 1,999,999
⊕ 2,000,000 - 4,999,999   ○ UNDER 500,000

SCALE 1:79,500,000   ROBINSON PROJECTION   STANDARD PARALLELS 38°N AND 38°S
MILES 0 1000 2000 3000 4000
KILOMETERS 0 1000 2000 4000

World - Physical

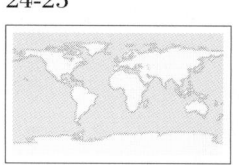

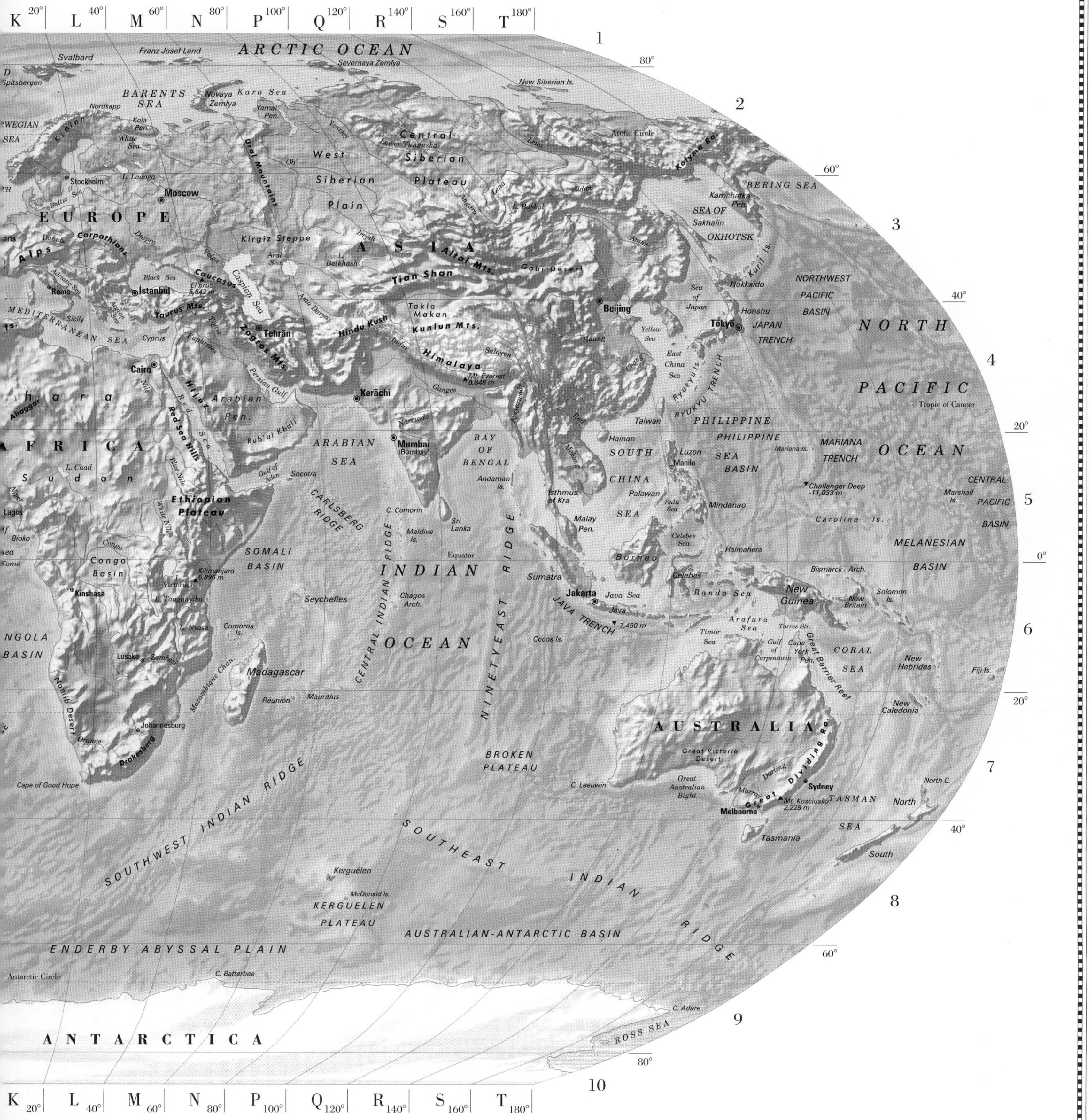

K 20° L 40° M 60° N 80° P 100° Q 120° R 140° S 160° T 180°

1

ARCTIC OCEAN

2

Svalbard Franz Josef Land Severnaya Zemlya
Spitsbergen
80°
D New Siberian Is.
Novaya Kara Sea
BARENTS Zemlya Yamal Arctic Circle
SEA Pen. Lena 60°
Nordkapp Kola White Yenisey Central Kolyma Ra.
WEGIAN Pen. Sea West Lower Tunguska Siberian BERING SEA 3
SEA Kielen Stockholm Siberian Plateau Kamchatka Aldan SEA OF Pen.
L. Ladoga Ob' Plain Lena Aldan OKHOTSK
EUROPE Moscow Vilyuy Amur Sakhalin
aris Donets Dnipro Kirgiz Steppe Irtysh Kuril Is. NORTHWEST
Alps Carpathians Volga Aral Angara L. Baykal Hokkaido PACIFIC 40°
Rome Black Sea Caucasus Sea Altai Mts. Gobi Desert Sea of BASIN
Istanbul El'brus Caspian Balkhash Tian Shan Japan Honshu NORTH
5,642 m Sea Beijing Tōkyō JAPAN
Taurus Mts. Amu Darya Takla Kunlun Mts. Huang Yellow TRENCH PACIFIC 4
Cyprus Zagros Mts. Makan Sea East
MEDITERRANEAN SEA Tehrān Hindu Kush Himalaya Saluseen China RYUKYU TRENCH OCEAN 20°
Is. Sicily Euphrates Indus Ganges Mt. Everest Okang Sea Taiwan PHILIPPINE Tropic of Cancer
Cairo Hllaz Persian Gulf 8,848 m Red Hainan PHILIPPINE SEA MARIANA CENTRAL
Karāchi South BASIN TRENCH PACIFIC 5
hara Nile Arabian Rub'al Khali Normada ARABIAN Mumbai BAY CHINA Luzon Mariana Is. Mariana Is. BASIN
Ahaggar Pen. SEA (Bombay) OF Manila
AFRICA Red Sea Hills SEA BENGAL SEA Palawan Challenger Deep Marshall
Sudan Blue Nile Ethiopian Andaman Malay Pen. Mindanao -11,033 m Is. MELANESIAN
L. Chad Plateau CARLSBERG C. Comorin Is. Isthmus Celebes Caroline Is. BASIN 0°
Lagos White Nile RIDGE Maldive of Kra Sea Sulu Halmahera
Bioko Congo Kilimanjaro Sri Lanka INDIAN Sumatra Sea Borneo Bismarck Arch.
Kinshasa 5,895 m Seychelles Chagos Arch. Java Sea Celebes New
Congo Victoria Equator OCEAN Jakarta Banda Sea Guinea New
Basin L. Tanganyika Java Solomon Is. Britain 6
ea JAVA TRENCH Arafura New
NGOLA L. Nyasa Comoros Cocos Is. -7,450 m Sea Hebrides Fiji Is.
BASIN Lusaka Zambezi Is. Timor Gulf of Cape CORAL 20°
Madagascar Mozambique Chan. Sea Carpentaria York SEA New
Johannesburg Réunion Mauritius NINETYEAST Great Barrier Reef Caledonia
Namib Desert Drakesberg SOUTHWEST INDIAN RIDGE CENTRAL INDIAN RIDGE RIDGE AUSTRALIA
Orange BROKEN Great Victoria Darling Great Dividing Ra. 7
Cape of Good Hope PLATEAU Desert Sydney North C.
C. Leeuwin Great Mt. Kosciusko TASMAN North
Australian 2,228 m
Bight Melbourne SEA South 40°
SOUTHEAST Murray Tasmania
Kerguélen
INDIAN
McDonald Is.
KERGUELEN
PLATEAU RIDGE 8
AUSTRALIAN-ANTARCTIC BASIN 60°
ENDERBY ABYSSAL PLAIN
Antarctic Circle C. Batterbee
C. Adare 9
ANTARCTICA ROSS SEA
80°
10

K 20° L 40° M 60° N 80° P 100° Q 120° R 140° S 160° T 180°

POPULATION OF CITIES AND TOWNS
⊛ OVER 5,000,000 ⊙ 500,000 - 1,999,999
⊚ 2,000,000 - 4,999,999 ○ UNDER 500,000

SCALE 1:81,700,000 ROBINSON PROJECTION STANDARD PARALLELS 38°N AND 38°S
MILES 0 1000 2000 3000 4000
KILOMETERS 0 1000 2000 3000 4000

Europe

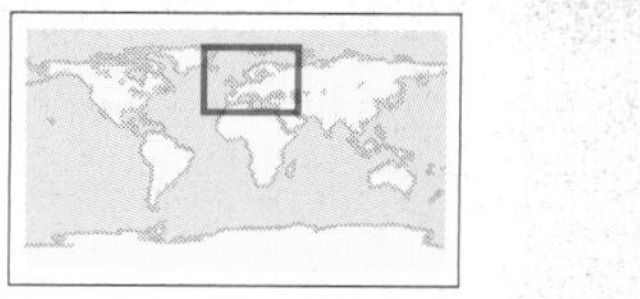

The terrain in this high-oblique, northwest-looking image, is indicative of the rugged, mountainous landscape characterizing most of Greece. Two major landform regions are captured in this image: the northwest to southeast-trending Mountains of Pindus in central Greece (north of the Gulf of Corinth), and the Peloponnisos Peninsula (south of the Gulf of Corinth). The Pindus, a massive continuation of the Dinaric Alps of Albania and the former Yugoslavia, make the land inhospitable and travel difficult. This rugged terrain caused the Greeks to become a seafaring people.

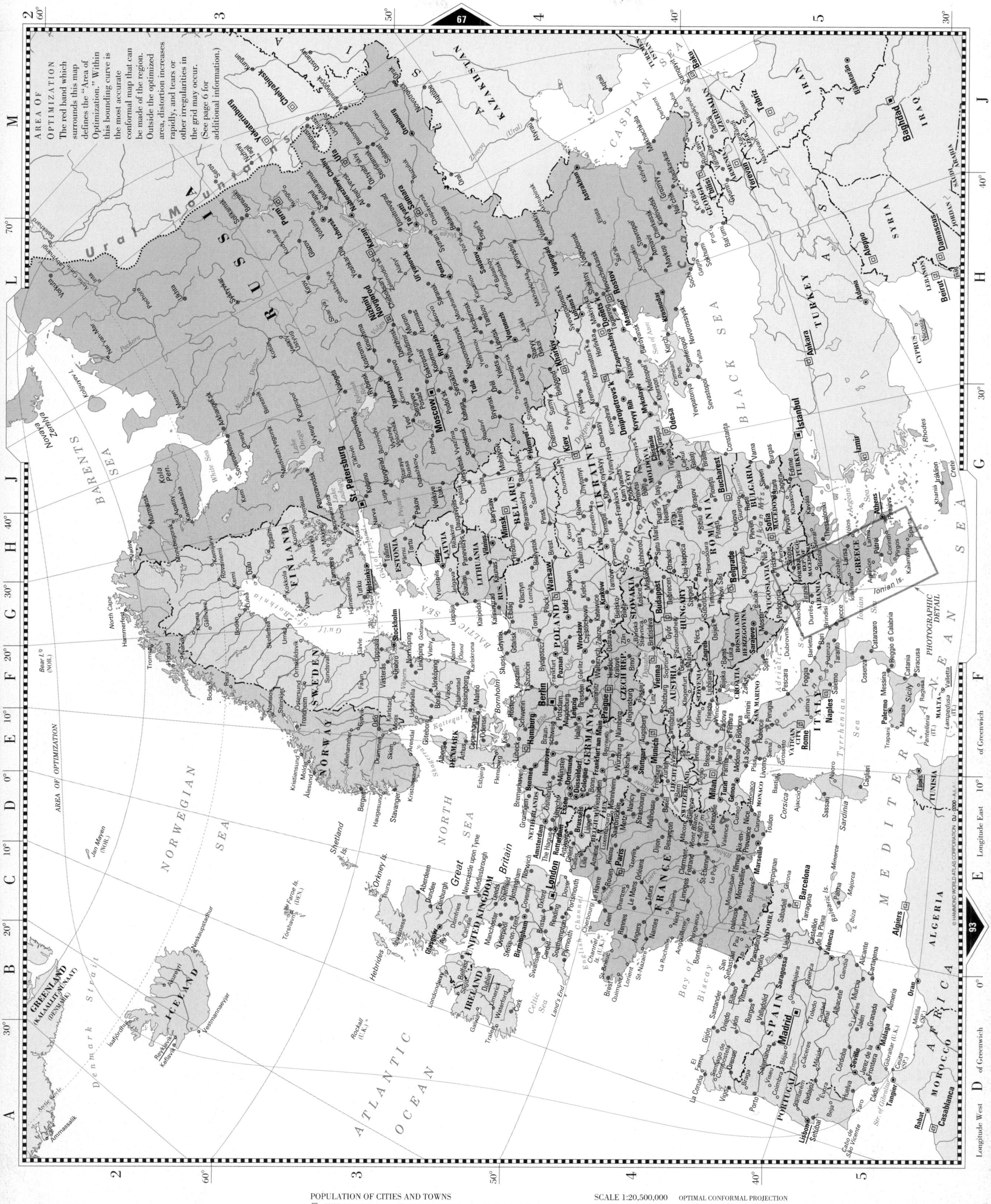

AREA OF OPTIMIZATION The red band which surrounds this map defines the "Area of Optimization." Within this bounding curve is the most accurate conformal map that can be made of the region. Outside the optimized area, distortion increases rapidly, and tears or other irregularities in the grid may occur. (See page 6 for additional information.)

AREA OF OPTIMIZATION

POPULATION OF CITIES AND TOWNS

- ■ OVER 3,000,000
- ◼ 1,000,000 - 2,999,999
- ⬟ 500,000 - 999,999
- ● 100,000 - 499,999
- ○ UNDER 100,000

SCALE 1:20,500,000   OPTIMAL CONFORMAL PROJECTION

MILES 0 300 600 900

KILOMETERS 0 300 600 900

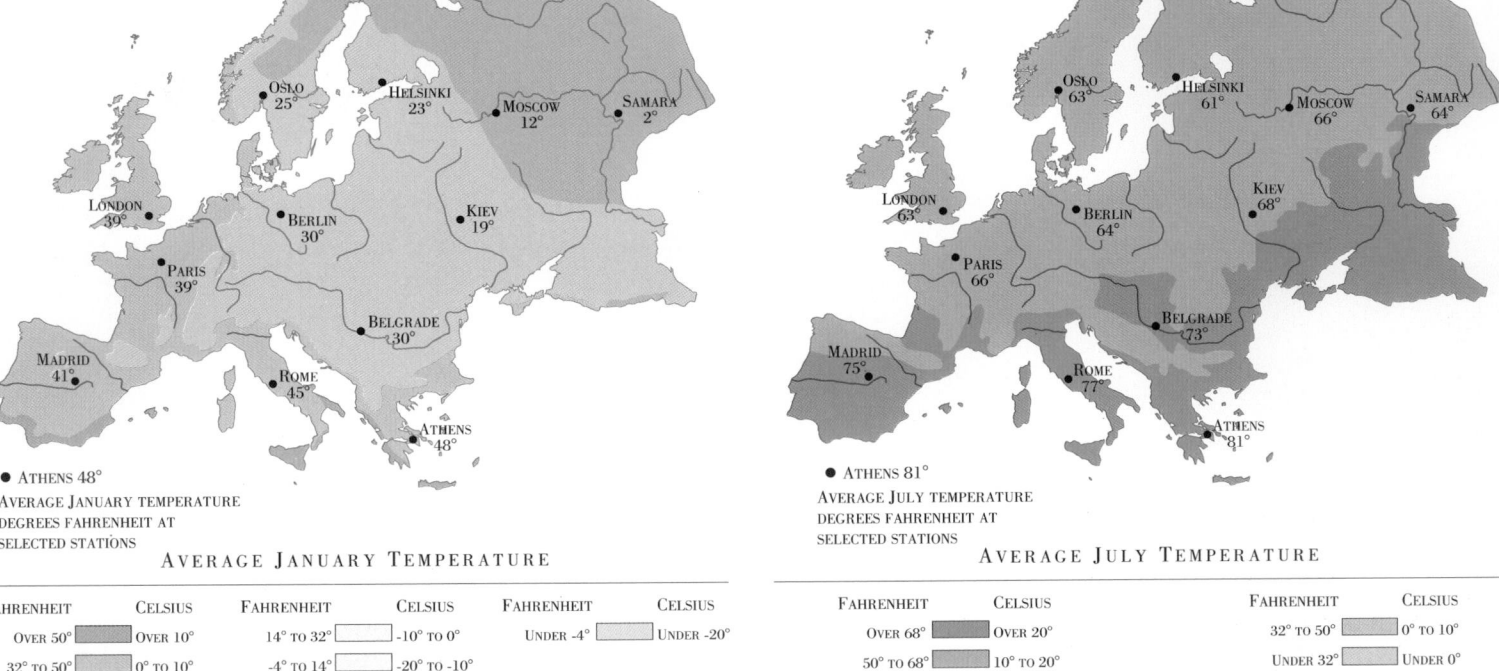

AVERAGE JANUARY TEMPERATURE

● Athens 48°
Average January temperature
degrees Fahrenheit at
selected stations

FAHRENHEIT	CELSIUS	FAHRENHEIT	CELSIUS	FAHRENHEIT	CELSIUS
OVER 50°	OVER 10°	14° TO 32°	-10° TO 0°	UNDER -4°	UNDER -20°
32° TO 50°	0° TO 10°	-4° TO 14°	-20° TO -10°		

AVERAGE JULY TEMPERATURE

● Athens 81°
Average July temperature
degrees Fahrenheit at
selected stations

FAHRENHEIT	CELSIUS	FAHRENHEIT	CELSIUS
OVER 68°	OVER 20°	32° TO 50°	0° TO 10°
50° TO 68°	10° TO 20°	UNDER 32°	UNDER 0°

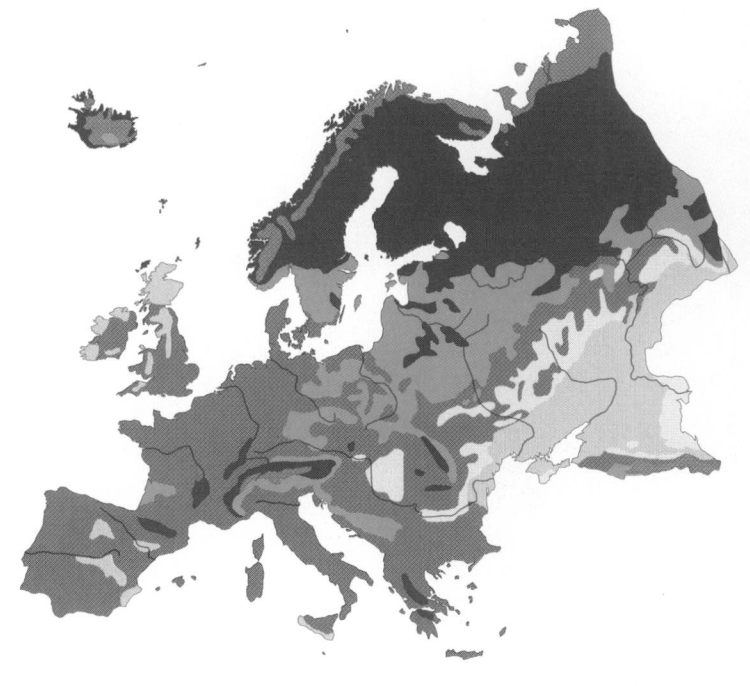

CLIMATE

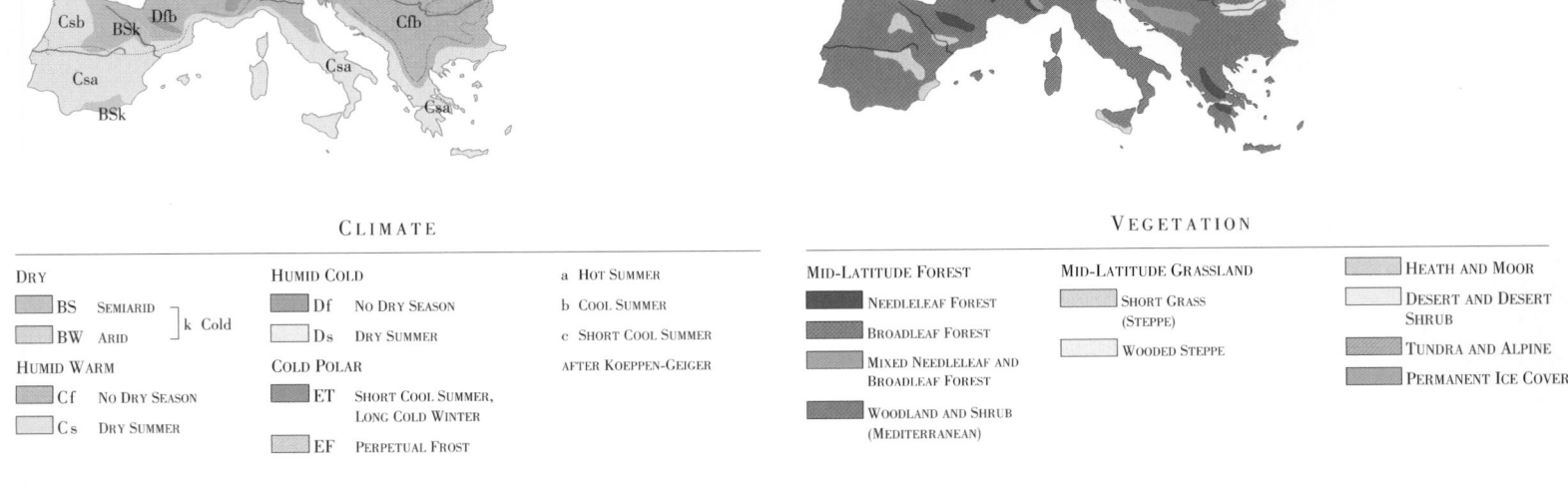

DRY
- BS SEMIARID
- BW ARID   } k COLD

HUMID WARM
- Cf NO DRY SEASON
- Cs DRY SUMMER

HUMID COLD
- Df NO DRY SEASON
- Ds DRY SUMMER

COLD POLAR
- ET SHORT COOL SUMMER, LONG COLD WINTER
- EF PERPETUAL FROST

a HOT SUMMER
b COOL SUMMER
c SHORT COOL SUMMER

AFTER KOEPPEN-GEIGER

VEGETATION

MID-LATITUDE FOREST
- NEEDLELEAF FOREST
- BROADLEAF FOREST
- MIXED NEEDLELEAF AND BROADLEAF FOREST
- WOODLAND AND SHRUB (MEDITERRANEAN)

MID-LATITUDE GRASSLAND
- SHORT GRASS (STEPPE)
- WOODED STEPPE

- HEATH AND MOOR
- DESERT AND DESERT SHRUB
- TUNDRA AND ALPINE
- PERMANENT ICE COVER

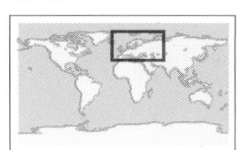

Europe – Geographical Comparisons

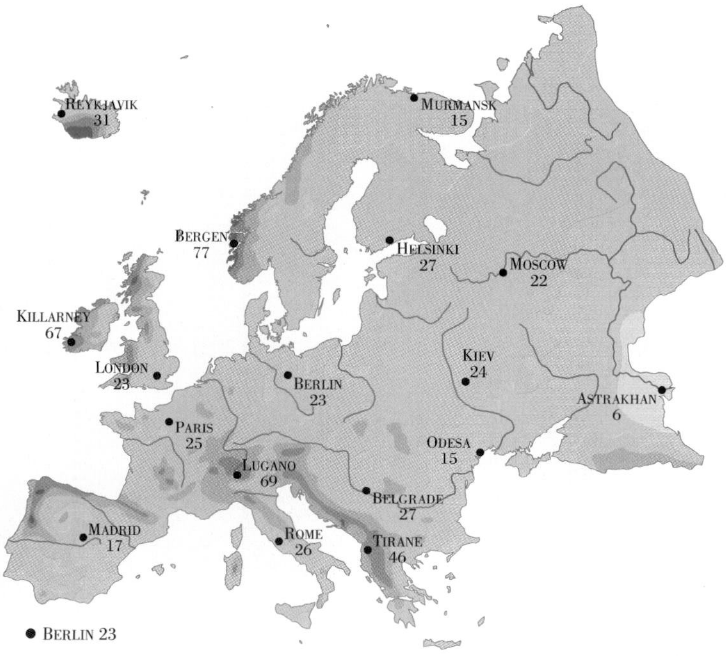

AVERAGE ANNUAL RAINFALL

REYKJAVIK 31

MURMANSK 15

BERGEN 77

HELSINKI 27

MOSCOW 22

KILLARNEY 67

LONDON 23

BERLIN 23

KIEV 24

ASTRAKHAN 6

PARIS 25

ODESA 15

LUGANO 69

BELGRADE 27

MADRID 17

ROME 26

TIRANE 46

● BERLIN 23

AVERAGE ANNUAL RAINFALL
IN INCHES AT SELECTED STATIONS

INCHES	CM	INCHES	CM	INCHES	CM
OVER 80	OVER 200	40 TO 60	100 TO 150	10 TO 20	25 TO 50
60 TO 80	150 TO 200	20 TO 40	50 TO 100	UNDER 10	UNDER 25

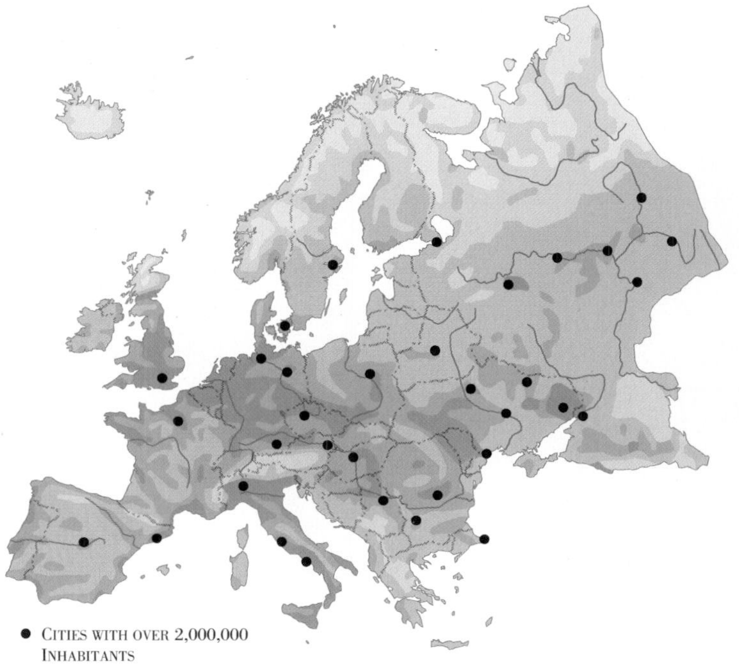

POPULATION DISTRIBUTION

● CITIES WITH OVER 2,000,000
INHABITANTS

DENSITY PER		SQ. MI.	SQ. KM.	SQ. MI.	SQ. KM.
SQ. MI.	SQ. KM.	130 TO 260	50 TO 100	3 TO 25	1 TO 10
OVER 260	OVER 100	25 TO 130	10 TO 50	UNDER 3	UNDER 1

LAND USE

FURS

FURS

FURS

FLAX

OATS

RYE

RYE

HEMP

WHEAT

DAIRY

RYE

DAIRY

RYE

POTATOES

WHEAT

DAIRY

RYE

POTATOES

SUGAR BEETS

CATTLE

WHEAT

OATS

HOGS

OATS

WHEAT

CORN

CORN

HOGS

SHEEP

DAIRY

DAIRY

WHEAT

WINE

BARLEY

CORN

TOBACCO

TEA

WINE

WINE

WINE

CORN

WHEAT

WHEAT

CORN

SHEEP

OLIVES

WINE

SHEEP

FRUIT

SHEEP

TOBACCO

OLIVES

	CEREALS, LIVESTOCK		FRUIT AND TRUCK FARMING		GENERAL FARMING, LIVESTOCK
	DAIRY, LIVESTOCK		PASTURE LIVESTOCK		FORESTS
	LIVESTOCK HERDING		DAIRY, CEREALS		NONPRODUCTIVE
	SPECIAL CROPS				

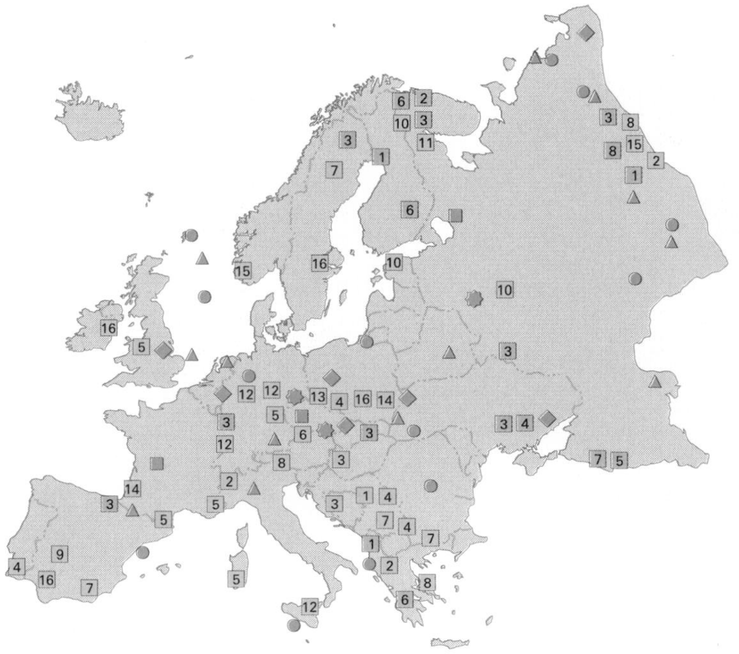

MINERAL RESOURCES

ENERGY & FUELS	IRON & FERROALLOYS	OTHER MAJOR RESOURCES		
◆ COAL	1 CHROMIUM	1 ANTIMONY	7 LEAD	13 SILVER
⬟ LIGNITE	2 COBALT	2 ASBESTOS	8 MAGNESITE	14 SULFER
▲ NATURAL GAS	3 IRON ORE	3 BAUXITE	9 MERCURY	15 TITANIUM
● PETROLEUM	4 MANGANESE	4 COPPER	10 PHOSPHATES	16 ZINC
▪ URANIUM	5 MOLYBDENUM	5 FLORSPAR	11 PLATINUM	
	6 NICKEL	6 GRAPHITE	12 POTASH	
	7 TUNGSTEN			
	8 VANADIUM			

London, Paris

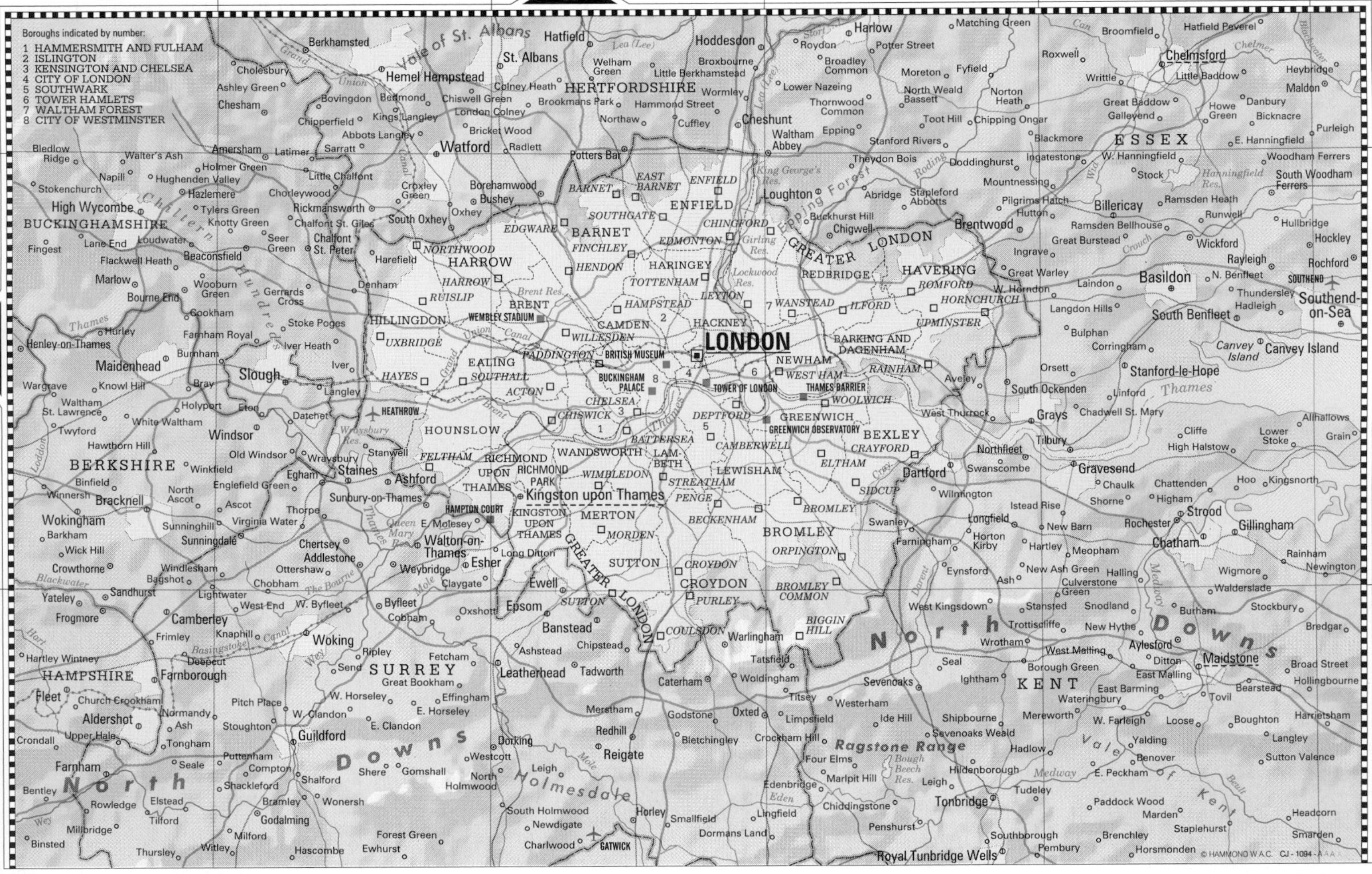

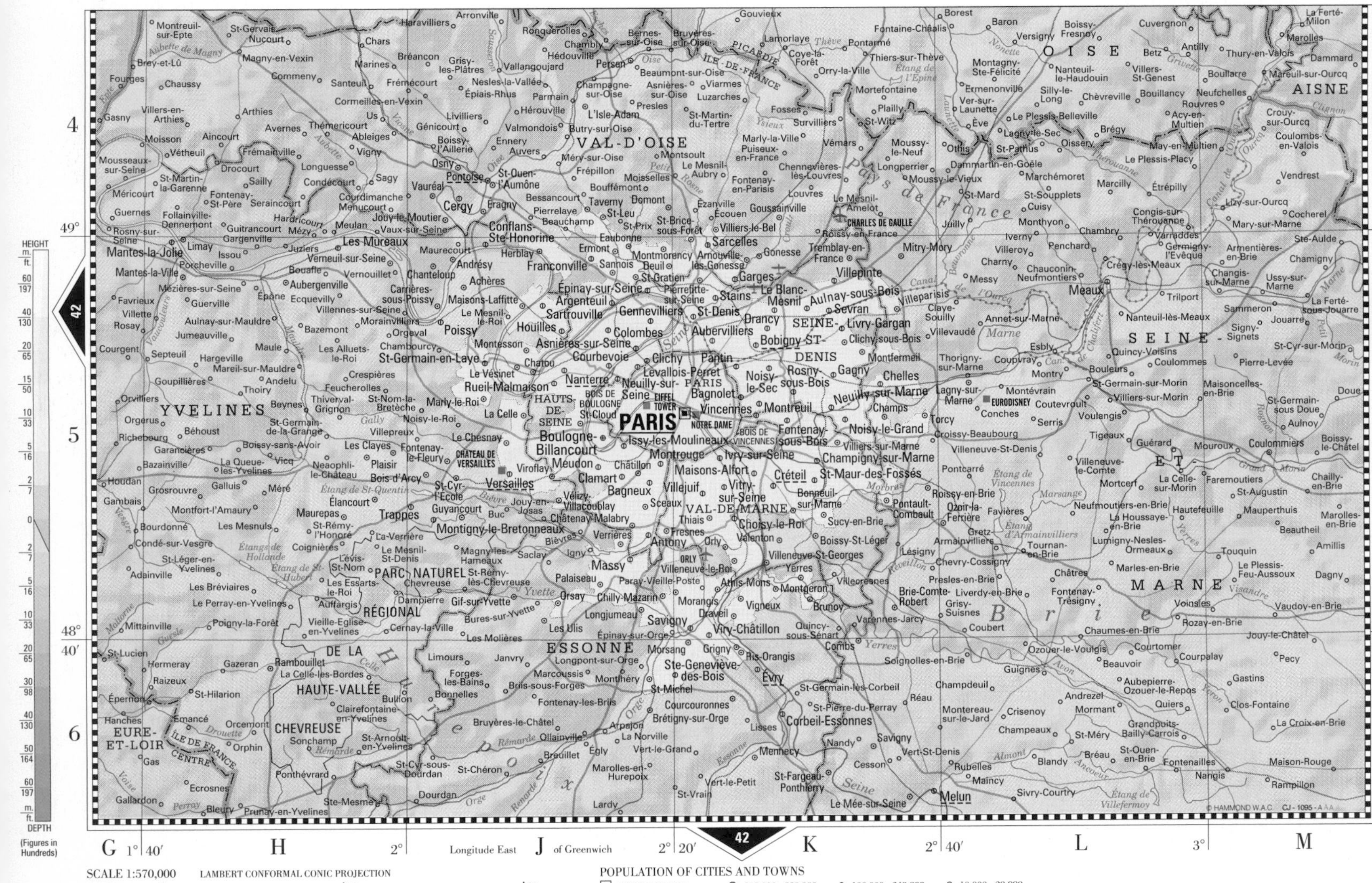

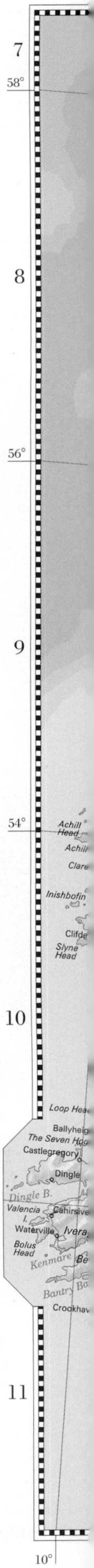

Boroughs indicated by number:
1 HAMMERSMITH AND FULHAM
2 ISLINGTON
3 KENSINGTON AND CHELSEA
4 CITY OF LONDON
5 SOUTHWARK
6 TOWER HAMLETS
7 WALTHAM FOREST
8 CITY OF WESTMINSTER

© HAMMOND W.A.C. CJ – 1094 – AAA

© HAMMOND W.A.C. CJ – 1095 – AAU

SCALE 1:570,000 LAMBERT CONFORMAL CONIC PROJECTION

MILES 0 ___ 10 ___ 20
KILOMETERS 0 __ 10 __ 20

HEIGHT m./ft.

DEPTH (Figures in Hundreds)

POPULATION OF CITIES AND TOWNS

■ OVER 2,000,000
▣ 1,000,000 – 1,999,999
● 500,000 – 999,999
● 250,000 – 499,999
● 100,000 – 249,999
● 30,000 – 99,999
○ 10,000 – 29,999
○ UNDER 10,000

United Kingdom, Ireland

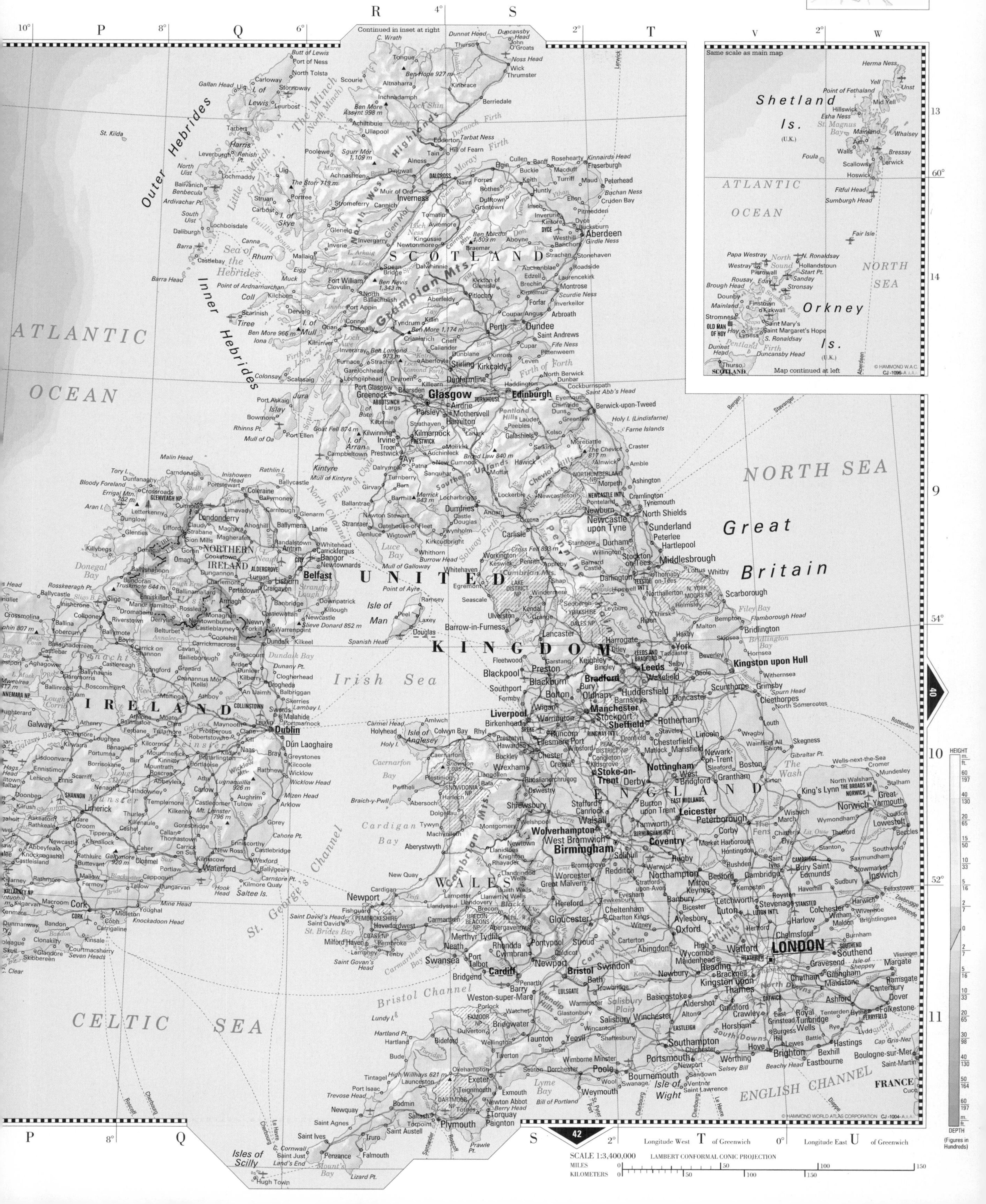

Inset map (top right): Same scale as main map

Shetland Is. (U.K.)

Orkney Is. (U.K.)

ATLANTIC OCEAN

NORTH SEA

SCOTLAND

Grampian Mts.

North West Highlands

NORTHERN IRELAND

Belfast

IRELAND

Dublin

UNITED KINGDOM

Glasgow

Edinburgh

Southern Uplands

Pennines

Cheviot Hills

ATLANTIC OCEAN

CELTIC SEA

Irish Sea

St. George's Channel

Cardigan Bay

WALES

ENGLAND

Great Britain

NORTH SEA

Isle of Man

Liverpool

Manchester

Leeds

Sheffield

Birmingham

Coventry

Leicester

Nottingham

Stoke-on-Trent

Bristol

Cardiff

Swansea

LONDON

ENGLISH CHANNEL

FRANCE

Isle of Wight

SCALE 1:3,400,000 LAMBERT CONFORMAL CONIC PROJECTION

MILES 0 50 100 150

KILOMETERS 0 50 100 150

Longitude West of Greenwich | Longitude East of Greenwich

HEIGHT (m.) / DEPTH (Figures in Hundreds)

© HAMMOND WORLD ATLAS CORPORATION CJ-1004-A-A-A

Southern England and Wales

Northeastern Ireland, Northern England and Wales

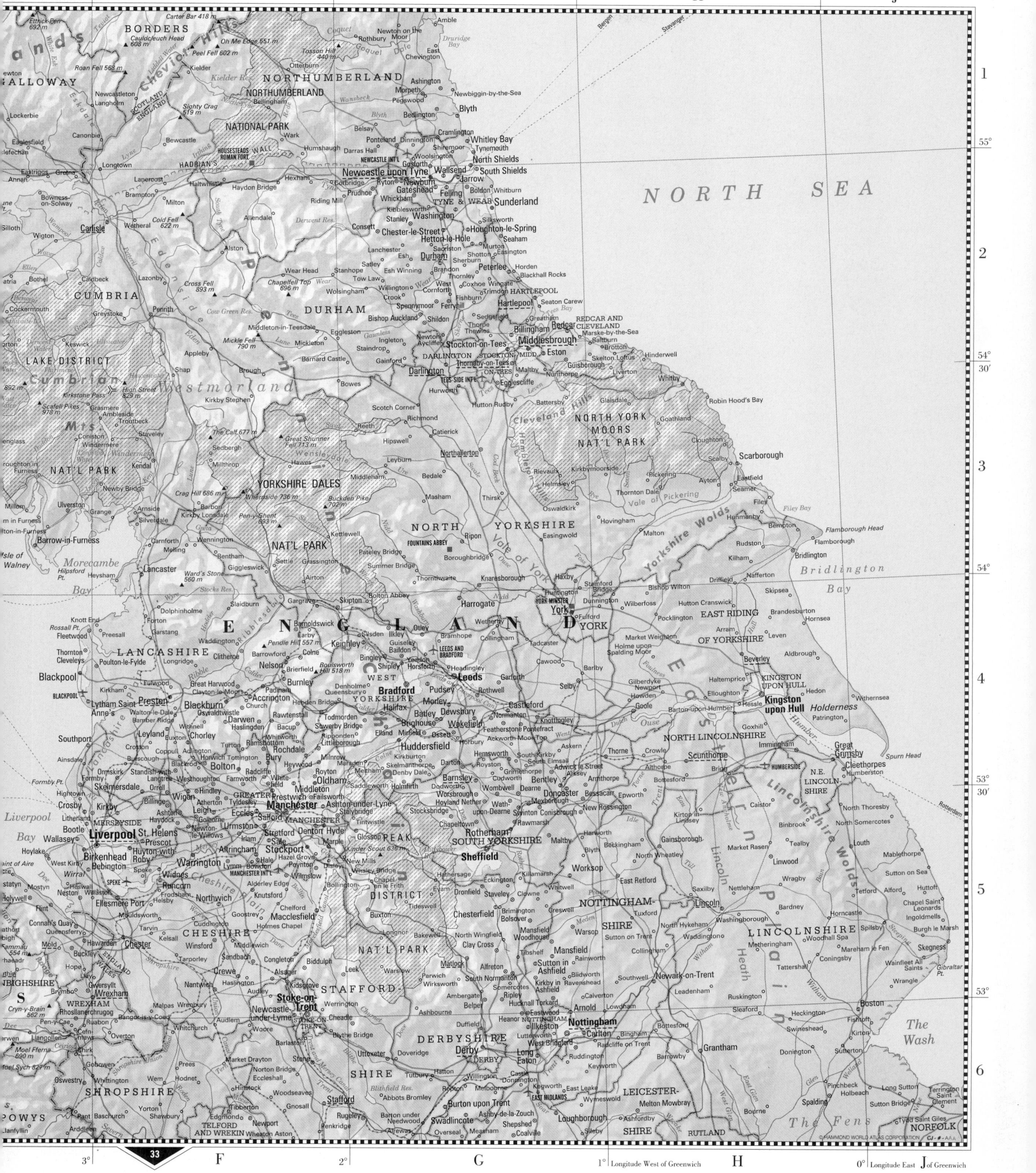

Central Scotland

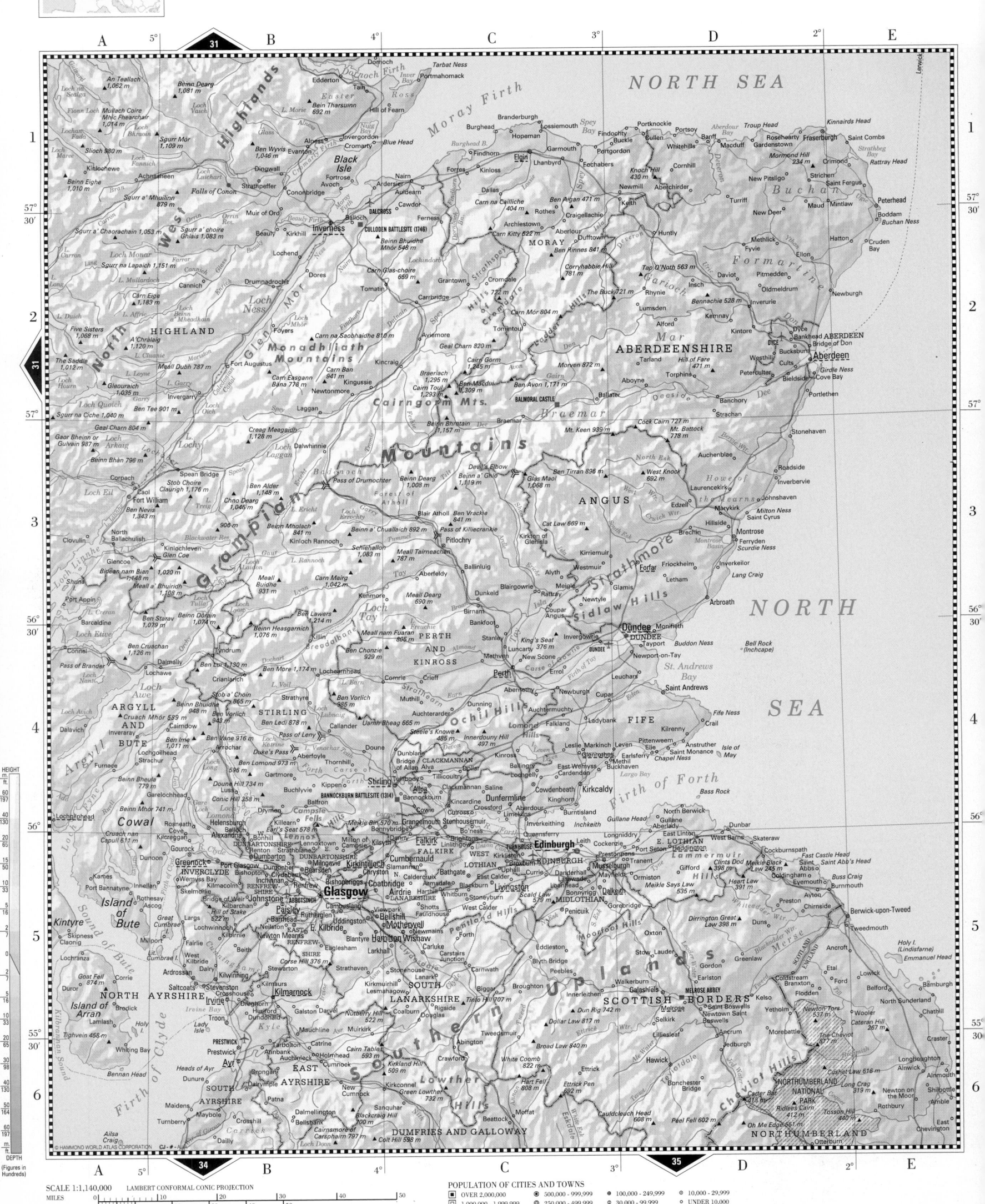

SCALE 1:1,140,000   LAMBERT CONFORMAL CONIC PROJECTION

MILES   0   10   20   30   40   50

KILOMETERS   0   10   20   30

POPULATION OF CITIES AND TOWNS

■	OVER 2,000,000	●	500,000 - 999,999	●	100,000 - 249,999	●	10,000 - 29,999
▢	1,000,000 - 1,999,999	◉	250,000 - 499,999	●	30,000 - 99,999	●	UNDER 10,000

Scandinavia and Finland, Iceland

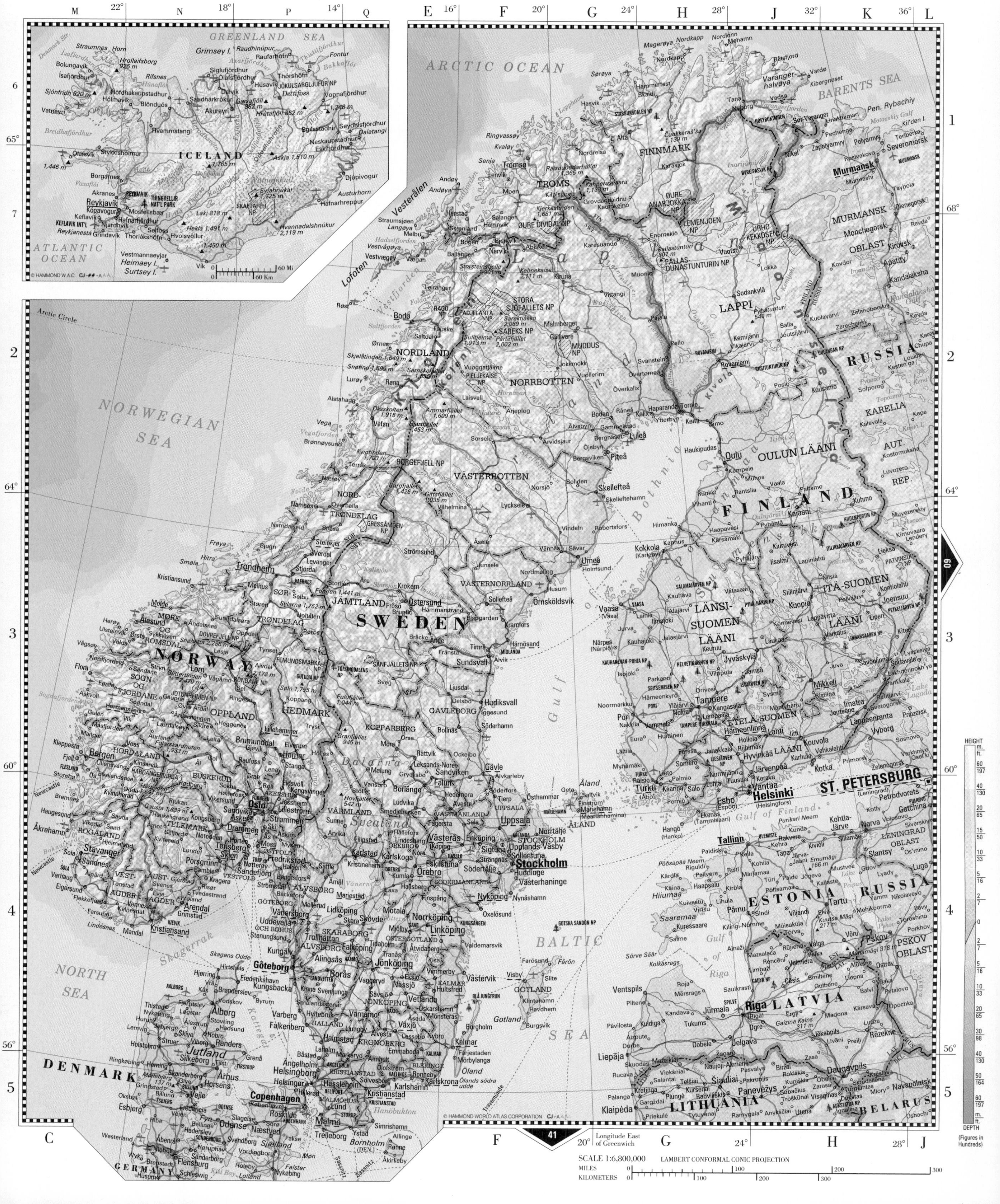

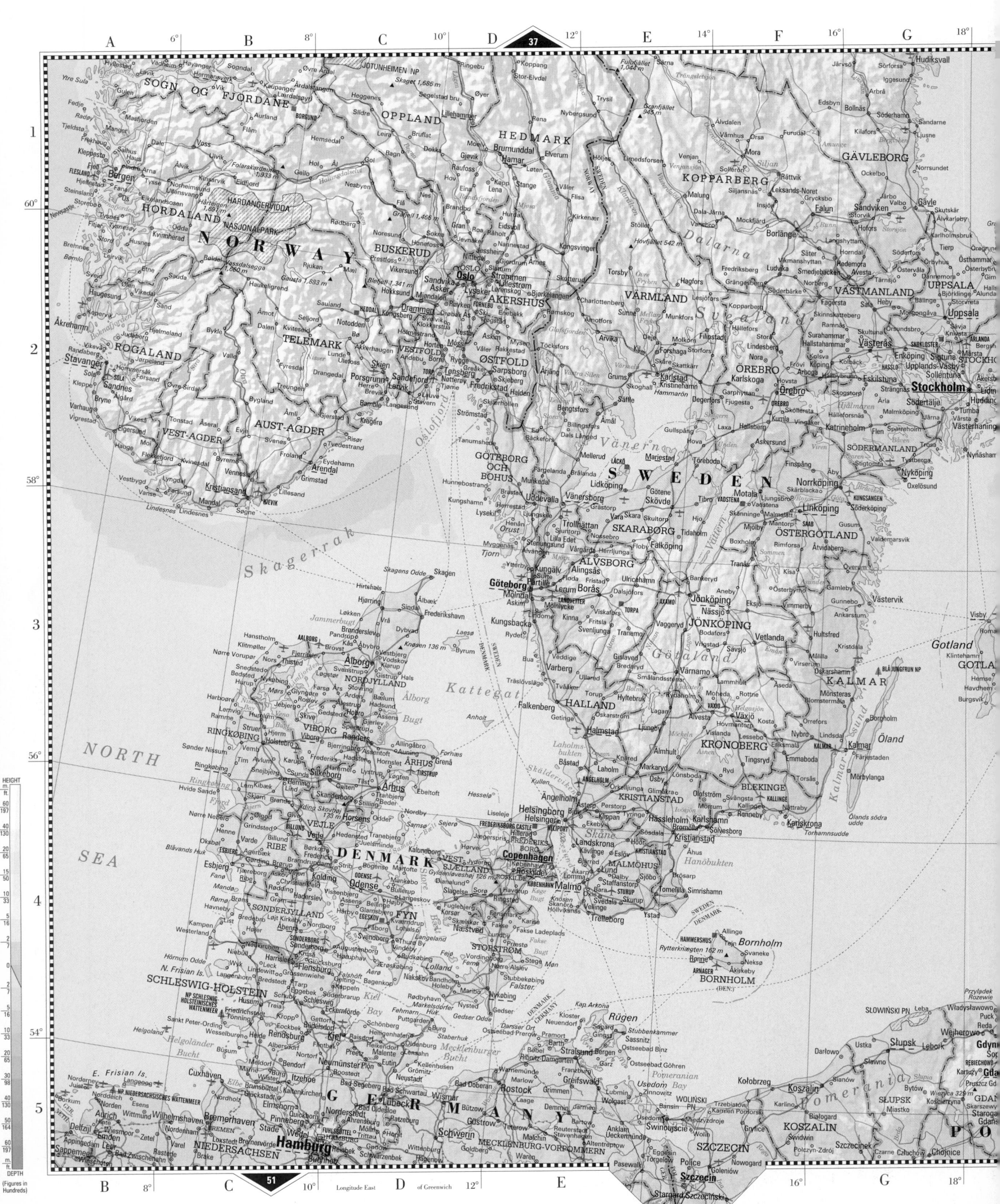

Baltic Region

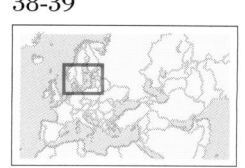

POPULATION OF CITIES AND TOWNS
- ● OVER 2,000,000
- ◉ 500,000 - 999,999
- ● 100,000 - 249,999
- ● 10,000 - 29,999
- ☐ 1,000,000 - 1,999,999
- ● 250,000 - 499,999
- ● 30,000 - 99,999
- ○ UNDER 10,000

SCALE 1:3,400,000   LAMBERT CONFORMAL CONIC PROJECTION

MILES 0   50   100   150
KILOMETERS 0   50   100   150

© HAMMOND WORLD ATLAS CORPORATION

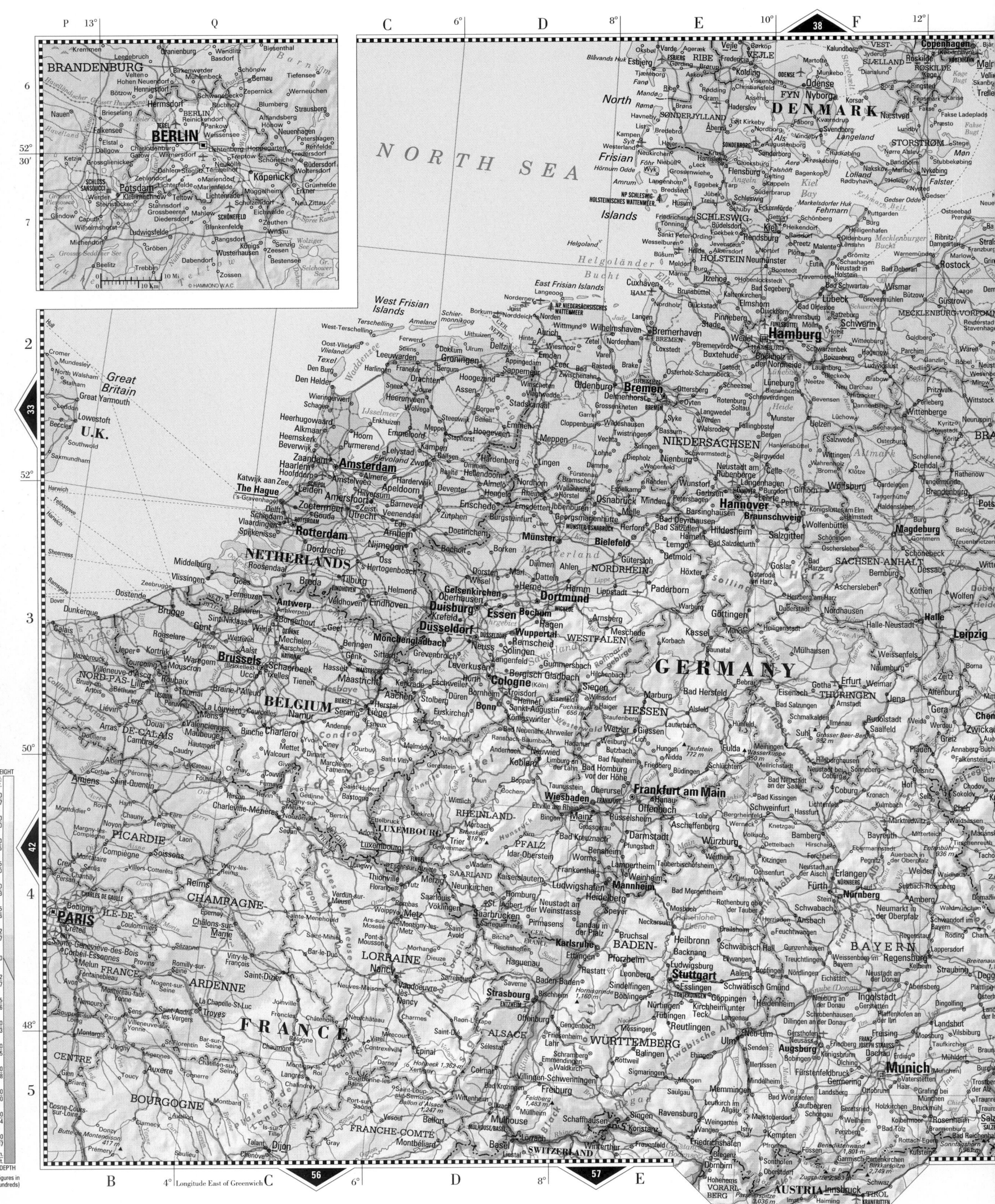

North Central Europe

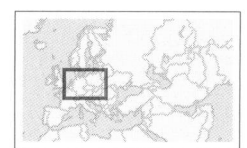

POPULATION OF CITIES AND TOWNS

- ■ OVER 2,000,000
- ⊡ 1,000,000 - 1,999,999
- ● 500,000 - 999,999
- ◉ 250,000 - 499,999
- ● 100,000 - 249,999
- ● 30,000 - 99,999
- ○ 10,000 - 29,999
- ○ UNDER 10,000

SCALE 1:3,400,000   LAMBERT CONFORMAL CONIC PROJECTION

MILES 0   50   100   150
KILOMETERS 0   50   100   150

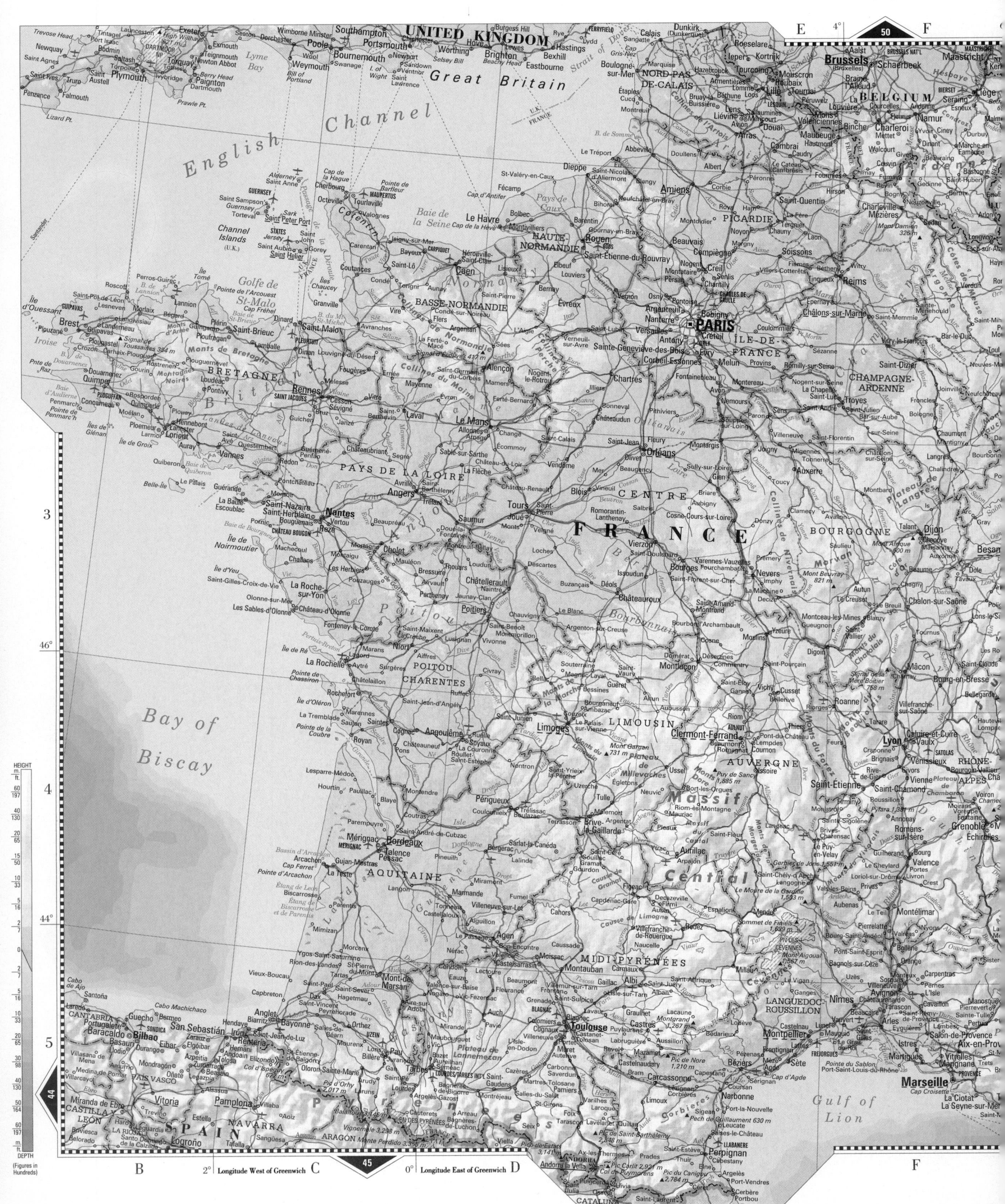

West Central Europe

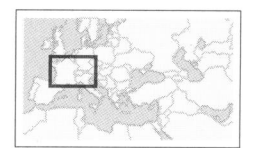

POPULATION OF CITIES AND TOWNS

- ■ OVER 2,000,000
- ◉ 1,000,000 - 1,999,999
- ● 500,000 - 999,999
- ● 250,000 - 499,999
- ● 100,000 - 249,999
- ● 30,000 - 99,999
- ◉ 10,000 - 29,999
- ○ UNDER 10,000

SCALE 1:3,400,000 LAMBERT CONFORMAL CONIC PROJECTION

MILES 0   50   100

KILOMETERS 0   50   100   150

HAMMOND WORLD ATLAS CORPORATION   CJ-1015-AAA

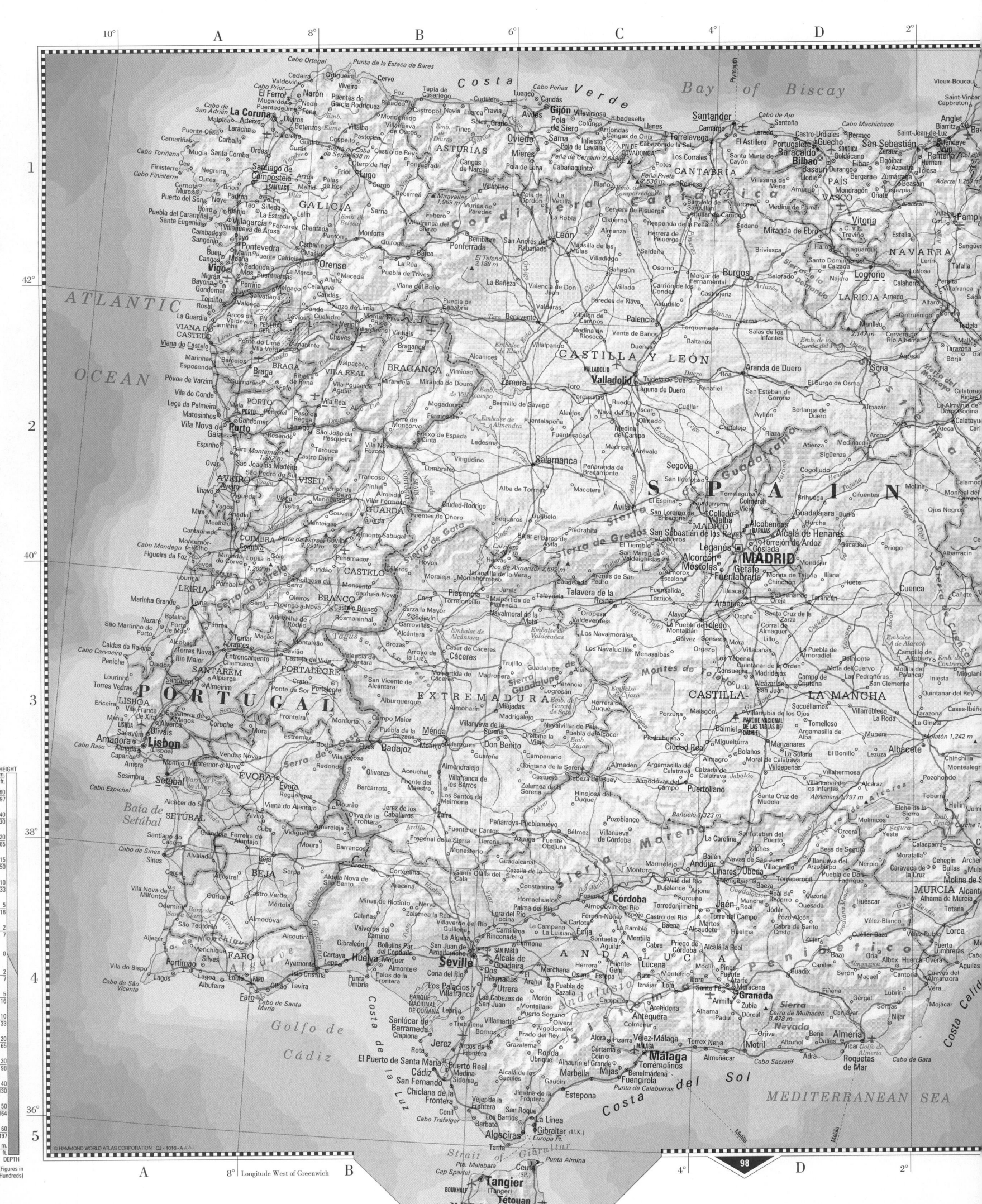

Spain, Portugal

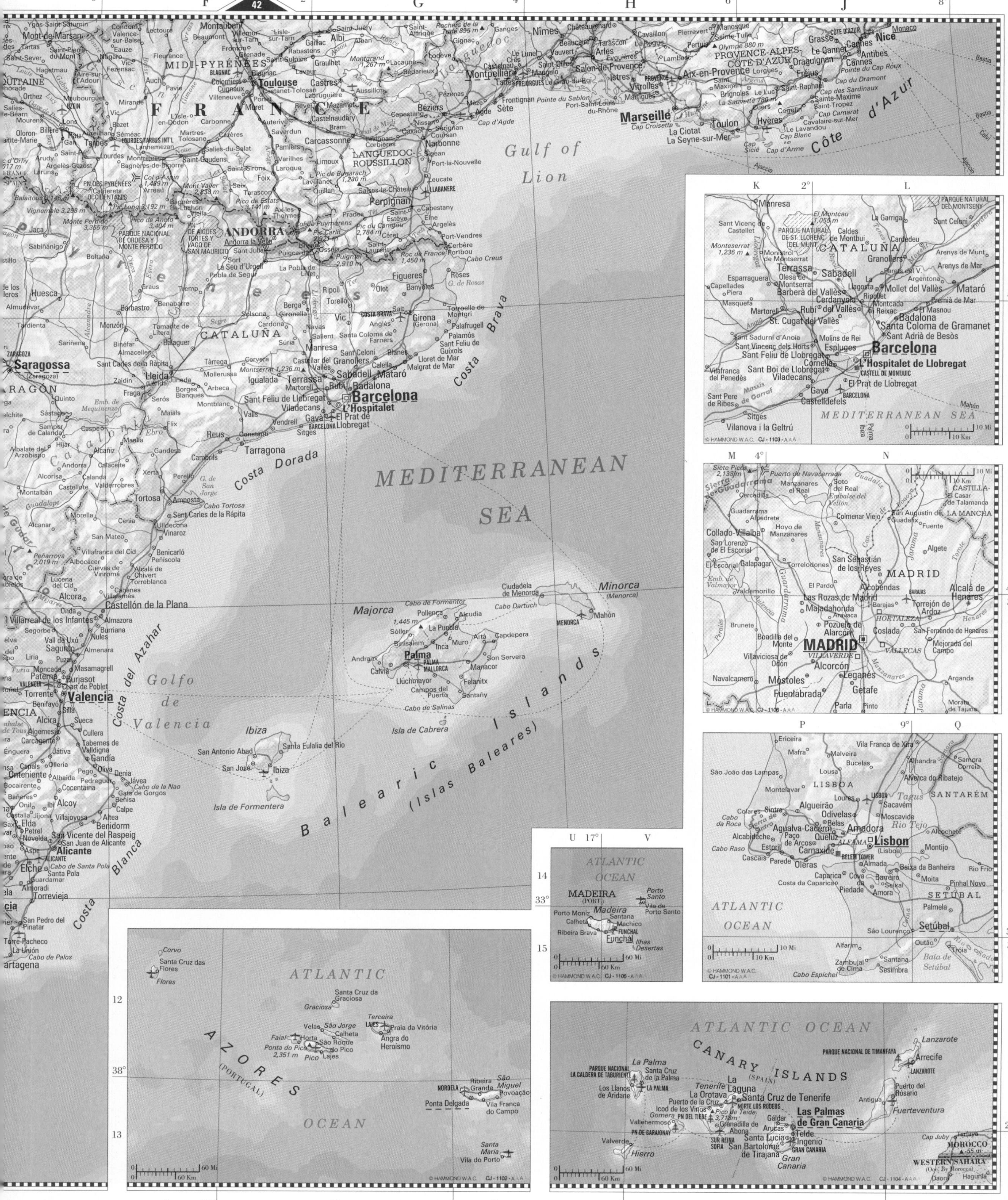

42

POPULATION OF CITIES AND TOWNS

- ■ OVER 2,000,000
- ■ 1,000,000 - 1,999,999
- ● 500,000 - 999,999
- ● 250,000 - 499,999
- ● 100,000 - 249,999
- ● 30,000 - 99,999
- ● 10,000 - 29,999
- ○ UNDER 10,000

SCALE 1:3,400,000   LAMBERT CONFORMAL CONIC PROJECTION

MILES 0 ————— 50 ————— 100 ————— 150

KILOMETERS 0 ————— 100 ————— 150

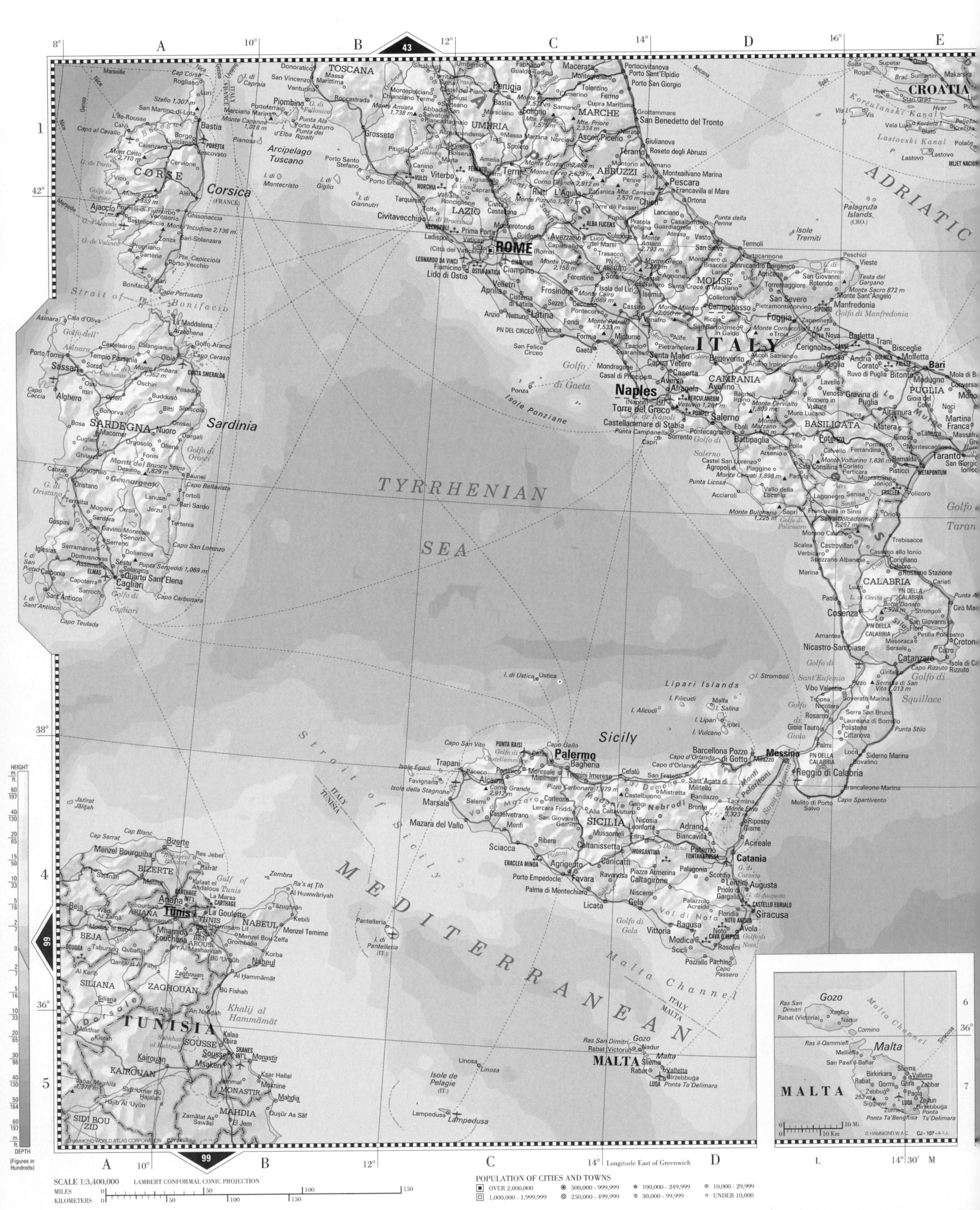

Southern Italy, Albania, Greece

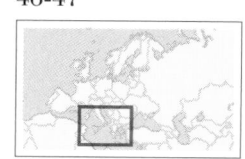

Netherlands, Northwestern Germany

NORTH SEA

West Frisian Islands

Waddenzee

GRONINGEN

FRIESLAND

DRENTHE

NOORD-HOLLAND

IJsselmeer

FLEVOLAND

OVERIJSSEL

Amsterdam

NATIONAAL PARK DE KENNEMERDUINEN

Haarlem

GELDERLAND

Apeldoorn

UTRECHT

Utrecht

Amersfoort

NP DE HOGE VELUWE

NATIONAAL PARK VELUWEZOOM

The Hague
('s-Gravenhage)

Leiden

Arnhem

Nijmegen

NETHERLANDS

Enschede

ZUID HOLLAND

Rotterdam

Dordrecht

Hoekse Waard

Overflakkee

Schouwen

ZEELAND

Middelburg

Vlissingen

Breda

Tilburg

NOORD-BRABANT

's Hertogenbosch

Eindhoven

LIMBURG

Venlo

Duisburg

GERMANY

Mönchengladbach

Düsseldorf

ANTWERPEN

Antwerp
(Antwerpen)

OOST-VLAANDEREN

Ghent
(Gent)

BELGIUM

LIMBURG

Longitude East of Greenwich

H

38

Frisian Islands

NP NIEDERSÄCHSISCHE WATTENMEER

Ostfriesland

SCHLESWIG-
HOLSTEIN

MECKLENBURG-
VORPOMMERN

BREMEN

Hamburg

HAMBURG

BREMEN

Bremen

NIEDERSACHSEN

Lüneburger

Heide

G E R M A N Y

Hannover

BRAUNSCHWEIG

Braunschweig

Münsterland

Teutoburger Wald

Wesergebirge

Wiehengebirge

Osnabrück

Bielefeld

Münster

NORDRHEIN-

Dortmund

Wuppertal

WESTFALEN

Paderborn

Sauerland

Rothaargebirge

Eggegebirge

Solling

Harz
Brocken 1,142 m

SACHSEN-
ANHALT

Göttingen

Kassel

HESSEN

THÜRINGEN

Harz

© HAMMOND WORLD ATLAS CORPORATION C.J.

POPULATION OF CITIES AND TOWNS

□ OVER 2,000,000
▣ 1,000,000 - 1,999,999
● 500,000 - 999,999
◉ 250,000 - 499,999
⊛ 100,000 - 249,999
⊙ 30,000 - 99,999
○ 10,000 - 29,999
○ UNDER 10,000

SCALE 1:1,140,000   LAMBERT CONFORMAL CONIC PROJECTION

MILES   0   10   20   30   40   50
KILOMETERS 0   10   20   30   40   50

E   8°   F   9°   G   10°   H

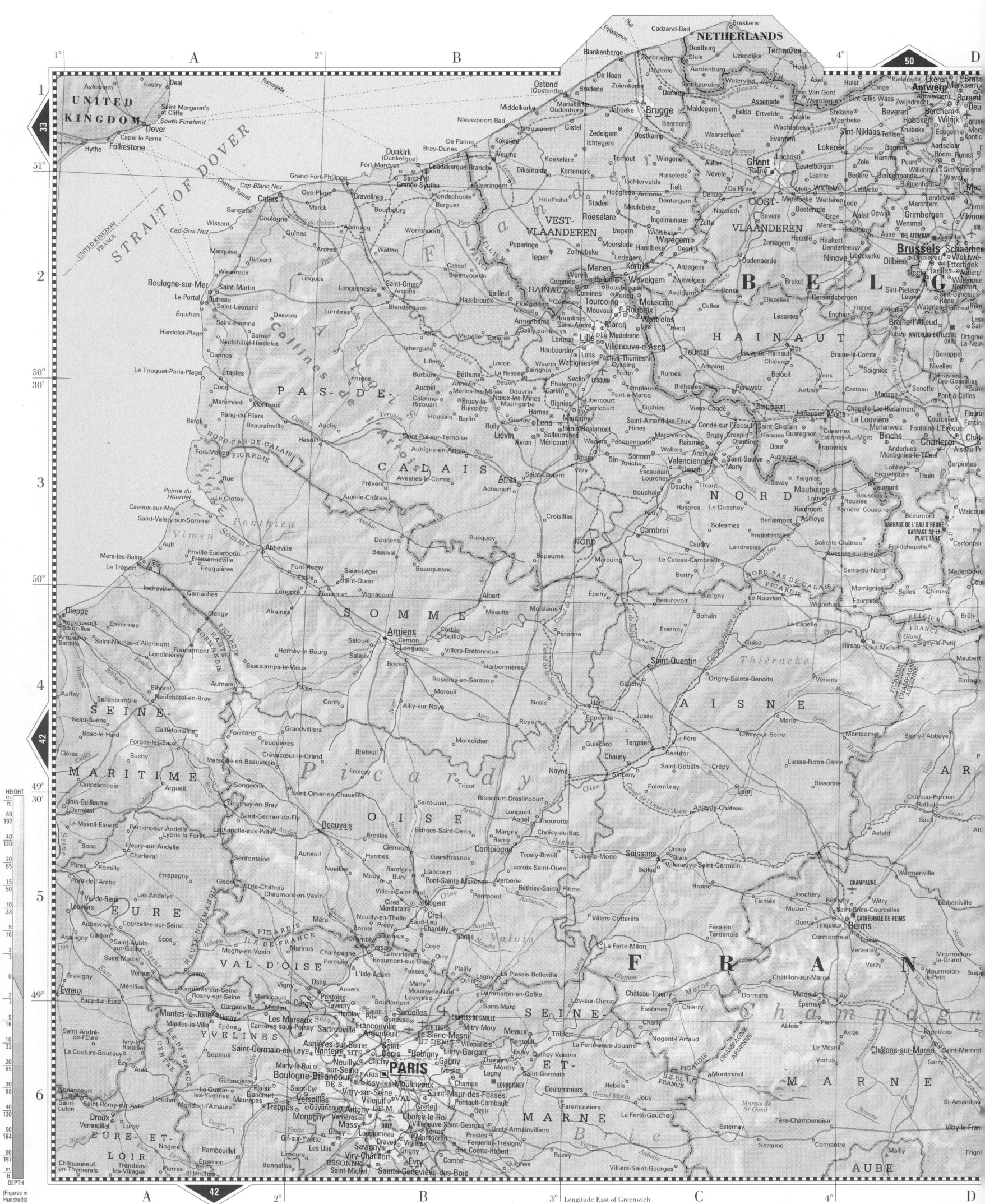

Belgium, Northern France, Western Germany

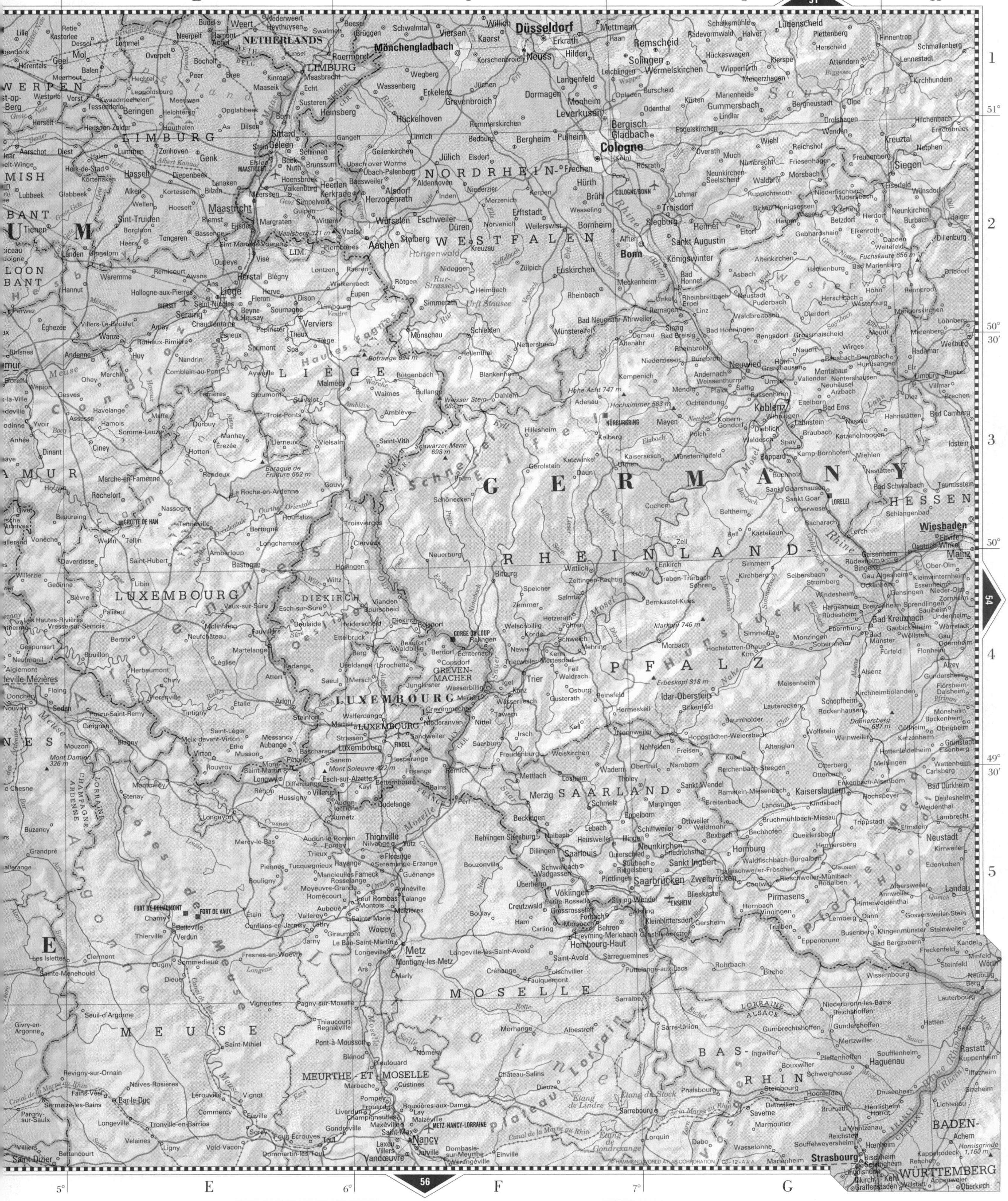

POPULATION OF CITIES AND TOWNS

■ OVER 2,000,000 ● 500,000 - 999,999 ● 100,000 - 249,999 ○ 10,000 - 24,999
□ 1,000,000 - 1,999,999 ● 250,000 - 499,999 ● 30,000 - 99,999 ○ UNDER 10,000

SCALE 1:1,140,000   LAMBERT CONFORMAL CONIC PROJECTION

MILES 0 10 20 30 40 50

KILOMETERS 0 10 20 30 40 50

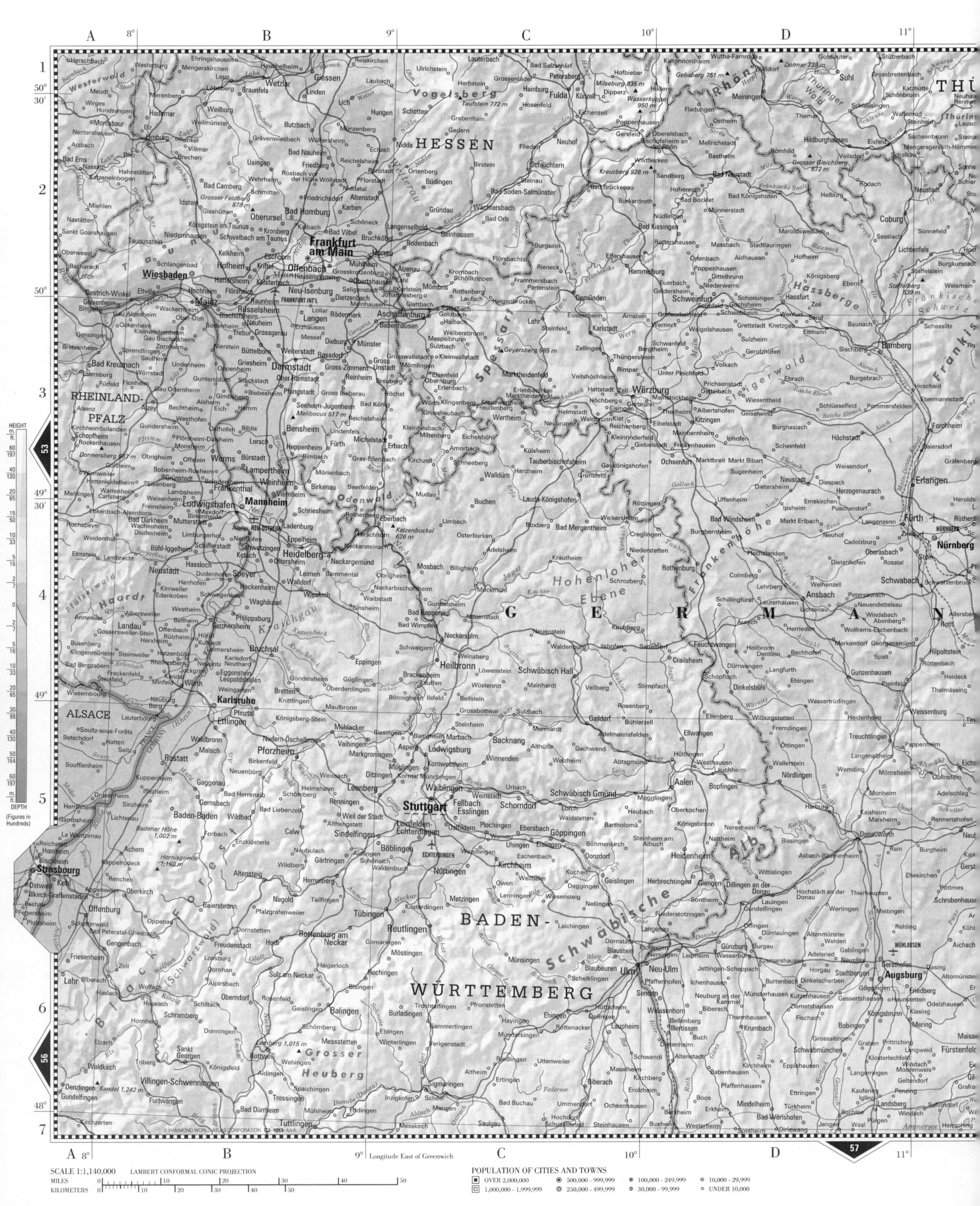

POPULATION OF CITIES AND TOWNS

- ☐ OVER 2,000,000
- ☐ 1,000,000 - 1,999,999
- ● 500,000 - 999,999
- ● 250,000 - 499,999
- ● 100,000 - 249,999
- ● 30,000 - 99,999
- ○ 10,000 - 29,999
- ○ UNDER 10,000

Southern Germany, Czech Republic, Upper Austria

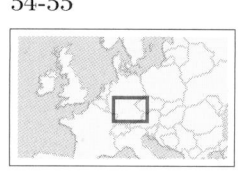

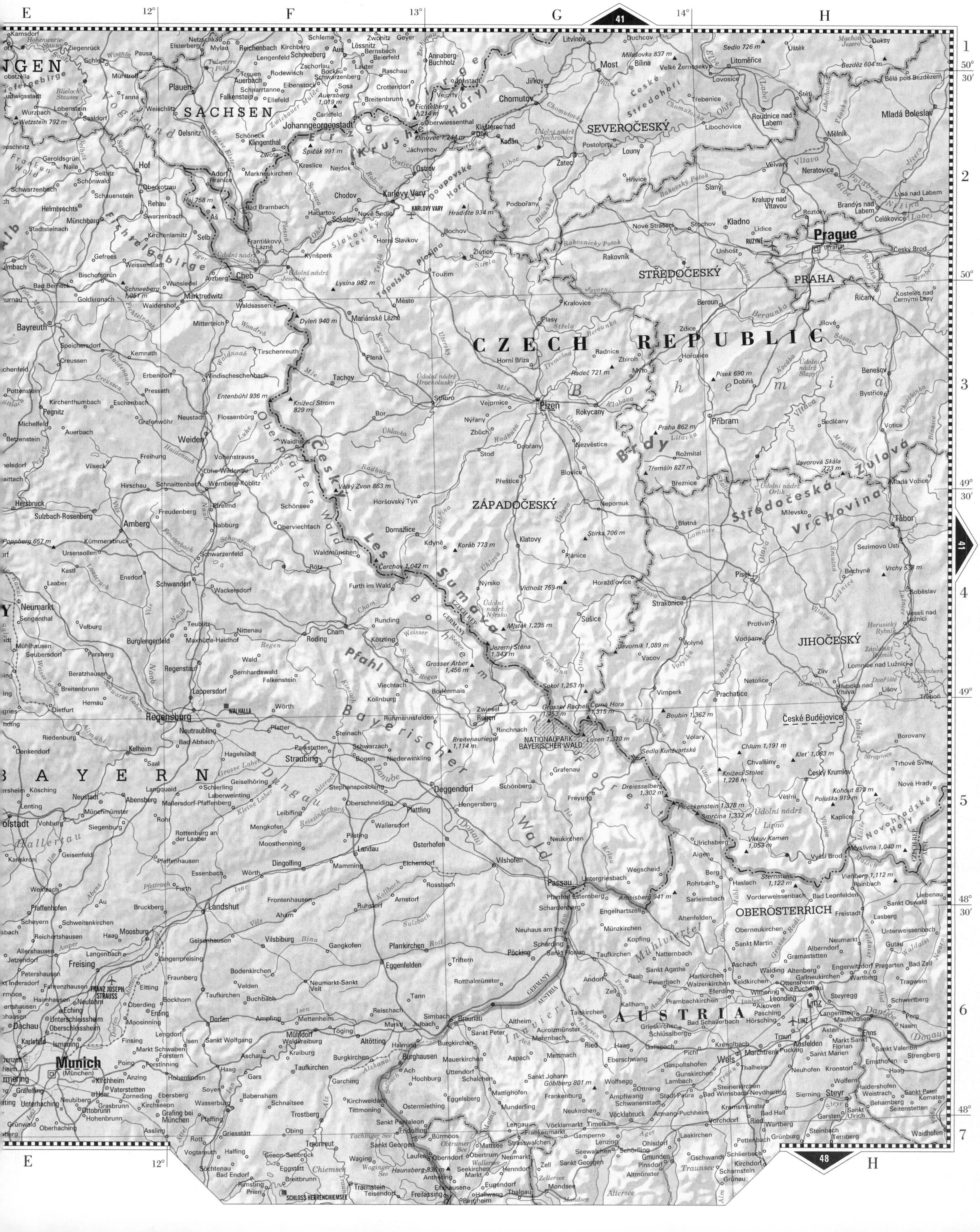

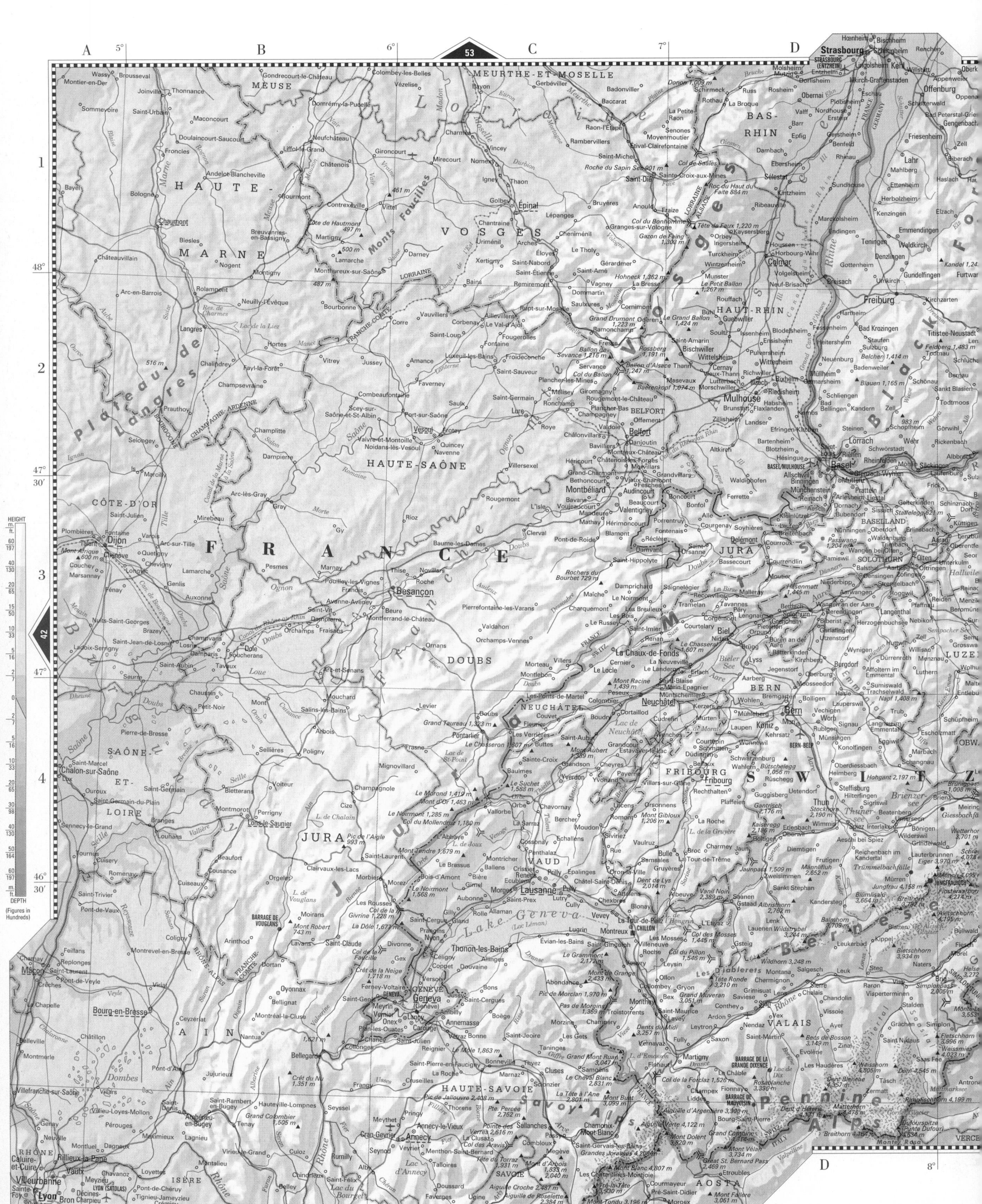

Central Alps Region

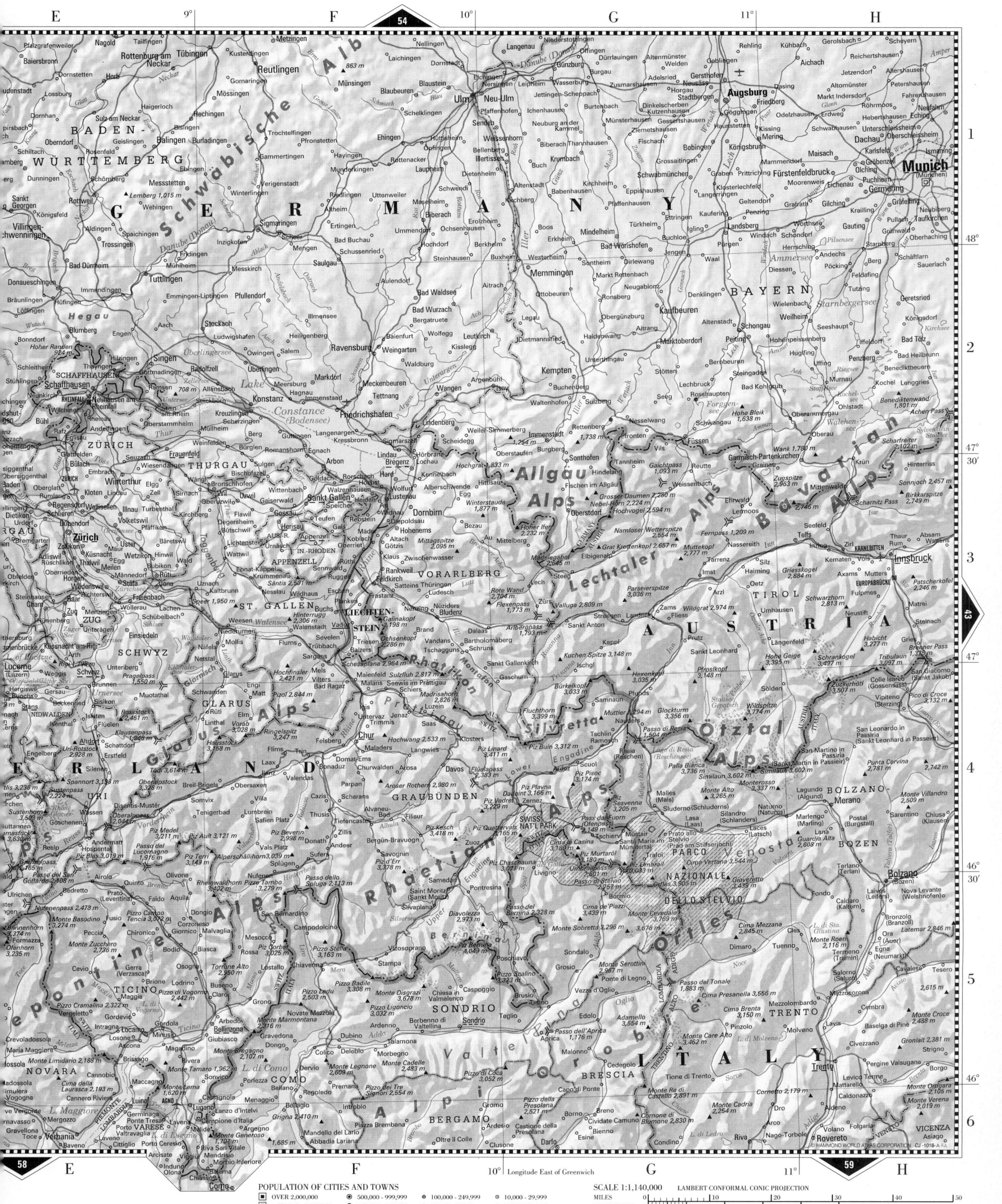

POPULATION OF CITIES AND TOWNS

■ OVER 2,000,000   ● 500,000 - 999,999   ● 100,000 - 249,999   ○ 10,000 - 29,999

□ 1,000,000 - 1,999,999   ● 250,000 - 499,999   ○ 30,000 - 99,999   ○ UNDER 10,000

Longitude East of Greenwich

SCALE 1:1,140,000   LAMBERT CONFORMAL CONIC PROJECTION

MILES 0   10   20   30   40   50

KILOMETERS 0   10   20   30   40   50

HAMMOND WORLD ATLAS CORPORATION   CJ-1018-A AA

Northern Italy

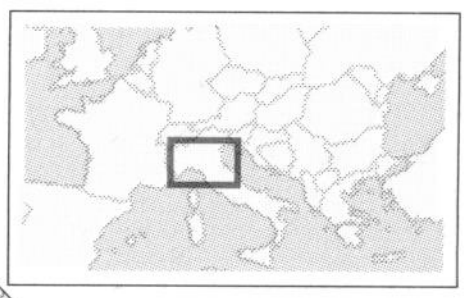

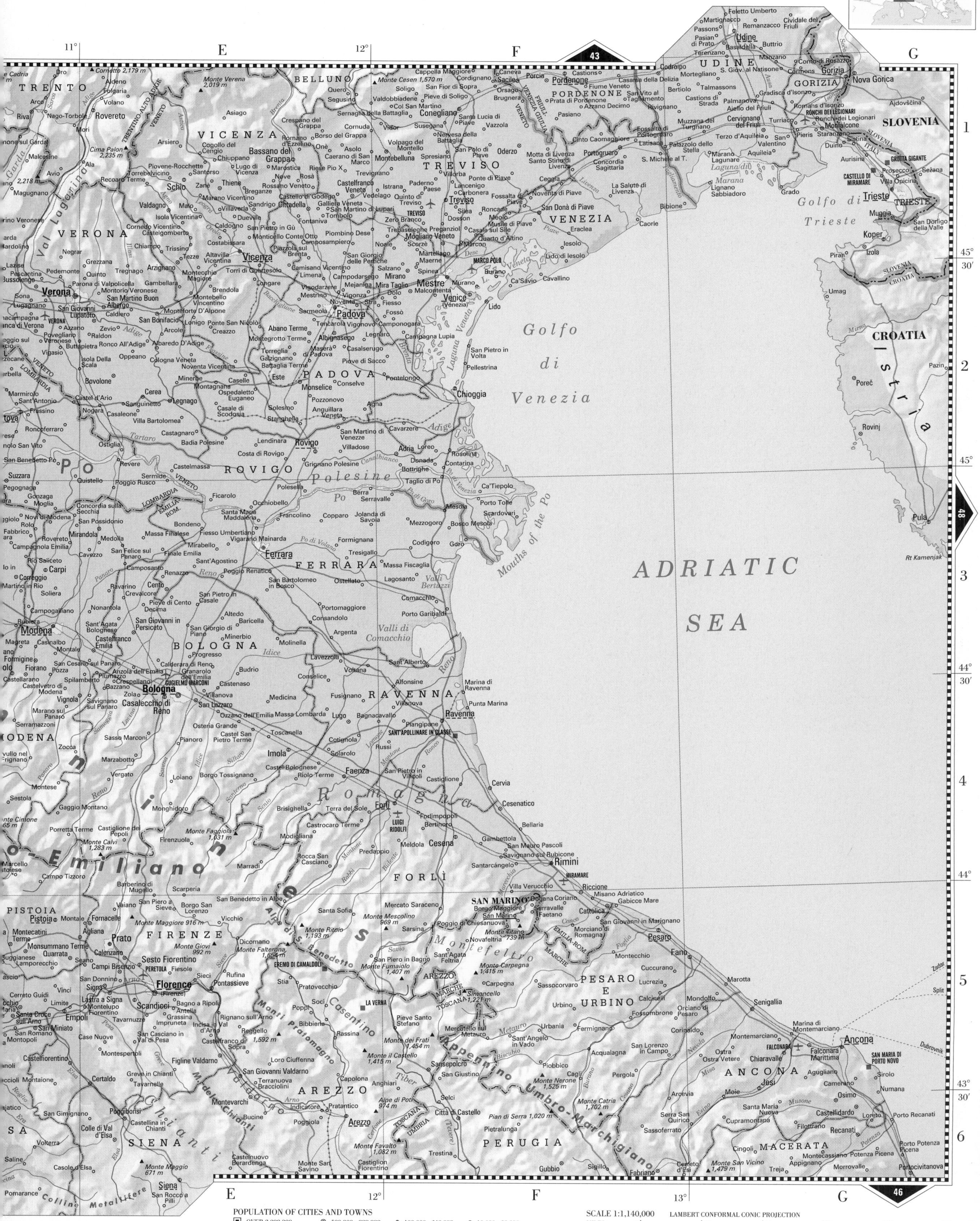

Major labels

TRENTO · VICENZA · BELLUNO · VERONA · TREVISO · VENEZIA · UDINE · PORDENONE · GORIZIA · SLOVENIA · CROATIA · Istria

Verona · Vicenza · Padova · Mestre · Venice (Venezia) · Trieste · Koper

PADOVA · ROVIGO · Polesine · Po · FERRARA · Ferrara · BOLOGNA · Bologna · MODENA · Modena · Carpi

RAVENNA · Ravenna · ROMAGNA · FORLÌ · Forlì · Rimini · SAN MARINO · San Marino

Golfo di Venezia

ADRIATIC SEA

Mouths of the Po

PISTOIA · Pistoia · FIRENZE · Firenze · Florence (Firenze) · Prato · AREZZO · Arezzo · SIENA · Siena

PESARO E URBINO · Pesaro · Fano · ANCONA · Ancona · MARCHE · PERUGIA · MACERATA

Appennino Umbro-Marchigiano

Monti Pratomagno · Casentino · Chianti · Tiber

Legend

POPULATION OF CITIES AND TOWNS

- ■ OVER 2,000,000
- ▣ 1,000,000 – 1,999,999
- ● 500,000 – 999,999
- ◉ 250,000 – 499,999
- ● 100,000 – 249,999
- ○ 30,000 – 99,999
- ○ 10,000 – 29,999
- ○ UNDER 10,000

SCALE 1:1,140,000   LAMBERT CONFORMAL CONIC PROJECTION

MILES 0 10 20 30 40 50

KILOMETERS 0 10 20 30 40 50

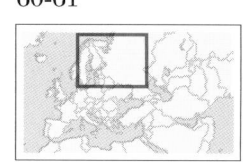

Southeastern Europe

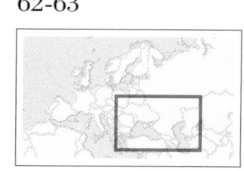

RUSSIA

KAZAKHSTAN

UZBEKISTAN

TURKMENISTAN

GEORGIA

ARMENIA

AZERBAIJAN

IRAN

CASPIAN SEA

Aral Sea

Russia and Neighboring Countries

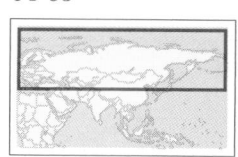

POPULATION OF CITIES AND TOWNS

■ OVER 2,000,000	● 500,000 - 999,999	○ 50,000 - 99,999
▣ 1,000,000 - 1,999,999	● 100,000 - 499,999	○ UNDER 50,000

SCALE 1:20,500,000   LAMBERT CONFORMAL CONIC PROJECTION

MILES   0   300   600   900
KILOMETERS   0   300   600   900

RUSSIA
(Administrative divisions are named only when
they differ from their respective capitals.)

1. RESPUBLIKA ADYGEYA
2. RESPUBLIKA KARACHAYEVO-CHERKESIYA
3. RESPUBLIKA KABARDINO-BALKARIYA
4. RESPUBLIKA SEVERNAYA OSETIYA-ALANIYA
5. RESPUBLIKA INGUSHETIYA
6. RESPUBLIKA CHECHNYA
7. RESPUBLIKA DAGESTAN
8. RESPUBLIKA MORDOVIYA
9. RESPUBLIKA CHUVASHIYA
10. RESPUBLIKA MARIY-EL
11. RESPUBLIKA TATARSTAN
12. RESPUBLIKA BASHKORTOSTAN
13. RESPUBLIKA UDMURTIYA
14. KOMI-PERMYATSKIY AVTONOMNYY OKRUG
15. RESPUBLIKA KHAKASIYA
16. UST-ORDYNSKIY BURYATSKIY AVT. OKRUG
17. AGINSKIY BURYATSKIY AVT. OKRUG

© HAMMOND WORLD ATLAS CORPORATION   CJ-29-A

Asia

The delta of the Indus River, the longest river in southwest Asia, is the highlight of this southeast-looking, low-oblique image. Fed by snowmelt and glacial meltwater from the mountains of the Tibet Plateau, the Indus River flows nearly 1800 miles (2897 km.) before emptying into the Arabian Sea. After leaving the Tibet Plateau, the river flows onto the Punjab Plains of western Pakistan and through a vast alluvial lowland where it receives its major tributary, the Panjnad (five streams). In this severely arid landscape the rivers form precarious strips of fertile land.

AREA OF OPTIMIZATION

The red band which surrounds this map defines the "Area of Optimization." Within this bounding curve is the most accurate conformal map that can be made of the region. Outside the optimized area, distortion increases rapidly, and tears or other irregularities in the grid may occur. (See page 6 for additional information.)

POPULATION OF CITIES AND TOWNS

| ■ OVER 3,000,000 | ● 500,000 - 999,999 | ○ UNDER 100,000 |
| □ 1,000,000 - 2,999,999 | ● 100,000 - 499,999 | |

SCALE 1:47,700,000   OPTIMAL CONFORMAL PROJECTION

Longitude East of Greenwich

© HAMMOND WORLD ATLAS CORPORATION   CJ · 1030 · A A

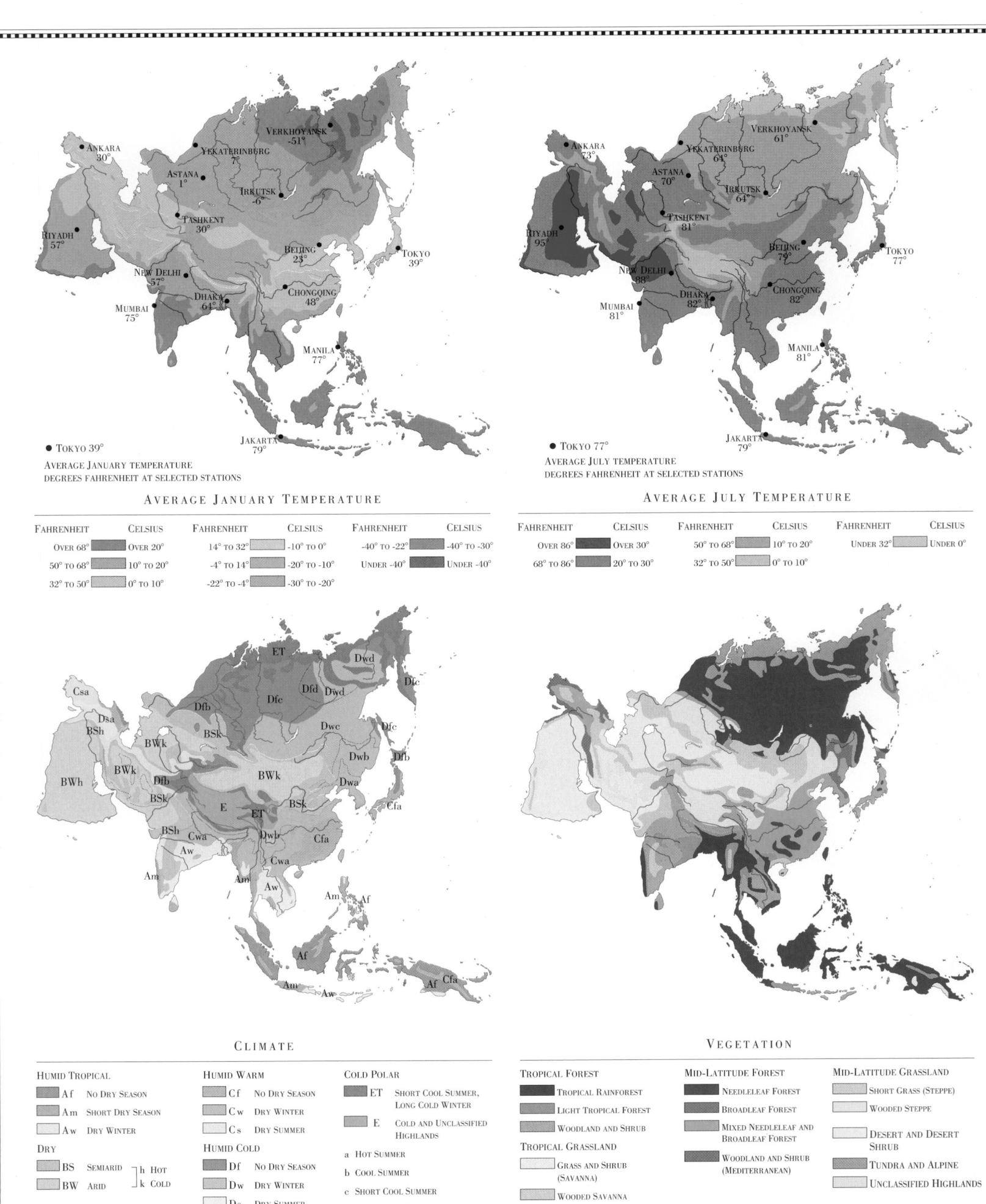

AVERAGE JANUARY TEMPERATURE

● TOKYO 39°
AVERAGE JANUARY TEMPERATURE
DEGREES FAHRENHEIT AT SELECTED STATIONS

FAHRENHEIT	CELSIUS	FAHRENHEIT	CELSIUS	FAHRENHEIT	CELSIUS
OVER 68°	OVER 20°	14° TO 32°	-10° TO 0°	-40° TO -22°	-40° TO -30°
50° TO 68°	10° TO 20°	-4° TO 14°	-20° TO -10°	UNDER -40°	UNDER -40°
32° TO 50°	0° TO 10°	-22° TO -4°	-30° TO -20°		

AVERAGE JULY TEMPERATURE

● TOKYO 77°
AVERAGE JULY TEMPERATURE
DEGREES FAHRENHEIT AT SELECTED STATIONS

FAHRENHEIT	CELSIUS	FAHRENHEIT	CELSIUS	FAHRENHEIT	CELSIUS
OVER 86°	OVER 30°	50° TO 68°	10° TO 20°	UNDER 32°	UNDER 0°
68° TO 86°	20° TO 30°	32° TO 50°	0° TO 10°		

CLIMATE

HUMID TROPICAL
Af NO DRY SEASON
Am SHORT DRY SEASON
Aw DRY WINTER

DRY
BS SEMIARID   ⌉h HOT
BW ARID   ⌋k COLD

AFTER KOEPPEN-GEIGER

HUMID WARM
Cf NO DRY SEASON
Cw DRY WINTER
Cs DRY SUMMER

HUMID COLD
Df NO DRY SEASON
Dw DRY WINTER
Ds DRY SUMMER

COLD POLAR
ET SHORT COOL SUMMER,
    LONG COLD WINTER
E   COLD AND UNCLASSIFIED
    HIGHLANDS

a HOT SUMMER
b COOL SUMMER
c SHORT COOL SUMMER
d VERY COLD WINTER

VEGETATION

TROPICAL FOREST
TROPICAL RAINFOREST
LIGHT TROPICAL FOREST
WOODLAND AND SHRUB

TROPICAL GRASSLAND
GRASS AND SHRUB
(SAVANNA)
WOODED SAVANNA

MID-LATITUDE FOREST
NEEDLELEAF FOREST
BROADLEAF FOREST
MIXED NEEDLELEAF AND
BROADLEAF FOREST
WOODLAND AND SHRUB
(MEDITERRANEAN)

MID-LATITUDE GRASSLAND
SHORT GRASS (STEPPE)
WOODED STEPPE
DESERT AND DESERT
SHRUB
TUNDRA AND ALPINE
UNCLASSIFIED HIGHLANDS

Asia - Geographical Comparisons

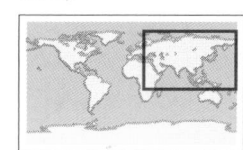

Map 1: Average Annual Rainfall

VERKHOYANSK 6
ANKARA 13
ASTANA 12
TEHRAN 9
TASHKENT 17
ULAANBAATR 7
RIYADH 4
BEIJING 25
TOKYO 61
NEW DELHI 28
CHONGQING 43
MUMBAI 82
CHERRAPUNJI 449
MANILA 82
PADANG 151

● TOKYO 61

AVERAGE ANNUAL RAINFALL
IN INCHES AT SELECTED STATIONS

AVERAGE ANNUAL RAINFALL

INCHES	CM	INCHES	CM	INCHES	CM
OVER 80	OVER 200	40 TO 60	100 TO 150	10 TO 20	25 TO 50
60 TO 80	150 TO 200	20 TO 40	50 TO 100	UNDER 10	UNDER 25

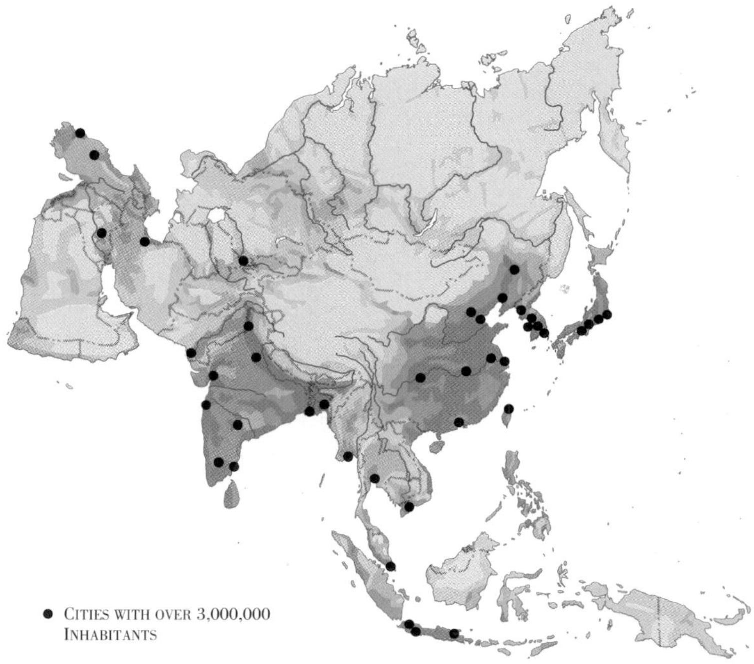

Map 2: Population Distribution

● CITIES WITH OVER 3,000,000
INHABITANTS

POPULATION DISTRIBUTION

DENSITY PER		SQ. MI.	SQ. KM.	SQ. MI.	SQ. KM.
SQ. MI.	SQ. KM.	130 TO 260	50 TO 100	3 TO 25	1 TO 10
OVER 260	OVER 100	25 TO 130	10 TO 50	UNDER 3	UNDER 1

Map 3: Land Use

TOBACCO
WHEAT
OLIVES
FRUIT
SHEEP
SHEEP
DATES
SHEEP
OATS
WHEAT
CATTLE
FURS
POTATOES
OATS WHEAT
FURS
OATS
SHEEP
COTTON
SHEEP
WHEAT
SHEEP
WHEAT
POTATOES
SOYBEANS
RICE
TEA
DATES
PEANUTS
COTTON
CATTLE
WHEAT
RICE
TEA
RICE
SOYBEANS
CORN
RICE COTTON
TEA
HOGS
SUGARCANE
FRUIT
RICE
JUTE
RICE
CASSAVA
CORN
RICE
SUGAR
RUBBER
FRUIT
RICE
TEA
RUBBER
COCONUTS
RUBBER
COCONUTS
SPICES
SPICES
COCONUTS
COCONUTS
COCOA
RICE
COFFEE

LAND USE

- CEREALS, LIVESTOCK
- CASH CROPS, MIXED FARMING
- DAIRY, LIVESTOCK
- DIVERSIFIED TROPICAL & SUBTROPICAL CROPS
- LIVESTOCK RANCHING & HERDING
- SPECIAL CROPS
- FORESTS
- NONPRODUCTIVE

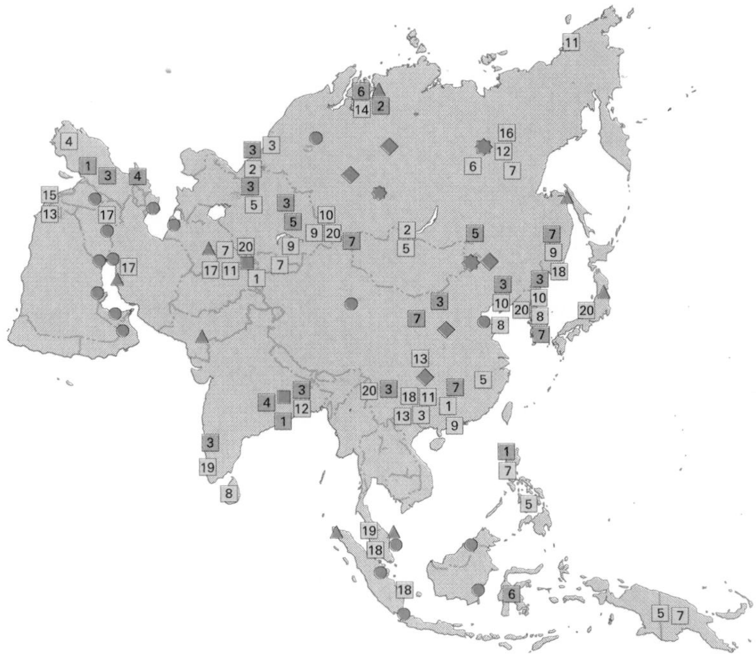

Map 4: Mineral Resources

MINERAL RESOURCES

ENERGY & FUELS
- ◆ COAL
- ⬢ LIGNITE
- ▲ NATURAL GAS
- ● PETROLEUM
- ▪ URANIUM

IRON & FERROALLOYS
- 1 CHROMIUM
- 2 COBALT
- 3 IRON ORE
- 4 MANGANESE
- 5 MOLYBDENUM
- 6 NICKEL
- 7 TUNGSTEN

OTHER MAJOR RESOURCES
- 1 ANTIMONY
- 2 ASBESTOS
- 3 BAUXITE
- 4 BORAX
- 5 COPPER
- 6 DIAMONDS
- 7 GOLD
- 8 GRAPHITE
- 9 LEAD
- 10 MAGNESITE
- 11 MERCURY
- 12 MICA
- 13 PHOSPHATES
- 14 PLATINUM
- 15 POTASH
- 16 SILVER
- 17 SULFER
- 18 TIN
- 19 TITANIUM
- 20 ZINC

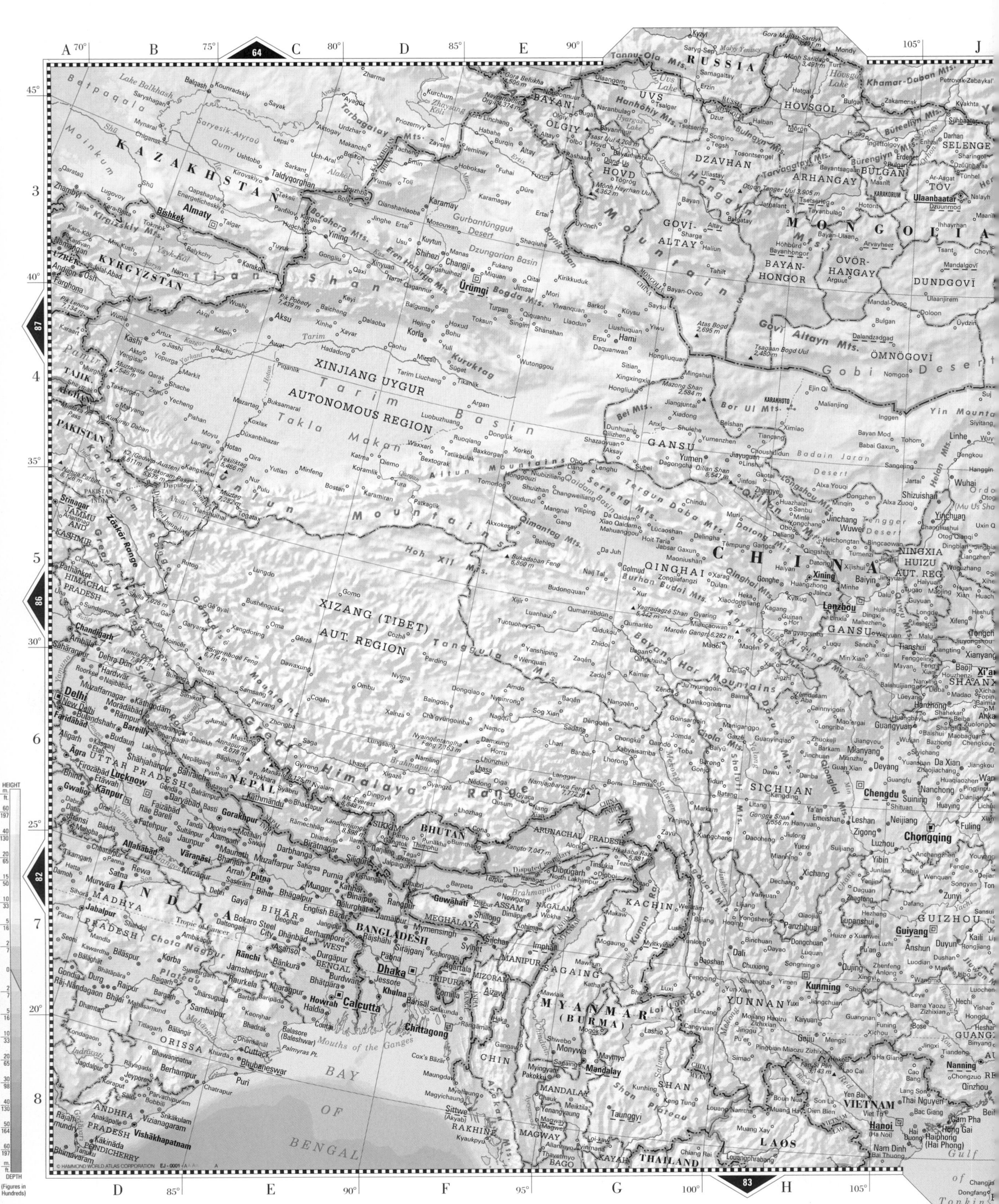

Eastern Asia

Northeastern China

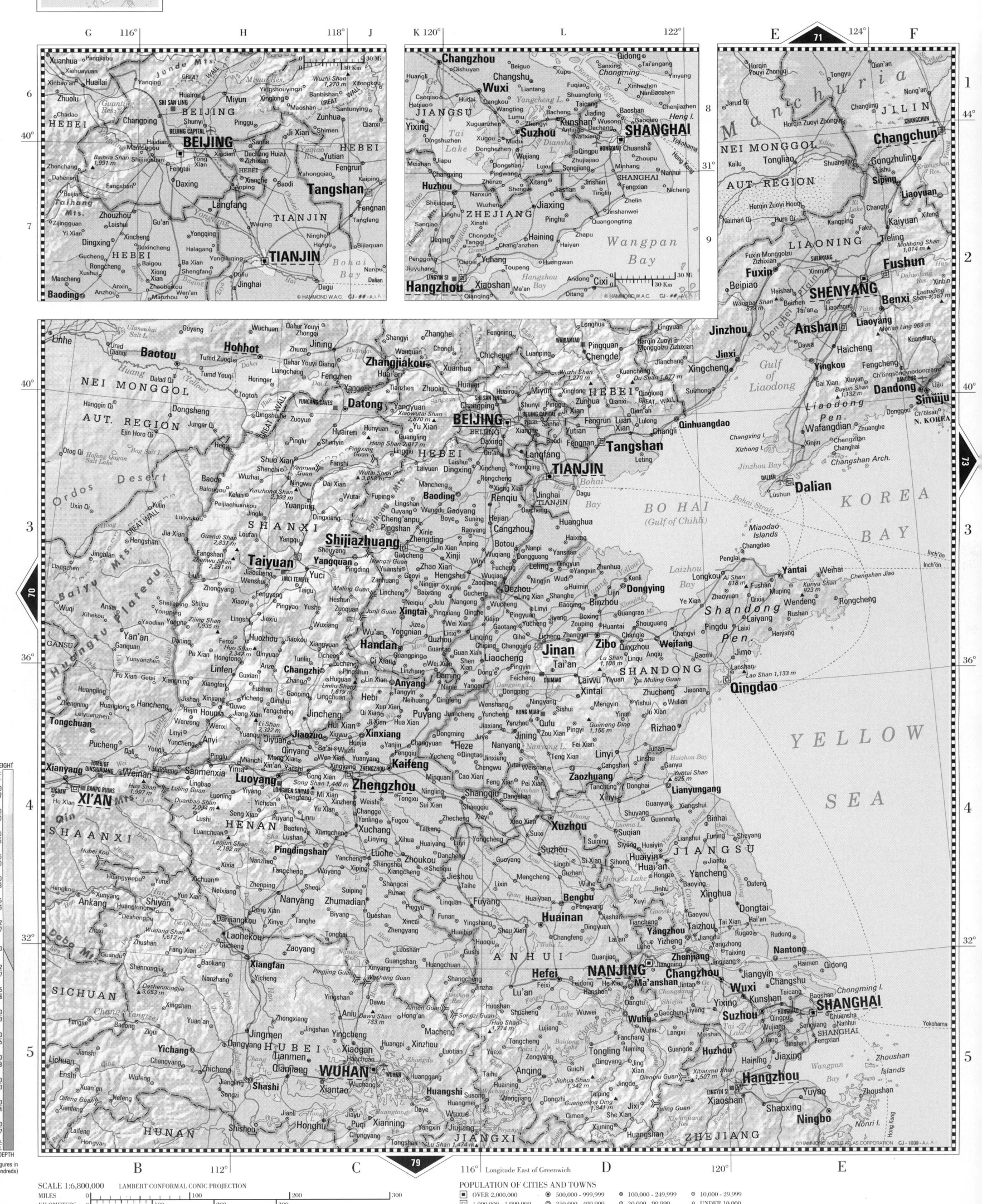

SCALE 1:6,800,000   LAMBERT CONFORMAL CONIC PROJECTION

MILES

KILOMETERS

POPULATION OF CITIES AND TOWNS

■ OVER 2,000,000   ● 500,000 - 999,999   ⊕ 100,000 - 249,999   ○ 10,000 - 29,999

▣ 1,000,000 - 1,999,999   ⊙ 250,000 - 499,999   ⊛ 30,000 - 99,999   ○ UNDER 10,000

Longitude East of Greenwich

Korea

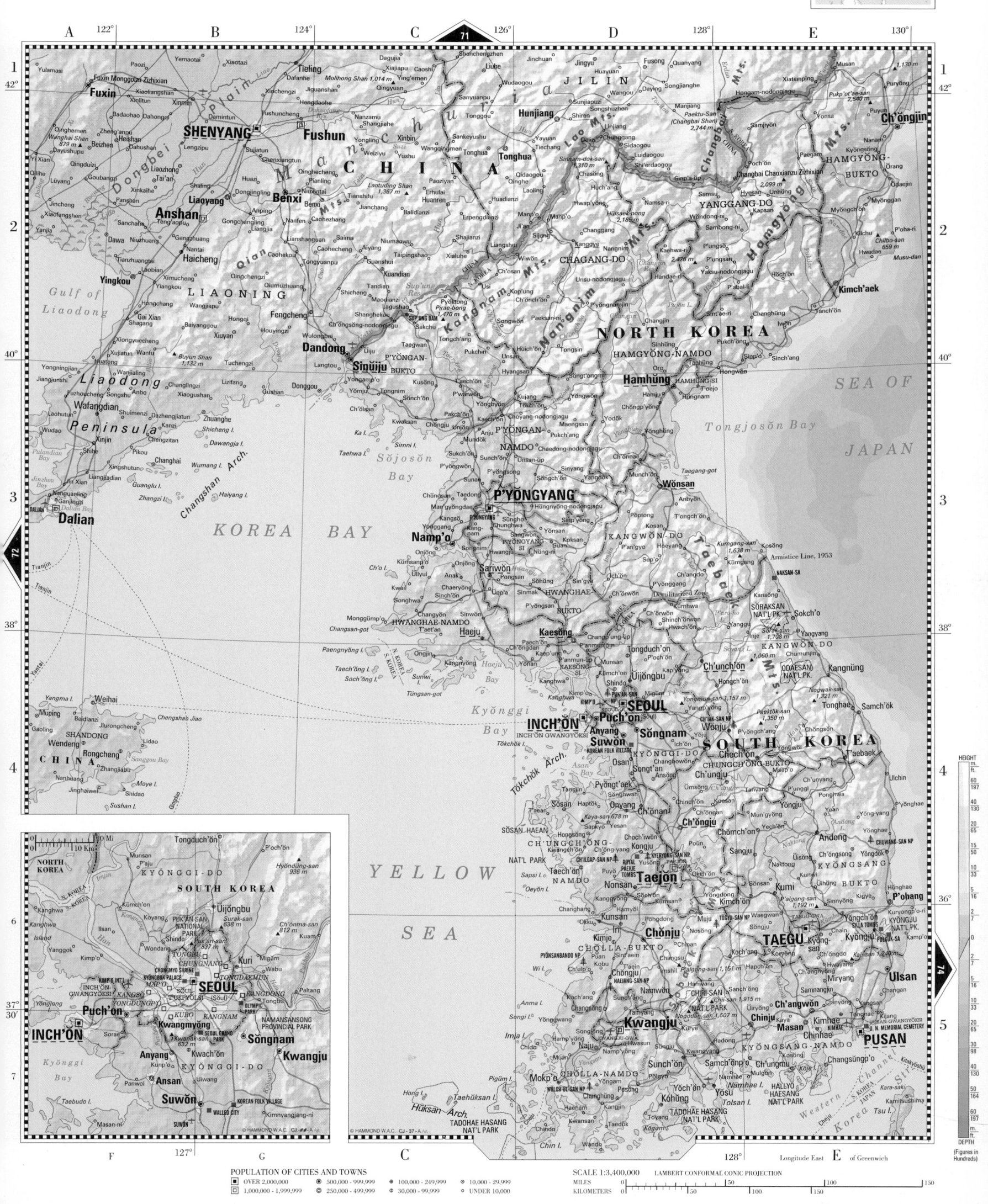

POPULATION OF CITIES AND TOWNS

- ■ OVER 2,000,000
- □ 1,000,000 - 1,999,999
- ● 500,000 - 999,999
- ○ 250,000 - 499,999
- ◉ 100,000 - 249,999
- ◎ 30,000 - 99,999
- ○ 10,000 - 29,999
- ○ UNDER 10,000

SCALE 1:3,400,000 LAMBERT CONFORMAL CONIC PROJECTION

MILES 0 ... 50 ... 100 ... 150

KILOMETERS 0 ... 50 ... 100 ... 150

Longitude East of Greenwich

HEIGHT
m. / ft.
60 / 197
40 / 130
20 / 65
15 / 50
10 / 33
7 / 23
0 / 0
7 / 23
15 / 50
30 / 98
40 / 164
60 / 197
DEPTH
m. / ft.
(Figures in Hundreds)

Central and Southern Japan

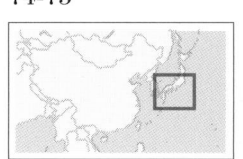

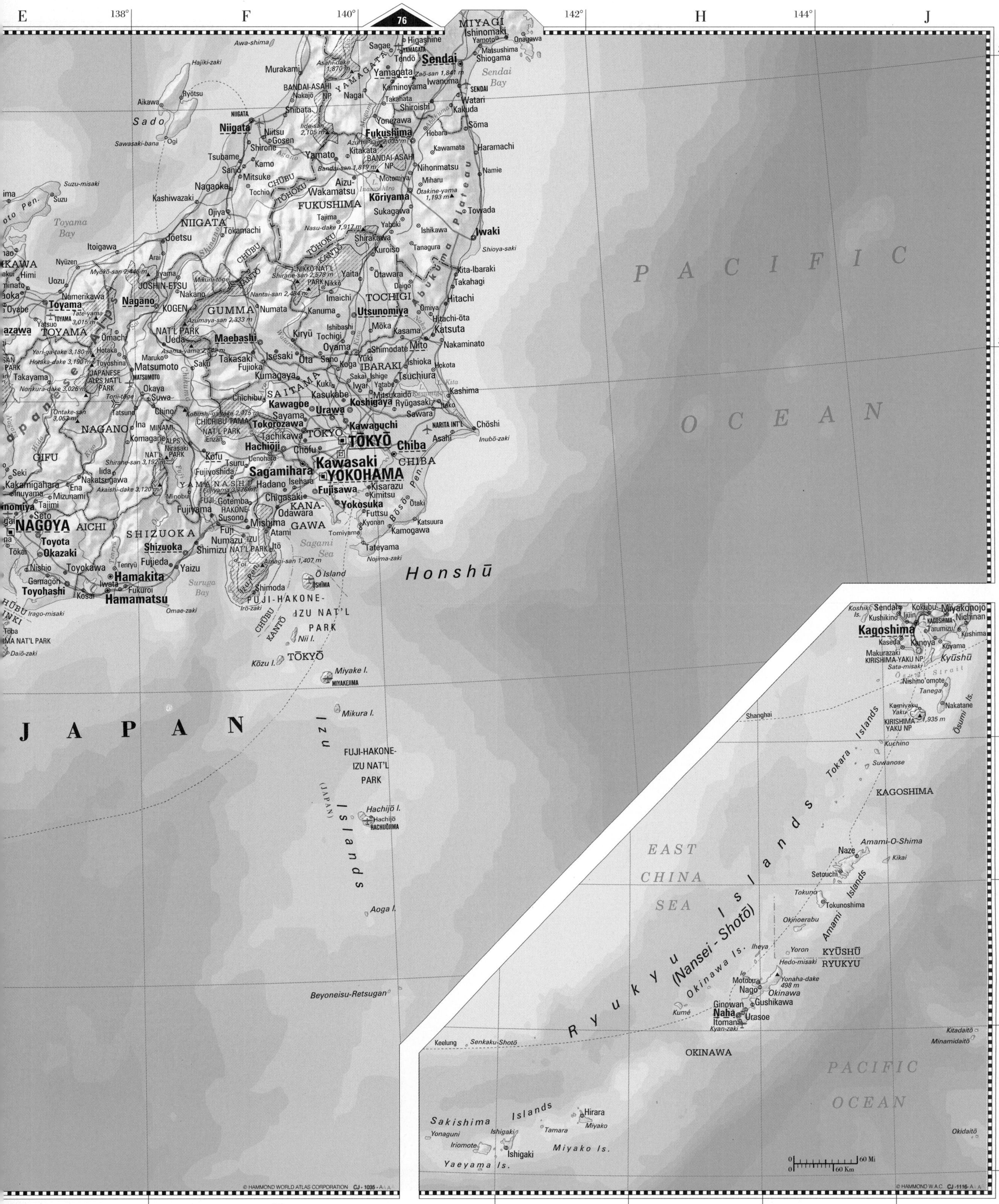

E 138° F 140° 76 142° H 144° J

38°

Awa-shima
Higashine
MIYAGI
Ishinomaki
Onagawa
Yamoto
Matsushima
Sagae
Tendo
Shiogama
Murakami
Asahi-dake 1,870 m
Yamagata
Sendai
Kaminoyama
Iwanuma
SENDAI
Sendai Bay
Nakajo
Zaō-san 1,841 m
Shiroishi
YAMAGATA
Shibata
Kakuda
Ryotsu
Watari
NIIGATA
Niigata
Nitsu
Yonezawa
Sōma
Sado
Iide-san 2,105 m
Fukushima
Haramachi
Gosen
Yamato
Kitakata
BANDAI-ASAHI NP
Sawasaki-bana
Ogi
Tsubame
Shirone
Aizu-wakamatsu
Bandai-san 1,819 m
Motomiya
Namie
Sanjō
Kamo
BANDAI-ASAHI
Nihonmatsu
Mitsuke
Tochio
Kōriyama
Miharu
Ōtakine-yama 1,193 m
Nagaoka
FUKUSHIMA
CHŪBU
Tajima
Sukagawa
Ojiya
Kashiwazaki
Jōetsu
Tōkamachi
TŌHOKU
Nasu-dake 1,917 m
Shirakawa
Ishikawa
Tanagura
Iwaki
2
Shioya-saki
Myōko-san 2,446 m
Iiyama
Nakano
NIKKŌ-NAT'L
Shirane-san 2,578 m
Nikkō
Kuroiso
Toyama Bay
Itoigawa
PARK
Imaichi
Kita-Ibaraki
Nameikawa
JOSHIN-ETSU
Nakano
Nantai-san 2,484 m
Daigo
Takahagi
Nyūzen
KOGEN
Numata
Kanuma
Ōmiya
Hitachi
Toyama
Nagano
Ueda
Asama-yama 2,542 m
Kiryū
TOCHIGI
Mōka
Hitachi-ōta
Hotaka
Yari-ga-take 3,180 m
NAT'L PARK
Azumaya-san 2,333 m
Tochigi
Utsunomiya
Kasama
Nakaminato
TOYAMA
GUMMA
Takasaki
Ishibashi
Oyama
PARK
Maebashi
Ōta
Mito
Hotaka-dake 3,190 m
Saku
Isesaki
Sano
Shimodate
IBARAKI
Ishioka
Takayama
MATSUMOTO
Maruko
Fujioka
Koga
Yuki
Norikura-dake 3,026 m
Matsumoto
JAPANESE
Kumagaya
Sakai
Ishige
Tsuchiura
ALPS NAT'L
Okaya
Chichibu
Kukki
Mitsukaido
36°
Ontake-san 3,063 m
Suwa
Kasukabe
Ryūgasaki
Kashima
Chino
CHICHIBU-TAMA
SAITAMA
Sayama
Yatabe
Sawara
NAGANO
Ina
Minami
Kobushi-gatake 2,475 m
Kawagoe
Urawa
Koshigaya
Komagane
NAT'L PARK
Tokorozawa
Kawaguchi
Chōshi
GIFU
Kōfu
Enzan
Tachikawa
TŌKYŌ
Kaida
YAMANASHI
Chōfu
TŌKYŌ
Chiba
Seki
Kofu
Tsuru
Hachiōji
Narita Int'l
Tajimi
Uenohara
Sagamihara
Asahi
Inubō-zaki
Kakamigahara
Iida
Shirane-san 3,192 m
FUJI
Hadano
Isehara
Kawasaki
YOKOHAMA
Inuyama
Minami ALPS NAT'L
Fujiyoshida
Fujisawa
Kisarazu
Akaishi-dake 3,120 m
PARK
KANA-
Yokosuka
NAGOYA
AICHI
Susono
HAKONE
Odawara
Kimitsu
3
Toyota
Shizuoka
Fuji-Gotemba
Mishima
GAWA
Yokosuka
Futtsu
Ōtaki
Okazaki
Fujieda
Numazu
Izu
Atami
Kyonan
Katsuura
Seto
Tōkai
Toyokawa
Shimizu
FUJI-HAKONE
Tomiyama
Kamogawa
Gamagōri
Yaizu
IZU NAT'L PARK
Itō
Tateyama
HINO
Nishio
Tenryu
SHIZUOKA
Nojima-zaki
Toba
Hamakita
Fukuroi
Suruga Bay
Shimoda
Ō Island
Honshū
IMA NAT'L PARK
Toyohashi
Hamamatsu
Kosai
Iwata
Omae-zaki
Irō-zaki
Daiō-zaki
Irago-misaki
FUJI-HAKONE-
IZU NAT'L
PARK
Nii I.
Kōzu I.
TŌKYŌ
Miyake I.
MIYAKEJIMA

PACIFIC

OCEAN

JAPAN

Izu
Mikura I.

FUJI-HAKONE-
IZU NAT'L
PARK

(JAPAN)
Islands

Hachijō I.
Hachijō
HACHIJŌJIMA

Aoga I.

Beyonesu-Retsugan

OCEAN

Inset: Kyūshū and Ryukyu Islands

Koshiki Is.
Sendai
Kokubu
Miyakonojō
Kushikino
Ijūin
KAGOSHIMA
Nichinan
Kaseda
Kagoshima
Kanoya
Koyama
Kushima
Makurazaki
Kyūshū
KIRISHIMA-YAKU NP
Sata-misaki
Ōsumi Strait
Nishino'omote
5
Shanghai
Tanega
Kamiyaku
Yaku
Nakatane
KIRISHIMA-
YAKU NP
1,935 m
Ōsumi Is.
Kuchino
30°
Tokara Islands
Suwanose
KAGOSHIMA
6
EAST
Naze
Amami-O-Shima
CHINA
Setouchi
Kikai
SEA
Amami Islands
28°
Tokuno
Ryukyu (Nansei-Shotō)
Okinoerabu
Amami
Tokunoshima
Iheya
Yoron
KYŪSHŪ
7
Okinawa Is.
Hedo-misaki
RYUKYU
Ryukyu Islands
Motobu
Yonaha-dake 498 m
Nago
Okinawa
Ie
Ginowan
Gushikawa
Kumé
Naha
Urasoe
Keelung
Itoman
Kyan-zaki
Kitadaitō
Senkaku-Shotō
26°
Minamidaitō
OKINAWA
PACIFIC
Sakishima Islands
Hirara
OCEAN
Yonaguni
Tamara
Miyako
Okidaitō
Ishigaki
Iriomote
Ishigaki
Miyako Is.
Yaeyama Is.
24°

E 138° F G 124° H 126° J 128° K 130° L

POPULATION OF CITIES AND TOWNS

■	OVER 2,000,000
□	1,000,000 - 1,999,999
●	500,000 - 999,999
●	250,000 - 499,999
●	100,000 - 249,999
●	30,000 - 99,999
○	10,000 - 29,999
○	UNDER 10,000

SCALE 1:3,400,000   LAMBERT CONFORMAL CONIC PROJECTION

MILES 0   50   100   150
KILOMETERS 0   50   100   150

Northern Japan

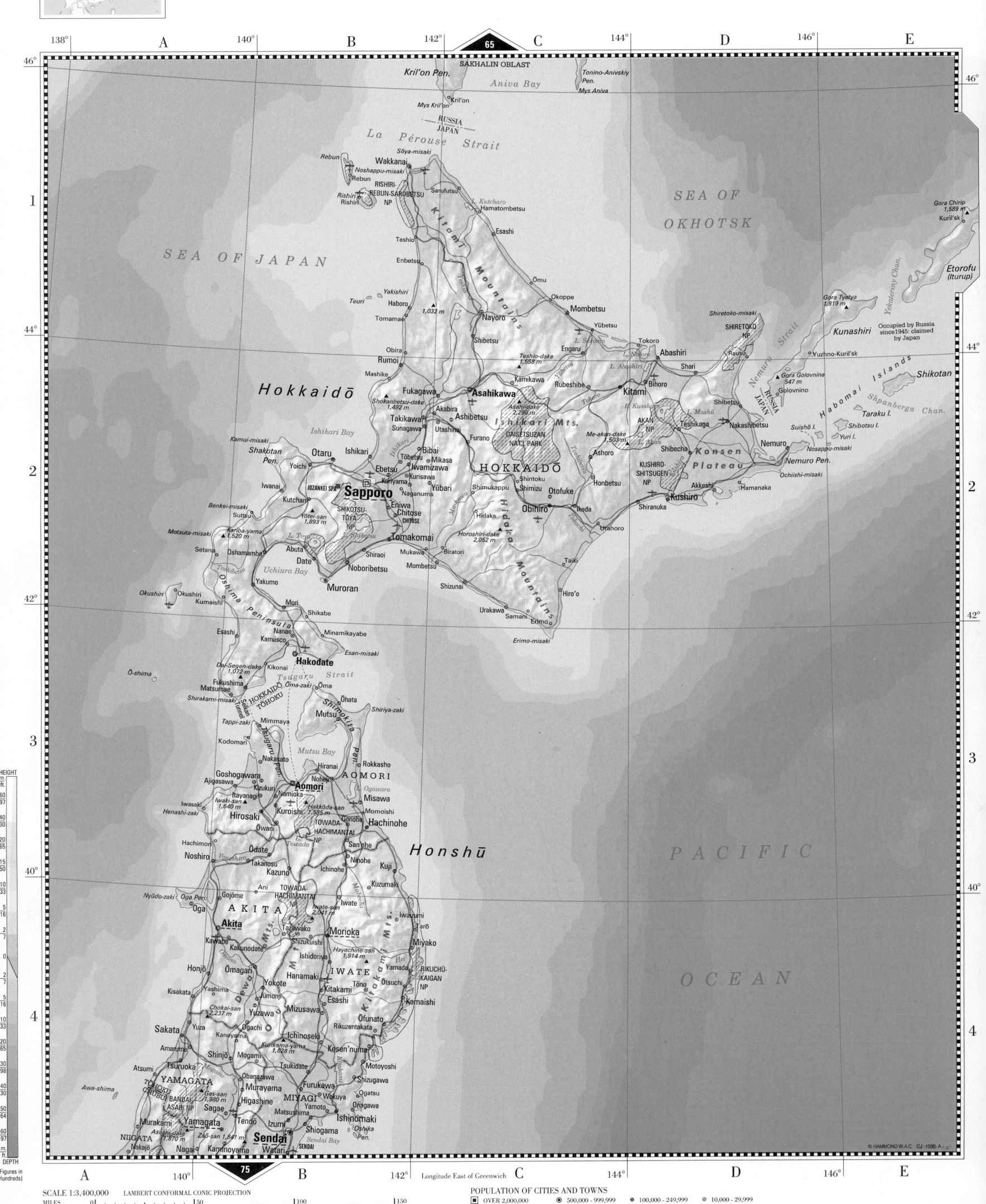

SCALE 1:3,400,000   LAMBERT CONFORMAL CONIC PROJECTION

MILES
KILOMETERS

Longitude East of Greenwich

POPULATION OF CITIES AND TOWNS

■ OVER 2,000,000	● 500,000 - 999,999	● 100,000 - 249,999	○ 10,000 - 29,999
▣ 1,000,000 - 1,999,999	◉ 250,000 - 499,999	● 30,000 - 99,999	○ UNDER 10,000

HEIGHT
m.
ft.

DEPTH
m.
ft.

(Figures in Hundreds)

© HAMMOND W.A.C. CJ-1036-A

Tōkyō-Yokohama, Ōsaka-Nagoya

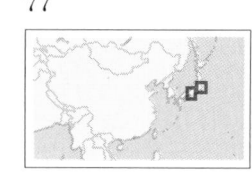

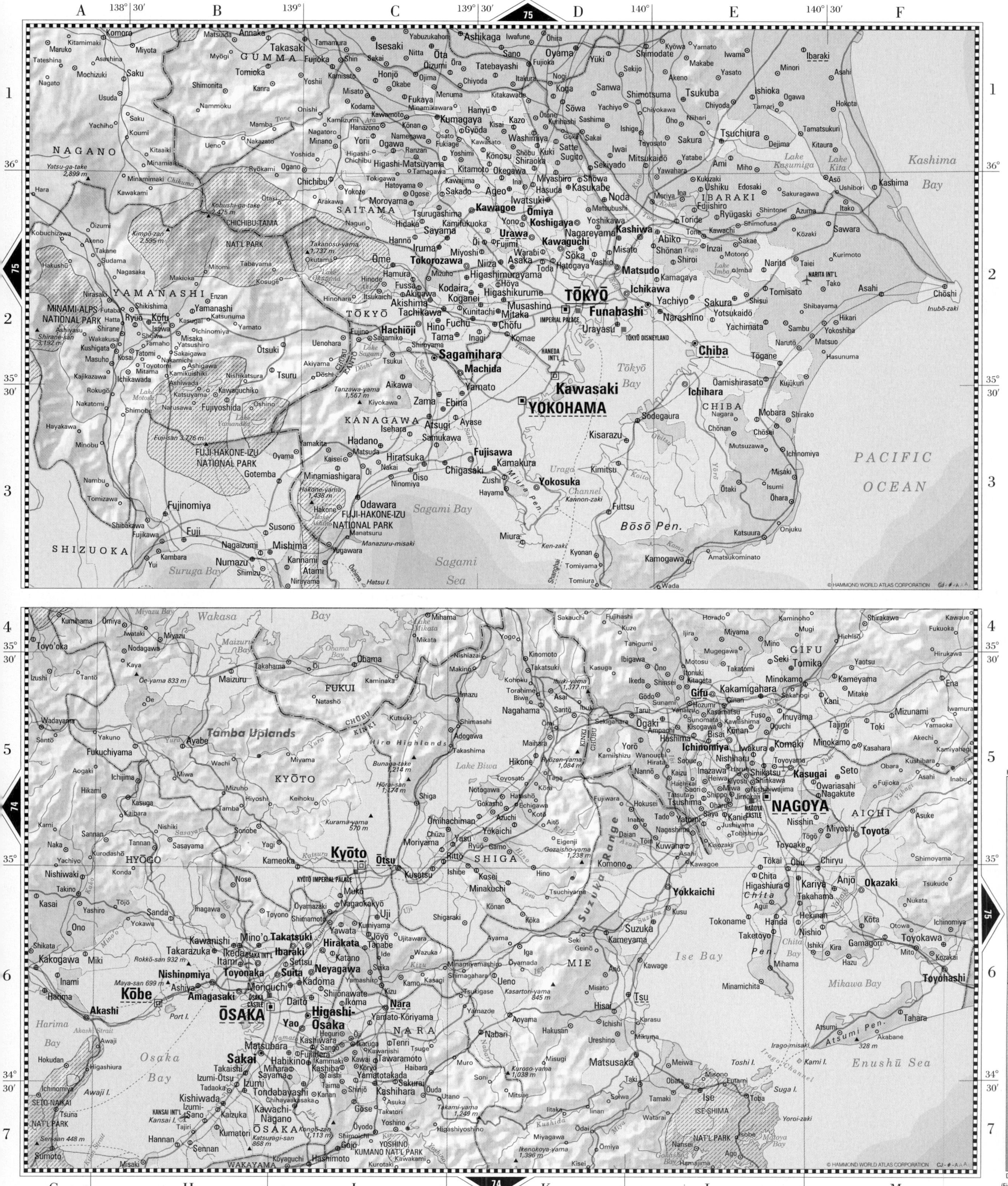

Indochina

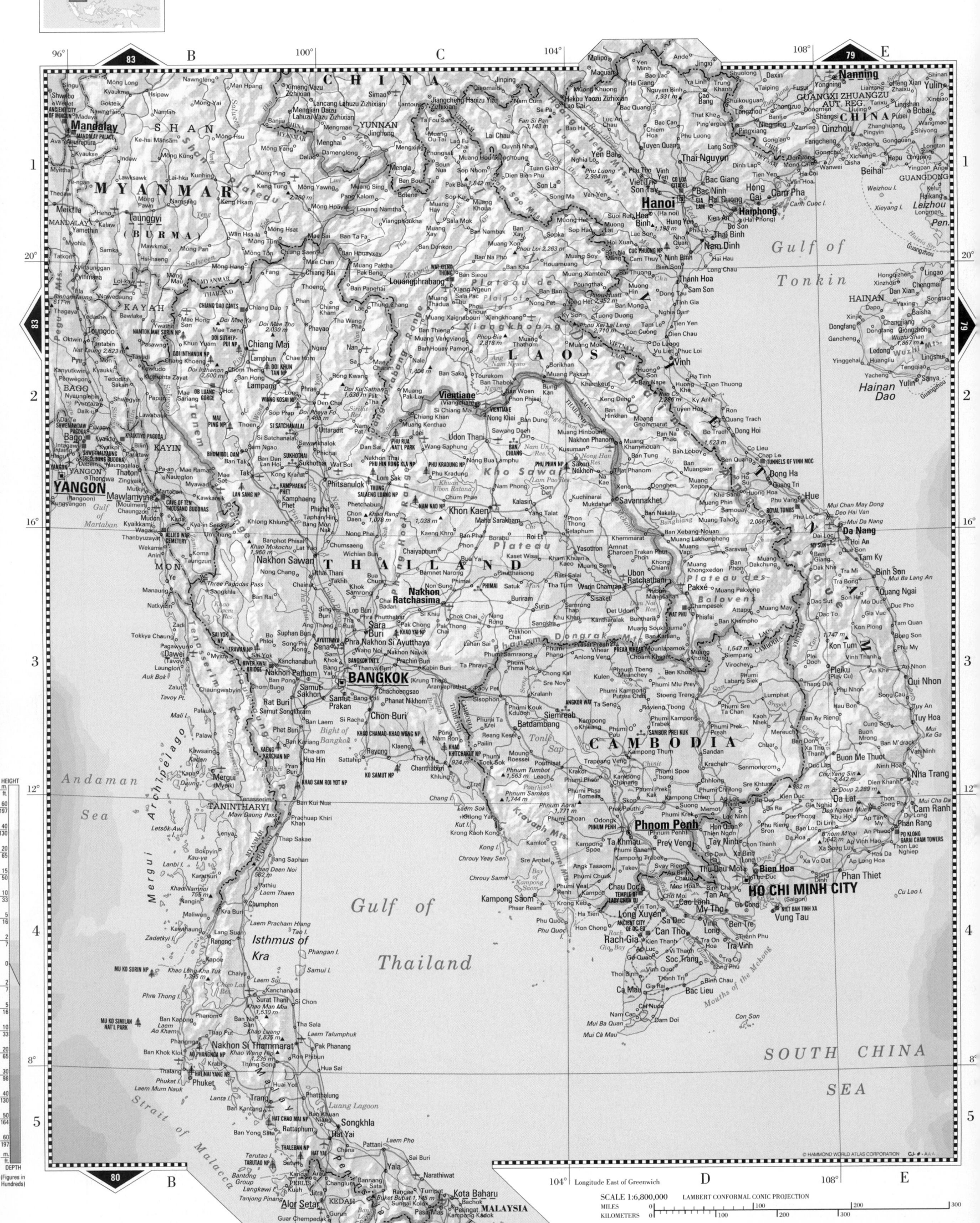

SCALE 1:6,800,000   LAMBERT CONFORMAL CONIC PROJECTION

MILES 0   100   200   300

KILOMETERS 0   100   200   300

Longitude East of Greenwich

Southeastern China, Taiwan, Philippines

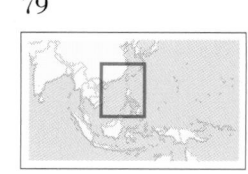

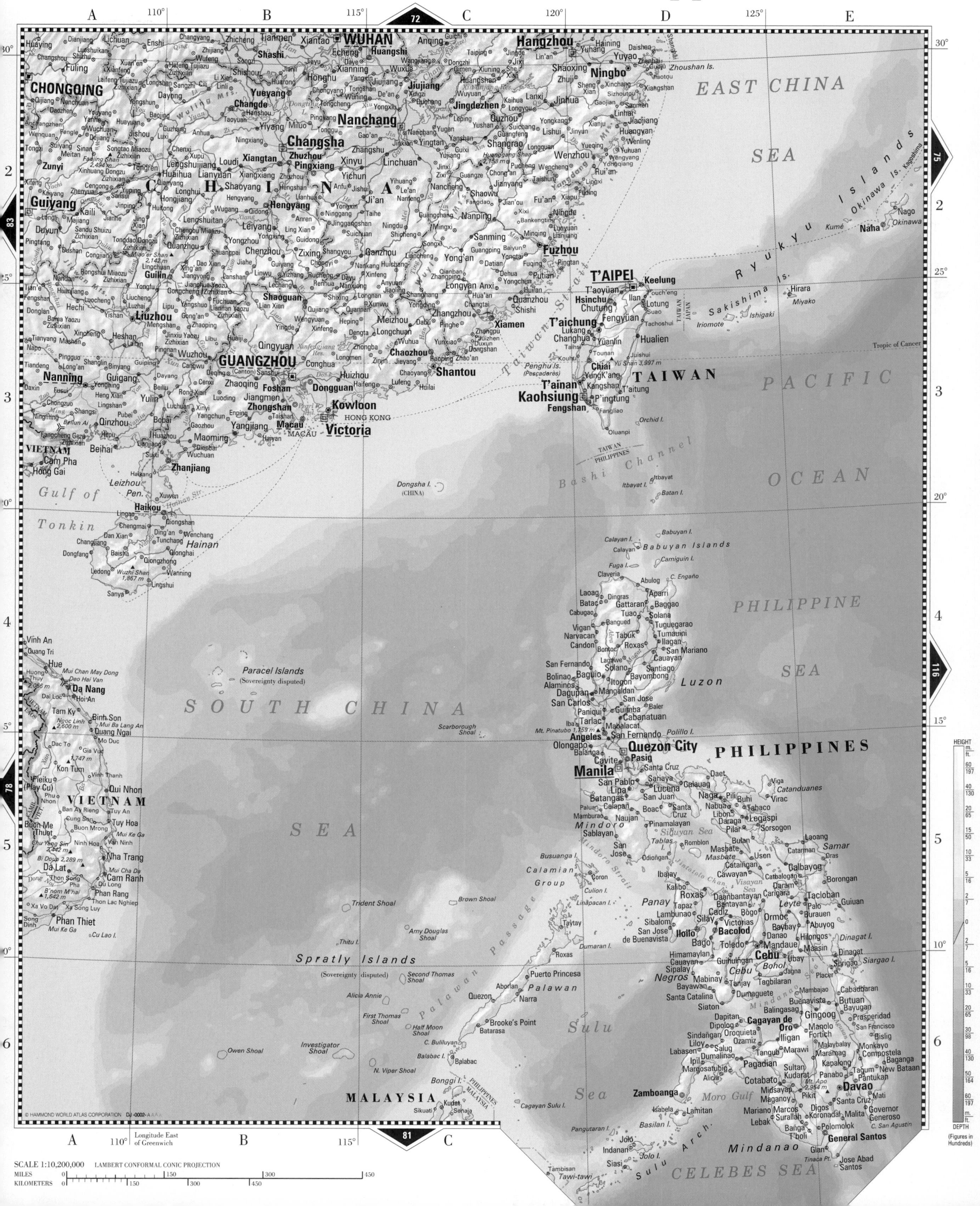

CHONGQING · **WUHAN** · **Hangzhou** · **Ningbo**

CHINA

Guiyang · **Changsha** · **Nanchang** · **Fuzhou**

Guilin · **Liuzhou** · **Shaoguan** · **Xiamen**

Nanning · **GUANGZHOU** · **Shantou** · **T'AIPEI** · **Keelung**

Zhanjiang · **Dongguan** · **Kowloon** · **HONG KONG** · **Victoria** · **Macau** · **T'aichung**

Haikou · **Hainan** · **Kaohsiung** · **TAIWAN**

EAST CHINA SEA

Ryukyu Islands · *Okinawa Is.* · *Naha* · *Okinawa*

PACIFIC OCEAN

Tropic of Cancer

TAIWAN PHILIPPINES

Bashi Channel · *Dongsha I. (CHINA)*

VIETNAM

Gulf of Tonkin

SOUTH CHINA SEA

Paracel Islands (Sovereignty disputed)

Scarborough Shoal

Da Nang · **Luzon** · *PHILIPPINE SEA*

Mt. Pinatubo 1,759 m · **Angeles** · **Quezon City** · **Pasig** · **Manila** · **PHILIPPINES**

Mindoro · *Sibuyan Sea*

Spratly Islands (Sovereignty disputed)

Palawan Passage

Iloilo · **Bacolod** · *Negros* · **Cebu** · *Bohol* · *Samar* · *Leyte*

Palawan · **Puerto Princesa**

Sulu Sea

Zamboanga · **Cagayan de Oro** · **Davao** · *Mt. Apo 2,954 m*

Mindanao · *Moro Gulf* · **General Santos**

MALAYSIA

Sulu Arch. · *CELEBES SEA*

SCALE 1:10,200,000   LAMBERT CONFORMAL CONIC PROJECTION

MILES 0 — 150 — 300 — 450
KILOMETERS 0 — 150 — 300 — 450

Longitude East of Greenwich

HEIGHT / DEPTH (Figures in Hundreds)

© HAMMOND WORLD ATLAS CORPORATION

Andaman

Sea

MYANMAR
(BURMA)

THAILAND

Isthmus of
Kra

Gulf of

Thailand

CAMBODIA

Phnom Penh
(Phnum Pénh)

VIETNAM

Ho Chi Minh City
(Saigon)

Bien Hoa

SOUTH   CHIN

SEA

Spratly

MALAYSIA

Banda Aceh

Strait of Malacca

Songkhla

Hat Yai

Alor Setar

George Town
Butterworth

Medan

Kota Baharu

Kuala Terengganu

Ipoh

Malaya

Peninsula

Shah Alam
Kelang

Kuala Lumpur

Singapore

Johor Baharu

SINGAPORE

BRUNEI
Bandar Seri Begawan

Sarawak

Sibu

Kuching

Borneo

Karimantan

Pakanbaru

Sumatra

Jambi

Pontianak

Palembang

Banjarmasin

Padang

INDIAN

Equator

Greater   Sunda

Java   Sea

Bengkulu

Tanjungkarang-
Telukbetung

JAKARTA
Bekasi
Depok
Bogor   Karawang   Cirebon
Klangenan

BANDUNG

Semarang

Surakarta

Yogyakarta

SURABAYA

Malang

Madura

Java

OCEAN

SCALE 1:10,200,000   LAMBERT CONFORMAL CONIC PROJECTION

MILES   0 ‖‖‖‖‖ 150   300   450
KILOMETERS 0 ‖‖‖‖‖ 150   300   450

Longitude East of Greenwich

POPULATION OF CITIES AND TOWNS
□ OVER 2,000,000   ● 500,000 - 999,999   ● 100,000 - 249,999   ○ 10,000 - 29,999
▣ 1,000,000 - 1,999,999   ◉ 250,000 - 499,999   ● 30,000 - 99,999   ○ UNDER 10,000

HEIGHT
m. ft.
60/197
40/130
20/65
15/50
10/33
2/7
0
2/7
5/16
10/33
20/65
30/98
40/130
60/197
m. ft.
DEPTH

(Figures in
Hundreds)

Indonesia, Malaysia

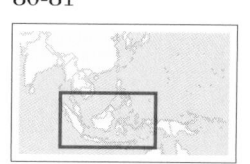

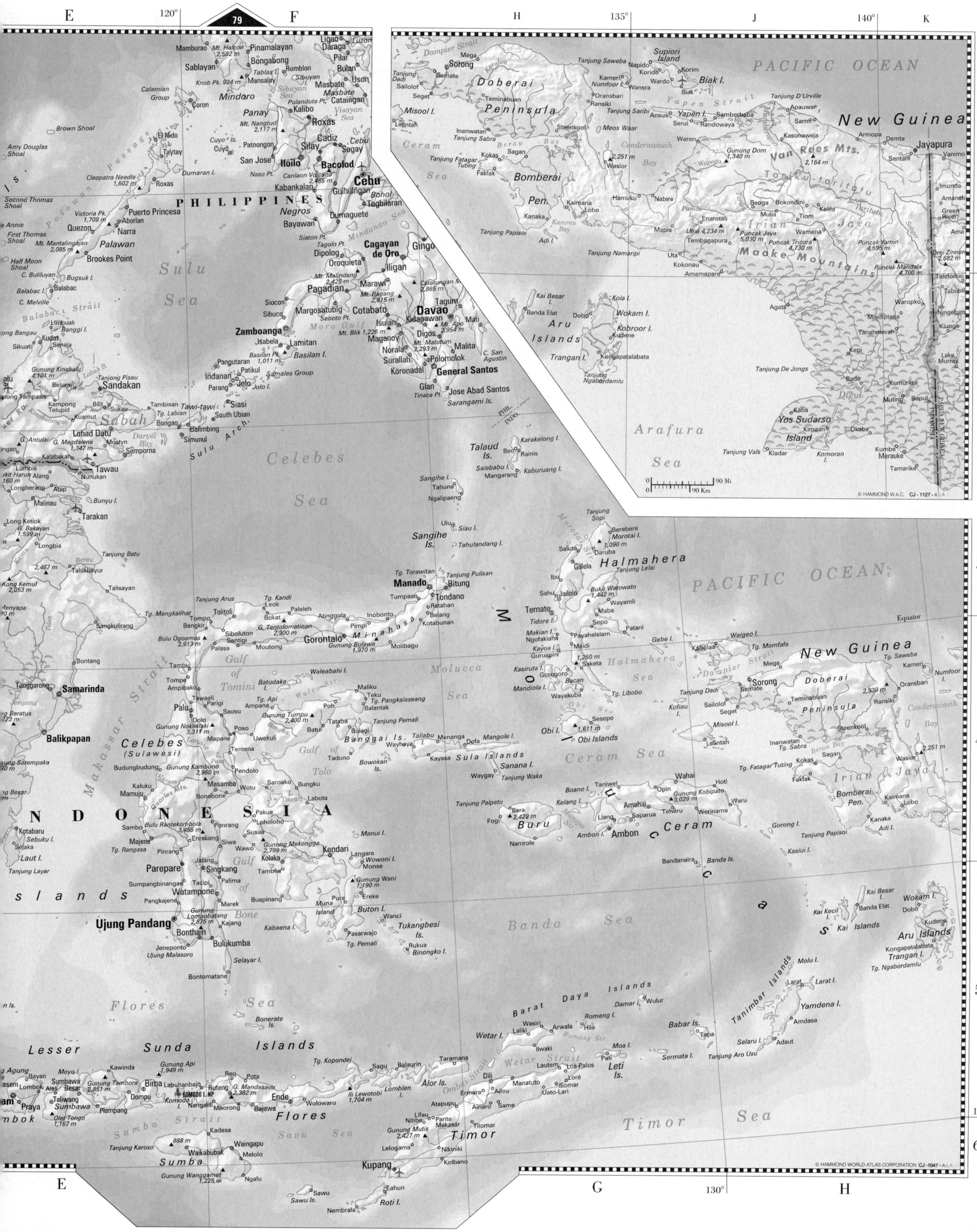

79

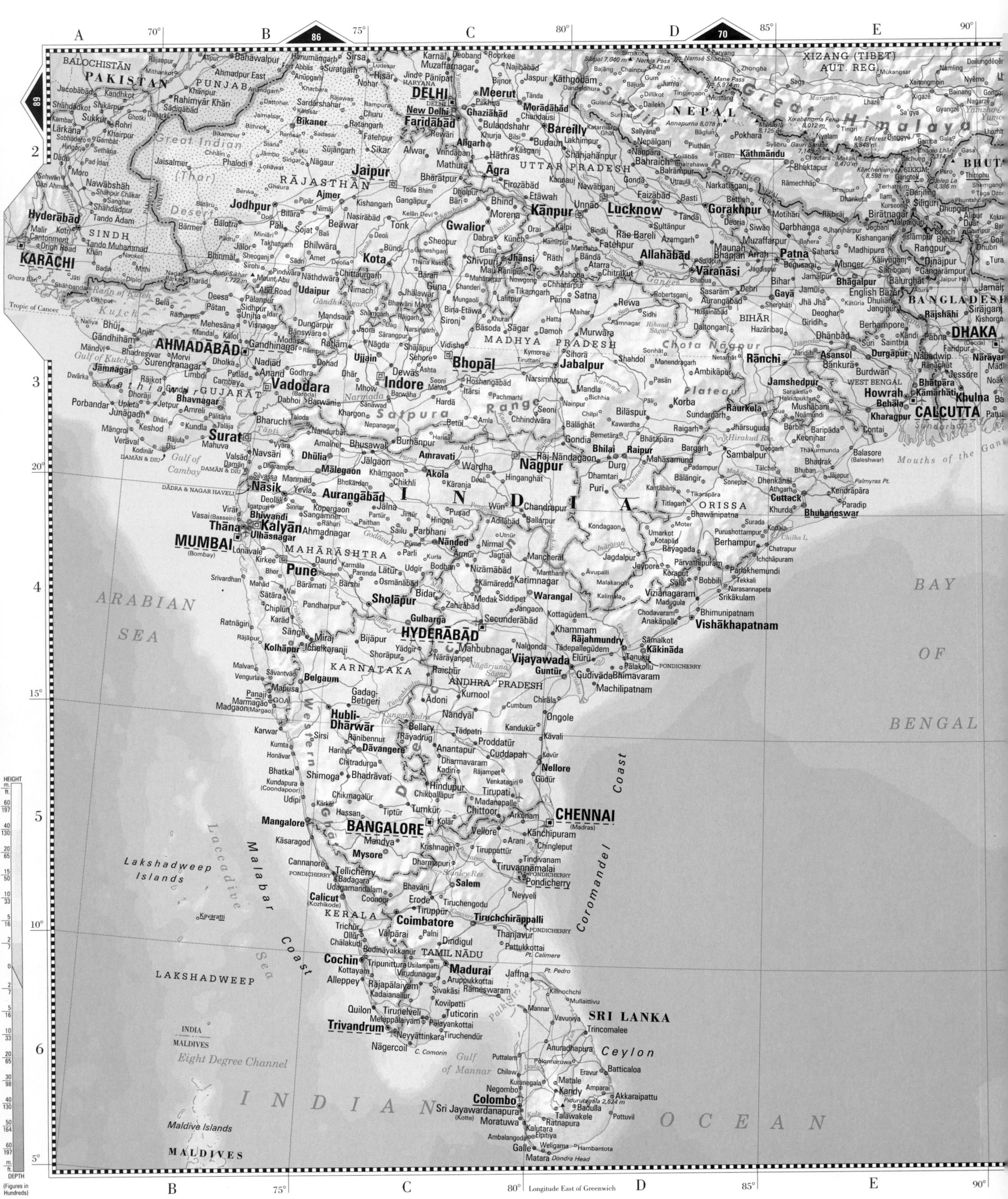

Southern Asia

POPULATION OF CITIES AND TOWNS

SCALE 1:10,200,000   LAMBERT CONFORMAL CONIC PROJECTION

■ OVER 2,000,000	● 500,000 - 999,999	◉ 100,000 - 249,999	○ 10,000 - 29,999
□ 1,000,000 - 1,999,999	◉ 250,000 - 499,999	○ 30,000 - 99,999	• UNDER 10,000

MILES   0   150   300   450
KILOMETERS   0   150   300   450

© HAMMOND WORLD ATLAS CORPORATION   CJ-#-AJA

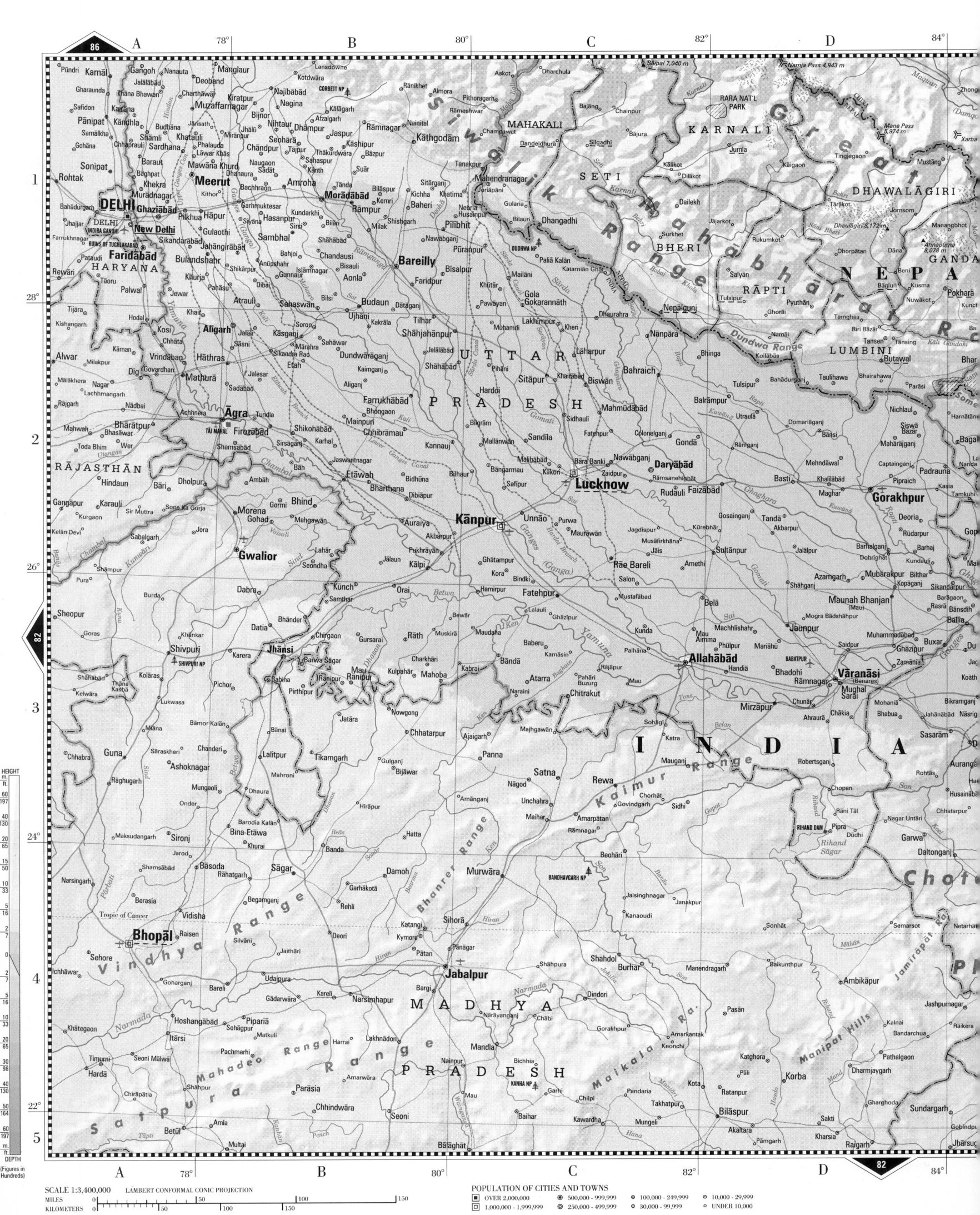

A · 78° · B · 80° · C · 82° · D · 84°

SCALE 1:3,400,000   LAMBERT CONFORMAL CONIC PROJECTION

MILES   0   50   100   150

KILOMETERS   0   50   100   150

POPULATION OF CITIES AND TOWNS

▣ OVER 2,000,000	■ 500,000 - 999,999	● 100,000 - 249,999	○ 10,000 - 29,999
▢ 1,000,000 - 1,999,999	□ 250,000 - 499,999	• 30,000 - 99,999	○ UNDER 10,000

HEIGHT

m. / ft.
60 / 197
40 / 130
20 / 65
15 / 50
10 / 33
5 / 16
2 / 7
0
2 / 7
5 / 16
10 / 33
20 / 65
30 / 98
40 / 130
50 / 164
60 / 197

m.
ft.
DEPTH
(Figures in Hundreds)

Ganges Plain

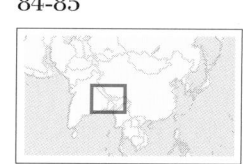

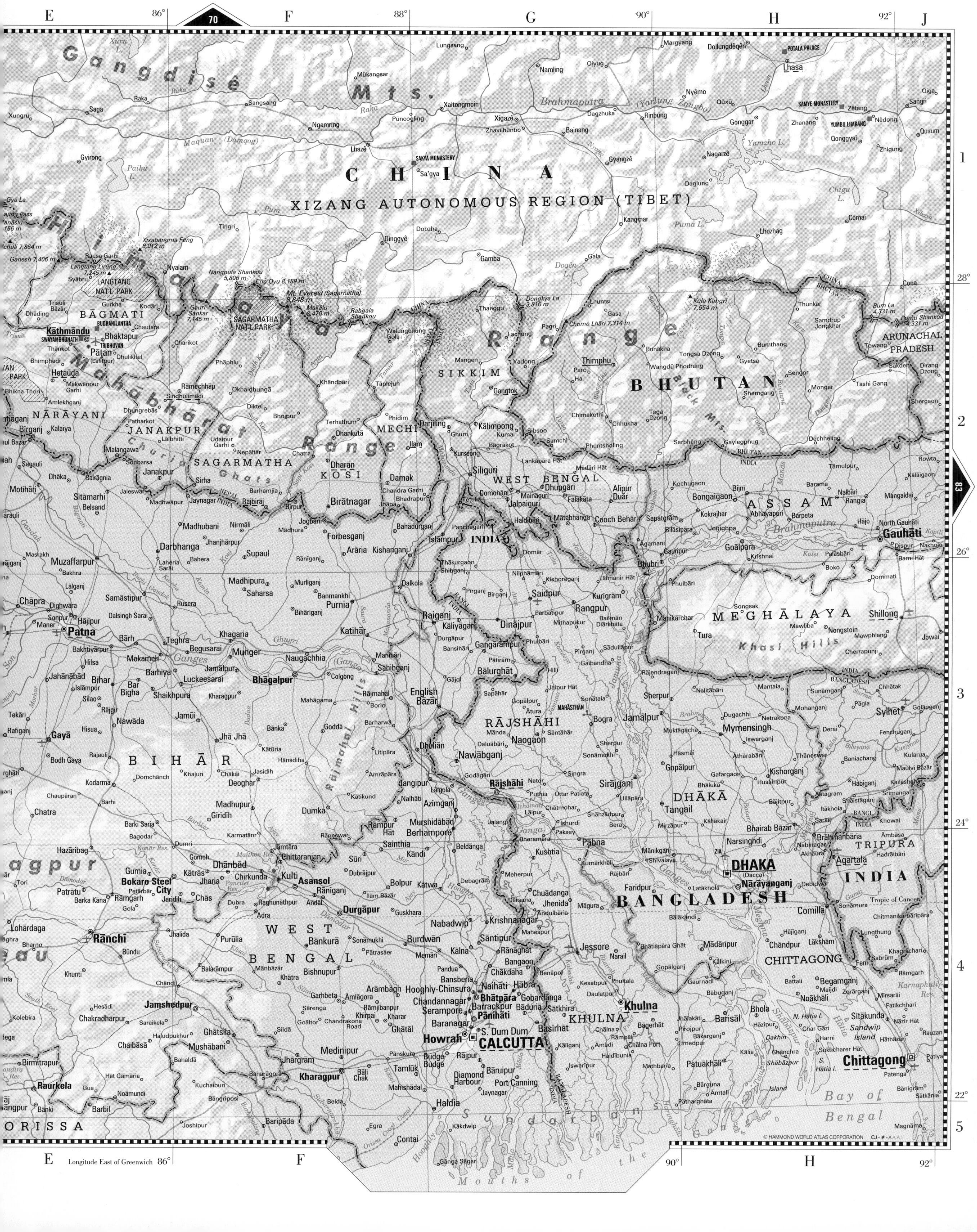

E 86° 70 F 88° G 90° H 92° J

Gangdisê Mts.

Himalaya Mahābhārat Range Churia Ghats

CHINA

XIZANG AUTONOMOUS REGION (TIBET)

Xuru L. · Mükangsar · Lungsang · Namling · Oiyug · Margyang · Doilungdêqên · POTALA PALACE · Lhasa

Saga · Sangsang · Raka · Brahmaputra (Yarlung Zangbo) · Xaitongmoin · Xigazê · Dagzhuka · Rinbung · Bainang · Zhanang · Nêdong · Gonggar · Qüxü · SAMYE MONASTERY · Zêtang · Sangri · Oiga

Xungru · Gyirong · Paikü L. · Ngamring · Püncogling · Lhazê · Zhaxilhünbo · Nagarzê · Yamzho L. · Qonggyai · Qusum

Gya La · Raung Garhi · Tingri · Dobzha · Dinggyê · SAKYA MONASTERY · Sa'gya · Pum · Daglung · Kangmar · Lhozhag · Chigu L. · Xibaxa

Himalaya

Xixabangma Feng 8,012 m · Nangpula Shankou 5,806 m · Cho Oyu 8,189 m · Gamba · Doqên · Gala · Puma L. · Comai

Nyalam · Langtang Lirung 7,245 m · Gauri Sankar 7,145 m · Mt. Everest (Sagarmatha) 8,848 m · Makalu 8,470 m · Rahgala Shankou · Walungchung Gola · Thanggu · Dongkya La 3,810 m · Lhuntsi · Gasa · Chomo Lhāri 7,314 m · Kula Kabgri 7,554 m · Thunkar · Samdrup Jongkhar · Bum La 4,331 m · Pumu Shankou 4,331 m · Cona

NEPAL · LANGTANG NAT'L PARK · SAGARMATHA NAT'L PARK · **SIKKIM** · Pagri · Punakha · Tongsa Dzong · Bumthang · **ARUNACHAL PRADESH**

BĀGMATI · Kathmāndu · SWAYAMBHUNATH · Bhaktapur · Patan · Mangen · Yadong · Thimphu · Paro · Ha · Wangdü Phodrang · Gyetsa · Tawang · Dirang Dzong

BHUTAN · Tongsa Dzong · Sengor · Mongar · Tashi Gang · Shergaon

NĀRĀYANI · JANAKPUR · **MECHI** · Darjiling · Kalimpong · Sibsoo · Chimakothi · Chhukha · Shemgang · Sakden · Rowta

SAGARMATHA · **KOSI** · Dhankuta · Ilam · Ghum · Kurseong · Gangtok · Samchi · Phuntsholing · Sarbhāng · Gaylegphug · Dechheling · Tāmulpur · Kalāigaon

ASSAM · Abhayapuri · Barama · Nalbari · Rangia · Mangaldai

Siliguri · **WEST BENGAL** · Dhupgāri · Alipur Duār · Kochugaon · Bijni · North Gauhāti · **Gauhāti** · Dispur · Nakholi

Birātnagar · Chandra Garhi · Jhāpa · Tetulia · Jalpaiguri · Falākata · Mādāri Hāt · Mātābhānga · Cooch Behār · Sapatgrām · Bilāsipāra · Hājo · Jogighopā

KOSI · Damak · Bahādurgānj · Panchagarh · Haldibāri · Domohāni · Mainaguri · **INDIA** · Agamāni · Gauripur · Krishnai · Goalpāra · Boko · Barni Hāt · Dommati

BIHĀR · Darbhanga · Madhubani · Nirmāli · Madhura · Forbesganj · Araria · Kishanganj · Thākurgaon · Shibganj · Nilphāmāri · Kishoreganj · Lālmanir Hāt · Phulbāri · **MEGHĀLAYA** · Shillong

Muzaffarpur · Samāstipur · Madhipura · Saharsa · Murliganj · Purnia · Dalkola · Pirganj · Birganj · Saidpur · Kurigrām · Bailmāri · Songsak · Tura · Mawliba · Nongstoin · Mawphlang

Patna · Begusarai · Khagaria · Katihār · Raiganj · Kāliyaganj · Dinajpur · Pārbatipur · Rangpur · Bailmān · Dlārkhāta · Manikarchar · **Khasi Hills** · Cherrapunji

Ganges · Munger · Naugachhia · Manihāri · Durgāpur · Bansihāri · Gangarāmpur · Phulbāri · Gaibandha · Rājendraganj · Nālitābāri · Mantala · **BANGLADESH** · Chhātak · Sylhet · Golāpganj

Bhāgalpur · Colgong · Sāhibganj · Gājol · Bālurghāt · Pātiram · Jaipur Hāt · Hili · Sādullāpur · Sherpur · Dugachhi · Netrakona · Derai · Fenchuganj

English Bāzār · Rājmahal · Borio · Sapāhār · Gopālpur · Atura · Bogra · Jamālpur · Muktāgācha · Mymensingh · Iswarganj · Husāmpur · Kulāura · Maulvi Bāzār · Kailāshahr

RĀJSHĀHI · Mānda · Naogaon · Daluābāri · Sāntāhar · MAHĀSTHĀN · Sherpur · Gopālpur · Gafargaon · Kishorganj · Bhāluka · Bājitpur · Āstagrām · Shāistāganj · Hābiganj · Simāngal

Gayā · Nawābganj · Litipāra · Amrapāra · Dhulian · Godāgāri · Nator · Puthia · Chātmohar · Ishurdi · Singra · Sonāmukhi · Ullāpāra · Sirājganj · Tangail · Kālia · Kāliākair · Ishkhola · **DHĀKĀ** · Bhairab Bāzār · **TRIPURA**

RĀNCHI · Hazāribag · Dumka · Jāngipur · Lālgola · Nalhāti · Azimganj · Rājshāhi · Jalangi · Lālpur · Shāhzādpur · Bera · Pābna · Mirzāpur · Nabinagar · Narsinghdi · Brāhmanbāria · Āmbāsa · Agartala

INDIA · Dhānbād · Kātrās · Jhariā · Kulti · Rānigānj · Sūri · Drājpur · Kāndi · Beldānga · Meherpur · Kushtia · Kumārkhāli · Rājbāri · Mānikganj · Shivālaya · Narayanganj · ZIA · Comilla

Bokaro Steel City · Asansol · Chittaranjan · Sainthia · Berhampore · Bheramāra · Paksey · Kumārkhāli · **Ganges** · **DHAKA** (Dacca) · Faridpur · Latākhola · Balākāndi · Chitmanikcharipāra

Durgāpur · Bolpur · Katwa · Debagram · Chuādanga · Jhenida · Māgura · Andulbāria · Dasuma · **BANGLADESH** · Chāndpur · Lākshām · Hājiganj · Lungthung

WEST BENGAL · Nabadwip · Krishnanagar · Mahespur · Jessore · Narail · Madāripur · Khāgrāchari · Ramgarh · Sabrūm

Jamshedpur · Bānkura · Sonāmukhi · Burdwān · Rānāghāt · Benāpol · Kesabpur · Khulna · Phultala · Gopālganj · Gaurnadi · Bābuganj · Noākhāli · Begamganj · Maijdi · Zorārganj · Mirsarāi

CHITTAGONG · Battali · Fatikchhari · Sītākunda · Nāzir Hāt

Kharagpur · Bishnupur · Arāmbāgh · Hooghly-Chinsura · Chandannagar · Serampore · Bhātpāra · Barrackpore · Bādurīa · Sātkhira · **KHULNA** · Chālna · Bāgerhāt · N. Hātia I. · Sandwip Island · Hātia I.

Medinipur · Garhbeta · Chandrakona Road · Baranagar · Pānihāti · S. Dum Dum · Basirhāt · Chālna Port · Pirojpur · Barguna · Barisāl · Bhola · Dakhin · Harni

Howrah · **CALCUTTA** · Budge Budge · Bāruipur · Port Canning · Jaynagar · Basirhāt · Patuākhāli · Shābāzpur · **Chittagong** · Patenga

ORISSA · Contai · Haldia · *Sundarbans* · Diamond Harbour · Mahishadal · Tamlūk · *Hooghly* · Kākdwip · Ganga Sāgar · *Bay of Bengal*

Mouths of the · Tropic of Cancer

1 · 28° · 83 · 26° · 3 · 24° · 4 · 22° · 5

© HAMMOND WORLD ATLAS CORPORATION CJ-F-AA

Punjab Plain

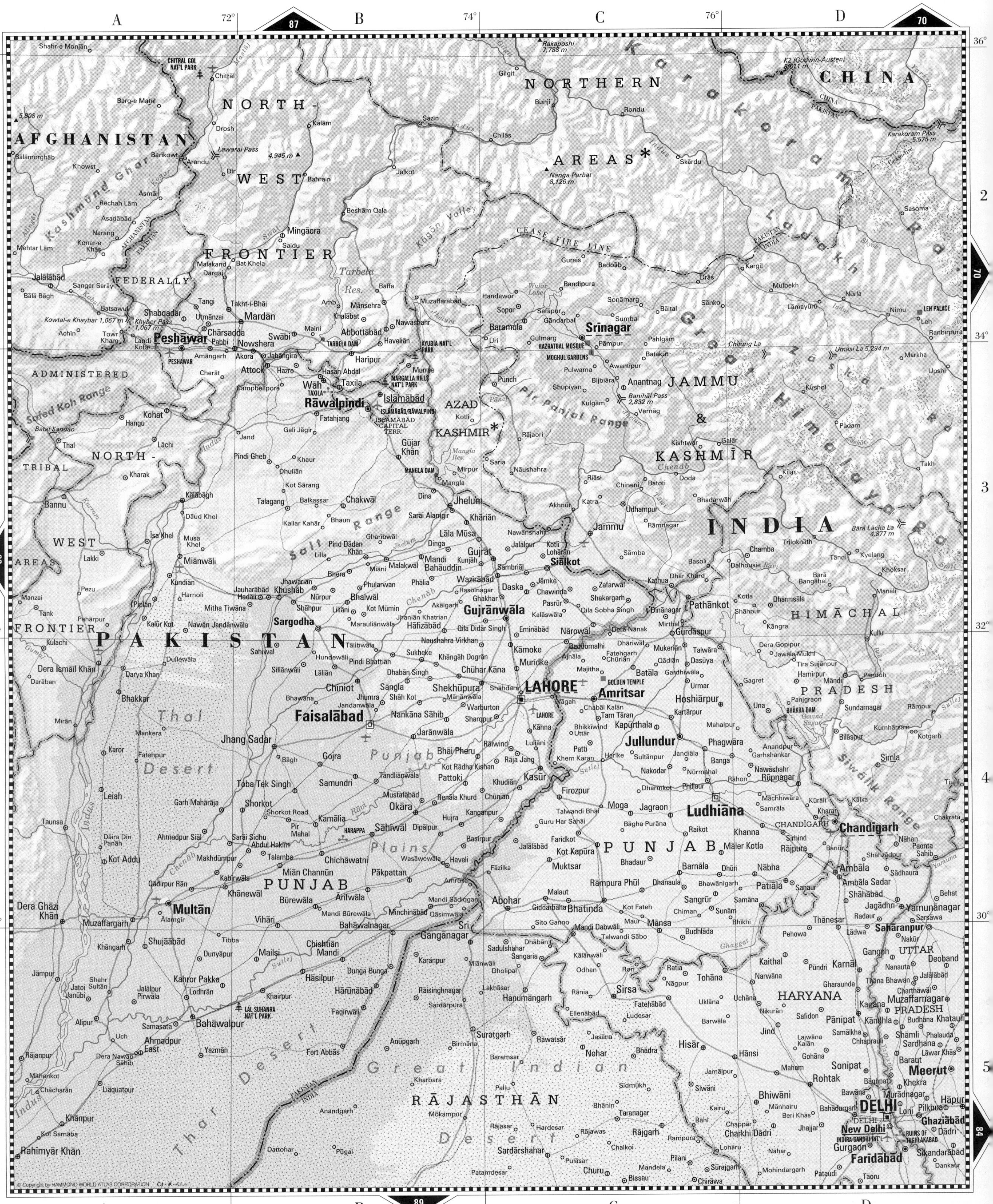

A   72°   **87**   B   74°   C   76°   D   **70**

36°

Shahr-e Monjan

NORTHERN

Rakaposhi
7,788 m

K2 (Godwin-Austen)
8,611 m

CHINA

Gilgit

AFGHANISTAN

5,808 m

Chitral

Barg-e Matal

Drosh

Kalām

Sazin

Chilās

Bunji

Rondu

Skārdu

Karakoram Pass
5,575 m

NORTH-

Lawarai Pass

4,945 m

Bālāmorghāb

Barikowt

Arandu

Khowst

WEST

AREAS*

Nanga Parbat
8,126 m

Sasoma

2

Dir

Bahrain

Besham Qala

Rēchah Lām

Asadābād

Narang

Mingāora

Saidu

Skardu

Konar-e
Khās

Mehtar Lām

FRONTIER

Malakand
Bat Khela

Dargai

Tarbela
Res.

Baffa

Kāgān Valley

CEASE FIRE LINE

Gurais

Badoāb

Drās

Kargil

Mulbekh

2

70

Jalālābād

Sangar Saraý

Bālā Bāgh

FEDERALLY

Batsawul

Kowtal-e Khaybar 1,067 m
Khyber Pass
1,067 m

Tangi

Takht-i-Bhai

Utmānzai

Mardan

Amb

Mānsehra

Khalābat

Nawāshahr

Muzaffarābād

Handawor

Sopor

Safāpūr

Sonāmarg

Wular
Lake

Gāndarbal

Bāltal

Sānko

Nūrla

LEH PALACE

34°

Āchin

Towr
Kham

Peshāwar

Shabqadar

Charsadda

Nowshera

Swābi

Maini

Abbottābad

Haveliān

Uri

Gulmarg

Bāramūla

HAZRATBAL MOSQUE

Srinagar

Pāmpur

Batakūt

Chilung La

Umāsi La 5,294 m

Leh

Ranbirpur

Markha

Upshi

34°

ADMINISTERED

PESHAWAR

Pabbi

Jahāngīra

Akora

Haripur

Hasan Abdāl

Murree

AYUBIA NAT'L
PARK

MARGALLA HILLS
NAT'L PARK

MOGHUL GARDENS

Awantipur

Pulwama

Shupiyan

Bijbiāra

Anantnag

JAMMU

Kūshel

Kārgil

Sufed Koh Range

Kohat

Hangu

Cherāt

Wah

Campbellpore

Taxila

TAXILA

Attock

Hazro

Islāmābād

ISLĀMĀBĀD/RĀWALPINDI

Rāwalpindi

Fatehjang

Jand

Gali Jāgīr

Punch

Pir Panjal Range

Kulgām

Vernāg

Banihāl Pass
2,832 m

Kishtwar

Padam

Galār

Takh

Bāṭal Kandao

Lāchi

Thal

Kharak

Khaur

Dhulian

Khyber
ISLĀMĀBĀD
CAPITAL
TERR.

AZAD

Gūjar
Khān

Mangla
Res.

Mirpur

Rājaori

Nāushahra

Riāsi

Chineni

Batoti

Doda

Bhadarwāh

Kilar

Bārā Lācha La
4,877 m

3

Bannu

Karrak

Kālābagh

Pindi Gheb

Kot Sārang

Talagang

Balkassar

Chakwāl

Dina

MANGLA DAM

Mangla

Saria

KASHMIR*

Udhampur

Rāmnagar

Sāmba

Chamba

Triloknāth

Dhār Khurd

Dalhousie

Basoli

Barā
Bangāhal

Kyelang

Khoksar

Manāli

HIMĀCHAL

3

89

WEST

Isa Khel

Mitha Tiwāna

Pind Dādan
Khān

Jhelum

Khārian

Jammu

Jalālpur

Kathua

Pathānkot

Mīrthal

Kāngra

Dharmsāla

Mandi

Pāndoh

AREAS

Musa
Khel

Hadāli

Jauhārābād
Khushāb

Sali

Lilla

Bhera

Mandi
Bahāuddin

Kunjah

Kotli
Lohārān

Sambriāl

Siālkot

Zafarwal

Qila Sobha Singh

Qādiān

Gurdāspur

Dasūya

Talwāra

Tira Sujānpur

Hamirpur

Gagret

Jawāla
Mukhi

Dera Gopipur

PRADESH

Kullu

Una

Sundarnagar

Rāmpur

32°

Manzai

Pezu

Kundiān

Nūrpur

Range

Miāni

Phularwan

Malakwāl

Phālia

Wazirābād

Daska

Jāmke

Chawinda

Pasrūr

Shakargarh

Dinānagar

Baddomalhi

Ajnāla

Dharīwāl

Batāla

Gandhiwāla

Mukerian

Hoshiārpur

Urmar

Garhshankar

Banga

Nawāshahr
Rūpnagar

Nurmāhal

Bilāspur

Simla

Kotgarh

32°

Tānk

Piplan

Bhakkar

Mianwāli

Jhawariān

Daudu Khel

Bhaun

Sargodha

Bhalwāl

Kalūr Kot

Nawān Jandānwāla

Chenāb

Kot Mūmin

Liāni

Jhānian Khatrian

Qila Didār Singh

Emīnābād

Narowāl

Majitha

Dera Nānak

Gujrānwāla

Kālāswāla

Nārowal

Dera
Dhāriwāl

Fatehgarh
Chūrian

Kāmoke

Muridke

Talwandi

BHĀKRA DAM

Kumhārsain

INDIA

PAKISTAN

Kulachi

Dulewāla

Tāilbwāla

Sukheke

Khāngāh Dogrān

Chūhar Kāna

Shāhdara

Ghakhar

Maralianwāla

Hāfizābad

Naushahra Virkhan

Govind
Sagar

PRADESH

30°

Dera Ismāil Khān

Darāban

Darya Khan

Miān

Chīniot

Jhumra

Sāngla

Shāh Kot

Shekhūpura

Mānanwāla

Warburton

LAHORE

GOLDEN TEMPLE

Wāgha

Amritsar

Chābāl Kalān

Kāhna

Kapūrthala

Mahilpur

Kartārpur

Anandpur
Sāhib

Nawāshahr

Jandiāla

Garhdiwāla

Phagwāra

Māchhiwāra

Samrāla

5

PUNJAB

4

Mīrān

Bhakkar

Karor

Mankera

Fatehpur

Faisalābad

Jhang Sadar

Bāgh

Gojra

Jandānwāla

Jullundur

Nānkāna Sāhib

Jarānwāla

Bhāi Pheru

Raiwind

Lulliāni

Patti

Sultānpur

Nakodar

Phillaur

Kūrāli

Kālka

Paonta
Sāhib

Chakrāta

4

Leiah

Tausa

Garh Mahārāja

Tōba Tek Singh

Shorkot

Samundri

Punjab

Kot Rādha Kishan

Khudian

Khem Karan

Harike

Hārfke

Dharmkot

Moga

Jagraon

Bāgha Purāna

Ludhiāna

Raikot

Khanna

Sirhind

Rājpura

Banūr

Nāhan

Shāhzādpur

CHANDĪGARH

Chandigarh

Ambāla

Nālāgarh

Sādhaura

Behat

Shorkot Road

Kamālia

Ahmadpur Siāl

Sārai Sidhu

Pir
Mahal

Mustafābad

Renāla Khurd

Chūniān

Hujra

Kanganpur

Basirpur

HARAPPA

Okāra

Sāhiwāl

Dipālpur

Firozpur

Talwandi Bhāi

Guru Har Sahāi

Faridkot

Kot Kapūra

Bhadaur

Barnāla

Dhūri

Nābha

Mālēr Kotla

Sanaur

Ambāla Sadar

Jagādhri

Yamunānagar

30°

PUNJAB

Dāira Din
Panāh

Kot Addu

Abdul Hakim

Talamba

Plains

Makhdūmpur

Chichāwatni

Wasāwewāla

Haveli

Fāzilka

Kot
Kapūra

Muktsar

Malaut

Rāmpura Phūl

Dhānaula

Bhawānigarh

Patiāla

Samāna

Thānesar

UTTAR

Pehowa

Gangoh

Karnāl

Ladwa

Nānauta

Deoband

Jalālābād

84

Dera Ghāzi
Khān

Muzaffargarh

Multān

Alamgīr

Mīan Channūn

Khānewāl

Bürewāla

Arifwāla

Pākpattan

Mandi Sādiqganj

Abohar

Giddarbāha

Bhatinda

Kot Fateh

Sangrūr

Chiman

Māmsa

Bhikhi

Budhlāda

Talwandi Sābo

HARYANA

Jind

Safidon

Nikurān

Uchāna

Narwāna

Thāna Bhawan

Budhāna

Kairāna

Shāmli

Kāndhla

Muzaffarnagar

Charthāwal

Phalauda

Sardhāna

Lāwar Khās

PRADESH

5

Khāngarh

Shujāābad

Tibba

Vihāri

Mailsi

Dunyāpur

Chishtiān
Mandi

Bahāwalnagar

Mandi
Sādiqganj

Minchinābad

Qāsimwāla

Sri

Gangānagar

Sadulshahr

Karānpur

Sangariā

Kālānwāli

Dābwāli

Maur

Dhābān

Sito Ganno

Mandi Dabwāli

Ratia

Tohāna

Nāgpur

Ludesar

Barwāla

Fatehābad

Lajwāna
Kalān

Shāhpur

Samālkha

Bhiwāni

Bāwana

Khekra

30°

Jāmpur

Jatoi
Janūbi

Shahr
Sultān

Jalālpur
Pirwāla

Lodhrān

Khairpur

Hārūnābad

Raisinghnagar

Dholipal

Dunga Bunga

Rāisinghnagar

Hanumāngarh

Sardārpura

Rāni

Odhan

Ellenābād

Ukāna

Hisār

Hānsi

Maham

Rohtak

Bahādurgarh

Sonipat

Murthal

DELHI

Hāpur

DELHI

Ghaziābad

Dādri

5

Rājanpur

Mithankot

Kot Samāba

Rahimyār Khān

Kahror
Pakka

Alipur

Uch

Samasata

Bahāwalpur

Ahmadpur
East

Dera Nawāb
Sāhib

LAL SUHANRA
NAT'L PARK

Khānpur

Yazmān

Ahmadpur

Faqirwāli

Fort Abbās

Thar Desert

Great Indian

Kharbara

Baramsar

Pallu

Sidmukh

Nohar

Bhādra

Taranagar

Churu

Siwāni

Jamālpur

Bhiwāni

Mānheru

Beri Khās

Jhajjar

Charkhi Dādri

RUINS OF
TUGHLAKABAD

New Delhi

INDIRA GANDHI INT'L

Gurgaon

Loni

RUINS OF
DĀDRI

Sikandarābād

Dankaur

Paṭaudi

Faridabad

Chācharān

Liāquatpur

Khānpur

Kot Samāba

Dattohar

Pūgal

Great Indian Desert

Bissau

Chirāwa

Pilāni

Mahendragarh

Mohindargarh

Tāoru

60°

58°

RĀJASTHĀN

Mōkampur

Rājasar

Hardesar

Bhāli

Rājawas

Rājgarh

Rāmpura

Chalōki

Sūrajgarh

30°

Sardārshahr

Desert

Anandgarh

Pataundesar

Sūratgarh

Birmāna

Anūpgarh

Rāwatsar

Mānaksar

A   Longitude East of Greenwich 72°   B   **89**   74°   C   76°   D

© Copyright by HAMMOND WORLD ATLAS CORPORATION

SCALE 1:3,400,000   LAMBERT CONFORMAL CONIC PROJECTION

MILES   0   50   100   150

KILOMETERS   0   50   100   150

POPULATION OF CITIES AND TOWNS

■ OVER 2,000,000   ● 500,000 - 999,999   ● 100,000 - 249,999   ○ 10,000 - 29,999

□ 1,000,000 - 1,999,999   ● 250,000 - 499,999   ● 30,000 - 99,999   ○ UNDER 10,000

*AZAD KASHMIR AND THE NORTHERN AREAS ARE ADMINISTERED
BY PAKISTAN BUT DO NOT HAVE PROVINCIAL STATUS.

HEIGHT
m. / ft.

60 / 197
40 / 130
20 / 65
15 / 50
10 / 33
0
2 / 7
5 / 16
10 / 33
20 / 65
30 / 98
40 / 130
50 / 164
60 / 197
m. / ft.
DEPTH
(Figures in
Hundreds)

Central Asia

POPULATION OF CITIES AND TOWNS

■ OVER 2,000,000
▣ 1,000,000 - 1,999,999
● 500,000 - 999,999
◉ 250,000 - 499,999
◌ 100,000 - 249,999
○ 30,000 - 99,999
○ 10,000 - 29,999
○ UNDER 10,000

SCALE 1:10,200,000   LAMBERT CONFORMAL CONIC PROJECTION

MILES 0 . . . 150 . . . 300 . . . 450

KILOMETERS 0 . . . 150 . . . 300 . . . 450

Longitude East of Greenwich

© HAMMOND WORLD ATLAS CORPORATION

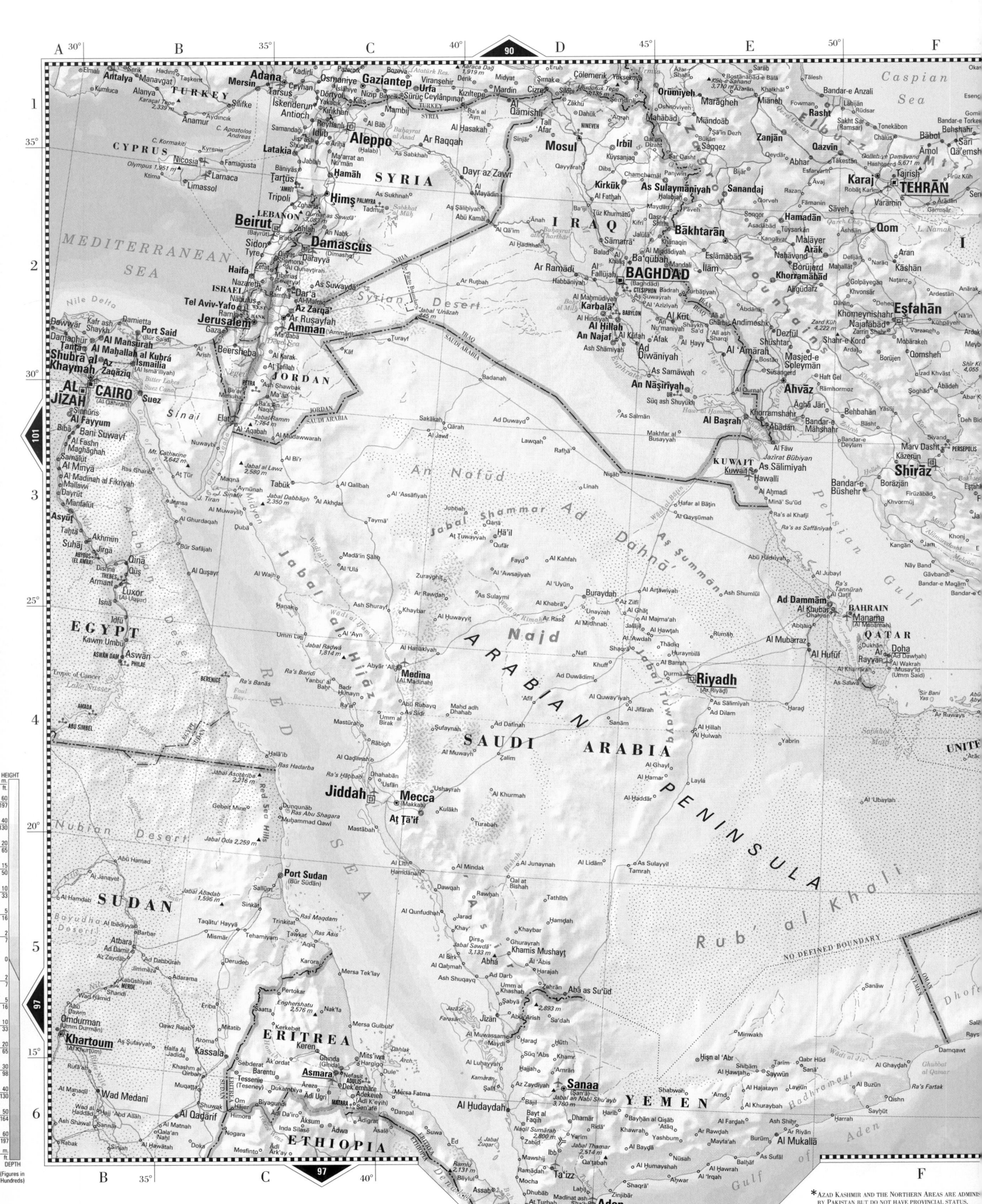

Southwestern Asia

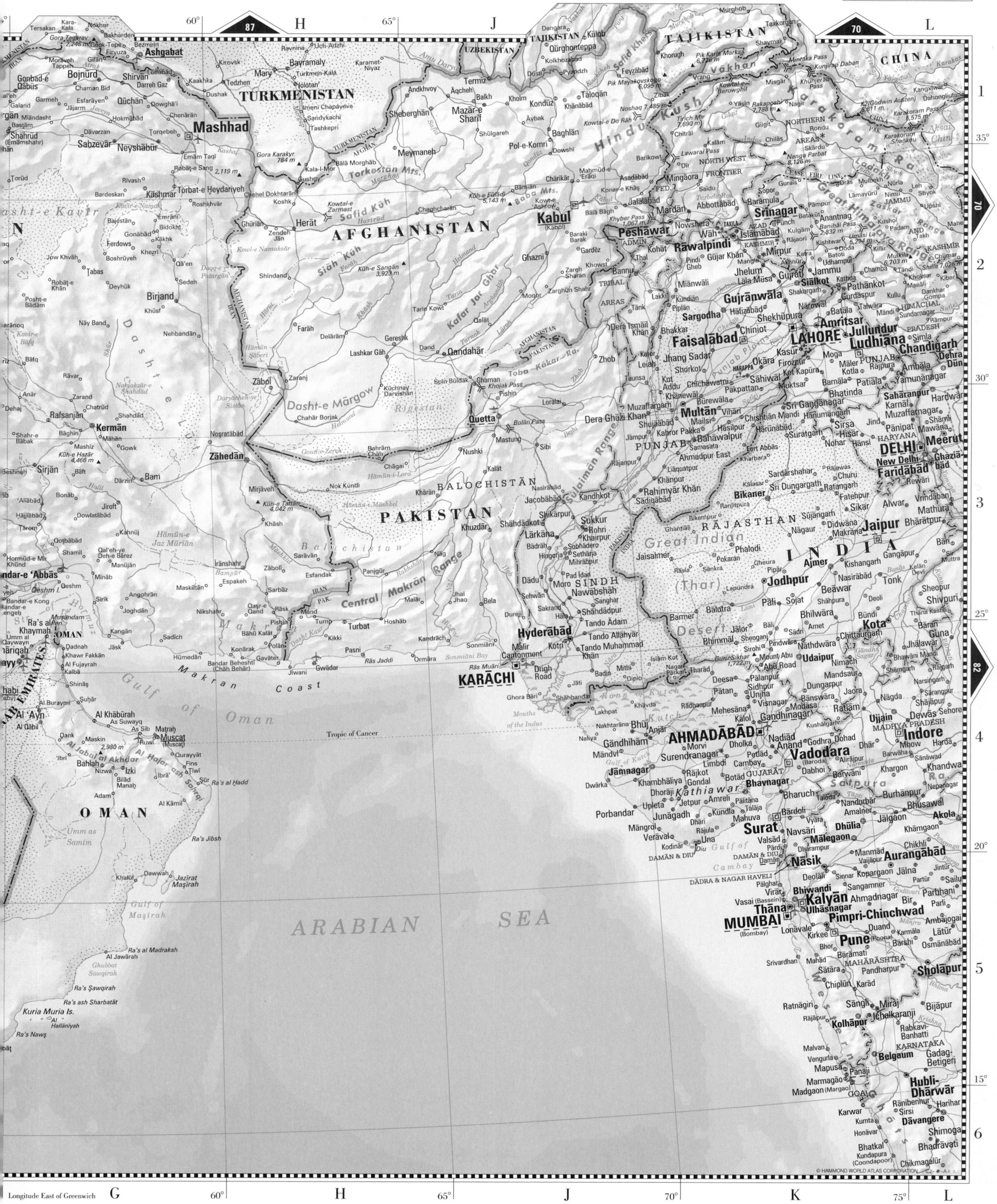

TURKMENISTAN
UZBEKISTAN
TAJIKISTAN
CHINA
AFGHANISTAN
Kabul
IRAN
PAKISTAN
Hindu Kush
Karakoram Rge.
KASHMIR
NORTHERN AREAS
NORTH WEST FRONTIER
TRIBAL AREAS
PUNJAB
BALOCHISTAN
Baluchistan
SINDH
INDIA
RĀJASTHĀN
HARYANA
DELHI
New Delhi
HIMĀCHAL PRADESH
PUNJAB
MADHYA PRADESH
GUJARĀT
MAHĀRĀSHTRA
GOA
KARNĀTAKA
OMAN
UNITED ARAB EMIRATES
Gulf of Oman
Gulf of Maşīrah
ARABIAN SEA
Great Indian Desert (Thar)
Dasht-e Kavīr
Dasht-e Lūt
Makran Coast
Gulf of Cambay
Kathiawar
Tropic of Cancer

Mashhad
Ashgabat
Bojnūrd
Kermān
Sīrjān
Zāhedān
Bandar-e ʻAbbās
Muscat
Herāt
Qandahār
Quetta
Karachi
Hyderābād
Peshāwar
Rāwalpindi
Srīnagar
Jammu
Siālkot
Gujrānwāla
Amritsar
LAHORE
Faisalābād
Ludhiāna
Chandigarh
Multān
Jaipur
Jodhpur
Udaipur
AHMADĀBĀD
Vadodara
Surat
MUMBAI (Bombay)
Pune
Nasik
Kalyān
Thāna
Pimpri-Chinchwad
Sholāpur
Kolhāpur
Belgaum
Hubli-Dhārwār

Longitude East of Greenwich

POPULATION OF CITIES AND TOWNS

- ■ OVER 2,000,000
- ◻ 1,000,000 - 1,999,999
- ● 500,000 - 999,999
- ◉ 250,000 - 499,999
- ● 100,000 - 249,999
- ● 30,000 - 99,999
- ● 10,000 - 29,999
- ● UNDER 10,000

SCALE 1:10,200,000   LAMBERT CONFORMAL CONIC PROJECTION

MILES   0   150   300   450
KILOMETERS   0   150   300   450

Northern Middle East

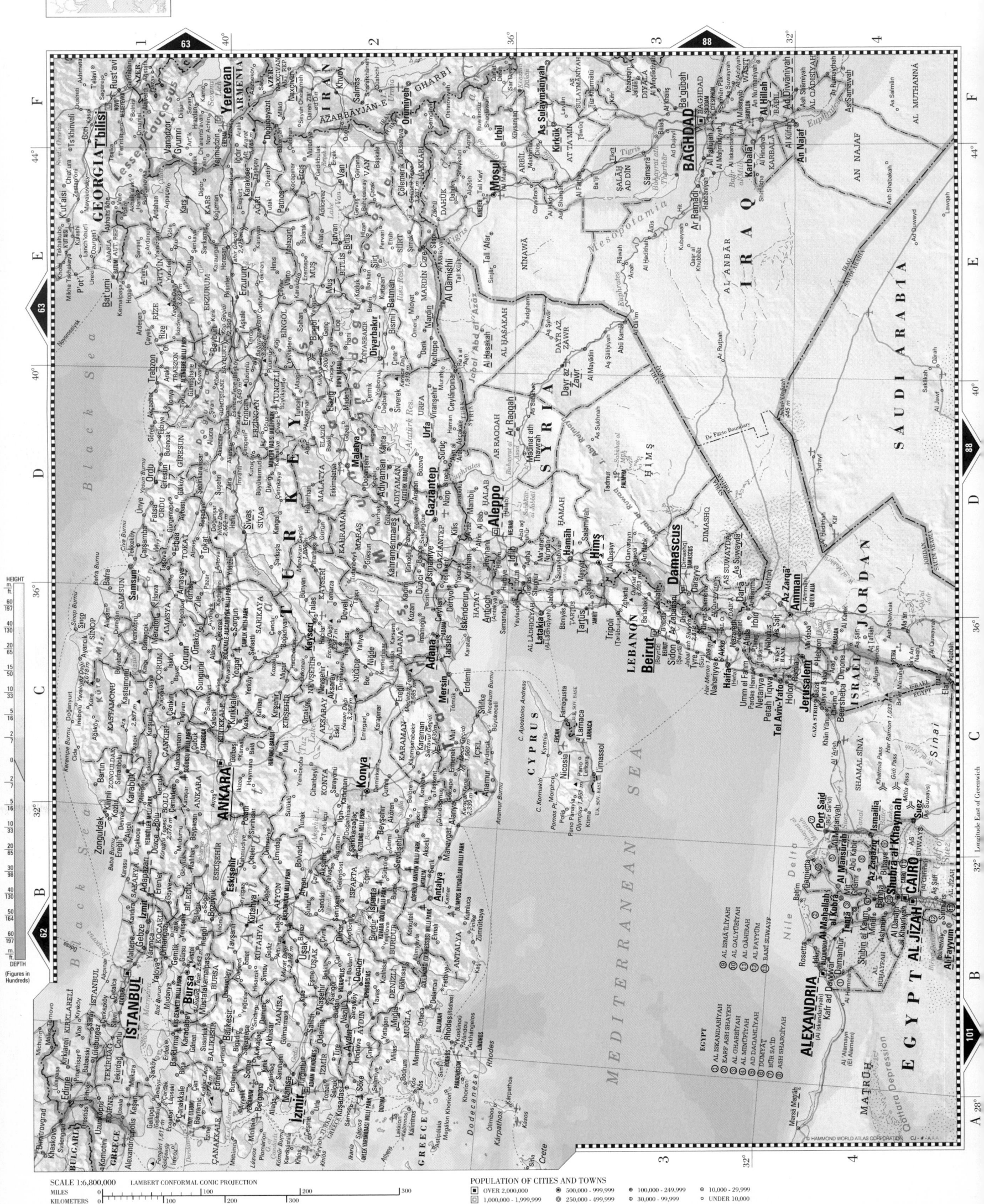

POPULATION OF CITIES AND TOWNS

| ▪ OVER 2,000,000 | ● 500,000 - 999,999 | ● 100,000 - 249,999 | ○ 10,000 - 29,999 |
| ▫ 1,000,000 - 1,999,999 | ● 250,000 - 499,999 | ○ 30,000 - 99,999 | ○ UNDER 10,000 |

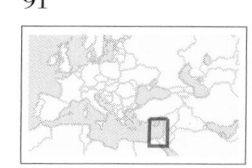

MEDITERRANEAN SEA

CYPRUS

TURKEY

SYRIA

LEBANON

ISRAEL

JORDAN

EGYPT

SAUDI ARABIA

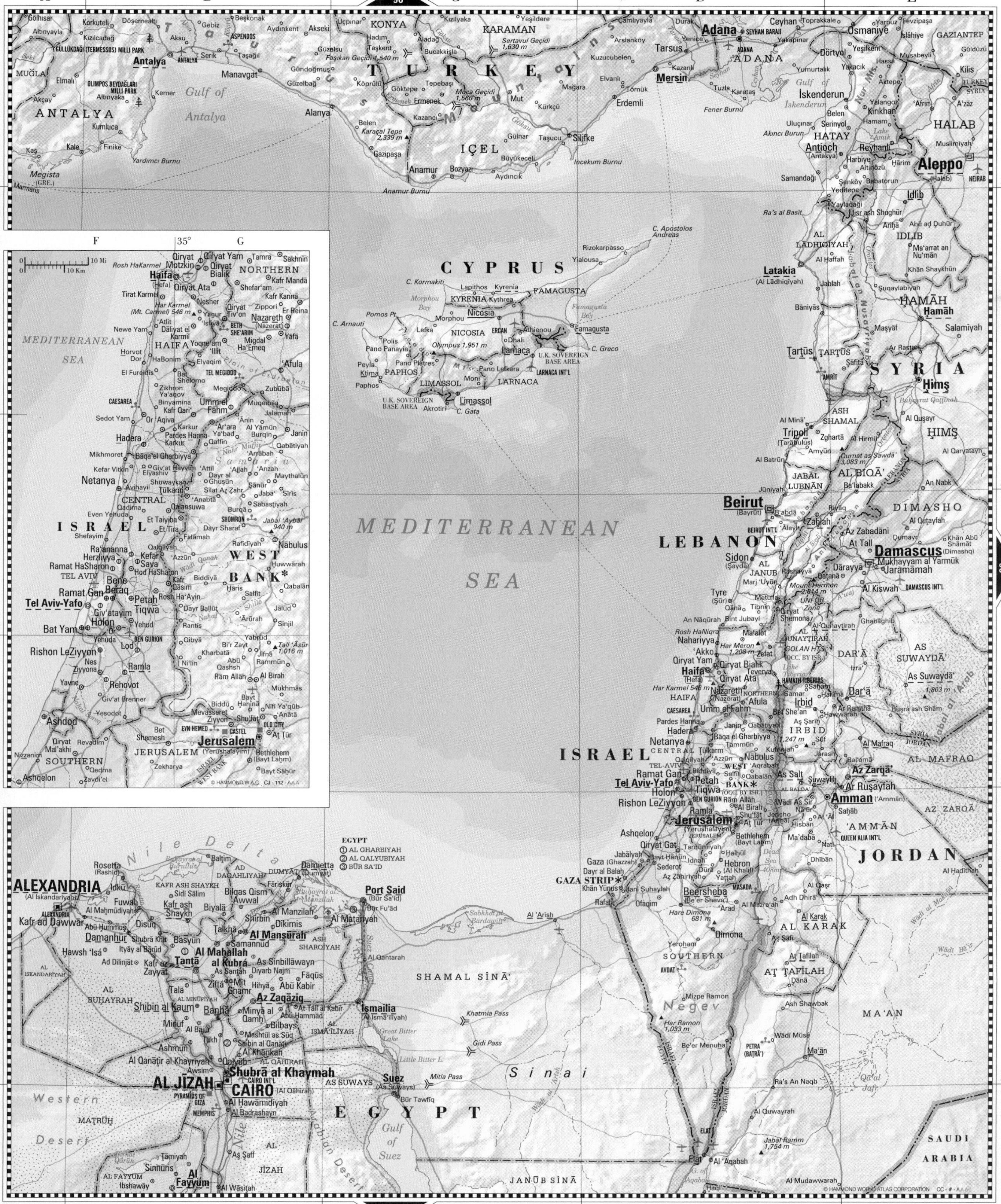

* WEST BANK AND GAZA STRIP ARE ISRAELI OCCUPIED WITH CURRENT STATUS SUBJECT TO THE ISRAELI-PALESTINIAN INTERIM AGREEMENT – PERMANENT STATUS TO BE DETERMINED

POPULATION OF CITIES AND TOWNS

| ■ OVER 2,000,000 | ⊛ 500,000 - 999,999 | ⊙ 100,000 - 249,999 | ○ 10,000 - 29,999 |
| ▫ 1,000,000 - 1,999,999 | ⊙ 250,000 - 499,999 | ○ 30,000 - 99,999 | ○ UNDER 10,000 |

SCALE 1:3,400,000   LAMBERT CONFORMAL CONIC PROJECTION
Longitude East of Greenwich

MILES 0   50   100   150
KILOMETERS 0   50   100   150

HEIGHT / DEPTH (Figures in Hundreds)

© HAMMOND WORLD ATLAS CORPORATION

Africa

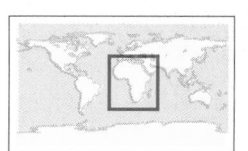

Several physiographic features are captured in this southeast-looking, high-oblique image. The Nile River Delta, the large, dark area at the bottom of the image, extends from the capital city of Cairo at the apex of the delta to the Suez Canal. The entire region is classified as desert (less than 10 inches [25 cm.] of rainfall per year). Desert-like areas are visible southwest of the delta and in the northwestern Sinai. Major rock outcrops (darker areas) are seen encircling the Red Sea. The two bodies of water flanking the southern end of the Sinai Peninsula are the Gulf of Suez and the Gulf of Aqaba.

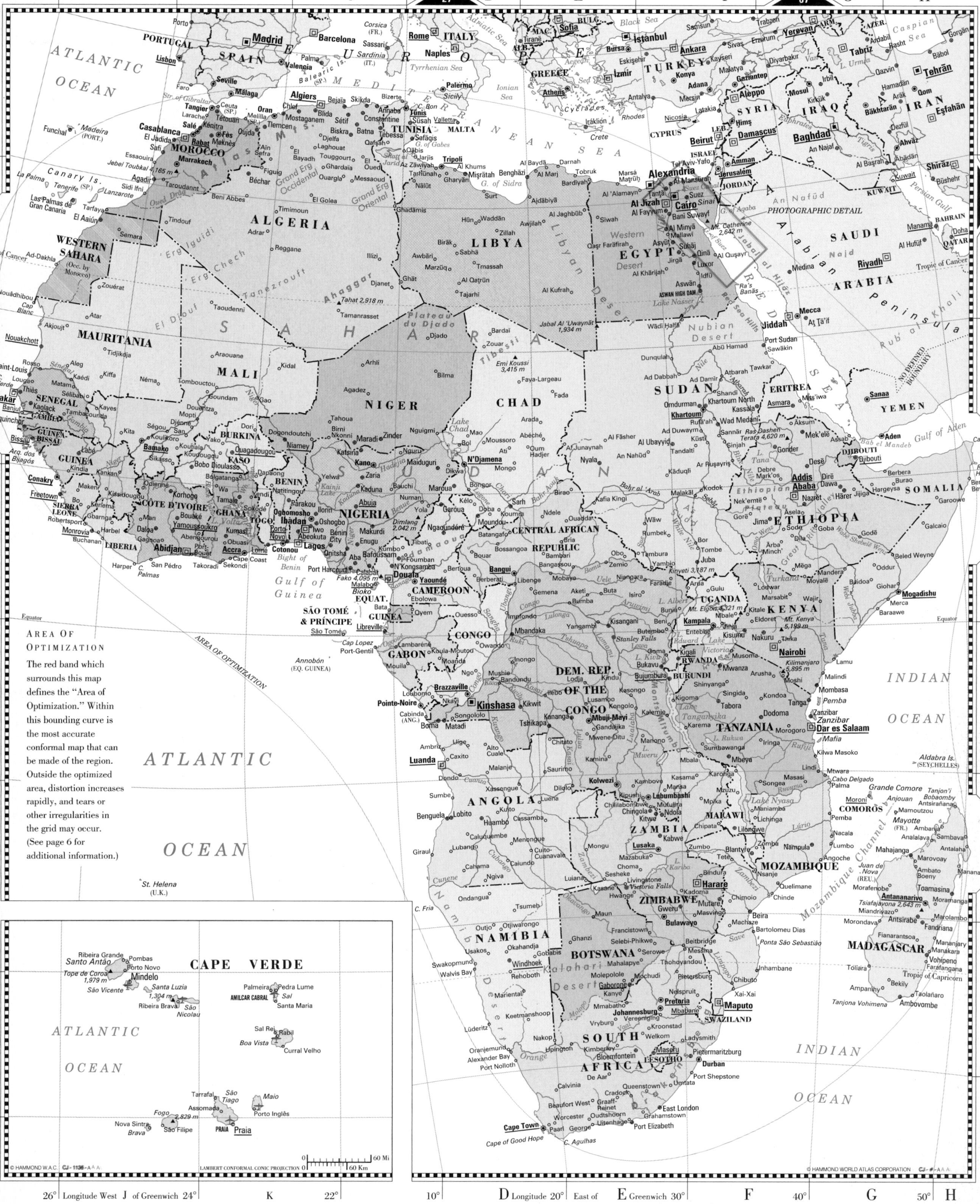

AREA OF OPTIMIZATION

The red band which surrounds this map defines the "Area of Optimization." Within this bounding curve is the most accurate conformal map that can be made of the region. Outside the optimized area, distortion increases rapidly, and tears or other irregularities in the grid may occur. (See page 6 for additional information.)

CAPE VERDE

POPULATION OF CITIES AND TOWNS
- ◻ OVER 3,000,000
- ⬚ 1,000,000 - 2,999,999
- ● 500,000 - 999,999
- ● 100,000 - 499,999
- ○ UNDER 100,000

SCALE 1:34,100,000   OPTIMAL CONFORMAL PROJECTION

LAMBERT CONFORMAL CONIC PROJECTION

© HAMMOND WORLD ATLAS CORPORATION

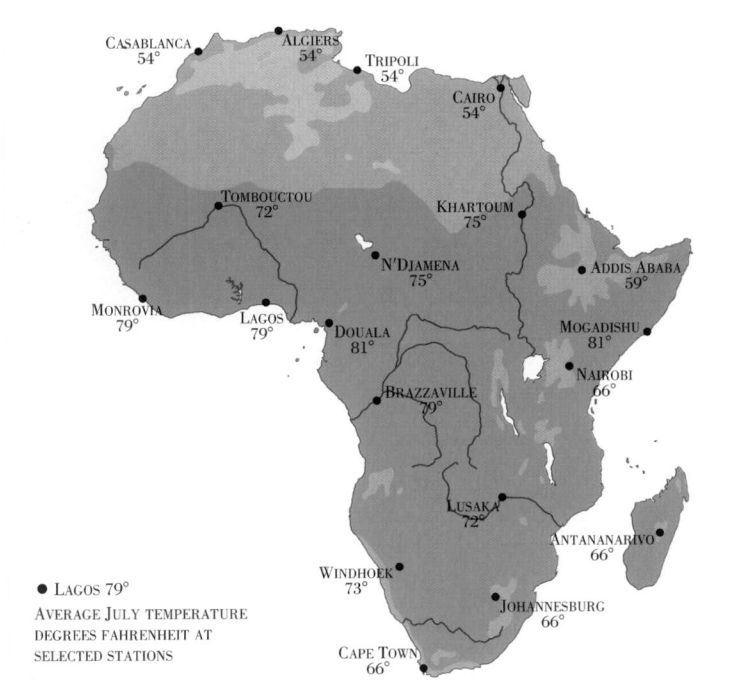

CASABLANCA 54° ALGIERS 54° TRIPOLI 54° CAIRO 54° TOMBOUCTOU 72° KHARTOUM 75° N'DJAMENA 75° ADDIS ABABA 59° MONROVIA 79° LAGOS 79° DOUALA 81° MOGADISHU 81° NAIROBI 66° BRAZZAVILLE 79° LUSAKA 72° ANTANANARIVO 66° WINDHOEK 73° JOHANNESBURG 66° CAPE TOWN 66°

● LAGOS 79°
AVERAGE JULY TEMPERATURE
DEGREES FAHRENHEIT AT
SELECTED STATIONS

AVERAGE JANUARY TEMPERATURE

CASABLANCA 72° ALGIERS 77° TRIPOLI 79° CAIRO 82° TOMBOUCTOU 90° KHARTOUM 90° N'DJAMENA 82° ADDIS ABABA 59° MONROVIA 77° LAGOS 75° DOUALA 77° MOGADISHU 77° NAIROBI 61° BRAZZAVILLE 72° LUSAKA 61° ANTANANARIVO 57° WINDHOEK 57° JOHANNESBURG 50° CAPE TOWN 57°

● LAGOS 75°
AVERAGE JULY TEMPERATURE
DEGREES FAHRENHEIT AT
SELECTED STATIONS

AVERAGE JULY TEMPERATURE

FAHRENHEIT | CELSIUS
OVER 68° | OVER 20°
50° TO 68° | 10° TO 20°
32° TO 50° | 0° TO 10°
UNDER 32° | UNDER 0°

FAHRENHEIT | CELSIUS
OVER 86° | OVER 30°
68° TO 86° | 20° TO 30°
50° TO 68° | 10° TO 20°
UNDER 50° | UNDER 10°

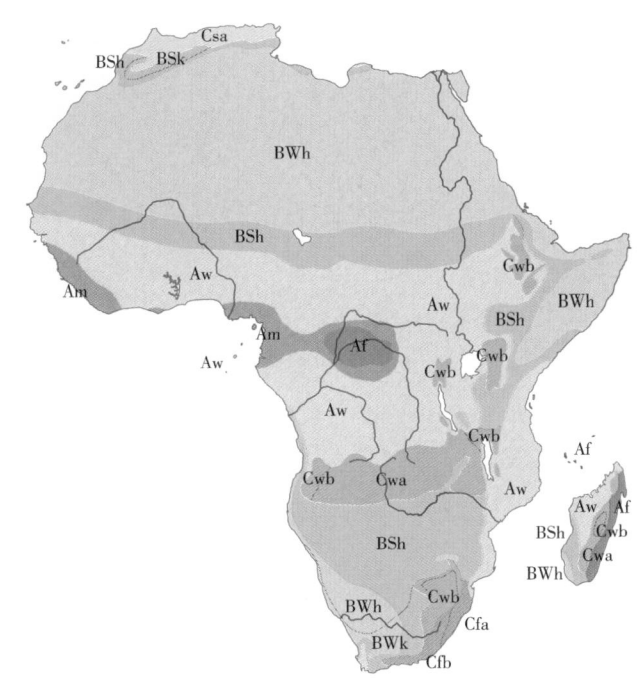

BSh BSk Csa BWh BSh Am Aw Aw Am Af Cwb Aw BWh BSh Cwb Cwb Aw Cwb Cwa Aw Af Aw Af BSh Cwb Cwa BWh Cwb BWh BWk Cfa Cfb

CLIMATE

VEGETATION

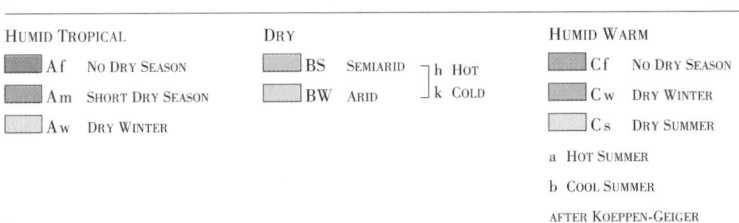

HUMID TROPICAL
Af NO DRY SEASON
Am SHORT DRY SEASON
Aw DRY WINTER

DRY
BS SEMIARID
BW ARID
h HOT
k COLD

HUMID WARM
Cf NO DRY SEASON
Cw DRY WINTER
Cs DRY SUMMER
a HOT SUMMER
b COOL SUMMER
AFTER KOEPPEN-GEIGER

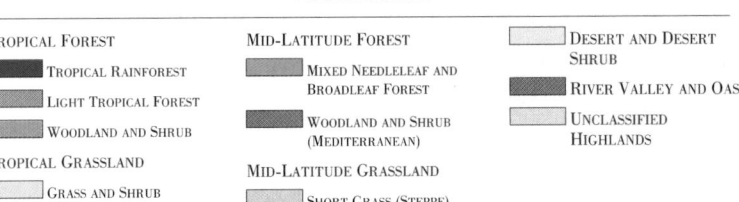

TROPICAL FOREST
TROPICAL RAINFOREST
LIGHT TROPICAL FOREST
WOODLAND AND SHRUB

TROPICAL GRASSLAND
GRASS AND SHRUB (SAVANNA)
WOODED SAVANNA

MID-LATITUDE FOREST
MIXED NEEDLELEAF AND BROADLEAF FOREST
WOODLAND AND SHRUB (MEDITERRANEAN)

MID-LATITUDE GRASSLAND
SHORT GRASS (STEPPE)

DESERT AND DESERT SHRUB
RIVER VALLEY AND OASIS
UNCLASSIFIED HIGHLANDS

Africa – Geographical Comparisons

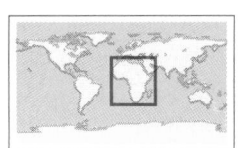

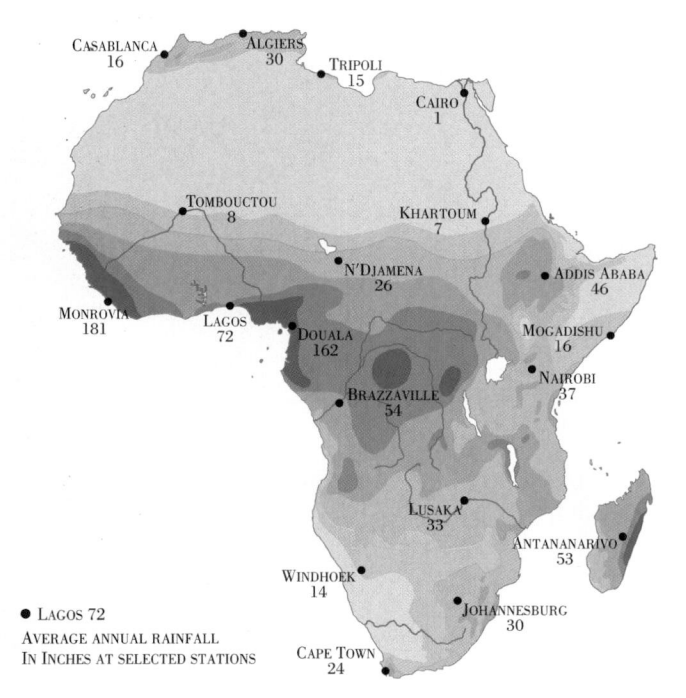

● LAGOS 72
AVERAGE ANNUAL RAINFALL
IN INCHES AT SELECTED STATIONS

AVERAGE ANNUAL RAINFALL

INCHES	CM	INCHES	CM	INCHES	CM
OVER 80	OVER 200	40 TO 60	100 TO 150	10 TO 20	25 TO 50
60 TO 80	150 TO 200	20 TO 40	50 TO 100	UNDER 10	UNDER 25

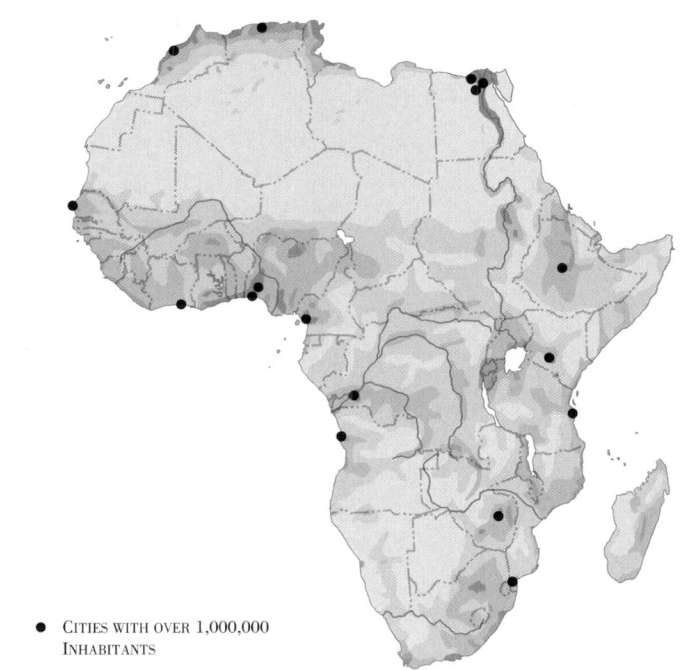

● CITIES WITH OVER 1,000,000
INHABITANTS

POPULATION DISTRIBUTION

DENSITY PER		SQ. MI.	SQ. KM.	SQ. MI.	SQ. KM.
SQ. MI.	SQ. KM.	130 TO 260	50 TO 100	3 TO 25	1 TO 10
OVER 260	OVER 100	25 TO 130	10 TO 50	UNDER 3	UNDER 1

LAND USE

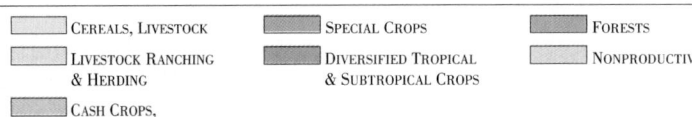

CEREALS, LIVESTOCK		SPECIAL CROPS		FORESTS	
LIVESTOCK RANCHING & HERDING		DIVERSIFIED TROPICAL & SUBTROPICAL CROPS		NONPRODUCTIVE	
CASH CROPS, MIXED FARMING					

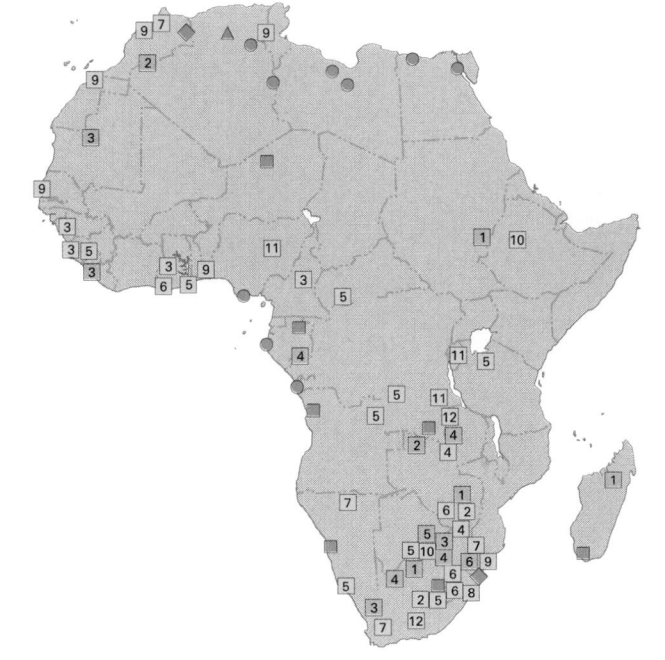

MINERAL RESOURCES

ENERGY & FUELS	IRON & FERROALLOYS	OTHER MAJOR RESOURCES	
◆ COAL	1 CHROMIUM	1 ANTIMONY	7 LEAD
▲ NATURAL GAS	2 COBALT	2 ASBESTOS	8 MICA
● PETROLEUM	3 IRON ORE	3 BAUXITE	9 PHOSPHATES
■ URANIUM	4 MANGANESE	4 COPPER	10 PLATINUM
	5 NICKEL	5 DIAMONDS	11 TIN
	6 VANADIUM	6 GOLD	12 ZINC

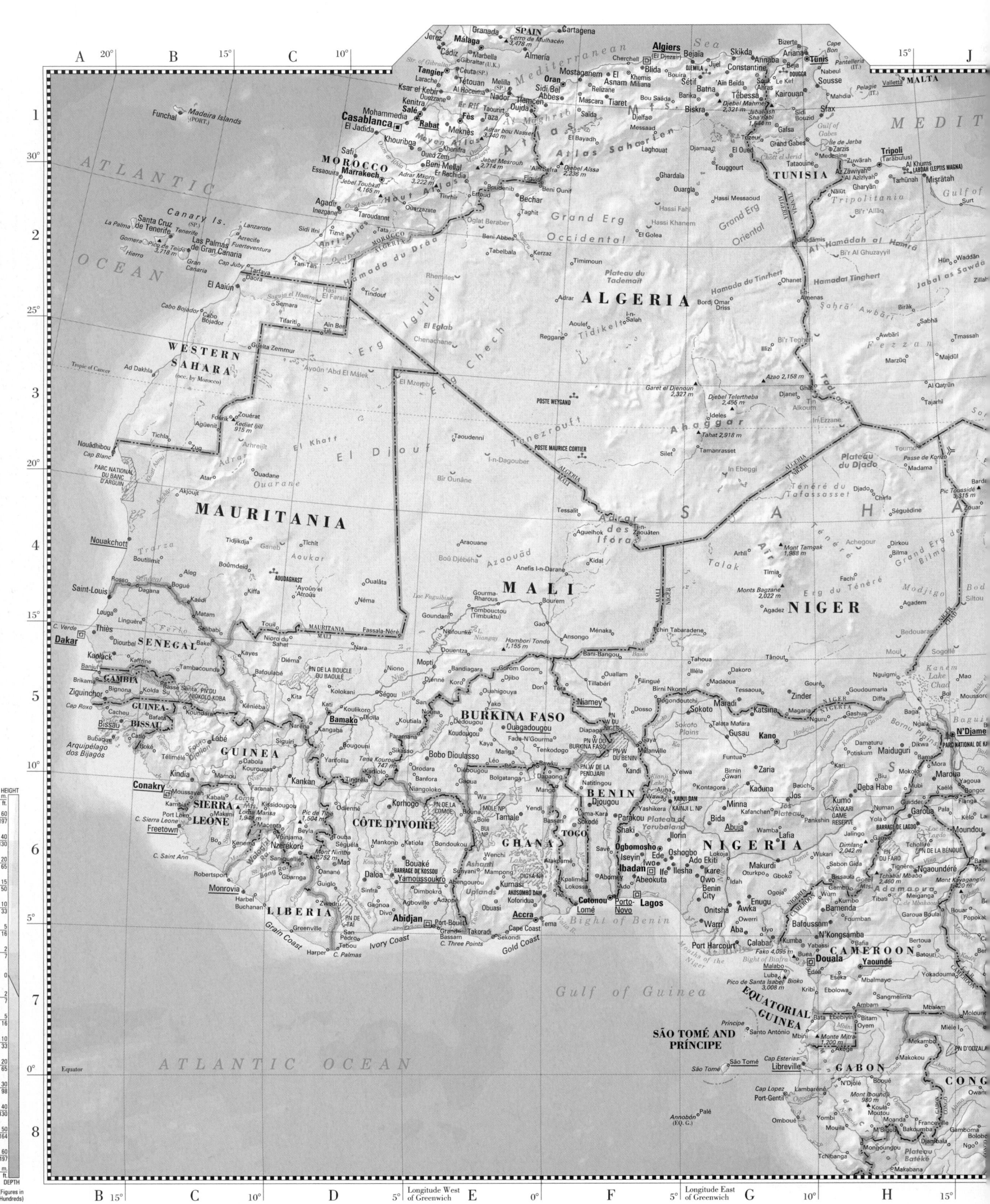

Northern Africa

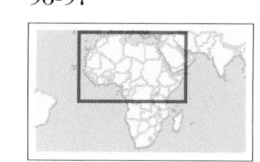

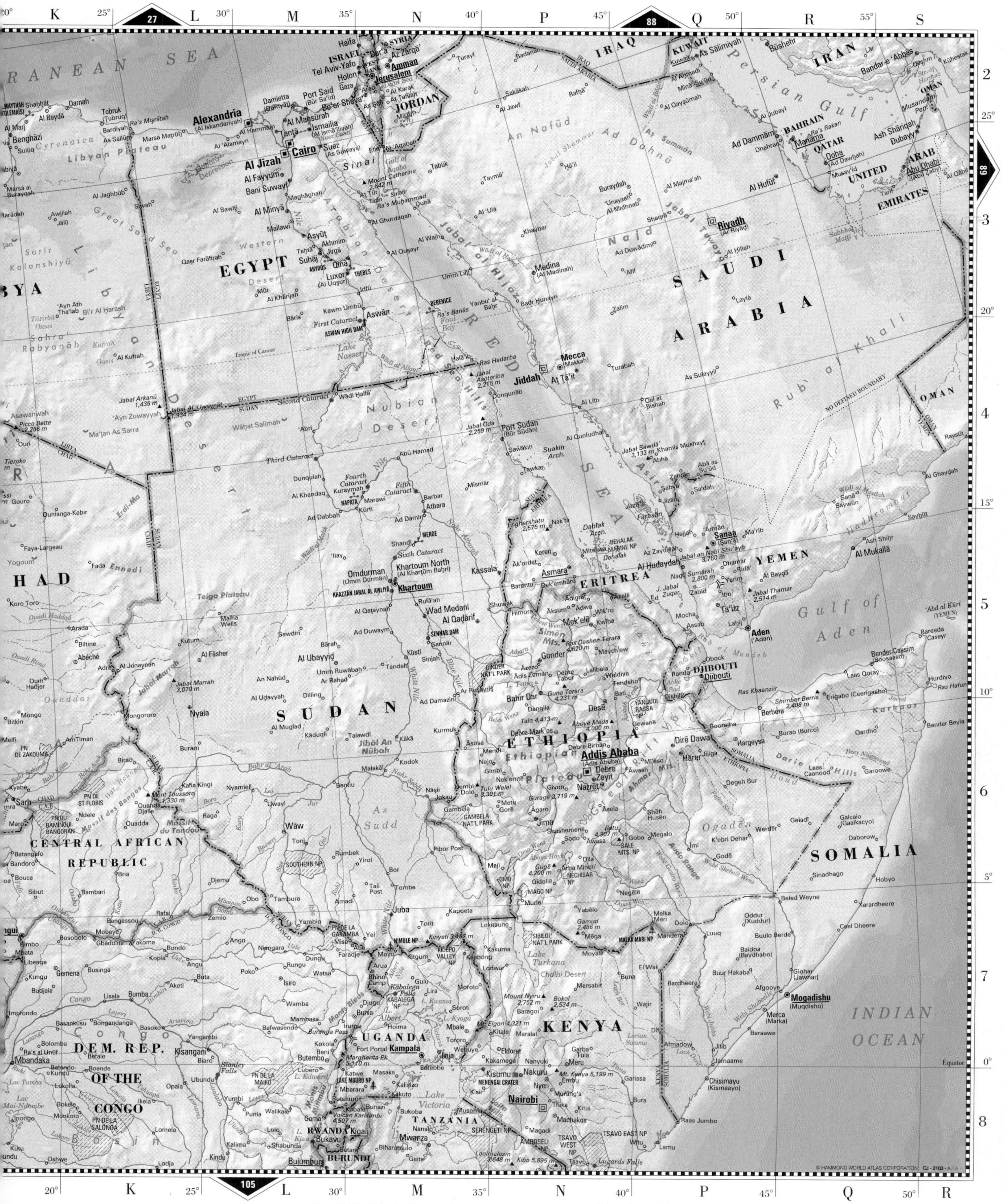

MEDITERRANEAN SEA

Countries and regions: LIBYA, EGYPT, SUDAN, CHAD, CENTRAL AFRICAN REPUBLIC, DEM. REP. OF THE CONGO, UGANDA, KENYA, TANZANIA, RWANDA, BURUNDI, ETHIOPIA, ERITREA, DJIBOUTI, SOMALIA, SAUDI ARABIA, YEMEN, OMAN, UNITED ARAB EMIRATES, QATAR, BAHRAIN, KUWAIT, IRAQ, IRAN, JORDAN, ISRAEL, SYRIA

Major cities: Alexandria, Cairo, Al Jizah, Khartoum, Omdurman, Addis Ababa, Nairobi, Mogadishu, Kampala, Djibouti, Asmara, Sanaa, Aden, Mecca, Jiddah, Riyadh, Abu Dhabi, Doha, Manama, Amman, Jerusalem, Kuwait

Seas and waters: RED SEA, Gulf of Aden, Persian Gulf, Gulf of Aqaba, INDIAN OCEAN, Lake Nasser, Lake Victoria, Lake Turkana, L. Albert, L. Edward, L. Kyoga, Nile, Blue Nile, White Nile

POPULATION OF CITIES AND TOWNS

■ OVER 2,000,000	● 500,000 - 999,999
▣ 1,000,000 - 1,999,999	● 100,000 - 499,999
● 50,000 - 99,999	○ UNDER 50,000

SCALE 1:17,000,000   POLYCONIC PROJECTION

MILES 0 — 250 — 500 — 750

KILOMETERS 0 — 250 — 500 — 750

A 16° **B** 12° **C** 8° **D** 4°

SPAIN
Cádiz
Chiclana de la Frontera
Barbate de Franco
Mijas
Marbella
Málaga
Algeciras
La Línea de la Concepción
Gibraltar (U.K.)
Punta Almina
Cap Spartel (BOUKHALF)
Ceuta (SP.)
TANGIER (BOUKHALF)
Cap de Trois Four
Tangier
(Tanger)
Tétouan
Asilah
Al Hoceima
Larache
Chechaouene
Jebel Bouhalla
2,170 m
AL HOCEIMA
(CÔTE DU RIF)
Na
Zelo
Na
Ksar el Kebir
Bab
Taza Boureit
Targuist
Akroul
Midar
Souk el
Arba du Rharb
Ouezzane
Taounate
Maoun
Gue
Kenitra
Sidi Kacem
(VOLUBILIS)
Karia Ba
Mohammed
Tissa
Salé
RABAT (SALE)
Moulay Idrisse
Taza
Rabat
Ain el
Moulay Yakoub
Sefrou
CASABLANCA
(Dar-El-Beida)
Mohammedia
Ben
Slimane
Khemisset
Tiflet
FES (SASS)
Fes
CENTRE-
Meknes
El Hajeb
Ifrane
NORD
CASABLANCA (MOHAMED V)
Mediouna
Azrou
Adrar bou Nasser
3,340 m
El Jadida
Azemmour
Berrechid
Imouzzer des
Marmoucha
Settat
Benahmed
Ifrane
Boulemane
Oualidia
Boulaouane
Khouribga
Oued Zem
Khenifra
Midelt
Moyen Atlas
Cap Safi
El Had
Harrara
Sidi
Bennour
El Kbab
Jebel Mesrouh
2,714 m
CENTRE
Boujad
Safi
Jemaa Sahim
Kasba Tadla
Beni Mellal
Jebel Masker
3,277 m
Beni
Chemaia
Youssoufia
Benguerir
El Borouj
Azilal
Rich
Oued Ziz
GORGES DU ZIZ
El Kelaa
des Srarhna
MOROCCO
Er Rachidia
Bouder
Essaouira
Marrakech
Ait Ourir
Jebel Azourki
3,690 m
Adrar Mkorn
3,222 m
Cap Sim
Chichaoua
MARRAKECH (MENARA)
Jebel Rhat
3,825 m
Irhil M'goun
4,071 m
CENTRE-SUD
Tinerhir
Goulmima
Oued Rheris
Erfoud
TENSIFT
Ounara
Tahnaout
Boumalne
Oued Dades
Tamanar
Imi n'Tanout
Jebel Toubkal
4,165 m
Igldet 3,615 m
PN DU
TOUBKAL
Jebel Sirwa
3,304 m
Agdz
Tazenakht
Jebel Rhart
1,650 m
Cap Rhir
Djebel Tichka
3,348 m
Ait Ben
Haddou
Ouarzazate
Jebel Saghro
Zagora
Agadir (INEZGANE)
AGADIR (INEZGANE)
Taroudannt
Oued Sous
Taliouine
Tinzouline
Oued el Draa
1,730 m
Agadir
Inezgane
Oulad Teima
Tagounit
Biougra
Irherm
2,531 m
Foum Zguid
Tiznit
Irherm n'Ougdal
SUD
Jebel Lkst
2,359 m
Jebel Bani
Tafraout
Akka
Oued Draa
Tata
BE
Sidi Ifni
Bou Izakarn
Foum el
Hassane
Tebelbala
Assa
Hamada du Drâa
Cap Drâa
Goulimine
Ben Zohra
Rhemfles
TINDOUF
Tan-Tan
Oued Drâa
Jebel Ouarkziz
Bou Laber
Maligat
Daraini
Cap Juby
Tarfaya
55 m
Tindouf
BORDJ FLYE SAINTE-
Daora
Hagunía
ALGERIA
MAURITANIA
El Aaiún
EL AAIÚN (HASSANI)
Edchera
Hasi el Farsia
El Eglab
Lemsid
Saguia el Hamra
Yetti
Cabo Bojador
Semara
Bu Craa
Chenachane
Sebjet
Aridol
Tifariti
Sebjet
Aarreid
Ain Ben Tili
WESTERN
Bir Aidiat
Bir Bel
Guerdâne
Bir Zimła
Aaglet Yeraifia
Guelta Zemmur
Bir Moghrein
Sebkhet
Iguetti
SAHARA
(Occupied by Morocco)
'Ayoun 'Abd
el Malek
El Mzereb
S
Oued Assag
Sebkhet Ounm
ed Droûs Telli
Toutfourine
A
Tropic of Cancer
TIRIS ZEMMOUR
Ad Dakhla
El Aotf
Buir Taiaret
Sebkhet Ounm
ed Droûs Guebli
'Erg el
Ahmar
Punta Durnford
El Aargub
Fuch
Karet
Sebkhet de ?
Rhallaouane
'Erg
Aaglet Tennuaca
Tiris
Rhallamane
Cabo Barbas
366 m
Sebkhet
Tidsit
Hamada Safia
Sebkhet
Ijill
Hamoûni
El Khatt
Majabda
Taoudenni
Ausert
Fderik
Zouérat
Kediet Ijill
915 m
Télig
Cabo Blanco
Tichla
Zug
Galb
Azefal
Touâjîl
Zemlet Toftal
330 m
'Erg
Iioubhane
MAURITANIA
MAL
Guerguerat
Bou Lanour
Buir Amraou
Afhrelijt
Chreïtik
Guelb er Richât
519 m
El Mraye
El Khnâchi
NOUADHIBOU
Cansado
Ben Ama
El Diouf
TOMBOUCT
Nouâdhibou
DAKHLET
INCHIRI
Ahmeyim
Choûm
Ouadane
Bïr Ounân
Güera
Cabo Blanco
NOUADHIBOU
Dhar er
HODH
Cap d'Arguin
ADRAR
ECH
Erg Atouila
PARC NATIONAL
DU BANC D'ARGUIN
Chinguetti
CHARGUI

MOROCCO is divided into 7 non-administrative regions shown here. Scale does not permit showing the boundaries and names of Morocco's provinces and prefectures.

ATLANTIC

OCEAN

Madeira Is.
(PORT.)
Porto Santo
Vila de
Porto Santo
Madeira
Santana
Machico
Calheta
FUNCHAL
Ribeira Brava
Funchal
Ilhas Desertas

Ilhas
Selvagens
(PORT.)

Canary Islands
(SPAIN)
PN DE TIMANFAYA
Lanzarote
PN LA CALDERA
DE TABURIENTE
La Palma
Arrecife
LANZAROTE
Santa Cruz
de la Palma
Los Llanos
de Aridane
Tenerife
Santa Cruz
La Laguna de Tenerife
Fuerteventura
La Orotava
NORTE LOS RODEOS
Icod de los Vinos
Puerto de la Cruz
Antigua
Puerto del
Rosario
Vallehermoso
Pico de Teide
3,718 m
Las Palmas
de Gran Canaria
PN DEL TEIDE
Arucas
Valverde
Granadilla
Santa Lucía
PN DE GARAJONAY
de Abona SUR REINA
Telde
Gomera
SOFIA
Ingenio
Hierro
San Bartolomé
de Tirajana
GRAN CANARIA
Gran Canaria

HEIGHT
m.
ft.
60 197
40 130
20 65
15 50
10 33
5 16
0
2 7
5 16
10 33
20 65
40 130
50 164
60 197
m.
ft.
DEPTH
(Figures in
Hundreds)

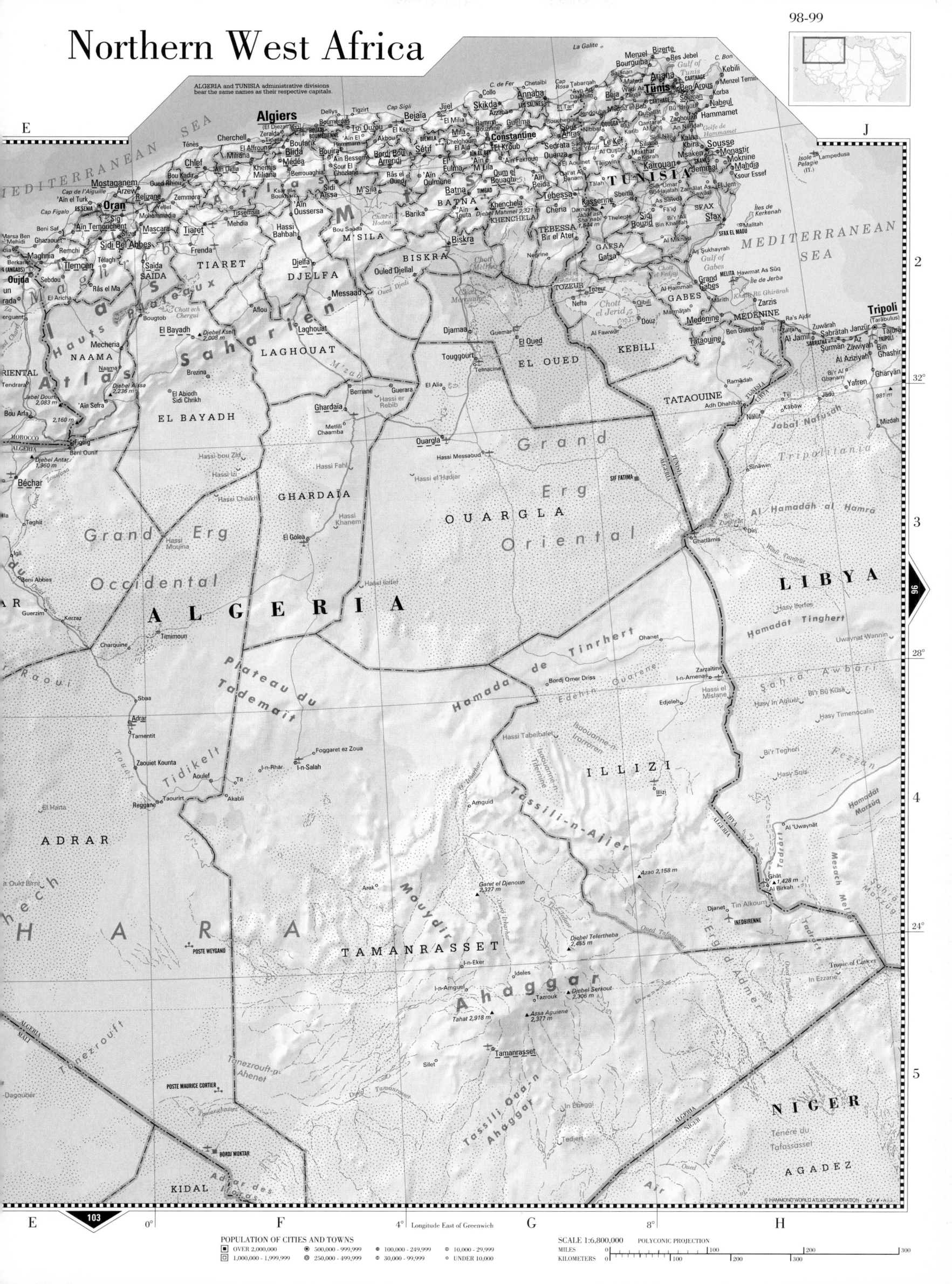

Northern West Africa

ALGERIA and TUNISIA administrative divisions
bear the same names as their respective capitals.

POPULATION OF CITIES AND TOWNS

■ OVER 2,000,000	● 500,000 - 999,999	● 100,000 - 249,999	● 10,000 - 29,999
□ 1,000,000 - 1,999,999	● 250,000 - 499,999	● 30,000 - 99,999	● UNDER 10,000

SCALE 1:6,800,000   POLYCONIC PROJECTION

MILES 0   50   100   200   300
KILOMETERS 0   100   200   300

Longitude East of Greenwich

© HAMMOND WORLD ATLAS CORPORATION

Northern Morocco, Algeria, Tunisia

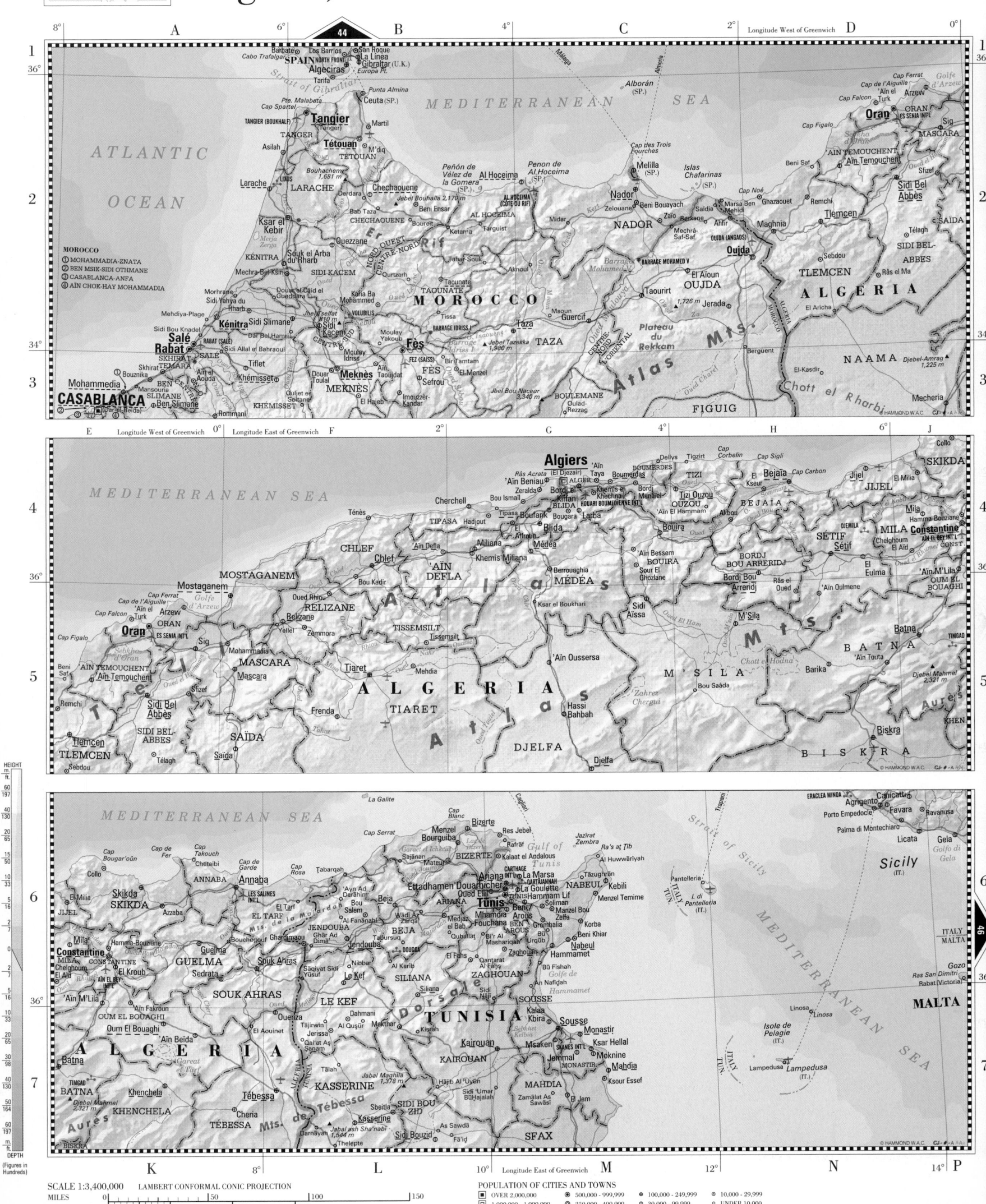

SCALE 1:3,400,000   LAMBERT CONFORMAL CONIC PROJECTION

MILES 0   50   100   150

KILOMETERS 0   50   100   150

POPULATION OF CITIES AND TOWNS

Symbol	Population	Symbol	Population
■ OVER 2,000,000	◉ 500,000 - 999,999	◉ 100,000 - 249,999	◉ 10,000 - 29,999
□ 1,000,000 - 1,999,999	◉ 250,000 - 499,999	◉ 30,000 - 99,999	◦ UNDER 10,000

HEIGHT
m. ft.
60 197
40 130
20 65
10 33
5 16
2 7
0
2 7
5 16
10 33
20 65
30 98
40 130
50 164
60 197
m. ft.
DEPTH
(Figures in Hundreds)

Northeastern Africa

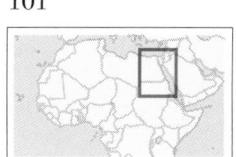

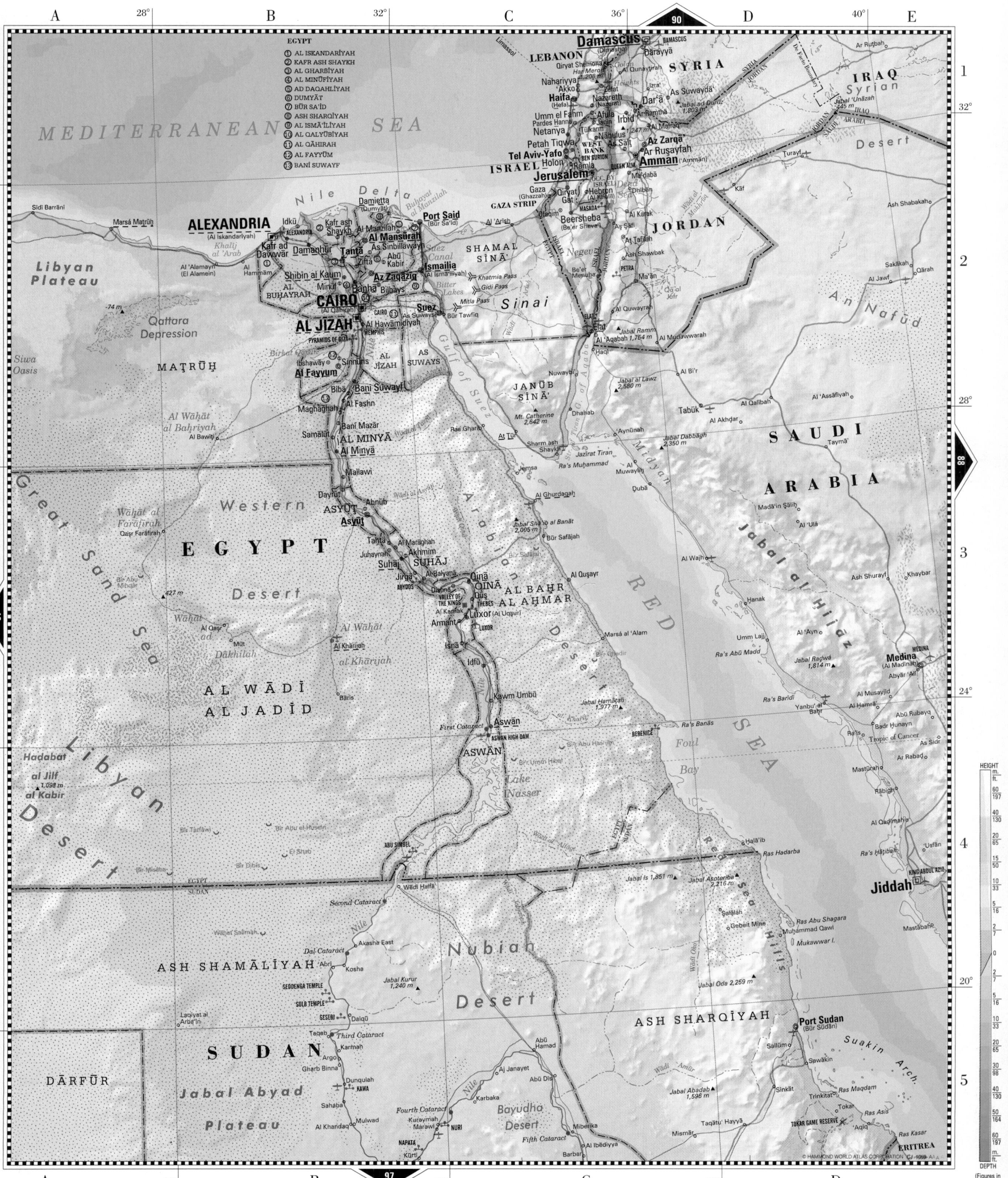

EGYPT
1. AL ISKANDARĪYAH
2. KAFR ASH SHAYKH
3. AL GHARBĪYAH
4. AL MINŪFĪYAH
5. AD DAQAHLĪYAH
6. DUMYĀT
7. BŪR SAʿĪD
8. ASH SHARQĪYAH
9. AL ISMĀʿĪLĪYAH
10. AL QALYŪBĪYAH
11. AL QĀHIRAH
12. AL FAYYŪM
13. BANĪ SUWAYF

MEDITERRANEAN SEA

Sidi Barrāni
Marsá Matrūḥ
Al ʿAlamayn (El Alamein)

Libyan Plateau

Siwa Oasis

-74 m

Qattara Depression

MAṬRŪḤ

EGYPT

Western Desert

AL WĀDĪ AL JADĪD

Ḥaḍabat al Jilf al Kabir
1,098 m

Libyan Desert

Great Sand Sea

Waḥāt al Farāfirah
Qaṣr Farāfirah

427 m

Bir Abū Minḡār

Al Qaṣr
Mūt
Dākhilah

Bāris

DĀRFŪR

SUDAN

Jabal Abyad Plateau

ASH SHAMĀLĪYAH

Nubian Desert

NILE Delta

ALEXANDRIA (Al Iskandarīyah)
Kafr ad Dawwār
Damanhūr
Idkū
Kafr ash Shaykh
Al Manzilah
Damietta (Dumyāt)
Port Said (Būr Saʿīd)

AL BUHAYRAH
Shibin al Kaum
Minūf
Ṭanṭā
Zifta
Āṣ Sinbillāwayn
Al Mansūrah
Al Kabir
Ismailia (Al Ismāʿīlīyah)
Az Zaqāzīq
Bilbays
Banha

CAIRO (Al Qāhirah)
AL JIZAH
PYRAMIDS OF GIZA
MEMPHIS
Al Ḥawāmidīyah
Suez (As Suways)
Būr Tawfiq
Bitter Lakes
Suez Canal

AL JIZAH
AS SUWAYS
Al Fayyūm
Sinnūris
Biba
Bani Suwayf
Al Fashn
Maghāghah
Banī Mazār
Samalūt
AL MINYĀ
Al Minyā
Mallawi

Dayrūt
Ahnūb
ASYŪṬ
Asyūṭ
Juhaynah
Tahta
Al Maraghah
Akhmim
Suhaj
SUHĀJ
Jirga
Al Balyana
ABYDOS
QINĀ
Qūs
Nag Hammadi
VALLEY OF THE KINGS
AL BAHR AL AHMAR
THEBES
Luxor (Al Uqṣur)
LUXOR
Armant
Isnā
Idfū

Kawm Umbū
First Cataract
Aswān
ASWĀN
ASWAN HIGH DAM
Abū Simbel
Lake Nasser

EGYPT
SUDAN

Wādī Halfa
Second Cataract
Akasha East
Waḥāt Salīmah
Dal Cataract
Abri
Kosha

SEDEINGA TEMPLE
SOLB TEMPLE
SESEBI
Dalqū
Laqiyat al Arbaʿīn

Ṭaqab
Third Cataract
Karmah
Gharb Binna
Dunqulah
Argo
Kawa
Sahaba

NAPATA
Kūrti
Marawi
NURI
Al Khandaq
Mulwad
Fourth Cataract
Kutaymih
Karbaka

Bayudha Desert
Fifth Cataract
Miberika
Abū Ḥamad
Al Janayet
Abū Diss

Jabal Kurur 1,240 m

Jabal Oda 2,259 m

SHAMAL SĪNĀ

GAZA STRIP
Al ʿArīsh

Khatmia Pass
Gidi Pass
Mitla Pass

Sinai

JANŪB SĪNĀ

Mt. Catherine 2,642 m
At Ṭūr
Sharm ash Shaykh
Ras Muḥammad
Jazirat Tiran

Gulf of Suez

Rās Gharib

At Tūr

Jemsa

Al Ghurdaqah

Arabian Desert

Jabal Shāʾib al Banāt 2,005 m

Būr Safājah

Safājah

Al Quṣayr

Marsá al ʿAlam

Jabal Hamātah 1,977 m

Ra's Banās
BERENICE
Bir Umm Hibal
Bir Abū Ḥaṣwah

Foul Bay

RED SEA

Red Sea Hills

Halāʾib
Ras Hadarba
Jabal Is 1,851 m
Jabal Asoteriba 2,216 m

Jabal Abādab 1,596 m

Gebeit Mine
Muḥammad Qawl
Mukawwar I.
Ras Abu Shagara

ASH SHARQĪYAH

Port Sudan (Būr Sūdān)
Sallūm
Sawākin
Sinkāt
Ras Asis
Aqiq
Ras Kasar

Suakin Arch.

TOKAR GAME RESERVE

Mismār
Al Ibēdīyya
Barbar

Qabāb
Ṭaqatu Ḥayya
Tokar
Trinkitat

ERITREA

LEBANON
Damascus (Dimashq)
Limassol
Darayyā
SYRIA
Qiryat Shemona
Har Meron 2,205 m
Golan Heights
Nahariyya
Akko
Haifa (Hefa)
Umm el Fahm
Pardes Hanna
Nazareth
Netanya
Nablus
Tūlkarm
Petaḥ Tiqwa
Tel Aviv-Yafo
Holon
Ramla
Jerusalem
Gaza (Ghazzah)
Qiryat Gat
ISRAEL
Beersheba (Beʾer Sheva)
MASADA
Aṣ Ṣafi
Negev

Dead Sea

Dar'ā
Al Mafraq
Ar Ramtha
Irbid
As Salt
Az Zarqa
Amman (ʿAmmān)
Mādabā
Dhiban
Al Karak
Aṭ Ṭafilah
Ash Shawbak
PETRA
Maʿān

As Suwayda

Ar Rutbah

IRAQ

Syrian Desert

Jabal ʿUnāzah 745 m
Turayf

Kāf

Ash Shabakah

Al Jawf
Qārah

Sakākah

An Nafūd

JORDAN

Elat
Jabal Ramm 1,754 m
Al Quwayrah
Ḥaql
Jabal al Lawz 2,580 m
Nuwaybi
Jabal Dabbāgh 2,350 m
Duba
Muwayliḥ
Aynūnah
Tabūk
Al Qalibah
Al Akhḍar
Al ʿAssāfiyah

SAUDI ARABIA

Taymāʾ

Madā'in Ṣāliḥ
Al ʿUlā

Al ʿAyn
Umm Lajj
Jabal al Hijāz
Al Wajh
Ḥanak
Ash Shurayf
Khaybar
Jabal Ragwa 1,814 m
Yanbuʿ al Baḥr
Abyār ʿAli
Badr Ḥunayn
Medina (Al Madīnah)

Ra's Baridi
Ra's Abū Madd
Al Ḥamra
Al Muṣayjid

Rabigh
Mastūrah
Al Qaḍīmah

Jiddah
KING ABDUL AZIZ
Usfān

Limassol

POPULATION OF CITIES AND TOWNS
- ■ OVER 2,000,000
- □ 1,000,000 - 1,999,999
- ● 500,000 - 999,999
- ◉ 250,000 - 499,999
- ● 100,000 - 249,999
- ◎ 30,000 - 99,999
- ○ 10,000 - 29,999
- ○ UNDER 10,000

Longitude East of Greenwich

SCALE 1:6,800,000 POLYCONIC PROJECTION

MILES 0 ... 100 ... 200 ... 300
KILOMETERS 0 ... 100 ... 200 ... 300

© HAMMOND WORLD ATLAS CORPORATION

HEIGHT
m. / ft.
6000 / 19700
4000 / 13000
2000 / 6500
1500 / 5000
1000 / 3300
500 / 1600
200 / 650
50 / 160
0
DEPTH
(Figures in Hundreds)

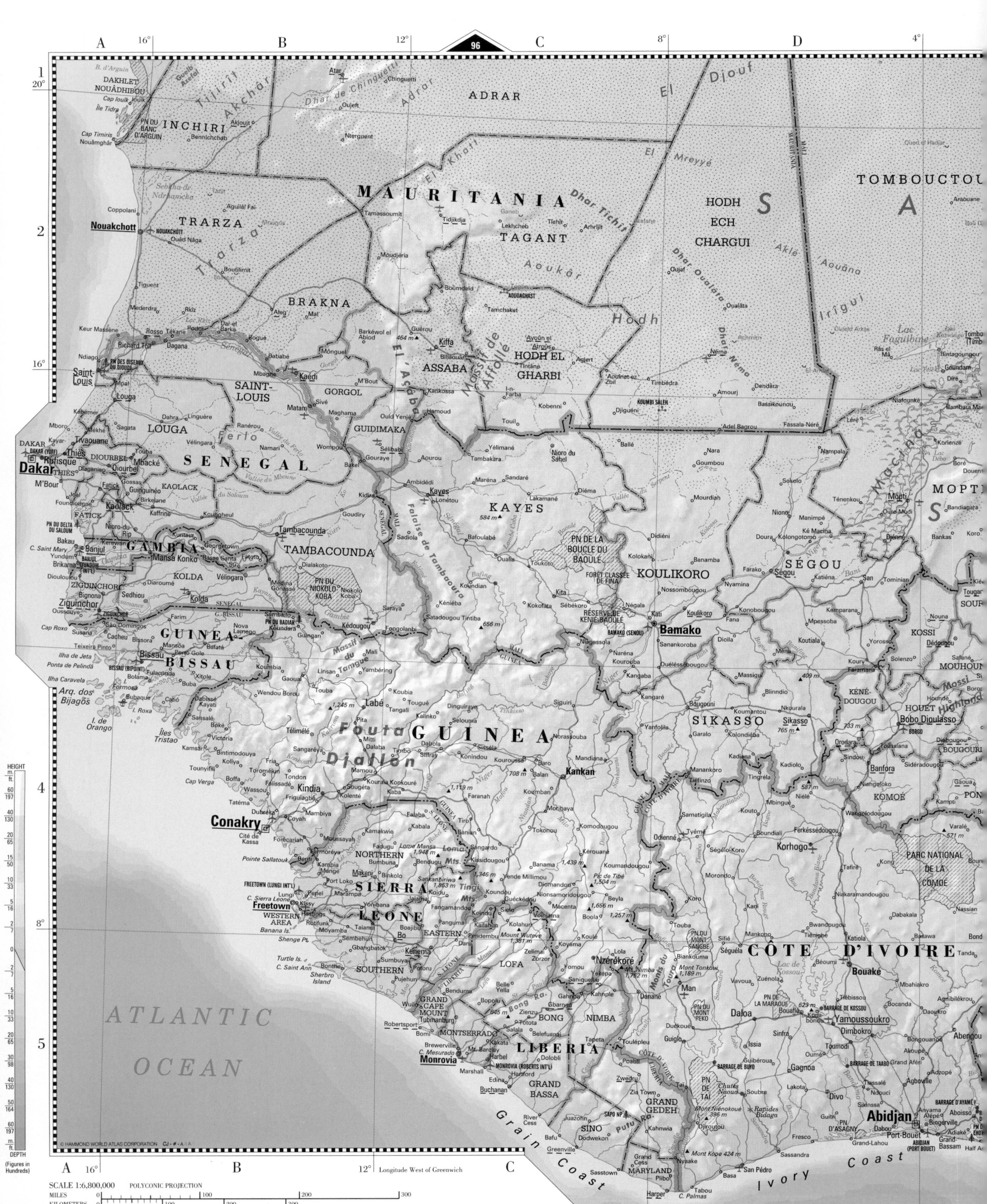

Southern West Africa

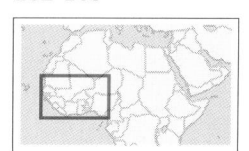

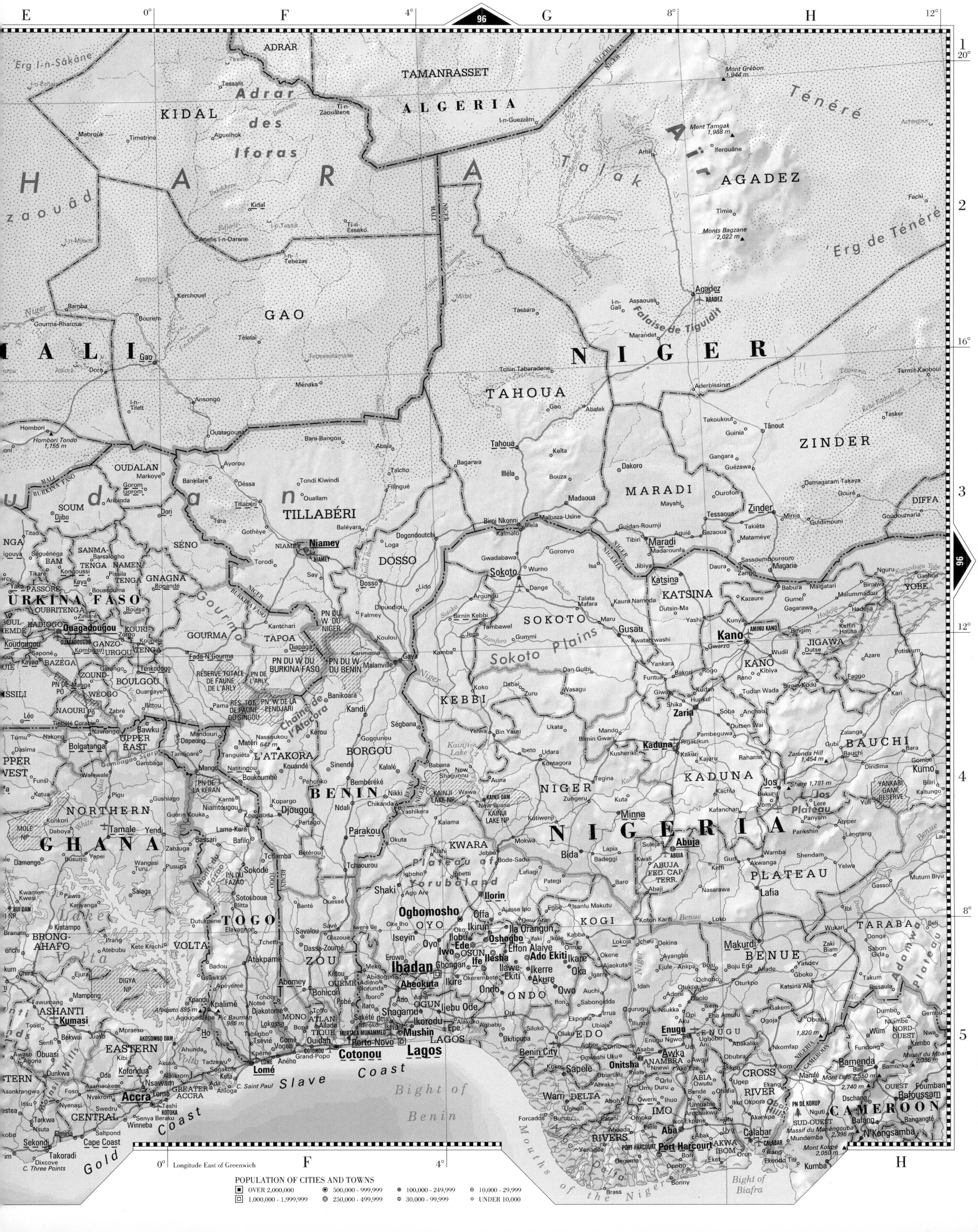

POPULATION OF CITIES AND TOWNS
- ■ OVER 2,000,000
- □ 1,000,000 - 1,999,999
- ● 500,000 - 999,999
- ● 250,000 - 499,999
- ● 100,000 - 249,999
- ● 30,000 - 99,999
- ○ 10,000 - 29,999
- ○ UNDER 10,000

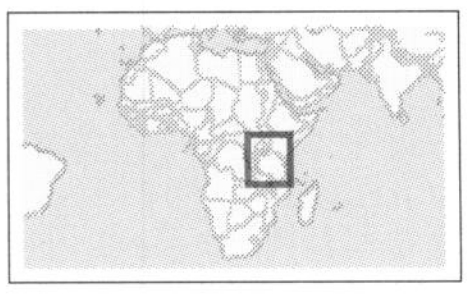

East Africa

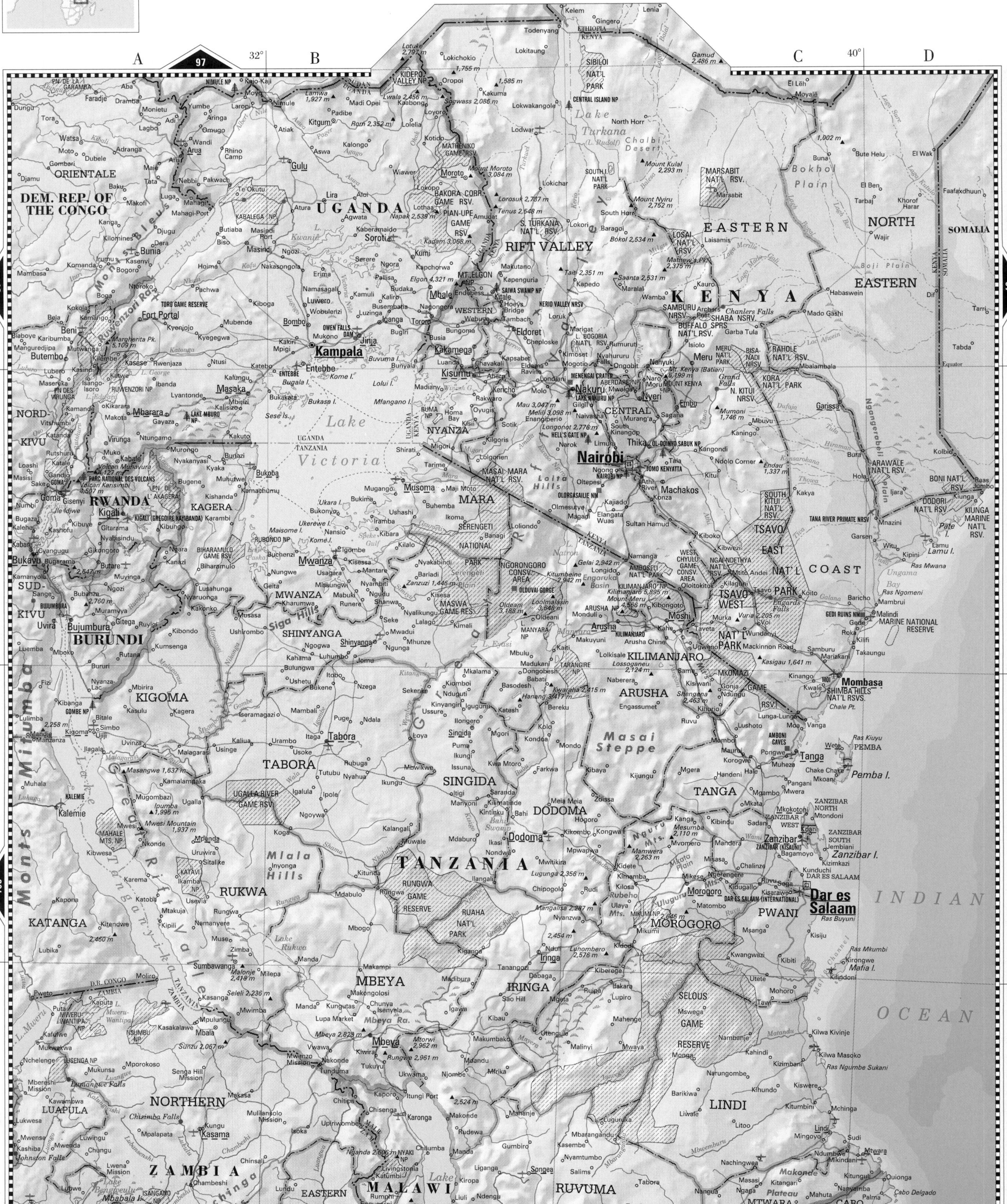

DEM. REP. OF THE CONGO

ORIENTALE

UGANDA

RIFT VALLEY

EASTERN

NORTH EASTERN

SOMALIA

KENYA

Lake Turkana (L. Rudolf)

Chalbi Desert

Bokol Plain

Kampala

ETHIOPIA / KENYA

NORD-KIVU

NYANZA

WESTERN

CENTRAL

Nairobi

Lake Victoria

MARA

RWANDA

KAGERA

Kigali

SUD-KIVU

BURUNDI

Bujumbura

SERENGETI NATIONAL PARK

NGORONGORO CONSV. AREA

COAST

TSAVO EAST NAT'L PARK

TSAVO WEST

MWANZA

SHINYANGA

KIGOMA

TABORA

SINGIDA

ARUSHA

KILIMANJARO

Mombasa

PEMBA

Pemba I.

TANGA

Masai Steppe

DODOMA

Dodoma

ZANZIBAR NORTH

ZANZIBAR SOUTH

Zanzibar I.

RUKWA

KATANGA

TANZANIA

MOROGORO

PWANI

Dar es Salaam

INDIAN OCEAN

MBEYA

IRINGA

SELOUS GAME RESERVE

D.R. CONGO

ZAMBIA

LINDI

LUAPULA

NORTHERN

MALAWI

Lake Nyasa (L. Malawi)

RUVUMA

MTWARA

Makonde Plateau

CABO DELGADO

ZAMBIA

NIASSA

MOZAMBIQUE

Archipélago de Quirimba

HEIGHT
m. / ft.
60 / 197
40 / 130
20 / 65
15 / 50
10 / 33
5 / 16
2 / 7
0
2 / 7
5 / 16
10 / 33
20 / 65
30 / 98
40 / 130
50 / 164
60 / 197
m.
DEPTH
(Figures in Hundreds)

SCALE 1:6,800,000   POLYCONIC PROJECTION

MILES   0   100   200   300

KILOMETERS   0   100   200   300

Longitude East of Greenwich

POPULATION OF CITIES AND TOWNS

■ OVER 2,000,000   ● 500,000 - 999,999   ● 100,000 - 249,999   ○ 10,000 - 29,999
□ 1,000,000 - 1,999,999   ● 250,000 - 499,999   ● 30,000 - 99,999   ○ UNDER 10,000

© HAMMOND WORLD ATLAS CORPORATION   CJ-2102-A

Southern Africa

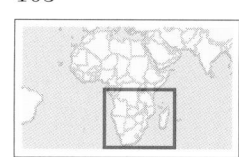

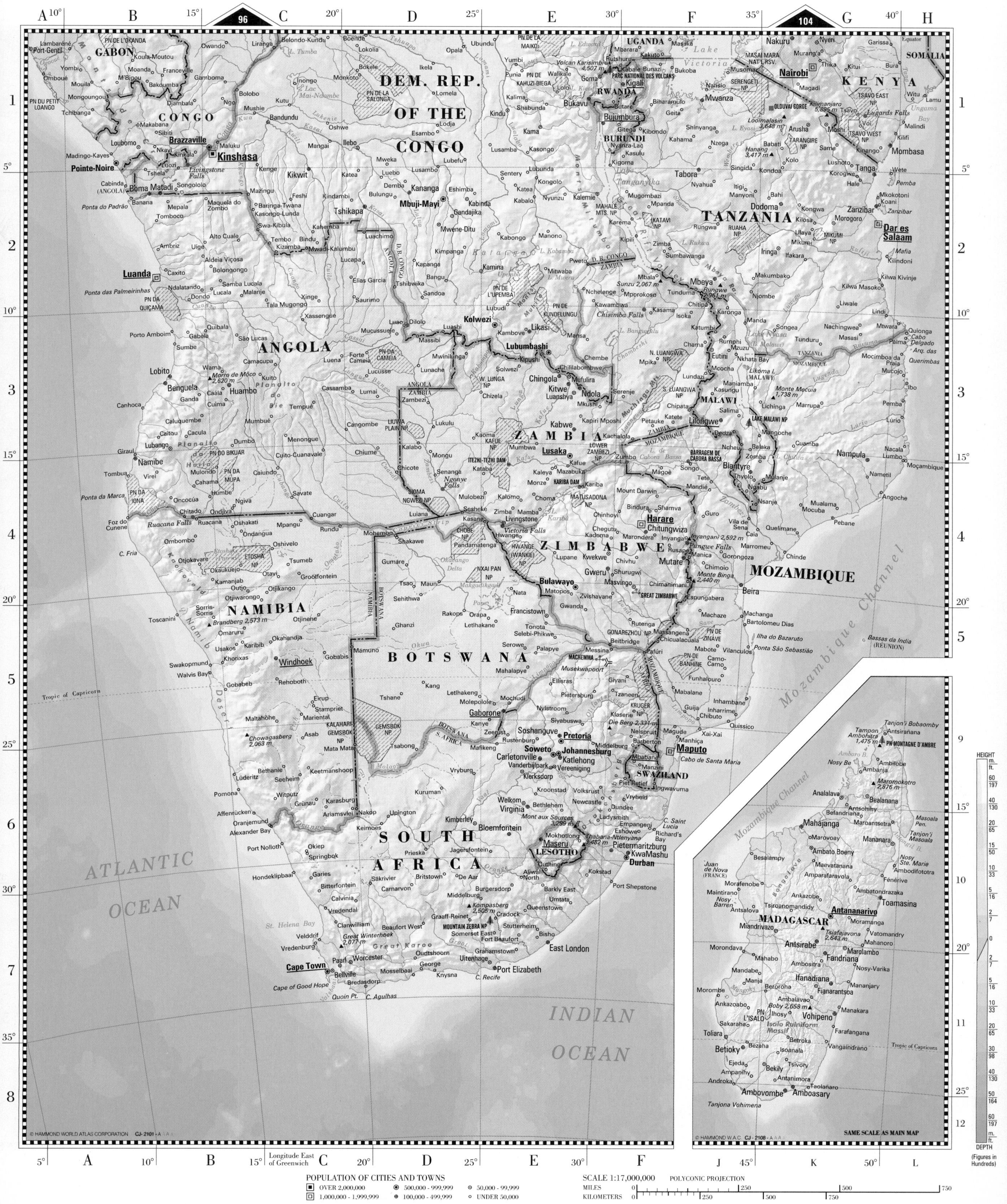

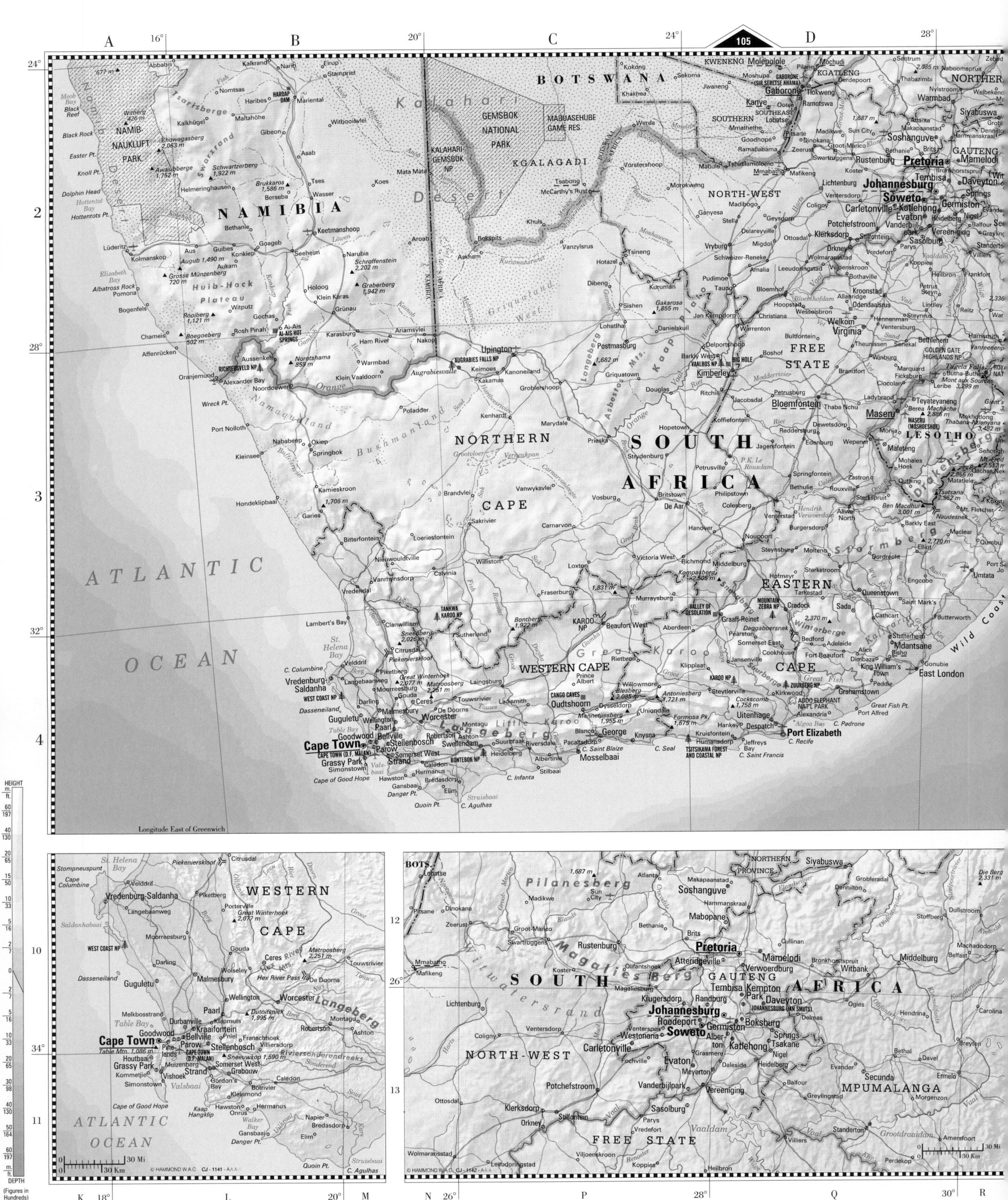

South Africa

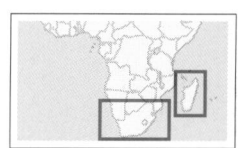

POPULATION OF CITIES AND TOWNS
■ OVER 2,000,000 ● 500,000 - 999,999 ◉ 100,000 - 249,999 ⊙ 10,000 - 29,999
▣ 1,000,000 - 1,999,999 ◉ 250,000 - 499,999 ⊙ 30,000 - 99,999 ∘ UNDER 10,000

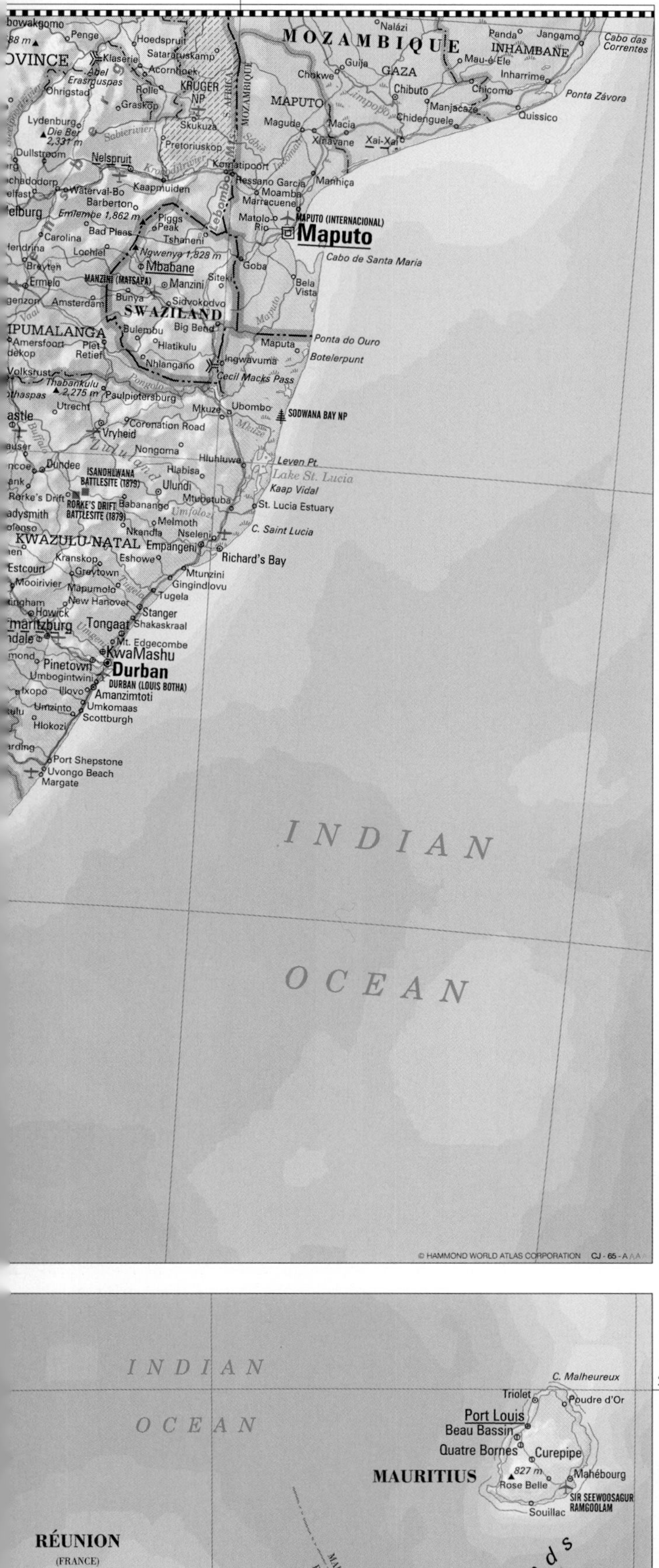

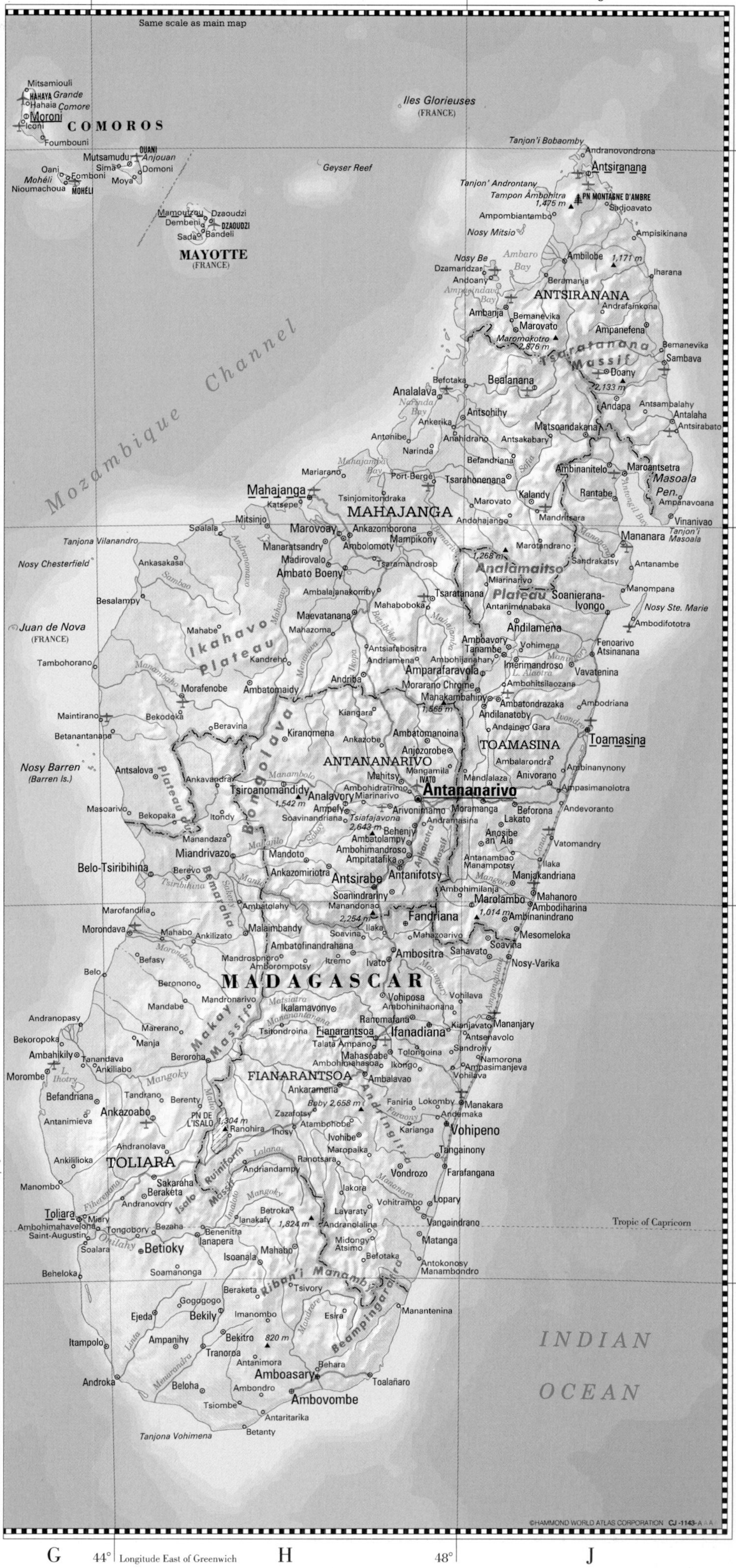

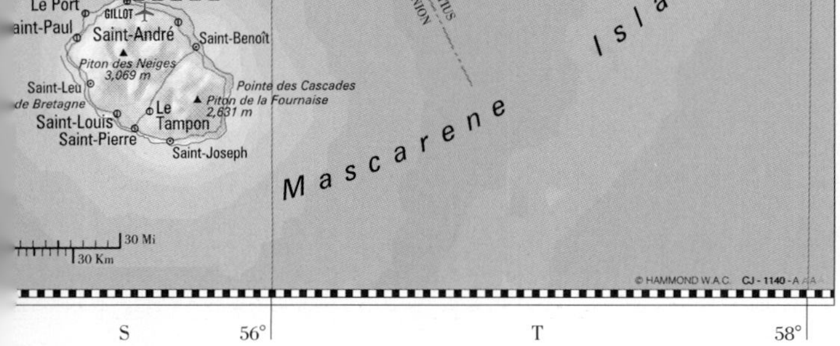

SCALE 1:6,800,000   LAMBERT CONFORMAL CONIC PROJECTION
MILES 0   100   200   300
KILOMETERS 0   100   200   300

Australia

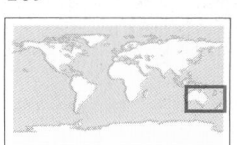

The Lake Eyre Basin is located in the arid interior of south central Australia. This basin is one of the largest areas of internal drainage in the world. It consists of two distinct, but interrelated basins: the north basin and the south basin. The much larger north basin shown here (the highly reflective areas) consists of two very large, normally dry lakebeds. The western lobe (bottom of the image) is Belt Bay, and the eastern lobe is Madigan Bay. The color change, especially in the Madigan Bay lobe, indicates that there was some water in this lobe at the time the image was taken.

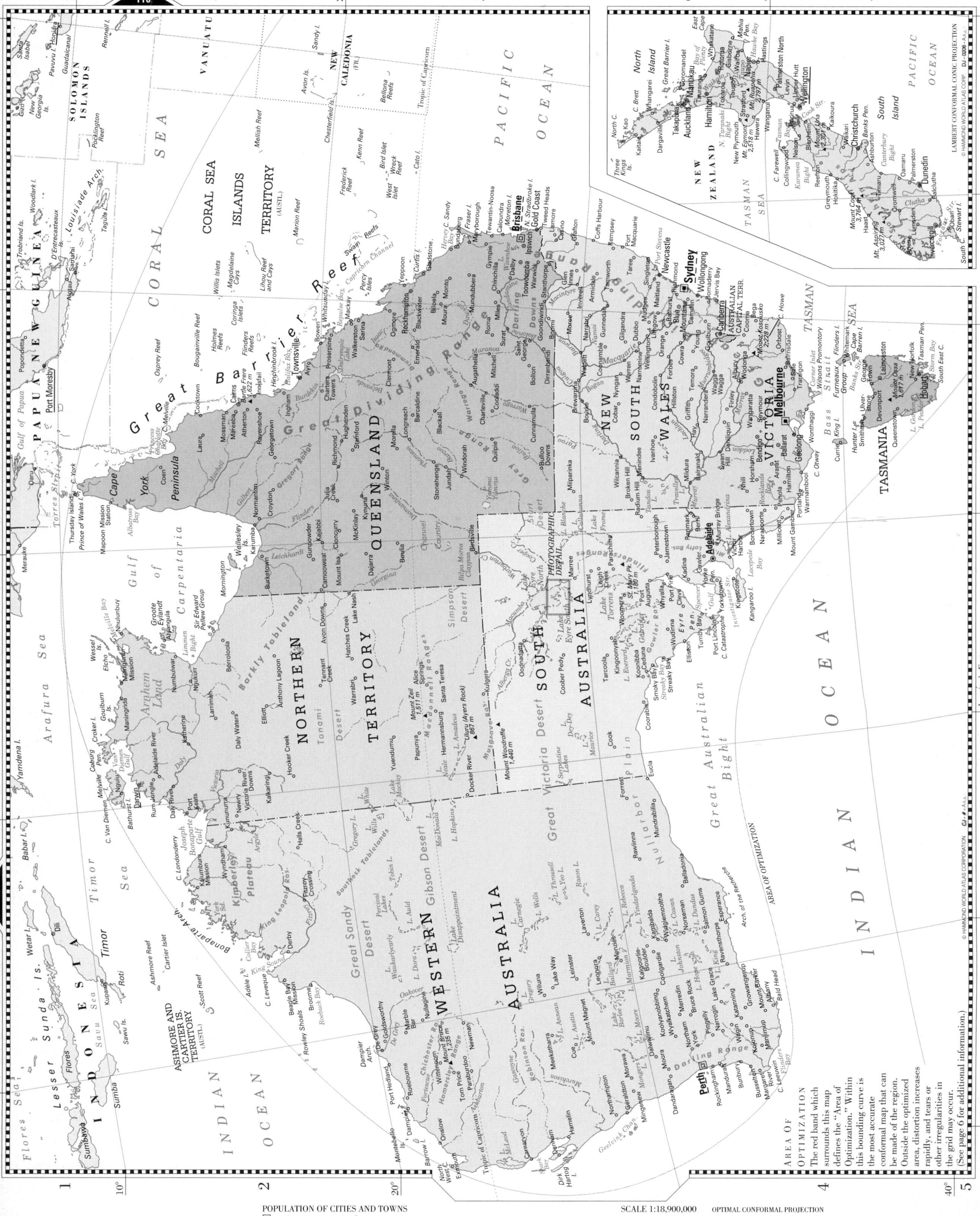

NEW ZEALAND

North Island

South Island

TASMAN SEA

PACIFIC OCEAN

LAMBERT CONFORMAL CONIC PROJECTION
© HAMMOND WORLD ATLAS CORP

Mt. Cook 3,764 m
Mt. Aspiring 3,027 m

AUSTRALIA

PAPUA NEW GUINEA

INDONESIA

CORAL SEA

CORAL SEA ISLANDS TERRITORY (AUSTL.)

PACIFIC OCEAN

SOLOMON ISLANDS

VANUATU

NEW CALEDONIA (FR.)

Great Barrier Reef

Cape York Peninsula

Gulf of Carpentaria

Arafura Sea

Timor Sea

Arnhem Land

NORTHERN TERRITORY

Barkly Tableland

Tanami Desert

QUEENSLAND

Great Dividing Range

Simpson Desert

Brisbane
Gold Coast
Newcastle
Sydney
Wollongong
Canberra
AUSTRALIAN CAPITAL TERR.

NEW SOUTH WALES

VICTORIA

Melbourne
Geelong

TASMANIA
Hobart
Launceston

Bass Strait

TASMAN SEA

Gibson Desert

Great Sandy Desert

Great Victoria Desert

WESTERN AUSTRALIA

SOUTH AUSTRALIA

Nullarbor Plain

Great Australian Bight

Kimberley Plateau

L. Eyre
Lake Eyre South
Lake Torrens
Lake Gairdner

Adelaide

PHOTOGRAPHIC DETAIL

AREA OF OPTIMIZATION

Perth

INDIAN OCEAN

Timor

Uluru (Ayers Rock) 867 m

Mount Woodroffe 1,440 m

Mount Zeil 1,511 m

POPULATION OF CITIES AND TOWNS

■ OVER 2,000,000
□ 1,000,000 - 1,999,999
● 500,000 - 999,999
◉ 100,000 - 499,999
○ 50,000 - 99,999
○ UNDER 50,000

SCALE 1:18,900,000   OPTIMAL CONFORMAL PROJECTION

MILES 0   250   500   750
KILOMETERS 0   250   500   750

Longitude East of Greenwich

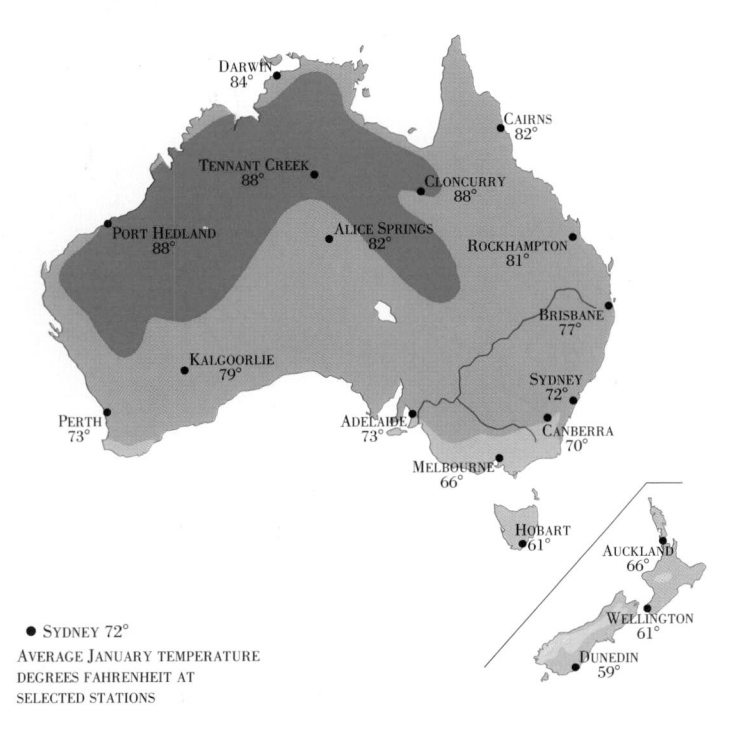

AVERAGE JANUARY TEMPERATURE

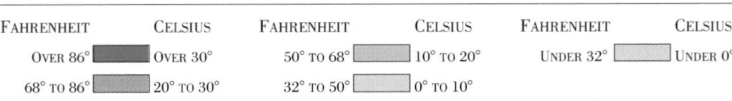

FAHRENHEIT	CELSIUS	FAHRENHEIT	CELSIUS	FAHRENHEIT	CELSIUS
OVER 86°	OVER 30°	50° TO 68°	10° TO 20°	UNDER 32°	UNDER 0°
68° TO 86°	20° TO 30°	32° TO 50°	0° TO 10°		

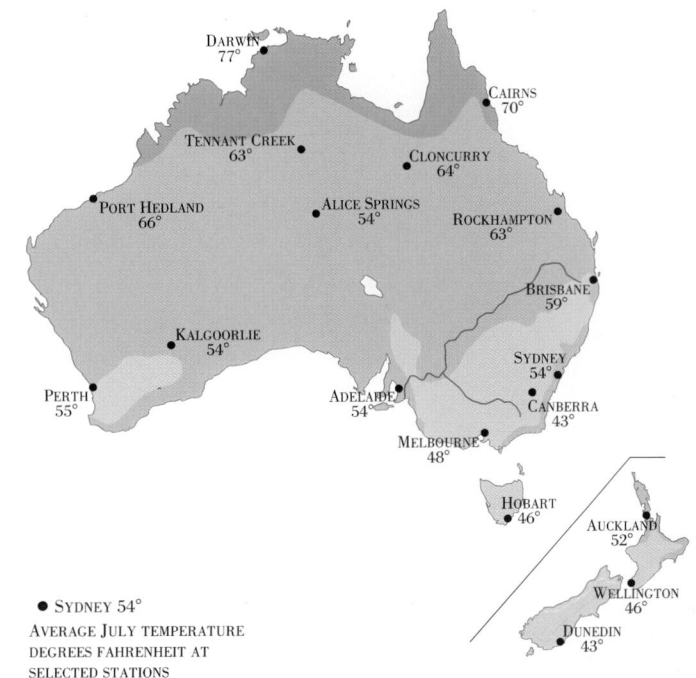

AVERAGE JULY TEMPERATURE

FAHRENHEIT	CELSIUS	FAHRENHEIT	CELSIUS
OVER 68°	OVER 20°	32° TO 50°	0° TO 10°
50° TO 68°	10° TO 20°	UNDER 32°	UNDER 0°

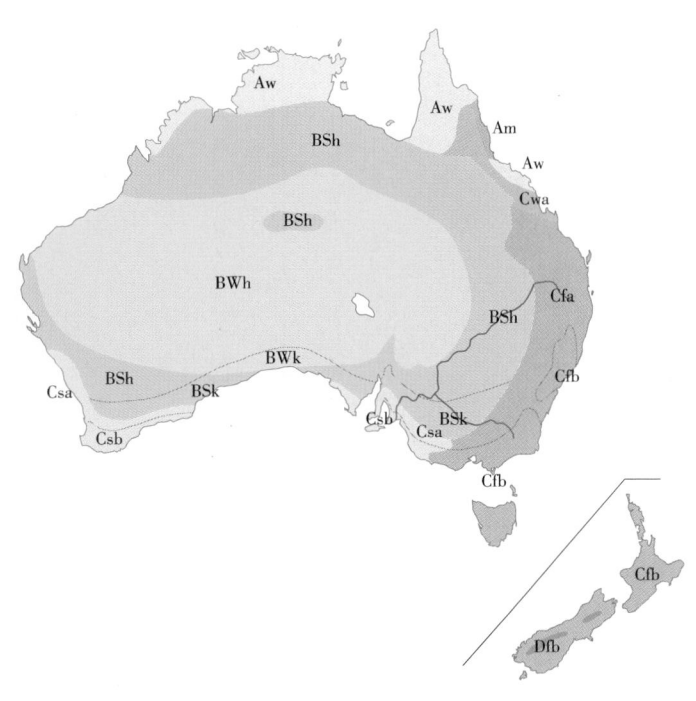

CLIMATE

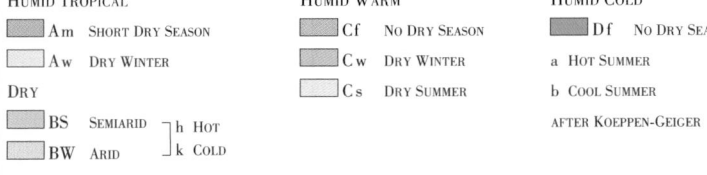

HUMID TROPICAL

Am SHORT DRY SEASON

Aw DRY WINTER

DRY

BS SEMIARID   ⎱ h HOT
BW ARID   ⎰ k COLD

HUMID WARM

Cf NO DRY SEASON

Cw DRY WINTER

Cs DRY SUMMER

HUMID COLD

Df NO DRY SEASON

a HOT SUMMER

b COOL SUMMER

AFTER KOEPPEN-GEIGER

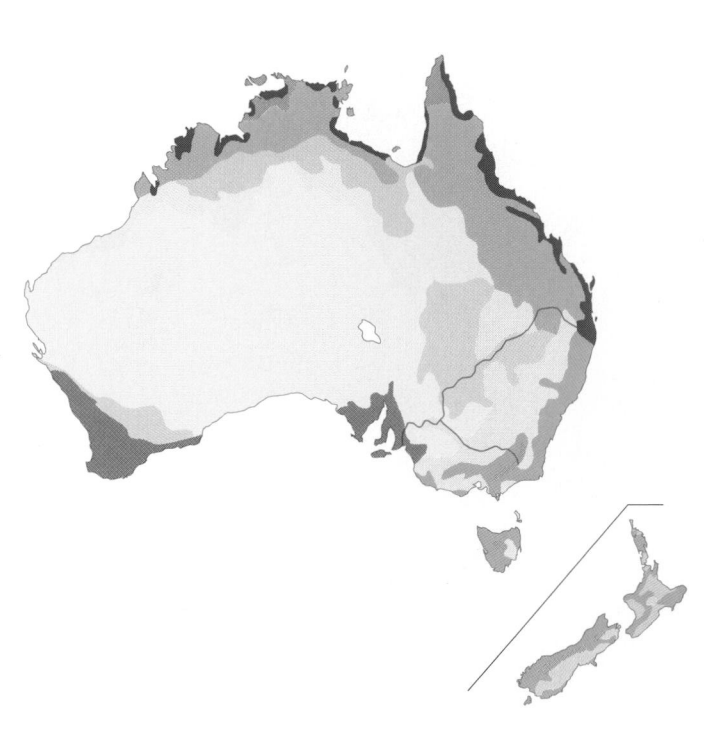

VEGETATION

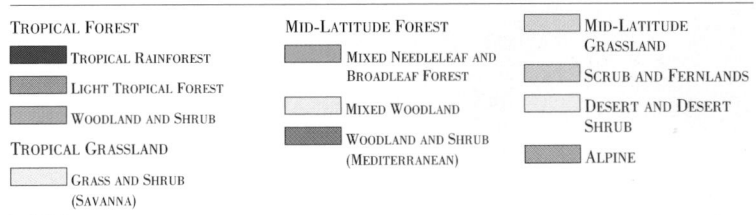

TROPICAL FOREST

TROPICAL RAINFOREST

LIGHT TROPICAL FOREST

WOODLAND AND SHRUB

TROPICAL GRASSLAND

GRASS AND SHRUB
(SAVANNA)

WOODED SAVANNA

MID-LATITUDE FOREST

MIXED NEEDLELEAF AND
BROADLEAF FOREST

MIXED WOODLAND

WOODLAND AND SHRUB
(MEDITERRANEAN)

MID-LATITUDE
GRASSLAND

SCRUB AND FERNLANDS

DESERT AND DESERT
SHRUB

ALPINE

Australia, New Zealand- Geographical Comparisons

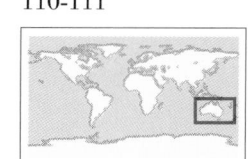

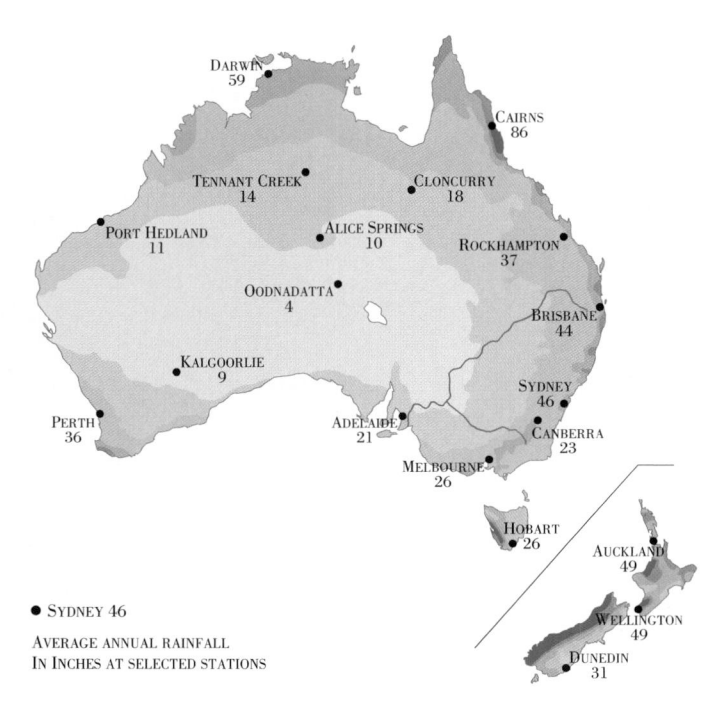

SYDNEY 46

AVERAGE ANNUAL RAINFALL
IN INCHES AT SELECTED STATIONS

AVERAGE ANNUAL RAINFALL

INCHES	CM	INCHES	CM	INCHES	CM
OVER 80	OVER 200	40 TO 60	100 TO 150	10 TO 20	25 TO 50
60 TO 80	150 TO 200	20 TO 40	50 TO 100	UNDER 10	UNDER 25

CITIES WITH OVER 500,000
INHABITANTS

POPULATION DISTRIBUTION

DENSITY PER		SQ. MI.	SQ. KM.	SQ. MI.	SQ. KM.
SQ. MI.	SQ. KM.	25 TO 130	10 TO 50	UNDER 3	UNDER 1
OVER 130	OVER 50	3 TO 25	1 TO 10		

LAND USE

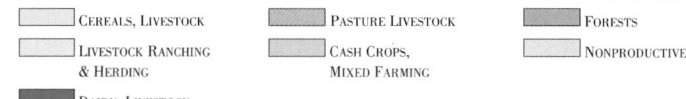

CEREALS, LIVESTOCK	PASTURE LIVESTOCK	FORESTS
LIVESTOCK RANCHING & HERDING	CASH CROPS, MIXED FARMING	NONPRODUCTIVE
DAIRY, LIVESTOCK		

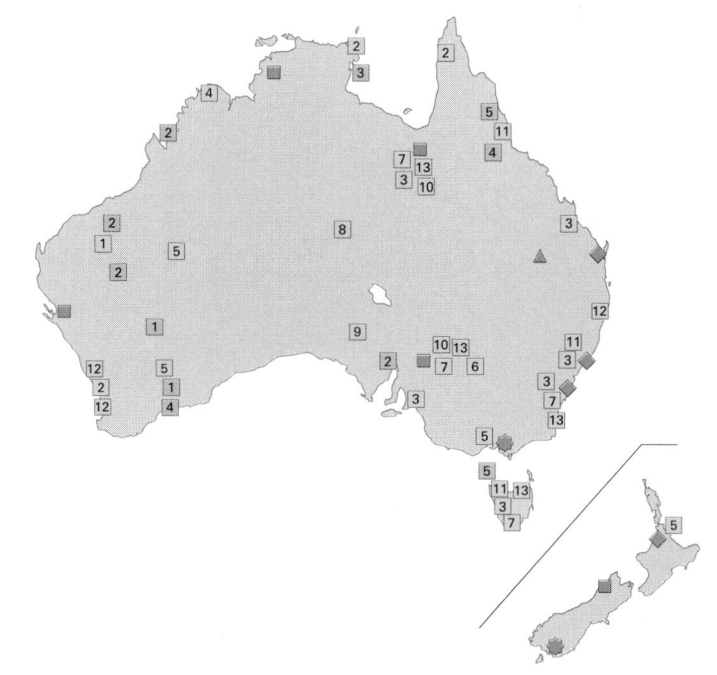

MINERAL RESOURCES

ENERGY & FUELS	IRON & FERROALLOYS	OTHER MAJOR RESOURCES		
COAL	1 COBALT	1 ASBESTOS	6 GYPSUM	11 TIN
LIGNITE	2 IRON ORE	2 BAUXITE	7 LEAD	12 TITANIUM
NATURAL GAS	3 MANGANESE	3 COPPER	8 MICA	13 ZINC
URANIUM	4 NICKEL	4 DIAMONDS	9 OPALS	
	5 TUNGSTEN	5 GOLD	10 SILVER	

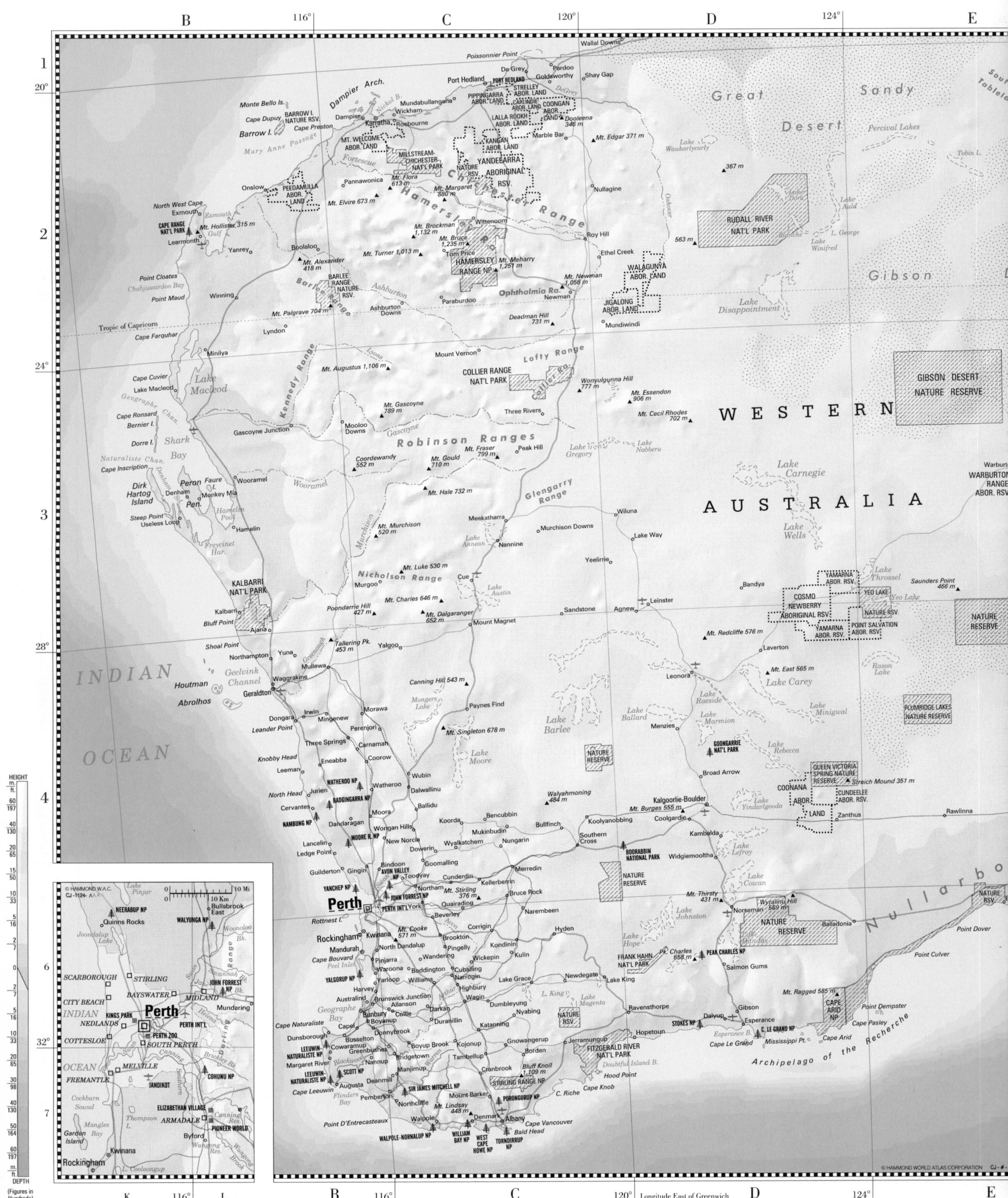

Western and Central Australia

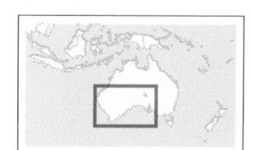

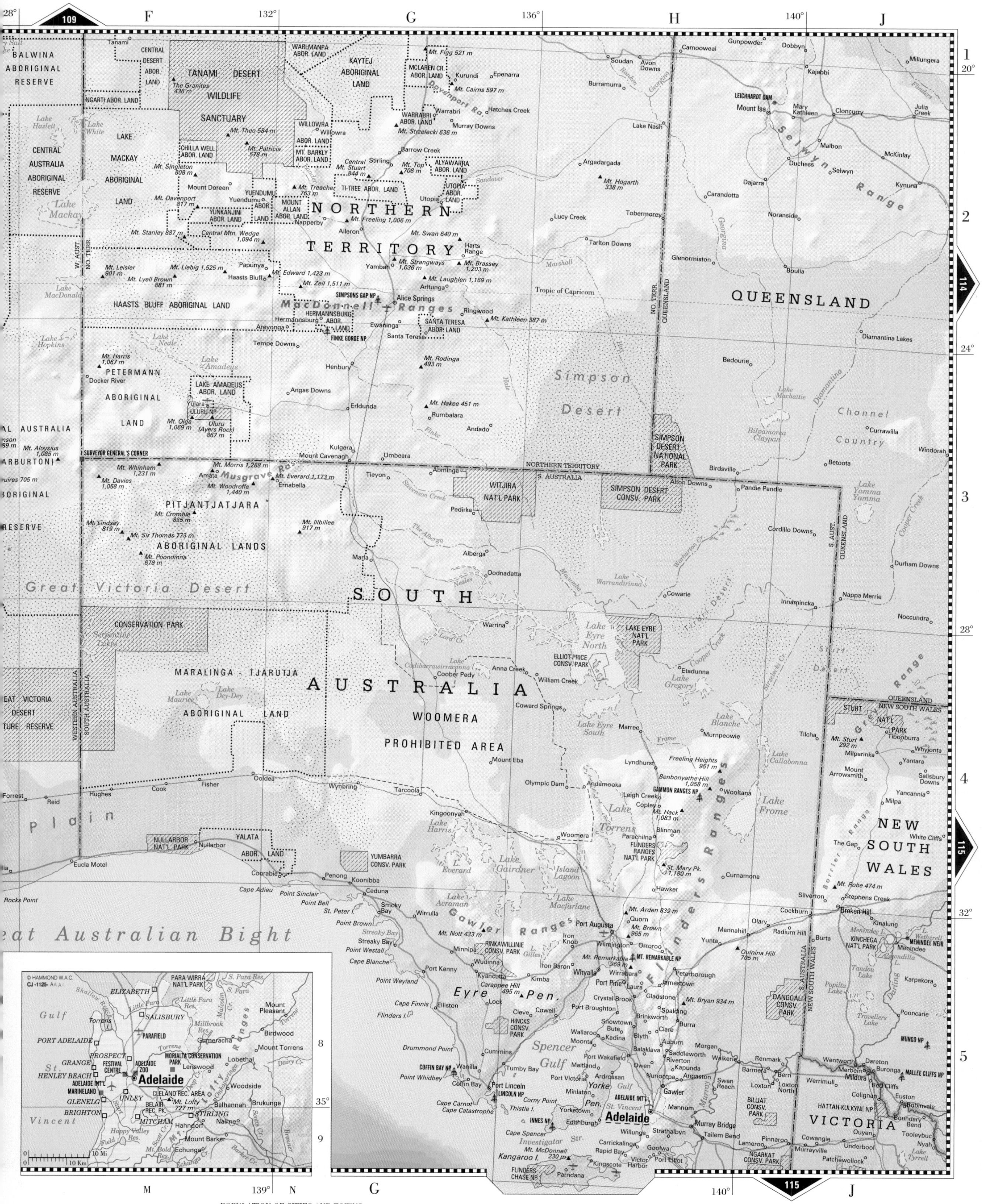

109 F 132° G 136° H 140° J

NORTHERN TERRITORY

QUEENSLAND

SOUTH AUSTRALIA

NEW SOUTH WALES

VICTORIA

Simpson Desert

Great Victoria Desert

WOOMERA PROHIBITED AREA

MARALINGA - TJARUTJA ABORIGINAL LAND

PITJANTJATJARA ABORIGINAL LANDS

HAASTS BLUFF ABORIGINAL LAND

PETERMANN ABORIGINAL LAND

LAKE AMADEUS ABOR. LAND

MacDonnell Ranges

TANAMI DESERT WILDLIFE SANCTUARY

Great Australian Bight

Eyre Pen.

Spencer Gulf

Flinders Ranges

Selwyn Range

Channel Country

Sturt Desert

Tropic of Capricorn

POPULATION OF CITIES AND TOWNS

- ■ OVER 2,000,000
- ● 500,000 – 999,999
- ● 100,000 – 249,999
- ● 10,000 – 29,999
- □ 1,000,000 – 1,999,999
- ● 250,000 – 499,999
- ● 30,000 – 99,999
- ○ UNDER 10,000

SCALE 1:6,800,000 LAMBERT CONFORMAL CONIC PROJECTION

MILES 0 100 200 300
KILOMETERS 0 100 200 300

Adelaide (inset map)

© HAMMOND W.A.C.
CJ-1125 AA A

Northeastern Australia

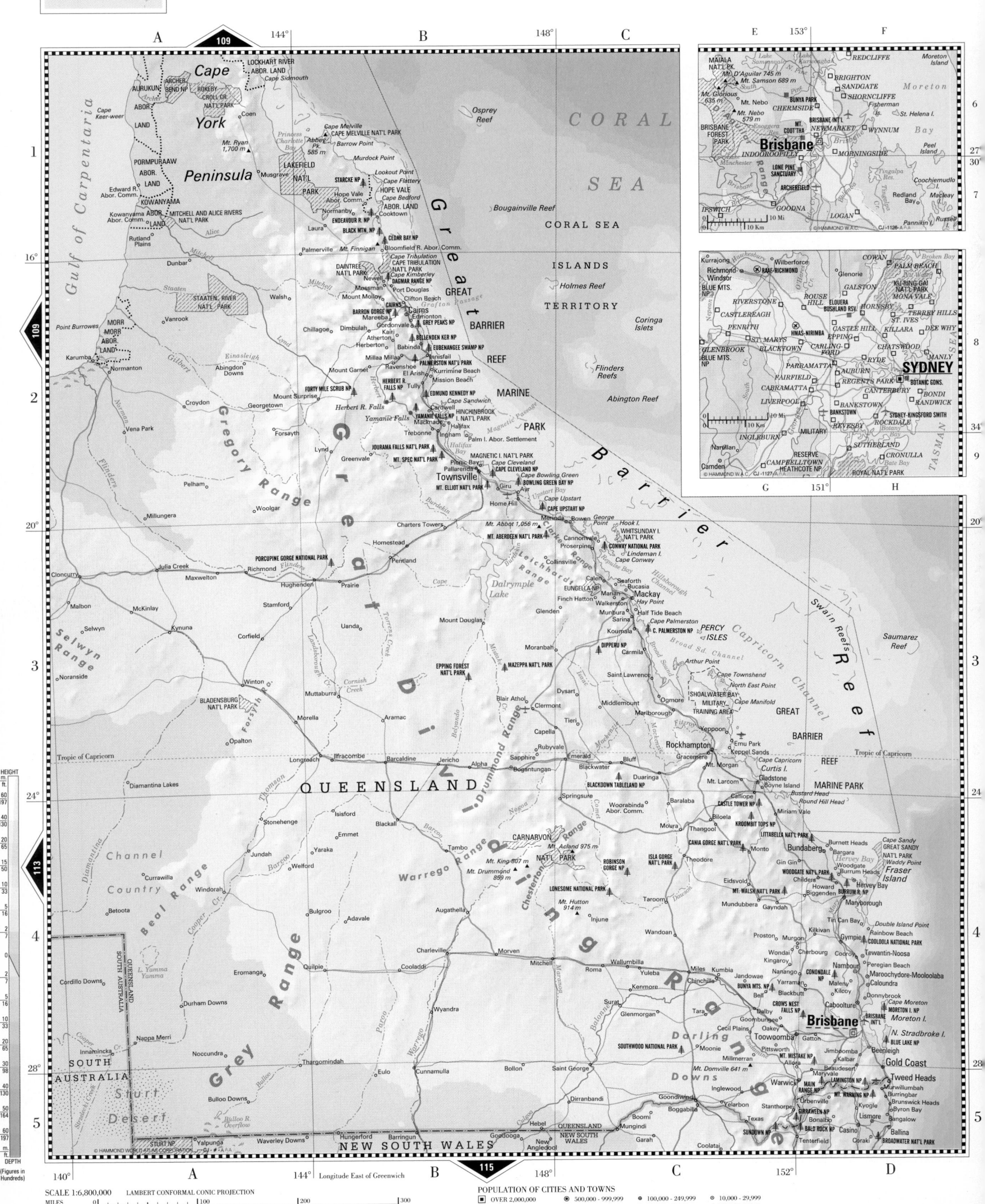

POPULATION OF CITIES AND TOWNS

Southeastern Australia

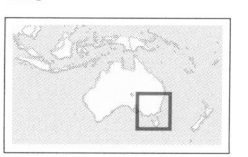

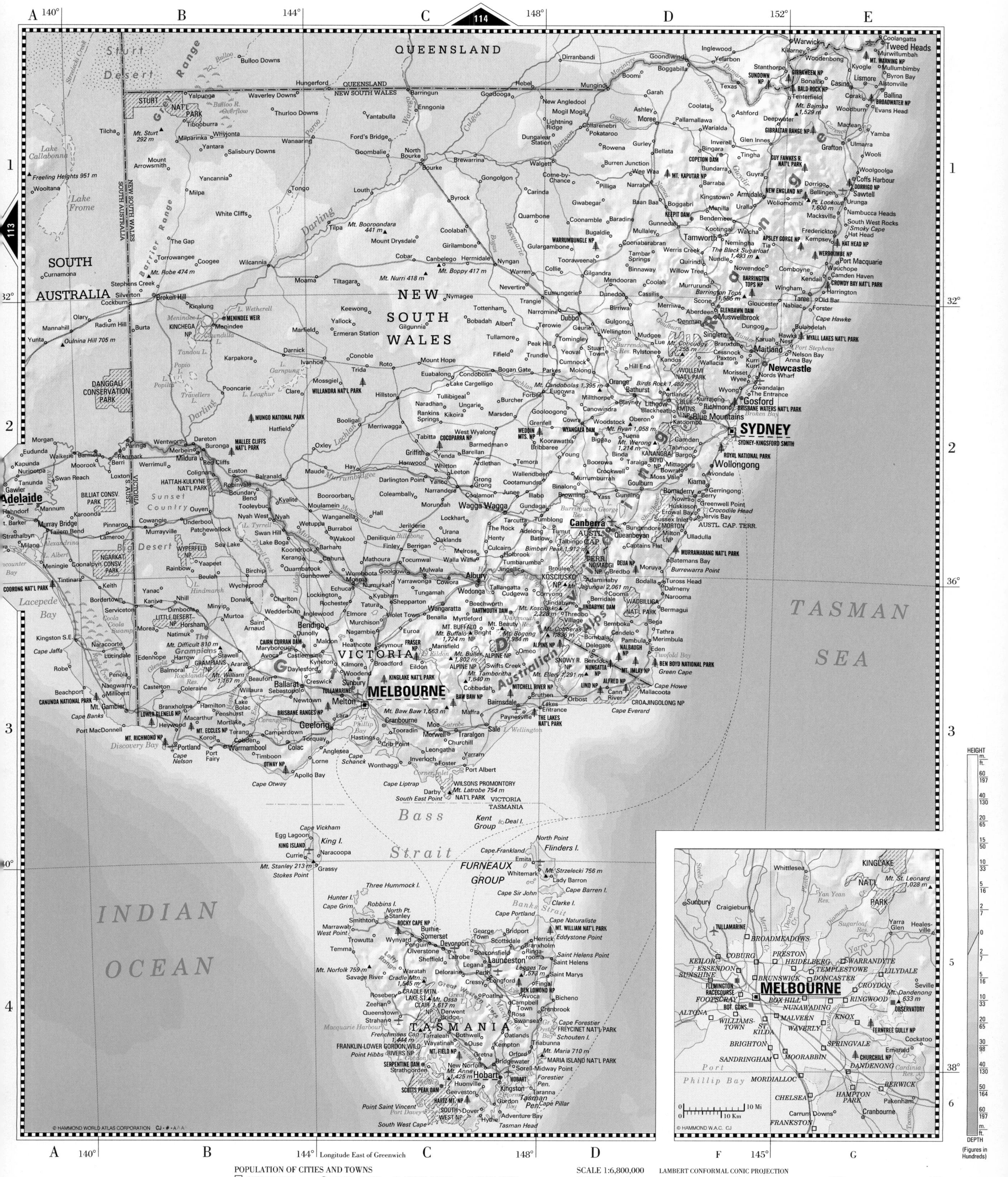

POPULATION OF CITIES AND TOWNS

■ OVER 2,000,000   ● 500,000 - 999,999   ● 100,000 - 249,999   ● 10,000 - 29,999

▢ 1,000,000 - 1,999,999   ● 250,000 - 499,999   ● 30,000 - 99,999   ○ UNDER 10,000

SCALE 1:6,800,000   LAMBERT CONFORMAL CONIC PROJECTION

MILES 0   100   200   300

KILOMETERS 0   100   200   300

HEIGHT
m. / ft.
60 / 197
40 / 130
20 / 65
15 / 49
10 / 33
5 / 16
0
7 / 16
30 / 98
40 / 130
50 / 164
60 / 197
m. / ft.
DEPTH
(Figures in Hundreds)

© HAMMOND WORLD ATLAS CORPORATION CJ

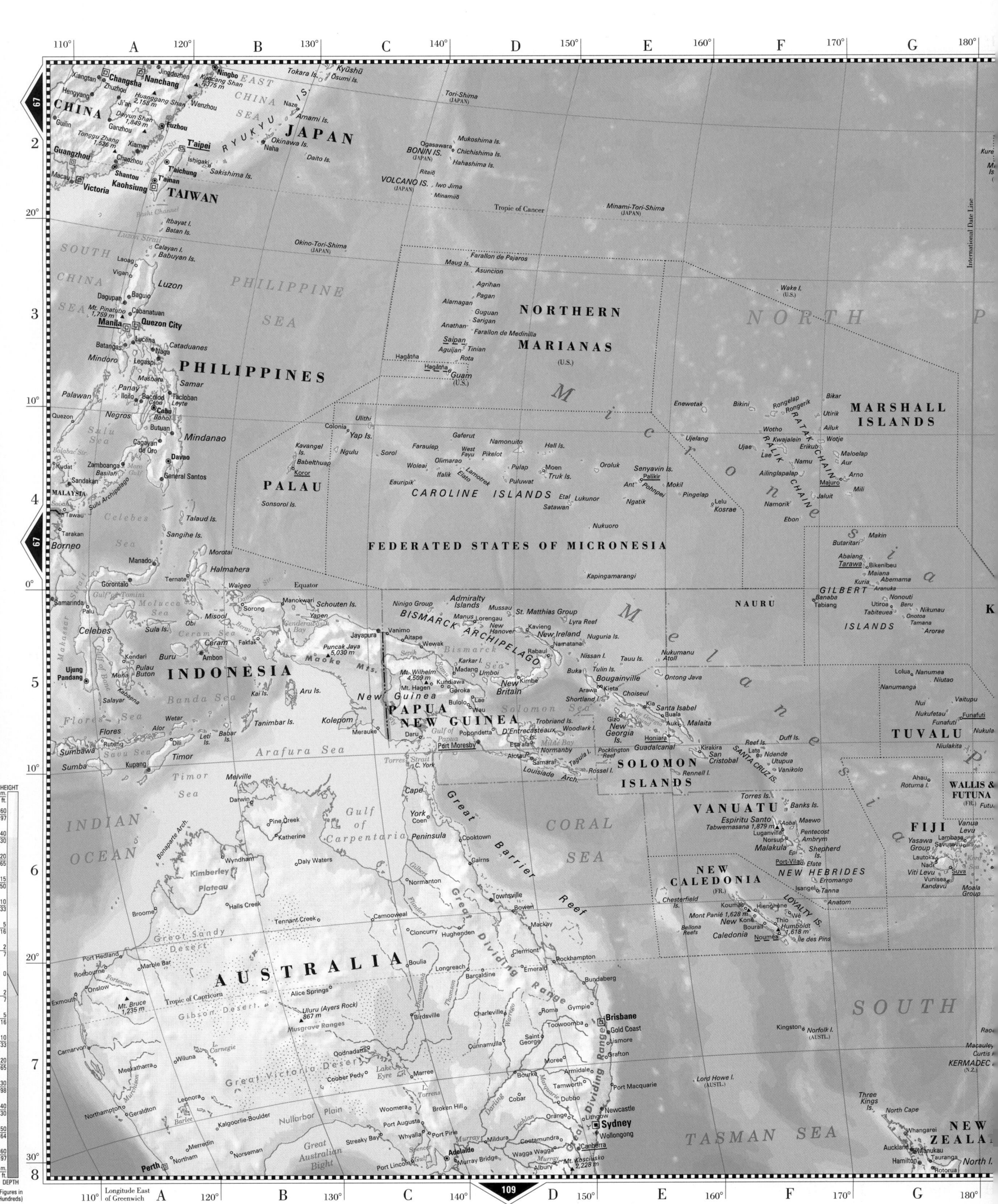

Central Pacific Ocean, New Zealand

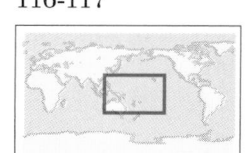

Hawaiian Islands area

HAWAII (U.S.)

Pearl and Hermes Reef · Lisianski I. · Laysan I. · Maro Reef · French Frigate Shoals · Necker I. · Nihoa · Niihau · Kauai · Oahu · Honolulu · Molokai · Lanai · Maui · Hilo · Hawaii

HAWAIIAN ISLANDS

Johnston Atoll (U.S.)

PACIFIC OCEAN

Tropic of Cancer

Kingman Reef (U.S.) · Palmyra (U.S.) · Teraina (Washington I.) · Tabuaeran (Fanning I.) · Kiritimati (Christmas I.)

Equator · Jarvis I. (U.S.)

International Date Line

LINE ISLANDS · Malden I. · Starbuck I. · Vostok I. · Caroline I. · Flint I.

KIRIBATI · PHOENIX IS. · Abariringa (Canton) · Enderbury · Birnie · Rawaki (Phoenix) · McKean · Orona (Hull) · Manra (Sydney)

POLYNESIA

Samoa / Tonga / Cook Islands / French Polynesia area

TOKELAU (N.Z.) · Atafu · Nukunonu · Fakaofo · Swains I.

SAMOA · AMERICAN SAMOA · Mt. Silisili 1,858 m · Asau · Savai'i · Apia · Upolu · Pago Pago · Tutuila · Manu'a Is. · Rose I.

Niuatoputapu Group · Nelafu · Vava'u Group · Alofi · Niue · NIUE (N.Z.) · Pangai · Ha'apai Group · Nuku'alofa · 'Eua · TONGA

NORTHERN COOK IS. · Tongareva (Penrhyn) · Rakahanga · Manihiki · Pukapuka · Nassau · Suwarrow

COOK ISLANDS (N.Z.) · Palmerston Atoll · Aitutaki Atoll · Manuae Atoll · Amuri · Mitiaro · Atiu · Mauke · SOUTHERN COOK IS. · Avarua · Rarotonga · Mangaia

Bellingshausen · Îles Sous-le-Vent · Maupiti · Tupai · Bora Bora · Huahine · Raiatea · Uturoa · Moorea · Tahaa · Tahiti · Papeete · Faaa · Tetiaroa · Makatea · SOCIETY IS. · Îles du Vent · Hereheretue

King George Is. · Tikehau · Rangiroa · Manihi · Takaroa · Takapoto · Tepoto · Napuka · Pukapuka · Disappointment Is. · Tiputa · Arutua · Apataki · Kaukura · Toau · Fakarava · Anaa · Tahanea · Hikueru · Marokau · Otepa · Hao · Tatakoto · Fakahina · Raroia · Makemo · Taenga · Amanu · Vahitahi · Reao · Pukarua · Nukutavake

TUAMOTU ARCHIPELAGO

FRENCH POLYNESIA · Duke of Gloucester Is. · Vanavaro · Tureia · Marutea · Actaeon Group · Mururoa · Maria · Fangataufa · Morane · Tenarunga · Temoe · Rikitea · Mangareva · GAMBIER IS.

Maria I. · Moerai · Rurutu · Rimatara · Mataura · Tubuai · Raivavae · AUSTRAL ISLANDS (Tubuaï Islands) · Rapa · Marotiri (Bass Is.)

MARQUESAS IS.

PITCAIRN ISLANDS (U.K.) · Oeno I. · Adamstown · Pitcairn I. · Henderson I. · Ducie I.

Tropic of Capricorn

Easter Island (Isla de Pascua) (CHILE)

PACIFIC OCEAN

New Zealand

TASMAN SEA

Three Kings Is. · C. Maria van Diemen · North C. · Te Kao · C. Kerikeri · Kaitaia · Kaikohe · C. Brett · Whangarei · Dargaville · Warkworth · Great Barrier I. · Kaipara Har. · Hauraki Gulf · Coromandel Pen.

Takapuna · Auckland · Manukau · Huntly · Te Aroha · Thames · Bay of Plenty · Hamilton · Tauranga · Te Awamutu · Cambridge · Whakatane · Te Araroa · East C. · Te Kuiti · Tokoroa · Rotorua · Kawerau · Hikurangi 1,754 m · Murupara · UREWERA NP

North Island

NEW ZEALAND

North Taranaki Bight · New Plymouth · Mt. Egmont 2,518 m · C. Egmont · Waitara · Stratford · Hawera · Taumarunui · Turangi · Mt. Ruapehu 2,797 m · TONGARIRO NP · Taupo · Wairoa · Gisborne · Mahia Pen. · Napier · Hawke Bay · Hastings · Waipukurau

South Taranaki Bight · Wanganui · Dannevirke · Ashhurst · Palmerston North · Levin · Masterton · Porirua · Upper Hutt · Wellington · Lower Hutt · C. Palliser

C. Farewell · Collingwood · Tasman Bay · Motueka · Karamea Bight · Karamea · Nelson · Blenheim · Ward · Westport · Mt. Owen 1,875 m · Murchison · NELSON LAKES NP · Mt. Una 2,301 m · Clarence · Reefton · Lewis Pass · Kaikoura · Greymouth · Hokitika · Waikari · Rangiora · Otira · ARTHUR'S PASS NP · Arthur's Pass · Kaiapoi · Fox Glacier · WESTLAND NP · Mt. Cook 3,764 m · MT. COOK NP · Darfield · Christchurch · Banks Pen. · Haast · Geraldine · Ashburton · MT. ASPIRING NP · Mt. Aspiring 3,027 m · Twizel · Temuka · Timaru · Canterbury Bight · Wanaka · Cromwell · Waimate · Queenstown · Alexandra · Oamaru · FIORDLAND NAT'L PARK · Te Anau · Lumsden · Palmerston · West C. · Gore · Mosgiel · Milton · Dunedin · Riverton · Balclutha · Invercargill · Bluff · Mt. Anglem 980 m · Oban · South C. · Stewart I. · Snares Is. · Foveaux Strait

South Island

PACIFIC OCEAN

© HAMMOND W.A.C.

LAMBERT CONFORMAL CONIC PROJECTION

0 · 90 Mi · 0 · 90 Km

Bottom margin

POPULATION OF CITIES AND TOWNS
- OVER 3,000,000
- 1,000,000 – 2,999,999
- 500,000 – 999,999
- 100,000 – 499,999
- UNDER 100,000

SCALE 1:30,700,000 · LAMBERT AZIMUTHAL EQUAL-AREA PROJECTION

MILES 0 · 400 · 800 · 1200
KILOMETERS 0 · 400 · 800 · 1200

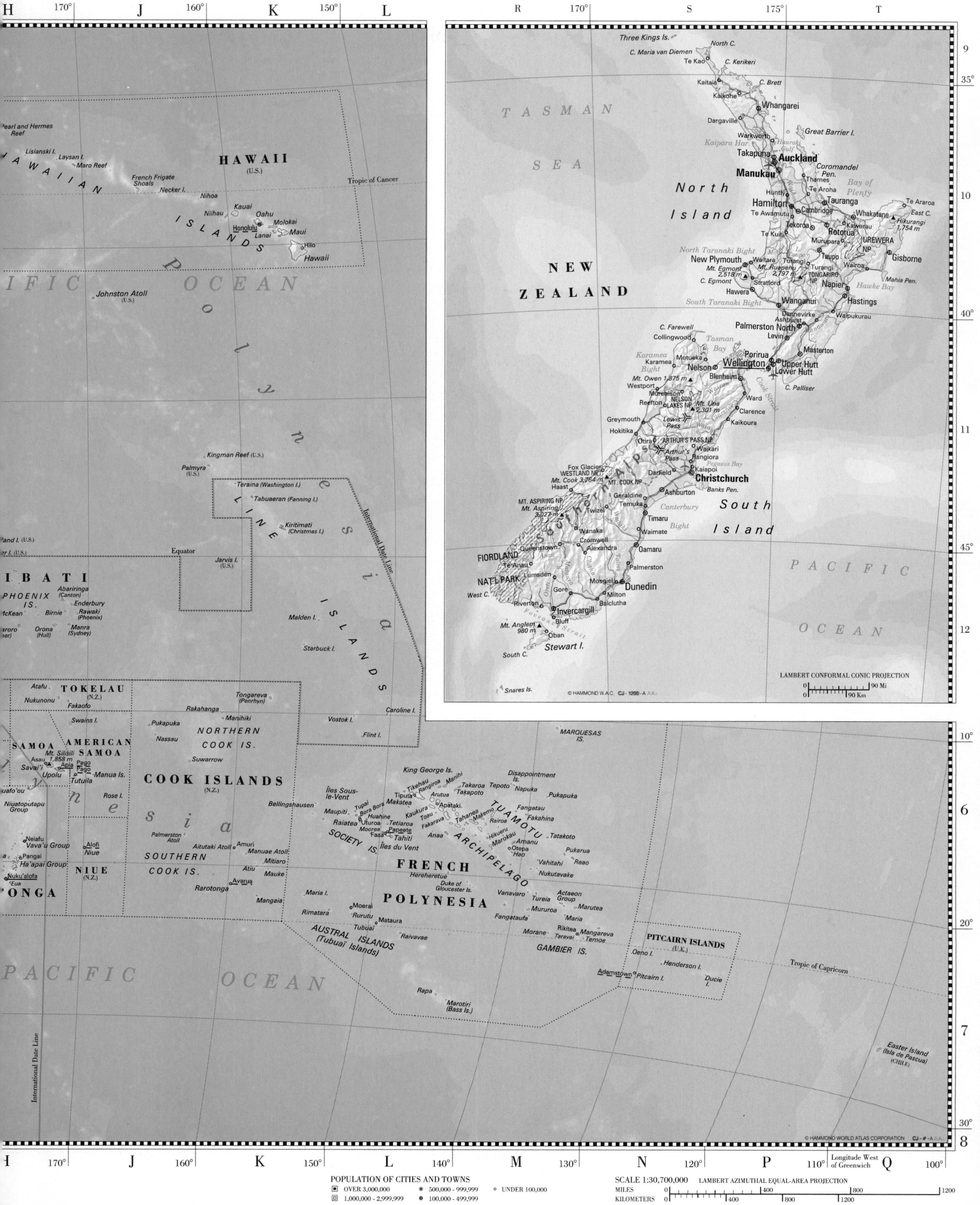

Longitude West of Greenwich

North America

The Grand Canyon, one of the deepest canyons in the world, with a depth of 1 mile (1.6 km.), can be seen in this spectacular, west-looking, low-oblique image. The Colorado River cut through rocks billions of years old to create this canyon. The Grand Canyon is 277 miles (466 km.) long and averages nearly 10 miles (16 km.) in width. The snow-covered, forested Kaibab Plateau (north of the canyon) and the Coconino Plateau (south of the canyon) are visible. Western portions of the Painted Desert can be seen east of the canyon where the Little Colorado joins the Colorado River.

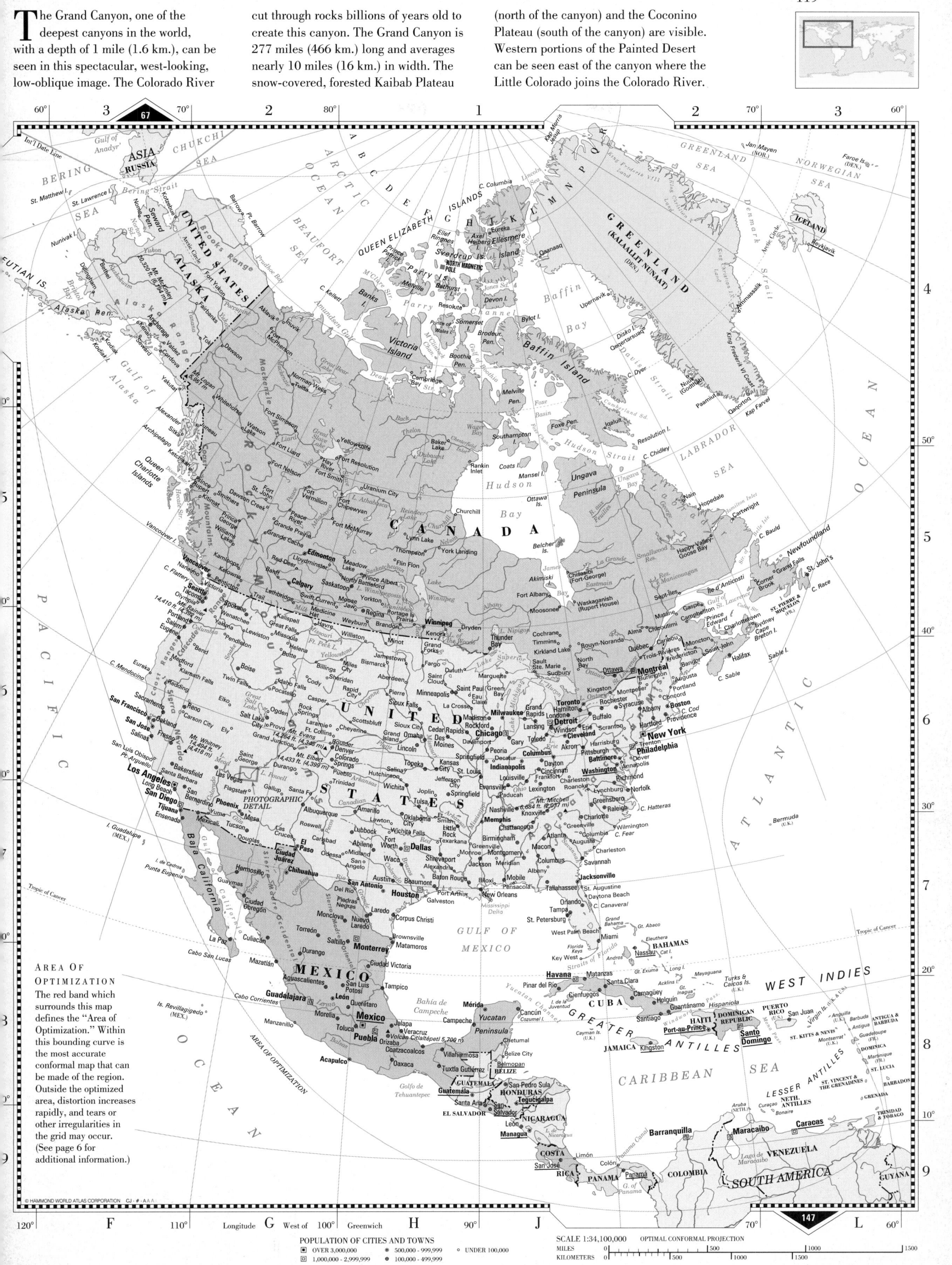

AREA OF OPTIMIZATION
The red band which surrounds this map defines the "Area of Optimization." Within this bounding curve is the most accurate conformal map that can be made of the region. Outside the optimized area, distortion increases rapidly, and tears or other irregularities in the grid may occur. (See page 6 for additional information.)

© HAMMOND WORLD ATLAS CORPORATION   CJ - # - AAA

POPULATION OF CITIES AND TOWNS

SCALE 1:34,100,000   OPTIMAL CONFORMAL PROJECTION

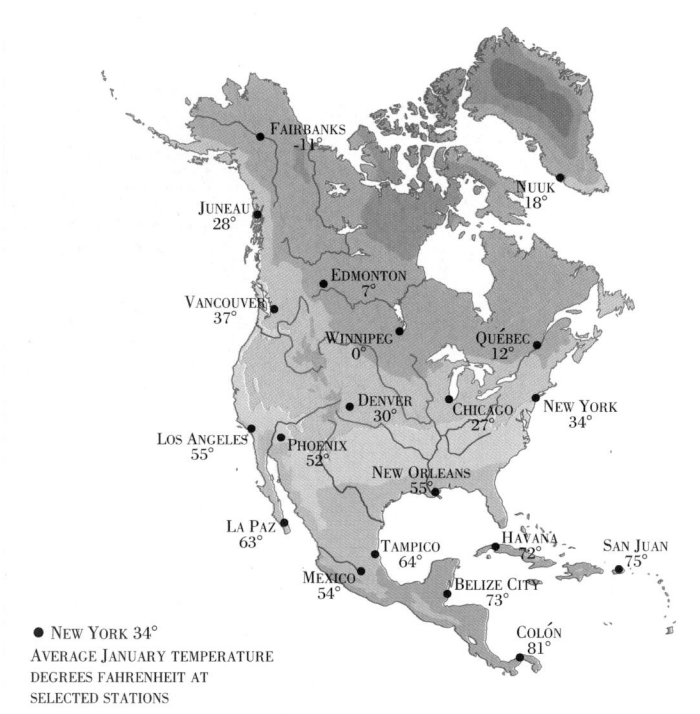

FAIRBANKS
-11°

JUNEAU
28°

NUUK
18°

VANCOUVER
37°

EDMONTON
7°

WINNIPEG
0°

QUÉBEC
12°

DENVER
30°

CHICAGO
27°

NEW YORK
34°

LOS ANGELES
55°

PHOENIX
52°

NEW ORLEANS
55°

LA PAZ
63°

TAMPICO
64°

HAVANA
72°

SAN JUAN
75°

MEXICO
54°

BELIZE CITY
73°

COLÓN
81°

● NEW YORK 34°
AVERAGE JANUARY TEMPERATURE
DEGREES FAHRENHEIT AT
SELECTED STATIONS

AVERAGE JANUARY TEMPERATURE

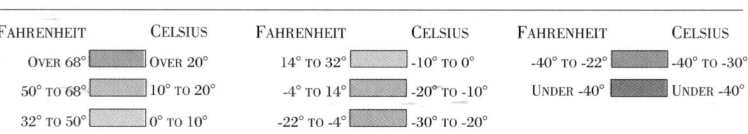

FAHRENHEIT	CELSIUS	FAHRENHEIT	CELSIUS	FAHRENHEIT	CELSIUS
OVER 68°	OVER 20°	14° TO 32°	-10° TO 0°	-40° TO -22°	-40° TO -30°
50° TO 68°	10° TO 20°	-4° TO 14°	-20° TO -10°	UNDER -40°	UNDER -40°
32° TO 50°	0° TO 10°	-22° TO -4°	-30° TO -20°		

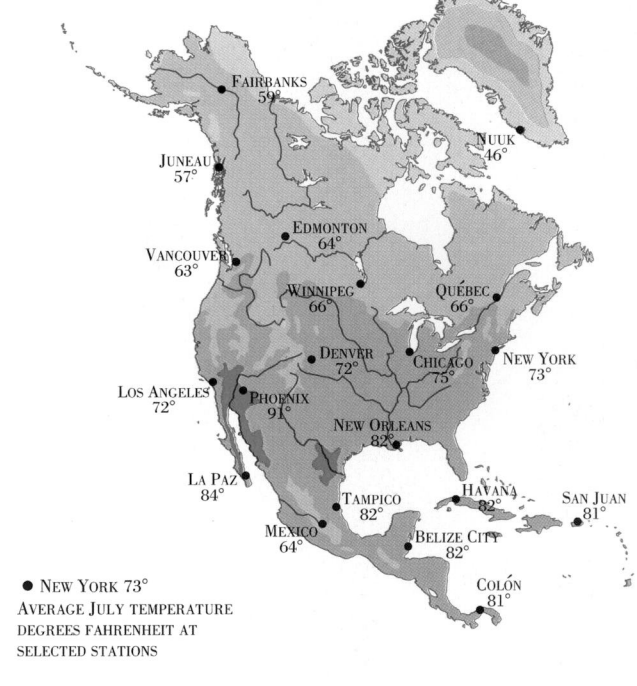

FAIRBANKS
59°

JUNEAU
57°

NUUK
46°

VANCOUVER
63°

EDMONTON
64°

WINNIPEG
66°

QUÉBEC
66°

DENVER
72°

CHICAGO
75°

NEW YORK
73°

LOS ANGELES
72°

PHOENIX
91°

NEW ORLEANS
82°

LA PAZ
84°

TAMPICO
82°

HAVANA
82°

SAN JUAN
81°

MEXICO
64°

BELIZE CITY
82°

COLÓN
81°

● NEW YORK 73°
AVERAGE JULY TEMPERATURE
DEGREES FAHRENHEIT AT
SELECTED STATIONS

AVERAGE JULY TEMPERATURE

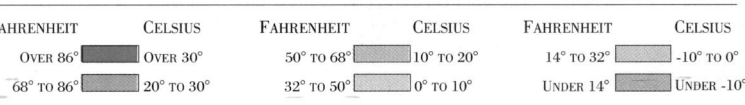

FAHRENHEIT	CELSIUS	FAHRENHEIT	CELSIUS	FAHRENHEIT	CELSIUS
OVER 86°	OVER 30°	50° TO 68°	10° TO 20°	14° TO 32°	-10° TO 0°
68° TO 86°	20° TO 30°	32° TO 50°	0° TO 10°	UNDER 14°	UNDER -10°

EF

ET

Dfc

ET

Cfc

Dfc

ET

Cfb

ET

Dfc

Csa

Dsb

Dfb

BSk

Dfb

BWk

Dfa

Cfb

Dfb

BWh

BSk

Cfa

BSh

BWh

Aw

BSh

Cw

Aw

Aw

Am

Af

BSh

Af

CLIMATE

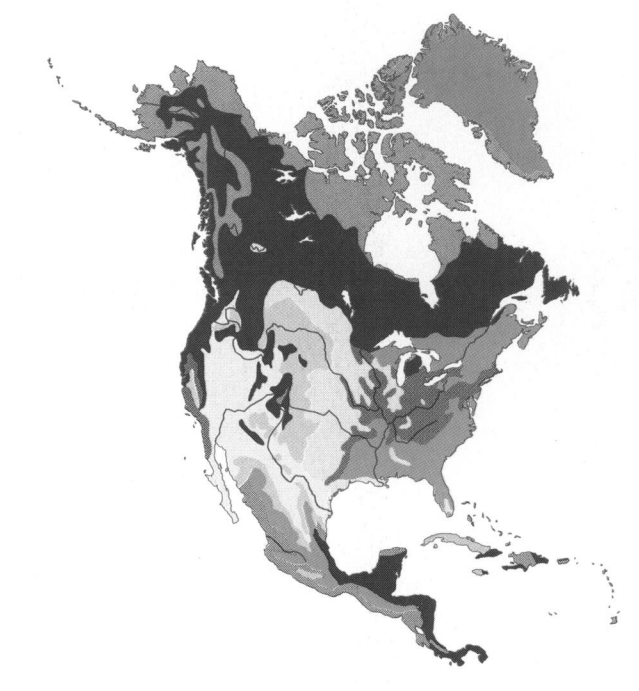

VEGETATION

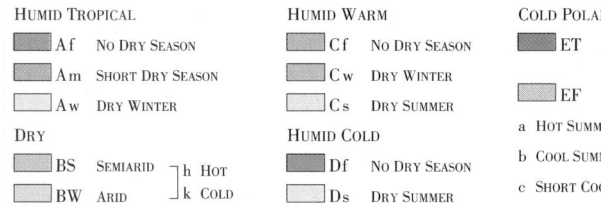

HUMID TROPICAL
- Af NO DRY SEASON
- Am SHORT DRY SEASON
- Aw DRY WINTER

DRY
- BS SEMIARID ⎤ h HOT
- BW ARID ⎦ k COLD

HUMID WARM
- Cf NO DRY SEASON
- Cw DRY WINTER
- Cs DRY SUMMER

HUMID COLD
- Df NO DRY SEASON
- Ds DRY SUMMER

COLD POLAR
- ET SHORT COOL SUMMER, LONG COLD WINTER
- EF PERPETUAL FROST

a HOT SUMMER
b COOL SUMMER
c SHORT COOL SUMMER

AFTER KOEPPEN-GEIGER

TROPICAL FOREST
- TROPICAL RAINFOREST
- LIGHT TROPICAL FOREST

TROPICAL GRASSLAND
- WOODED SAVANNA

MID-LATITUDE FOREST
- NEEDLELEAF FOREST
- BROADLEAF FOREST
- MIXED NEEDLELEAF AND BROADLEAF FOREST
- WOODLAND AND SHRUB (MEDITERRANEAN)

MID-LATITUDE GRASSLAND
- SHORT GRASS (STEPPE)
- TALL GRASS (PRAIRIE)
- DESERT AND DESERT SHRUB
- TUNDRA AND ALPINE
- PERMANENT ICE COVER

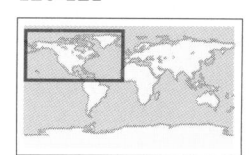

North America – Geographical Comparisons

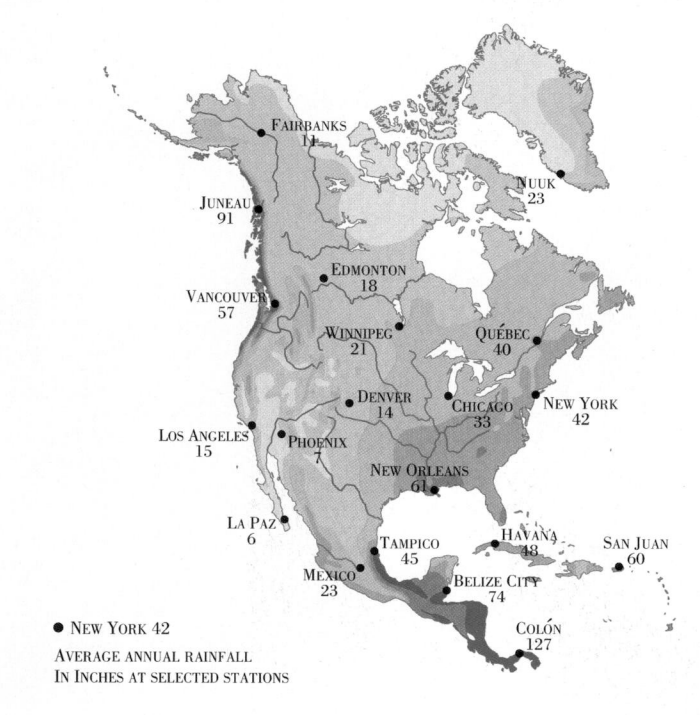

- FAIRBANKS 11
- JUNEAU 91
- NUUK 23
- VANCOUVER 57
- EDMONTON 18
- WINNIPEG 21
- QUÉBEC 40
- DENVER 14
- CHICAGO 33
- NEW YORK 42
- LOS ANGELES 15
- PHOENIX 7
- NEW ORLEANS 61
- LA PAZ 6
- TAMPICO 45
- HAVANA 48
- SAN JUAN 60
- MEXICO 23
- BELIZE CITY 74
- COLÓN 127

● NEW YORK 42
AVERAGE ANNUAL RAINFALL
IN INCHES AT SELECTED STATIONS

AVERAGE ANNUAL RAINFALL

INCHES	CM	INCHES	CM	INCHES	CM
OVER 80	OVER 200	40 TO 60	100 TO 150	10 TO 20	25 TO 50
60 TO 80	150 TO 200	20 TO 40	50 TO 100	UNDER 10	UNDER 25

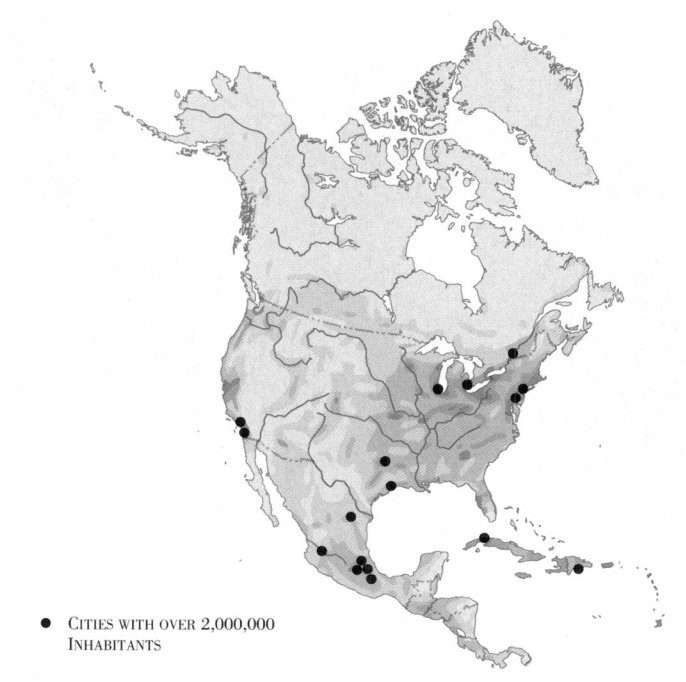

● CITIES WITH OVER 2,000,000 INHABITANTS

POPULATION DISTRIBUTION

DENSITY PER		SQ. MI.	SQ. KM.	SQ. MI.	SQ. KM.
SQ. MI.	SQ. KM.	130 TO 260	50 TO 100	3 TO 25	1 TO 10
OVER 260	OVER 100	25 TO 130	10 TO 50	UNDER 3	UNDER 1

Labels on map: FURS, BARLEY, OATS, FLAX, WHEAT, FURS, OATS, WINE, SHEEP, CATTLE, CORN, CORN, WHEAT, FRUIT, CATTLE, SOYBEANS, COTTON, TOBACCO, COTTON, COTTON, PEANUTS, GOATS, FRUIT, CORN, CATTLE, HOGS, SUGARCANE, COFFEE

LAND USE

- CEREALS, LIVESTOCK
- LIVESTOCK RANCHING & LIMITED AGRICULTURE
- FRUIT, TRUCK & MIXED FARMING
- COTTON & SPECIAL CROPS
- DIVERSIFIED TROPICAL CROPS
- GENERAL FARMING
- DAIRY
- FORESTS
- UNPRODUCTIVE

MINERAL RESOURCES

ENERGY & FUELS
- ◆ COAL
- ▲ NATURAL GAS
- ● PETROLEUM
- ■ URANIUM

IRON & FERROALLOYS
- 1 COBALT
- 2 IRON ORE
- 3 MANGANESE
- 4 MOLYBDENUM
- 5 NICKEL
- 6 TUNGSTEN
- 7 VANADIUM

OTHER MAJOR RESOURCES
- 1 ANTIMONY
- 2 ASBESTOS
- 3 BAUXITE
- 4 BORAX
- 5 COPPER
- 6 FLUORSPAR
- 7 GOLD
- 8 GRAPHITE
- 9 LEAD
- 10 MERCURY
- 11 MICA
- 12 PHOSPHATES
- 13 PLATINUM
- 14 POTASH
- 15 SILVER
- 16 SULFUR
- 17 TITANIUM
- 18 ZINC

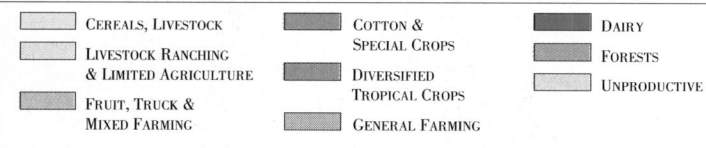

Canada

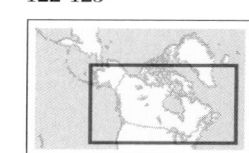

POPULATION OF CITIES AND TOWNS
- ■ OVER 2,000,000
- ● 500,000 - 999,999
- ○ 50,000 - 99,999
- ☐ 1,000,000 - 1,999,999
- ◉ 100,000 - 499,999
- ○ UNDER 50,000

SCALE 1:13,600,000   LAMBERT CONFORMAL CONIC PROJECTION

MILES 0   200   400   600

KILOMETERS 0   200   400   600

© HAMMOND WORLD ATLAS CORPORATION

United States

POPULATION OF CITIES AND TOWNS

■ OVER 2,000,000   ● 500,000 - 999,999   • 50,000 - 99,999
▢ 1,000,000 - 1,999,999   ● 100,000 - 499,999   ∘ UNDER 50,000

SCALE 1:13,600,000   LAMBERT CONFORMAL CONIC PROJECTION

MILES   0   200   400   600
KILOMETERS   0   200   400   600

© HAMMOND WORLD ATLAS CORPORATION

CJ-1079-A

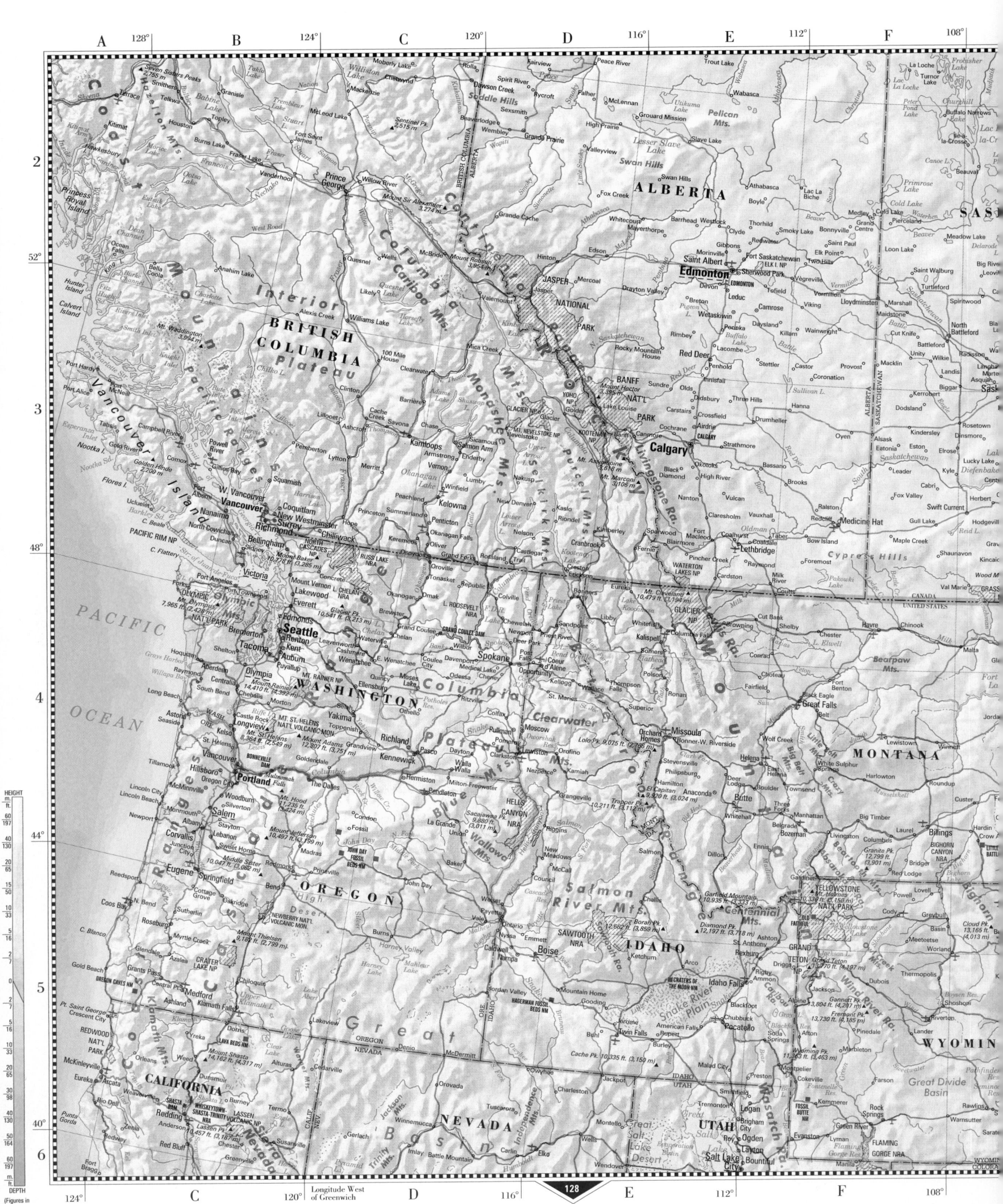

Southwestern Canada, Northwestern United States

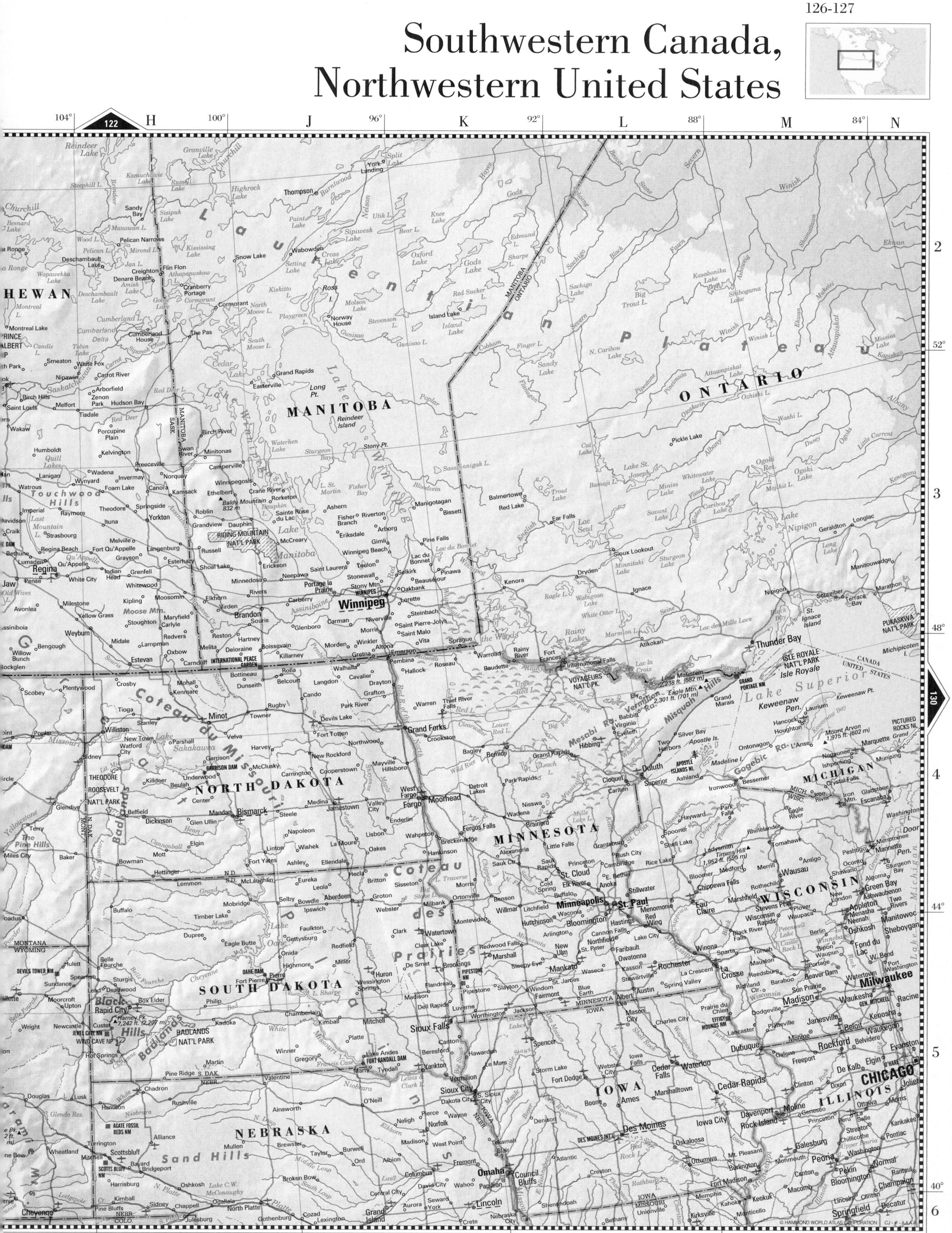

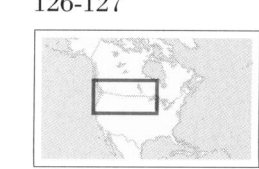

POPULATION OF CITIES AND TOWNS
- ■ OVER 2,000,000
- □ 1,000,000 - 1,999,999
- ◉ 500,000 - 999,999
- ◎ 250,000 - 499,999
- ● 100,000 - 249,999
- ⊙ 30,000 - 99,999
- • 10,000 - 29,999
- ○ UNDER 10,000

SCALE 1:6,800,000   LAMBERT CONFORMAL CONIC PROJECTION

MILES 0   100   200   300
KILOMETERS 0   100   200   300

© HAMMOND WORLD ATLAS CORPORATION

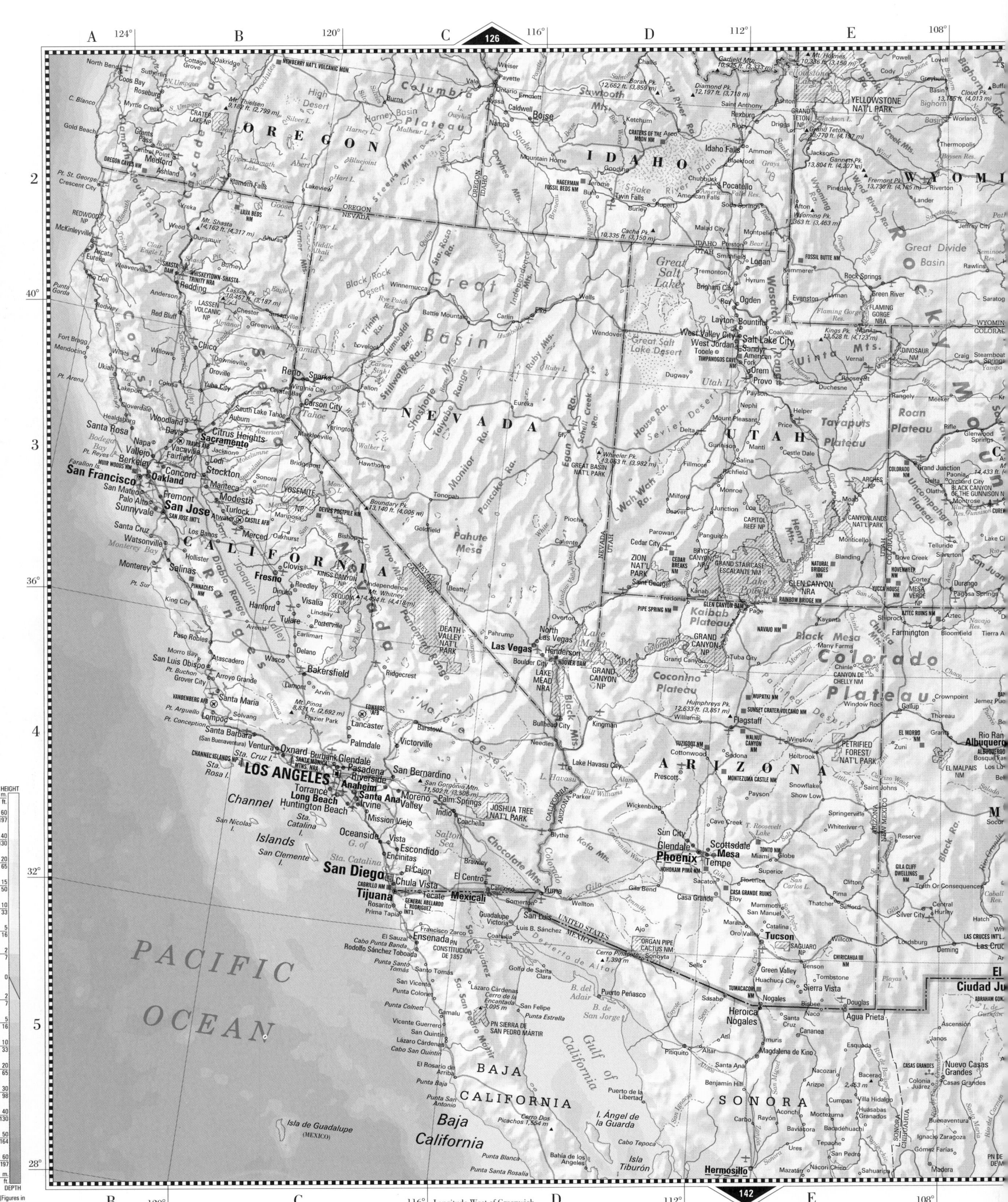

Southwestern United States

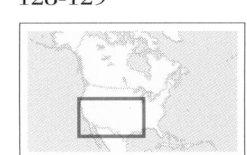

Southeastern Canada, Northeastern United States

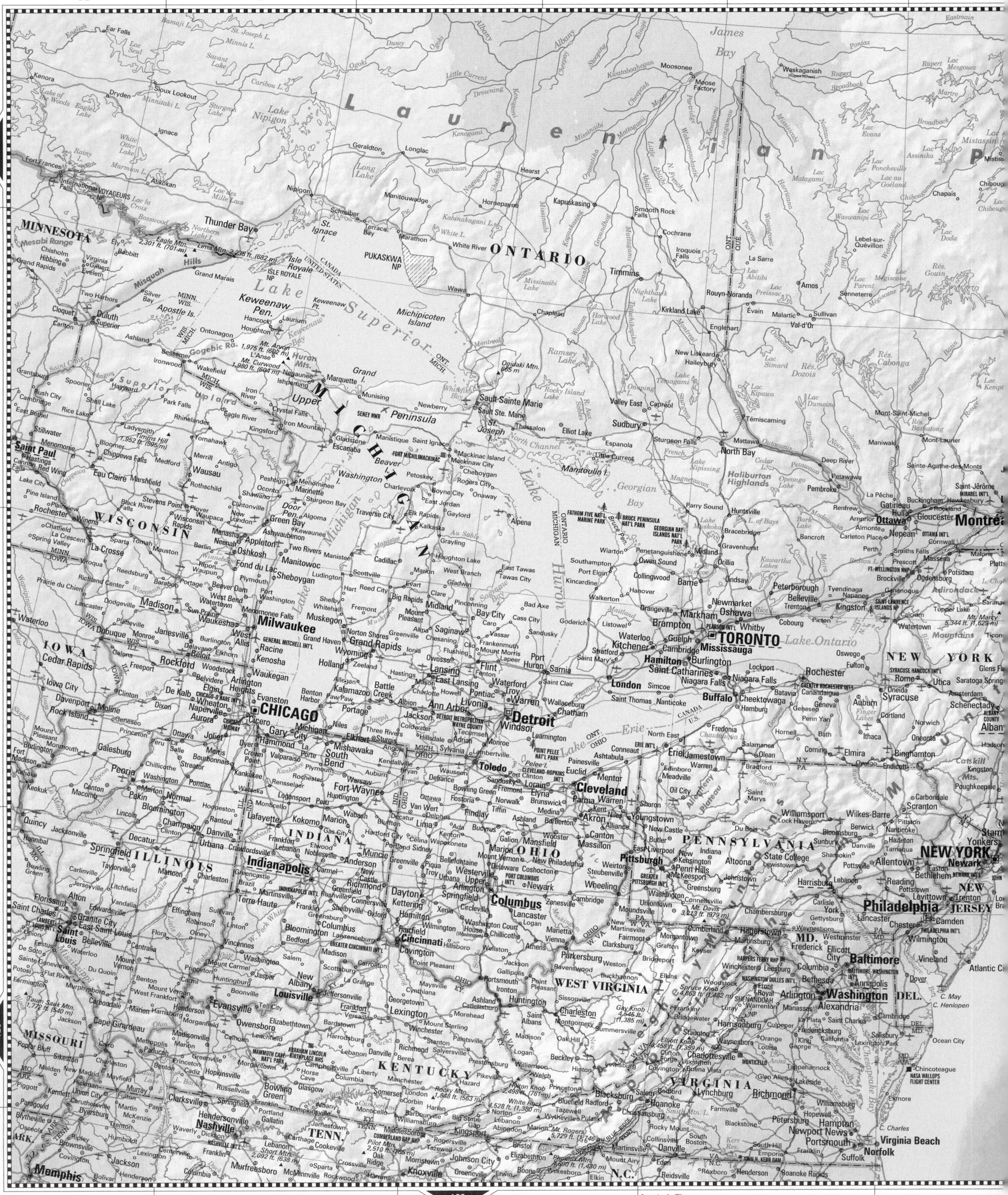

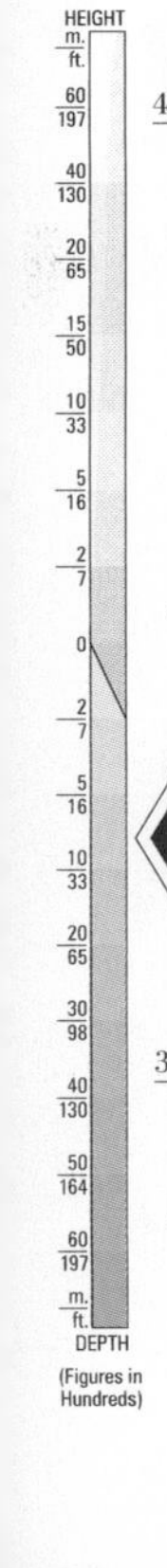

Map Labels

72° G **68°** H **64°** J **60°** K **52°** L

Plateau Laurentien

QUÉBEC

Lac Plétipi
Petit Lac Manicouagan
Rés. Manicouagan
Lac Magpie
Rés. Outardes Quatre
Lac Péribonka
Lac Monogne
Lac Onistagane

Newfoundland

L'ANSE AUX MEADOWS NHP
Saint Anthony
C. Bauld
Str. of Belle Isle
Hare Bay
Roddickton
Port au Choix
La Tabatière
PORT AU CHOIX NHP
White Bay
La Scie
Baie Verte
Musgrave Harbour
Notre Dame Bay
Springdale
GROS MORNE NP
Gros Morne 806m
Rocky Harbour
Botwood
Lewisporte
Deer Lake
Bishop's Falls
Gander Lake
Gander
Glovertown
TERRA NOVA NP
Bonavista Bay
C. Bonavista
Bonavista
Clarenville

Sept-Îles
Port-Cartier
Havre-Saint-Pierre
PN DE FORILLON
Port-Menier
Île d'Anticosti
Pte. Heath
Honguedo Passage
Jupiter R.

Gulf of St. Lawrence

Long Range Mts.
NEWFOUNDLAND
Corner Brook
Bay of Islands
Pasadena
Humber R.
Red Indian L.
Grand L.
Stephenville
St. George's Bay
C. St. George
St. George's
Saint George's Bay
Burgeo
C. Ray
Channel-Port aux Basques

St. Lawrence

Dolbeau
Mistassini
Alma
Chicoutimi
Jonquière
La Baie
Rivière-du-Loup
Hauterive
Baie-Comeau
Cap-Chat
Sainte-Anne-des-Monts
Murdochville
Matane
Mont-Joli
Mont Jacques Cartier 1,268 m
York
Gaspé
Cap de Gaspé
Gaspé Peninsula
Percé
Chandler

Québec
Lévis-Lauzon
Trois-Pistoles
Rimouski
Amqui
Notre Dame Mts.
New Richmond
Dalhousie
Carleton
Bonaventure
Chaleur Bay
Shippegan
Île Lamèque

Îles de la Madeleine (QUÉ.)

Cabot Strait

CAPE BRETON HIGHLANDS NP
Cape Breton I.
532 m
Cheticamp
Ingonish
New Waterford
Glace Bay
Sydney Mines
Sydney
ALEXANDER GRAHAM BELL NHP
FORTRESS OF LOUISBOURG NHP

ST. PIERRE & MIQUELON (FRANCE)
Grande Miquelon
Miquelon
Petite Miquelon
St-Pierre
St. Pierre I.
Fortune
Burgeo
Harbour Breton
Grand Bank
Fortune Bay
Burin Pen.
Burin
Marystown
Placentia
Placentia Bay
CASTLE HILL NHP
Avalon Peninsula
Harbour Grace
Bay Roberts
Carbonear
Torbay
St. John's
Mount Pearl
Mistaken Pt.
C. Race

Campbellton
Beresford
Bathurst
Tracadie
Nepisiguit R.
Mt. Carleton 820 m
North C.
KOUCHIBOUGUAC NP
Blackville
Saint-Louis-de-Kent
Buctouche
Miramichi

NEW BRUNSWICK

Edmundston
Madawaska
Van Buren
Grand Falls
Fort Kent
Caribou
Presque Isle
Houlton
Woodstock
QUE. N.B.
Cabano
Dégelis
Fort Kent

Stanley
Minto
Riverview
Petitcodiac
Sussex
Dorchester
Moncton
Sackville
Amherst
Shediac
Cornwall
Summerside
St. Eleanors

PRINCE EDWARD ISLAND
Charlottetown
PRINCE EDWARD ISLAND NAT'L PARK
Montague
Souris
Inverness

Northumberland Str.
St. George's Bay
Antigonish
Pictou
New Glasgow
Stellarton
Port Hawkesbury
Chedabucto Bay
C. Breton
C. Canso

Fredericton
Oromocto
Grand L.
Chipman
Chamberlain L.
Chesuncook L.
Mt. Katahdin 5,268 ft (1,606 m)
East Millinocket
Millinocket
Lincoln
Old Town
Orono
Bangor
Brewer

MAINE

Saint John
Saint George
Saint Stephen
Eastport
Grand Manan
Machias

FUNDY NP
FORT BEAUSÉJOUR NHP
Springhill
Truro
Caledonia Hills

NOVA SCOTIA

GRAND PRÉ NHP
HALIFAX NHP
Dartmouth
Halifax
Lunenburg
Bridgewater
KEJIMKUJIK NP
Liverpool
Shelburne
Yarmouth
Digby
South Mtn.
Bay of Fundy

Sable I. (CAN.)

© HAMMOND WORLD ATLAS CORPORATION   CJ-2111-A

New England Inset

NEW HAMPSHIRE
Mt. Washington 6,288 ft (1,917 m)
Berlin
Littleton
Conway
Plymouth
Lebanon
Hanover
Concord
Claremont
Keene
Manchester
Nashua
VERMONT
Montpelier
Rutland
Middlebury
Newport
Saint Johnsbury
St. Albans
Burlington

Rochester
Dover
Portsmouth
Somersworth
Sanford
Biddeford
Saco
Portland
PORTLAND INT'L JETPORT
Brunswick
Bath
Boothbay Harbor
Rockland
Camden
Belfast
Ellsworth
Bar Harbor
ACADIA NP
Augusta
Gardiner
Waterville
Skowhegan
Farmington
Rumford
Dexter
Foxcroft
Dover

Gulf of Maine

MASS.
Lowell
Lawrence
Haverhill
Merrimack
Cambridge
Newton
Boston
GEN. E. L. LOGAN INT'L
Quincy
Brockton
Worcester
Chicopee
Springfield
Pittsfield

C. Ann
Lynn
C. Cod
CAPE COD NAT'L SEASHORE

CONNECTICUT
Hartford
New Britain
Waterbury
New Haven
Bridgeport
RHODE ISLAND
Providence
Pawtucket
Warwick
Fall River
New Bedford
Newport
Nantucket I.
Martha's Vineyard
Block I.
New London
Long Island

Montréal Inset (lower left)

74° M **73° 30'** N P

Saint-Sauveur-des-Monts
LES PAYS-D'EN-HAUT
LA RIVIÈRE-DU-NORD
Prévost
Lafontaine
Sainte-Adèle
Lac-Alouette
Saint-Antoine
Mirabel
MIRABEL INT'L
Saint-Augustin
Saint-Hermas
Saint-Benoît
St-Eustache
DEUX-MONTAGNES
Pointe-Calumet
Oka
Hudson
Saint-Lazare
VAUDREUIL-SOULANGES
Les Cèdres
Coteau-du-Lac
Coteau-Landing
BEAUHARNOIS-SALABERRY

MONTCALM
Saint-Esprit
Laurentides
New Glasgow
L'Épiphanie
L'ASSOMPTION
Contrecoeur
Saint-Jérôme
Sainte-Anne-des-Plaines
LES MOULINS
Mascouche
Terrebonne
THÉRÈSE
Sainte-Thérèse
Blainville
BLAINVILLE
Rosemère
Boisbriand
LAVAL
Laval
LAJEMMERAIS
Verchères
Repentigny
Charlemagne
Montréal-Est
Anjou
Saint-Léonard
Boucherville
Sainte-Julie-de-Verchères
St-Amable
Varennes
Pointe-aux-Trembles
Saint-Marc-sur-Richelieu
Calixa-Lavallée
St-Arnaud
Beloeil
Saint-Bruno-de-Montarville

L. des Deux Montagnes
L. St-Louis
Île Bizard
Dollard-des-Ormeaux
Pierrefonds
Kirkland
Beaconsfield
Pointe-Claire
Dorval
Lachine
Saint-Laurent
Mont-Royal
Outremont
COMMUNAUTÉ URBAINE DE MONTRÉAL
Montréal
Westmount
Verdun
LaSalle
Kahnawake
Côte-Saint-Luc
Saint-Lambert
Longueuil
Saint-Hubert
Greenfield Park
CHAMPLAIN
Brossard
LA VALLÉE-DU-RICHELIEU
Chambly
FORT CHAMBLY NAT'L HISTORIC PARK
Carignan
St-Jacques-le-Mineur

Chateauguay
Mercier
Sainte-Martine
Ste-Martine
LES JARDINS-DE-NAPIERVILLE
Napierville
St-Blaise
Saint-Rémi
LE HAUT-RICHELIEU
Saint-Édouard
St-Philippe-de-Laprairie
La Prairie
Candiac
Delson
Saint-Constant
Sainte-Catherine
Roussillon
Île Perrot
Notre-Dame-de-l'Île-Perrot
Pincourt
Beauharnois
Saint-Timothée
Maple Grove
Coteau

© HAMMOND WORLD ATLAS CORPORATION   CJ-2163-A

Toronto–Niagara Inset (lower right)

Q **79° 30'** R **79°** S

King City
Nobleton
Oak Ridges
Gormley
Greenwood
Brougham
Kinsale
Taunton
Bowmanville
Caledon East
Bolton
Mono Road
Elgin Mills
Unionville
Green River
Pickering
Whitby
Oshawa
Courtice
DURHAM
Port Darlington
Caledon
Sandhill
Kleinburg
Maple
Richmond Hill
Langstaff
Markham
METRO TORONTO ZOO
Ajax
Ross Pt.
Raby Head
Frenchman's Bay

PEEL
Cheltenham
Victoria
Terra Cotta
Brampton
Snelgrove
Bramalea
PEARSON
Woodbridge
NORTH YORK
SCARBOROUGH
EAST YORK
YORK
Georgetown
Norval
Huttonville
Meadowvale
Malton
ETOBICOKE
Toronto
CN TOWER
Toronto I.

Halton Hills
Ashgrove
Hornby
Streetsville
Port Credit
Mississauga
Lorne Park
Clarkson
HALTON
Milton

ONTARIO
Lowville
Palermo
Kilbride
Oakville
Flamborough
Bronte
Millgrove
Waterdown
Aldershot
ROYAL BOT. GARDEN
Burlington
Dundas
Hamilton Harbour
Hamilton
HAMILTON-WENTWORTH
Stoney Creek
Mt. Hope
Fruitland
Winona
Grimsby
Beamsville
Vineland Station
Jordan
Jordan Station
Vineland
Lincoln
Campden
Smithville
Caistor Centre
St. Anns
North Pelham
Effingham
Pelham
Thorold South
Thorold
Fonthill

Lake Ontario

CANADA
UNITED STATES

NEW YORK
Olcott
Wilson
Burt
Appleton
Somerset
Barker
Newfane
NIAGARA
Lockport
Gasport
Ransomville
Youngstown
OLD FORT NIAGARA
Niagara-on-the-Lake
FT. GEORGE
Virgil
Saint Catharines
Queenston
Lewiston
Niagara Falls
Niagara Falls
Power Res.
TUSCARORA IND. RES.
Sanborn
Wolcottsville
N. Tonawanda
Tonawanda
Amherst
Williamsville
ALBRIGHT KNOX ART GALLERY
GREATER BUFFALO INT'L
Cheektowaga
Depew
Lancaster
Elma
West Seneca
ERIE
Kenmore

NIAGARA
Welland
Wellandport
Port Colborne
Fort Erie
Dunnville
Wainfleet
Long Beach
Pt. Abino
Buffalo
Lackawanna
Cayuga Cr.

HALDIMAND-NORFOLK
Haldimand
Winger
Caistorville
Bismarck
Woodburn
Binbrook
Elfrida

Lake Erie

POPULATION OF CITIES AND TOWNS
- ■ OVER 2,000,000
- ☐ 1,000,000 - 1,999,999
- ● 500,000 - 999,999
- ◉ 250,000 - 499,999
- ● 100,000 - 249,999
- ● 30,000 - 99,999
- ● 10,000 - 29,999
- • UNDER 10,000

SCALE 1:6,800,000   LAMBERT CONFORMAL CONIC PROJECTION
MILES   0 ___ 100 ___ 200 ___ 300
KILOMETERS   0 ___ 100 ___ 200 ___ 300

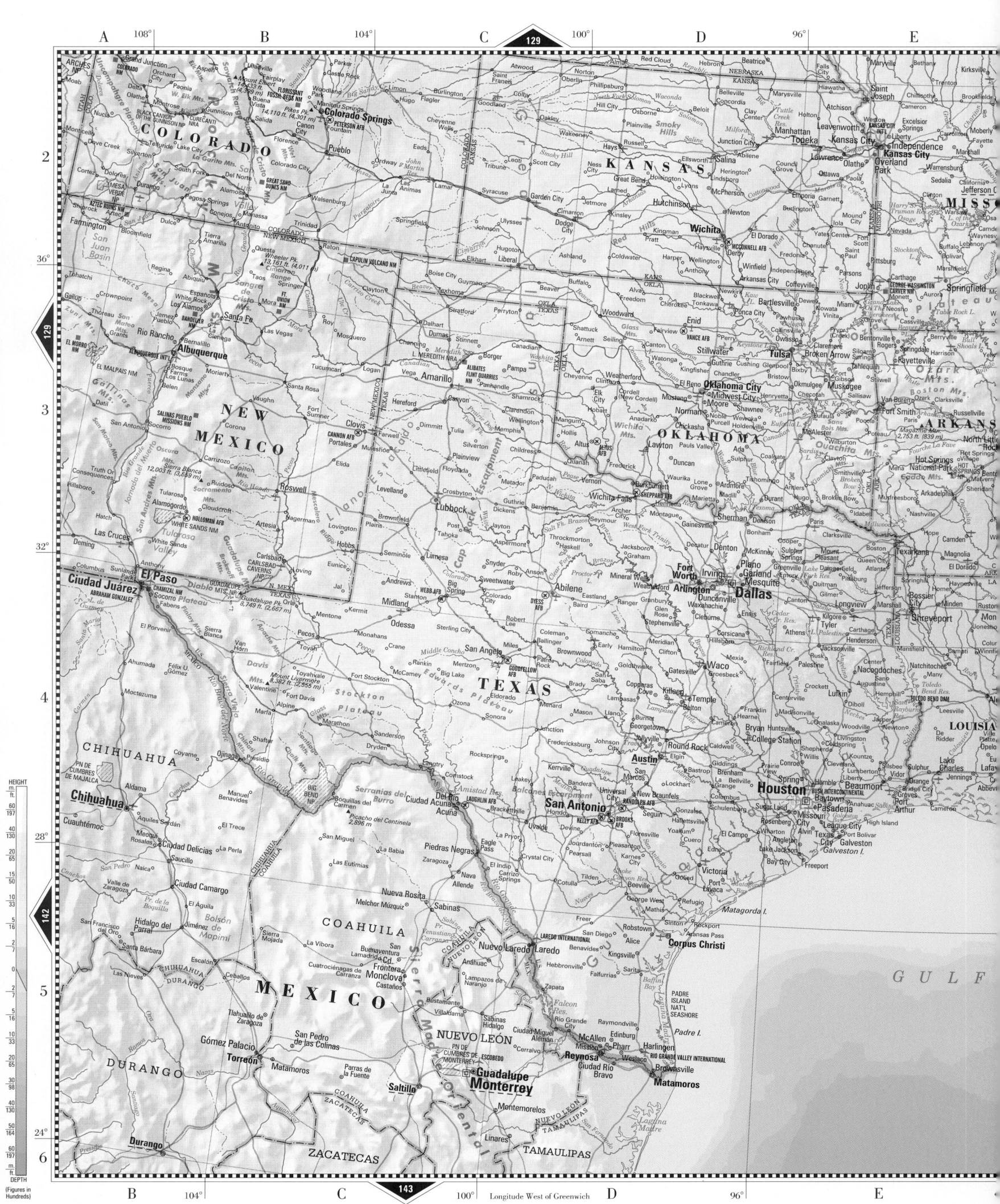

Southeastern United States

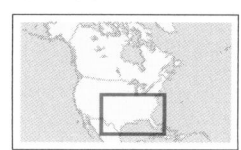

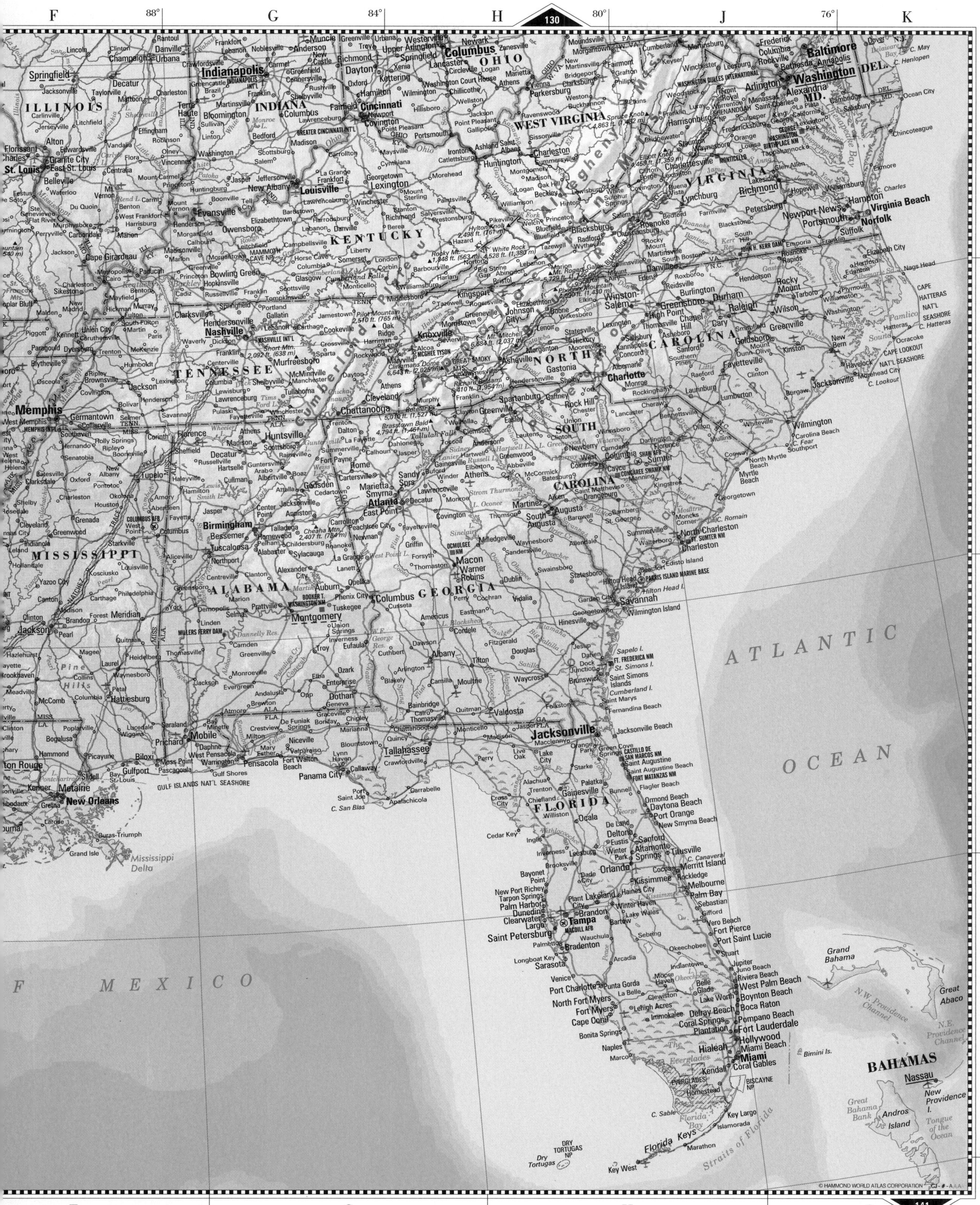

POPULATION OF CITIES AND TOWNS

☐ OVER 2,000,000 ⊙ 500,000 - 999,999 ⦿ 100,000 - 249,999 ⊙ 10,000 - 29,999
☐ 1,000,000 - 1,999,999 ⊙ 250,000 - 499,999 ⊙ 30,000 - 99,999 ∘ UNDER 10,000

SCALE 1:6,800,000   LAMBERT CONFORMAL CONIC PROJECTION

MILES 0   100   200   300
KILOMETERS 0   100   200

© HAMMOND WORLD ATLAS CORPORATION

Alaska

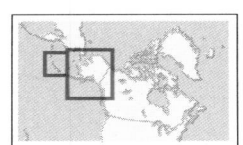

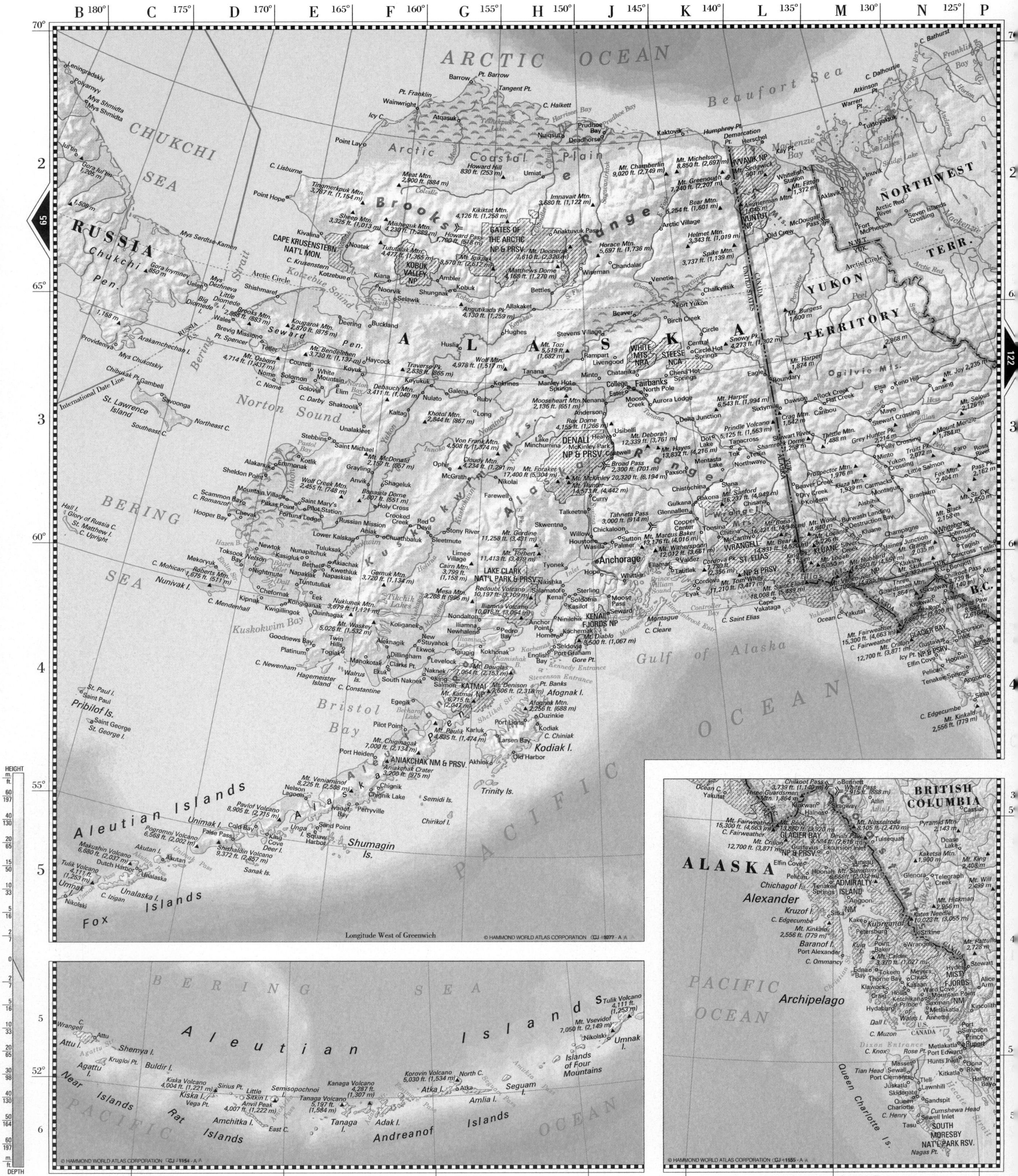

Seattle, San Francisco, Detroit, Chicago

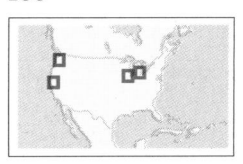

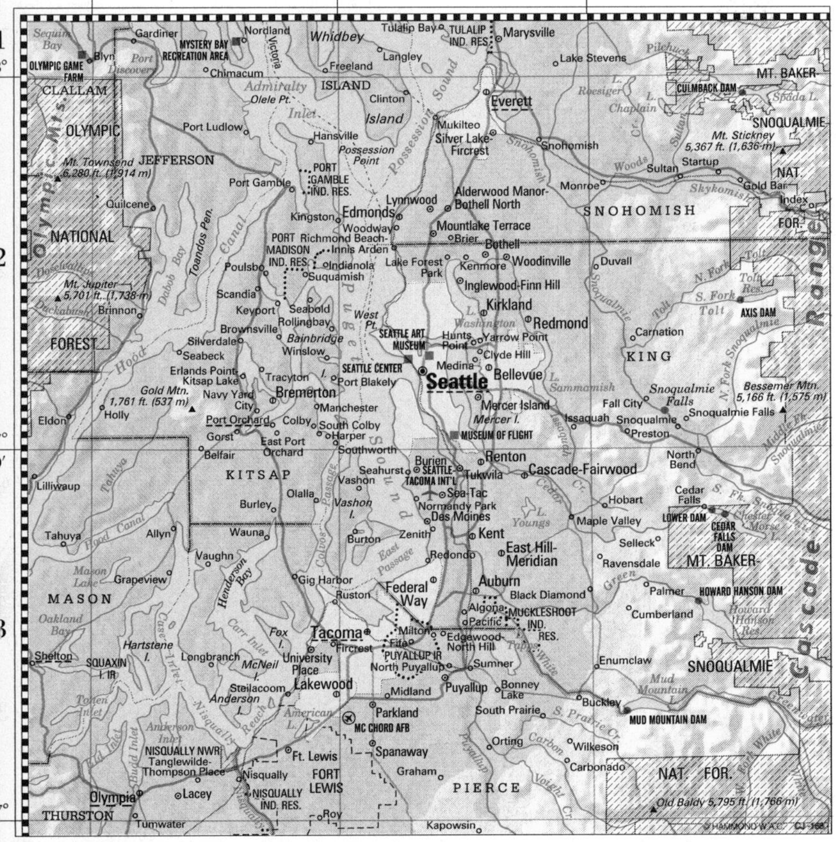

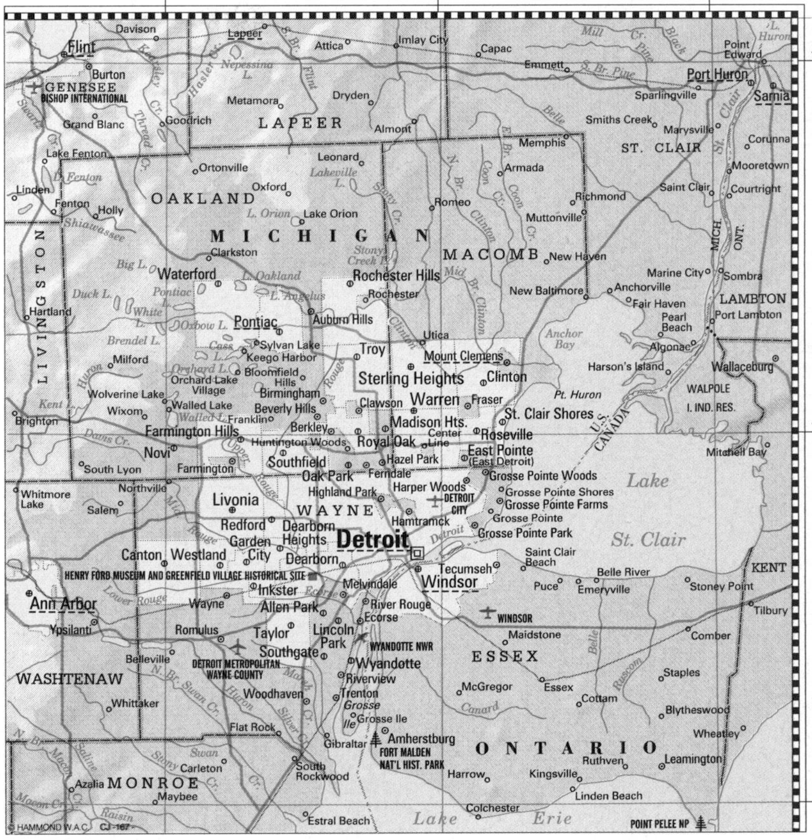

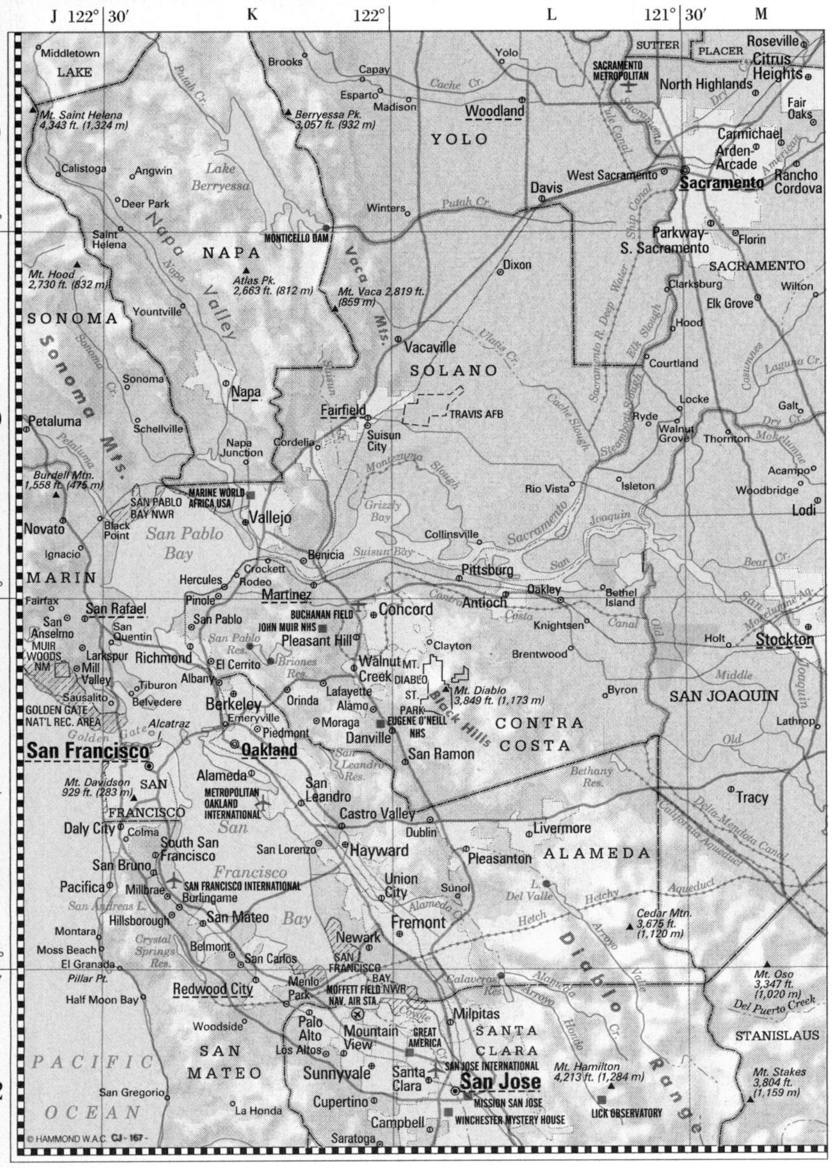

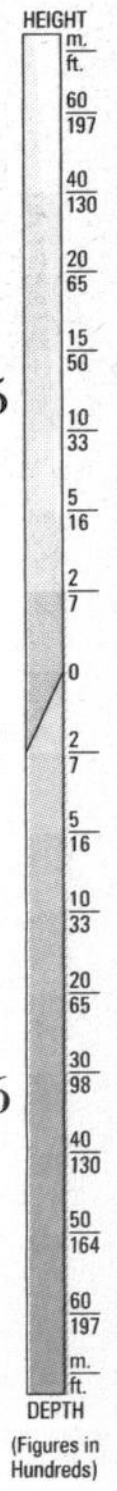

SCALE 1:1,140,000   LAMBERT CONFORMAL CONIC PROJECTION

Longitude West of Greenwich

MILES 0 10 20 30 40 50

KILOMETERS 0 10 20 30 40 50

HEIGHT

m. ft.

DEPTH (Figures in Hundreds)

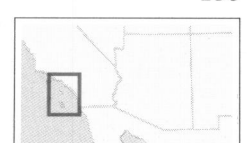

Los Angeles-San Diego

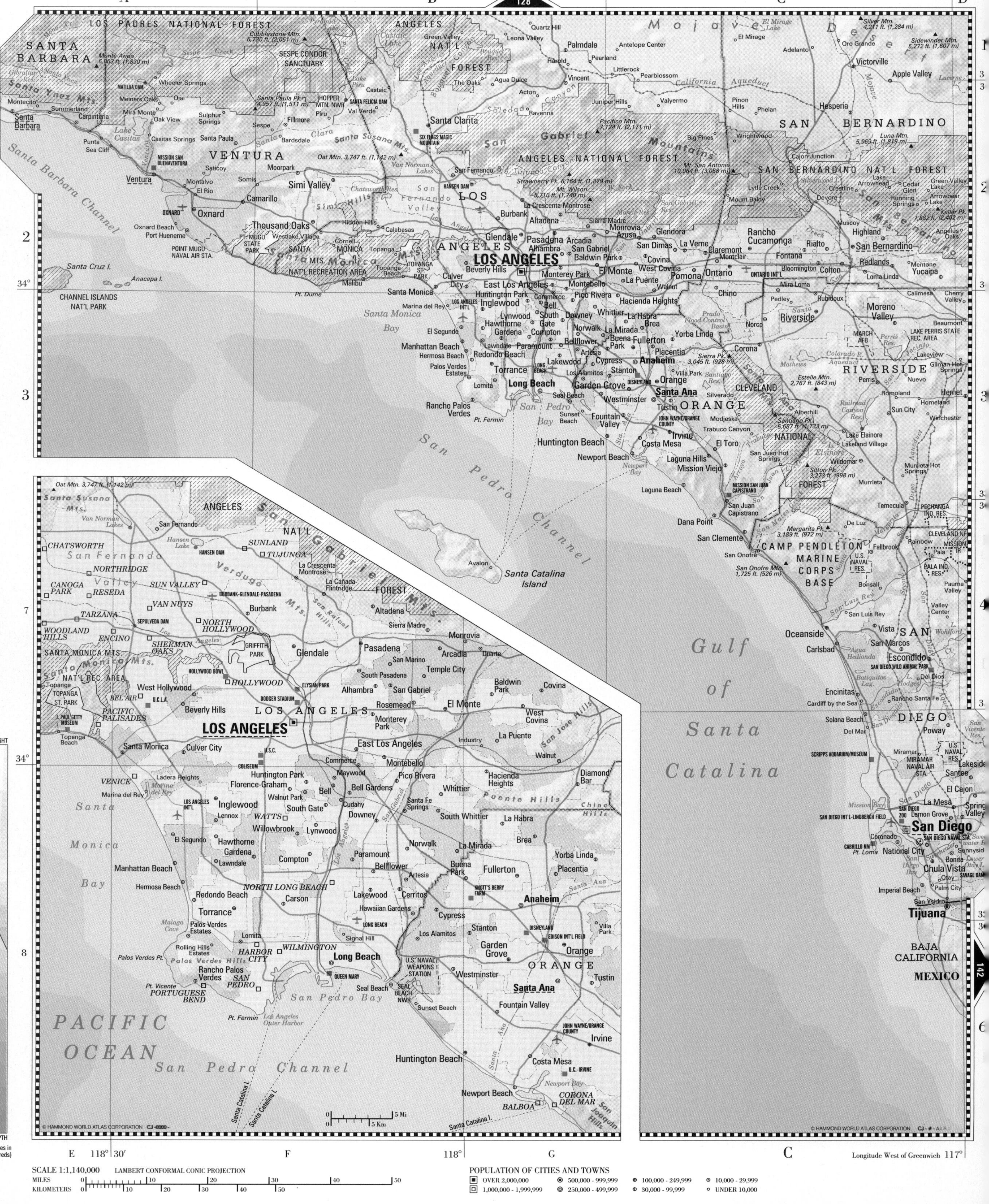

Phoenix, Salt Lake City, Denver, Oklahoma City, Kansas City, St. Louis, San Antonio, New Orleans

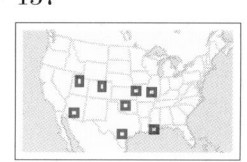

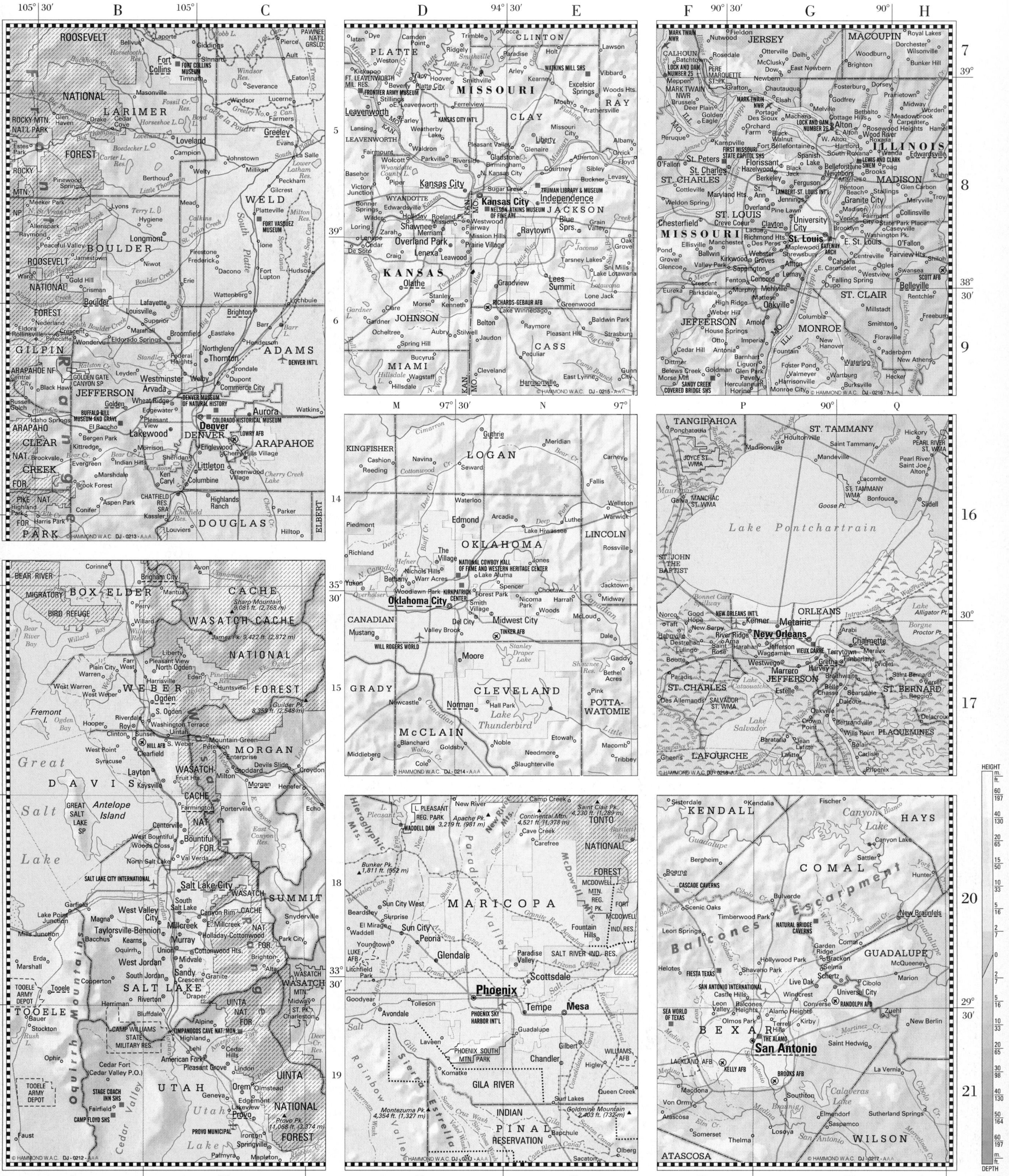

POPULATION OF CITIES AND TOWNS

- ■ OVER 2,000,000
- □ 1,000,000 - 1,999,999
- ◉ 500,000 - 999,999
- ◎ 250,000 - 499,999
- ● 100,000 - 249,999
- ○ 30,000 - 99,999
- ○ 10,000 - 29,999
- ○ UNDER 10,000

SCALE 1:1,140,000   LAMBERT CONFORMAL CONIC PROJECTION

MILES 0 10 20 30 40 50

KILOMETERS 0 10 20 30 40 50

HEIGHT

m. ft.
60 197
40 130
20 65
15 50
10 33
5 16
2 7
0 0
5 16
10 33
20 65
30 98
40 130
50 164
60 197

DEPTH
(Figures in Hundreds)

New York-Philadelphia-Washington

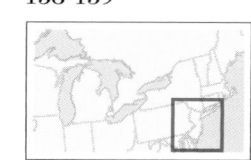

POPULATION OF CITIES AND TOWNS

■	OVER 2,000,000	⬤	500,000 - 999,999	⊙	100,000 - 249,999	◦	10,000 - 29,999
▣	1,000,000 - 1,999,999	◉	250,000 - 499,999	●	30,000 - 99,999	·	UNDER 10,000

SCALE 1:1,140,000   LAMBERT CONFORMAL CONIC PROJECTION

MILES 0 10 20 30 40 50

KILOMETERS 0 10 20 30 40 50

© HAMMOND WORLD ATLAS CORPORATION   CJ-#-AAA

© HAMMOND W.A.C. CJ-1171

Middle America

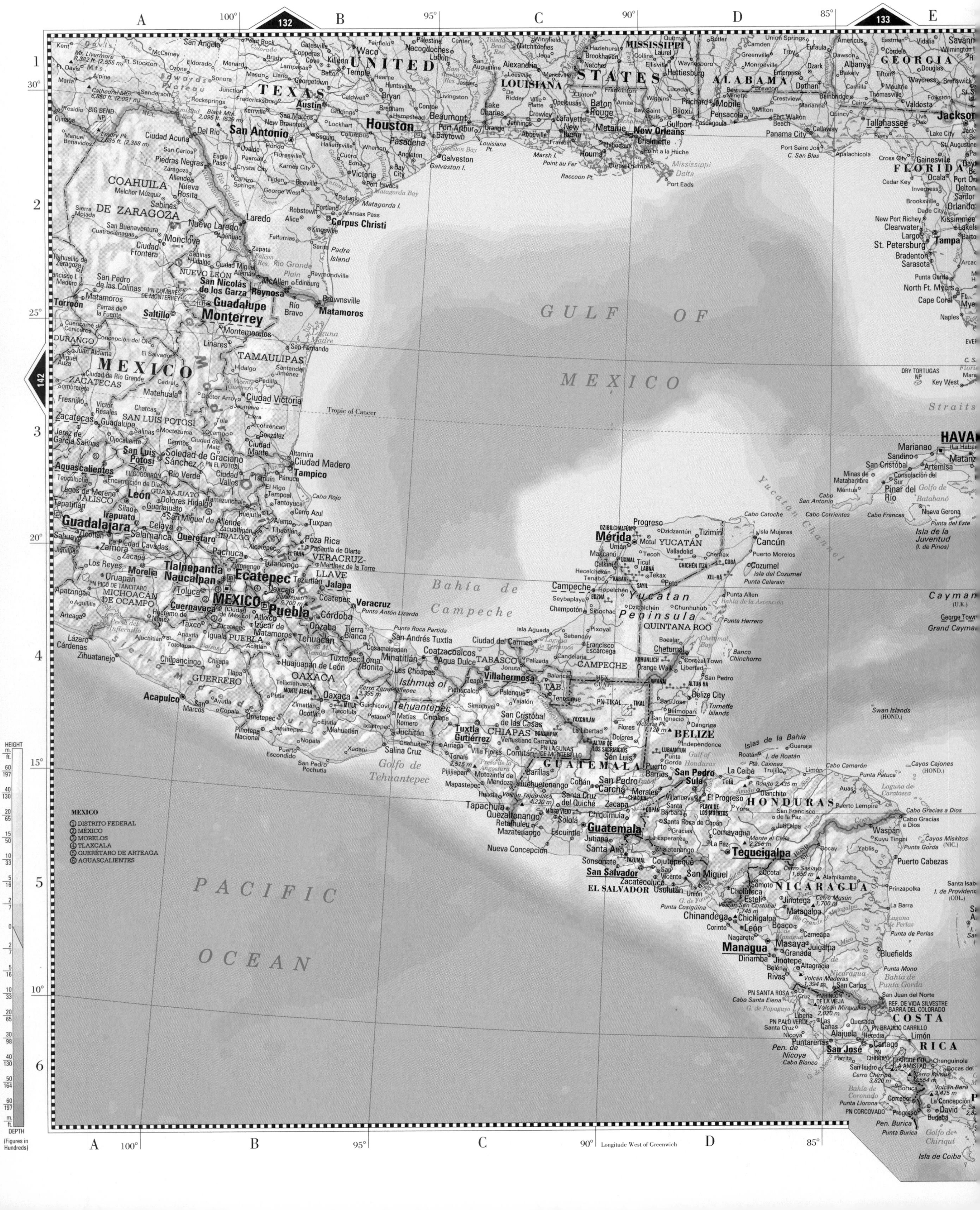

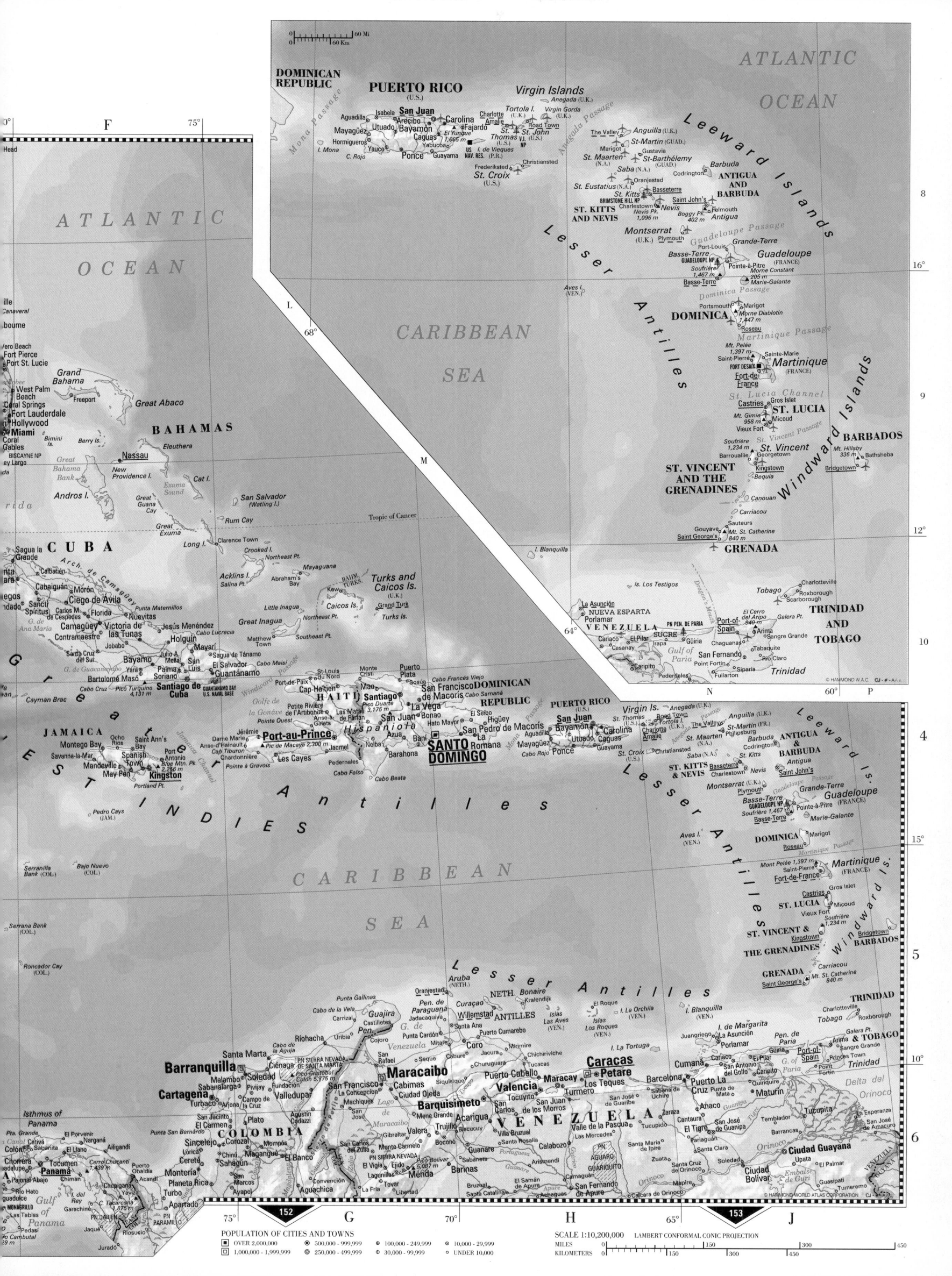

ATLANTIC OCEAN

DOMINICAN REPUBLIC

PUERTO RICO (U.S.)
Virgin Islands

60 Mi
60 Km

San Juan
Aguadilla
Isabela
Arecibo
Carolina
Mayagüez
Utuado
Bayamón
Caguas
El Yunque
1,065 m
Charlotte
Amalie
St. Thomas
(U.S.)
Road Town
Tortola I.
(U.K.)
Virgin Gorda
(U.K.)
Anegada (U.K.)
Hormigueros
Yauco
San Juan
Ponce
Guayama
Yabucoa
Fajardo
St. John
(U.S.)
The Valley
Anguilla
(U.K.)
I. Mona
C. Rojo
US
NAV. RES. (P.R.)
I. de Vieques
Marigot
St-Martin
(N.A.)
St-Barthélemy
(GUAD.)
Gustavia
Codrington
Barbuda

Frederiksted
Christiansted
St. Croix
(U.S.)
Saba (N.A.)
St. Eustatius (N.A.)
Oranjestad
St. Kitts
Basseterre
Saint John's
ANTIGUA AND BARBUDA

ST. KITTS AND NEVIS
BRIMSTONE HILL NP
Charlestown
Nevis
Nevis Pk.
1,096 m
Boggy Pk.
402 m
Falmouth
Antigua

Montserrat (U.K.)
Plymouth
Port-Louis
Basse-Terre
GUADELOUPE NP
Soufrière
1,467 m
Grande-Terre
Pointe-à-Pitre
Morne Constant
205 m
Guadeloupe (FRANCE)
Marie-Galante
Basse-Terre

Aves I. (VEN.)

Dominica Passage

Portsmouth
Marigot
Morne Diablotin
1,447 m
Roseau
DOMINICA

Martinique Passage

Mt. Pelée
1,397 m
Sainte-Marie
Saint-Pierre
FORT DESAIX
Martinique (FRANCE)
Fort-de-France

St. Lucia Channel
Castries
Gros Islet
Mt. Gimie
958 m
ST. LUCIA
Micoud
Vieux Fort

Soufrière
1,234 m
St. Vincent Passage
Barrouallie
Georgetown
St. Vincent
Kingstown
Mt. Hillaby
336 m
BARBADOS
Bridgetown
Bathsheba

ST. VINCENT AND THE GRENADINES
Bequia
Canouan
Carriacou
Sauteurs
Gouyave
Saint George's
Mt. St. Catherine
840 m
GRENADA

I. Blanquilla

Is. Los Testigos
Tobago
Charlotteville
Roxborough
Scarborough
La Asunción
NUEVA ESPARTA
Porlamar
El Cerro
del Aripo
940 m
Galera Pt.
TRINIDAD AND TOBAGO
VENEZUELA
PN PEN. DE PARIA
Port-of-Spain
Arima
Sangre Grande
Cariaco
El Pilar
SUCRE
Irapa
Güiria
Chaguanas
Tabaquite
Río Claro
Casanay
San Fernando
Point Fortin
Siparia
Fullarton
Trinidad
Pedernales

© HAMMOND W.A.C.
CJ - # - A · A

ATLANTIC OCEAN

Head

F
75°

Canaveral

ville

bourne

Vero Beach
Fort Pierce
Port St. Lucie

Grand
Bahama
Freeport
Great Abaco

West Palm
Beach
Coral Springs
Fort Lauderdale
Hollywood
Miami
Coral
Gables
BISCAYNE NP
Key Largo
Bimini
Is.
Berry Is.
Eleuthera
New Providence I.
Nassau
BAHAMAS
Great
Guana
Cay
Andros I.
Great
Bahama
Bank
Great
Exuma
Exuma
Sound
Cat I.
San Salvador
(Watling I.)

da

rida

Long I.
Clarence Town
Rum Cay
Crooked I.
Northeast Pt.
Tropic of Cancer

CUBA
Sagua la
Grande
Caibarién
BAHM.
TURKS.
Acklins I.
Salina Pt.
Kew
Turks and
Caicos Is.
(U.K.)
Caicos Is.
Grand Turk
Turks Is.

nta
ara
Morón
Ciego de Ávila
Punta Maternillos
Little Inagua
Matthew
Town
Great Inagua
Northeast Pt.
Southeast Pt.
Carlos M.
de Céspedes
egos
ndo
Sancti
Spíritus
Florida
Santa Cruz
del Sur
G. de
Ana María
Camagüey
Victoria de
las Tunas
Jobabo
Jesús Menéndez
Holguín
Mayarí
Sagua de Tánamo
Cabo Lucrecia
Cabo Maisí
Contramaestre
Julio A.
Mella
San
Luis
El Salvador
Soriano
Cabo Francés Viejo
DOMINICAN
Bayamo
Yara
Palma
Guantánamo
Cap-Haïtien
Cabo Samaná
Bartolomé Masó
Pico Turquino
1,974 m
Santiago de
Cuba
GUANTÁNAMO BAY
U.S. NAVAL BASE
Port-de-Paix
Mao
Santiago
Pico Duarte
3,175 m
San Francisco
de Macorís
Cabo Cabrón
Cabo Cruz
G. de Guacanayabo
REPUBLIC
Petite Rivière
de l'Artibonite
Las Matas
de Farfán
La Vega
Bonao
Higüey
PUERTO RICO
(U.S.)

Cayman Brac
Golfe de
la Gonâve
HAITI
Port-au-Prince
Pointe Ouest
Hispaniola
Azua
El Seibo
San Pedro de Macorís
Virgin Is.
(U.S.)
Anegada (U.K.)
Road Town
Tortola I. (U.K.)
JAMAICA
Ocho
Rios
Montego Bay
Saint Ann's
Bay
Jérémie
Dame Marie
Anse-d'Hainault
Cap
Tiburon
Chardonnière
Port
Antonio
Dominican
Jacmel
Neiba
La
Romana
SANTO
DOMINGO
Bani
St. Thomas
(U.S.)
Charlotte
Amalie
San Juan
Bayamón
Utuado
Carolina
Caguas
St. John
(U.S.)
The Valley
Anguilla (U.K.)
St-Martin (F.R.)
Philipsburg
St. Maarten (N.A.)
Codrington
Barbuda
ANTIGUA & BARBUDA
Mandeville
Spanish
Town
Blue Mtn. Pk.
2,256 m
Pedernales
Barahona
Cabo Falso
Les Cayes
Pointe à Gravois
Cabo Beata
Mayagüez
Ponce
Guayama
Christiansted
St. Croix (U.S.)
Saba (N.A.)
ST. KITTS & NEVIS
Basseterre
St. Kitts
Saint John's
Antigua
May Pen
Kingston
Portland Pt.
Charlestown
Nevis
Montserrat (U.K.)
Plymouth
Basse-Terre
GUADELOUPE NP
Soufrière 1,467 m
Grande-Terre
Pointe-à-Pitre
Guadeloupe (FRANCE)
Basse-Terre
Marie-Galante
Pedro Cays
(JAM.)

WEST
INDIES
Greater
Antilles
Lesser
Antilles
Aves I. (VEN.)
DOMINICA
Roseau
Marigot
Mont Pelée 1,397 m
Saint-Pierre
Martinique (FRANCE)
Fort-de-France
Castries
Gros Islet
ST. LUCIA
Micoud
Vieux Fort
Soufrière 1,234 m
ST. VINCENT &
THE GRENADINES
Kingstown
Bridgetown
BARBADOS
Carriacou
GRENADA
Saint George's
Mt. St. Catherine 840 m
Windward Is.
Leeward Is.

CARIBBEAN SEA
Serranilla
Bank (COL.)
Bajo Nuevo
(COL.)

Serrana
Bank
(COL.)

Roncador Cay
(COL.)

Isthmus of
Panama
Pta. Grande
Colón
Cativá
PANAMA
Río Hato
Chorrera
Tocumen
Pajonal Abajo
Carrol Chucunci
1,439 m
Gulf of
Panama
Pedasí
29 m
PN DARIÉN
2,075 m
PN PARAMILLO
Jaqué
Jurado

COLOMBIA
Barranquilla
Cartagena
Santa Marta
Ríohacha
Uribia
Cabo de
la Vela
Punta Gallinas
Guajira
Pen. de
Paraguaná
Aruba (NETH.)
Oranjestad
NETH. Curaçao
Kralendijk
ANTILLES
Willemstad
Bonaire
El Roque
I. La Orchila (VEN.)
Islas
Las Aves
(VEN.)
Islas
Los Roques
(VEN.)
I. La Tortuga
(VEN.)
I. Blanquilla
(VEN.)
Juangriego
La Asunción
Porlamar
I. de Margarita
(VEN.)
Pen. de
Paria
Güiria
Port-of-Spain
TRINIDAD
Tobago
Charlotteville
Roxborough
& TOBAGO
Galera Pt.
Arima
Sangre Grande
Trinidad
Pta.
Cojoro
San
Rafael
Coro
Maracaibo
Caracas
Petare
Valencia
Maracay
Los Teques
Barcelona
Puerto La
Cruz
Cumaná
San Antonio
del Golfo
Carúpano
Río Caribe
Maturín
Delta del
Orinoco

VENEZUELA
Barquisimeto
Barinas
Mérida
Pico Bolívar
5,007 m
Ciudad Guayana
Ciudad Bolívar
Embalse
de Gurí
El Tigre
El Palmar
Upata

F 75° G 70° H 65° J 60°

POPULATION OF CITIES AND TOWNS
▪ OVER 2,000,000   ◉ 500,000 - 999,999   ◉ 100,000 - 249,999   ○ 10,000 - 29,999
▫ 1,000,000 - 1,999,999   ◉ 250,000 - 499,999   ○ 30,000 - 99,999   ○ UNDER 10,000

SCALE 1:10,200,000   LAMBERT CONFORMAL CONIC PROJECTION
MILES 0   150   300   450
KILOMETERS 0   150   300   450

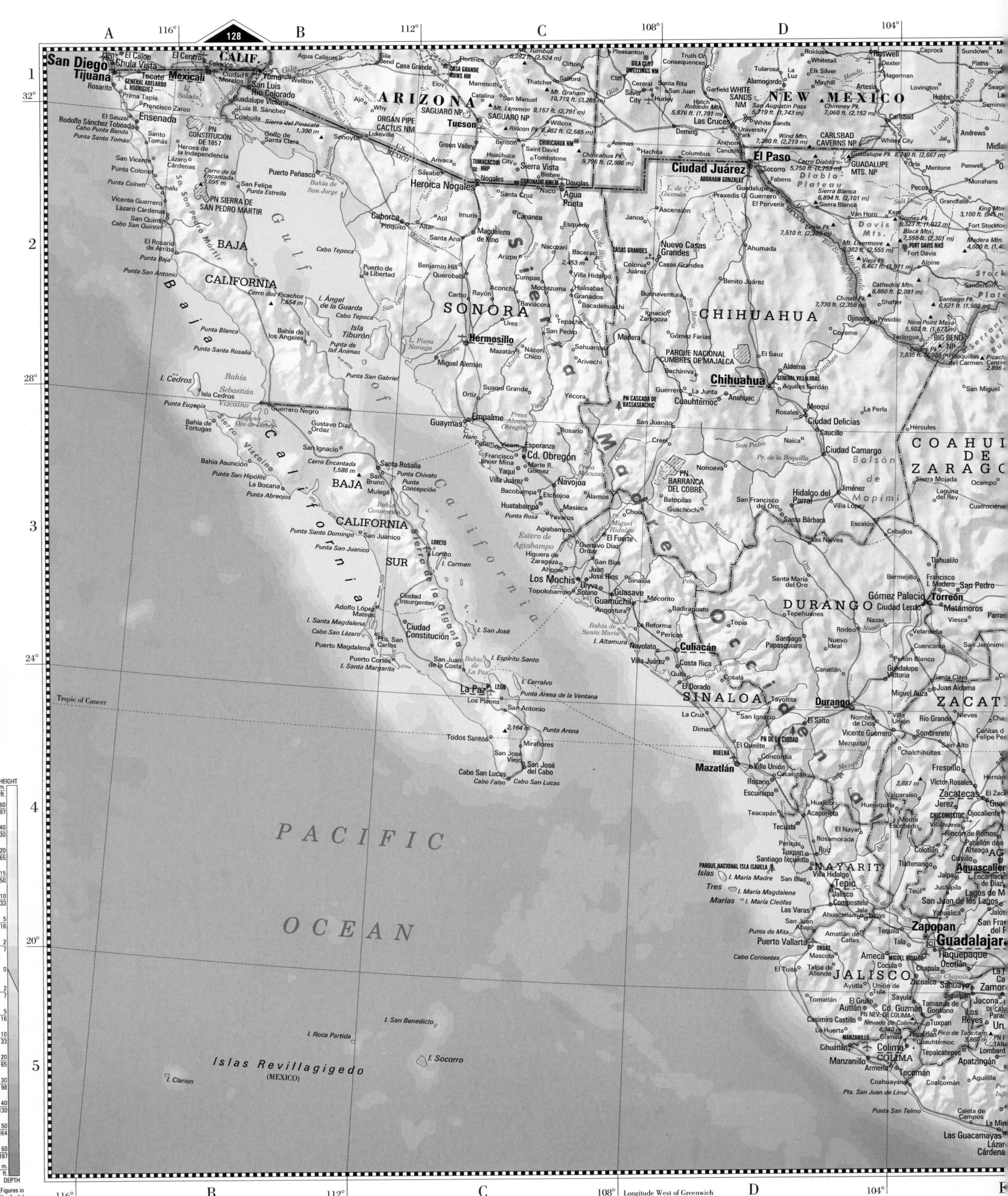

Northern and Central Mexico

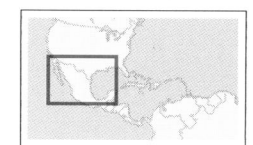

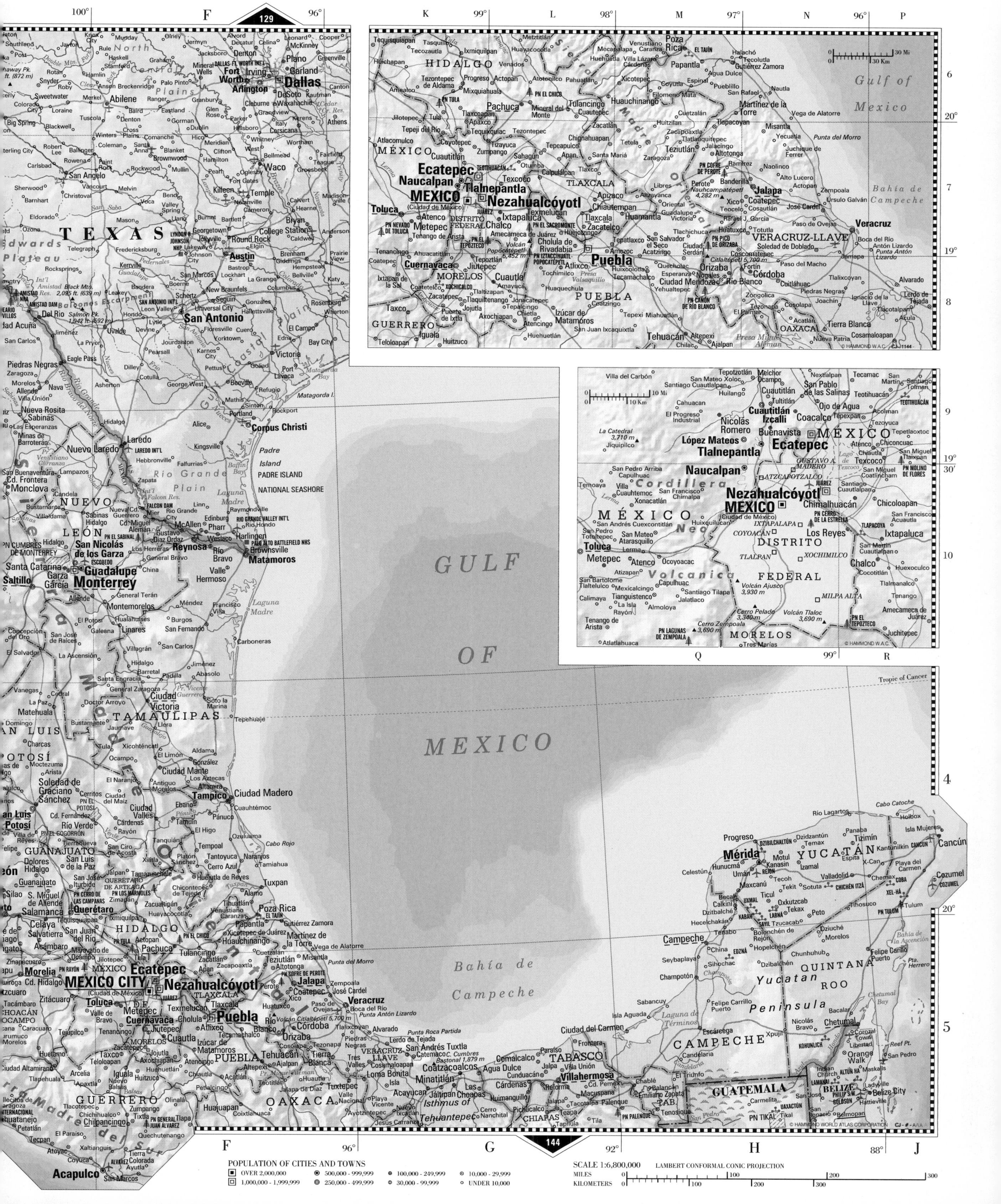

POPULATION OF CITIES AND TOWNS
- ☐ OVER 2,000,000
- ☐ 1,000,000 - 1,999,999
- ● 500,000 - 999,999
- ● 250,000 - 499,999
- ● 100,000 - 249,999
- ● 30,000 - 99,999
- ● 10,000 - 29,999
- ○ UNDER 10,000

SCALE 1:6,800,000   LAMBERT CONFORMAL CONIC PROJECTION

MILES   0   50   100   200   300
KILOMETERS   0   100   200   300

© HAMMOND WORLD ATLAS CORPORATION

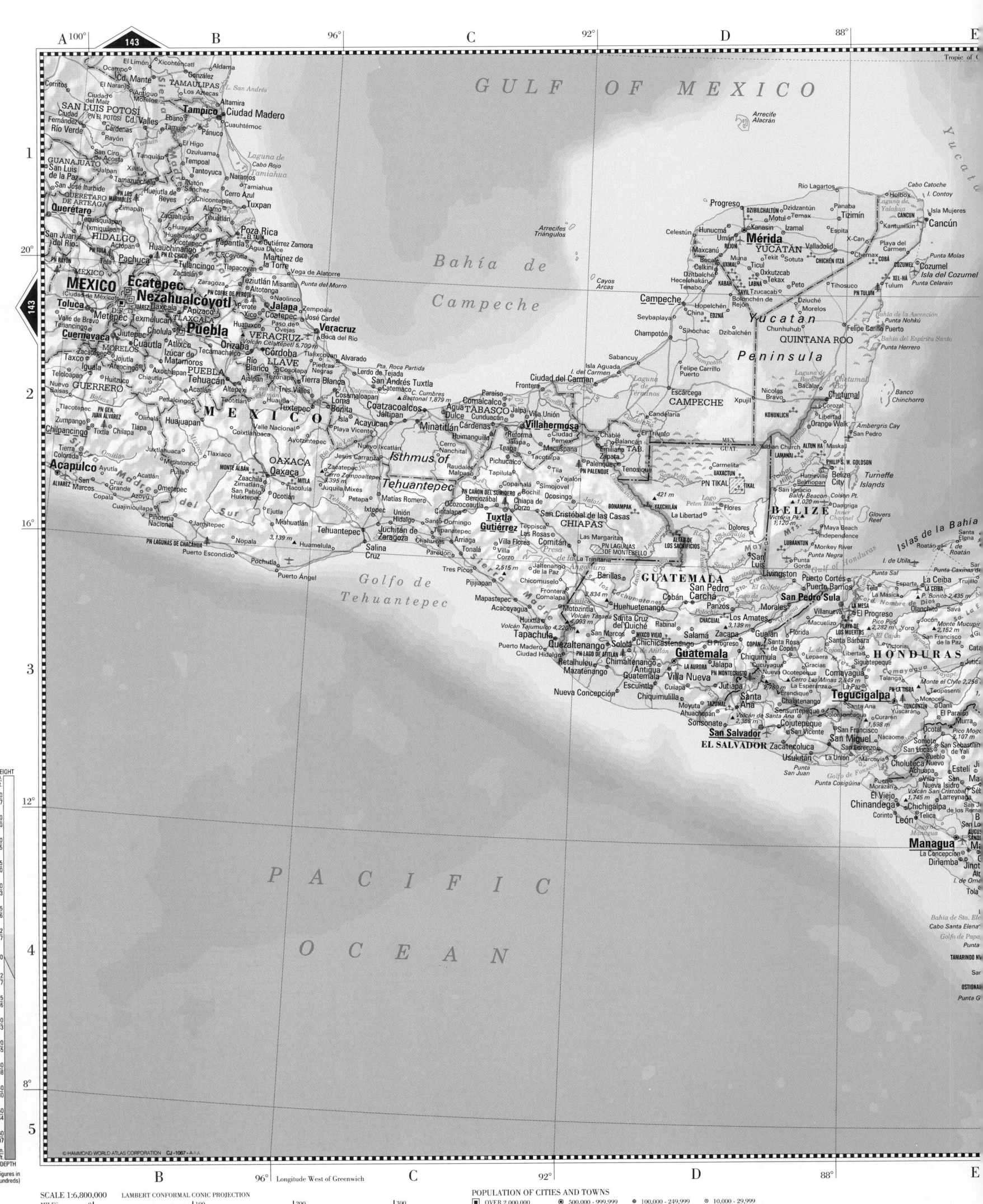

GULF OF MEXICO

Tropic of C

Bahía de

Campeche

Arrecife Alacrán

Yucata

GUANAJUATO

SAN LUIS POTOSÍ

Tampico
Ciudad Madero

HIDALGO

Querétaro

20°

MEXICO
Ecatepec
Nezahualcóyotl

Toluca

TLAXCALA

Jalapa

Cuernavaca

MORELOS

Puebla

VERACRUZ

Córdoba

Orizaba

LLAVE

Río Blanco

PUEBLA

Tehuacán

GUERRERO

MEXICO

OAXACA

Oaxaca

MONTE ALBÁN

Acapulco

Sierra Madre del Sur

Progreso

Mérida
YUCATÁN

CHICHÉN ITZÁ

Cancún

COZUMEL

Cozumel

Campeche

Yucatán

Peninsula

QUINTANA ROO

CAMPECHE

Chetumal

Banco
Chinchorro

Coatzacoalcos

TABASCO

Villahermosa

TAB.

Isthmus of

Tehuantepec

Tuxtla
Gutiérrez

CHIAPAS

MEX.
GUAT.

PN PALENQUE

PN TIKAL

TIKAL

BELIZE

16°

Tehuantepec

Salina
Cruz

Golfo de
Tehuantepec

GUATEMALA

San Pedro Sula

La Ceiba

Islas de la Bahía

Tapachula

Quezaltenango

Guatemala

HONDURAS

3

Tegucigalpa

San Salvador

EL SALVADOR

12°

Chinandega

León

Managua

P A C I F I C

O C E A N

SCALE 1:6,800,000   LAMBERT CONFORMAL CONIC PROJECTION

MILES

KILOMETERS

Longitude West of Greenwich

POPULATION OF CITIES AND TOWNS

OVER 2,000,000   500,000 - 999,999   100,000 - 249,999   10,000 - 29,999

1,000,000 - 1,999,999   250,000 - 499,999   30,000 - 99,999   UNDER 10,000

Southern Mexico, Central America, Western Caribbean

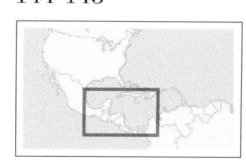

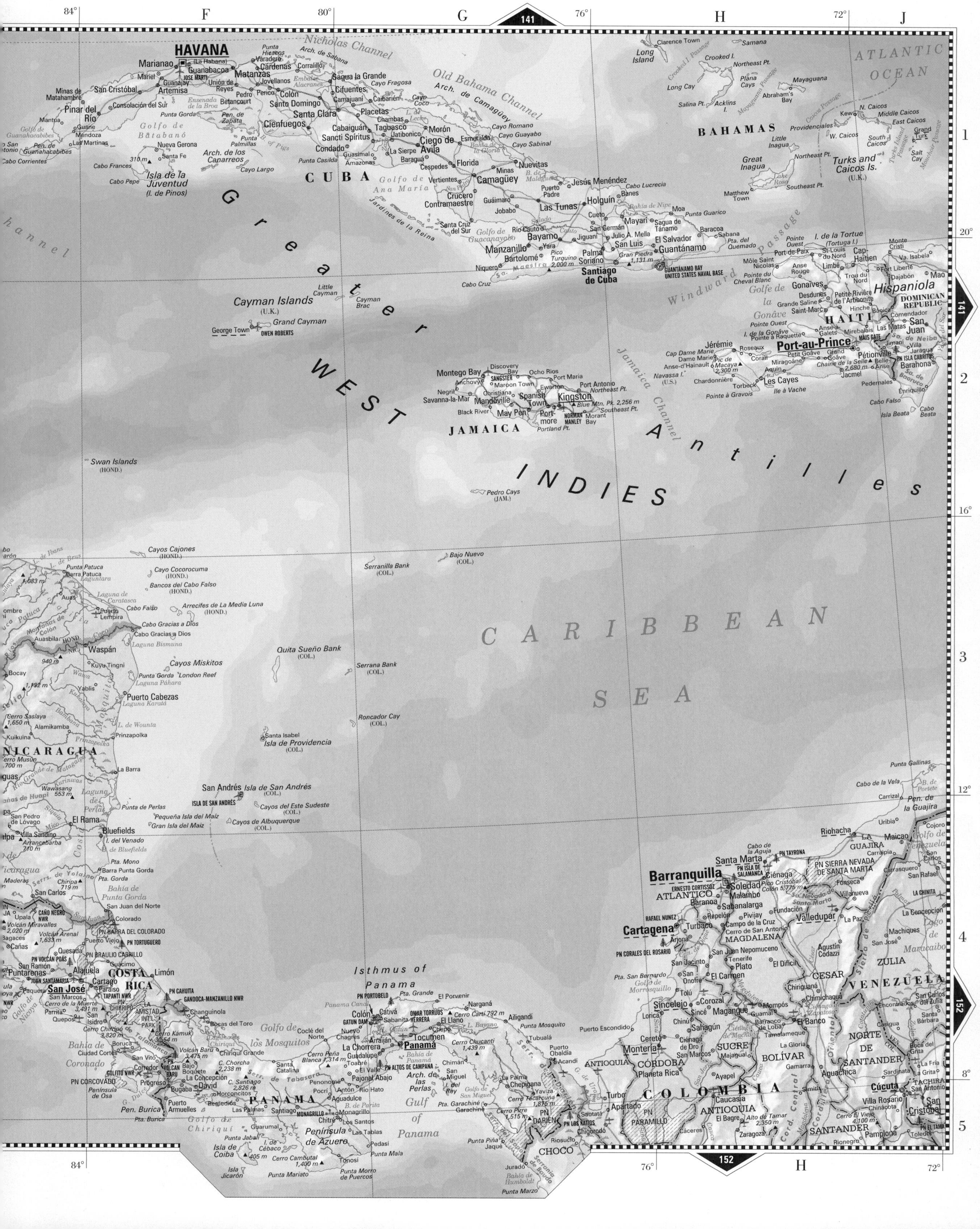

South America

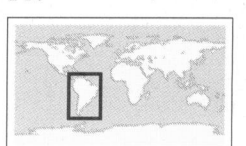

The highest mountain peak in the Americas, Mount Aconcagua, at 22,831 feet (6959 m.) above sea level, is visible in this northeast-looking, low-oblique image. Several major snow-covered peaks with summits exceeding 20,000 feet (6100 m.) rise along the north-south axis of the cohesive and massive structure of the Andes Mountains through this area of Argentina and Chile. The narrow east-west valley immediately south of Mount Aconcagua contains a section of the American Highway that connects Mendoza, Argentina, with Santiago, Chile.

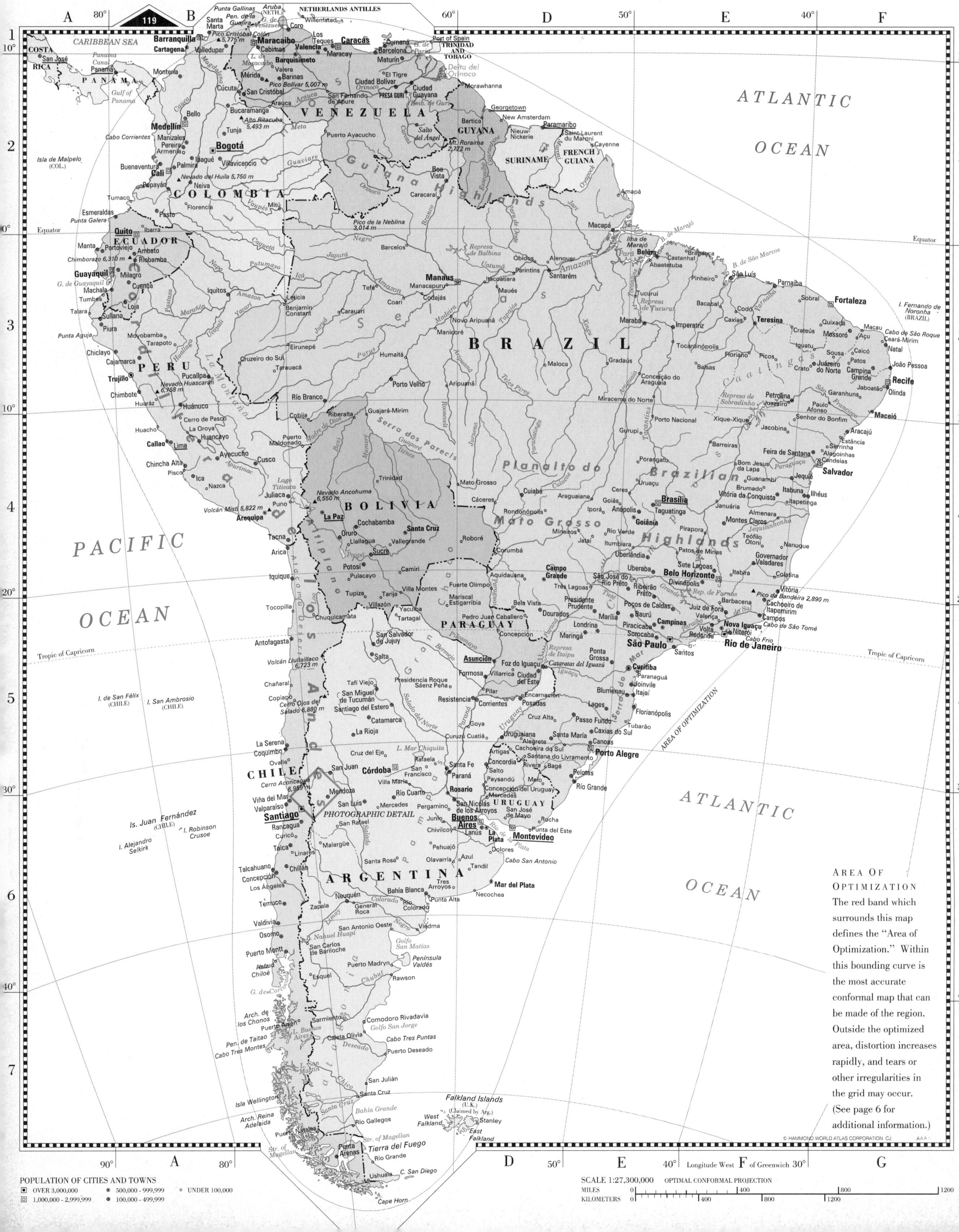

AREA OF OPTIMIZATION
The red band which surrounds this map defines the "Area of Optimization." Within this bounding curve is the most accurate conformal map that can be made of the region. Outside the optimized area, distortion increases rapidly, and tears or other irregularities in the grid may occur. (See page 6 for additional information.)

POPULATION OF CITIES AND TOWNS
■ OVER 3,000,000   ● 500,000 - 999,999   ○ UNDER 100,000
□ 1,000,000 - 2,999,999   ● 100,000 - 499,999

SCALE 1:27,300,000   OPTIMAL CONFORMAL PROJECTION
MILES   0   400   800   1200
KILOMETERS   0   400   800   1200

© HAMMOND WORLD ATLAS CORPORATION, CJ

AVERAGE JANUARY TEMPERATURE

Barranquilla 79°
Caracas 66°
Paramaribo 79°
Quibdó 79°
Bogotá 57°
Quito 55°
Manaus 79°
Fortaleza 81°
Lima 72°
La Paz 52°
Brasilia 73°
Antofagasta 68°
Asunción 84°
Río de Janeiro 79°
Curitiba 68°
Santiago 66°
Buenos Aires 73°
Comodoro Rivadavia 64°
Río Grande 48°

● Lima 72°
AVERAGE JANUARY TEMPERATURE
DEGREES FAHRENHEIT AT
SELECTED STATIONS

AVERAGE JANUARY TEMPERATURE

FAHRENHEIT	CELSIUS	FAHRENHEIT	CELSIUS	FAHRENHEIT	CELSIUS
OVER 86°	OVER 30°	50° TO 68°	10° TO 20°	UNDER 32°	UNDER 0°
68° TO 86°	20° TO 30°	32° TO 50°	0° TO 10°		

AVERAGE JULY TEMPERATURE

Barranquilla 82°
Caracas 70°
Paramaribo 81°
Quibdó 77°
Bogotá 57°
Quito 55°
Manaus 81°
Fortaleza 79°
Lima 59°
La Paz 46°
Brasilia 64°
Antofagasta 55°
Asunción 64°
Río de Janeiro 66°
Curitiba 55°
Santiago 46°
Buenos Aires 52°
Comodoro Rivadavia 45°
Río Grande 34°

● Lima 59°
AVERAGE JULY TEMPERATURE
DEGREES FAHRENHEIT AT
SELECTED STATIONS

AVERAGE JULY TEMPERATURE

FAHRENHEIT	CELSIUS	FAHRENHEIT	CELSIUS	FAHRENHEIT	CELSIUS
OVER 86°	OVER 30°	50° TO 68°	10° TO 20°	UNDER 32°	UNDER 0°
68° TO 86°	20° TO 30°	32° TO 50°	0° TO 10°		

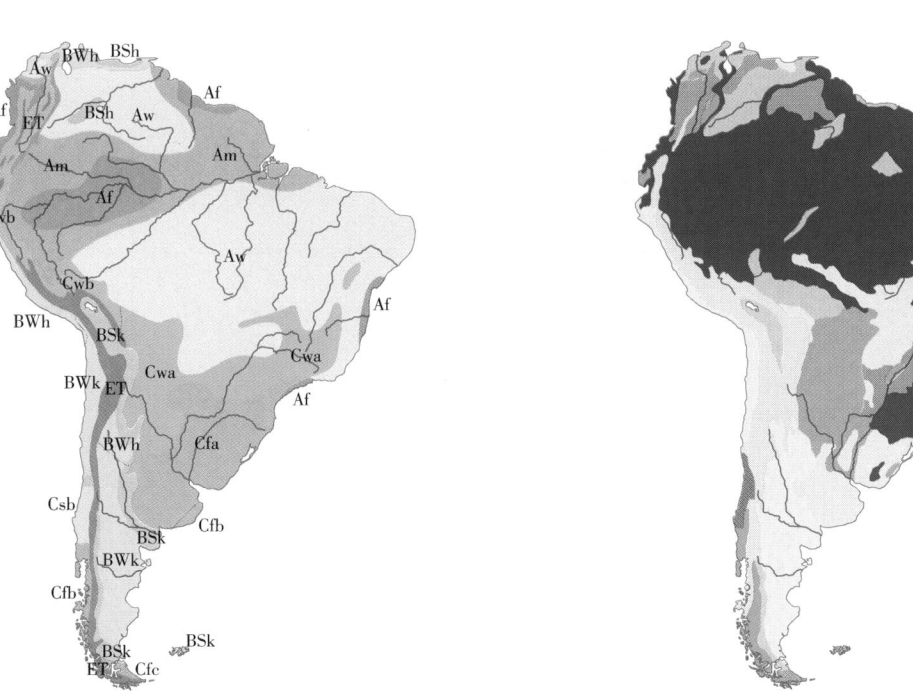

CLIMATE

HUMID TROPICAL
- Af — No Dry Season
- Am — Short Dry Season
- Aw — Dry Winter

DRY
- BS — Semiarid
- BW — Arid
  - h HOT
  - k COLD

HUMID WARM
- Cf — No Dry Season
- Cw — Dry Winter
- Cs — Dry Summer

COLD POLAR
- ET — Short Cool Summer, Long Cold Winter

- a HOT SUMMER
- b COOL SUMMER
- c SHORT COOL SUMMER

AFTER KOEPPEN-GEIGER

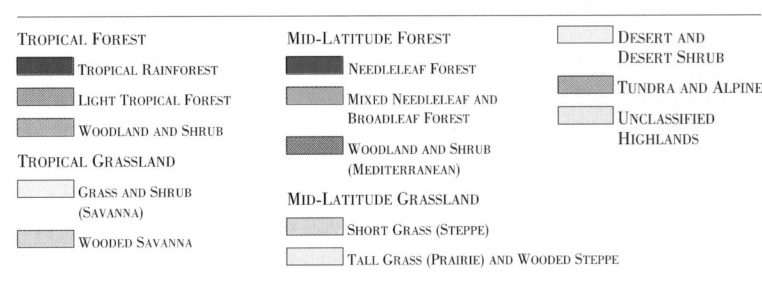

VEGETATION

TROPICAL FOREST
- Tropical Rainforest
- Light Tropical Forest
- Woodland and Shrub

TROPICAL GRASSLAND
- Grass and Shrub (Savanna)
- Wooded Savanna

MID-LATITUDE FOREST
- Needleleaf Forest
- Mixed Needleleaf and Broadleaf Forest
- Woodland and Shrub (Mediterranean)

MID-LATITUDE GRASSLAND
- Short Grass (Steppe)
- Tall Grass (Prairie) and Wooded Steppe

- Desert and Desert Shrub
- Tundra and Alpine
- Unclassified Highlands

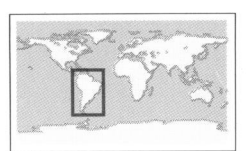

South America - Geographical Comparisons

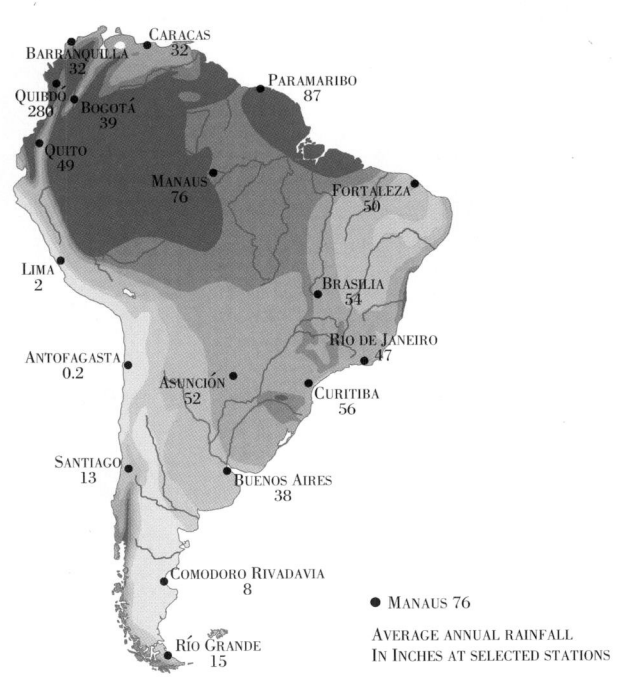

BARRANQUILLA 32
CARACAS 32
PARAMARIBO 87
QUIBDO 280
BOGOTÁ 39
QUITO 49
MANAUS 76
FORTALEZA 50
LIMA 2
BRASILIA 54
RÍO DE JANEIRO 47
ANTOFAGASTA 0.2
ASUNCIÓN 52
CURITIBA 56
SANTIAGO 13
BUENOS AIRES 38
COMODORO RIVADAVIA 8
RÍO GRANDE 15

● MANAUS 76
AVERAGE ANNUAL RAINFALL
IN INCHES AT SELECTED STATIONS

● CITIES WITH OVER 1,000,000
INHABITANTS

AVERAGE ANNUAL RAINFALL

INCHES	CM	INCHES	CM	INCHES	CM
OVER 80	OVER 200	40 TO 60	100 TO 150	10 TO 20	25 TO 50
60 TO 80	150 TO 200	20 TO 40	50 TO 100	UNDER 10	UNDER 25

POPULATION DISTRIBUTION

DENSITY PER	SQ. MI.	SQ. KM.	SQ. MI.	SQ. KM.
SQ. MI.	SQ. KM.	130 TO 260	50 TO 100	3 TO 25	1 TO 10
OVER 260	OVER 100	25 TO 130	10 TO 50	UNDER 3	UNDER 1

RICE
HOGS
COCOA
CATTLE COFFEE
COFFEE CATTLE
BANANAS
VANILLA
BRAZIL NUTS
BANANAS
CORN
COTTON
SISAL
WILD RUBBER
SHEEP
CATTLE
TOBACCO
SUGARCANE
SHEEP CORN
CATTLE
CATTLE HOGS
CITRUS
COCOA
COTTON
TOBACCO
COTTON
COFFEE
TEA BANANAS SUGARCANE
CATTLE HOGS
TOBACCO
WINE
SHEEP
QUEBRACHO
SOYBEANS
CORN SHEEP RICE CORN
FLAX CORN
CATTLE
WHEAT
SHEEP
SHEEP

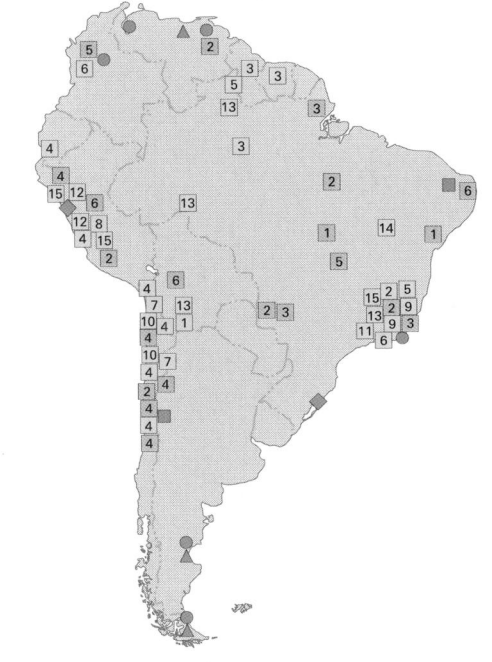

LAND USE

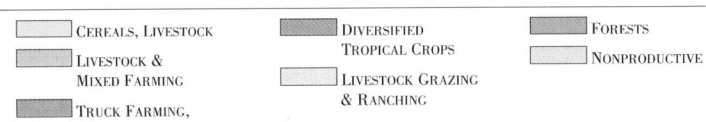

	CEREALS, LIVESTOCK		DIVERSIFIED TROPICAL CROPS		FORESTS
	LIVESTOCK & MIXED FARMING		LIVESTOCK GRAZING & RANCHING		NONPRODUCTIVE
	TRUCK FARMING, SPECIAL CROPS				

MINERAL RESOURCES

ENERGY & FUELS
◆ COAL
▲ NATURAL GAS
● PETROLEUM
■ URANIUM

IRON & FERROALLOYS
1 CHROMIUM
2 IRON ORE
3 MANGANESE
4 MOLYBDENUM
5 NICKEL
6 TUNGSTEN

OTHER MAJOR RESOURCES
1 ANTIMONY
2 ASBESTOS
3 BAUXITE
4 COPPER
5 DIAMONDS
6 GOLD
7 IODINE
8 LEAD
9 MICA
10 NITRATES
11 PHOSPHATES
12 SILVER
13 TIN
14 TITANIUM
15 ZINC

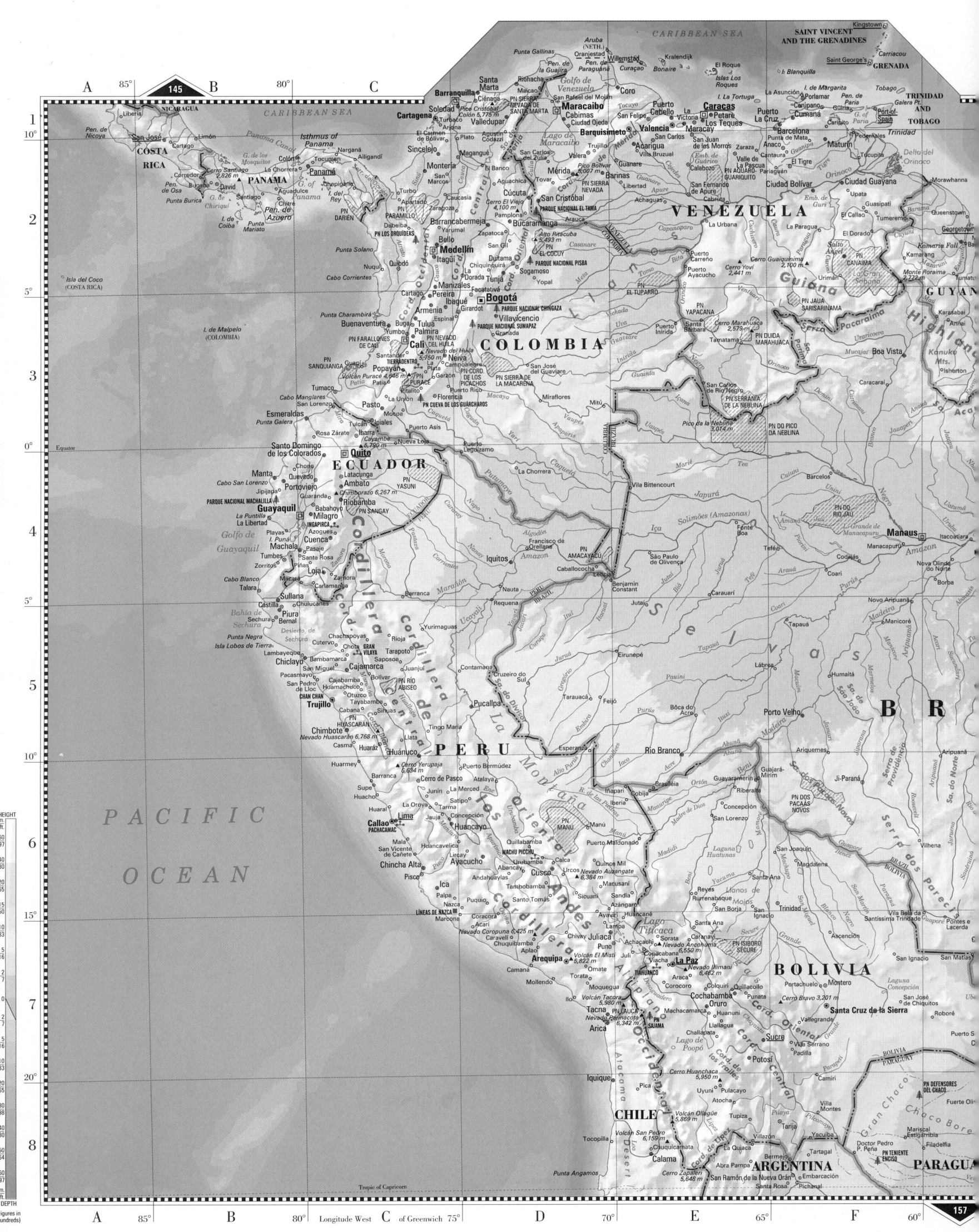

Northern South America

POPULATION OF CITIES AND TOWNS

■ OVER 2,000,000   ● 500,000 - 999,999   ◦ 50,000 - 99,999
▣ 1,000,000 - 1,999,999   ◉ 100,000 - 499,999   ∘ UNDER 50,000

SCALE 1:14,800,000   LAMBERT CONFORMAL CONIC PROJECTION

MILES   0   200   400   600
KILOMETERS   0   200   400   600

© HAMMOND WORLD ATLAS CORPORATION   CJ-2107-A

Colombia, Venezuela, Ecuador

E 64° F 60° G 56° H

CARIBBEAN SEA

ATLANTIC OCEAN

DEPENDENCIAS FEDERALES (VEN.)

GRENADA
Carriacou
Victoria
Sauteurs
Saint George's
Mt. St. Catherine 840 m
POINT SALINES

I. Blanquilla (VEN.)

El Roque
Roques
(VEN.)

I. La Orchila (VEN.)

Is. Los Testigos (VEN.)
I. de Margarita (VEN.)

Tobago
576 m
Charlotteville
Roxborough
Scarborough
CROWN POINT

NUEVA ESPARTA
Juangriego
La Asunción
Porlamar
PN LAGUNA DE LA RESTINGA
I. Coche
I. Cubagua

Caracas
Petare
Los Teques MIRANDA
ctoria
Ocumare del Tuy
PN GUATOPO
ARAGUA
Juan de Torres
El Sombrero

Cumaná
PN MOCHIMA
San Antonio del Golfo
PN CERRO EL COPEY
PN PENÍNSULA DE PARIA
PN CERRO EL COPEY
Carúpano
Casanay
Irapa
Güiria
PN EL GUACHARO
Blanchisseuse
Toco
Pta. Galera
El Cerro del Aripo 940 m
Arima

TRINIDAD AND TOBAGO

SUCRE
Cariaco
Pen. de Araya
El Pilar
Dragon's Mouth
Port-of-Spain
Chaguanas
PIARCO
Sangre Grande

Puerto La Cruz
Barcelona
Pozuelos
Puerto Píritu
GRAL. J. A. ANZOÁTEGUI
San Antonio
Areo
Caicara
Quiriquire
San Fernando
Couva
Río Claro
Siparia
Point Fortin
Pta. Galeota
Eullarton

Gulf of Paria
Serpent's Mouth

Guanape
Onoto
Aguasay
Punta de Mata
Maturín
San Antonio de Tabasca
Uracoa

ANZOÁTEGUI
El Tigre
San Tomé
San José de Guanipa
Temblador
La Horqueta
Tucupita

MONAGAS

DELTA

Delta del Orinoco

Santa María de Ipire
Pariaguán
El Pao
Zuata
Santa Clara
La Canoa
Barrancas
Macareo
Santo Niño
La Esperanza

UÁRICO
San Mauricio
Santa María
San Antonio
Los Castillos
Piacoa
El Toro
San José de Amacuro

PN AGUARO GUARIQUITO
Uverito
Boca del Pao
Almacén
Soledad
Ciudad Guayana
La Margarita
Las Piedras

AMACURO

Cabruta
Santa Cruz de Orinoco
Moitaco
Ciudad Bolívar
El Pao
Upata

Mapire
Caicara
Santa Rosalía
Puruey
Cerro Bolívar 802 m
Ciudad Piar
El Manteco

VENEZUELA

PRESA GURI
Embalse de Guri

Mabaruma
Baramanni
Mount Everard
La Horqueta

BARIMA-WAINI
Charity
Barama
Baramita
Anna Regina
Suddie
POMEROON-SUPENAAM
Queenstown

Las Lajitas
Mantecal
Las Trincheras
La Paragua
El Miamo
Tumeremo

Serranía de la Cerbatana
Guiana
San Pedro de las Bocas

El Casabe
El Dorado

VENEZUELA
GUYANA

Aurora
ESSEQUIBO IS.-W. DEMERARA
Vrood-en-Hoop
Georgetown
Mahaica
Mahaicony Village

BOLÍVAR

CUYUNI-MAZARUNI
Cataratas de Kamaria
Tumereng
Bartica
DEMERARA-MAHAICA
Fort Wellington
TIMEHRI
Paradise
New Amsterdam

Salto Pará
Parque
Salto Hacha
Carabobo
Cataratas de Surwakwima
Kamarang
MAHAICA-BERBICE
Linden
Corriverton
Nieuw-Nickerie
Totness
Nieuw Amsterdam

Highlands
Salto del Angel (Angel Falls)
Auyán-Tepuí 2,950 m
Cerro Venamo 1,890 m
Monte Ayanganna 2,042 m
UPPER DEMERARA-BERBICE
Kangaruma
Rockstone
Kwakwani
E. BER. COR.
NICKERIE
CORONIE
Groningen
Lelydorp
Zanderij
SARAMACCA
Paramaribo

Cerro Yaví 2,300 m
Cerro Guaiquinima 2,100 m
Uruyén
NACIONAL
Chimantá-Tepuí 2,342 m
Tematumari
Oreallo
Epira
PARA
Brokopondo

Cerro Guanay 2,441 m
Urimán
Aparurén
Monte Roraima 2,772 m
PN KAIETEUR
Cataratas de Kaieteur
POTARO-SIPARUNI
Mahdia
Kurupukari
Bitagron
PRESA AFOBAKA

Santa María de Erebató
Guaina
La Gran Sabana
Péra-tepuí
Uonquén
Arabopó

SURINAME
Cataratas Tönckens
Hendrik Top 975 m
Paul Isnard

AMAZONAS
PN JAUA SARISARINAMA
Yerichaña
Uriranteriña
Guaña
CANAIMA
Icabarú
Santa Elena de Uairén
Rera
Apoteri
Kumaka
Juliana Top 1,230 m
Orealla
BROKO PONDO

FRENCH GUTANA

PN YAPACANA
Cerro Marahuaca 2,579 m
PN DUIDA MARAHUACA
Karasabai
Annai
Yupukari
Lethem
Wilhelmina Gebergte
SIPALIWINI

Puruname
Tarnatama
Cerro Duida 2,400 m
La Esmeralda
Urbana
Kanuku Mts.
Apoteri
Kayser Gebergte
Alalapadu

Buenos Aires
Pamoni
Serra Pacaraima
Uraricoera
GUYANA
Wichabai
EAST BERBICE-CORENTYNE
Biloku
Paruintins

comunidad
Capibara
Esperanza
Mucajai
UPPER TAKUTU-UPPER ESSEQUIBO
Isherton
Kuyuwini
Tumuc-Humac Mts.
AMAPÁ

Serra Parima
BOA-VISTA
Boa Vista
Caracaraí
Kassikaityu
1,009 m
Serra Acaraí
BRAZIL
Porto Poet

Solano
Guayabal
San Carlos de Río Negro
RORAIMA
Catrimani

PARQUE NACIONAL SERRANÍA DE LA NEBLINA
El Carmen
Santa Isabel
VENEZUELA
BRAZIL

Pico de la Neblina 3,014 m
PARQUE NACIONAL DO PICO DA NEBLINA

PARÁ
Equator 0°

B R A Z I L

Negro
Barcelos

AMAZONAS

PARQUE NACIONAL DO RIO JAÚ

Represa de Balbina
Sauiá
Nhamundá
Oriximiná
Óbidos
Santarém
Monte Alegre
Alenquer
L. Grande do Curuaí

L. do Erepecu

Lago Amaná
Fonte Boa

L. Grande de Manacapuru

Itapiranga
Urucará
Urucurituba
Parintins
Barreirinha

EDUARDO GOMES
Manaus
© HAMMOND WORLD ATLAS CORPORATION

Amazon

E 64° F 60° G 56° H

POPULATION OF CITIES AND TOWNS
■ OVER 2,000,000   ⊙ 500,000 - 999,999   ⊙ 100,000 - 249,999   ⊙ 10,000 - 29,999
□ 1,000,000 - 1,999,999   ⊙ 250,000 - 499,999   ⊙ 30,000 - 99,999   ⊙ UNDER 10,000

SCALE 1:6,800,000   LAMBERT CONFORMAL CONIC PROJECTION
MILES 0   100   200   300
KILOMETERS 0   100   200   300

Northeastern Brazil

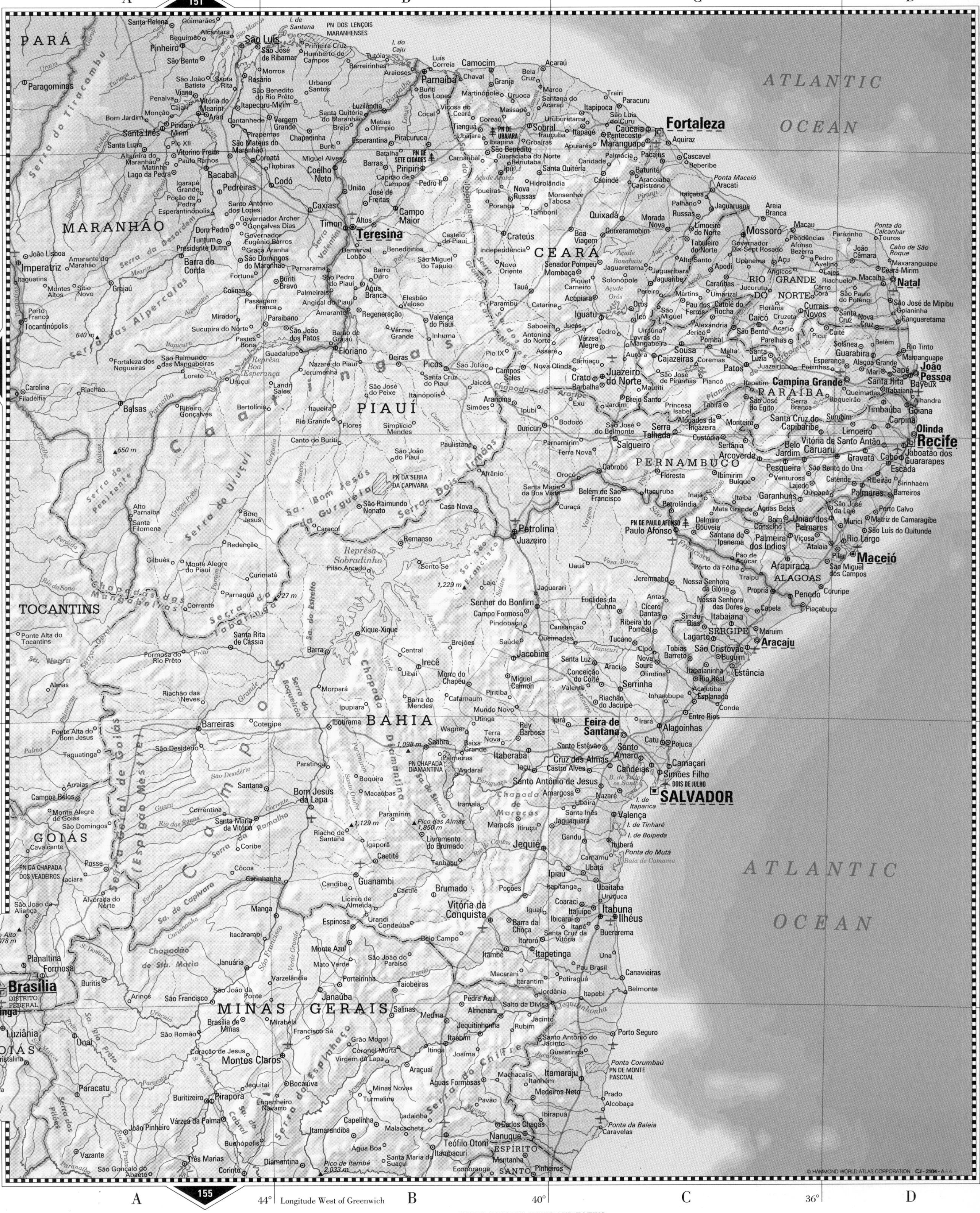

ATLANTIC OCEAN

ATLANTIC OCEAN

HEIGHT
m. ft.
60 197
40 130
20 65
15 50
10 33
5 16
2 7
0
2 7
5 16
10 33
20 65
30 98
40 130
50 164
60 197
m. ft.
DEPTH
(Figures in Hundreds)

SCALE 1:6,800,000 LAMBERT CONFORMAL CONIC PROJECTION
MILES 0   100   200   300
KILOMETERS 0   100   200   300

Longitude West of Greenwich

POPULATION OF CITIES AND TOWNS
■ OVER 2,000,000   ● 500,000 - 999,999   ◉ 100,000 - 249,999   ⊙ 10,000 - 29,999
▣ 1,000,000 - 1,999,999   ◎ 250,000 - 499,999   ⊚ 30,000 - 99,999   ○ UNDER 10,000

© HAMMOND WORLD ATLAS CORPORATION   CJ-2104-A-A

Southeastern Brazil

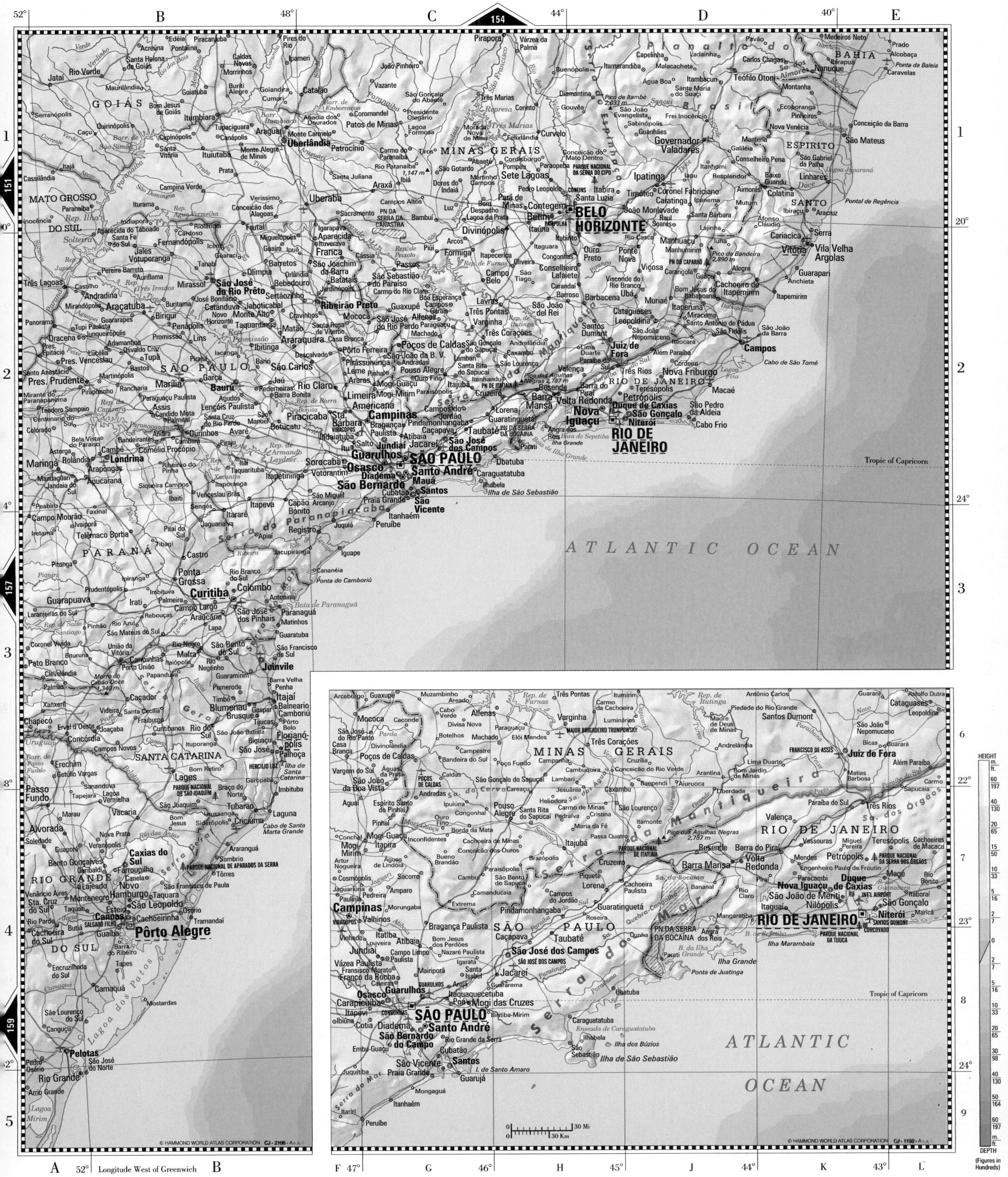

POPULATION OF CITIES AND TOWNS

| ■ OVER 2,000,000 | ● 500,000 - 999,999 | ● 100,000 - 249,999 | ○ 10,000 - 29,999 |
| □ 1,000,000 - 1,999,999 | ● 250,000 - 499,999 | ● 30,000 - 99,999 | ○ UNDER 10,000 |

SCALE 1:6,800,000   LAMBERT CONFORMAL CONIC PROJECTION

Longitude West of Greenwich

© HAMMOND WORLD ATLAS CORPORATION   CJ - 2106 - A
© HAMMOND WORLD ATLAS CORPORATION   CJ - 1150 - A

HEIGHT
m. / ft.
6000 / 197
2000 / 130
1000 / 65
500 / 33
200 / 16
100 / 7
Sea Level

DEPTH
m. / ft.
0 / 7
200 / 16
1000 / 33
2000 / 65
3000 / 98
4000 / 130
5000 / 164
6000 / 197

(Figures in Hundreds)

Peru

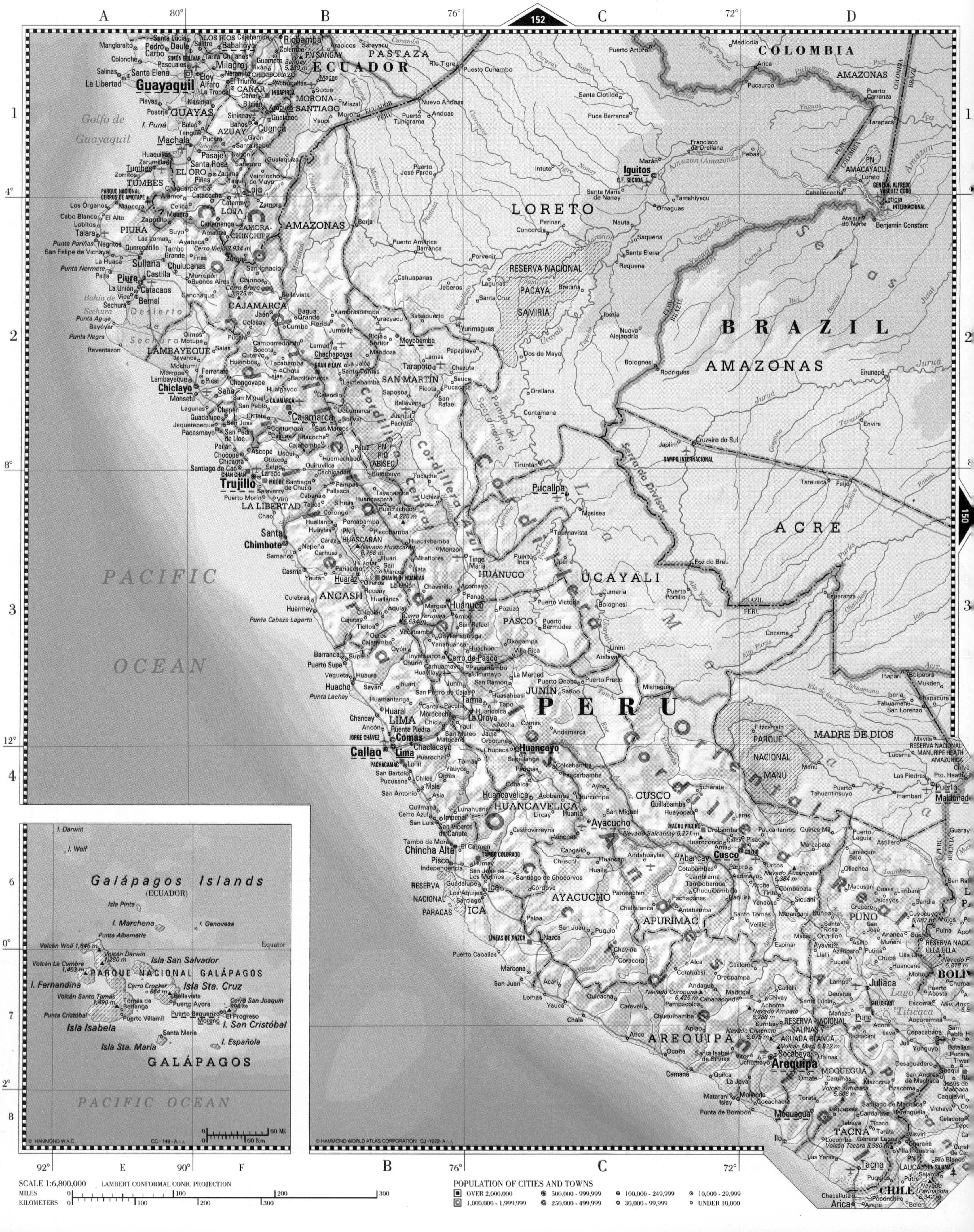

Southern South America

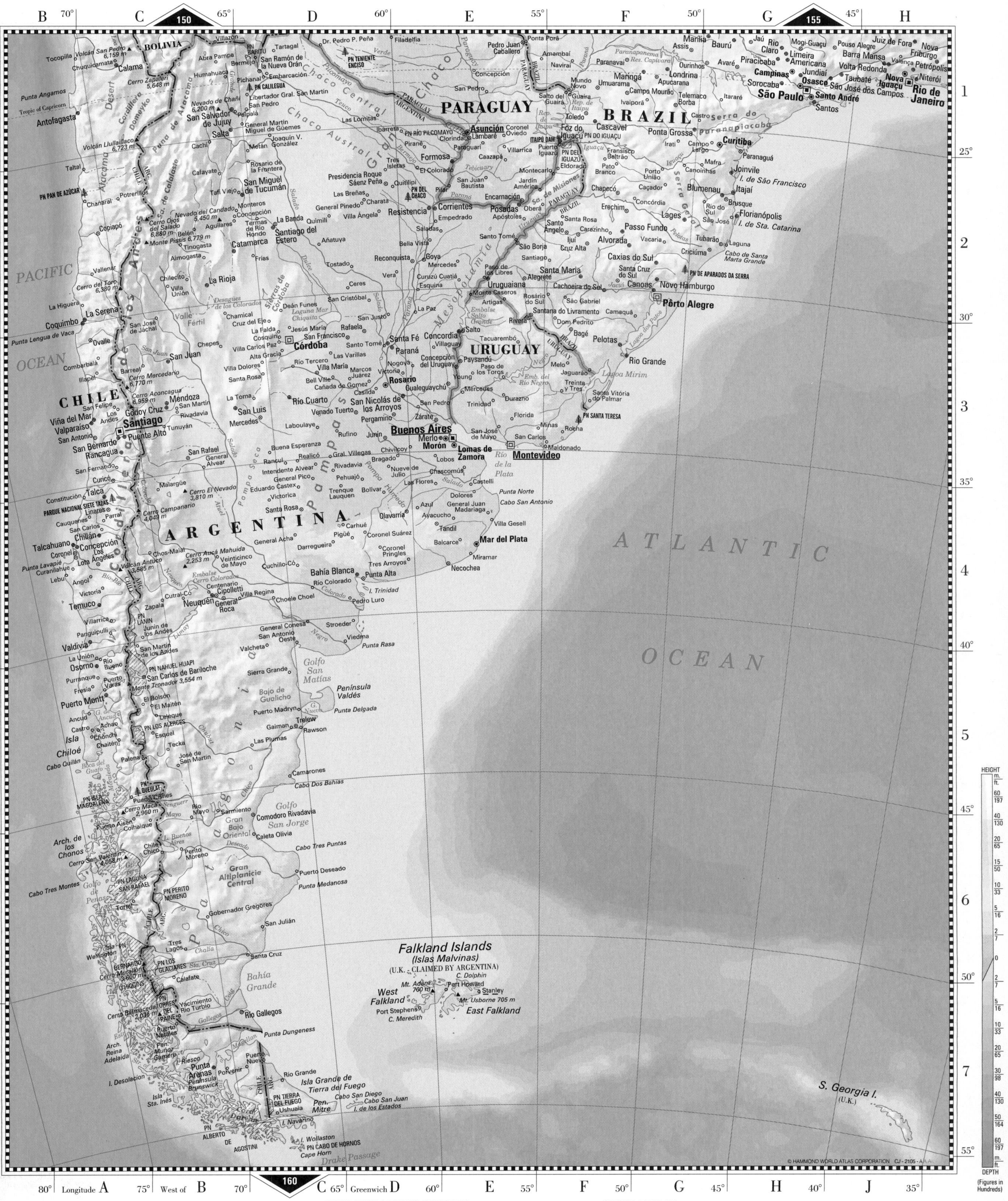

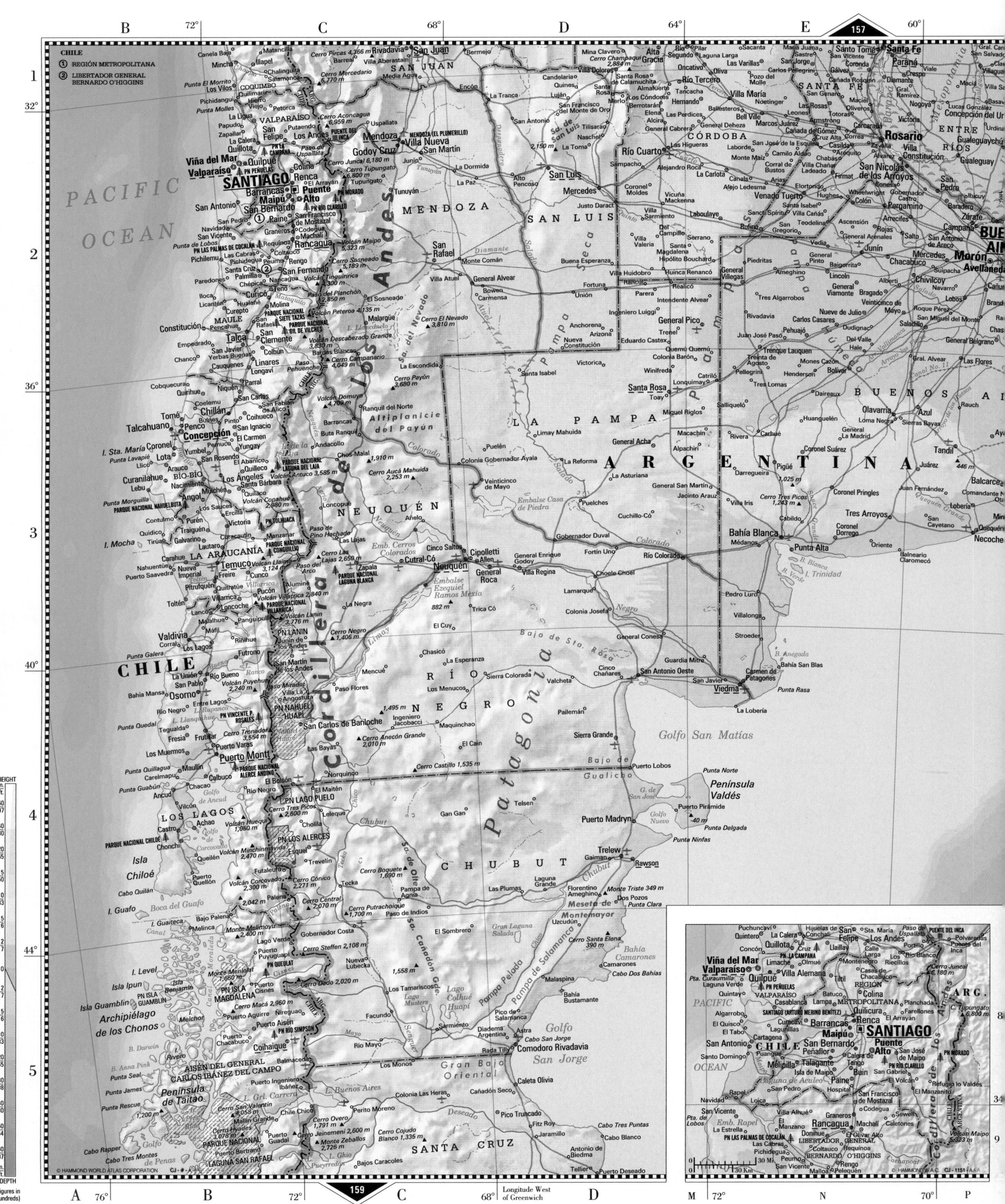

Southern Chile and Argentina

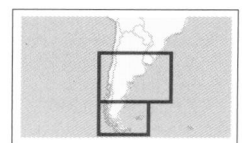

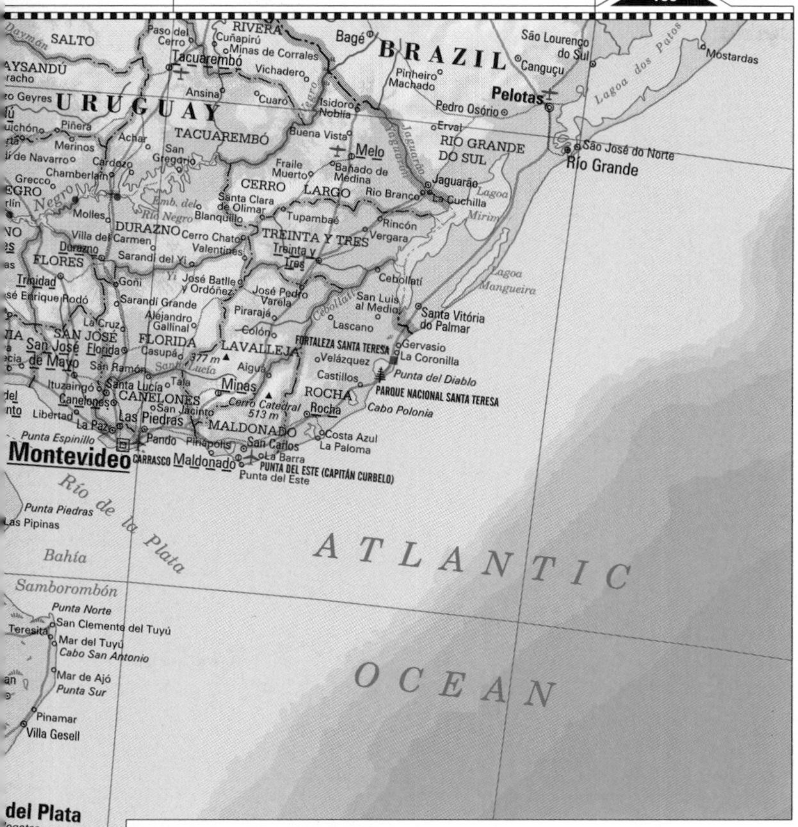

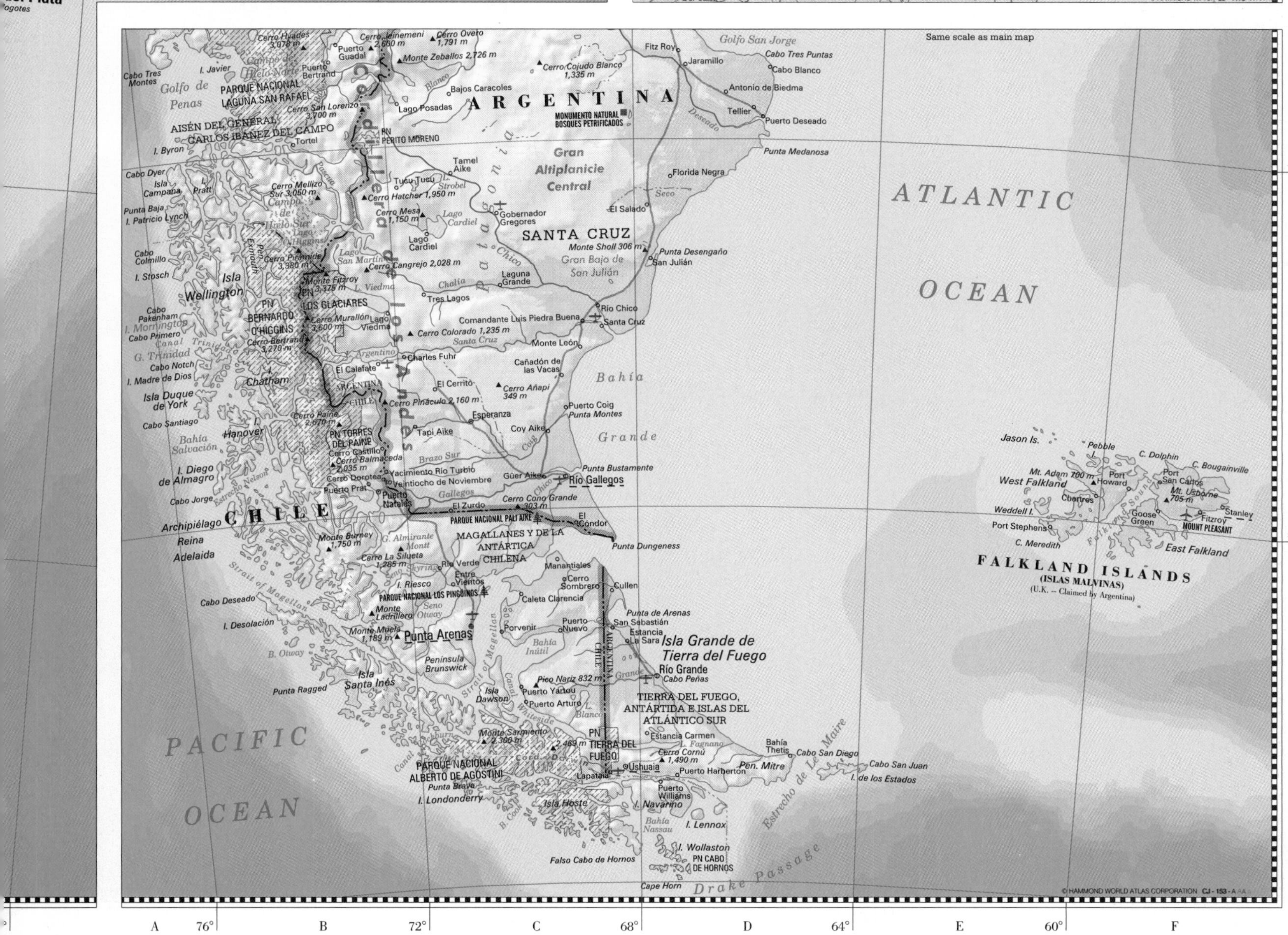

Main map labels (Uruguay / southern Brazil / Río de la Plata):

URUGUAY — BRAZIL — RIVERA — TACUAREMBÓ — CERRO LARGO — RÍO GRANDE DO SUL — Pelotas — Rio Grande — São José do Norte — Canguçu — Bagé — Melo — TREINTA Y TRES — DURAZNO — FLORES — FLORIDA — LAVALLEJA — Minas — MALDONADO — ROCHA — Cerro Catedral 513 m — PARQUE NACIONAL SANTA TERESA — Cabo Polonio — Punta del Este (Capitán Curbelo) — La Paloma — CANELONES — Montevideo — Maldonado — Punta del Diablo

ATLANTIC OCEAN — Bahía Samborombón — Río de la Plata — del Plata

Upper-right map (Entre Ríos / Buenos Aires / Uruguay):

ENTRE RÍOS — PAYSANDÚ — RÍO NEGRO — DURAZNO — TACUAREMBÓ — SORIANO — FLORES — COLONIA — SAN JOSÉ — FLORIDA — CANELONES — URUGUAY — ARGENTINA — BUENOS AIRES — Concepción del Uruguay — Gualeguaychú — Gualeguay — Fray Bentos — Mercedes — Nueva Palmira — Carmelo — Colonia — Colonia del Sacramento — Zárate — Campana — Belén de Escobar — Tigre — San Fernando — Vicente López — General San Martín — Luján — Morón — Merlo — BUENOS AIRES — Avellaneda — Lanús — Lomas de Zamora — La Plata — Montevideo — Ensenada — Brandsen — Lobos — Salado — Cañuelas — ATLANTIC OCEAN

SCALE 1:6,800,000 — LAMBERT CONFORMAL CONIC PROJECTION

MILES 0 100 200 300
KILOMETERS 0 100 200 300

© HAMMOND W.A.C. CJ-1175-A-AA

Lower map (Patagonia / Tierra del Fuego / Falkland Islands):

ARGENTINA — CHILE — SANTA CRUZ — Golfo San Jorge — Cabo Tres Puntas — Puerto Deseado — Punta Medanosa — Puerto San Julián — San Julián — Gran Bajo de San Julián — Río Chico — Santa Cruz — Comandante Luis Piedra Buena — Monte León — Bahía Grande — Puerto Coig — Punta Montes — Río Gallegos — Punta Dungeness — Cabo Vírgenes

Golfo de Penas — PARQUE NACIONAL LAGUNA SAN RAFAEL — AISÉN DEL GENERAL CARLOS IBÁÑEZ DEL CAMPO — Puerto Guadal — Lago Posadas — Cerro San Lorenzo 3,700 m — PN PERITO MORENO — Lago Buenos Aires — Gran Altiplanicie Central — Cerro Cojudo Blanco 1,335 m — Fitz Roy — Jaramillo

Isla Wellington — PN BERNARDO O'HIGGINS — PN LOS GLACIARES — El Chaltén — Lago Viedma — Lago Argentino — El Calafate — Cerro Fitzroy 3,375 m — Cerro Murallón 2,600 m — Tres Lagos — Lago San Martín — Lago Cardiel — El Salado

Isla Diego de Almagro — Hanover — PN TORRES DEL PAINE — Puerto Natales — El Zurdo — Cerro Cono Grande 303 m — PARQUE NACIONAL PALI AIKE

MAGALLANES Y DE LA ANTÁRTICA CHILENA — Punta Arenas — Strait of Magellan — Estrecho de Magallanes — Porvenir — Bahía Inútil — Isla Grande de Tierra del Fuego — Río Grande — Cabo Peñas — San Sebastián — TIERRA DEL FUEGO, ANTÁRTIDA E ISLAS DEL ATLÁNTICO SUR — Ushuaia — PN TIERRA DEL FUEGO — Puerto Williams — Isla Navarino — Cabo San Juan — I. de los Estados — Estrecho de Le Maire — Pen. Mitre — Bahía San Diego — I. Hoste — I. Lennox — I. Wollaston — PN CABO DE HORNOS — Cabo de Hornos — Cape Horn — Drake Passage

PACIFIC OCEAN — ATLANTIC OCEAN

FALKLAND ISLANDS (ISLAS MALVINAS) (U.K.) — Claimed by Argentina — West Falkland — East Falkland — Mt. Adam 700 m — Mt. Usborne 705 m — Stanley — MOUNT PLEASANT — Port Howard — Port San Carlos — Goose Green — Jason Is. — Pebble — C. Dolphin — C. Bougainville — Weddell I. — Port Stephens — C. Meredith

Same scale as main map

© Hammond World Atlas Corporation CJ-153-A-AA

Arctic Regions, Antarctica

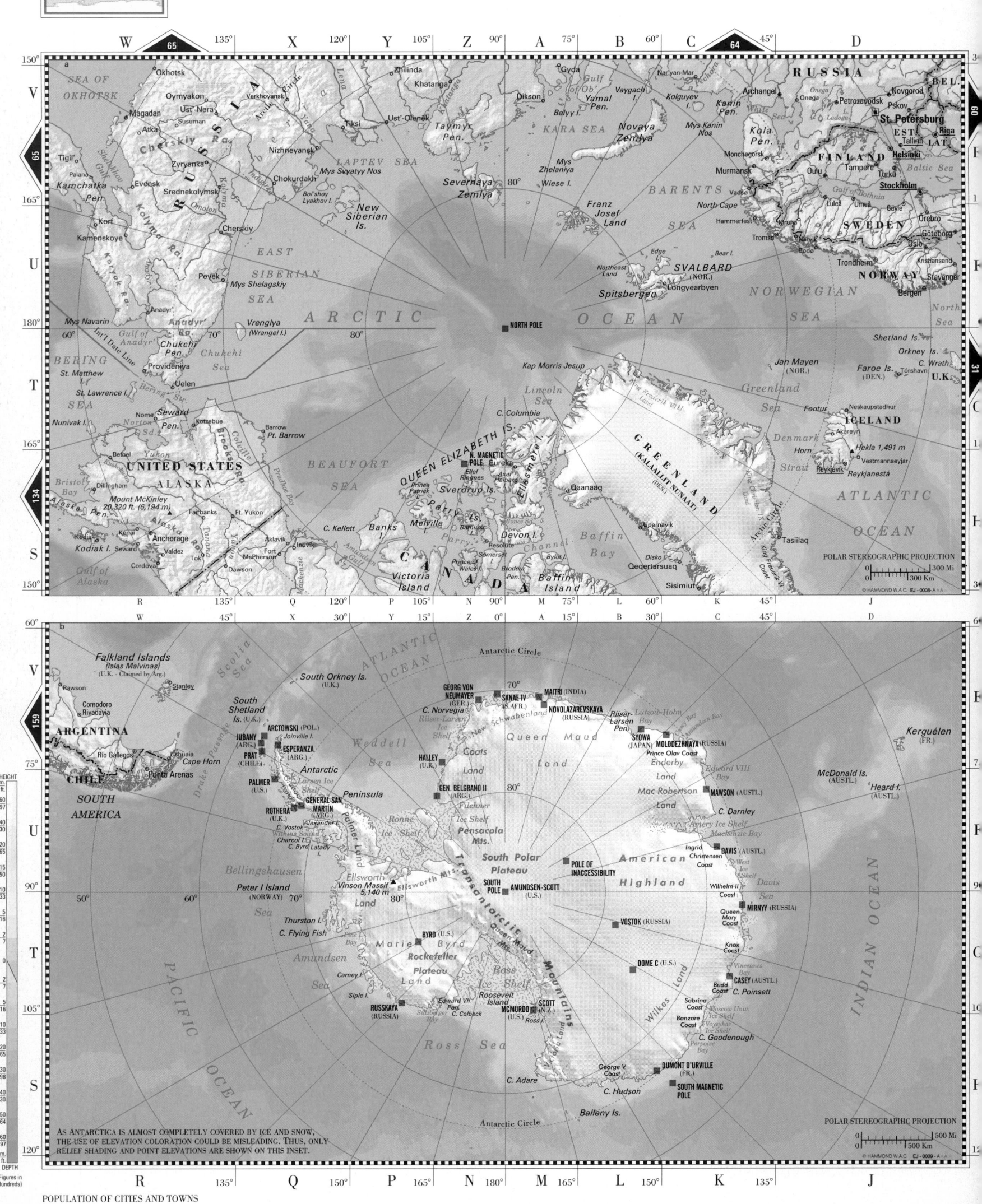

Statistical Tables and Index

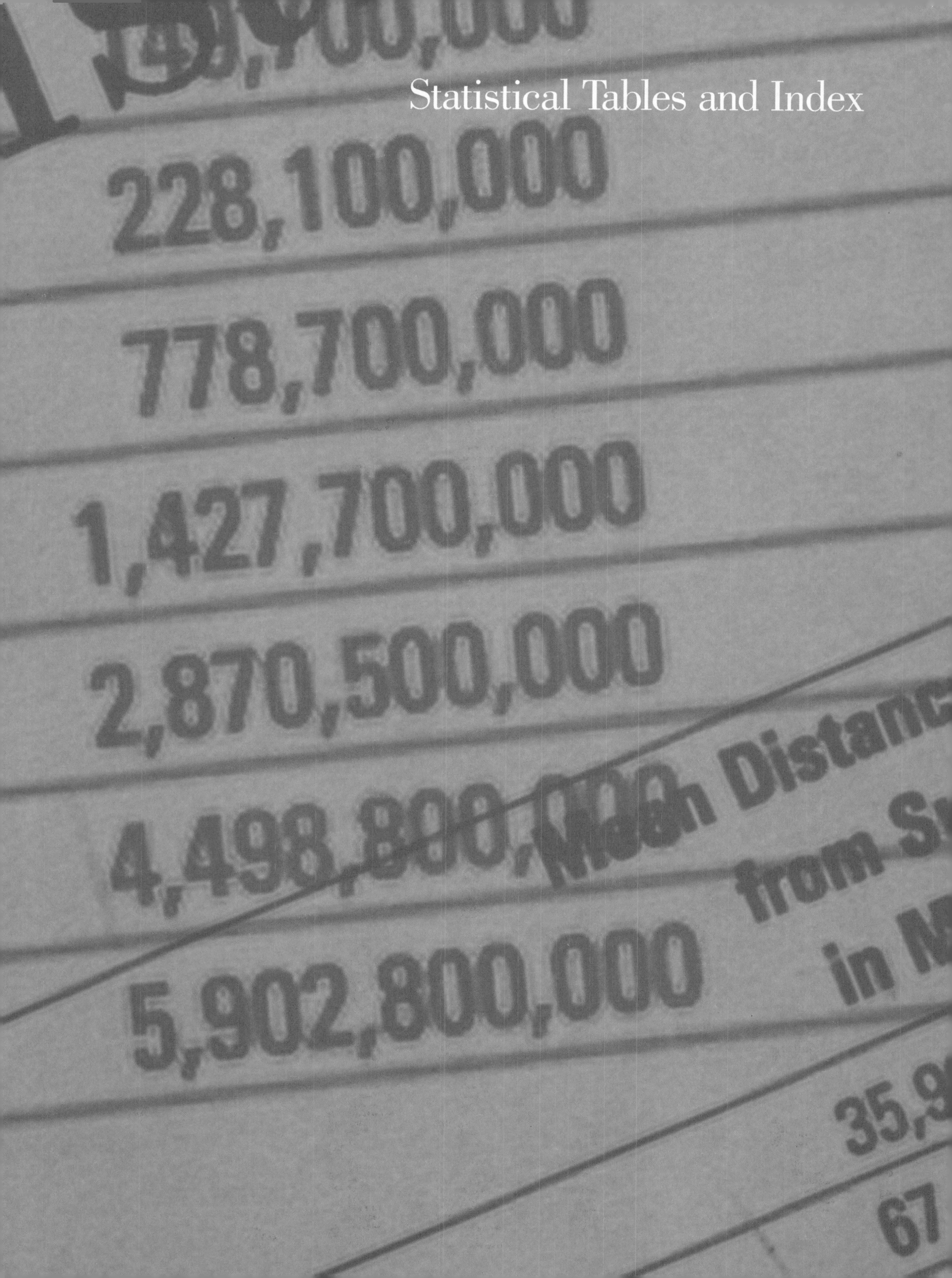

World Statistics

ELEMENTS OF THE SOLAR SYSTEM

	Mean Distance from Sun: in Miles	in Kilometers	Period of Revolution around Sun	Period of Rotation on Axis	Equatorial Diameter in Miles	in Kilometers	Surface Gravity (Earth = 1)	Mass (Earth = 1)	Mean Density (Water = 1)	Number of Satellites
Mercury	35,990,000	57,900,000	87.97 days	58.7 days	3,032	4,880	0.38	0.055	5.4	0
Venus	67,240,000	108,200,000	224.70 days	243.7 days†	7,521	12,104	0.91	0.815	5.2	0
Earth	93,000,000	149,700,000	365.26 days	23h 56m	7,926	12,755	1.00	1.00	5.5	1
Mars	141,610,000	227,900,000	686.98 days	24h 37m	4,221	6,794	0.38	0.107	3.9	2
Jupiter	483,675,000	778,400,000	11.86 years	9h 55m	88,846	142,984	2.36	317.8	1.3	16
Saturn	886,572,000	1,426,800,000	29.46 years	10h 30m	74,898	120,536	0.92	95.2	0.7	18
Uranus	1,783,957,000	2,871,000,000	84.01 years	17h 14m†	31,763	51,118	0.89	14.5	1.3	15
Neptune	2,795,114,000	4,498,300,000	164.79 years	16h 6m	30,778	49,532	1.13	17.1	1.6	8
Pluto	3,670,000,000	5,906,400,000	247.70 years	6.4 days†	1,413	2,274	0.07	0.002	2.1	1

† Retrograde motion

Source: NASA, National Space Science Center

DIMENSIONS OF THE EARTH

	Area in: Sq. Miles	Sq. Kilometers
Superficial area	196,939,000	510,072,000
Land surface	57,506,000	148,940,000
Water surface	139,433,000	361,132,000

	Distance in: Miles	Kilometers
Equatorial circumference	24,902	40,075
Polar circumference	24,860	40,007
Equatorial diameter	7,926.4	12,756.4
Polar diameter	7,899.8	12,713.6
Equatorial radius	3,963.2	6,378.2
Polar radius	3,949.9	6,356.8

Volume of the Earth	2.6×10^{11} cubic miles	10.84×10^{11} cubic kilometers
Mass or weight	6.6×10^{21} short tons	6.0×10^{21} metric tons
Maximum distance from Sun	94,600,000 miles	152,000,000 kilometers
Minimum distance from Sun	91,300,000 miles	147,000,000 kilometers

OCEANS AND MAJOR SEAS

	Area in: Sq. Miles	Sq. Kms.	Greatest Depth in: Feet	Meters
Pacific Ocean	63,855,000	165,384,000	36,198	11,033
Atlantic Ocean	31,744,000	82,217,000	28,374	8,648
Indian Ocean	28,417,000	73,600,000	25,344	7,725
Arctic Ocean	5,427,000	14,056,000	17,880	5,450
Caribbean Sea	970,000	2,512,300	24,720	7,535
Mediterranean Sea	969,000	2,509,700	16,896	5,150
South China Sea	895,000	2,318,000	15,000	4,600
Bering Sea	875,000	2,266,250	15,800	4,800
Gulf of Mexico	600,000	1,554,000	12,300	3,750
Sea of Okhotsk	590,000	1,528,100	11,070	3,370
East China Sea	482,000	1,248,400	9,500	2,900
Yellow Sea	480,000	1,243,200	350	107
Sea of Japan	389,000	1,007,500	12,280	3,740
Hudson Bay	317,500	822,300	846	258
North Sea	222,000	575,000	2,200	670
Black Sea	185,000	479,150	7,365	2,245
Red Sea	169,000	437,700	7,200	2,195
Baltic Sea	163,000	422,170	1,506	459

THE CONTINENTS

	Area in: Sq. Miles	Sq. Kms.	Percent of World's Land
Asia	17,128,500	44,362,815	29.5
Africa	11,707,000	30,321,130	20.2
North America	9,363,000	24,250,170	16.2
South America	6,879,725	17,818,505	11.9
Antarctica	5,405,000	14,000,000	9.4
Europe	4,057,000	10,507,630	7.0
Australia	2,967,893	7,686,850	5.1

MAJOR SHIP CANALS

	Length in: Miles	Kms.	Minimum Depth in: Feet	Meters
Volga-Baltic, Russia	225	362	–	–
Baltic-White Sea, Russia	140	225	16	5
Suez, Egypt	100.76	162	42	13
Albert, Belgium	80	129	16.5	5
Moscow-Volga, Russia	80	129	18	6
Volga-Don, Russia	62	100	–	–
Göta, Sweden	54	87	10	3
Kiel (Nord-Ostsee), Germany	53.2	86	38	12
Panama Canal, Panama	50.72	82	41.6	13
Houston Ship, U.S.A.	50	81	36	11

LARGEST ISLANDS

	Area in: Sq. Miles	Sq. Kms.
Greenland	840,000	2,175,600
New Guinea	305,000	789,950
Borneo	286,000	740,740
Madagascar	226,656	587,040
Baffin, Canada	195,928	507,454
Sumatra, Indonesia	164,000	424,760
Honshu, Japan	88,000	227,920
Great Britain	84,400	218,896
Victoria, Canada	83,896	217,290
Ellesmere, Canada	75,767	196,236
Celebes, Indonesia	72,986	189,034
South I., New Zealand	58,393	151,238
Java, Indonesia	48,842	126,501
North I., New Zealand	44,187	114,444
Cuba	42,803	110,860
Newfoundland, Canada	42,031	108,860
Luzon, Philippines	40,420	104,688
Iceland	39,768	103,000
Mindanao, Philippines	36,537	94,631
Ireland	32,589	84,406
Hokkaidō, Japan	30,436	78,829
Sakhalin, Russia	29,500	76,405

	Area in: Sq. Miles	Sq. Kms.
Hispaniola, Haiti & Dom. Rep.	29,399	76,143
Banks, Canada	27,038	70,028
Ceylon, Sri Lanka	25,332	65,610
Tasmania, Australia	24,600	63,710
Svalbard, Norway	23,957	62,049
Devon, Canada	21,331	55,247
Novaya Zemlya (north isl.), Russia	18,600	48,200
Marajó, Brazil	17,991	46,597
Tierra del Fuego, Chile & Argentina	17,900	46,360
Alexander, Antarctica	16,700	43,250
Axel Heiberg, Canada	16,671	43,178
Melville, Canada	16,274	42,150
Southampton, Canada	15,913	41,215
New Britain, Papua New Guinea	14,100	36,519
Taiwan	13,836	35,835
Kyushu, Japan	13,770	35,664
Hainan, China	13,127	33,999
Prince of Wales, Canada	12,872	33,338
Spitsbergen, Norway	12,355	31,999
Vancouver, Canada	12,079	31,285
Timor, Indonesia	11,527	29,855
Sicily, Italy	9,926	25,708

	Area in: Sq. Miles	Sq. Kms.
Somerset, Canada	9,570	24,786
Sardinia, Italy	9,301	24,090
Shikoku, Japan	6,860	17,767
New Caledonia, France	6,530	16,913
Nordaustlandet, Norway	6,409	16,599
Samar, Philippines	5,050	13,080
Negros, Philippines	4,906	12,707
Palawan, Philippines	4,550	11,785
Panay, Philippines	4,446	11,515
Jamaica	4,232	10,961
Hawaii, United States	4,038	10,458
Viti Levu, Fiji	4,010	10,386
Cape Breton, Canada	3,981	10,311
Mindoro, Philippines	3,759	9,736
Kodiak, Alaska, U.S.A.	3,670	9,505
Cyprus	3,572	9,251
Puerto Rico, U.S.A.	3,435	8,897
Corsica, France	3,352	8,682
New Ireland, Papua New Guinea	3,340	8,651
Crete, Greece	3,218	8,335
Anticosti, Canada	3,066	7,941
Wrangel, Russia	2,819	7,301

PRINCIPAL MOUNTAINS

	Height in : Feet	Meters
Everest, Nepal-China	29,028	8,848
K2 (Godwin Austen), Pakistan-China	28,250	8,611
Kånchenjunga, Nepal-India	28,208	8,598
Lhotse, Nepal-China	27,923	8,511
Makalu, Nepal-China	27,789	8,470
Dhaulagiri, Nepal	26,810	8,172
Nanga Parbat, Pakistan	26,660	8,126
Annapurna, Nepal	26,504	8,078
Nanda Devi, India	25,645	7,817
Rakaposhi, Pakistan	25,550	7,788
Kongur Shan, China	25,325	7,719
Tirich Mir, Pakistan	25,230	7,690
Gongga Shan, China	24,790	7,556
Communism Peak, Tajikistan	24,590	7,495
Pobedy Peak, Kyrgyzstan	24,406	7,439
Chomo Lhari, Bhutan-China	23,997	7,314
Muztag, China	23,891	7,282
Cerro Aconcagua, Argentina	22,831	6,959
Ojos del Salado, Chile-Argentina	22,572	6,880
Bonete, Chile-Argentina	22,546	6,872
Tupungato, Chile-Argentina	22,310	6,800
Pissis, Argentina	22,241	6,779
Mercedario, Argentina	22,211	6,770
Huascarán, Peru	22,205	6,768
Llullaillaco, Chile-Argentina	22,057	6,723
Nevada Ancohuma, Bolivia	21,489	6,550
Chimborazo, Ecuador	20,561	6,267
McKinley, Alaska	20,320	6,194
Logan, Yukon, Canada	19,524	5,951
Cotopaxi, Ecuador	19,347	5,897
Kilimanjaro, Tanzania	19,340	5,895
El Misti, Peru	19,101	5,822
Pico Cristóbal Colón, Colombia	18,947	5,775
Huila, Colombia	18,865	5,750
Citlaltépetl (Orizaba), Mexico	18,700	5,700
Damavand, Iran	18,605	5,671
El'brus, Russia	18,510	5,642
St. Elias, Alaska, U.S.A.-Yukon, Canada	18,008	5,489
Dykh-tau, Russia	17,070	5,203
Batian (Kenya), Kenya	17,058	5,199
Ararat, Turkey	16,946	5,165
Vinson Massif, Antarctica	16,864	5,140
Margherita (Ruwenzori), Africa	16,795	5,119
Kazbek, Georgia-Russia	16,558	5,047
Puncak Jaya, Indonesia	16,503	5,030
Blanc, France	15,771	4,807
Klyuchevskaya Sopka, Russia	15,584	4,750
Fairweather, Br. Col., Canada	15,300	4,663
Dufourspitze (Mte. Rosa), Italy-Switzerland	15,203	4,634
Ras Dashen, Ethiopia	15,157	4,620
Matterhorn, Switzerland	14,691	4,478
Whitney, California, U.S.A.	14,494	4,418
Elbert, Colorado, U.S.A.	14,433	4,399
Rainier, Washington, U.S.A.	14,410	4,392
Shasta, California, U.S.A.	14,162	4,317
Pikes Peak, Colorado, U.S.A.	14,110	4,301
Finsteraarhorn, Switzerland	14,022	4,274
Mauna Kea, Hawaii, U.S.A.	13,796	4,205
Mauna Loa, Hawaii, U.S.A.	13,677	4,169
Jungfrau, Switzerland	13,642	4,158
Grossglockner, Austria	12,457	3,797
Fujiyama, Japan	12,389	3,776
Cook, New Zealand	12,349	3,764

LONGEST RIVERS

	Length in: Miles	Kms.
Nile, Africa	4,145	6,671
Amazon, S. America	4,007	6,448
Mississippi-Missouri-Red Rock, U.S.A.	3,710	5,971
Chang Jiang (Yangtze), China	3,500	5,633
Ob'-Irtysh, Russia-Kazakhstan	3,362	5,411
Yenisey-Angara, Russia	3,100	4,989
Huang He (Yellow), China	2,950	4,747
Congo, Africa	2,780	4,474
Amur-Shilka-Onon, Asia	2,744	4,416
Lena, Russia	2,734	4,400
Mackenzie-Peace-Finlay, Canada	2,635	4,241
Paraná-La Plata, S. America	2,630	4,232
Mekong, Asia	2,610	4,200
Niger, Africa	2,580	4,152
Missouri-Red Rock, U.S.A.	2,564	4,125
Yenisey, Russia	2,500	4,028
Mississippi, U.S.A.	2,348	3,778
Murray-Darling, Australia	2,310	3,718
Volga, Russia	2,290	3,685
Madeira, S. America	2,013	3,240
Purus, S. America	1,995	3,211
Yukon, Alaska-Canada	1,979	3,185
Zambezi, Africa	1,950	3,138
São Francisco, Brazil	1,930	3,106
St. Lawrence, Canada-U.S.A.	1,900	3,058
Rio Grande, Mexico-U.S.A.	1,885	3,034
Syrdarïya-Naryn, Asia	1,859	2,992
Indus, Asia	1,800	2,897
Danube, Europe	1,775	2,857
Brahmaputra, Asia	1,700	2,736
Tocantins, Brazil	1,677	2,699
Salween, Asia	1,675	2,696
Euphrates, Asia	1,650	2,655
Xi (Si), China	1,650	2,655
Amu Darya, Asia	1,616	2,601
Nelson-Saskatchewan, Canada	1,600	2,575
Orinoco, S. America	1,600	2,575
Paraguay, S. America	1,584	2,549
Kolyma, Russia	1,562	2,514
Ganges, Asia	1,550	2,494
Zhayyq (Ural), Kazakhstan-Russia	1,509	2,428
Japurá, S. America	1,500	2,414
Arkansas, U.S.A.	1,450	2,334
Colorado, U.S.A.-Mexico	1,450	2,334
Negro, S. America	1,400	2,253
Dnepr (Dnyapro, Dnipro), Russia-Belarus-Ukraine	1,368	2,202
Orange, Africa	1,350	2,173
Ayeyarwady, Myanmar	1,325	2,132
Brazos, U.S.A.	1,309	2,107
Ohio-Allegheny, U.S.A.	1,306	2,102
Kama, Russia	1,252	2,031
Don, Russia	1,222	1,967
Red, U.S.A.	1,222	1,966
Columbia, U.S.A.-Canada	1,214	1,953
Tigris, Asia	1,181	1,901
Darling, Australia	1,160	1,867
Angara, Russia	1,135	1,827
Sungari, Asia	1,130	1,819
Pechora, Russia	1,124	1,809
Snake, U.S.A.	1,038	1,670
Churchill, Canada	1,000	1,609
Pilcomayo, S. America	1,000	1,609
Uruguay, S. America	994	1.600
Platte-N. Platte, U.S.A.	990	1,593
Ohio, U.S.A.	981	1,578
Magdalena, Colombia	956	1,538
Pecos, U.S.A.	926	1,490
Oka, Russia	918	1,477
Canadian, U.S.A.	906	1,458
Colorado, Texas, U.S.A.	894	1,439
Dnister (Nistru), Ukraine-Moldova	876	1,410
Fraser, Canada	850	1,369
Rhine, Europe	820	1,319
Northern Dvina, Russia	809	1,302
Ottawa, Canada	790	1,271

PRINCIPAL NATURAL LAKES

	Area in: Sq. Miles	Sq. Kms.	Max. Depth in: Feet	Meters
Caspian Sea, Asia	143,243	370,999	3,264	995
Lake Superior, U.S.A.-Canada	31,820	82,414	1,329	405
Lake Victoria, Africa	26,628	69,215	270	82
Lake Huron, U.S.A.-Canada	23,010	59,596	748	228
Lake Michigan, U.S.A.	22,400	58,016	923	281
Aral Sea, Kazakhstan-Uzbekistan	15,830	41,000	213	65
Lake Tanganyika, Africa	12,650	32,764	4,700	1,433
Lake Baykal, Russia	12,162	31,500	5,316	1,620
Great Bear Lake, Canada	12,096	31,328	1,356	413
Lake Nyasa (Malawi), Africa	11,555	29,928	2,320	707
Great Slave Lake, Canada	11,031	28,570	2,015	614
Lake Erie, U.S.A.-Canada	9,940	25,745	210	64
Lake Winnipeg, Canada	9,417	24,390	60	18
Lake Ontario, U.S.A.-Canada	7,540	19,529	775	244
Lake Balkhash, Kazakhstan	7,081	18,340	87	27
Lake Chad, Africa*	7,000	18,130	25	8
Lake Ladoga, Russia	6,900	17,871	738	225
Lake Maracaibo, Venezuela	5,120	13,261	100	31
Lake Onega, Russia	3,761	9,741	377	115
Lake Eyre, Australia*	3,500-0	9,065-0	–	–
Lake Titicaca, Peru-Bolivia	3,200	8,288	1,000	305
Lake Nicaragua, Nicaragua	3,100	8,029	230	70
Lake Athabasca, Canada	3,064	7,936	400	122
Reindeer Lake, Canada*	2,568	6,651	–	–
Lake Turkana (Rudolf), Africa	2,463	6,379	240	73
Ysyk-Köl, Kyrgyzstan	2,425	6,281	2,303	702
Lake Torrens, Australia*	2,230	5,776	–	–
Vänern, Sweden	2,156	5,584	328	100
Nettilling Lake, Canada*	2,140	5,543	–	–
Lake Winnipegosis, Canada	2,075	5,374	38	12
Lake Albert, Africa	2,075	5,374	160	49
Kariba Lake, Zambia-Zimbabwe	2,050	5,310	295	90
Lake Nipigon, Canada	1,872	4,848	540	165
Lake Mweru, Africa	1,800	4,662	60	18
Lake Manitoba, Canada	1,799	4,659	12	4
Lake Taymyr, Russia	1,737	4,499	85	26
Lake Khanka, China-Russia	1,700	4,403	33	10
Lake Kioga, Uganda	1,700	4,403	25	8
Lake of the Woods, U.S.A.-Canada	1,679	4,349	70	21

* Figures subject to great seasonal variations.

Time Zones of the World

165° W	150° W	135° W	120° W	105° W	90° W	75° W	60° W	45° W	30° W	15° W	0°
1 A.M.	2 A.M.	3 A.M.	4 A.M.	5 A.M.	6 A.M.	7 A.M.	8 A.M.	9 A.M.	10 A.M.	11 A.M.	NOON

ARCTIC OCEAN

GREENLAND

NOON

11 A.M.

3 A.M.
ALASKA

Anchorage

Nuuk

Reykjavík

ICELAND

Whitehorse

CANADA

NOR

UNITED
KINGDOM

IRELAND

London

Paris

FRANCE

NET
BELG.

Edmonton

Winnipeg

Montréal

Seattle

1 A.M.

Boise

Chicago

Detroit

Halifax

NEWFOUNDLAND
8:30 A.M.

ST. PIERRE
& MIQUELON
9 A.M.

PORTUGAL

Madrid

SPAIN

Alg

San Francisco

UNITED   STATES

Denver

New York
Washington

AZORES

BERMUDA

MOROCCO

Los Angeles

Phoenix

Atlanta

CANARY IS.

ALGERI

Houston

ATLANTIC

W. SAHARA

Honolulu

Miami

BAHAMAS

MAURITANIA

HAWAII

MEXICO

CUBA

PUERTO
RICO

ANTIGUA & BARBUDA

CAPE
VERDE

Dakar

SENEGAL

MALI

PACIFIC

Mexico

HALF DOM.
REP.

DOMINICA

GAMBIA

1 A.M.

JAMAICA

BELIZE

GUATEMALA   HONDURAS

GRENADA   BARBADOS

TRINIDAD & TOBAGO

GUINEA-BISSAU

BURKINA
FASO

N

EL SALVADOR   NICARAGUA

GUINEA

BENIN

COSTA RICA

PANAMA

SIERRA LEONE

CÔTE
D'IVOIRE

GHANA

La

1 A.M.

COLOMBIA

VENEZUELA

GUYANA

LIBERIA

TOGO

INT'L DATE LINE

Bogotá

SUR.   FR. GUIANA

SÃO TOMÉ
PRÍNCIPI

MIDNIGHT

KIRIBATI

EGUADOR

GÁLAPAGOS IS.

Manaus

OCEAN

MARQUESAS IS.
2:30 A.M.

Lima

PERU

BRAZIL

Recife

ASCENSION

FRENCH   POLYNESIA

La Paz

BOLIVIA

OCEAN

PITCAIRN IS.

EASTER I.

PARAGUAY

Rio de
Janeiro

CHILE

TRISTAN DA CUNHA

Santiago

Buenos
Aires

URUGUAY

ARGENTINA

TIME ZONES OF THE WORLD

STANDARD TIME ZONES	3 A.M.	4 A.M.	5 A.M.	6 A.M.
AREAS USING HALF HOUR DEVIATIONS	5:30 P.M.		

FALKLAND IS.

S. GEORGIA

1 A.M.	2 A.M.	3 A.M.	4 A.M.	5 A.M.	6 A.M.	7 A.M.	8 A.M.	9 A.M.	10 A.M.	11 A.M.	NOON

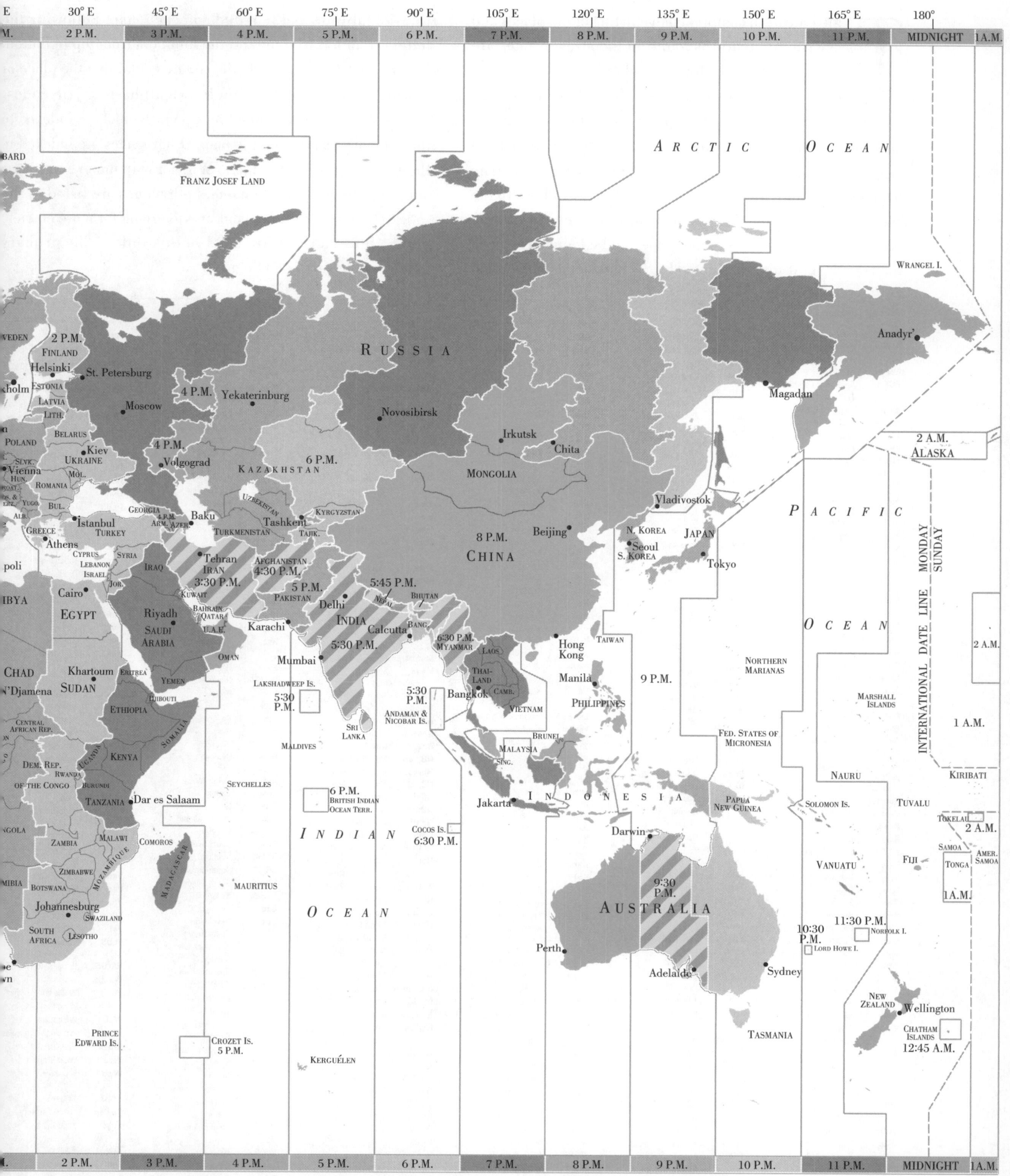

ARCTIC OCEAN

FRANZ JOSEF LAND

WRANGEL I.

RUSSIA

Anadyr'

2 P.M.
FINLAND
Helsinki
ESTONIA
St. Petersburg
kholm
LATVIA
LITH.
Moscow
4 P.M.
Yekaterinburg
Novosibirsk
Magadan

POLAND
BELARUS
Irkutsk
Chita
2 A.M.
ALASKA
SLVK.
Vienna
Kiev
UKRAINE
4 P.M.
Volgograd
KAZAKHSTAN
6 P.M.
MONGOLIA
Vladivostok

HUN.
ROMANIA
MOL.
CROAT.
YUGO.
BUL.
GEORGIA
Baku
UZBEKISTAN
KYRGYZSTAN
Tashkent
8 P.M.
Beijing
N. KOREA
Seoul
S. KOREA
JAPAN
PACIFIC

ALB.
GREECE
İstanbul
TURKEY
ARM. AZER.
TURKMENISTAN
TAJIK.
CHINA
Tokyo

Athens
CYPRUS
SYRIA
Tehran
IRAN
AFGHANISTAN
4:30 P.M.
2 A.M.

poli
LEBANON
ISRAEL
IRAQ
JOR.
3:30 P.M.
5 P.M.
PAKISTAN
5:45 P.M.
NEPAL
BHUTAN

IBYA
Cairo
KUWAIT
BAHRAIN
QATAR
Delhi
Calcutta
BANG.
Hong
Kong
TAIWAN

EGYPT
Riyadh
SAUDI
ARABIA
U.A.E.
Karachi
INDIA
5:30 P.M.
6:30 P.M.
MYANMAR
LAOS
OCEAN

CHAD
Khartoum
ERITREA
OMAN
Mumbai
THAI-
LAND
CAMB.
Manila
9 P.M.
NORTHERN
MARIANAS

N'Djamena
SUDAN
YEMEN
LAKSHADWEEP IS.
5:30
P.M.
Bangkok
VIETNAM
PHILIPPINES

DJIBOUTI
ETHIOPIA
5:30
P.M.
MYANMAR
6:30 P.M.
ANDAMAN &
NICOBAR IS.
MARSHALL
ISLANDS

CENTRAL
AFRICAN REP.
SRI
LANKA
BRUNEI

KENYA
SOMALIA
MALDIVES
MALAYSIA
FED. STATES OF
MICRONESIA

DEM. REP.
OF THE CONGO
BURUNDI
RWANDA
UGANDA
SEYCHELLES
SING.

TANZANIA
Dar es Salaam
6 P.M.
BRITISH INDIAN
OCEAN TERR.
INDONESIA
PAPUA
NEW GUINEA
NAURU
KIRIBATI

NGOLA
ZAMBIA
MALAWI
COMOROS
Jakarta
SOLOMON IS.
TUVALU

MOZAMBIQUE
COCOS IS.
6:30 P.M.
Darwin
TOKELAU
2 A.M.

MIBIA
ZIMBABWE
BOTSWANA
MADAGASCAR
INDIAN
9:30
P.M.
VANUATU
FIJI
SAMOA
TONGA
AMER.
SAMOA

Johannesburg
MAURITIUS
AUSTRALIA
11:30 P.M.
1 A.M.

SOUTH
AFRICA
SWAZILAND
LESOTHO
OCEAN
10:30
P.M.
NORFOLK I.

e
wn
Perth
LORD HOWE I.

PRINCE
EDWARD IS.
CROZET IS.
5 P.M.
Adelaide
Sydney

KERGUÉLEN
NEW
ZEALAND
Wellington
TASMANIA
CHATHAM
ISLANDS
12:45 A.M.

INTERNATIONAL DATE LINE
MONDAY
SUNDAY

Index of the World

This index is a comprehensive listing of the places and geographic features found in the atlas. Names are arranged in strict alphabetical order, without regard to hyphens or spaces. Every name is followed by the country or area to which it belongs. Except for cities, towns, countries and cultural areas, all entries include a reference to feature type, such as province, river, island, peak, and so on. The page number and alpha-numeric code appear in blue to the right of each listing. The page number directs you to the largest scale map on which the name can be found. The code refers to the grid squares formed by the horizontal and vertical lines of latitude and longitude on each map. Following the letters from left to right and the numbers from top to bottom helps you to locate quickly the square containing the place or feature. Inset maps have their own alpha-numeric codes. Names that are accompanied by a point symbol are indexed to the symbol's location on the map. Other names are indexed to the initial letter of the name. When a map name contains a subordinate or alternate name, both names are listed in the index. To conserve space and provide room for more entries, many abbreviations are used in this index. The primary abbreviations are listed below.

Index Abbreviations

A
Ab,Can	Alberta
Abor.	Aboriginal
Acad.	Academy
ACT	Australian Capital Territory
A.F.B.	Air Force Base
Afld.	Airfield
Afg.	Afghanistan
Afr.	Africa
Ak,US	Alaska
Al,US	Alabama
Alb.	Albania
Alg.	Algeria
Amm. Dep.	Ammunition Depot
And.	Andorra
Ang.	Angola
Angu.	Anguilla
Ant.	Antarctica
Anti.	Antigua and Barbuda
Ar,US	Arkansas
Arch.	Archipelago
Arg.	Argentina
Arm.	Armenia
Arpt.	Airport
Aru.	Aruba
ASam.	American Samoa
Ash.	Ashmore and Cartier Islands
Aus.	Austria
Austl.	Australia
Aut.	Autonomous
Az,US	Arizona
Azer.	Azerbaijan
Azor.	Azores

B
Bahm.	Bahamas, The
Bahr.	Bahrain
Bang.	Bangladesh
Bar.	Barbados
BC,Can	British Columbia
Bela.	Belarus
Belg.	Belgium
Belz.	Belize
Ben.	Benin
Berm.	Bermuda
Bfld.	Battlefield
Bhu.	Bhutan
Bol.	Bolivia
Bor.	Borough
Bosn.	Bosnia and Herzegovina
Bots.	Botswana
Braz.	Brazil
BrIn.	British Indian Ocean Territory
Bru.	Brunei
Bul.	Bulgaria
Burk.	Burkina Faso
Buru.	Burundi
BVI	British Virgin Islands

C
Ca,US	California
CAfr.	Central African Republic
Camb.	Cambodia
Camr.	Cameroon
Can.	Canada
Can.	Canal
Canl.	Canary Islands
Cap.	Capital
Cap. Dist.	Capital District
Cap. Terr.	Capital Territory
Cay.	Cayman Islands
C.d'Iv.	Côte d'Ivoire
C.G.	Coast Guard
Chan.	Channel
Chl.	Channel Islands
Co.	County
Co,US	Colorado
Col.	Colombia
Com.	Comoros
Cont.	Continent
CpV.	Cape Verde Islands
CR	Costa Rica
Cr.	Creek
Cro.	Croatia
CSea.	Coral Sea Islands Territory
Ct,US	Connecticut
Ctr.	Center
Ctry.	Country
Cyp.	Cyprus
Czh.	Czech Republic

D
DC,US	District of Columbia
De,US	Delaware
Den.	Denmark
Depr.	Depression
Dept.	Department
Des.	Desert
DF	Distrito Federal
Dist.	District
Djib.	Djibouti
Dom.	Dominica
Dpcy.	Dependency
D.R.Congo	Democratic Republic of the Congo
DRep.	Dominican Republic

E
Ecu.	Ecuador
Emb.	Embankment
Eng.	Engineering
Eng,UK	England
EqG.	Equatorial Guinea
Erit..	Eritrea
ESal.	El Salvador
Est.	Estonia
Eth.	Ethiopia
Eur.	Europe

F
Falk.	Falkland Islands
Far.	Faroe Islands
Fed. Dist.	Federal District
Fin.	Finland
Fl,US	Florida
For.	Forest
Fr.	France
FrAnt.	French Southern and Antarctic Lands
FrG.	French Guiana
FrPol.	French Polynesia
FYROM	Former Yugoslav Rep. of Macedonia

G
Ga,US	Georgia
Galp.	Galapagos Islands
Gam.	Gambia, The
Gaza	Gaza Strip
GBis.	Guinea-Bissau
Geo.	Georgia
Ger.	Germany
Gha.	Ghana
Gib.	Gibraltar
Glac.	Glacier
Gov.	Governorate
Govt.	Government
Gre.	Greece
Grld.	Greenland
Gren.	Grenada
GrsId.	Grassland
Guad.	Guadeloupe
Guat.	Guatemala
Gui.	Guinea
Guy.	Guyana

H
Har.	Harbor
Hi,US	Hawaii
Hist.	Historic(al)
Hon.	Honduras
Hts.	Heights
Hun.	Hungary

I
Ia,US	Iowa
Ice.	Iceland
Id,US	Idaho
Il,US	Illinois
IM	Isle of Man
In,US	Indiana
Ind. Res.	Indian Reservation
Indo.	Indonesia
Int'l	International
Ire.	Ireland
Isl., Isls.	Island, Islands
Isr.	Israel
Isth.	Isthmus
It.	Italy

J
Jam.	Jamaica
Jor.	Jordan

K
Kaz.	Kazakhstan
Kiri.	Kiribati
Ks,US	Kansas
Kuw.	Kuwait
Ky,US	Kentucky
Kyr.	Kyrgyzstan

L
La,US	Louisiana
Lab.	Laboratory
Lag.	Lagoon
Lakesh.	Lakeshore
Lat.	Latvia
Lcht.	Liechtenstein
Ldg.	Landing
Leb.	Lebanon
Les.	Lesotho
Libr.	Liberia
Lith.	Lithuania
Lux.	Luxembourg

M
Ma,US	Massachusetts
Madg.	Madagascar
Madr.	Madeira
Malay.	Malaysia
Mald.	Maldives
Malw.	Malawi
Mart.	Martinique
May.	Mayotte
Mb,Can	Manitoba
Md,US	Maryland
Me,US	Maine
Mem.	Memorial
Mex.	Mexico
Mi,US	Michigan
Micr.	Micronesia, Federated States of
Mil.	Military
Mn,US	Minnesota
Mo,US	Missouri
Mol.	Moldova
Mon.	Monument
Mona.	Monaco
Mong.	Mongolia
Monts.	Montserrat
Mor.	Morocco
Moz.	Mozambique
Mrsh.	Marshall Islands
Mrta.	Mauritania
Mrts.	Mauritius
Ms,US	Mississippi
Mt.	Mount
Mt,US	Montana
Mtn., Mts.	Mountain, Mountains
Mun. Arpt.	Municipal Airport
Myan.	Myanmar

N
NAm.	North America
Namb.	Namibia
NAnt.	Netherlands Antilles
Nat'l	National
Nav.	Naval
NB,Can	New Brunswick
Nbrhd.	Neighborhood
NC,US	North Carolina
NCal.	New Caledonia
ND,US	North Dakota
Ne,US	Nebraska
Neth.	Netherlands
Nf,Can	Newfoundland
Nga.	Nigeria
NH,US	New Hampshire
NI,UK	Northern Ireland
Nic.	Nicaragua
NJ,US	New Jersey
NKor.	North Korea
NM,US	New Mexico
NMar.	Northern Mariana Islands
Nor.	Norway
NS,Can	Nova Scotia
Nv,US	Nevada
Nun.,Can	Nunavut
NW,Can	Northwest Territories
NY,US	New York
NZ	New Zealand

O
Obl.	Oblast
Oh,US	Ohio
Ok,US	Oklahoma
On,Can	Ontario
Or,US	Oregon

P
Pa,US	Pennsylvania
PacUS	Pacific Islands, U.S.
Pak.	Pakistan
Pan.	Panama
Par.	Paraguay
Par.	Parish
PE,Can	Prince Edward Island
Pen.	Peninsula
Phil.	Philippines
Phys. Reg.	Physical Region
Pitc.	Pitcairn Islands
Plat.	Plateau
PNG	Papua New Guinea
Pol.	Poland
Port.	Portugal
Poss.	Possession
Pkwy.	Parkway
PR	Puerto Rico
Pref.	Prefecture
Prov.	Province
Prsv.	Preserve
Pt.	Point

Q
Qu,Can	Quebec

R
Rec.	Recreation(al)
Ref.	Refuge
Reg.	Region
Rep.	Republic
Res.	Reservoir, Reservation
Reun.	Réunion
RI,US	Rhode Island
Riv.	River
Rom.	Romania
Rsv.	Reserve
Rus.	Russia
Rvwy.	Riverway
Rwa.	Rwanda

S
SAfr.	South Africa
Sam.	Samoa
SAm.	South America
SaoT.	São Tomé and Príncipe
SAr.	Saudi Arabia
Sc,UK	Scotland
SC,US	South Carolina
SD,US	South Dakota
Seash.	Seashore
Sen.	Senegal
Sey.	Seychelles
SGeo.	South Georgia and Sandwich Islands
Sing.	Singapore
Sk,Can	Saskatchewan
SKor.	South Korea
SLeo.	Sierra Leone
Slov.	Slovenia
Slvk.	Slovakia
SMar.	San Marino
Sol.	Solomon Islands
Som.	Somalia
Sp.	Spain
Spr., Sprs.	Spring, Springs
SrL.	Sri Lanka
Sta.	Station
StH.	Saint Helena
Str.	Strait
StK.	Saint Kitts and Nevis
StL.	Saint Lucia
StP.	Saint Pierre and Miquelon
StV.	Saint Vincent and the Grenadines

(continued)
Sur.	Suriname
Sval.	Svalbard
Swaz.	Swaziland
Swe.	Sweden
Swi.	Switzerland

T
Tah.	Tahiti
Tai.	Taiwan
Taj.	Tajikistan
Tanz.	Tanzania
Ter.	Terrace
Terr.	Territory
Thai.	Thailand
Tn,US	Tennessee
Tok.	Tokelau
Trg.	Training
Trin.	Trinidad and Tobago
Trkm.	Turkmenistan
Trks.	Turks and Caicos Islands
Tun.	Tunisia
Tun.	Tunnel
Turk.	Turkey
Tuv.	Tuvalu
Twp.	Township
Tx,US	Texas

U
UAE	United Arab Emirates
Ugan.	Uganda
UK	United Kingdom
Ukr.	Ukraine
Uru.	Uruguay
US	United States
USVI	U.S. Virgin Islands
Ut,US	Utah
Uzb.	Uzbekistan

V
Va,US	Virginia
Val.	Valley
Van.	Vanuatu
VatC.	Vatican City
Ven.	Venezuela
Viet.	Vietnam
Vill.	Village
Vol.	Volcano
Vt,US	Vermont

W
Wa,US	Washington
Wal,UK	Wales
Wall.	Wallis and Futuna
WBnk.	West Bank
Wi,US	Wisconsin
Wild.	Wildlife, Wilderness
WSah.	Western Sahara
WV,US	West Virginia
Wy,US	Wyoming

Y
Yem.	Yemen
Yk,Can	Yukon Territory
Yugo.	Yugoslavia

Z
Zam.	Zambia
Zim.	Zimbabwe

A

100 Mile House, BC, Can. 126/C3
Aa (riv.), Ger. 50/D5
Aach (riv.), Ger. 57/F2
Aach, Ger. 57/E2
Aachen, Ger. 53/F2
Aalbach (riv.), Ger. 54/C3
Aalborg (int'l arpt.), Den. 38/C3
Aalburg, Neth. 50/C5
Aalen, Ger. 54/D5
Aalsmeer, Neth. 50/B4
Aalst, Belg. 52/D2
Aalten, Neth. 50/D5
Aalter, Belg. 52/C1
Aar (riv.), Ger. 53/H3
Aarau, Swi. 56/E3
Aarberg, Swi. 56/D3
Aarburg, Swi. 56/D3
Aardenburg, Neth. 52/C1
Aare (riv.), Swi. 43/H3
Aargau (canton), Swi. 57/E3
Aarred (lake), WSah. 98/B4
Aarschot, Belg. 53/D2
Aartselaar, Belg. 53/D1
Aarwangen, Swi. 56/D3
Aba, D.R. Congo 104/A2
Aba, China 70/H5
Aba, Nga. 103/G5
Abā as Su'ūd, SAr. 88/D5
Abacaxis (riv.), Braz. 150/G5
Abadab (peak), Sudan 101/C5
Ābādān, Iran 88/E2
Ābādeh, Iran 88/F2
Abadia dos Dourados, Braz. 155/C1
Abadla, Alg. 99/E3
Abádszalók, Hun. 48/E2
Abaeté, Braz. 155/C1
Abaetetuba, Braz. 151/J4
Abaiang (isl.), Kiri. 116/G4
Abakan, Rus. 64/K4
Abancay, Peru 156/C4
Abano Terme, It. 59/E2
Abar Kūh, Iran 88/F2
Abarán, Sp. 44/E3
Abashiri (lake), Japan 76/C2
Abashiri, Japan 76/D1
Abasolo, Mex. 143/E4
Abasolo, Mex. 143/F3
Abay, Kaz. 87/F3
Ābaya Hayk (lake) 97/N6
Abbadia Lariana, It. 57/F6
Abbadia San Salvatore, It. 43/J5
Abbeville, La, US 129/J5
Abbeville, SC, US 133/H3
Abbeville, Fr. 52/A3
Abbey (peak), Austl. 114/B1
Abbeyfeale, Ire. 31/P10
Abbeyleix, Ire. 31/Q10
Abbiategrasso, It. 58/B2
Abbot (mt.), Austl. 114/B3
Abbotsinch (int'l arpt.), Sc, UK 36/B5
Abbottābād, Pak. 86/B2
Abbottstown, Pa, US 138/B4
Abcoude, Neth. 50/B4
Abdul Hakīm, Pak. 86/B4
Abdulino, Rus. 63/K1
Abéché, Chad 97/K5
Abemama (isl.), Kiri. 116/G4
Abenberg, Ger. 54/D4
Abengourou, C.d'Iv. 102/E5
Åbenrå, Den. 38/C4
Abens (riv.), Ger. 40/F4
Abensberg, Ger. 55/E5
Abeokuta, Nga. 103/F5
Abercarn, Wal, UK 32/C3
Aberchirder, Sc, UK 36/D1
Aberdare, Wal, UK 32/C3
Aberdare NP, Kenya 104/C3
Aberdeen, Austl. 115/D2
Aberdeen, SD, US 127/J4
Aberdeen, Wa, US 126/C4
Aberdeen, Ms, US 133/F3
Aberdeen, SAfr. 106/D4
Aberdeen (lake), Nun., Can. 122/F2
Aberdeen, Md, US 138/B5
Aberdeen, Sc, UK 36/D2
Aberdeen (pol. reg.), Sc, UK 36/D2
Aberdeen Proving Ground, Md, US 138/B5
Aberdeenshire, Sc, UK 36/D2
Aberdeenshire (pol. reg.), Sc, UK 36/D2
Aberdour, Sc, UK 36/C4
Aberdour (bay), Sc, UK 36/D1
Aberfeldy, Sc, UK 36/C3
Aberfoyle, Sc, UK 36/B4
Abergavenny, Wal, UK 32/C3
Abergele, Wal, UK 34/E5
Aberlour, Sc, UK 36/C2
Abernethy, Sc, UK 36/C4
Abert (lake), Or, US 126/C5
Abertillery, Wal, UK 32/C3
Aberystwyth, Wal, UK 32/B2
Abhā, SAr. 88/D5
Abhar, Iran 88/E1
Abhayāpuri, India 85/H2
Abhe Bad (lake), Djib.,Eth 97/P5
Abia (prov.), Nga. 103/G5
Abidjan, C.d'Iv. 102/D5
Abiko, Japan 77/E2
Abilene, Tx, US 129/H4
Abilene, Ks, US 129/H3
Abingdon, Eng, UK 33/E3
Abingdon, Md, US 138/B5
Abington (reef), Austl. 114/C2
Abington, Sc, UK 36/C6
Abino (pt.), On, Can. 131/R10
Abiquiu, NM, US 132/B2
Abitibi (lake), On,Qu, Can. 123/H4
Abitibi (riv.), On, Can. 123/H4
Abkhazia Aut. Rep., Geo. 63/G4
Ableiges, Fr. 30/H4
Abnūb, Egypt 101/B3
Åbo (Turku), Fin. 39/K1
Abohar, India 86/C4
Aboisso, C.d'Iv. 102/E5
Abomey, Ben. 103/F5
Abondance, Fr. 56/C5
Abony, Hun. 48/D2
Aboyne, Sc, UK 36/D2
Abra (riv.), Phil. 79/D4
Abra Pampa, Arg. 157/C1
Abraham Gonzalez (int'l arpt.), Mex. 128/F5
Abrantes, Port. 44/A3
Abreojos (pt.), Mex. 142/B3
Abrud, Rom. 49/F2
Abruzzi (prov.), It. 43/K5
Abruzzo, PN de, It. 46/C2
Absam, Aus. 57/H3
Absaroka (range), Mt,Wy, US 126/F4
Absecon, NJ, US 138/D5
Abtsgmünd, Ger. 54/D5
Abu el-Husein (well), Egypt 101/B4
Abū Ḩammād, Egypt 91/B4
Abu Hashim (well), Egypt 101/C4
Abū Ḩummuş, Egypt 91/B4
Abū Kabīr, Egypt 91/B4
Abū Kamāl, Syria 90/E3
Abū Qashsh, WBnk. 91/G8
Abu Shagara (cape), Sudan 101/D4
Abu Simbel (ruin), Egypt 101/B4
Abū Z̧aby (Abu Dhabi) (cap.), UAE 89/F4
Abuja (cap.), Nga. 103/G4
Abuja (int'l arpt.), Nga. 103/G4
Abuja Capital Territory, Nga. 103/G4
Abukuma (riv.), Japan 75/G2
Abukuma (plat.), Japan 75/G2
Abulog, Phil. 79/D4
Abunã (riv.), Braz. 150/E6
Abuta, Japan 76/B2
Ābuyē Mēda (peak), Eth. 97/N5
Abuyog, Phil. 79/E5
Åby, Swe. 38/G2
Åbybro, Den. 38/C3
Abydos (ruin), Egypt 101/B3
Acacías, Col. 152/C4
Acacoyagua, Mex. 144/C3
Acadia NP, Me, US 131/G2
Acadian Village, La, US 129/J5
Acajutiba, Braz. 154/C3
Acámbaro, Mex. 143/E4
Acampo, Ca, US 135/M10
Acandí, Col. 152/B2
Acaponeta (riv.), Mex. 142/D4
Acaponeta, Mex. 142/D4
Acapulco de Juárez, Mex. 140/B4
Acaraí (mts.), Braz.,Guy. 153/G4
Acaraí, Serra (mts.), Braz. 150/G3
Acaraú (riv.), Braz. 154/B1
Acaraú, Braz. 154/B1
Acari (riv.), Braz. 150/G5
Acari, Braz. 154/C2
Acarí, Peru 156/C4
Acarigua, Ven. 152/D2
Acatlán de Osorio, Mex. 144/B2
Acatlán de Pérez Figueroa, Mex. 143/N8
Acatzingo, Mex. 143/M7
Acayucan, Mex. 144/C2
Accha, Peru 156/D4
Acciaroli, It. 46/D2
Accra (cap.), Gha. 103/E5
Accrington, Eng, UK 35/F4
Aceuchal, Sp. 44/B3
Ach (riv.), Aus. 55/G6
Achacachi, Bol. 150/E7
Achaguas, Ven. 152/D3
Achao, Chile 158/B4
Achar, Uru. 159/K10
Achegour (well), Niger 96/H4
Achen (pass), Ger. 57/H2
Acheng, China 71/N2
Achères, Fr. 30/J5
Achhnera, India 84/A2
Achicourt, Fr. 52/B3
Achill (isl.), Ire. 30/N10
Achill Head (pt.), Ire. 30/N9
Achiltibuie, Sc, UK 31/R7
Achinsk, Rus. 64/K4
Achmîm (well), Mrta. 102/D2
Achnasheen, Sc, UK 36/A1
Achoma, Peru 156/D4
A'chràlaig (peak), Sc, UK 36/A2
Achuapa, Nic. 144/E3
Achupallas, Ecu. 156/B1
Acireale, It. 46/D4
Acklins (isl.), Bahm. 141/G3
Acland (mt.), Austl. 114/C4
Acobamba, Peru 156/C4
Acolla, Peru 156/C3
Acolman, Mex. 143/R9
Acomayo, Peru 156/D4
Acomayo, Peru 156/B3
Aconcagua (peak), Arg. 158/C2
Aconchi, Mex. 142/C2
Acopiara, Braz. 154/C2
Acora, Peru 156/D4
Acqualagna, It. 59/F5
Acquanegra sul Chiese, It. 58/D2
Acquapendente, It. 46/B1
Acqui Terme, It. 58/B3
Acraman (lake), Austl. 113/G5
Acrata (pt.), Alg. 100/G4
Acre (riv.), Braz. 150/E6
Acre (state), Braz. 156/D3
Acreúna, Braz. 155/B1
Acropolis, Gre. 47/N9
Actaeon Group (isls.), FrPol. 117/M7
Acton, Ca, US 136/B2
Actopan, Mex. 143/N7
Actopan, Mex. 143/L6
Açu, Braz. 154/C2
Açude Aratas (res.), Braz. 154/B2
Açude Banabuiu (res.), Braz. 154/C2
Acula, Mex. 143/P8
Aculeo (lag.), Chile 158/N8
Acy-en-Multien, Fr. 30/L4
Ad Dahnā' (des.), SAr. 88/D3
Ad-Dakhla, WSah. 98/B5
Ad Damazin, Sudan 97/M5
Ad Damīr, Sudan 88/B5
Ad Dammām, SAr. 88/F3
Ad Daqahlīyah (gov.), Egypt 101/B1
Ad Dilinjāt, Egypt 91/B4
Ad Dīwānīyah, Iraq 90/F4
Ad Dujayl, Iraq 90/F3
Ad Duwaym, Sudan 97/M5
Ada, Ok, US 129/H4
Ada, Oh, US 130/D3
Ada, Gha. 103/F5
Ada, Yugo. 48/E3
Adainville, Fr. 30/G5
Adair (cape), Nun., Can. 123/J1
Adair, Bahia del (bay), Mex. 128/D5
Adaja (riv.), Sp. 44/C2
Adak (str.), Ak, US 134/C6
Adak (isl.), Ak, US 65/U4
Adam (mt.), UK 159/E6
Adamantina, Braz. 155/B2
Adamaoua (plat.), Camr.,Nga. 93/D4
Adamello (peak), It. 57/G5
Adaminaby, Austl. 115/D3
Adams (lake), BC, Can. 126/D3
Adams (mt.), Wa, US 126/C4
Adams (co.), Co, US 137/C3
Adams (co.), Pa, US 138/A4
Adamstown (cap.), Pitc. 117/M7
Adamstown, Pa, US 138/B3
Adamwa (plat.), Nga. 103/H5
'Adan, Yem. 88/D6
Adana (prov.), Turk. 90/C2
Adana, Turk. 91/D1
Adana (int'l arpt.), Turk. 91/D1
Adapazarı, Turk. 49/K5
Adare, Ire. 31/P10
Adare (cape), Ant. 160/M
Adarza (peak), Fr. 44/E1
Add (riv.), Sc, UK 36/A4
Adda (riv.), It. 43/J4
Addison, Il, US 135/P16
Addlestone, Eng, UK 30/B2
Addo Elephant NP, SAfr. 106/D4
Adekeieh (Ādī K'eyih), Erit. 88/C6
Adelaide, SAfr. 106/D4
Adelaide (pen.), Nun., Can. 122/G2
Adelaide (int'l arpt.), Austl. 113/M8
Adelaide, Austl. 113/M8
Adelaide Zoo, Austl. 113/M8
Adelanto, Ca, US 136/C1
Adelebsen, Ger. 51/G5
Adelheidsdorf, Ger. 51/H3
Adelmannsfelden, Ger. 54/D5
Adelong, Austl. 115/D2
Adelschlag, Ger. 54/E5
Adelsheim, Ger. 54/C4
Adelsried, Ger. 54/D6
Aden (gulf), Afr.,Asia 67/D8
Adenau, Ger. 53/F3
Adendorf, Ger. 51/H2
Adh Dhirā', Jor. 91/D4
Adi (isl.), Indo. 81/H4
Ādī Ugrī, Erit. 88/C6
Adieu (cape), Austl. 113/G5
Adige (riv.), It. 43/J4
Adige (Etsch) (riv.), It. 57/G4
Ādīgrat, Eth. 88/C6
Adilābād, India 82/C4
Adilcevaz, Turk. 90/E2
Adiora (well), Mali 103/E2
Adirondack (mts.), NY, US 125/L3
Ādīs Ābeba (Addis Ababa) (cap.), Eth. 97/N6
Adiyaman, Turk. 90/D2
Adiyaman (prov.), Turk. 90/D2
Adjud, Rom. 49/H2
Adjuntas, Presa de la (res.), Mex. 143/F4
Adler/Sochi (int'l arpt.), Rus. 62/F4
Adliswil, Swi. 57/E3
Admiralty (inlet), Nun., Can. 123/H1
Admiralty (isl.), Ak, US 122/C3
Admiralty Island Nat'l Mon., Ak, US 134/M4
Admiralty (isls.), PNG 116/D5
Admiralty (inlet), Wa, US 135/B2
Adnan Menderes (int'l arpt.), Turk. 62/C5
Ado (riv.), Japan 77/J5
Ado Ekiti, Nga. 103/G5
Ado Odo, Nga. 103/F5
Adogawa, Japan 77/K5
Adolfo López Mateos, Mex. 142/B3
Ādoni, India 82/C4
Adour (riv.), Fr. 42/C5
Adra, India 85/F4
Adra, Sp. 44/D4
Adrano, It. 46/D4
Adrar (phys. reg.), Mrta. 96/C3
Adrar, Alg. 99/E4
Adrar (pol. reg.), Mrta. 102/C1
Adrar (prov.), Alg. 99/E4
Adrar (reg.), Mrta. 98/C5
Adrar bou Nasser (peak), Mor. 98/E2
Adrar Sotuf (mts.), WSah. 98/B5
Adria, It. 59/F2
Adrian, Mi, US 130/C3
Adriatic (sea), Eur. 27/F4
Adro, It. 58/C1
Aduana del Sásabe, Mex. 128/E5
Adulis (ruin), Erit. 88/C5
Adur (riv.), Eng, UK 33/F5
Ādwa, Eth. 88/C6
Adwick le Street, Eng, UK 35/G4
Adycha (riv.), Rus. 65/P3
Adygea (aut. rep.), Rus. 62/F3
Adz'va (riv.), Rus. 61/P2
Aegean (sea), Gre.,Turk 62/C5
Aerø (isl.), Den. 38/D4
Aeron (riv.), Wal, UK 32/B2
Aesch, Swi. 56/D3
Aeschi bei Spiez, Swi. 56/D4
Äetsä, Fin. 39/K1
Afadjoto (peak), Gha. 103/F5
'Afak, Iraq 88/E2
Afándou, Gre. 90/B2
Aff (riv.), Fr. 42/B3
Affoltern im Emmental, Swi. 56/D3
Affric (lake), Sc, UK 36/A2
Affton, Mo, US 137/G8
Afghanistan (ctry.) 89/H2
Afmadow, Som. 97/P7
Afogados da Ingàzeira, Braz. 154/C2
Afognak (mtn.), Ak, US 134/H4
Afognak (isl.), Ak, US 134/H4
Afollé, Massif de (phys. reg.), Mrta. 102/C2
Afonso Bezerra, Braz. 154/C2
Afonso Cláudio, Braz. 155/D2
Afragola, It. 46/D2
Afrânio, Braz. 154/B3
Africa (cont.) 93
Afrin (riv.), Turk. 91/E1
'Afrīn, Syria 91/E1
Afrique (peak), Fr. 56/A3
Afsluitdijk (dam), Neth. 50/C2
Afte (riv.), Ger. 51/F5
Afton, Wy, US 126/F5
Afuidich (lake), WSah. 98/B5
'Afula, Isr. 91/G6
Afyon, Turk. 62/D5
Afyon (prov.), Turk. 62/D5
Afzalgarh, India 84/B1
Agadem (well), Niger 96/H5
Agades (int'l arpt.), Niger 103/G2
Agadez, Niger 103/G2
Agadez (dept.), Niger 99/H5
Agadir, Mor. 98/C3
Agago (riv.), Ugan. 104/B2
Agamor (well), Mali 103/F2
Agano (riv.), Japan 75/F2
Agassiz Ice Cap (ice field), Nun., Can. 123/T6
Agattu (str.), Ak, US 134/A5
Agattu (isl.), Ak, US 65/T4
Agbabu, Nga. 103/G5
Agboville, C.d'Iv. 102/D5
Ağdam, Azer. 63/H5
Agde, Fr. 42/E5
Agen, Fr. 42/D4
Ageo, Japan 77/D2
Ager (riv.), Aus. 55/G7
Agerbæk, Den. 38/C4
Agerisee (lake), Swi. 57/E3
Agger (riv.), Ger. 53/G1
Aggteleki NP, Slvk. 48/E1
Āghā Jārī, Iran 88/E2
Aghagallon, NI, UK 34/B3
Aghagower, Ire. 31/P10
Agiabampo, Mex. 142/C3
Aginskiy Buryatskiy (aut. okrug), Rus. 65/Q7
Aginskoye, Rus. 71/K1
Agliana, It. 59/D5
Ağlıköy, Turk. 62/E4
Agly (riv.), Fr. 42/E5
Agna, It. 59/E2
Agnanderón, Gre. 47/G3
Agnita, Rom. 49/G3
Agno (riv.), It. 59/E1
Agno (int'l arpt.), Swi. 57/E6
Agnone, It. 46/D2
Ago, Japan 77/L7
Agogna (riv.), It. 43/H4
Agordo, It. 43/K3
Agout (riv.), Fr. 42/D5
Āgra, India 84/B2
Agraciada, Uru. 159/J10
Agrado, Col. 152/C4
Āgreda, Sp. 44/E2
Ağrı (peak), Turk. 63/H5
Ağrı (prov.), Turk. 63/G5
Agriá, Gre. 47/H3
Agrigento, It. 46/C4
Agrihan (isl.), NMar. 116/D3
Agrínion, Gre. 47/G3
Agrio (riv.), Arg. 158/C3
Agropoli, It. 46/D2
Agryz, Rus. 61/M4
Agsumal (dry lake), WSah. 98/B4
Água Boa, Braz. 154/B5
Água Branca, Braz. 154/B2
Agua Dulce, Ca, US 136/B2
Agua Dulce, Mex. 144/C2
Agua Fria (riv.), Az, US 137/R19
Agua Hedionda (lake), Ca, US 136/C4
Agua Larga, Ven. 152/D2
Agua Prieta, Mex. 128/E5
Aguachica, Col. 152/C2
Aguadilla, PR 141/M8
Aguadulce, Pan. 152/A2
Aguaí, Braz. 211/G7
Agualva-Cacém, Port. 45/P10
Aguan (riv.), Hon. 140/D4
Aguanus (riv.), Qu, Can. 131/J1
Aguapeí (riv.), Braz. 155/B2
Aguarico (riv.), Peru 152/B5
Águas Belas, Braz. 154/C3
Águas Corrientes, Uru. 159/K11
Águas da Prata, Braz. 211/G6
Águas de Lindóia, Braz. 211/G7
Águas Formosas, Braz. 154/B5
Águas, Serra das (hills), Braz. 211/H7
Aguasay, Ven. 153/F2
Aguascalientes, Mex. 142/E4
Aguascalientes (state), Mex. 140/A3
Águavermelha, Represa (res.), Braz. 155/B1
Aguaytía (riv.), Peru 156/C3
Agudos, Braz. 155/B2
Agueda (riv.), Sp. 44/B2
Águeda, Port. 44/A2
Aguêraktem (well), Mali 98/D5
Agugliano, It. 59/G5
Agui, Japan 77/L6
Aguijan (isl.), NMar. 116/D3
Aguilar, Sp. 44/C4
Aguilar de Campóo, Sp. 44/C1
Aguilares, Arg. 157/C2
Aguilas, Sp. 44/E4
Aguililla, Mex. 142/E5
Aguja (pt.), Peru 156/A2
Agulhas (cape), SAfr. 106/M11
Agulhas Negras, Pico das (peak), Braz. 211/J7
Agung (vol.), Indo. 81/E5
Agusan (riv.), Phil. 79/E6
Agustín Codazzi, Col. 152/C2
Ahaggar (plat.), Alg. 96/F3
Ahaggar (mts.), Alg. 99/G5
Ahal (pol. reg.), Trkm. 87/C5
Aham, Ger. 55/F5
Ahar, Iran 63/H5
Ahaus, Ger. 50/E4
Ahfir, Mor. 100/C2
Ahlat, Turk. 90/E2
Ahlen, Ger. 51/E5
Ahlerstedt, Ger. 51/G2
Ahmadābād, India 89/K4
Ahmadpur East, Pak. 86/A5
Ahmadpur Siāl, Pak. 86/A4
Ahmar (mts.), Eth. 97/P6
Ahmar, 'Erg el (des.), Mali 98/D4
Ahmed (well), WSah. 98/B5
Ahmeyine (well), Mrta. 98/B5
Ahoghill, NI, UK 34/B2
Ahome, Mex. 142/C3
Ahr (riv.), Ger. 43/G1
Ahraura, India 84/D3
Ahrensburg, Ger. 51/H1
Ahse (riv.), Ger. 51/F5
Ahuacatlán, Mex. 143/K8
Ahuacatlán, Mex. 142/D4
Ahuachapán, ESal. 144/D3
Ahualulco, Mex. 143/E4
Ahuimanu, Hi, US 124/W13
Ahumada, Mex. 128/F5
Ahun, Fr. 42/E3
Åhus, Swe. 38/F4
Ahvāz, Iran 88/E2
Ahvenanmaa (prov.), Fin. 37/F4
Ai (riv.), China 73/C2
Ai (mtn.), China 72/E3
Ai-Ais Hot Springs, Namb. 106/B2
Ai-shima (isl.), Japan 74/B3
Aibag Gol (riv.), China 72/B2
Aichach, Ger. 54/E6
Aichi (pref.), Japan 75/E3
Aidhausen, Ger. 54/D2
Aidlingen, Ger. 54/B5
Aiea, Hi, US 124/W13
Aiello del Friuli, It. 59/G1
Aiffres, Fr. 42/C3
Aigen im Mühlkreis, Aus. 55/G5
Aigle, Pic de l' (peak), Fr. 56/B4
Aiglemont, Fr. 53/D4
Aigoual (peak), Fr. 42/E4
Aiguá, Uru. 159/G2
Aigues (riv.), Fr. 42/F4
Aigües Tortes y Lago de San Mauricio, PN de, Sp. 45/F1
Aiguille, Cap de l' (cape), Alg. 100/E5
Aiguillon, Fr. 42/D4
Aikawa, Japan 75/F1
Aikawa, Japan 77/C2
Aiken, SC, US 133/H3
Ailigandí, Pan. 152/B2
Ailinglapalap (isl.), Mrsh. 116/F4
Aillevillers-et-Lyaumont, Fr. 56/C2
Ailly-sur-Noye, Fr. 52/B4
Ailsa Craig (isl.), Sc, UK 36/A6
Ailuk (isl.), Mrsh. 116/G3
Aimen (pass), China 72/C5
Aimogasta, Arg. 157/C2
Aimorés, Braz. 155/D1
Aimorés, Serra dos (mts.), Braz. 155/D1
Ain (riv.), Fr. 42/F4
'Aïn Beïda, Alg. 100/K7
'Aïn Beniau, Alg. 100/G4
'Aïn Bessem, Alg. 100/G4
Aïn Chok-Hay Mohammadia (prov.), Mor. 100/A2
'Aïn Defla, Alg. 100/F4
'Aïn Defla (prov.), Alg. 100/F4
Aïn el Aouda, Mor. 100/A3
'Aïn el Bey (int'l arpt.), Alg. 100/K6
'Aïn el Hammam, Alg. 100/H4
'Aïn el Turk, Alg. 100/D2
'Aïn Fakroun, Alg. 100/K6
'Aïn M'lila, Alg. 100/K6
'Aïn Oulmene, Alg. 100/H5
'Aïn Oussersa, Alg. 100/G5
'Aïn Sefra, Alg. 99/E2
Aïn Taoujdat, Mor. 100/B3
'Aïn Taya, Alg. 100/G4
'Aïn Temouchent, Alg. 100/D2
'Aïn Touta, Alg. 100/H5
Aina Haina, Hi, US 124/W13
Aincourt, Fr. 30/H4
Aínos (peak), Gre. 47/G3
Aínos NP, Gre. 47/G3
Aipe, Col. 152/C4
Aïr (plat.), Niger 96/G4
Air Force (isl.), Nun., Can. 123/J2
Airaines, Fr. 52/A4
Airdrie, Ab, Can. 126/E3
Airdrie, Sc, UK 36/C5
Aire (riv.), Fr. 42/F2
Aire, Canal d' (canal), Fr. 52/B2
Aire-sur-la-Lys, Fr. 52/B2
Aire-sur-l'Adour, Fr. 42/C5
Airolo, Swi. 57/E4
Airvault, Fr. 42/C3
Aisch (riv.), Ger. 43/J2
Aiseau-Presles, Belg. 53/D3
Aisén del General Carlos Ibáñez del Campo (pol. reg.), Chile 158/B5
Aisne (riv.), Fr. 40/B4
Aïssa (peak), Alg. 99/E2
Aist (riv.), Aus. 55/H6
Aït Ourir, Mor. 98/D3
Aitape, PNG 116/D5
Aitō, Japan 77/K5
Aitolikón, Gre. 47/G3
Aitrach, Ger. 57/G2
Aitrang, Ger. 57/G2
Aitutaki Atoll (isl.), Cookls. 117/J6
Aiud, Rom. 49/F2
Aiuruoca, Braz. 211/J6
Aiuruoca (riv.), Braz. 211/J7
Aix-en-Provence, Fr. 42/F5
Aiyina, Gre. 47/H4
Aiyínion, Gre. 47/H2
Aiyion, Gre. 47/H3
Aīzawl, India 83/F3
Aizu-Wakamatsu, Japan 75/F2
Ajaccio, Fr. 46/A2
Ajaccio, Golfe d' (gulf), It. 46/A2
Ajaigarh, India 84/C3
Ajalpan, Mex. 143/M8
Ajaria Aut. Rep., Geo. 63/G4
Ajax, On, Can. 131/R8
Ajay (riv.), India 85/F3
Ajdābiyā, Libya 97/K1
Ajdovščina, Slov. 43/K4
Ajigasawa, Japan 76/B3
'Ajjah, WBnk. 91/G7
Ajka, Hun. 48/C2
Ajo, Az, US 128/D4
Ajo (cape), Sp. 44/D1
Ajuchitlán del Progreso, Mex. 140/A4
Ajusco (vol.), Mex. 143/Q10
Aka (riv.), Japan 75/F1
Akabane, Japan 77/M6
Akabira, Japan 76/C2
Akaishi-dake (peak), Japan 75/F3
Akaltara, India 84/D4
Akan (lake), Japan 76/D2
Akan NP, Japan 76/D2
Åkarp, Swe. 38/E4
Akarsu, Turk. 62/F5
Akashi (str.), Japan 77/G6
Akashi, Japan 77/G6
Akbarpur, India 84/D2
Akbarpur, India 84/B2
Akbaytal (pass), Taj. 87/F5
Akbou, Alg. 100/H4
Akçaabat, Turk. 62/F4
Akçakale, Turk. 90/D2
Akçakoca, Turk. 49/K5
Akçaova, Turk. 49/J5
Akçapınar, Turk. 90/D2
Akçay, Turk. 91/A1
Akchâr (riv.), Mrta. 96/B4
Akchâr (phys. reg.), Mrta. 98/B5
Akdağmadeni, Turk. 62/E5
Akechi, Japan 77/M5
Akeno, Japan 77/E1
Akeno, Japan 77/A2
Åkersberga, Swe. 38/H2
Akershus (co.), Nor. 37/D3
Aketi, D.R. Congo 97/K7
Akhalts'ikhe, Geo. 63/G4
Akharnaí, Gre. 47/N8
Akhelóos (riv.), Gre. 47/G3
Akhiok, Ak, US 134/H4
Akhisar, Turk. 62/C5
Akhnūr, India 86/C3
Akhtopol, Bul. 49/H4
Akhtuba (riv.), Rus. 63/H3
Akhtubinsk, Rus. 63/H2
Aki, Japan 74/C4
Aki (riv.), Japan 77/C2
Akiachak, Ak, US 134/F3
Akigawa, Japan 77/C2
Akimiski (isl.), On, Can. 123/H3
Akıncı (pt.), Turk. 91/D1
Akıncılar, Turk. 62/F4
Åkirkeby, Den. 38/F4
Akishima, Japan 77/C2
Akita (pref.), Japan 76/B4
Akita, Japan 76/B4
Akiyama, Japan 77/C2
Akjoujt, Mrta. 102/B2
Akka, Mor. 98/C3
Akkaraipattu, SrL. 82/D6
Akkerhaugen, Nor. 38/C2
Akkeshi, Japan 76/D2
'Akko, Isr. 91/D3
Akkrum, Neth. 50/C2
Aklavik, NW, Can. 134/L2
Akō, Japan 74/D3
Akora, Pak. 86/B2
Āk'ordat, Erit. 88/C5
Akören, Turk. 90/C2
Akosombo (dam), Gha. 103/F5
Akpatok (isl.), Qu, Can. 123/K2
Akpınar, Turk. 49/J5
Akqi, China 87/G3
Akranes, Ice. 37/M7
Åkrathos (cape), Gre. 47/J2
Åkrehamn, Nor. 38/A2
Akrítas (cape), Gre. 47/G4
Akron, Co, US 129/G2
Akron, Oh, US 130/D3
Akron, Pa, US 138/B3
Aksai Chin (reg.), China,India 70/C4
Aksaray, Turk. 90/C2
Aksaray (prov.), Turk. 90/C2
Aksay Kazakzu Zizhixian, China 70/F4
Akşehir, Turk. 90/B2
Akşehir Lake (lake), Turk. 90/B2
Akseki, Turk. 91/B1
Aksoran (peak), Kaz. 87/G3
Aksu, China 70/D3
Aksu (riv.), Turk. 91/B1
Aksu, Turk. 91/B1
Āksum, Eth. 88/C6
Aktepe, Turk. 91/E1
Aktí (pen.), Gre. 62/C4
Akto, China 87/G5
Akune, Japan 74/B4
Akure, Nga. 103/G5
Akureyri, Ice. 37/N6
Akuse, Gha. 103/F5
Akutan (isl.), Ak, US 134/E5
Akutan, Ak, US 134/E5
Akutan Pass (chan.), Ak, US 134/E5
Akwa Ibom (state), Nga. 103/G5
Akyab (Sittwe), Myan. 83/F3
Akyazı, Turk. 49/K5
Ål, Nor. 38/C1
Al 'āl, Jor. 91/D4
Al 'Amārah, Iraq 88/E2
Al Anbār (gov.), Iraq 90/E3
Al 'Aqabah, Jor. 91/D5
Al 'Arīsh, Egypt 91/C4
Al 'Ayn, UAE 89/G4
Al 'Azīzīyah, Libya 96/H1
Al 'Azīzīyah, Iraq 90/F3
Al Bāb, Syria 90/D2
Al Badrashayn, Egypt 91/B5
Al Baḩr Al Aḩmar (gov.), Egypt 101/C3
Al Bājūr, Egypt 91/B4
Al Balqā' (gov.), Jor. 91/D4
Al Balyanā, Egypt 101/B3
Al Başrah, Iraq 88/E2
Al Batrūn, Leb. 91/D2
Al Baydā, Libya 97/K1
Al Biqā' (valley), Leb. 91/D3
Al Biqā' (gov.), Leb. 91/E2
Al Bīrah, WBnk. 91/G8
Al Birkah, Libya 99/H4
Al Buḩayrah (gov.), Egypt 101/B2
Al Fāsher, Sudan 97/L5
Al Fatḩah, Iraq 90/E3
Al Fāw, Iraq 88/E3
Al Fayyūm (gov.), Egypt 101/B1
Al Fayyum, Egypt 91/B5
Al Ghurdaqah, Egypt 101/C3
Al Ḩadīthah, Iraq 90/E3
Al Ḩaḑr, Iraq 90/E3
Al Ḩaffah, Syria 91/E2
Al Ḩajar ash Sharqī (mts.), Oman 89/G4
Al Hamādah al Ḩamrā (upland), Libya 96/H2
Al Ḩammāmāt, Tun. 46/B4
Al Ḩasakah, Syria 90/E2
Al Ḩasakah (prov.), Syria 90/E2
Al Ḩawāmidīyah, Egypt 91/B5
Al Ḩayy, Iraq 88/E2
Al Ḩillah, Iraq 88/E2
Al Hindīyah, Iraq 90/F3
Al Hirmil, Leb. 91/E2
Al Hoceima (prov.), Mor. 100/B2
Al Hoceima, Mor. 100/C2
Al Ḩudaydah, Yem. 88/D6
Al Hufūf, SAr. 88/E3
Al Iskandarīyah, Iraq 90/F3
Al Iskandarīyah, Egypt 91/A4
Al Iskandarīyah (gov.), Egypt 101/B1
Al Ismā'īlīyah, Egypt 91/C4
Al Ismā'īlīyah (gov.), Egypt 91/C4
Al Jabal Akaur (mts.), Oman 89/G4
Al Jaghbūb, Libya 97/K2
Al Jamm, Tun. 46/B5
Al Janub (gov.), Leb. 91/D3
Al Jifārah (plain), Libya 99/H2
Al Jīzah, Egypt 91/B4
Al Junaynah, Sudan 97/K5
Al Kāf, Tun. 100/L6
Al Kāf (gov.), Tun. 100/L6
Al Karak (gov.), Jor. 91/D4
Al Karak, Jor. 91/D4
Al Khābūrah, Oman 89/G4
Al Khalīl (Hebron), WBnk. 91/D4
Al Khāliş, Iraq 90/F3
Al Khānkah, Egypt 91/B4
Al Khārijah, Egypt 101/B3
Al Kharţūm Baḩrī (Khartoum North), Sudan 97/M4
Al Khubar, SAr. 88/F3
Al Khums, Libya 96/H1
Al Kiswah, Syria 91/E3
Al Kūfah, Iraq 90/F3
Al Kufrah, Libya 97/K3
Al Lādhiqīyah (prov.), Syria 90/C3
Al Lādhiqīyah (Latakia), Syria 91/D2
Al Madīnah, SAr. 88/C4
Al Madīnah al Fikrīyah, Egypt 88/B3
Al Mafraq (gov.), Jor. 91/E3
Al Mafraq, Jor. 91/E3
Al Maghrib (reg.), Mor. 96/E1
Al Maḩallah al Kubrá, Egypt 91/B4
Al Mahdīyah, Tun. 46/B5

Al Mahdīyah (prov.), Tun. 100/M7
Al Maḩmūdīyah, Egypt 91/B4
Al Mālikīyah, Syria 90/E2
Al Manşūrah, Egypt 91/B4
Al Manzilah, Egypt 91/B4
Al Marāghah, Egypt 101/B3
Al Marj, Libya 97/K1
Al Marsá, Tun. 46/B4
Al Maţarīyah, Egypt 91/C4
Al Mawşil (Mosul), Iraq 90/E2
Al Mayādin, Syria 90/E3
Al Mazra'ah, Jor. 91/D4
Al Minyā (gov.), Egypt 101/B2
Al Miqdādīyah, Iraq 90/F3
Al Mubarraz, SAr. 88/E4
Al Mudawwarah, Jor. 91/D5
Al Mukallā, Yem. 88/E6
Al Muknīn, Tun. 46/B5
Al Munastīr, Tun. 46/B5
Al Munastīr (prov.), Alg. 100/M7
Al Murnāqīyah, Tun. 46/B4
Al Musayyib, Iraq 90/F3
Al Muthanná (gov.), Iraq 90/F4
Al Qābil, Oman 89/G4
Al Qaḑārif, Sudan 88/C6
Al Qādisīyah (gov.), Iraq 90/F4
Al Qāhirah (gov.), Egypt 101/B1
Al Qāhirah (Cairo) (cap.), Egypt 91/B5
Al Qā'im, Iraq 90/E3
Al Qāmishlī, Syria 90/E2
Al Qanāţir al Khayrīyah, Egypt 91/B4
Al Qantarah, Egypt 91/C4
Al Qaşr, Jor. 91/D4
Al Qaşrayn (gov.), Tun. 100/L7
Al Qaşrayn, Tun. 100/L7
Al Qayrawān, Tun. 46/B5
Al Qayrawān (gov.), Tun. 46/A5
Al Qunayţirah (prov.), Syria 91/D3
Al Qunayţirah, Syria 91/D3
Al Qurnah, Iraq 88/E2
Al Quşayr, Syria 91/E2
Al Quţayfah, Syria 91/E3
Al Quwayrah, Jor. 91/D5
Al Ubayyiḑ, Sudan 97/M5
Al 'Uwaynāt (peak), Sudan 97/L3
Al Wādī Al Jadīd (gov.), Egypt 101/B3
Al Wāḩāt al Baḩrīyah (oasis), Egypt 101/B2
Al Wāḩāt al Khārijah (oasis), Egypt 101/B3
Al Wāsiţah, Egypt 91/B5
Al Yāmūn, WBnk. 91/G7
Ala (pt.), It. 46/B1
Ala, It. 59/E1
Alabama (riv.), Al,Ga, US 133/G4
Alabama (state), US 133/G3
Alabaster, Al, US 133/G3
Alaca, Turk. 62/E4
Alacalı, Turk. 49/J5
Alaçam, Turk. 62/E4
Alaçatı, Turk. 47/K3
Alachua, Fl, US 133/H4
Alacrán (reef), Mex. 144/D1
Alacranes (res.), Cuba 145/F1
Aladağ, Turk. 91/C1
Alaejos, Sp. 44/C2
Alagir, Rus. 63/H4
Alagna Valsesia, It. 58/A1
Alagnon (riv.), Fr. 42/E4
Alagoa Grande, Braz. 154/D2
Alagoas (state), Braz. 154/C3
Alagoinhas, Braz. 154/C4
Alagón (riv.), Sp. 44/C2
Alagón, Sp. 45/E2
Alajärvi, Fin. 60/D3
Alajuela, CR 145/E4
Alakanuk, Ak, US 134/F3
Alakol' (lake), Kaz. 70/D2
Alakol (lake), Kaz. 64/J5
Alalaú (riv.), Braz. 153/F5
Alamagan (isl.), NMar. 116/D3
'Alāmarvdasht (riv.), Iran 88/F3
Alameda, Ca, US 135/K11
Alaminos, Phil. 79/C4
Alamo (lake), Az, US 128/D4
Alamo, Mex. 144/B1
Alamo, Ca, US 135/K11
Alamo Heights, Tx, US 137/U21
Alamogordo, NM, US 129/F4
Alamor, Ecu. 156/A2
Álamos, Mex. 142/C3
Åland (isl.), Fin. 37/G3
Aland (riv.), Ger. 40/F2
Alanya, Turk. 91/C1
Alaotra (lake), Madg. 107/J7
Alapaha (riv.), Fl,Ga, US 133/H4
Alaplı, Turk. 49/K5
Alarcón, Embalse de (res.), Sp. 44/D3
Alaşehir, Turk. 90/B2
Alaska (state), US 134/G2
Alaska (range), Ak, US 134/G4
Alaska (pen.), Ak, US 134/G4
Alaska, Gulf of (gulf), Ak, US 134/J4
Alaska Maritime NWR, Ak, US 134/D3
Alaska Peninsula NWR, US 134/G4
Alassio, It. 58/B5
Alatyr', Rus. 61/K5
Alaverdi, Arm. 63/H4
Alavus, Fin. 60/D3
Alaw (riv.), Wal, UK 34/D5
Alaw, Llyn (lake), Wal, UK 34/D5
Alayor, Sp. 44/C3
Alayskiy (mts.), Kyr. 87/F5
Alazeya (riv.), Rus. 65/R3
Alb (riv.), Ger. 54/B5
Alba, It. 43/H4
Alba (prov.), Rom. 49/F2
Alba de Tormes, Sp. 44/C2
Alba Fucens (ruin), It. 46/C1
Alba Iulia, Rom. 49/F2
Albacete, Sp. 44/E3
Albaida, Sp. 45/E3
Albairate, It. 58/B2
Albæk, Den. 38/D3
Albalate del Arzobispo, Sp. 45/E2
Alban, Fr. 42/E5
Albanel (lake), Qu, Can. 130/F1
Albania (ctry.) 75/F2
Albany, Or, US 126/C4
Albany, Ky, US 130/C4
Albany (cap.), NY, US 130/F3
Albany, Ga, US 133/G4
Albany, Mo, US 137/E5
Albany, Austl. 112/C5
Albany (riv.), On, Can. 122/H3
Albany, Ca, US 135/K11
Albany County (int'l arpt.), NY, US 130/F3
Albaredo d'Adige, It. 59/E2
Albarine (riv.), Fr. 56/B5
Albarracín, Sp. 44/E2
Albatross (bay), Austl. 109/D2
Albatross Rock (pt.), Namb. 106/A2
Albbruck, Ger. 56/E2
Albemarle (sound), NC, US 133/J2
Albemarle, NC, US 133/H3
Albemarle (pt.), Ecu. 156/E6
Alben (peak), It. 43/H4
Albenga, It. 58/B4
Alberche (riv.), Sp. 44/C2
Alberhill, Ca, US 136/C3
Alberndorf in der Riedmark, Aus. 55/H6
Alberschwende, Aus. 57/F3
Albersdorf, Ger. 38/C4
Albersweiler, Ger. 54/B4
Albert (lake), Austl. 115/A2
Albert (lake), Ugan.,D.R. 93/E4
Albert, Fr. 52/B3
Albert Kanaal (riv.), Belg. 53/E2
Albert Nile (riv.), Ugan. 97/M7
Alberta (prov.), Can. 122/E3
Alberti, Arg. 158/E2
Albertinia, SAfr. 106/C4
Albertirsa, Hun. 48/D2
Alberto de Agostini, PN, Chile 157/B7
Alberton, SAfr. 106/Q13
Albertshofen, Ger. 54/D3
Albertville, Al, US 133/G3
Albertville, Fr. 43/G4
Albestroff, Fr. 53/F6
Albeuve, Swi. 56/D4
Albi, Fr. 42/E5
Albignasego, It. 59/E2
Albina, Sur. 151/H2
Albinea, It. 58/D3
Albino, It. 58/C1
Albion, Mi, US 130/C3
Albisola Marina, It. 58/B4
Albisola Superiore, It. 58/B4
Alblasserdam, Neth. 50/B5
Albocácer, Sp. 45/E2
Alborán (isl.), Mor. 98/E2
Ålborg (bay), Den. 38/D3
Ålborg, Den. 38/C3
Albox, Sp. 44/D4
Albright-Knox Art Gallery, NY, US 131/S10
Albristhorn (peak), Swi. 56/D5
Albufeira, Port. 44/A4
Albula (riv.), Swi. 43/H3
Albuñol, Sp. 44/D4
Albuquerque (int'l arpt.), NM, US 128/F4
Albuquerque, NM, US 128/F4
Albuquerque, Cayos de (isls.), Col. 145/F3
Alburquerque, Sp. 44/B3
Alburtis, Pa, US 138/C3
Albury, Austl. 115/C3
Alby-sur-Chéran, Fr. 56/C6
Alca, Peru 156/C4
Alcabideche, Port. 45/P10
Alcácer do Sal, Port. 44/A3
Alcalá de Chivert, Sp. 45/F2
Alcalá de Guadaira, Sp. 44/C4
Alcalá de Henares, Sp. 45/N9
Alcalá de los Gazules, Sp. 44/C4
Alcalá la Real, Sp. 44/D4
Alcamo, It. 46/C4
Alcanadre (riv.), Sp. 45/E2
Alcanar, Sp. 45/E2
Alcañices, Sp. 44/B2
Alcañiz, Sp. 45/E2
Alcântara, Braz. 154/A1
Alcántara, Sp. 44/B3
Alcántara, Embalse de (res.), Sp. 44/B3
Alcantarilla, Sp. 44/E4
Alcaraz, Sp. 44/D3
Alcaraz, Sierra de (range), Sp. 44/D3
Alcatraz (isl.), Ca, US 135/K11
Alcatrazes, Ilha de (isl.), Braz. 211/H9
Alcaudete, Sp. 44/C4
Alcázar de San Juan, Sp. 44/D3
Alcira, Sp. 45/E3
Alcira, Arg. 158/D2
Alçıtepe, Turk. 47/K2
Alcoa, Tn, US 133/H3
Alcobaça, Braz. 154/C5
Alcobaça, Port. 44/A3
Alcobendas, Sp. 45/N8
Alcochete, Port. 45/Q10
Alcora, Sp. 45/E2
Alcorcón, Sp. 45/N9
Alcorisa, Sp. 45/E2
Alcoutim, Port. 44/B4
Alcoy, Sp. 45/E3
Alcúdia, Sp. 45/G3
Aldabra (isls.), Sey. 93/G5
Aldama, Mex. 132/B4
Aldama, Mex. 143/F4
Aldan (plat.), Rus. 65/N4
Aldan, Rus. 65/N4
Aldan (riv.), Rus. 67/N3
Alde (riv.), Eng, UK 33/H2
Aldeburgh, Eng, UK 33/H2
Aldeia Nova de São Bento, Port. 44/B4
Alden, Il, US 135/N15
Aldenhoven, Ger. 53/F2
Aldeno, It. 57/H6
Aldergrove (int'l arpt.), NI, UK 34/B2
Aldergrove, NI, UK 34/B2
Alderley Edge, Eng, UK 35/F5
Alderney (isl.), Chl, UK 42/B2
Aldershot, Eng, UK 33/F4
Alderwood Manor-Bothell North, Wa, US 135/C2
Aldine, Tx, US 129/J5
Aldingen, Ger. 57/E1
Aldred (lake), Pa, US 138/B4
Aldridge, Eng, UK 33/E1
Ale Water (riv.), Sc, UK 36/D6
Aleg, Mrta. 102/B2
Alegre, Braz. 155/D2
Alegrete, Braz. 157/E2
Alejandro Gallinal, Uru. 159/G2
Alejandro Roca, Arg. 158/E2
Alejandro Selkirk (isl.), Chile 147/A6
Alejo Ledesma, Arg. 158/E2
Aleknagik, Ak, US 134/G4
Aleksandrov, Rus. 60/H4
Aleksandrovac, Yugo. 48/E4
Aleksandrovsk, Rus. 61/N4
Aleksandrów Kujawski, Pol. 41/K2
Aleksandrów Lódzki, Pol. 41/K3
Alekseyevka, Kaz. 87/F2
Alekseyevka, Kaz. 87/E2
Alekseyevka, Rus. 62/F2
Aleksin, Rus. 60/H5
Aleksinac, Yugo. 48/E4
Além Paraíba, Braz. 211/L6
Alençon, Fr. 42/D2
Alenquer, Braz. 151/H4
Alenuihaha (chan.), US 124/T10
Alerce Andino, PN, Chile 158/B4
Aléria, Fr. 46/A1
Alert (pt.), Nun., Can. 123/S6
Aleşd, Rom. 48/F2
Alessandria (prov.), It. 58/B3
Alessandria, It. 58/B3
Ålestrup, Den. 38/C3
Ålesund, Nor. 37/C3
Aletschhorn (peak), Swi. 56/D5
Aleutian (range), Ak, US 134/G4
Aleutian (isls.), Ak, US 134/B5
Alexander (mt.), Austl. 112/B2
Alexander (arch.), Ak, US 134/L4
Alexander (isl.), Ant. 160/V
Alexander Bay, SAfr. 106/B3
Alexander City, Al, US 133/G3
Alexander Nevsky Abbey, Rus. 61/T7
Alexandra, NZ 117/R12
Alexandria, La, US 129/J5
Alexandria, Braz. 154/C2
Alexandria, Mn, US 127/K4
Alexandria, SAfr. 106/D4
Alexándria, Gre. 47/H2
Alexandria, Rom. 49/G4
Alexandria (int'l arpt.), Egypt 91/A4
Alexandria, Va, US 138/A6
Alexandria, Sc, UK 36/B5
Alexandrina (lake), Austl. 109/C4
Alexandroúpolis, Gre. 47/J2
Alexis Creek, BC, Can. 126/C2
Alfaro, Sp. 44/E1
Alfatar, Bul. 49/H4
Alfbach (riv.), Ger. 53/F3
Alfeld, Ger. 51/G5
Alfenas, Braz. 211/H6
Alfhausen, Ger. 51/E3
Alfiós (riv.), Gre. 47/G4
Alfonsine, It. 59/F3
Alfonso Bonilla Aragón (int'l arpt.), Col. 152/B4
Alfred NP, Austl. 115/D3
Alfreton, Eng, UK 35/G5
Alfter, Ger. 53/G2
Alga, Kaz. 63/L2
Ålgård, Nor. 38/A2
Algarrobo, Chile 158/N8
Algarve (reg.), Port. 44/A4
Algeciras, Sp. 44/C4
Algeciras, Col. 152/C4
Algemesí, Sp. 45/E3
Alger (prov.), Alg. 100/G4
Algeria (ctry.) 96/F2
Algermissen, Ger. 51/G4
Algete, Sp. 45/N8
Alghero, It. 46/A2
Algiers (El Djezair) (cap.), Alg. 100/G4
Algoa (bay), SAfr. 106/D4
Algodón (riv.), Peru 150/D4
Algodonales, Sp. 44/C4
Algoma, Wi, US 127/M4
Algona, Wa, US 135/C3
Algonac, Mi, US 135/G6
Algonquin, Il, US 135/P14
Algorta, Uru. 159/K10
Algueirão, Port. 45/P10
Algund (Lagundo), It. 57/H4
Alhama de Granada, Sp. 44/D4
Alhama de Murcia, Sp. 44/E4
Alhambra, Ca, US 136/F7
Alhandra, Braz. 154/D2
Alhandra, Port. 45/P10
Alhaurín el Grande, Sp. 44/C4
'Alī al Gharbī, Iraq 88/E2
'Alī ash Sharqī, Iraq 88/E2
Āli Bayramlı, Azer. 63/J5
Alia, It. 46/C4
Alía, Sp. 44/C3
Aliağa, Turk. 62/C5
Aliákmon (riv.), Gre. 47/G2
Aliákmonos (lake), Gre. 47/G2
Aliartos, Gre. 47/H3
Alibates Flint Quarries Nat'l Mon., Tx, US 129/G4
Alibey (lake), Ukr. 49/K3
Alibeyköy, Turk. 49/J5
Alicante, Sp. 45/E3
Alicante (int'l arpt.), Sp. 45/E3
Alice, Tx, US 132/D5
Alice (pt.), It. 47/E3
Alice Arm, BC, Can. 134/N4
Alice Springs, Austl. 113/G2
Aliceville, Al, US 133/F3
Alicia, Phil. 79/D6
Alicudi (isl.), It. 46/D3
Alicurá (res.), Arg. 158/C4
Alife, It. 46/D2
Alīganj, India 84/B2
Alijó, Port. 44/B2
Alima (riv.), Congo 96/J8
Alingār (riv.), Afg. 86/A2
Alingsås, Swe. 38/E3
Alīpur, Pak. 86/A5
Alīpur Duār, India 85/G2
Alīrājpur, India 89/K4
Alisos (riv.), Mex. 128/E5
Alistráti, Gre. 47/H2
Alivérion, Gre. 47/J3
Aliwal North, SAfr. 106/D3
Aljezur, Port. 44/A4
Aljustrel, Port. 44/A4
Alken, Belg. 53/E2
Alkmaar, Neth. 50/B3
Alkoum (well), Alg. 99/H4
Alkoven, Aus. 55/H6
Allada, Ben. 103/F5
Allahābād, India 84/C3
Allakaket, Ak, US 134/H2
Allaman, Swi. 56/C5
Allan (hills), Sk, Can. 127/G3
Allan, Sk, Can. 127/G3
Alland, Aus. 49/N7
Allanmyo, Myan. 83/G4
Allanridge, SAfr. 106/D2
Allanson, Austl. 112/C5
'Allāq (well), Libya 96/H1
Allariz, Sp. 44/B1
Alle, Swi. 56/D3
Allegan, Mi, US 130/C3
Allegheny (plat.), US 130/E3
Allegheny (riv.), US 130/E3
Allegheny (mts.), US 125/K4
Allen (riv.), Eng, UK 32/B5
Allen, Arg. 158/D3
Allen Park, Mi, US 135/F7
Allendale, SC, US 133/H3
Allendale, NJ, US 139/J7
Allende, Mex. 132/C4
Allende, Mex. 143/E3
Allendorf, Ger. 51/F6
Allensbach, Ger. 57/F2
Allenspark, Co, US 137/A2
Allentown, Pa, US 138/C2
Allentsteig, Aus. 41/H4
Allenwood, Pa, US 138/B1
Alleppey, India 82/C6
Aller (riv.), Ger. 51/H3
Allerkanal (canal), Ger. 51/H4
Allersberg, Ger. 54/E4
Allershausen, Ger. 55/E6
Allgäu Alps (range), Aus.,Ger. 40/F5
Alliance, Ne, US 127/H5
Alliance, Oh, US 130/D3
Allied War Cemetery, Myan. 78/B2
Allier (riv.), Fr. 42/E3
Alligator (pt.), La, US 137/Q16
Allingåbro, Den. 38/D3
Allinges, Fr. 56/C5
Alloa, Sc, UK 36/C4
Allonnes, Fr. 42/D3
Allora, Austl. 114/C5
Allos, Fr. 43/G4
Alloway, NJ, US 138/C4
Allschwil, Swi. 56/D2
Alm (riv.), Aus. 55/G7
Alma, Mi, US 130/C3
Alma, Qu, Can. 131/G1
Almacelles, Sp. 45/F2
Almada, Port. 45/P10
Almadén, Sp. 44/C3
Almafuerte, Arg. 158/D2
Almagro, Sp. 44/D3
Almanor (lake), Ca, US 128/B2
Almansa, Sp. 45/E3
Almanza, Sp. 44/C1
Almanzor, Pico de (peak), Sp. 44/C2
Almanzora (riv.), Sp. 44/D4
Almas (riv.), Braz. 151/J6
Almas, Braz. 154/A3
Almas, Pico das (peak), Braz. 154/B4
Almaty (int'l arpt.), Kaz. 87/G4
Almaty, Kaz. 87/G4
Almazán, Sp. 44/D2
Almazora, Sp. 45/E3
Almeida, Port. 44/B2
Almeirim, Braz. 151/H4
Almeirim, Port. 44/A3
Almelo, Neth. 50/D4
Almenara, Braz. 154/B5
Almenara (peak), Sp. 44/D3
Almenara, Sp. 45/E3
Almendra, Embalse de (res.), Sp. 44/B2
Almendralejo, Sp. 44/B3
Almenno San Salvatore, It. 58/C1
Almere, Neth. 50/C4
Almería, Sp. 44/D4
Almería, Golfo de (gulf), Sp. 44/D4
Al'met'yevsk, Rus. 61/M5
Älmhult, Swe. 38/F3
Almina (pt.), Sp. 100/B2
Almirós, Gre. 47/H3
Almiroú (gulf), Gre. 47/J5
Almodôvar, Port. 44/A4
Almodóvar del Campo, Sp. 44/C3
Almodóvar del Río, Sp. 44/C4
Almoharín, Sp. 44/B3
Almond (riv.), Sc, UK 36/C4
Almont (riv.), Fr. 30/L6
Almonte, On, Can. 130/E2
Almonte, Sp. 44/B4
Almora, India 84/B1
Almoradí, Sp. 45/E3
Almorox, Sp. 44/C2
Almte. Montt (gulf), Chile 159/B7
Almudévar, Sp. 45/E1
Almuñécar, Sp. 44/D4
Almus, Turk. 62/F4
Alness, Sc, UK 36/B1
Alness (riv.), Sc, UK 36/B1
Alnwick, Eng, UK 36/E6
Alofi (isl.), Wall. 116/H6
Alofi, NZ 117/J6
Along, India 83/G2
Alónnisos (isl.), Gre. 47/H3
Alor (isls.), Indo. 81/F5
Alor (isl.), Indo. 116/B5
Alor Setar, Malay. 83/H6
Álora, Sp. 44/C4
Alotau, PNG 116/E6
Aloysius (mt.), Austl. 113/F3
Alpachiri, Arg. 158/E3
Alpe di Poti (peak), It. 59/E6
Alpedrete, Sp. 45/M8
Alpen, Ger. 50/D5
Alpena, Mi, US 130/D2
Alpercatas (riv.), Braz. 154/A2
Alpercatas, Serra das (mts.), Braz. 151/J5
Alperschällihorn (peak), Swi. 57/F4
Alpes de Provence (range), Fr. 43/G5
Alpha, Austl. 114/B3
Alpha, NJ, US 138/C2
Alphen aan de Rijn, Neth. 50/B4
Alpi Apuane (range), It. 43/J4
Alpi Dolomitiche (range), It. 43/J4
Alpi Orobie (range) It. 43/J3
Alpiarça, Port. 44/A3
Alpine, Wy, US 126/F5
Alpine, Ut, US 137/K13
Alpine, NJ, US 139/K8
Alpirsbach, Ger. 57/E1
Alpnach, Swi. 57/E4
Alps (mts.), Eur. 27/E4
Alqōsh, Iraq 90/E2
Als (isl.), Den. 40/F1
Alsace (pol. reg.), Fr. 40/D4
Alsager, Eng, UK 35/F5
Alsask, Sk, Can. 126/F3
Alsasua, Sp. 44/D1
Alsdorf, Ger. 53/F2
Alsenz (riv.), Ger. 53/G4
Alsenz, Ger. 53/G4
Alsfeld, Ger. 43/H1
Alsheim, Ger. 54/B3
Alsip, Il, US 135/Q16
Alstahaug, Nor. 37/E2
Alster (riv.), Ger. 51/H1
Alsting, Fr. 53/F5
Alstonville, Austl. 115/E1
Alt (riv.), Eng, UK 35/E4
Alta, Ut, US 137/K12
Alta, Nor. 37/G1
Alta Floresta, Braz. 151/G5
Alta Gracia, Arg. 157/D3
Altach, Aus. 57/F3
Altadena, Ca, US 136/F7
Altagracia, Nic. 144/E4
Altai (mts.), Asia 70/E2
Altamaha (riv.), Ga, US 140/E1
Altamira, Braz. 151/H4
Altamira, Mex. 144/B1
Altamira do Maranhão, Braz. 154/A2
Altamonte Springs, Fl, US 133/H4
Altamura, It. 46/E2
Altar, Mex. 142/C2
Altar (vol.), Ecu. 152/B5
Altar de los Sacrificios (ruin), Guat. 144/D2
Altar, Desierto de (des.), Mex. 128/D4
Altare, It. 58/B4
Altavilla Vicentina, It. 59/E1
Altay, China 70/E2
Altay, Mong. 70/E2
Altay, Mong. 70/G2
Altay (aut. rep.), Rus. 64/J4
Altayskiy (kray), Rus. 87/G2
Altdorf, Swi. 57/E4
Altdorf bei Nürnberg, Ger. 55/E4
Altea, Sp. 45/E3
Altedo, It. 59/E3
Altena, Ger. 51/E6
Altenahr, Ger. 53/G2
Altenau, Ger. 51/H5
Altenau (riv.), Ger. 51/F5
Altenbeken, Ger. 51/F5
Altenberg bei Linz, Aus. 55/H6
Altenburg, Ger. 40/G3
Altenfelden, Aus. 55/G6
Altenglan, Ger. 53/G4
Altengottern, Ger. 51/H6
Altenkirchen, Ger. 53/G2
Altenmünster, Ger. 54/D6
Altenstadt, Ger. 57/G1
Altenstadt, Ger. 54/B2
Altensteig, Ger. 54/B5
Altentreptow, Ger. 38/E5
Altepexi, Mex. 143/M8
Alter Rhein (riv.), Ger. 50/D5
Altes Land (phys. reg.), Ger. 51/G1
Altheim, Aus. 55/G6
Althengstett, Ger. 54/B5
Althofen, Aus. 43/L3
Althütte, Ger. 54/C5
Altındere NP, Turk. 62/F4
Altınözü, Turk. 91/E1
Altıntaş, Turk. 62/D5
Altınyaka, Turk. 91/B1
Altınyayla, Turk. 91/A1
Altiplano (plat.), Bol.,Peru 147/C4
Altkirch, Fr. 56/D2
Altlandsberg, Ger. 40/Q6
Altmark (phys. reg.), Ger. 40/F2
Altmühl (riv.), Ger. 43/J2
Altmünster, Aus. 55/G7
Altnaharra, Sc, UK 31/R7
Alto (peak), Braz. 154/A4
Alto (peak), It. 57/G4
Alto Araguaia, Braz. 151/H7
Alto de Tamar (peak), Col. 152/C3
Alto Garças, Braz. 151/H7
Alto Lucero, Mex. 143/N7
Alto Parnaíba, Braz. 154/A3
Alto Purús (riv.), Peru 150/D6
Alto Santo, Braz. 154/C2
Alto Yuruá (riv.), Peru 156/C3
Altomünster, Ger. 54/E6
Alton, La, US 137/Q16
Alton, Il, US 137/G8
Alton, Eng, UK 33/F4
Altona, Mb, Can. 127/J3
Altoona, Pa, US 130/E3
Altopascio, It. 59/D5
Altos, Braz. 154/B2
Altos de Campana NP, Pan. 152/B2
Altotonga, Mex. 143/M7
Altötting, Ger. 55/F6
Altrincham, Eng, UK 35/F5
Altrip, Ger. 54/B4
Altun (mts.), China 67/H6
Altun Ha (ruin), Belz. 144/D2
Alturas, Ca, US 126/C5
Altus (res.), Ok, US 129/H4
Altus, Ok, US 129/H4
Altzayanca, Mex. 143/M7
Alucra, Turk. 62/F4
Aluminé, Arg. 158/C3
Alunda, Swe. 38/H1
Ālūs, Iraq 90/E3
Alushta, Ukr. 62/E3
Alva, Ok, US 129/H3
Alva, Sc, UK 36/C4
Alvalade, Port. 44/A4
Älvängen, Swe. 38/E3
Alvarado, Mex. 143/P8
Álvarez, Arg. 158/E2
Alvaro Obregón, Presa (dam), Mex. 142/C2
Alvdal, Nor. 37/D3
Älvdalen, Swe. 38/F1
Alverca, Port. 45/P10
Alveringem, Belg. 52/B1
Alvesta, Swe. 38/F3
Ålvik, Nor. 38/B1
Alvin, Tx, US 129/J5
Alvito, Port. 44/B3
Älvkarleby, Swe. 38/G1
Alvorada, Braz. 155/A4
Alvorada do Norte, Braz. 154/A4
Älvsborg (co.), Swe. 37/E4
Älvsbyn, Swe. 37/G2
Alwen (riv.), Wal, UK 34/E5
Alxa Youqi, China 70/H4
Alxa Zuoqi, China 70/J4
Alyawarra Abor. Land, Austl. 113/G2
Alyth, Sc, UK 36/C3
Alytus, Lith. 39/L4
Alz (riv.), Ger. 43/K2
Alzano Lombardo, It. 58/C1
Alzenau in Unterfranken, Ger. 54/C2
Alzette (riv.), Lux. 53/F4
Alzey, Ger. 54/B3
Am Timan, Chad 97/K5
Ama, La, US 137/P17
Amacayacú, PN, Col. 150/D4
Amacuro (riv.), Ven. 153/F2
Amacuro (delta), Ven. 153/F2
Amacuzac (riv.), Mex. 143/K8
Amadeus (lake), Austl. 109/C3
Amadjuak (lake), Nun., Can. 123/J2
Amadora, Port. 45/P10
Amagansett, NY, US 139/F2
Amagansett NWR, NY, US 139/F2
Amagasaki, Japan 77/H6
Amagi, Japan 74/B4
Amagi-san (peak), Japan 75/F3
Amaguaña, Ecu. 152/B5
Amajac (riv.), Mex. 143/N7
Åmål, Swe. 38/E2
Amala (riv.), Kenya 104/B3
Amalfi, Col. 152/C3
Amalia, SAfr. 106/D2
Amaliás, Gre. 47/G4
Amaluza, Ecu. 152/B5
Amambaí, Braz. 157/E1
Amambaí (riv.), Braz. 151/H8
Amami (isls.), Japan 67/M7
Amami-O-Shima (isl.), Japan 75/K6
Amanā (lake), Braz. 150/F4
Amance, Fr. 56/C2
Amānganj, India 84/C3
Amāngarh, Pak. 86/A2
Amantea, It. 46/E3
Amanu (isl.), FrPol. 117/L6
Amanzimtoti, SAfr. 107/E3
Amapá, Braz. 151/H3
Amapá (state), Braz. 153/H4
Amarante, Braz. 154/B2
Amarante, Port. 44/A2
Amarante do Marahão, Braz. 154/A2
Amarapura, Myan. 83/G3
Amareleja, Port. 44/B3
Amargosa, Braz. 154/C4
Amargosa (riv.), Ca, US 128/C3
Amarillo, Tx, US 129/G4
Amaro (peak), It. 46/D1
Amarpātan, India 84/C3
Amarume, Japan 76/A4
Amarwāra, India 84/B4
Amasra, Turk. 49/L5
Amasya, Turk. 62/E4
Amasya (prov.), Turk. 62/E4
Amata, Austl. 113/F3
Amatlán de Cañas, Mex. 142/D4
Amatsukominato, Japan 77/E3
Amawalk (res.), NY, US 139/E1
Amay, Belg. 53/E2
Amayuca, Mex. 143/L8
Amazon (Amazonas) (riv.), Braz.,Per 156/C1
Amazonas, Cuba 145/G1
Amazonas (state), Braz. 152/C5
Amazonas (Amazon) (riv.), Braz.,Per 156/C1
Amazônia, PN da (Tapajós), Braz. 151/G4
Ambāh, India 84/B2
Ambahikily, Madg. 107/G8
Ambajogai, India 89/L5
Ambāla Sadar, India 86/D4
Ambalangoda, SrL. 82/D6
Ambalavao, Madg. 107/H8
Ambam, Camr. 96/H7
Ambanja, Madg. 107/J6
Ambaro (bay), Madg. 107/J6
Ambato, Ecu. 152/B5
Ambato Boeny, Madg. 107/H7
Ambatofinandrahana, Madg. 107/H8
Ambatolampy, Madg. 107/H7
Ambatomaidy, Madg. 107/H7
Ambatomanoina, Madg. 107/H7
Ambatondrazaka, Madg. 107/J7
Ambazac, Fr. 42/D4
Ámbelos (cape), Gre. 47/H3
Amberg, Ger. 55/E4
Ambergris Cay (isl.), Belz. 144/E2
Ambérieu-en-Bugey, Fr. 56/B6
Amberloup, Belg. 53/E3
Ambikāpur, India 84/D4
Ambilobe, Madg. 107/J6
Ambinanindrano, Madg. 107/J8
Ambinanitelo, Madg. 107/J6
Ambler, Ak, US 134/G2
Ambler, Pa, US 138/C3
Amblève (riv.), Belg. 40/C3
Amblève, Belg. 53/F3
Ambo, Peru 156/B3
Amboasary, Madg. 107/H9
Amboavory, Madg. 107/J7
Ambodifototra, Madg. 107/J7
Ambodiharina, Madg. 107/J8
Ambohidratrimo, Madg. 107/H7
Ambohijanahary, Madg. 107/J7
Ambohimahasoa, Madg. 107/H8
Ambohimandroso, Madg. 107/H7
Ambohinihaonana, Madg. 107/H8
Ambohitsilaozana, Madg. 107/J7
Ambolomoty, Madg. 107/H7
Ambon (isl.), Indo. 81/G4
Ambon, Indo. 81/G4
Ambondro, Madg. 107/H9
Amboni Caves, Tanz. 104/C4
Amborompotsy, Madg. 107/H8
Amboseli NP, Kenya 104/C3
Ambositra, Madg. 107/H8
Ambovombe, Madg. 107/H9
Ambrym (isl.), Van. 116/F6
Amchitka (isl.), Ak, US 65/T4
Amchitka Pass (chan.), Ak, US 134/B6
Amealco, Mex. 143/K6
Ameca, Mex. 142/D4
Amecameca de Juárez, Mex. 143/R10
Ameghino, Arg. 158/E2
Ameglia, It. 58/C4
Ameisberg (peak), Aus. 55/G5
Ameland (isl.), Neth. 50/C2
Amelia, It. 46/C1
Amelinghausen, Ger. 51/H2
Amer (chan.), Neth. 50/B5
American (lake), Wa, US 135/B3
American (riv.), Ca, US 135/M9
American Falls (mts.), Id, US 128/D2
American Fork, Ut, US 137/K13
American, North Fork (riv.), Ca, US 128/B3
American Samoa (dpcy.), US 117/H6
American, South Fork (riv.), Ca, US 128/B3
Americana, Braz. 155/C2
Americus, Ga, US 133/G3
Ameringkogel (peak), Aus. 43/L3
Amersfoort, SAfr. 107/E2
Amersfoort, Neth. 50/C4
Amersham, Eng, UK 33/F3
Amery Ice Shelf, Ant. 160/E
Amesbury, Eng, UK 33/E4
Amet, India 89/K3
Amethi, India 84/C2
Amfíklia, Gre. 47/G3
Amfilokhía, Gre. 47/G3
Ámfissa, Gre. 47/H3
Amga (riv.), Rus. 65/N3
Amguema (riv.), Rus. 65/T3
Amgun' (riv.), Rus. 65/P4
Amherst, NS n. 131/H2
Amherst, NY, US 131/S10
Amherstburg, On, Can. 135/F7
Ami, Japan 77/E1
Amiata (peak), It. 43/J5
Amiens, Fr. 52/B4
Amik (lake), Turk. 90/D2
Amila (isl.), Ak, US 65/U4
Amilcar Cabral (int'l arpt.), CpV. 93/K10
Amillis, Fr. 30/M5
Amíndaion, Gre. 47/G2

169

Aminu – Argen

Aminu Kano (int'l arpt.), Nga. 103/H3
Amisk (lake), Sk, Can. 127/H2
Amistad (res.), Mex.,US 140/A2
Amistad Nat'l Rec. Area, Tx, US 129/G5
Amite, La, US 129/K5
Amityville, NY, US 139/M9
Amla, India 84/B5
Āmlāgora, India 85/F4
Åmli, Nor. 38/C2
'Ammān (gov.), Jor. 91/E4
Amman (riv.), Wal, UK 32/C3
Amman ('Ammān) (cap.), Jor. 91/D4
Ammanford, Wal, UK 32/C3
Ammarfjället (peak), Swe. 37/E2
Ammassalik, Grld 160/J
Ammer (riv.), Ger. 54/B5
Ammerman (mtn.), Yk, Can. 134/K2
Ammersee (lake), Ger. 43/J3
Amnéville, Fr. 53/F5
Āmol, Iran 88/F1
Amora, Port. 45/P10
Amorbach, Ger. 54/C3
Amorgós, Gre. 47/J4
Amorgós (isl.), Gre. 47/J4
Amory, Ms, US 133/F3
Amos, Qu, Can. 130/E1
Åmot, Nor. 38/B2
Amotfors, Swe. 38/E2
Amozoc, Mex. 143/L7
Ampachi, Japan 77/L5
Ampanefena, Madg. 107/J6
Ampangalana (canal), Madg. 107/J8
Ampanihy, Madg. 107/H9
Amparafaravola, Madg. 107/J7
Amparai, SrL. 82/D6
Amparo, Braz. 211/G7
Ampasindava (bay), Madg. 107/H6
Ampato (peak), Peru 156/D4
Ampefy, Madg. 107/H7
Amper (riv.), Ger. 55/E6
Ampfing, Ger. 55/F6
Ampflwang im Hausruckwald, Aus. 55/G6
Ampitatafika, Madg. 107/H7
Amposta, Sp. 45/F2
Amqui, Qu, Can. 131/H1
Amravati, India 82/C3
Amreli, India 89/K4
'Amrīt (ruin), Syria 91/D2
Amritsar, India 86/C4
Amroha, India 84/B1
Amrum (isl.), Ger. 40/E1
Amstel (riv.), Neth. 50/B4
Amstelveen, Neth. 50/B4
Amsterdam, NY, US 130/F3
Amsterdam, SAfr. 107/E2
Amsterdam (cap.), Neth. 50/B4
Amsterdam (isl.), Fr. 23/N7
Amsterdam Rijnkanaal (riv.), Neth. 50/C4
Amsterdam (Schipol) (int'l arpt.), Neth. 50/B4
Amstetten, Aus. 43/L2
Amu Darya (riv.), Asia 67/F8
Amudat, Ugan. 104/B2
Amukta Pass (chan.), Ak, US 134/D5
Amuku (mts.), Guy. 153/G4
Amund Ringnes (isl.), Nun., Can. 123/S7
Amundsen (gulf), NW, Can. 122/D1
Amundsen (bay), Ant. 160/D
Amundsen (sea), Ant. 160/S
Amundsen-Scott, US, Ant. 160/A
Amunge (lake), Swe. 38/F1
Amur (riv.), Rus. 71/P2
Amurrio, Sp. 44/D1
Amurskaya (obl.), Rus. 65/N4
Amyūn, Leb. 91/D2
An Nabk, Syria 91/E2
An Nahūd, Sudan 97/L5
An Najaf, Iraq 90/F4
An Najaf (gov.),Iraq 90/E4
An Nāşirīyah,Iraq 88/E2
An Nu'manīyah,Iraq 90/F3
An Teallach (peak), Sc, UK 36/A1
An Uaimh, Ire. 31/Q10
Ana María (gulf), Cuba 141/F3
Anaa (isl.), FrPol. 117/L6
Anabar (riv.), Rus. 65/L3
'Anabtā, WBnk. 91/G7
Anachucuna (mtn.), Pan. 152/B2
Anaco, Ven. 153/E2
Anaconda-Deer Lodge County, Mt, US 126/E4
Anadarko, Ok, US 129/H4
Anadyr' (range), Rus. 160/U
Anadyr' (riv.), Rus. 67/S3
Anadyr' (gulf), Rus. 67/T3
Anadyr', Rus. 65/T3
Anáfi (isl.), Gre. 47/J4
Anaheim, Ca, US 136/G8
Anahim Lake, BC, Can. 126/B2
Anáhuac, Mex. 132/C5
Anahuac, Tx, US 132/E4
Anahuac, Mex. 142/D2
Anak, NKor. 73/C3
Anakāpalle, India 82/D4
Anaktuvuk Pass, Ak, US 134/H2
Analalava, Madg. 107/H6
Analamaitso (plat.), Madg. 107/J7
Analavory, Madg. 107/H7
Anambas (isls.), Indo. 80/C3
Anambra (state), Nga. 103/G5
Anamur, Turk. 91/C1
Anamur (pt.), Turk. 91/C1
Anan, Japan 74/D4
Anand, India 89/K4
Ananea, Peru 156/D4
Ananea, Bol. 156/D4
Anantapur, India 82/C5
Anantnag, India 86/C3
Anapa, Rus. 62/F3
Añapi (peak), Arg. 159/C6
Anápolis, Braz. 151/J7
Anapu (riv.), Braz. 151/H4
Anār, Iran 89/G2
Anārak, Iran 88/F2
Anastácio, Braz. 151/G8
'Anātā, WBnk. 91/G8
Anathan (isl.), NMar. 116/D3
Anatolia (reg.), Turk. 62/D5
Añatuya, Arg. 157/D2
Anauá (riv.), Braz. 150/F3
Ancash (dept.), Peru 156/B3
Anchieta, Braz. 155/D2
Anchor (bay), Mi, US 135/G6
Anchor Point, Ak, US 134/H4
Anchorage, Ak, US 134/J3
Anchorville, Mi, US 135/G6
Anchovy, Jam. 145/G2
Ancient City of Oc-Eo, Viet. 78/D4
Ancoeur (riv.), Fr. 30/L6
Ancohuma (peak), Bol. 156/D4
Ancón, Peru 156/B3
Ancón de Sardinas (bay), Col. 152/B4
Ancona (prov.), It. 59/G5
Ancona, It. 59/G5
Ancoraimes, Bol. 156/D4
Ancre (riv.), Fr. 52/B3
Ancrum, Sc, UK 36/D5
Ancud, Chile 158/B4
Ancud, Golfo de (gulf), Chile 157/B5
Anda, China 71/N2
Andacollo, Arg. 158/C3
Andagua, Peru 156/C4
Andahuaylas, Peru 156/C4
Andāl, India 85/F4
Åndalsnes, Nor. 37/C3
Andalucia (aut. comm.), Sp. 44/C4
Andalusia, Al, US 133/G4
Andalusia (reg.), Sp. 44/C4
Andaman (sea), Asia 67/J8
Andaman (isls.), India 67/H8
Andaman and Nicobar (isls.), India 83/F5
Andamarca, Peru 156/C3
Andamooka, Austl. 113/H4
Andapa, Madg. 107/J6
Andaraí, Braz. 154/B4
Andau, Aus. 43/M3
Andebu, Nor. 38/D2
Andechs, Ger. 57/H2
Andeer, Swi. 57/F4
Andelfingen, Swi. 57/E2
Andelle (riv.), Fr. 52/A5
Andelot-Blancheville, Fr. 56/B1
Andelsbach (riv.), Ger. 57/F2
Andelu, Fr. 30/H5
Andemaka, Madg. 107/H8
Andenne, Belg. 53/E3
Anderlues, Belg. 53/D3
Andermatt, Swi. 57/E4
Andernach, Ger. 53/G3
Anderson, Ak, US 134/J3
Anderson, Tx, US 129/J5
Anderson, Ca, US 128/B2
Anderson, SC, US 133/H3
Anderson, In, US 130/C3
Anderson (riv.), NW, Can. 122/D2
Anderson (inlet), Wa, US 135/B3
Anderson (isl.), Wa, US 135/B3
Andes (mts.), SAm. 147/C5
Andes, Cordillera de los (mts.), SAm. 157/B4
Andevoranto, Madg. 107/J7
Andfjorden (chan.), Nor. 37/F1
Andhra Pradesh (state), India 70/D8
Andijk, Neth. 50/C3
Andijon (pol. reg.), Uzb. 87/F4
Andijon, Uzb. 87/F4
Andikíthira (isl.), Gre. 47/H5
Andilamena, Madg. 107/J7
Andilanatoby, Madg. 107/J7
Andīmeshk, Iran 88/E2
Andíparos (isl.), Gre. 47/J4
Andira, Braz. 155/B2
Ándissa, Gre. 47/J3
Andkhvoy, Afg. 87/E5
Andohajango, Madg. 107/J6
Andong, SKor. 74/A2
Andorf, Aus. 55/G6
Andorno Micca, It. 58/B1
Andorra, Sp. 45/E2
Andorra (ctry.) 73/F1
Andorra la Vella (cap.), And. 42/D5
Andover, Eng, UK 33/E4
Andover, NJ, US 138/D2
Andøy, Nor. 37/F1
Andøya (isl.), Nor. 37/E1
Andradas, Braz. 211/G7
Andradina, Braz. 155/B2
Andraitx, Sp. 45/G3
Andramasina, Madg. 107/H7
Andranolava, Madg. 107/H8
Andranomavo (riv.), Madg. 107/H7
Andranopasy, Madg. 107/G8
Andreanof (isls.), Ak, US 134/C6
Andrelândia, Braz. 211/J6
Andrespol, Pol. 41/K3
Andrésy, Fr. 30/J5
Andrezel, Fr. 30/L6
Andria, It. 46/E2
Andriba, Madg. 107/H7
Andringitra (mts.), Madg. 107/H8
Andrítsaina, Gre. 47/G4
Androka, Madg. 107/H9
Androntany (cape), Madg. 107/J6
Ándros, Gre. 47/J4
Ándros (isl.), Gre. 47/J4
Andros (isl.), Bahm. 141/F3
Androscoggin (riv.), US 131/G2
Andújar, Sp. 44/C3
Aneby, Swe. 38/F3
Anecón Grande (peak), Arg. 158/C4
Anegada (isl.), UK 141/J4
Anegada (bay), Arg. 158/E4
Anegada Passage (chan.), NAm. 141/J4
Anécho, Togo 103/F5
Aneityum (isl.), Van. 116/F7
Añelo, Arg. 158/C3
Aneto, Pico de (peak), Sp. 45/F1
Anfu, China 83/K2
Ang Nam Ngum (res.), Laos 83/H4
Ang Thong, Thai. 78/C3
Angamos (pt.), Chile 157/B1
Angara (riv.), Rus. 67/J4
Angaston, Austl. 113/H5
Angel (riv.), Ger. 51/E5
Ángel (falls), Ven. 153/F3
Angeles, Phil. 79/D4
Angeles National Forest, Ca, US 136/B1
Ängelholm, Swe. 38/E3
Angelholm (int'l arpt.), Swe. 38/E3
Angelina (riv.), Tx, US 129/J5
Angeln (reg.), Ger. 40/E1
Angelus (lake), Mi, US 135/F6
Angera, It. 58/B1
Ångermanalven (riv.), Swe. 37/E2
Angermünde, Ger. 41/H2
Angers, Fr. 42/C3
Anghiari, It. 59/F5
Angical do Piauí, Braz. 154/B2
Angicos, Braz. 154/C2
Angkor (ruin), Camb. 78/C3
Anglem (mt.), NZ 117/R12
Anglès, Sp. 45/G2
Anglesea, Austl. 115/C3
Anglesey (co.), Wal, UK 34/D5
Anglesey (isl.), Wal, UK 34/D5
Anglet, Fr. 42/C5
Angleton, Tx, US 129/J5
Anglin (riv.), Fr. 42/D3
Angoche, Moz. 105/G4
Angol, Chile 158/B3
Angola, Afr. 105/B2
Angola, In, US 130/C3
Angola (ctry.) 105/C3
Angoon, Ak, US 134/M4
Angostura (res.), Mex. 140/C4
Angostura, Mex. 142/C3
Angoulême, Fr. 42/D4
Angra do Heroísmo, Azor., Port. 45/S12
Angra dos Reis, Braz. 211/J7
Angren, Uzb. 87/F4
Anguilla (isl.), UK 141/N8
Anguillara Veneta, It. 59/E2
Angus (pol. reg.), Sc,UK, 36/C3
Angutikada (peak), Ak, US 134/G2
Anhanduí (riv.), Braz. 151/H8
Anhée, Belg. 53/D3
Anholt (isl.), Den. 38/D3
Anhui (prov.), China 71/L5
Ani, Japan 76/B4
Aniak, Ak, US 134/G3
Aniakchak (crater), Ak, US 134/G4
Aniakchak Nat'l Mon. and Prsv., Ak, US 134/F4
Aniche, Fr. 52/C3
Animas (riv.), Co,NM, US 128/F3
Ánimas, Punta De Las (pt.), Mex. 142/B2
'Ānīn, Isr. 91/G6
Anina, Rom. 48/E3
Aniva (cape), Rus. 71/R2
Aniva (bay), Rus. 76/C1
Anivorano, Madg. 107/J7
Anizy-le-Château, Fr. 52/C4
Anjalankoski, Fin. 39/M1
Anjār, India 89/K4
Anjō, Japan 77/M6
Anjou (reg.), Fr. 42/C3
Anjou, Qu, Can. 131/N6
Anjouan (isl.), Com. 107/H6
Anjozorobe, Madg. 107/H7
Anju, NKor. 73/C3
Ankang, China 70/J5
Ankara (prov.), Turk. 62/E5
Ankara (cap.), Turk. 62/E5
Ankaramena, Madg. 107/H8
Ankaratra (mass.), Madg. 107/H7
Ankarsrum, Swe. 38/G3
Ankavandra, Madg. 107/H7
Ankazoabo, Madg. 107/H8
Ankazobe, Madg. 107/H7
Ankazomborona, Madg. 107/H7
Ankazomiriotra, Madg. 107/H7
Ankerika, Madg. 107/H6
Ankililioka, Madg. 107/G8
Ankilizato, Madg. 107/H8
Anklam, Ger. 38/E5
Ankum, Ger. 51/E3
Anlong, China 83/J2
Anloo, Neth. 50/D2
Anlu, China 72/C5
Anma (isl.), SKor. 73/D5
Ann (cape), Ma, US 131/G3
Ann Arbor, Mi, US 130/D3
Anna (lake), Va, US 130/E4
Anna Bay, Austl. 115/E2
Anna Pavlowna, Neth. 50/B3
Anna Pink (bay), Chile 158/B5
Anna Regina, Guy. 153/G3
Annaba, Alg. 100/K6
Annaba (prov.), Alg. 100/K6
Annaberg-Buchholz, Ger. 55/G1
Annaclone, NI, UK 34/B3
Annai, Guy. 153/G4
Annaka, Japan 77/B1
Annalong, NI, UK 34/C3
Annan, Sc, UK 35/E2
Annan (riv.), Sc, UK 36/C6
Annandale, Va, US 138/A6
Annandale, NJ, US 138/D2
Annapolis (cap.), Md, US 138/B6
Annapurna (peak), Nepal 84/D1
Annbank Station, Sc, UK 36/B6
Anne (mt.), Austl. 115/C4
Anne Arundel (co.), Md, US 138/B6
Annean (lake), Austl. 109/A3
Annecy, Fr. 56/C6
Annecy (lake), Fr. 56/C6
Annecy-le-Vieux, Fr. 56/C6
Annemasse, Fr. 56/C5
Annet-sur-Marne, Fr. 30/L5
Annette, Ak, US 134/M4
Annezin, Fr. 52/B2
Anniston, Al, US 133/G3
Annobón (isl.), EqG. 93/C5
Annonay, Fr. 42/F4
Annville, Pa, US 138/B3
Annweiler, Ger. 53/G5
Anō, Japan 77/K6
Áno Viánnos, Gre. 47/J5
Anoia (riv.), Sp. 45/K7
Anoka, Mn, US 127/K4
Anosibe An' Ala, Madg. 107/J7
Ânou-Zeggarene (riv.), Niger 103/G2
Anould, Fr. 56/C1
Anóyia, Gre. 47/J5
Anping, China 72/C3
Anqiu, China 72/D3
Anren, China 83/K2
Anrhomer (peak), Mor. 98/D3
Anröchte, Ger. 51/F5
Ans, Belg. 53/E2
Ansai, China 72/B3
Ansan, SKor. 73/F7
Ansbach, Ger. 54/D4
Anse-à-Galets, Haiti 145/H2
Anse-d'Hainault, Haiti 145/H2
Anse Rouge, Haiti 145/H2
Ansfelden, Aus. 55/H6
Anshan, China 73/B2
Anshun, China 83/J2
Anson, Tx, US 129/H4
Ansŏng, SKor. 73/D4
Ansongo, Mali 103/F3
Ant (riv.), Eng, UK 33/H1
Ant (isl.), Anti. 116/E4
Anta, Peru 156/C4
Antabamba, Peru 156/C4
Antakya, Turk. 91/E1
Antalaha, Madg. 107/J6
Antalya (prov.), Turk. 90/B2
Antalya (int'l arpt.), Turk. 91/B1
Antalya, Turk. 91/B1
Antalya, Gulf of (gulf), Turk. 91/B1
Antanambao Manampotsy, Madg. 107/J7
Antananarivo (prov.), Madg. 107/H7
Antananarivo (cap.), Madg. 107/H7
Antanifotsy, Madg. 107/H7
Antanimieva, Madg. 107/G8
Antanimora, Madg. 107/H9
Antar (peak), Alg. 99/E3
Antarctic (pen.), Ant. 160/W
Antarctic Circle 160/Z
Antarctica (cont.) 160
Antas, Braz. 154/C3
Antas, Rio das (riv.), Braz. 155/B4
Antella, It. 59/E5
Antelope (isl.), Ut, US 137/J12
Antelope Center, Ca, US 136/C1
Antequera, Sp. 44/C4
Antes Fort, Pa, US 138/A1
Anthering, Aus. 55/G7
Anthony, NM, US 128/F4
Anti-Atlas (mts.), Mor. 96/C2
Anti-Lebanon (mts.), Leb. 91/D3
Antibes, Fr. 43/G5
Anticosti, Île d' (isl.), Qu, Can. 123/K4
Antiesen (riv.), Aus. 55/G6
Antifer, Cap d' (cape), Fr. 42/D2
Antigo, Wi, US 127/L4
Antigonish, NS, Can. 131/J2
Antigua, Sp. 98/B3
Antigua (isl.), Anti. 141/N8
Antigua and Barbuda (ctry.) 141/N8
Antigua Guatemala, Guat. 144/D3
Antiguo Morelos, Mex. 143/F4
Antilly, Fr. 30/L4
Antioquia (dept.), Col. 145/H5
Antioquia, Col. 152/C3
Antipodes (isls.), NZ 23/T8
Antisana (vol.), Ecu. 152/B5
Antlers, Ok, US 129/J4
Antofagasta, Chile 157/B1
Antoing, Belg. 52/C2
Antokonosy Manambondro, Madg. 107/H8
Antón, Pan. 152/A2
Antón Lizardo, Mex. 143/P7
Anton Lizardo (pt.), Mex. 143/P7
Antongil (bay), Madg. 105/K10
Antonia, Mo, US 137/G9
Antonibe, Madg. 107/H6
Antoniesberg (peak), SAfr. 106/C4
Antonina, Braz. 155/B3
Antonina do Norte, Braz. 154/C2
Antônio Carlos, Braz. 211/K6
Antonito, Co, US 132/B2
Antonovo, Bul. 49/H4
Antony, Fr. 30/J5
Antrim, NI, UK 34/B2
Antrim (mts.), NI, UK 34/B1
Antrim (dist.), NI, UK 34/B2
Antronapiana, It. 56/E5
Antsalova, Madg. 107/H7
Antsambalahy, Madg. 107/J6
Antsenavolo, Madg. 107/J8
Antsirabe, Madg. 107/H7
Antsirañana, Madg. 107/J6
Antsiranana (prov.), Madg. 107/J6
Antsohihy, Madg. 107/H6
Antuco (vol.), Chile 158/C3
Antulai (mtn.), Malay. 81/E3
Antwerp (Deurne) (int'l arpt.), Belg. 50/B6
Antwerpen, Belg. 50/B6
Anūpgarh, India 86/B5
Anūpshahr, India 84/B1
Anuradhapura, SrL. 82/D6
Anvik, Ak, US 134/F3
Anvil Peak (vol.), Ak, US 134/B6
Anxi, China 79/C2
Anxi, China 70/G3
Anyang, China 72/C3
Anyang, SKor. 73/F7
A'nyêmaqên (mts.), China 70/G4
Anyi, China 72/B4
Anyuan, China 79/C2
Anza (riv.), It. 56/E6
'Anzah, WBnk. 91/G7
Anze, China 72/C3
Anzegem, Belg. 52/C2
Anzhero-Sudzhensk, Rus. 64/J4
Anzin, Fr. 52/C3
Anzing, Ger. 55/E6
Anzio, It. 46/C2
Anzoátegui, Ven. 152/D2
Anzoátegui (state), Ven. 153/E2
Anzoátegui (int'l arpt.), Ven. 153/E2
Anzola dell'Emilia, It. 59/E3
Ao Kham (pt.), Thai. 78/B4
Ao Phangnga NP, Thai. 78/B4
Aoba (isl.), Van. 116/F6
Aoga (isl.), Japan 75/F4
Aogaki, Japan 77/H5
Aoiz, Sp. 44/E1
Aomori (pref.), Japan 76/B3
Aomori, Japan 76/B3
Aonla, India 84/B1
Aoral (peak), Camb. 78/D3
Áos, Gre. 47/J4
Aosta, It. 43/G4
Aosta, Valle d' (valley), It. 58/A1
Aoudaghast (ruin), Mrta. 102/C2
Aouk, Bahr (riv.), Chad 93/D4
Aoukar (pol. reg.), Mrta. 96/D4
Aoulef, Alg. 99/F4
Aoyama, Japan 77/K6
Apache (mts.), Tx, US 132/B4
Apache (peak), Az, US 137/R18
Apalachicola, Fl, US 133/G4
Apan, Mex. 143/L7
Apaporis (riv.), Col. 150/D3
Aparados da Serra, PN de, Braz. 155/B4
Aparecida, Braz. 155/C2
Aparecida do Taboado, Braz. 155/B2
Aparición, Ven. 152/D2
Aparri, Phil. 79/D4
Apartadó, Col. 152/B3
Apátfalva, Hun. 48/E2
Apatin, Yugo. 48/D3
Apatity, Rus. 60/G2
Apatzingán de la Constitución, Mex. 142/E5
Apaxco, Mex. 143/K7
Apaxtla de Castrejon, Mex. 143/F5
Apeldoorn, Neth. 50/C4
Apelern, Ger. 51/G4
Apen, Ger. 51/E2
Apennines (mts.), It. 27/F4
Apensen, Ger. 51/G2
Aphrodisias (ruin), Turk. 90/B2
Api (peak), Indo. 81/E5
Api (cape), Indo. 81/F4
Api (cape), Indo. 80/C3
Apiacás, Serra dos (mts.), Braz. 150/G6
Apiaí, Braz. 155/B3
Apizaco, Mex. 143/L7
Aplao, Peru 156/C5
Apo (mt.), Phil. 81/G2
Apodi, Braz. 154/C2
Apodi (riv.), Braz. 154/C2
Apollo Bay, Austl. 115/B3
Apollonía, Gre. 47/J4
Apolo, Bol. 156/D4
Aporé (riv.), Braz. 151/H7
Apore (riv.), Braz. 155/B1
Apostle (isls.), Wi, US 127/L4
Apostle Islands Nat'l Lakeshore, Wi, US 127/L4
Apóstoles, Arg. 157/E2
Apostolos Andreas (cape), Cyp. 91/D2
Apoteri, Guy. 153/G3
Appalachian (mts.), US 125/K4
Appen, Ger. 51/G1
Appennino Ligure (mts.), It. 43/H4
Appennino Tosco-Emiliano (mts.), It. 43/J4
Appennino Umbro-Marchigiano (mts.), It. 43/K5
Appenweier, Ger. 56/D1
Appenzell, Swi. 57/F3
Appenzell (canton), Swi. 57/F3
Appignano, It. 59/G6
Appingedam, Neth. 50/D2
Apple Valley, Ca, US 136/C1
Appleton, NY, US 131/S9
Aprica, It. 57/G5
Aprica, Passo dell' (pass), It. 57/G5
Aprilia, It. 46/C2
Apriltsi, Bul. 47/J1
Apsheronsk, Rus. 62/F3
Apsley Gorge NP, Austl. 115/E1
Apua (pt.), Hi, US 124/U11
Apucarana, Braz. 155/B2
Apuiarés, Braz. 154/C1
Apure (riv.), Ven. 150/E2
Apure (prov.), Ven. 152/D3
Apurímac (dept.), Peru 156/C4
Apurímac (riv.), Peru 147/B4
Aqaba (gulf), Asia 67/B7
Aqmola (obl.), Kaz. 87/E2
'Aqrabah, WBnk. 91/D3
'Aqrah, Iraq 90/E2
Aqsay, Kaz. 63/K2
Aqtaū, Kaz. 63/J4
Aqtöbe (int'l arpt.), Kaz. 87/C2
Aqtöbe (obl.), Kaz. 87/C3
Aqtöbe, Kaz. 63/L2
Aquanaval (riv.), Mex. 142/E3
Aquaro-Guariquito, PN, Ven. 150/E2
Aquia, Peru 156/B3
Aquidauana, Braz. 151/G8
Aquidauana (riv.), Braz. 151/G8
Aquila, Swi. 57/E5
Aquileia, It. 59/G1
Aquiles Serdán, Mex. 132/B4
Aquin, Haiti 145/H2
Aquiraz, Braz. 154/C1
Aquitaine (pol. reg.), Fr. 42/C4
Ar-Asgat, Mong. 70/J2
Ar Horqin Qi, China 72/E2
Ar Ramādī, Iraq 90/E3
Ar Ramthā, Jor. 91/D3
Ar Raqqah, Syria 90/D3
Ar Raqqah (prov.), Syria 90/D2
Ar Rastan, Syria 91/E2
Ar Rayyān, Qatar 88/F3
Ar Riyāḑ (Riyadh) (cap.), SAr. 88/E4
Ar Rumaythah, Iraq 90/F4
Ar Ruşayfah, Jor. 91/E3
Ar Ruţbah, Iraq 90/E3
Ara (riv.), Japan 75/F2
Arab, Al, US 133/G3
'Arab, Baḩr al (riv.), Sudan 93/E3
Araban, Turk. 90/D2
Arabi, La, US 137/Q17
Arabian (des.), Egypt 97/M2
Arabian (pen.), SAr. 88/D3
Arabian (sea), Asia 67/F8
Araç (riv.), Turk. 62/E4
Araç, Turk. 62/E4
Araca, Bol. 150/E7
Araça (riv.), Braz. 153/F4
Aracaju, Braz. 154/C3
Aracataca, Col. 152/C2
Aracati, Braz. 154/C2
Araçatuba, Braz. 155/B2
Aracena, Sp. 44/B4
Araci, Braz. 154/C3
Aračinovo, FYROM 47/G1
Aracoiaba, Braz. 154/C2
Aracruz, Braz. 155/D1
Araçuaí, Braz. 154/B5
Araçuaí (riv.), Braz. 154/B5
Arad, Rom. 48/E2
Arad (prov.), Rom. 48/E2
'Arad, Isr. 91/D4
Ārādān, Iran 88/F1
Arafura (sea), Austl.,Indo. 116/C5
Aragarças, Braz. 151/H7
Aragats (peak), Arm. 63/H4
Aragón (aut. comm.), Sp. 45/E2
Aragón (riv.), Sp. 45/E1
Aragua (state), Ven. 153/E2
Araguaia (riv.), Braz. 147/D3
Araguaia, PN do, Braz. 151/H6
Araguaiana, Braz. 151/H7
Araguaína, Braz. 151/J5
Araguari (riv.), Braz. 151/H3
Araguari, Braz. 155/B1
Araguatins, Braz. 151/J5
Arai, Japan 75/F2
Araioses, Braz. 154/B1
Arāk, Iran 88/E2
Arakamchechan (isl.) 134/D3
Arakan (mts.), Myan. 70/F7
Arakawa, Japan 77/C2
Árakhthos (riv.), Gre. 47/G3
Araklı, Turk. 62/G4
Aral (sea), Asia 87/C3
Aral, Kaz. 87/D3
Aral Mangy Qaraqumy (des.), Kaz. 87/D3
Aralık, Turk. 63/H5
Aralsor (lake), Kaz. 63/H2
Aramac, Austl. 114/B3
Arāmbāgh, India 85/F4
Aran (isls.), Ire. 31/P10
Aran Fawddwy (peak), Wal, UK 34/E6
Aranda de Duero, Sp. 44/D2
Arandelovac, Yugo. 48/E3
Arani, India 82/C5
Aranjuez, Sp. 44/D2
Aransas Pass, Tx, US 132/D5
Arantina, Braz. 211/J6
Aranuka (isl.), Kiri. 116/G5
Arapahoe NWR, Co, US 137/C3
Arapiraca, Braz. 154/C3
Arapiuns (riv.), Braz. 153/H5
Arapongas, Braz. 155/B2
'Ar'ara, Isr. 91/G7
Araranguá, Braz. 155/B4
Araraquara, Braz. 155/B2
Araras, Braz. 155/C2
Ararat, Austl. 115/B3
Arari, Braz. 154/A1
Arāria, India 85/F2
Araripe, Chapada do (uplands), Braz. 154/B2
Araripina, Braz. 154/B2
Aras (riv.), Iran 63/H5
Aratane (well), Mrta. 102/C2
Aratoca, Col. 152/C3
Arauá (riv.), Braz. 150/F4
Arauca, Col. 152/D3
Arauca (riv.), Col.,Ven. 153/E3
Arauca (dept.), Col. 152/D3
Araucária, Braz. 155/B3
Arauco, Chile 158/B3
Arauquita, Col. 152/D3
Araure, Ven. 152/D2
Aravis, Col des (pass), Fr. 56/C6
Arawa, PNG 116/E5
Arawale Nat'l Rsv., Kenya 104/D3
Araxá, Braz. 155/C1
Araya (pen.), Ven. 153/E2
Ārba Minch', Eth. 97/N6
Arbeca, Sp. 45/F2
Arbīl (gov.), Iraq 90/E3
Arboga, Swe. 38/F2
Arbois, Fr. 56/B4
Arbois, Mont d' (peak), Fr. 56/C6
Arboletes, Col. 152/B2
Arbon, Swi. 57/F2
Arborfield, Sk, Can. 127/H2
Arborg, Mb, Can. 127/J3
Arbrå, Swe. 38/G1
Arbroath, Sc, UK 36/D3
Arc (riv.), Fr. 42/F5
Arc-en-Barrois, Fr. 56/B2
Arc-et-Senans, Fr. 56/B3
Arc-lès-Gray, Fr. 56/B3
Arc-sur-Tille, Fr. 56/B3
Arcachon, Fr. 42/C4
Arcachon, Bassin d' (lag.), Fr. 42/C4
Arcachon, Pointe d' (pt.), Fr. 42/C4
Arcadia, Fl, US 133/H5
Arcadia, Ok, US 137/N14
Arcadia, Ca, US 136/F7
Arcas, Cayos (isl.), Mex. 144/D1
Arcata, Ca, US 126/B5
Arceburgo, Braz. 211/G6
Arcelia, Mex. 143/E5
Arcene, It. 58/C1
Arceto, It. 59/D3
Archena, Sp. 44/E3
Archer City, Tx, US 129/H4
Arches, Fr. 56/C1
Arches NP, Ut, US 128/E3
Archidona, Sp. 44/C4
Archman, Trkm. 63/L5
Arcipelago Toscano (isl.), It. 43/H5
Arcisate, It. 57/E6
Arco, It. 57/G6
Arco, Paso del (pass), Arg. 158/C3
Arcola, It. 58/C4
Arcole, It. 59/E2
Arcos, Braz. 155/C2
Arcos de Jalón, Sp. 44/D2
Arcos de la Frontera, Sp. 44/C4
Arcos de Valdevez, Port. 44/A2
Arcoverde, Braz. 154/C3
Arctic (plain), Ak, US 134/F2
Arctic (ocean) 160/U
Arctic Bay, Nun., Can. 123/H1
Arctic Circle 160/J
Arctic NWR, US 134/J2
Arctic Red (riv.), NW, Can. 134/M2
Arctic Village, Ak, US 134/J2
Arctowski, Pol., Ant. 160/W
Arda (riv.), Bul. 62/C4
Ardabīl, Iran 63/J5
Ardahan, Turk. 63/G4
Ardal, Iran 88/F2
Årdalstangen, Nor. 38/B1
Ardanuç, Turk. 63/G4
Ardèche (riv.), Fr. 42/F4
Ardee, Ire. 34/B4
Arden (mt.), Austl. 113/H5
Arden, De, US 138/C4
Arden, Den. 38/C3
Arden-Arcade, Ca, US 135/M9
Ardennes (for.), Belg. 42/F1
Ardennes (dept.), Fr. 53/D4
Ardennes, Canal des (canal), Fr. 53/D4
Ardenno, It. 57/F5
Ardersier, Sc, UK 36/B1
Ardeşen, Turk. 63/G4
Ardesio, It. 57/F6
Ardestān, Iran 88/F2
Ardez, Swi. 57/G4
Ardila (riv.), Sp. 44/B3
Ardino, Bul. 49/G5
Ardivachar (pt.), Sc, UK 31/Q8
Ardle (riv.), Sc, UK 36/C3
Ardlethan, Austl. 115/C2
Ardmore, Ok, US 129/H4
Ardmore, Pa, US 138/C4
Ardnamurchan (pt.), Sc, UK 31/Q8
Ardon, Swi. 56/D5
Ardooie, Belg. 52/C2
Ardres, Fr. 52/A2
Ardrossan, Austl. 113/H5
Ardrossan, Sc, UK 36/B5
Ards (pen.), Sc, UK 34/C3
Ards (dist.), NI, UK 34/C2
Ardsley, NY, US 139/K7
Åre, Swe. 37/E3
Areado, Braz. 211/G6
Arecibo, PR 141/M8
Areia Branca, Braz. 154/C2
Arena (pt.), Ca, US 128/B3
Arena de la Ventana Punta (pt.), Mex. 142/C3
Arenal (vol.), CR 145/E4
Arenápolis, Braz. 151/G6
Arenas de San Pedro, Sp. 44/C2
Arenas, Punta de (pt.), Arg. 159/C7
Arendal, Nor. 38/C2
Arendonk, Belg. 50/C6
Arendtsville, Pa, US 138/A4
Arenig Fawr (peak), Wal, UK 34/E6
Arenys de Mar, Sp. 45/L6
Arenzano, It. 58/B4
Areo, Ven. 153/F2
Areópolis, Gre. 47/H4
Arequipa (dept.), Peru 156/C5
Arequipa, Peru 156/D5
Arequito, Arg. 158/E2
Aresing, Ger. 54/E5
Arévalo, Sp. 44/C2
Arezzo, It. 59/E6
Arezzo (prov.), It. 59/E5
Arga (riv.), Sp. 44/E1
Argalastí, Gre. 47/H3
Argamasilla de Alba, Sp. 44/D3
Argamasilla de Calatrava, Sp. 44/C3
Arganda, Sp. 45/N9
Argegno, It. 57/F6
Argelès-Gazost, Fr. 42/C5
Argelès-sur-Mer, Fr. 42/E5
Argen (riv.), Ger. 57/F2
Argenbühl, Ger. 57/F2

170

Argen – Ayabe

Argens (riv.), Fr. 43/G5
Argenta, It. 59/E3
Argentan, Fr. 42/C2
Argentat, Fr. 42/D4
Argentera (peak), It. 43/G4
Argenteuil, Fr. 30/J5
Argentière, Aiguille d' (peak), Swi. 56/D6
Argentina (ctry.), Arg. 157/C4
Argentina (riv.), It. 58/A5
Argentino (lake), Arg. 159/B6
Argenton-sur-Creuse, Fr. 42/D3
Argentona, Sp. 45/L6
Argeş (prov.), Rom. 49/G3
Argeş (riv.), Rom. 62/C3
Arghandab (riv.), Afg. 89/J2
Argıthanı, Turk. 90/B2
Argolis (gulf), Gre. 47/H4
Argonne (for.), Fr. 40/C4
Argonne National Laboratory, Il, US 135/P16
Árgos, Gre. 47/H4
Árgos Orestikón, Gre. 47/G2
Argostólion, Gre. 47/G3
Arguello (pt.), Ca, US 128/B4
Arguin, Cap d' (cape), Mrta. 98/A5
Argun' (riv.), Rus. 65/M4
Arguut, Mong. 70/H2
Argyle (lake), Austl. 109/B2
Argyll and Bute (pol. reg.), Sc, UK 36/A4
Arhangay (prov.), Mong. 70/G2
Arhreijît (well), Mrta. 98/B5
Århus (co.), Den. 38/D3
Århus, Den. 38/D3
Ariano Irpino, It. 46/D2
Ariari (riv.), Col. 152/C4
Arias, Arg. 158/E2
Arica, Chile 156/D5
Arıcak, Turk. 90/E2
Arid (cape), Austl. 112/D5
Arida, Japan 74/D3
Aridhaía, Gre. 47/H2
Arido (peak), Ca, US 136/A1
Aridol (lake), WSah. 98/B4
Ariège (riv.), Fr. 42/D5
Arifiye, Turk. 49/K5
Ārifwāla, Pak. 86/B4
Arīḩā, Syria 91/E2
Arikaree (riv.), Co, US 129/G3
Arilje, Yugo. 48/E4
Arima, Trin. 153/F2
Arinos (riv.), Braz. 151/G6
Arinos, Braz. 154/A4
Arinthod, Fr. 56/B5
Ario de Rosales, Mex. 143/E5
Aripao, Ven. 153/E3
Aripuanã, Braz. 150/G6
Aripuanã (riv.), Braz. 147/C3
Ariquemes, Braz. 150/F5
Arish, Austl. 114/B2
Arismendi, Ven. 152/D2
Arivechi, Mex. 142/C2
Arivonimamo, Madg. 107/H7
Ariza, Sp. 44/D2
Arizona (canal), Az, US 137/R18
Arizona (state), US 128/D4
Arizona, Arg. 158/D2
Arizpe, Mex. 142/C2
Årjäng, Swe. 38/E2
Arjeplog, Swe. 37/F2
Arjona, Sp. 44/C4
Arjona, Col. 152/C2
Arkadelphia, Ar, US 129/J4
Arkaig (lake), Sc, UK 36/A3
Arkalokhórion, Gre. 47/J5
Arkansas (riv.), US 132/E3
Arkansas (state), US 132/E3
Arkansas City, Ar, US 129/K4
Arkansas City, Ks, US 129/H3
Arkanū (peak), Libya 97/K3
Arkhángelos, Gre. 90/B2
Arkhangel'sk (int'l arpt.), Rus. 60/J2
Arkhangel'sk (Archangel), Rus. 60/J2
Arkhangel'skaya (obl.), Rus. 60/H3
Arkhangel'skoye, Rus. 61/W9
Arklow, Ire. 34/B6
Arkona (cape), Ger. 38/E4
Arkonam, India 82/C5
Arkticheskiy Institut (isls.), Rus. 64/H2
Ärla, Swe. 38/G2
Arlan (peak), Trkm. 87/B5
Arlanda (int'l arpt.), Swe. 38/G2
Arlanza (riv.), Sp. 44/C1
Arlazón (riv.), Sp. 44/D1
Arlbergpass (pass), Aus. 57/G3
Arles, Fr. 42/F5
Arlesheim, Swi. 56/D3
Arley, Mo, US 137/E5
Arlington, Mn, US 127/K4
Arlington, Ga, US 133/G4
Arlington, Va, US 138/A6
Arlington Heights, Il, US 130/C3
Arló, Hun. 41/L4
Arlon, Belg. 53/E4
Arluno, It. 58/B1
Arly (riv.), Fr. 56/C6
Arly, PN de l', Burk. 103/F4
Arly, Réserve Totale de Faune de l', Burk. 103/F4
Armada, Mi, US 135/G6
Armadale, Sc, UK 36/C5
Armagh (dist.), NI, UK 34/B3
Armagh, NI, UK 34/B3
Armançon (riv.), Fr. 42/F3
Armando Laydner, Represa de (res.), Braz. 155/B2
Armant, Egypt 101/C3
Armavir, Rus. 63/G3
Arme, Cap d' (cape), Fr. 43/G5
Armenia, Col. 150/C3
Armenia (ctry.) 63/H5
Armentières, Fr. 52/B2
Armentières-en-Brie, Fr. 30/M5
Armería, Mex. 142/E5
Armidale, Austl. 115/D1
Armilla, Sp. 44/D4
Armstrong, BC, Can. 126/D3
Armstrong, Arg. 158/E2
Armthorpe, Eng, UK 35/G4
Ārmūr, India 82/C4
Armutlu, Turk. 49/J5
Army Ordnance Museum, Md, US 138/B5
Arnage, Fr. 42/D3
Arnager (int'l arpt.), Den. 38/F4
Arnaía, Gre. 47/H2
Arnaud (riv.), Qu, Can. 123/J3
Arnauti (cape), Cyp. 91/C2
Arnedo, Sp. 44/D1
Arnett, Ok, US 129/H3
Arnhem, Neth. 50/C5
Arnhem Land (reg.), Austl. 109/C2
Arno (riv.), It. 43/J5
Arno (isl.), Mrsh. 116/G4
Arnold, Mo, US 137/G9
Arnold, Md, US 138/B5
Arnold, Eng, UK 35/G6
Arnoldstein, Aus. 43/K3
Arnon (riv.), Fr. 42/E3
Arnouville-lès-Gonesse, Fr. 30/K5
Arnprior, On, Can. 130/E2
Arnsberg, Ger. 51/F6
Arnstadt, Ger. 43/J1
Arnstein, Ger. 54/C3
Arnstorf, Ger. 55/F5
Aro Usu (cape), Indo. 81/H5
Aroab, Namb. 106/B2
Aroche, Sp. 44/B4
Arolsen, Ger. 51/G6
Aron (riv.), Fr. 42/E3
Arona, Canl. 45/X16
Arona, It. 58/B1
Aronde (riv.), Fr. 52/B5
Arorae (isl.), Kiri. 116/G5
Arosa, Swi. 57/F4
Aroser Rothern (peak), Swi. 57/F4
Ærøskøbing, Den. 38/D4
Arpaçay, Turk. 63/G4
Arpajon, Fr. 30/J6
Arpajon-sur-Cère, Fr. 42/E4
Arqalyq, Kaz. 87/E2
Arquata Scrivia, It. 58/B3
Arques, Fr. 52/B2
'Arrābah, WBnk. 91/G7
Arrah, India 85/E3
Arraias (riv.), Braz. 151/H6
Arraias, Braz. 154/A4
Arraiján, Pan. 152/B2
Arran (isl.), Sc, UK 31/R8
Arrancabarba (peak), Nic. 145/E4
Arras, Fr. 52/B3
Arreau, Fr. 42/D5
Arrecife, Sp. 98/B3
Arrecifes, Arg. 158/E2
Arrée, Monts d' (mts.), Fr. 42/B2
Arriaga, Mex. 144/C2
Arriondas, Sp. 44/C1
Arrochar, Sc, UK 36/B4
Arroio Grande, Braz. 155/A5
Arronville, Fr. 30/J4
Arroscia (riv.), It. 58/B4
Arroux (riv.), Fr. 42/F3
Arrow (riv.), Eng, UK 32/C2
Arrowbear Lake, Ca, US 136/C2
Arroyo de la Luz, Sp. 44/B3
Arroyo Grande, Ca, US 128/B4
Arroyo Hondo (riv.), Ca, US 135/L12
Arroyo Trabuco (riv.), Ca, US 136/C3
Års, Den. 38/C3
Ars-sur-Moselle, Fr. 53/F5
Arsen'yev, Rus. 71/P3
Arsiero, It. 59/E1
Arslanköy, Turk. 91/D1
Arta (gulf), Gre. 47/G3
Árta, Gre. 47/G3
Artá, Sp. 45/G3
Arteaga, Mex. 142/E5
Arteixo, Sp. 44/A1
Artem, Rus. 71/P3
Artemisa, Cuba 145/F1
Artesia, NM, US 129/F4
Artesia, Ca, US 136/F8
Arth, Swi. 57/E3
Arthies, Fr. 30/H4
Arthur (pt.), Austl. 114/C3
Arthur (riv.), Austl. 112/C5
Arthur Kill (riv.), NJ,NY, US 139/J9
Arthur's (pass), NZ 117/S11
Arthur's Pass NP, NZ 117/S11
Artigas, Uru. 157/E3
Artogne, It. 58/D1
Artois (reg.), Fr. 40/A3
Artova, Turk. 62/F4
Artur Nogueira, Braz. 211/F7
Arturo Merino Benitez (Santiago) (int'l arpt.), Chile 158/N8
Artux, China 87/G5
Artvin (prov.), Turk. 63/G4
Artvin, Turk. 63/G4
Aru (isls.), Indo. 116/C5
Arua, Ugan. 104/A2
Aruba (isl.), Aru., Neth. 147/B1
Arucas, Sp. 98/B3
Arudy, Fr. 42/C5
Arujá, Braz. 211/G8
Arun (riv.), China 85/F2
Arunāchal Pradesh (state), India 70/F6
Arundel, Eng, UK 33/F5
Aruppukkottai, India 82/C6
'ārūrah, WBnk. 91/G7
Arus (cape), Indo. 81/F3
Arusha, Tanz. 104/C3
Arusha (pol. reg.), Tanz. 104/C4
Arusha NP, Tanz. 104/C3
Arutua (isl.), FrPol. 117/L6
Aruwimi (riv.), D.R. Congo 93/E4
Arvada, Co, US 137/B3
Arvayheer, Mong. 70/H2
Arve (riv.), Fr. 56/C6
Arviat, Nun., Can. 122/G2
Arvidsjaur, Swe. 37/F2
Arvika, Swe. 38/E2
Arvin, Ca, US 128/C4
Arvon (mt.), Mi, US 127/L4
Aryānah, Tun. 46/B4
Aryānah (gov.), Tun. 46/A4
Arys', Kaz. 87/E4
Arz (riv.), Fr. 42/B3
Arzachena, It. 46/A2
Arzamas, Rus. 61/K5
Arzbach, Ger. 53/G3
Arzberg, Ger. 55/F2
ärzen, Ger. 51/G4
Arzew, Alg. 100/E5
Arzignano, It. 59/E1
Arzl im Pitztal, Aus. 57/G3
Arzúa, Sp. 44/A1
Ås, Nor. 38/D2
As, Belg. 53/E1
Aš, Czh. 55/F2
As Sabkhah, Syria 90/D3
Aş Şaff, Egypt 91/B5
Aş Şāfī, Jor. 91/D4
As Sālimīyah, Kuw. 88/E3
As Sallūm, Egypt 97/L1
As Salmān, Iraq 90/F4
As Salţ, Jor. 91/D3
As Sanţah, Egypt 91/B4
Aş Şarīḩ, Jor. 91/D3
As Sinbillāwayn, Egypt 91/B4
As Sudd (reg.), Sudan 93/F4
As Sulaymānīyah (gov.), Iraq 90/F3
As Sulaymānīyah, Iraq 90/F3
As Suwaydā' (prov.), Syria 90/D3
As Suwaydā', Syria 91/E3
Aş Şuwayrah, Iraq 90/F3
As Suways (gov.), Egypt 101/C2
As Suways, Egypt 91/C4
Asaba, Nga. 103/G5
Asadābād, Afg. 86/A2
Asadābād, Iran 88/E2
Asagny, PN d', C.d'Iv. 102/D5
Asahan (riv.), Indo. 80/A3
Asahi, Japan 75/G3
Asahi (riv.), Japan 74/C3
Asahi, Japan 77/F1
Asahi, Japan 77/L5
Asahi, Japan 77/M5
Asahi-dake (peak), Japan 76/C2
Asahikawa, Japan 76/C2
Asai, Japan 77/K5
Asaka, Japan 77/D2
Asake (riv.), Japan 77/K5
Asama-yama (peak), Japan 75/F2
Asan (bay), SKor. 73/D4
Asansol, India 85/F4
Asashi-dake (peak), Japan 75/F1
Asashina, Japan 77/A1
Asawanwah (well), Libya 96/J3
Asbach, Ger. 53/G2
Asbach-Bäumenheim, Ger. 54/D5
Asbest, Rus. 61/P4
Asbestos (mts.), SAfr. 106/C3
Asbury Park, NJ, US 138/D3
Ascención, Bol. 150/F7
Ascención (bay), Mex. 140/D4
Ascensión, Mex. 128/F5
Ascensión, Arg. 158/E2
Aschach (riv.), Aus. 55/G6
Aschach an der Donau, Aus. 55/H6
Aschaffenburg, Ger. 54/C3
Aschau am Inn, Ger. 55/F6
Ascheberg, Ger. 51/E5
Aschendorf, Ger. 51/E2
Aschersleben, Ger. 40/F3
Ascoli Piceno, It. 43/K5
Ascoli Satriano, It. 46/D2
Ascona, Swi. 57/E5
Ascope, Peru 156/B2
Åseda, Swe. 38/F3
Āsela, Eth. 97/N6
Åsele, Swe. 37/F2
Asendorf, Ger. 51/G2
Asendorf, Ger. 51/F3
Asenovgrad, Bul. 47/J1
Åseral, Nor. 38/B2
Aserei (peak), It. 58/C3
Asfeld, Fr. 53/D5
Ash, Eng, UK 30/D3
Ash, Eng, UK 30/A3
Ash Shabakah, Iraq 90/E4
Ash Shamal (gov.), Leb. 91/E2
Ash Shāmīyah, Iraq 90/F4
Ash Shāriqah, UAE 89/G3
Ash Sharqāt, Iraq 90/E3
Ash Sharqīyah (state), Sudan 101/C5
Ash Shawbak, Jor. 91/D4
Asha, Nga. 103/F5
Ashanti (uplands), C.d'Iv.. 96/E6
Ashanti (pol. reg.), Gha. 103/E5
Asharoken, NY, US 139/M8
Ashbourne, Ire. 34/B4
Ashbourne, Eng, UK 35/G5
Ashburton (riv.), Austl. 109/A3
Ashburton, NZ 117/S11
Ashby (canal), Eng, UK 33/E1
Ashby-de-la-Zouch, Eng, UK 33/E1
Ashcroft, BC, Can. 126/C3
Ashdod, Isr. 91/F8
Asheboro, NC, US 133/J3
Ashern, Mb, Can. 127/J3
Asheville, NC, US 133/H3
Asheweig (riv.), On, Can. 127/M2
Ashford, Austl. 115/D1
Ashford, Eng, UK 33/G4
Ashford, Eng, UK 30/B2
Ashford, Ire. 34/B5
Ashgabat (cap.), Trkm. 89/G1
Ashhurst, NZ 117/T11
Ashibetsu, Japan 76/C2
Ashigawa, Japan 77/B2
Ashikaga, Japan 77/C1
Ashington, Eng, UK 35/G1
Ashino (lake), Japan 77/C3
Ashiwada, Japan 77/B3
Ashiya, Japan 77/H6
Ashiyasu, Japan 77/A2
Ashizuri-misaki (cape), Japan 74/C4
Ashkal (lake), Tun. 100/L6
Ashland, Ks, US 129/H3
Ashland, Or, US 126/C5
Ashland, Ky, US 130/D4
Ashland, Oh, US 130/D3
Ashland, Pa, US 138/B2
Ashley, ND, US 127/J4
Ashley, Pa, US 138/C1
Ashmore (reef), Austl. 109/B2
Ashmore and Cartier Islands Territory (dpcy.), Austl. 109/B2
Ashmūn, Egypt 91/B4
Ashoknagar, India 84/A3
Ashoro, Japan 76/C2
Ashqelon, Isr. 91/F8
Ashta, India 82/C3
Ashtabula, Oh, US 130/D3
Ashton, Id, US 126/F4
Ashton, SAfr. 106/M10
Ashton-in-Makerfield, Eng, UK 35/F5
Ashton-under-Lyne, Eng, UK 35/F5
Asia, Peru 156/B4
Asia (cont.) 67
Asiago, It. 57/H6
Asikkala, Fin. 39/L1
Asilah, Mor. 100/A2
Asillo, Peru 156/D4
Asinara (isl.), It. 46/A2
Asinara, Golfo dell' (gulf), It. 46/A2
Asino, Rus. 64/J4
Asipovichy, Bela. 62/D1
'Asīr (mts.), SAr. 88/D5
Asis (cape), Sudan 101/D5
Aşkale, Turk. 63/G5
Askeaton, Ire. 31/P10
Asker, Nor. 38/D2
Askersund, Swe. 38/F2
Askim, Nor. 38/D2
Askim, Swe. 38/D3
Áskion (peak), Gre. 47/G2
Askja (crater), Ice. 37/P6
Askov, Den. 38/C4
Askvoll, Nor. 37/C3
Asmara (cap.), Erit. 88/C5
Asnen (lake), Swe. 38/F3
Asnières-sur-Oise, Fr. 30/K4
Asnières-sur-Seine, Fr. 30/J5
Asō, Japan 77/E2
Aso NP, Japan 74/B4
Aso-san (peak), Japan 74/B4
Asola, It. 58/D2
Asolo, It. 59/E1
Āsosa, Eth. 97/M5
Asoteriba (peak), Sudan 101/D4
Aspach, Aus. 55/G6
Aspe, Sp. 45/E3
Aspen, Co, US 128/F3
Aspen Hill, Md, US 138/A5
Aspen Park, Co, US 137/B3
Aspendos (ruin), Turk. 91/B1
Asperg, Ger. 54/C5
Aspermont, Tx, US 129/G4
Aspers, Pa, US 138/A4
Aspetuck (riv.), Ct, US 139/E1
Aspiring (mt.), NZ 117/R11
Asprópirgos, Gre. 47/H3
Asquith, Sk, Can. 126/G2
Assa, Mor. 98/C3
Assa Aguiene (peak), Alg. 99/G5
Assab, Erit. 88/D6
Assaba (pol. reg.), Mrta. 102/C2
Assam (state), India 70/F6
Assaré, Braz. 154/C2
Asse, Belg. 53/D2
Assemini, It. 46/A3
Assen, Neth. 50/D3
Assenede, Belg. 52/C1
Assens, Den. 38/C4
Assens, Den. 38/D3
Assentoft, Den. 38/D3
Assesse, Belg. 53/E3
Assiniboia, Sk, Can. 127/G3
Assiniboine (mt.), BC, Can. 126/E3
Assiniboine (riv.), Mb,Sk, Can. 127/H3
Assinika (lake), Qu, Can. 130/F1
Assis, Braz. 155/B2
Assling, Ger. 55/F6
Asso, It. 58/C1
Assomada, CpV. 93/K10
Astakós, Gre. 47/G3
Astana (cap.), Kaz. 87/F2
Asten, Neth. 50/C6
Asten, Aus. 55/H6
Asti (prov.), It. 58/B3
Asti, It. 43/H4
Astico (riv.), It. 59/E1
Astipálaia, Gre. 90/A2
Astolfo Dutra, Braz. 211/L6
Astorga, Braz. 155/B2
Astoria, Or, US 126/C4
Åstorp, Swe. 38/E3
Astrakhan', Rus. 63/J3
Astrakhanskaya (obl.), Rus. 63/H3
Ástros, Gre. 47/H4
Astudillo, Sp. 44/C1
Asturias (aut. comm.), Sp. 44/B1
Asuka, Japan 77/J7
Asuke, Japan 77/M5
Asunción (cap.), Par. 157/E2
Asuncion (isl.), NMar. 116/D3
Asunción Ixtaltepec, Mex. 140/B4
Asunden (lake), Swe. 38/F3
Aswa (riv.), Ugan. 97/M7
Aswān (gov.), Egypt 101/C4
Aswān, Egypt 101/C3
Aswan High (dam), Egypt 101/C4
Asyūţ (gov.), Egypt 101/B3
Asyūţ, Egypt 101/B3
Aszód, Hun. 49/R9
Aţ Ţafīlah, Jor. 91/D4
Aţ Ţafīlah (gov.), Jor. 91/D4
Aţ Ţā'if, SAr. 88/D4
At Tall, Syria 91/E3
At Tall al Kabīr, Egypt 91/B4
At Ta'mīn (gov.), Iraq 90/E3
Aţ Ţūr, WBnk. 91/G8
Atabapo (riv.), Ven. 153/E4
Atacama (des.), Chile 147/B4
Atacames, Ecu. 152/B4
Atafu (isl.), Tok. 117/H5
Atakpamé, Togo 103/F5
Atalaia, Braz. 154/C3
Atalaia do Norte, Braz. 156/D2
Atalándi, Gre. 47/H3
Atalaya, Peru 156/C3
Atami, Japan 75/F3
Atar, Mrta. 96/C3
Atarfe, Sp. 44/D4
Atarra, India 84/C3
Atas Bogd (peak), Mong. 70/G3
Atascadero, Ca, US 128/B4
Atascosa (co.), Tx, US 137/T21
Atascosa, Tx, US 137/T21
Atatürk (dam), Turk. 90/D2
Atatürk (res.), Turk. 90/D2
Ataturk (int'l arpt.), Turk. 49/J5
Atbara (riv.), Eth. 97/N5
Atbara, Sudan 97/M4
Atbasar, Kaz. 87/E2
Atchafalaya (riv.), La, US 129/K5
Atchafalaya (bay), La, US 129/K5
Atchison, Ks, US 129/J3
Atco, NJ, US 138/D4
Atebubu, Gha. 103/E5
Ateca, Sp. 44/E2
Ateelva (riv.), Nor. 37/G1
Atén, Bol. 156/D4
Atencingo, Mex. 143/L8
Atenco, Mex. 143/Q10
Atenco, Mex. 143/R9
Atengo (riv.), Mex. 142/D4
Atessa, It. 46/D1
Atglen, Pa, US 138/C4
Ath, Belg. 52/C2
Athabasca, Ab, Can. 126/E2
Athabasca (riv.), Ab, Can. 122/E3
Athabasca (lake), Ab,Sk, Can. 122/E3
Athapapuskow (lake), Mb, Can. 127/H2
Āthār Ţulmaythah (Ptolemaïs) (ruin), Libya 97/K1
Athboy, Ire. 31/Q10
Athenry, Ire. 31/P10
Athens, Tx, US 129/J4
Athens, Ga, US 133/H3
Athens, Al, US 133/G3
Athens, Tn, US 133/G3
Atherstone, Eng, UK 33/E1
Atherton, Mo, US 137/E5
Atherton, Austl. 114/B2
Atherton, Eng, UK 35/F4
Athgarh, India 82/E3
Athi (riv.), Kenya 104/C3
Athínai (Athens) (cap.), Gre. 47/N9
Athis-Mons, Fr. 30/K5
Athlone, Ire. 31/Q10
Atholl (for.), Sc, UK 36/B3
Áthos (peak), Gre. 47/J2
Athy, Ire. 31/Q10
Ati, Chad 96/J5
Atibaia (riv.), Braz. 211/G7
Atibaia, Braz. 211/G8
Atico, Peru 156/C5
Atienza, Sp. 44/D2
Atikokan, On, Can. 127/L3
Atil, Mex. 142/C2
Atitlán (lake), Guat. 144/D3
Atiu (isl.), Cookls. 117/K7
Atizapan, Mex. 143/Q10
Atka, Ak, US 134/D5
Atka (isl.), Ak, US 65/U4
Atkarsk, Rus. 63/H2
Atkinson (pt.), NW, Can. 134/M2
Atlacomulco de Fabela, Mex. 143/K7
Atlanta (cap.), Ga, US 133/G3
Atlantic (co.), NJ, US 138/D4
Atlantic (ocean) 22/G3
Atlantic Beach, NY, US 139/L9
Atlantic City, NJ, US 138/D5
Atlantic Highlands, NJ, US 139/J10
Atlantico (dept.), Col. 145/H4
Atlántida, Uru. 159/L11
Atlantique (prov.), Ben. 103/F5
Atlas (mts.), Mor. 96/E1
Atlas (peak), Ca, US 135/K10
Atlas Saharien (mts.), Alg. 96/E1
Atlatlahuaca, Mex. 143/Q10
Atlin, BC, Can. 134/M3
'Atlit, Isr. 91/F6
Atlixco, Mex. 143/L8
Atmore, Al, US 133/G4
Atocha, Bol. 150/E8
Atomium, The, Belg. 53/D2
Atotonilco, Mex. 143/L6
Atouila, 'Erg (des.), Mali 98/D5
Atoyac, Mex. 143/E5
Atoyac (riv.), Mex. 144/B2
Atqasuk, Ak, US 134/G1
Atrai (riv.), Bang. 85/G3
Atrak (riv.), Iran 64/F6
Ätran (riv.), Swe. 38/E3
Atrato (riv.), Col. 150/C2
Atrauli, India 84/B1
Atsugi, Japan 77/C3
Atsumi, Japan 77/M6
Atsumi (pen.), Japan 77/M6
Attalens, Swi. 56/C4
Attalla, Al, US 133/G3
Attapu, Laos 78/D3
Attawapiskat (lake), On, Can. 127/L2
Attawapiskat (riv.), On, Can. 123/H3
Attel (riv.), Ger. 55/F7
Attendorn, Ger. 51/E6
Atteridgeville, SAfr. 106/Q12
Attersee (lake), Aus. 43/K3
Attert, Belg. 53/E4
Attica, Mi, US 135/F5
Attigny, Fr. 53/D5
'Attīl, WBnk. 91/G7
Attock, Pak. 86/B3
Attu, Ak, US 134/A5
Attu (isl.), Ak, US 65/T4
Atuel (riv.), Arg. 157/C4
Atuntaqui, Ecu. 152/B4
Åtvidaberg, Swe. 38/G2
Atwater, Ca, US 128/B3
Atyraū (obl.), Kaz. 87/B3
Atyraū, Kaz. 63/J3
Atyraū (int'l arpt.), Kaz. 63/J3
Au, Swi. 57/F3
Au, Aus. 57/F3
Au in der Hallertau, Ger. 55/E5
Au Sable (riv.), Mi, US 130/C2
Auari (riv.), Braz. 153/E3
Aubange, Belg. 53/E4
Aube (dept.), Fr. 53/D6
Aube (riv.), Fr. 40/C4
Aubenas, Fr. 42/F4
Aubepierre-Ozouer-le-Repos, Fr. 30/L6
Aubergenville, Fr. 30/H5
Aubert (peak), Swi. 56/C4
Aubervilliers, Fr. 30/K5
Aubetin (riv.), Fr. 52/C6
Aubette (riv.), Fr. 52/A5
Aubette de Magny (riv.), Fr. 30/H4
Aubigny-en-Artois, Fr. 52/B3
Aubigny-sur-Nère, Fr. 42/E3
Aubin, Fr. 42/E4
Aubonne, Swi. 56/C5
Auboué, Fr. 53/E5
Aubrac, Monts du (mts.), Fr. 42/E4
Aubrives, Fr. 53/D3
Aubry, Ks, US 137/D6
Auburn, Wa, US 126/C4
Auburn, Ne, US 129/J2
Auburn, Ca, US 128/B3
Auburn, Me, US 131/G2
Auburn, NY, US 130/E3
Auburn, In, US 130/C3
Auburn, Al, US 133/G3
Auburn, Austl. 113/H5
Auburn, Pa, US 138/B2
Auburn Hills, Mi, US 135/F6
Aubusson, Fr. 42/E4
Aucá Mahuida (peak), Arg. 158/C3
Auch, Fr. 42/D5
Auchel, Fr. 52/B3
Auchinleck, Sc, UK 36/B6
Auchterarder, Sc, UK 36/C4
Auchtermuchty, Sc, UK 36/C4
Auchy-lès-Hesdin, Fr. 52/B3
Auckland, NZ 117/S10
Auckland (int'l arpt.), NZ 117/S10
Auckland (isls.), NZ 23/T8
Aude (riv.), Fr. 42/E5
Auderghem, Belg. 53/D2
Audeux (riv.), Fr. 56/C3
Audierne (bay), Fr. 42/A3
Audincourt, Fr. 56/C3
Audo (range), Eth. 97/P6
Audruicq, Fr. 52/B2
Audun-le-Roman, Fr. 53/E5
Audun-le-Tiche, Fr. 53/E5
Aue (riv.), Ger. 51/E2
Aue, Ger. 55/F1
Auer (Ora), It. 57/H5
Auerbach, Ger. 55/F1
Auerbach in der Oberpfalz, Ger. 55/E3
Auersberg (peak), Ger. 55/F2
Aufess (riv.), Ger. 54/E3
Auffargis, Fr. 30/H5
Augathella, Austl. 114/B4
Augher, NI, UK 34/A3
Aughnacloy, NI, UK 34/B3
Aughrim, Ire. 34/B6
Augrabies Falls NP, SAfr. 106/C3
Augrabiesvalle (falls), SAfr. 106/C3
Augsburg, Ger. 54/D6
Augub (peak), Namb. 106/A2
Augusta, Ga, US 133/H3
Augusta (cap.), Me, US 131/G2
Augusta, It. 46/D4
Augusta, Austl. 112/B5
Augusta, NJ, US 138/D1
Augusta, Golfo di (gulf), It. 46/D4
Augustdorf, Ger. 51/F5
Augustenborg, Den. 38/C4
Augusto César Sandino (int'l arpt.), Nic. 144/E3
Augustów, Pol. 39/K5
Augustus (mt.), Austl. 112/C3
Auk Bok (isl.), Myan. 78/B3
Auki, Sol. 116/F5
Aukstatija NP, Lith. 39/M4
Auld (lake), Austl. 109/B3
Aulencia (riv.), Sp. 45/M9
Aulendorf, Ger. 57/F2
Aulla, It. 58/C4
Aulnay-sous-Bois, Fr. 30/K5
Aulnay-sur-Mauldre, Fr. 30/H5
Aulne (riv.), Fr. 42/A2
Aulnoy, Fr. 30/M5
Aulnoye-Aymeries, Fr. 52/C3
Aulnut (int'l arpt.), Fr. 42/E4
Ault, Co, US 137/C1
Ault (peak), Swi. 57/F4
Ault, Fr. 52/A3
Aumale, Fr. 52/A4
Aumetz, Fr. 53/E5
Aumühle, Ger. 51/H1
Aunay-sur-Odon, Fr. 42/C2
Aunette (riv.), Fr. 52/B5
Auneuil, Fr. 52/B5
Auning, Den. 38/D3
Aur (isl.), Mrsh. 116/G4
Aura, NJ, US 138/C4
Aurach, Ger. 54/D4
Aurach (riv.), Ger. 54/D3
Auraiya, India 84/B2
Aurangābād, India 85/E3
Aurangābād, India 89/L5
Auray, Fr. 42/B3
Aureilhan, Fr. 42/D5
Aurich, Ger. 51/E2
Auriflama, Braz. 155/B2
Aurillac, Fr. 42/E4
Aurisina, It. 59/G1
Aurland, Nor. 38/B1
Aurolzmünster, Aus. 55/G6
Aurora, Braz. 154/C2
Aurora, Mo, US 129/J3
Aurora, Il, US 129/K2
Aurora, Co, US 137/C3
Aurora, Guy. 153/G3
Aurora Lodge, Ak, US 134/J3
Aus, Namb. 106/B2
Ausa (riv.), It. 59/G1
Aussillon, Fr. 42/E5
Aust-Agder (co.), Nor. 37/C4
Austin, Nv, US 128/C3
Austin (lake), Austl. 109/A3
Austin (isl.), Nun., Can. 122/G2
Austral (Tubuaï Islands) (isls.), FrPol. 117/K7
Australia (cont.) 109
Australian Alps (range), Austl. 115/C3
Australian Capital Territory (cap. terr.), Austl. 109/D4
Australind, Austl. 112/B5
Austria (ctry.) 43/L3
Austurhorn (pt.), Ice. 37/P7
Auterive, Fr. 42/D5
Authie (riv.), Fr. 42/D1
Autlán de Navarro, Mex. 142/D5
Automne (riv.), Fr. 52/B5
Autreppe, Belg. 52/C3
Autun, Fr. 42/F3
Auvergne (pol. reg.), Fr. 42/E4
Auvers-sur-Oise, Fr. 30/J4
Auvézère (riv.), Fr. 42/D4
Aux Sables (riv.), On, Can. 130/D2
Auxerre, Fr. 42/E3
Auxi-le-Château, Fr. 52/B3
Auxonne, Fr. 56/B3
Auyán-Tepuí (peak), Ven. 153/F3
Auyuittuq NP, Nun., Can. 123/K2
Auzangate (peak), Peru 156/D4
Āvaj, Iran 88/E1
Avallon, Fr. 42/E3
Avalon, Ca, US 136/B4
Avalon, NJ, US 138/D5
Avalon (pen.), Nf, Can. 123/L4
Avanne-Aveney, Fr. 56/B3
Avaré, Braz. 155/B2
Avarua, NZ 117/K7
Avdat (ruin), Isr. 91/D4
Avebury Stone Circle, Eng, UK 33/E4
Aveiro, Port. 44/A2
Aveiro (dist.), Port. 44/A2
Aveley, Eng, UK 30/D2
Avelgem, Belg. 52/C2
Avellaneda, Arg. 159/J11
Avellino, It. 46/D2
Avelon (riv.), Fr. 52/A5
Avenal, Ca, US 128/B3
Avenches, Swi. 56/D4
Avenel, NJ, US 139/H9
Avernes, Fr. 30/H4
Aversa, It. 46/D2
Aves (isl.), Ven. 141/J4
Avesnes-le-Comte, Fr. 52/B3
Avesnes-sur-Helpe, Fr. 52/C3
Avesta, Swe. 38/G1
Aveyron (riv.), Fr. 42/D4
Avezzano, It. 46/C1
Avich (lake), Sc, UK 36/A4
Aviemore, Sc, UK 36/C2
Avignon, Fr. 42/F5
Aviḥayil, Isr. 91/F7
Ávila de los Caballeros, Sp. 44/C2
Avilés, Sp. 44/C1
Avio, It. 59/D1
Avion, Fr. 52/B3
Avis, Pa, US 138/A1
Avisio (riv.), It. 57/H5
Avize, Fr. 52/D6
Avlum, Den. 38/C3
Avoca, Austl. 115/C4
Avoca, Austl. 115/B3
Avoca (riv.), Ire. 34/B6
Avoch, Sc, UK 36/B1
Avola, It. 46/D4
Avon, Fr. 42/E2
Avon (riv.), Eng, UK 32/C6
Avon (riv.), Fr. 30/L6
Avon (riv.), Sc, UK 36/C1
Avon Valley NP, Austl. 112/C4
Avon Water (riv.), Sc, UK 36/B5
Avonbeg (riv.), Ire. 34/B6
Avondale, Austl. 115/D2
Avondale, Az, US 137/R19
Avondale, Pa, US 138/C4
Avonlea, Sk, Can. 127/G3
Avonmore (riv.), Ire. 34/B5
Avranches, Fr. 42/C2
Avre (riv.), Fr. 40/B4
Avrillé, Fr. 42/C3
Awa-shima (isl.), Japan 76/A4
A'waj (riv.), Syria 91/E3
Awaji, Japan 77/H6
Awans, Belg. 53/E2
Āwasa, Eth. 97/N6
Āwash, Eth. 97/P6
Āwash Wenz (riv.), Eth. 97/P5
Awaso, Gha. 103/E5
Awat, China 70/D3
Awbārī, Libya 96/H2
Awbārī (des.), Libya 99/H4
Awe (lake), Sc, UK 36/A4
Awjilah, Libya 97/K2
Awka, Nga. 103/G5
Awsīm, Egypt 91/B4
Ax-les-Thermes, Fr. 42/D5
Axamo (int'l arpt.), Swe. 38/F3
Axams, Aus. 57/H3
Axarfjördhur (inlet), Ice. 37/N6
Axel, Neth. 50/A6
Axel Heiberg (isl.), Nun., Can. 123/S7
Axim, Gha. 103/E5
Axios (riv.), Gre. 47/H2
Axis (dam), Wa, US 135/D2
Axminster, Eng, UK 32/D5
Axochiapan, Mex. 143/L8
Ay (riv.), Rus. 61/N5
Ay, Fr. 52/C5
Ayabaca, Peru 156/B2
Ayabe, Japan 77/H5

171
Ayacu – Baoji

Ayacucho, Peru 156/C4
Ayacucho (dept.), Peru 156/C4
Ayacucho, Arg. 158/F3
Ayagöz, Kaz. 70/D2
Ayaguz (riv.), Kaz. 70/C2
Ayama, Japan 77/K6
Ayamé I, Barrage d' (dam), C.d'Iv. 102/E5
Ayamé II, Barrage d' (dam), C.d'Iv. 102/E5
Ayamonte, Sp. 44/B4
Ayancık, Turk. 62/E4
Ayanganna (mtn.), Guy. 153/G3
Ayapel, Col. 152/C2
Ayaş, Turk. 62/E4
Ayase, Japan 77/C3
Ayaviri, Peru 156/D4
Āybak, Afg. 87/E5
'Aybāl, Jabal (peak), WBnk. 91/G7
Aybastı, Turk. 62/F4
Aydar Köli (lake), Trkm. 87/E4
Aydın, Turk. 90/A2
Aydin (prov.), Turk. 90/B2
Aydıncık, Turk. 62/E4
Aydıncık, Turk. 91/C1
Aydınkent, Turk. 91/B1
Ayer, Swi. 56/D5
Ayers Rock (Uluru) (peak), Austl. 113/F3
Ayeyarwady (state), Myan. 83/F4
Ayeyarwady (Irrawaddy), (riv.) Myan. 67/J7
Ayiá, Gre. 47/H3
Ayía Paraskeví, Gre. 47/K3
Ayiásos, Gre. 47/K3
Áyios Ioánnis (cape), Gre. 47/J5
Áyios Kírikos, Gre. 47/K4
Áyios Konstandínos, Gre. 47/H3
Áyios Matthaíos, Gre. 47/F3
Áyios Nikólaos, Gre. 47/J5
Aylesbury, Eng, UK 33/F3
Aylesford, Eng, UK 33/G4
Ayllón, Sp. 44/D2
Aylmer (lake), NW, Can. 122/F2
'Ayn al 'Arab, Syria 90/D2
'Ayn Zuwayyah (well), Libya 97/K3
Ayna, Peru 156/C4
Ayon (isl.), Rus. 65/S3
Ayora, Sp. 45/E3
Ayotzintepec, Mex. 144/B2
'Ayoûn 'Abd el Mâlek (well), Mrta. 98/D4
'Ayoûn el 'Atroûs, Mrta. 102/C2
Ayr, Austl. 114/B2
Ayr, Sc, UK 36/B6
Ayr (riv.), Sc, UK 36/B5
Aytré, Fr. 42/C3
Ayubia NP, Pak. 86/B3
Ayutla, Mex. 142/D4
Ayutla de los Libres, Mex. 140/B4
Ayutthaya (ruin), Thai. 78/C3
Ayvacık, Turk. 47/K3
Ayvalık, Turk. 62/C5
Aywaille, Belg. 53/E3
Az Zabadānī, Syria 91/E3
Az Ẕāhirīyah, WBnk. 91/D4
Az Zaqāzīq, Egypt 91/B4
Az Zarqā' (gov.), Jor. 91/E3
Az Zarqā', Jor. 91/E3
Az Zāwiyah, Libya 96/H1
Az Zaydīyah, Yem. 88/D5
Azad Kashmir (terr.), Pak. 86/B3
Azahar (coast), Sp. 45/F3
Azalea, Or, US 126/C5
Azalia, Mi, US 135/E7
Azamgarh, India 84/D2
Azángaro (riv.), Peru 156/D4
Azángaro, Peru 156/D4
Azao (peak), Alg. 99/H4
Azaouād (phys. reg.), Mali 96/E4
Āzarbān, Iran 88/E1
Āzarbāyjān-e Gharbī (prov.), Iran 90/F2
A'zāz, Syria 91/E1
Azemmour, Mor. 98/C2
Azerbaijan (ctry.) 63/H4
Azilal, Mor. 98/D3
Azīmganj, India 85/G3
Azogues, Ecu. 152/B5
Azores (dpcy.), Port. 45/R12
Azourki (peak), Mor. 98/D3
Azov, Rus. 62/F3
Azov (sea), Ukr.,Rus. 64/D5
Azoyú, Mex. 144/B2
Azpeitia, Sp. 44/D1
Azrou, Mor. 98/D2
Aztec, NM, US 128/F3
Aztec Ruins Nat'l Mon., NM, US 128/E3
Azua de Compostela, DRep. 141/G4
Azuaga, Sp. 44/C3
Azuara, Sp. 45/E2
Azuay (dept.), Ecu. 152/B5
Azuchi, Japan 77/K5
Azuero, Peninsula de (pen.), Pan. 150/B2
Azuga, Rom. 49/G3
Azul (mtn.), CR 144/E4
Azul (riv.), Guat. 144/D2
Azul, Arg. 158/F3
Azul, Cordillera (mts.), Peru 156/B2
Azuma, Japan 77/E2
Azuma-san (peak), Japan 75/G2
Azumaya-san (peak), Japan 75/F2
Azur, Côte d' (coast), Fr. 43/G5
Azusa, Ca, US 136/C2
Azzaba, Alg. 100/K6
Azzano Decimo, It. 59/F1
Azzano San Paolo, It. 58/C1
Azzate, It. 58/B1
'Azzūn, WBnk. 91/G7

B

Ba (riv.), Viet. 79/A5
Bà (riv.), Viet. 83/J5
Ba Lang An (cape), Viet. 78/E3
Ba Quan (cape), Viet. 78/D4
Baar, Swi. 57/E3
Baarle-Hertog, Belg. 50/B6
Baarle-Nassau, Neth. 50/B6
Baarn, Neth. 50/C4
Bab el Mandeb (str.), Asia 88/D6
Baba (peak), Bul. 47/H1
Baba (pt.), Turk. 49/K5
Baba (mts.), Afg. 89/J2
Baba Burnu (pt.), Turk. 47/K3
Babadag, Rom. 49/J3
Babaeski, Turk. 49/H5
Babahoyo, Ecu. 152/B5
Babai Khola (riv.), Nepal 84/C1
Babakale, Turk. 47/K3
Babar (isls.), Indo. 116/B5
Babatorun, Turk. 91/E1
Babatpur (int'l arpt.), India 84/D3
Babbacombe (bay), Eng, UK 32/C6
Babbitt, Mn, US 127/L4
B'abdā, Leb. 91/D3
Babelthuap (isl.), Palau 116/C4
Babenhausen, Ger. 57/G1
Babenhausen, Ger. 54/B3
Babensham, Ger. 55/F6
Baberu, India 84/C3
Babia (peak), Pol. 62/A2
Babian (riv.), China 83/H3
Bābil (gov.), Iraq 90/F3
Bābil (Babylon) (ruin), Iraq 90/F3
Babīna, India 84/B3
Babinda, Austl. 114/B2
Babine (riv.), BC, Can. 122/D3
Bābol, Iran 88/F1
Babruysk, Bela. 62/D1
Babuyan (isl.), Phil. 67/M8
Babylon, NY, US 139/E2
Bac Giang, Viet. 78/D1
Bac Lieu, Viet. 78/D4
Bac Ninh, Viet. 83/J3
Bacabal, Braz. 154/A2
Bacadéhuachi, Mex. 142/C2
Bacajá (riv.), Braz. 151/H4
Bacalar, Mex. 144/D2
Bacalar (lag.), Mex. 144/D2
Bacan (isl.), Indo. 81/G4
Bacău (prov.), Rom. 49/H2
Bacău, Rom. 49/H2
Baccarat, Fr. 56/C1
Bacchiglione (riv.), It. 59/E2
Bacchus, Ut, US 137/J12
Bacerac, Mex. 142/C2
Bacharach, Ger. 53/G3
Bachhraon, India 84/B1
Bachíniva, Mex. 142/D2
Back (riv.), Md, US 138/B5
Back (riv.), Nun., Can. 122/F2
Bačka (reg.), Yugo. 48/D3
Bačka Palanka, Yugo. 48/D3
Bačka Topola, Yugo. 48/D3
Bäckefors, Swe. 38/E2
Backnang, Ger. 54/C5
Bacobampa, Mex. 142/C3
Bacolod, Phil. 81/F1
Bács-Kiskun (prov.), Hun. 48/D2
Bácsalmás, Hun. 48/D2
Bacup, Eng, UK 35/F4
Bad (riv.), SD, US 127/H5
Bad Abbach, Ger. 55/F5
Bad Axe, Mi, US 130/D3
Bad Bellingen, Ger. 56/D2
Bad Bergzabern, Ger. 54/A4
Bad Berneck, Ger. 55/E2
Bad Bocklet, Ger. 54/D2
Bad Brambach, Ger. 55/F2
Bad Breisig, Ger. 53/G3
Bad Brückenau, Ger. 54/C2
Bad Buchau, Ger. 57/F1
Bad Camberg, Ger. 54/B2
Bad Doberan, Ger. 38/D4
Bad Driburg, Ger. 51/G5
Bad Dürkheim, Ger. 54/B4
Bad Dürrheim, Ger. 57/E1
Bad Ems, Ger. 53/G3
Bad Endorf, Ger. 55/F7
Bad Essen, Ger. 51/F4
Bad Freienwalde, Ger. 41/H2
Bad Gandersheim, Ger. 51/H5
Bad Goisern, Aus. 43/K3
Bad Grund, Ger. 51/H5
Bad Hall, Aus. 55/H6
Bad Harzburg, Ger. 51/H5
Bad Heilbrunn, Ger. 57/H2
Bad Herrenalb, Ger. 54/B5
Bad Hersfeld, Ger. 43/H1
Bad Hofgastein, Aus. 43/K3
Bad Homburg vor der Höhe, Ger. 54/B2
Bad Honnef, Ger. 53/G2
Bad Hönningen, Ger. 53/G2
Bad Ischl, Aus. 43/K3
Bad Karlshafen, Ger. 51/G5
Bad Kissingen, Ger. 54/D2
Bad Kohlgrub, Ger. 57/H2
Bad König, Ger. 54/C3
Bad Königshofen, Ger. 54/D2
Bad Kreuznach, Ger. 53/G4
Bad Krozingen, Ger. 56/D2
Bad Langensalza, Ger. 51/H6
Bad Lauterberg, Ger. 51/H5
Bad Leonfelden, Aus. 55/H5
Bad Liebenzell, Ger. 54/B5
Bad Lippspringe, Ger. 51/F3
Bad Marienberg, Ger. 53/G2
Bad Mergentheim, Ger. 54/C4
Bad Munder am Deister, Ger. 51/G4
Bad Nauheim, Ger. 54/B2
Bad Nenndorf, Ger. 51/G4
Bad Neuenahr-Ahrweiler, Ger. 53/G2
Bad Neustadt an der Saale, Ger. 54/D2
Bad Oeynhausen, Ger. 51/F4
Bad Orb, Ger. 54/C2
Bad Peterstal-Griesbach, Ger. 56/E1
Bad Plaas, SAfr. 107/E2
Bad Pyrmont, Ger. 51/G5
Bad Ragaz, Swi. 57/F4
Bad Rappenau, Ger. 54/C4
Bad Reichenhall, Ger. 43/K3
Bad Rothenfelde, Ger. 51/F4
Bad Sachsa, Ger. 51/H5
Bad Salzdetfurth, Ger. 51/G4
Bad Salzschlirf, Ger. 54/C1
Bad Salzuflen, Ger. 51/F4
Bad Salzungen, Ger. 40/F3
Bad Sankt-Leonhard im Lavanttal, Aus. 43/L3
Bad Sassendorf, Ger. 51/F5
Bad Schallerbach, Aus. 55/G6
Bad Schwalbach, Ger. 53/H3
Bad Schwartau, Ger. 38/D5
Bad Segeberg, Ger. 38/D5
Bad Soden-Salmünster, Ger. 54/C2
Bad Sooden-Allendorf, Ger. 51/G6
Bad Tölz, Ger. 57/H2
Bad Vilbel, Ger. 54/B2
Bad Vöslau, Aus. 43/M3
Bad Waldsee, Ger. 57/F2
Bad Wildungen, Ger. 51/G6
Bad Wimpfen, Ger. 54/C4
Bad Wimsbach-Neydharting, Aus. 55/G6
Bad Windsheim, Ger. 54/D3
Bad Wörishofen, Ger. 57/G1
Bad Wurzach, Ger. 57/F2
Bad Zell, Aus. 55/H6
Bad Zwischenahn, Ger. 51/F2
Badagara, India 82/C5
Badain Jaran (des.), China 70/H3
Badajoz, Sp. 44/B3
Badalona, Sp. 45/L7
Badalucco, It. 58/A5
Badbergen, Ger. 51/E3
Baddeckenstedt, Ger. 51/H4
Baddomalhi, Pak. 86/C4
Baden, Aus. 43/M2
Baden, Swi. 57/E3
Baden-Baden, Ger. 54/B5
Baden-Württemberg (state), Ger. 43/H2
Badener (peak), Ger. 54/B5
Badenoch (reg.), Sc, UK 36/B3
Badenweiler, Ger. 56/D2
Badgastein, Aus. 43/K3
Badgingarra NP, Austl. 112/B4
Badia Polesine, It. 59/E2
Badiar, PN du, Gui. 102/B3
Badile (peak), It. 57/F5
Badīn, Pak. 89/J4
Badiraguato, Mex. 142/D3
Badlands (plat.), SD, US 127/H5
Badlands NP, SD, US 127/H5
Badonviller, Fr. 56/C1
Badou, Togo 103/F5
Badovinci, Yugo. 48/D3
Badrāh, Pak. 89/J3
Badrah, Iraq 88/E2
Badua (riv.), India 85/F3
Badulla, SrL. 82/D6
Baduriā, India 85/G4
Baena, Sp. 44/C4
Baependi, Braz. 211/J6
Baerenkopf (peak), Fr. 56/C2
Baesweiler, Ger. 53/F2
Baeza, Sp. 44/D4
Baffa, Pak. 86/B2
Baffin (bay), Tx, US 132/D5
Baffin (bay), Can.,Grld. 119/K2
Baffin (isl.), Nun., Can. 123/H1
Bafia, Camr. 96/H7
Bafilo, Togo 103/F4
Bafing (riv.), Gui. 96/C5
Bafoulabé, Mali 102/C3
Bafoussam, Camr. 96/H6
Bāfq, Iran 89/G2
Bafra, Turk. 62/E4
Bafra (cape), Turk. 62/E4
Bāft, Iran 89/G3
Bag Salt (lake), China 72/B3
Bagaces, CR 144/E4
Bagadó, Col. 152/B3
Bagaha, India 85/E2
Bagamoyo, Tanz. 104/C4
Baganga, Phil. 81/G2
Bagda (mts.), China 70/E3
Bagé, Braz. 157/F3
Bagenkop, Den. 38/D4
Baggao, Phil. 79/D4
Baggy (pt.), Eng, UK 32/B4
Bāgh, Pak. 86/B4
Baghain (riv.), India 84/C3
Baghdād (Baghdad) (cap.), Iraq 90/F3
Bagheria, It. 46/C3
Baghlān, Afg. 89/J1
Bāghpat, India 86/D5
Bağırpaşa (peak), Turk. 90/E2
Bagley, Mn, US 127/K4
Bāglun, Nepal 84/D1
Bāgmati (riv.), India 85/E2
Bāgmati (zone), Nepal 85/E2
Bagn, Nor. 38/C1
Bagnacavallo, It. 59/F4
Bagnasco, It. 58/B4
Bagnères-de-Bigorre, Fr. 42/D5
Bagnères-de-Luchon, Fr. 42/D5
Bagneux, Fr. 30/J5
Bagni di Lucca, It. 58/D4
Bagno a Ripoli, It. 59/E5
Bagnolet, Fr. 30/K5
Bagnoli Irpino, It. 46/D2
Bagnolo Cremasco, It. 58/C2
Bagnolo in Piano, It. 59/D3
Bagnolo Mella, It. 58/D2
Bagnolo San Vito, It. 59/D2
Bagnols-sur-Cèze, Fr. 42/F4
Bagnone, It. 58/C4
Bago, Phil. 79/D5
Bago (div.), Myan. 70/G8
Bago (Pegu), Myan. 83/G4
Bagoe (riv.), Mali 96/D5
Bagolino, It. 58/D1
Bagshot, Eng, UK 30/A3
Bagua Grande, Peru 156/B2
Baguio, Phil. 79/D4
Baguirmi (reg.), Chad 96/J5
Bagzane (peak), Niger 103/H2
Bāh, India 84/B2
Bahādurganj, India 85/F2
Bahādurgarh, India 86/D5
Bahamas (ctry.) 141/F2
Bahāwalnagar, Pak. 86/B5
Bahāwalpur, Pak. 86/A5
Bahçe, Turk. 90/D2
Bahçesaray, Turk. 90/E2
Baheri, India 84/B1
Bahi (swamp), Tanz. 104/B4
Bahia (state), Braz. 154/B4
Bahía Asunción, Mex. 142/B3
Bahía Blanca, Arg. 158/E3
Bahía de Caráquez, Ecu. 152/A5
Bahía de los Angeles, Mex. 142/B2
Bahía de Tortugas, Mex. 142/B3
Bahía, Islas de la (isls.), Hon. 140/D4
Bahía Solano, Col. 152/B3
Bahir Dar, Eth. 97/N5
Bahjoi, India 84/B1
Bahlah, Oman 89/G4
Bahr al 'Arab (riv.), Sudan 97/L6
Baḩr al Milḩ (lake), Iraq 90/E3
Bahraich, India 84/C2
Bahrain (ctry.) 88/F3
Bahrain, Gulf of (gulf), Asia 88/F3
Baia de Aramă, Rom. 49/F3
Baia Mare, Rom. 49/F2
Baia Sprie, Rom. 49/F2
Baïbokoum, Chad 96/J6
Baicheng, China 70/F3
Baicheng, China 71/M2
Băicoi, Rom. 49/G3
Baidong (lake), China 72/D5
Baie-Comeau, Qu, Can. 131/G1
Baie-Saint-Paul, Qu, Can. 131/G2
Baienfurt, Ger. 57/F2
Baiersbronn, Ger. 54/B5
Baiersdorf, Ger. 54/E3
Baigorrita, Arg. 158/E2
Baigou (riv.), China 72/G7
Baihar, India 84/C4
Baihe (riv.), China 72/G7
Ba'ījī, Iraq 90/E3
Baikunthpur, India 84/D4
Bailadores, Ven. 152/D2
Baildon, Eng, UK 35/G4
Băile Govora, Rom. 49/G3
Băile Herculane, Rom. 48/F3
Băile Olăneşti, Rom. 49/G3
Băile Tuşnad, Rom. 49/G2
Bailén, Sp. 44/D3
Băileşti, Rom. 49/F3
Bailieborough, Ire. 31/Q10
Bailleul, Fr. 52/B2
Bailong (riv.), China 70/H5
Bailu (riv.), China 72/C4
Baima, China 70/H5
Bain (riv.), Eng, UK 35/H5
Bainang, China 85/G1
Bainbridge, Ga, US 133/G4
Bainbridge, Pa, US 138/B3
Bainbridge (isl.), Wa, US 135/B2
Bainbridge Naval Training Sta., Md, US 138/B4
Baingoin, China 70/E5
Bains-les-Bains, Fr. 56/C2
Bairāgnia, India 85/E2
Baird (inlet), Ak, US 134/F3
Baird, Tx, US 129/H4
Bairin Youqi, China 71/L3
Bairnsdale, Austl. 115/C3
Baïse (riv.), Fr. 42/D5
Baixa da Banheira, Port. 45/P10
Baixa Grande, Braz. 154/B4
Baixiang, China 72/C3
Baixo Guandu, Braz. 155/D1
Baiyin, China 70/H4
Baiyu (mts.), China 72/B3
Baiyun (int'l arpt.), China 79/B3
Baja (pt.), Mex. 142/B2
Baja, Hun. 48/D2
Baja (pt.), Chile 159/B6
Baja California (state), Mex. 142/B2
Baja California (pen.), Mex. 142/B2
Baja California Sur (state), Mex. 142/B3
Bājah (gov.), Tun. 46/A4
Bājah, Tun. 100/L6
Bajánsenye, Hun. 43/M3
Bajestān, Iran 89/G2
Bājil, Yem. 88/D5
Bajina Bašta, Yugo. 48/D4
Bajmbat (mt.), Austl. 115/E1
Bajmok, Yugo. 48/D3
Bajo Boquete, Pan. 145/F4
Bajo de Gualicho (plain), Arg. 157/C5
Bajram Curri, Alb. 47/G1
Bakanas (riv.), Kaz. 87/G3
Bakau, Gam. 102/A3
Bakayan (peak), Indo. 81/E3
Bakel, Sen. 102/B3
Baker, Mt, US 127/G4
Baker, La, US 129/K5
Baker (mt.), Wa, US 126/C3
Baker (isl.), Pac., US 117/H4
Baker (lake), Nun., Can. 122/G2
Baker (riv.), Chile 159/B5
Baker City, Or, US 126/D4
Baker Lake, Nun., Can. 122/G2
Bakersfield, Ca, US 128/C4
Bakhchysaray, Ukr. 62/E3
Bakhmach, Ukr. 62/E2
Bākhtarān, Iran 88/E2
Bakhtiyārpur, India 85/E3
Bakhuis (mts.), Sur. 153/G4
Bakkaflói (bay), Ice. 37/P6
Baklan, Turk. 90/B2
Bakonyszombathely, Hun. 48/C2
Bakora Corridor Game Rsv., Ugan. 104/B2
Bakovský Potok (riv.), Czh. 55/G2
Bakoye (riv.), Gui. 102/C3
Baku (int'l arpt.), Azer. 63/J4
Baku (cap.), Azer. 63/J4
Bala, Turk. 62/E5
Bala, Wal, UK 34/E6
Balabac, Phil. 81/E2
Balabac (str.), Malay.,Ph 81/E2
Balabac (isl.), Phil. 81/E2
Ba'labakk, Leb. 91/E2
Bālāghāt, India 84/C5
Balaguer, Sp. 45/F2
Balaïtous (peak), Fr. 42/C5
Balaka, Malw. 105/F3
Balakhna, Rus. 61/J4
Balaklava, Austl. 113/H5
Balakovo, Rus. 63/H1
Bal'amā, Jor. 91/E3
Bălan, Rom. 49/G2
Balancán, Mex. 144/D2
Balanga, Phil. 79/D5
Balāngir, India 82/D3
Balao, Ecu. 156/B1
Balarāmpur, India 85/F4
Balashikha, Rus. 61/W9
Balashov, Rus. 63/G2
Balasore (Baleshwar), India 82/E3
Balassagyarmat, Hun. 41/K4
Balaton (lake), Cro. 48/C2
Balatonföldvár, Hun. 48/C2
Balatonfüred, Hun. 48/C2
Balatonszabadi, Hun. 48/D2
Balatonszentgyörgy, Hun. 48/C2
Balbina (res.), Braz. 147/D3
Balbriggan, Ire. 34/B4
Balcarce, Arg. 158/F3
Balcary (pt.), Sc, UK 34/E2
Balchik, Bul. 49/J4
Balclutha, NZ 117/R12
Balcones Escarpment (plat.), Tx, US 137/T20
Balcones Heights, Tx, US 137/T21
Bald (pt.), Austl. 112/C5
Bald Eagle Mtn. (mtn.), Pa, US 138/A1
Bald Rock NP, Austl. 115/E1
Baldock, Eng, UK 33/F3
Baldwin, NY, US 139/L9
Baldwin Harbour, NY, US 139/L9
Baldwin Park, Mo, US 137/E6
Baldwin Park, Ca, US 136/G7
Baldy (mtn.), Mb, Can. 127/H3
Baldy Beacon (peak), Belz. 144/D2
Bale Mountains NP, Eth. 97/N6
Baleares (Balearic) (isls.), Sp. 45/G3
Baleia, Ponta da (pt.), Braz. 154/C5
Baleine, Grand Rivière de la (riv.), Qu, Can. 123/J3
Baleine, Petite Rivière de la (riv.), Qu, Can. 123/J3
Baleine, Rivière à la (riv.), Qu, Can. 123/K3
Balen, Belg. 53/E1
Baler, Phil. 79/D4
Balerna, Swi. 57/F6
Balesa (riv.), Kenya 104/C2
Baleshwar (Balasore), India 82/E3
Balfour, SAfr. 106/E2
Balfron, Sc, UK 36/B4
Balgatay, Mong. 70/G2
Balhannah, Austl. 113/M8
Bali (sea), Indo. 80/D5
Bali (isl.), Indo. 67/L10
Bāli Chak, India 85/F4
Balice (int'l arpt.), Pol. 41/K3
Baliem (riv.), Indo. 81/J4
Balıkesir, Turk. 62/C5
Balıkesir (prov.), Turk. 62/C5
Balikpapan, Indo. 81/E4
Balimbing, Phil. 81/E2
Baling, Malay. 83/H6
Balingasag, Phil. 79/D6
Bālinge, Swe. 38/G2
Balingen, Ger. 57/E1
Balk, Neth. 50/C3
Balkan (pol. reg.), Trkm. 87/B4
Balkan (mts.), Bul.,Yugo. 27/F3
Balkhash (lake), Kaz. 67/G5
Ballagan (pt.), Ire. 34/B4
Ballaghaderreen, Ire. 31/P10
Ballangen, Nor. 37/F1
Ballantrae, Sc, UK 34/C1
Ballarat, Austl. 115/B3
Ballard (lake), Austl. 109/B3
Ballarpur, India 82/C4
Ballater, Sc, UK 36/C2
Ballaugh, IM, UK 34/D3
Ballens, Swi. 56/B5
Balleny (isls.), Ant. 160/L
Ballia, India 85/E3
Ballina, Austl. 115/E1
Ballinamallard, NI, UK 31/Q9
Ballinasloe, Ire. 31/P10
Ballinderry (riv.), NI, UK 34/B2
Ballinger, Tx, US 129/H5
Ballingry, Sc, UK 36/C4
Ballinrobe, Ire. 31/P10
Balloch, Sc, UK 36/B2
Ballon, Col du (pass), Fr. 56/C2
Ballon d'Alsace (peak), Fr. 56/C2
Ballon de Sevance (peak), Fr. 56/C2
Ballwin, Mo, US 137/F8
Bally, Pa, US 138/C3
Ballycarry, NI, UK 34/B2
Ballycastle, NI, UK 34/B1
Ballycastle, Ire. 31/P9
Ballyclare, NI, UK 34/B2
Ballyeaston, NI, UK 34/B2
Ballygawley, NI, UK 34/A3
Ballygeary, Ire. 31/Q10
Ballygowan, NI, UK 34/C3
Ballyhaunis, Ire. 31/P10
Ballyheigue, Ire. 30/P10
Ballyliffin, Ire. 34/A1
Ballymena (dist.), NI, UK 34/B2
Ballymena, NI, UK 34/B2
Ballymoney (dist.), NI, UK 34/B1
Ballymoney, NI, UK 34/B1
Ballynahinch, NI, UK 34/C3
Ballynure, NI, UK 34/C2
Ballyquintin (pt.), NI, UK 34/C3
Ballyshannon, Ire. 31/P9
Balmaceda (peak), Chile 159/B6
Balmazújváros, Hun. 41/L5
Balmhorn (peak), Swi. 56/D5
Balmoral, Austl. 115/B3
Balmoral Castle, Sc, UK 36/C2
Balneário Camboriú, Braz. 155/B3
Balneario Claromecó, Arg. 158/E3
Balneario de los Novillos, PN, Mex. 129/G5
Balochistān (reg.), Pak. 89/J3
Balonne (riv.), Austl. 109/D3
Bālotra, India 89/K3
Balqash, Kaz. 87/G3
Balrāmpur, India 84/D2
Balranald, Austl. 115/B2
Balş, Rom. 49/G3
Bálsamo (pt.), Ecu. 152/A5
Balsapuerto, Peru 156/B2
Balsas, Braz. 154/A2
Balsas (riv.), Mex. 143/F5
Balsthal, Swi. 56/D3
Baltanás, Sp. 44/C2
Bălţi, Mol. 49/H2
Baltic (sea), Swe. 37/F5
Baltic (plain), Rus. 61/S7
Baltic Spit (bar), Pol.,Rus. 39/H4
Balṭīm, Egypt 91/B4
Baltimore, Md, US 138/B5
Baltimore (co.), Md, US 138/B4
Baltimore-Washington (int'l arpt.), Md, US 138/B5
Baltiysk, Rus. 39/H4
Baltray, Ire. 34/B4
Baltrum (isl.), Ger. 51/E1
Bælum, Den. 38/D3
Bālurghāt, India 85/G3
Balve, Ger. 51/E6
Balya, Turk. 62/C5
Balykshi, Kaz. 63/J3
Balzar, Ecu. 152/B5
Balzers, Lcht. 57/F3
Bam (prov.), Burk. 103/E3
Bam, Iran 89/G3
Bama Yaozu Zizhixian, China 83/J3
Bamaji (lake), On, Can. 127/K3
Bamako (cap.), Mali 102/D3
Bamako (Senou) (int'l arpt.), Mali 102/D3
Bambamarca, Peru 156/B2
Bambana (riv.), Nic. 145/E3
Bambari, CAfr. 97/K6
Bamberg, SC, US 133/H3
Bamberg, Ger. 54/D3
Bamble, Nor. 38/C2
Bambuí, Braz. 155/C2
Bamenda, Camr. 103/H5
Bāmīān, Afg. 87/E6
Bamingui-Bangoran, PN du, CAfr. 97/J6
Bammental, Ger. 54/B4
Bampūr (riv.), Iran 89/H3
Ban Boun Tai, Laos 83/H3
Ban Chiang (ruin), Thai. 78/C2
Ban Houayxay, Laos 83/H3
Ban Kantang, Thai. 78/B5
Ban Kengkok, Laos 83/J4
Ban Pak Phanang, Thai. 78/C4
Banaba (isl.), Kiri. 116/F5
Banagher, Ire. 31/Q10
Banamba, Mali 102/D3
Banana (isls.), SLeo. 102/B4
Bananal, Braz. 211/J7
Bananal, Ilha do (isl.), Braz. 151/H6
Banar (riv.), Bang. 85/H3
Banarlı, Turk. 49/H5
Banās (pt.), Egypt 101/C4
Banās (riv.), India 89/L3
Banat (reg.), Bosn. 48/E3
Banatsko Novo Selo, Yugo. 48/E3
Banaz, Turk. 62/D5
Banbar, China 70/G5
Banbridge, NI, UK 34/B3
Banbridge (dist.), NI, UK 34/B3
Banbury, Eng, UK 33/E2
Banc d'Arguin, Mrta. 98/A5
Banc d'Arguin, PN du, Mrta. 96/B3
Banc d'Arguin, PN du, Mrta. 102/A2
Banchette, It. 58/A2
Banchory, Sc, UK 36/D2
Banco Chinchorro (isls.), Mex. 140/D4
Bancroft, On, Can. 130/E2
Banda (isls.), Indo. 81/H4
Bāndā, India 84/C3
Banda, India 84/B3
Banda (sea), Indo. 67/M10
Banda Aceh, Indo. 80/A2
Bandai-san (peak), Japan 75/G2
Bandama (riv.), C.d'Iv. 96/D6
Bandama Blanc (riv.), C.d'Iv. 102/D4
Bandama Rouge (riv.), C.d'Iv. 102/D4
Bandar Beheshtī, Iran 89/H3
Bandar-e 'Abbās, Iran 89/G3
Bandar-e Anzalī, Iran 88/E1
Bandar-e Deylam, Iran 88/F2
Bandar-e Lengeh, Iran 89/F3
Bandar-e Māhshahr, Iran 88/E2
Bandar-e Torkeman, Iran 88/F1
Bandar Seri Begawan (cap.),Bru. 80/D3
Bande, Sp. 44/B1
Bandeira do Sul, Braz. 211/G6
Bandeira, Pico da (peak), Braz. 155/D2
Bandeirantes, Braz. 155/B2
Bandelier Nat'l Mon., NM, US 129/F4
Bandera, Tx, US 129/H5
Banderilla, Mex. 143/N7
Bandhavgarh NP, India 84/C4
Bandholm, Den. 38/D4
Bandiagara, Mali 102/E3
Bandipura, India 86/C2
Bandirma (gulf), Turk. 49/H5
Bandırma, Turk. 49/H5
Bandon, Ire. 31/P11
Bandon (riv.), Ire. 31/P11
Bandundu, D.R. Congo 105/C1
Bandung, Indo. 80/C5
Bañeres, Sp. 45/E3
Banes, Cuba 145/H1
Banff, Ab, Can. 126/E3
Banff, Sc, UK 36/D1
Banff NP, Ab, Can. 126/E3
Banfora, Burk. 102/D4
Bang Lang (res.), Thai. 78/C5
Banga, Phil. 79/D6
Banga, India 86/C4
Bangalore, India 82/C5
Bangalow, Austl. 114/D5
Bangaon, India 85/G4
Bāngarmau, India 84/C2
Bangassou, CAfr. 97/K7
Bangau (cape), Malay. 81/E2
Banggai (isls.), Indo. 81/F4
Banghiang (riv.), Laos 78/D2
Bangka (str.), Indo. 80/B4
Bangka (isl.), Indo. 67/K10
Bangkok (int'l arpt.), Thai. 78/C3
Bangkok, Bight of (bay), Thai. 83/H5
Bangkok (Krung Thep) (cap.),Thai. 78/C3
Bangladesh (ctry.) 82/E3
Bangor (int'l arpt.), Me, US 131/G2
Bangor, Me, US 131/G2
Bangor, Pa, US 138/C2
Bangor, Wal, UK 34/D5
Bangor, NI, UK 34/C2
Bangued, Phil. 79/D4
Bangui (cap.), CAfr. 97/J7
Bangweulu (swamp), Zam. 104/A5
Bangweulu (lake), Zam. 105/E3
Banhā, Egypt 91/B4
Banhine, PN de, Moz. 105/F5
Bani (riv.), Mali 96/D5
Baní, DRep. 141/G4
Banī Mazār, Egypt 101/B2
Banī Suhaylah, Gaza 91/D4
Banī Suwayf (gov.), Egypt 101/B1
Banī Suwayf, Egypt 101/B2
Bánica, DRep. 145/J2
Banifing (riv.), Mali 102/D3
Banihāl (pass), India 86/C3
Banikoara, Ben. 103/F4
Banister (riv.), Va, US 133/J2
Bāniyās, Syria 91/D2
Banja Koviljača, Yugo. 48/D3
Banja Luka, Bosn. 48/C3
Banjarmasin, Indo. 80/D4
Banjul (cap.), Gam. 102/A3
Bānka, India 85/F3
Bankas, Mali 102/E3
Bankeryd, Swe. 38/F3
Bankfoot, Sc, UK 36/C3
Bankhead, Sc, UK 36/D2
Bānki, India 85/E4
Banks (cape), Austl. 115/B3
Banks (pt.), Ak, US 134/H4
Banks (lake), Wa, US 126/D4
Banks (str.), Austl. 109/D5
Banks (isls.), Van. 116/F6
Banks (isl.), NW, Can. 122/D2
Banks (pen.), NZ 109/H7
Bānkurā, India 85/F4
Bankya, Bul. 47/H1
Banmankhi, India 85/F3
Bann (riv.), Ire. 31/Q10
Bann (riv.), NI, UK 34/B3
Banna (riv.), It. 58/A3
Bannockburn, Sc, UK 36/C4
Bannockburn Battlesite, Sc, UK 36/C4
Bannu, Pak. 86/A3
Baños, Ecu. 156/B1
Banpo Ruins, China 72/B4
Bansberia, India 85/G4
Bānsdīh, India 85/E3
Bānsi, India 84/D2
Bansin, Ger. 38/F5
Banská Bystrica, Slvk. 62/A2
Banská Štiavnica, Slvk. 48/D1
Bansko, Bul. 47/H2
Banstead, Eng, UK 30/C3
Bānswāra, India 89/K4
Bantayan, Phil. 79/D5
Banté, Ben. 103/F4
Bantenan (cape), Indo. 80/D5
Bantong Group (isls.), Thai. 78/B5
Bantry, Ire. 31/P11
Bañuelo (peak), Sp. 44/C3
Banyak (isls.), Indo. 80/A3
Banyoles, Sp. 45/G1
Banyuwangi, Indo. 80/D5
Banzare (coast), Ant. 160/J
Banzart (gov.), Tun. 46/A4
Banzart (Bizerte), Tun. 46/A4
Baode, China 72/B3
Baodi, China 72/H7
Baoding, China 72/G7
Baofeng, China 72/C4
Baoji, China 70/J5
Baojing, China 83/J2

172

Baoka – Beliz

Baokang, China 72/B5
Baoruco (mts.), DRep. 145/J2
Baoshan, China 83/G2
Baoshan, China 72/L8
Baotou, China 72/B2
Baoulé (riv.), Mali 96/D5
Baoying, China 72/D4
Bapaume, Fr. 52/B3
Bapchule, Az, US 137/S19
Baptistown, NJ, US 138/C2
Bāqa el Gharbiyya, Isr. 91/G7
Baqên, China 70/F5
Ba'qūbah, Iraq 90/F3
Bar, Yugo. 47/F1
Bar (riv.), Fr. 40/C4
Bar Bigha, India 85/E3
Bar el Ksaïb (well), Mali 98/D5
Bar Harbor, Me, US 131/G2
Bar-le-Duc, Fr. 53/E6
Bar-sur-Aube, Fr. 42/F2
Bar-sur-Seine, Fr. 42/F2
Bara, Swe. 38/E4
Bāra Banki, India 84/C2
Bārā Lācha La (pass), India 86/D3
Barabai, Indo. 80/E4
Barabinsk, Rus. 87/G1
Baraboo, Wi, US 127/L5
Baracaldo, Sp. 44/D1
Baracoa, Cuba 145/H1
Barada (riv.), Syria 91/E3
Baradero, Arg. 159/J10
Baradine, Austl. 115/D1
Baragoi, Kenya 104/C2
Baraguá, Cuba 145/G1
Baragua, Ven. 152/D2
Barajas (int'l arpt.), Sp. 45/N9
Barajevo, Yugo. 48/E3
Barākar (riv.), India 85/F3
Barakī Barak, Afg. 89/J2
Baralaba, Austl. 114/C4
Baram (cape), Malay. 80/D3
Baram (riv.), Malay. 80/D3
Barama (riv.), Guy. 150/F2
Baramanni, Guy. 153/G3
Baramula, India 86/C2
Bāran, India 89/L3
Baranagar, India 85/G4
Baranavichy, Bela. 62/C1
Barani (well), Alg. 98/E4
Baranoa, Col. 152/C2
Baranof (isl.), Ak, US 122/C3
Baranya (prov.), Hun. 48/C3
Barão de Cocais, Braz. 155/D1
Barão de Grajaú, Braz. 154/B2
Baraolt, Rom. 49/G2
Baraque de Fraiture (hill), Belg. 53/E3
Barat Daya (isls.), Indo. 81/G5
Barataria, La, US 137/P17
Barauli, India 85/E2
Baraut, India 86/D5
Baraya, Col. 152/C4
Barbacena, Braz. 155/D2
Barbacoas, Col. 152/B4
Barbados (ctry.) 141/P9
Barbalha, Braz. 154/C2
Barbaros, Turk. 49/H5
Barbas (cape), Mor. 98/A5
Barbastro, Sp. 45/F1
Barbate de Franco, Sp. 44/C4
Barbeau (peak), Nun., Can. 123/T6
Barberà del Vallès, Sp. 45/L6
Barberino di Mugello, It. 59/E5
Barbers (pt.), Hi, US 124/V13
Barberton, Oh, US 130/D3
Barberton, SAfr. 107/E2
Barbona (peak), It. 58/D5
Barbosa, Col. 152/C3
Barbourville, Ky, US 130/D4
Barbuda (isl.), Anti. 141/N8
Barcaldine, Austl. 114/B3
Barcarrota, Sp. 44/B3
Barcău (riv.), Rom. 48/F2
Barcellona Pozzo di Gotto, It. 46/D3
Barcelona, Ven. 153/E2
Barcelona, Sp. 45/L7
Barcelona (int'l arpt.), Sp. 45/L7
Barcelos, Port. 44/A2
Barcelos, Braz. 153/F5
Barcin, Pol. 41/J2
Barcoo (riv.), Austl. 109/D3
Barcs, Hun. 48/C3
Barczewo, Pol. 39/J5
Bardejov, Slvk. 41/L4
Bardi, It. 58/C3
Bardīyah, Libya 97/L1
Bārdoli, India 89/K4
Bardolino, It. 59/D1
Bardonia, NY, US 139/K7
Bardsdale, Ca, US 136/B2
Bardsey (isl.), Wal, UK 34/D6
Bardstown, Ky, US 130/C4
Bareggio, It. 58/B2
Bareli, India 84/B4
Barellan, Austl. 115/C2
Barendrecht, Neth. 50/B5
Barentin, Fr. 42/D2
Barents (sea), Eur. 27/H1
Barentu, Erit. 88/C5
Bäretswil, Swi. 57/E3
Barfleur, Pointe de (pt.), Fr. 42/C2
Barga, It. 58/D4
Bargara, Austl. 114/D4
Bargarh, India 82/D3
Bargfeld-Stegen, Ger. 51/H1
Bargi, India 84/B4
Bargo, Austl. 115/D2
Bargteheide, Ger. 51/H1
Bārh, India 85/E3
Barhaj, India 84/D2
Barhalganj, India 84/D2
Barham, Austl. 115/C2
Barhiya, India 85/F3
Bāri, India 84/A2
Bari, It. 46/E2
Bari Sardo, It. 46/A3
Bariano, It. 58/C1
Baricella, It. 59/E3
Barichara, Col. 152/C3
Barīdī (pt.), SAr. 88/C4
Barigazzo (peak), It. 58/C3
Barika, Alg. 100/H5
Barillas, Guat. 144/D3
Barima (riv.), Guy. 153/G2
Barima-Waini (pol. reg.), Guy. 153/F3
Barinas (state), Ven. 152/D2
Barinas, Ven. 152/D2
Barinitas, Ven. 152/D2
Bariri, Braz. 155/B2
Barisāl (pol. reg.), Bang. 85/H4
Barisan Mountains (mts.), Indo. 80/B4
Barito (riv.), Indo. 80/D4
Baritu, PN, Arg. 157/D1
Bark (lake), On, Can. 130/E2
Bark (riv.), Wi, US 135/N13
Barka Kāna, India 85/E4
Barker, NY, US 131/S9
Barki Saria, India 85/E3
Barking and Dagenham (bor.), Eng, UK 30/D2
Barkley (sound), BC, Can. 126/B3
Barkley (lake), Ky,Tn, US 133/G2
Barkly East, SAfr. 106/D3
Barkly Tableland (plat.), Austl. 109/C2
Barkly West, SAfr. 106/D3
Barkol Kazak Zizhixian, China 70/F3
Barlee (lake), Austl. 109/A3
Barlee (range), Austl. 112/B2
Barlee Range Nature Rsv., Austl. 112/B2
Barletta, It. 46/E2
Barlin, Fr. 52/B3
Barlinek, Pol. 41/H2
Barmedman, Austl. 115/C2
Barmera, Austl. 113/J5
Barmstedt, Ger. 51/G1
Barnāla, India 86/C4
Bärnbach, Aus. 43/L3
Barnegat (inlet), NJ, US 138/D4
Barnegat (bay), NJ, US 138/D4
Barnegat, NJ, US 138/D4
Barnegat Light, NJ, US 138/D4
Barneveld, Neth. 50/C4
Barnhart, Mo, US 137/G9
Barnoldswick, Eng, UK 35/F4
Barnsley, Eng, UK 35/G4
Barnstaple, Eng, UK 32/B4
Barnstaple (Bideford) (bay), Eng, UK 32/B4
Barnstorf, Ger. 51/F3
Barntrup, Ger. 51/G5
Barnwell, SC, US 133/H3
Baroghil (pass), Pak. 87/F5
Baron, Fr. 30/L4
Barone (peak), It. 58/B1
Barow (riv.), Ire. 34/A5
Barowghīl (pass), Afg. 89/K1
Barquisimeto, Ven. 152/D2
Barquisimeto (int'l arpt.), Ven. 152/D2
Barr (lake), Co, US 137/C3
Barr, Co, US 137/C3
Barr, Fr. 56/D1
Barra, Braz. 154/B3
Barra (isl.), Sc, UK 31/Q8
Barra Bonita, Braz. 155/B2
Barra Bonita, Represa de (res.), Braz. 155/B2
Barra da Choça, Braz. 154/B4
Barra del Colorado, PN, CR 140/E5
Barra do Bugres, Braz. 150/G7
Barra do Corda, Braz. 154/A2
Barra do Garças, Braz. 151/H7
Barra do Mendes, Braz. 154/B3
Barra do Piraí, Braz. 211/K7
Barra do Ribeiro, Braz. 155/B4
Barra Head (pt.), Sc, UK 31/Q8
Barra Mansa, Braz. 211/J7
Barra Velha, Braz. 155/B3
Barraba, Austl. 115/D1
Barrackpur, India 85/G4
Barrage de Lagdo (dam), Camr. 96/H6
Barranca, Peru 156/B3
Barranca, Peru 156/B2
Barranca de Upía, Col. 152/C3
Barranca del Cobre PN, Mex. 142/D3
Barrancabermeja, Col. 152/C3
Barrancas, Ven. 153/F2
Barrancas, Col. 152/C2
Barrancas, Chile 158/N8
Barranco de Loba, Col. 152/C2
Barrancos, Port. 44/B3
Barranquilla, Col. 152/C2
Barras, Braz. 154/B2
Barreal, Arg. 157/C3
Barreiras, Braz. 154/A4
Barreirinhas, Braz. 154/B1
Barreiro, Port. 45/P10
Barreiros, Braz. 154/D3
Barren (isls.), Madg. 105/J10
Barren (isl.), Madg. 107/G7
Barren, Nosy (Barren Islands) (isls.), Madg. 107/G7
Barretal, Mex. 143/F3
Barretos, Braz. 155/B2
Barrhead, Ab, Can. 126/E2
Barrhead, Sc, UK 36/B5
Barrie, On, Can. 130/E2
Barrier (range), Austl. 113/J4
Barrington, Il, US 135/P15
Barrington Hills, Il, US 135/P15
Barrington Tops (peak), Austl. 115/D1
Barrington Tops NP, Austl. 115/D1
Barro Duro, Braz. 154/B2
Barron Gorge NP, Austl. 114/B2
Barroso, Braz. 155/D2
Barrouallie, StV. 141/N9
Barrow, Ak, US 134/G1
Barrow (pt.), Ak, US 134/G1
Barrow (isl.), Austl. 109/A3
Barrow (riv.), Ire. 31/Q10
Barrow (pt.), Austl. 114/B1
Barrow (str.), Nun., Can. 122/G1
Barrow-in-Furness, Eng, UK 35/E3
Barrow Island, Austl. 112/B2
Barrowford, Eng, UK 35/F4
Barruelo de Santullán, Sp. 44/C1
Barry, Wal, UK 32/C4
Barsakel'mes (lake), Uzb. 87/C4
Barsinghausen, Ger. 51/G4
Barssel, Ger. 51/E2
Barstow, Ca, US 128/C4
Bartang (riv.), Taj. 87/F5
Bartenheim, Fr. 56/D2
Barth, Ger. 38/E4
Bartholomä, Ger. 54/C5
Bartholomäberg, Aus. 57/F3
Bartica, Guy. 153/G3
Bartın, Turk. 49/L5
Bartle Frere (peak), Austl. 109/D2
Bartlesville, Ok, US 129/J3
Bartlett, Tx, US 129/H5
Bartlett (dam), Az, US 137/S18
Bartlett (res.), Az, US 137/S18
Bartlett, Il, US 135/P16
Bartolomé Masó, Cuba 145/G1
Bartolomeu Dias, Moz. 105/G5
Bartonsville, Pa, US 138/C2
Bartoszyce, Pol. 39/J4
Bartow, Fl, US 133/H5
Bartow, Ger. 38/E5
Barú (vol.), Pan. 145/F4
Bāruipur, India 85/G4
Barumun (riv.), Indo. 80/B3
Barus, Indo. 80/A3
Baruun-Urt, Mong. 71/K2
Barwa Sāgar, India 84/B3
Barwāha, India 89/L4
Barwāla, India 86/C5
Barwon (riv.), Austl. 109/D3
Barycz (riv.), Pol. 41/J3
Barysaw, Bela. 39/N4
Barysh, Rus. 63/H1
Barzanò, It. 58/C1
Bas-Rhin (dept.), Fr. 56/D1
Basaldella, It. 59/G1
Basauri, Sp. 44/D1
Basavilbaso, Arg. 159/J10
Bascharage, Lux. 53/E4
Basehor, Ks, US 137/D5
Basel, Swi. 56/D2
Basel/Mulhouse (int'l arpt.), Fr. 56/D2
Baselga di Pinè, It. 57/H5
Baselland (canton), Swi. 56/D3
Bashee (riv.), SAfr. 106/E3
Bashi (chan.), Phil.,Tai. 116/A2
Bashi Channel (chan.), Phil.,Tai. 79/C3
Bashkortostan (aut. rep.), Rus. 64/Q6
Bāsht, Iran 88/F2
Basilan (peak), Phil. 81/F2
Basilan (isl.), Phil. 116/B4
Basildon, Eng, UK 33/G3
Basilica di Fieschi, It. 58/C4
Basilicata (reg.), It. 46/D2
Basingstoke, Eng, UK 33/E4
Basingstoke (canal), Eng, UK 30/A3
Basīrhāt, India 85/G4
Basīrpur, Pak. 86/B4
Başkale, Turk. 90/F2
Baskatong (res.), Qu, Can. 130/F2
Baskil, Turk. 90/D2
Başkomutan NP, Turk. 62/D5
Bāsoda, India 84/A4
Basodino (peak), It. 57/E5
Basoko, D.R. Congo 97/K7
Basoli, India 86/C3
Bass (str.), Austl. 109/D4
Bass Rock (isl.), Sc, UK 36/D4
Bassae (Vassés) (ruin), Gre. 47/G4
Bassano, Ab, Can. 126/E3
Bassano del Grappa, It. 59/E1
Bassari, Togo 103/F4
Bassas da India (isl.), Reun. 105/G5
Basse-Normandie (pol. reg.), Fr. 42/C2
Basse Santa Su, Gam. 102/B3
Basse-Terre (isl.), Guad. 141/J4
Basse-Terre, Fr. 141/N8
Bassecourt, Swi. 56/D3
Bassein (riv.), Myan. 83/F4
Bassein (Vasai), India 89/K5
Bassenge, Belg. 53/E2
Bassenheim, Ger. 53/G3
Bassenthwaite (lake), Eng, UK 35/E2
Basseterre (cap.), StK. 141/N8
Bassum, Ger. 51/F3
Basswood (lake), US,Can. 130/B1
Båstad, Swe. 38/E3
Bastak, Iran 89/F3
Bastām, Iran 89/G1
Bastelicaccia, Fr. 46/A2
Bastheim, Ger. 54/D2
Bastī, India 84/D2
Bastia, Fr. 46/A1
Bastia, It. 43/K5
Bastogne, Belg. 53/E4
Bastos, Braz. 155/B2
Bastrop, Tx, US 129/H5
Basyūn, Egypt 91/B4
Bat Shelomo, Isr. 91/F6
Bat Yam, Isr. 91/F7
Bata, EqG. 96/G7
Batabanó (gulf), Cuba 140/E3
Batac, Phil. 79/D4
Batagay, Rus. 65/P3
Batai (pass), Pak. 86/A3
Batalha, Braz. 154/B2
Batalha, Port. 44/A3
Batan (isls.), Phil. 67/M7
Batang, China 70/G6
Batangafo, CAfr. 96/J6
Batangas, Phil. 79/D5
Batarasa, Phil. 79/C6
Batatais, Braz. 155/C2
Batavia, NY, US 130/E3
Batavia, Il, US 135/P16
Bataysk, Rus. 62/F3
Batchtown, Il, US 137/F7
Bătdâmbâng, Camb. 78/C3
Bate (bay), Austl. 114/H9
Batéké (plat.), Congo 96/H8
Batemans Bay, Austl. 115/D2
Batesburg-Leesville, SC, US 133/H3
Batesville, Ms, US 129/K4
Bath, Me, US 131/G3
Bath, NY, US 130/E3
Bath, Eng, UK 32/D4
Bath, Pa, US 138/C2
Bath and Northeast Somerset (co.), Eng, UK 32/D4
Bathgate, Sc, UK 36/C5
Bathmen, Neth. 50/D4
Bathurst, Austl. 115/D2
Bathurst (cape), NW, Can. 134/N1
Bathurst, NB, Can. 131/H2
Bathurst (isl.), Nun., Can. 123/R7
Bathurst (inlet), Nun., Can. 122/F2
Bathurst Inlet, Nun., Can. 122/F2
Batian (Mt. Kenya) (peak), Kenya 104/C3
Batiquitos (lag.), Ca, US 136/C4
Batiscan (riv.), Qu, Can. 131/F2
Batley, Eng, UK 35/G4
Batlow, Austl. 115/D2
Batman, Turk. 90/E2
Batman (dam), Turk. 90/E2
Batna (prov.), Alg. 99/G2
Batna, Alg. 100/J5
Baton Rouge (cap.), La, US 129/K5
Batopilas, Mex. 142/D3
Batoti, India 86/C3
Batouri, Camr. 96/H7
Baṭrā' (ruin), Jor. 91/D4
Båtsfjord, Nor. 37/J1
Batsto (riv.), NJ, US 138/D4
Batsto, NJ, US 138/D4
Batsto Historic Village, NJ, US 138/D4
Battaglia Terme, It. 59/E2
Battenberg, Ger. 51/F6
Bätterkinden, Swi. 56/D3
Batticaloa, SrL. 82/D6
Battipaglia, It. 46/D2
Battle, Eng, UK 33/G5
Battle (riv.), Ab,Can. 122/E3
Battle Creek, Mi, US 130/C3
Battle Mountain, Nv, US 126/D5
Battleford, Sk, Can. 126/F2
Battock (mt.), Sc, UK 36/D3
Batu (bay), Malay. 80/D3
Batu (peak), Malay. 80/D3
Batu (isls.), Indo. 80/A4
Batu (peak), Eth. 97/N6
Batu (cape), Indo. 81/E3
Batu Gajah, Malay. 80/B3
Batu Pahat, Malay. 80/B3
Batu Puteh (peak), Malay. 80/B3
Batudaka (isl.), Indo. 81/F4
Batuensambang (peak), Indo. 80/D3
Bat'umi (int'l arpt.), Geo. 63/G4
Bat'umi, Geo. 63/G4
Baturaja, Indo. 80/B4
Baturité, Braz. 154/C2
Batys Qazaqstan, Kaz. 64/E5
Bauchi (state), Nga. 103/H4
Bauchi, Nga. 103/H4
Baudette, Mn, US 127/K3
Baudó (mts.), Col. 145/G5
Baudó (riv.), Col. 152/B3
Bauer, Ut, US 137/J13
Bauld (cape), Nf, Can. 131/L1
Baulmes, Swi. 56/C4
Bauman (peak), Togo 103/F5
Baume-les-Dames, Fr. 56/C3
Baumholder, Ger. 53/G4
Baunach (riv.), Ger. 54/D2
Baunach, Ger. 54/D3
Baunatal, Ger. 51/G6
Baunei, It. 46/A2
Baurú, Braz. 155/B2
Bautzen, Ger. 41/H3
Bavans, Fr. 56/C3
Bavarian Alps (mts.), Aus.,Ger. 57/G3
Bavay, Fr. 52/C3
Båven (lake), Swe. 38/G2
Baveno, It. 57/E6
Baviácora, Mex. 142/C2
Bavilliers, Fr. 56/C2
Bavispe, Río de (riv.), Mex. 142/C2
Baw Baw (mt.), Austl. 115/C3
Baw Baw NP, Austl. 115/C3
Bawāna, India 86/D5
Bawang (cape), Indo. 80/C4
Bawean (isl.), Indo. 80/D5
Bawku, Gha. 103/E4
Baxoi, China 83/G2
Bay City, Tx, US 129/J5
Bay City, Mi, US 130/D3
Bay Minette, Al, US 133/G4
Bay Roberts, Nf, Can. 131/L2
Bay Saint Louis, Ms, US 133/F4
Bayamo, Cuba 145/G1
Bayamón, PR 141/M8
Bayan, Mong. 70/G2
Bayan Har (mts.), China 70/G5
Bayan-Hongor (prov.), Mong. 70/G2
Bayan-Ölgiy (prov.), Mong. 70/E2
Bayan-Ulaan, Mong. 70/H2
Bayanaul'skiy NP, Kaz. 87/G2
Bayanhongor, Mong. 70/H2
Bayanhushuu, Mong. 70/F2
Bayannuur, Mong. 70/F2
Bayano (lake), Pan. 145/G4
Bayanterem, Mong. 71/K2
Bayantsagaan, Mong. 70/H2
Bayard, Ne, US 127/H5
Bayat, Turk. 62/E4
Bayawan, Phil. 81/F2
Baybach (riv.), Ger. 53/G3
Baybay, Phil. 79/D5
Bayburt, Turk. 62/G4
Bayburt (prov.), Turk. 62/F4
Baydaratskaya (bay), Rus. 64/G2
Baydhabo (Baidoa), Som. 97/P7
Bayel, Fr. 56/A1
Bayerischer Wald (hills), Ger. 55/F4
Bayerischer Wald NP, Ger. 55/G5
Bayern (state), Ger. 40/F4
Bayeux, Braz. 154/D2
Bayeux, Fr. 42/C2
Baygorria (res.), Uru. 159/K10
Baykal (mts.), Rus. 65/L4
Baykal (lake), Rus. 67/L4
Baykan, Turk. 90/E2
Bayombong, Phil. 79/D4
Bayon, Fr. 56/C1
Bayona, Sp. 44/A1
Bayonet Point, Fl, US 133/H4
Bayonne, Fr. 42/C5
Bayonne, NJ, US 139/J9
Bayport, NY, US 139/E2
Bayramaly, Trkm. 89/H1
Bayramiç, Turk. 47/K3
Bayreuth, Ger. 55/E3
Bayrūt (cap.), Leb. 91/D3
Bays, Lake of (lake), On, Can. 130/E2
Bayşehir (lake), Turk. 90/B2
Bayt Ḩanīnā, WBnk. 91/G8
Bayt Ḩānūn, Gaza 91/D4
Bayt Laḩm (Bethlehem), WBnk. 91/G8
Bayt Sāḩūr, WBnk. 91/G8
Baytik Shan (mts.), China,Mon 70/E2
Baytown, Tx, US 129/J5
Bayudha (des.), Sudan 101/C5
Bayugan, Phil. 79/E6
Bayville, NY, US 139/L8
Baza, Sp. 44/D4
Bazainville, Fr. 30/G5
Bazardüzü (peak), Azer. 63/H4
Bazaruto, Ilha do (isl.), Moz. 105/G5
Bazèga (prov.), Burk. 103/E4
Bazemont, Fr. 30/H5
Bazet, Fr. 42/D5
Bazhong, China 70/J5
Bazin (riv.), Qu, Can. 130/F2
Bāzpur, India 84/B1
Bazzano, It. 59/E3
Be, Nosy (isl.), Madg. 107/H6
Beach Haven, NJ, US 138/D4
Beachport, Austl. 115/B3
Beachwood, NJ, US 138/D4
Beachy (head), Eng, UK 33/G5
Beachy Head (pt.), Eng, UK 42/D1
Beacon (peak), Wal, UK 32/C2
Beaconsfield, Austl. 115/C4
Beaconsfield, Eng, UK 33/F3
Beaconsfield, Qu, Can. 131/N7
Beal (range), Austl. 114/A4
Bealanana, Madg. 107/J6
Beale (cape), BC, Can. 126/B3
Beampingaratra (ridge), Madg. 107/H9
Bear (isl.), Nor. 160/E
Bear (mt.), Ak, US 134/K3
Bear (mtn.), Ak, US 134/K3
Bear (riv.), US 128/E2
Bear, De, US 138/C4
Bear (lake), Ut, US 124/D3
Bear Creek (lake), Co, US 137/B3
Bear River (bay), Ut, US 137/J11
Bear River Migratory Bird Refuge (nat'l wild. ref.), Ut, US 137/J10
Beardsley, Az, US 137/R18
Beardsley (canal), Az, US 137/R18
Bearfort (mtn.), NJ, US 139/H7
Bearma (riv.), India 84/B4
Bearpaw (mts.), Mt, US 126/F3
Bearsden, Sc, UK 36/B5
Beartooth (mts.), Mt,Wy, US 126/F4
Beās (riv.), India 84/B3
Beas de Segura, Sp. 44/D3
Beasain, Sp. 44/D1
Beata (cape), DRep. 141/G4
Beata (isl.), Thai. 145/J2
Beata (pt.), DRep. 145/J2
Beatenberg, Swi. 56/D4
Beatty, Nv, US 128/C3
Beattystown, NJ, US 138/D2
Beau Bassin-Rose Hill, Mrts. 107/T15
Beaucaire, Fr. 42/F5
Beaucamps-le-Vieux, Fr. 52/A4
Beauchamp, Fr. 30/J4
Beaucourt, Fr. 56/C3
Beaudesert, Austl. 114/D4
Beaufort, Austl. 115/B3
Beaufort, SC, US 133/H3
Beaufort, Fr. 56/B4
Beaufort (sea), Can.,US 119/C2
Beaufort, Lux. 53/F4
Beaufort West, SAfr. 106/C4
Beaugency, Fr. 42/D3
Beaujolais, Monts du (mts.), Fr. 42/F4
Beauly (riv.), Sc, UK 36/B2
Beauly, Sc, UK 36/B2
Beauly Firth (lake), Sc, UK 36/B2
Beaumaris, Wal, UK 34/D5
Beaume, Fr. 42/F3
Beaumont, Tx, US 129/J5
Beaumont, Ca, US 136/D3
Beaumont, Fr. 42/E4
Beaumont, Belg. 53/D3
Beaumont-de-Lomagne, Fr. 42/D5
Beaumont-sur-Oise, Fr. 30/J4
Beaupréau, Fr. 42/C3
Beauquesne, Fr. 52/B3
Beauraing, Belg. 53/D3
Beaurainville, Fr. 52/A3
Beaurevoir, Fr. 52/C4
Beausejour, Mb, Can. 127/J3
Beautheil, Fr. 30/M5
Beautor, Fr. 52/C4
Beauvais, Fr. 52/B5
Beauval, Sk, Can. 126/G2
Beauval, Fr. 52/B3
Beauvoir, Fr. 30/L6
Beaver, Ak, US 134/J2
Beaver (riv.), Ok, US 128/G3
Beaver (riv.), On, Can. 127/L2
Beaver, Ut, US 128/D3
Beaver (isl.), Mi, US 130/C2
Beaver (lake), Ar, US 132/E2
Beaver (riv.), Yk, Can. 122/D2
Beaver Creek, Yk, Can. 134/K3
Beaver Meadows, Pa, US 138/C2
Beaver Springs, Pa, US 138/A2
Beaverhead (riv.), Mt, US 126/E4
Beaverlodge, Ab, Can. 126/D2
Beavertown, Pa, US 138/A2
Bebedouro, Braz. 155/B2
Beberibe, Braz. 154/C2
Bebington, Eng, UK 35/E5
Bebra, Ger. 51/G7
Becal, Mex. 144/D1
Beccles, Eng, UK 33/H2
Bečej, Yugo. 48/E3
Becerreá, Sp. 44/B1
Bechar (prov.), Alg. 98/E3
Bechar, Alg. 99/E3
Becharof (lake), Ak, US 134/G4
Becharof NWR, Ak, US 134/G4
Bechhofen, Ger. 53/G5
Bechtheim, Ger. 54/B3
Bechyně, Czh. 55/H4
Beckdorf, Ger. 51/G2
Beckenried, Swi. 57/E4
Beckingen, Ger. 53/F5
Beckley, WV, US 130/D4
Beckum, Ger. 51/F5
Beclean, Rom. 49/G2
Becs de Bosson (peak), Swi. 56/D5
Bédarieux, Fr. 42/E5
Bedburg, Ger. 53/F2
Bedburg-Hau, Ger. 50/D5
Beder, Den. 38/D3
Bedford, In, US 130/C4
Bedford, Va, US 130/E4
Bedford, Qu, Can. 130/F2
Bedford, SAfr. 106/D4
Bedford, Eng, UK 33/F2
Bedford (cape), Austl. 114/B1
Bedford Hills, NY, US 139/E1
Bedford Level (phys. reg.), Eng, UK 33/F2
Bedford Park, Il, US 135/Q16
Bedfordshire (co.), Eng, UK 33/F2
Bedlington, Eng, UK 35/G1
Bedonia, It. 58/C3
Bedouaram (well), Niger 96/H4
Bedretto, Swi. 57/E5
Bedsted, Den. 38/C3
Bedum, Neth. 50/D2
Bedworth, Eng, UK 33/E2
Beebe Seep (canal), Co, US 137/C2
Beechworth, Austl. 115/C3
Beek, Neth. 53/E2
Beelen, Ger. 51/F5
Beelitz, Ger. 40/P7
Beenleigh, Austl. 114/D4
Beer (pt.), Eng, UK 32/C5
Be'er Sheva', Isr. 91/D4
Beerfelden, Ger. 54/B3
Beernem, Belg. 52/C1
Beerzel, Belg. 53/D1
Beesel, Neth. 50/D6
Beeville, Tx, US 132/D4
Befandriana, Madg. 107/J6
Befandriana, Madg. 107/G8
Beforona, Madg. 107/J7
Befotaka, Madg. 107/J6
Beg (lake), NI, UK 34/B2
Bega, Austl. 115/D3
Bega (riv.), Ger. 51/F5
Bega Veche (riv.), Cro. 48/E3
Begamganj, Bang. 85/H4
Begamganj, India 84/B4
Bégard, Fr. 42/B2
Begarslan (peak), Trkm. 63/K4
Begejci, Yugo. 48/E3
Begichev (isl.), Rus. 65/M2
Begna (riv.), Nor. 37/D3
Begusarai, India 85/F3
Béhague (pt.), FrG. 151/H3
Behāla (str.), Indo. 80/B4
Behāla, India 85/G4
Behamberg, Aus. 55/H6
Behat, India 86/D4
Behbahān, Iran 88/F2
Behenjy-Afovany, Madg. 107/H7
Béhoust, Fr. 30/H5
Behren-lès-Forbach, Fr. 53/F5
Behrī (riv.), Nepal 84/C1
Behshahr, Iran 88/F1
Bei (riv.), China 79/A2
Bei (mts.), China 64/K5
Bei'an, China 71/N2
Beierfeld, Ger. 55/F1
Beigua (peak), It. 58/B4
Beijing (mun.), China 71/L3
Beijing (cap.), China 72/H7
Beijing Capital (int'l arpt.), China 72/H6
Beilen, Neth. 50/D3
Beiliu, China 83/K3
Beilngries, Ger. 55/E4
Beilstein, Ger. 54/C4
Beilun (pass), China 79/A3
Bein Tharsuinn (peak), Sc, UK 36/B1
Beindersheim, Ger. 54/B3
Beinn a' Chuallaich (peak), Sc, UK 36/B3
Beinn a' Ghlò (peak), Sc, UK 36/C3
Beinn a' Mheadhoin (lake), Sc, UK 36/B2
Beinn Bhàn (peak), Sc, UK 36/A3
Beinn Bheula (peak), Sc, UK 36/B4
Beinn Bhrotain (peak), Sc, UK 36/C2
Beinn Bhuidhe (peak), Sc, UK 36/B4
Beinn Bhuidhe Mhór (peak),Sc, UK 36/B2
Beinn Dearg (peak), Sc, UK 36/B1
Beinn Dearg (peak), Sc, UK 36/C3
Beinn Dòrain (peak), Sc, UK 36/B4
Beinn Eighe (peak), Sc, UK 36/A1
Beinn Heasgarnich (peak), Sc, UK 36/B3
Beinn Mholach (peak), Sc, UK 36/B3
Beinn Mhór (peak), Sc, UK 36/A4
Beinwil am See, Swi. 56/E3
Beipiao, China 72/E2
Beira, Moz. 105/F4
Beiru (riv.), China 72/C4
Beirut (int'l arpt.), Leb. 91/D3
Beitbridge, Zim. 105/E5
Beith, Sc, UK 36/B5
Beiuş, Rom. 48/F2
Beizhen, China 73/A2
Beja, Port. 44/B3
Beja (dist.), Port. 44/A4
Bejaïa (prov.), Alg. 100/H4
Bejaïa, Alg. 100/H4
Béjar, Sp. 44/C2
Bejhi (riv.), Pak. 89/J3
Bekabad, Uzb. 87/E4
Bekasi, Indo. 80/C5
Békés (prov.), Hun. 48/E2
Békés, Hun. 48/E2
Békéscsaba, Hun. 48/E2
Bekilli, Turk. 90/B2
Bekily, Madg. 107/H9
Bekitro, Madg. 107/H9
Bekwai, Gha. 103/E5
Bel Air, Md, US 138/B4
Bel Air South, Md, US 138/B5
Bela, Pak. 89/J3
Belā, India 82/D2
Belá, Slvk. 41/K4
Bela Crkva, Yugo. 48/E3
Bela Cruz, Braz. 154/B1
Bela Palanka, Yugo. 47/H1
Bělá pod Bezdězem, Czh. 55/H1
Belā Pratāpgarh, India 84/C3
Bela Vista, Braz. 151/G8
Bela Vista, Moz. 107/F2
Bela Vista do Paraíso, Braz. 155/B2
Belair, La, US 137/Q17
Belair Rec. Pk., Austl. 113/M9
Belan (riv.), India 84/D3
Belarus (ctry.) 27/G3
Belas, Port. 45/P10
Belaya (riv.), Rus. 64/F4
Belbo (riv.), It. 58/B3
Bełchatów, Pol. 41/K3
Belchen (peak), Ger. 56/D2
Belcher (chan.), Nun., Can. 123/S7
Belcher (isls.), On, Can. 123/H3
Belchite, Sp. 45/E2
Belcourt, ND, US 127/J3
Beldānga, India 85/G4
Belebey, Rus. 61/M5
Beled Weyne, Som. 97/Q7
Belém, Braz. 151/J4
Belém, Braz. 154/D2
Belém de São Francisco, Braz. 154/C3
Belem Tower, Port. 45/P10
Belén, Arg. 157/C2
Belen, NM, US 128/F4
Belén, Chile 156/D5
Belén, Nic. 140/D5
Belen, Turk. 91/E1
Belen, Turk. 91/C1
Belén de Escobar, Arg. 159/J11
Belene, Bul. 49/G4
Beles Wenz (riv.), Eth. 97/N5
Belesar, Embalse de (res.), Sp. 44/B1
Belev, Rus. 62/F1
Belews Creek, Mo, US 137/F9
Belfair, Wa, US 135/B3
Belfast, Me, US 131/G2
Belfast, SAfr. 107/E2
Belfast (dist.), NI, UK 34/B2
Belfast (cap.), NI, UK 34/C2
Belfast Lough (bay), NI, UK 34/C2
Belfaux, Swi. 56/D4
Belfield, ND, US 127/H4
Belfort (dept.), Fr. 56/C2
Belfort, Fr. 56/C2
Belgioioso, It. 58/C2
Belgium (ctry.) 40/C3
Belgorod, Rus. 62/F2
Belgorodskaya (obl.), Rus. 62/F2
Belgrade, Mt, US 126/F4
Belgrade (Beograd) (cap.),Yugo. 48/E4
Beli Drim (riv.), Yugo. 47/G1
Beli Manastir, Cro. 48/D3
Beli Timok (riv.), Yugo. 48/F4
Belitsa, Bul. 47/H2
Belitung (isl.), Indo. 80/C4
Belize (riv.), Belz. 144/D2
Belize (ctry.) 144/D2

173
Beliz – Bipoi

Belize City, Belz. 144/D2
Beljanica (peak), Yugo. 48/E3
Bel'kovskiy (isl.), Rus. 65/N2
Bell (pt.), Austl. 113/G5
Bell, Austl. 114/C4
Bell (riv.), Qu, Can. 123/J4
Bell (pen.), Nun., Can. 123/H2
Bell, Ca, US 136/F8
Bell, Ger. 53/G3
Bell Gardens, Ca, US 136/F8
Bell Rock (Inchcape) (isl.), Sc, UK 36/D4
Bell Ville, Arg. 157/D3
Bella Coola, BC, Can. 126/B2
Bella Vista, Arg. 157/E2
Bellac, Fr. 42/D3
Bellaghy, NI, UK 34/B2
Bellagio, It. 57/F6
Bellano, It. 57/F5
Bellary, India 82/C4
Bellavista, Peru 156/B2
Bellavista, Peru 156/B2
Bellavista (cape), It. 46/A3
Bellavista, Ecu. 156/E7
Belle (riv.), On, Can. 135/G7
Belle-Anse, Haiti 145/H2
Belle Chasse, La, US 137/Q17
Belle Fourche (riv.), Wy, US 127/G5
Belle Glade, Fl, US 133/H5
Belle Haven, Va, US 138/A6
Belle-Île (isl.), Fr. 42/B3
Belle Isle (str.), NF, Can. 131/K1
Belle Terre, NY, US 139/E2
Belleek, NI, UK 34/B3
Bellefontaine, Oh, US 130/D3
Bellefonte, De, US 138/C4
Bellegarde-sur-Valserine, Fr. 56/B5
Bellenberg, Ger. 57/G1
Bellenden Ker NP, Austl. 114/B2
Belleplain, NJ, US 138/D5
Bellerive-sur-Allier, Fr. 42/E3
Bellerose, NY, US 139/L9
Belleu, Fr. 52/C5
Belleville, On, Can. 130/E2
Belleville, Il, US 137/H8
Belleville, Fr. 56/A5
Belleville, NJ, US 139/J8
Belleville, Mi, US 135/E7
Belleville-sur-Meuse, Fr. 53/E5
Bellevue, Md, US 138/B6
Belley, Fr. 56/B6
Bellflower, Ca, US 136/F8
Bellheim, Ger. 54/B4
Bellignat, Fr. 56/B5
Bellinge, Den. 38/D4
Bellingen, Austl. 115/E1
Bellingham, Wa, US 126/C3
Bellingshausen (isl.), FrPol. 117/K6
Bellingshausen (sea), Ant. 160/U
Bellingwolde, Neth. 51/E2
Bellinzago Novarese, It. 58/B1
Bellinzona, Swi. 57/F5
Bellmawr, NJ, US 138/C4
Bellmead, Tx, US 129/H5
Bellmore, NY, US 139/L9
Bello, Col. 150/C2
Bellona Reefs (reef), NCal. 116/E7
Bellot (str.), Nun., Can. 122/G1
Bellport, NY, US 139/F2
Bellshill, Sc, UK 36/B5
Belluno (prov.), It. 59/E1
Belluno, It. 43/K3
Bellville, Tx, US 129/H5
Bellville, SAfr. 106/L10
Bellvue, Co, US 137/B1
Bellwald, Swi. 56/E5
Belm, Ger. 51/F4
Belmar, NJ, US 138/D3
Bélmez, Sp. 44/C3
Belmont, Ca, US 135/K11
Belmonte, Braz. 154/C4
Belmonte, Sp. 44/D3
Belmonte, Port. 44/B2
Belmopan (cap.), Belz. 144/D2
Belmullet, Ire. 31/P9
Belo Campo, Braz. 154/B4
Belo Horizonte, Braz. 155/D1
Belo Jardim, Braz. 154/C3
Belo-Tsiribihina, Madg. 107/H7
Beloeil, Qu, Can. 131/P6
Beloeil, Belg. 52/C2
Belogorsk, Rus. 71/N1
Beloha, Madg. 107/H9
Beloit, Wi, US 127/L5
Beloit, Ks, US 129/H3
Belomorsk, Rus. 60/G2
Belorado, Sp. 44/D1
Belorechensk, Rus. 62/F3
Belören, Turk. 90/C2
Beloretsk, Rus. 61/N5
Beloslav, Bul. 49/H4
Belovo, Bul. 47/J1
Belovo, Rus. 64/J4
Beloye (lake), Rus. 64/D3
Belper, Eng, UK 35/G5
Belsand, India 85/E2
Belt, Mt, US 126/F4
Belterwijde (lake), Neth. 50/D3
Beltheim, Ger. 53/G3
Belton, Tx, US 129/H5
Belton, Mo, US 137/D6
Beltsville, Md, US 138/B5
Beltzville (lake), Pa, US 138/C2
Belukha (peak), Rus. 70/E2
Belvedere, Ca, US 135/K11
Belvidere, NJ, US 138/C2
Belyando (riv.), Austl. 109/D3
Belyy (isl.), Rus. 160/A
Belzig, Ger. 40/G2
Bełżyce, Pol. 41/M3
Bemaraha (plat.), Madg. 107/H7
Bemarivo (riv.), Madg. 107/H7
Bembéréké, Ben. 103/F4
Bembibre, Sp. 44/B1
Bemboka, Austl. 115/D3
Bemetāra, India 82/D3
Bemidji, Mn, US 127/K4
Bemmel, Neth. 50/C5
Ben Aigan (hill), Sc, UK 36/C1
Ben Alder (peak), Sc, UK 36/B3
Ben Améra (well), Mrta. 98/B5
Ben Avon (peak), Sc, UK 36/C2
Ben Boyd NP, Austl. 115/D3
Ben Chonzie (peak), Sc, UK 36/C4
Ben Cleuch (peak), Sc, UK 36/C4
Ben Cruachan (peak), Sc, UK 36/A4
Ben Davis (pt.), NJ, US 138/C5
Ben Gurion (int'l arpt.), Isr. 91/F7
Ben Hope (peak), Sc, UK 31/R7
Ben Ime (peak), Sc, UK 36/B4
Ben Lawers (peak), Sc, UK 36/B3
Ben Ledi (peak), Sc, UK 36/B4
Ben Lomond (peak), Sc, UK 36/B4
Ben Lomond NP, Austl. 115/C4
Ben Lui (peak), Sc, UK 36/B4
Ben Macdui (peak), Sc, UK 36/C2
Ben More (peak), Sc, UK 31/Q8
Ben More (peak), Sc, UK 36/B4
Ben More Assynt (peak), Sc, UK 31/R7
Ben Msik-Sidi Othmane (prov.), Mor. 100/A2
Ben Nevis (peak), Sc, UK 36/B3
Ben Rinnes (peak), Sc, UK 36/C2
Ben Slimane, Mor. 98/D2
Ben Slimane (prov.), Mor. 100/A3
Ben Starav (peak), Sc, UK 36/A3
Ben Tee (peak), Sc, UK 36/B2
Ben Tirran (peak), Sc, UK 36/C3
Ben Tre, Viet. 78/D4
Ben Vane (peak), Sc, UK 36/B4
Ben Vorlich (peak), Sc, UK 36/B4
Ben Vrackie (peak), Sc, UK 36/C3
Ben Wyvis (peak), Sc, UK 36/B1
Ben Zohra (well), Alg. 98/E3
Benabarre, Sp. 45/F1
Benahmed, Mor. 98/D2
Benalla, Austl. 115/C3
Benalmádena, Sp. 44/C4
Benavente, Sp. 44/C1
Benavides, Tx, US 132/D5
Benbane (pt.), NI, UK 34/B1
Benbecula (isl.), Sc, UK 31/Q8
Benbonyathe (peak), Austl. 113/H4
Benburb, NI, UK 34/B3
Bend, Or, US 126/C4
Bendeleben (mt.), Ak, US 134/F2
Bendemeer, Austl. 115/D1
Bendersville, Pa, US 138/A4
Bendigo, Austl. 115/C3
Bendorf, Ger. 38/C4
Bene Beraq, Isr. 91/F7
Benedict (mt.), Nf, Can. 123/L3
Benediktbeuern, Ger. 57/H2
Benediktenwand (peak), Ger. 57/H2
Beneditinos, Braz. 154/B2
Benenitra, Madg. 107/H8
Benešov, Czh. 55/H3
Benevento, It. 46/D2
Benfeld, Fr. 56/D1
Bengal (bay), Asia 67/H8
Bengal, Bay of (gulf), Asia 70/E7
Bengbu, China 72/D4
Benghāzī, Libya 96/K1
Bengkalis, Indo. 80/B3
Bengkalis (isl.), Indo. 80/B3
Bengkayang, Indo. 80/C3
Bengkulu, Indo. 80/B4
Bengough, Sk, Can. 127/G3
Bengtsfors, Swe. 38/E2
Benguela, Ang. 105/B3
Benguerir, Mor. 98/D2
Beni, D.R. Congo 104/A2
Beni (riv.), Bol. 147/C4
Beni Abbes, Alg. 99/E3
Beni Bouayach, Mor. 100/C2
Beni Ensar, Mor. 100/B2
Beni Khiar, Tun. 100/M6
Beni Mellal, Mor. 98/D2
Beni Ounif, Alg. 99/E2
Benicarló, Sp. 45/F2
Benicia, Ca, US 135/K10
Benidorm, Sp. 45/E3
Benifayó, Sp. 45/E3
Benin (ctry.) 103/F4
Benin, Bight of (bay), Afr. 93/C4
Benin City, Nga. 103/G5
Benisa, Sp. 45/F3
Benito Juárez, Mex. 142/D2
Benjamin, Tx, US 129/H4
Benjamin Constant, Braz. 156/D2
Benjamín Hill, Mex. 142/C2
Benjamin, Isla (isl.), Chile 158/B5
Benkei-misaki (cape), Japan 76/B2
Benkelman, Ne, US 129/G2
Bennachie (hill), Sc, UK 36/D2
Bennan (pt.), Sc, UK 36/A6
Bennett (isl.), Rus. 65/Q2
Bennettsville, SC, US 133/J3
Bennington, Vt, US 130/F3
Bénoue, PN de la, Camr. 96/H6
Bensenville, Il, US 135/Q16
Bensheim, Ger. 54/B3
Benson, Mn, US 127/K4
Benson, Az, US 128/E5
Benta (riv.), Hun. 49/Q10
Bentheim, Ger. 51/E4
Bentley, Eng, UK 35/G4
Bento Gonçalves, Braz. 155/B4
Benton, La, US 129/J4
Benton, Ar, US 129/J4
Benton, Pa, US 138/B1
Benton Harbor, Mi, US 130/C3
Bentong, Malay. 80/B3
Benue (state), Nga. 103/H5
Benue (riv.), Nga. 93/C4
Benxi, China 73/B2
Benxi, China 73/C2
Beočin, Yugo. 48/D3
Beograd (int'l arpt.), Yugo. 48/E3
Beohāri, India 84/C3
Beppu (bay), Japan 74/B4
Beppu, Japan 74/B4
Bequia (isl.), StV. 141/N9
Bequimão, Braz. 154/A1
Beraber (well), Alg. 96/E1
Beragh, NI, UK 34/A2
Beraketa, Madg. 107/H8
Berasia, India 84/A4
Berat, Alb. 47/F2
Beratus (peak), Indo. 81/E4
Beratzhausen, Ger. 55/E4
Berau (riv.), Indo. 81/E3
Berau (bay), Indo. 116/C5
Berbenno di Valtellina, It. 57/F5
Berbera, Som. 97/Q5
Berbérati, CAfr. 96/J7
Berbice (riv.), Guy. 150/G2
Berceto, It. 58/C3
Berchem, Belg. 50/B6
Bercher, Swi. 56/C4
Berching, Ger. 55/E4
Berchtesgaden, Ger. 43/K3
Berchtesgaden, NP, Ger. 43/K3
Berck, Fr. 52/A3
Berdorf, Lux. 53/F4
Berdsk, Rus. 87/H2
Berdyans'k, Ukr. 62/F3
Berdychiv, Ukr. 62/D2
Berea, Ky, US 130/C4
Bereguardo, It. 58/C2
Berehove, Ukr. 41/M4
Berekum, Gha. 103/E5
Berenguela, Bol. 156/D5
Berenice (ruin), Egypt 101/C4
Beresford, SD, US 127/J5
Beresford, NB, Can. 131/H2
Bereşti, Rom. 49/H2
Berettyóújfalu, Hun. 48/E2
Berevo, Madg. 107/H7
Berezina (riv.), Bela. 62/D1
Berezniki, Rus. 61/N4
Berezovo, Rus. 64/G3
Berg (riv.), SAfr. 106/B4
Berg, Swi. 57/F2
Berg, Lux. 53/F4
Berg, Ger. 54/B5
Berg bei Rohrbach, Aus. 55/G5
Berga, Sp. 45/F1
Bergama, Turk. 62/C5
Bergamo, It. 58/C1
Bergamo (prov.), It. 57/F6
Bergara, Sp. 44/D1
Bergatreute, Ger. 57/F2
Bergen, Neth. 50/B3
Bergen, Ger. 51/G3
Bergen (co.), NJ, US 138/D2
Bergen, Nor. 38/A1
Bergen, Ger. 38/E4
Bergen op Zoom, Neth. 50/B5
Bergen Park, Co, US 137/B3
Bergenfield, NJ, US 139/K8
Bergerac, Fr. 42/D4
Bergeyk, Neth. 50/C6
Bergheim, Tx, US 137/T20
Bergheim, Aus. 55/G7
Bergheim, Ger. 53/F2
Bergisch Gladbach, Ger. 53/G2
Bergkamen, Ger. 51/E5
Bergnäset, Swe. 60/D2
Bergneustadt, Ger. 53/G1
Bergrheinfeld, Ger. 40/F4
Bergse Maas (riv.), Neth. 50/B5
Bergshamra, Swe. 38/H2
Bergsviken, Swe. 37/G2
Bergtheim, Ger. 54/D3
Berguent, Mor. 100/C2
Bergues, Fr. 52/B2
Bergum, Neth. 50/D2
Bergumermeer (lake), Neth. 50/D2
Bergün-Bravuogn, Swi. 57/F4
Bergviken (lake), Swe. 38/G1
Berh, Mong. 71/K2
Berikat (cape), Indo. 80/C4
Bering (isl.), Rus. 65/S4
Bering (sea), Asia,NAm. 65/U4
Bering (str.), Rus.,US 67/U3
Bering Land Bridge Nat'l Prsv., Ak, US 134/E2
Beringen, Belg. 53/E1
Beritarikap (cape), Indo. 80/B4
Berja, Sp. 44/D4
Berkel, Neth. 50/B5
Berkel (riv.), Ger. 40/D2
Berkeley, Ca, US 128/B3
Berkeley, Mo, US 137/G8
Berkeley Heights, NJ, US 139/H9
Berkhamsted, Eng, UK 30/B1
Berkheim, Ger. 57/G1
Berkhout, Neth. 50/B3
Berkley, Mi, US 135/F6
Berkovitsa, Bul. 47/H1
Berks (co.), Pa, US 138/C3
Berkshire (co.), Eng, UK 33/E3
Berkshire Downs (hills), Eng, UK 33/E3
Berlaimont, Fr. 52/C3
Berlanga de Duero, Sp. 44/D2
Berlare, Belg. 52/D1
Berleburg, Ger. 51/F6
Berlicum, Neth. 50/C5
Berlin, Wi, US 127/L5
Berlin, NH, US 131/G2
Berlin (cap.), Ger. 40/G6
Berlin (state), Ger. 40/G6
Berlin, NJ, US 138/D4
Bermagui, Austl. 115/D3
Bermejo, Bol. 157/D1
Bermejo (riv.), Arg. 147/D5
Bermeo, Sp. 44/D1
Bermillo de Sayago, Sp. 44/B2
Bermuda (isl.), UK 119/L6
Bern (canton), Swi. 56/D4
Bern (cap.), Swi. 56/D4
Bern-Belp (int'l arpt.), Swi. 56/D4
Bernal, Peru 156/A2
Bernalda, It. 46/E2
Bernalillo, NM, US 128/F4
Bernard (riv.), NW, Can. 122/D1
Bernardo O'Higgins, PN, Chile 157/B6
Bernardsville, NJ, US 138/D2
Bernau, Ger. 56/E2
Bernau, Ger. 40/G6
Bernay, Fr. 42/D2
Bernbeuren, Ger. 57/G2
Bernburg, Ger. 40/F3
Berne (riv.), Ger. 51/F2
Bernes-sur-Oise, Fr. 30/J4
Bernese Alps (mtn.), Swi. 43/G3
Bernhardswald, Ger. 55/F4
Bernice, La, US 129/J4
Bernier (isl.), Austl. 112/B3
Bernier (bay), Nun., Can. 122/G1
Bernina (peak), Swi. 57/F5
Bernina (mtn.), Swi. 57/F5
Bernina, Passo del (pass), Swi. 57/G5
Bernissart, Belg. 52/C3
Bernkastel-Kues, Ger. 53/G4
Bernsbach, Ger. 55/F1
Bernville, Pa, US 138/B3
Beromünster, Swi. 56/E3
Beroroha, Madg. 107/H8
Beroun, Czh. 55/H3
Berounka (riv.), Czh. 41/G4
Berovo, FYROM 47/H2
Berra, It. 59/E3
Berre, Étang de (lake), Fr. 42/F5
Berrechid, Mor. 98/D2
Berri, Austl. 113/J5
Berriane, Alg. 99/F2
Berridale, Austl. 115/D3
Berriedale, Sc, UK 31/S7
Berrigan, Austl. 115/C2
Berriozábal, Mex. 144/C2
Berrotarán, Arg. 158/D2
Berrouaghia, Alg. 100/G4
Berry, Austl. 115/D2
Berry (isls.), Bahm. 141/F2
Berry (reg.), Fr. 42/D3
Berry (pt.), Eng, UK 32/C6
Berry (mtn.), Pa, US 138/A2
Berryessa (peak), Ca, US 135/K9
Bersenbrück, Ger. 51/E3
Berthoud, Co, US 137/B2
Bertinoro, It. 59/F4
Bertiolo, It. 59/G1
Bertogne, Belg. 53/E3
Bertolínia, Braz. 154/B2
Bertoua, Camr. 96/H7
Bertrand (peak), Arg. 159/B6
Bertrandville, La, US 137/Q17
Bertrix, Belg. 53/E4
Bertry, Fr. 52/C3
Beru (isl.), Kiri. 116/G5
Beruit (isl.), Malay. 80/D3
Bervie Water (riv.), Sc, UK 36/D3
Berwick, NS, Can. 131/H2
Berwick, Pa, US 138/B1
Berwick-upon-Tweed, Eng, UK 36/D5
Berwyn, Il, US 135/Q16
Berwyn (mts.), Wal, UK 34/E6
Berzence, Hun. 48/C2
Bès (riv.), Fr. 42/E2
Besalampy, Madg. 107/H7
Besançon, Fr. 56/C3
Besar (peak), Indo. 81/E4
Besbre (riv.), Fr. 42/E3
Beşiri, Turk. 90/E2
Beška, Yugo. 48/E3
Beskids (mts.), Pol. 41/L4
Beşkonak, Turk. 91/B1
Beslan, Rus. 63/H4
Besna Kobila (peak), Yugo. 47/H1
Besozzo, It. 58/B1
Bessacarr, Eng, UK 35/G5
Bessancourt, Fr. 30/J4
Bessarabia (reg.), Mol. 49/J2
Bessbrook, NI, UK 34/B3
Bessemer, Al, US 133/G3
Bessemer (mtn.), Wa, US 135/D2
Bessines-sur-Gartempe, Fr. 42/D3
Best, Neth. 50/C5
Bestensee, Ger. 40/Q7
Bestwig, Ger. 51/F6
Bet She'an, Isr. 91/D3
Bet Shemesh, Isr. 91/F8
Betanantanana, Madg. 107/H7
Betanzos, Sp. 44/A1
Beth She'arim (ruin), Isr. 91/G6
Bethal, SAfr. 106/E2
Bethalto, Il, US 137/G8
Bethanie, Namb. 106/B2
Bethany, Mo, US 127/K5
Bethany, Ok, US 137/M14
Bethany (res.), Ca, US 135/L11
Bethel, Ak, US 134/F3
Bethel, Pa, US 138/B3
Bethel Acres, Ok, US 137/N15
Bethel Island, Ca, US 135/L10
Béthenville, Fr. 53/D5
Bétheny, Fr. 52/D5
Bethesda, Md, US 138/A6
Bethesda, Wal, UK 34/D5
Béthisy-Sainte-Pierre, Fr. 52/B5
Bethlehem, SAfr. 106/E3
Bethlehem, Pa, US 138/C2
Bethlehem, Md, US 138/C6
Bethoncourt, Fr. 56/C2
Bethpage, NY, US 139/M9
Bethulie, SAfr. 106/D3
Béthune, Sk, Can. 127/G3
Béthune (riv.), Fr. 42/D2
Béthune, Fr. 52/B2
Betim, Braz. 155/C1
Betioky, Madg. 107/H8
Betpaqala (plain), Kaz. 70/A2
Betroka, Madg. 107/H8
Betschdorf, Fr. 54/A5
Betsiamites (riv.), Qu, Can. 131/G1
Betsiboka (riv.), Madg. 107/H7
Bettancourt-la-Ferrée, Fr. 53/D6
Bette (peak), Libya 97/J3
Bettembourg, Lux. 53/F4
Betterton, Md, US 138/B5
Bettiah, India 85/E2
Bettlach, Swi. 56/D3
Bettles, Ak, US 134/H2
Betuwe (phys. reg.), Neth. 50/C5
Betwa (riv.), India 84/B3
Betz, Fr. 30/L4
Betzdorf, Ger. 53/G2
Betzenstein, Ger. 55/E3
Beulah, Austl. 115/B2
Beulah, ND, US 127/H4
Beulah (lake), Wi, US 135/P14
Beulakerwijde (lake), Neth. 50/C3
Beuningen, Neth. 50/C5
Beure, Fr. 56/C3
Beuvray (peak), Fr. 42/F3
Beuvron (riv.), Fr. 42/D3
Beuvronne (riv.), Fr. 30/L5
Beuvry, Fr. 52/B2
Bevensen, Ger. 51/H2
Bever (riv.), Ger. 51/E4
Beveren, Belg. 50/B6
Beverin (peak), Swi. 57/F4
Beverley, Austl. 112/C5
Beverley, Eng, UK 35/H4
Beverly, Mo, US 137/D5
Beverly Hills, Ca, US 136/F7
Beverly Hills, Mi, US 135/F6
Beverstedt, Ger. 51/F2
Beverungen, Ger. 51/G5
Beverwijk, Neth. 50/B4
Bewār, India 84/B3
Bewl Bridge (res.), Eng, UK 33/G4
Bex, Swi. 56/D5
Bexar (co.), Tx, US 137/T21
Bexbach, Ger. 53/G5
Bexhill, Eng, UK 33/G5
Bexley (bor.), Eng, UK 30/D2
Beyçayırı, Turk. 49/H5
Beycuma, Turk. 49/K5
Beyne-Heusay, Belg. 53/E2
Beynes, Fr. 30/H5
Beyoneisu-Retsugan (isl.), Japan 75/F5
Beypazarı, Turk. 49/K5
Beyşehir, Turk. 90/B2
Bezaha, Madg. 107/H8
Bezau, Aus. 57/F3
Bezdan, Yugo. 48/D3
Bezděz (peak), Czh. 55/H1
Bezdrev (lake), Czh. 55/H4
Bezhetsk, Rus. 60/H4
Béziers, Fr. 42/E5
Bhabua, India 84/D3
Bhadarwāh, India 86/C3
Bhadaur, India 86/C4
Bhadohī, India 84/D3
Bhādra, India 86/C5
Bhadreswar, India 82/A3
Bhāgalpur, India 85/F3
Bhāi Pheru, Pak. 86/B4
Bhairab (riv.), Bang. 85/G4
Bhairab Bāzār, Bang. 85/H3
Bhakkar, Pak. 86/A4
Bhākra (dam), India 86/D4
Bhaktapur, Nepal 85/E2
Bhalwāl, Pak. 86/B3
Bhamo, Myan. 83/G3
Bhānder, India 84/B3
Bhānrer (range), India 84/B4
Bhānwad, India 82/A3
Bharatpur, Nepal 85/E2
Bharātpur, India 84/A2
Bharthana, India 84/B2
Bharuch, India 89/K4
Bhasāwar, India 84/A2
Bhātāpāra, India 82/D3
Bhatinda, India 86/C4
Bhatkal, India 89/K6
Bhātpāra, India 85/G4
Bhavāni, India 82/C5
Bhavnagar, India 89/K4
Bhawāna, Pak. 86/B4
Bhawāni Mandi, India 89/L4
Bhera, Pak. 86/B3
Bheri (zone), Nepal 84/C1
Bhilai, India 82/D3
Bhīlwāra, India 89/K3
Bhīma (riv.), India 89/L5
Bhima (riv.), India 82/C4
Bhīmavaram, India 82/D4
Bhimunipatnam, India 82/D4
Bhinga, India 84/C2
Bhiwandi, India 89/K5
Bhiwāni, India 86/D5
Bhojpur, Nepal 85/F2
Bhokardan, India 82/C3
Bhola, Bang. 85/H4
Bhongaon, India 84/B2
Bhopāl, India 82/C3
Bhor, India 89/K5
Bhraoin (lake), Sc, UK 36/A1
Bhuban, India 82/E3
Bhumibol (dam), Thai. 78/B2
Bhusawal, India 89/L4
Bhutan (ctry.) 82/E2
Bi Doup (peak), Viet. 78/E3
Biá (riv.), Braz. 150/E4
Bia (riv.), C.d'Iv. 102/E5
Biafra, Bight of (bay), Camr. 96/G7
Biak (isl.), Indo. 81/J4
Biak (int'l arpt.), Indo. 81/J4
Biała Podlaska (prov.), Pol. 41/M3
Biała Podlaska, Pol. 41/M2
Białobrzegi, Pol. 41/L3
Białogard, Pol. 38/G4
Białowieski NP, Pol. 62/B1
Białowieski NP, Pol. 41/K4
Białowieski NP, Pol. 41/M2
Białystok (prov.), Pol. 41/M2
Białystok, Pol. 41/M2
Bianca (peak), It. 57/G4
Biancavilla, It. 46/D4
Biandrate, It. 58/B2
Biandronno, It. 58/B1
Bianze, It. 58/B2
Biarritz, Fr. 42/C5
Biasca, Swi. 57/E5
Bibā, Egypt 101/B2
Bibai, Japan 76/B2
Bibbiano, It. 58/D3
Bibbiena, It. 59/E5
Biberach, Ger. 56/E1
Biberach, Ger. 57/G1
Biberach an der Riss, Ger. 57/F1
Biberist, Swi. 56/D3
Bibione, It. 59/G1
Biblián, Ecu. 152/B5
Biblis, Ger. 54/B3
Bicas, Braz. 211/K6
Bicaz, Rom. 49/H2
Bicester, Eng, UK 33/E3
Bicheno, Austl. 115/D4
Bicknacre, Eng, UK 30/E1
Bicske, Hun. 48/D2
Bida, Nga. 103/G4
Bīdar, India 82/C4
Biddeford, Me, US 131/G3
Biddiyā, WBnk. 91/G7
Biddū, WBnk. 91/G8
Biddulph, Eng, UK 35/F5
Bidean nam Bian (peak), Sc, UK 36/A3
Bideford, Eng, UK 32/B4
Bidente (riv.), It. 59/F4
Bidhūna, India 84/B2
Bīdokht, Iran 89/G2
Biebesheim am Rhein, Ger. 54/B3
Biebrza (riv.), Pol. 41/M2
Biel, Swi. 56/D3
Bielawa, Pol. 41/J3
Bieldside, Sc, UK 36/D2
Bielefeld, Ger. 51/F4
Bieler (lake), Swi. 56/D3
Bieler (lake), Nun., Can. 123/J1
Biella, It. 58/B1
Bielsk Podlaski, Pol. 41/M2
Bielsko (prov.), Pol. 41/K4
Bielsko-Biała, Pol. 41/K4
Bien Hoa, Viet. 78/D4
Bienenbüttel, Ger. 51/H2
Bienne (riv.), Fr. 56/B5
Bienno, It. 57/G6
Bientina, It. 58/D5
Bienville (lake), Qu, Can. 123/J3
Bière, Swi. 56/C4
Bierset (int'l arpt.), Belg. 53/E2
Bierum, Neth. 50/D2
Bierutów, Pol. 41/J3
Biesbosch (reg.), Neth. 50/B5
Biesenthal, Ger. 40/Q6
Biesles, Fr. 56/B1
Biesme (riv.), Fr. 53/D5
Bieszczadzki NP, Pol. 62/B2
Bieszczadzki NP, Pol. 41/M4
Bietigheim, Ger. 54/C5
Bietschhorn (peak), Swi. 56/D5
Bièvre (riv.), Fr. 30/J5
Bièvre, Belg. 53/E4
Bièvres, Fr. 30/J5
Big (des.), Austl. 115/B2
Big (riv.), Mo, US 137/F9
Big (isl.), On, Can. 122/G4
Big (riv.), Nun., Can. 122/D1
Big (lake), Mi, US 135/E6
Big Belt (mts.), Mt, US 126/F4
Big Bend, Swaz. 107/E2
Big Bend, Wi, US 135/P14
Big Bend NP, Tx, US 140/A2
Big Blue (riv.), Ks,Ne, US 129/H2
Big Diomede (isl.) 134/E2
Big Fork (riv.), Mn, US 127/K4
Big Hole (riv.), Mt, US 126/E4
Big Hole, SAfr. 106/D3
Big Lake, Tx, US 129/G5
Big Lost (riv.), Id, US 128/D2
Big Muskego (lake), Wi, US 135/P14
Big Pine (hill), Pa, US 138/C1
Big Pines, Ca, US 136/C2
Big Rapids, Mi, US 130/C3
Big River, Sk, Can. 126/G2
Big Rock, Il, US 135/N16
Big Sandy (riv.), Wy, US 128/E2
Big Sioux (riv.), Ia,SD, US 127/J5
Big Spring, Tx, US 129/G4
Big Stone (lake), Mn,SD, US 127/J4
Big Thompson (riv.), Co, US 137/B2
Big Thompson, North Fork (riv.), Co, US 137/A2
Big Timber, Mt, US 126/F4
Big Trout (lake), On, Can. 122/H3
Big Tujunga Canyon (canyon), Ca, US 136/B2
Big Wood (riv.), Id, US 128/D2
Biga, Turk. 49/H5
Bigadiç, Turk. 62/D5
Bigbury (bay), Eng, UK 32/C6
Biggar, Sk, Can. 126/G2
Biggar, Sc, UK 36/C5
Bigge (riv.), Ger. 53/G1
Biggenden, Austl. 114/D4
Biggleswade, Eng, UK 33/F2
Bighorn (basin), Wy, US 128/E1
Bighorn (lake), Mt,Wy, US 126/F4
Bighorn (mts.), Wy, US 124/E3
Bighorn (riv.), Wy, US 122/F4
Biglerville, Pa, US 138/A4
Bignona, Sen. 102/A3
Biguaçu, Braz. 155/B3
Bihać, Bosn. 43/L4
Bihar, India 85/E3
Biharamulo, Tanz. 104/A3
Biharamulo Game Rsv., Tanz. 104/A3
Bihārīganj, India 85/F3
Biharkeresztes, Hun. 48/E2
Bihor (co.), Rom. 41/M5
Bihorel, Fr. 42/D2
Bihoro, Japan 76/D2
Bijagós, Arquipélago do (isl.) 96/B5
Bījār, Iran 88/E1
Bijāwar, India 84/B3
Bijbiāra, India 86/C3
Bijeljina, Bosn. 48/D3
Bijelo Polje, Yugo. 47/F1
Bijiang, China 83/G2
Bijie, China 83/J2
Bijni, India 85/H2
Bijnor, India 84/B1
Bīkaner, India 89/K3
Bikar (isl.), Mrsh. 116/G3
Bikin, Rus. 71/P2
Bikin (riv.), Rus. 71/Q2
Bikini (isl.), Mrsh. 116/F3
Bikramganj, India 85/E3
Bikuar, PN do, Ang. 105/C4
Bila Tserkva, Ukr. 62/D2
Bilāra, India 82/B2
Bilāri, India 84/B1
Bilāsipāra, India 85/H2
Bilāspur, India 84/D4
Bilāspur, India 84/B1
Bilāspur, India 86/D4
Bilaukraung (range), Myan. 83/G5
Bilauktaung (range), Myan.,Thai 78/B3
Bilba Morea Claypan (lake),Austl. 109/C3
Bilbao, Sp. 44/D1
Bilbays, Egypt 91/B4
Bileća, Bosn. 47/F1
Bilecik (prov.), Turk. 90/B1
Bilecik, Turk. 62/D4
Biłgoraj, Pol. 41/M3
Bilgrām, India 84/C2
Bilhaur, India 84/C2
Bilhorod-Dnistrovs'kyy, Ukr. 49/K2
Bilibino, Rus. 65/S3
Bilin, Myan. 83/G4
Bilin (riv.), Myan. 78/B2
Bílina (riv.), Czh. 55/G2
Bílina, Czh. 55/G1
Biliu (riv.), China 73/B3
Bill of Portland (pt.), Eng, UK 32/D5
Bill Williams (riv.), Az, US 128/D4
Bille (riv.), Ger. 51/H1
Billerbeck, Ger. 51/E5
Billère, Fr. 42/C5
Billericay, Eng, UK 30/E2
Billiat Conservation Park, Austl. 115/B2
Billiat Consv. Park, Austl. 113/J5
Billigheim, Ger. 54/C4
Billinge, Eng, UK 35/F4
Billingham, Eng, UK 35/G2
Billings, Mt, US 126/F4
Billingsfors, Swe. 38/E2
Billiton (isl.), Indo. 67/K10
Billund (int'l arpt.), Den. 38/C4
Billund, Den. 38/C4
Bilma, Niger 96/H4
Biloela, Austl. 114/C4
Biloku, Guy. 153/G4
Biloxi, Ms, US 133/F4
Bilpa Morea Claypan (lake), Austl. 113/H3
Bilqas Qism Awwal, Egypt 91/B4
Bilsi, India 84/B1
Bilthar, India 84/D2
Biltine, Chad 97/K5
Bilzen, Belg. 53/E2
Bima, Indo. 81/E5
Bimberi (peak), Austl. 115/D2
Bimbo, CAfr. 97/J7
Bimini (isls.), Bahm. 141/F2
Bin 'Arūs, Tun. 46/B4
Bin 'Arus (gov.), Tun. 46/B4
Bina (riv.), Ger. 55/F6
Bina-Etāwa, India 84/B3
Binalong, Austl. 115/D2
Binasco, It. 58/C2
Binbrook, On, Can. 131/Q9
Binche, Belg. 53/D3
Binchuan, China 83/H2
Bindki, India 84/C2
Bindura, Zim. 105/F4
Binéfar, Sp. 45/F2
Binga (mtn.), Moz. 105/F4
Bingara, Austl. 115/D1
Bingen, Ger. 53/G4
Bingerville, C.d'Iv. 102/E5
Binghamton, NY, US 130/F3
Bingley, Eng, UK 35/G4
Bingöl, Turk. 90/E2
Bingöl (prov.), Turk. 90/E2
Binh Son, Viet. 78/E3
Binhai, China 72/D4
Binhon, Myan. 83/G4
Binisalem, Sp. 45/G3
Binjai, Indo. 80/A3
Binkılıç, Turk. 49/J5
Binnaway, Austl. 115/D1
Binningen, Swi. 56/D2
Binongko (isl.), Indo. 81/F5
Bintang (peak), Malay. 80/B2
Binyamina, Isr. 91/F6
Bío-Bío (riv.), Chile 157/B4
Bío-Bío (pol. reg.), Chile 158/B3
Biograd, Cro. 48/B4
Biogradska Gora NP, Yugo. 47/F1
Biogradska NP, Yugo. 48/D4
Bioko (isl.), EqG. 93/C4
Biougra, Mor. 98/C3
Bipoint (Bissau) (int'l arpt.), GBis. 102/B4

174

Bippe – Born

Bippen, Ger. 51/E3
Bi'r, India 89/L5
Bîr Abu Minqâr (well), Egypt 101/A3
Bir Aïdiat (well), Mrta. 98/C4
Bir Bel Guerdâne (well), Mrta. 98/C4
Bi'r Ghadir (well), Egypt 101/C3
Bîr Ounâne (well), Mali 98/E5
Bi'r Zayt, WBnk. 91/G8
Birāk, Libya 96/H2
Birao, CAfr. 97/K5
Birātnagar, Nepal 85/F2
Biratori, Japan 76/C2
Birch (mts.), Ab, Can. 122/E3
Birch Creek, Ak, US 134/J2
Birch Hills, Sk, Can. 127/G2
Birch River, Mb, Can. 127/H2
Birchip, Austl. 115/B2
Bird Islet (isl.), Austl. 109/E3
Birds Rock (peak), Austl. 115/D2
Birdsboro, Pa, US 138/C3
Birdwood, Austl. 113/M8
Birecik, Turk. 90/D2
Bīrganj, Nepal 85/E2
Biritiba-Mirim, Braz. 211/G8
Bīrjand, Iran 89/G2
Birkat Qārūn (lake), Egypt 90/B4
Birken-Honigsessen, Ger. 53/G2
Birkenau, Ger. 54/B3
Birkenfeld, Ger. 53/G4
Birkenhead, Eng, UK 35/E5
Birkenheide, Ger. 54/B4
Birkenwerder, Ger. 40/D6
Birkirkara, Malta 46/L7
Birkkarspitze (peak), Aus. 57/H3
Bîrlad, Rom. 49/H2
Birmingham, Al, US 133/G3
Birmingham, Mo, US 137/E5
Birmingham (int'l arpt.), Eng, UK 33/E2
Birmingham, Eng, UK 33/E2
Birmingham, Mi, US 135/F6
Birmitrapur, India 85/E4
Birnam, Sc, UK 36/C3
Birnhorn (peak), Aus. 43/K3
Birni Nkonni, Niger 103/G3
Birnie (isl.), Kiri. 117/H5
Birnin Kebbi, Nga. 103/G3
Birobijan, Rus. 71/P2
Bīrpur, India 85/F2
Birr, Ire. 31/Q10
Birs (riv.), Swi. 43/G3
Birsk, Rus. 61/M5
Birstein, Ger. 54/C2
Biruaca, Ven. 153/E3
Biržai, Lith. 39/L3
Birżebbuġa, Malta 46/M7
Bis (lake), Rom. 49/F4
Bisa-Nadi Nat'l Rsv., Kenya 104/C2
Bisai, Japan 77/L5
Bīsalpur, India 84/B1
Bisamberg, Aus. 49/N7
Bisauli, India 84/B1
Bisbee Douglas (int'l arpt.), Az, US 142/C2
Biscarrosse, Fr. 42/C4
Biscarrosse,Étang de (lake), Fr. 42/C4
Biscay (bay), Fr.,Sp. 27/D4
Biscayne NP, Fl, US 141/E2
Bisceglie, It. 46/E2
Bischberg, Ger. 54/D3
Bischheim, Fr. 53/G6
Bischofsgrün, Ger. 55/E2
Bischofsheim, Ger. 54/B3
Bischofsheim an der Rhön, Ger. 54/D2
Bischofshofen, Aus. 43/K3
Bischofszell, Swi. 57/F3
Bischwiller, Fr. 56/D2
Biscubio (riv.), It. 59/F5
Biscucuy, Ven. 152/D2
Bīshah (riv.), SAr. 88/D4
Bishkek (cap.), Kyr. 87/F4
Bishnupur, India 85/F4
Bishop, Ca, US 128/C3
Bishop Auckland, Eng, UK 35/G2
Bishopbriggs, Sc, UK 36/B5
Bishop's Falls, Nf, Can. 131/L1
Bishop's Stortford, Eng, UK 33/G3
Bishopton, Sc, UK 36/B5
Bisingen, Ger. 54/B6
Biskra, Alg. 100/H5
Biskupiec, Pol. 39/J5
Bislig, Phil. 81/G2
Bismarck (cap.), ND, US 127/H4
Bismarck, On, Can. 131/Q9
Bismarck (arch.), PNG 116/D5
Bismarck (sea), PNG 116/D5
Bismil, Turk. 90/E2
Bismuna (lag.), Nic. 145/F3
Bispgarden, Swe. 37/F3
Bispingen, Ger. 51/G2
Bissau (cap.), GBis. 102/B4
Bissau, India 86/C5
Bissendorf, Ger. 51/F4
Bissett, Mb, Can. 127/K3
Bissingen, Ger. 54/D5
Bistagno, It. 58/B3
Bistrița (riv.), Rom. 49/G2
Bistrița, Rom. 49/G2
Bistrița-Năsăud (prov.), Rom. 49/G2
Biswān, India 84/C2
Bita (riv.), Col. 150/E2
Bitam, Gabon 96/H7
Bitburg, Ger. 53/F4
Bitche, Fr. 53/G5
Bitkin, Chad 96/J5
Bitlis (prov.), Turk. 90/E2
Bitlis, Turk. 90/E2
Bitola, FYROM 47/G2
Bitonto, It. 46/E2
Bitter (lakes), Egypt 101/C2
Bitterfontein, SAfr. 106/B3
Bitterroot (range), Id,Mt, US 126/E4
Bitti, It. 46/A2
Bitung, Indo. 81/G3
Bituruna, Braz. 155/B3
Biwa, Japan 77/K5
Bixby, Ok, US 132/E3
Biyalā, Egypt 91/B4
Biyang, China 72/C4
Bizard (isl.), Qu, Can. 131/M7
Bjärred, Swe. 38/E4
Bjelovar, Cro. 48/C3
Bjerkvik, Nor. 37/F1
Bjerringbro, Den. 38/C3
Bjørkelangen, Nor. 38/D2
Björklinge, Swe. 38/G1
Bjørnafjorden (estu.), Nor. 38/A1
Bjorne (pen.), Nun., Can. 123/S7
Bjugn, Nor. 37/D3
Bjuv, Swe. 38/E3
Blå Jungfrun NP, Swe. 38/G3
Blace, Yugo. 47/G1
Blachownia, Pol. 41/K3
Black (bay), On, Can. 127/L3
Black (for.), Ger. 40/D5
Black (hills), SD, US 124/F3
Black (isl.), Sc, UK 36/B1
Black (mesa), Az, US 128/E3
Black (mt.), Yk, Can. 134/M3
Black (mtn.), Wal, UK 32/C3
Black (mts.), Az, US 129/D4
Black (mts.), Wal, UK 32/C3
Black (pt.), Eng, UK 32/A6
Black (pt.), Ct, US 139/F1
Black (pt.), NI, UK 34/C2
Black (range), NM, US 128/F4
Black (riv.), On, Can. 127/L2
Black (riv.), Wi, US 127/L4
Black (riv.), China,Vie 70/H7
Black (riv.), NY, US 130/F3
Black (sea), Asia,Eur. 67/C5
Black Canyon of the Gunnison Nat'l Park, Co, US 128/F3
Black Diamond, Ab, Can. 126/E3
Black Diamond, Wa, US 135/C3
Black Eagle, Mt, US 126/F4
Black Forest (Schwarzwald) (for.), Ger. 54/B6
Black Hawk, Co, US 137/B3
Black Jack, Mo, US 137/G8
Black Mountain NP, Austl. 114/B1
Black Mtn. (mtn.), Wal, UK 32/C3
Black Point, Ca, US 135/K10
Black River, Jam. 145/G2
Black River Falls, Wi, US 127/L4
Black Rock (des.), Nv, US 128/C2
Black Rock (pt.), RI, US 139/G1
Black Sea Lowland (reg.), Mol.,Ukr. 49/J3
Black Sugarloaf (peak), Austl. 115/D1
Black Volta (riv.), Burk. 93/B4
Black Walnut, Mo, US 137/G8
Black Warrior (riv.), Al, US 133/G3
Blackadder Water (riv.), Sc, UK 36/D5
Blackall, Austl. 114/B4
Blackburn, Eng, UK 35/F4
Blackburn, Sc, UK 36/C5
Blackbutt, Austl. 114/D4
Blackcraig (peak), Sc, UK 36/B6
Blackdown (hills), Eng, UK 32/C5
Blackdown (hill), Eng, UK 33/F4
Blackdown Tableland NP, Austl. 114/C3
Blackfoot (res.), Id, US 126/F5
Blackheath, Austl. 115/D2
Blackmoor (upland), Eng, UK 32/B5
Blackpool, Eng, UK 35/E4
Blackrod, Eng, UK 35/F4
Blackshear (lake), Ga, US 133/H3
Blackstone, Va, US 130/E4
Blackville, NB, Can. 131/H2
Blackwater (riv.), Mo, US 129/J3
Blackwater (riv.), Ire. 31/P10
Blackwater, Austl. 114/C3
Blackwater (riv.), Eng, UK 30/A2
Blackwater (res.), Sc, UK 36/B3
Blackwell, Ok, US 129/H3
Blackwood (riv.), Austl. 112/B5
Blackwood, NJ, US 138/C4
Bladensburg, Md, US 138/B6
Bladensburg NP, Austl. 114/A3
Bladnoch (riv.), Sc, UK 34/D2
Blaenau Gwent (co.), Wal, UK 32/C3
Blagnac, Fr. 42/D5
Blagnac (int'l arpt.), Fr. 42/D5
Blagny, Fr. 53/E4
Blagoevgrad, Bul. 47/H1
Blagoveshchensk, Rus. 71/N1
Blaine Lake, Sk, Can. 126/G2
Blainville, Qu, Can. 131/N6
Blair, Ne, US 127/J5
Blair (hill), Pa, US 138/C1
Blair Atholl, Sc, UK 36/C3
Blairstown, NJ, US 138/D2
Blaise (riv.), Fr. 42/F2
Blaj, Rom. 49/F2
Blakely, Ga, US 133/G4
Blakeslee, Pa, US 138/C1
Blamont, Fr. 56/C3
Blanc (cape), Mrta. 96/B3
Blanc (cape), Fr. 43/G5
Blanc (peak), Fr. 56/C6
Blanc, Cap (cape), Tun. 46/A4
Blanc Nez (cape), Fr. 52/A2
Blanca (peak), NM, US 129/F4
Blanca (pt.), Mex. 142/B2
Blanca (bay), Arg. 147/C6
Blanca, Cordillera (mts.), Peru 150/C5
Blanca, Costa (coast), Sp. 45/E4
Blanchard, Ok, US 137/M15
Blanche (lake), Austl. 109/D3
Blanche (peak), Swi. 56/D5
Blanche (cape), Austl. 113/G5
Blanco (cape), CR 144/E4
Blanco (cape), Mor. 98/A5
Blanco (cape), Peru 150/B4
Blanco (lake), Chile 159/C7
Blanco (riv.), Bol. 150/F6
Blanco (riv.), Tx, US 129/H5
Blanding, Ut, US 128/E3
Blandy, Fr. 30/L6
Blanes, Sp. 45/G2
Blangy-sur-Bresle, Fr. 52/A4
Blankenberge, Belg. 52/C1
Blankenfelde, Ger. 40/Q7
Blankenheim, Ger. 53/F3
Blanquilla (isl.), Ven. 150/F1
Blanquillo, Uru. 159/G2
Blansko, Czh. 41/J4
Blantyre, Malw. 105/G4
Blantyre, Sc, UK 36/B5
Blanzy, Fr. 42/F3
Blaricum, Neth. 50/C4
Blas (peak), Swi. 57/E4
Blatná, Czh. 55/G4
Blato, Cro. 46/E1
Blatten, Swi. 56/D5
Blau (riv.), Ger. 54/C6
Blaubeuren, Ger. 54/C6
Blauen (peak), Ger. 56/D2
Blaustein, Ger. 54/C6
Blauvelt, NY, US 139/K7
Blåvands (pt.), Den. 38/C4
Blavet (riv.), Fr. 42/B3
Blaye, Fr. 42/C4
Blayney, Austl. 115/D2
Bleckede, Ger. 51/H2
Bled, Slov. 43/L3
Blefjell (peak), Nor. 38/C2
Blégny, Belg. 53/E2
Bléharies, Belg. 52/C2
Bleiburg, Aus. 48/B2
Bleicherode, Ger. 51/H6
Bleik (peak), Ger. 57/G2
Bleiswijk, Neth. 50/B4
Blekinge (co.), Swe. 37/E4
Blendecques, Fr. 52/B2
Blender, Ger. 51/G3
Blenheim, NZ 117/S11
Blénod-lès-Pont-à-Mousson, Fr. 53/F6
Bléone (riv.), Fr. 43/G4
Blesberg (peak), SAfr. 106/C4
Blessington, Ire. 34/B5
Bletterans, Fr. 56/B4
Bleury, Fr. 30/H6
Bleus (mts.), D.R. Congo 97/L7
Bleus, Monts (mts.), D.R. Congo 104/A2
Blida (prov.), Alg. 100/G4
Blida, Alg. 100/G4
Blies (riv.), Ger. 53/G5
Blieskastel, Ger. 53/G5
Blik (mt.), Phil. 81/F2
Blinnenhorn (peak), Swi. 57/E5
Blithe (riv.), Eng, UK 35/F6
Blithfield (res.), Eng, UK 35/G6
Block (isl.), RI, US 131/G3
Block Island C. G. Sta., RI, US 139/G1
Block Island (New Shoreham), RI, US 139/G1
Block Island NWR, RI, US 139/G1
Blodelsheim, Fr. 56/D2
Bloemendaal, Neth. 50/B4
Bloemfontein, SAfr. 106/D3
Bloemhof, SAfr. 106/D2
Bloemhofdam (res.), SAfr. 106/D2
Blois, Fr. 42/D3
Blomberg, Ger. 51/E1
Blomberg, Ger. 51/G5
Blomstermåla, Swe. 38/G3
Blonay, Swi. 56/C5
Blönduós, Ice. 37/N6
Bloodvein (riv.), Mb,On, Can. 122/G3
Bloody Foreland (pt.), Ire. 31/P9
Bloomfield, NM, US 128/F3
Bloomfield, NJ, US 139/J8
Bloomfield Hills, Mi, US 135/F6
Bloomingdale, NJ, US 139/H7
Bloomingdale, Il, US 135/P16
Bloomington, Mn, US 127/K4
Bloomington, Il, US 127/L5
Bloomington, Ca, US 136/C2
Bloomsburg, Pa, US 138/B2
Bloomsbury, NJ, US 138/C2
Blora, Indo. 80/D5
Blotzheim, Fr. 56/D2
Blountstown, Fl, US 133/G4
Blovice, Czh. 55/G3
Blšanka (riv.), Czh. 43/K1
Bludenz, Aus. 57/F3
Blue (riv.), Ok, US 132/D3
Blue (mtn.), India 83/F3
Blue (mts.), Or,Wa, US 124/C2
Blue Head (pt.), Sc, UK 36/C1
Blue Island, Il, US 135/Q16
Blue Lake NP, Austl. 114/D4
Blue Marsh Lake (res.), Pa, US 138/B3
Blue Mesa (res.), Co, US 128/F3
Blue Mountain (peak), Jam. 145/G2
Blue Mountain (ridge), Pa, US 138/A3
Blue Mountains, Austl. 115/D2
Blue Mountains NP, Austl. 115/D2
Blue Nile (riv.), Sudan, Et 97/M5
Blue Ridge (mts.), US 133/H3
Blue Ridge Parkway, US 130/D4
Blue Springs, Mo, US 137/E5
Bluefield, WV, US 130/D4
Bluefields, Nic. 145/F4
Bluefields (bay), Nic. 145/F4
Bluejoint (lake), Or, US 128/C2
Bluenose (lake), Nun., Can. 122/E2
Bluff, NZ 117/R12
Bluff (pt.), Austl. 112/B3
Bluff, Austl. 114/C3
Bluff (peak), Austl. 112/C5
Bluffdale, Ut, US 137/K13
Bluffton, In, US 130/C3
Blumberg, Ger. 57/E2
Blümlisalp (peak), Swi. 56/D5
Blyn, Wa, US 135/B1
Blyth, Austl. 113/H5
Blyth, Eng, UK 35/G1
Blythe, Ca, US 128/D4
Blytheville, Ar, US 129/K4
Bnom Mhai (peak), Viet. 78/D4
Bo, SLeo. 102/C5
Bø, Nor. 38/C2
Bo Hai (Chihli) (gulf), China 65/M6
Bo Hai (Gulf of Chihli) (gulf), China 71/L4
Boa Esperança, Braz. 155/C2
Boa Esperança, Reprêsa (res.), Braz. 151/J5
Boa Viagem, Braz. 154/C2
Boa Vista, Braz. 153/F4
Boa Vista (int'l arpt.), Braz. 153/F4
Boa Vista (isl.), CpV. 93/K10
Boac, Phil. 79/D5
Boaco, Nic. 144/E3
Boadilla del Monte, Sp. 45/N9
Bo'ai, China 72/C4
Boano (isl.), Indo. 81/G4
Boas (riv.), Nun., Can. 123/H2
Boavita, Col. 152/C3
Boaz, Al, US 133/G3
Boba, Hun. 48/C2
Bobai, China 83/J3
Bobaomby (cape), Madg. 107/J5
Bobbili, India 82/D4
Bobbio, It. 58/C3
Bobenheim-Roxheim, Ger. 54/B3
Bobigny, Fr. 30/K5
Bobingen, Ger. 57/G1
Böblingen, Ger. 54/C5
Bobo Dioulasso, Burk. 102/D4
Boboshevo, Bul. 47/H1
Bobotov Kuk (peak), Yugo. 47/F1
Bobovdol, Bul. 47/H1
Bóbr (riv.), Pol. 41/H3
Bobrov, Rus. 62/G2
Bobures, Ven. 152/D2
Boby (peak), Madg. 107/H8
Boca de Aroa, Ven. 152/D2
Boca del Guafo (chan.), Chile 158/B4
Boca del Pao, Ven. 153/E2
Boca del Río, Mex. 143/N7
Boca do Acre, Braz. 150/E5
Boca Raton, Fl, US 133/H5
Bocaina, Serra da (mts.), Braz. 211/J7
Bocairente, Sp. 45/E3
Bocas del Toro, Pan. 145/F4
Bocay (riv.), Nic. 144/E3
Bochil, Mex. 144/C2
Bochnia, Pol. 41/L4
Bocholt, Ger. 50/D5
Bocholt, Belg. 53/E1
Bochum, Ger. 51/E6
Bockau, Ger. 55/F1
Bockenem, Ger. 51/H4
Bockenheim an der Weinstrasse, Ger. 53/H4
Bockhorn, Ger. 51/F2
Bockhorn, Ger. 55/E6
Boconó, Ven. 152/D2
Bocq (riv.), Belg. 53/D3
Boda, CAfr. 96/J7
Bodafors, Swe. 38/F3
Bodalla, Austl. 115/D3
Bodaybo, Rus. 65/M4
Boddam, Sc, UK 36/E2
Boddington, Austl. 112/C5
Bode (riv.), Ger. 40/F3
Bodega (bay), Ca, US 128/B3
Bodegraven, Neth. 50/B4
Bodélé (reg.), Chad 96/J4
Bodenheim, Ger. 54/B3
Bodenkirchen, Ger. 55/F6
Bodenmais, Ger. 55/G4
Bodensee (Constance) (lake), Swi 43/H3
Bodenteich, Ger. 51/H3
Bodh Gaya, India 85/E3
Bodhan, India 82/C4
Bodināyakkanūr, India 82/C5
Bodio, Swi. 57/E5
Bodkin (pt.), Md, US 138/B5
Bodmin, Eng, UK 32/B6
Bodmin Moor (upland), Eng, UK 32/B6
Bodø, Nor. 37/E2
Bodocó, Braz. 154/C2
Bodrog (riv.), Hun.,Slvk. 41/L4
Bodrum, Turk. 90/A2
Bódvaszilas, Hun. 41/L4
Boedecker (lake), Co, US 137/B2
Boëge, Fr. 56/C5
Boegoeberg (peak), Namb. 106/A2
Boekel, Neth. 50/C5
Boende, D.R. Congo 97/K8
Boerne, Tx, US 137/T20
Boeuf (riv.), La, US 129/K4
Bog of Allen (swamp), Ire. 34/A5
Bogalusa, La, US 133/F4
Bogan (riv.), Austl. 109/D4
Bogan Gate, Austl. 115/C2
Bogandé, Burk. 103/E3
Bogatić, Yugo. 48/D3
Bogatynia, Pol. 41/H3
Boğazkale-Alacahöyük NP, Turk. 62/E4
Boğazlıyan, Turk. 62/E5
Bogdanci, FYROM 47/H2
Bogen, Nor. 37/F1
Bogen, Ger. 55/F5
Bogense, Den. 38/D4
Boggabilla, Austl. 114/C5
Boggabri, Austl. 115/D1
Boggy (peak), Anti. 141/N8
Boglárlelle, Hun. 48/C2
Bogliasco, It. 58/C4
Bognor Regis, Eng, UK 33/F5
Bogny-sur-Meuse, Fr. 53/D4
Bogo, Phil. 79/D5
Bogong (mt.), Austl. 115/C3
Bogong NP, Austl. 115/C3
Bogor, Indo. 80/C5
Bogotá (cap.), Col. 150/D3
Bogota, NJ, US 139/J8
Bogovino, FYROM 47/G2
Bogra (pol. reg.), Bang. 85/G3
Bogra, Bang. 85/G3
Bogué, Mrta. 102/B2
Bohai (bay), China 72/D3
Bohain-en-Vermandois, Fr. 52/C4
Bohemia (reg.), Czh. 41/G4
Bohemian (for.), Czh.,Ger. 40/G4
Bohicon, Ben. 103/F5
Böhl-Iggelheim, Ger. 54/B4
Böhme (riv.), Ger. 51/G3
Böhmenkirch, Ger. 54/C5
Bohmte, Ger. 51/F4
Bohners Lake, Wi, US 135/P14
Bohol (isl.), Phil. 116/B4
Böhönye, Hun. 48/C2
Bohu, China 70/E3
Boiling Springs, Pa, US 138/A3
Boipeda, Ilha de (isl.), Braz. 154/C4
Boiro, Sp. 44/A1
Bois-d'Amont, Fr. 56/C4
Bois-d'Arcy, Fr. 30/J5
Bois de Boulogne (dept.), Fr. 30/J5
Bois de Vincennes (dept.), Fr. 30/K5
Bois-des-Filion, Qu, Can. 131/N6
Bois, Rio dos (riv.), Braz. 155/B1
Boisbriand, Qu, Can. 131/N6
Boise (riv.), Id, US 126/E5
Boise City, Ok, US 129/G3
Boissevain, Mb, Can. 127/H3
Boissy-Fresnoy, Fr. 30/L4
Boissy-L'Aillerie, Fr. 30/J4
Boissy-le-Châtel, Fr. 30/M5
Boissy-Saint-Léger, Fr. 30/K5
Boissy-Sans-Avoir, Fr. 30/H5
Boizenburg, Ger. 51/H2
Bojador (cape), Mor. 96/C2
Bojano, It. 48/B5
Boji (plain), Kenya 104/C2
Bojkovice, Czh. 41/J4
Bojnūrd, Iran 89/G1
Bokaro Steel City, India 85/F4
Boké (pol. reg.), Gui. 102/B4
Boké, Gui. 102/B4
Bokhol (plain), Kenya 104/C2
Boknafjorden (estu.), Nor. 37/C4
Bokol (peak), Kenya 104/C2
Bokoro, Chad 96/J5
Bokpyin, Myan. 78/B4
Boksburg, SAfr. 106/Q13
Bokspits, Bots. 106/C2
Bol, Chad 96/H5
Bolama, GBis. 102/B4
Bolān (pass), Pak. 89/J3
Bolaños de Calatrava, Sp. 44/D3
Bolayır, Turk. 47/K2
Bolbec, Fr. 42/D2
Boldeşti-Scăeni, Rom. 49/H3
Boldon, Eng, UK 35/G2
Bole, China 70/D3
Bole, Gha. 103/E4
Bolesławiec, Pol. 41/H3
Bolgatanga, Gha. 103/E4
Boli, China 71/P2
Boliden, Swe. 37/G2
Bolinao, Phil. 79/C4
Bolivar, Mo, US 129/J3
Bolívar, Peru 156/B2
Bolívar, Ecu. 152/A4
Bolívar (dept.), Col. 152/C2
Bolívar (peak), Ven. 152/D2
Bolívar, Col. 152/B3
Bolívar (peak), Ven. 153/F3
Bolívar (state), Ven. 153/E3
Bolívar, Arg. 158/E3
Bolivia (ctry.), Bol. 150/F7
Bollate, It. 58/C1
Bollène, Fr. 42/F4
Bolligen, Swi. 56/D4
Bollin (riv.), Eng, UK 35/F5
Bollnäs, Swe. 38/G1
Bollullos Par del Condado, Sp. 44/B4
Bolmen (lake), Swe. 38/E3
Bolobo, D.R. Congo 96/J8
Bologna, It. 59/E4
Bologna (prov.), It. 59/E3
Bologne, Fr. 56/B1
Bolognesi, Peru 156/C3
Bologoye, Rus. 60/G4
Bolomba, D.R. Congo 97/J7
Bolonchén de Rejón, Mex. 144/D2
Bolovens (plat.), Laos 78/D3
Bolpur, India 85/F4
Bolsena, It. 46/B1
Bolsena (lake), It. 46/B1
Bol'shaya Kinel' (riv.), Rus. 63/K1
Bol'shaya Rogovaya (riv.), Rus. 61/P2
Bol'shaya Synya (riv.), Rus. 61/N2
Bol'shevik (isl.), Rus. 67/H2
Bol'shezemel'skaya (tundra), Rus. 61/M2
Bol'shoy Bolvanskiy Nos (pt.), Rus. 64/F2
Bol'shoy Irgiz (riv.), Rus. 63/J1
Bol'shoy Lyakhov (isl.), Rus. 67/P2
Bol'shoy Lyakhovskiy (isl.), Rus. 65/Q2
Bol'shoy Uzen' (riv.), Rus. 63/J2
Bolsover, Eng, UK 35/G5
Bolsward, Neth. 50/C2
Bolt (pt.), Eng, UK 32/C6
Boltaña, Sp. 45/F1
Boltigen, Swi. 56/D4
Bolton, Eng, UK 35/F4
Bolu, Turk. 49/K5
Bolu (prov.), Turk. 62/D4
Bolungavík, Ice. 37/M6
Bolus Head (pt.), Ire. 30/N11
Bolvadin, Turk. 90/B2
Bóly, Hun. 48/D3
Bolzano, It. 57/H5
Bolzano-Bozen (prov.), It. 57/H4
Bom Conselho, Braz. 154/C3
Bom Despacho, Braz. 155/C1
Bom Jardim, Braz. 154/A1
Bom Jardim de Minas, Braz. 211/J6
Bom Jesus, Braz. 155/B4
Bom Jesus, Braz. 154/A3
Bom Jesus da Gurguéia, Serra (mts.), Braz. 151/K5
Bom Jesus de Goiás, Braz. 155/B1
Bom Jesus do Itabapoana, Braz. 155/D2
Bom Jesus dos Perdões, Braz. 211/G8
Bom Retiro, Braz. 155/B3
Boma, D.R. Congo 105/B2
Bomaderry, Austl. 115/D2
Bombala, Austl. 115/D3
Bombay Hook NWR, De, US 138/C5
Bombay (Mumbai), India 89/K5
Bomberai (pen.), Indo. 81/H4
Bombo, Ugan. 104/B2
Bomi, China 83/G2
Bomlitz, Ger. 51/G3
Bømlo (isl.), Nor. 38/A2
Bomu (riv.), D.R. Congo 93/E4
Bon-Encontre, Fr. 42/D4
Bona (mt.), Ak, US 134/K3
Bonaduz, Swi. 57/F4
Bonaire (isl.), NAnt. 141/H5
Bonalbo, Austl. 115/E1
Bonampak (ruin), Mex. 144/D2
Bonao, DRep. 141/G4
Bonaparte (isls.), Austl. 109/B2
Bonaparte (arch.), Austl. 116/B6
Bonasila (mtn.), Ak, US 134/F3
Bonaventure, Qu, Can. 131/H1
Bonaventure (riv.), Qu, Can. 131/H1
Bonavista (bay) Nf, Can. 131/L1
Bonavista, Nf, Can. 131/L1
Bonavista (cape) Nf, Can. 131/L1
Boncourt, Swi. 56/D3
Bondeno, It. 59/E3
Bondo, D.R. Congo 97/K7
Bondoukou, C.d'Iv. 102/E4
Bondowoso, Indo. 80/D5
Bone (gulf), Indo. 67/M10
Bönen, Ger. 51/E5
Bonerate (isls.), Indo. 81/F5
Bonfol, Swi. 56/D3
Bonfouca, La, US 137/Q16
Bong (range), Libr. 96/C6
Bong (co.), Libr. 102/C5
Bongabong, Phil. 81/F1
Bongaigaon, India 85/H2
Bongandanga, D.R. Congo 97/K7
Bongao, Phil. 81/E2
Bonggi (isl.), Malay. 81/E2
Bongka (riv.), Indo. 81/F4
Bongo, Massif des (plat.), CAfr. 97/K6
Bongolava (uplands), Madg. 105/K10
Bongor, Chad 96/J5
Bonham, Tx, US 129/H4
Bonheiden, Belg. 53/D1
Bonhill, Sc, UK 36/B5
Bonhomme, Col du (pass), Fr. 56/D1
Boni Nat'l Rsv., Kenya 104/D3
Bonifacio, Fr. 46/A2
Bonifacio (str.), It. 46/A2
Bonifay, Fl, US 133/G4
Bönigen, Swi. 56/D4
Bonin (isls.), Japan 116/C2
Bonita, Ca, US 136/C5
Bonita Springs, Fl, US 133/H5
Bonito (peak), Hon. 144/E3
Bonn, Ger. 53/G2
Bonndorf im Schwarzwald, Ger. 57/E2
Bonne, Fr. 56/C5
Bonnelles, Fr. 30/J6
Bonner Springs, Ks, US 137/D5
Bonner-West Riverside, Mt, US 126/E4
Bonners Ferry, Id, US 126/D3
Bonnet Carré Spillway, La, US 137/P16
Bonnet, Lac du (lake), Mb, Can. 127/K3
Bonneuil-sur-Marne, Fr. 30/K5
Bonneval, Fr. 42/D2
Bonneville (dam), Wa,Or, US 126/C4
Bonneville, Fr. 56/C5
Bonney Lake, Wa, US 135/C3
Bönnigheim, Ger. 54/C4
Bonnybridge, Sc, UK 36/C5
Bonorva, It. 46/A2
Bons-en-Chablais, Fr. 56/C5
Bonsall, Ca, US 136/C4
Bontberg (peak), SAfr. 106/C4
Bontebok NP, SAfr. 106/C4
Bonthain, Indo. 81/E5
Bonthe, SLeo. 102/B5
Bontoc, Phil. 79/D4
Bonyhád, Hun. 48/D2
Bonzart (lake), Tun. 100/L6
Booker T. Washington Nat'l Mon., Va, US 133/J2
Boom, Belg. 53/D1
Boone, Ia, US 127/K5
Boone, NC, US 130/D4
Booneville, Ms, US 133/F3
Boonton, NJ, US 139/H8
Boorabbin NP, Austl. 112/D4
Boorama, Som. 97/P6
Booroondara (mt.), Austl. 115/C1
Boorowa, Austl. 115/D2
Boos (int'l arpt.), Fr. 42/D2
Boos, Ger. 57/G1
Boosaaso (Bender Cassim), Som. 97/Q5
Boostedt, Ger. 38/D4
Boothbay Harbor, Me, US 131/G3
Boothia (pen.), Nun., Can. 122/G1
Boothia (gulf), Nun., Can. 122/G1
Bootle, Eng, UK 35/E5
Booué, Gabon 96/H8
Bopa, Ben. 103/F5
Bopfingen, Ger. 54/D5
Boppard, Ger. 53/G3
Boppy (mt.), Austl. 115/C1
Boqueirão, Braz. 154/C2
Boqueirão, Serra do (mts.), Braz. 154/B3
Boquete (peak), Arg. 158/C4
Boquilla (res.), Mex. 142/D3
Boquillas del Carmen, Mex. 132/C4
Boquira, Braz. 154/B4
Bor, Turk. 90/C2
Bor, Yugo. 48/F3
Bor, Rus. 61/K4
Bor, Czh. 55/F3
Bor Ul (mts.), China 64/K5
Bora Bora (isl.), FrPol. 117/K6
Borah (peak), Id, US 126/E4
Borås, Swe. 38/E3
Borāzjān, Iran 88/F3
Borba, Braz. 150/G4
Borba, Port. 44/B3
Borbera (riv.), It. 58/B3
Borbore (riv.), It. 58/B3
Borborema, Planalto da (plat.), Braz. 151/L5
Borča, Yugo. 48/E3
Borcea Branch (riv.), Rom. 49/H3
Borchen, Ger. 51/F5
Borçka, Turk. 63/G4
Borculo, Neth. 50/D4
Borda da Mata, Braz. 211/G7
Bordeaux, Fr. 42/C4
Borden (isl.), NW,Nun., Can. 123/R7
Borden (pen.), Nun., Can. 123/H1
Bordentown, NJ, US 138/D3
Bordertown, Austl. 115/B3
Bordj Bou Arreridj, Alg. 100/H4
Bordj Bou Arreridj (prov.), Alg. 100/H4
Bordj el Kiffan, Alg. 100/G4
Bordj Manaïel, Alg. 100/G4
Bordj Moktar, Alg. 99/F5
Bordj Omar Driss, Alg. 99/G3
Bordj Sainte-Marie, Alg. 98/E4
Borehamwood, Eng, UK 30/C2
Borest, Fr. 30/L4
Boretto, It. 58/D3
Borgå (Porvoo), Fin. 39/L1
Borgaretto, It. 58/A2
Borgarnes, Ice. 37/N7
Børgefjell NP, Nor. 37/E2
Borgentreich, Ger. 51/G5
Borger, Tx, US 129/G4
Börger, Ger. 51/E3
Borger, Neth. 50/D3
Borgerhout, Belg. 50/B6
Borges Blanques, Sp. 45/F2
Borghetto Lodigiano, It. 58/C2
Borghetto Santo Spirito, It. 58/B4
Borgholm, Swe. 38/G3
Borgholzhausen, Ger. 51/F4
Borghorst, Ger. 51/E4
Borgloon, Belg. 53/E2
Borgne (lake), La, US 137/Q17
Borgne (riv.), Swi. 56/D5
Borgo (int'l arpt.), Burk. 102/D4
Borgo, Fr. 46/A1
Borgo, It. 57/H5
Borgo a Mozzano, It. 58/D5
Borgo San Dalmazzo, It. 43/G4
Borgo San Giacomo, It. 58/C2
Borgo San Lorenzo, It. 59/E5
Borgo Tossignano, It. 59/E4
Borgo Val di Taro, It. 58/C4
Borgo Vercelli, It. 58/B2
Borgofranco d'Ivrea, It. 58/A1
Borgomanero, It. 58/B1
Borgonovo Val Tidone, It. 58/C2
Borgosatollo, It. 58/D2
Borgosesia, It. 58/B1
Borgou (prov.), Ben. 103/F4
Borgund, Nor. 38/B1
Borio, India 85/F3
Borisoglebsk, Rus. 63/G2
Borispol (int'l arpt.), Ukr. 62/D2
Borja, Peru 156/B2
Borja, Sp. 44/E2
Borken, Ger. 50/D5
Borken, Ger. 51/G6
Borkop, Den. 38/C4
Borkum, Ger. 50/D1
Borkum (isl.), Ger. 50/D1
Borlänge, Swe. 38/F1
Bormida (riv.), It. 43/H4
Bormida, It. 58/B4
Bormida di Millesimo (riv.), It. 58/B4
Bormio, It. 57/G5
Born, Neth. 53/E1

175
Borna – Bruma

Borna, Ger. 40/G3
Borndiep (chan.), Neth. 50/C2
Borne, Neth. 50/D4
Borne (riv.), Fr. 56/C6
Bornel, Fr. 52/B5
Bornem, Belg. 53/D1
Bornemouth (co.), Eng, UK 33/E5
Borneo (isl.), Indo.,Malay. 67/L9
Bornheim, Ger. 53/G2
Bornholm (isl.), Den., Swe. 27/F3
Bornholm (co.), Den. 38/F4
Bornholmsgat (chan.), Den.,Swi. 41/H1
Borno, It. 57/G6
Bornos, Sp. 44/C4
Börnsen, Ger. 51/H2
Bornu (plain), Nga. 96/H5
Boro (riv.), Sudan 97/L6
Borohoro (mts.), China 70/D3
Borongan, Phil. 79/E5
Borough Green, Eng, UK 30/D3
Borovany, Czh. 55/H5
Borovichi, Rus. 60/G4
Borovo, Cro. 48/D3
Borovo, Bul. 49/G4
Borre, Nor. 38/D2
Borrisokane, Ire. 31/P10
Bornida (riv.), It. 58/B3
Borşa, Rom. 49/F2
Borsec, Rom. 49/G2
Borso del Grappa, It. 59/E1
Borsod-Abaúj-Zemplén (co.), Hun. 48/E1
Borssele, Neth. 50/A6
Borstel, Ger. 51/F3
Bort-les-Orgues, Fr. 42/E4
Boruca, CR 145/F4
Borūjerd, Iran 88/E2
Boryslav, Ukr. 41/M4
Borzonasca, It. 58/C4
Borzya, Rus. 71/L1
Bosa, It. 46/A2
Bosanska Dubica, Bosn. 48/C3
Bosanska Gradiška, Bosn. 48/C3
Bosanska Kostajnica, Bosn. 48/C3
Bosanska Krupa, Bosn. 48/C3
Bosanski Brod, Bosn. 48/D3
Bosanski Petrovac, Bosn. 48/C3
Bosanski Šamac, Bosn. 48/D3
Bosco Mesola, It. 59/F3
Bosconero, It. 58/A2
Bose, China 83/J3
Boshof, SAfr. 106/D3
Boskoop, Neth. 50/B4
Boskovice, Czh. 41/J4
Bosna (riv.), Bosn. 48/D3
Bosnia and Herzegovina (ctry.) 48/C3
Bošnjaci, Cro. 48/D3
Bōsō (pen.), Japan 75/G3
Bosobolo, D.R. Congo 97/J7
Bosporus (str.), Turk. 62/D4
Bosque Farms, NM, US 128/F4
Bosques Petrificados, Mon. Natural, Arg. 159/C5
Bossangoa, CAfr. 96/J6
Bossier City, La, US 129/J4
Bostān, Iran 88/E2
Bostānābād-e Bālā, Iran 88/E1
Boston (mts.), Ar, US 129/J4
Boston (cap.), Ma, US 131/G3
Boston, Eng, UK 35/H6
Bosut (riv.), Cro. 48/D3
Boswil, Swi. 57/E3
Botād, India 89/K4
Boteler (peak), NC, US 133/H3
Botelerpunt (pt.), SAfr. 107/F2
Botelhos, Braz. 211/G6
Botev (peak), Bul. 47/J1
Botevgrad, Bul. 47/H1
Bothaspas (pass), SAfr. 107/E2
Bothaville, SAfr. 106/D2
Bothel, Ger. 51/G2
Bothell, Wa, US 135/C2
Bothnia (gulf), Swe.,Fin. 160/E
Bothwell, Austl. 115/C4
Botoşani (prov.), Rom. 49/H2
Botoşani, Rom. 49/H2
Botou, China 72/D3
Botrange (peak), Belg. 53/F3
Botrivier, SAfr. 106/L11
Botsford, Ct, US 139/E1
Botswana (ctry.) 105/D5
Bottanuco, It. 58/C1
Botte Donato (peak), It. 46/E3
Botticino, It. 58/D1
Bottineau, ND, US 127/H3
Bottrighe, It. 59/F2
Bottrop, Ger. 50/D5
Botucatu, Braz. 155/B2
Botwood, Nf, Can. 131/L1
Bou (riv.), C.d'Iv. 102/D4
Bou Arfa, Mor. 99/E2
Boû Djébéha (well), Mali 102/E2
Bou Hamdane, Oued (riv.), Alg. 100/K6
Bou Ismaïl, Alg. 100/G4
Bou Izakarn, Mor. 98/C3
Bou Kadir, Alg. 100/F4
Bou Laber (well), Alg. 98/D4
Bou Naceur (peak), Mor. 100/C3
Bou Regreg (riv.), Mor. 100/A3
Bou Salem, Tun. 100/L6
Bou Sellam, Oued (riv.), Alg. 100/H4
Bouaflé, C.d'Iv. 102/D5
Bouafle, Fr. 30/H5
Bouaké, C.d'Iv. 102/D5
Bouar, CAfr. 96/J6
Boubín (peak), Czh. 55/G5
Bouca, CAfr. 96/J6
Bouchain, Fr. 52/C3
Bouchegouf, Alg. 100/K6
Boucherville, Qu, Can. 131/P6
Boucle du Baoulé, PN de la, Mali 96/D5
Boucle Du Baoulé, PN de la, Mali 102/C3
Boudry, Swi. 56/C4
Boufarik, Alg. 100/G4
Bouffémont, Fr. 30/J4
Bougainville (reef), Austl. 109/D2
Bougainville (isl.), PNG 116/E5
Bougainville (cape), UK 159/F6
Bougara, Alg. 100/G4
Bougar'oûn (cape), Alg. 100/K6
Bough Beech (res.), Eng, UK 30/D3
Bougouni, Mali 102/D4
Bougouriba (prov.), Burk. 102/E4
Bouguenais, Fr. 42/C3
Bouhachem (peak), Mor. 100/B2
Bouhalla (peak), Mor. 100/B2
Bouillancy, Fr. 30/L4
Bouillon, Belg. 53/E4
Bouira (prov.), Alg. 100/G4
Bouira, Alg. 100/G4
Boujad, Mor. 98/D2
Boukhalf (Tangier) (int'l arpt.), Mor. 100/B2
Boukoumbé, Ben. 103/F4
Boulaide, Lux. 53/E4
Boulaouane, Mor. 98/C2
Boulay-Moselle, Fr. 53/F5
Boulazac, Fr. 42/D4
Boulder, Mt, US 126/E4
Boulder (co.), Co, US 137/B2
Boulder, Co, US 137/B2
Boulder City, Nv, US 128/D4
Boulder Hill, Il, US 135/P16
Boulemane, Mor. 98/D2
Boulemane (prov.), Mor. 100/C3
Bouleurs, Fr. 30/L5
Boulgo (prov.), Burk. 103/E4
Boulia, Austl. 113/H2
Bouligny, Fr. 53/E5
Boulkiemde (prov.), Burk. 103/E3
Boullarre, Fr. 30/M4
Boulogne (riv.), Fr. 42/C3
Boulogne-Billancourt, Fr. 30/J5
Boulogne-sur-Mer, Fr. 52/A2
Boulsworth (hill), Eng, UK 35/F4
Boumalne, Mor. 98/D3
Boumerdas (prov.), Alg. 100/G4
Boumerdas, Alg. 100/G4
Boun Nua, Laos 83/H3
Bouna, C.d'Iv. 102/E4
Bound Brook, NJ, US 138/D2
Boundary (peak), Nv, US 128/C3
Boundiali, C.d'Iv. 102/D4
Bountiful, Ut, US 137/K12
Bouquet (res.), Ca, US 136/B1
Bouquet (canyon), Ca, US 136/B2
Bourbon l'Archambault, Fr. 42/E3
Bourbonnais (reg.), Fr. 42/D3
Bourbonne-les-Bains, Fr. 56/B2
Bourbourg, Fr. 52/B2
Bourdonné, Fr. 30/G5
Bourem, Mali 103/E2
Bouressa (riv.), Mali 103/F2
Bourg-en-Bresse, Fr. 56/B5
Bourg-lès-Valence, Fr. 42/F4
Bourg-Saint-Andéol, Fr. 42/F4
Bourg-Saint-Maurice, Fr. 43/G4
Bourg-Saint-Pierre, Swi. 56/D6
Bourganeuf, Fr. 42/D4
Bourges, Fr. 42/E3
Bourget (lake), Fr. 56/B6
Bourgneuf (bay), Fr. 42/B3
Bourgogne (pol. reg.), Fr. 42/F3
Bourgogne (canal), Fr. 56/B3
Bourgoin-Jallieu, Fr. 42/F4
Bourke, Austl. 115/C1
Bourmont, Fr. 56/B1
Bourne (riv.), Eng, UK 33/E4
Bourne End, Eng, UK 33/F3
Bourne, The (riv.), Eng, UK 30/B3
Bournemouth, Eng, UK 33/E5
Bourscheid, Lux. 53/F4
Bourtanger Moor (reg.), Ger. 51/E3
Bousbecque, Fr. 52/C2
Bousso, Chad 96/J5
Boussois, Fr. 52/D3
Boutilimit, Mrta. 102/B2
Boutte, La, US 137/P17
Bouvard (cape), Austl. 112/B5
Bouvet (isl.), Nor. 23/K8
Bouxières-aux-Dames, Fr. 53/F6
Bouxwiller, Fr. 53/G6
Bouznika, Mor. 100/A3
Bouzonville, Fr. 53/F5
Bovalino, It. 46/E3
Bovegno, It. 58/D1
Boven Tapanahoni (riv.), Sur. 153/H4
Bovenden, Ger. 51/G5
Bovenwijde (lake), Neth. 50/D3
Boves, Fr. 52/B4
Bovezzo, It. 58/D1
Bovingdon, Eng, UK 30/B1
Bovino, It. 48/B5
Bovolone, It. 59/E2
Bow (riv.), Ab, Can. 122/E3
Bow Island, Ab, Can. 126/F3
Bowdle, SD, US 127/J4
Bowdon, Eng, UK 35/F5
Bowen, Austl. 114/C3
Bowen, Arg. 158/D2
Bowers Beach, De, US 138/C5
Bowie, Az, US 128/E4
Bowie, Md, US 138/B6
Bowling Green, Mo, US 129/K3
Bowling Green, Ky, US 130/C4
Bowling Green, Oh, US 130/D3
Bowling Green (cape), Austl. 114/B2
Bowling Green Bay NP, Austl. 114/B2
Bowman, ND, US 127/H4
Bowman (bay), Nun., Can. 123/J2
Bowmansdale, Pa, US 138/B3
Bowmanstown, Pa, US 138/C2
Bowmansville, Pa, US 138/B3
Bowmore, Sc, UK 31/Q9
Bowokan (isls.), Indo. 81/F4
Bowral, Austl. 115/D2
Bowron (riv.), BC, Can. 126/C2
Box Elder (co.), Ut, US 137/J11
Boxberg, Ger. 54/C4
Boxholm, Swe. 38/F2
Boxing, China 72/D3
Boxmeer, Neth. 50/C5
Boxtel, Neth. 50/C5
Boyabat, Turk. 62/E4
Boyaca (dept.), Col. 152/C3
Boyanup, Austl. 112/B5
Boychinovtsi, Bul. 49/F4
Boyd (lake), Co, US 137/B2
Boye, China 72/C3
Boyer (riv.), Ia, US 127/K5
Boyertown, Pa, US 138/C3
Boyle, Ab, Can. 126/E2
Boyle, Ire. 31/P10
Boyne (riv.), Ire. 31/Q10
Boyne City, Mi, US 130/C2
Boyne Island, Austl. 114/C3
Boynton Beach, Fl, US 133/H5
Boysen (res.), Wy, US 126/F5
Boyup Brook, Austl. 112/C5
Boz (pt.), Turk. 49/J5
Bozashchy Tübegi (pen.), Kaz. 63/J3
Bozcaada (isl.), Gre. 47/J3
Bozcaada, Turk. 47/K3
Bozeman, Mt, US 126/F4
Bozkir, Turk. 90/C2
Bozkurt, Turk. 62/E4
Bozman, Md, US 138/B6
Bozoum, CAfr. 96/J6
Bozova, Turk. 90/D2
Bozüyük, Turk. 62/D5
Bozyazı, Turk. 91/C1
Bozzolo, It. 58/D2
Bra, It. 58/A3
Braan (riv.), Sc, UK 36/C3
Brač (isl.), Cro. 46/E1
Bracciano (lake), It. 46/B1
Bracebridge, On, Can. 130/E2
Brackel, Ger. 51/H2
Bracken, Tx, US 137/U20
Brackenheim, Ger. 54/C4
Brackettville, Tx, US 129/G5
Bracknell, Eng, UK 33/F4
Braço do Norte, Braz. 155/B4
Brad, Rom. 49/F2
Bradano (riv.), It. 48/B5
Bradda (pt.), IM, UK 34/D3
Bradenton, Fl, US 133/H5
Bradford, Pa, US 130/E3
Bradford, Eng, UK 35/G4
Bradley (int'l arpt.), Ct, US 131/F3
Bradley Beach, NJ, US 138/D3
Brady, Tx, US 129/H5
Braemar (reg.), Sc, UK 36/C2
Braeriach (peak), Sc, UK 36/C2
Braga (dist.), Port. 44/A2
Braga, Port. 44/A2
Bragado, Arg. 158/E2
Bragança, Braz. 151/J4
Bragança (dist.), Port. 44/B2
Bragança, Port. 44/B2
Brāhmanbāria, Bang. 85/H4
Brahmaputra (riv.), Asia 67/J7
Braich-y-Pwll (pt.), Wal, UK 34/D6
Braid (riv.), NI, UK 34/B2
Brăila (prov.), Rom. 49/H3
Brăila, Rom. 49/H3
Brainards, NJ, US 138/C2
Braine, Fr. 52/C5
Braine-l'Alleud, Belg. 53/D2
Braine-le-Comte, Belg. 53/D2
Brainerd, Mn, US 127/K4
Braintree, Eng, UK 33/G3
Braithwaite, La, US 137/Q17
Brak (riv.), SAfr. 106/C3
Brake, Ger. 51/F2
Brakel, Ger. 51/G5
Brakel, Neth. 50/C5
Brakel, Belg. 52/C2
Brakna (pol. reg.), Mrta. 102/B2
Brålanda, Swe. 38/E2
Bram, Fr. 42/E5
Bramdrupdam, Den. 38/C4
Bramley, Eng, UK 30/B3
Brampton, On, Can. 131/Q8
Bramsche, Ger. 51/F4
Bramstedt, Ger. 51/F2
Bran (riv.), Sc, UK 36/A1
Brancaleone-Marina, It. 46/E4
Branch Dale, Pa, US 138/B2
Branchville, NJ, US 138/D1
Branchville, Ct, US 139/E1
Branco (riv.), Braz. 147/C2
Brand, Aus. 57/F3
Brandberg (peak), Namb. 105/B5
Brandbu, Nor. 38/D1
Brande, Den. 38/C4
Brandenburg (state), Ger. 40/P6
Brandenburg, Ger. 40/G2
Brander, Pass of (pass), Sc, UK 36/A4
Brandfort, SAfr. 106/D3
Brandizzo, It. 58/A2
Brandon, Mb, Can. 127/J3
Brandon, Fl, US 133/H5
Brandon, Ms, US 133/F3
Brandsen, Arg. 159/J11
Brandvlei, SAfr. 106/C3
Brandýs nad Labem, Czh. 55/H2
Brandywine, Md, US 138/B6
Brandywine (riv.), Pa, US 138/C4
Branford, Ct, US 139/F1
Branges, Fr. 56/B4
Braniewo, Pol. 39/H4
Brannenburg, Ger. 43/K3
Brant Beach, NJ, US 138/D4
Branxholm, Austl. 115/C4
Branzoll (Bronzolo), It. 57/H4
Bras d'Or (lake), NS, Can. 131/J2
Brasiléia, Braz. 150/E6
Brasília de Minas, Braz. 154/A5
Brasília, PN de, Braz. 151/J7
Braşov, Rom. 49/G3
Braşov (prov.), Rom. 49/G3
Brasschaat, Belg. 50/B6
Brassey (mt.), Austl. 113/G2
Brasstown Bald (peak), Ga, US 133/H3
Brastad, Swe. 38/D2
Bratislava (cap.), Slvk. 43/M2
Bratislava (pol. reg.), Slvk. 41/J4
Bratislava (Ivanka) (int'l arpt.), Slvk. 48/C1
Bratsk, Rus. 65/L4
Brattleboro, Vt, US 131/F3
Bratunac, Bosn. 48/D3
Braubach, Ger. 53/G3
Braulio Carrillo, PN, CR 140/E5
Braunau am Inn, Aus. 55/G6
Braunfels, Ger. 54/B1
Braunig (lake), Tx, US 137/U21
Braunlage, Ger. 51/H5
Bräunlingen, Ger. 57/E2
Braunschweig, Ger. 51/H4
Brava (isl.), CpV. 93/J11
Brava (pt.), Chile 159/C7
Brava (pt.), Uru. 159/K11
Brava, Costa (coast), Sp. 45/G2
Bråviken (inlet), Swe. 38/G2
Bravo (peak), Bol. 150/F7
Bravo (peak), Peru 156/B2
Bravo del Norte (riv.), Mex. 140/A2
Brawley, Ca, US 128/D4
Bray (isl.), Nun., Can. 123/J2
Bray, Ire. 34/B5
Bray (pt.), Ire. 34/B5
Bray-Dunes, Fr. 52/B1
Braye (riv.), Fr. 42/D3
Brazey-en-Plaine, Fr. 56/B3
Brazil (ctry.) 150/F5
Brazilian Highlands (uplands), Braz. 147/E4
Brazo Casiquiare (riv.), Ven. 153/E4
Brazo Sur (riv.), Arg. 159/C6
Brazópolis, Braz. 211/H7
Brazos (riv.), Tx, US 132/D3
Brazos, Salt Fork (riv.), Tx, US 132/C3
Brazzaville (cap.), Congo 105/C1
Brčko, Bosn. 48/D3
Brda (riv.), Pol. 38/G5
Brdy (mts.), Czh. 41/G4
Brea, Ca, US 136/G8
Breadalbane (dist.), Sc, UK 36/B4
Breamish (riv.), Eng, UK 36/D6
Bréancon, Fr. 30/J4
Bréau, Fr. 30/L6
Breaza, Rom. 49/G3
Brebbia, It. 58/B1
Brêche (riv.), Fr. 52/B5
Brechen, Ger. 54/B2
Brechin, Sc, UK 36/D3
Brecht, Belg. 50/B6
Breckenridge, Mn, US 127/J4
Breckenridge, Tx, US 129/H4
Breckerfeld, Ger. 51/E6
Breckland (phys. reg.), Eng, UK 33/G2
Brecknock (pen.), Chile 159/C7
Břeclav, Czh. 43/M2
Brecon, Wal, UK 32/C3
Brecon Beacons (mts.), Wal, UK 32/C3
Breda, Neth. 50/B5
Bredaryd, Swe. 38/E3
Bredasdorp, SAfr. 106/M11
Bredebro, Den. 38/C4
Bredene, Belg. 52/B1
Bredstedt, Ger. 38/C4
Breë (riv.), SAfr. 106/B4
Bree, Belg. 53/E1
Breg (riv.), Ger. 40/E5
Bregagno (peak), It. 57/F5
Bregalnica (riv.), FYROM 47/H2
Breganze, It. 59/E1
Bregenz, Aus. 57/F3
Bregenzer Ache (riv.), Aus. 57/F3
Bregovo, Bul. 48/F3
Brégy, Fr. 30/L4
Breidhafjördhur (bay), Ice. 37/M6
Breil-Brigels, Swi. 57/F4
Breisach, Ger. 56/D1
Breitbrunn am Chiemsee, Ger. 55/F7
Breitenauriegel (peak), Ger. 55/G5
Breitenbach, Swi. 56/D3
Breitenbrunn, Ger. 55/E4
Breitenfurt bei Wien, Aus. 49/N7
Breitenworbis, Ger. 51/H6
Breithorn (peak), Swi. 56/D5
Breithorn (peak), Swi. 56/D6
Brejo, Braz. 154/B1
Brejo Santo, Braz. 154/C2
Brejões, Braz. 154/B3
Brembate di Sopra, It. 58/C1
Brembilla, It. 58/C1
Brembio, It. 58/C2
Brembo (riv.), It. 57/F6
Bremen (int'l arpt.), Ger. 51/F2
Bremen, Ger. 51/F2
Bremen (state), Ger. 38/C5
Bremer (riv.), Austl. 114/E7
Bremerhaven, Ger. 51/F1
Bremerton, Wa, US 126/C4
Bremervörde, Ger. 51/G2
Bremgarten, Swi. 57/E3
Bremgarten bei Bern, Swi. 56/D4
Bremnes, Nor. 38/A2
Brend (riv.), Ger. 54/D2
Brendel (lake), Mi, US 135/E7
Brendola, It. 59/E2
Brendon (hills), Eng, UK 32/C4
Brenig, Llyn (lake), Wal, UK 34/E5
Brenne (riv.), Fr. 40/C5
Brenner (pass), Aus. 57/H4
Brenner (riv.), Austl. 113/N9
Brenno (riv.), Swi. 57/E5
Breno, It. 57/G6
Brent (bor.), Eng, UK 30/C2
Brent (res.), Eng, UK 30/C2
Brent (riv.), Eng, UK 30/B2
Brenta (riv.), It. 43/J4
Brenta (peak), It. 57/G5
Brentwood, NY, US 139/E2
Brentwood, Ca, US 135/L11
Brentwood, Eng, UK 30/D2
Brenz (riv.), Ger. 54/D5
Brescello, It. 58/D3
Brescia, It. 58/D1
Brescia (prov.), It. 57/G6
Bresle (riv.), Fr. 42/D1
Bresles, Fr. 52/B5
Bressana, It. 58/C2
Bressanone, It. 43/J3
Bressay (isl.), Sc, UK 31/W13
Bressuire, Fr. 42/C3
Brest, Fr. 42/A2
Brest, Bela. 41/M2
Brest (int'l arpt.), Bela. 41/M2
Brestskaya (obl.), Bela. 62/C1
Bretagne (pol. reg.), Fr. 42/B2
Bretagne, Monts de (mts.), Fr. 42/B2
Bretagne, Pointe de (pt.), Reun. 107/S15
Bretaña, Peru 156/C2
Breteuil, Fr. 52/B4
Brétigny-sur-Orge, Fr. 30/J6
Breton, Ab, Can. 126/E2
Breton (cape), NS, Can. 131/K2
Brett (cape), NZ 117/S10
Brett (riv.), Eng, UK 33/G2
Brettach (riv.), Ger. 54/C4
Bretten, Ger. 54/B4
Bretzenheim, Ger. 53/G4
Breuberg, Ger. 54/C3
Breuillet, Fr. 30/J6
Breukelen, Neth. 50/B4
Breuna, Ger. 51/G6
Breuvannes-en-Bassigny, Fr. 56/B1
Breves, Braz. 151/H4
Brevig Mission, Ak, US 134/E2
Brevik, Nor. 38/C2
Brevoort (isl.), Nun., Can. 123/K2
Brewarrina, Austl. 115/C1
Brewer, Me, US 131/G2
Brewster, Ne, US 127/J5
Brewton, Al, US 133/G4
Brey-et-Lû, Fr. 30/G4
Breyten, SAfr. 107/E2
Brežice, Slov. 43/L4
Březnice, Czh. 55/G3
Breznik, Bul. 48/F4
Brezoi, Rom. 49/G3
Brezovo, Bul. 47/J1
Bria, CAfr. 97/K6
Briançon, Fr. 43/G4
Brianne, Llyn (res.), Wal, UK 32/C2
Briar Creek, Pa, US 138/B1
Briare, Fr. 42/E3
Brickerville, Pa, US 138/B3
Bricktown, NJ, US 138/D3
Bride (riv.), Ire. 31/P10
Bride, IM, UK 34/D3
Bridge City, Tx, US 132/E4
Bridge of Allan, Sc, UK 36/C4
Bridge of Don, Sc, UK 36/D2
Bridge of Weir, Sc, UK 36/B5
Bridgehampton, NY, US 139/F2
Bridgend, Wal, UK 32/C3
Bridgend (co.), Wal, UK 32/C3
Bridgeport, Ca, US 128/C3
Bridgeport, Ne, US 127/H5
Bridgeport, NJ, US 138/C4
Bridgeport, Ct, US 139/E1
Bridger, Mt, US 126/F4
Bridgeton, NJ, US 138/C5
Bridgetown (cap.), Bar. 141/P9
Bridgetown, Austl. 112/C5
Bridgeville, De, US 138/C6
Bridgewater, Austl. 115/C4
Bridgewater, NS, Can. 131/H2
Bridgnorth, Eng, UK 32/D1
Bridgton, Me, US 131/G2
Bridgwater, Eng, UK 32/D4
Bridgwater (bay), Eng, UK 32/C4
Bridlington, Eng, UK 35/H3
Bridlington (bay), Eng, UK 35/H3
Bridport, Austl. 115/C4
Bridport, Eng, UK 32/D5
Brie (reg.), Fr. 40/B4
Brie-Comte-Robert, Fr. 30/K5
Brieg Brzeg, Pol. 41/J3
Brielle, Neth. 50/B5
Brielle, NJ, US 138/D3
Brienz, Swi. 56/E4
Brier, Wa, US 135/C2
Brierfield, Eng, UK 35/F4
Brieselang, Ger. 40/Q6
Brig, Swi. 56/D5
Brigach (riv.), Ger. 54/B7
Brigantine, NJ, US 138/D5
Brigend (co.), Wal, UK 32/C3
Brigham City, Ut, US 137/J10
Brighouse, Eng, UK 35/G4
Bright, Austl. 115/C3
Brightlingsea, Eng, UK 33/H3
Brighton, Il, US 137/G7
Brighton, Ut, US 137/K12
Brighton, Co, US 137/C3
Brighton, Eng, UK 33/F5
Brighton, Wi, US 135/P14
Brignais, Fr. 42/F4
Brignoles, Fr. 42/G5
Brihuega, Sp. 44/D2
Briis-sous-Forges, Fr. 30/J6
Brikama, Gam. 102/A3
Brilhante (riv.), Braz. 151/G8
Brilon, Ger. 51/F6
Brimstone Hill NP, StK. 141/N8
Brindisi, It. 47/E2
Brinkworth, Austl. 113/H5
Brinnon, Wa, US 135/B2
Brión, Sp. 44/A1
Brione, Swi. 57/E5
Briones (res.), Ca, US 135/K11
Brisbane, Austl. 114/F6
Brisbane (int'l arpt.), Austl. 114/F6
Brisbane (riv.), Austl. 114/E7
Brisbane Forest Park, Austl. 114/E6
Brisbane Ranges NP, Austl. 115/C3
Brisbane Water NP, Austl. 115/D2
Brisighella, It. 59/E4
Brissago, Swi. 57/E5
Bristol, Tn, US 130/D4
Bristol (chan.), Eng,Wal, UK 32/B4
Bristol, Eng, UK 32/D4
Bristol (co.), Eng, UK 32/D4
Bristol (bay), Ak, US 134/F4
Bristol, Pa, US 138/D3
Bristow, Ok, US 129/H4
British (mts.), Ak, US 134/K2
British Columbia (prov.), Can. 122/D3
British Empire (range), Nun., Can. 123/S6
British Indian Ocean Territory (dpcy.), UK 67/G10
British Museum, Eng, UK 30/C2
Britstown, SAfr. 106/C3
Brittany (reg.), Fr. 42/B3
Britton, SD, US 127/J4
Brive-la-Gaillarde, Fr. 42/D4
Brives-Charensac, Fr. 42/E4
Briviesca, Sp. 44/D1
Brivio, It. 58/C1
Brnik (int'l arpt.), Slov. 43/L3
Brno, Czh. 41/J4
Broa (bay), Cuba 145/F1
Broad (pass), Ak, US 134/J3
Broad (riv.), NC,SC, US 133/H3
Broad Law (peak), Sc, UK 36/C6
Broad Sound (isls.), Austl. 114/C2
Broadback (riv.), Qu, Can. 130/E1
Broadford, Austl. 115/C3
Broadkill (riv.), De, US 138/C6
Broads NP, The, Eng, UK 33/H1
Broadstairs, Eng, UK 33/H4
Broadus, Mt, US 127/G4
Broadwater NP, Austl. 115/E1
Broadway (hill), Eng, UK 33/E3
Broadway, NJ, US 138/C2
Broc, Swi. 56/D4
Brochet, Mb, Can. 122/F3
Brock (isl.), NW, Can. 123/R7
Brocken (peak), Ger. 51/H5
Brockman (mt.), Austl. 112/C2
Brockton, Ma, US 131/G3
Brockville, On, Can. 130/F2
Brodeur (pen.), Nun., Can. 122/G1
Brodheadsville, Pa, US 138/C2
Brodnica, Pol. 41/K2
Broek in Waterland, Neth. 50/B4
Broek Op Langedijk, Neth. 50/B3
Bröhn (peak), Ger. 51/G4
Broken (bay), Austl. 115/D2
Broken Arrow, Ok, US 129/J3
Broken Bow (lake), Ok, US 129/J4
Broken Bow, Ok, US 129/J3
Broken Bow, Ne, US 127/J5
Broken Hill, Austl. 115/B1
Brokeoff (mts.), NM, US 132/B3
Brokopondo, Sur. 151/G2
Brokopondo (dist.), Sur. 153/H3
Brome, Ger. 40/F2
Bromölla, Swe. 38/F3
Bromsgrove, Eng, UK 32/D2
Bromskirchen, Ger. 51/F6
Bron, Fr. 56/A6
Brønderslev, Den. 38/C3
Brong-Ahafo (pol. reg.), Gha. 103/E5
Broni, It. 58/C2
Bronkhorstspruit, SAfr. 106/E2
Brønnøy, Nor. 37/E2
Brøns, Den. 38/C4
Bronschhofen, Swi. 57/F3
Bronte, It. 46/D4
Bronx (bor.), NY, US 139/E2
Bronx Zoo, NY, US 139/K8
Bronxville, NY, US 139/K8
Brook Forest, Co, US 137/B3
Brooke's Point, Phil. 81/E2
Brookfield, Il, US 135/Q16
Brookhaven, Ms, US 129/K5
Brooklyn (bor.), NY, US 138/D2
Brooklyn, Il, US 137/G8
Brooklyn Park, Md, US 138/B5
Brookmans Park, Eng, UK 30/C1
Brooks (mtn.), Ak, US 134/E2
Brooks, Ab, Can. 126/F3
Brooks, Il, US 137/G8
Brooks (range), Ak, US 134/F2
Brookside, De, US 138/C4
Brooksville, Fl, US 133/H4
Brookton, Austl. 112/C5
Brookvale, Co, US 137/B3
Brookville, NY, US 139/L8
Broomall, Pa, US 138/C4
Broomfield, Co, US 137/B3
Brørup, Den. 38/C4
Brösarp, Swe. 38/F4
Brossard, Qu, Can. 131/P7
Brough (pt.), Sc, UK 31/V14
Broughshane, NI, UK 34/B2
Brousseval, Fr. 56/A1
Brouwersdam (dam), Neth. 50/A5
Brouwershaven, Neth. 50/A5
Brovst, Den. 38/C3
Brown (mt.), Austl. 113/H5
Brown (pt.), Austl. 113/G5
Brown Clee (hill), Eng, UK 32/D2
Brown Shoal (bar) 79/C5
Brownfield, Tx, US 129/G4
Brownhills, Eng, UK 33/E1
Browning, Mt, US 126/E3
Browns Mills, NJ, US 138/D4
Brownsea (isl.), Eng, UK 33/E5
Brownsville, Tn, US 130/B5
Brownsville, Tx, US 132/D5
Brownsville, Wa, US 135/B2
Broxburn, Sc, UK 36/C5
Broye (riv.), Swi. 56/C4
Brozas, Sp. 44/B3
Bruay-la-Buissière, Fr. 52/B3
Bruay-sur-L'Escaut, Fr. 52/C3
Bruce (pen.), On, Can. 130/D2
Bruce (mt.), Austl. 112/C2
Bruce Rock, Austl. 112/C4
Bruchberg (peak), Ger. 51/H5
Bruche (riv.), Fr. 43/G2
Bruchhausen-Vilsen, Ger. 51/G3
Bruchköbel, Ger. 54/B2
Bruchmühlbach-Miesau, Ger. 53/G5
Bruchsal, Ger. 54/B4
Brucht (riv.), Ger. 51/G5
Bruck, Aus. 49/P7
Bruck an der Grossglocknerstrasse, Aus. 43/K3
Bruck an der Mur, Aus. 43/L3
Bruckberg, Ger. 55/F5
Bruckmühl, Ger. 43/J3
Brue (riv.), Eng, UK 32/D4
Bruflat, Nor. 38/C1
Brügg, Swi. 56/D3
Brugg, Swi. 56/E3
Brugge, Belg. 52/C1
Brüggen, Ger. 50/D6
Brugnera, It. 59/F1
Brühl, Ger. 53/F2
Bruinisse, Neth. 50/B5
Brukkaros (peak), Namb. 106/B2
Brungle, Austl. 113/M8
Brumado, Braz. 154/B4

176
Bruma – Calho

Brumath, Fr. 53/G6
Brummen, Neth. 50/D4
Brumunddal, Nor. 38/D1
Brune (riv.), Fr. 52/C4
Bruneau (riv.), Id,Nv, US 126/E5
Brunei (ctry.) 80/D2
Brunete, Sp. 45/M9
Brunflo, Swe. 37/E3
Brunico, It. 43/J3
Brünigpass (pass), Swi. 56/E4
Brunn am Gebirge, Aus. 49/N7
Brunoy, Fr. 30/K5
Brunsbüttel, Ger. 51/G1
Brunssum, Neth. 53/E2
Brunstatt, Fr. 56/D2
Brunswick, Ga, US 133/H4
Brunswick, Me, US 131/G3
Brunswick, Oh, US 130/D3
Brunswick Heads, Austl. 114/D5
Brunswick Junction, Austl. 112/B5
Brunswick, Peninsula de (pen.), Chile 157/B7
Brus (lake), Nic. 145/E3
Brusartsi, Bul. 48/F4
Brushy Creek, Tx, US 129/J5
Brusio, Swi. 57/G5
Brussels, Il, US 137/F8
Brussels (int'l arpt.), Belg. 53/D2
Brussels (Bruxelles) (cap.), Belg. 53/D2
Brusson, It. 58/A1
Bruthen, Austl. 115/C3
Bruyères, Fr. 56/C1
Bruyères-le-Châtel, Fr. 30/J6
Bruyères-sur-Oise, Fr. 30/J4
Bruz, Fr. 42/C2
Bruzual, Ven. 152/D2
Bryan, Tx, US 129/H5
Bryan, Oh, US 130/C3
Bryan (mt.), Austl. 113/H5
Bryansk, Rus. 62/E1
Bryanskaya (obl.), Rus. 62/E1
Bryce Canyon NP, Ut, US 128/D3
Bryn Brawd (peak), Wal, UK 32/C2
Bryn Mawr, Pa, US 138/C3
Bryne, Nor. 38/A2
Brzeg Dolny, Pol. 41/J3
Brzesko, Pol. 41/L4
Brzozów, Pol. 41/M4
Bua, Swe. 38/E3
Buala, Sol. 116/E5
Buba, GBis. 102/B4
Bubaque, GBis. 102/B4
Bubendorf, Swi. 56/D3
Bubikon, Swi. 57/E3
Bubu (riv.), Tanz. 104/B4
Buc, Fr. 30/J5
Bucak, Turk. 90/B2
Bucakkişla, Turk. 91/C1
Bucaramanga, Col. 152/C3
Bucasia, Austl. 114/C3
Bucelas, Port. 45/P10
Buch, Ger. 57/G1
Buchan (gulf), Nun., Can. 123/J1
Buchan (reg.), Sc, UK 36/D1
Buchan Ness (pt.), Sc, UK 36/E2
Buchanan (lake), Tx, US 129/H5
Buchanan, Libr. 102/C5
Buchans, Nf, Can. 131/K1
Bucharest (Bucureşti) (cap.), Rom. 49/H4
Buchbach, Ger. 55/F6
Büchen, Ger. 51/H2
Buchen, Ger. 54/C3
Buchenberg, Ger. 57/G2
Buchholz, Ger. 53/G3
Buchholz in der Nordheide, Ger. 51/G2
Buchloe, Ger. 57/G1
Buchon (pt.), Ca, US 128/B4
Buchs, Swi. 57/F3
Bucine, It. 59/E6
Buck, The (peak), Sc, UK 36/D2
Buckden Pike (peak), Eng, UK 35/F3
Bückeburg, Ger. 51/G4
Buckie, Sc, UK 36/D1
Buckingham, Qu, Can. 130/F2
Buckingham, Eng, UK 33/F3
Buckingham Palace, Eng, UK 30/C2
Buckland, Ak, US 134/F2
Buckley, Wa, US 135/C3
Buckley, Wal, UK 35/E5
Buckner, Mo, US 137/E5
Bucks (co.), Pa, US 138/C3
Bucksburn, Sc, UK 36/D2
Bucquoy, Fr. 52/B3
Buctouche, NB, Can. 131/H2
Bucureşti (co.), Rom. 49/G3
Bucy-le-Long, Fr. 52/C5
Bucyrus, Oh, US 130/D3
Bucyrus, Ks, US 137/D6
Budai hegy (hill), Hun. 49/Q9
Budakeszi, Hun. 49/Q9
Budaörs, Hun. 49/R10
Budapest (co.), Hun. 49/R9
Budapest (cap.), Hun. 49/R9
Budaun, India 84/B1
Budd (coast), Ant. 160/H
Budd (inlet), Wa, US 135/B3
Budd Lake, NJ, US 138/D2
Buddon Ness (pt.), Sc, UK 36/D4
Buddusò, It. 46/A2
Bude, Eng, UK 32/B5
Bude (bay), Eng, UK 32/B5
Budel, Neth. 50/C6
Büdelsdorf, Ger. 38/C4
Budge-Budge, India 85/G4
Budhāna, India 86/D5
Budhanilantha, Nepal 85/E2
Budhlāda, India 86/C5
Budia, Sp. 44/D2
Büdingen, Ger. 54/C2
Budrio, It. 59/E3
Budva, Yugo. 47/F1
Budzhak (reg.), Mol. 49/J2
Buea, Camr. 96/G7
Buelna (int'l arpt.), Mex. 142/D4
Buena, NJ, US 138/D4
Buena Esperanza, Arg. 158/D2
Buena Fe, Ecu. 152/B5
Buena Park, Ca, US 136/G8
Buena Vista, Co, US 129/F3
Buenaventura, Mex. 142/D2
Buenaventura, Col. 152/B4
Buenavista, Phil. 79/E6
Buenavista, Mex. 143/Q9
Bueno (riv.), Chile 158/B4
Bueno Brandão, Braz. 211/G7
Buenópolis, Braz. 154/A5
Buenos Aires, Peru 156/B2
Buenos Aires, Col. 152/B4
Buenos Aires (lake), Arg.,Chile 147/B7
Buenos Aires (prov.), Arg. 158/E3
Buenos Aires (cap.), Arg. 159/J11
Buenos Aires (Jorge Newbery) (int'l arpt.), Arg. 159/J11
Buenos Aires (Ministro Pistarini) (int'l arpt.), Arg. 159/J11
Buerarema, Braz. 154/C4
Buesaco, Col. 152/B4
Buet (peak), Fr. 56/C5
Bueu, Sp. 44/A1
Buffalo (mt.), Austl. 115/C3
Buffalo, Ok, US 129/H3
Buffalo, Mn, US 127/K4
Buffalo, Wy, US 126/G4
Buffalo (lake), Ab, Can. 126/E2
Buffalo, SD, US 127/H4
Buffalo (riv.), Ar, US 132/E3
Buffalo (riv.), SAfr. 107/E3
Buffalo, NY, US 131/S10
Buffalo Bill Museum and Grave, Co, US 137/B3
Buffalo Narrows, Sk, Can. 126/F2
Buffalo Springs Nat'l Rsv., Kenya 104/C2
Buffelsrivier (riv.), SAfr. 106/B3
Buford, Ga, US 133/G3
Buftea, Rom. 49/G3
Bug (riv.), Pol. 64/C4
Buga, Col. 152/B4
Bugaba, Pan. 145/F4
Bugac, Hun. 48/D2
Bugala (isl.), Ugan. 104/B3
Bugalagrande, Col. 152/B3
Bugat, Mong. 70/F2
Buğdaylı, Turk. 49/H5
Bugel (pt.), Indo. 80/D5
Buggenhout, Belg. 53/D1
Bugojno, Bosn. 48/C3
Bugosa (prov.), Ugan. 104/B2
Bugsuk (isl.), Phil. 81/E2
Bugul'ma, Rus. 61/M5
Buguruslan, Rus. 63/K1
Buh (riv.), Ukr. 41/M3
Buḩayrat al Asad (lake), Syria 90/D2
Buḩayrat ath Tharthār (res.), Iraq 90/E3
Buḩayrat Banzart (lake), Tun. 46/A4
Buhi, Phil. 79/D5
Buhl, Fr. 56/D2
Bühl, Ger. 57/E2
Bühler (riv.), Ger. 54/C4
Bühlerzell, Ger. 54/C5
Buhuşi, Rom. 49/H2
Bui (dam), Gha. 103/E4
Bui Gorge (res.), Gha. 103/E4
Bui NP, Gha. 103/E4
Buin (peak), Swi. 57/G4
Buin, Chile 158/N8
Buíque, Braz. 154/C3
Bujalance, Sp. 44/C4
Bujanovac, Yugo. 47/G1
Bujumbura (cap.), Buru. 104/A3
Bujumbura (int'l arpt.), Buru. 104/A3
Buk, Pol. 41/J2
Buka (isl.), PNG 116/E5
Bukadaban (peak), China 70/F4
Būkān, Iran 88/E1
Bukasa (isl.), Ugan. 104/B3
Bukavu, D.R. Congo 104/A3
Bukene, Tanz. 104/B4
Buket Bubat (peak), Malay. 83/H6
Bukhoro (pol. reg.), Uzb. 87/D5
Bukhoro, Uzb. 87/D5
Bukhovo, Bul. 47/H1
Bukittinggi, Indo. 80/B4
Bükki NP, Hun. 62/B2
Bukoba, Tanz. 104/A3
Buku (cape), Indo. 80/B4
Bülach, Swi. 57/E2
Bulahdelah, Austl. 115/E2
Bulan, Phil. 81/F1
Bulancak, Turk. 62/F4
Bulandshahr, India 84/A1
Bulanık, Turk. 90/E2
Bulawa (peak), Indo. 81/F3
Bulawayo, Zim. 105/E5
Buldan, Turk. 90/B2
Buldibuyo, Peru 156/B3
Bulgan, Mong. 70/H1
Bulgan (prov.), Mong. 70/H2
Bulgan, Mong. 70/H2
Bulgan, Mong. 70/H3
Bulgaria (ctry.) 62/C4
Bŭlgarovo, Bul. 49/H4
Bulgheria (peak), It. 46/D2
Bululiyan (cape), Phil. 81/E2
Bulkley (riv.), BC, Can. 126/B2
Bull (pt.), NI, UK 34/B1
Bull Shoals (lake), Ar,Mo, US 129/J3
Bullange, Belg. 53/F3
Bullas, Sp. 44/E3
Bulle, Swi. 56/D4
Buller (isl.), NZ 117/S11
Bullerup, Den. 38/D4
Bullhead City, Az, US 128/D4
Bullion, Fr. 30/H6
Bulloo (riv.), Austl. 109/D3
Bulloo River Overflow (swamp), Austl. 114/A5
Bully-les-Mines, Fr. 52/B3
Bulnayn (mts.), Mong. 70/G2
Bulnes, Chile 158/B3
Bultfontein, SAfr. 106/D3
Bulukumba, Indo. 81/F5
Bulverde, Tx, US 137/U20
Bumba, D.R. Congo 97/K7
Bumtang (riv.), Bhu. 85/H2
Bumthang, Bhu. 85/H2
Bunaga-take (peak), Japan 77/J5
Bunbury, Austl. 112/B5
Bundaberg, Austl. 114/D4
Bundarra, Austl. 115/D1
Bünde, Ger. 51/F4
Bunde, Ger. 51/E2
Bundoran, Ire. 31/P9
Bündu, India 85/E4
Bungendore, Austl. 115/D2
Bunguran (isl.), Indo. 80/C3
Bunia, D.R. Congo 104/A2
Bunker (peak), Az, US 137/R18
Bunker Hill, Il, US 137/H7
Bunkie, La, US 129/J5
Bunnell, Fl, US 133/H4
Bunnik, Neth. 50/C4
Buñol, Sp. 45/E3
Bunschoten, Neth. 50/C4
Bunya, Austl. 114/E6
Bunya Mountains NP, Austl. 114/C4
Bünyan, Turk. 90/C2
Bunyu (isl.), Indo. 81/E3
Buochs, Swi. 57/E4
Buon Me Thuot, Viet. 78/E3
Buonconvento, It. 43/J5
Buquim, Braz. 154/C3
Būr Sa'īd (gov.), Egypt 90/C4
Būr Sa'īd (gov.), Egypt 91/C4
Būr Sa'īd (Port Said), Egypt 91/C4
Būr Sūdān (Port Sudan), Sudan 101/D5
Burang, China 70/D5
Buranga (pass), Ugan. 97/M7
Burano (riv.), It. 59/F5
Burano, It. 59/F2
Buras-Triumph, La, US 133/F4
Burauen, Phil. 79/D5
Buraydah, SAr. 88/D3
Burbach, Ger. 53/H2
Burbank, Ca, US 136/F7
Burbure, Fr. 52/B2
Burco (Burao), Som. 97/Q6
Burdekin (riv.), Austl. 109/D2
Burdell (mtn.), Ca, US 135/J10
Burdur (lake), Turk. 90/B2
Burdur (prov.), Turk. 90/B2
Burdur, Turk. 90/B2
Burdwān, India 85/F4
Bure (riv.), Eng, UK 33/H1
Büren, Ger. 51/F5
Buren, Neth. 50/C5
Büren an der Aare, Swi. 56/D3
Bürengiyn (mts.), Mong. 70/H2
Bures-sur-Yvette, Fr. 30/J5
Būrewāla, Pak. 86/B4
Bureya (riv.), Rus. 65/P4
Burg, Ger. 38/C4
Burg, Ger. 40/F2
Burg, Ger. 38/D4
Burgas (prov.), Bul. 47/K1
Burgas (bay), Bul. 49/H4
Burgas (int'l arpt.), Bul. 49/H4
Burgau, Ger. 54/D6
Burgaw, NC, US 133/J3
Burgberg im Allgäu, Ger. 57/G2
Burgbernheim, Ger. 54/D4
Burgbrohl, Ger. 53/G3
Burgdorf, Ger. 51/H4
Burgdorf, Swi. 56/D3
Burgebrach, Ger. 54/D3
Burgenland (prov.), Aus. 41/J5
Burgeo, Nf, Can. 131/K2
Burgersdorp, SAfr. 106/D3
Burges (mt.), Austl. 112/D4
Burgess (mt.), Yk, Can. 134/L2
Burgess Hill, Eng, UK 33/F5
Burgfjället (peak), Swe. 37/E2
Burghaslach, Ger. 54/D3
Burghausen, Ger. 55/F6
Burghead (bay), Sc, UK 36/C1
Burghead, Sc, UK 36/C1
Burgheim, Ger. 54/E5
Burgkirchen, Aus. 55/G6
Burgkirchen an der Alz, Ger. 55/F6
Burgkunstadt, Ger. 54/E2
Bürglen, Swi. 57/F2
Burglengenfeld, Ger. 55/F4
Burgos, Mex. 143/F3
Burgos, Sp. 44/D1
Burgsinn, Ger. 54/C2
Burgstall (Postal), It. 57/H4
Burgsteinfurt, Ger. 51/E4
Burgsvik, Swe. 38/H3
Burgundy (reg.), Fr. 42/F3
Burgwedel, Ger. 51/G3
Burhābalang (riv.), India 85/F4
Burhan Budai (mts.), China 70/G4
Burhaniye, Turk. 62/C5
Burhānpur, India 89/L4
Burhar-Dhanpuri, India 84/C4
Burhi Gandok (riv.), India 85/E2
Burica (pen.), Pan. 140/E6
Burica (pt.), Pan. 145/F4
Burin, Nf, Can. 131/L2
Burin (pen.), Nf, Can. 123/L4
Buriram, Thai. 78/C3
Buritama, Braz. 155/B2
Buriti, Braz. 154/B1
Buriti Alegre, Braz. 155/B1
Buriti Bravo, Braz. 154/B2
Buriti dos Lopes, Braz. 154/B1
Buritis, Braz. 154/A4
Buritizeiro, Braz. 154/A5
Burjasot, Sp. 45/E3
Burkardroth, Ger. 54/C2
Burke (chan.), BC, Can. 126/B2
Bürkelkopf (peak), Aus. 57/G4
Burkina Faso (ctry.) 141/E3
Burksville, Il, US 137/G9
Burladingen, Ger. 57/F1
Burley, Wa, US 135/B3
Burlingame, Ca, US 135/K11
Burlington, Ia, US 127/L5
Burlington, Co, US 129/G3
Burlington, Ks, US 129/J3
Burlington, Wi, US 130/B3
Burlington, NC, US 133/J2
Burlington, Vt, US 130/F2
Burlington, On, Can. 131/Q9
Burlington (co.), NJ, US 138/D4
Burlington, NJ, US 138/D3
Burlington, Il, US 135/N15
Burma (Myanmar) (ctry.) 83/G3
Bürmoos, Aus. 55/F7
Burnas (lake), Ukr. 49/K3
Burnet, Tx, US 129/H5
Burnett Heads, Austl. 114/D4
Burney, Ca, US 128/B2
Burney (peak), Chile 159/B7
Burnham, Il, US 135/Q16
Burnham-on-Sea, Eng, UK 32/D4
Burnie-Somerset, Austl. 115/C4
Burnley, Eng, UK 35/F4
Burns, Or, US 126/D5
Burns Lake, BC, Can. 126/B2
Burnside (riv.), Nun., Can. 122/E2
Burntisland, Sc, UK 36/C4
Burntwood, Eng, UK 33/E1
Burntwood (riv.), Mb, Can. 122/G3
Buronga, Austl. 115/B2
Buronzo, It. 58/B2
Burqā, WBnk. 91/G7
Burqīn, WBnk. 91/G7
Burr Ridge, Il, US 135/Q16
Burra, Austl. 113/H5
Burrel, Alb. 47/G2
Burrendong (res.), Austl. 115/D2
Burrewarra (pt.), Austl. 115/D2
Burriana, Sp. 45/E3
Burringbar, Austl. 114/D5
Burrinjuck (res.), Austl. 115/D2
Burrow (pt.), Sc, UK 34/D2
Burrowes (pt.), Austl. 114/A2
Burrum Heads, Austl. 114/D4
Burrum River NP, Austl. 114/D4
Burry (inlet), Wal, UK 32/B3
Bursa (prov.), Turk. 62/D5
Bursa, Turk. 62/D4
Burscheid, Ger. 53/G1
Bürstadt, Ger. 54/B3
Burt, NY, US 131/S9
Burtenbach, Ger. 54/D6
Burton, Wa, US 135/C3
Burton Latimer, Eng, UK 33/F2
Burton upon Trent, Eng, UK 33/E1
Buru (isl.), Indo. 67/M10
Burullus, Buḩayrat al (lake), Egypt 91/B4
Burundi (ctry.) 104/A3
Bururi, Buru. 104/A3
Buruticupu (riv.), Braz. 154/A2
Burwash Landing, Yk, Can. 134/L3
Bury, Eng, UK 35/F4
Bury, Fr. 52/B5
Buryatiya (aut. rep.), Rus. 65/M4
Bury Saint Edmunds, Eng, UK 33/G2
Burynshyk (pt.), Kaz. 63/J3
Busalla, It. 58/B3
Busembatia, Ugan. 104/B2
Busenberg, Ger. 53/G5
Buseno, Swi. 57/F5
Bush (riv.), Md, US 138/B5
Bush Kill (riv.), Pa, US 138/C1
Bushey, Eng, UK 30/B2
Bushkill, Pa, US 138/C1
Bushkill Falls, Pa, US 138/C1
Bushmanland (reg.), SAfr. 106/B3
Bushmills, NI, UK 34/B1
Busigny, Fr. 52/C3
Businga, D.R. Congo 97/K7
Buskerud (co.), Nor. 37/D3
Busko-Zdrój, Pol. 41/L3
Buss Craig (pt.), Sc, UK 36/D5
Busselton, Austl. 112/B5
Busseri (riv.), Sudan 97/L6
Busseto, It. 58/D3
Bussolengo, It. 59/D2
Bussum, Neth. 50/C4
Bustamante, Mex. 132/C5
Bustamante, Mex. 143/F4
Bustamante (pt.), Arg. 159/C6
Bustard (pt.), Austl. 114/C4
Buşteni, Rom. 49/G3
Busto Arsizio, It. 58/B1
Busto Garolfo, It. 58/B1
Busuanga (isl.), Phil. 79/C5
Büsum, Ger. 38/C4
Buta, D.R. Congo 97/K7
Buta Ranquil, Arg. 158/C3
Butare, Rwa. 104/A3
Butaritari (isl.), Kiri. 116/G4
Butawal, Nepal 84/D2
Bute (inlet), BC, Can. 126/B3
Bute, Austl. 113/H5
Bute (isl.), Sc, UK 36/A5
Bute, Sound of (sound), Sc, UK 36/A5
Büteeliyn (mts.), Mong. 70/H2
Butembo, D.R. Congo 104/A2
Bütgenbach, Belg. 53/F3
Buti, It. 58/D5
Butiá, Braz. 155/B4
Butiaba, Ugan. 104/A2
Butler, Pa, US 130/E3
Butler, NJ, US 139/H8
Butmir (int'l arpt.), Bosn. 48/D4
Butry-sur-Oise, Fr. 30/J4
Bütschelegg (peak), Swi. 56/D4
Bütschwil, Swi. 57/F3
Butt of Lewis (pt.), Sc, UK 31/Q7
Buttapietra, It. 59/D2
Butte-Silver Bow County, Mt, US 126/E4
Büttelborn, Ger. 54/B3
Butterworth, Malay. 80/B2
Buttes, Swi. 56/C4
Buttevant, Ire. 31/P10
Buttrio, It. 59/G1
Butuan, Phil. 81/G2
Butung (isl.), Indo. 67/M10
Buturlinovka, Rus. 63/G2
Butzbach, Ger. 54/B2
Bützow, Ger. 38/D5
Buëch (riv.), Fr. 42/F4
Buulo Berde, Som. 97/Q7
Buvuma (isl.), Ugan. 104/B2
Buxar, India 84/D3
Buxheim, Ger. 57/G2
Buxtehude, Ger. 51/G2
Buxton, Eng, UK 35/F5
Buy, Rus. 60/J4
Buyant-Uhaa, Mong. 71/K3
Buynaksk, Rus. 63/H4
Buyo, Barrage de (dam), C.d'Iv. 102/D5
Büyük Anafarta, Turk. 47/K2
Büyükarmutlu, Turk. 62/F5
Büyükçekmece, Turk. 49/J5
Büyükeceli, Turk. 91/C1
Büyükkarıştıran, Turk. 49/H5
Büyükyurt, Turk. 90/D2
Buyun Shan (peak), China 73/B2
Buyuni (pt.), Tanz. 104/C4
Buzançais, Fr. 42/D3
Buzancy, Fr. 53/D5
Buzău, Rom. 49/H3
Buzău (prov.), Rom. 49/H3
Buzău (riv.), Rom. 62/C3
Buziaş, Rom. 48/E3
Búzios, Ilha dos (isl.), Braz. 211/H8
Buz'kyy Lyman (estu.), Ukr. 49/K2
Buzsák, Hun. 48/C2
Buzuluk, Rus. 63/K1
Byala, Bul. 49/G4
Byala, Bul. 49/H4
Byala Slatina, Bul. 49/F4
Byam Martin (chan.), Nun., Can. 123/R7
Byam Martin (isl.), Nun., Can. 123/R7
Byarezina (riv.), Bela. 60/E5
Bydgoszcz, Pol. 41/J2
Bydgoszcz (prov.), Pol. 41/J2
Byfleet, Eng, UK 30/B3
Byford, Austl. 112/L7
Bygland, Nor. 38/B2
Bykhov, Bela. 39/P5
Bykle, Nor. 38/B2
Bykovo (int'l arpt.), Rus. 61/X9
Bylot (isl.), Nun., Can. 123/J1
Bynum Run (riv.), Md, US 138/B4
Byram (riv.), Ct, US 139/E1
Byram (pt.), Ct, US 139/L7
Byram (lake), NY, US 139/L7
Byrd, US, Ant. 160/S
Byrd (cape), Ant. 160/U
Byremo, Nor. 38/B2
Byron, Ca, US 135/L11
Byron (isl.), Chile 159/B5
Byron Bay, Austl. 114/D5
Byrranga (mts.), Rus. 64/K2
Byrum, Den. 38/D3
Bystice (riv.), Czh. 55/F2
Bystrá (peak), Slvk. 41/K4
Bystřice, Czh. 55/H3
Bytantay (riv.), Rus. 65/N3
Bytom, Pol. 41/K3
Bytów, Pol. 38/G4

C

C.F. Secada (int'l arpt.), Peru 156/C1
Ca (riv.), Viet. 83/J4
Ca Mau, Viet. 78/D4
Ca Mau (cape), Viet. 78/D4
Caála, Ang. 105/C3
Caatingas (phys. reg.), Braz. 147/E3
Caazapá, Par. 157/E2
Cabadbaran, Phil. 79/E6
Cabaiguán, Cuba 145/G1
Caballo (res.), NM, US 128/F4
Caban-Coch (res.), Wal, UK 32/C2
Cabana, Peru 156/B3
Cabanaconde, Peru 156/D4
Cabañaquinta, Sp. 44/C1
Cabanatuan, Phil. 79/D4
Cabanes, Sp. 45/F2
Cabano, Qu, Can. 131/G2
Cabella Ligure, It. 58/C3
Cabestany, Fr. 42/E5
Cabeza del Buey, Sp. 44/C3
Cabeza Lagarto (pt.), Peru 156/B3
Cabezón de la Sal, Sp. 44/C1
Cabildo, Arg. 158/E3
Cabimas, Ven. 152/D2
Cabinda, Ang. 105/B2
Cabo, Braz. 154/D3
Cabo Corrientes, Cabo (cape), Mex. 142/D4
Cabo de Hornos, PN, Chile 157/C8
Cabo Delgado (prov.), Moz. 104/C5
Cabo Frio, Braz. 155/D2
Cabo Gracias a Dios, Nic. 145/F3
Cabo Orange, PN do, Braz. 151/H3
Cabo San Lucas, Mex. 142/C4
Cabo Verde, Braz. 211/G6
Cabonga (res.), Qu, Can. 123/J4
Caboolture, Austl. 114/D4
Cabora Bassa (lake), Moz. 105/F4
Cabora Bassa, Barragem de (dam), Moz. 105/F4
Cabot (str.), NS,NF, Can. 123/K4
Cabra, Sp. 44/C4
Cabra de Santo Cristo, Sp. 44/D4
Cabral, Serra do (range), Braz. 154/A5
Cabras, It. 46/A3
Cabrera, Isla de (isl.), Sp. 45/G3
Cabri, Sk, Can. 126/F3
Cabriel (riv.), Sp. 44/E3
Cabrillo Nat'l Mon., Ca, US 136/C5
Cabrobó, Braz. 154/C3
Cabruta, Ven. 153/E3
Cabudare, Ven. 152/D2
Cabugao, Phil. 79/D4
Cabure, Ven. 152/D2
Caçador, Braz. 155/B3
Čačak, Yugo. 48/E4
Cacalotán, Mex. 142/D4
Caccia (cape), It. 46/A2
Cáceres, Braz. 150/G7
Cáceres, Sp. 44/B3
Cáceres, Col. 152/C3
Cachapoal (riv.), Chile 158/N9
Cachari, Arg. 159/J12
Cache (peak), Id, US 126/E5
Cache (co.), Ut, US 137/K11
Cache Creek, BC, Can. 126/C3
Cache la Poudre (riv.), Co, US 137/C2
Cache Slough (riv.), Ca, US 135/L10
Cacheu, GBis. 102/A3
Cachí, Arg. 157/C2
Cachicadán, Peru 156/B3
Cachimbo, Serra do (mts.), Braz. 150/G5
Cachipo, Ven. 153/E2
Cachoeira de Minas, Braz. 211/H7
Cachoeira do Sul, Braz. 155/A4
Cachoeira Paulista, Braz. 211/H7
Cachoeiras de Macacu, Braz. 211/L7
Cachoeirinha, Braz. 155/B4
Caconde, Braz. 211/G6
Caçu, Braz. 155/B1
Caculé, Braz. 154/B4
Čadca, Slvk. 41/K4
Caddo (mts.), Ar, US 132/E3
Cadelbosco di Sopra, It. 58/D3
Cadelle (peak), It. 57/F5
Cadenberge, Ger. 51/G1
Cader Idris (peak), Wal, UK 32/C1
Cadibarrawirracanna (lake), Austl. 113/G4
Cadillac, Mi, US 130/C2
Cadiz, Phil. 81/F1
Cadiz, Ky, US 130/C4
Cádiz, Sp. 44/B4
Cádiz, Golfo de (gulf), Port.,Sp. 44/B4
Cadolzburg, Ger. 54/D4
Cadria (peak), It. 57/G6
Caen, Fr. 42/C2
Caerano di San Marco, It. 59/F1
Caernarfon (bay), Wal, UK 34/D5
Caernarfon, Wal, UK 34/D5
Caernarfon Castle, Wal, UK 34/D5
Caerphilly, Wal, UK 32/C3
Caerphilly (co.), Wal, UK 32/C3
Caesarea (ruin), Isr. 91/G6
Caesarea (ruin), Isr. 91/D3
Caetité, Braz. 154/B4
Cafarnaum, Braz. 154/B3
Cafayate, Arg. 157/C2
Cagayan Sulu (isl.), Phil. 79/C6
Cagli, It. 59/F5
Cagliari, It. 46/A3
Cagliari, Golfo di (gulf), It. 46/A3
Cagnes-sur-Mer, Fr. 43/G5
Caguán (riv.), Col. 150/D3
Caguas, PR 141/M8
Caher, Ire. 31/Q10
Cahirsiveen, Ire. 30/N11
Cahokia, Il, US 137/G8
Cahore (pt.), Ire. 31/Q10
Cahors, Fr. 42/D4
Cahuacan, Mex. 143/Q9
Cahuapanas, Peru 156/B2
Cahuinari (riv.), Col. 152/D5
Cahuita, PN, CR 145/F4
Cahul, Mol. 49/J3
Cai (riv.), Braz. 155/G4
Caia, Moz. 105/G4
Caiapó (riv.), Braz. 151/H7
Caiapó, Serra (mts.), Braz. 151/H7
Caibarién, Cuba 145/G1
Caicara, Ven. 153/F2
Caicara, Ven. 153/E3
Caicó, Braz. 154/C2
Caicos (isls.), Uk 141/G3
Caicos Passage (chan.), Bahm. 145/H1
Caieiras, Braz. 211/G8
Cailloma, Peru 156/D4
Cailly (riv.), Fr. 52/A4
Caio (peak), It. 58/D3
Cairate, It. 58/B1
Cairn (mtn.), Ak, US 134/G3
Cairn Curran (dam), Austl. 115/B3
Cairn Gorm (peak), Sc, UK 36/C2
Cairn Table (peak), Sc, UK 36/B6
Cairn Toul (peak), Sc, UK 36/C2
Cairndow, Sc, UK 36/B4
Cairngorm (mts.), Sc, UK 36/B2
Cairns (int'l arpt.), Austl. 114/B2
Cairns (mt.), Austl. 113/G2
Cairns, Austl. 114/B2
Cairnsmore of Carsphairn (peak), Sc, UK 36/B6
Cairo, Ga, US 133/G4
Cairo (peak), It. 46/C2
Cairo (int'l arpt.), Egypt 91/B4
Cairo Montenotte, It. 58/B4
Caistor Centre, On, Can. 131/Q9
Caistorville, On, Can. 131/Q9
Caizi (lake), China 72/D5
Cajabamba, Peru 156/B3
Cajabamba, Ecu. 152/B5
Cajacay, Peru 156/B3
Cajamarca (ruin), Peru 156/B3
Cajamarca, Peru 156/B2
Cajamarca (dept.), Peru 156/B2
Cajari, Braz. 154/A1
Cajatambo, Peru 156/B3
Cajazeiras, Braz. 154/C2
Cajibío, Col. 152/B4
Cajón (pt.), Cuba 145/E1
Cajon Junction, Ca, US 136/C2
Cajones, Cayos (isl.), Hon. 140/E4
Caju (isl.), Braz. 154/B1
Çal, Turk. 90/B2
Cala d'Oliva, It. 46/A2
Calabar, Nga. 103/H5
Calabar (int'l arpt.), Nga. 103/H5
Calabasas, Ca, US 136/B2
Calabozo, Ven. 153/E2
Calabria, PN della, It. 46/D3
Calaburras (pt.), Sp. 44/C4
Calaceite, Sp. 45/F2
Calacoto, Bol. 156/D5
Calafat, Rom. 48/F4
Calahorra, Sp. 44/E1
Calais, Me, US 131/H2
Calais, Fr. 52/A2
Calais, Canal de (canal), Fr. 52/A2
Calalaste, Sierra de (mts.), Arg. 157/C2
Calama, Chile 157/C1
Calamar, Col. 152/C2
Calamian Group (isls.), Phil. 81/E1
Calamocha, Sp. 44/E2
Calamonte, Sp. 44/B3
Calañas, Sp. 44/B4
Calanda, Sp. 45/E2
Calangianus, It. 46/A2
Calapan, Phil. 79/D5
Călăraşi (prov.), Rom. 49/H3
Călăraşi, Rom. 49/H3
Calasparra, Sp. 44/E3
Calatayud, Sp. 44/E2
Calatorao, Sp. 44/E2
Calauag, Phil. 79/D5
Calaveras (lake), Tx, US 137/U21
Calaveras (res.), Ca, US 135/L12
Calayan, Phil. 79/D4
Calayan (isl.), Phil. 116/B3
Calbayog, Phil. 81/F1
Calberlah, Ger. 51/H4
Calbuco, Chile 158/B4
Calca, Peru 156/D4
Calcanhar, Ponta do (pt.), Braz. 154/D2
Calcasieu (riv.), La, US 129/J5
Calceta, Ecu. 152/A5
Calci, It. 58/D5
Calcinate, It. 58/C1
Calcinato, It. 58/D2
Calcinelli, It. 59/F5
Calcio, It. 58/C2
Calçoene, Braz. 151/H3
Calcutta, India 85/G4
Calcutta (int'l arpt.), India 85/G4
Calcutta, Sur. 153/H3
Caldaro (Kaltern), It. 43/J3
Caldas, Braz. 211/G6
Caldas (dept.), Col. 152/C3
Caldas da Rainha, Port. 44/A3
Caldas Novas, Braz. 155/B1
Calden, Ger. 51/G6
Calder (mt.), Ak, US 134/M4
Calder (riv.), Eng, UK 35/F4
Caldera de Taburiente, PN de la, Sp. 98/A3
Calderara di Reno, It. 59/E3
Calderas, Ven. 152/D2
Caldercruix, Sc, UK 36/C5
Caldes de Montbui, Sp. 45/L6
Caldew (riv.), Eng, UK 35/F2
Caldicot, Wal, UK 32/D3
Caldiero, It. 59/E2
Çaldıran, Turk. 63/G5
Caldonazzo, It. 57/H6
Caldono, Col. 152/B4
Caldwell, Tx, US 129/H5
Caldwell, NJ, US 139/H8
Caldwell, Wi, US 135/P14
Caldy (isl.), Eng, UK 32/B3
Caledon (riv.), SAfr. 106/D3
Caledon, On, Can. 131/Q8
Caledon, SAfr. 106/L11
Caledon, NI, UK 34/B3
Caledonia (hills), NB, Can. 131/H2
Caledonia, Wi, US 135/P14
Caledonian (canal), Sc, UK 36/B2
Calella, Sp. 45/G2
Calen, Austl. 114/C3
Calenzana, Fr. 46/A1
Calenzano, It. 59/E5
Calera de Tango, Chile 158/N8
Calestano, It. 58/D3
Caleta de Campos, Mex. 142/E5
Caleta Olivia, Arg. 158/D5
Calexico, Ca, US 128/D4
Calf of Man (isl.), IM, UK 34/C3
Calf, The (peak), Eng, UK 35/F3
Calgary (int'l arpt.), Ab, Can. 126/E3
Calgary, Ab, Can. 126/E3
Calheta, Azor., Port. 45/S12
Calhoun, Ga, US 133/G3
Calhoun, Ky, US 130/C4

Casa – Chapa

179

Chape – Ciadî

Chapel Hill, NC, US 133/J3
Chapel Ness (pt.), Sc, UK 36/D4
Chapelfell Top (peak), Eng, UK 35/F2
Chapelle-lez-Herlaimont, Belg. 53/D3
Chapeltown, Eng, UK 35/G5
Chaplain (lake), Wa, US 135/D2
Chapleau, On, Can. 130/D2
Chaplin, Sk, Can. 126/G3
Chāpra, India 85/E3
Char (well), Mrta. 98/B5
Chara (riv.), Rus. 65/M4
Charambirá (pt.), Col. 152/B3
Charaña, Bol. 156/D5
Charandra (riv.), Gre. 47/N8
Charata, Arg. 157/D2
Charcas, Mex. 143/E4
Charcot (isl.), Ant. 160/U
Chardonnière, Haiti 145/H2
Charente (riv.), Fr. 42/C4
Chari (riv.), Chad 93/D3
Chārīkār, Afg. 89/J1
Chariton (riv.), Ia,Mo, US 129/J2
Charity, Guy. 153/G3
Chärjew, Trkm. 87/D5
Charkhāri, India 84/B3
Charkhi Dādri, India 86/D5
Charlemagne, Qu, Can. 131/P6
Charlemont, NI, UK 34/B3
Charleroi, Belg. 53/D3
Charleroi à Bruxelles, Canal de (canal), Belg. 53/D2
Charles (peak), Austl. 112/D5
Charles (mt.), Austl. 112/C3
Charles (isl.), Qu, Can. 123/J2
Charles City, Ia, US 127/K5
Charles de Gaulle (int'l arpt.), Fr. 30/K4
Charleston, Nv, US 126/E5
Charleston, Ms, US 129/K4
Charleston (cap.), WV, US 130/D4
Charleston, SC, US 133/J3
Charleston, Ut, US 137/L13
Charlestown, StK. 141/N8
Charlestown, Md, US 138/C4
Charleville, Austl. 114/B4
Charleville-Mézières, Fr. 53/D4
Charlevoix, Mi, US 130/C2
Charlotte (lake), BC, Can. 126/B2
Charlotte, Mi, US 130/C3
Charlotte, NC, US 133/H3
Charlotte Amalie, USVI 141/M8
Charlotte/Douglas (int'l arpt.), NC, US 133/H3
Charlottenberg, Swe. 38/E2
Charlottenburg, Ger. 40/Q6
Charlottetown (cap.), PE, Can. 131/J2
Charlton, Austl. 115/B3
Charlton (isl.), On, Can. 123/H3
Charlton Kings, Eng, UK 32/D3
Charly, Fr. 52/C6
Charmes (res.), Fr. 56/B2
Charmes, Fr. 56/C1
Charmey, Swi. 56/D4
Charnay-lès-Mâcon, Fr. 42/F3
Charny, Fr. 30/L5
Charny-sur-Meuse, Fr. 53/E5
Charolais, Monts du (mts.), Fr. 42/F3
Charouine, Alg. 99/E3
Charquemont, Fr. 56/C3
Chars, Fr. 30/H4
Chārsadda, Pak. 86/A2
Charters Towers, Austl. 114/B3
Charthāwāl, India 86/D5
Chartres, Fr. 42/D2
Chās, India 85/F4
Chaschauna (peak), Swi. 57/G4
Chascomús, Arg. 158/F2
Chase, BC, Can. 126/D3
Chasŏng, NKor. 73/D2
Chassezac (riv.), Fr. 42/F4
Chastre-Villeroux-Blanmont, Belg. 53/D2
Chatanika, Ak, US 134/J2
Château Bougon (int'l arpt.), Fr. 42/C3
Chateau de Versailles, Fr. 30/J5
Château-d'Olonne, Fr. 42/C3
Château-du-Loir, Fr. 42/D3
Château-Porcien, Fr. 53/D4
Château-Renault, Fr. 42/D3
Château-Salins, Fr. 53/F6
Château-Thierry, Fr. 52/C5
Châteaubriant, Fr. 42/C3
Châteaudun, Fr. 42/D2
Châteauguay, Qu, Can. 131/N7
Châteauneuf-sur-Charente, Fr. 42/C4
Châteaurenard, Fr. 42/F5
Châteauroux, Fr. 42/D3
Châteauvillain, Fr. 56/A1
Châtel-Saint-Denis, Swi. 56/C4
Châtelaillon-Plage, Fr. 42/C3
Châtelet, Belg. 53/D3
Châtellerault, Fr. 42/D3
Châtenay-Malabry, Fr. 30/J5
Châtenois, Fr. 56/B1
Châtenois-les-Forges, Fr. 56/C2
Chatfield (res.), Co, US 137/B3
Chatham, On, Can. 130/D3
Chatham, Eng, UK 33/G4
Chatham (isls.), Chile 159/B6
Chatham, NJ, US 139/H9
Châtillon, It. 43/G4
Châtillon, Fr. 30/J5
Châtillon-sur-Chalaronne, Fr. 56/A5
Châtillon-sur-Marne, Fr. 52/C5
Châtillon-sur-Seine, Fr. 42/F3
Chatkal (riv.), Kyr. 87/F4
Chatou, Fr. 30/J5
Chatra, India 85/E3
Chatrapur, India 82/E4
Châtres, Fr. 30/L5
Chatsworth (res.), Ca, US 136/B2
Chatsworth, NJ, US 138/D4
Chattahoochee (riv.),US 133/G4
Chattahoochee, Fl, US 133/G4
Chattanooga, Tn, US 133/G3
Chatteris, Eng, UK 33/G2
Chau Doc, Viet. 78/D4
Chaucey, Îles (isls.), Fr. 42/C2
Chauconin-Neufmontiers, Fr. 30/L5
Chaudfontaine, Belg. 53/E2
Chaudière (riv.), Qu, Can. 131/G2
Chauk, Myan. 83/F3
Chaukan (pass), India 83/G2
Chaumes-en-Brie, Fr. 30/L5
Chaumont, Fr. 56/B1
Chaumont-en-Vexin, Fr. 52/A5
Chaunskaya (bay), Rus. 65/T3
Chauny, Fr. 52/C4
Chaussin, Fr. 56/B4
Chaussy, Fr. 30/H4
Chautauqua (lake), NY, US 130/E3
Chautauqua, Il, US 137/G8
Chauvigny, Fr. 42/D3
Chaval, Braz. 154/B1
Chavanoz, Fr. 56/B6
Chaves, Port. 44/B2
Chavín de Huantar (ruin), Peru 156/B3
Chaviña, Peru 156/C4
Chavinillo, Peru 156/B3
Chavornay, Swi. 56/C4
Chawinda, Pak. 86/C3
Chay (riv.), Viet. 78/D1
Chayana (riv.), Bol. 150/E7
Chaykovskiy, Rus. 61/M4
Chazuta, Peru 156/B2
Cheadle, Eng, UK 35/G6
Cheaha (mtn.), Al, US 133/G3
Cheb, Czh. 55/F2
Cheboksary, Rus. 61/K4
Cheboksary (res.), Rus. 61/K4
Cheboygan, Mi, US 130/C2
Chechaouene, Mor. 100/B2
Chechaouene (prov.), Mor. 100/B2
Chechen' (isl.), Rus. 63/H3
Chechnya (aut. rep.), Rus. 64/Q6
Chech'ŏn, SKor. 73/E4
Checotah, Ok, US 129/J4
Chedabucto (bay), NS, Can. 131/J2
Cheduba (isl.), Myan. 83/F4
Cheektowaga, NY, US 131/S10
Cheepash (riv.), On, Can. 130/D1
Cheepay (riv.), On, Can. 130/D1
Chefornak, Ak, US 134/F3
Chegutu, Zim. 105/F4
Chehalis, Wa, US 126/C4
Cheïkh (well), Alg. 99/F3
Cheju, SKor. 71/N5
Cheju (str.), SKor. 71/N5
Cheju (isl.), SKor. 71/N5
Cheka (peak), Rus. 87/C2
Chelan, Wa, US 126/C4
Chelan (lake), Wa, US 126/C4
Chelghoum El Aïd, Alg. 100/J4
Chelles, Fr. 30/K5
Chełm (prov.), Pol. 41/M3
Chełm, Pol. 41/M3
Chełmno, Pol. 41/K2
Chelmsford, Eng, UK 33/G3
Chełmża, Pol. 41/K2
Cheltenham, Eng, UK 32/D3
Chelva, Sp. 45/E3
Chelyabinsk (int'l arpt.), Rus. 61/P5
Chelyabinsk, Rus. 61/P5
Chelyabinskaya (obl.), Rus. 87/D2
Chelyuskina (cape), Rus. 65/L2
Chemaïa, Mor. 98/C2
Chemax, Mex. 144/E1
Chemnitz, Ger. 40/G3
Chen (riv.), China 79/A2
Chena Hot Springs, Ak, US 134/J2
Chenāb (riv.), Pak. 89/K2
Chenachane (well), Alg. 98/D4
Cheney, Wa, US 126/D4
Cheng'anpu, China 72/C3
Chengbu Miaozu Zizhixian, China 83/K2
Chengde, China 72/D2
Chengdu, China 70/H5
Chengkou, China 70/J5
Chengmai, China 83/J4
Chengshan Jiao (cape), China 73/B4
Chengwu, China 72/C4
Cheniménil, Fr. 56/C1
Chennai (Madras), India 82/D5
Chennevières-lès-Louvres, Fr. 30/K4
Chenôve, Fr. 56/A3
Chenxi, China 83/K2
Chenzhou, China 83/K2
Chep Lak Kok (int'l arpt.), China 71/T10
Chepelare, Bul. 47/J2
Chepén, Peru 156/B2
Chepes, Arg. 157/C3
Chépica, Chile 158/C2
Chepigana, Pan. 152/B2
Chepo, Pan. 152/B2
Chepstow, Wal, UK 32/D3
Cheptsa (riv.), Rus. 61/M4
Cher (riv.), Fr. 42/E3
Chéran (riv.), Fr. 56/C6
Cherasco, It. 58/A3
Cherāt, Pak. 86/A3
Cheraw, SC, US 133/J3
Cherbourg, Fr. 42/C2
Cherbourg, Austl. 114/C4
Cherchell, Alg. 100/G4
Cherepovets, Rus. 60/H4
Cherfi, Oued (riv.), Alg. 100/K6
Cheria, Alg. 100/K7
Cherkas'ka (obl.), Ukr. 62/D2
Cherkasy, Ukr. 62/E2
Cherkessk, Rus. 63/G3
Chermignon, Swi. 56/D5
Chernaya (riv.), Rus. 61/N1
Cherni Lom (riv.), Bul. 49/H4
Cherni Vrŭkh (peak), Bul. 47/H1
Chernihiv, Ukr. 62/D2
Chernihivs'ka (obl.), Ukr. 62/D2
Chernivets'ka (obl.), Ukr. 62/C2
Chernivtsi, Ukr. 49/G1
Chernushka, Rus. 61/N4
Cherokee, Ok, US 129/H3
Cherry Creek (dam), Co, US 137/C3
Cherry Creek (lake), Co, US 137/C3
Cherry Hill, Md, US 138/C4
Cherry Hill, NJ, US 138/C4
Cherry Valley, Ca, US 136/D3
Cherski (range), Rus. 67/P3
Chertsey, Eng, UK 30/B2
Cherven Bryag, Bul. 49/G4
Chervonohrad, Ukr. 62/C2
Cherwell (riv.), Eng, UK 33/E3
Chesaning, Mi, US 130/C3
Chesapeake (bay), US 130/E4
Chesapeake and Delaware (canal), De,Md, US 138/C4
Chesapeake Bay Maritime Museum, Md, US 138/B6
Chesapeake City, Md, US 138/C4
Chesham, Eng, UK 33/F3
Cheshire (co.), Eng, UK 35/F5
Cheshire (plain), Eng, UK 35/F5
Cheshskaya (bay), Rus. 64/E3
Cheshunt, Eng, UK 30/C1
Chesilhurst, NJ, US 138/D4
Chester, Mt, US 126/F3
Chester, Ca, US 126/C5
Chester, SC, US 133/H3
Chester, Pa, US 138/C4
Chester, NJ, US 138/C2
Chester (co.), Pa, US 138/C4
Chester (riv.), Md, US 138/B5
Chester, Eng, UK 35/F5
Chester Heights, Pa, US 138/C4
Chester-le-Street, Eng, UK 35/G2
Chester Morse (lake), Wa, US 135/D3
Chesterfield, Eng, UK 35/G5
Chesterfield, Mo, US 137/F8
Chesterfield (isls.), NCal. 116/E6
Chesterfield (inlet), Nun., Can. 122/G2
Chesterfield Inlet, Nun., Can. 122/G2
Chesterfield, Nosy (isl.), Madg. 107/G7
Chesterton (range), Austl. 114/B4
Chestertown, Md, US 138/B5
Chesuncook (lake), Me, US 131/G2
Cheswold, De, US 138/C5
Chetumal (bay), Mex. 140/D4
Chetumal, Mex. 144/D2
Chetwynd, BC, Can. 126/C2
Cheung Chau (isl.), China 71/T11
Chevak, Ak, US 134/E3
Cheval Blanc (pt.), Haiti 145/H2
Chevigny-Saint-Sauveur, Fr. 56/B3
Cheviot (hills), Sc, UK 36/D6
Cheviot, The (peak), Eng, UK 36/D6
Chevreuse, Fr. 30/J5
Chevry-Cossigny, Fr. 30/K5
Chew (riv.), Eng, UK 32/D4
Chew Valley (lake), Eng, UK 32/D4
Chewelah, Wa, US 126/D3
Chexbres, Swi. 56/C5
Cheyenne (riv.), SD,Wy, US 127/H5
Cheyenne (cap.), Wy, US 127/G5
Cheyenne, Ok, US 129/H4
Cheyenne Wells, Co, US 129/G3
Cheyres, Swi. 56/C4
Chhabra, India 84/A3
Chhaprauli, India 86/D5
Chhāta, India 84/A2
Chhatarpur, India 84/B3
Chhibrāmau, India 84/B2
Chhindwāra, India 84/B4
Chi (riv.), Thai. 83/H4
Chiai, Tai. 79/D3
Ch'iak-san NP, SKor. 73/E4
Chiampo, It. 59/E1
Chianciano Terme, It. 43/J5
Chiang Kai Shek (int'l arpt.), Tai. 79/D2
Chiang Mai, Thai. 83/G4
Chiang Rai, Thai. 83/G4
Chianti (reg.), It. 59/E5
Chianti, Monti del (mts.), It. 59/E5
Chiapa de Corzo, Mex. 144/C2
Chiapas (state), Mex. 140/C4
Chiappa (pt.), It. 58/C4
Chiaravalle, It. 59/G5
Chiari, It. 58/C1
Chiasso, Swi. 57/F6
Chiat'ura, Geo. 63/G4
Chiautempan, Mex. 143/L7
Chiautla, Mex. 143/R9
Chiautla de Tapia, Mex. 144/B2
Chiavari, It. 58/C4
Chiavenna, It. 57/F5
Chiba, Japan 75/G3
Chibougamau, Qu, Can. 130/F1
Chibougamau (riv.), Qu, Can. 130/F1
Chibougamau (lake), Qu, Can. 130/F1
Chibukak (pt.), Ak, US 134/D3
Chibuto, Moz. 105/F5
Chicago, Il, US 127/M5
Chicago Heights, Il, US 135/Q16
Chicago Midway (int'l arpt.), Il, US 129/L2
Chicago, North Branch (riv.), Il, US 135/Q15
Chicago-O'Hare (int'l arpt.), Il, US 127/M5
Chicago Ridge, Il, US 135/Q16
Chicago Sanitary and Ship Canal, Il, US 135/P16
Chicama, Peru 156/B2
Chichagof (isl.), Ak, US 122/C3
Chichaoua, Mor. 98/C3
Chīchāwatni, Pak. 86/B4
Chichén Itzá (ruin), Mex. 144/D1
Chicheng, China 71/L3
Chichester (range), Austl. 109/A3
Chichester, Eng, UK 33/F5
Chichibu, Japan 75/F3
Chichicastenango, Guat. 144/D3
Chichigalpa, Nic. 144/E3
Chichihualco, Mex. 143/F5
Chichiriviche, Ven. 152/D2
Chichishima (isls.), Japan 116/D2
Chickaloon, Ak, US 134/J3
Chickamauga (lake), Tn, US 133/G3
Chickasaw Nat'l Rec. Area, Ok, US 129/H4
Chickasha, Ok, US 129/H4
Chicla, Peru 156/B3
Chiclana de la Frontera, Sp. 44/B4
Chiclayo, Peru 156/B2
Chico, Ca, US 128/B3
Chico (riv.), Arg. 147/B7
Chicoloapan, Mex. 143/R10
Chicomostoc (ruin), Mex. 142/E4
Chicomuselo, Mex. 144/C3
Chiconcuac, Mex. 143/R9
Chicontepec de Tejeda, Mex. 144/B1
Chicopee, Ma, US 131/F3
Chicoutimi, Qu, Can. 131/G1
Chicualacuala, Moz. 105/F5
Chidley (cape), Nf, Can. 123/K2
Chido, SKor. 73/D5
Chiefland, Fl, US 133/H4
Chiemsee (lake), Ger. 43/K3
Chieo Lan (res.), Thai. 83/G6
Chieri, It. 58/A2
Chierry, Fr. 52/C5
Chiers (riv.), Fr. 53/E5
Chiesa in Valmalenco, It. 57/F5
Chiese (riv.), It. 43/J3
Chieti, It. 46/D1
Chietla, Mex. 143/L8
Chièvres, Belg. 52/C2
Chifeng, China 71/L3
Chifre, Serra do (mts.), Braz. 151/K7
Chigasaki, Japan 75/F3
Chiginagak (mt.), Ak, US 134/G4
Chignahuapan, Mex. 143/L7
Chignecto (bay), NB,NS, Can. 131/H2
Chignik, Ak, US 134/G4
Chignik Lake, Ak, US 134/G4
Chigorodó, Col. 152/B3
Chigu (lake), China 85/H1
Chigwell, Eng, UK 30/D2
Chihayaakasaka, Japan 77/J7
Chihuahua, Mex. 132/B4
Chihuahua (state), Mex. 142/D2
Chikaskia (riv.), Ks,Ok, US 129/H3
Chikballāpur, India 82/C5
Chikhli, India 89/L4
Chikmagalūr, India 89/L6
Chikoy (riv.), Rus. 65/L5
Chikugo (riv.), Japan 74/B4
Chikuma (riv.), Japan 75/F2
Chilac, Mex. 143/M8
Chilaw, SrL. 82/C6
Chilbo-san (peak), NKor. 73/E2
Chilca, Peru 156/B4
Chilcotin (riv.), BC, Can. 122/D3
Childers, Austl. 114/D4
Childersburg, Al, US 133/G3
Childress, Tx, US 129/G4
Chile (ctry.) 157/B3
Chile Chico, Chile 158/C5
Chile, Monte el (peak), Hon. 144/E3
Chilecito, Arg. 157/C2
Chilete, Peru 156/B2
Ch'ilgap-san NP, SKor. 73/D4
Chililabombwe, Zam. 105/E3
Chilka (lake), India 82/E4
Chilko (lake), BC, Can. 122/D3
Chilkoot (pass), Can.,US 134/L4
Chilkoot (pass), Ak, US 134/L3
Chilla Well Abor. Land, Austl. 113/F2
Chillán, Chile 158/B3
Chillanes, Ecu. 156/B1
Chillicothe, Il, US 127/L5
Chilliwack, BC, Can. 126/C3
Chillon, Swi. 56/C5
Chilly-Mazarin, Fr. 30/J5
Chiloé (isl.), Chile 147/B7
Chiloé, PN, Chile 158/B4
Chiloquin, Or, US 126/C5
Chilpancingo de los Bravos, Mex. 143/F5
Chiltern (hills), Eng, UK 33/E3
Chiltern Hundreds (reg.), Eng, UK 30/A2
Chilung La (pass), India 86/D3
Chilwa (lake), Malw. 105/G4
Chimacum, Wa, US 135/B1
Chimalhuacán, Mex. 143/R10
Chimaliro (hill), Malw. 104/B5
Chimaltenango, Guat. 144/D3
Chimán, Pan. 152/B2
Chimanimani, Zim. 105/F4
Chimantá-Tepuí (peak), Ven. 153/F3
Chimay, Belg. 53/D3
Chimbay, Uzb. 87/C4
Chimborazo (dept.), Ecu. 152/B5
Chimborazo (vol.), Ecu. 152/B5
Chimbote, Peru 156/B3
Chimichaqua, Col. 152/C2
Chimoio, Moz. 105/F4
Chimtarga (peak), Taj. 87/E5
Chin (state), Myan. 70/F7
China, Mex. 143/F3
China, Mex. 144/D2
China (ctry.) 70/G4
Chinácota, Col. 152/C3
Chinan, SKor. 73/D5
Chinandega, Nic. 144/E3
Chinati (mts.), Tx, US 132/B4
Chincha Alta, Peru 156/B4
Chinchaga (riv.), Ab,BC, Can. 122/E3
Chinchilla, Sp. 44/E3
Chinchilla, Austl. 114/C4
Chinch'ŏn, SKor. 73/D4
Chinchón, Sp. 44/D2
Chincoteague, Va, US 130/F4
Chinde, Moz. 105/G4
Chindo, SKor. 73/D5
Chindrieux, Fr. 56/B6
Chindu, China 70/G4
Chindwin (riv.), Myan. 70/F7
Chingaza, PN, Col. 152/C3
Chingleput, India 82/C5
Chingola, Zam. 105/E3
Chinguetti, Dhar de (cliff), Mrta. 98/B5
Chinhae, SKor. 73/E5
Chinhoyi, Zim. 105/F4
Chiniak (cape), Ak, US 134/H4
Chiniot, Pak. 86/B4
Chinit (riv.), Camb. 78/D3
Chinju, SKor. 73/E5
Chinko (riv.), CAfr. 97/K6
Chinle, Az, US 128/E3
Chinnor, Eng, UK 33/F3
Chino, Japan 75/F3
Chino, Ca, US 136/C2
Chino (hills), Ca, US 136/G8
Chinook, Mt, US 126/F3
Chinsali, Zam. 104/B5
Chinú, Col. 152/C2
Chiny, Belg. 53/E4
Chinyŏng, SKor. 73/E5
Chioggia, It. 59/F2
Chipata, Zam. 105/F3
Chipatá, Col. 152/C3
Chiping, China 72/D3
Chipiona, Sp. 44/B4
Chipley, Fl, US 133/G4
Chiplūn, India 89/K5
Chippenham, Eng, UK 32/D4
Chippewa (riv.), Wi, US 127/L4
Chippewa (co.), Wi, US 127/L4
Chipping Ongar, Eng, UK 30/D1
Chiprovtsi, Bul. 48/F4
Chiputneticook (lakes), US,Can. 131/H2
Chiquián, Peru 156/B3
Chiquimula, Guat. 144/D3
Chiquimulilla, Guat. 144/D3
Chiquinquirá, Col. 150/D2
Chiquita (sea), Arg. 147/C6
Chīrāla, India 82/D4
Chirāwa, India 86/C5
Chirchiq, Uzb. 87/E4
Chīrgaon, India 84/B3
Chiri-san (peak), SKor. 73/D5
Chiri-san NP, SKor. 73/D5
Chiricahua Nat'l Mon., Az, US 142/C1
Chiriguaná, Col. 152/C2
Chirikof (isl.), Ak, US 134/G4
Chirinos, Peru 156/B2
Chirip (peak), Rus. 76/E1
Chiripa (peak), Nic. 145/E4
Chiriquí (lag.), Pan. 145/F4
Chiriquí, Golfo de (gulf), Pan. 150/B2
Chirkunda, India 85/F4
Chirnside, Sc, UK 36/D5
Chironico, Swi. 57/E5
Chirpan, Bul. 47/J1
Chirripó (mtn.), CR 145/F4
Chirripó, PN, CR 140/E6
Chiryu, Japan 77/M6
Chisana, Ak, US 134/K3
Chisasibi (Fort-George), Qu, Can. 123/J3
Chisholm, Mn, US 130/A2
Chishtiān Mandi, Pak. 86/B5
Chisimba (falls), Zam. 104/A5
Chişinău (cap.), Mol. 49/J2
Chişinău (int'l arpt.), Mol. 49/J2
Chişineu Criş, Rom. 48/E2
Chistochina, Ak, US 134/K3
Chistopol', Rus. 61/L5
Chita, Col. 152/C3
Chita (bay), Japan 77/L6
Chita, Japan 77/L6
Chita (pen.), Japan 77/L6
Chitina, Ak, US 134/K3
Chitipa, Malw. 104/B5
Chitose (int'l arpt.), Japan 76/B2
Chitose, Japan 76/B2
Chitradurga, India 82/C5
Chitrakut, India 84/C3
Chitral Gol NP, Pak. 86/A2
Chitré, Pan. 152/A3
Chittagong (pol. div.), Bang. 85/H4
Chittagong, Bang. 83/F3
Chittaranjan, India 85/F4
Chittoor, India 82/C5
Chitungwiza, Zim. 105/F4
Chiuduno, It. 58/C1
Chiuppano, It. 59/E1
Chiusa di Pesio, It. 58/A4
Chiusella (riv.), It. 58/A1
Chiusi, It. 43/J5
Chivacoa, Ven. 152/D2
Chivasso, It. 58/A2
Chivato (pt.), Mex. 142/C3
Chivay, Peru 156/D4
Chivé, Bol. 156/D4
Chivhu, Zim. 105/F4
Chivilcoy, Arg. 158/E2
Chixoy (riv.), Guat. 144/D3
Chiyoda, Japan 77/C1
Chiyoda, Japan 77/E1
Chiyokawa, Japan 77/D1
Chizela, Zam. 105/E3
Chlef (riv.), Alg. 100/F4
Chlef (prov.), Alg. 100/F4
Chlef, Alg. 100/F4
Chlum (peak), Czh. 55/H5
Chno Dearg (peak), Sc, UK 36/B3
Ch'o (isl.), NKor. 73/C3
Cho Oyu (peak), Nepal 85/F1
Chobe NP, Bots. 105/D4
Chobham, Eng, UK 30/B3
Choceň, Czh. 41/J4
Choch'iwŏn, SKor. 73/D4
Chocianów, Pol. 41/H3
Chocó (dept.), Col. 145/G5
Chocolate (mts.), Ca, US 128/D4
Chocontá, Col. 152/C3
Chocope, Peru 156/B2
Choctaw, Ok, US 137/N15
Chodavaram, India 82/D4
Chodov, Czh. 55/F2
Chodzież, Pol. 41/J2
Choele Choel, Arg. 158/D3
Chōfu, Japan 75/F3
Choiseul (isl.), Sol. 116/E5
Choisy-au-Bac, Fr. 52/B5
Choisy-le-Roi, Fr. 30/K5
Choix, Mex. 142/C3
Chojna, Pol. 41/H2
Chojnice, Pol. 38/G5
Chojnów, Pol. 41/H3
Chokai-san (peak), Japan 76/B4
Choke Canyon (res.), Tx, US 132/D4
Chola (mts.), China 70/G5
Cholet, Fr. 42/C3
Cholila, Arg. 158/C4
Chŏlla-bukto (prov.), SKor. 73/D5
Ch'ŏlla-namdo (prov.), SKor. 73/D5
Cholula de Rivadabia, Mex. 143/L7
Choluteca (riv.), Hon. 140/D5
Choluteca, Hon. 144/E3
Choma, Zam. 105/E4
Chŏmch'on, SKor. 73/E4
Chomo Lhāri (peak), Bhu. 85/G2
Chomutov, Czh. 55/G2
Chomutovka (riv.), Czh. 55/G2
Chon Buri, Thai. 78/C3
Ch'ŏnan, SKor. 73/D4
Chōnan, Japan 77/E3
Chonchi, Chile 158/B4
Ch'ŏnch'ŏn, NKor. 73/D2
Chone, Ecu. 152/A5
Ch'ŏng-yang, SKor. 73/D4
Chong'an, China 79/C2
Ch'ŏngch'ŏn (riv.), NKor. 73/D2
Ch'ŏngdo, SKor. 73/D5
Ch'ŏngjin, NKor. 73/E2
Ch'ŏngjin -si (prov.), NKor. 73/E2
Chŏngju, SKor. 73/D4
Chŏngju, SKor. 73/D5
Chŏngju, NKor. 73/C3
Chongli, China 72/C2
Chongmyo Shrine, SKor. 73/G6
Chongoyape, Peru 156/B2
Chŏngsŏn, SKor. 73/E4
Ch'ŏngsong, SKor. 74/A2
Chongyi, China 83/K2
Chongzuo, China 83/J3
Chŏnju, SKor. 73/D5
Ch'ŏnma-san (peak), SKor. 73/G6
Chonos, Archipiélago de los (arch.), Chile 158/B5
Chopan, India 84/D3
Chorcha (mtn.), Pan. 145/F4
Chorley, Eng, UK 35/F4
Chorleywood, Eng, UK 30/B2
Choroszcz, Pol. 41/M2
Chortkiv, Ukr. 62/C2
Ch'ŏrwŏn, SKor. 73/D3
Chorzele, Pol. 41/L2
Chorzów, Pol. 41/K3
Chos-Malal, Arg. 158/C3
Ch'osan, NKor. 73/C2
Chōsei, Japan 77/E3
Chōshi, Japan 75/G3
Choszczno, Pol. 41/H2
Chota, Peru 156/B2
Chota Nāgpur (plat.), India 82/D3
Choteau, Mt, US 126/E4
Chott el Rharbi (depr.), Alg. 100/D3
Chotýšanka (riv.), Czh. 55/H3
Chowagasberg (peak), Namb. 105/C6
Chowan (riv.), NC, US 133/J2
Choybalsan, Mong. 71/K2
Choyr, Mong. 70/J2
Chreïrik (well), Mrta. 98/B5
Christchurch (int'l arpt.), NZ 117/S11
Christchurch, NZ 117/S11
Christchurch (bay), Eng, UK 33/E5
Christchurch, Eng, UK 33/E5
Christian (sound), Ak, US 134/M4
Christiana, SAfr. 106/D2
Christiana, Jam. 145/G2
Christiana, De, US 138/C4
Christiana, Pa, US 138/C4
Christiansfeld, Den. 38/C4
Christiansted, USVI 141/M8
Christina (riv.), De, US 138/C5
Christmas (isl.), Austl. 67/K11
Chrudim, Czh. 41/H4
Chryston, Sc, UK 36/B5
Chrzanów, Pol. 41/K3
Chu Yang Sin (peak), Viet. 78/E3
Chuādanga, Bang. 85/G4
Chuansha, China 72/L8
Chuathbaluk, Ak, US 134/G3
Chubut (riv.), Arg. 147/C7
Chubut (prov.), Arg. 158/C4
Chucanti (peak), Pan. 152/B2
Chūgoku (mts.), Japan 74/C3
Chūgoku (prov.), Japan 74/B4
Chūhar Kāna, Pak. 86/B4
Chukai, Malay. 80/B3
Chukchi (sea), Rus. 67/T3
Chukchi (pen.), Rus. 67/T3
Chukotskiy (aut. okrug), Rus. 65/S3
Chukotskiy (cape), Rus. 134/D3
Chula Vista, Ca, US 136/C5
Ch'ulp'o, SKor. 73/D5
Chulucanas, Peru 156/A2
Chulym (riv.), Rus. 64/J4
Chuma, Bol. 156/D4
Chumerna (peak), Bul. 47/J1
Chumphon, Thai. 78/B4
Chuna (riv.), Rus. 64/K4
Chunār, India 84/D3
Ch'unch'ŏn, SKor. 73/D4
Ch'ungch'ŏng-bukto (prov.), SKor. 73/D4
Ch'ungch'ŏng-namdo (prov.), SKor. 73/D4
Ch'ungju (lake), SKor. 74/A2
Ch'ungju, SKor. 73/D4
Ch'ungman (riv.), NKor. 73/C2
Ch'ungmu, SKor. 73/E5
Chŭngsan, NKor. 73/C3
Chunhuhub, Mex. 144/D2
Chūniān, Pak. 86/B4
Chunya, Tanz. 104/B5
Chunya (riv.), Rus. 65/L3
Ch'unyang, SKor. 73/E4
Chupa, Peru 156/D4
Chupaca, Peru 156/C4
Chuquibamba, Peru 156/C4
Chuquibambilla, Peru 156/C4
Chuquicamata, Chile 157/C1
Chur, Swi. 57/F4
Churachandpur, India 83/F3
Churcampa, Peru 156/C4
Church, Eng, UK 35/F4
Church Hill, Md, US 138/C5
Churchill, Austl. 115/C3
Churchill (lake), Sk, Can. 122/F3
Churchill, Mb, Can. 122/G3
Churchill (riv.), Mb,Sk, Can. 122/F3
Churchill (cape), Mb, Can. 122/G3
Churchill (peak), BC, Can. 122/D3
Churchill Falls, Nf, Can. 123/K3
Churchill NP, Austl. 115/G5
Churchville, Md, US 138/B4
Churia Ghats (mts.), Nepal 85/E2
Churín, Peru 156/B3
Churnet (riv.), Eng, UK 35/G5
Churu, India 86/C5
Churuguara, Ven. 152/D2
Churumuco de Morelos, Mex. 143/E5
Churwalden, Swi. 57/F4
Chuschi, Peru 156/C4
Chuska (mts.), Az,NM, US 128/E3
Chusovaya (riv.), Rus. 61/N4
Chusovoy, Rus. 61/N4
Chutung, Tai. 79/D3
Chuvashiya (aut. rep.), Rus. 64/Q6
Chuwang-san NP, SKor. 74/A2
Chuxiong, China 83/H2
Chüy (obl.), Kyr. 87/F4
Chuzhou, China 71/L5
Chūzu, Japan 77/K5
Ci Xian, China 72/C3
Ciadîr-Lunga, Mol. 49/J2

180

Ciami – Congu

Ciamis, Indo. 80/C5
Ciampino (int'l arpt.), It. 46/C2
Ciampino, It. 46/C2
Cianjur, Indo. 80/C5
Cibolo, Tx, US 137/U20
Cicagna, It. 58/C4
Cicero, Il, US 130/C3
Cícero Dantas, Braz. 154/C3
Ćićevac, Yugo. 48/E4
Cide, Turk. 62/E4
Ciechanow (prov.), Pol. 41/L2
Ciechanów, Pol. 41/L2
Ciechocinek, Pol. 41/K2
Ciego de Ávila, Cuba 145/G1
Ciénaga, Col. 152/C2
Ciénaga de Oro, Col. 152/C2
Cienfuegos, Cuba 145/F1
Cieplice Śląskie Zdrój, Pol. 41/H3
Cieszyn, Pol. 41/K4
Cieza, Sp. 44/E3
Çifteler, Turk. 62/D5
Cifuentes, Sp. 44/D2
Cifuentes, Cuba 145/F1
Cigánd, Hun. 41/L4
Cigliano, It. 58/B2
Cigüela (riv.), Sp. 44/D3
Cihanbeyli, Turk. 90/C2
Cihuatlán, Mex. 142/D5
Cijara, Embalse de (res.), Sp. 44/C3
Cijulang, Indo. 80/C5
Cilacap, Indo. 80/C5
Cilavegna, It. 58/B2
Çıldır (lake), Turk. 63/G4
Cilfaesty (peak), Wal, UK 32/C2
Cili, China 79/B2
Cilleros, Sp. 44/B2
Cima della Laurasca (peak), It. 57/E5
Cima de'Piazzi (peak), It. 57/G5
Cima la Casina (peak), It. 57/G4
Cimarron (range), NM, US 132/B2
Cimarron (riv.), Ks,Ok, US 124/G4
Cime du Cheiron (peak), Fr. 43/G5
Cime du Diable (peak), Fr. 43/G4
Cimone (peak), It. 59/D4
Cîmpeni, Rom. 49/F2
Cîmpia Turzii, Rom. 49/F2
Cîmpina, Rom. 49/G3
Cîmpulung, Rom. 49/G3
Cîmpulung Moldovenesc, Rom. 49/G2
Çınar, Turk. 90/E2
Çınarcık, Turk. 49/J5
Cinaruco (riv.), Ven. 152/D3
Cinca (riv.), Sp. 45/F1
Cincar (peak), Bosn. 48/C4
Cincinnati, Oh, US 130/C4
Cinco Saltos, Arg. 158/C3
Cîndrelu (peak), Rom. 49/F3
Çine, Turk. 90/B2
Ciney, Belg. 53/E3
Cingia de'Botti, It. 58/D2
Cingoli, It. 59/G6
Cinisello Balsamo, It. 58/C1
Cinnaminson, NJ, US 138/D4
Cintalapa de Figueroa, Mex. 144/C2
Cinto (peak), Fr. 46/A1
Cinto Caomaggiore, It. 59/F1
Cintruénigo, Sp. 44/E1
Čiovo (isl.), Cro. 48/C4
Cipó, Braz. 154/C3
Cipolletti, Arg. 158/D3
Circeo, PN del, It. 46/C2
Circle, Ak, US 134/K2
Circle, Mt, US 127/G4
Circle Hot Springs, Ak, US 134/K2
Cirebon, Indo. 80/C5
Cirencester, Eng, UK 32/E3
Cires-lès-Mello, Fr. 52/B5
Cirò Marina, It. 47/E3
Ciron (riv.), Fr. 42/C4
Ciserano, It. 58/C1
Cisnădie, Rom. 49/G3
Cisneros, Col. 152/C3
Cisnes (riv.), Chile 158/B5
Cisse (riv.), Fr. 42/D3
Cisterna di Latina, It. 46/C2
Cistierna, Sp. 44/C1
Citlaltépetl (vol.),Mex. 143/M7
Citrus Heights, Ca, US 128/B3
Citrusdal, SAfr. 106/L10
Città del Vaticano (Vatican City) (cap.), VatC. 46/C2
Città di Castello, It. 59/F6
Citta di Torino (int'l arpt.), It. 43/G4
Cittadella, It. 59/E1
Cittanova, It. 46/E3
Cittiglio, It. 57/E6
City (isl.), NY, US 139/K8
City (int'l arpt.), NI, UK 34/C2
Ciudad Acuña, Mex. 129/G5
Ciudad Altamirano, Mex. 143/E5
Ciudad Bolívar, Ven. 153/F2
Ciudad Bolivia, Ven. 152/D2
Ciudad Camargo, Mex. 142/D3
Ciudad Constitución, Mex. 142/C3
Ciudad Cortés, CR 145/F4
Ciudad Cuauhtémoc, Mex. 144/B1
Ciudad de Dolores Hidalgo, Mex. 143/E4
Ciudad de México (Mexico) (cap.), Mex. 143/Q10
Ciudad de Nutrias, Ven. 152/D2
Ciudad de Río Grande, Mex. 142/E4
Ciudad del Carmen, Mex. 144/D2
Ciudad del Maíz, Mex. 143/F4
Ciudad Delicias, Mex. 132/B4
Ciudad Fernández, Mex. 143/E4
Ciudad Frontera, Mex. 132/C5
Ciudad Guayana, Ven. 153/F2
Ciudad Guzmán, Mex. 142/E5
Ciudad Hidalgo, Mex. 143/E5
Ciudad Hidalgo, Mex. 144/C3
Ciudad Insurgentes, Mex. 142/C3
Ciudad Ixtepec, Mex. 144/C2
Ciudad Juárez, Mex. 128/F5
Ciudad Lerdo, Mex. 142/E3
Ciudad Madero, Mex. 144/B1
Ciudad Mante, Mex. 143/F4
Ciudad Mendoza, Mex. 143/M8
Ciudad Miguel Alemán, Mex. 132/D5
Ciudad Obregón, Mex. 142/C3
Ciudad Ojeda, Ven. 152/D2
Ciudad Pemex, Mex. 144/C2
Ciudad Piar, Ven. 153/F3
Ciudad, PN de la, Mex. 142/D4
Ciudad Real, Sp. 44/D3
Ciudad Rodrigo, Sp. 44/B2
Ciudad Serdán, Mex. 143/M8
Ciudad Valles, Mex. 144/B1
Ciudad Victoria, Mex. 143/F4
Ciutadella de Menorca, Sp. 45/G3
Civa Burnu (pt.), Turk. 62/F4
Civate, It. 58/C1
Civezzano, It. 57/H5
Cividale del Friuli, It. 43/K3
Cividate Camuno, It. 57/G6
Civita Castellana, It. 46/C1
Civitavecchia, It. 46/B1
Civray, Fr. 42/D3
Çivril, Turk. 90/B2
Cixi, China 72/L9
Cize, Fr. 56/B4
Cizre, Turk. 90/E2
Cizre (dam), Turk. 90/E2
Cizur, Sp. 44/E1
Clackmannan, Sc, UK 36/C4
Clackmannan, (pol. reg.), Sc, UK 36/C4
Claerwen (res.), Wal, UK 32/C2
Claiborne, Md, US 138/B6
Clain (riv.), Fr. 42/D3
Clair Engle (lake), Ca, US 128/B2
Claire (lake), Ab, Can. 122/E3
Clairefontaine-en-Yvelines, Fr. 30/H6
Clairvaux-les-Lacs, Fr. 56/B4
Claise (riv.), Fr. 42/D3
Clallam (co.), Wa, US 135/A2
Clamart, Fr. 30/J5
Clamecy, Fr. 42/E3
Clane, Ire. 31/Q10
Clanton, Al, US 133/G3
Clanwilliam, SAfr. 106/B4
Clara, Ire. 31/Q10
Clara (pt.), Arg. 158/D4
Clare, Mi, US 130/C3
Clare, Ks, US 137/D6
Clare (riv.), Ire. 31/P10
Clare, Austl. 113/H5
Clare (isl.), Ire. 30/N10
Claremont, NH, US 131/F3
Claremont, Ca, US 136/C2
Claremore, Ok, US 129/J3
Claremorris, Ire. 31/P10
Clarence, NZ 117/S11
Clarence (riv.), NZ 117/S11
Clarence, NY, US 131/S9
Clarence (pt.), Nun., Can. 123/T7
Clarence Town, Bahm. 141/G3
Clarendon, Tx, US 129/G4
Clarenville, Nf, Can. 131/L1
Claresholm, Ab, Can. 126/E3
Clarion (isl.), Mex. 142/B5
Clark, SD, US 127/J4
Clark, NJ, US 139/H9
Clark Fork (riv.), Mt, US 126/E3
Clark Fork (riv.), Id, US 122/E4
Clarke (isl.), Austl. 115/D4
Clarke (lake), Pa, US 138/B4
Clarks Point, Ak, US 134/G4
Clarksburg, WV, US 130/D4
Clarksburg, NJ, US 138/D3
Clarksburg, Ca, US 135/L10
Clarksdale, Ms, US 129/K4
Clarkston, Wa, US 126/D4
Clarkston, Mi, US 135/F6
Clarksville, Tx, US 129/J4
Clarksville, Ar, US 129/J4
Clarksville, Tn, US 130/C4
Claro (riv.), Braz. 151/H7
Claro, Swi. 57/F5
Clatteringshaws Loch (lake), Sc, UK 34/D1
Claudy, NI, UK 34/A2
Clausen, Ger. 53/G5
Clausthal-Zellerfeld, Ger. 51/H5
Claveria, Phil. 79/D4
Clawson, Mi, US 135/F6
Clay (co.), Mo, US 137/E5
Clay (pt.), IM, UK 34/D3
Clay Center, Ks, US 129/H3
Clay Cross-North Wingfield, Eng, UK 35/G5
Claye-Souilly, Fr. 30/L5
Claymont, De, US 138/C4
Clayton, NM, US 129/G3
Clayton, Ok, US 132/E3
Clayton, Ga, US 133/H3
Clayton, Mo, US 137/G8
Clayton, De, US 138/C5
Clayton, NJ, US 138/C4
Clayton, Ca, US 135/L11
Clayton-le-Moors, Eng, UK 35/F4
Clear (lake), Ca, US 128/B3
Clear (hills), Ab, Can. 122/E3
Clear (cape), Ire. 31/P11
Clear Fork (riv.), Tx, US 143/E1
Clear Fork Brazos (riv.), Tx, US 129/H4
Clear Lake, SD, US 127/J4
Cleare (cape), Ak, US 134/J4
Clearfield, Ut, US 137/J11
Clearwater (riv.), Mn, US 127/K4
Clearwater, BC, Can. 126/C3
Clearwater, Fl, US 133/H5
Clearwater (mts.), Id, US 124/C2
Cleburne, Tx, US 129/H4
Cleethorpes, Eng, UK 35/H4
Cleeve (hill), Eng, UK 32/D3
Cleland Rec. Area, Austl. 113/M8
Clementon, NJ, US 138/D4
Clemson, SC, US 133/H3
Cleona, Pa, US 138/B3
Cleopatra Needle (peak), Phil. 81/E1
Clermont, Austl. 114/B3
Clermont, Fr. 52/B5
Clermont-en-Argonne, Fr. 53/E5
Clermont-Ferrand, Fr. 42/E4
Clerval, Fr. 56/C3
Clervaux, Lux. 53/F3
Cles, It. 57/H5
Cleve, Austl. 113/H5
Clevedon, Eng, UK 32/D4
Cleveland, Tx, US 129/J5
Cleveland (mt.), Mt, US 126/E3
Cleveland, Ms, US 129/K4
Cleveland, Tn, US 133/G3
Cleveland, Oh, US 130/D3
Cleveland, Mo, US 137/D6
Cleveland (co.), Ok, US 137/N15
Cleveland (cape), Austl. 114/B2
Cleveland (hills), Eng, UK 35/G3
Cleveland-Hopkins (int'l arpt.), Oh, US 130/D3
Cleveland National Forest, Ca, US 136/C3
Clevelândia, Braz. 155/A3
Clew (bay), Ire. 31/P10
Clewiston, Fl, US 133/H5
Clichy, Fr. 30/J5
Clichy-sous-Bois, Fr. 30/K5
Clifden, Ire. 30/F10
Cliffside Park, NJ, US 139/K8
Cliffwood, NJ, US 139/J10
Clifton, Az, US 128/E4
Clifton, NJ, US 139/J8
Clifton Beach, Austl. 114/B2
Clifton Forge, Va, US 133/J2
Clignon (riv.), Fr. 52/C5
Clingmans (peak), NC,Tn, US 133/H3
Clinton, BC, Can. 126/C3
Clinton, Ia, US 127/L5
Clinton, Ok, US 129/H4
Clinton, Mo, US 129/J3
Clinton, Ms, US 129/K4
Clinton, La, US 129/K5
Clinton, NC, US 133/J3
Clinton, SC, US 133/H3
Clinton (co.), Mo, US 137/E5
Clinton, Ut, US 137/J11
Clinton, NJ, US 138/D2
Clinton (res.), NJ, US 138/D1
Clinton (co.), Pa, US 138/A1
Clinton, Ct, US 139/F1
Clinton, Wa, US 135/C2
Clinton, Mi, US 135/G6
Clinton (riv.), Mi, US 135/F6
Clinton-Colden (lake), NW, Can. 122/F2
Clinton, Middle Branch (riv.), Mi, US 135/G6
Clinton, North Branch (riv.), Mi, US 135/G6
Clintonville, Wi, US 130/B2
Clints Dod (hill), Sc, UK 36/D5
Clio, Mi, US 130/D3
Clitheroe, Eng, UK 35/F4
Cloates (pt.), Austl. 112/B2
Clocolan, SAfr. 106/D3
Clogherhead, Ire. 34/B4
Clonakilty, Ire. 31/P11
Cloncurry, Austl. 114/A3
Clondalkin, Ire. 34/B5
Clonmany, Ire. 34/A1
Clonmel, Ire. 31/Q10
Cloppenburg, Ger. 51/F3
Clorinda, Arg. 157/E2
Clos-Fontaine, Fr. 30/M6
Closter, NJ, US 139/K8
Cloudcroft, NM, US 132/B3
Cloudy (mtn.), Ak, US 134/G3
Cloughmills, NI, UK 34/B2
Cloverdale, Ca, US 128/B3
Clovis, NM, US 129/G4
Clovis, Ca, US 128/C3
Cluanie (lake), Sc, UK 36/A2
Cluj (co.), Rom. 49/F2
Cluj-Napoca, Rom. 49/F2
Cluses, Fr. 56/C5
Clusone, It. 57/F6
Clutha (riv.), NZ 109/G7
Clwyd (riv.), Wal, UK 35/E5
Clwyd (co.), Wal, UK 35/E5
Clwydian (range), Wal, UK 35/E5
Clyde (riv.), NS, Can. 131/H2
Clyde (riv.), Sc, UK 36/B5
Clyde, Firth of (inlet), Sc, UK 31/R8
Clyde Hill, Wa, US 135/C2
Clydesdale (valley), Sc, UK 36/C5
Clywedog (riv.), Wal, UK 32/C2
CN Tower, On, Can. 131/R8
Co Loa Citadel, Viet. 78/D1
Côa (riv.), Port. 44/B2
Coacalco, Mex. 143/Q9
Coachella, Ca, US 128/C4
Coagh, NI, UK 34/B2
Coahuayana de Hidalgo, Mex. 142/E5
Coahuila (state), Mex. 132/C5
Coahuila, Mex. 142/B1
Coalburn, Sc, UK 36/C5
Coalcomán de Matamoros, Mex. 142/E5
Coaldale, Ab, Can. 126/E3
Coaldale, Pa, US 138/C2
Coalgate, Ok, US 129/H4
Coalhurst, Ab, Can. 126/E3
Coalisland, NI, UK 34/B2
Coalville, Ut, US 128/E2
Coalville, Eng, UK 33/E1
Coaraci, Braz. 154/C4
Coari, Braz. 150/F4
Coari (riv.), Braz. 150/F5
Coasa, Peru 156/D4
Coast (mts.), Can.,US 122/C2
Coast (prov.), Kenya 104/C3
Coast (ranges), Ca, US 126/C5
Coatbridge, Sc, UK 36/B5
Coatepec, Mex. 143/N7
Coatepec Harinas, Mex. 143/K8
Coatesville, Pa, US 138/C4
Coatetelco, Mex. 143/K8
Coaticook, Qu, Can. 131/G2
Coats (isl.), Nun., Can. 123/H2
Coats Land (pol. reg.), Ant. 160/Y
Coatzacoalcos, Mex. 144/C2
Coatzingo, Mex. 143/L8
Coba (ruin), Mex. 144/E1
Coba de Serpe, Sierra de (peak), Sp. 44/B1
Cobán, Guat. 144/D3
Cobar, Austl. 115/C1
Cobb (lake), Co, US 137/C1
Cobberas (mt.), Austl. 115/D3
Cobblestone (mtn.), Ca, US 136/B1
Cobden, Austl. 115/B3
Cóbh, Ire. 31/P11
Cobham (riv.), Mb,On, Can. 127/K2
Cobija, Bol. 150/E6
Cobourg, On, Can. 130/E3
Cobquecura, Chile 158/B3
Coburg (pen.), Austl. 109/C2
Coburg (isl.), Nun., Can. 123/T7
Coburg, Ger. 54/D2
Coca, Ecu. 152/B5
Coca (riv.), Ecu. 152/B5
Cocachacra, Peru 156/D5
Cocal, Braz. 154/B1
Coccaglio, It. 58/C1
Cocentaina, Sp. 45/E3
Cochabamba, Bol. 150/E7
Coche (isl.), Ven. 153/F2
Cochem, Ger. 53/G3
Cocherel, Fr. 30/M4
Cochin, India 82/C6
Cochran, Ga, US 133/H3
Cochrane, Ab, Can. 126/E3
Cochrane, On, Can. 130/D1
Cock Cairn (peak), Sc, UK 36/D3
Cockatoo, Austl. 115/G5
Cockburn (sound), Austl. 112/K7
Cockburn (chan.), Chile 159/B7
Cockeysville, Md, US 138/B5
Cockscomb (peak), SAfr. 106/D4
Coclé del Norte, Pan. 145/F4
Coco (riv.), Hon. 140/E5
Coco, Cayo (isl.), Cuba 145/G1
Coco, Isla del (isl.), CR 150/A2
Cocoa, Fl, US 133/H4
Coconino (plat.), Az, US 128/D4
Cocoparra NP, Austl. 115/C2
Cocorocuma, Cayo (isl.), Hon. 145/F3
Côcos, Braz. 154/A4
Cocos (isls.), Austl. 67/J11
Cocotitlán, Mex. 143/R10
Cocula, Mex. 142/E4
Cod (isl.), Nf, Can. 123/K3
Codajás, Braz. 150/F4
Codegua, Chile 158/N9
Codigoro, It. 59/F3
Codlea, Rom. 49/G3
Codogno, It. 58/C2
Codsall, Eng, UK 32/D1
Coelemu, Chile 158/B3
Coelho Neto, Braz. 154/B2
Coesfeld, Ger. 51/E5
Coeur d'Alene (lake), Id, US 126/D4
Coeur d'Alene, Id, US 126/D4
Coevorden, Neth. 50/D3
Coffin Bay, Austl. 113/G5
Coffin Bay NP, Austl. 113/G5
Coffs Harbour, Austl. 115/E1
Cofre de Perote, PN, Mex. 143/M7
Coggiola, It. 58/B1
Coghinas (lake), It. 46/A2
Cognac, Fr. 42/C4
Cogoleto, It. 58/B4
Cogolin, Fr. 43/G5
Cogollo del Cengio, It. 59/E1
Cogolludo, Sp. 44/D2
Cohansey (riv.), NJ, US 138/C5
Cohuna, Austl. 115/C2
Cohunu NP, Austl. 112/L7
Coiba, Isla de (isl.), Pan. 150/B2
Coig (riv.), Arg. 157/C7
Coignières, Fr. 30/H5
Coihaique, Chile 158/B5
Coihueco, Chile 158/C3
Coimbatore, India 82/C5
Coimbra (dist.), Port. 44/A2
Coimbra, Port. 44/A2
Coín, Sp. 44/C4
Coina (riv.), Port. 45/P10
Coise (riv.), Fr. 42/F4
Cojedes (riv.), Ven. 150/E2
Cojedes (state), Ven. 152/D2
Cojimíes, Ecu. 152/A4
Cojudo Blanco (peak), Arg. 159/C5
Cojutepeque, ESal. 144/D3
Čoka, Yugo. 48/E3
Cokeville, Wy, US 126/F5
Col d'Ispéguy (pass), Fr. 42/C5
Col San Martino, It. 59/F1
Colac, Austl. 115/B3
Colares, Port. 45/P10
Colasay, Peru 156/B2
Colatina, Braz. 155/D1
Colbeck (cape), Ant. 160/P
Colbún, Chile 158/C2
Colby, Wa, US 135/B2
Colca (riv.), Peru 156/D4
Colcabamba, Peru 156/C4
Colchester, Eng, UK 33/G3
Cold Bay, Ak, US 134/F4
Cold Fell (peak), Eng, UK 35/F2
Cold Lake, Ab, Can. 126/F2
Cold Spring, Mn, US 127/K4
Cold Spring Harbor, NY, US 139/M8
Coldstream, Sc, UK 36/D5
Coldwater, Ks, US 129/H3
Coldwater, Mi, US 130/C3
Cole, Ok, US 137/M15
Cole (riv.), Eng, UK 33/E3
Coleambally, Austl. 115/C2
Coleman, Tx, US 129/H5
Çölemerik, Turk. 90/E2
Colenso, SAfr. 107/E3
Coleraine, Austl. 115/B3
Coleraine (dist.), NI, UK 34/B1
Coleraine, NI, UK 34/B1
Colesberg, SAfr. 106/D3
Colesville, Md, US 138/A5
Colfax, Wa, US 126/D4
Colgate (cape), Nun., Can. 123/S6
Colgong, India 85/F3
Colhué Huapí (lake), Arg. 158/C5
Colico, It. 57/F5
Coligny, SAfr. 106/D2
Coligny, Fr. 56/B5
Colima, Mex. 142/E5
Colima (state), Mex. 142/D5
Colima, Nevado de (peak), Mex. 142/E5
Colina, Chile 158/N8
Coliseum, Ca, US 136/F8
Coll (isl.), Sc, UK 31/Q8
Collado-Villalba, Sp. 45/N8
Collagna, It. 58/D4
Collarenebri, Austl. 115/D1
Colle di Val d'Elsa, It. 59/E6
Collecchio, It. 58/D3
College, Ak, US 134/J3
College Park, Md, US 138/B6
College Station, Tx, US 129/H5
Collegeville, Pa, US 138/C3
Collegno, It. 43/G4
Collesalvetti, It. 58/D5
Colletorto, It. 46/D2
Collie, Austl. 112/C5
Collier (bay), Austl. 109/B2
Collier (range), Austl. 112/C3
Collier Range NP, Austl. 112/C3
Collierville, Tn, US 129/K4
Colliford (res.), Eng, UK 32/B5
Collingwood, On, Can. 130/D2
Collins, Ms, US 133/F4
Collinstown (int'l arpt.), Ire. 34/B5
Collinsville, Ok, US 132/E2
Collinsville, Il, US 137/H8
Collinsville, Austl. 114/B3
Collinsville, Ca, US 135/L10
Collo, Alg. 100/K6
Collombey, Swi. 56/C5
Collon, Ire. 34/B4
Collonges, Fr. 56/B5
Colma, Ca, US 135/K11
Colmar, Fr. 56/D1
Colmar, Pa, US 138/C3
Colmberg, Ger. 54/D4
Colmenar, Sp. 44/C4
Colmenar de Oreja, Sp. 44/D2
Colmenar Viejo, Sp. 45/N8
Colmillo (cape), Chile 159/B6
Colne (riv.), Eng, UK 35/G4
Colne, Eng, UK 35/F4
Cologna Veneta, It. 59/E2
Cologne, It. 58/C1
Cologne, NJ, US 138/D5
Cologne/Bonn (int'l arpt.), Ger. 53/G2
Cologno Monzese, It. 58/C1
Colombes, Fr. 30/J5
Colombey-les-Belles, Fr. 56/B1
Colombia (ctry.) 150/D3
Colombia, Col. 152/C4
Colombier, Swi. 56/C4
Colombine (peak), It. 58/D1
Colombo, Braz. 155/B3
Colombo (cap.), SrL. 82/C6
Colomiers, Fr. 42/D5
Colomoncagua, Hon. 144/D3
Colón, Pan. 145/G4
Colón (mts.), Hon. 145/E3
Colón, Cuba 145/F1
Colón, Uru. 159/G2
Colón, Arg. 158/E2
Colonche, Ecu. 156/A1
Colonelganj, India 84/C2
Colonia, Micr. 116/C4
Colonia (dept.), Uru. 158/F2
Colonia, NJ, US 139/H9
Colonia Barón, Arg. 158/E3
Colonia del Sacramento, Uru. 159/K11
Colonia Juárez, Mex. 142/C2
Colonia Las Heras, Arg. 158/C5
Colonial Park, Pa, US 138/B3
Colonsay (isl.), Sc, UK 31/Q8
Colorado (riv.), Arg. 157/C4
Colorado, Braz. 155/B2
Colorado (peak), Arg. 159/C6
Colorado (plat.), US 128/E3
Colorado (riv.), US 128/D4
Colorado (state), US 128/F3
Colorado City, Tx, US 129/G4
Colorado Historical Museum, Co, US 137/C3
Colorado Springs, Co, US 129/F3
Colorno, It. 58/D3
Colotlán, Mex. 142/E4
Colquiri, Bol. 150/E7
Colson (pt.), Belz. 144/D2
Colstrip, Mt, US 126/G4
Colt (hill), Sc, UK 36/B6
Coltauco, Chile 158/N9
Colton, Ca, US 136/C2
Colts Neck, NJ, US 138/D3
Coluene (riv.), Braz. 147/D4
Columbe, Ecu. 156/B1
Columbia, La, US 129/J4
Columbia (plat.), US 126/C4
Columbia (cap.), SC, US 133/H3
Columbia, Tn, US 130/C5
Columbia, Ky, US 130/C4
Columbia, Ms, US 133/F4
Columbia, Il, US 137/G9
Columbia (riv.), Can.,US 126/C4
Columbia (co.), Pa, US 138/B1
Columbia, NJ, US 138/C2
Columbia, Md, US 138/B5
Columbia, Pa, US 138/B3
Columbia Falls, Mt, US 126/E3
Columbine (cape), SAfr. 106/K10
Columbus, Ne, US 127/J5
Columbus, Tx, US 129/H5
Columbus, Mt, US 126/F4
Columbus, NM, US 132/B4
Columbus, In, US 130/C4
Columbus (cap.), Oh, US 130/D4
Columbus, Ms, US 133/F3
Columbus, Ga, US 133/G3
Columbus, NJ, US 138/D3
Colunga, Sp. 44/C1
Colusa, Ca, US 128/B3
Colville (riv.), Ak, US 134/G2
Colville, Wa, US 126/D3
Colville (lake), NW, Can. 122/D2
Colvos (passg.), Wa, US 135/B3
Colwyn Bay, Wal, UK 34/E5
Comacchio, It. 59/F3
Comacchio, Valli di (lag.), It. 43/K4
Comai, China 85/H1
Comal (co.), Tx, US 137/U20
Comal, Tx, US 137/U20
Comala, Mex. 142/E5
Comalcalco, Mex. 144/C2
Comanche, Tx, US 129/H5
Comandante Luis Piedra Buena, Arg. 159/C6
Comandante Nicanor Otamendi, Arg. 158/F3
Comănești, Rom. 49/H2
Comarnic, Rom. 49/G3
Comas, Peru 156/C3
Comas, Peru 156/B3
Comayagua, Hon. 144/E3
Comayagua (mts.), Hon. 144/D3
Combapata, Peru 156/D4
Combarbalá, Chile 157/B3
Combeaufontaine, Fr. 56/B2
Comber, On, Can. 135/G7
Comber, NI, UK 34/C2
Comblain-au-Pont, Belg. 53/E3
Combloux, Fr. 56/C6
Combs-la-Ville, Fr. 30/K6
Comé, Ben. 103/F5
Comendador, DRep. 145/J2
Comilla (pol. reg.), Bang. 85/H4
Comines, Fr. 52/C2
Comines, Belg. 52/B2
Comino (isl.), Malta 46/L6
Comitán de Domínguez, Mex. 144/C2
Commack, NY, US 139/E2
Commentry, Fr. 42/E3
Commeny, Fr. 30/H4
Commerce, Ca, US 136/F7
Commerce City, Co, US 137/C3
Commercy, Fr. 53/E6
Commewijne (dist.), Sur. 153/H3
Committee (bay), Nun., Can. 123/H2
Como (lake), It. 43/H3
Como, It. 57/F6
Como, Wi, US 135/P14
Comodoro Rivadavia, Arg. 158/D5
Comoé (prov.), Burk. 102/D4
Comoe, PN de la, C.d'Iv. 96/E6
Comoé, PN de la, C.d'Iv. 102/D4
Comorin (cape), India 82/C6
Comoros (ctry.) 107/G5
Comox, BC, Can. 126/B3
Compiègne, Fr. 52/B5
Compostela, Phil. 79/E6
Compostela, Mex. 142/D4
Compton, Ca, US 136/F8
Comrat, Mol. 49/J2
Comrie, Sc, UK 36/C4
Comstock, Tx, US 132/C4
Con Son (isl.), Viet. 83/J6
Cona, China 83/F2
Conaica, Peru 156/C4
Conakry (pol. reg.), Gui. 102/B4
Conakry (cap.), Gui. 102/B4
Conakry (int'l arpt.), Gui. 102/B4
Conambo (riv.), Ecu. 152/B5
Conca (riv.), It. 59/F5
Concarneau, Fr. 42/B3
Conceição da Barra, Braz. 155/E1
Conceição das Alagoas, Braz. 155/B1
Conceição do Araguaia, Braz. 151/J5
Conceição do Coité, Braz. 154/C3
Conceição do Mato Dentro, Braz. 155/D1
Conceição do Rio Verde, Braz. 211/H6
Conceição dos Ouros, Braz. 211/H7
Concepción (lake), Bol. 150/F7
Concepción, Arg. 157/C2
Concepción, Par. 157/E1
Concepción, Bol. 150/E6
Concepción, Peru 150/C6
Concepción (pt.), Mex. 142/C3
Concepción (bay), Mex. 142/B3
Concepción, Chile 158/B3
Concepción de La Vega, DRep. 141/G4
Concepción del Oro, Mex. 143/E3
Concepción del Uruguay, Arg. 159/J10
Conception (pt.), Ca, US 128/B4
Concesio, It. 58/D1
Conchal, Braz. 211/F7
Conchas (lake), NM, US 129/F4
Conches, Fr. 30/L5
Conchillas, Uru. 159/J11
Concho (riv.), Tx, US 129/G5
Conchos (riv.), Mex. 142/D2
Concord, Ca, US 128/B3
Concord, NC, US 133/H3
Concord (cap.), NH, US 131/G3
Concord, Wi, US 135/N13
Concordia, Arg. 157/E3
Concórdia, Braz. 155/A3
Concordia, Peru 156/C2
Concordia, Mex. 142/D4
Concordia Sagittaria, It. 59/F1
Concordia sulla Secchia, It. 59/D3
Concrete, Wa, US 126/C3
Condado, Cuba 145/G1
Condamine (riv.), Austl. 109/E3
Condamine, Austl. 114/C3
Conde, Braz. 154/C3
Condé-sur-L'Escaut, Fr. 52/C3
Condé-sur-Noireau, Fr. 42/C2
Condé-sur-Vesgre, Fr. 30/G5
Condé-sur-Vire, Fr. 42/C2
Condécourt, Fr. 30/H4
Condeúba, Braz. 154/B3
Condino, It. 57/G6
Condobolin, Austl. 115/C2
Condom, Fr. 42/D5
Condon, Or, US 126/C4
Condroz (plat.), Belg. 40/C3
Conecuh (riv.), Al, US 133/G4
Conegliano, It. 59/F1
Conejos, Co, US 129/F3
Conesa, Arg. 158/E2
Conestoga (riv.), Pa, US 138/B3
Conewago (lake), Pa, US 138/A3
Confins (int'l arpt.), Braz. 155/D1
Conflans-en-Jarnisy, Fr. 53/E5
Conflans-Sainte-Honorine, Fr. 30/J5
Congaree Swamp Nat'l Mon., SC, US 133/H3
Congers, NY, US 139/K7
Congis-sur-Thérouanne, Fr. 30/L4
Congjiang, China 83/J2
Congleton, Eng, UK 35/F5
Congo (basin), D.R. Congo 97/K7
Congo (ctry.) 93/D4
Congo (riv.), Afr. 93/D4
Congo, Democratic Republic of the (ctry.) 93/E5
Congonhal, Braz. 211/G7
Congonhas, Braz. 155/D2
Congonhas (int'l arpt.), Braz. 211/G8
Conguillío, PN, Chile 158/C3

181
Conic – Çubuk

Conic (hill), Sc, UK 36/B4
Cónico (peak), Arg. 158/C4
Conifer, Co, US 137/B3
Conil de la Frontera, Sp. 44/B4
Conisbrough, Eng, UK 35/G5
Conlig, NI, UK 34/C2
Conn (lake), Nun., Can. 123/J1
Connacht (reg.), Ire. 31/P10
Connah's Quay, Wal, UK 35/E5
Connantre, Fr. 52/C6
Conneaut, Oh, US 130/D3
Connecticut (riv.), US 131/G2
Connecticut (state), US 131/F3
Connellsville, Pa, US 130/E3
Connemara NP, Ire. 31/P10
Connersville, In, US 130/C4
Cono Grande (peak), Arg. 159/C6
Conocoto, Ecu. 152/B5
Conon, Falls of (falls), Sc, UK 36/B1
Cononbridge, Sc, UK 36/B1
Conondale NP, Austl. 114/D4
Čonoplja, Yugo. 48/D3
Conrad, Mt, US 126/F3
Conroe, Tx, US 129/J5
Consandolo, It. 59/E3
Conscience Point NWR, NY, US 139/F2
Consdorf, Lux. 53/F4
Conselheiro Pena, Braz. 155/D1
Conselice, It. 59/E3
Conselve, It. 59/E2
Conservation Park, Austl. 113/F4
Consett, Eng, UK 35/G2
Conshohocken, Pa, US 138/C3
Consolación del Sur, Cuba 145/F1
Consolidated (canal), Az, US 137/S19
Constance (lake), Swi. 43/H3
Constance (Bodensee) (lake), Swi. 43/H3
Constant (mtn.), Fr. 141/N9
Constanţa (prov.), Rom. 49/H3
Constanţa, Rom. 49/J3
Constantí, Sp. 45/F2
Constantina, Sp. 44/C4
Constantine (cape), Ak, US 134/G4
Constantine, Alg. 100/K6
Constitución, Chile 158/B2
Constitución (res.), Uru. 159/K10
Constitución de 1857, PN, Mex. 128/C5
Consuegra, Sp. 44/D3
Contai, India 85/F5
Contamana, Peru 156/C2
Contarina, It. 59/F2
Contas, Rio de (riv.), Braz. 151/K6
Contegem, Braz. 155/C1
Contes, Fr. 43/G5
Conthey, Swi. 56/D5
Continental (range), Ab,BC, Can. 126/C2
Continental (mtn.), Az, US 137/S18
Contoy (isl.), Mex. 144/E1
Contra Costa (canal), Ca, US 135/L10
Contra Costa (co.), Ca, US 135/L11
Contramaestre, Cuba 145/G1
Contratación, Col. 152/C3
Contrecoeur, Qu, Can. 131/P6
Contreras, Embalse de (res.), Sp. 44/E3
Contrexéville, Fr. 56/B1
Controller (bay), Ak, US 134/J3
Contulmo, Chile 158/B3
Contumazá, Peru 156/B2
Contwig, Ger. 53/G5
Contwoyto (lake), Nun., Can. 122/F2
Conty, Fr. 52/B4
Convención, Col. 152/C2
Conversano, It. 47/E2
Converse, Tx, US 137/U20
Conway, Ar, US 129/J4
Conway, SC, US 133/J3
Conway, NH, US 131/G3
Conway (cape), Austl. 114/C3
Conway NP, Austl. 114/C3
Conwy (bay), Wal, UK 34/D5
Conwy (riv.), Wal, UK 34/E5
Conwy (co.), Wal, UK 34/E5
Conwy, Vale of (valley), Wal, UK 34/E5
Conyngham, Pa, US 138/B2
Coober Pedy, Austl. 113/G4
Cooch Behār, India 85/G2
Coochiemudlo (isl.), Austl. 114/F7
Cook (mt.), NZ 117/S11
Cook (inlet), Ak, US 122/A3
Cook (co.), Il, US 135/Q16
Cook (bay), Chile 159/C7
Cook (str.), NZ 109/H7
Cook Islands (dpcy.), NZ 117/J6
Cooke (mt.), Austl. 112/C5
Cookeville, Tn, US 130/C4
Cookham, Eng, UK 30/A2
Cookhouse, SAfr. 106/D4
Cookstown, NI, UK 34/B2
Cookstown (dist.), NI, UK 34/B2
Cooksville, Md, US 138/A5
Cooktown, Austl. 114/B1
Coola Coola (swamp), Austl. 115/B3
Coolah, Austl. 115/D1
Coolamon, Austl. 115/C2
Coolangatta, Austl. 115/E1
Cooley (pt.), Ire. 34/B4
Coolgardie, Austl. 112/D4
Cooloola NP, Austl. 114/D4
Cooloongup (lake), Austl. 112/K7
Cooma, Austl. 115/D3
Coonabarabran, Austl. 115/D1
Coonalpyn, Austl. 115/A2
Coonamble, Austl. 115/D1
Coonana Abor. Land, Austl. 112/D4
Coondapoor (Kundapura), India 89/K6
Coongan Abor. Land, Austl. 112/C2
Coonoor, India 82/C5
Cooper, Tx, US 129/J4
Coopersburg, Pa, US 138/C2
Cooperstown, ND, US 127/J4
Coordewandy (peak), Austl. 112/C3
Coorong NP, Austl. 115/A3
Coorow, Austl. 112/C4
Cooroy, Austl. 114/D4
Coosa (riv.), Al, US 133/G3
Cootamundra, Austl. 115/D2
Coot'tha (mt.), Austl. 114/E6
Copacabana, Bol. 156/D5
Copahué (vol.), Chile 158/C3
Copainalá, Mex. 144/C2
Copala, Mex. 140/B4
Copán (ruin), Hon. 144/D3
Cope (cape), Sp. 44/E4
Copeland (isl.), NI, UK 34/C2
Copenhagen (København) (cap.), Den. 38/E4
Copertino, It. 47/F2
Copeton (dam), Austl. 115/D1
Copiague, NY, US 139/M9
Copiapó, Chile 157/B2
Coplay, Pa, US 138/C2
Copparo, It. 59/E3
Coppename (riv.), Sur. 153/H3
Coppenbrügge, Ger. 51/G4
Copper (riv.), Ak, US 122/B2
Copper Center, Ak, US 134/J3
Copperas Cove, Tx, US 129/H5
Coppermine (riv.), NW,Nun., Can. 122/E2
Copperton, Ut, US 137/J12
Coppet, Swi. 56/C5
Copşa Mică, Rom. 49/G2
Coqên, China 70/E5
Coquet (riv.), Eng, UK 36/D6
Coquet Dale (valley), Eng, UK 35/G1
Coquimbo, Chile 157/B2
Coquitlam, BC, Can. 126/C3
Corabia, Rom. 49/G4
Coração de Jesus, Braz. 154/A5
Coracora, Peru 156/C4
Corail, Haiti 145/H2
Coraki, Austl. 115/E1
Coral (sea) 109/D2
Coral Gables, Fl, US 133/H5
Coral Harbour, Nun., Can. 123/H2
Coral Sea Islands Territory (dpcy.), Austl. 109/E2
Coral Springs, Fl, US 133/H5
Corales del Rosario, PN, Col. 152/C2
Coram, NY, US 139/E2
Corato, It. 46/E2
Corbeil-Essonnes, Fr. 30/K6
Corbelin (cape), Alg. 100/H4
Corbenay, Fr. 56/C2
Corbet (peak), Swi. 57/F5
Corbett NP, India 84/B1
Corbetta, It. 58/B2
Corbie, Fr. 52/B5
Corbieres (mts.), Fr. 42/E5
Corbin, Ky, US 130/C4
Corbin City, NJ, US 138/D5
Corby, Eng, UK 33/F2
Corcovado, Braz. 211/K7
Corcovado, CR 145/E4
Corcovado (vol.), Chile 158/B4
Corcovado (gulf), Chile 147/B7
Corcovado, PN, CR 140/E6
Cordeiro, Braz. 155/D2
Cordele, Ga, US 133/H4
Cordelia, Ca, US 135/K10
Cordell, Ok, US 129/H4
Cordenons, It. 43/K4
Cordignano, It. 59/F1
Cordillera de Los Picachos, PN, Col. 150/D3
Cordillera Oriental (mts.), SAm. 152/B5
Cordisburgo, Braz. 155/C1
Córdoba, Arg. 157/D3
Córdoba, Sp. 44/C4
Córdoba, Mex. 143/N8
Córdoba (dept.), Col. 145/H4
Córdoba (plain), SAm. 158/E2
Córdoba, Sierra de (mts.), Arg. 157/D3
Cordova, Ak, US 134/J3
Cordova (peak), Ak, US 134/J3
Cordova, Md, US 138/C6
Coreaú, Braz. 154/B1
Corella, Sp. 44/E1
Coremas, Braz. 154/C2
Corentyne (riv.), Guy. 150/G3
Corfu (Kérika) (isl.), Gre. 47/F3
Corgémont, Swi. 56/D3
Corgo, Sp. 44/B1
Coria, Sp. 44/B3
Coria del Río, Sp. 44/B4
Coriano, It. 59/F5
Coribe, Braz. 154/A4
Coricudgy (mt.), Austl. 115/D2
Corigliano Calabro, It. 46/E3
Corinaldo, It. 59/G5
Coringa Islets (isls.), Austl. 114/C2
Corinne, Ut, US 137/J10
Corinth, Ms, US 133/F3
Corinth (gulf), Gre. 47/H3
Corinth (Kórinthos) (ruin), Gre. 47/H4
Corinto, Nic. 144/E3
Cork, Ire. 31/P11
Corleone, It. 46/C4
Corleto Perticara, It. 46/E2
Çorlu, Turk. 49/H5
Cormeilles-en-Vexin, Fr. 30/J4
Cormons, It. 59/G1
Cormontreuil, Fr. 52/D5
Cormorant, Mb, Can. 127/H2
Cormorant (lake), Mb, Can. 127/H2
Cornacchia (peak), It. 46/D2
Cornaredo, It. 58/C2
Cornberg, Ger. 51/G6
Corndon (peak), Wal, UK 32/C1
Cornedo Vicentino, It. 59/E1
Cornélio Procópio, Braz. 155/B2
Cornelius Grinnell (bay), Nun., Can. 123/K2
Cornell, Ca, US 136/B2
Cornella, Sp. 45/L7
Corner (inlet), Austl. 109/D4
Corner Brook, Nf, Can. 131/K1
Cornetto (peak), It. 57/H6
Cornfield (pt.), Ct, US 139/F1
Corniglio, It. 58/D4
Cornimont, Fr. 56/C2
Corning, NY, US 130/E3
Corno alle Scale (peak), It. 43/J4
Corno di Rosazzo, It. 59/G1
Cornone di Blumone (peak), It. 57/G6
Cornú (peak), Arg. 159/D7
Cornuda, It. 59/F1
Cornwall, PE, Can. 131/J2
Cornwall, On, Can. 131/G2
Cornwall (isl.), Nun., Can. 123/S7
Cornwall (cape), Eng, UK 32/A6
Cornwall (co.), Eng, UK 32/A6
Cornwall, Pa, US 138/B3
Cornwallis (isl.), Nun., Can. 123/S7
Corny (pt.), Austl. 113/H5
Coro, Ven. 152/D2
Coroatá, Braz. 154/A2
Corocoro, Bol. 156/D5
Coromandel, Braz. 155/C1
Coromandel (pen.), NZ 117/T10
Coromandel (coast), India 82/D5
Coron, Phil. 81/F1
Corona, Ca, US 136/C3
Coronado (bay), CR 140/E6
Coronado, Ca, US 136/C5
Coronation, Ab, Can. 126/F2
Coronation (gulf), Nun., Can. 122/E2
Coronel, Chile 158/B3
Coronel Dorrego, Arg. 158/E3
Coronel Fabriciano, Braz. 155/D1
Coronel Moldes, Arg. 158/D2
Coronel Murta, Braz. 154/B5
Coronel Oviedo, Par. 157/E2
Coronel Pringles, Arg. 158/E3
Coronel Suárez, Arg. 158/E3
Coronel Vidal, Arg. 158/F3
Coronel Vivida, Braz. 155/A3
Corongo, Peru 156/B3
Coronie (dist.), Sur. 153/G3
Coropuna (peak), Peru 156/C4
Çorovodë, Alb. 47/G2
Corozal, Col. 152/C2
Corozal, Belz. 144/D2
Corpach, Sc, UK 36/A3
Corpus Christi, Tx, US 132/D5
Corpus Christi (int'l arpt.), Tx, US 143/F3
Corral, Chile 158/B3
Corral de Almaguer, Sp. 44/D3
Corral de Bustos, Arg. 158/E2
Corrales, Col. 152/C3
Corralillo, Cuba 145/F1
Corre, Fr. 56/C2
Correa, Arg. 158/E2
Corredor, CR 145/F4
Correggio, It. 59/D3
Corrente (riv.), Braz. 154/A4
Corrente, Braz. 154/A3
Correntina, Braz. 154/A4
Corrib (lake), Ire. 31/P10
Corrientes (riv.), Peru 150/C4
Corrientes, Arg. 157/E2
Corrientes (cape), Cuba 145/E1
Corrientes (pt.), Col. 152/B3
Corrigan, Tx, US 129/J5
Corrigin, Austl. 112/C5
Corriverton, Guy. 153/G3
Corryhabbie (peak), Sc, UK 36/C2
Corryong, Austl. 115/C3
Corse (dept.), Fr. 43/H5
Corse (cape), Fr. 43/H5
Corse (hill), Sc, UK 36/B5
Corserine (peak), Sc, UK 34/D1
Corsewall (pt.), NI, UK 34/C1
Corsham, Eng, UK 32/D4
Corsica (isl.), Fr. 27/E4
Corsicana, Tx, US 129/H4
Corsico, It. 58/C2
Corsons (inlet), NJ, US 138/D5
Cortaillod, Swi. 56/C4
Cortegana, Sp. 44/B4
Cortemaggiore, It. 58/C3
Cortemilia, It. 58/B3
Cortez, Co, US 128/E3
Cortina d'Ampezzo, It. 43/K3
Cortines, Arg. 159/J11
Cortland, NY, US 130/E3
Corubal (riv.), GBis. 102/B3
Coruche, Port. 44/A3
Çoruh (riv.), Turk. 63/G4
Çorum (prov.), Turk. 62/E4
Çorum, Turk. 62/E4
Corumbá (riv.), Braz. 151/J7
Corumbá, Braz. 150/G7
Corumbaú (pt.), Braz. 154/C5
Coruripe, Braz. 154/C3
Corvallis, Or, US 126/C4
Corve (riv.), Eng, UK 32/D2
Corvo (peak), It. 46/C1
Corvo (isl.), Azor., Port. 45/R12
Corzoneso, Swi. 57/E5
Cosalá, Mex. 142/D3
Cosamaloapan, Mex. 143/P8
Cosautlán, Mex. 143/N7
Coscomatepec, Mex. 143/M7
Cosenza, It. 46/E3
Coshocton, Oh, US 130/D3
Cosigüina (pt.), Nic. 144/E3
Coslada, Sp. 45/N9
Cosmo Newberry Abor. Rsv., Austl. 112/D3
Cosmópolis, Braz. 211/F7
Cosne-Cours-sur-Loire, Fr. 42/E3
Cosne d'Allier, Fr. 42/E3
Cosolapa, Mex. 143/N8
Cospeito, Sp. 44/B1
Cosquín, Arg. 157/D3
Cossato, It. 58/B1
Cosson (riv.), Fr. 42/D3
Cossonay, Swi. 56/C4
Costa Azul, Uru. 159/G2
Costa Brava (int'l arpt.), Sp. 45/G2
Costa da Caparica, Port. 45/P10
Costa de Mosquitos (phys. reg.), Nic. 145/E4
Costa di Rovigo, It. 59/E2
Costa Masnaga, It. 58/C1
Costa Mesa, Ca, US 136/G8
Costa Rica (ctry.) 145/F4
Costa Smeralda (int'l arpt.), It. 46/A2
Costa Volpino, It. 58/D1
Costabissara, It. 59/E1
Costeşti, Rom. 49/G3
Costigliole d'Asti, It. 58/B3
Cotabambas, Peru 156/C4
Cotabato, Phil. 81/F2
Cotacachi (peak), Ecu. 152/B4
Cotahuasi, Peru 156/C4
Cotatumbo (riv.), Col. 145/H4
Côte d'Azur (int'l arpt.), Fr. 43/G5
Côte de Hautmont (hill), Fr. 56/B1
Côte d'Ivoire (ctry.) 102/D5
Côte d'Or (uplands), Fr. 42/F3
Côte du Rif (Al Hoceima) (int'l arpt.), Mor. 100/C2
Côte-Saint-Luc, Qu, Can. 131/N7
Coteau des Prairies (plat.), SD, US 127/J4
Coteau-du-Lac, Qu, Can. 131/M7
Coteau du Missouri (plat.), ND, US 127/H3
Coteau-Landing, Qu, Can. 131/M7
Cotegipe, Braz. 154/A4
Cotentin (pen.), Fr. 42/C2
Côtes de Meuse (uplands), Fr. 42/F2
Cothi (riv.), Wal, UK 32/B3
Cotia, Braz. 211/G8
Cotignola, It. 59/E4
Cotonou, Ben. 103/F5
Cotonou (int'l arpt.), Ben. 103/F5
Cotopaxi (dept.), Ecu. 152/B5
Cotopaxi (vol.), Ecu. 152/B5
Cotopaxi, PN, Ecu. 152/B5
Cotswolds (hills), Eng, UK 32/D3
Cottage Grove, Or, US 126/C5
Cottage Hills, Il, US 137/G8
Cottbus, Ger. 41/H3
Cottian Alps (mts.), Fr. 43/G4
Cottleville, Mo, US 137/F8
Cottonport, La, US 129/J5
Cottonwood, Az, US 128/D4
Cottonwood (riv.), Tx, US 129/F5
Cotulla, Tx, US 132/D4
Coubert, Fr. 30/L6
Coubre, Pointe de la (pt.), Fr. 42/C4
Couchey, Fr. 56/A3
Coudekerque-Branche, Fr. 52/B1
Coulee City, Wa, US 126/D4
Coulee Dam Nat'l Rec. Area, Wa, US 126/D3
Coulogne, Fr. 52/A2
Coulombs-en-Valois, Fr. 30/M4
Coulommes, Fr. 30/L5
Coulommiers, Fr. 52/C6
Coulonge (riv.), Qu, Can. 130/E2
Coulounieix-Chamiers, Fr. 42/D4
Council, Ak, US 134/F3
Council, Id, US 126/D4
Council Grove, Ks, US 129/H3
Coupar Angus, Sc, UK 36/C3
Coupvray, Fr. 30/L5
Courantyne (riv.), Guy.,Sur. 147/D2
Courbevoie, Fr. 30/J5
Courcelles, Belg. 53/D3
Courcouronnes, Fr. 30/K6
Courdimanche, Fr. 30/H4
Courgenay, Swi. 56/D3
Courgent, Fr. 30/G5
Courmayeur, It. 56/C6
Cournon-d'Auvergne, Fr. 42/E4
Courpalay, Fr. 30/L6
Courrendlin, Swi. 56/D3
Courroux, Swi. 56/D3
Coursan, Fr. 42/E5
Courtelary, Swi. 56/D3
Courtepin, Swi. 56/D4
Courtice, On, Can. 131/S8
Courtisols, Fr. 53/D6
Courtland, Ca, US 135/L10
Courtmacsherry, Ire. 31/P11
Courtney, Mo, US 137/E5
Courtomer, Fr. 30/L6
Cousance, Fr. 56/B4
Coushatta, La, US 129/J4
Cousolre, Fr. 53/D3
Coutances, Fr. 42/C2
Coutevroult, Fr. 30/L5
Coutras, Fr. 42/C4
Coutts, Ab, Can. 126/F3
Couva, Trin. 153/F2
Couvet, Swi. 56/C4
Couvin, Belg. 53/D3
Covadonga NP, Sp. 44/C1
Covasna, Rom. 49/H3
Covasna (prov.), Rom. 49/G3
Cove Bay, Sc, UK 36/D2
Cove Neck, NY, US 139/L8
Coventry (canal), Eng, UK 33/E1
Coventry, Eng, UK 33/E2
Covilhã, Port. 44/B2
Covina, Ca, US 136/G7
Covington, Tn, US 129/K4
Covington, Ga, US 133/H3
Covo, It. 58/C2
Cow Green (res.), Eng, UK 35/F2
Cowal (reg.), Sc, UK 36/A4
Cowan (lake), Austl. 109/B4
Cowdenbeath, Sc, UK 36/C4
Cowell, Austl. 113/H5
Cowes, Eng, UK 33/E5
Cowie, Sc, UK 36/C4
Cowlitz (riv.), Wa, US 126/C4
Cowra, Austl. 115/D2
Coxim, Braz. 151/H7
Cox's Bāzār, Bang. 83/F3
Coyame, Mex. 129/F5
Coye-la-Forêt, Fr. 30/K4
Coyotepec, Mex. 143/K7
Coyuca de Benítez, Mex. 143/E5
Coyutla, Mex. 143/M6
Cozumel, Mex. 144/E1
Cozumel (int'l arpt.), Mex. 144/E1
Cozumel (isl.), Mex. 144/E1
Cradle (mtn.), Austl. 115/C4
Cradle Mountain-Lake Saint Clair NP, Austl. 115/C4
Cradock, SAfr. 106/D4
Crag (mtn.), Yk, Can. 134/K3
Crag (peak), Eng, UK 35/F3
Craig, Co, US 128/F2
Craig, Ak, US 134/M4
Craig, Ks, US 137/D6
Craigavon (dist.), NI, UK 34/B3
Craigavon, NI, UK 34/B3
Craigieburn, Austl. 115/F5
Craik, Sk, Can. 127/G3
Crail, Sc, UK 36/D4
Crailsheim, Ger. 54/D4
Craiova, Rom. 49/F3
Cramalina (peak), Swi. 57/E5
Cramlington, Eng, UK 35/G1
Cran-Gevrier, Fr. 56/C6
Crana (riv.), Ire. 34/A1
Cranberry Portage, Mb, Can. 127/H2
Cranborne Chase (for.), Eng, UK 32/D5
Cranbourne, Austl. 115/G6
Cranbrook, BC, Can. 126/E3
Cranbrook, Austl. 112/C5
Cranbury, NJ, US 138/D3
Crane, Tx, US 132/C4
Crane Neck (pt.), NY, US 139/E2
Crane River, Mb, Can. 127/J3
Cranford, NJ, US 139/H9
Cranleigh, Eng, UK 33/F4
Craponne, Fr. 42/F4
Crasna (riv.), Rom. 48/F2
Crater (lake), Or, US 128/B2
Crater Lake NP, Or, US 128/B2
Craters of the Moon Nat'l Mon., Id, US 128/D2
Crateús, Braz. 154/B2
Crati (riv.), It. 46/E3
Crato, Port. 44/B3
Cravinhos, Braz. 155/C2
Crawfordsville, In, US 130/C3
Crawfordville, Fl, US 133/G4
Crawley, Eng, UK 33/F4
Cray (riv.), Eng, UK 30/D2
Crazy (mts.), Mt, US 126/F4
Creag Meagaidh (peak), Sc, UK 36/B3
Creagerstown, Md, US 138/A4
Creasy (Mifflinville), Pa, US 138/B1
Creazzo, It. 59/E2
Crêches-sur-Saône, Fr. 56/A5
Crécy-sur-Serre, Fr. 52/C4
Credit (riv.), On, Can. 131/Q8
Cree (lake), Sk, Can. 122/F3
Cree (riv.), Sk, Can. 122/F3
Cree (riv.), Sc, UK 34/D2
Creel, Mex. 142/D3
Creetown, Sc, UK 34/D2
Creglingen, Ger. 54/D4
Crégy-lès-Meaux, Fr. 30/L5
Créhange, Fr. 53/F5
Creighton, Sk, Can. 127/H2
Creil, Fr. 52/B5
Crema, It. 58/C2
Crémieu, Fr. 56/B6
Cremlingen, Ger. 51/H4
Cremona (prov.), It. 58/C2
Cremona, It. 58/D2
Crepaja, Yugo. 48/E3
Crépy, Fr. 52/C4
Creran (lake), Sc, UK 36/A3
Cres (isl.), Cro. 48/B3
Crescent, Mo, US 137/F8
Crescent, Co, US 137/B3
Crescent, Ut, US 137/K12
Crescent City, Ca, US 126/B5
Crescentino, It. 58/B2
Cresco, Pa, US 138/C1
Crespano del Grappa, It. 59/E1
Crespellano, It. 59/E3
Crespières, Fr. 30/H5
Crespin, Fr. 52/C3
Cresskill, NJ, US 139/K8
Cressona, Pa, US 138/B2
Cressy, Austl. 115/C4
Crest, Fr. 42/F4
Crest Hill, Il, US 135/P16
Crestline, Ca, US 136/C2
Creston, Ia, US 127/K5
Creston, BC, Can. 126/D3
Crestview, Fl, US 133/G4
Crestwood Village, NJ, US 138/D4
Creswick, Austl. 115/B3
Crete (sea), Gre. 47/J4
Crete (isl.), Gre. 27/G5
Créteil, Fr. 30/K5
Creuch (hill), Sc, UK 36/B5
Creus (cape), Sp. 45/G1
Creuse (riv.), Fr. 42/D3
Creussen, Ger. 55/E3
Creussen (riv.), Ger. 55/E3
Creutzwald-la-Croix, Fr. 53/F5
Creuzburg, Ger. 51/H6
Crevacuore, It. 58/B1
Crevalcore, It. 59/E3
Creve Coeur, Mo, US 137/G8
Crèvecœur-le-Grand, Fr. 52/B4
Crevillente, Sp. 45/E3
Crevoladossola, It. 57/E5
Crewe, Eng, UK 35/F5
Crib Point, Austl. 115/C3
Criciúma, Braz. 155/B4
Crieff, Sc, UK 36/C4
Criffell (hill), Sc, UK 34/E2
Crikvenica, Cro. 48/B3
Crillon (mt.), Ak, US 134/L4
Crimean (pen.), Ukr. 49/L3
Crimeanpen (pen.), Ukr. 62/E3
Crimond, Sc, UK 36/E1
Crisenoy, Fr. 30/L6
Crisman, Co, US 137/B2
Crissier, Swi. 56/C4
Cristal, Monts de (mts.), Gabon 105/B1
Cristalina, Braz. 154/A5
Cristina, Braz. 211/H7
Cristóbal (pt.), Ecu. 156/E7
Cristóbal Colón (peak), Col. 152/C2
Cristoforo Colombo (int'l arpt.), It. 58/B4
Cristuru Secuiesc, Rom. 49/G2
Crişul Alb (riv.), Rom. 48/F2
Crişul Negru (riv.), Rom. 48/E2
Crixás-Açu (riv.), Braz. 151/H6
Crna Reka (riv.), FYROM 47/G2
Črnomelj, Slov. 43/L4
Croajingolong NP, Austl. 115/D3
Croatia (ctry.) 48/B3
Croce (peak), It. 57/H5
Croce, Pico di (peak), It. 57/H4
Croche (peak), Fr. 56/C6
Croche (riv.), Qu, Can. 131/F2
Crocker (range), Malay. 81/E3
Crocker (peak), Ecu. 156/E7
Crockett, Tx, US 129/J5
Crockett, Ca, US 135/K10
Crocodile Head (pt.), Austl. 115/D2
Crodo, It. 57/E5
Crofton, Md, US 138/B6
Croghan (mts.), Ire. 34/B6
Croisette (cape), Fr. 42/F5
Croisilles, Fr. 52/B3
Croissy-Beaubourg, Fr. 30/K5
Croker (isl.), Austl. 109/C2
Cromarty Firth (bay), Sc, UK 36/B1
Crombie (mt.), Austl. 113/F3
Cromdale (hills), Sc, UK 36/C2
Cromwell, NZ 117/R12
Crong A Na (riv.), Viet. 78/D3
Crooked (isl.), Bahm. 141/G3
Crooked Creek, Ak, US 134/G3
Crooked Island Passage (chan.), Bahm. 145/H1
Crookston, Mn, US 127/J4
Crookwell, Austl. 115/D2
Croom, Ire. 31/P10
Crosby, ND, US 127/H3
Crosby, Eng, UK 35/E5
Crosbyton, Tx, US 129/G4
Cross (lake), Mb, Can. 127/J2
Cross City, Fl, US 133/H4
Cross Fell (peak), Eng, UK 35/F2
Cross Plains, Tx, US 129/H4
Cross River (state), Nga. 103/H5
Cross River (res.), NY, US 139/E1
Cross Roads, Pa, US 138/B4
Crossfield, Ab, Can. 126/E3
Crossford, Sc, UK 36/C4
Crosshouse, Sc, UK 36/B5
Crossroads, Ire. 31/P9
Crossville, Tn, US 133/G3
Crostolo (riv.), It. 58/D3
Croton-on-Hudson (Croton-Harmon), NY, US 139/E1
Crotone, It. 47/E3
Crottendorf, Ger. 55/F1
Croult (riv.), Fr. 30/K5
Crouy, Fr. 52/C5
Crouy-sur-Ourcq, Fr. 30/M4
Crow Agency, Mt, US 126/G4
Crowborough, Eng, UK 33/G4
Crowdy Bay NP, Austl. 115/E1
Crowe (riv.), On, Can. 130/E2
Crowley, La, US 129/J5
Crowley's (ridge), Ar, US 133/F3
Crown Point, In, US 130/C3
Crown Point, La, US 137/P17
Crown Point (int'l arpt.), Trin. 153/F2
Crown Prince Frederik (isl.), Nun., Can. 123/H1
Crownpoint, NM, US 128/E4
Crows Nest Falls NP, Austl. 114/D4
Crowthorne, Eng, UK 33/F4
Croydon, Austl. 114/A2
Croydon (bor.), Eng, UK 30/C2
Croydon, Pa, US 138/D3
Croydon, Ut, US 137/K11
Crozet (isls.), Fr. 23/M8
Crozon, Fr. 42/A2
Cruach Mhór (peak), Sc, UK 36/A4
Cruach nan Capull (peak), Sc, UK 36/A5
Crucero, Peru 156/D4
Cruden Bay, Sc, UK 36/E2
Cruick Water (riv.), Sc, UK 36/D3
Crumlin, NI, UK 34/B2
Crummock Water (lake), Eng, UK 35/E2
Crumpton, Md, US 138/C5
Cruseilles, Fr. 56/C5
Crusnes (riv.), Fr. 53/E5
Cruz (cape), Cuba 145/G2
Cruz Alta, Braz. 157/F2
Cruz Alta, Arg. 158/E2
Cruz Alta (peak), Port. 45/P10
Cruz das Almas, Braz. 154/C4
Cruz del Eje, Arg. 157/D3
Cruz Grande, Mex. 144/B2
Cruzeiro, Braz. 211/J7
Cruzeiro do Sul, Braz. 156/C2
Cruzeta, Braz. 154/C2
Cruzília, Braz. 211/J6
Crvenka, Yugo. 48/D3
Cryn-y-Brain (peak), Wal, UK 35/E5
Crystal (lake), Pa, US 138/C1
Crystal Bay, Nv, US 128/C3
Crystal Brook, Austl. 113/H5
Crystal Cave, Pa, US 138/C2
Crystal City, Tx, US 132/D4
Crystal Springs, Ms, US 129/K5
Crystal Springs (res.), Ca, US 135/K11
Csenger, Hun. 41/M5
Csepreg, Hun. 43/M3
Csongrád, Hun. 48/E2
Csorna, Hun. 48/C2
Csorvás, Hun. 48/E2
Csóványos (peak), Hun. 48/D2
Csurgó, Hun. 48/C2
Cu Lao (isl.), Viet. 79/A5
Cuajinicuilapa, Mex. 144/B2
Cualedro, Sp. 44/B2
Cuamba, Moz. 105/G3
Cuando (riv.), Ang. 105/D4
Cuango (riv.), Ang. 105/C2
Cuanza (riv.), Ang. 93/D6
Cuart de Poblet, Sp. 45/E3
Cuarto (riv.), Arg. 158/D2
Cuatrociénagas de Carranza, Mex. 132/C5
Cuauhtémoc, Mex. 142/E5
Cuauhtémoc, Mex. 142/D2
Cuautepec, Mex. 143/L6
Cuautitlán, Mex. 143/Q9
Cuautitlán Izcalli, Mex. 143/Q9
Cuautla, Mex. 143/L8
Cuba, Mo, US 129/K3
Cuba, Port. 44/B3
Cuba (ctry.) 145/F1
Cubagua (isl.), Ven. 153/E2
Cuballing, Austl. 112/C5
Cubango (riv.), Ang. 93/D6
Çubuk, Turk. 62/E4

182
Cucam – Dell

Cucamonga (Rancho Cucamonga), Ca, US 136/C2
Cuccurano, It. 59/F5
Cuchivero (riv.), Ven. 150/E2
Cuchumatanes (mts.), Guat. 144/D3
Cuckmere (riv.), Eng, UK 33/G5
Cucq, Fr. 42/D1
Cúcuta, Col. 152/C3
Cucuyagua, Hon. 144/D3
Cudahy, Ca, US 136/F8
Cuddapah, India 82/C5
Cudgewa, Austl. 115/C3
Cudillero, Sp. 44/B1
Cudrefin, Swi. 56/D4
Cudworth, Eng, UK 35/G4
Cue, Austl. 112/C3
Cuéllar, Sp. 44/C2
Cuéllar-Baza, Sp. 44/D4
Cuenca, Sp. 44/D2
Cuenca, Ecu. 152/B5
Cuenca, Sierra de (range), Sp. 44/E2
Cuencamé de Ceniceros, Mex. 142/E3
Cuernavaca, Mex. 143/K8
Cuero, Tx, US 129/H5
Cuers, Fr. 42/G5
Cueto, Cuba 145/H1
Cuetzalán, Mex. 143/M6
Cueva de los Guácharos, PN, Col. 150/C3
Cuevas de Vinromá, Sp. 45/F2
Cuevas del Almanzora, Sp. 44/E4
Cuffley, Eng, UK 30/C1
Cufré, Uru. 159/K11
Cugir, Rom. 49/F3
Cuglieri, It. 46/A2
Cugnaux, Fr. 42/D5
Cuiabá (riv.), Braz. 151/G7
Cuiabá, Braz. 151/G7
Cuicas, Ven. 152/D2
Cuijk, Neth. 50/C5
Cuilapa, Guat. 144/D3
Cuilco (riv.), Guat. 144/C3
Cuillin (sound), Sc, UK 31/Q8
Cuilo (riv.), Ang. 105/C2
Cuisance (riv.), Fr. 56/B4
Cuise-la-Motte, Fr. 52/C5
Cuiseaux, Fr. 56/B5
Cuisery, Fr. 56/A4
Cuisy, Fr. 30/L4
Cuité, Braz. 154/C2
Cuitláhuac, Mex. 143/N8
Cuito (riv.), Ang. 105/C4
Cuiuni (riv.), Braz. 150/F4
Culcairn, Austl. 115/C2
Culdaff (riv.), Ire. 34/A1
Culemborg, Neth. 50/C5
Culgoa (riv.), Austl. 109/D3
Culiacán Rosales, Mex. 142/D3
Culion (isl.), Phil. 79/D5
Cullen, Sc, UK 36/D1
Cullera, Sp. 45/E3
Culleredo, Sp. 44/A1
Cullman, Al, US 133/G3
Culloden Battlesite, Sc, UK 36/B2
Cully, Swi. 56/C5
Cullybackey, NI, UK 34/B2
Culmback (dam), Wa, US 135/D2
Culmore, NI, UK 34/A1
Culoz, Fr. 56/B6
Culpeper, Va, US 130/E4
Culross, Sc, UK 36/C4
Cults, Sc, UK 36/D2
Culver (pt.), Austl. 112/E5
Culver City, Ca, US 136/F7
Culvers (lake), NJ, US 138/D1
Cumaná, Ven. 153/E2
Cumari, Braz. 155/B1
Cumba, Peru 156/B2
Cumbal, Col. 152/B4
Cumbal, Nevado de (peak), Col. 152/B4
Cumberland (lake), Sk, Can. 127/H2
Cumberland (lake), Ky, US 130/C4
Cumberland (plat.), US 133/G3
Cumberland, Md, US 130/E4
Cumberland (falls), Ky, US 133/G2
Cumberland (isl.), Ga, US 133/H4
Cumberland (pen.), Nun., Can. 123/K2
Cumberland (co.), NJ, US 138/A3
Cumberland (sound), Nun., Can. 123/K2
Cumberland (riv.), Ky,Tn, US 125/J4
Cumberland, Wa, US 135/D3
Cumberland House, Sk, Can. 127/H2
Cumbernauld, Sc, UK 36/C5
Cumbres Bastonal, Cerro (peak), Mex. 144/C2
Cumbres de Majalca, PN, Mex. 142/D2
Cumbres de Monterrey, PN de, Mex. 143/E3
Cumbria (co.), Eng, UK 35/E2
Cumbrian (mts.), Eng, UK 35/E2
Cumbum, India 82/C4
Cummins, Austl. 113/G5
Cumnock, Austl. 115/D2
Cumpas, Mex. 142/C2
Çumra, Turk. 90/C2
Cumshewa (pt.), BC, Can. 134/M5
Cunaviche, Ven. 153/E3
Cunco, Chile 158/B3
Cundeelee Abor. Rsv., Austl. 112/D4
Cunderdin, Austl. 112/C4
Cundinamarca (dept.), Col. 152/C3
Cunduacán, Mex. 144/C2
Cunene (riv.), Ang. 93/D6
Cuneo (prov.), It. 58/A3
Cuneo, It. 43/G4
Cunha, Braz. 211/J8
Cunnamulla, Austl. 114/B5
Cunninghame (reg.), Sc, UK 36/B5
Čuokkarašša (peak), Nor. 37/H1
Cuorgnè, It. 43/G4
Cupar, Sc, UK 36/C4
Cupertino, Ca, US 135/K12
Cupra Marittima, It. 43/K5
Cupramontana, It. 59/G6
Cuprija, Yugo. 48/E4
Čuprija, Yugo. 48/E4
Cuquenán (riv.), Ven. 153/F3
Curaçá, Braz. 154/C3
Curaçao (isl.), NAnt. 150/E1
Curacautín, Chile 158/C3
Curacaví, Chile 158/N8
Curahuara de Carangas, Bol. 156/D5
Curanilahue, Chile 158/B3
Curaray (riv.), Ecu. 150/C4
Curaray (riv.), Ecu.,Peru 152/C5
Curarén, Hon. 144/E3
Curaumilla (pt.), Chile 158/N8
Curcubăta (peak), Rom. 49/F2
Cure (riv.), Fr. 40/B5
Curecanti Nat'l Rec. Area, Co, US 132/B2
Curepipe, Mrts. 107/T15
Curepto, Chile 158/B2
Curicó, Chile 158/C2
Curimatá, Braz. 154/A3
Curitibanos, Braz. 155/B3
Curno, It. 58/C1
Curone (riv.), It. 58/C3
Curral Velho, CpV. 93/K10
Current (riv.), Ar,Mo, US 129/K3
Currie, Austl. 115/B3
Currie, Sc, UK 36/C5
Curry, Ak, US 134/H3
Curtea de Argeş, Rom. 49/G3
Curtici, Rom. 48/E2
Curtis, Sp. 44/A1
Curtis (isl.), NZ 116/G8
Curtis (riv.), Austl. 114/D4
Curtis (pt.), Md, US 138/B6
Curú NWR, CR 145/E4
Curuá (riv.), Braz. 151/G4
Curuá Una (riv.), Braz. 153/H5
Curuçú (riv.), Braz. 150/D5
Curup, Indo. 80/B4
Cururupu, Braz. 151/K4
Curuzú Cuatiá, Arg. 157/E2
Curvelo, Braz. 155/C1
Cusco (dept.), Peru 156/C4
Cusco, Peru 156/D4
Cusher (riv.), NI, UK 34/B3
Cushet Law (peak), Eng, UK 36/D6
Cushing, Ok, US 129/H4
Cusna (peak), It. 58/D4
Cusset, Fr. 42/E3
Cusseta, Ga, US 133/G3
Custer, Mt, US 126/G4
Custer, SD, US 127/H5
Custines, Fr. 53/F6
Custódia, Braz. 154/C3
Cut (hill), Eng, UK 32/C5
Cut Bank, Mt, US 126/E3
Cut Knife, Sk, Can. 126/F2
Cutchogue, NY, US 139/F2
Cutervo, Peru 156/B2
Cuthbert, Ga, US 133/G4
Cutral-Có, Arg. 158/C3
Cutro, It. 47/E3
Cuttack, India 82/E3
Cuvergnon, Fr. 30/L4
Cuvier (cape), Austl. 112/B3
Cuxhaven, Ger. 51/F1
Cuyabeno, Ecu. 152/C5
Cuyama (riv.), Ca, US 128/C4
Cuyo (isls.), Phil. 81/F1
Cuyo, Phil. 81/F1
Cuyocuyo, Peru 156/D4
Cuyuni (riv.), Ven. 150/F2
Cuyuni (riv.), Guy., Ven. 153/G3
Cuyuni-Mazaruni (pol. reg.), Guy. 153/F3
Cuzco (ruin), Peru 156/D4
Cwmbran, Wal, UK 32/C3
Cyangugu, Rwa. 104/A3
Cyclades (isls.), Gre. 47/J4
Cypress (hills), Ab,Sk, Can. 126/F3
Cypress, Ca, US 136/F8
Cyprus (ctry.) 91/C2
Cyrenaica (reg.), Libya 97/K1
Cysoing, Fr. 52/C2
Cywyn (riv.), Wal, UK 32/B3
Czaplinek, Pol. 41/J2
Czarna Białostocka, Pol. 41/M2
Czarnków, Pol. 41/J2
Czech Republic (ctry.) 41/H4
Częstochowa, Pol. 41/K3
Częstochowa (prov.), Pol. 41/K3
Człuchów, Pol. 38/G5

D

Da (riv.), China 79/D2
Da Hinggan (mts.), China 67/M5
Da Lat, Viet. 78/E4
Da Nang (cape), Viet. 78/E2
Da Nang, Viet. 78/E2
Da Xian, China 70/J5
Daaden, Ger. 53/G2
Da'an, China 71/M2
Daanbantayan, Phil. 79/D5
Daba (mts.), China 70/J5
Dabajuro, Ven. 152/D2
Dabakala, C.d'Iv. 102/D4
Dabas, Hun. 48/D2
Dabbāgh, Jabal (peak), SAr. 88/C3
Dabeiba, Col. 152/B3
Dabo, Fr. 53/G6
Dabob (bay), Wa, US 135/B2
Dabou, C.d'Iv. 102/D5
Daboya, Gha. 103/E4
Dabra, India 84/B3
Dąbrowa Białostocka, Pol. 39/K5
Dąbrowa Górnicza, Pol. 41/K3
Dabu, China 79/C3
Dachang Huizu Zizhixian, China 72/H7
Dachau, Ger. 55/E6
Dacono, Co, US 137/C2
Dade City, Fl, US 133/H4
Dades, Oued (riv.), Mor. 98/D3
Dadi (cape), Indo. 81/H4
Dādra and Nagar Haveli (state), India 82/B4
Dādri, India 86/D5
Dādu, Pak. 89/J3
Daduru (riv.), SrL. 82/C6
Daen Noi (peak), Thai. 78/B4
Daet, Phil. 79/D5
Dafang, China 83/J2
Dafeng, China 72/E4
Dagana, Sen. 102/B2
Dağardı, Turk. 62/D5
Dağbaşı, Turk. 90/D2
Dagestan (aut. rep.), Rus. 63/H4
Daggaboersnek (pass), SAfr. 106/D4
Dagmar Range NP, Austl. 114/B2
Dagneux, Fr. 56/B6
Dagny, Fr. 30/M5
Dagu, China 72/H7
Daguan, China 83/H2
D'Aguilar (range), Austl. 114/E6
D'Aguilar (mt.), Austl. 114/E6
Dagupan, Phil. 79/D4
Dahana (des.), SAr. 67/D7
Daharki, Pak. 82/A2
Dahei (riv.), China 72/B2
Dahlak (arch.), Erit. 97/N4
Dahlem, Ger. 53/F3
Dahlenburg, Ger. 51/H2
Dahlonega, Ga, US 133/H3
Dahmani, Tun. 100/L7
Dahme (riv.), Ger. 41/G3
Dahn, Ger. 53/G5
Dahūk, Iraq 90/E2
Dahūk (gov.), Iraq 90/E2
Dahuofang (res.), China 72/D2
Dai (lake), China 72/C2
Dai-Segen-dake (peak), Japan 76/B3
Dai-sen (peak), Japan 74/C3
Dai Xian, China 72/C3
Daian, Japan 77/L5
Daicheng, China 72/D3
Daigo, Japan 75/G2
Dailekh, Nepal 84/C1
Dailly, Sc, UK 36/B6
Daimiao, China 72/D3
Daimiel, Sp. 44/D3
Daingerfield, Tx, US 129/J4
Daiō-zaki (pt.), Japan 75/E3
Dāira Dīn Panāh, Pak. 86/A4
Daireaux, Arg. 158/E3
Daisen-Oki NP, Japan 74/C3
Daisetsuzan NP, Japan 76/C2
Daishan, China 79/D1
Daito (isl.), Japan 67/N7
Daitō, Japan 77/J6
Daiyun (peak), China 71/L6
Dajabón, DRep. 145/J2
Dakar (cap.), Sen. 102/A3
Dakar (pol. reg.), Sen. 102/A3
Dākhilah, Wāḩāt ad (oasis), Egypt 101/B3
Dakhin Shābāzpur (isl.), Bang. 85/H4
Dakhlet Nouadhibou (pol. reg.), Mrta. 98/A5
Dakoro, Niger 103/G3
Dakota City, Ne, US 127/J5
Đakovica, Yugo. 47/G1
Đakovo, Cro. 48/D3
Dal (falls), Sudan 101/B4
Dal (riv.), Swe. 64/B3
Dala-Järna, Swe. 38/F1
Dalaas, Aus. 57/F3
Dalad Qi, China 72/B2
Dalaman, Turk. 90/B2
Dalaman (int'l arpt.), Turk. 90/B2
Dalandzadgad, Mong. 70/H3
Dalandzadgad, Mong. 65/L5
Dalarna (reg.), Swe. 37/E3
Dalatangi (pt.), Ice. 37/Q6
Dalbeattie, Sc, UK 34/E2
Dalby, Austl. 114/C4
Dalby, Swe. 38/E4
Dalcour, La, US 137/Q17
Dalcross (int'l arpt.), Sc, UK 36/B1
Dale, Ok, US 137/N15
Dale, Nor. 38/A1
Dalen, Neth. 50/D3
Dalen, Nor. 38/C2
Dalfsen, Neth. 50/D3
Dalgaranger (mt.), Austl. 112/C3
Dalhart, Tx, US 129/G3
Dalhousie (cape), NW, Can. 134/N1
Dalhousie, NB, Can. 131/H1
Dalhousie, India 86/C3
Dali, China 83/H2
Dali, China 72/B4
Dalian (bay), China 73/A3
Dalian, China 73/A3
Dalian (int'l arpt.), China 72/E3
Dalías, Sp. 44/D4
Dalidag (peak), Azer. 63/H5
Dāliyat el Karmil, Isr. 91/G6
Dalj, Cro. 48/D3
Dalkeith, Sc, UK 36/C5
Dalkola, India 85/F3
Dall (lake), Ak, US 134/F3
Dall (isl.), Ak, US 122/C3
Dallas, Tx, US 129/H4
Dallas-Fort Worth (int'l arpt.), Tx, US 129/H4
Dallastown, Pa, US 138/B4
Dallgow, Ger. 40/Q6
Dallol Bosso (riv.), Niger,Mali 103/F3
Dalmatia (reg.), Cro. 48/B3
Dalmatia, Pa, US 138/B2
Dalmellington, Sc, UK 36/B6
Dalmeny, Austl. 115/D3
Dalmine, It. 58/C1
Dal'negorsk, Rus. 71/Q3
Dal'nerechensk, Rus. 71/P2
Daloa, C.d'Iv. 102/D5
Dalry, Sc, UK 36/B5
Dalrymple (lake), Austl. 109/D3
Dalrymple, Sc, UK 36/B6
Dals Långed, Swe. 38/E2
Dalsingh Sarai, India 85/E3
Dalsjöfors, Swe. 38/E3
Dalton, Ga, US 133/G3
Daltonganj, India 85/E3
Dalvík, Ice. 37/N6
Dalwallinu, Austl. 112/C4
Daly (riv.), Austl. 109/C2
Daly (bay), Nun., Can. 122/G2
Damak, Nepal 85/F2
Damān, India 82/B3
Damān and Diu (state), India 82/B3
Damanhūr, Egypt 91/B4
Damar (isl.), Indo. 81/G5
Damascus (int'l arpt.), Syria 91/E3
Damascus, Md, US 138/A5
Damascus (Dimashq) (cap.), Syria 91/E3
Damaturu, Nga. 96/H5
Damavānd (mtn.), Iran 88/F1
Dambach-la-Ville, Fr. 56/D1
Dambaslar, Turk. 49/H5
Dame Marie (cape), Haiti 145/H2
Dame Marie, Haiti 145/H2
Dāmghān, Iran 89/F1
Damietta (riv.), Egypt 91/B4
Damietta (Dumyāţ), Egypt 91/B4
Daming, China 72/C3
Damion (peak), Fr. 53/D4
Dammard, Fr. 30/M4
Dammartin-en-Goële, Fr. 30/L4
Dammastock (peak), Swi. 57/E4
Damme, Ger. 51/F3
Damme, Belg. 52/C1
Dāmodar (riv.), India 82/E3
Damoh, India 84/B4
Damongo, Gha. 103/E4
Damparis, Fr. 56/B3
Dampier (str.), Indo. 81/H4
Dampier (arch.), Austl. 109/A2
Dampier, Austl. 112/C2
Dampierre, Fr. 30/H5
Dampierre-sur-Salon, Fr. 56/B2
Damprichard, Fr. 56/C3
Damrei (mts.), Camb. 78/C4
Damsterdiep (riv.), Neth. 50/D2
Damvant, Swi. 56/C3
Damxung, China 70/F5
Dan (riv.), NC,Va, US 133/H2
Dan Xian, China 83/J4
Dānā, Jor. 91/D4
Dana Point, Ca, US 136/C4
Danané, C.d'Iv. 102/C5
Danao, Phil. 79/D5
Danba, China 70/H5
Danbury, Eng, UK 33/G3
Dancheng, China 72/C4
Dandaragan, Austl. 112/B4
Dandeldhurā, Nepal 84/C1
Dandenong (mt.), Austl. 115/G5
Danderhall, Sc, UK 36/C5
Dandong, China 73/C2
Dane (riv.), Eng, UK 35/F5
Danger (pt.), SAfr. 106/L11
Danggali Conservation Park, Austl. 115/B2
Dangriga, Belz. 144/D2
Dangshan, China 72/D4
Dangtu, China 72/D5
Dangyang, China 71/K5
Danielskuil, SAfr. 106/C3
Danielsville, Pa, US 138/C2
Danilov, Rus. 60/J4
Daning, China 72/B3
Danjoutin, Fr. 56/C2
Dankaur, India 86/D5
Dankov, Rus. 62/F1
Dankova (peak), Kyr. 87/G4
Danlí, Hon. 144/E3
Dannelly (res.), Al, US 133/G3
Dannemora, Swe. 38/G1
Dannenberg, Ger. 40/F2
Dannes, Fr. 52/A2
Dannevirke, NZ 117/T11
Dannhauser, SAfr. 107/E3
Danube (riv.), Eur. 27/F4
Danube, Delta of the (delta), Rom. 49/J3
Danube (Donau) (riv.), Ger. 43/H2
Danube, Mouths of the (delta), Rom.,Ukr. 62/D3
Danville, Il, US 130/C3
Danville, Ky, US 130/C4
Danville, Pa, US 138/B2
Dao Xian, China 83/K2
Daoura, Oued ed (riv.), Alg. 98/D3
Daozhen, China 83/J2
Dapaong, Togo 103/F4
Daphne, Al, US 133/G4
Dapitan, Phil. 79/D6
Daqing, China 71/N2
Daqing (riv.), China 72/H7
Dar-el-Beida (Casablanca), Mor. 98/D2
Dar es Salaam (int'l arpt.), Tanz. 104/C4
Dar es Salaam (pol. reg.), Tanz. 104/C4
Dar es Salaam (cap.), Tanz. 104/C4
Dar Rounga (reg.), CAfr. 97/K6
Darʿā (prov.), Syria 90/C3
Darʿā (prov.), Syria 91/E3
Darʿā, Syria 91/E3
Dārāb, Iran 89/F3
Darabani, Rom. 49/H1
Daraga, Phil. 81/F1
Daram, Phil. 79/D5
Dārān, Iran 88/F2
Đaravica (peak), Yugo. 47/G1
Dārayyā, Syria 91/E3
Darbhanga, India 85/E2
Darby (cape), Ak, US 134/F3
Darby, Pa, US 138/C4
Darda, Cro. 48/D3
Dardanelle (lake), Ar, US 129/J4
Dardanelles (str.), Turk. 62/C4
Darent (riv.), Eng, UK 30/D3
Dareton, Austl. 115/B2
Darfield, NZ 117/S11
Darfo, It. 57/G6
Dārfūr (state), Sudan 101/A5
Dargaville, NZ 117/S10
Dargle (riv.), Ire. 34/B5
D'Arguin (bay), Mrta. 102/A1
Darhan, Mong. 70/J2
Darie (hills), Som. 97/Q6
Darien, Ga, US 133/H4
Darien, Ct, US 139/M7
Darien, Il, US 135/P16
Darién, PN, Pan. 150/C2
Darién, Serranía del (mts.), Pan. 150/C2
Darkan, Austl. 112/C5
Darlag, China 70/G5
Darling (range), Austl. 109/A4
Darling (riv.), Austl. 109/D4
Darling, SAfr. 106/L10
Darling Downs (reg.), Austl. 109/D3
Darling Downs (range), Austl. 114/C3
Darlington, SC, US 133/J3
Darlington, Md, US 138/B4
Darlington, Eng, UK 35/G2
Darlington (co.), Eng, UK 35/G2
Darlington Point, Austl. 115/C2
Darłowo, Pol. 38/G4
Darmstadt, Ger. 54/B3
Darnah, Libya 97/K1
Darney, Fr. 56/C1
Darnley (bay), NW, Can. 122/D2
Darnley (cape), Ant. 160/E
Daroca, Sp. 44/E2
Darregueira, Arg. 158/E3
Darsser (cape), Ger. 38/E4
Dart (riv.), Eng, UK 32/C6
Dart, West (riv.), Eng, UK 32/C6
Dartford, Eng, UK 30/D2
Dartmoor (upland), Eng, UK 32/B5
Dartmoor NP, Eng, UK 42/A1
Dartmouth (dam), Austl. 115/C3
Dartmouth (res.), Austl. 115/C3
Dartmouth, NS, Can. 131/J2
Dartmouth, Eng, UK 32/C6
Darton, Eng, UK 35/G4
Dartuch (cape), Sp. 45/G3
Daruvar, Cro. 48/C3
Darvel (bay), Malay. 81/E3
Darvel, Sc, UK 36/B5
Darwen, Eng, UK 35/F4
Darwin (bay), Chile 158/B5
Darwin (isl.), Ecu. 156/E6
Darwin (vol.), Ecu. 156/E7
Darwin, Cordillera (mts.), Chile 157/B7
Darya Khan, Pak. 86/A4
Daryābād, India 84/C2
Dashennongjia (peak), China 72/B5
Dashkhovuz, Trkm. 87/C4
Dashkhovuz (pol. reg.), Trkm. 87/C4
Dashkhovuz (int'l arpt.), Trkm. 87/C4
Dasht-e Kavīr (des.), Iran 64/F6
Dasht-e Lūt (des.), Iran 64/F6
Dasht-e Mārgow (des.), Afg. 89/H2
Dasht Kaur (riv.), Pak. 89/H3
Dasing, Ger. 54/E6
Daska, Pak. 86/C3
Dassa-Zoumé, Ben. 103/F5
Dassel, Ger. 51/G5
Dassendorf, Ger. 51/H1
Dasseneiland (isl.), SAfr. 106/B4
Dasūya, India 86/C4
Dātāganj, India 84/B1
Datchet, Eng, UK 30/B2
Date, Japan 76/B2
Datia, India 84/B3
Datian, China 79/C2
Datil, NM, US 132/B3
Datong (mts.), China 70/G4
Datong, China 70/H4
Datong, China 72/C2
Datteln, Ger. 51/E5
Datu (cape), Indo. 80/C3
Datuk (cape), Indo. 80/B3
Daugava (riv.), Lat. 64/C4
Daugavpils, Lat. 39/M4
Daule, Ecu. 152/B5
Daule (riv.), Ecu. 152/B5
Daun, Ger. 53/F3
Daund, India 89/K5
Daung (isl.), Myan. 78/B3
Dauphin, Mb, Can. 127/H3
Dauphin (lake), Mb, Can. 127/J3
Dauphin (co.), Pa, US 138/B3
Dauphin, Pa, US 138/B3
Dauphiné (reg.), Fr. 42/F4
Dauphiné, Alpes du (range), Fr. 42/F4
Dāvangere, India 89/L6
Davao, Phil. 81/G2
Davel, SAfr. 107/E2
Davenport, Wa, US 126/D4
Davenport, Ia, US 127/L5
Davenport (mt.), Austl. 113/F2
Daventry, Eng, UK 33/E2
Daverdisse, Belg. 53/E3
Daveyton, SAfr. 106/E2
Davgaard-Jensen Land (phys. reg.), Grld. 123/T6
David, Pan. 145/F5
David City, Ne, US 127/J5
Davidson, Sk, Can. 127/G3
Davidson (mt.), Ca, US 135/J11
Davies (mt.), Austl. 113/F3
Davis (mt.), Pa, US 130/E4
Davis, Ca, US 128/B3
Davis (mts.), Tx, US 132/B4
Davis (str.), Can.,Grld. 123/L2
Davis (sea), Ant. 160/F
Davis, Austl., Ant. 160/F
Davlekanovo, Rus. 61/M5
Davo (riv.), C.d'Iv. 102/D5
Davos, Swi. 57/F4
Dawa, China 73/B2
Dawa Wenz (riv.), Eth. 97/N7
Dawangjia (isl.), China 73/B3
Dawson, Yk, Can. 134/L3
Dawson, Ga, US 133/G4
Dawson (riv.), Austl. 109/D3
Dawson (isl.), Chile 159/C7
Dawson Creek, BC, Can. 126/C2
Dawu, China 70/H5
Dawu (mtn.), China 72/C5
Dawu, China 72/C5
Dax, Fr. 42/C5
Daxing, China 72/H7
Daxue (mts.), China 70/H5
Dayang (riv.), China 73/B2
Dayao, China 83/H2
Daye, China 79/B1
Daying (riv.), China 83/G3
Daylesford, Austl. 115/C3
Dayong, China 79/B2
Dayr al Balaḩ, Gaza 91/D4
Dayr al Ghuşūn, WBnk. 91/G7
Dayr Az Zawr (prov.), Syria 90/E3
Dayr Ballūţ, WBnk. 91/G7
Dayr Sharaf, WBnk. 91/G7
Dayrūţ, Egypt 101/B3
Daysland, Ab, Can. 126/E2
Dayton, Wa, US 126/D4
Dayton, Tn, US 133/G3
Dayton, NJ, US 138/D3
Daytona Beach, Fl, US 133/H4
Dayu, China 83/K2
Dazhizhu Dau (isl.), China 71/T11
De Aar, SAfr. 106/D3
De Bilt, Neth. 50/C4
De Doorns, SAfr. 106/L10
De Funiak Springs, Fl, US 133/G4
De Grey (riv.), Austl. 109/A3
De Haan, Belg. 52/C1
De Hart (res.), Pa, US 138/B3
De Hoge Veluwe, NP, Neth. 50/C4
De Kalb (co.), Il, US 135/N16
De Land, Fl, US 133/H4
De Leijen (lake), Neth. 50/D2
De Lier, Neth. 50/B5
De Luz, Ca, US 136/C4
De Panne, Belg. 52/B1
De Peel (phys. reg.), Neth. 50/C6
De Pinte, Belg. 52/C2
De Ridder, La, US 129/J5
De Soto, Mo, US 129/K3
De Soto, Ks, US 137/D6
De Wijk, Neth. 50/D3
Dead Sea (sea), Jor.,Isr. 90/C4
Deadhorse, Ak, US 134/J1
Deadman (peak), Austl. 112/C2
Deadwood, SD, US 127/H4
Deal (isl.), Austl. 115/C3
Deal, NJ, US 138/D3
Deale, Md, US 138/B6
Dean (riv.), BC, Can. 126/B2
Dean (chan.), BC, Can. 126/B2
De'an, China 79/C2
Dean (for.), Eng, UK 32/D3
Deán Funes, Arg. 157/D3
Deanmill, Austl. 112/C5
Dearborn Heights, Mi, US 135/F7
Dearne, Eng, UK 35/G4
Dease (str.), Nun., Can. 122/F2
Dease (riv.), BC, Can. 122/D3
Dease Lake, BC, Can. 134/M4
Death Valley NP, Ca, US 128/C3
Debar, FYROM 47/G2
Debauch (mtn.), Ak, US 134/G3
Debe Habe, Nga. 96/H5
Debelets, Bul. 47/J1
Deben (riv.), Eng, UK 33/H2
Dębica, Pol. 41/L3
Dęblin, Pol. 41/L3
Dębno, Pol. 41/H2
Deborah (mt.), Ak, US 134/J3
Debre Birhan, Eth. 97/N6
Debre Mark'os, Eth. 97/N5
Debre Tabor, Eth. 97/N5
Debre Zeyit, Eth. 97/N6
Debrecen, Hun. 41/L5
Decatur, Il, US 127/L6
Decatur, Tx, US 129/H4
Decatur, Al, US 133/G3
Decatur, Ga, US 133/G3
Decatur, In, US 130/C3
Decazeville, Fr. 42/E4
Deccan (plat.), India 82/C5
Decima, It. 59/E3
Děčín, Czh. 41/H3
Décines-Charpieu, Fr. 56/A6
Decize, Fr. 42/E3
Dedemsvaart, Neth. 50/D3
Dedo (peak), Arg. 158/C5
Dédougou, Burk. 102/E3
Dedza, Malw. 105/F3
Dee (riv.), Sc, UK 36/C3
Deel (riv.), Ire. 34/A4
Deep Fork (riv.), Ok, US 137/N14
Deep River, On, Can. 130/E2
Deepcut, Eng, UK 30/F3
Deepwater, Austl. 115/D1
Deepwater, NJ, US 138/C4
Deepwater (pt.), De, US 138/C5
Deer (isl.), Ak, US 134/F5
Deer Creek (res.), Ut, US 137/L13
Deer Lake, Nf, Can. 131/K1
Deer Lake, Pa, US 138/B2
Deer Lodge, Mt, US 126/E4
Deer Park, Wa, US 126/D4
Deer Park, NY, US 139/E2
Deer Park, Md, US 138/B5
Deer Park, Il, US 135/P15
Deer Plain, Il, US 137/F8
Deerfield, Il, US 135/P15
Deering, Ak, US 134/F2
Deerlijk, Belg. 52/C2
Deeside (valley), Sc, UK 36/D2
Deex Nugaaleed (riv.), Som. 97/Q6
Defensores del Chaco, PN, Par. 150/F8
Defiance, Oh, US 130/C3
Dégelis, Qu, Can. 131/G2
Degerfors, Swe. 38/F2
Degersheim, Swi. 57/F3
Deggendorf, Ger. 55/F5
Deggingen, Ger. 54/C5
Dego, It. 58/B4
DeGrey (riv.), Austl. 112/C2
Deh Bīd, Iran 88/F2
Dehalak (isl.), Erit. 97/P4
Dehalak Marine NP, Erit. 97/P4
Deheq, Iran 88/F2
Dehra Dūn, India 89/L2
Dehri, India 85/E3
Dehua, China 79/C2
Deidesheim, Ger. 54/B4
Deinste, Ger. 51/G1
Deinze, Belg. 52/C2
Deister (mts.), Ger. 51/G4
Deiva Marina, It. 58/C4
Dej, Rom. 49/F2
Deje, Swe. 38/E2
Dejiang, China 83/J2
Dejima, Japan 77/E1
Dekemhare (Dek'emhāre), Erit. 88/C5
Del Campillo, Arg. 158/D2
Del Carril, Arg. 159/J11
Del City, Ok, US 137/N15
Del Dios, Ca, US 136/C5
Del Gran Paradiso, It. 58/A2
Del Mar, Ca, US 136/C5
Del Norte, Co, US 132/B2
Del Rio, Tx, US 129/G5
Del Valle, Arg. 158/E2
Del Valle (lake), Ca, US 135/L11
Delacroix, La, US 137/Q17
Delafield, Wi, US 135/P13
Delano, Ca, US 128/C4
Delareyville, SAfr. 106/D2
Delarode (lake), Sk, Can. 126/G2
Delavan, Wi, US 129/K2
Delavan (lake), Wi, US 135/P14
Delavan Lake, Wi, US 135/N14
Delaware (riv.), US 130/F3
Delaware, Oh, US 130/D3
Delaware (bay), NJ, US 130/F4
Delaware (state), US 130/F4
Delaware (pass), Pa, US 138/C2
Delaware, NJ, US 138/C2
Delaware (co.), Pa, US 138/C4
Delaware City, De, US 138/C4
Delaware Water Gap Nat'l Rec. Area, Pa, US 130/F3
Delbrück, Ger. 51/F5
Delčevo, FYROM 47/H2
Delden, Neth. 50/D4
Delebio, It. 57/F5
Delegate, Austl. 115/D3
Delémont, Swi. 56/D3
Delft, Neth. 50/B4
Delfzijl, Neth. 50/D2
Delgada (pt.), Arg. 158/E4
Delgado (cape), Moz. 104/D5
Delhi, La, US 129/K4
Delhi, India 86/D5
Delhi, Il, US 137/G7
Delhi (state), India 82/C2
Delice, Turk. 62/E5
Delice (riv.), Turk. 62/E5
Delījān, Iran 88/F2
Déljne, NW, Can. 122/D2
Delisle, Sk, Can. 127/G3
Dell Rapids, SD, US 127/J5

183

Delli – Dortm

Delligsen, Ger. 51/G5
Delmas, SAfr. 106/Q13
Delme (riv.), Ger. 51/F3
Delmenhorst, Ger. 51/F2
Delmiro Gouveia, Braz. 154/C3
Delmont, NJ, US 138/D5
Delnice, Cro. 48/B3
Deloraine, Austl. 115/C4
Deloraine, Mb, Can. 127/H3
Delphi (Dhelfoi) (ruin), Gre. 47/H3
Delphos, Oh, US 130/C3
Delportshoop, SAfr. 106/D3
Delran, NJ, US 138/D4
Delray Beach, Fl, US 133/H5
Delson, Qu, Can. 131/N7
Delta, Ut, US 128/D3
Delta (state), Nga. 103/G5
Delta, Pa, US 138/B4
Delta del Tigre, Uru. 159/K11
Delta du Saloum, PN du, Sen. 102/A3
Delta Junction, Ak, US 134/J3
Delta-Mendota (canal), Ca, US 135/M11
Deltona, Fl, US 133/H4
Delvinë, Alb. 47/G3
Dëma (riv.), Rus. 87/C2
Demanda, Sierra de la (range), Sp. 44/D1
Demarcation (pt.), Ak, US 134/K2
Demarest, NJ, US 139/K8
Demba, D.R. Congo 105/D2
Dembī Dolo, Eth. 97/M6
Demer (riv.), Belg. 40/C3
Demerara (riv.), Guy. 153/G3
Demerara-Mahaica (pol. reg.), Guy. 153/G3
Demerval Lobão, Braz. 154/B2
Deming, NM, US 132/B3
Demini (riv.), Braz. 150/F3
Demirci, Turk. 62/D5
Demirkent, Turk. 90/C2
Demirköprü (dam), Turk. 90/B2
Demirköy, Turk. 49/H5
Demirtaş, Turk. 49/J5
Demmin, Ger. 38/E5
Democratic Republic of the Congo (ctry.) 93/E5
Demone (valley), It. 46/D4
Demopolis, Al, US 133/G3
Dempo (peak), Indo. 80/B4
Dempster (pt.), Austl. 112/D5
Den Burg, Neth. 50/B2
Den Ham, Neth. 50/D4
Den Helder, Neth. 50/B3
Den Oever, Neth. 50/C3
Denain, Fr. 52/C3
Denakil (reg.), Djib.,Eth. 97/P5
Denali NP and Prsv., Ak, US 134/H3
Denare Beach, Sk, Can. 127/H2
Denbigh, Wal, UK 35/E5
Denbighshire (co.), Wal, UK 35/E5
Dender (riv.), Belg. 40/B3
Denderleeuw, Belg. 53/D2
Dendermonde, Belg. 53/D1
Denekamp, Neth. 50/E4
Deng Xian, China 72/C4
Dengfeng, China 72/C4
Dengkou, China 70/J3
Dengta, China 79/B3
Denham (sound), Austl. 112/B3
Denham, Austl. 112/B3
Denholme, Eng, UK 35/G4
Denia, Sp. 45/F3
Deniliquin, Austl. 115/C2
Denio, Nv, US 126/D5
Denison (mt.), Ak, US 134/H4
Denison, Ia, US 127/K5
Denison, Tx, US 129/H4
Denizli, Turk. 90/B2
Denizli (prov.), Turk. 90/B2
Denkendorf, Ger. 55/E5
Denklingen, Ger. 57/G2
Denman, Austl. 115/D2
Denmark, Austl. 112/C5
Denmark (str.), Grld.,Ice. 119/R3
Denmark (ctry.) 38/C4
Dennisville, NJ, US 138/D5
Denpasar, Indo. 80/E5
Dent de Lys (peak), Swi. 56/C4
Dent d'Hérens (peak), It. 56/D6
Dentergem, Belg. 52/C2
Dentlein am Forst, Ger. 54/D4
Denton, Tx, US 132/D3
Denton, Tx, US 129/H4
Denton, Md, US 138/C6
Denton, Eng, UK 35/F5
D'Entrecasteaux (isls.), PNG 116/D5
D'Entrecasteaux (pt.), Austl. 112/B5
Dents du Midi (peak), Swi. 56/C5
Denver (cap.), Co, US 137/C3
Denver (co.), Co, US 137/B3
Denver, Pa, US 138/B3
Denver International (int'l arpt.), Co, US 137/C3
Denver Museum of Natural History, Co, US 137/C3
Denville, NJ, US 138/D2
Denzlingen, Ger. 56/D1
Deoband, India 86/D5
Deogarh, India 82/D3
Deoghar, India 85/F3
Deohā (riv.), India 84/B1
Deolāli, India 89/K5
Deoli, India 82/C3
Déols, Fr. 42/D3
Deorī, India 84/B4
Deoria, India 84/D2
Dependencias Federales (state), Ven. 153/E1
Depew, NY, US 131/S10
Depok, Indo. 80/C5
Deqing, China 79/B3
Deqing, China 72/L9
Dera Ghāzi Khān, Pak. 86/A4
Dera Gopipur, India 86/D4
Dera Ismāīl Khān, Pak. 86/A4
Derbent, Rus. 63/J4
Derby, Ct, US 139/E1
Derby, Eng, UK 35/G6
Derby (co.), Eng, UK 35/G6
Derbyshire (co.), Eng, UK 35/G6
Derdap NP, Yugo. 62/B3
Derecske, Hun. 48/E2
Dereköy, Turk. 49/H5
Derendingen, Swi. 56/D3
Derg, Lough (lake), Ire. 31/P10
Derik, Turk. 90/E2
Derinkuyu, Turk. 90/C2
Dernau, Ger. 53/G2
Déroute, Passage de la (chan.), Fr. 42/B2
Derravaragh (lake), Ire. 34/A4
Derry, NH, US 131/G3
Derryboy, NI, UK 34/C3
Dervaig, Sc, UK 31/Q8
Derventa, Bosn. 48/C3
Dervio, It. 57/F5
Derwent (riv.), Austl. 115/C4
Derwent (riv.), Eng, UK 35/E2
Derwent (res.), Eng, UK 35/F2
Derwent Water (lake), Eng, UK 35/E2
Des Allemands, La, US 137/P17
Des Moines (cap.), Ia, US 127/K5
Des Moines (riv.), Ia,Mn, US 125/H3
Des Peres, Mo, US 137/G8
Desaguadero (riv.), Bol. 150/E7
Desaguadero, Peru 156/D5
Desagües de los Colorados (dry lake), Arg. 157/C2
Desana, It. 58/B2
Descabezado Grande (vol.), Chile 158/C2
Descalvado, Braz. 155/C2
Descartes, Fr. 42/D3
Deschambault (lake), Sk, Can. 127/H2
Deschambault Lake, Sk, Can. 127/H2
Deschutes (riv.), Or, US 126/C4
Desdunes, Haiti 145/H2
Desē, Eth. 97/N5
Dese (riv.), It. 59/F2
Deseado (riv.), Arg. 147/C7
Deseado (cape), Chile 159/B7
Desengaño (pt.), Arg. 159/D6
Desenzano del Garda, It. 58/D2
Désertines, Fr. 42/E3
Desio, It. 58/C1
Desna (riv.), Ukr. 62/D2
Desolación (isl.), Chile 157/A7
Desordem, Serra da (range), Braz. 154/A2
Despatch, SAfr. 106/D4
Dessau, Ger. 40/G3
Dessel, Belg. 50/C6
Dessoubre (riv.), Fr. 56/C3
Destelbergen, Belg. 52/C1
Destrehan, La, US 137/P17
Destruction Bay, Yk, Can. 134/L3
Desulo, It. 46/A2
Desvres, Fr. 52/A2
Deta, Rom. 48/E3
Detern, Ger. 51/E2
Detmold, Ger. 51/F5
Detroit (riv.), Can.,US 135/F7
Detroit Lakes, Mn, US 127/K4
Detroit Metropolitan Wayne County (int'l arpt.), Mi, US 130/D3
Dettelbach, Ger. 54/D3
Dettifoss (falls), Ice. 37/P6
Dettwiller, Fr. 53/G6
Deua NP, Austl. 115/D2
Deuil-la-Barre, Fr. 30/J5
Deûle (riv.), Fr. 52/B2
Deurne, Belg. 50/B6
Deurne, Neth. 50/C6
Deustua, Peru 156/D4
Deutsch Evern, Ger. 51/H2
Deutsch Wagram, Aus. 49/P7
Deutschkreutz, Aus. 43/M3
Deutschlandsberg, Aus. 43/L3
Deux-Montagnes, Qu, Can. 131/N6
Deux-Montagnes (co.), Qu, Can. 131/M6
Deux-Montagnes, Lac des (lake), Qu, Can. 131/M7
Deva, Rom. 48/F3
Dévaványa, Hun. 48/E2
Develi, Turk. 90/C2
Deventer, Neth. 50/D4
Deveron (riv.), Sc, UK 36/D2
Deville, Fr. 53/D4
Devil's (isl.), FrG. 151/H2
Devils (riv.), Mex. 143/E2
Devil's Elbow (pass), Sc, UK 36/C3
Devils Lake, ND, US 127/J3
Devils Paw (peak), Ak, US 134/M4
Devils Postpile Nat'l Mon., Ca, US 128/C3
Devils Slide, Ut, US 137/K11
Devine, Tx, US 129/H5
Devizes, Eng, UK 32/E4
Devnya, Bul. 49/H4
Devoll (riv.), Alb.,Gre. 48/E5
Devon, Ab, Can. 126/E2
Devon (co.), Eng, UK 32/C5
Devon (isl.), Nun., Can. 123/S7
Devon (riv.), Sc, UK 36/C4
Devon-Berwyn, Pa, US 138/C3
Devonport, Austl. 115/C4
Devore, Ca, US 136/C2
Devrek, Turk. 49/K5
Devrek (riv.), Turk. 62/D4
Devrez (riv.), Turk. 62/E4
Dewa (pt.), Indo. 80/A3
Dewa (mts.), Japan 76/B4
Dewās, India 89/L4
Dewetsdorp, SAfr. 106/D3
Dewsbury, Eng, UK 35/G4
Dexter, Me, US 131/G2
Dey-Dey (lake), Austl. 109/C3
Deyang, China 70/H5
Dez (riv.), Iran 64/E6
Dezfūl, Iran 88/E2
Dezhneva (cape), Rus. 134/E2
Dezhou, China 72/D3
Dhabān Singh, Pak. 86/B4
Dhākā (div.), Bang. 85/H4
Dhāka, India 85/E2
Dhaleswari (riv.), Bang. 85/H4
Dhali, Cyp. 91/C2
Dhāmpur, India 84/B1
Dhamtari, India 82/D3
Dhanaula, India 86/C4
Dhanaura, India 84/B1
Dhānbād, India 85/F4
Dhangadhī, Nepal 84/C1
Dhankutā, Nepal 85/F2
Dhār, India 89/L4
Dharampur, India 89/K4
Dharān, Nepal 85/F2
Dhāri, India 89/K4
Dhārīwāl, India 86/C4
Dharmapuri, India 82/C5
Dharmavaram, India 82/C5
Dharmjaygarh, India 84/D4
Dharmsāla, India 86/D3
Dhasan (riv.), India 84/B3
Dhaulāgiri (peak), Nepal 84/D1
Dhaulāgiri (zone), Nepal 84/D1
Dhaurahra, India 84/C1
Dhelfoí, Gre. 47/H3
Dhelvinákion, Gre. 47/G3
Dheskáti, Gre. 47/G3
Dheune (riv.), Fr. 56/A4
Dhībān, Jor. 91/D4
Dhidhimótikhon, Gre. 47/K2
Dhíkaia, Gre. 47/K2
Dhílos (ruin), Gre. 47/J4
Dhimitsána, Gre. 47/H4
Dhírfis (peak), Gre. 47/H3
Dhístomon, Gre. 47/H3
Dhofar (reg.), Oman 88/F5
Dhokímion, Gre. 47/G3
Dholka, India 89/K4
Dhomokós, Gre. 47/H3
Dhonoúsa (isl.), Gre. 47/J4
Dhorāji, India 89/K4
Dhronbach (riv.), Ger. 53/F4
Dhūlia, India 89/K4
Dhuliān, India 85/F3
Dhulikhel, Nepal 85/E2
Dhupgāri, India 85/G2
Dhūri, India 86/C4
Di Linh, Viet. 78/E4
Dia (isl.), Gre. 47/J5
Diablo (mt.), Ak, US 134/H4
Diablo (range), Ca, US 128/B3
Diablo (plat.), China 132/B4
Diablo, Punta del (pt.), Uru. 159/G2
Diablotin (peak), Dom. 141/N9
Diadema, Braz. 211/G8
Diadema Argentina, Arg. 158/D5
Diamante (riv.), Arg. 158/D2
Diamantina, Braz. 154/B5
Diamantina (riv.), Austl. 109/D3
Diamantina, Chapada (hills), Braz. 151/K6
Diamantino, Braz. 151/G6
Diamond Bar, Ca, US 136/G8
Diamond Harbour, India 85/G4
Diamond Head (pt.), Hi, US 124/W13
Dianalund, Den. 38/D4
Dianbai, China 83/K3
Dianjiang, China 79/A1
Diano Marina, It. 58/B5
Dianshan (lake), China 72/L8
Diapaga, Burk. 103/F3
Dias Creek, NJ, US 138/D5
Diavolezza (peak), Swi. 57/F5
Dibai, India 84/B1
Dibeng, SAfr. 106/C2
Dibiāpur, India 84/B2
Dibis (well), Egypt 101/B4
Dibs, Iraq 90/F3
Dickens, Tx, US 129/G4
Dickens (pt.), RI, US 139/G1
Dickinson, ND, US 127/H4
Dickson, Tn, US 130/C4
Dicle (dam), Turk. 90/E2
Dicomano, It. 59/E5
Didam, Neth. 50/D5
Didcot, Eng, UK 33/E3
Didsbury, Ab, Can. 126/E3
Dīdwāna, India 89/K3
Didyma (ruin), Turk. 90/A2
Die Berg (peak), SAfr. 105/F6
Dieblich, Ger. 53/G3
Diébougou, Burk. 102/E4
Dieburg, Ger. 54/B3
Diedersdorf, Ger. 40/Q7
Diefenbaker (lake), Sk, Can. 126/G3
Diego de Almagro (isl.), Chile 159/B6
Diego Garcia (isl.), UK 67/G10
Diekirch (dist.), Lux. 53/E4
Diekirch, Lux. 53/F4
Diemen, Neth. 50/B4
Diemtigen, Swi. 56/D4
Diepenbeek, Belg. 53/E2
Diepenveen, Neth. 50/D4
Diepholz, Ger. 51/F3
Diepoldsau, Swi. 57/F3
Dieppe, Fr. 42/D2
Dierdorf, Ger. 53/G2
Diespeck, Ger. 54/D3
Diessen am Ammersee, Ger. 57/H2
Diest, Belg. 53/E2
Dietenheim, Ger. 57/G1
Dietenhofen, Ger. 54/D4
Dietersheim, Ger. 54/D3
Dietfurt an der Altmühl, Ger. 55/E4
Dietikon, Swi. 57/E3
Dietmannsried, Ger. 57/G2
Dietzenbach, Ger. 54/B2
Dieue-sur-Meuse, Fr. 53/E5
Dieulouard, Fr. 53/E6
Dieuze, Fr. 53/F6
Diever, Neth. 50/D3
Diez, Ger. 54/B2
Diffa, Niger 96/H5
Diffa (dept.), Niger 103/H3
Differdange, Lux. 53/E4
Difficult (mt.), Austl. 115/B3
Dīg, India 84/A2
Digboi, India 83/G2
Digby, NS, Can. 131/H2
Dighwāra, India 85/E3
Digne-les-Bains, Fr. 43/G4
Digoin, Fr. 42/E3
Digor, Turk. 63/G4
Digul (riv.), Indo. 81/K4
Digya NP, Gha. 103/E5
Dijon, Fr. 56/A3
Dikirnis, Egypt 91/B4
Diklosmta (peak), Geo. 63/H4
Diksmuide, Belg. 52/B1
Dīla, Eth. 97/N6
Dilbeek, Belg. 53/D2
Dilek Yarımadası NP, Turk. 90/A2
Dili, Indo. 81/G5
Dillenburg, Ger. 53/H2
Dillendorf, Ger. 53/F5
Dillingen an der Donau, Ger. 54/D5
Dillingham, Ak, US 134/G4
Dillon, Mt, US 126/E4
Dillon, SC, US 133/J3
Dillsburg, Pa, US 138/A3
Dilolo, D.R. Congo 105/D3
Dilsen, Belg. 53/E1
Dimāpur, India 83/F2
Dimaro, It. 57/G5
Dimas, Mex. 142/D4
Dimashq (prov.), Syria 90/D3
Dimbokro, C.d'Iv. 102/D5
Dimboola, Austl. 115/B3
Dîmbovița (prov.), Rom. 49/G3
Dimbulah, Austl. 114/B2
Dimitriya Lapteva (str.), Rus. 65/P2
Dimitrovgrad, Bul. 47/J1
Dimitrovgrad, Yugo. 47/H1
Dimitrovgrad, Rus. 63/J1
Dimlang (peak), Nga. 96/H6
Dimmitt, Tx, US 129/G4
Dimona, Isr. 91/D4
Dimovo, Bul. 49/F4
Dina, Pak. 86/B3
Dinagat (isl.), Phil. 81/G1
Dinagat, Phil. 79/E6
Dinājpur (pol. reg.), Bang. 85/G3
Dinan, Fr. 42/B2
Dīnānagar, India 86/C3
Dinant, Belg. 53/D3
Dinar, Turk. 90/B2
Dinard, Fr. 42/B2
Dinaric Alps (mts.), Cro. 48/C3
Dinas (pt.), Wal, UK 32/B2
Dinder NP, Sudan 97/N5
Dindigul, India 82/C5
Dindori, India 84/C4
Dinga, Pak. 86/B3
Ding'an, China 83/K4
Dingbian, China 70/J4
Dingelstädt, Ger. 51/H6
Dinggyê, China 85/F1
Dingle, Ire. 30/F10
Dingle (bay), Ire. 30/N10
Dingmans Ferry, Pa, US 138/D1
Dingnan, China 79/C3
Dingolfing, Ger. 55/F5
Dingras, Phil. 79/D4
Dingtao, China 72/C4
Dingwall, Sc, UK 36/B1
Dingxi, China 70/H4
Dingxiang, China 72/C3
Dingxing, China 72/G7
Dingyuan, China 72/D4
Dinkel (riv.), Ger. 51/E4
Dinkelsbühl, Ger. 54/D4
Dinkelscherben, Ger. 54/D6
Dinklage, Ger. 51/F3
Dinosaur Nat'l Mon., US 128/E2
Dinslaken, Ger. 50/D5
Dinsmore, Sk, Can. 126/G3
Dintel Mark (riv.), Neth. 50/B5
Dinuba, Ca, US 128/C3
Dinxperlo, Neth. 50/D5
Dioïla, Mali 102/D3
Dion (riv.), Gui. 102/C4
Diósd, Hun. 49/Q10
Diourbel (pol. reg.), Sen. 102/A3
Diourbel, Sen. 102/A3
Dīpālpur, Pak. 86/B4
Diphu, India 83/F2
Diplo, Pak. 89/J4
Dipni (dam), Turk. 90/E2
Dipperu NP, Austl. 114/C3
Dipperz, Ger. 54/C1
Dique (canal), Col. 145/H4
Diré, Mali 102/E2
Dirē Dawa, Eth. 97/P6
Diriamba, Nic. 144/E4
Dirj, Libya 99/H3
Dirk Hartog (isl.), Austl. 109/A3
Dirksland, Neth. 50/B5
Dirlewang, Ger. 57/G2
Dirranbandi, Austl. 114/C5
Dirrington Great Law (hill), Sc, UK 36/D5
Dirty Devil (riv.), Ut, US 128/E3
Disappointment (lake), Austl. 109/B3
Disappointment (isls.), FrPol. 117/L6
Discovery (bay), Austl. 115/B3
Discovery Bay, Jam. 145/G2
Disentis-Mustér, Swi. 57/E4
Disgrazi (peak), It. 57/F5
Disko (isl.), Grld. 119/M3
Disko (Qeqertarsuaq) (isl.), Grld. 123/L2
Disneyland, Ca, US 136/G8
Dison, Belg. 53/E2
Dispur, India 83/F2
Disraëli, Qu, Can. 131/G2
Dissen am Teutoburger Wald, Ger. 51/F4
Distrito Féderal (fed. dist.), Braz. 154/A4
Distrito Federal (fed. dist.), Mex. 140/A5
Distrito Federal (fed. dist.), Ven. 153/E2
Distrito Federal (fed. dist.), Col. 152/C3
Disūq, Egypt 91/B4
Ditching Beacon (hill), Eng, UK 33/F5
Dittaino (riv.), It. 46/D4
Dittelbrunn, Ger. 54/D2
Dittmer, Mo, US 137/F9
Ditzingen, Ger. 54/C5
Diu, India 89/K4
Diva (riv.), Yugo. 48/D4
Dive (riv.), Fr. 42/D3
Dividing Creek, NJ, US 138/C5
Divinolândia, Braz. 211/G6
Divinópolis, Braz. 155/C2
Divisa Nova, Braz. 211/G6
Divisor, Serra do (mts.), Braz. 150/D5
Divo, C.d'Iv. 102/D5
Divonne-les-Bains, Fr. 56/C5
Divriği, Turk. 62/F5
Dix (lake), Swi. 56/D5
Dixmoor, Il, US 135/Q16
Dixon, Il, US 127/L5
Dixon Entrance (chan.), Can.,US 134/M4
Diyadin, Turk. 63/G5
Diyāla (gov.), Iraq 90/F3
Diyarb Najm, Egypt 91/B4
Diyarbakir (prov.), Turk. 90/E2
Diyarbakır, Turk. 90/E2
Djado (plat.), Niger 93/D2
Djakotomé, Ben. 103/F5
Djamaa, Alg. 99/G2
Djambala, Congo 96/H8
Djanet, Alg. 99/H4
Djebel-Amrag (mtn.), Alg. 100/D3
Djebel Tichka (peak), Mor. 98/C3
Djedi, Oued (riv.), Alg. 99/G2
Djelfa, Alg. 96/F1
Djéma, CAfr. 97/L6
Djemila (ruin), Alg. 100/H4
Djénné, Mali 102/D3
Djibo, Burk. 103/E3
Djibouti (cap.), Djib. 97/P5
Djibouti (ctry.) 97/P5
Djougou, Ben. 103/F4
Djúpivogur, Ice. 37/P7
Dnepr (riv.), Rus. 62/D1
Dnipro (riv.), Ukr. 27/H3
Dniprodzerzhyns'k, Ukr. 62/E2
Dnipropetrovs'k, Ukr. 62/E2
Dnipropetrovs'ka (obl.), Ukr. 62/E2
Dniprovs'kyy Lyman (estu.), Ukr. 49/K2
Dnister (riv.), Ukr. 40/M4
Dnistrovs'kyy Lyman (estu.), Ukr. 49/K2
Dnyapro (riv.), Bela. 39/P4
Do (lake), Mali 103/E3
Do Rāh (pass), Afg. 89/K1
Do Son, Viet. 78/D1
Doany, Madg. 107/J6
Doba, Chad 96/J6
Dobbs Ferry, NY, US 139/K7
Dobele, Lat. 39/K3
Döbeln, Ger. 40/G3
Doberai (pen.), Indo. 81/H4
Dobiegniew, Pol. 41/H2
Dobogó-kő (peak), Hun. 49/Q9
Doboj, Bosn. 48/D3
Dobřany, Czh. 55/G3
Dobre Miasto, Pol. 39/J5
Dobrich, Bul. 49/H4
Dobříš, Czh. 55/H3
Dobruja (reg.), Bul. 49/H4
Dobrush, Bela. 62/D1
Dobryanka, Rus. 61/N4
Doce (riv.), Braz. 151/K7
Dochart (riv.), Sc, UK 36/B4
Dock Junction, Ga, US 133/H4
Docker River, Austl. 113/F3
Doctor Arroyo, Mex. 143/E4
Doctor Pedro P. Peña, Par. 157/D1
Doctor Petru Groza, Rom. 48/F2
Doda (lake), Qu, Can. 130/F1
Doda, India 86/C3
Doda (riv.), India 86/D3
Dodder (riv.), Ire. 34/B5
Doddinghurst, Eng, UK 30/D2
Dodecanese (isl.), Gre. 90/A2
Dodge City, Ks, US 129/G3
Dodger Stadium, Ca, US 136/F7
Dodgeville, Wi, US 127/L5
Dodman (pt.), Eng, UK 32/B6
Dodoma, Tanz. 104/B4
Dodoma (pol. reg.), Tanz. 104/B4
Dodori Nat'l Rsv., Kenya 104/D3
Dodsland, Sk, Can. 126/F3
Dodworth, Eng, UK 35/G4
Doesburg, Neth. 50/D4
Doetinchem, Neth. 50/D5
Doğanhisar, Turk. 90/B2
Doğankent (riv.), Turk. 62/F4
Doğanşar, Turk. 90/D1
Doğanşehir, Turk. 90/D2
Doğanyurt, Turk. 62/E4
Döğer, Turk. 62/D5
Dogliani, It. 58/A3
Dogondoutchi, Niger 103/G3
Doğubayazıt, Turk. 63/H5
Doğukaradeniz (mts.), Turk. 63/G4
Dohad, India 89/K4
Dohrīghāt, India 84/D2
Doi Khun Tan NP, Thai. 78/B2
Doilungdêqên, China 82/F2
Doiras, Embalse de (res.), Sp. 44/B1
Dois de Julho (int'l arpt.), Braz. 154/C4
Dois Irmãos, Serra (mts.), Braz. 151/K5
Doische, Belg. 53/D3
Dokka, Nor. 38/D1
Dokkum, Neth. 50/D2
Dokkumer Ee (riv.), Neth. 50/C2
Doksy, Czh. 55/H1
Dolbeau, Qu, Can. 131/F1
Dolcedorme (peak), It. 46/E3
Dole, Fr. 56/B3
Dolent (peak), Swi. 56/D6
Dolgellau, Wal, UK 32/C1
Dolgoprudnyy, Rus. 61/W9
Dolianova, It. 46/A3
Dolinsk, Rus. 71/R2
Dolj (prov.), Rom. 49/F3
Dollar, Sc, UK 36/C4
Dollar Law (peak), Sc, UK 36/C5
Dollard-des-Ormeaux, Qu, Can. 131/N7
Dollard (Dollart) (bay), Neth.,Ger. 51/E2
Doller (riv.), Fr. 40/D5
Dollnstein, Ger. 54/E5
Dolmar (peak), Ger. 54/D1
Dolmen (ruin), It. 46/E2
Dolna Banya, Bul. 47/H1
Dolni Dŭbnik, Bul. 49/G4
Dolo, Eth. 97/P7
Dolo, It. 59/F2
Dolo (riv.), It. 58/D4
Doloon, Mong. 70/J3
Dolores, Arg. 158/F3
Dolores, Guat. 144/D2
Dolores (riv.), Co, US 128/E3
Dolores, Co, US 132/A2
Dolores, Uru. 159/J10
Dolores, Ven. 152/D2
Dolphin (cape), UK 159/F6
Dolphin and Union (str.), Nun., Can. 122/E2
Dölsach, Aus. 43/K3
Dolton, Il, US 135/Q16
Dom (peak), Swi. 56/D5
Dom (peak), Indo. 81/J4
Dom Noi (res.), Thai. 78/D3
Dom Pedrito, Braz. 157/F3
Dom Pedro, Braz. 154/A2
Domat-Ems, Swi. 57/F4
Domažlice, Czh. 55/F4
Dombasle-sur-Meurthe, Fr. 53/F6
Dombay-Ul'gen (peak), Geo. 63/G4
Dombes (lake), Fr. 56/B5
Dombóvár, Hun. 48/D2
Dombrád, Hun. 48/E1
Domburg, Neth. 50/A5
Dome C, US, Ant. 160/J
Domérat, Fr. 42/E3
Domeyko, Cordillera (mts.), Chile 157/C1
Dominica (ctry.) 141/N9
Dominica Passage (chan.), Dom.,Guad. 141/N9
Dominican Republic (ctry.) 141/H4
Dommartin-lès-Remiremont, Fr. 56/C2
Dommartin-lès-Toul, Fr. 53/E6
Dommel (riv.), Belg. 53/E1
Domodedovo (int'l arpt.), Rus. 61/W9
Domodossola, It. 57/E5
Domohāni, India 85/G2
Domont, Fr. 30/J4
Dompu, Indo. 81/E5
Domrémy-la-Pucelle, Fr. 56/B1
Dömsöd, Hun. 48/D2
Domusnovas, It. 46/A3
Domuyo (vol.), Arg. 158/C3
Domvilk (mt.), Austl. 114/C5
Domžale, Slov. 43/L3
Don (ridge), Rus. 64/E5
Don (riv.), Rus. 27/J4
Don (riv.), Eng, UK 35/G5
Don Benito, Sp. 44/C3
Donabate, Ire. 34/B5
Donada, It. 59/F2
Donaghadee, NI, UK 34/C2
Donaghmore, NI, UK 34/B2
Donald, Austl. 115/B3
Donaldsonville, La, US 129/K5
Doñana NP, Sp. 44/B4
Donath, Swi. 57/F4
Donau (Danube) (riv.), Ger. 43/H2
Donaueschingen, Ger. 57/E2
Donauwörth, Ger. 54/D5
Doncaster, Eng, UK 35/G4
Donchery, Fr. 53/D4
Dondra Head (pt.), SrL. 82/D6
Donegal, Ire. 31/P9
Donegal (dist.), Ire. 34/A1
Donegal (bay), Ire. 31/P9
Donets (riv.), Ukr. 64/D5
Donets'k, Ukr. 62/F2
Donets'k (int'l arpt.), Ukr. 62/F2
Donets'ka (obl.), Ukr. 62/F3
Dong (riv.), Viet. 83/J5
Dong Ha, Viet. 78/D2
Dong Hoi, Viet. 78/D2
Dong Noi (riv.), Viet. 79/A5
Donga (riv.), Nga. 103/H4
Dongar Parāsia, India 84/B4
Dongara, Austl. 112/B4
Dongbei (plain), China 72/E2
Dongchuan, China 83/H2
Dong'e, China 72/D3
Dongen, Neth. 50/B5
Dongfang, China 83/J4
Donggou, China 73/C3
Dongguan, China 83/K3
Dongguang, China 72/D3
Donghai, China 72/D4
Dongio, Swi. 57/E5
Dongkya (pass), China 85/G2
Donglan, China 79/A3
Dongliao (riv.), China 72/F2
Dongming, China 72/C4
Dongo, It. 57/F5
Dongping, China 72/D4
Dongsha (isl.), China 79/C3
Dongshan, China 79/C3
Dongtai, China 72/E4
Dongtiao (riv.), China 72/L9
Dongting (lake), China 79/B2
Dongzhi, China 79/C1
Donihue, Chile 158/N9
Donjek (riv.), Yk, Can. 122/C2
Donji Komren, Yugo. 47/G1
Donji Vakuf, Bosn. 48/C3
Donnas, It. 58/A1
Donnersberg (peak), Ger. 53/G4
Donnybrook, Austl. 114/D4
Donnybrook, Austl. 112/B5
Donon (peak), Fr. 56/D1
Donoratico, It. 43/J5
Donzdorf, Ger. 54/C5
Donzy, Fr. 42/E3
Dooleena (peak), Austl. 112/C2
Doon (riv.), Sc, UK 36/B6
Doon (lake), Sc, UK 36/B6
Doonbeg, Ire. 31/P10
Doonerak (mt.), Ak, US 134/H2
Door (pen.), Wi, US 127/M4
Doorn (riv.), SAfr. 106/B3
Doorn, Neth. 50/C4
Doppo (peak), It. 58/D1
Doqên (lake), China 85/G1
Dora (lake), Austl. 109/B3
Dora Riparia (riv.), It. 43/G4
Dorada (coast), Sp. 45/F2
Dorchester, NB, Can. 131/H2
Dorchester, Il, US 137/H7
Dorchester, Eng, UK 32/D5
Dorchester (cape), Nun., Can. 123/J2
Dorchester, NJ, US 138/D5
Dordogne (riv.), Fr. 42/D4
Dordrecht, SAfr. 106/D3
Dordrecht, Neth. 50/B5
Dore (lake), Sk, Can. 126/G2
Dore, Monts (mts.), Fr. 42/E4
Dores do Indaiá, Braz. 155/C1
Dorfen, Ger. 55/F6
Dorfen (riv.), Ger. 55/E6
Dorgali, It. 46/A2
Dori, Burk. 103/E3
Dorion, Qu, Can. 131/M7
Dorking, Eng, UK 30/C3
Dorlisheim, Fr. 56/D1
Dormagen, Ger. 53/F1
Dormans, Fr. 52/C5
Dornach, Swi. 56/D3
Dornbirn, Aus. 57/F3
Dorney Park/Wildwater Kingdom, Pa, US 138/C2
Dornhan, Ger. 57/E1
Dorno, It. 58/B2
Dornoch Firth (inlet), Sc, UK 36/B1
Dornod (prov.), Mong. 71/K2
Dornogovĭ (prov.), Mong. 71/J3
Dornstadt, Ger. 54/C6
Dornstetten, Ger. 54/B6
Dorog, Hun. 49/Q9
Dorothy, NJ, US 138/D5
Dörpen, Ger. 51/E3
Dorre (isl.), Austl. 112/B3
Dorrigo, Austl. 115/E1
Dorrigo NP, Austl. 115/E1
Dorsale (mts.), Tun. 46/A5
Dorsbach (riv.), Ger. 54/B2
Dorset (co.), Eng, UK 32/D5
Dorsey, Il, US 137/G8
Dorsten, Ger. 50/D5
Dortan, Fr. 56/B5
Dortmund, Ger. 51/E5
Dortmund-Ems (canal), Ger. 51/E4

184

Dortm – Edwar

Dortmund (Wickede) (int'l arpt.), Ger. 51/E5
Dörtyol, Turk. 91/E1
Dorum, Ger. 51/F1
Dorval, Qu, Can. 131/N7
Dörverden, Ger. 51/G3
Dos Bahías (cape), Arg. 158/D5
Dos de Mayo, Peru 156/C2
Dos Hermanas, Sp. 44/C4
Döşemealtı, Turk. 91/B1
Dosewallips (riv.), Wa, US 135/A2
Dōshi, Japan 77/C2
Dōshi (riv.), Japan 77/C2
Dosse (riv.), Ger. 40/G2
Dosso, Niger 103/F3
Dosso (dept.), Niger 103/F3
Dosson, It. 59/F1
Dossor, Kaz. 63/K3
Dot Lake, Ak, US 134/K3
Dothan, Al, US 133/G4
Dötlingen, Ger. 51/F3
Döttingen, Swi. 57/E2
Douai, Fr. 52/C3
Douala, Camr. 96/G7
Douar el Càïd el Gueddara, Mor. 100/A2
Douar Toulal, Mor. 100/B3
Douarnenez, Fr. 42/A2
Douarnenez, Baie de (bay), Fr. 42/A2
Double Island (pt.), Austl. 114/D4
Double Mountain Fork Brazos (riv.), Tx, US 129/G4
Double Mtn. Fork (riv.), Tx, US 143/E1
Doubs (riv.), Fr. 42/F3
Doubs (dept.), Fr. 56/C3
Doubs, Fr. 56/C4
Doubtful Island (bay), Austl. 112/C5
Douchy-les-Mines, Fr. 52/C3
Doue, Fr. 30/M5
Doué-la-Fontaine, Fr. 42/C3
Douentza, Mali 102/E3
Dougga (ruin), Tun. 100/L6
Douglas (mt.), Ak, US 134/H4
Douglas, Wy, US 127/G5
Douglas, Ga, US 133/H4
Douglas, SAfr. 106/C3
Douglas (co.), Co, US 137/C4
Douglas, Sc, UK 36/C5
Douglas (cap.), IM, UK 34/D3
Douglassville, Pa, US 138/C3
Doulaincourt-Saucourt, Fr. 56/B1
Doullens, Fr. 52/B3
Doune, Sc, UK 36/B4
Doune (peak), Sc, UK 36/B4
Doupovské Hory (mts.), Czh. 43/K1
Dour, Belg. 52/C3
Dourados, Braz. 151/H8
Dourdan, Fr. 30/J6
Dourdou (riv.), Fr. 42/E4
Dourh (peak), Mor. 99/E2
Douro (riv.), Port. 44/B2
Dousman, Wi, US 135/P13
Doussard, Fr. 56/C6
Douvaine, Fr. 56/C5
Douvrin, Fr. 52/B2
Doux (riv.), Fr. 42/F4
Douze (riv.), Fr. 42/C4
Dove Creek, Co, US 128/E3
Dover, Austl. 115/C4
Dover, Eng, UK 33/H4
Dover (pt.), Austl. 112/E5
Dover, Pa, US 138/B4
Dover, NJ, US 138/D2
Dover (cap.), De, US 138/C5
Dover-Foxcroft, Me, US 131/G2
Dover, Strait of (str.), Fr.,UK 42/D1
Dovrefjell NP, Nor. 37/D3
Dow, Il, US 137/G7
Dowerin, Austl. 112/C4
Dowlatābād, Iran 89/G3
Down (dist.), NI, UK 34/C3
Downers Grove, Il, US 135/P16
Downey, Ca, US 136/F8
Downieville, Ca, US 128/B3
Downingtown, Pa, US 138/C4
Downpatrick, NI, UK 34/C3
Doylestown, Pa, US 138/C3
Dōzen (isl.), Japan 74/C3
Dozois (res.), Qu, Can. 130/E2
Drâa (cape), Mor. 98/C3
Drâa, Oued (riv.), Mor. 93/B2
Drac (riv.), Fr. 42/F4
Dracena, Braz. 155/B2
Drachten, Neth. 50/D2
Drăgănești-Olt, Rom. 49/G3
Dragoman, Bul. 47/H1
Dragon's Mouth (str.), Trin.,Ven. 153/F2
Draguignan, Fr. 43/G5
Drake (passg.) 157/C8
Drake, Co, US 137/B2
Drake (passg.), SAm. 159/D8
Drakensberg (mts.), SAfr. 93/E8
Dráma, Gre. 47/J2
Drammen, Nor. 38/D2
Drance (riv.), Swi. 56/D5
Drancy, Fr. 30/K5
Drangedal, Nor. 38/C2
Dranse (riv.), Fr. 56/C5
Dransfeld, Ger. 51/G5
Draper, Ut, US 137/K12
Drau (riv.), Aus. 43/K3
Drava (riv.), Slov. 43/L3
Dráva (riv.), Aus. 48/C3
Draveil, Fr. 30/K5
Drawa (riv.), Pol. 41/H2
Drawieński NP, Pol. 41/H2
Drawsko Pomorskie, Pol. 41/H2
Drayton, ND, US 127/J3
Drayton Valley, Ab, Can. 126/E2
Dreghorn, Sc, UK 36/B5
Drei Zinnen (peak), PNG 81/K4
Dreiesselberg (peak), Ger. 55/G5
Dreisam (riv.), Ger. 56/D2
Drensteinfurt, Ger. 51/E5
Drenthe (prov.), Neth. 50/D3
Drentse Hoofdvaart (riv.), Neth. 50/D3
Drentwede, Ger. 51/F3
Dresano, It. 58/C2
Dresden, Ger. 64/B4
Drezdenko, Pol. 41/H2
Driebergen, Neth. 50/C4
Driedorf, Ger. 53/H2
Drigh Road, Pak. 89/J4
Drimoleague, Ire. 31/P11
Drin (gulf), Alb. 47/F2
Drin (riv.), Alb. 47/F1
Drina (riv.), Bosn. 48/D4
Drniš, Cro. 48/C4
Dro, It. 57/G6
Drøbak, Nor. 38/D2
Drobeta-Turnu Severin, Rom. 48/F3
Drochtersen, Ger. 51/G1
Drocourt, Fr. 30/H4
Drogheda, Ire. 34/B4
Drohobych, Ukr. 62/B2
Droitwich, Eng, UK 32/D2
Drolshagen, Ger. 53/G1
Dromiskin, Ire. 34/B4
Dromore (riv.), Ire. 34/A3
Dromore, NI, UK 34/B3
Dronero, It. 43/G4
Dronfield, Eng, UK 35/G5
Drongan, Sc, UK 36/B6
Dronne (riv.), Fr. 42/D4
Dronten, Neth. 50/C3
Dropt (riv.), Fr. 42/D4
Drouette (riv.), Fr. 52/A6
Drowning (riv.), On, Can. 130/C1
Drumbeg, NI, UK 34/C2
Drumcar, Ire. 34/B4
Drumheller, Ab, Can. 126/E3
Drumleck (pt.), Ire. 34/B5
Drummond (range), Austl. 109/D3
Drummond (pt.), Austl. 113/G5
Drummond (mt.), Austl. 114/B4
Drummondville, Qu, Can. 131/F2
Drumochter, Pass of (pass), Sc, UK 36/B3
Drunen, Neth. 50/C5
Druridge (bay), Eng, UK 35/G1
Drusenheim, Fr. 53/G6
Druskininkai, Lith. 39/K4
Druten, Neth. 50/C5
Drvar, Bosn. 48/C3
Drwęca (riv.), Pol. 41/K2
Dry Fork Cheyenne (riv.), Wy, US 129/F2
Dry Tortugas (isl.), Fl, US 133/H5
Dry Tortugas NP, Fl, US 133/H5
Dryanovo, Bul. 47/J1
Dryden, On, Can. 127/K3
Dryden, Tx, US 132/C4
Dryden, Mi, US 135/F6
Drygarn Fawr (peak), Wal, UK 32/C2
Du Bois, Pa, US 130/E3
Du Page (riv.), Il, US 135/P16
Du Page (co.), Il, US 135/P16
Du Page, East Br. (riv.), Il, US 135/P16
Du Quoin, Il, US 129/K3
Duaringa, Austl. 114/C3
Duarte (peak), DRep. 141/G4
Duarte, Ca, US 136/G7
Dubawnt (riv.), NW, Can. 122/F2
Dubawnt (lake), Nun., Can. 122/F2
Dubayy, UAE 89/G3
Dubbo, Austl. 115/D2
Dübendorf, Swi. 57/E3
Dübener Heide (phys. reg.), Ger. 40/G3
Dubino, It. 57/F5
Dublin, Ga, US 133/H3
Dublin, Pa, US 138/C3
Dublin, Md, US 138/B4
Dublin, Ca, US 135/L11
Dublin (co.), Ire. 34/B5
Dublin (cap.), Ire. 34/B5
Dubna, Rus. 60/H4
Dubnica nad Váhom, Slvk. 41/K4
Dubno, Ukr. 62/C2
Dubois, Wy, US 126/F5
Duboistown, Pa, US 138/A1
Dubossary (res.), Mol. 49/J2
Dubrājpur, India 85/F4
Dubrovnik, Cro. 47/F1
Dubrovnik (int'l arpt.), Cro. 47/F1
Dubuque, Ia, US 127/L5
Duchang, China 79/C2
Duchcov, Czh. 55/G1
Duchesne (riv.), Ut, US 128/E2
Duchesne, Ut, US 128/E2
Ducie (isl.), Pitc. 117/N7
Duck (riv.), Tn, US 130/C5
Duck (lake), Mi, US 135/E7
Duckabush (riv.), Wa, US 135/A2
Duda (riv.), Col. 152/C4
Duddon (riv.), Eng, UK 35/E3
Dudelange, Lux. 53/F5
Dudenhofen, Ger. 54/B4
Duderstadt, Ger. 51/H5
Dudh Kosi (riv.), Nepal 85/F2
Dūdhi, India 84/D3
Dudhwa NP, India 84/C1
Dudignac, Arg. 158/E2
Düdingen, Swi. 56/D4
Dudinka, Rus. 64/J3
Dudley, Eng, UK 32/D1
Dueñas, Sp. 44/C2
Duero (riv.), Sp. 44/C2
Dueville, It. 59/E1
Dufaja (riv.), Kenya 104/C3
Duff (isls.), Sol. 116/F5
Duffel, Belg. 53/D1
Dufftown, Sc, UK 36/C2
Dufour (Dufourspitze) (peak), Swi. 58/A1
Dufourspitze (peak), Swi. 43/G4
Dugi Otok (isl.), Cro. 48/B3
Dugny-sur-Meuse, Fr. 53/E5
Dugo Selo, Cro. 48/C3
Dugway, Ut, US 128/D2
Duich (lake), Sc, UK 36/A2
Duida (peak), Ven. 153/E4
Duida Marahuaca, PN, Ven. 150/E3
Duingen, Ger. 51/G4
Duisburg, Ger. 50/D6
Duitama, Col. 152/C3
Duiven, Neth. 50/D5
Duke of Gloucester (isls.), FrPol. 117/L7
Duke's (pass), Sc, UK 36/B4
Dukielska (Dukla Pass) (pass), Pol. 41/L4
Dulan, China 70/G4
Dulce (riv.), Arg. 157/D2
Dulce, NM, US 128/F3
Dulce (gulf), Pan. 145/F4
Dulce Nombre de Culmí, Hon. 144/E3
Duleek, Ire. 34/B4
Dŭlgopol, Bul. 49/H4
Duliu (riv.), China 83/J2
Dullewāla, Pak. 86/A4
Dülmen, Ger. 51/E5
Dulnain (riv.), Sc, UK 36/C2
Dulovo, Bul. 49/H4
Dumalinao, Phil. 79/D6
Dumaran (isl.), Phil. 81/E1
Dumaresq (riv.), Austl. 115/D1
Dumas, Ar, US 129/K4
Dumas, Tx, US 129/G4
Dumbarton, Sc, UK 36/B5
Ďumbier (peak), Slvk. 41/K4
Dumbleyung, Austl. 112/C5
Dumbrăveni, Rom. 49/G2
Dume (pt.), Ca, US 136/B2
Dumfries, Sc, UK 34/E1
Dumfries and Galloway (pol. reg.), Sc, UK 36/C6
Dumka, India 85/F3
Dumlu, Turk. 63/G4
Dümmer (lake), Ger. 51/F3
Dumoine (riv.), Qu, Can. 130/E2
Dumoine (lake), Qu, Can. 123/J4
Dumont, NJ, US 139/K8
Dumont d'Urville, Fr., Ant. 160/K
Dumraon, India 85/E3
Dumyāṭ (gov.), Egypt 101/B1
Dún Laoghaire, Ire. 34/B5
Dun Rig (peak), Sc, UK 36/C5
Dunaföldvár, Hun. 48/D2
Dunaharaszti, Hun. 49/R10
Dunajec (riv.), Pol. 41/L4
Dunakeszi, Hun. 49/R9
Dunany (pt.), Ire. 34/B4
Dunaszekcső, Hun. 48/D2
Dunaújváros, Hun. 48/D2
Dunavecse, Hun. 48/D2
Dunavtsi, Bul. 48/F4
Dunbar, Sc, UK 36/D5
Dunblane, Sc, UK 36/C4
Dunboyne, Ire. 34/B5
Duncan, BC, Can. 126/C3
Duncan, Ok, US 129/H4
Duncannon, Pa, US 138/A3
Duncansby Head (pt.), Sc, UK 31/V14
Duncanville, Tx, US 132/D3
Dund-Us, Mong. 70/F2
Dundalk (bay), Ire. 31/Q10
Dundalk, Md, US 138/B5
Dundalk, Ire. 34/B4
Dundas (lake), Austl. 109/B4
Dundas, On, Can. 131/Q9
Dundas (pen.), NW, Can. 123/R7
Dundee, SAfr. 107/E3
Dundee, Sc, UK 36/D4
Dundee (pol. reg.), Sc, UK 36/D4
Dundgovĭ (prov.), Mong. 70/J2
Dundonald, Sc, UK 36/B5
Dundrum, NI, UK 34/C3
Dundrum (bay), NI, UK 34/C3
Dundurn, Sk, Can. 126/G3
Dundwa (range), Nepal 84/D2
Dundwārāganj, India 84/B2
Dunedin, Fl, US 133/H4
Dunedin, NZ 117/S12
Dunedoo, Austl. 115/D2
Dunellen, NJ, US 139/H9
Dunfanaghy, Ire. 31/Q9
Dunfermline, Sc, UK 36/C4
Dunga Bunga, Pak. 86/B5
Dungannon (co.), NI, UK 34/B3
Dungannon, NI, UK 34/B3
Dungarpur, India 89/K4
Dungarvan, Ire. 31/Q10
Dungau (reg.), Ger. 55/F5
Dungeness (pt.), Eng, UK 33/G5
Dungeness (pt.), Arg. 159/C7
Dungiven, NI, UK 34/B2
Dunglow, Ire. 31/P9
Dungog, Austl. 115/D2
Dungu, D.R. Congo 104/A2
Dungu (riv.), D.R. Congo 104/A2
Dunhua, China 71/N3
Dunhuang, China 70/F3
Dunkeld, Sc, UK 36/C3
Dunkerque (Dunkirk), Fr. 42/E1
Dunkery (hill), Eng, UK 32/C4
Dunkirk (Dunkerque), Fr. 42/E1
Dunkwa, Gha. 103/E5
Dunleer, Ire. 34/B4
Dunloy, NI, UK 34/B2
Dunmanway, Ire. 31/P11
Dunmurry, NI, UK 34/B2
Dunn, NC, US 133/J3
Dunnamanagh, NI, UK 34/A2
Dünnern (riv.), Swi. 56/D3
Dunnet Head (pt.), Sc, UK 31/V14
Dunningen, Ger. 57/E1
Dunnville, On, Can. 131/Q10
Dunolly, Austl. 115/B3
Dunoon, Sc, UK 36/B5
Dunqulah, Sudan 101/B5
Duns, Sc, UK 36/D5
Dunsborough, Austl. 112/B5
Dunseith, ND, US 127/H3
Dunshaughlin, Ire. 34/B4
Dunsmuir, Ca, US 128/B2
Dunstable, Eng, UK 33/F3
Dunyāpur, Pak. 86/A5
Duolun, China 71/L3
Dupo, Il, US 137/G8
Dupont, Pa, US 138/C1
Dupree, SD, US 127/H4
Dupuy (cape), Austl. 112/B2
Duque de Caxias, Braz. 211/K7
Duque de York (isl.), Chile 159/A6
Dūrā, WBnk. 91/D4
Durağan, Turk. 62/E4
Durak, Turk. 91/D1
Durance (riv.), Fr. 42/F5
Durango (state), Mex. 140/A3
Durango, Sp. 44/D1
Durango de Victoria, Mex. 142/D3
Durant, Ok, US 129/H4
Durazno (dept.), Uru. 159/F2
Durazno, Uru. 159/K10
Durban, SAfr. 107/E3
Durbanville, SAfr. 106/L10
Durbion (riv.), Fr. 56/C1
Durbuy, Belg. 53/E3
Dúrcal, Sp. 44/D4
Durdevac, Cro. 48/C2
Durdevo, Yugo. 48/E3
Düren, Ger. 53/F2
Durg, India 82/D3
Durgāpur, India 85/F4
Durham, NH, US 131/G3
Durham, NC, US 133/J3
Durham (co.), Eng, UK 35/F2
Durham, Eng, UK 35/G2
Durlston (pt.), Eng, UK 32/E5
Durmitor NP, Yugo. 47/F1
Durnford (pt.), WSah. 98/B5
Dürrenroth, Swi. 56/D3
Durrës, Alb. 47/F2
Dürrlauingen, Ger. 54/D6
Dürrwangen, Ger. 54/D4
Dursunbey, Turk. 62/D5
Durūz (peak), Syria 91/E3
D'Urville (cape), Indo. 81/J4
Dusanovo, Yugo. 47/G1
Dusey (riv.), On, Can. 127/M3
Dushan, China 83/J2
Dushanbe (cap.), Taj. 87/E5
Dushanbe (int'l arpt.), Taj. 87/E5
Düsseldorf (int'l arpt.), Ger. 50/D6
Düsseldorf, Ger. 50/D6
Duszniki-Zdrój, Pol. 41/J3
Dutch (riv.), Eng, UK 35/H4
Dutch Harbor, Ak, US 134/E5
Dutch Wonderland, Pa, US 138/B3
Dutoitspiek (peak), SAfr. 106/L10
Dutse, Nga. 103/H4
Duvall, Wa, US 135/D2
Duvno, Bosn. 48/C4
Duyun, China 83/J2
Düzce, Turk. 49/K5
Düzici, Turk. 90/D2
Dve Mogili, Bul. 49/G4
Dvina (bay), Rus. 60/H2
Dvořiště (lake), Czh. 55/H4
Dwārka, India 89/J4
Dwārkeswar (riv.), India 85/F4
Dworshak (res.), Id, US 126/D4
Dwyfor (riv.), Wal, UK 34/D6
Dwyka (riv.), SAfr. 106/C4
Dyat'kovo, Rus. 62/E1
Dybvad, Den. 38/D3
Dyce (int'l arpt.), Sc, UK 36/D2
Dyce, Sc, UK 36/D2
Dye, Mo, US 137/D5
Dyer, In, US 130/C3
Dyer (cape), Nun., Can. 123/K2
Dyer (cape), Chile 159/B6
Dyfi (riv.), Wal, UK 32/C1
Dyje (riv.), Czh. 41/J4
Dykh-tau (peak), Rus. 63/G4
Dyle (riv.), Belg. 40/C3
Dyleň (peak), Czh. 55/F3
Dylewska (peak), Pol. 41/K2
Dysart, Austl. 114/C3
Dysseldorp, SAfr. 106/C4
Dyul'tydag (peak), Rus. 63/H4
Dzaoudzi (int'l arpt.), May. 107/H6
Dzaoudzi (cap.), May. 107/H6
Dzavhan (prov.), Mong. 70/G2
Dzavhan (riv.), Mong. 70/F2
Dzenzik (pt.), Ukr. 62/F3
Dzerzhinsk, Rus. 60/J4
Dzhankoy, Ukr. 62/E3
Dzharylgach (gulf), Ukr. 49/L2
Dzhebel, Bul. 47/J2
Dzhugdzhur (range), Rus. 67/N4
Działdowo, Pol. 41/L2
Dzibalchén, Mex. 144/D2
Dzibilchaltún (ruin), Mex. 144/D1
Dzidzantún, Mex. 144/D1
Dzierżoniów, Pol. 41/J3
Dzitbalché, Mex. 144/D1
Dziuché, Mex. 144/D2
Dzukija NP, Lith. 39/L4
Dzungarian (basin), China 64/J5
Dzur, Mong. 70/G2
Dzüünbayan, Mong. 71/K3
Dzüünbulag, Mong. 71/K2
Dzüünharaa, Mong. 70/J2
Dzuunmod, Mong. 70/J2

E

Eads, Co, US 129/G3
Eagle, Ak, US 134/K3
Eagle (lake), Wi, US 127/K3
Eagle (mtn.), Mn, US 127/L4
Eagle (lake), Ca, US 126/C5
Eagle, Co, US 128/F3
Eagle (lake), On, Can. 130/A1
Eagle (riv.), Nf, Can. 123/L3
Eagle, Wi, US 135/P14
Eagle Butte, SD, US 127/H4
Eagle Pass, Tx, US 132/C4
Eagle River, Wi, US 127/L4
Eaglesham, Sc, UK 36/B5
Ealing (bor.), Eng, UK 30/B2
Ear Falls, On, Can. 127/K3
Earle Naval Weapons Center, NJ, US 138/D3
Earlimart, Ca, US 128/C4
Earl's Seat (peak), Sc, UK 36/B4
Earlston, Sc, UK 36/D5
Earn (riv.), Sc, UK 36/C4
Earn (lake), Sc, UK 36/B4
Easley, SC, US 133/H3
East (cape), NZ 117/T10
East (cape), Ak, US 134/B6
East (mt.), Austl. 112/D4
East (pt.), NJ, US 138/C5
East (passg.), Wa, US 135/C3
East (riv.), NY, US 139/K8
East Alton, Il, US 137/G8
East Anglia (reg.), Eng, UK 33/H2
East Angus, Qu, Can. 131/G2
East Ayrshire (pol. reg.), Sc, UK 36/B6
East Bangor, Pa, US 138/C2
East Berbice-Corentyne (pol. reg.), Guy. 153/G3
East Berlin, Pa, US 138/B4
East Berwick, Pa, US 138/B1
East Brunswick, NJ, US 139/H10
East Caicos (isl.), UK 145/J1
East Canyon (res.), Ut, US 137/K12
East Carondelet, Il, US 137/G8
East China (sea), Asia 67/M6
East Dart (riv.), Eng, UK 32/C5
East Dereham, Eng, UK 33/G1
East Dunbartonshire (pol. reg.), Sc, UK 36/B5
East Falkland (isl.), UK 147/D8
East Farmingdale, NY, US 139/M9
East Frisian (isls.), Ger. 40/D2
East Glen (riv.), Eng, UK 35/H6
East Greenville, Pa, US 138/C3
East Grinstead, Eng, UK 33/F4
East Hampton, NY, US 139/F2
East Haven, Ct, US 139/F1
East Helena, Mt, US 126/F4
East Hill-Meridian, Wa, US 135/C3
East Hills, NY, US 139/L8
East Jordan, Mi, US 130/C2
East Kilbride, Sc, UK 36/B5
East Korea (bay), NKor. 71/N4
East Lamma (chan.), China 71/U11
East Lansing, Mi, US 130/C3
East Leavenworth, Mo, US 137/D5
East Linton, Sc, UK 36/D5
East Liverpool, Oh, US 130/D3
East London, SAfr. 106/D4
East Los Angeles, Ca, US 136/F7
East Lothian (pol. reg.), Sc, UK 36/D5
East Lynne, Mo, US 137/E6
East Meadow, NY, US 139/L9
East Midlands (int'l arpt.), Eng, UK 35/G6
East Millcreek, Ut, US 137/K12
East Millinocket, Me, US 131/G2
East Newark, NJ, US 139/J9
East Newbern, Il, US 137/G7
East Nishnabotna (riv.), Ia, US 129/J2
East Northport, NY, US 139/E2
East Orange, NJ, US 139/J8
East Peckham, Eng, UK 30/E3
East Petersburg, Pa, US 138/B3
East Point, Ga, US 133/G3
East Pointe (East Detroit), Mi, US 135/G7
East Port Orchard, Wa, US 135/B2
East Prospect, Pa, US 138/B4
East Quogue, NY, US 139/F2
East Renfrewshire (pol. reg.), Sc, UK 36/B5
East Retford, Eng, UK 35/H5
East Riding of Yorkshire (co.), Eng, UK 35/H4
East Rockaway, NY, US 139/L9
East Rutherford, NJ, US 139/J8
East Saint Louis, Il, US 137/G8
East Siberian (sea), Rus. 65/S2
East Side, Pa, US 138/C1
East Stroudsburg, Pa, US 138/C2
East Sussex (co.), Eng, UK 33/G5
East Tawas, Mi, US 130/D2
East Troy, Wi, US 135/P14
East Wemyss, Sc, UK 36/C4
East Wenatchee, Wa, US 126/C4
East Windsor, NJ, US 138/D3
East York, Can. 131/R8
Eastbourne, Eng, UK 33/G5
Eastern (prov.), Zam. 104/B5
Eastern (pol. reg.), Gha. 103/E5
Eastern (chan.), Japan 74/A4
Eastern (prov.), SLeo. 102/C4
Eastern (bay), Md, US 138/B6
Eastern (plain), Eng, UK 35/H4
Eastern Ghats (mts.), India 82/C5
Eastern Neck Island NWR, Md, US 138/B5
Eastern Sayans (mts.), Rus. 64/K4
Easterville, Mb, Can. 127/J2
Eastlake, Co, US 137/C3
Eastleigh (int'l arpt.), Eng, UK 33/E5
Eastleigh, Eng, UK 33/E5
Eastmain (riv.), Qu, Can. 123/J3
Eastman, Ga, US 133/H3
Easton (res.), Ct, US 139/E1
Easton, Pa, US 138/C2
Easton, Ct, US 139/E1
Eastport, Me, US 131/H2
Eastport, NY, US 139/F2
Eastriggs, Sc, UK 35/E2
Eastwood, Eng, UK 35/G6
Eaton, Co, US 137/C1
Eatonia, Sk, Can. 126/F3
Eatons Neck (pt.), NY, US 139/M8
Eatontown, NJ, US 138/D3
Eau (riv.), Eng, UK 35/H5
Eau Claire (lake), Qu, Can. 123/J3
Eau d'Heure (riv.), Belg. 53/D3
Eau d'Heure, Barrage de l' (dam), Belg. 53/D3
Eaubonne, Fr. 30/J5
Eaulne (riv.), Fr. 52/A4
Eauripik (isl.), Micr. 116/D4
Eauze, Fr. 42/D5
Ebano, Mex. 144/B1
Ebble (riv.), Eng, UK 33/E4
Ebbw Vale, Wal, UK 32/C3
Ebebiyin, EqG. 96/H7
Ebeggi (well), Alg. 99/G5
Ebeleben, Ger. 51/H6
Ebeltoft, Den. 38/D3
Ebensee, Aus. 43/K3
Eberbach, Ger. 54/B4
Ebergassing, Aus. 49/P7
Ebergötzen, Ger. 51/H5
Ebermannstadt, Ger. 54/E3
Ebern, Ger. 54/D2
Ebersbach an der Fils, Ger. 54/C5
Ebersberg, Ger. 55/E6
Eberschwang, Aus. 55/G6
Ebersheim, Fr. 56/D1
Eberswalde-Finow, Ger. 41/G2
Ebetsu, Japan 76/B2
Ebian, China 83/H2
Ebina, Japan 77/C3
Ebnat-Kappel, Swi. 57/F3
Ebo (lake), Mali 102/E3
Eboli, It. 46/D2
Ebolowa, Camr. 96/H7
Ebon (isl.), Mrsh. 116/F4
Ebrach, Ger. 54/D3
Ebreichsdorf, Aus. 49/N8
Ebro (riv.), Sp. 27/D4
Ebstorf, Ger. 51/H2
Ecatepec, Mex. 143/Q9
Ecclefechan, Sc, UK 35/E1
Eccles, Eng, UK 35/F5
Eceabat, Turk. 49/H5
Echallens, Swi. 56/C4
Echarate, Peru 156/C4
Echaz (riv.), Ger. 54/C6
Éché Fadadinga (riv.), Niger 103/H3
Echigawa, Japan 77/K5
Eching, Ger. 55/E6
Échirolles, Fr. 42/F4
Echo, Ut, US 137/L12
Echo (lake), NJ, US 138/D1
Echoing (riv.), Mb,On, Can. 127/L2
Echt, Neth. 53/E1
Echterdingen (int'l arpt.), Ger. 54/C5
Echternach, Lux. 53/F4
Echuca, Austl. 115/C3
Echunga, Austl. 113/M9
Echzell, Ger. 54/B2
Écija, Sp. 44/C4
Ećka, Yugo. 48/E3
Eckernförde, Ger. 38/C4
Eckerö (isl.), Fin. 39/H1
Eckerö, Fin. 39/H1
Eclipse Sound (bay), Nun., Can. 123/H1
Écommoy, Fr. 42/D3
Ecoporanga, Braz. 154/B5
Ecorse (riv.), Mi, US 135/F7
Ecorse, Mi, US 135/F7
Écouen, Fr. 30/K4
Ecquevilly, Fr. 30/H5
Ecrins, PN des, Fr. 43/G4
Écrosnes, Fr. 30/H6
Écrouves, Fr. 53/E6
Ecuador (ctry.) 150/C4
Ecublens, Swi. 56/C4
Ed, Swe. 38/D2
Eday (isl.), Sc, UK 31/V14
Eddystone (pt.), Austl. 115/D4
Eddystone Rocks (isls.), Eng, UK 32/B6
Ede, Nga. 103/G5
Ede, Neth. 50/C4
Edéa, Camr. 96/H7
Edegem, Belg. 53/D1
Edehin Ouarene (des.), Alg. 99/G4
Edéia, Braz. 155/B1
Edelény, Hun. 41/L4
Edemissen, Ger. 51/H4
Eden, Austl. 115/D3
Eden, NC, US 130/E4
Eden, Ut, US 137/K11
Eden (riv.), Sc, UK 36/D4
Edenbridge, Eng, UK 30/D3
Edenburg, SAfr. 106/D3
Edendale, SAfr. 107/E3
Edenhope, Austl. 115/B3
Edenkoben, Ger. 54/B4
Edenside (valley), Eng, UK 35/F2
Edenton, NC, US 133/J2
Eder (riv.), Ger. 40/E3
Eder-Stausee (lake), Ger. 51/F6
Edewecht, Ger. 51/E2
Edgar (mt.), Austl. 112/D2
Edge (isl.), Sval. 160/E
Edgecumbe (cape), Ak, US 134/L4
Edgell (isl.), Nun., Can. 123/K2
Edgemere, Md, US 138/B5
Edgemont, Ut, US 137/K13
Edgerton, Wy, US 127/G5
Edgewater, Co, US 137/B3
Edgewater Park, NJ, US 138/D3
Edgewood, Pa, US 138/B2
Edgewood, Md, US 138/B5
Edgewood Arsenal, Md, US 138/B5
Edgewood-North Hill, Wa, US 135/C3
Édhessa, Gre. 47/H2
Edinboro, Pa, US 130/D3
Edinburg, Tx, US 132/D5
Edinburgh (cap.), Sc, UK 36/C5
Edinburgh (pol. reg.), Sc, UK 36/C5
Edirne (prov.), Turk. 62/C4
Edirne, Turk. 47/K2
Edison, NJ, US 139/H9
Edison International Field, Ca, US 136/G8
Edison Nat'l Hist. Site, NJ, US 139/J8
Edisto Island, SC, US 133/H3
Edisto, South Fork (riv.), SC, US 133/H3
Edithburgh, Austl. 113/H5
Édjérir (riv.), Mali 103/F2
Edmond, Ok, US 137/N14
Edmonds, Wa, US 126/C4
Edmonton (int'l arpt.), Ab, Can. 126/E2
Edmonton (cap.), Ab, Can. 126/E2
Edmund Kennedy NP, Austl. 114/B2
Edmundston, NB, Can. 131/G2
Edna, Tx, US 129/H5
Edna Bay, Ak, US 134/M4
Edo (state), Nga. 103/G5
Edo (riv.), Japan 77/D2
Edolo, It. 57/G5
Edosaki, Japan 77/E2
Edremit, Turk. 62/C5
Edremit (gulf), Gre.,Turk 62/C5
Edsbyn, Swe. 38/E1
Edson, Ab, Can. 126/D2
Eduardo Castex, Arg. 158/D2
Edward (mt.), Austl. 113/F2
Edward (lake), D.R. Congo 93/E5
Edward River Aboriginal Community, Austl. 114/A1

185

Edwar – Erlan

Edward VII (pen.), Ant. 160/P
Edward VIII (bay), Ant. 160/D
Edwards (riv.), Il, US 129/K2
Edwards (plat.), Tx, US 124/F5
Edwardsville, Il, US 137/H8
Edwardsville, Ks, US 137/D5
Edwardsville, Pa, US 138/C1
Edzell, Sc, UK 36/D3
Edzná (ruin), Mex. 144/D2
Eek, Ak, US 134/F3
Eeklo, Belg. 52/C1
Eel (riv.), Ca, US 128/B3
Eelde-Paterswolde, Neth. 50/D2
Eem (riv.), Neth. 50/C4
Eemenes, Neth. 50/C4
Eems (Ems) (riv.), Ger., Neth 50/D2
Eemshaven (har.), Neth. 50/D2
Eemskanaal (riv.), Neth. 50/D2
Eersel, Neth. 50/C6
Efate (isl.), Van. 116/F6
Eferding, Aus. 55/H6
Effigy Mounds Nat'l Mon., Ia, US 127/L5
Effingham, Il, US 129/K3
Effingham, On, Can. 131/R9
Effon Alaiye, Nga. 103/G5
Effort, Pa, US 138/C2
Eforie, Rom. 49/J3
Efringen-Kirchen, Ger. 56/D2
Efyrnwy, Llyn (lake), Wal, UK 34/E6
Egadi (isls.), It. 46/B3
Egan (range), Nv, US 128/D3
Egan (riv.), Ger. 54/D5
Egaña, Uru. 159/K10
Egegik, Ak, US 134/G4
Eger (riv.), Ger. 40/G3
Eger, Hun. 41/L5
Egeskov, Den. 38/D4
Egestorf, Ger. 51/H2
Egg, Aus. 57/F3
Egg, Swi. 57/E3
Egg Harbor City, NJ, US 138/D4
Egg Island (pt.), NJ, US 138/C5
Eggebek, Ger. 38/C4
Eggegebirge (ridge), Ger. 51/F5
Eggelsberg, Aus. 55/F6
Eggenburg, Aus. 43/L2
Eggenfelden, Ger. 55/F6
Eggenstein-Leopoldshafen, Ger. 54/B4
Eggesin, Ger. 38/F5
Eggiwil, Swi. 56/D4
Egglescliffe, Eng, UK 35/G3
Eggstätt, Ger. 55/F7
Egham, Eng, UK 30/B2
Éghezée, Belg. 53/D2
Egilsstadhir, Ice. 37/P6
Égletons, Fr. 42/E4
Eglinton (isl.), NW, Can. 123/R7
Eglinton, NI, UK 34/A1
Eglisau, Swi. 57/E2
Égly, Fr. 30/J6
Egmond aan Zee, Neth. 50/B3
Egmont (cape), NZ 117/S10
Egmont (mt.), NZ 117/S10
Egna (Neumarkt), It. 57/H5
Egnach, Swi. 57/F2
Eğridir, Turk. 90/B2
Eğridir (lake), Turk. 90/B2
Éguas, Rio das (riv.), Braz. 154/A4
Egypt (ctry.) 97/L2
Ehebach (riv.), Ger. 54/D3
Ehekirchen, Ger. 54/D5
Ehime (pref.), Japan 74/C4
Ehingen, Ger. 57/F1
Ehingen, Ger. 54/D4
Ehringshausen, Ger. 54/B1
Ehrwald, Aus. 57/G3
Eibar, Sp. 44/D1
Eibelstadt, Ger. 54/C3
Eibenstock, Ger. 55/F1
Eibergen, Neth. 50/D4
Eich, Ger. 54/B3
Eichel (riv.), Fr. 53/G6
Eichenau, Ger. 54/E6
Eichenbühl, Ger. 54/C3
Eichendorf, Ger. 55/F5
Eichenzell, Ger. 54/C2
Eichstätt, Ger. 54/E5
Eichwalde, Ger. 40/Q7
Eicklingen, Ger. 51/H3
Eid, Nor. 37/C3
Eidfjord, Nor. 38/B1
Eidsvold, Austl. 114/C4
Eidsvoll, Nor. 38/D1
Eifel (plat.), Ger. 40/D3
Eiffel Tower, Fr. 30/J5
Eigenji, Japan 77/K5
Eiger (peak), Swi. 56/D4
Eigersund, Nor. 38/A2
Eigg (isl.), Sc, UK 31/Q8
Eight Degree (chan.), India,Mal 82/B6
Eijerlandse Gat (chan.), Neth. 50/B2
Eijsden, Neth. 53/E2
Eikelandsosen, Nor. 38/A1
Eil, Loch (inlet), Sc, UK 36/A3
Eildon (lake), Austl. 115/C3
Eildon, Austl. 115/C3
Eilerts de Haan (mts.), Sur. 153/G4
Einbeck, Ger. 51/G5
Eindhoven (int'l arpt.), Neth. 50/C6
Eindhoven, Neth. 50/C6
Einsiedeln, Swi. 57/E3
Einville-au-Jard, Fr. 53/F6
Eirunepé, Braz. 156/D2
Eisch (riv.), Lux. 53/E4
Eisenach, Ger. 51/H7
Eisenberg, Ger. 54/B3
Eisenhower Nat'l Hist. Site, Pa, US 138/A4
Eisenhüttenstadt, Ger. 41/H2
Eiserfeld, Ger. 53/G2
Eisfeld, Ger. 54/D2
Eisingen, Ger. 54/C3
Eislingen, Ger. 54/C5
Eitelborn, Ger. 53/G3
Eiter (riv.), Ger. 51/F3
Eitorf, Ger. 53/G2
Eitting, Ger. 55/E6
Ejea de los Caballeros, Sp. 45/E1
Ejeda, Madg. 107/H9
Ejido, Ven. 152/D2
Ejin Horo Qi, China 72/B3
Ejin Qi, China 70/H3
Ejutla de Crespo, Mex. 144/B2
Ekeby, Swe. 38/E3
Ekenäs (Tammisaari), Fin. 39/K2
Ekeren, Belg. 50/B6
Ekhínos, Gre. 47/J2
Ekibastuz, Kaz. 87/G2
Eksjö, Swe. 38/F3
Ekuk, Ak, US 134/G4
Ekwan (riv.), On, Can. 123/H3
Ekwok, Ak, US 134/G4
El Aaiún, WSah. 98/B4
El Aatf (reg.), WSah. 98/B5
El Abiodh Sidi Chrikh, Alg. 99/F2
El 'Açâba (mass.), Mrta. 102/C2
El Affroun, Alg. 100/G4
El Águila, Mex. 132/B5
El Aioun, Mor. 100/C2
El Alto, Peru 156/A2
El Amparo de Apure, Ven. 152/D3
El Anegado, Ecu. 152/A5
El Aouinet, Alg. 100/K7
El Arahal, Sp. 44/C4
El Arhlaf (well), Mrta. 102/D2
El Astillero, Sp. 44/D1
El Bagre, Col. 152/C3
El Banco, Col. 152/C2
El Barco, Sp. 44/B1
El Barco de Ávila, Sp. 44/C2
El Baúl, Ven. 152/D2
El Bayadh (prov.), Alg. 99/F2
El Bayadh, Alg. 99/F2
El Bolsón, Arg. 158/C4
El Bonillo, Sp. 44/D3
El Borouj, Mor. 98/D2
El Burgo de Osma, Sp. 44/D2
El Cajon, Ca, US 136/D5
El Cajón (res.), Hon. 144/E3
El Calafate, Arg. 159/B6
El Callao, Ven. 153/F3
El Capitan (peak), Mt, US 126/E4
El Carmen, Peru 156/B4
El Carmen, Chile 158/B3
El Carmen, Col. 152/B3
El Carmen de Bolívar, Col. 152/C2
El Casar de Talamanca, Sp. 45/N8
El Cerrito, Ca, US 128/D4
El Cerrito, Col. 152/B4
El Cerrito, Ca, US 135/K11
El Cerro del Aripo (peak), Trin. 153/F2
El Cerrón (peak), Ven. 152/D2
El Chico, PN, Mex. 143/L6
El Cocuy, Col. 152/C3
El Cocuy, PN, Col. 150/D2
El Colorado, Arg. 157/E2
El Difícil, Col. 152/C2
El Djouf (des.), Mrta. 96/D3
El Dorado, Ks, US 129/H3
El Dorado, Ar, US 129/J4
El Dorado, Mex. 142/D3
El Dorado, Ven. 153/F3
El Eglab (plat.), Alg. 96/D2
El Empedrado, Ven. 152/D2
El Escorial, Sp. 45/M8
El Espinar, Sp. 44/C2
El Eulma, Alg. 100/H4
El Fahs, Tun. 100/L6
El Ferrol, Sp. 44/A1
El Fuerte, Mex. 142/C3
El Fureidīs, Isr. 91/F6
El Gogorrón, PN, Mex. 140/A3
El Golea, Alg. 99/F3
El Golfete (lake), Guat. 144/D3
El Granada, Ca, US 135/K11
El Grullo, Mex. 142/D5
El Guachara, PN, Ven. 153/F2
El Hajeb, Mor. 100/B3
El Hank (cliff), Mali, 98/D4
El Harino, Pan. 152/A2
El Harta (well), Alg. 99/E4
El Higo, Mex. 144/B1
El Indio, Tx, US 132/C4
El Jadida, Mor. 98/C2
El Kelaâ des Srarhna, Mor. 98/D2
El Khatt (cliff), Mrta. 96/C3
El Khatt (depr.), Mrta. 102/C2
El Khnâchîch (cliff), Mali 98/E5
El Kroub, Alg. 100/K6
El Kseur, Alg. 100/H4
El Libertador General Bernardo O'Higgins (pol. reg.), Chile 158/N8
El Limón, Mex. 143/F4
El Mahia (phys. reg.), Mali 99/E5
El Maitén, Arg. 158/C4
El Malpais Nat'l Mon., NM, US 128/F4
El Manteco, Ven. 153/F3
El-Menzel, Mor. 100/B3
El Miamo, Ven. 153/F3
El Milia, Alg. 100/J4
El Mirage, Az, US 137/R18
El Mirage, Ca, US 136/C1
El Montcau (peak), Sp. 45/K6
El Monte, Ca, US 136/F7
El Morrito (pt.), Chile 158/C1
El Mrâyer (well), Mrta. 98/C5
El Mreyyé (phys. reg.), Mrta. 102/C2
El Mzereb (well), Mali 98/D4
El Naranjo de Carlos Sarabia, Mex. 143/F4
El Nayar, Mex. 142/D4
El Nevado (peak), Arg. 158/C2
El Nido, Phil. 81/E1
El Olivar Alto, Chile 158/N9
El Oro (prov.), Ecu. 156/A1
El Oued (prov.), Alg. 99/G2
El Oued, Alg. 99/G2
El Palmar, Ven. 153/F3
El Pao, Ven. 153/F2
El Pao, Ven. 153/E2
El Paraíso, Mex. 143/E5
El Paraíso, Hon. 144/E3
El Paso, Tx, US 128/F5
El Paso International (int'l arpt.), Tx, US 129/F5
El Pilar, Ven. 153/F2
El Porvenir, Mex. 129/F5
El Porvenir, Pan. 152/B2
El Potosí, Mex. 143/E3
El Potosí, PN, Mex. 140/B3
El Prat de Llobregat, Sp. 45/L7
El Progreso, Hon. 144/E3
El Progreso, Guat. 144/D3
El Progreso, Ecu. 156/F7
El Progreso Industrial, Mex. 143/Q9
El Puerto de Santa María, Sp. 44/B4
El Quelite, Mex. 142/D4
El Quisco, Chile 158/N8
El Rama, Nic. 145/E3
El Rancho, Co, US 137/B3
El Reno, Ok, US 129/H4
El Rio, Ca, US 136/A2
El Roble, Pan. 152/A2
El Rosario de Arriba, Mex. 142/B2
El Sacromonte, PN, Mex. 143/L7
El Salto, Mex. 142/D4
El Salvador, Mex. 143/E3
El Salvador, Cuba 145/H1
El Salvador (ctry.) 144/D3
El Salvador (int'l arpt.), ESal. 144/D3
El Samán de Apure, Ven. 152/D3
El Sauz, Mex. 129/F5
El Sauzal, Mex. 142/A2
El Segundo, Ca, US 136/F8
El Shab (well), Egypt 101/B4
El Tabo, Chile 158/N8
El Tajín (ruin), Mex. 143/M6
El Tama, PN, Ven. 152/C3
El Tambo, Ecu. 152/B5
El Tarf (prov.), Alg. 100/K6
El Tarf, Alg. 100/L6
El Teleno (peak), Sp. 44/B1
El Tepozteco, PN, Mex. 143/R10
El Tiemblo, Sp. 44/C2
El Tigre, Ven. 153/E2
El Tocuyo, Ven. 152/D2
El Toro, Ca, US 136/C3
El Triunfo, Ecu. 152/B5
El Triunfo, Mex. 144/D2
El Tucuche (peak), Trin. 153/F2
El Tuito, Mex. 142/D4
El Tuparro, PN, Col. 150/E3
El Valle, Pan. 152/A2
El Venado (isl.), Nic. 145/F4
El Viejo, Nic. 144/E3
El Viejo (peak), Col. 152/C3
El Vigía, Ven. 152/D2
El Yagual, Ven. 152/D3
El Yunque (peak), PR 141/M8
El Zacatón, Mex. 142/E4
Elan (riv.), Wal, UK 32/C2
Élancourt, Fr. 30/H5
Elandsrivier (riv.), SAfr. 106/Q12
Elassón, Gre. 47/H3
Elat (int'l arpt.), Isr. 91/D5
Elat, Isr. 91/D5
Elátia, Gre. 47/H3
Elato (isl.), Micr. 116/D4
Elazığ, Turk. 90/D2
Elazig (prov.), Turk. 90/D2
Elba, Al, US 133/G4
Elba (isl.), It. 43/H5
Elbasan, Alb. 47/G2
Elbbach (riv.), Ger. 53/G2
Elbe (riv.), Ger. 27/F3
Elbe (Labe) (riv.), Czh.,Ger. 41/H2
Elbe-Seitenkanaal (canal), Ger. 51/H2
Elbert (co.), Co, US 137/C4
Elberton, Ga, US 133/H3
Elbeuf, Fr. 42/D2
Elbigenalp, Aus. 57/G3
Elbląg, Pol. 39/H4
Elblag (prov.), Pol. 39/H4
Elbow, Sk, Can. 126/G3
El'brus (peak), Rus. 63/G4
Elburg, Neth. 50/C4
Elburn, Il, US 135/N16
Elburz (mts.), Iran 64/E6
Elche, Sp. 45/E3
Elche de la Sierra, Sp. 44/D3
Elchingen, Ger. 54/D6
Elcho (isl.), Austl. 109/C2
Eld (inlet), Wa, US 135/A3
Elda, Sp. 45/E3
Elde (riv.), Ger. 40/G2
Eldersburg, Md, US 138/B5
Eldivan, Turk. 62/E4
Eldon, Wa, US 135/A2
Eldora, Co, US 137/A3
Eldora, NJ, US 138/D5
Eldorado, Arg. 157/F2
Eldorado, Tx, US 129/G5
Eldorado Springs, Co, US 137/B3
Eldoret, Kenya 104/B2
Eleao (peak), Hi, US 124/W13
Elefsís, Gre. 47/H3
Elek, Hun. 48/E2
Elektrostal', Rus. 61/X9
Elena, Arg. 158/D2
Elesbão Veloso, Braz. 154/B2
Eleşkirt, Turk. 63/G5
Eleuthera (isl.), Bahm. 141/F2
Eleven Point (riv.), Mo, US 129/K3
Elevsís (ruin), Gre. 47/N8
Elevtheroúpolis, Gre. 47/J2
Elfershausen, Ger. 54/C2
Elgg, Swi. 57/E3
Elgin, ND, US 127/H4
Elgin, Il, US 127/L5
Elgin, Tx, US 129/H5
Elgin, Sc, UK 36/C1
Elgóibar, Sp. 44/D1
Elgon (Wagagai) (peak), Ugan. 104/B2
Elida, NM, US 132/C3
Elim, Ak, US 134/F3
Elimäki, Fin. 39/M1
Elista, Rus. 63/H3
Elixhausen, Aus. 55/G7
Elizabeth (bay), Namb. 106/A2
Elizabeth, NJ, US 139/J9
Elizabeth City, NC, US 133/J2
Elizabethan Village Hist. Site, Austl. 112/L7
Elizabethton, Tn, US 130/D4
Elizabethtown, Pa, US 138/B3
Elizabethville, Pa, US 138/B2
Elk (mts.), Co, US 132/B2
Elk (riv.), WV, US 133/H2
Ełk, Pol. 39/K5
Elk City, Ok, US 129/H4
Elk Grove, Ca, US 135/M10
Elk Grove Village, Il, US 135/P16
Elk Island NP, Ab, Can. 126/E2
Elk Mills, Md, US 138/C4
Elk Point, Ab, Can. 126/F2
Elk Rapids, Mi, US 130/C2
Elk Ridge, Md, US 138/B5
Elk River, Mn, US 127/K4
Elk Slough (riv.), Ca, US 135/L10
Elkenroth, Ger. 53/G2
Elkhart, In, US 130/C3
Elkhart, Ks, US 129/G3
Elkhart, Tx, US 129/J5
Elkhorn, Mb, Can. 127/H3
Elkhorn, Wi, US 130/B3
Elkhorn (riv.), Ne, US 125/G3
Elkhovo, Bul. 47/K1
Elkin, NC, US 130/D4
Elko, Nv, US 126/E5
Elkton, Md, US 138/C4
Ellamar, Ak, US 134/J3
Elland, Eng, UK 35/G4
Elle (riv.), Ger. 53/F2
Ellef Ringnes (isl.), Nun., Can. 123/R7
Ellefeld, Ger. 55/F2
Ellen (riv.), Eng, UK 35/E2
Ellenberg, Ger. 54/D4
Ellendale, ND, US 127/J4
Ellendale, De, US 138/C6
Ellensburg, Wa, US 126/C4
Eller (riv.), Ger. 51/H5
Ellerbach (riv.), Ger. 53/G4
Ellero (riv.), It. 58/A4
Ellery (mt.), Austl. 115/D3
Ellesmere (isl.), Nun., Can. 123/S6
Ellesmere Port, Eng, UK 35/F5
Ellezelles, Belg. 52/C2
Ellice (riv.), Nun., Can. 122/F2
Ellicott City, Md, US 138/B5
Ellinikón (int'l arpt.), Gre. 47/N9
Elliot, SAfr. 106/D3
Elliot Lake, On, Can. 130/D2
Elliot Price Consv. Park, Austl. 113/H4
Elliott (peak), Va, US 133/J2
Ellis Island, NJ,NY, US 139/J9
Ellisras, SAfr. 105/E5
Elliston, Austl. 113/G5
Ellisville, Mo, US 137/F8
Ellon, Sc, UK 36/D2
Ellrich, Ger. 51/H5
Ellsworth, Me, US 131/G2
Ellsworth, Wi, US 130/A2
Ellsworth, Ks, US 129/H3
Ellsworth (mts.), Ant. 160/U
Ellsworth Land (phys. reg.), Ant. 160/U
Ellwangen, Ger. 54/D5
Elm, Swi. 57/F4
Elm Grove, Wi, US 135/P13
Elma, NY, US 131/S10
Elmadağ, Turk. 62/E5
Elmalı, Turk. 91/A1
Elmas (int'l arpt.), It. 46/A3
Elmendorf, Tx, US 137/U21
Elmer, NJ, US 138/C4
Elmhurst, Il, US 135/Q16
Elmina, Gha. 103/E5
Elmira, NY, US 130/E3
Elmont, NY, US 139/L9
Elmore, Austl. 115/C3
Elmsford, NY, US 139/K7
Elmshorn, Ger. 51/G1
Elmstein, Ger. 53/G5
Elmwood Park, Wi, US 135/Q14
Elmwood Park, NJ, US 139/J8
Elmwood Park, Il, US 135/Q16
Elne, Fr. 42/E5
Elói Mendes, Braz. 211/H6
Élorn (riv.), Fr. 42/A2
Elortondo, Arg. 158/E2
Elorza, Ven. 152/D3
Elouera Nat'l Rsv., Austl. 114/H8
Eloy, Az, US 128/E4
Eloy Alfaro, Ecu. 152/B5
Éloyes, Fr. 56/C1
Elpitiya, SrL. 82/D6
Elrose, Sk, Can. 126/F3
Elsa, Yk, Can. 134/L3
Elsa (riv.), It. 43/J5
Elsa, Embalse de (res.), Sp. 44/B2
Elsah, Il, US 137/G8
Elsdorf, Ger. 51/G2
Elsdorf, Ger. 53/F2
Else (riv.), Ger. 51/F4
Elsenfeld, Ger. 54/C3
Elsenz (riv.), Ger. 54/B4
Elsfleth, Ger. 51/F2
Elsinore (lake), Ca, US 136/C3
Elsmere, De, US 138/C4
Elst, Neth. 50/C5
Elstal, Ger. 40/Q6
Elstead, Eng, UK 33/F4
Elsterberg, Ger. 55/F1
Eltmann, Ger. 54/D3
El'ton (lake), Rus. 63/H2
Eltville am Rhein, Ger. 54/B2
Elūrū, India 82/D4
Elvanlı, Turk. 91/D1
Elvas, Port. 44/B3
Elverum, Nor. 38/D1
Elvire (mt.), Austl. 112/C2
Elvo (riv.), It. 58/B2
Elwell (lake), Mt, US 126/F3
Elwood, In, US 130/C3
Elwood-Magnolia, NJ, US 138/D4
Elwy (riv.), Wal, UK 34/E5
Ely, Nv, US 128/D3
Ely, Eng, UK 33/G2
Elyaqim, Isr. 91/G6
Elyashiv, Isr. 91/F7
Elyria, Oh, US 130/D3
Elysburg, Pa, US 138/B2
Elysian Park, Ca, US 136/F7
Elz (riv.), Ger. 54/B6
Elz, Ger. 54/B2
Elzach, Ger. 56/E1
Elzbach (riv.), Ger. 53/G3
Elze, Ger. 51/G4
Emajõgi (riv.), Est. 39/M2
Emāmshahr (Shāhrūd), Iran 89/F1
Emån (riv.), Swe. 38/F3
Emancé, Fr. 30/H6
Emas, PN das, Braz. 151/H7
Emba (riv.), Kaz. 62/K3
Embarcación, Arg. 157/D1
Embarras (riv.), Il, US 133/F2
Embi, Kaz. 63/L2
Embi (riv.), Kaz. 64/F5
Embira (riv.), Braz. 150/D5
Emborcação, Barragem de (res.), Braz. 155/C1
Embrach, Swi. 57/E3
Embrun, Fr. 43/G4
Embsen, Ger. 51/H2
Embu, Kenya 104/C3
Emden, Ger. 51/E2
Emeishan, China 83/H2
Emerald, Austl. 114/C3
Emerald, Austl. 115/G5
Emerson, Mb, Can. 127/J3
Emerson, NJ, US 139/J8
Emeryville, Ca, US 135/K11
Emet, Turk. 62/D5
Emigsville, Pa, US 138/B3
Emilia-Romagna (pol. reg.), It. 43/J4
Emiliano Zapata, Mex. 144/D2
Emin, China 70/D2
Emīnābād, Pak. 86/C3
Eminence, Mo, US 129/K3
Emir Pasha (gulf), Tanz. 104/A3
Emirdağ, Turk. 62/D5
Emirgazi, Turk. 90/C2
Emlembe (peak), Swaz. 107/E2
Emlichheim, Ger. 50/D3
Emma (riv.), Sur. 153/H4
Emmaboda, Swe. 38/F3
Emmanuel Head (pt.), Eng, UK 36/E5
Emmaus, Pa, US 138/C2
Emme (riv.), Swi. 56/D4
Emmeloord, Neth. 50/C3
Emmen, Neth. 50/D3
Emmendingen, Ger. 56/D1
Emmental (valley), Swi. 56/D3
Emmer (riv.), Ger. 51/G4
Emmerbach (riv.), Ger. 51/E5
Emmerich, Ger. 50/D5
Emmett, Mi, US 135/G6
Emmingen-Liptingen, Ger. 57/E2
Emmitsburg, Md, US 138/A4
Emmonak, Ak, US 134/F3
Emneth, Eng, UK 33/G1
Emőd, Hun. 48/E2
Emory, Tx, US 129/J4
Emosson (lake), Swi. 56/C5
Empalme, Mex. 142/C3
Empangeni, SAfr. 107/E3
Empedrado, Arg. 157/E2
Empedrado, Chile 158/B2
Empoli, It. 59/D5
Emporia, Ks, US 129/H3
'Emrānī, Iran 89/G2
Ems (Eems) (riv.), Ger.,Neth. 50/D2
Ems-Jade (canal), Ger. 51/E2
Emsbüren, Ger. 51/E4
Emsdetten, Ger. 51/E4
Emskirchen, Ger. 54/D3
Emsland (reg.), Ger. 40/D2
Emstek, Ger. 51/F3
Emu Park, Austl. 114/C3
Emumägi (hill), Est. 39/M2
Emyvale, Ire. 34/B3
Ena, Japan 75/E3
Enbetsu, Japan 76/B1
Encantada, Cerro (peak), Mex. 142/B3
Encantada, Cerro de la (peak), Mex. 142/B2
Encarnación, Par. 157/E2
Encarnación de Díaz, Mex. 142/E4
Enchi, Gha. 102/E5
Encinitas, Ca, US 136/C4
Enciso, Col. 152/C3
Encontrados, Ven. 152/C2
Encounter (bay), Austl. 115/A2
Encruzilhada do Sul, Braz. 155/A4
Encs, Hun. 41/L4
Endau (peak), Kenya 104/C3
Ende, Indo. 81/F5
Endeavour River NP, Austl. 114/B1
Enderbury (isl.), Kiri. 117/H5
Enderby, BC, Can. 126/D3
Enderby Land (phys. reg.), Ant. 160/D
Enderlin, ND, US 127/J4
Endicott, NY, US 130/E3
Endingen, Ger. 56/D1
Ene (riv.), Peru 150/D6
Eneabba, Austl. 112/B4
Enebakk, Nor. 38/D2
Enewetak (isl.), Mrsh. 116/F3
Enez, Turk. 47/K2
Enfield (bor.), Eng, UK 30/C2
Engaño (cape), Phil. 79/D4
Engaru, Japan 76/C1
Engaruka (basin), Tanz. 104/B3
Engelberg, Swi. 57/E4
Engelhartszell, Aus. 55/G5
Engel's, Rus. 63/H2
Engelskirchen, Ger. 53/G2
Engelsmanplaat (isl.), Neth. 50/D2
Engen, Ger. 57/E2
Engenheiro Navarro, Braz. 154/B5
Engenheiro Paulo de Frontin, Braz. 211/K7
Enger, Ger. 51/F4
Engerwitzdorf, Aus. 55/H6
Enggano (isl.), Indo. 80/B5
Enghershatu (peak), Erit. 88/C5
Enghien, Belg. 52/D2
Engi, Swi. 57/F4
England, UK 32/D2
Englefontaine, Fr. 52/C3
Englehart, On, Can. 130/E2
Englewood, Co, US 137/C3
Englewood, NJ, US 139/K8
Englewood Cliffs, NJ, US 139/K8
English (riv.), On, Can. 127/K3
English (chan.), UK,Fr. 27/D4
English Bay, Ak, US 134/H4
English Bāzār, India 85/G3
English Creek, NJ, US 138/D5
Englishtown, NJ, US 138/D3
Énguera, Sp. 45/E3
Enguri (riv.), Geo. 63/G4
Enhtal, Mong. 70/J2
Enid, Ok, US 129/H3
Eniwa, Japan 76/B2
Enkenbach-Alsenborn, Ger. 53/G5
Enkhuizen, Neth. 50/C3
Enkirch, Ger. 53/G4
Enköping, Swe. 38/G2
Enna, It. 46/D4
Ennedi (plat.), Chad 97/K4
Ennepe (riv.), Ger. 51/E6
Ennepetal, Ger. 51/E6
Ennery, Fr. 30/J4
Enningerloh, Ger. 51/F5
Ennis, Mt, US 126/F4
Ennis, Tx, US 129/H4
Ennis, Ire. 31/P10
Enniscorthy, Ire. 31/Q10
Enniskerry, Ire. 34/B5
Enniskillen, NI, UK 31/Q9
Ennistimon, Ire. 31/P10
Enns, Aus. 55/H6
Enns (riv.), Aus. 41/H5
Enogger (res.), Austl. 114/E6
Enola, Pa, US 138/B3
Enontekiö, Fin. 37/G1
Enoree (riv.), SC, US 133/H3
Enping, China 83/K3
Enrick (riv.), Sc, UK 36/B2
Enrique Carbó, Arg. 159/J10
Enriquillo, DRep. 145/J2
Enschede, Neth. 50/D4
Ensdorf, Ger. 55/E4
Ense, Ger. 51/E5
Enseleni, SAfr. 107/F3
Ensenada, Mex. 142/A2
Ensenada, Arg. 159/K11
Enshi, China 79/A1
Ensisheim, Fr. 56/D2
Entebbe (int'l arpt.), Ugan. 104/B2
Entebbe, Ugan. 104/B2
Entenbühl (peak), Ger. 55/F3
Enterprise, Al, US 133/G4
Enterprise, Ut, US 137/K11
Entlebuch, Swi. 56/E4
Entre Rios, Braz. 154/C3
Entre Ríos (mts.), Hon. 144/E3
Entroncamento, Port. 44/A3
Entzheim, Fr. 56/D1
Enugu, Nga. 103/G5
Enugu (state), Nga. 103/G5
Enumclaw, Wa, US 135/D3
Enushū (sea), Japan 77/M6
Envira, Braz. 156/D2
Enz (riv.), Ger. 43/H2
Enza (riv.), It. 58/D4
Enzan, Japan 75/F3
Enzbach (riv.), Ger. 53/F4
Enzersdorf an der Fischa, Aus. 49/P7
Enzklösterle, Ger. 54/B5
Epalinges, Swi. 56/C4
Epáno Arkhánai, Gre. 47/J5
Epanomí, Gre. 47/H2
Epe, Nga. 103/F5
Epe, Neth. 50/C4
Epehy, Fr. 52/C3
Epernay, Fr. 52/C5
Epfig, Fr. 56/D1
Ephrata, Pa, US 138/B3
Epi (isl.), Van. 116/F6
Epiais-Rhus, Fr. 30/J4
Epídhavros (Epidaurus) (ruin), Gre. 47/H4
Épinal, Fr. 56/C1
Épinay-sur-Orge, Fr. 30/J6
Épinay-sur-Seine, Fr. 30/J5
Epira, Guy. 153/G3
Epirus (reg.), Gre. 47/G3
Épône, Fr. 52/A6
Eppelborn, Ger. 53/F5
Eppelheim, Ger. 54/B4
Eppenbrunn, Ger. 53/G5
Eppeville, Fr. 52/C4
Epping (for.), Eng, UK 30/D2
Epping, Eng, UK 30/D1
Epping Forest NP, Austl. 114/B3
Eppingen, Ger. 54/B4
Eppishausen, Ger. 57/G1
Epsom, Eng, UK 30/C3
Epsom and Ewell, Eng, UK 33/F4
Epte (riv.), Fr. 52/A4
Equator (fall), Ecu. 152/A4
Equatorial Guinea (ctry.) 96/G7
Équihen-Plage, Fr. 52/A2
Er (lake), China 83/H2
Er Rachidia, Mor. 98/D3
Er Reina, Isr. 91/G6
Er Rif (mts.), Mor. 96/D1
Era (riv.), It. 59/D6
Eraclea, It. 59/F1
Eraclea (ruin), It. 46/E2
Eraclea Minoa (ruin), It. 46/C4
Éragny, Fr. 30/J4
Erandique, Hon. 144/D3
Eravur, SrL. 82/D6
Erawan NP, Thai. 78/B3
Erba, It. 58/C1
Erbaa, Turk. 62/F4
Erbach, Ger. 54/B3
Erbendorf, Ger. 55/F3
Erbeskopf (peak), Ger. 53/G4
Ercan (int'l arpt.), Cyp. 91/C2
Erçek, Turk. 90/E2
Erçek (lake), Turk. 90/E2
Ercilla, Chile 158/B3
Erciş, Turk. 90/E2
Erciyes (peak), Turk. 90/C2
Erclin (riv.), Fr. 52/C3
Érd, Hun. 49/Q10
Erda, Ut, US 137/J12
Erdek (gulf), Turk. 49/H5
Erdek, Turk. 49/H5
Erdemli, Turk. 91/D1
Erdenet, Mong. 70/H2
Erdi-Ma (plat.), Chad 97/K4
Erding, Ger. 55/E6
Erdre (riv.), Fr. 42/C3
Erdweg, Ger. 54/E6
Erechim, Braz. 155/A3
Ereen Davaanï (mts.), Mong. 71/K2
Ereğli, Turk. 90/C2
Ereğli, Turk. 49/K5
Eremo di Camaldoli, It. 59/E5
Erenhaberga (mts.), China 70/D3
Erenhot, China 71/K3
Erenler, Turk. 49/K5
Erentepe, Turk. 90/E2
Erepecu, Lago do (lake), Braz. 151/G4
Eresma (riv.), Sp. 44/C2
Erétria, Gre. 47/H3
Ereymentaū, Kaz. 87/F2
Erezée, Belg. 53/E3
Erfa (riv.), Ger. 54/C3
Erfoud, Mor. 98/D3
Erft (riv.), Ger. 40/D3
Erftstadt, Ger. 53/F2
Erfurt, Ger. 40/F3
'Erg Chech (des.), Mali,Alg. 93/B2
'Erg Iguidi (des.), Alg.,Mrta. 98/D4
Ergene Nehri (riv.), Turk. 49/H5
Erguig (riv.), Chad 96/J5
Ergun Youqi, China 71/M1
Ergun Zuoqi, China 71/M1
Ericeira, Port. 45/P10
Ericht (lake), Sc, UK 36/B3
Ericht (riv.), Sc, UK 36/B3
Erickson, Mb, Can. 127/J3
Erickson, BC, Can. 126/D3
Erie (int'l arpt.), Pa, US 130/D3
Erie, Pa, US 130/D3
Erie, Co, US 137/B2
Erie (co.), NY, US 131/S10
Erie (canal), NY, US 131/S9
Erie (lake), Can.,US 130/D3
Eriksdale, Mb, Can. 127/J3
Eriksmålå, Swe. 38/F3
Erikub (isl.), Mrsh. 116/F4
Erimanthos (peak), Gre. 47/G4
Erimo, Japan 76/C2
Erimo-misaki (cape), Japan 76/C3
Erithraí, Gre. 47/H3
Eritrea (ctry.) 97/N5
Erkelenz, Ger. 53/F1
Erken (isl.), Swe. 39/H1
Erkheim, Ger. 57/G1
Erkner, Ger. 40/Q7
Erkrath, Ger. 50/D6
Erlach, Swi. 56/D3
Erlands Point-Kitsap Lake, Wa, US 135/B2

186

Erlan – Ferra

Erlangen, Ger. 54/E3
Erlau (riv.), Ger. 55/G5
Erlenbach (riv.), Ger. 54/B4
Erlenbach am Main, Ger. 54/C3
Erlenbach bei Marktheidenfeld, Ger. 54/C3
Erlenbach im Simmental, Swi. 56/D4
Erlinsbach, Swi. 56/E3
Erlongshan (res.), China 72/F2
Erme (riv.), Eng, UK 32/C6
Ermelo, SAfr. 107/E2
Ermelo, Neth. 50/C4
Ermenek (riv.), Turk. 91/C1
Ermenek, Turk. 91/C1
Ermenonville, Fr. 30/L4
Ermióni, Gre. 47/H4
Ermont, Fr. 30/J5
Ermoúpolis, Gre. 47/J4
Erms (riv.), Ger. 54/C6
Erndtebrück, Ger. 53/H2
Ernée (riv.), Fr. 42/C2
Ernée, Fr. 42/C2
Ernesto Cortissoz (int'l arpt.), Col. 152/C2
Ernsthofen, Aus. 55/H6
Erode, India 82/C5
Erolzheim, Ger. 57/G1
Erowal Bay, Austl. 115/D2
Erpel, Ger. 53/G2
Erquelinnes, Belg. 53/D3
Errigal (mtn.), Ire. 31/P9
Erris Head (pt.), Ire. 31/P9
Erro (riv.), It. 58/B4
Errochty (lake), Sc, UK 36/B3
Erromango (isl.), Van. 116/F6
Erse (riv.), Ger. 51/H4
Ersekë, Alb. 47/G2
Erstein, Fr. 56/D1
Erstfeld, Swi. 57/E4
Ertingen, Ger. 57/F1
Ertis (riv.), Kaz. 64/H4
Ertix (riv.), China 70/E2
Eruh, Turk. 90/E2
Eruwa, Nga. 103/F5
Erwin, Tn, US 130/D4
Erwitte, Ger. 51/F5
Eryuan, China 83/G2
Erzegebirge (Krušné Hory) (mts.), Czh.,Ger. 43/K1
Erzen (riv.), Alb. 47/F2
Erzhausen, Ger. 54/B3
Erzincan, Turk. 62/F5
Erzurum (prov.), Turk. 63/G4
Erzurum, Turk. 63/G5
Es Senia (int'l arpt.), Alg. 100/E5
Esan-misaki (cape), Japan 76/B3
Esashi, Japan 76/C1
Esashi, Japan 76/B3
Esashi, Japan 76/B4
Esbiye, Turk. 62/F4
Esbjerg, Den. 38/C4
Esbjerg (int'l arpt.), Den. 38/C4
Esbly, Fr. 30/L5
Esbo (Espoo), Fin. 39/L1
Escada, Braz. 154/D3
Escalante (riv.), Ut, US 128/E3
Escalón, Mex. 142/D3
Escalona, Sp. 44/C2
Escambia (riv.), Fl, US 133/G4
Escaudain, Fr. 52/C3
Escaut (riv.), Fr. 40/B3
Esch (riv.), Fr. 53/E6
Esch-sur-Alzette, Lux. 53/E4
Esch-sur-Sure, Lux. 53/E4
Eschach (riv.), Ger. 57/E1
Eschau, Fr. 56/D1
Eschborn, Ger. 54/B2
Eschede, Ger. 51/H3
Eschen, Lcht. 57/F3
Eschenbach, Ger. 54/C5
Eschenbach in der Oberpfalz, Ger. 55/E3
Eschershausen, Ger. 51/G5
Esches (riv.), Fr. 52/B5
Escholzmatt, Swi. 56/D4
Eschwege, Ger. 51/H6
Eschweiler, Ger. 53/F2
Escobedo (int'l arpt.), Mex. 132/C5
Escoma, Bol. 156/D4
Escondido, Ca, US 136/C4
Escuinapa de Hidalgo, Mex. 142/D4
Escuintla, Guat. 144/D3
Esdraelon, Plain of (plain), Isr. 91/G6
Eséka, Camr. 96/H7
Esenboga (int'l arpt.), Turk. 62/E4
Esence (peak), Turk. 62/F5
Esens, Ger. 51/E1
Esera (riv.), Sp. 45/F1
Eşfahān, Iran 88/F2
Esfandak, Iran 89/H3
Esgair Ddu (peak), Wal, UK 32/C1
Esha Ness (cape), Sc, UK 31/W13
Esher, Eng, UK 30/B2
Eshowe, SAfr. 107/E3
Esil, Kaz. 87/E2
Esil (riv.), Kaz. 67/F4
Esine, It. 57/G6
Esino (riv.), It. 59/G6
Esk (riv.), Eng, UK 35/E2
Eskdale (valley), Sc, UK 36/C6
Eskifjördhur, Ice. 37/Q6
Eskil, Turk. 90/C2
Eskilstuna, Swe. 38/G2
Eskimalatya, Turk. 90/D2
Eskimo (lakes), NW, Can. 122/C2
Eskipazar, Turk. 62/E4
Eskişehir, Turk. 62/D5
Eskişehir (prov.), Turk. 62/D5
Esla (riv.), Sp. 44/C1
Eslāmābād, Iran 88/E2
Eslohe, Ger. 51/F6
Eslöv, Swe. 38/E4
Eşme, Turk. 90/B2
Esmeralda, Cuba 145/G1
Esmeraldas, Ecu. 152/B4
Esmeraldas (dept.), Ecu. 152/B4
Esneux, Belg. 53/E2
Espada (pt.), Col. 152/D1
Espalion, Fr. 42/E4
Española, NM, US 129/F4
Espanola, On, Can. 130/D2
Española (isl.), Ecu. 156/F7
Esparraguera, Sp. 45/K6
Esparta, Hon. 144/E3
Esparto, Ca, US 135/K9
Espejo, Sp. 44/C4
Espelkamp, Ger. 51/F4
Esperança, Braz. 154/D2
Esperance (bay), Austl. 112/D5
Esperance, Austl. 112/D5
Esperantina, Braz. 154/B1
Esperantinópolis, Braz. 154/A2
Esperanza (inlet), BC, Can. 126/B3
Esperanza, Peru 156/D3
Esperanza, Mex. 142/C3
Esperanza, Mex. 143/M8
Esperanza (mts.), Hon. 144/E3
Esperanza, Arg., Ant. 160/W
Espichel (cape), Port. 45/P11
Espinal, Mex. 143/M6
Espinal, Col. 152/C3
Espinar, Peru 156/D4
Espinhaço, Serra do (mts.), Braz. 151/K7
Espinho, Port. 44/A2
Espinillo (pt.), Uru. 159/F2
Espinosa, Braz. 154/B4
Espírito Santo (state), Braz. 155/D2
Espiritu Santo (isl.), Van. 116/F6
Espíritu Santo (bay), Cuba 144/E2
Espita, Mex. 144/D1
Esplanada, Braz. 154/C3
Espluga de Francolí, Sp. 45/E2
Espluges, Sp. 45/L7
Esposende, Port. 44/A2
Espungabera, Moz. 105/F5
Espy, Pa, US 138/B1
Esqueda, Mex. 142/C2
Esquel, Arg. 158/C4
Esquina, Arg. 157/E3
Essaouira, Mor. 98/C3
Esse (riv.), Ger. 51/G5
Essen, Belg. 50/B6
Essen, Ger. 50/E6
Essen, Ger. 51/E3
Essenbach, Ger. 55/F5
Essendon (mt.), Austl. 112/D3
Essenheim, Ger. 53/H4
Essequibo (riv.), Guy. 147/D2
Essequibo Island-West Demerara (pol. reg.), Guy. 153/G3
Essex (co.), NJ, US 138/D2
Essex, Md, US 138/B5
Essex (co.), On, Can. 135/G7
Essex, On, Can. 135/G7
Essex (co.), Eng, UK 30/E1
Essex Fells, NJ, US 139/H8
Esslingen, Ger. 54/C5
Essômes-sur-Marne, Fr. 52/C5
Essonne (riv.), Fr. 42/E2
Est, Canal de l' (canal), Fr. 53/E5
Estaca de Bares, Punta de la (cape), Sp. 44/B1
Estación Santa Engracia, Mex. 143/F3
Estados, Isla de los (isl.), Arg. 157/D7
Eşţahbān, Iran 88/F3
Estaires, Fr. 52/B2
Estância, Braz. 154/C3
Estats, Pico de (peak), Sp. 45/F1
Estavayer-le-Lac, Swi. 56/C4
Estcourt, SAfr. 107/E3
Este, It. 59/E2
Este, Punta del (pt.), Cuba 140/E3
Este Sudeste, Cayos del (isls.), Col. 145/F3
Esteio, Braz. 155/B4
Esteli, Nic. 144/E3
Estell Manor (Risley), NJ, US 138/D5
Estella, Sp. 44/D1
Estelle (mtn.), Ca, US 136/C3
Estelle, La, US 137/P17
Estepa, Sp. 44/C4
Estepona, Sp. 44/C4
Ester, Ak, US 134/J3
Esterhazy, Sk, Can. 127/H3
Esterias (cape), Gabon 96/G7
Esternay, Fr. 52/C6
Estero de Agiabampo (lag.), Mex. 142/C3
Estéron (riv.), Fr. 43/G5
Esterwegen, Ger. 51/E3
Estes Park, Co, US 137/A2
Estevan, Sk, Can. 127/H3
Estinnes-au-Mont, Belg. 53/D3
Eston, Sk, Can. 126/F3
Eston and South Bank, Eng, UK 35/G2
Estonia (ctry.) 39/M2
Estoril, Port. 45/P10
Estral Beach, Mi, US 135/F8
Estrées-Saint-Denis, Fr. 52/B5
Estrela, Serra da (mts.), Port. 44/A3
Estrela, Serra da (peak), Port. 44/B2
Estrella (pt.), Mex. 142/B2
Estrelto, Serra do (range), Braz. 154/B3
Estremoz, Port. 44/B3
Estrondo, Serra do (mts.), Braz. 151/J5
Esztergom, Hun. 48/D2
Eţ Taiyiba, Isr. 91/G7
Eţ Tīra, Isr. 91/F7
Etah, India 84/B2
Étain, Fr. 53/E5
Etal (isl.), Micr. 116/E4
Étalle, Belg. 53/E4
Étaples, Fr. 52/A2
Etāwah, India 84/B2
Etāwah Branch (riv.), India 84/B2
Etchojoa, Mex. 142/C3
Ethelbert, Mb, Can. 127/H3
Ethiopia (ctry.) 97/N5
Ethiopian (plat.), Eth. 97/N6
Eti (riv.), Japan 77/K5
Etili, Turk. 49/H6
Étival-Clairefontaine, Fr. 56/C1
Etive, Loch (inlet), Sc, UK 36/A4
Etna (peak), It. 46/D4
Etna, Monte (Mount Etna) (vol.), It. 46/D4
Etne, Nor. 38/A2
Etobicoke, Can. 131/Q8
Etolin (str.), Ak, US 134/E3
Eton, Eng, UK 30/B2
Etorofu (isl.), Japan 71/S2
Etorofu (isl.), Rus. 67/P5
Etosha (salt pan), Namb. 105/C4
Etosha NP, Namb. 105/C4
Etowah, Ok, US 137/N15
Étrépilly, Fr. 30/L4
Etropole, Bul. 47/J1
Etroubles, It. 56/D6
Ettadhamen Douarhicher, Tun. 100/M6
Ettelbruck, Lux. 53/F4
Etten-Leur, Neth. 50/B5
Ettenheim, Ger. 56/D1
Etterbeek, Belg. 53/D2
Etters (Goldsboro), Pa, US 138/B3
Ettlingen, Ger. 54/B5
Ettrick Pen (peak), Sc, UK 36/C6
Ettrick Water (riv.), Sc, UK 36/C5
Ettringen, Ger. 57/G1
Eu, Fr. 52/A3
'Eua (isl.), Tonga 117/H7
Eubenangee Swamp NP, Austl. 114/B2
Euclid, Oh, US 130/D3
Euclides da Cunha, Braz. 154/C3
Eudora, Ar, US 129/K4
Eudunda, Austl. 115/A2
Euerbach, Ger. 54/D2
Eufaula, Al, US 133/G4
Eufaula (lake), Ok, US 125/G4
Eugendorf, Aus. 55/G7
Eugene, Or, US 126/C4
Eugene O'Neill NHS, Ca, US 135/L11
Eugenia (pt.), Mex. 142/B3
Eugowra, Austl. 115/D2
Eume, Embalse de (res.), Sp. 44/B1
Eungella NP, Austl. 114/C3
Eunice, La, US 129/J5
Eunice, NM, US 129/G4
Eupen, Belg. 53/F2
Euphrates (riv.), Iraq,Syria 67/D6
Eura, Fin. 39/K1
Eurajoki, Fin. 39/J1
Eure (riv.), Fr. 42/D2
Eure (dept.), Fr. 52/A5
Eure-et-Loir (dept.), Fr. 52/A6
Eureka, SD, US 127/J4
Eureka, Mt, US 126/E3
Eureka, Ca, US 126/B5
Eureka, Nv, US 128/D3
Eureka, Mo, US 137/F9
Eureka (sound), Nun., Can. 123/S7
Euroa, Austl. 115/C3
Eurodisney, Fr. 30/L5
Euron (riv.), Fr. 56/C1
Europa (pt.), Gib. 44/C4
Europabrücke, Aus. 57/H3
Europe (cont.) 27
Europoort, Neth. 50/B5
Euskirchen, Ger. 53/F2
Eussenheim, Ger. 54/C3
Eustis, Fl, US 133/H4
Euston, Austl. 115/B2
Eutin, Ger. 38/D4
Eutini, Malw. 104/B5
Eutsuk (lake), BC, Can. 126/B2
Euville, Fr. 53/E6
Évain, Qu, Can. 130/E1
Evander, SAfr. 106/E2
Evans (mt.), Co, US 129/F3
Evans (lake), Qu, Can. 130/E1
Evans, Co, US 137/C2
Evans (str.), Nun., Can. 123/H2
Evans Head, Austl. 115/E1
Evanston, Wy, US 126/F5
Evansville, Wy, US 129/F2
Evansville, In, US 130/C4
Evaporation (basin), Ut, US 126/E5
Evart, Mi, US 130/C3
Evaton, SAfr. 106/D2
Evaz, Iran 88/F3
Ève, Fr. 30/L4
Even Yehuda, Isr. 91/F7
Evenlode (riv.), Eng, UK 33/E3
Evenkiyskiy (aut. okrug), Rus. 64/K3
Everard (cape), Austl. 115/D3
Everard (lake), Austl. 109/C4
Everard (mt.), Austl. 113/G3
Everest (peak), China, Nepal 82/E2
Everest (Sagarmatha) (mtn.), China,Nepal 85/F2
Everett, Wa, US 126/C4
Evergem, Belg. 52/C1
Everglades (swamp), Fl, US 133/H5
Everglades NP, Fl, US 133/H5
Evergreen, Al, US 133/G4
Evergreen, Co, US 137/C2
Evergreen Park, Il, US 135/Q16
Everswinkel, Ger. 51/E5
Evesham, Eng, UK 33/E2
Evesham, Vale of (valley), Eng, UK 32/D2
Évian-les-Bains, Fr. 56/C5
Évinos (riv.), Gre. 47/G3
Evje, Nor. 38/B2
Evolène, Swi. 56/D5
Évora, Port. 44/B3
Évora (dist.), Port. 44/A3
Évreux, Fr. 42/D2
Évron, Fr. 42/C2
Evrótas (riv.), Gre. 47/H4
Évry, Fr. 30/K6
Évvoia (isl.), Gre. 47/H3
Évvoia (gulf), Gre. 47/H3
Évvoia (gulf), Gre. 62/B5
Evvoia (isl.), Gre. 62/B5
Evxinoúpolis, Gre. 47/H3
Ewa Beach, Hi, US 124/V13
Ewa Villages, Hi, US 124/V13
Ewan, NJ, US 138/C4
Ewarton, Jam. 145/G2
Ewaso Ng'iro (riv.), Kenya 104/C2
Ewell, Eng, UK 30/C3
Ewing, NJ, US 138/D3
Exaplátanos, Gre. 47/H2
Excelsior Springs, Mo, US 137/E5
Excursion Inlet, Ak, US 134/L4
Exe (riv.), Eng, UK 32/C4
Exeter, NH, US 131/G3
Exmoor (upland), Eng, UK 32/C4
Exmoor NP, Eng, UK 32/C4
Exmore, Va, US 133/K2
Exmouth, Austl. 112/B2
Exmouth (gulf), Austl. 112/B2
Exmouth (pen.), Chile 159/B6
Extrema, Braz. 211/G7
Extremadura (reg.), Sp. 44/B3
Exu, Braz. 154/C2
Exuma (sound), Bahm. 141/F3
Eyach (riv.), Ger. 54/B6
Eyak, Ak, US 134/J3
Eyasi (lake), Tanz. 105/F1
Eyb (riv.), Ger. 54/C5
Eydehamn, Nor. 38/C2
Eyemouth, Sc, UK 36/D5
Eyguières, Fr. 42/F5
Eyn Hemed (ruin), Isr. 91/G8
Eyre (pen.), Austl. 109/C4
Eyre (lake), Austl. 116/C7
Eyre North (lake), Austl. 109/C3
Eyre South (lake), Austl. 109/C3
Ézanville, Fr. 30/K4
Ezequiel Ramos Mexía (res.), Arg. 158/C3
Ezhou, China 79/B1
Ezine, Turk. 47/K3
Ezzane (well), Alg. 96/H3

F

F.E. Walter (res.), Pa, US 138/C1
Fabbrico, It. 59/D3
Fabens, Tx, US 132/B4
Fabero, Sp. 44/B1
Fåborg, Den. 38/D4
Fabriano, It. 43/K5
Facatativá, Col. 150/D3
Faches-Thumesnil, Fr. 52/C2
Fada (lake), Sc, UK 36/A1
Fada-N'Gourma, Burk. 103/F3
Faenza, It. 59/E4
Fafa (riv.), CAfr. 97/J6
Fafe, Port. 44/A2
Fafen Shet' (riv.), Eth. 97/P6
Făgăraş, Rom. 49/G3
Fagersta, Swe. 38/F2
Faggiola (peak), It. 59/E4
Fagnano (lake), Arg. 159/D7
Fagnano Olona, It. 58/B1
Fagnières, Fr. 53/D6
Faguibine (lake), Mali 96/D4
Fahl (well), Alg. 99/F3
Fahrenzhausen, Ger. 55/E6
Faial (isl.), Azor., Port. 45/S12
Faido, Swi. 57/E5
Failsworth, Eng, UK 35/F4
Fains-Véel, Fr. 53/E6
Fair Haven, Vt, US 130/F3
Fair Haven, Mi, US 135/G6
Fair Hill, Md, US 138/C4
Fair Isle (isl.), Sc, UK 31/W14
Fair Lawn, NJ, US 139/J8
Fair Oaks, Ca, US 135/M9
Fairbanks, Ak, US 134/J3
Fairfax (co.), Va, US 138/A6
Fairfax, Va, US 138/A6
Fairfax, Ca, US 135/J11
Fairfield, Mt, US 126/F4
Fairfield, Tx, US 129/H5
Fairfield, Ca, US 128/B3
Fairfield, Ut, US 137/J13
Fairfield, Pa, US 138/A4
Fairfield, Ct, US 139/E1
Fairfield (co.), Ct, US 139/L7
Fairfield, NJ, US 139/H8
Fairland, Md, US 138/B5
Fairlee, Md, US 138/B5
Fairless Hills, Pa, US 138/D3
Fairlie, Sc, UK 36/B5
Fairmont, WV, US 130/D4
Fairmont City, Il, US 137/G8
Fairmount, Ks, US 137/D5
Fairplay, Co, US 132/B2
Fairton, NJ, US 138/C5
Fairview, Ok, US 129/H3
Fairview, NJ, US 139/K8
Fairview Heights, Il, US 137/G8
Fairway, Ks, US 137/D5
Fairweather (mt.), Ak, US 134/L4
Fairweather (cape), Ak, US 134/L4
Fairweather (mt.), BC, Can. 122/C3
Faisalābād, Pak. 86/B4
Faistós (ruin), Gre. 47/J5
Faizābād, India 84/D2
Fajardo, PR 141/M8
Fakahina (isl.), FrPol. 117/M6
Fakaofo (isl.), Tok. 117/H5
Fakarava (isl.), FrPol. 117/L6
Fako (peak), Camr. 96/G7
Fakse, Den. 38/E4
Fakse Ladeplads, Den. 38/E4
Faku, China 72/E2
Fal (riv.), Eng, UK 32/B6
Fālākāta, India 85/G2
Falāmah, WBnk. 91/G7
Fálanna, Gre. 47/H3
Falcon (res.), Mex.,US 140/B2
Falcon (cape), Alg. 100/D2
Falcón (state), Ven. 152/D2
Falconara Marittima, It. 59/G5
Falémé (riv.), Mali 96/C5
Falfurrias, Tx, US 132/D5
Falher, Ab, Can. 126/D2
Falkenberg, Swe. 38/E3
Falkensee, Ger. 40/G6
Falkenstein, Ger. 55/F4
Falkenstein, Ger. 55/F2
Falkirk, Sc, UK 36/C5
Falkirk (pol. reg.), Sc, UK 36/C5
Falkland (isls.), UK 147/C8
Falkland, Sc, UK 36/C4
Falkland Sound (str.), UK 159/E7
Falköping, Swe. 38/E2
Fall City, Wa, US 135/D2
Fall River, Ma, US 131/G3
Fallbrook, Ca, US 136/C4
Fallere (peak), It. 56/D6
Falling Spring, Il, US 137/G8
Fallingbostel, Ger. 51/G3
Fallis, Ok, US 137/N14
Fallon, Nv, US 128/C3
Falls Church, Va, US 138/A6
Fallston, Md, US 138/B4
Falmouth, Anti. 141/N8
Falmouth, Eng, UK 32/A6
Falmouth (bay), Eng, UK 32/A6
False Pass, Ak, US 134/F5
Falshöft (pt.), Ger. 38/C4
Falso (cape), Hon. 145/F3
Falso, Cabo (cape), Mex. 142/C4
Falso Cabo de Hornos (cape), Chile 159/C7
Falster (isl.), Den. 37/E5
Falterona (peak), It. 59/E5
Fălticeni, Rom. 49/H2
Falun, Swe. 38/F1
Famagusta (bay), Cyp. 91/C2
Famagusta (dist.), Cyp. 91/C2
Famagusta, Cyp. 91/C2
Fameck, Fr. 53/F5
Famenne (reg.), Belg. 53/E3
Fammau, Moel (peak), Wal, UK 35/E5
Fan Si Pan (peak), Viet. 83/H3
Fana, Nor. 38/A1
Fanchang, China 72/D5
Fandriana, Madg. 107/H8
Fang Xian, China 72/B4
Fangatau (isl.), FrPol. 117/L6
Fangataufa (isl.), FrPol. 117/L7
Fangcheng, China 72/C4
Fangcheng Gezu Zizhixian, China 83/J3
Fangshan, China 72/B3
Fanjing (peak), China 83/J2
Fannich (lake), Sc, UK 36/A1
Fanning (Tabuaeran) (isl.), Kiri. 117/K4
Fano, It. 59/G5
Fanø (isl.), Den. 38/C4
Fanshi, China 72/C3
Fanwood, NJ, US 139/H9
Faqīrwāli, Pak. 86/B5
Fāqūs, Egypt 91/B4
Fara Novarese, It. 58/B1
Faradje, D.R. Congo 104/A2
Farafangana, Madg. 107/H8
Farāfirah, Wāḩāt al (oasis), Egypt 101/A3
Farāh, Afg. 64/G6
Farāh (riv.), Afg. 64/G6
Farallon (isls.), Ca, US 128/B3
Farallon de Medinilla (isl.), NMar. 116/D3
Farallon de Pajaros (isl.), NMar. 116/D2
Farallones de Cali, PN, Col. 150/C3
Faranah (pol. reg.), Gui. 102/C4
Faranah, Gui. 102/C4
Farángi Samariás NP, Gre. 47/H5
Faraony (riv.), Madg. 107/H8
Faraulep (isl.), Micr. 116/D4
Farciennes, Belg. 53/D3
Fareham, Eng, UK 33/E5
Faremoutiers, Fr. 52/C6
Farewell, Ak, US 134/H3
Farewell (cape), NZ 117/S11
Färgelanda, Swe. 38/D2
Farghona (pol. reg.), Uzb. 87/F4
Farghona, Uzb. 87/F4
Fargo, ND, US 127/J4
Faribault, Mn, US 127/K4
Farīdābād, India 86/D5
Farīdkot, India 86/C4
Farīdpur, Bang. 85/G4
Farīdpur (pol. reg.), Bang. 85/G4
Farīdpur, India 84/B1
Fāriskūr, Egypt 91/B4
Färjestaden, Swe. 38/G3
Farkadhón, Gre. 47/H3
Farkasgyepü, Hun. 48/C2
Farley, Mo, US 137/D5
Farmers, Co, US 137/C2
Farmingdale, NJ, US 138/D3
Farmingdale, NY, US 139/M9
Farmington, Me, US 131/G2
Farmington, NM, US 128/E3
Farmington, Mo, US 129/K3
Farmington, Ut, US 137/K12
Farmington, De, US 138/C6
Farmington, Mi, US 135/F7
Farmington Hills, Mi, US 135/E6
Farnborough, Eng, UK 33/F4
Farnham, Eng, UK 33/F4
Farnham Royal, Eng, UK 30/B2
Farnworth, Eng, UK 35/F4
Faro, Yk, Can. 134/M3
Faro (dist.), Port. 44/A4
Faro, Port. 44/B4
Faro (int'l arpt.), Port. 44/B4
Faro, PN du, Camr. 96/H6
Faroe (isls.), Den. 160/G
Fåron (isl.), Swe. 39/H3
Farösund, Swe. 39/H3
Farquhar (cape), Austl. 112/B2
Farr West, Ut, US 137/J11
Farroupilha, Braz. 155/B4
Farrukhābād, India 84/B2
Fársala, Gre. 47/H3
Farsø, Den. 38/C3
Farson, Wy, US 126/F5
Farsund, Nor. 38/B2
Fartak, Ras (pt.), Yem. 88/F5
Farwell, Tx, US 129/G4
Fasā, Iran 88/F3
Fasano, It. 47/E2
Faşıkan (pass), Turk. 91/C1
Fassberg, Ger. 51/H3
Fast Castle (pt.), Sc, UK 36/D5
Fastiv, Ukr. 62/D2
Fatagar Tuting (cape), Indo. 81/H4
Fatahjang, Pak. 86/B3
Fatehābād, India 86/C5
Fatehpur, India 84/C3
Fatehpur, India 84/C2
Fatehpur, India 89/K3
Fatick (pol. reg.), Sen. 102/A3
Fatick, Sen. 102/A3
Fátima, Port. 44/A3
Fatsa, Turk. 62/F4
Fatu Hiva (isl.), FrPol. 117/M6
Faucille, Col de la (pass), Fr. 56/C5
Faucilles (mts.), Fr. 40/C4
Faughan (riv.), NI, UK 34/A2
Fauglia, It. 58/D5
Fauldhouse, Sc, UK 36/C5
Faulkton, SD, US 127/J4
Faulquemont, Fr. 53/F5
Faure (isl.), Austl. 112/B3
Făurei, Rom. 49/H3
Fauske, Nor. 37/E2
Faust, Ut, US 137/J13
Fauvillers, Belg. 53/E4
Faux, Tête de (peak), Fr. 56/D1
Favalto (peak), It. 59/F6
Favara, It. 46/C4
Fave (riv.), Fr. 56/C1
Faverges, Fr. 56/C6
Faverney, Fr. 56/C2
Faversham, Eng, UK 33/G4
Favières, Fr. 30/L5
Favignana, It. 46/C4
Favria, It. 58/A2
Favrieux, Fr. 30/G5
Fawn (riv.), On, Can. 127/L2
Fawn Grove, Pa, US 138/B4
Faxaflói (bay), Ice. 37/M7
Faxinal, Braz. 155/B2
Faya-Largeau, Chad 97/J4
Fayette, Al, US 133/G3
Fayette, Ms, US 129/K5
Fayetteville, Tn, US 133/G3
Fayetteville, Ga, US 133/G3
Fayetteville, NC, US 133/J3
Fayl-la-Forêt, Fr. 56/B2
Fazao, Monts du (mts.), Togo 103/F4
Fazao, PN du, Togo 103/F4
Fdérik, Mrta. 98/B5
Feale (riv.), Ire. 31/P10
Fear (cape), NC, US 133/J3
Feasterville-Trevose, Pa, US 138/D3
Feather (riv.), Ca, US 128/B3
Featherstone, Eng, UK 35/G4
Fécamp, Fr. 42/D2
Fecht (riv.), Fr. 56/D1
Federal Hall Nat'l Mem., NY, US 139/K9
Federal Heights, Co, US 137/B3
Federally Admin. Tribal Areas, Pak. 86/A2
Federsee (lake), Ger. 54/C6
Fedje, Nor. 38/A1
Feeny, NI, UK 34/A2
Fegersheim, Fr. 54/A6
Fehérgyarmat, Hun. 48/F2
Fehmarn (isl.), Den. 38/D4
Fehmarn Belt (str.), Den. 40/F1
Fei Huang (riv.), China 72/D4
Fei Xian, China 72/D4
Feia, Lagoa (lake), Braz. 155/D2
Feicheng, China 72/D3
Feidong, China 72/D5
Feignies, Fr. 52/C3
Feijó, Braz. 156/D3
Feillans, Fr. 56/A5
Feira, Port. 44/A2
Feira de Santana, Braz. 154/C4
Feistritz (riv.), Aus. 43/L3
Feixi, China 72/D5
Fejér (co.), Hun. 48/D2
Fejø (isl.), Ger. 38/D4
Feke, Turk. 90/C2
Feketić, Yugo. 48/D3
Felanitx, Sp. 45/G3
Feldafing, Ger. 57/H2
Feldaist (riv.), Aus. 55/H6
Feldberg (peak), Ger. 56/E2
Feldkirch, Aus. 57/F3
Feldkirchen an der Donau, Aus. 55/H6
Feldkirchen bei Graz, Aus. 48/B2
Feldkirchen in Kärnten, Aus. 43/L3
Feletto, It. 58/A2
Feletto Umberto, It. 59/G1
Felino, It. 58/D3
Felipe Carillo Puerto, Mex. 144/D2
Felixdorf, Aus. 48/C2
Felixlândia, Braz. 155/C1
Felixstowe, Eng, UK 33/H3
Felizzano, It. 58/B3
Fell, Ger. 53/F4
Fellbach, Ger. 54/C5
Felling, Eng, UK 35/G2
Felsberg, Ger. 51/G6
Felsberg, Swi. 57/F4
Felton, Pa, US 138/B4
Felton, De, US 138/C5
Fema (peak), It. 43/K5
Femø (isl.), Den. 38/D4
Femundsmarka NP, Nor. 37/D3
Fénay, Fr. 56/B3
Fene, Sp. 44/A1
Fener (pt.), Turk. 91/D1
Fénérive, Madg. 105/K10
Feng Xian, China 72/D4
Fengári (peak), Gre. 47/J2
Fengcheng, China 71/L6
Fengcheng, China 73/C2
Fengcheng, China 83/J2
Fengle (riv.), China 72/D5
Fengnan, China 72/J7
Fengning, China 72/D2
Fengqing, China 83/G3
Fengqiu, China 72/C4
Fengrun, China 72/J7
Fengshan, Tai. 79/D3
Fengtai, China 72/H7
Fengxian, China 72/L9
Fengyang, China 72/D4
Fengyüan, Tai. 79/D3
Fengzhen, China 72/C2
Fenimore Pass (chan.), Ak, US 134/C5
Fenoarivo Atsinanana, Madg. 107/J7
Fens (phys. reg.), Eng, UK 33/G1
Fensmark, Den. 38/D4
Fensterbach (riv.), Ger. 55/F4
Fenton, Mi, US 130/D3
Fenton, Mo, US 137/G8
Fenton (lake), Mi, US 135/E7
Fenxi, China 72/B3
Feodosiya, Ukr. 62/E3
Fer, Cap de (cape), Alg. 100/K6
Ferbane, Ire. 31/Q10
Ferdinandshof, Ger. 41/G2
Fère-Champenoise, Fr. 52/C6
Fère-en-Tardenois, Fr. 52/C5
Ferentino, It. 46/C2
Ferento (ruin), It. 46/C1
Fergus Falls, Mn, US 127/J4
Ferguson, Mo, US 137/G8
Ferguson (lake), Nun., Can. 122/F2
Ferihegy (int'l arpt.), Hun. 48/D2
Ferkéssédougou, C.d'Iv. 102/D4
Ferlach, Aus. 43/L3
Fermanagh (dist.), NI, UK 34/A3
Fermi National Accelerator Laboratory, Il, US 135/P16
Fermignano, It. 59/F5
Fermin (pt.), Ca, US 136/F8
Fermo, It. 43/K5
Fermoselle, Sp. 44/B2
Fermoy, Ire. 31/P10
Fernán-Núñez, Sp. 44/C4
Fernandina (isl.), Ecu. 156/E7
Fernandina Beach, Fl, US 133/H4
Fernando de Noronha (isl.), Braz. 147/F3
Fernandópolis, Braz. 155/B2
Ferndale, Md, US 138/B5
Ferndale, Mi, US 135/F7
Ferney-Voltaire, Fr. 56/C5
Fernie, BC, Can. 126/E3
Fernpass (pass), Aus. 57/G3
Ferntree Gully NP, Austl. 115/G5
Ferrandina, It. 46/E2
Ferrara (prov.), It. 59/E3

Free State (prov.), SAfr. 106/P13
Freeburg, Il, US 137/H9
Freeburg, Pa, US 138/B2
Freedom, Ok, US 132/D2
Freehold, NJ, US 138/D3
Freeland, Pa, US 138/C1
Freeland, Md, US 138/B4
Freeland, Wa, US 135/B1
Freeling (mt.), Austl. 113/G2
Freeling Heights (peak), Austl. 113/H4
Freemansburg, Pa, US 138/C2
Freeport, Il, US 127/L5
Freeport, Tx, US 129/J5
Freeport, Bahm. 141/F2
Freeport, NY, US 139/L9
Freer, Tx, US 132/D5
Freetown (cap.), SLeo. 102/B4
Fregenal de la Sierra, Sp. 44/B3
Fréhel (cape), Fr. 42/B2
Frei Inocêncio, Braz. 155/D1
Freib Mulde (riv.), Ger. 40/G3
Freiberg, Ger. 41/G3
Freiburg, Ger. 51/G1
Freiburg, Ger. 56/D2
Freienbach, Swi. 57/E3
Freihung, Ger. 55/E3
Freilassing, Ger. 55/F7
Freinsheim, Ger. 54/B3
Freire, Chile 158/B3
Freisen, Ger. 53/G4
Freising, Ger. 55/E6
Freistadt, Aus. 55/H5
Freital, Ger. 41/G3
Freixo de Espada à Cinta, Port. 44/B2
Frejorgues (int'l arpt.), Fr. 42/E5
Fréjus, Fr. 43/G5
Frekhaug, Nor. 38/A1
Frémainfille, Fr. 30/H4
Fremdingen, Ger. 54/D5
Frémécourt, Fr. 30/J4
Fremont (riv.), Ut, US 128/E3
Fremont, Oh, US 130/D3
Fremont, Mi, US 130/C3
Fremont, Ca, US 128/B3
Fremont (isl.), Ut, US 137/J11
French (riv.), On, Can. 130/D2
French Creek State Park, Pa, US 138/C3
French Frigate Shoals (bar), Hi, US 117/J2
French Guiana (dpcy.), Fr. 151/H3
French Polynesia (terr.), Fr. 117/L6
Frenchman (riv.), Can.,US 122/F4
Frenchman's (bay), On, Can. 131/R8
Frenchmans Cap (peak), Austl. 115/C4
Frenchtown, NJ, US 138/C2
Frenda, Alg. 100/F5
Frépillon, Fr. 30/J4
Freren, Ger. 51/E4
Fresco (riv.), Braz. 151/H5
Fresco, C.d'Iv. 102/D5
Fresia, Chile 158/B4
Fresnes, Fr. 30/J5
Fresnes-en-Woëvre, Fr. 53/E5
Fresnillo, Mex. 142/E4
Fresno, Ca, US 128/C3
Fresnoy-le-Grand, Fr. 52/C4
Fresse-sur-Moselle, Fr. 56/C2
Fressenneville, Fr. 52/A3
Fretin, Fr. 52/C2
Freuchie (lake), Sc, UK 36/C3
Freudenberg, Ger. 55/E4
Freudenberg, Ger. 53/G2
Freudenburg, Ger. 53/F4
Freudenstadt, Ger. 57/E1
Frévent, Fr. 52/B3
Freycinet (har.), Austl. 112/B3
Freycinet NP, Austl. 115/D4
Freyming-Merlebach, Fr. 53/F5
Freystadt, Ger. 55/E4
Freyung, Ger. 55/G5
Fria (cape), Namb. 105/B4
Frías, Arg. 157/C2
Frías, Peru 156/B2
Fribourg, Swi. 56/D4
Fribourg (canton), Swi. 56/D4
Frick, Swi. 56/E3
Frickenhausen am Main, Ger. 54/D3
Fridingen an der Donau, Ger. 57/E1
Fridolfing, Ger. 55/F6
Friedberg, Ger. 54/B2
Friedberg, Ger. 54/D6
Friedeburg, Ger. 51/E2
Friedrichsdorf, Ger. 54/B2
Friedrichshafen, Ger. 57/F2
Friedrichstadt, Ger. 38/C4
Friedrichsthal, Ger. 53/G5
Frielendorf, Ger. 51/G7
Friesenhagen, Ger. 53/G2
Friesenheim, Ger. 56/D1
Friesland (prov.), Neth. 50/C2
Friesoythe, Ger. 51/E2
Frignicourt, Fr. 53/D6
Frio (riv.), Tx, US 143/F2
Friockheim, Sc, UK 36/D3
Friol, Sp. 44/B1
Frisange, Lux. 53/F4
Fristad, Swe. 38/E3
Fritsla, Swe. 38/E3
Fritzlar, Ger. 51/G6
Friuli-Venezia Giulia (prov.), It. 43/K3
Friville-Escarbotin, Fr. 52/A3
Frobisher (bay), Nun., Can. 123/K2
Frogmore, Eng, UK 30/A3
Frohavel (inlet), Nor. 37/D3
Frohnleiten, Aus. 43/L3
Froid-Chapelle, Belg. 53/D3
Froideconche, Fr. 56/C2
Froissy, Fr. 52/B4
Froland, Nor. 38/C2
Frolovo, Rus. 63/G2
Frome (lake), Austl. 109/D4
Frome (riv.), Eng, UK 32/D5
Frome, Eng, UK 32/D4
Frome (riv.), Austl. 113/H4
Froncles, Fr. 56/B1
Front (range), Co, US 129/F2
Fronteira, Port. 44/B3
Frontenhausen, Ger. 55/F5
Frontera, Mex. 144/C2
Frontera Comalapa, Mex. 144/C3
Frontier Army Museum, Ks, US 137/D5
Frontignan, Fr. 42/E5
Fronton, Fr. 42/D5
Frosinone, It. 46/C2
Frösö, Swe. 37/E3
Frotey-lès-Vesoul, Fr. 56/C2
Frouard, Fr. 53/F6
Frövi, Swe. 38/F2
Frøya (isl.), Nor. 37/D3
Frozen (str.), Nun., Can. 123/H2
Fruges, Fr. 52/B2
Fruit Heights, Ut, US 137/K11
Fruška Gora NP, Cro. 48/D3
Frutal, Braz. 155/B1
Frutigen, Swi. 56/D4
Frutillar, Chile 158/B4
Fryazino, Rus. 61/X9
Frýdek-Místek, Czh. 41/K4
Fu Xian, China 72/B4
Fu'an, China 79/C2
Fucecchio, It. 59/D5
Fucheng, China 72/D3
Fuchskaute (peak), Ger. 43/H1
Fuchū, Japan 74/C3
Fuchū, Japan 77/C2
Fuchuan, China 79/B3
Fuchun (riv.), China 72/D5
Fuding, China 79/D2
Fuengirola, Sp. 44/C4
Fuenlabrada, Sp. 45/N9
Fuensalida, Sp. 44/C2
Fuente, Sp. 45/N8
Fuente de Cantos, Sp. 44/B3
Fuente del Maestre, Sp. 44/B3
Fuente Obejuna, Sp. 44/C3
Fuentelapeña, Sp. 44/C2
Fuentes de Oñoro, Sp. 44/B2
Fuentesaúco, Sp. 44/C2
Fuerte (riv.), Mex. 142/C3
Fuerte Olimpo, Par. 150/G8
Fuerteventura (isl.) 96/C2
Fuga (isl.), Phil. 79/D4
Fuglebjerg, Den. 38/D4
Fugong, China 83/G2
Fugou, China 72/C4
Fuhai, China 70/E2
Fuhne (riv.), Ger. 40/F3
Fuhse (riv.), Ger. 51/H4
Fuji (riv.), Japan 75/F3
Fuji, Japan 75/F3
Fuji-Hakone-Izu NP, Japan 75/F3
Fuji-san (peak), Japan 75/F3
Fujian (prov.), China 71/L6
Fujieda, Japan 75/F3
Fujihashi, Japan 77/K4
Fujiidera, Japan 77/J6
Fujikawa, Japan 77/B3
Fujimi, Japan 77/D2
Fujino, Japan 77/C2
Fujinomiya, Japan 77/B3
Fujioka, Japan 75/F2
Fujioka, Japan 77/D1
Fujioka, Japan 77/M5
Fujisawa, Japan 75/F3
Fujishiro, Japan 77/E2
Fujiwara, Japan 77/K5
Fujiyoshida, Japan 77/B3
Fukagawa, Japan 76/C2
Fukang, China 70/E3
Fukaya, Japan 77/C1
Fukiage, Japan 77/C1
Fukuchiyama, Japan 77/H5
Fukue, Japan 74/A4
Fukui (pref.), Japan 74/E3
Fukui, Japan 74/E2
Fukuoka, Japan 74/B4
Fukuoka (int'l arpt.), Japan 74/B4
Fukuoka (pref.), Japan 74/B4
Fukuoka, Japan 77/M4
Fukuroi, Japan 75/E3
Fukushima, Japan 75/G2
Fukushima (pref.), Japan 75/F2
Fukushima, Japan 76/B3
Fukuyama, Japan 74/C3
Fūlādī (mtn.), Afg. 89/J2
Fulda (riv.), Ger. 40/E3
Fulda, Ger. 54/C1
Fullerton, Ca, US 136/G8
Fullerton (Whitehall), Pa, US 138/C2
Fully, Swi. 56/D5
Fulpmes, Aus. 57/H3
Fulton, Mo, US 129/K3
Fulton, NY, US 130/E3
Fulton, Ky, US 130/B4
Fulufjället (peak), Swe. 38/E1
Fumaiolo (peak), It. 59/F5
Fumay, Fr. 53/D4
Fumel, Fr. 42/D4
Fumin, China 83/H2
Funabashi, Japan 77/D2
Funafuti (cap.), Tuv. 116/G5
Funafuti (isl.), Tuv. 116/G5
Funan, China 72/C4
Funchal, Port. 98/A2
Funchal (int'l arpt.), Port. 98/A2
Fundación, Col. 152/C2
Fundão, Port. 44/B2
Fundy (bay), US,Can. 131/H2
Fundy NP, NB, Can. 131/H2
Funhalouro, Moz. 105/F5
Funing, China 83/J3
Funing, China 72/D4
Fuorn, Pass dal (Ofenpass) (pass), Swi. 57/G4
Fuping, China 72/C3
Fuqing, China 79/C2
Fuquan, China 83/J2
Fur (riv.), China 73/C2
Furan (riv.), Fr. 56/B6
Furano, Japan 76/C2
Fürfeld, Ger. 53/G4
Furmanov, Rus. 60/J4
Furnas (res.), Braz. 147/E5
Furneaux Group (isls.), Austl. 109/D4
Fürstenau, Ger. 51/E3
Fürstenfeld, Aus. 43/M3
Fürstenfeldbruck, Ger. 54/E6
Fürstenwalde, Ger. 41/H2
Fürth, Ger. 54/B3
Fürth, Ger. 54/D4
Furth, Ger. 55/F5
Furth im Wald, Ger. 55/F4
Furtwangen im Schwarzwald, Ger. 56/E1
Furudal, Swe. 38/F1
Furukawa, Japan 76/B4
Fury and Hecla (str.), Nun., Can. 123/H2
Fushan, China 72/B4
Fushan, China 72/E3
Fushun, China 73/B2
Fushun, China 83/J2
Fusignano, It. 59/E4
Fusio, Swi. 57/E5
Fuso, Japan 77/L5
Fussa, Japan 77/C2
Füssen, Ger. 57/G2
Fusui, China 78/D1
Futaba, Japan 77/A2
Futaleufú, Chile 158/C4
Futami, Japan 77/L7
Futog, Yugo. 48/D3
Futrono, Chile 158/B4
Futtsu, Japan 75/F3
Futuna (isl.), Wall. 116/H6
Fuwah, Egypt 91/B4
Fuxian (lake), China 83/H3
Fuxin, China 72/E2
Fuxin Monggolzu Zizhixian, China 72/E2
Fuyang, China 72/C4
Fuyi (riv.), China 79/B2
Fuyu, China 71/M2
Fuyu, China 71/M2
Fuyuan, China 83/H2
Fuyun, China 70/E2
Füzesabony, Hun. 48/E2
Fuzhou, China 79/C2
Fyn (co.), Den. 38/D4
Fyn (isl.), Den. 37/D5
Fyne, Loch (inlet), Sc, UK 36/A5
Fyresdal, Nor. 38/C2

G

Ga Vache (isl.), Haiti 145/H2
Gaast, Neth. 50/C2
Gabas (riv.), Fr. 42/C5
Gabela, Ang. 105/B3
Gabes (gulf), Tun. 93/D1
Gabicce Mare, It. 59/F5
Gablingen, Ger. 54/D6
Gablitz, Aus. 49/N7
Gabon (ctry.) 96/H7
Gaborone (cap.), Bots. 105/E5
Gabriel Leyva Solano, Mex. 142/C3
Gabrovo, Bul. 47/J1
Gaby, It. 58/A1
Gacko, Bosn. 47/F1
Gādarwāra, India 84/B4
Gaddy, Ok, US 137/N15
Gadmen, Swi. 57/E4
Gadsden, Al, US 133/G3
Găeşti, Rom. 49/G3
Gaeta, It. 46/C2
Gaeta, Golfo di (gulf), It. 46/C2
Gaferut (isl.), Micr. 116/D4
Gaffney, SC, US 133/H3
Gagarin, Rus. 60/G5
Gaggenau, Ger. 54/B5
Gaggio Montano, It. 59/D4
Gaglianico, It. 58/B1
Gagnoa, C.d'Iv. 102/D5
Gagny, Fr. 30/K5
Gagra, Geo. 62/G4
Gagret, India 86/D4
Gai Xian, China 73/B2
Gaichtpass (pass), Aus. 57/G3
Gail (riv.), Aus. 43/K3
Gaildorf, Ger. 54/C5
Gaillac, Fr. 42/D5
Gailtaler (mts.), Aus. 43/K3
Gaiman, Arg. 158/D4
Gaimersheim, Ger. 55/E5
Gainesville, Tx, US 129/H4
Gainesville, Ga, US 133/H3
Gainesville, Fl, US 133/H4
Gainsborough, Eng, UK 35/H5
Gairdner (lake), Austl. 109/C4
Gairn (riv.), Sc, UK 36/C2
Gais, Swi. 57/F3
Gaiserwald, Swi. 57/F3
Gaizina (peak), Lat. 39/L3
Gakarosa (peak), SAfr. 106/C2
Gakona, Ak, US 134/J3
Galana (riv.), Kenya 104/C3
Galand, Iran 89/G1
Galapagar, Sp. 45/M8
Galápagos (isls.), Ecu. 156/E6
Galápagos (dept.), Ecu. 156/E7
Galápagos, PN, Ecu. 156/E7
Galashiels, Sc, UK 36/D5
Galaţi (prov.), Rom. 49/H3
Galaţi, Rom. 49/J3
Galatina, It. 47/F2
Galatiní, Gre. 47/G2
Galátista, Gre. 47/H2
Galatone, It. 47/F2
Galb Azefal (hill), WSah. 98/B5
Galbiate, It. 58/C1
Galdácano, Sp. 44/D1
Gáldar, Sp. 98/B3
Galeana, Mex. 143/E3
Galela, Indo. 81/G3
Galena, Ak, US 134/G3
Galena, Md, US 138/C5
Galeota (pt.), Trin. 153/F2
Galera (pt.), Ecu. 152/A4
Galera (pt.), Trin. 153/F2
Galera (pt.), Chile 158/B3
Galesburg, Il, US 127/L5
Galey (riv.), Ire. 31/P10
Galga (riv.), Hun. 49/R9
Galgamácsa, Hun. 49/R9
Galgorm, NI, UK 34/B2
Galich, Rus. 60/J4
Galicia (aut. comm.), Sp. 44/A1
Galičica NP, FYROM 47/G2
Galiléia, Braz. 155/D1
Galileo Galilei (int'l arpt.), It. 58/D5
Galinakopf (peak), Aus. 57/F3
Galion, Oh, US 130/D3
Gallan Head (pt.), Sc, UK 31/Q7
Gallarate, It. 58/B1
Gallatin, Tn, US 130/C4
Galle, SrL. 82/D6
Gallegos (riv.), Arg. 157/B7
Galliate, It. 58/B2
Gallicano, It. 58/D4
Galliera Veneta, It. 59/E1
Gallinas (mts.), NM, US 132/B3
Gallinas (pt.), Col. 152/D1
Gallipoli, It. 47/E2
Gallipoli (pen.), Turk. 49/H5
Gällivare, Swe. 37/G2
Gallneukirchen, Aus. 55/H6
Gallo (cape), It. 46/C3
Gallo (lake), It. 57/G4
Gallspach, Aus. 55/G6
Galluis, Fr. 30/H5
Gallup, NM, US 128/E4
Gallur, Sp. 44/E2
Gally (riv.), Fr. 30/H5
Galston, Sc, UK 36/B5
Galten, Den. 38/C3
Galtymore (peak), Ire. 31/P10
Galva, La, US 137/P16
Galvarino, Chile 158/B3
Galveston, Tx, US 129/J5
Galveston (bay), Tx, US 140/C2
Galveston (isl.), Tx, US 140/C2
Gálvez, Sp. 44/C3
Galway, Ire. 31/P10
Galway (bay), Ire. 31/P10
Galzignano, It. 59/E2
Gam (riv.), Viet. 83/J3
Gamaches, Fr. 52/A4
Gamagara (riv.), SAfr. 106/C2
Gamagōri, Japan 77/M6
Gamarra, Col. 152/C2
Gamba, China 85/G1
Gambaga, Gha. 103/E4
Gambaga Scarp (cliff), Gha. 103/E4
Gambais, Fr. 30/H5
Gambara, It. 58/D2
Gambat, Pak. 82/A2
Gambela NP, Eth. 97/M6
Gambell, Ak, US 134/D3
Gambellara, It. 59/E2
Gamber, Md, US 138/B5
Gambettola, It. 59/F4
Gambia (riv.), Gam. 102/A3
Gambia (ctry.) 102/B3
Gambier (isls.), FrPol. 117/M7
Gámbita, Col. 152/C3
Gambo, Nf, Can. 131/L1
Gambolò, It. 58/B2
Gambsheim, Fr. 54/A5
Gaming, Aus. 43/L3
Gamka (riv.), SAfr. 106/C4
Gamkab (riv.), Namb. 106/B3
Gamleby, Swe. 38/G3
Gammelstad, Swe. 60/D2
Gammertingen, Ger. 57/F1
Gammon Ranges NP, Austl. 113/H4
Gamo, Japan 77/K5
Gampern, Aus. 55/G7
Gamud (peak), Eth. 104/C1
Gan (riv.), China 71/L6
Gan, Fr. 42/C5
Gananoque, On, Can. 130/E2
Gäncä, Azer. 63/H4
Ganda, Ang. 105/B3
Gandajika, D.R. Congo 105/D2
Gandak (riv.), India 85/E2
Gandaki (zone), Nepal 84/D1
Gander (lake), Nf, Can. 131/L1
Gander, Nf, Can. 131/L1
Ganderkesee, Ger. 51/F2
Gandesa, Sp. 45/F2
Gāndhi Sāgar (res.), India 82/B3
Gāndhīhām, India 89/K4
Gāndhinagar, India 89/K4
Gandía, Sp. 45/E3
Gandino, It. 58/C1
Gandoca-Manzanillo NWR, CR 145/F4
Gandu, Braz. 154/C4
Ganeb (well), Mrta. 102/C2
Ganesh (mtn.), China 85/E1
Gangāpur, India 89/L3
Gangārāmpur, India 85/G3
Gangaw, Myan. 83/F3
Gangca, China 70/H4
Gangdisê (mts.), China 70/D5
Gangelt, Ger. 53/F2
Ganges, Fr. 42/E5
Ganges (riv.), Asia 67/A5
Ganges (Ganga) (riv.), India 84/B1
Ganges, Mouths of the (delta), Bang. 70/E7
Gangi, It. 46/D4
Gangkofen, Ger. 55/F6
Gangoh, India 86/D5
Gangtok, India 85/G2
Ganluo, China 83/H2
Gannat, Fr. 42/E3
Ganquan, China 72/B3
Gansbaai, SAfr. 106/L11
Gänserndorf, Aus. 49/P7
Gansu (prov.), China 70/H4
Gantrisch (peak), Swi. 56/D4
Ganyu, China 72/D4
Ganzhou, China 79/B2
Ganzlin, Ger. 40/G2
Ganzourgou (prov.), Burk. 103/E3
Gao (pol. reg.), Mali 103/F2
Gao, Mali 103/E2
Gao'an, China 79/C2
Gaocheng, China 72/C3
Gaochun, China 72/D5
Gaomi, China 72/D3
Gaoping, China 72/C4
Gaoqing, China 72/D3
Gaor Bheinn (Gulvain) (peak), Sc, UK 36/A3
Gaotai, China 70/G4
Gaotang, China 72/D3
Gaoua, Burk. 102/E4
Gaoyang, China 72/C3
Gaoyi, China 72/C3
Gaoyou, China 72/D4
Gaozhou, China 83/K3
Gap, Fr. 43/G4
Gap, Pa, US 138/B4
Gar, China 70/C5
Garabogazköl Aylagy (gulf), Trrkm. 63/K4
Garachiné, Pan. 152/B2
Garachiné (pt.), Pan. 145/G4
Garai (riv.), Bang. 82/E3
Garajonay, PN de, Sp. 98/A3
Garamba, PN de la, D.R. Congo 97/L7
Garancières, Fr. 52/A6
Garanhuns, Braz. 154/C3
Garbsen, Ger. 51/G4
Garça, Braz. 155/B2
Garças (riv.), Braz. 151/H7
Garching an der Alz, Ger. 55/F6
Garcia de Sota, Embalse de (res.), Sp. 44/C3
Gard (riv.), Fr. 42/F4
Garda (lake), It. 43/J4
Garda, It. 59/D1
Garde, Cap de (cape), Alg. 100/K6
Gardelegen, Ger. 40/F2
Garden (isl.), Austl. 112/K7
Garden City, Ga, US 133/H3
Garden City, NY, US 139/L9
Garden City, Mi, US 135/F7
Garden City Park, NY, US 139/L9
Garden Grove, Ca, US 136/G8
Garden Ridge, Tx, US 137/U20
Garden View, Pa, US 138/A1
Gardena, Ca, US 136/F8
Gardenstown, Sc, UK 36/D1
Gardēz, Afg. 89/J2
Gardiner, Mt, US 126/F4
Gardiner, Me, US 131/G2
Gardiner, Wa, US 135/B1
Gardiners (isl.), NY, US 139/F1
Gardiners (bay), NY, US 139/F1
Gardner (lake), Ks, US 137/D6
Gardner, Ks, US 137/D6
Gardone val Trompia, It. 58/D1
Gare Loch (inlet), Sc, UK 36/B4
Gareat el Tarf (salt pan), Alg. 100/K7
Garelochhead, Sc, UK 36/B4
Garessio, It. 58/B4
Garet el Djenoun (peak), Alg. 99/G4
Garfield (mtn.), Mt, US 126/E4
Garfield, Ut, US 137/J12
Garfield, NJ, US 139/J8
Garforth, Eng, UK 35/G4
Gargaliánoi, Gre. 47/G4
Gargan (peak), Fr. 42/D4
Gargenville, Fr. 52/A6
Garges-lès-Gonesse, Fr. 30/K5
Gargnano, It. 59/D1
Garh Mahārāja, Pak. 86/A4
Garhākotā, India 84/B4
Garhbeta, India 85/F4
Garhmuktesar, India 84/B1
Garibaldi, Braz. 155/B4
Garies, SAfr. 106/B3
Garioch (reg.), Sc, UK 36/D2
Garissa, Kenya 104/C3
Garland, Tx, US 129/H4
Garlasco, It. 58/B2
Garmisch-Partenkirchen, Ger. 57/H3
Garmsār, Iran 88/F1
Garnpung (lake), Austl. 115/B2
Garonne (riv.), Fr. 42/D4
Garopaba, Braz. 155/B4
Garou (lake), Mali 103/E2
Garoua, Camr. 96/H6
Garphyttan, Swe. 38/F2
Garraf (mts.), Sp. 45/K7
Garrel, Ger. 51/F3
Garrison (dam), ND, US 127/H4
Garrison, ND, US 127/H4
Garron (pt.), NI, UK 34/C1
Garrovillas, Sp. 44/B3
Garry (bay), Nun., Can. 123/H2
Garry (lake), Nun., Can. 122/F2
Garry (lake), Sc, UK 36/B2
Garry (riv.), Sc, UK 36/A2
Gars am Inn, Ger. 55/F6
Garsten, Aus. 55/H6
Garte (riv.), Ger. 51/H6
Gartempe (riv.), Fr. 42/D3
Gärtringen, Ger. 54/B5
Garut, Indo. 80/C5
Garvagh, NI, UK 34/B2
Garwa, India 84/D3
Garwolin, Pol. 41/L3
Garwood, NJ, US 139/H9
Gary, In, US 130/C3
Garza García, Mex. 143/E3
Garzê, China 70/H5
Garzón, Col. 152/C4
Gas, Fr. 30/G6
Gas City, In, US 130/C3
Gas-san (peak), Japan 76/B4
Gæsafjöll (peak), Ice. 37/P6
Gaschurn, Aus. 57/G4
Gasconade (riv.), Mo, US 129/J3
Gascony (reg.), Fr. 42/C5
Gascoyne (riv.), Austl. 109/A3
Gascoyne (mt.), Austl. 112/C3
Gaspar (str.), Indo. 80/C4
Gaspar, Braz. 155/B3
Gaspé, Qu, Can. 131/H1
Gaspé (pen.), Qu, Can. 131/H1
Gaspé, Cap de (cape), Qu, Can. 131/H1
Gaspoltshofen, Aus. 55/G6
Gasport, NY, US 131/S9
Gassino Torinese, It. 58/A2
Gastins, Fr. 30/M6
Gaston (lake), NC, US 133/J2
Gastonia, NC, US 133/H3
Gastoúni, Gre. 47/G4
Gata (cape), Sp. 44/D4
Gata (cape), Cyp. 91/C2
Gata de Gorgos, Sp. 45/F3
Gata, Sierra de (mts.), Sp. 44/B2
Gatchina, Rus. 39/P2
Gatehouse-of-Fleet, Sc, UK 34/D2
Gates of the Arctic NP and Prsv., Ak, US 134/G2
Gateshead (isl.), Nun., Can. 122/F1
Gateshead, Eng, UK 35/G2
Gatesville, Tx, US 132/D4
Gateway Arch (arch), Mo, US 137/G8
Gateway NRA, NJ,NY, US 139/K9
Gatineau, Qu, Can. 130/F2
Gatineau (riv.), Qu, Can. 123/J4
Gatow, Ger. 40/Q7
Gattaran, Phil. 79/D4
Gattendorf, Aus. 43/M2
Gattinara, It. 58/B1
Gatton, Austl. 114/D4
Gatún (dam), Pan. 145/G4
Gatún (lake), Pan. 145/G4
Gatwick (int'l arpt.), Eng, UK 30/C3
Gau Algesheim, Ger. 54/B3
Gau Bischofsheim, Ger. 54/B3
Gau Odernheim, Ger. 54/B3
Gaubickelheim, Ger. 53/H4
Gauchy, Fr. 52/C4
Gauja (riv.), Est.,Lat. 39/L3
Gauja NP, Lat. 39/L3
Gaukönigshofen, Ger. 54/C3
Gaunless (riv.), Eng, UK 35/G2
Gaupne, Nor. 37/C3
Gaur (riv.), Sc, UK 36/B3
Gauri Sankar (peak), Nepal 85/F2
Gauripur, India 85/G2
Gausta (peak), Nor. 38/C2
Gauting, Ger. 55/E6
Gavà, Sp. 45/L7
Gávdhos (isl.), Gre. 47/J5
Gavere, Belg. 52/C2
Gavi, It. 58/B3
Gavião, Port. 44/B3
Gavirate, It. 58/B1
Gävle, Swe. 38/G1
Gävleborg (co.), Swe. 37/E3
Gawler (ranges), Austl. 109/C4
Gawler, Austl. 113/H5
Gay (peak), WV, US 130/D4
Gay, Rus. 62/J1
Gaya, Niger 103/F4
Gayaza, Ugan. 104/A3
Gaylord, Mi, US 130/C2
Gayndah, Austl. 114/C4
Gaza Strip, Isr. 90/C4
Gazeran, Fr. 30/H6
Gaziantep (prov.), Turk. 90/D2
Gaziantep, Turk. 90/D2
Gaziköy, Turk. 49/H5
Gazipaşa, Turk. 91/C1
Gazon de Faing (peak), Fr. 56/D1
Gazzaniga, It. 58/C1
Gbadolite, D.R. Congo 97/K7
Gbarnga, Libr. 102/C5
Gbongan, Nga. 103/G5
Gdansk (gulf), Pol. 41/K1
Gdańsk, Pol. 38/H4
Gdańsk (prov.), Pol. 38/H4
Gdynia, Pol. 38/H4
Ge (lake), China 72/D5
Geal Charn (peak), Sc, UK 36/C2
Geal Charn (peak), Sc, UK 36/A3
Gebaberg (peak), Ger. 54/D1
Gebe (isl.), Indo. 81/G3
Gebhardshain, Ger. 53/G2
Gebiz, Turk. 91/B1
Gebze, Turk. 49/J5
Gede (peak), Indo. 80/C5
Gedern, Ger. 54/C2
Gedi Ruins Nat'l Mon., Kenya 104/D3
Gedikbulak, Turk. 90/E2
Gedinne, Belg. 53/D4
Gediz (riv.), Turk. 90/A2
Gediz, Turk. 62/D5
Gedser (cape), Den. 38/D4
Gedser, Den. 38/D4
Gedsted, Den. 38/C3
Geel, Belg. 53/E1
Geelong, Austl. 115/C3
Geelvink (chan.), Austl. 109/A3
Geertruidenberg, Neth. 50/B5
Geeste (riv.), Ger. 51/F1
Geeste, Ger. 51/E3
Geesthacht, Ger. 51/H2
Geeveston, Austl. 115/C4
Gefrees, Ger. 55/E2
Gê'gyai, China 70/D5
Gehrde, Ger. 51/F3
Gehrden, Ger. 51/G4
Geifas (peak), Wal, UK 32/C2
Geikie (riv.), Sk, Can. 122/F3
Geilenkirchen, Ger. 53/F2
Geilo, Nor. 38/C1
Geinō, Japan 77/K6
Geiselhöring, Ger. 55/F5
Geiselwind, Ger. 54/D3
Geisenfeld, Ger. 55/E5
Geisenhausen, Ger. 55/F6
Geisenheim, Ger. 53/G4
Geislingen, Ger. 57/E1
Geislingen an der Steige, Ger. 54/C5
Geita, Tanz. 104/B3
Gejiu, China 83/H3
Gela, It. 46/D4
Gela, Golfo di (gulf), It. 46/D4
Gelai (peak), Tanz. 104/C3
Gelderland (prov.), Neth. 50/C4
Geldermalsen, Neth. 50/C5
Geldern, Ger. 50/D5
Geldersheim, Ger. 54/D2
Geldrop, Neth. 50/C6
Geleen, Neth. 53/E2
Gelendost, Turk. 90/B2
Gelendzhik, Rus. 62/F3
Gelibolu (Gallipoli), Turk. 47/K2
Gelibolu Yarımadas NP, Turk. 47/K2
Gelincik (peak), Turk. 90/E2
Gelligaer, Wal, UK 32/C3
Gelnhausen, Ger. 54/C2
Gelsenkirchen, Ger. 50/E5
Geltendorf, Ger. 57/H1
Gelterkinden, Swi. 56/D3
Gelting, Ger. 38/C4
Gemas, Malay. 80/B3
Gembloux, Belg. 53/D2
Gemena, D.R. Congo 97/J7
Gemert, Neth. 50/C5
Gemlik (gulf), Turk. 49/J5
Gemlik, Turk. 49/J5
Gemona del Friuli, It. 43/K3
Gemsbok NP, Bots. 105/D6
Gemuk (mtn.), Ak, US 134/G3
Gemünden am Main, Ger. 54/C2
Genalē Wenz (riv.), Eth. 97/N6
Genappe, Belg. 53/D2
Genay, Fr. 56/A6
Genç, Turk. 90/E2
Gendringen, Neth. 50/D5
Gendt, Neth. 50/C5
Genemuiden, Neth. 50/D3
General Abelardo L. Rodriguez (int'l arpt.), Mex. 128/C4
General Acha, Arg. 158/D3
General Alfredo Vasquez Cobo (int'l arpt.), Col. 156/D2
General Alvear, Arg. 158/D2
General Alvear, Arg. 158/E3
General Arenales, Arg. 158/E2
General Belgrano, Arg. 158/F2
General Belgrano II, Arg., Ant. 160/X
General Cabrera, Arg. 158/E2
General Carrera (lake), Chile 157/B6
General Cepeda, Mex. 143/E3
General Conesa, Arg. 158/D4
General Deheza, Arg. 158/E2
General Edward Lawrence Logan (Logan Int'l) (int'l arpt.), Ma, US 131/G3
General Enrique Godoy, Arg. 158/D3
General Francisco Villa, Mex. 143/F3
General Galarza, Arg. 159/J10
General Grant Nat'l Mem., NY, US 139/K8
General Juan Álvarez, PN, Mex. 143/F5
General Juan José Ríos, Mex. 142/C3
General Juan Madariaga, Arg. 159/F3
General La Madrid, Arg. 158/E3
General Lagos, Chile 156/D5
General Las Heras, Arg. 159/J11
General Lavalle, Arg. 159/K12
General Martín Miguel de Güemes, Arg. 157/C1
General Pico, Arg. 158/E2
General Pinedo, Arg. 157/D2
General Pinto, Arg. 158/E2
General Roca, Arg. 158/D3
General San Martín, Arg. 158/E3
General San Martín, Arg. 159/J11
General San Martín, Arg., Ant. 160/V
General Santiago Marino (int'l arpt.),Ven. 153/F2
General Terán, Mex. 143/F3
General-Toshevo, Bul. 49/J4

189
Gener – Gourm

General Viamonte, Arg. 158/E2
General Villalobas (int'l arpt.), Mex. 132/B4
General Villegas, Arg. 158/E2
General Zaragoza, Mex. 143/F4
Generoso (peak), Swi. 57/F6
Genesee (riv.), NY, US 130/E3
Genesee (co.), Mi, US 135/E6
Genesee, Wi, US 135/P14
Genesee Depot, Wi, US 135/P14
Geneseo, Il, US 127/L5
Geneseo, NY, US 130/E3
Geneva, Al, US 133/G4
Geneva, NY, US 130/E3
Geneva, Ne, US 129/H2
Geneva, Ut, US 137/K13
Geneva (int'l arpt.), Swi. 56/C5
Geneva (Genève), Swi. 43/G3
Geneva (Léman) (lake), Fr. 43/G3
Genève (canton), Swi. 56/C5
Genève, Swi. 56/C5
Gengenbach, Ger. 56/E1
Génicourt, Fr. 30/J4
Genk, Belg. 53/E2
Genlis, Fr. 56/B3
Gennach (riv.), Ger. 57/G2
Gennargentu (mts.), It. 46/A2
Gennep, Neth. 50/C5
Gennevilliers, Fr. 30/J5
Genoa City, Wi, US 135/P14
Genoa (Genova), It. 43/H4
Genova (prov.), It. 58/C4
Genova (Genoa), It. 58/B4
Genova, Golfo di (gulf), It. 43/H4
Genovesa (isl.), Ecu. 156/F6
Gensingen, Ger. 53/G4
Gent-Brugge Kanaal (canal), Belg. 52/C1
Gent (Ghent), Belg. 52/C1
Genteng (cape), Indo. 80/C5
Genteng, Indo. 80/D5
Geographe (bay), Austl. 112/B5
Geographe (chan.), Austl. 112/B3
Georg von Neumayer, Ger., Ant. 160/Z
George (lake), Ugan. 104/A3
George (lake), Fl, US 133/H4
George, SAfr. 106/C4
George (pt.), Austl. 114/C3
George (lake), Austl. 113/D2
George (riv.), Qu, Can. 123/K3
George Land (isl.), Rus. 64/E2
George Town, Malay. 80/B2
George Town, Austl. 115/C4
George Town (cap.), Cay. 145/F2
George V (coast), Ant. 160/L
George Washington Birthplace Nat'l Mon., Va, US 133/J2
George West, Tx, US 132/D4
Georgensgmünd, Ger. 54/E4
Georges (riv.), Austl. 114/G9
Georgetown, Ga, US 133/H4
Georgetown, SC, US 133/J3
Georgetown, Tx, US 129/H5
Georgetown, Ky, US 130/C4
Georgetown, Gam. 102/B3
Georgetown, StV. 141/N9
Georgetown (cap.), Guy. 153/G3
Georgetown, Austl. 114/A2
Georgetown, Ct, US 139/E1
Georgi Traykov, Bul. 49/H4
Georgia (ctry.) 63/G4
Georgia (state), US 133/G3
Georgia, Strait of (str.), BC, Can. 126/B3
Georgian (bay), On, Can. 123/H4
Georgian Bay Islands NP, On, Can. 130/D2
Georgina (riv.), Austl. 109/C3
Georgsmarienhütte, Ger. 51/F4
Gepatsch (lake), Aus. 57/G4
Gera, Ger. 40/G3
Geraardsbergen, Belg. 52/C2
Geral de Goiás, Serra (mts.), Braz. 151/J6
Geral, Serra (mts.), Braz. 157/F2
Geraldine, NZ 117/S11
Geraldton, Austl. 112/B4
Gérardmer, Fr. 56/C1
Gerasdorf bei Wien, Aus. 49/N7
Gerbéviller, Fr. 56/C1
Gerbier de Jonc (peak), Fr. 42/F4
Gerbrunn, Ger. 54/C3
Gerdau (riv.), Ger. 51/H3
Gerdine (mt.), Ak, US 134/H3
Gerede, Turk. 49/L5
Geretsried, Ger. 57/H2
Gergal, Sp. 44/D4
Gerger, Turk. 90/D2
Gerlach, Nv, US 126/D5
Gerlachovský Štít (peak), Slvk. 41/L4
Gerlafingen, Swi. 56/D3
Germantown, Tn, US 129/K4
Germantown, Md, US 138/A5
Germany (ctry.) 40/E3
Germering, Ger. 55/E6
Germersheim, Ger. 54/B4
Germigny-l'Evêque, Fr. 30/L5
Germinaga, It. 57/E6
Germiston, SAfr. 106/E2
Gernsbach, Ger. 54/B5
Geroldsgrün, Ger. 55/E2
Gerolsbach, Ger. 55/E5
Gerolstein, Ger. 53/F3
Gerolzhofen, Ger. 54/D3
Gerpinnes, Belg. 53/D3
Gerra (Verzasca), Swi. 57/E5
Gerringong, Austl. 115/D2
Gers (riv.), Fr. 42/D5
Gersau, Swi. 57/E4
Gersfeld, Ger. 54/C2
Gersheim, Ger. 53/G5
Gerspenz (riv.), Ger. 54/B3
Gerstetten, Ger. 54/E5
Gerstheim, Fr. 56/D1
Gersthofen, Ger. 54/D6
Gerstungen, Ger. 51/H7
Gêrzê, China 70/D5
Gerze, Turk. 62/E4
Gescher, Ger. 50/E5
Geseke, Ger. 51/F5
Gespunsart, Fr. 53/D4
Gessertshausen, Ger. 54/D6
Gestro Wenz (riv.), Eth. 97/P6
Gesves, Belg. 53/E3
Geta, Fin. 39/H1
Getafe, Sp. 45/N9
Gete (riv.), Belg. 53/E2
Getinge, Swe. 38/E3
Gettorf, Ger. 38/C4
Gettysburg, SD, US 127/J4
Gettysburg, Pa, US 130/E4
Gettysburg Nat'l Mil. Park, Pa, US 138/A4
Getúlio Vargas, Braz. 155/A3
Geul (riv.), Neth. 53/E2
Geureudong (peak), Indo. 80/A3
Geurie, Austl. 115/D2
Gevaş, Turk. 90/E2
Gevelsberg, Ger. 51/E6
Gevgelija, FYROM 47/H2
Gex, Fr. 56/C5
Geyer, Ger. 55/F1
Geyersberg (peak), Ger. 54/C3
Geyikli, Turk. 47/K3
Geyser (reef), Madg. 107/H6
Geyve, Turk. 49/K5
Gez (riv.), China 87/F5
Ghadāmis, Libya 99/H3
Ghaggar (riv.), India 86/C5
Ghaghara (riv.), India 84/C2
Ghakhar, Pak. 86/C3
Ghana (ctry.) 103/E4
Ghanzi, Bots. 105/D5
Gharaunda, India 86/D5
Ghardaïa, Alg. 99/F2
Ghardaïa (prov.), Alg. 99/F3
Ghardimaou, Tun. 100/L6
Gharghoda, India 84/D4
Gharyān, Libya 96/H1
Ghāt, Libya 99/H4
Ghātāl, India 85/F4
Ghātampur, India 84/C2
Ghātsīla, India 85/F4
Ghazal, Bahr el (riv.), Chad 96/J5
Ghazaouet, Alg. 100/D2
Ghāzīpur, India 84/D3
Ghaznī, Afg. 89/J2
Ghedi, It. 58/D2
Gheens, La, US 137/P17
Ghemme, It. 58/B1
Ghenghis Khan, Wall of, Mong. 71/K2
Gheorghe Gheorghiu-Dej, Rom. 49/H2
Gheorgheni, Rom. 49/G2
Gherla, Rom. 49/F2
Ghilarza, It. 46/A2
Ghinda (Gīnda), Erit. 88/C5
Ghio (lake), Arg. 158/C5
Ghirārah (gulf), Gabon 99/H2
Ghisalba, It. 58/C1
Ghisonaccia, Fr. 46/A1
Ghotki, Pak. 82/A2
Ghugri (riv.), India 85/F3
Ghūrīān, Afg. 89/H2
Ghuzayyil, Bi'r al (well), Libya 96/H2
Giannutri (isl.), It. 46/B1
Giant's Castle (peak), SAfr. 106/E3
Giant's Causeway, NI, UK 34/B1
Giarre, It. 46/D4
Gibbons, Ab, Can. 126/E2
Gibbstown, NJ, US 138/C4
Gibloux (peak), Swi. 56/D4
Gibraleón, Sp. 44/B4
Gibraltar, Ven. 141/G6
Gibraltar (res.), Ca, US 136/A1
Gibraltar (cap.), Gib. 44/C4
Gibraltar (str.), Mor.,Sp. 27/D5
Gibraltar, Mi, US 135/F7
Gibraltar (pt.), Eng, UK 35/J5
Gibraltar Range NP, Austl. 115/E1
Gibson (des.), Austl. 109/B3
Gibson Desert Nature Reserve, Austl. 112/E3
Giddarbāha, India 86/C4
Giddings, Tx, US 129/H5
Giddings, Co, US 137/B1
Gidi (pass), Egypt 91/C4
Giebelstadt, Ger. 54/C3
Gieboldehausen, Ger. 51/H5
Gien, Fr. 42/E3
Giengen an der Brenz, Ger. 54/D5
Gier (riv.), Fr. 42/F4
Giessbachfälle (falls), Swi. 56/E4
Giessen (riv.), Fr.,Ger. 56/D1
Giessen, Ger. 54/B1
Giessendam, Neth. 50/B5
Gieten, Neth. 50/D2
Gif-sur-Yvette, Fr. 30/J5
Gīfān, Iran 63/L5
Gifford, Fl, US 133/H5
Gifford (riv.), Nun., Can. 123/H1
Giffre (riv.), Fr. 56/C5
Gifhorn, Ger. 51/H4
Gifu, Japan 77/L5
Giganta, Sierra de la (mts.), Mex. 142/C3
Gigante, Col. 152/C4
Giglio (isl.), It. 46/B1
Gijón, Sp. 44/C1
Gil de Vilches, PN, Chile 158/C2
Gila (riv.), Az, US 128/D4
Gila Bend, Az, US 128/D4
Gila Cliff Dwellings Nat'l Mon., NM, US 128/E4
Gila River Ind. Res., Az, US 137/R19
Gilbert, Mn, US 130/A2
Gilbert (riv.), Austl. 109/D2
Gilbert, Az, US 137/S19
Gilbert (isls.), Kiri. 116/G5
Gilberts, Il, US 135/P15
Gilbués, Braz. 154/A3
Gilching, Ger. 54/E6
Gilcrest, Co, US 137/C2
Gilford, NI, UK 34/B3
Gilford Park, NJ, US 138/D4
Gilgandra, Austl. 115/D1
Gilgil, Kenya 104/C3
Gilgit (riv.), Pak. 87/F5
Gilles (lake), Austl. 113/H5
Gillette, Wy, US 127/G4
Gillies Bay, BC, Can. 126/B3
Gillingham, Eng, UK 33/G4
Gillot (int'l arpt.), Reun. 107/S15
Gilly, Swi. 56/C5
Gilman Hot Springs, Ca, US 136/D3
Gilmer, Tx, US 129/J4
Gilpin, Co, US 137/A3
Gilqit (riv.), Pak. 89/K1
Gilze, Neth. 50/B5
Gīmbī, Eth. 97/N6
Gimbsheim, Ger. 54/B3
Gimel, Swi. 56/C4
Gimie (mt.), StL. 141/N9
Gimli, Mb, Can. 127/J3
Gimo, Swe. 38/H1
Gin Gin, Austl. 114/C4
Ginan, Japan 77/L5
Gingelom, Belg. 53/E2
Gingin, Austl. 112/B4
Gingindlovu, SAfr. 107/E3
Gingoog, Phil. 81/G2
Gingst, Ger. 38/E4
Ginosa, It. 46/E2
Ginowan, Japan 75/J7
Gioia (gulf), It. 46/D3
Gioia del Colle, It. 46/E2
Gioia Tauro, It. 46/D3
Giornico, Swi. 57/E5
Gioüra (isl.), Gre. 47/J3
Gioveretto (peak), It. 57/G5
Giovi (peak), It. 59/E5
Gipping (riv.), Eng, UK 33/G2
Girardot, Col. 150/D3
Girardville, Pa, US 138/B2
Giraumont, Fr. 53/E5
Girdle Ness (pt.), Sc, UK 36/D2
Giresun (prov.), Turk. 62/F4
Giresun, Turk. 62/F4
Girgnasco, It. 58/B1
Gīrīdīh, India 85/F3
Girifalco, It. 46/E3
Girling (res.), Eng, UK 30/C2
Giromagny, Fr. 56/C2
Girón, Ecu. 152/B5
Girón, Col. 152/C3
Girona, Sp. 45/G2
Gironcourt-sur-Vraine, Fr. 56/B1
Gironde (riv.), Fr. 42/C4
Gironella, Sp. 45/F1
Girraween NP, Austl. 115/D1
Giru, Austl. 114/B2
Girvan, Sc, UK 34/D1
Gisborne, NZ 117/T10
Gisenyi, Rwa. 104/A3
Gislaved, Swe. 38/E3
Gisors, Fr. 52/A5
Gistel, Belg. 52/B1
Gistrup, Den. 38/D3
Gitega, Buru. 104/A3
Gittsfjället (peak), Swe. 37/E2
Giubiasco, Swi. 57/F5
Giugliano in Campania, It. 48/B5
Giulianova, It. 43/K5
Giurgiu (prov.), Rom. 49/G3
Giurgiu, Rom. 49/G4
Giussano, It. 58/C1
Giv'at Brenner, Isr. 91/F8
Giv'at Ḩayyim, Isr. 91/F7
Giv'atayim, Isr. 91/F7
Give, Den. 38/C4
Givet, Fr. 53/D3
Givors, Fr. 42/F4
Givrine, Col de la (pass), Swi. 56/C5
Giyani, SAfr. 105/F5
Gizhiga (bay), Rus. 65/R3
Gizo, Sol. 116/E5
Giżycko, Pol. 39/J4
Gjerdrum, Nor. 38/D1
Gjerlev, Den. 38/D3
Gjerstad, Nor. 38/C2
Gjirokastër, Alb. 47/G2
Gjoa Haven, Nun., Can. 122/G2
Gjøvik, Nor. 38/D1
Glabbeek, Belg. 53/E2
Glace Bay, NS, Can. 131/K2
Glacier (peak), Wa, US 126/C3
Glacier Bay NP and Prsv., Ak, US 134/L4
Glacier NP, BC, Can. 126/D3
Gladbeck, Ger. 50/D5
Gladewater, Tx, US 129/J4
Gladstone, Mo, US 137/D5
Gladstone, Austl. 114/C3
Gladstone, Austl. 113/H5
Gladwin, Mi, US 130/C3
Glafsfjorden (lake), Swe. 38/D2
Glåma (riv.), Nor. 37/D3
Glamis, Sc, UK 36/D3
Glamsbjerg, Den. 38/D4
Glan, Phil. 81/G2
Glan (riv.), Ger. 40/D4
Glanamman, Wal, UK 32/C3
Gland, Swi. 56/C5
Gland (riv.), Fr. 53/D4
Glandorf, Ger. 51/F4
Glärnisch (range), Swi. 57/E3
Glarus, Swi. 57/F3
Glarus (canton), Swi. 57/E4
Glarus Alps (range), Swi. 43/H3
Glas Maol (peak), Sc, UK 36/C3
Glasgow, Mt, US 126/G3
Glasgow, Ky, US 130/C4
Glasgow, De, US 138/C4
Glasgow, Sc, UK 36/B5
Glashütten, Ger. 54/B2
Glaslyn (riv.), Wal, UK 34/D6
Glass (mts.), Ok, US 132/D2
Glass (lake), Sc, UK 36/B1
Glass (riv.), Sc, UK 36/B2
Glassboro, NJ, US 138/C4
Glastonbury, Eng, UK 32/D4
Glatt (riv.), Ger. 54/B6
Glattbach, Ger. 54/C3
Glattfelden, Swi. 57/E2
Glavinitsa, Bul. 49/H4
Glazoué, Ben. 103/F5
Glazov, Rus. 61/M4
Glems (riv.), Ger. 54/C5
Glen (riv.), Eng, UK 35/H6
Glen Burnie, Md, US 138/B5
Glen Canyon (dam), Az, US 128/E3
Glen Canyon Nat'l Rec. Area, US 128/E3
Glen Carbon, Il, US 137/H8
Glen Coe (pass), Sc, UK 36/B3
Glen Cove, NY, US 139/L8
Glen Gardner, NJ, US 138/D2
Glen Haven, Co, US 137/B2
Glen Innes, Austl. 115/D1
Glen Lyon, Pa, US 138/B1
Glen Mòr (valley), Sc, UK 36/B2
Glen Park, Mo, US 137/G9
Glen Ridge, NJ, US 139/J8
Glen Rock, Pa, US 138/B4
Glen Rock, NJ, US 139/J8
Glen Ullin, ND, US 127/H4
Glenaire, Mo, US 137/E5
Glénan, Îles de (isls.), Fr. 42/A3
Glenarm, NI, UK 34/C2
Glenarm (riv.), NI, UK 34/C2
Glenavy, NI, UK 34/B2
Glenbawn (dam), Austl. 115/D2
Glenboro, Mb, Can. 127/J3
Glencoe, SAfr. 107/E3
Glencoe, Mo, US 137/F8
Glencoe, Il, US 135/Q15
Glencoe, Sc, UK 36/A3
Glendale, Or, US 126/C5
Glendale, Az, US 137/R18
Glendale, Ca, US 136/F7
Glendale Heights, Il, US 135/P16
Glenden, Austl. 114/C3
Glendive, Mt, US 127/G4
Glendo (res.), Wy, US 127/G5
Glendora, Ca, US 136/C2
Glendun (riv.), NI, UK 34/B1
Glenealy, Ire. 34/B6
Glenelg (riv.), Austl. 115/B3
Glenelg, Md, US 138/B5
Glenelg, Sc, UK 31/R8
Glenelly (riv.), NI, UK 34/A2
Glengarry (range), Austl. 112/C3
Glenluce, Sc, UK 34/D2
Glenmere (lake), NY, US 138/D1
Glennallen, Ak, US 134/J3
Glenolden, Pa, US 138/C4
Glenorie, Austl. 114/H8
Glenpool, Ok, US 129/H4
Glenrothes, Sc, UK 36/C4
Glens Falls, NY, US 130/F3
Glenshane (pass), NI, UK 34/B2
Glenside, Pa, US 138/C3
Glenties, Ire. 31/P9
Glenveagh NP, Ire. 31/Q9
Glenview, Il, US 135/Q15
Glenwood, NJ, US 138/D1
Glenwood Springs, Co, US 128/F3
Gleouraich (peak), Sc, UK 36/A2
Glifádha, Gre. 47/N9
Glimåkra, Swe. 38/E3
Glina, Cro. 48/C3
Glinde, Ger. 51/H1
Glindow, Ger. 40/P7
Gliwice, Pol. 41/K3
Globe, Az, US 128/E4
Glockturm (peak), Aus. 57/G4
Gloggnitz, Aus. 41/H5
Głogów, Pol. 41/J3
Głogówek, Pol. 41/J3
Glonn (riv.), Ger. 54/E6
Gloria (bay), Cuba 145/G1
Glorieuses, Îles (isls.), Reun. 107/H5
Glorious (mt.), Austl. 114/E6
Glory of Russia (cape), Ak, US 134/D3
Glossop, Eng, UK 35/G5
Gloster, Ms, US 129/K5
Gloucester, Austl. 115/D1
Gloucester, On, Can. 130/F2
Gloucester, Eng, UK 32/D3
Gloucester (co.), NJ, US 138/C4
Gloucester City, NJ, US 138/C4
Gloucestershire (co.), Eng, UK 32/D3
Glovers Reef (reef), Belz. 144/E2
Glovertown, Nf, Can. 131/L1
Głowno, Pol. 41/K3
Głubczyce, Pol. 41/J3
Głuchołazy, Pol. 41/J3
Glücksburg, Ger. 38/C4
Glückstadt, Ger. 51/G1
Glyndon, Md, US 138/B5
Glyngøre, Den. 38/C3
Glynn, NI, UK 34/C2
Gmünd, Aus. 41/H4
Gmunden, Aus. 55/G7
Gnagna (prov.), Burk. 103/E3
Gnarrenburg, Ger. 51/G2
Gniew, Pol. 39/H5
Gniezno, Pol. 41/J2
Gnjilane, Yugo. 47/G1
Gnowangerup, Austl. 112/C5
Gō (riv.), Japan 74/C3
Go Cong, Viet. 78/D4
Goa (state), India 82/B4
Goālpāra, India 85/H2
Goat Fell (peak), Sc, UK 36/A5
Goba, Eth. 97/N6
Gobabis, Namb. 105/C5
Gobardānga, India 85/G4
Gobernador Castro, Arg. 158/F2
Gobernador Costa, Arg. 158/C5
Gobernador Gregores, Arg. 159/C6
Gobernador Mansilla, Arg. 159/J10
Gobi (des.), China,Mon 67/K5
Göblberg (peak), Aus. 55/G6
Gobō, Japan 74/D4
Goch, Ger. 50/D5
Gochsheim, Ger. 54/D2
Godalming, Eng, UK 33/F4
Godāvari (riv.), India 67/G8
Goddā, India 85/F3
Godeanu (peak), Rom. 48/F3
Godech, Bul. 47/H1
Goderich, On, Can. 130/D3
Godfrey, Il, US 137/G8
Gōdo, Japan 77/L5
Gödöllő, Hun. 41/K5
Godoy Cruz, Arg. 158/C2
Gods (riv.), Mb, Can. 122/G3
Gods (lake), Mb, Can. 122/G3
Gods Mercy (bay), Nun., Can. 123/H2
Godthåb (Nuuk), Grld. 119/M3
Godwin Austen (K2) (peak), Pak. 86/D2
Goéland (lake), Qu, Can. 130/E1
Goeree (isl.), Neth. 50/A5
Goes, Neth. 50/A5
Gogebic (range), Mi, US 127/L4
Göggingen, Ger. 54/D6
Gogland (isl.), Rus. 39/M1
Gogōme, Japan 76/B4
Gogounou, Ben. 103/F4
Gogra (riv.), India 82/D2
Gohad, India 84/B2
Gohāna, India 86/D5
Gohbach (riv.), Ger. 51/G3
Goiana, Braz. 154/D2
Goiandira, Braz. 155/B1
Goiânia, Braz. 151/J7
Goianinha, Braz. 154/D2
Goiás, Braz. 151/H7
Goiás (state), Braz. 154/A5
Goiatuba, Braz. 155/B1
Goil (lake), Sc, UK 36/B4
Goirle, Neth. 50/C5
Góis, Port. 44/A2
Goito, It. 59/D2
Gojō, Japan 74/D3
Gojra, Pak. 86/B4
Gok (riv.), Turk. 62/E4
Goka, Japan 77/D1
Gokase (riv.), Japan 74/B4
Gokashō, Japan 77/K5
Gokasho (bay), Japan 77/L7
Gökçeada (isl.), Turk. 90/A1
Gökçebey, Turk. 49/L5
Gökçekaya (dam), Turk. 90/B1
Göksu (riv.), Turk. 90/D2
Göksun, Turk. 90/D2
Göktepe, Turk. 91/C1
Gol, Nor. 38/C1
Gola Gokarannāth, India 84/C1
Golan Hts. (reg.), Syria 91/D3
Golasecca, It. 58/B1
Gölbaşı, Turk. 90/D2
Gölbaşı, Turk. 62/E5
Golbey, Fr. 56/C1
Golborne, Eng, UK 35/F5
Gölcük, Turk. 49/J5
Gold (coast), Gha. 96/E7
Gold (mtn.), Wa, US 135/B2
Gold Bar, Wa, US 135/B2
Gold Beach, Or, US 126/B5
Gold Coast, Austl. 114/D5
Gold Hill, Co, US 137/B2
Gold River, BC, Can. 126/B3
Goldach, Swi. 57/F3
Gołdap, Pol. 39/K4
Goldbach, Ger. 54/C3
Goldberg, Ger. 38/E5
Golden, BC, Can. 126/D3
Golden, Co, US 137/B3
Golden Eagle, Il, US 137/F8
Golden Gate (chan.), Ca, US 135/J11
Golden Gate Highlands NP, SAfr. 106/D3
Golden Hinde (peak), BC, Can. 126/B3
Golden Temple, India 86/C4
Goldendale, Wa, US 126/C4
Goldene Aue (reg.), Ger. 40/F3
Goldenstedt, Ger. 51/F3
Goldkronach, Ger. 55/E2
Goldman, Mo, US 137/F9
Goldmine (mtn.), Az, US 137/S19
Goldsboro, NC, US 133/J3
Goldsboro, Md, US 138/C5
Goldsby, Ok, US 137/N15
Goldsworthy, Austl. 112/C2
Goldthwaite, Tx, US 132/D4
Göle, Turk. 63/G4
Goleniów, Pol. 38/F5
Golfito NWR, CR 145/F4
Golfo Aranci, It. 46/A2
Golfo de Santa Clara, Mex. 142/B2
Gölhisar, Turk. 91/A1
Goliad, Tx, US 129/H5
Gölköy, Turk. 62/F4
Gollach (riv.), Ger. 54/D3
Göllheim, Ger. 54/B3
Gölmarmara, Turk. 62/C5
Golmud, China 70/F4
Golovin, Ak, US 134/F3
Golovnina (peak), Rus. 76/D2
Golpāyegān, Iran 88/F2
Gölpazarı, Turk. 49/K5
Gols, Aus. 43/M3
Golts, Md, US 138/C5
Golub-Dobrzyń, Pol. 41/K2
Golubovci (int'l arpt.), Yugo. 47/F1
Golyam Perelik (peak), Bul. 47/J2
Golyama Kamchiya (riv.), Bul. 49/H4
Golyama Syutkya (peak), Bul. 47/J2
Goma, D.R. Congo 104/A3
Goma (int'l arpt.), D.R. Congo 104/A3
Gomaringen, Ger. 54/C6
Gomati (riv.), India 84/C2
Gombe (riv.), Tanz. 104/A4
Gombe NP, Tanz. 104/A4
Gomera (isl.) 96/B2
Gómez Farías, Mex. 142/D2
Gómez Palacio, Mex. 142/E3
Gomīshān, Iran 88/F1
Gommern, Ger. 40/F2
Gomoh, India 85/F4
Goms (valley), Swi. 56/E5
Gonābād, Iran 89/G2
Gonaïves, Haiti 145/H2
Gonarezhou NP, Zim. 105/F5
Gonâve (gulf), Haiti 141/G4
Gonâve (isl.), Haiti 145/H2
Gonbad-e Qābūs, Iran 89/G1
Gonbadī, Iran 87/D5
Gönc, Hun. 41/L4
Gonçalves Dias, Braz. 154/A2
Gondelsheim, Ger. 54/B4
Gonder, Eth. 97/N5
Gondia, India 82/D3
Gondomar, Sp. 44/A1
Gondomar, Port. 44/A2
Gondrecourt-le-Château, Fr. 56/B1
Gondreville, Fr. 53/E6
Gondrexange (lake), Fr. 53/F6
Gönen, Turk. 49/H5
Gonesse, Fr. 30/K5
Gong Xian, China 83/H2
Gong Xian, China 72/C4
Gong'an, China 83/K3
Gongbo'gyamda, China 83/F2
Gongcheng, China 79/B3
Gongga (peak), China 83/H2
Gonggar, China 85/H1
Gonghe, China 70/H4
Gongliu, China 70/D3
Gongola (riv.), Nga. 96/H5
Gongshan Drungzu Nuzu Zizhixian, China 83/G2
Gongzhuling, China 72/F2
Goñi, Uru. 159/K10
Gonjo, China 70/G5
Gónnoi, Gre. 47/H3
Gonohe, Japan 76/B3
Gonubie, SAfr. 106/D4
Gönyű, Hun. 48/C2
Gonzaga, It. 59/D3
Gonzales, Tx, US 129/H5
González, Mex. 143/F4
Good Hope, La, US 137/P17
Good Hope, Cape of (cape), SAfr. 106/L11
Goodenough (cape), Ant. 160/J
Goodnews Bay, Ak, US 134/F4
Goodooga, Austl. 115/C1
Goodrich, Mi, US 135/F6
Goodwick, Wal, UK 32/B2
Goodwood, SAfr. 106/L10
Goodyear, Az, US 137/R19
Gooimeer (lake), Neth. 50/C4
Goole, Eng, UK 35/H4
Goolgowi, Austl. 115/C2
Gooloogong, Austl. 115/D2
Goolwa, Austl. 113/H5
Goomalling, Austl. 112/C4
Goombungee, Austl. 114/C4
Goondiwindi, Austl. 114/C5
Goongarrie NP, Austl. 112/D4
Goor, Neth. 50/D4
Goose (lake), Mb, Can. 127/H2
Goose (pt.), La, US 137/Q16
Goose (lake), Ca, US 124/B3
Goose (pt.), De, US 138/C5
Gopālganj, India 85/E2
Gopālpur, Bang. 85/G3
Gopat (riv.), India 84/D3
Göppingen, Ger. 54/C5
Góra, Pol. 41/J3
Góra Kalwaria, Pol. 41/L3
Goražde, Bosn. 48/D4
Gorczański NP, Pol. 41/L4
Gorda (pt.), Nic. 145/F3
Gorda (pt.), Cuba 145/F1
Gorda (pt.), Nic. 145/F4
Gordevio, Swi. 57/E5
Gørding, Den. 38/C4
Gordola, Swi. 57/E5
Gordon, Austl. 115/C4
Gordon (lake), Austl. 109/D5
Gordonsbaai, SAfr. 106/L11
Gordonvale, Austl. 114/B2
Gore (pt.), Ak, US 134/H4
Goré, Chad 96/J6
Gorē, Eth. 97/N6
Gore, NZ 117/R12
Gorebridge, Sc, UK 36/C5
Görele, Turk. 62/F4
Goresbridge, Ire. 31/Q10
Gorey, Chl, UK 42/B2
Gorey, Ire. 31/Q10
Gorgān, Iran 89/F1
Gorge du Loup, Lux. 53/F4
Gorges du Ziz, Mor. 98/D2
Gorgol (pol. reg.), Mrta. 102/B3
Gorgol (riv.), Mrta. 102/B2
Gorgona, Isola di (isl.), It. 58/C6
Gorgonzola, It. 58/C1
Gori, Geo. 63/H4
Gorinchem, Neth. 50/B5
Gorizia, It. 59/G1
Gorizia (prov.), It. 59/G1
Gorj (prov.), Rom. 49/F3
Gorki, Bela. 62/D1
Gor'kiy (res.), Rus. 60/J4
Gorlice, Pol. 41/L4
Görlitz, Ger. 41/H3
Gorllwyn (peak), Wal, UK 32/C2
Gorman, Tx, US 129/H4
Gormanstown, Ire. 34/B4
Gormī, India 84/B2
Gorner (glacier), Swi. 56/D6
Gornji Milanovac, Yugo. 48/E3
Gornji Vakuf, Bosn. 48/C4
Gorno-Altay Aut. Rep., Rus. 64/J4
Goro, It. 59/F3
Gorodets, Rus. 61/J4
Gorom Gorom, Burk. 103/E3
Gorong (isl.), Indo. 81/H4
Gorongoza, Moz. 105/F4
Gorontalo, Indo. 81/F3
Gorssel, Neth. 50/D4
Gorst, Wa, US 135/B2
Gortin, NI, UK 34/A2
Görwihl, Ger. 56/E2
Goryn' (riv.), Ukr. 62/C2
Gorzano (peak), It. 43/K5
Gorzów Wielkopolski, Pol. 41/H2
Gosainganj, India 84/D2
Göschenen, Swi. 57/E4
Gōse, Japan 77/J7
Gosen, Japan 75/F2
Gosford, Austl. 115/D2
Gosforth, Eng, UK 35/G2
Goshen, NJ, US 138/D5
Goshogawara, Japan 76/B3
Goslar, Ger. 51/H5
Gospić, Cro. 48/B3
Gosport, Eng, UK 33/E5
Gossas, Sen. 102/A3
Gossau, Swi. 57/F3
Gossersweiler-Stein, Ger. 53/G5
Gostivar, FYROM 47/G2
Gostyń, Pol. 41/J3
Gostynin, Pol. 41/K2
Göta (riv.), Swe. 38/E2
Götaland (reg.), Swe. 38/E3
Göteborg, Swe. 38/D3
Göteborg Och Bohus (co.), Swe. 37/D4
Gotel (mts.), Nga. 96/H6
Gotemba, Japan 75/F3
Götene, Swe. 38/E2
Gotha, Ger. 51/H7
Gotland (isl.), Swe. 64/B4
Gotland (co.), Swe. 37/F4
Gotse Delchev, Bul. 47/H2
Gotska Sandön (isl.), Swe. 39/H2
Gotska Sandön NP, Swe. 39/H2
Gōtsu, Japan 74/C3
Gottenheim, Ger. 56/D1
Göttingen, Ger. 51/G5
Gottmadingen, Ger. 57/E2
Gottolengo, It. 58/D2
Götzis, Aus. 57/F3
Gouda, Neth. 50/B4
Gouda, SAfr. 106/L10
Gough (isl.), StH 22/J7
Gouin (res.), Qu, Can. 123/J4
Goulais (riv.), On, Can. 130/C2
Goulburn (riv.), Austl. 115/D2
Goulburn, Austl. 115/D2
Goulburn (isls.), Austl. 109/C2
Gould, Ar, US 132/F3
Gould (mt.), Austl. 112/C3
Gouldsboro, Pa, US 138/C1
Goulimine, Mor. 98/C3
Goulmima, Mor. 98/D3
Goundam, Mali 102/E2
Goupillières, Fr. 30/H5
Gourdon, Fr. 42/D4
Gouré, Niger 103/H3
Gourin, Fr. 42/B2
Gourits (riv.), SAfr. 106/C4
Gourma (phys. reg.), Burk. 103/F3
Gourma (prov.), Burk. 103/F3

190

Gourm – Guala

Gourma Rharous, Mali 103/E2
Gournay-en-Bray, Fr. 52/A5
Gourock, Sc, UK 36/B5
Goussainville, Fr. 30/K4
Gouvêa, Braz. 155/D1
Gouveia, Port. 44/B2
Gouvieux, Fr. 30/K4
Gouvy, Belg. 53/E3
Gouyave, Gren. 141/N9
Govardhan, India 84/A2
Goverla (peak), Ukr. 49/G1
Governador Archer, Braz. 154/A2
Governador Dix-Sept Rosado, Braz. 154/C2
Governador Eugênio Barros, Braz. 154/A2
Governador Valadares, Braz. 155/D1
Governor Generoso, Phil. 79/E6
Governors (isl.), NY, US 139/J9
Govi-Altay (prov.), Mong. 70/F2
Govĭ Altayn (mts.), Mong. 65/K5
Govind Sāgar (res.), India 86/D4
Govindgarh, India 84/C3
Gower (pen.), Wal, UK 32/B3
Goya, Arg. 157/E2
Goyllarisquizga, Peru 156/B3
Göynük, Turk. 49/K5
Goyt (riv.), Eng, UK 35/F5
Gozaisho-yama (peak), Japan 77/K5
Gözeli, Turk. 90/D2
Gozo (isl.), Malta 46/D4
Gozzano, It. 58/B1
Graaff-Reinet, SAfr. 106/D4
Graafschap (phys. reg.), Neth. 50/D4
Graben, Ger. 57/G1
Graberberg (peak), Namb. 106/B2
Grabouw, SAfr. 106/L11
Grabow, Ger. 40/F2
Graça Aranha, Braz. 154/A2
Gračac, Cro. 48/B3
Gračanica, Bosn. 48/D3
Gracemere, Austl. 114/C3
Graceville, Fl, US 133/G4
Grächen, Swi. 56/D5
Gracias, Hon. 144/D3
Gracias a Dios (cape), Hon. 145/F3
Graciosa (isl.), Azor., Port. 45/S12
Grad Sofiya (prov.), Bul. 47/H1
Gradačac, Bosn. 48/D3
Gradisca d'Isonzo, It. 59/G1
Grado, It. 59/G1
Grado, Sp. 44/B1
Grady (co.), Ok, US 137/M15
Gräfelfing, Ger. 55/E6
Grafenau, Ger. 55/G5
Gräfenberg, Ger. 54/E3
Grafenrheinfeld, Ger. 54/D3
Gräfentonna, Ger. 51/H6
Grafenwöhr, Ger. 55/E3
Graffignana, It. 58/C2
Grafing bei München, Ger. 55/E6
Gråfjell (peak), Nor. 38/C1
Grafrath, Ger. 57/H1
Grafton, Austl. 115/E1
Grafton, ND, US 127/J3
Grafton, WV, US 130/D4
Grafton, Il, US 137/G8
Grafton Passage, Austl. 114/B2
Graham, Tx, US 129/H4
Graham (isl.), Nun., Can. 123/S7
Graham (isl.), BC, Can. 122/C3
Graham Bell (isl.), Rus. 64/G1
Graham Land (phys. reg.), Ant. 160/V
Grahamstown, SAfr. 106/D4
Graian Alps (range), It. 43/G4
Grain (coast), Libr. 96/D6
Grain Valley, Mo, US 137/E5
Grainau, Ger. 57/H3
Grajaú (riv.), Braz. 151/J5
Grajaú, Braz. 154/A2
Grajewo, Pol. 39/K5
Gram, Den. 38/C4
Gramada, Bul. 48/F4
Gramastetten, Aus. 55/H6
Gramat, Fr. 42/D4
Gramat, Causse de (plat.), Fr. 42/D4
Gramatneusiedl, Aus. 49/N7
Grampian (pol. reg.), Sc, UK 36/C2
Grampian (mts.), Sc, UK 36/B3
Grampians NP, Austl. 115/B3
Grampians, The (phys. reg.), Austl. 115/B3
Gramsbergen, Neth. 50/D3
Gramsh, Alb. 47/G2
Gran, Nor. 38/D1
Gran Altiplanicie Central (plat.), Arg. 157/C6
Gran Bajo de San Julián (plain),Arg. 159/C6
Gran Bajo Oriental (plain), Arg. 157/C6
Gran Canaria (isl.) 96/B2
Gran Canaria (int'l arpt.), Sp. 98/B4
Gran Chaco (plain), SAm. 147/C5
Gran Isla del Maíz (isl.), Nic. 145/F3
Gran Laguna Salada (lag.), Arg. 158/D5
Gran Paradiso, PN del, It. 43/G4
Gran Piedra (hill), Cuba 145/H2
Gran Pilastro (peak), It. 43/J3
Gran Vilaya (ruin), Peru 156/B2
Granada, Sp. 44/D4
Granada, Nic. 144/E4
Granada, Col. 152/C4
Granadilla de Abona, Sp. 98/A3
Granados, Mex. 142/C2
Granard, Ire. 31/Q10
Granarolo dell'Emilia, It. 59/E3
Granbury, Tx, US 129/H4
Grand (lake), Nf, Can. 123/L4
Grand (canal), China 72/D4
Grand (falls), Kenya 104/C3
Grand (canal), Az, US 137/R18
Grand (isl.), NY, US 127/M4
Grand (isl.), Mi, US 130/C2
Grand (riv.), Mo, US 132/E2
Grand (riv.), SD, US 127/H4
Grand Bahama (isl.), Bahm. 141/F2
Grand Bank, Nf, Can. 131/L2
Grand Bassa (co.), Libr. 102/C5
Grand-Bassam, C.d'Iv. 102/E5
Grand Bay, NB, Can. 131/H2
Grand Canal d'Alsace (canal), Fr. 56/D2
Grand Canyon, Az, US 128/D3
Grand Canyon NP, Az, US 128/D3
Grand Cape Mount (co.), Libr. 102/C5
Grand Cayman (isl.), Cay. 140/E4
Grand Centre, Ab, Can. 126/F2
Grand-Charmont, Fr. 56/C2
Grand Colombier (peak), Fr. 56/B6
Grand Combine (peak), Swi. 56/D6
Grand Coulee, Wa, US 126/D4
Grand Coulee (dam), Wa, US 126/D4
Grand Drumont (peak), Fr. 56/C2
Grand Erg de Bilma (des.), Niger 96/H4
Grand Erg Occidental (des.), Alg. 93/C1
Grand Erg Oriental (des.), Alg. 93/C1
Grand Falls, NB, Can. 131/H2
Grand Falls, Nf, Can. 131/L1
Grand Forks, ND, US 127/J4
Grand Forks, BC, Can. 126/D3
Grand-Fort-Philippe, Fr. 52/B2
Grand Goâve, Haiti 145/H2
Grand Haven, Mi, US 130/C3
Grand Isle, La, US 133/F4
Grand Jide (co.), Libr. 102/D5
Grand Junction, Co, US 128/E3
Grand-lahou, C.d'Iv. 102/D5
Grand Lake o' the Cherokees (lake), Ok, US 129/J3
Grand Manan (isl.), NB, Can. 131/H2
Grand-Mère, Qu, Can. 131/F2
Grand Mont Ruan (peak), Fr. 56/C5
Grand Muveran (peak), Swi. 56/D5
Grand-Popo, Ben. 103/F5
Grand Portage Nat'l Mon., Mn, US 127/L4
Grand Rapids, Mb, Can. 127/J2
Grand Rapids, Mi, US 130/C3
Grand Rhône (riv.), Fr. 42/F5
Grand Saint-Bernard, Col du (pass), Swi. 56/D6
Grand Staircase-Escalante Nat'l Mon., Ut, US 128/E3
Grand Taureau (peak), Fr. 56/C4
Grand Teton NP, Wy, US 128/E2
Grandcour, Swi. 56/C4
Grande (riv.), Braz. 150/J7
Grande (isl.), Braz. 155/C2
Grande (peak), It. 46/C1
Grande (peak), It. 46/C4
Grande (pt.), Pan. 145/G4
Grande (bay), Arg. 147/C8
Grande (lake), Braz. 153/H5
Grande Cache, Ab, Can. 126/D2
Grande Comore (isl.), Com. 93/G6
Grande de Gurupá, Ilha (isl.), Braz. 151/H4
Grande de Manacapuru, Lago (lake), Braz. 150/F4
Grande de Matagalpa (riv.), Nic. 140/D5
Grande de Santiago (riv.), Mex. 142/D4
Grande de Tierra del Fuego (isl.), Arg.,Chil 157/C7
Grande Dixence, Barrage de la (dam), Swi. 56/D5
Grande do Curuaí (lake), Braz. 153/H5
Grande Miquelon (isl.), StP. 131/K2
Grande Prairie, Ab, Can. 126/D2
Grande Saline, Haiti 145/H2
Grande, Serra (mts.), Braz. 153/F4
Grande-Synthe, Fr. 52/B1
Grande-Terre (isl.), Guad. 141/J4
Grandes Jorasses (peak), It. 56/D6
Grandfresnoy, Fr. 52/B5
Grândola, Port. 44/A3
Grandpuits-Bailly-Carrois, Fr. 30/L6
Grandson, Swi. 56/C4
Grandview, Wa, US 126/D4
Grandview, Mb, Can. 127/H3
Grandview, Tx, US 129/H4
Grandview, Mo, US 137/D6
Grandvillars, Fr. 56/C2
Grandvilliers, Fr. 52/A4
Graneros, Chile 158/N9
Granfjället (peak), Swe. 38/E1
Grange, Mont de (peak), Fr. 56/C5
Grangemouth, Sc, UK 36/C4
Granger (mt.), Yk, Can. 134/L3
Granges-sur-Vologne, Fr. 56/C1
Grängesberg, Swe. 38/F1
Grangeville, Id, US 126/D4
Granisle, BC, Can. 126/B2
Granite (peak), Mt, US 126/F4
Granite, Ut, US 137/K12
Granite City, Il, US 137/G8
Granite Reef Aqueduct, Az, US 137/S18
Granites, The (peak), Austl. 113/F2
Granja, Braz. 154/B1
Granollers, Sp. 45/L6
Grantham, Eng, UK 35/H6
Grantown-on-Spey, Sc, UK 36/C2
Grants, NM, US 128/F4
Grants Pass, Or, US 126/C5
Granville, Fr. 42/C2
Granville (lake), Mb, Can. 122/F3
Grão Mogol, Braz. 154/B5
Grapeview, Wa, US 135/B3
Gras-Ellenbach, Ger. 54/B3
Grasberg, Ger. 51/F2
Grasbrunn, Ger. 55/E6
Grasø (isl.), Swe. 38/H1
Grasonville, Md, US 138/B6
Grass (lake), Il, US 135/P15
Grasse, Fr. 43/G5
Grassie, On, Can. 131/Q9
Grasslands NP, Sk, Can. 126/G3
Grassy, Austl. 115/C4
Grassy Park, SAfr. 106/L11
Grästorp, Swe. 38/E2
Gratkorn, Aus. 43/L3
Gratz, Pa, US 138/B2
Graubünden (canton), Swi. 57/F4
Graulhet, Fr. 42/E5
Graus, Sp. 45/F1
Gravatá, Braz. 154/D3
Grave, Neth. 50/C5
Gravedona, It. 57/F5
Gravelbourg, Sk, Can. 126/G3
Gravelines, Fr. 52/B2
Gravellona Toce, It. 57/E6
Gravenhurst, On, Can. 130/E2
Grävenwiesbach, Ger. 54/B2
Gravesend, Eng, UK 30/E2
Gravina di Puglia, It. 46/E2
Gravois (pt.), Haiti 145/H2
Gray, Fr. 56/B3
Grayling, Ak, US 134/F3
Grayling, Mi, US 130/C2
Grays (har.), Wa, US 126/B4
Grays (lake), Id, US 126/F5
Grays, Eng, UK 30/E2
Grayslake, Il, US 135/P15
Grayson, Sk, Can. 127/H3
Graz, Aus. 43/L3
Grazalema, Sp. 44/C4
Great (lake), Austl. 115/C4
Great (plain), Can.,US 127/G3
Great (basin), Nv, US 124/C4
Great (falls), NJ, US 139/J8
Great Abaco (isl.), Bahm. 141/F2
Great Alfold (plain), Yugo. 48/D2
Great America, Ca, US 135/L12
Great Australian Bight (bay), Austl. 109/B4
Great Barrier (reef), Austl. 109/D2
Great Barrier (isl.), NZ 109/H6
Great Basin NP, Nv, US 128/D3
Great Bear (lake), NW, Can. 122/D2
Great Bend, Ks, US 129/H3
Great Bitter (lake), Egypt 91/C4
Great Brak (riv.), SAfr. 106/C3
Great Britain (isl.), UK 27/D3
Great Cedar (swamp), NJ, US 138/D5
Great Coco (isl.), Myan. 83/F5
Great Cumbrae (isl.), Sc, UK 36/B5
Great Divide (basin), Wy, US 126/F5
Great Dividing (range), Austl. 109/D2
Great Egg (har.), NJ, US 138/D5
Great Egg Harbor (riv.), NJ, US 138/D4
Great Exuma (isl.), Bahm. 141/F3
Great Falls, Mt, US 126/F4
Great Fish (riv.), SAfr. 106/D4
Great Fish (pt.), SAfr. 106/D4
Great Guana Cay (isl.), Bahm. 141/F3
Great Harwood, Eng, UK 35/F4
Great Himalaya (range), Asia 70/D6
Great Inagua (isl.), Bahm. 141/G3
Great Indian (des.), India, Pak. 82/B2
Great Karoo (plat.), SAfr. 105/D7
Great Kei (riv.), SAfr. 106/D4
Great Mis Tor (hill), Eng, UK 32/B5
Great Missenden, Eng, UK 33/F3
Great Neck, NY, US 139/L8
Great Nicobar (isl.), India 83/F6
Great Ouse (riv.), Eng, UK 33/E2
Great Oyster (bay), Austl. 115/D4
Great Palace, Rus. 61/T7
Great Palace, Rus. 61/S7
Great Peconic (bay), NY, US 139/F2
Great Pee Dee (riv.), SC, US 133/J3
Great Piece Meadows (swamp), NJ, US 139/H8
Great Rift (valley), Afr. 105/F1
Great Ruaha (riv.), Tanz. 105/F2
Great Salt (lake), Ut, US 128/D2
Great Salt Lake (riv.), Ut, US 137/J11
Great Salt Lake (des.), Ut, US 124/D3
Great Sand Sea (des.), Egypt, Li 97/K2
Great Sandy (des.), Austl. 109/B2
Great Scarcies (riv.), SLeo. 102/B4
Great Shunner Fell (peak), Eng, UK 35/F3
Great Slave (lake), NW, Can. 122/E2
Great Smoky Mountains NP, NC,Tn, US 133/H3
Great South (bay), NY, US 139/F2
Great Stour (riv.), Eng, UK 33/G4
Great. Tenasserim (riv.), Myan. 78/B3
Great Victoria (des.), Austl. 109/B3
Great Victoria Desert Nature Rsv., Austl. 113/E4
Great Wall, China 70/J4
Great Western Tiers (mts.),Austl. 115/C4
Great Winterhoek (peak), SAfr. 106/L10
Great Yarmouth, Eng, UK 33/H1
Great Zab (riv.), Iraq 90/E2
Great Zimbabwe (ruin), Zim. 105/F5
Greater Accra (pol. reg.), Gha. 103/F5
Greater Antilles (isls.), NAm. 141/F3
Greater Buffalo (int'l arpt.), NY, US 131/S10
Greater Cincinnati (int'l arpt.), Ky, US 130/C4
Greater London (co.), Eng, UK 30/D2
Greater Manchester (co.), Eng, UK 35/F4
Greater Pittsburgh (int'l arpt.), Pa, US 130/D3
Greater Rochester (int'l arpt.), NY, US 130/E3
Greater Sunda (isls.), Indo. 80/C4
Grebenhain, Ger. 54/C2
Grebenstein, Ger. 51/G6
Grébon (peak), Niger 103/H2
Grecco, Uru. 159/K10
Greco (peak), It. 46/C2
Greco (cape), Cyp. 91/D2
Greding, Ger. 55/E4
Gredos, Sierra de (mts.), Sp. 44/C2
Greece (ctry.) 47/G3
Greeley, Co, US 137/C2
Greeley Number 2 (canal), Co, US 137/C2
Greely (fjord), Nun., Can. 123/S6
Green (cape), Austl. 115/D3
Green (bay), Mi,Wi, US 127/M4
Green (riv.), Ky, US 130/C4
Green (mts.), Vt, US 130/F3
Green (riv.), Ut,Wy, US 124/E4
Green Cove Springs, Fl, US 133/H4
Green Creek, NJ, US 138/D5
Green Haven, Md, US 138/B5
Green Lane (res.), Pa, US 138/C3
Green Lowther (peak), Sc, UK 36/C6
Green Pond, NJ, US 138/D1
Green River, Wy, US 126/F5
Green Valley, Az, US 128/E5
Green Valley, Ca, US 136/B1
Green Valley Lake, Ca, US 136/C2
Green Village, NJ, US 139/H9
Greenbelt, Md, US 138/B6
Greenbushes, Austl. 112/C5
Greencastle, In, US 130/C4
Greencastle, Ire. 34/B1
Greendale, Wi, US 135/Q14
Greeneville, Tn, US 130/D4
Greenfield, Ma, US 131/F3
Greenfield, In, US 130/C4
Greenfield, Wi, US 135/P14
Greenfield Park, Qu, Can. 131/P7
Greenisland, NI, UK 34/C2
Greenland (sea) 119/R2
Greenmount, Md, US 138/B4
Greenock, Sc, UK 36/B5
Greenough (mt.), Ak, US 134/K2
Greenough (riv.), Austl. 112/B4
Greenport, NY, US 139/F1
Greensboro, NC, US 133/J2
Greensboro, Al, US 133/G3
Greensboro, Md, US 138/C6
Greensburg, In, US 130/C4
Greensburg, Pa, US 130/E3
Greenvale, Austl. 114/B2
Greenville, Ca, US 126/C5
Greenville, SC, US 133/H3
Greenville, Al, US 133/G4
Greenville, Mi, US 130/C3
Greenville, NC, US 133/J3
Greenville, Tx, US 129/H4
Greenville, Ms, US 129/K4
Greenville, Oh, US 130/C3
Greenville, Libr. 102/C5
Greenwater (riv.), Wa, US 135/D3
Greenwell Point, Austl. 115/D2
Greenwich, Ct, US 139/L7
Greenwich (bor.), Eng, UK 30/D2
Greenwich (pt.), Ct, US 139/L8
Greenwich Observatory, Eng, UK 30/D2
Greenwood (lake), SC, US 133/H3
Greenwood, SC, US 133/H3
Greenwood, Ms, US 129/K4
Greenwood, Mo, US 137/E6
Greenwood, De, US 138/C6
Greenwood Lake, NY, US 138/D1
Greers Ferry (lake), Ar, US 129/J4
Grefrath, Ger. 50/D6
Gregório (riv.), Braz. 150/D5
Gregory, SD, US 127/J5
Gregory (range), Austl. 109/D2
Gregory (lake), Austl. 109/B3
Greifswald, Ger. 38/E4
Greifwalder Bodden (bay), Ger. 41/G1
Greimberg (peak), Aus. 43/L3
Greiz, Ger. 43/K1
Gremyachinsk, Rus. 61/N4
Grenå, Den. 38/D3
Grenada, Ms, US 129/K4
Grenada (ctry.) 141/N10
Grenade, Fr. 42/D5
Grenay, Fr. 52/B3
Grenchen, Swi. 56/D3
Grenfell, Austl. 115/D2
Grenfell, Sk, Can. 127/H3
Grennach (riv.), Ger. 54/D6
Grenoble, Fr. 42/F4
Grenzach-Wyhlen, Ger. 56/D2
Gressåmoen NP, Nor. 37/E2
Greta (riv.), Eng, UK 35/E2
Gretna, Mb, Can. 127/J3
Gretna, La, US 137/P17
Gretna, Sc, UK 35/E2
Grettstadt, Ger. 54/D3
Gretz-Armainvilliers, Fr. 30/L5
Greve (riv.), It. 59/E5
Greve in Chianti, It. 59/E5
Grevelingendam (dam), Neth. 50/B5
Greven, Ger. 51/E4
Grevená, Gre. 47/G2
Grevenbroich, Ger. 53/F1
Grevenmacher (dist.), Lux. 53/F4
Grevenmacher, Lux. 53/F4
Grevesmühlen, Ger. 40/F2
Grevlingen (chan.), Neth. 50/A5
Grey (range), Austl. 109/D3
Grey (riv.), Nf, Can. 131/K2
Grey (pt.), NI, UK 34/C2
Grey Abbey, NI, UK 34/C2
Grey Hunter (peak), Yk, Can. 134/L3
Grey Peaks NP, Austl. 114/B2
Greybull, Wy, US 126/F4
Greylingstad, SAfr. 106/E2
Greymouth, NZ 117/S11
Greystones, Ire. 34/B5
Greytown, SAfr. 107/E3
Grez-Doiceau, Belg. 53/D2
Grezzana, It. 59/E1
Gribbin (pt.), Eng, UK 32/B6
Griefensee (lake), Swi. 57/E3
Griekwastad, SAfr. 106/C3
Griend (isl.), Neth. 50/C2
Gries am Brenner, Aus. 57/H3
Griesheim, Ger. 54/B3
Grieskirchen, Aus. 55/G6
Griesskogel (peak), Aus. 57/H3
Griesstätt, Ger. 55/F7
Griffin, Ga, US 133/G3
Griffith, Austl. 115/C2
Griffith, In, US 135/R16
Griffith Park, Ca, US 136/F7
Grigna (peak), It. 57/F6
Grignano Polesine, It. 59/E2
Grigny, Fr. 30/K6
Grijalva (riv.), Mex. 144/C2
Grijpskerk, Neth. 50/D2
Grim (cape), Austl. 115/C4
Grimbergen, Belg. 53/D2
Grimisuat, Swi. 56/D5
Grimmen, Ger. 38/E4
Grimsby, On, Can. 131/Q9
Grimsby, Eng, UK 35/H4
Grimselpass (pass), Swi. 57/E4
Grimsey (isl.), Ice. 37/N6
Grimstad, Nor. 38/C2
Grindavík, Ice. 37/M7
Grindelwald, Swi. 56/E4
Grindsted, Den. 38/C4
Grinnell (pen.), Nun., Can. 123/S7
Grintavec (peak), Slov. 43/L3
Griqualand East (reg.), SAfr. 106/E3
Griqualand West (reg.), SAfr. 106/C2
Gris-Nez (cape), Fr. 52/A2
Grise Fiord, Nun., Can. 123/S7
Grisslehamn, Swe. 39/H1
Grisy-les-Plâtres, Fr. 30/J4
Grisy-Suisnes, Fr. 30/L5
Grivette (riv.), Fr. 30/L4
Grizzly (bay), Ca, US 135/K10
Grmeč (mts.), Bosn. 48/C3
Groaíras, Braz. 154/B1
Grobbendonk, Belg. 50/B6
Gröbenzell, Ger. 55/E6
Groblershoop, SAfr. 106/C3
Grodków, Pol. 41/J3
Grodzisk Wielkopolski, Pol. 41/J2
Groenlo, Neth. 50/D4
Groesbeck, Tx, US 132/D4
Groesbeek, Neth. 50/C5
Groix (isl.), Fr. 42/B3
Grójec, Pol. 41/L3
Grömitz, Ger. 38/D4
Gromo, It. 57/F6
Gronau, Ger. 50/E4
Gronau, Ger. 51/G4
Groningen, Neth. 50/D2
Groningen (prov.), Neth. 50/D2
Gronlait (peak), It. 57/H5
Grono, Swi. 57/F5
Groot (riv.), SAfr. 105/D7
Groot-Marico (riv.), SAfr. 106/D2
Grootdraaidam (res.), SAfr. 106/Q13
Groote Eylandt (isl.), Austl. 109/C2
Grootegast, Neth. 50/D2
Grootfontein, Namb. 105/C4
Grootvloer (salt pan), SAfr. 106/C3
Gropello Cairoli, It. 58/B2
Gros Islet, StL. 141/N9
Gros Morne (peak), Nf, Can. 131/K1
Gros Morne NP, Nf, Can. 131/K1
Grosbliederstroff, Fr. 53/G5
Grosio, It. 57/G5
Grosne (riv.), Fr. 42/F3
Grosrouvre, Fr. 30/H5
Gross Bieberau, Ger. 54/B3
Gross-Enzersdorf, Aus. 49/P7
Gross-Gerungs, Aus. 41/H4
Gross Oesingen, Ger. 51/H3
Gross Unstadt, Ger. 54/B3
Gross-Zimmern, Ger. 54/B3
Grossaitingen, Ger. 57/G1
Grossalmerode, Ger. 51/G6
Grossbeeren, Ger. 40/Q7
Grossbottwar, Ger. 54/C5
Grossbreitenbach, Ger. 54/D1
Grosse (isl.), Mi, US 135/F7
Grosse Aue (riv.), Ger. 51/F4
Grosse Ile, Mi, US 135/F7
Grosse Laber (riv.), Ger. 55/F5
Grosse Mühl (riv.), Aus. 55/G6
Grosse Münzenberg (peak), Namb. 106/A2
Grosse Nister (riv.), Ger. 53/G2
Grosse Pointe, Mi, US 135/G7
Grosse Pointe Farms, Mi, US 135/G7
Grosse Pointe Park, Mi, US 135/G7
Grosse Pointe Shores, Mi, US 135/G7
Grosse Pointe Woods, Mi, US 135/G7
Grosse Rodl (riv.), Aus. 55/H6
Grossengottern, Ger. 51/H6
Grossenkneten, Ger. 51/F3
Grossenlüder, Ger. 54/C1
Grossenwiehe, Ger. 38/C4
Grosser Ahrensberg (peak), Ger. 51/G5
Grosser Aletsch (glacier), Swi. 56/D5
Grosser Arber (peak), Ger. 55/G4
Grosser Beer-Berg (peak), Ger. 43/J1
Grosser Bösenstein (peak), Aus. 43/L3
Grosser Daumen (peak), Ger. 57/G3
Grosser Feldberg (peak), Ger. 54/B2
Grosser Gleichberg (peak), Ger. 54/D2
Grosser Heuberg (mts.), Ger. 54/B6
Grosser Knechtsand (isl.), Ger. 51/F1
Grosser Peilstein (peak), Aus. 41/H4
Grosser Plessower (lake), Ger. 40/P7
Grosser Priel (peak), Aus. 43/L3
Grosser Rachel (peak), Ger. 55/G5
Grosser Seddiner (lake), Ger. 40/P7
Grosser Selchower (lake), Ger. 40/Q7
Grosses Meer (lake), Ger. 51/E2
Grosses Moor (swamp), Ger. 51/H3
Grosseto, It. 43/J5
Grossgerau, Ger. 54/B3
Grossglienicke, Ger. 40/Q7
Grossglockner (peak), Aus. 43/K3
Grosshansdorf, Ger. 51/H1
Grossheubach, Ger. 54/C3
Grosskrotzenburg, Ger. 54/B2
Grossmaischeid, Ger. 53/G3
Grosso (cape), Fr. 43/H5
Grossrosseln, Ger. 53/F5
Grosssiegharts, Aus. 41/H4
Grosswallstadt, Ger. 54/C3
Grosswangen, Swi. 56/E3
Grosuplje, Slov. 43/L4
Grote Gete (riv.), Belg. 53/D2
Groton, SD, US 127/J4
Grotta Gigante, It. 59/G1
Grottaglie, It. 47/E2
Grottammare, It. 43/K5
Grotte de Han, Belg. 53/E3
Grouard Mission, Ab, Can. 126/D2
Groundhog (riv.), On, Can. 130/D1
Grouw, Neth. 50/C2
Grovdageaidnu-Kautokeino, Nor. 37/G1
Grove, Ok, US 129/J3
Grove (pt.), Md, US 138/B5
Grover, Mo, US 137/F8
Grover City, Ca, US 128/B4
Groves, Tx, US 129/J5
Groveton, Va, US 138/A6
Groznyy, Rus. 63/H4
Grudovo, Bul. 49/H4
Grudziądz, Pol. 41/K2
Grumeti (riv.), Tanz. 104/B3
Grums, Swe. 38/E2
Grünau im Almtal, Aus. 55/G7
Grünburg, Aus. 55/H7
Gründau, Ger. 54/C2
Grune (pt.), Eng, UK 35/E2
Grünsfeld, Ger. 54/C3
Grünstadt, Ger. 54/B3
Grünwald, Ger. 55/E6
Gruyères, Swi. 56/D4
Gryazi, Rus. 62/F1
Grycksbo, Swe. 38/F1
Gryfice, Pol. 38/F5
Gryfino, Pol. 41/H2
Gryon, Swi. 56/D5
Gschwandt, Aus. 55/G7
Gschwend, Ger. 54/C5
Gsteig, Swi. 56/D5
Gua, India 85/E4
Guabún (pt.), Chile 158/B4
Guaca, Col. 152/C3
Guacanayabo (gulf), Cuba 141/F3
Guacarí, Col. 152/B4
Guachochi, Mex. 142/D3
Guácimo, CR 145/F4
Guaçuí, Braz. 155/D2
Guadalajara, Mex. 142/E4
Guadalajara, Sp. 44/D2
Guadalcanal, Sp. 44/C3
Guadalcanal (isl.), Sol. 116/E6
Guadalentín (riv.), Sp. 44/D4
Guadalimar (riv.), Sp. 44/D3
Guadalix (riv.), Sp. 45/N8
Guadalope (riv.), Sp. 45/E2
Guadalquivir (riv.), Sp. 44/D4
Guadalupe, Peru 156/C4
Guadalupe, Peru 156/B2
Guadalupe (peak), Tx, US 129/F5
Guadalupe, Braz. 154/B2
Guadalupe (mts.), NM,Tx, US 132/B3
Guadalupe, Mex. 142/E4
Guadalupe (co.), Tx, US 137/U20
Guadalupe, Mex. 143/E3
Guadalupe (riv.), Tx, US 140/B2
Guadalupe, Sp. 44/C3
Guadalupe, Pan. 152/B2
Guadalupe, Col. 152/C4
Guadalupe (isl.), Mex. 119/E7
Guadalupe Mountains NP, Tx, US 129/F5
Guadalupe, Sierra de (mts.), Sp. 44/C3
Guadalupe Victoria, Mex. 142/B1
Guadalupe Victoria, Mex. 142/D3
Guadalupe Victoria, Mex. 143/M7
Guadarrama (riv.), Sp. 44/C3
Guadarrama, Ven. 152/D2
Guadarrama, Sp. 45/M8
Guadarrama, Sierra de (mts.), Sp. 44/C2
Guadeloupe (isl.), Fr. 141/N8
Guadeloupe NP, Fr. 141/N8
Guadeloupe Passage (chan.), Fr. 141/J4
Guadiana (riv.), Port.,Sp. 44/B3
Guadiana Menor (riv.), Sp. 44/D4
Guadix, Sp. 44/D4
Guafo (isl.), Chile 158/B4
Guafo, Boca del (mouth) 157/B5
Guagua Pichincha (peak), Ecu. 152/B5
Guaíba, Braz. 155/B4
Guaíba (riv.), Braz. 155/B4
Guáimaro, Cuba 145/G1
Guainía (riv.), Col. 150/E3
Guainía (dept.), Col. 152/D4
Guaiquinima (peak), Ven. 153/F3
Guaíra, Braz. 157/F1
Guaíra, Braz. 155/B2
Guaiteca (isl.), Chile 158/B4
Guajará-Mirim, Braz. 150/E6
Guajira (pen.), Col. 147/B1
Gualaceo, Ecu. 152/B5
Gualaco, Hon. 144/E3
Gualán, Guat. 144/D3
Gualaquiza, Ecu. 156/B1

Gualeguay, Arg. 159/J10
Gualeguaychú, Arg. 159/J10
Gualtieri, It. 58/D3
Guam (isl.), Pac., US 116/D3
Guamal, Col. 152/C2
Guamblin, Isla (isl.), Chile 158/A5
Guamote, Ecu. 156/B1
Guamúchil, Mex. 142/C3
Gu'an, China 72/H7
Guan Xian, China 70/H5
Guan Xian, China 72/C3
Guanabacoa, Cuba 145/F1
Guanabara (bay), Braz. 211/K7
Guanahacabibes (gulf), Cuba 144/E1
Guanahacabibes (pen.), Cuba 145/E1
Guanaja (isl.), Hon. 144/E2
Guanaja, Hon. 144/E2
Guanajay, Cuba 145/F1
Guanajuato, Mex. 143/E4
Guanajuato (state), Mex. 140/A3
Guanambi, Braz. 154/B4
Guanape, Ven. 153/E2
Guanare (riv.), Ven. 150/E2
Guanare, Ven. 152/D2
Guanarito, Ven. 152/D2
Guanay (peak), Ven. 153/E3
Guandi (mtn.), China 72/B3
Guane, Cuba 145/E1
Guangchang, China 79/C2
Guangde, China 72/D5
Guangdong (prov.), China 71/K7
Guangfeng, China 79/C2
Guangling, China 72/C3
Guanglu (isl.), China 73/B3
Guangnan, China 83/J3
Guangping, China 79/C2
Guangping, China 72/C3
Guangrao, China 72/D3
Guangshan, China 72/C4
Guangxi Zhuangzu (aut. reg.), China 70/J7
Guangyuan, China 70/J5
Guangze, China 79/C2
Guangzhou, China 83/K3
Guanhães, Braz. 155/D1
Guanipa (riv.), Ven. 150/F2
Guannan, China 72/D4
Guantánamo, Cuba 145/H1
Guantánamo Bay U.S. Naval Base, Cuba 145/H2
Guantao, China 72/C3
Guanting (res.), China 72/G6
Guanujo, Ecu. 152/B5
Guanyun, China 72/D4
Guapí, Col. 152/B4
Guaporé, Braz. 155/B4
Guaporé (riv.), Braz. 147/C4
Guaqui, Bol. 156/D5
Guarabira, Braz. 154/D2
Guaraci, Braz. 155/B2
Guaraciaba do Norte, Braz. 154/B2
Guaraí, Braz. 151/J5
Guaramirim, Braz. 155/B3
Guaranda, Ecu. 152/B5
Guarani, Braz. 211/K6
Guarapari, Braz. 155/D2
Guarapuava, Braz. 155/B3
Guarará, Braz. 211/K6
Guararapes (int'l arpt.), Braz. 154/D3
Guararapes, Braz. 155/B2
Guararema, Braz. 211/G8
Guaratinga, Braz. 154/C5
Guaratinguetá, Braz. 211/H7
Guaratuba, Braz. 155/B3
Guarda (dist.), Port. 44/B2
Guarda, Port. 44/B2
Guardamar, Sp. 45/E3
Guardamiglio, It. 58/C2
Guardarrama (riv.), Sp. 45/N8
Guardia Alta (peak), It. 57/H4
Guardia Mitre, Arg. 158/E4
Guardia Sanframondi, It. 48/B5
Guardiagrele, It. 46/D1
Guareña, Sp. 44/B3
Guárico (riv.), Ven. 141/H6
Guárico (state), Ven. 153/E2
Guarico (pt.), Cuba 145/H1
Guárico, Embalse de (res.), Ven. 150/E2
Guarujá, Braz. 211/G9
Guarulhos (int'l arpt.), Braz. 211/G8
Guarulhos, Braz. 211/G8
Guarumal, Pan. 152/A3
Guasave, Mex. 142/C3
Guasdualito, Ven. 152/D3
Guasimal, Cuba 145/G1
Guasipati, Ven. 153/F3
Guastalla, It. 58/D3
Guatemala (cap.), Guat. 144/D3
Guatemala (ctry.) 144/D3
Guateque, Col. 152/C3
Guaviare (dept.), Col. 152/C4
Guaviare (riv.), Col. 147/C2
Guaxupé, Braz. 211/G6
Guayabero (riv.), Col. 152/C4
Guayabo, Cayo (isl.), Cuba 145/G1
Guayalejo (riv.), Mex. 143/F4
Guayama, PR 141/M8
Guayape (riv.), Hon. 144/E3
Guayaquil (gulf), Ecu.,Peru 147/A3
Guayaquil, Ecu. 152/B5
Guayaquil, Gulf of (gulf), Ecu.,Peru 156/A1
Guayaramerín, Bol. 150/E6
Guayas, Ecu. 152/B5
Guayas (prov.), Ecu. 152/A5
Guayas (riv.), Col. 152/C4
Guaymas, Mex. 142/C3
Gubakha, Rus. 61/N4
Gubbio, It. 59/F6
Guben, Ger. 41/H3
Gubin, Pol. 41/H3
Gubkin, Rus. 62/F2
Gucheng, China 72/B4
Gucheng, China 72/C3
Gúdar, Sierra de (range), Sp. 45/E2
Gudenå (riv.), Den. 38/D3
Gudensberg, Ger. 51/G6
Gudermes, Rus. 63/H4
Gudivāda, India 82/D4
Gudow, Ger. 51/H1
Güdül, Turk. 49/L5
Gūdūr, India 82/C5
Guebli (lake), Mrta. 98/B5
Guebwiller, Fr. 56/D2
Guecho, Sp. 44/D1
Guelb Azefal (hill), Mrta. 98/B5
Guelb er Rîchât (peak), Mrta. 98/C5
Guelma, Alg. 100/K6
Guelma (prov.), Alg. 100/K6
Guelph, On, Can. 130/D3
Guémené-Penfao, Fr. 42/C3
Guénange, Fr. 53/F5
Guérande, Fr. 42/B3
Guerara, Alg. 99/G2
Guérard, Fr. 30/L5
Guercif, Mor. 100/C2
Guéret, Fr. 42/D3
Guernes, Fr. 30/G4
Guernsey (int'l arpt.), Chl, UK 42/B2
Guernsey (isl.), Chl, UK 42/B2
Guerrero (state), Mex. 140/B4
Guerrero, Mex. 142/D2
Guerrero Negro, Mex. 142/B3
Guerville, Fr. 30/H5
Guesle (riv.), Fr. 30/H6
Gueugnon, Fr. 42/F3
Gueux, Fr. 52/C5
Gugē (peak), Eth. 97/N6
Guggisberg, Swi. 56/D4
Gugielmo Marconi (int'l arpt.), It. 59/E3
Güglingen, Ger. 54/B4
Guguan (isl.), NMar. 116/D3
Guguletu, SAfr. 106/L10
Gui (riv.), China 79/B3
Guiana Highlands (uplands), SAm. 147/C2
Guichen, Fr. 42/C3
Guichón, Uru. 159/K10
Guidder, Camr. 96/H6
Guidimaka (pol. reg.), Mrta. 102/B3
Guiding, China 83/J2
Guidizzolo, It. 58/D2
Guidong, China 83/K2
Guidonia, It. 46/C2
Guiglo, C.d'Iv. 102/D5
Guignes-Rabutin, Fr. 30/L6
Guihulngan, Phil. 81/F1
Guija, Moz. 105/F5
Guijuelo, Sp. 44/C2
Guilder (peak), Ut, US 137/L11
Guilderton, Austl. 112/B4
Guildford, Eng, UK 30/B3
Guilherand, Fr. 42/F4
Guilin (int'l arpt.), China 79/B2
Guilin, China 83/K2
Guillaume-Delisle (lake), Qu, Can. 123/J3
Guillena, Sp. 44/B4
Guimarães, Braz. 154/A1
Guimarães, Port. 44/A2
Guimba, Phil. 79/D4
Guimeng (mtn.), China 72/D4
Guinan, China 70/H4
Guinard (riv.), Sc, UK 36/A1
Guinea (ctry.) 102/C4
Guinea (gulf), Afr. 93/C4
Guinea-Bissau (ctry.) 102/B3
Guînes, Fr. 52/A2
Guingamp, Fr. 42/B2
Guinguinéo, Sen. 102/B3
Guiones (pt.), CR 144/E4
Guipavas, Fr. 42/A2
Guipavas (int'l arpt.), Fr. 42/A2
Guir, Oued (riv.), Alg. 98/E2
Guiratinga, Braz. 151/H7
Güiria, Ven. 153/F2
Guisborough, Eng, UK 35/G2
Guiscard, Fr. 52/C4
Guise, Fr. 52/C4
Guitiriz, Sp. 44/B1
Guitrancourt, Fr. 30/H4
Guiuan, Phil. 79/E5
Güiza (riv.), Col. 152/B4
Guizhou (prov.), China 70/J6
Gujan-Mestras, Fr. 42/C4
Gūjar Khān, Pak. 86/B3
Gujarāt (state), India 82/B3
Gujrānwāla, Pak. 86/C3
Gujrāt, Pak. 86/C3
Gukovo, Rus. 62/F2
Gulaothi, India 84/A1
Gulargambone, Austl. 115/D1
Gulbarga, India 82/C4
Guldenbach (riv.), Ger. 53/G3
Güldüzü, Turk. 91/E1
Gulen, Nor. 38/A1
Gulf Coastal (plain), Tx, US 132/D5
Gulf Islands Nat'l Seashore, US 133/F4
Gulf Shores, Al, US 133/G4
Gulfport, Ms, US 133/F4
Gulgong, Austl. 115/D2
Guliston, Uzb. 87/E4
Gulkana, Ak, US 134/J3
Gull Lake, Sk, Can. 126/F3
Gulladuff, NI, UK 34/B2
Gullane, Sc, UK 36/D4
Gullane (pt.), Sc, UK 36/D4
Gullspång, Swe. 38/F2
Güllükdağı (Termessos) NP, Turk. 91/B1
Gulmarg, India 86/C2
Gülnar, Turk. 91/C1
Gulpen, Neth. 53/E2
Gülpınar, Turk. 47/K3
Gulu, Ugan. 104/B2
Gulyantsi, Bul. 49/G4
Gumal (riv.), Pak. 86/A4
Gumare, Bots. 105/D4
Gumbrechtshoffen, Fr. 53/G6
Gumdag, Trkm. 63/K5
Gumeracha, Austl. 113/M8
Gumia, India 85/E4
Gumla, India 85/E4
Gumma (pref.), Japan 75/F2
Gummersbach, Ger. 53/G1
Gumpoldskirchen, Aus. 49/N7
Gumti (riv.), India 85/H4
Gümüşhacıköy, Turk. 62/E4
Gümüşhane, Turk. 62/F4
Gümüşhane (prov.), Turk. 62/F4
Guna (peak), Eth. 97/N5
Gunbower, Austl. 115/C2
Gundagai, Austl. 115/D2
Gundelfingen, Ger. 56/D1
Gundelfingen an der Donau, Ger. 54/D5
Gundelsheim, Ger. 54/C4
Gundersheim, Ger. 54/B3
Gundershoffen, Fr. 53/G6
Gündoğmuş, Turk. 91/C1
Güneydogu Toroslar (mts.), Turk. 90/D2
Gunisao (riv.), Mb, Can. 127/J2
Gunisao (lake), Mb, Can. 127/J2
Gunja, Cro. 48/D3
Gunn City, Mo, US 137/E6
Gunnaur, India 84/B1
Gunnebo, Swe. 38/G3
Gunnedah, Austl. 115/D1
Gunning, Austl. 115/D2
Gunnison (riv.), Co, US 128/F3
Gunnison, Ut, US 128/E3
Gunpowder (riv.), Md, US 138/B5
Gunpowder Falls State Park, Md, US 138/B4
Gunskirchen, Aus. 55/G6
Guntersblum, Ger. 54/B3
Guntersville, Al, US 133/G3
Guntersville (lake), Al, US 133/G3
Guntramsdorf, Aus. 49/N7
Guntūr, India 82/D4
Günz (riv.), Ger. 40/F4
Günzburg, Ger. 54/D6
Gunzenhausen, Ger. 54/D4
Guoyang, China 72/D4
Gura Humorului, Rom. 49/G2
Guragē (peak), Eth. 97/N6
Gurbantünggut (des.), China 70/E2
Gurdāspur, India 86/C3
Gurgaon, India 86/D5
Gürgentepe, Turk. 62/F4
Gurguéia (riv.), Braz. 151/K6
Guri (res.), Ven. 147/C2
Guri (dam), Ven. 153/F3
Gurk (riv.), Aus. 43/L3
Gurkthaler Alpen (mts.), Aus. 43/K3
Gurnee, Il, US 135/Q15
Guro, Moz. 105/F4
Gürpınar, Turk. 90/E2
Gursarai, India 84/B3
Gürsu, Turk. 62/D4
Guru Sikhar (peak), India 89/K4
Gürün, Turk. 90/D2
Gurupi, Braz. 151/J6
Gurupi (riv.), Braz. 151/J4
Gurupi, Serra do (mts.), Braz. 151/J4
Gus'-Khrustal'nyy, Rus. 60/J5
Gusau, Nga. 103/G3
Gushi, China 72/C4
Gushikawa, Japan 75/J7
Gusinje, Yugo. 47/F1
Guskhara, India 85/F4
Guspini, It. 46/A3
Gussola, It. 58/D3
Gustavo Díaz Ordaz, Mex. 142/C3
Gustavo Díaz Ordaz, Mex. 142/B3
Gusterath, Ger. 53/F4
Güstrow, Ger. 38/E5
Gusum, Swe. 38/G2
Gutau, Aus. 55/H6
Gütersloh, Ger. 51/F5
Guthrie, Tx, US 129/G4
Guthrie, Ok, US 137/N14
Gutiérrez Zamora, Mex. 143/M6
Guttannen, Swi. 57/E4
Guttenberg, NJ, US 139/K8
Guttingen, Swi. 57/F2
Gutulia NP, Nor. 37/E3
Guwāhati, India 83/F2
Guxhagen, Ger. 51/G6
Guxian, China 72/B3
Guy Fawkes River NP, Austl. 115/E1
Guyana (ctry.) 153/G3
Guyancourt, Fr. 30/J5
Guyandotte (riv.), WV, US 133/H2
Guyang, China 72/B2
Guyenne (reg.), Fr. 42/C4
Guymon, Ok, US 129/G3
Guyra, Austl. 115/D1
Guyuan, China 70/J4
Güzelbağ, Turk. 91/B1
Güzelsu, Turk. 91/B1
Guzhang, China 83/J2
Guzhen, China 72/D4
Guzmán (lake), Mex. 142/D2
Gwādar, Pak. 89/H3
Gwaii Haanas NP, BC, Can. 122/C3
Gwalior, India 84/B2
Gwanda, Zim. 105/E5
Gwandalan, Austl. 115/D2
Gwash (riv.), Eng, UK 33/F1
Gwaunceste (peak), Wal, UK 32/C2
Gwda (riv.), Pol. 41/J2
Gwersyllt, Wal, UK 35/E5
Gweru, Zim. 105/E4
Gwydir (riv.), Austl. 115/D1
Gwynedd (co.), Wal, UK 34/D5
Gwyrfai (riv.), Wal, UK 34/D5
Gy, Fr. 56/B3
Gya (pass), China 85/E1
Gyaca, China 83/F2
Gyál, Hun. 49/R10
Gyasikan, Gha. 103/F5
Gyda (pen.), Rus. 67/G2
Gyhum, Ger. 51/G2
Gyirong, China 85/E1
Gyldenløveshøj (peak), Den. 38/D4
Gympie, Austl. 114/D4
Gyōda, Japan 77/C1
Gyoma, Hun. 48/E2
Gyömrő, Hun. 49/R10
Győr, Hun. 48/C2
Győr-Moson-Sopron (co.), Hun. 41/J5
Győrújbarát, Hun. 48/C2
Gyumri, Arm. 63/G4
Gyzylarbat, Trkm. 63/L5
Gżira, Malta 46/L7

H

Hå, Nor. 38/A2
Ha Giang, Viet. 83/H3
Ha Noi (Hanoi) (cap.), Viet. 83/J3
Haacht, Belg. 53/D2
Haag, Aus. 55/H6
Haag am Hausruck, Aus. 55/G6
Haag an der Amper, Ger. 55/E6
Haag in Oberbayern, Ger. 55/F6
Haaksbergen, Neth. 50/D4
Haaltert, Belg. 52/D2
Haamstede, Neth. 50/A5
Haan, Ger. 50/E6
Ha'apai Group (isl.), Tonga 117/H7
Haapavesi, Fin. 60/E2
Haapsalu, Est. 39/K2
Haar, Ger. 55/E6
Haardt (mts.), Ger. 43/G2
Haarlem, Neth. 50/B4
Haast, NZ 117/R11
Haasts Bluff Abor. Land, Austl. 113/F2
Hab (riv.), Pak. 89/J3
Habahe, China 70/E2
Habartov, Czh. 55/F2
Habbānīyah, Iraq 90/E3
Habicht (peak), Aus. 57/H3
Habiganj, Bang. 85/H3
Habikino, Japan 77/J6
Habomai (isls.), Rus. 76/D2
HaBonim, Isr. 91/F6
Haboro, Japan 76/B1
Hābra, India 85/G4
Habsheim, Fr. 56/D2
Hacha (falls), Ven. 153/F3
Hache (riv.), Ger. 51/F3
Hachenburg, Ger. 53/G2
Hachijō, Japan 75/F4
Hachikai, Japan 77/L5
Hachimori, Japan 76/B3
Hachinohe, Japan 76/B3
Hachiōji, Japan 75/F3
Hacıbektaş, Turk. 90/C2
Hacienda Heights, Ca, US 136/G8
Hacılar, Turk. 90/C2
Hack (mt.), Austl. 113/H4
Hackensack, NJ, US 139/J8
Hackensack (riv.), NJ, US 139/J9
Hackettstown, NJ, US 138/D2
Hackney (bor.), Eng, UK 30/C2
Ḥaḍabat al Jilf al Kabīr (plat.), Egypt 101/A4
Hadāli, Pak. 86/B3
Hadamar, Ger. 54/B2
Hadano, Japan 75/F3
Hadarba (cape), Sudan 101/D4
Ḥadd, Ra's al (pt.), Oman 89/G4
Haddenham, Eng, UK 33/F3
Haddington, Sc, UK 36/D5
Haddonfield, NJ, US 138/C4
Hadejia (riv.), Nga. 93/C3
Hadelner (canal), Ger. 51/F1
Ḥadera, Isr. 91/F7
Haderslev, Den. 38/C4
Hadhramaut (reg.), Yem. 88/E6
Hadım, Turk. 91/C1
Hadjout, Alg. 100/G4
Hadleigh, Eng, UK 30/E2
Hadley (bay), Nun., Can. 122/F1
Hadlow, Eng, UK 30/E3
Hadrian's Wall, Eng, UK 35/F1
Hadselfjorden (inlet), Nor. 37/E1
Hadsten, Den. 38/D3
Hadsund, Den. 38/D3
Haeju (bay), NKor. 73/C4
Haeju, NKor. 73/C3
Haena (pt.), Hi, US 124/S9
Haenam, SKor. 73/D5
Hafik, Turk. 62/F5
Hāfizābād, Pak. 86/B3
Hāflong, India 83/F2
Hafnarfjördhur, Ice. 37/N7
Hafnarhreppur, Ice. 37/P7
Haft Gel, Iran 88/E2
Hafun (pt.), Som. 97/R5
Hagåtña (cap.), Guam 116/D3
Hagelstadt, Ger. 55/F5
Hagemeister (isl.), Ak, US 134/F4
Hagen, Ger. 51/E6
Hagen am Teutoburger Wald, Ger. 51/E4
Hagen im Bremischen, Ger. 51/F2
Hagenow, Ger. 38/D5
Hagerman, NM, US 132/B3
Hagerstown, Md, US 130/E4
Hagetmau, Fr. 42/C5
Hagfors, Swe. 38/E1
Hagi, Japan 74/B3
Hagnau am Bodensee, Ger. 57/F2
Hags (pt.), Ire. 31/P10
Hague, Sk, Can. 127/G2
Hague, Cap de la (cape), Fr. 42/C2
Haguenau, Fr. 53/G6
Hahashima (isls.), Japan 116/D2
Hahaya (int'l arpt.), Com. 107/G5
Hahle (riv.), Ger. 51/H5
Hahndorf, Austl. 113/M9
Hahnenbach (riv.), Ger. 53/G4
Hahnstätten, Ger. 54/B2
Hahnville, La, US 137/P17
Ḥaḥrā Awbāri (des.), Libya 96/H2
Hai (riv.), China 72/D3
Hai Duong, Viet. 78/D1
Hai Phong, Viet. 83/J3
Hai Van (pass), Viet. 78/E2
Hai'an, China 72/E4
Haibach, Ger. 54/C3
Haibara, Japan 77/J6
Haicheng, China 73/B2
Haidenaab (riv.), Ger. 55/E3
Haidershofen, Aus. 55/H6
Haifa (dist.), Isr. 91/D3
Haifeng, China 79/C3
Haiger, Ger. 43/H1
Haigerloch, Ger. 54/B6
Haikou (int'l arpt.), China 79/B3
Haikou, China 83/K3
Haiku-Pauwela, Hi, US 124/T10
Ḥā'il, SAr. 88/D3
Hailākāndi, India 83/F3
Hailar (riv.), China 71/M2
Haileybury, On, Can. 130/E2
Hailsham, Eng, UK 33/G5
Hailun, China 71/N2
Haimen, China 72/E5
Haimhausen, Ger. 55/E6
Haiming, Aus. 57/G3
Haiming, Ger. 55/F6
Haina, Ger. 51/F6
Hainan (prov.), China 70/J8
Hainan (str.), China 83/K3
Hainan (isl.), China 67/L8
Hainaut (prov.), Belg. 52/B2
Hainburg, Ger. 54/C1
Haines, Ak, US 134/L3
Haines City, Fl, US 133/H4
Haines Junction, Yk, Can. 134/L3
Hainesville, NJ, US 138/D1
Hainesville, Il, US 135/P15
Hainich (mts.), Ger. 40/F3
Haining, China 72/L9
Haiti (ctry.) 145/H2
Haixia (str.), China 71/K7
Haixing, China 72/D3
Haiyan, China 79/B3
Haiyan, China 70/H4
Haiyang (isl.), China 73/B3
Haiyang, China 72/E3
Haiyuan, China 70/J4
Haizhou (bay), China 72/D4
Háj (peak), Czh. 55/F2
Hajdú-Bihār (co.), Hun. 70/E7
Hajdúboszormény, Hun. 41/L5
Hajdúdorog, Hun. 41/L5
Hajdúhadház, Hun. 48/E2
Hajdúnánás, Hun. 41/L5
Hajdúszoboszló, Hun. 41/L5
Hajiki-zaki (pt.), Japan 75/F1
Hājīpur, India 85/E3
Ḥajjah, Yem. 88/D5
Hajnówka, Pol. 41/M2
Hājo, India 85/H2
Hajós, Hun. 48/D2
Haka, Myan. 83/F3
Hakee (mt.), Austl. 113/G3
Hakkari (prov.), Turk. 90/E2
Hakken-san (peak), Japan 74/D3
Hakkōda-san (peak), Japan 76/B3
Hakodate, Japan 76/B3
Hakone, Japan 77/C3
Hakone-yama (peak), Japan 77/C3
Haku-san (peak), Japan 75/E2
Hakui, Japan 75/E2
Hakusan, Japan 77/K6
Hakusan NP, Japan 75/E2
Hakushū, Japan 77/A2
Hāla, Pak. 89/J3
Ḥalab (prov.), Syria 90/D2
Ḥalab (Aleppo), Syria 91/E1
Halabjah, Iraq 88/E1
Halachó, Mex. 143/M6
Halawa, Hi, US 124/T10
Halcon (mt.), Phil. 81/F1
Halden, Nor. 38/D2
Haldensleben, Ger. 40/F2
Haldenwang, Ger. 57/G2
Haldīa, India 85/G4
Haldībāri, India 85/G2
Haldimand, On, Can. 131/Q10
Haldimand-Norfolk (co.), On, Can. 131/Q10
Hale (riv.), Austl. 113/G3
Hale (mt.), Austl. 112/C2
Hale, Eng, UK 35/F5
Haleakala NP, Hi, US 124/T10
Haledon, NJ, US 139/J8
Haleiwa, Hi, US 124/V12
Halen, Belg. 53/E2
Hales Corners, Wi, US 135/P14
Halesowen, Eng, UK 32/D2
Haleyville, Al, US 133/G3
Half Assini, Gha. 102/E5
Half Falls (mt.), Pa, US 138/A3
Half Moon Bay, Ca, US 135/K12
Half Tide Beach, Austl. 114/C3
Halfing, Ger. 55/F7
Halfweg, Neth. 50/B4
Ḥalḥūl, WBnk. 91/D4
Haliburton Highlands (uplands), On, Can. 130/E2
Halifax (cap.), NS, Can. 131/J2
Halifax (int'l arpt.), NS, Can. 131/J2
Halifax (bay), Austl. 109/D2
Halifax, Austl. 114/B2
Halifax, Pa, US 138/B3
Halifax, Eng, UK 35/G4
Halikko, Fin. 39/K1
Halīl (riv.), Iran 89/G3
Haliun, Mong. 70/G2
Halkett (cape), Ak, US 134/H1
Hall, Austl. 115/C2
Hall (isl.) 123/J3
Hall (isls.), Micr. 116/E4
Hall (pen.), Nun., Can. 123/K2
Hall Beach, Nun., Can. 123/J2
Hall Park, Ok, US 137/N15
Halladale (riv.), Sc, UK 31/S7
Hallam (Hellam), Pa, US 138/B4
Halland (co.), Swe. 37/E4
Hällbybrunn, Swe. 38/G2
Halle, Ger. 51/F4
Halle, Ger. 64/B4
Halle, Belg. 53/D2
Halle-Neustadt, Ger. 40/F3
Hällefors, Swe. 38/F2
Hälleforsnäs, Swe. 38/G2
Hallein, Aus. 43/K3
Hallenberg, Ger. 51/F6
Hallertau (reg.), Ger. 55/E5
Hallettsville, Tx, US 129/H5
Halley, UK, Ant. 160/Y
Hallingdalselvi (riv.), Nor. 38/C1
Hallock, Mn, US 127/J3
Hallsberg, Swe. 38/F2
Hallstahammar, Swe. 38/G2
Hallstavik, Swe. 38/H1
Hallu (riv.), Fr. 40/B4
Halluin, Fr. 52/C2
Hallwang, Aus. 55/G7
Hallwilersee (lake), Swi. 56/E3
Hallyŏ Haesang NP, SKor. 74/A3
Halmahera (sea), Indo. 81/G4
Halmahera (isl.), Indo. 67/M9
Halmstad, Swe. 38/E3
Ḥalq al Wādī, Tun. 46/B4
Hals, Den. 38/D3
Hälsingborg (Helsingborg), Swe. 38/E3
Halsteren, Neth. 50/B5
Haltern, Ger. 51/E5
Halton (co.), On, Can. 131/Q8
Halton Hills, On, Can. 131/Q8
Halver, Ger. 51/E6
Halverder Aa (riv.), Ger. 51/E4
Ham, Fr. 52/C4
Ham, Oued El (riv.), Alg. 100/G5
Ham-sous-Varsberg, Fr. 53/F5
Hamada, Japan 74/C3
Hamada de Tinrhert (plat.), Alg. 99/G4
Hamada du Drâa (plat.), Alg. 96/D2
Hamada du Tinrhert (plat.), Arg. 96/G2
Hamada Safia (plat.), Mali 98/D5
Hamadān, Iran 88/E2
Hamādat Marzūq (plat.), Libya 99/H4
Hamadat Tinghert (uplands),Libya 96/H2
Ḥamādat Tinghert (uplands),Libya 99/H3
Ḥamāh (prov.), Syria 91/E2
Hamajima, Japan 77/L7
Hamakita, Japan 75/E3
Hamam, Turk. 91/E1
Hamamatsu, Japan 75/E3
Hamami (reg.), Mrta. 98/C5
Hamanaka, Japan 76/D2
Hamar, Nor. 38/D1
Ḥamāṭah (peak), Egypt 101/C3
Hamath Tiberias NP, Isr. 91/D3
Hamatombetsu, Japan 76/C1
Hambantota, SrL. 82/D6
Hambergen, Ger. 51/F2
Hambleton (hills), Eng, UK 35/G3
Hambühren, Ger. 51/G3
Hamburg, NY, US 130/E3
Hamburg, Ger. 51/G1
Hamburg, NJ, US 138/D1
Hamburg, Pa, US 138/C2
Hamburg (state), Ger. 38/D5
Hamburg (Fuhlsbüttel) (int'l arpt.), Ger. 51/G1
Häme (prov.), Fin. 37/G3
Hämeenkyrö, Fin. 39/K1
Hämeenlinna, Fin. 39/L1
Hamel, Il, US 137/H8
Hamelin Pool (bay), Austl. 112/B3
Hameln, Ger. 51/G4
Hamersley (range), Austl. 109/A3
Hamersley Range NP, Austl. 112/C2
Hamford Water (inlet), Eng, UK 33/H3
Hamgyŏng-bukto (prov.), NKor. 73/E2
Hamgyŏng-namdo (prov.), NKor. 73/D2
Ḥamh, Syria 90/D3
Hamhŭng, NKor. 73/D3
Hamhŭng-si (prov.), NKor. 73/D3
Hami, China 70/F3
Hamilton, Austl. 115/B3
Hamilton, Mt, US 126/E4
Hamilton, Tx, US 129/H5
Hamilton, Al, US 133/G3
Hamilton (har.), On, Can. 131/Q9
Hamilton, NZ 117/T10
Hamilton, On, Can. 131/Q9
Hamilton (inlet), Nf, Can. 123/L3
Hamilton (mt.), Ca, US 135/L12
Hamilton, Sc, UK 36/B5
Hamilton Mil. Res., NY, US 139/J9
Hamilton-Wentworth (co.), On, Can. 131/Q9
Hamina, Fin. 39/M1
Hamīrpur, India 84/B3
Hamīrpur, India 86/D4
Hamlin, Tx, US 129/G4
Hamm, Ger. 51/E5
Hamm, Ger. 54/B3
Hamm, Ger. 53/G2
Hamma-Bouziane, Alg. 100/K6
Ḥammām Al Anf, Tun. 46/B4
Ḥammāmāt (gulf), Gabon 99/H1
Hammarland, Fin. 39/H1
Hammarön (isl.), Swe. 38/E2
Hammarstrand, Swe. 37/F3
Hamme (riv.), Ger. 51/F2
Hamme, Belg. 53/D1
Hammel, Den. 38/C3
Hammelburg, Ger. 54/C2
Hammerfest, Nor. 37/G1
Hammershus, Den. 38/F4
Hammersmith and Fulham (bor.), Eng, UK 30/A1
Hamminkeln, Ger. 50/D5
Hammonasset (pt.), Ct, US 139/F1
Hammond, In, US 130/C3
Hammond, La, US 133/F4
Hammonton, NJ, US 138/D4
Hamnvik, Nor. 37/F1
Hamoir, Belg. 53/E3
Hamont-Achel, Belg. 50/C6
Hampshire Downs (hills), Eng, UK 33/E4
Hampstead, Md, US 138/B4
Hampton, Pa, US 138/A4
Hampton Bays, NY, US 139/F2
Hampton Court, Eng, UK 30/C2
Hampton Nat'l Hist. Site, Md, US 138/B5
Hamp'yŏng, SKor. 73/D5
Hamtramck, Mi, US 135/F7
Hamura, Japan 77/C2
Hamyang, SKor. 73/D5
Hamyŏl, SKor. 73/D4
Han (riv.), China 67/M6
Hana (riv.), India 84/C5
Hana, Hi, US 124/U10
Hanak, Turk. 63/G4
Hanamaki, Japan 76/B4
Hanamalo (pt.), Hi, US 124/U11
Hanang (peak), Tanz. 104/B4
Hanau, Ger. 54/B2
Hanazono, Japan 77/C1
Hancocks Bridge, NJ, US 138/C5
Handa, Japan 77/L6
Handawor, India 86/C2
Handeloh, Ger. 51/G2
Handiā, India 84/D3
Hanford, Ca, US 128/C3
Hangayn (mts.), Mong. 64/K5
Hangingstone (hill), Eng, UK 32/C5
Hangklip (cape), SAfr. 106/L11
Hangu, Pak. 86/A3
Hangzhou (bay), China 72/L9
Hanhofen, Ger. 54/B4
Hanhöhiy (mts.), Mong. 70/F2
Hani, Turk. 90/E2
Haninge, Swe. 38/H2
Hankensbüttel, Ger. 51/H3
Hankey, SAfr. 106/D4
Hankinson, ND, US 127/J4
Hanko (Hangö), Fin. 39/K2
Hanley, Sk, Can. 127/G3
Hanna, Ab, Can. 126/F3
Hannan, Japan 77/H7
Hanningfield (res.), Eng, UK 30/E2
Hannō, Japan 77/C2
Hannover (int'l arpt.), Ger. 51/G4
Hannover, Ger. 51/G4
Hannut, Belg. 53/E2
Hanōbukten (bay), Swe. 37/E5
Hanover, NH, US 131/F3
Hanover, On, Can. 130/D2
Hanover, SAfr. 106/D3
Hanover, Pa, US 138/B4
Hanover (isl.), Chile 159/B6
Hanover Park, Il, US 135/P16
Hansen (dam), Ca, US 136/F7
Hanshan, China 72/D5
Hanshou, China 79/B2
Hānsi, India 86/C5
Hanstedt, Ger. 51/H2
Hanstholm, Den. 38/C3
Hansville, Wa, US 135/B2
Hantzsch (riv.), Nun., Can. 123/J2
Hanumāngarh, India 86/C5
Hanwood, Austl. 115/C2
Hanyū, Japan 77/D1
Hanyuan, China 83/H2
Hanzhong, China 70/J5
Hao (isl.), FrPol. 117/L6
Haparanda, Swe. 60/E2
Hapch'ŏn, SKor. 73/E5
Happy Valley (res.), Austl. 113/M9
Happy Valley-Goose Bay, Nf, Can. 123/K3
Haptŏk, SKor. 73/D4
Hāpur, India 84/A1
Haquira, Peru 156/C4
Har-Ayrag, Mong. 71/J2

Har Karmel (Mount Carmel) (peak), Isr. 91/G6
Har Meron (peak), Isr. 91/D3
Har Ramon (peak), Isr. 91/D4
Hara, Japan 77/A2
Harahan, La, US 137/P17
Haramachi, Japan 75/G2
Harappa (ruin), Pak. 86/B4
Harare (cap.), Zim. 105/F4
Ḩarash, Bi'r al (well), Libya 97/K2
Haravilliers, Fr. 30/J4
Harbel, Libr. 102/C5
Harbeson, De, US 138/C6
Harbin, China 71/N2
Harbiye, Turk. 91/E1
Harbonnières, Fr. 52/B4
Harbour Breton, Nf, Can. 131/L2
Harbour Grace, Nf, Can. 131/L2
Hårby, Den. 38/D4
Hard, Aus. 57/F3
Hardā, India 89/L4
Hardangervidda NP, Nor. 38/B1
Hardau (riv.), Ger. 51/H3
Hardegsen, Ger. 51/G5
Hardenberg, Neth. 50/D3
Harderwijk, Neth. 50/C4
Hardheim, Ger. 54/C3
Hardin, Mt, US 126/G4
Harding, SAfr. 107/E3
Hardoi, India 84/C2
Hardoi Branch (riv.), India 84/C2
Hardricourt, Fr. 30/H4
Hardy (pen.), Chile 159/C7
Hare (bay), Nf, Can. 131/L1
Hare Dimona (peak), Isr. 91/D4
Harefield, Eng, UK 30/B2
Harelbeke, Belg. 52/C2
Haren, Ger. 51/E3
Haren, Neth. 50/D2
Hārer, Eth. 97/P6
Harford (co.), Md, US 138/B4
Hargesheim, Ger. 53/G4
Hargeville, Fr. 30/H5
Hargeysa, Som. 97/P6
Harghita (prov.), Rom. 49/G2
Harghita (peak), Rom. 49/G2
Hari (riv.), Indo. 80/B4
Hari (str.), Est. 39/K2
Harihar, India 89/L6
Ḩārim, Syria 91/E1
Harima (sea), Japan 74/D3
Ḩarīmā, Jor. 91/D3
Harima, Japan 77/G6
Harima (bay), Japan 77/G6
Haringey (bor.), Eng, UK 30/C2
Haringhāta (riv.), Bang. 85/G4
Haringvliet (chan.), Neth. 50/B5
Haringvlietdam (dam), Neth. 50/B5
Harīpur, Pak. 86/B3
Harīrūd (riv.), Afg. 67/F6
Ḩāris, WBnk. 91/G7
Harjavalta, Fin. 39/K1
Harlan, Ky, US 130/D4
Harlech, Wal, UK 34/D6
Harlingen, Tx, US 132/D5
Harlingen, Neth. 50/C2
Harlow, Eng, UK 30/D1
Harlowton, Mt, US 126/F4
Harmannsdorf, Aus. 49/N7
Harmelen, Neth. 50/B4
Harnes, Fr. 52/B3
Harney (basin), Or, US 128/C2
Harney (lake), Or, US 126/D5
Harney (peak), SD, US 127/H5
Harney (valley), Or, US 126/D5
Harney, Md, US 138/A4
Harnoli, Pak. 86/A3
Haro (cape), Mex. 142/C3
Haro, Sp. 44/D1
Harold, Ca, US 136/B1
Harpenden, Eng, UK 33/F3
Harper (mt.), Yk, Can. 134/L3
Harper (mt.), Ak, US 134/K3
Harper, Ks, US 129/H3
Harper, Libr. 102/D5
Harper, Wa, US 135/B2
Harper Woods, Mi, US 135/F7
Harpstedt, Ger. 51/F3
Harqin Zuoyi Monggolzu Zizhixian, China 72/D2
Harrah, Ok, US 137/N15
Harrai, India 84/B4
Harran, Turk. 90/D2
Harricana (riv.), Qu, Can. 123/J4
Harriman, Tn, US 130/C5
Harriman, NY, US 138/D1
Harrington, Austl. 115/E1
Harrington, De, US 138/C6
Harrington Park, NJ, US 139/K8
Harris (mt.), Austl. 113/F3
Harris (lake), Austl. 113/G4
Harris (isl.), Sc, UK 31/Q8
Harris Park, Co, US 137/B4
Harrisburg, Ne, US 127/H5
Harrisburg, Il, US 130/B4
Harrisburg (cap.), Pa, US 138/B3
Harrislee, Ger. 38/C4
Harrismith, SAfr. 106/E3
Harrison (bay), Ak, US 134/H1
Harrison, Ar, US 129/J3
Harrison, Mi, US 130/C2
Harrison, NY, US 139/L8
Harrison, NJ, US 139/J9
Harrison (cape), Nf, Can. 123/L3
Harrison (lake), BC, Can. 126/C3
Harrisonville, Il, US 137/G9
Harrisonville, Mo, US 137/E6
Harrisville, Ut, US 137/K11
Harrodsburg, Ky, US 130/C4
Harrogate, Eng, UK 35/G4
Harrow (bor.), Eng, UK 30/B2
Harry S Truman (res.), Mo, US 129/J3
Harsefeld, Ger. 51/G2
Harsewinkel, Ger. 51/F5
Harson's Island, Mi, US 135/G6
Hart (lake), Or, US 128/C2
Hart, Mi, US 130/C3
Hart (riv.), Yk, Can. 122/C2
Hart (riv.), Eng, UK 30/A3
Hart (isl.), NY, US 139/K8
Hart Fell (peak), Sc, UK 36/C6
Hartbeesrivier (riv.), SAfr. 106/C3
Hårteigen (peak), Nor. 38/B1
Hartelkanaal (riv.), Neth. 50/B5
Hartford (cap.), Ct, US 131/F3
Hartford, Il, US 137/G8
Hartford, NJ, US 138/D4
Hartford City, In, US 130/C3
Hartheim, Ger. 56/D2
Hartington, Ne, US 129/H2
Hartkirchen, Aus. 55/H6
Hartland (pt.), Eng, UK 32/B4
Hartland, Mi, US 135/E6
Hartlepool, Eng, UK 35/G2
Hartlepool (co.), Eng, UK 35/G2
Hartleton, Pa, US 138/A2
Hartley Wintney, Eng, UK 30/A3
Hartly, De, US 138/C5
Hartney, Mb, Can. 127/H3
Hartsdale, NY, US 139/K7
Hartselle, Al, US 133/G3
Hartshill, Eng, UK 33/E1
Hartstene (isl.), Wa, US 135/B3
Hartwell, Ga, US 133/H3
Hartwell (lake), Ga,SC, US 133/H3
Hartz Mountain NP, Austl. 115/C4
Haruhi, Japan 77/L5
Harun (peak), Indo. 81/E3
Hārūnābād, Pak. 86/B5
Hārūt (riv.), Afg. 89/H2
Harvey, ND, US 127/J4
Harvey, La, US 137/P17
Harvey, Austl. 112/B5
Harvey, Il, US 135/Q16
Harveys (lake), Pa, US 138/B1
Harwich, Eng, UK 33/H3
Haryana (state), India 82/C2
Harz (mts.), Ger. 40/F3
Hasan (peak), Turk. 90/C2
Hasan Abdāl, Pak. 86/B3
Hasanpur, India 84/B1
Hasbrouck Heights, NJ, US 139/J8
Hasdo (riv.), India 84/D4
Hase (riv.), Ger. 40/D2
Hasel (riv.), Ger. 54/D1
Haselünne, Ger. 51/E3
Hasenmatt (peak), Swi. 56/D3
Hashima, Japan 77/L5
Hashimoto, Japan 74/D3
Hasi el Farsia (well), WSah. 98/C4
Hāsilpur, Pak. 86/B5
Haskell, Tx, US 129/H4
Haslach an der Mühl, Aus. 55/H5
Haslach im Kinzigtal, Ger. 56/E1
Hasle bei Burgdorf, Swi. 56/D3
Haslemere, Eng, UK 33/F4
Haslingden, Eng, UK 35/F4
Hasloh, Ger. 51/G1
Haspres, Fr. 52/C3
Hassa, Turk. 91/E1
Hassan, India 82/C5
Hassan (El Aaiún) (int'l arpt.), WSah. 98/B4
Hassberge (hills), Ger. 54/D2
Hassel, Ger. 51/G3
Hassel Sound (str.), Nun., Can. 123/S7
Hasselt, Neth. 50/D3
Hasselt, Belg. 53/E2
Hassfurt, Ger. 54/D2
Hassi Bahbah, Alg. 100/G5
Hassi bou Zid (well), Alg. 99/F3
Hassi el Hadjar (well), Alg. 99/G3
Hassi el Mislane (well), Alg. 99/H4
Hassi er Rebib (well), Alg. 99/G2
Hässleholm, Swe. 38/E3
Hasslo (int'l arpt.), Swe. 38/G2
Hassloch, Ger. 54/B4
Haste, Ger. 51/G4
Hastings, Austl. 115/C3
Hastings, Ne, US 129/H2
Hastings, Mi, US 130/C3
Hastings, NZ 117/T10
Hastings, Eng, UK 33/G5
Hastings Battlesite, Eng, UK 33/G5
Hastings-On-Hudson, NY, US 139/K7
Hasuda, Japan 77/D2
Hasunuma, Japan 77/E2
Hasvik, Nor. 37/G1
Hat Chao Mai NP, Thai. 78/B5
Hat Head, Austl. 115/E1
Hat Head NP, Austl. 115/E1
Hat Nai Yang NP, Thai. 78/B5
Hat Yai, Thai. 78/C5
Hat Yai (int'l arpt.), Thai. 78/C5
Hatashō, Japan 77/K5
Hatavch, Mong. 71/K2
Hatay (prov.), Turk. 90/C2
Hatboro, Pa, US 138/C3
Hatch, NM, US 128/F4
Hatcher (peak), Arg. 159/B6
Haţeg, Rom. 48/F3
Hatfield, Pa, US 138/C3
Hatfield, Eng, UK 30/C1
Hatfield Peverel, Eng, UK 30/E1
Hatgal, Mong. 70/H1
Hāthras, India 84/B2
Hātia (riv.), Bang. 85/H4
Hātia, North (isl.), Bang. 85/H4
Hātia, South (isl.), Bang. 85/H4
Ḩaţibah, Ras (pt.), SAr. 88/C4
Hato (int'l arpt.), NAnt. 152/D1
Hato Corozal, Col. 152/D3
Hato Mayor, DRep. 141/H4
Hatogaya, Japan 77/D2
Hatoyama, Japan 77/C2
Hatsu (isl.), Japan 77/C3
Hatta, India 84/B3
Hatta, Japan 77/A2
Hattah-Kulkyne NP, Austl. 113/J5
Hattem, Neth. 50/D4
Hatten, Ger. 51/F2
Hatten, Fr. 53/G6
Hatteras, NC, US 133/K3
Hatteras (cape), NC, US 133/K3
Hattersheim am Mein, Ger. 54/B2
Hattiesburg, Ms, US 133/F4
Hattieville, Belz. 144/D2
Hattingen, Ger. 51/E6
Hattula, Fin. 39/L1
Hatvan, Hun. 48/D2
Hatzenbühl, Ger. 54/B4
Hatzfeld, Ger. 51/F6
Hau Giang (riv.), Viet. 78/D4
Haubourdin, Fr. 52/B2
Haud (reg.), Eth. 97/Q6
Hauge, Nor. 38/B2
Haugesund, Nor. 38/A2
Haukipudas, Fin. 60/E2
Haune (riv.), Ger. 40/E3
Haunsberg (peak), Aus. 55/F7
Hauppauge, NY, US 139/E2
Hauraki (gulf), NZ 117/S10
Haus, Nor. 38/A1
Hausach, Ger. 56/E1
Hausjärvi, Fin. 39/L1
Hausleiten, Aus. 49/N7
Hausstock (peak), Swi. 57/F4
Haut Atlas (mts.), Mor. 96/D1
Haut-Rhin (dept.), Fr. 56/D2
Haute-Normandie (pol. reg.), Fr. 42/D2
Haute-Saône (dept.), Fr. 56/B2
Haute-Savoie (dept.), Fr. 56/C5
Hautefeuille, Fr. 30/L5
Hautes Fagnes (uplands), Belg. 53/E3
Hauteurs de Gâtine (uplands), Fr. 42/C3
Hauteville-Lompnes, Fr. 56/B6
Hautmont, Fr. 52/C3
Hauts (plat.), Alg.,Mor. 99/E2
Hauula, Hi, US 124/W12
Havant, Eng, UK 33/F5
Havasu (lake), Az,Ca, US 128/D4
Havdhem, Swe. 38/H3
Havel (canal), Ger. 40/P6
Havel (riv.), Ger. 41/G2
Havelange, Belg. 53/E3
Haveli, Pak. 86/B4
Havelīān, Pak. 86/B2
Havelländischer Grosser Hauptkanal (canal), Ger. 40/P6
Havelock, NC, US 133/J3
Havelte, Neth. 50/D3
Havencore (isl.), Eng, UK 33/G3
Haverfordwest, Wal, UK 32/B3
Haverhill, Ma, US 131/G3
Haverhill, Eng, UK 33/G2
Havering (bor.), Eng, UK 30/D2
Havířov, Czh. 41/K4
Havixbeck, Ger. 51/E5
Havlíčkuv Brod, Czh. 41/H4
Havneby, Den. 38/C4
Havre, Mt, US 126/F3
Havre de Grace, Md, US 138/B4
Havre-Saint-Pierre, Qu, Can. 131/J1
Havsa, Turk. 47/K2
Havza, Turk. 62/E4
Haw (riv.), NC, US 133/J3
Hawaii (state), US 124/S10
Hawaii (isl.), Hi, US 117/K3
Hawaii Kai, Hi, US 124/W13
Hawaii Volcanoes NP, Hi, US 124/U11
Hawaiian (isls.), US 117/H2
Hawaiian Gardens, Ca, US 136/F8
Ḩawallī, Kuw. 88/E3
Hawarden, Wal, UK 35/E5
Hawera, NZ 117/S10
Haweswater (res.), Eng, UK 35/F2
Hawi, Hi, US 124/U10
Hawick, Sc, UK 36/D6
Hawke (cape), Austl. 115/E2
Hawke (bay), NZ 109/H6
Hawker, Austl. 113/H4
Hawkesbury (isl.), BC, Can. 126/A2
Hawkesbury, On, Can. 130/F2
Hawkesbury (riv.), Austl. 114/G8
Hawks Nest, Austl. 115/E2
Haworth, NJ, US 139/K8
Ḩawsh 'Īsá, Egypt 91/B4
Hawston, SAfr. 106/L11
Hawthorn Woods, Il, US 135/P15
Hawthorne, Nv, US 128/C3
Hawthorne, Ca, US 136/F8
Hawthorne, NJ, US 139/J8
Hawthorne, NY, US 139/K8
Ḩawwārah, Jor. 91/D3
Haxby, Eng, UK 35/G3
Hay, Austl. 115/C2
Hay (pt.), Austl. 114/C3
Hay (riv.), Ab,BC, Can. 122/E3
Hay River, NW, Can. 122/E2
Hayachine-san (peak), Japan 76/B4
Hayakawa, Japan 77/A3
Hayama, Japan 77/D3
Hayange, Fr. 53/F5
Haybes, Fr. 53/D4
Haycock, Ak, US 134/F2
Haydock, Eng, UK 35/F5
Hayes (mt.), Ak, US 134/J3
Hayes (pen.), Grld. 123/T7
Hayes (riv.), Mb, Can. 122/G3
Hayingen, Ger. 57/F1
Haylaastay, Mong. 71/K2
Hayle (riv.), Eng, UK 32/A6
Hayling (isl.), Eng, UK 33/F5
Haymana, Turk. 62/E5
Haynesville, La, US 129/J4
Hayrabolu, Turk. 49/H5
Hays, Ks, US 129/H3
Hays (co.), Tx, US 137/U20
Haysyn, Ukr. 62/D2
Hayward, Wi, US 127/L4
Hazār (mtn.), Iran 89/G3
Hazard, Ky, US 130/D4
Hazārībag, India 85/E4
Hazebrouck, Fr. 52/B2
Hazel Park, Mi, US 135/F7
Hazelwood, Mo, US 137/G8
Hazen (bay), Ak, US 134/E3
Hazen (str.), NW,Nun., Can. 123/R7
Hazlehurst, Ms, US 129/K5
Hazlemere, Eng, UK 30/A2
Hazlet, NJ, US 139/J10
Hazleton (mts.), BC, Can. 126/A2
Hazleton, Pa, US 138/C2
Hazlett (lake), Austl. 113/F2
Hazratbal Mosque, India 86/C2
Hazro, Pak. 86/B3
Hazu, Japan 77/M6
He (riv.), China 79/B3
He Xian, China 72/D5
Headcorn, Eng, UK 33/G4
Heads of Ayr (pt.), Sc, UK 36/B6
Healdsburg, Ca, US 128/B3
Healesville, Austl. 115/G5
Healy, Ak, US 134/J3
Heanor, Eng, UK 35/G6
Heard (isl.), Austl. 160/E
Hearst, On, Can. 130/D1
Heart (riv.), ND, US 127/H4
Heart Law (hill), Sc, UK 36/D5
Heath (pt.), Qu, Can. 131/J1
Heathcote, Austl. 115/C3
Heathcote NP, Austl. 114/G9
Heathrow (int'l arpt.), Eng, UK 30/B2
Hebbronville, Tx, US 132/D5
Hebei (prov.), China 71/K4
Hebertshausen, Ger. 55/E6
Hebrides (isls.), UK 27/D3
Hebrides (sea), Sc, UK 31/Q8
Hebron, Ne, US 129/H2
Hebron, Il, US 135/P15
Heby, Swe. 38/G2
Hecate (str.), BC, Can. 122/C3
Hecelchakán, Mex. 144/D1
Hechi, China 83/J3
Hechingen, Ger. 54/B6
Hechtel, Belg. 53/E1
Hechthausen, Ger. 51/G1
Hecker, Il, US 137/H9
Hecla, SD, US 127/J4
Hecla and Griper (bay), NW,Nun., Can. 123/R7
Hector (mt.), Ab, Can. 126/D3
Heddal, Nor. 38/C2
Hedel, Neth. 50/C5
Hedemora, Swe. 38/F1
Hedensted, Den. 38/C4
Hedmark (co.), Nor. 37/D3
Hedo-misaki (cape), Japan 75/K7
Hédouville, Fr. 30/J4
Heede, Ger. 51/E3
Heeia, Hi, US 124/W13
Heek, Ger. 51/E4
Heemskerk, Neth. 50/B3
Heemstede, Neth. 50/B4
Heerde, Neth. 50/D4
Heerenveen, Neth. 50/C3
Heerhugowaard, Neth. 50/B3
Heerlen, Neth. 53/E2
Heers, Belg. 53/E2
Heesch, Neth. 50/C5
Heeslingen, Ger. 51/G2
Heeze, Neth. 50/C6
Ḩefa (Haifa), Isr. 91/F6
Hefei, China 72/D5
Hefeng Tujiazu Zizhixian, China 79/B2
Hefner (lake), Ok, US 137/M14
Hegang, China 71/P2
Hegau (mts.), Ger. 43/H3
Hegau (reg.), Ger. 40/E5
Heggenes, Nor. 38/C1
Hegins, Pa, US 138/B2
Heguri, Japan 77/J6
Hei (riv.), Japan 76/B4
Heide, Ger. 38/C4
Heideck, Ger. 54/E4
Heidelberg, Ms, US 133/F4
Heidelberg, SAfr. 106/C4
Heidelberg, SAfr. 106/E2
Heidelberg, Ger. 54/B4
Heiden, Ger. 50/D5
Heiden, Swi. 57/F3
Heidenheim, Ger. 54/D4
Heidenheim, Ger. 54/D5
Heidenreichstein, Aus. 41/H4
Heiderscheid, Lux. 53/E4
Heigenbrücken, Ger. 54/C2
Heihe, China 71/N1
Heikendorf, Ger. 38/D4
Heilbron, SAfr. 106/D2
Heilbronn, Ger. 54/C4
Heilbronn, Ger. 54/D4
Heiligenberg, Ger. 57/F2
Heiligenblut, Aus. 43/K3
Heiligenhafen, Ger. 38/D4
Heiligenhaus, Ger. 50/D6
Heiligenstadt, Ger. 51/H6
Heilong (Amur) (riv.), China, Rus 65/N5
Heilongjiang (prov.), China 71/N2
Heiloo, Neth. 50/B3
Heimaey (isl.), Ice. 37/N7
Heimbach, Ger. 53/F2
Heimberg, Swi. 56/D4
Heimsheim, Ger. 54/B5
Heino, Neth. 50/D4
Heinola, Fin. 39/M1
Heinsberg, Ger. 53/F1
Heishan, China 73/B2
Heist-op-den-Berg, Belg. 53/D1
Heitersheim, Ger. 56/D2
Heiwa, Japan 77/L5
Hejian, China 72/D3
Hejin, China 72/B4
Hejing, China 70/E3
Hekimhan, Turk. 90/D2
Hekinan, Japan 77/L6
Hekla (vol.), Ice. 37/N7
Hekou, China 83/H3
Hel, Pol. 39/H4
Helan (mts.), China 70/J4
Helbe (riv.), Ger. 51/H6
Helden, Neth. 50/D6
Helena (cap.), Mt, US 126/E4
Helena (riv.), Austl. 112/L6
Helensburgh, Sc, UK 36/B4
Helgasjön (lake), Swe. 38/F3
Helgoland (isl.), Ger. 38/B4
Helgoländer (bay), Wa, US 135/B3
Helgoländer (bay), Ger. 38/C5
Heliodora, Braz. 211/H7
Heliport (int'l arpt.), Swe. 38/E3
Hellas (see Greece) 27/G5
Ḩelleh (riv.), Iran 88/F3
Hellendoorn, Neth. 50/D4
Hellenthal, Ger. 53/F3
Hellertown, Pa, US 138/C2
Hellevoetsluis, Neth. 50/B5
Hellín, Sp. 44/E3
Hells (canyon), Id, US 126/D4
Hells Canyon Nat'l Rec. Area, US 126/D4
Hell's Gate NP, Kenya 104/C3
Helmand (riv.), Afg. 67/F6
Helmbrechts, Ger. 55/E2
Helmet (mtn.), Ak, US 134/K2
Helmetta, NJ, US 139/H10
Helmond, Neth. 50/C6
Helmstadt, Ger. 54/C3
Helmstedt, Ger. 40/F2
Helong, China 71/N3
Helotes, Tx, US 137/T20
Helper, Ut, US 128/E3
Helsenhorn (peak), Swi. 56/E5
Helsingør, Den. 38/E3
Helsinki (Helsingfors) (cap.), Fin. 37/H3
Helsinki-Vantaa (int'l arpt.), Fin. 39/L1
Hem (riv.), Fr. 52/B2
Hemau, Ger. 55/E4
Hemel Hempstead, Eng, UK 30/B1
Hemer, Ger. 51/E6
Hemet, Ca, US 136/D3
Hemmingen, Ger. 51/G4
Hemmoor, Ger. 51/G1
Hemphill, Tx, US 132/E4
Hempstead, Tx, US 129/H5
Hempstead (har.), NY, US 139/L8
Hempstead, NY, US 139/L9
Hemse, Swe. 38/H3
Hemsedal, Nor. 38/C1
Hemsworth, Eng, UK 35/G4
Henan (prov.), China 71/K5
Henån, Swe. 38/D2
Henares (riv.), Sp. 44/D2
Henashi-zaki (pt.), Japan 76/A3
Hendaye, Fr. 42/C5
Hendek, Turk. 49/K5
Henderson, NC, US 130/E4
Henderson, Nv, US 128/D3
Henderson, Tn, US 130/B5
Henderson, Ky, US 130/C4
Henderson, Co, US 137/C3
Henderson (isl.), Pitc. 117/N7
Henderson, Arg. 158/E3
Henderson, Md, US 138/C5
Hendersonville, Tn, US 130/C4
Hendersonville, NC, US 133/H3
Hendrik-Ido-Ambacht, Neth. 50/B5
Hendrik Verwoerdam (res.), SAfr. 106/D3
Hendrina, SAfr. 107/E2
Henefer, Ut, US 137/L11
Heng (mtn.), China 72/C3
Heng (isl.), China 72/L8
Heng Xian, China 83/J3
Hengduan (mts.), China 70/G6
Hengelo, Neth. 50/D4
Hengersberg, Ger. 55/G5
Hengoed, Wal, UK 32/C3
Hengshan, China 79/B2
Hengshan, China 72/B3
Hengshui, China 72/C3
Hengyang, China 79/B2
Heniches'k, Ukr. 62/E3
Hénin-Beaumont, Fr. 52/B3
Henley-on-Thames, Eng, UK 33/F3
Henlopen (cape), De, US 138/C6
Henlopen Acres, De, US 138/C6
Henndorf am Wallersee, Aus. 55/G7
Henne, Den. 38/C4
Hennebont, Fr. 42/B3
Hennef, Ger. 53/G2
Hennenman, SAfr. 106/D2
Hennigsdorf, Ger. 40/Q6
Henrietta, Tx, US 129/H4
Henrietta Maria (cape), On, Can. 123/H3
Henry (cape), BC, Can. 134/M5
Henry (mts.), Ut, US 128/E3
Henry Ford Museum and Greenfield Village Historical Site, Mi, US 135/E7
Henryetta, Ok, US 129/J4
Henryville, Pa, US 138/C1
Hensies, Belg. 52/C3
Hentiy (prov.), Mong. 71/J2
Hentiyn (mts.), Mong. 70/J2
Henty, Austl. 115/C2
Henzada, Myan. 83/G4
Heping, China 79/B3
Heppenheim an der Bergstrasse, Ger. 54/B3
Hepu, China 83/J3
Heqing, China 83/H2
Hequ, China 72/B3
Heradhsvötn (riv.), Ice. 37/N6
Herāt, Afg. 89/H2
Herbert, Sk, Can. 126/G3
Herbert River (falls), Austl. 114/B2
Herbert River Falls NP, Austl. 114/B2
Herberton, Austl. 114/B2
Herbeumont, Belg. 53/E4
Herblay, Fr. 30/J5
Herbolzheim, Ger. 56/D1
Herbrechtingen, Ger. 54/D5
Herbstein, Ger. 54/C1
Hercegnovi, Yugo. 47/F1
Hercílio Luz (int'l arpt.), Braz. 155/B3
Herculaneum, Mo, US 137/G9
Herculaneum (ruin), It. 46/D2
Hercules, Ca, US 135/K10
Herdecke, Ger. 51/E6
Herdorf, Ger. 53/G2
Heredia, CR 145/E4
Hereford, Tx, US 129/G4
Hereford, Eng, UK 32/D2
Hereford, Pa, US 138/C3
Hereford (inlet), NJ, US 138/D5
Hereford, Md, US 138/B4
Hereford and Worcester (co.), Eng, UK 32/D2
Hereheretue (isl.), FrPol. 117/L7
Hereke, Turk. 49/J5
Herencia, Sp. 44/C3
Herentals, Belg. 50/B6
Herford, Ger. 51/F4
Hergiswil, Swi. 57/E4
Héricourt, Fr. 56/C2
Hérimoncourt, Fr. 56/C3
Herington, Ks, US 129/H3
Herisau, Swi. 57/F3
Herk (riv.), Belg. 53/E2
Herk-de-Stad, Belg. 53/E2
Hèrlèn Gol (Kerulen) (riv.), Mong. 71/K2
Herleshausen, Ger. 51/H6
Herma Ness (cape), Sc, UK 31/W13
Hermann, Mo, US 129/K3
Hermannsburg, Ger. 51/H3
Hermannsburg, Austl. 113/G2
Hermannsburg Abor. Land, Austl. 113/G2
Hermansverk, Nor. 38/B1
Hermanus, SAfr. 106/L11
Hermeray, Fr. 30/G6
Hermersberg, Ger. 53/G5
Hermes, Fr. 52/B5
Hermeskeil, Ger. 53/F4
Hermiston, Or, US 126/D4
Hermitage, Rus. 61/T7
Hermosa Beach, Ca, US 136/F8
Hermosillo, Mex. 142/C2
Hermsdorf, Ger. 40/G6
Hernández, Mex. 142/E4
Hernando, Ms, US 129/K4
Hernani, Sp. 44/E1
Herndon, Pa, US 138/B2
Herne, Ger. 51/E5
Herne, Belg. 52/D2
Herne Bay, Eng, UK 33/H4
Herning, Den. 38/C3
Heroes de la Independencia, Mex. 142/B2
Heroica Caborca, Mex. 142/B2
Heroica Ciudad de Tlaxiaco, Mex. 144/B2
Heroica Matamoros, Mex. 132/D5
Heroica Nogales, Mex. 128/E5
Heroldsberg, Ger. 54/E3
Hérouville, Fr. 30/J4
Hérouville-Saint-Clair, Fr. 42/C2
Herøy, Nor. 37/C3
Herpf (riv.), Ger. 54/D1
Herre, Nor. 38/C2
Herrenberg, Ger. 54/B5
Herrera, Sp. 44/C4
Herrera de Pisuerga, Sp. 44/C1
Herrera del Duque, Sp. 44/C3
Herrero (pt.), Mex. 144/E2
Herrestad, Swe. 38/D2
Herrieden, Ger. 54/D4
Herriman, Ut, US 137/J12
Herrlisheim, Fr. 53/G6
Herrljunga, Swe. 38/E2
Herrsching am Ammersee, Ger. 57/H2
Hers (riv.), Fr. 42/D5
Hersbruck, Ger. 55/E3
Herschbach, Ger. 53/G2
Herscheid, Ger. 51/E6
Herselt, Belg. 53/D1
Hershey, Pa, US 138/B3
Hersheypark, Pa, US 138/B3
Herstal, Belg. 53/E2
Herten, Ger. 51/E5
Hertford, NC, US 133/J2
Hertford, Eng, UK 33/F3
Herval d'Oeste, Braz. 155/B3
Hervás, Sp. 44/C2
Herve, Belg. 53/E2
Hervey (bay), Austl. 109/E3
Hervey Bay, Austl. 114/D4
Hervey Bay (reef), Austl. 114/D3
Herxheim bei Landau, Ger. 54/B4
Herzberg am Harz, Ger. 51/H5
Herzebrock-Clarholz, Ger. 51/F5
Herzele, Belg. 52/C2
Herzliyya, Isr. 91/F7
Herzogenaurach, Ger. 54/D3
Herzogenbuchsee, Swi. 56/D3
Herzogenburg, Aus. 48/B1
Herzogenrath, Ger. 53/F2
Hesbaye (plat.), Belg. 40/C3
Hesdin, Fr. 52/B3
Hesel, Ger. 51/E2
Heshui, China 70/J4
Heshun, China 72/C3
Hésingue, Fr. 56/D2
Hesperange, Lux. 53/F4
Hesperia, Ca, US 136/C2
Hess (riv.), Yk, Can. 122/C2
Hessel (riv.), Ger. 51/F5
Hesselø (isl.), Den. 38/D3
Hessen (state), Ger. 43/H1
Hessen, Ger. 51/H4
Hessisch Lichtenau, Ger. 51/G6
Hessisch Oldendorf, Ger. 51/G4
Hetauḍā, Nepal 85/E2
Heteren, Neth. 50/C5
Hettenleidelheim, Ger. 54/B3
Hettinger, ND, US 127/H4
Hetton-le-Hole, Eng, UK 35/G2
Hettstadt, Ger. 54/C3
Hetzerath, Ger. 53/F4
Heubach (riv.), Ger. 51/E5
Heubach, Ger. 54/C5
Heuchelheim, Ger. 54/B1
Heukuppe (peak), Aus. 41/H5
Heusden, Neth. 50/C5
Heusden-Zolder, Belg. 53/E1
Heusenstamm, Ger. 54/B2
Heusweiler, Ger. 53/F5
Hève, Cap de la (cape), Fr. 42/D2
Heves, Hun. 48/E2
Heves (co.), Hun. 41/L5
Hewitt, NJ, US 139/H7
Hewlett (pt.), NY, US 139/L8
Hewlett, NY, US 139/L9
Hex River (mts.), SAfr. 106/L10
Hex River (pass), SAfr. 106/L10
Hexenkopf (peak), Aus. 57/G3
Heyerode, Ger. 51/H6
Heythuysen, Neth. 50/C6
Heywood, Austl. 115/B3
Heywood, Eng, UK 35/F4
Heze, China 72/C4
Hialeah, Fl, US 133/H5
Hiawatha, Ks, US 129/J3
Hibbing, Mn, US 127/K4
Hibbs (pt.), Austl. 115/C4
Hicacos (pt.), Cuba 145/F1
Hichisō, Japan 77/M4
Hickman (mt.), BC, Can. 134/M4
Hickory, NC, US 133/H3
Hickory, La, US 137/Q16
Hickory Run State Park, Pa, US 138/C1
Hicksville, NY, US 139/L8
Hico, Tx, US 129/H5
Hida (riv.), Japan 75/E3
Hidaka (riv.), Japan 74/D4
Hidaka, Japan 76/C2
Hidaka (mts.), Japan 76/C2
Hidaka, Japan 77/C2
Hidalgo, Mex. 143/F3
Hidalgo (state), Mex. 140/B3
Hidalgo del Parral, Mex. 142/D3
Hidden Hills, Ca, US 136/B2
Hiddenhausen, Ger. 51/F4
Hidrolândia, Braz. 154/B2
Hierapolis (ruin), Turk. 90/B2
Hieroglyphic (mts.), Az, US 137/R18
Hierro (isl.) 96/B2
Hieve (lake), Ger. 51/E2
Higashi-Chichibu, Japan 77/C1
Higashi-Matsuyama, Japan 77/C1
Higashi-Ōsaka, Japan 77/J6
Higashikurume, Japan 77/D2
Higashimurayama, Japan 77/C2
Higashine, Japan 76/B4
Higashiura, Japan 77/G6
Higashiura, Japan 77/L6
Higashiyoshino, Japan 77/J7
High (des.), Or, US 126/C5
High (hill), Pa, US 138/C1
High (isl.), China 71/V10
High Bridge, NJ, US 138/D2
High Island, Tx, US 132/E4
High Level, Ab, Can. 122/E3
High Point, NC, US 133/H3
High Ridge, Mo, US 137/F9
High River, Ab, Can. 126/E3
High Street (peak), Eng, UK 35/F3
High Willhays (hill), Eng, UK 32/B5
High Wycombe, Eng, UK 33/F3
Higham, Eng, UK 30/E2
Higham Ferrers, Eng, UK 33/F2
Highland, Ca, US 136/C2
Highland, Ut, US 137/K13
Highland, In, US 135/R16
Highland (pol. reg.), Sc, UK 36/A2
Highland Lakes, NJ, US 138/D1
Highland Park, Co, US 137/A4

193

Highl – Humbo

Highland Park, NJ, US 139/H10
Highland Park, Mi, US 135/F7
Highlands, NJ, US 139/K10
Highrock (lake), Mb, Can. 127/H2
Highspire, Pa, US 138/B3
Hightstown, NJ, US 138/D3
Highwood, Il, US 135/Q15
Higley, Az, US 137/S19
Higuera de Zaragoza, Mex. 142/C3
Hihyā, Egypt 91/B4
Hiidenportin NP, Fin. 60/F3
Hiiumaa (isl.), Est. 60/D4
Híjar, Sp. 45/E2
Hijāz, Jabal al (mts.), SAr. 88/C3
Hiji, Japan 74/B4
Hijuelas de Conchali, Chile 158/N8
Hikami, Japan 77/H5
Hikari, Japan 77/F2
Hikone, Japan 77/K5
Hikueru (isl.), FrPol. 117/L6
Hikurangi (peak), NZ 117/T10
Hildburghausen, Ger. 54/D2
Hilden, Ger. 53/F1
Hilders, Ger. 54/C1
Hildesheim, Ger. 51/G4
Hilgermissen, Ger. 51/G3
Hill (isl.), Pa, US 138/B3
Hill City, Ks, US 129/H3
Hill of Fare (hill), Sc, UK 36/D2
Hill of Stake (hill), Sc, UK 36/B5
Hillaby (mt.), Bar. 141/P9
Hillburn, NY, US 139/J7
Hillcrest, NY, US 139/J7
Hille, Ger. 51/F4
Hillegom, Neth. 50/B4
Hillerød, Den. 38/E4
Hillesheim, Ger. 53/F3
Hillingdon (bor.), Eng, UK 30/B2
Hillsboro, ND, US 127/J4
Hillsboro, Or, US 126/C4
Hillsboro, Tx, US 129/H4
Hillsboro, Oh, US 130/D4
Hillsboro, Md, US 138/C6
Hillsborough (chan.), Austl. 114/C3
Hillsborough, NJ, US 138/D3
Hillsborough, Ca, US 135/K11
Hillsdale, Mi, US 130/C3
Hillsdale, Ks, US 137/D6
Hillsdale (lake), Ks, US 137/D6
Hillsdale, NJ, US 139/J7
Hillside, NJ, US 139/J9
Hillside, Sc, UK 36/D3
Hillston, Austl. 115/C2
Hillswick, Sc, UK 31/W13
Hilltop, Co, US 137/C4
Hilltown, NI, UK 34/B3
Hilo, Hi, US 124/U11
Hilonghilong (mt.), Phil. 81/G2
Hilongos, Phil. 79/D5
Hilpoltstein, Ger. 54/E4
Hilpsford (pt.), Eng, UK 35/E3
Hilsa, India 85/E3
Hilterfingen, Swi. 56/D4
Hilton Head (isl.), SC, US 133/H3
Hilton Head Island, SC, US 133/H3
Hilvarenbeek, Neth. 50/C6
Hilversum, Neth. 50/C4
Hilzingen, Ger. 57/E2
Himāchal Pradesh (state), India 70/C5
Himalaya (range), Asia 67/G6
Himālchuli (peak), Nepal 85/E1
Himamaylan, Phil. 79/D5
Himanka, Fin. 60/D2
Himberg, Aus. 49/N7
Himeji, Japan 74/D3
Himeji Castle, Japan 74/D3
Himi, Japan 75/E2
Himmelpforten, Ger. 51/G1
Ḩimş (prov.), Syria 90/D3
Ḩimş, Syria 91/E2
Hinche, Haiti 145/H2
Hinchinbrook (isl.), Austl. 109/D2
Hinchinbrook Entrance (chan.) 134/J3
Hinchinbrook Island, Austl. 114/B2
Hinckley, Eng, UK 33/E1
Hincks Conservation Park, Austl. 113/H5
Hindan (riv.), India 84/A1
Hindaun, India 84/A2
Hindelang, Ger. 57/G3
Hindeloopen, Neth. 50/C3
Hindley, Eng, UK 35/F4
Hindmarsh (lake), Austl. 115/B3
Hindu Kush (mts.), Asia 67/F6
Hindupur, India 82/C5
Hinesville, Ga, US 133/H4
Hinganghāt, India 82/C3
Hingol (riv.), Pak. 89/J3
Hingoli, India 82/C4
Hingorja, Pak. 89/J3
Hınıs, Turk. 63/G5
Hino, Japan 77/K5
Hino, Japan 77/C2
Hino (riv.), Japan 77/K5
Hino-misaki (cape), Japan 74/C3
Hinode, Japan 77/C2
Hinohara, Japan 77/C2
Hinojosa del Duque, Sp. 44/C3
Hinsdale, Il, US 135/Q16
Hinte, Ger. 51/E2
Hinterbrühl, Aus. 49/N7
Hinterrhein (riv.), Swi. 57/F4
Hinterrugg (peak), Swi. 57/F3
Hinterweidenthal, Ger. 53/G5
Hinton, Ab, Can. 126/D2
Hinton, WV, US 130/D4
Hinwil, Swi. 57/E3
Hipólito Bouchard, Arg. 158/E2
Hippolytushoef, Neth. 50/B3
Hipswell, Eng, UK 35/G3
Hira Highlands (uplands), Japan 77/J5
Hirado, Japan 74/A4
Hirakata, Japan 77/J6
Hirakud (res.), India 82/D3
Hiraman (riv.), Kenya 104/C3
Hiran (riv.), India 84/B4
Hiranai, Japan 76/B3
Hirara, Japan 75/H8
Hirata, Japan 74/C3
Hirata, Japan 77/L5
Hiratsuka, Japan 77/C3
Hirfanli (dam), Turk. 62/E5
Hîrlău, Rom. 49/H2
Hiro'o, Japan 76/C2
Hirosaki, Japan 76/B3
Hiroshima, Japan 74/C3
Hiroshima (pref.), Japan 74/C3
Hirschaid, Ger. 54/D3
Hirschau, Ger. 55/E3
Hirschhorn, Ger. 54/B4
Hirson, Fr. 53/D4
Hîrşova, Rom. 49/H3
Hirtshals, Den. 38/C3
Hirukawa, Japan 77/M4
Hisai, Japan 77/K6
Hisarcık, Turk. 62/D5
Ḩisbān, Jor. 91/D4
Ḩişn al 'Abr, Yem. 88/E5
Hispaniola (isl.), DRep.,Hait 141/G4
Historic Houses of Odessa, De, US 138/C5
Historic Towne of Smithville, NJ, US 138/D5
Hisua, India 85/E3
Hīt, Iraq 90/E3
Hitachi, Japan 75/G2
Hitachi-Ōta, Japan 75/G2
Hitchin, Eng, UK 33/F3
Hitoyoshi, Japan 74/B4
Hitra (isl.), Nor. 37/C3
Hittisau, Aus. 57/F3
Hitzacker, Ger. 40/F2
Hitzkirch, Swi. 57/E3
Hiyoshi, Japan 77/J5
Hizan, Turk. 90/E2
Hjålmaren (lake), Swe. 38/G2
Hjartfjellet (peak), Nor. 37/E2
Hjelmeland, Nor. 38/B2
Hjerm, Den. 38/C3
Hjo, Swe. 38/F2
Hjørring, Den. 38/C3
Hka (riv.), Myan. 78/B1
Hkakabo (peak), Myan. 83/G2
Hlabisa, SAfr. 107/E3
Hlohovec, Slvk. 48/C1
Hluboká nad Vltava, Czh. 55/H4
Hluhluwe, SAfr. 107/F3
Hlukhiv, Ukr. 62/E2
Hmawbi, Myan. 83/G4
Ho, Gha. 103/F5
Hoa Binh, Viet. 78/D1
Hoare (bay), Nun., Can. 123/K2
Hobara, Japan 75/G2
Hobart, Austl. 115/C4
Hobart (int'l arpt.), Austl. 115/C4
Hobart, Wa, US 135/D3
Hobbs, NM, US 129/G4
Hoboken, Belg. 50/B6
Hoboken, NJ, US 139/J9
Hoboksar Monggol Zizhixian, China 70/E2
Hobro, Den. 38/C3
Hochalmspitze (peak), Aus. 43/K3
Höchberg, Ger. 54/C3
Hochdorf, Ger. 57/F1
Hochfelden, Fr. 53/G6
Hochfinsler (peak), Swi. 57/F3
Hochgrat (peak), Ger. 57/G3
Hochheim am Main, Ger. 54/B2
Hochkönig (peak), Aus. 43/K3
Hŏch'ŏn (riv.), NKor. 73/D2
Hochschwab (peak), Aus. 43/L3
Hochsimmer (peak), Ger. 53/G3
Hochspeyer, Ger. 53/G5
Höchst, Aus. 57/F3
Höchst im Odenwald, Ger. 54/B3
Hochstadt am Main, Ger. 54/E2
Höchstadt an der Aisch, Ger. 54/D3
Hochstädt an der Donau, Ger. 54/D5
Hochstetten-Dhaun, Ger. 53/G4
Hochvogel (peak), Aus. 57/G3
Hochwang (peak), Swi. 57/F4
Hockenheim, Ger. 54/B4
Hockessin, De, US 138/C4
Hockley, Eng, UK 30/F2
Hod Hasharon, Isr. 91/F7
Hodal, India 84/A2
Hodder (riv.), Eng, UK 35/F4
Hoddesdon, Eng, UK 30/D1
Hodenhagen, Ger. 51/G3
Hodges (lake), Ca, US 136/C4
Hodgeville, Sk, Can. 126/G3
Hodh (phys. reg.), Mrta. 102/C2
Hodh El Gharbi (pol. reg.), Mrta. 102/C2
Hódmezővásáhely, Hun. 48/E2
Hodonín, Czh. 41/J4
Hoekse Waard (isl.), Neth. 50/B5
Hoensbroek, Neth. 53/E2
Hoeselt, Belg. 53/E2
Hoevelaken, Neth. 50/C4
Hoeven, Neth. 50/B5
Hoeybuktmoen (int'l arpt.), Nor. 37/J1
Hof, Ger. 55/E2
Hofbieber, Ger. 54/C1
Höfdhakaupstadhur, Ice. 37/N6
Hoffman Estates, Il, US 135/P15
Hofgeismar, Ger. 51/G6
Hofheim am Taunus, Ger. 54/B2
Hofheim in Unterfranken, Ger. 54/D2
Hofmeyr, SAfr. 106/D3
Hofong Qagan Salt (lake), China 72/B3
Hofors, Swe. 38/G1
Hofsá (riv.), Ice. 37/P6
Hofsjökull (glacier), Ice. 37/N7
Hōfu, Japan 74/B3
Hogarth (mt.), Austl. 113/H2
Hogyész, Hun. 48/D2
Hoh Xil (mts.), China 70/E4
Höhbürd, Mong. 70/H2
Hohe Acht (peak), Ger. 53/G3
Hohe Geige (peak), Aus. 57/G4
Hohe Tauern (mts.), Aus. 43/K3
Hohe Tauern NP, Aus. 43/K3
Hohegrass (peak), Ger. 51/G6
Hohen Neuendorf, Ger. 40/Q6
Hohenbrunn, Ger. 55/E6
Hohenems, Aus. 57/F3
Hohenhameln, Ger. 51/H4
Hohenlinden, Ger. 55/F6
Hohenlockstedt, Ger. 40/E2
Hohenloher Ebene (plain), Ger. 40/E4
Hohenpeissenberg, Ger. 57/G2
Hohenroth, Ger. 54/D2
Hoher Dachstein (peak), Aus. 43/K3
Hoher Ifen (peak), Ger. 57/G3
Hoher Randen (peak), Ger. 57/E2
Hohgant (peak), Swi. 56/D4
Hohhot, China 71/K3
Höhn, Ger. 53/G2
Hohneck (peak), Fr. 56/D1
Hohnstorf, Ger. 51/H2
Hohokam Pima Nat'l Mon., Az, US 128/E4
Höhr-Grenzhausen, Ger. 53/G3
Hoi An, Viet. 78/E3
Hoima, Ugan. 104/A2
Hoisington, Ks, US 129/H3
Højby, Den. 38/D4
Højer, Den. 38/C4
Hōjō, Japan 74/C4
Hokitika, NZ 117/S11
Hokkaidō (isl.), Japan 67/P5
Hokksund, Nor. 38/C2
Hokota, Japan 75/G2
Hokudan, Japan 77/G6
Hokusei, Japan 77/L5
Hol, Nor. 38/C1
Holbox, Mex. 144/E1
Holbrook, Austl. 115/C2
Holbrook, Az, US 128/E4
Holbrook, NY, US 139/E2
Holderness (pen.), Eng, UK 35/H4
Holdorf, Ger. 51/F3
Holdrege, Ne, US 129/H2
Holeby, Den. 38/D4
Holguín, Cuba 145/G1
Holiday Hills, Il, US 135/P15
Holitna (riv.), Ak, US 134/G3
Höljes, Swe. 38/E1
Holladay-Cottonwood, Ut, US 137/K12
Holland, Mi, US 130/C3
Holland (pt.), Md, US 138/B6
Hollandale, Ms, US 129/K4
Hollandse IJssel (riv.), Neth. 50/B5
Hollandstoun, Sc, UK 31/V14
Hollenstedt, Ger. 51/G2
Hollfeld, Ger. 54/E3
Holliday, Ks, US 137/D5
Hollis, Ok, US 129/H4
Hollis, Ak, US 134/M4
Hollister, Ca, US 128/B3
Hollister (mt.), Austl. 112/B2
Hollogne-aux-Pierres, Belg. 53/E2
Hollola, Fin. 39/L1
Höllviksnäs, Swe. 38/E4
Holly, Wa, US 135/B2
Holly Springs, Ms, US 133/F3
Hollywood, Fl, US 133/H5
Hollywood Bowl, Ca, US 136/F7
Hollywood Park, Tx, US 137/U20
Holm, Ger. 51/G1
Holman, NW, Can. 122/E1
Hólmavík, Ice. 37/N6
Holmdel, NJ, US 138/D3
Holmes (reefs), Austl. 109/D2
Holmesdale (valley), Eng, UK 30/C3
Holmestrand, Nor. 38/D2
Holmfirth, Eng, UK 35/G4
Holmsjön (lake), Swe. 37/F3
Holmsund, Swe. 37/G3
Ḥolon, Isr. 91/F7
Holstebro, Den. 38/C3
Holston (riv.), Tn, US 133/H2
Holt, Mo, US 137/E5
Holt, Ca, US 135/M11
Holtålen, Nor. 37/D3
Holten, Neth. 50/D4
Holtland, Ger. 51/E2
Holton, Ks, US 129/J3
Holtsville, NY, US 139/E2
Holy (isl.), Sc, UK 36/A5
Holy Cross, Ak, US 134/G3
Holyhead, Wal, UK 34/D5
Holyoke, Co, US 129/G2
Holyoke, Ma, US 131/F3
Holywell, Wal, UK 35/E5
Holywood, NI, UK 34/C2
Holzkirchen, Ger. 43/J3
Holzminden, Ger. 51/G5
Holzwickede, Ger. 51/E5
Hom (riv.), Namb. 106/B3
Homberg, Ger. 51/G6
Homberg, Ger. 50/D6
Hombori Tondo (peak), Mali 103/E3
Hombourg-Haut, Fr. 53/F5
Homburg, Ger. 53/G5
Home (bay), Nun., Can. 123/K2
Home Hill, Austl. 114/B2
Homécourt, Fr. 53/E5
Homeland, Ca, US 136/C3
Homer, Ak, US 134/H4
Homer, La, US 129/J4
Homestead, Fl, US 133/H5
Homestead Nat'l Mon. of America, Ne, US 129/H2
Homewood, Al, US 133/G3
Homewood, Il, US 135/Q16
Homib (riv.), Erit. 88/C5
Hommersåk, Nor. 38/A2
Homochitto (riv.), Ms, US 132/F4
Homyel', Bela. 62/D1
Homyel'skaya (prov.), Bela. 62/D1
Hon Quan, Viet. 78/D4
Honaunau-Napoopoo, Hi, US 124/U11
Honbetsu, Japan 76/C2
Honddu (riv.), Wal, UK 32/C2
Hondeklipbaai, SAfr. 106/B3
Hondo, Tx, US 129/H5
Hondo, Japan 74/B4
Hondo (riv.), Belz. 144/D2
Hondschoote, Fr. 52/B2
Hondsrug (reg.), Neth. 50/D3
Hondsrug (hills), Neth. 40/D2
Honduras (gulf), NAm. 144/E2
Honduras (ctry.) 144/D3
Honey (lake), Ca, US 126/C5
Honey Brook, Pa, US 138/C3
Honey Creek, Wi, US 135/P14
Hong (isl.), SKor. 73/C5
Hong (lake), China 72/C5
Hong (riv.), China 72/C4
Hong Gai, Viet. 83/J3
Hong Kong (dpcy.), China 67/L7
Hong Kong (isl.), China 71/U10
Hong'an, China 72/C5
Hongch'ŏn, SKor. 73/D4
Hongdu (riv.), China 83/J2
Honghu, China 79/B2
Hongjiang, China 83/J2
Hongqiao (int'l arpt.), China 72/L8
Hongshui (riv.), China 70/J6
Hongsŏng, SKor. 73/D4
Hongtong, China 72/B3
Honguedo (passg.), Qu, Can. 131/H1
Hongwŏn, NKor. 73/D2
Hongze, China 72/D4
Hœnheim, Fr. 53/G6
Honiara (cap.), Sol. 116/E5
Honjō, Japan 76/B4
Honjō, Japan 77/C1
Honolulu (cap.), Hi, US 124/T10
Honolulu (int'l arpt.), Hi, US 124/W13
Honolulu (co.), Hi, US 124/V13
Honouliuli, Hi, US 124/V13
Hönow, Ger. 40/Q6
Honshu (isl.), Japan 65/Q6
Honshū (isl.), Japan 67/P6
Hood (mt.), Or, US 126/C4
Hood (pt.), Austl. 112/C5
Hood, Ca, US 135/L10
Hood (mt.), Ca, US 135/J10
Hood Canal (str.), Wa, US 126/C4
Hoofddorp, Neth. 50/B4
Hoogeloon, Neth. 50/C6
Hoogeveen, Neth. 50/D3
Hoogeveense Vaart (canal), Neth. 50/D3
Hoogezand, Neth. 50/D2
Hooghly (riv.), India 85/F5
Hooghly-Chinsura, India 85/G4
Hoogkarspel, Neth. 50/C3
Hooglede, Belg. 52/C2
Hoogstraten, Belg. 50/B6
Hook (pt.), Ire. 31/Q10
Hook (sound), Austl. 114/C3
Hookena, Hi, US 124/U11
Hoonah, Ak, US 134/L4
Hooper, Ut, US 137/J11
Hooper Bay, Ak, US 134/E3
Hoopeston, Il, US 130/C3
Hoopstad, SAfr. 106/D2
Höör, Swe. 38/E4
Hoorn, Neth. 50/C3
Hoornse Hop (bay), Neth. 50/C3
Hoover (dam), Az, US 128/D3
Hoover, Mo, US 137/D5
Hopa, Turk. 63/G4
Hopatcong (lake), NJ, US 138/D2
Hopatcong, NJ, US 138/D2
Hope, Ak, US 134/J3
Hope, BC, Can. 126/C3
Hope (lake), Austl. 109/A4
Hope, NJ, US 138/D2
Hope Vale Aboriginal Community, Austl. 114/B1
Hopedale, Nf, Can. 123/K3
Hopelchén, Mex. 144/D2
Hopeman, Sc, UK 36/C1
Hopes Advance (cape), Qu, Can. 123/K2
Hope's Nose (pt.), Eng, UK 32/C6
Hopetown, SAfr. 106/D3
Hopewell, NJ, US 138/D3
Hopewell Furnace NHS, Pa, US 138/C3
Hopkins (riv.), Austl. 115/B3
Hopkins (lake), Austl. 109/B3
Hopkinsville, Ky, US 130/C4
Hoppecke (riv.), Ger. 51/F6
Hoppegarten, Ger. 40/Q6
Hopper Mtn. NWR, Ca, US 136/B2
Hoppstädten-Weiersbach, Ger. 53/G4
Hopsten, Ger. 51/E4
Hoquiam, Wa, US 126/C4
Horace (mtn.), Ak, US 134/J2
Horado, Japan 77/L4
Hōrai-san (peak), Japan 77/J5
Horasan, Turk. 63/G4
Horažďovice, Czh. 55/G4
Horb am Neckar, Ger. 54/B6
Horbourg-Wihr, Fr. 56/D1
Hörbranz, Aus. 57/F2
Horche, Sp. 44/D2
Horconcitos, Pan. 145/F4
Hordaland (co.), Nor. 37/C3
Hördt, Ger. 54/B4
Hœrdt, Fr. 53/G6
Horezu, Rom. 49/G3
Horgau, Ger. 54/D6
Horgen, Swi. 57/E3
Horine, Mo, US 137/G9
Horinger, China 72/B2
Horley, Eng, UK 30/C3
Horlivka, Ukr. 62/F2
Hormigüeros, PR 141/M8
Hormuz (str.), Oman 89/G3
Horn, Aus. 43/L2
Horn (pt.), Ice. 160/H
Horn-Bad Meinberg, Ger. 51/F5
Hornachuelos, Sp. 44/C4
Hornád (riv.), Slvk. 41/L4
Hornavan (lake), Swe. 37/F2
Hornbach, Ger. 53/G5
Hornberg, Ger. 57/E1
Horndal, Swe. 38/G1
Horneburg, Ger. 51/G1
Hornell, NY, US 130/E3
Horní Bříza, Czh. 55/G3
Horní Slavkov, Czh. 55/F2
Hornisgrinde (peak), Ger. 54/B5
Hornos (cape), Chile 159/D7
Hornoy-le-Bourg, Fr. 52/A4
Hornslet, Den. 38/D3
Hörnum (cape), Ger. 38/C4
Horoshiri-dake (peak), Japan 76/C2
Hořovice, Czh. 55/G3
Horqin Zuoyi Houqi, China 72/E2
Horqin Zuoyi Zhongqi, China 72/E1
Hörsching, Aus. 55/H6
Horse Cave, Ky, US 130/C4
Horsefly (lake), BC, Can. 126/C2
Horsens, Den. 38/C4
Horseshoe (lake), Il, US 137/G8
Horseshoe (lake), Co, US 137/B2
Horsetooth (res.), Co, US 137/B1
Horsey (isl.), Eng, UK 33/H3
Horsforth, Eng, UK 35/G4
Horsham, Austl. 115/B3
Horsham, Eng, UK 33/F4
Horsham, Pa, US 138/C3
Horšovský Týn, Czh. 55/F3
Horst, Neth. 50/D6
Hörstel, Ger. 51/E4
Horstmar, Ger. 51/E4
Horta, Azor., Port. 45/S12
Horten, Nor. 38/D2
Hortes, Fr. 56/B2
Hortobágyi NP, Hun. 62/B3
Horton (pt.), NY, US 139/F1
Horton (riv.), NW, Can. 122/D2
Høruphav, Den. 38/C4
Horusický Rybník (lake), Czh. 55/H4
Hørve, Den. 38/D4
Ḥorvot Dor, Isr. 91/F6
Horw, Swi. 57/E3
Horwich, Eng, UK 35/F4
Horwood (lake), On, Can. 130/D2
Hösbach, Ger. 54/C2
Hosenfeld, Ger. 54/C1
Hoshiārpur, India 86/C4
Hosingen, Lux. 53/F3
Hospental, Swi. 57/E4
Hosszúpereszteg, Hun. 48/C2
Hoste (isl.), Chile 159/C7
Hot Springs, SD, US 127/H5
Hot Springs NP, Ar, US 129/J4
Hotaka, Japan 75/E2
Hotaka-dake (peak), Japan 75/E2
Hotan, China 70/C4
Hotan (riv.), China 70/D4
Hotazel, SAfr. 106/C2
Hotont, Mong. 70/H2
Hottah (lake), NW, Can. 122/E2
Hottentot (bay), Namb. 106/A2
Hotton, Belg. 53/E3
Houari Boumedienne (int'l arpt.), Alg. 100/G4
Houdain, Fr. 52/B3
Houdan, Fr. 30/G5
Houet (prov.), Burk. 102/D4
Houffalize, Belg. 53/E3
Houghton Lake, Mi, US 130/C2
Houghton-le-Spring, Eng, UK 35/G2
Houilles, Fr. 30/J5
Houlton, Me, US 131/H2
Houma, China 72/B4
Houplines, Fr. 52/B2
Hourdel (pt.), Fr. 52/A3
Hourn, Loch (inlet), Sc, UK 36/A2
Hourtin, Fr. 42/C4
Housatonic (riv.), Ct, US 139/E1
House (range), Ut, US 128/D3
House Springs, Mo, US 137/F9
Housesteads Roman Fort, Eng, UK 35/F1
Houssen, Fr. 56/D1
Houston, Ak, US 134/J3
Houston, BC, Can. 126/B2
Houston, Mo, US 129/K3
Houston, Tx, US 129/J5
Houston, Ms, US 133/F3
Houston, De, US 138/C6
Houtbaai, SAfr. 106/L11
Houten, Neth. 50/C4
Houthulst, Belg. 52/B2
Houtman Abrolhos (isl.), Austl. 112/B4
Houtribdijk (dam), Neth. 50/C3
Houtskär (isl.), Fin. 39/J1
Houyet, Belg. 53/E3
Hov, Nor. 38/D1
Hova, Swe. 38/F2
Hovd (prov.), Mong. 70/F2
Hovd, Mong. 70/F2
Hövelhof, Ger. 51/F5
Hovenweep Nat'l Mon., Ut, US 128/E3
Hovfjället (peak), Swe. 38/E1
Hovmantorp, Swe. 38/F3
Hövsgöl (prov.), Mong. 70/G1
Hovsta, Swe. 38/F2
Howard (pass), Ak, US 134/G2
Howard (hill), Ak, US 134/H2
Howard, Austl. 114/D4
Howard (co.), Md, US 138/B5
Howard Hanson (res.), Wa, US 135/D3
Howard Hanson (dam), Wa, US 135/D3
Howe (cape), Austl. 115/D3
Howe of the Mearns (reg.), Sc, UK 36/D3
Howell, Mi, US 130/D3
Howell, NJ, US 138/D3
Howick, SAfr. 107/E3
Howland (isl.), Pac., US 117/H4
Höxter, Ger. 51/G5
Hoxud, China 70/E3
Hoy (isl.), Sc, UK 31/V14
Hoya, Ger. 51/G3
Hōya, Japan 77/D2
Høyanger, Nor. 38/B1
Hoyerswerda, Ger. 41/H3
Hoylake, Eng, UK 35/E5
Hoyland Nether, Eng, UK 35/G4
Hoyo de Manzanares, Sp. 45/N8
Hoyos, Sp. 44/B2
Hoyoux (riv.), Belg. 53/E3
Hozumi, Japan 77/L5
Hracholusky (res.), Czh. 55/F3
Hradec Králové, Czh. 41/H3
Hradište (peak), Czh. 55/G2
Hrasnica, Bosn. 48/D4
Hrastnik, Slov. 43/L3
Hrazdan, Arm. 63/H4
Hrodna, Bela. 39/K5
Hrodzyenskaya (obl.), Bela. 60/E5
Hrolleifsborg (peak), Ice. 37/M6
Hron (riv.), Slvk. 62/A2
Hronov, Czh. 41/J3
Hrubieszów, Pol. 41/M3
Hrubý Jeseník (mts.), Czh.,Pol. 41/J3
Hrútafjöll (peak), Ice. 37/P6
Hsinchu, Tai. 79/D3
Hua (peak), China 72/B4
Hua Hin, Thai. 78/B3
Hua Xian, China 72/C4
Hua'an, China 79/C2
Huacaybamba, Peru 156/B3
Huachi, China 70/J4
Huacho, Peru 156/B3
Huachón, Peru 156/C3
Huachuca City, Az, US 128/E5
Huacrachuco, Peru 156/B3
Huade, China 71/K3
Huahine (isl.), FrPol. 117/K6
Huai (riv.), China 72/C4
Huai'an, China 72/C2
Huai'an, China 72/D4
Huaibei, China 71/L5
Huaibin, China 72/C4
Huaiji, China 83/K3
Huailai, China 72/G6
Huainan, China 72/D4
Huairen, China 72/C3
Huairou, China 72/H6
Huaiyang, China 72/C4
Huaiyin, China 72/D4
Huaiyin, China 72/D4
Huaiyuan, China 72/D4
Huajicori, Mex. 142/D4
Huajuapan de León, Mex. 144/B2
Hualahuises, Mex. 143/F3
Hualañé, Chile 158/C2
Hualgayoc, Peru 156/B2
Hualien, Tai. 79/D3
Hualla, Peru 156/C4
Huallaga (riv.), Peru 147/B3
Huallanca, Peru 156/B3
Huallanca, Peru 156/B3
Huamachuco, Peru 156/B2
Huamantanga, Peru 156/B3
Huamantla, Mex. 143/M7
Huambo, Ang. 105/C3
Huambos, Peru 156/B2
Huan (riv.), China 72/C5
Huan Xian, China 70/J4
Huancané, Peru 156/D4
Huancapi, Peru 156/C4
Huancaspata, Peru 156/B3
Huancavelica (dept.), Peru 156/C4
Huancavelica, Peru 156/C4
Huancayo, Peru 156/C4
Huanchaca (peak), Bol. 150/E8
Huang (riv.), China 67/L6
Huangchuan, China 72/C4
Huanggang (peak), China 79/C2
Huanghua, China 72/D3
Huangling, China 72/B4
Huanglong, China 72/B4
Huangping, China 83/J2
Huangqi (lake), China 72/C2
Huangshan, China 79/C2
Huangtang (lake), China 72/C5
Huangtu (plat.), China 72/B4
Huanguelén, Arg. 158/E3
Huangyan, China 79/D2
Huangzhong, China 70/H4
Huanren, China 73/C2
Huanta, Peru 156/C4
Huantai, China 72/D3
Huántar, Peru 156/B3
Huánuco (dept.), Peru 156/C3
Huánuco, Peru 156/B3
Huanuni, Bol. 150/E7
Huapi (mts.), Nic. 144/E3
Huaquechula, Mex. 143/L8
Huaquillas, Ecu. 156/A1
Huaral, Peru 156/B3
Huaraz, Peru 156/B3
Huari, Peru 156/B3
Huaricolca, Peru 156/C3
Huarina, Bol. 156/D5
Huarmey, Peru 156/B3
Huarochirí, Peru 156/B4
Huarocondo, Peru 156/C4
Huarong, China 79/B2
Huásabas, Mex. 142/C2
Huasahuasi, Peru 156/C3
Huascarán (peak), Peru 156/B3
Huatabampo, Mex. 142/C3
Huatunas (lake), Bol. 150/E6
Huatuxco, Mex. 143/N7
Huauchinango, Mex. 143/L6
Huaura, Peru 156/B3
Huautla de Jiménez, Mex. 144/B2
Huayacocotla, Mex. 143/L6
Huaying, China 79/A1
Huaylas, Peru 156/B3
Huayllay, Peru 156/B3
Huayopata, Peru 156/C4
Huayuan, China 83/J2
Huazhou, China 83/K3
Hubbard (mt.), Ak, US 134/L3
Hubbard Creek (res.), Tx, US 129/H4
Hubei (prov.), China 71/K5
Hubei (pass), China 72/B4
Hubli-Dhārwār, India 89/L5
Huch'ang, NKor. 73/D2
Hückelhoven, Ger. 53/F1
Hückeswagen, Ger. 53/G1
Hucknall, Eng, UK 35/G5
Huddersfield, Eng, UK 35/G4
Huddinge, Swe. 38/G2
Hude, Ger. 51/F2
Hudiksvall, Swe. 38/G1
Hudson (riv.), NJ,NY, US 130/F3
Hudson, NY, US 130/F3
Hudson, Co, US 137/C2
Hudson (str.), Nun.,Qu, Can. 123/J2
Hudson (bay), Can. 123/H2
Hudson, Qu, Can. 131/M7
Hudson (cape), Ant. 160/L
Hudson (co.), NJ, US 139/J9
Hudson Bay, Sk, Can. 127/H2
Hudson's Hope, BC, Can. 122/D3
Hue, Viet. 78/D2
Huedin, Rom. 49/F2
Huehuetenango, Guat. 144/D3
Huehuetla, Mex. 143/L6
Huehuetlán, Mex. 143/L8
Huejotzingo, Mex. 143/L7
Huejuquilla el Alto, Mex. 142/E4
Huejutla de Reyes, Mex. 144/B1
Huelma, Sp. 44/D4
Huelva, Sp. 44/B4
Huelva (riv.), Sp. 44/B4
Huequi (vol.), Chile 158/B4
Huercal-Overa, Sp. 44/E4
Huerfano (riv.), Co, US 129/F3
Huesca, Sp. 45/E1
Huéscar, Sp. 44/D4
Huetamo de Nuñez, Mex. 143/E5
Huete, Sp. 44/D2
Huexoculco, Mex. 143/R10
Hüfingen, Ger. 57/E2
Hugh Town, Eng, UK 31/Q12
Hughenden, Austl. 114/B3
Hughenden Valley, Eng, UK 30/A2
Hughes, Ak, US 134/H2
Hughes, Arg. 158/E2
Hughesville, Pa, US 138/B1
Huglfing, Ger. 57/H2
Hugli (riv.), India 82/E3
Hugo, Ok, US 129/J4
Huguan, China 72/C3
Hui Xian, China 72/C4
Hui'an, China 79/C2
Huib-Hock (plat.), Namb. 106/B2
Huichang, China 79/C2
Huichapan, Mex. 143/K6
Hŭich'ŏn, NKor. 73/D2
Huila (dept.), Col. 152/C4
Huila, Nevado del (peak), Col. 152/C4
Huilai, China 79/C3
Huilango, Mex. 143/Q9
Huili, China 83/H2
Huimanguillo, Mex. 144/C2
Huimin, China 72/D3
Huinca Renancó, Arg. 158/D2
Huining, China 70/J4
Hŭisaek-pong (peak), NKor. 73/D2
Huishui, China 83/J2
Huisne (riv.), Fr. 42/D2
Huissen, Neth. 50/C5
Huitong, China 83/J2
Huittinen, Fin. 39/K1
Huitzilan, Mex. 143/M7
Huitzuco, Mex. 143/K8
Huixcolotla, Mex. 143/M8
Huixquilucan, Mex. 143/Q10
Huixtla, Mex. 144/C3
Huize, China 83/H2
Huizen, Neth. 50/C4
Hujra, Pak. 86/B4
Hulan, China 71/N2
Hulett, Wy, US 127/G4
Hull, Qu, Can. 130/F2
Hull (riv.), Eng, UK 35/H4
Hullbridge, Eng, UK 30/E2
Hüllhorst, Ger. 51/F4
Hulst, Neth. 50/B6
Hultsfred, Swe. 38/F3
Huma, China 71/N1
Huma (riv.), China 65/N4
Humahuaca, Arg. 157/C1
Humaitá, Braz. 150/F5
Humansdorp, SAfr. 106/D4
Humay, Peru 156/C4
Humber (riv.), Nf, Can. 131/K1
Humber (bay), On, Can. 131/R8
Humber (riv.), Eng, UK 35/H4
Humberto de Campos, Braz. 154/B1
Humble, Tx, US 129/J5
Humboldt, Sk, Can. 127/G2
Humboldt (range), Nv, US 128/C2
Humboldt, Tn, US 130/B5
Humboldt (bay), Col. 145/G5

194
Humbo – 'Isfiy

Humboldt (riv.), Nv, US 124/C3
Hume (lake), Austl. 115/C2
Húmeda, Pampa (plain), Arg. 158/E2
Humenné, Slvk. 41/L4
Humida, Pampa (plain), Arg. 157/D4
Humlum, Den. 38/C3
Hummels Wharf, Pa, US 138/B2
Hummelstown, Pa, US 138/B3
Humphrey (pt.), Ak, US 134/K2
Humphreys (peak), Az, US 128/E4
Hūn, Libya 96/J2
Húnaflói (bay), Ice. 37/N6
Hunan (prov.), China 71/K6
Hundsangen, Ger. 53/G3
Hunedoara, Rom. 48/F3
Hunedoara (prov.), Rom. 48/F3
Hünenberg, Swi. 57/E3
Hünfeld, Ger. 43/H1
Hung Yen, Viet. 78/D1
Hungaroring, Hun. 49/R9
Hungary (ctry.) 48/D2
Hungen, Ger. 54/B2
Hŭngnam, NKor. 73/D3
Hunjiang, China 73/D2
Hunnebostrand, Swe. 38/D2
Hunsel, Neth. 50/C6
Hunsrück (mts.), Ger. 40/D4
Hunte (riv.), Ger. 40/E2
Hunter (mt.), Ak, US 134/H3
Hunter (riv.), Austl. 115/D2
Hunter (isl.), Austl. 109/D5
Hunter, Tx, US 137/U20
Hunterdon (co.), NJ, US 138/C2
Huntingburg, In, US 130/C4
Huntingdon, Eng, UK 33/F2
Huntington, WV, US 130/D4
Huntington, In, US 130/C3
Huntington, NY, US 139/M8
Huntington (bay), NY, US 139/M8
Huntington Bay, NY, US 139/M8
Huntington Beach, Ca, US 136/G8
Huntington Park, Ca, US 136/F8
Huntington Station, NY, US 139/M8
Huntington Woods, Mi, US 135/F7
Huntley, Il, US 135/P15
Huntly, NZ 117/T10
Huntly, Sc, UK 36/D2
Hunts Inlet, BC, Can. 134/M4
Hunts Point, Wa, US 135/C2
Huntsville, Al, US 133/G3
Huntsville, On, Can. 130/E2
Huntsville, Ut, US 137/K11
Huntsville (res.), Pa, US 138/B1
Hunucmá, Mex. 144/D1
Hünxe, Ger. 50/D5
Hunyuan, China 72/C3
Huo (mtn.), China 72/B3
Huo (mtn.), China 72/D5
Huocheng, China 70/D3
Huojia, China 72/C4
Huolin Gol, China 71/L2
Huoqiu, China 72/D4
Huoshan, China 72/D5
Huozhou, China 72/B3
Hurdal, Nor. 38/D1
Hure Qi, China 72/E2
Hurepoix (reg.), Fr. 30/H6
Hurley, NM, US 128/E4
Hurley, Eng, UK 30/A2
Hurley (riv.), Ire. 34/B4
Hurlford, Sc, UK 36/B5
Huron (lake), Can.,US 130/D2
Huron (mts.), Mi, US 130/B2
Huron (pt.), Mi, US 135/G6
Huron (riv.), Mi, US 135/E7
Hurricane, WV, US 130/D4
Hurtaut (riv.), Fr. 52/D4
Hürtgenwald (reg.), Ger. 53/F2
Hürth, Ger. 53/F2
Hurup, Den. 38/C3
Husainābād, India 85/E3
Húsavík, Ice. 37/P6
Huscarán, PN, Peru 150/C5
Husher, Wi, US 135/Q14
Huşi, Rom. 49/J2
Huskisson, Austl. 115/D2
Huslia, Ak, US 134/G2
Husnes, Nor. 38/A2
Hussigny-Godbrange, Fr. 53/E5
Husum, Ger. 38/C4
Husum, Swe. 37/F3
Hutag, Mong. 70/H2
Hutchinson, Mn, US 127/K4
Hutchinson, Ks, US 129/H3
Hüttisheim, Ger. 57/F1
Hüttlingen, Ger. 54/D5
Hutton (mt.), Austl. 114/C4
Hutton, Eng, UK 30/E2
Huttwil, Swi. 56/D3
Hutuo (riv.), China 72/C3
Ḩuwwārah, WBnk. 91/G7
Huy, Belg. 53/E2
Huyton-with-Roby, Eng, UK 35/F5
Huzhou, China 72/L9
Hvammstangi, Ice. 37/N6
Hvannadalshnúkur (peak), Ice. 37/P7
Hvar (isl.), Cro. 46/E1
Hvide Sande, Den. 38/C4
Hvítá (riv.), Ice. 37/N7
Hvolsvöllur, Ice. 37/N7
Hwange, Zim. 105/E4
Hwange (Wankie) NP, Zim. 105/E4
Hwanghae-bukto (prov.), NKor. 73/D3
Hwanghae-namdo (prov.), NKor. 73/C3
Hwangju, NKor. 73/C3
Hwangju (riv.), NKor. 73/C3
Hwasun, SKor. 73/D5
Hyades (peak), Chile 158/B5
Hyattstown, Md, US 138/A5
Hyattsville, Md, US 138/B6
Hydaburg, Ak, US 134/M4
Hyde, Eng, UK 35/F5
Hyder, Ak, US 134/M4
Hyderābād, India 82/C4
Hyderābād, Pak. 89/J3
Hyères, Fr. 43/G5
Hyères, Îles d' (isls.), Fr 43/G5
Hyesan, NKor. 73/E2
Hygiene, Co, US 137/B2
Hyland (riv.), Yk, Can. 122/D2
Hyllestad, Nor. 38/A1
Hyltebruk, Swe. 38/E3
Hylton (hill), Ky, US 130/D4
Hyŏ-no-sen (peak), Japan 74/D3
Hyōgo (pref.), Japan 74/D3
Hyŏndŭng-san (peak), SKor. 73/G6
Hyrum, Ut, US 128/E2
Hythe, Eng, UK 33/H4
Hyūga, Japan 74/B4
Hyvinkää, Fin. 39/L1
Hywel, Moel (peak), Wal, UK 32/C2

I

I-n-Amenas, Alg. 99/H3
I-n-Azaoua, Oued (riv.), Niger 99/H5
I-n-Dagouber (well), Mali 99/E5
I-n-Échaï (well), Mali 103/E1
I-n-Gall, Niger 103/G2
I-n-Guezzâm, Alg. 103/G2
I-n-Milach (well), Mali 103/E2
I-n-Sâkâne, 'Erg (des.), Mali 103/E1
I-n-Salah, Alg. 99/F4
I-n-Tassik (well), Mali 103/F2
Iacanga, Braz. 155/B2
Iaciara, Braz. 154/A4
Iaco (riv.), Braz. 150/E6
Iaçu, Braz. 154/B4
Iâf di Montasio (peak), It. 43/K3
Iakora, Madg. 107/H8
Ialomiţa (riv.), Rom. 62/C3
Ialomiţa (prov.), Rom. 49/H3
Ianapera, Madg. 107/H8
Iapu, Braz. 155/D1
Iaşi (prov.), Rom. 49/H2
Iaşi, Rom. 49/H2
Iasmos, Gre. 47/J2
Iatan, Mo, US 137/D5
Iba, Phil. 79/C4
Ibadan, Nga. 103/F5
Ibagué, Col. 150/C3
Ibaiti, Braz. 155/B2
Ibajay, Phil. 79/D5
Ibanda, Ugan. 104/A3
Ibans (lake), Nic. 145/E3
Ibapaba, Serra da (range), Braz. 154/B1
Ibar (riv.), Yugo. 48/E4
Ibara, Japan 74/C3
Ibaraki (pref.), Japan 75/F2
Ibaraki, Japan 77/J6
Ibaraki, Japan 77/E1
Ibarra, Ecu. 152/B4
Ibarreta, Arg. 157/E2
Ibb, Yem. 88/D6
Ibba (riv.), Sudan 97/L6
Ibbenbüren, Ger. 51/E4
Ibdekkene (riv.), Mali 103/F2
Iberia, Peru 156/D3
Iberia, Peru 156/C2
Ibérico, Sistema (range), Sp. 44/D2
Iberville, Qu, Can. 131/P7
Ibi, Sp. 45/E3
Ibiá, Braz. 155/C1
Ibiapina, Braz. 154/B1
Ibicaraí, Braz. 154/C4
Ibicuy, Arg. 159/J10
Ibigawa, Japan 77/L5
Ibimirim, Braz. 154/C3
Ibiraçu, Braz. 155/D1
Ibirapuã, Braz. 154/B5
Ibitinga, Braz. 155/B2
Ibiúna, Braz. 211/F8
Ibiza (isl.) 45/F3
Ibiza, Sp. 45/F3
Ibo, Moz. 105/H3
Ibo (riv.), Japan 74/D3
Iboro, Nga. 103/F5
Ibotirama, Braz. 154/B4
Iboundji (peak), Gabon 96/H8
Ibrány, Hun. 41/L4
Ibshawāy, Egypt 91/B5
Ibuki, Japan 77/K5
Ibuki-yama (peak), Japan 77/K5
Ica (dept.), Peru 156/C4
Ica, Peru 156/C4
Iça (riv.), SAm. 147/D3
Içana (riv.), Braz. 150/E3
Icel (prov.), Turk. 90/C2
Iceland (ctry.) 37/N7
Icém, Braz. 155/B2
Ichalkaranji, India 89/K5
Ichāmati (riv.), Bang. 85/G3
Ichchāpuram, India 82/D4
Ichenhausen, Ger. 54/D6
Ichhāwar, India 84/A4
Ichihara, Japan 77/E3
Ichijima, Japan 77/H5
Ichikawa, Japan 77/D2
Ichikawada, Japan 77/B2
Ichinohe, Japan 76/B3
Ichinomiya, Japan 77/B2
Ichinomiya, Japan 77/E3
Ichinomiya, Japan 77/G7
Ichinomiya, Japan 77/M6
Ichinomiya, Japan 77/L5
Ichinoseki, Japan 76/B4
Ichishi, Japan 77/K6
Ich'ŏn, SKor. 73/D4
Ichtegem, Belg. 52/C1
Ickesburg, Pa, US 138/A3
Icó, Braz. 154/C2
Icod de los Vinos, Sp. 98/A3
Icy (cape), Ak, US 134/F1
Icy (pt.), Ak, US 134/L4
Icy (str.), Ak, US 134/L4
Icy (bay), Ak, US 122/B3
Idabel, Ok, US 129/J4
Idaho (state), US 126/E5
Idaho Springs, Co, US 137/A3
Idanha-a-Nova, Port. 44/B3
Idar, India 82/B3
Idar-Oberstein, Ger. 53/G4
Idarkopf (peak), Ger. 53/G4
Idaville, Pa, US 138/A3
Ide, Japan 77/J6
Ideles, Alg. 99/G5
Idfū, Egypt 101/C3
Ídhi (peak), Gre. 47/J5
Ídhra, Gre. 47/H4
Idice (riv.), It. 59/E4
Idjwe, Île (isl.), D.R.Congo 104/A3
Idkū, Egypt 91/B4
Idle (riv.), Eng, UK 35/H5
Idlib (prov.), Syria 90/D3
Idlib, Syria 91/E2
Idnah, WBnk. 91/D4
Idrija, Slov. 43/L4
Idriss I (dam), Mor. 100/B2
Idriss I, Barrage (res.), Mor. 100/B2
Idro, Lago d' (lake), It. 58/D1
Idstein, Ger. 54/B2
Ie (isl.), Japan 75/J7
Ieper, Belg. 52/B2
Ierápetra, Gre. 47/J5
Ierissós, Gre. 47/H2
Iesolo, It. 59/F1
Ifalik (isl.), Micr. 116/D4
Ifanadiana, Madg. 107/H8
Ife, Nga. 103/G5
Iferfes (well), Libya 99/H3
Iffeldorf, Ger. 57/H2
Iffezheim, Ger. 54/B5
Iforas, Adrar des (upland), Alg.,Mali 96/F4
Ifrane, Mor. 98/D2
Iga (riv.), Japan 77/K6
Iga, Japan 77/K6
Igal, Hun. 48/C2
Iganga, Ugan. 104/B2
Igaporã, Braz. 154/B4
Igara Paraná (riv.), Col. 152/C5
Igarapava, Braz. 155/C2
Igarapé Grande, Braz. 154/A2
Igarapé-Miri, Braz. 151/J4
Igaratá, Braz. 211/G8
Igarka, Rus. 64/J3
Igatpuri, India 82/B4
Igdet (peak), Mor. 98/C3
Iğdır, Turk. 63/H5
Igel, Ger. 53/F4
Iggesund, Swe. 38/G1
Ightham, Eng, UK 30/D3
Igikpak (mt.), Ak, US 134/H2
Igis, Swi. 57/F4
Igiugig, Ak, US 134/G4
Iglesias, It. 46/A3
Igli, Alg. 99/E3
Igling, Ger. 57/G1
Igloolik, Nun., Can. 123/H2
Ignace, On, Can. 127/L3
Ignacio, Ca, US 135/J10
Ignacio de la Llave, Mex. 143/P8
Ignacio Zaragoza, Mex. 142/D2
İğneada Burnu (cape), Turk. 49/J5
Igney, Fr. 56/C1
Ignon (riv.), Fr. 56/A2
Igny, Fr. 30/J5
Igombe (riv.), Tanz. 104/B4
Igora Paraná (riv.), Col. 156/C1
Igoumenítsa, Gre. 47/G3
Igra, Rus. 61/M4
Igreja, Morro da (peak), Braz. 155/B4
Iguaçu (riv.), Braz. 147/D5
Iguaçu, PN do, Braz. 157/F2
Iguaí, Braz. 154/B4
Iguala, Mex. 143/K8
Igualada, Sp. 45/F2
Iguape, Braz. 155/C3
Iguape (riv.), Braz. 155/B3
Iguatu, Braz. 154/C2
Iguazú, PN del, Arg. 157/F2
Iguetti (lake), Mrta. 98/C4
Iheya (isl.), Japan 75/J7
Ihhayrhan, Mong. 70/J2
Ihosy, Madg. 107/H8
Ihotry (lake), Madg. 107/G8
Ihuari, Peru 156/B3
Ii (riv.), Fin. 64/C3
Ii, Fin. 60/E2
Iida, Japan 75/E3
Iide-san (peak), Japan 75/F2
Iijoki (riv.), Fin. 60/F2
Iinan, Japan 77/K7
Iisalmi, Fin. 60/E3
Iitaka, Japan 77/K7
Iitti, Fin. 39/M1
Iiyama, Japan 75/F2
Iizuka, Japan 74/B4
Ijebu Ode, Nga. 103/F5
Ijill (peak), Mrta. 98/B5
Ijill (lake), Mrta. 98/B5
Ijira, Japan 77/L4
IJmeer (bay), Neth. 50/C4
IJmuiden, Neth. 50/B4
Ijnaoun (well), Mrta. 102/B2
Ijoki (riv.), Fin. 37/H2
Ijoubbane, 'Erg (des.), Mali 98/D5
IJssel (riv.), Neth. 50/C3
IJsselmeer (lake), Neth. 40/C2
IJsselmuiden, Neth. 50/C3
IJsselstein, Neth. 50/C4
Ijuí, Braz. 157/F2
Ijūin, Japan 74/B5
Ijzer (riv.), Belg. 40/A3
Ik (riv.), Rus. 61/M5
Ikahavo (plat.), Madg. 107/H7
Ikalamavony, Madg. 107/H8
Ikare, Nga. 103/G5
Ikaría, Gre. 90/A2
Ikaría (isl.), Gre. 47/J4
Ikaruga, Japan 77/J6
Ikeda, Japan 74/C3
Ikeda, Japan 76/C2
Ikeda, Japan 77/H6
Ikeda, Japan 77/L5
Ikeja, Nga. 103/F5
Ikenokoya-yama (peak), Japan 77/K7
Ikerre, Nga. 103/G5
Ikhtiman, Bul. 47/H1
Iki (isl.), Japan 74/A4
Iki (chan.), Japan 74/A4
Ikire, Nga. 103/G5
Ikirun, Nga. 103/G5
İkizce, Turk. 62/E5
İkizdere, Turk. 63/G4
Ikoma, Japan 77/J6
Ikongo, Madg. 107/H8
Ikopa (riv.), Madg. 107/H7
Ikorodu, Nga. 103/F5
Ikuno, Japan 74/D3
Ila Orangun, Nga. 103/G5
Ilabaya, Peru 156/D5
Ilagan, Phil. 79/D4
Ilam, Nepal 85/F2
Īlām, Iran 88/E2
Ilan, Tai. 79/D3
Ilanz, Swi. 57/F4
Ilaro, Nga. 103/F5
Ilave, Peru 156/D5
Iława, Pol. 41/K2
Ilawe-Ekiti, Nga. 103/G5
Ile (riv.), China.,Ka 70/C3
Île-à-la-Crosse, Sk, Can. 126/G2
Ile-a-la-Crosse (lake), Sk, Can. 126/G2
Île-de-France (pol. reg.), Fr. 52/A6
Ilebo, D.R. Congo 105/D1
Ilek (riv.), Rus. 63/K2
Îles Ehotilés, PN des, C.d'Iv. 102/E5
Iles Tristao, Îles (isls.), Gui. 102/B4
Ilesha, Nga. 103/G5
Ilfis (riv.), Swi. 56/D4
Ilgaz, Turk. 62/E4
Ilgın, Turk. 90/B2
Ilha Grande (bay), Braz. 211/J8
Ilha Grande, Baía de (bay), Braz. 155/C2
Ilha Solteira, Reprêsa (res.), Braz. 151/H7
Ilhabela, Braz. 211/H8
Ílhavo, Port. 44/A2
Ilhéus, Braz. 154/C4
Iliamna, Ak, US 134/H4
Iliamna (lake), Ak, US 134/G4
Iliamna (vol.), Ak, US 134/H3
İliç, Turk. 62/F5
Ilıca, Turk. 63/G5
Ilijaš, Bosn. 48/D4
Iliniza (peak), Ecu. 152/B5
Ilirska Bistrica, Slov. 43/L4
Ilısu (dam), Turk. 90/E2
Ilisu (res.), Turk. 90/E2
Ilium (Troy) (ruin), Turk. 47/K3
Ilkeston, Eng, UK 35/G6
Ilkley, Eng, UK 35/G4
Ill (riv.), Aus. 43/H3
Ill (riv.), Fr. 43/G3
Illana, Sp. 44/D2
Illapel, Chile 157/B3
Illasi (riv.), It. 59/E1
Illbillee (mt.), Austl. 113/G3
Illéla, Niger 103/G3
Iller (riv.), Ger. 43/J2
Illertissen, Ger. 57/G1
Illescas, Sp. 44/D2
Illiers-Combray, Fr. 42/D2
Illimani (peak), Bol. 150/E7
Illingen, Ger. 53/G5
Illinois (riv.), Il, US 130/B3
Illinois (state), US 130/B4
Illizi, Alg. 99/H4
Illizi (prov.), Alg. 99/G4
Illkirch-Graffenstaden, Fr. 56/D1
Illmensee, Ger. 57/F2
Illnau, Swi. 57/E3
Illora, Sp. 44/D4
Illovo, SAfr. 107/E3
Illzach, Fr. 56/D2
Ilm (riv.), Ger. 40/F4
Ilmajoki, Fin. 37/G3
Ilme (riv.), Ger. 51/G5
Il'men (lake), Rus. 64/D4
Ilmenau, Ger. 43/J1
Ilmenau (riv.), Ger. 51/H2
Ilo, Peru 156/D5
Ilobu, Nga. 103/G5
Ilorin, Nga. 103/G4
Ilovlya (riv.), Rus. 63/H2
Ilpendam, Neth. 50/B4
Ilse (riv.), Ger. 51/H5
Ilsede, Ger. 51/H4
Ilsenburg, Ger. 51/H5
Ilsfeld, Ger. 54/C4
Ilshofen, Ger. 54/C4
Ilyas Burnu (pt.), Turk. 49/H5
Ilych (riv.), Rus. 61/N3
Ilz (riv.), Ger. 41/G4
Imabari, Japan 74/C3
Imaichi, Japan 75/F2
Imaloto (riv.), Madg. 107/H8
İmamoğlu, Turk. 90/C2
Imandra (lake), Rus. 37/J2
Imari, Japan 74/A4
Imatra, Fin. 39/N1
Imazu, Japan 77/K5
Imba (lake), Japan 77/E2
Imba, Japan 77/E2
Imbabura (prov.), Ecu. 152/B4
Imbituba, Braz. 155/B4
Imbituva, Braz. 155/B3
Imeni Moskvy (canal), Rus. 61/W9
Imerimandroso, Madg. 107/J7
Imi n'tanout, Mor. 98/C3
İmişli, Azer. 63/J5
Imittós (peak), Gre. 47/N9
Imja (isl.), SKor. 73/C5
Imlay, Nv, US 126/D5
Immendingen, Ger. 57/E2
Immenhausen, Ger. 51/G6
Immenstaad am Bodensee, Ger. 57/F2
Immenstadt im Allgäu, Ger. 57/G2
Immingham, Eng, UK 35/H4
Immokalee, Fl, US 133/H5
Imnavait (mtn.), Ak, US 134/J2
Imo (state), Nga. 103/G5
Imola, It. 59/E4
Imouzzèr-Kandar, Mor. 100/B3
Imperatriz, Braz. 154/A2
Imperia, It. 58/B5
Imperial, Sk, Can. 127/G3
Imperial, Peru 156/B4
Imperial, Ne, US 129/G2
Imperial, Mo, US 137/G9
Imperial Beach, Ca, US 136/C5
Imperial Palace, Japan 77/D2
Impero (riv.), It. 58/B5
Impfondo, Congo 96/J7
Imphāl, India 83/F3
Imphy, Fr. 42/E3
Impruneta, It. 59/E5
İmralı (isl.), Turk. 49/J5
İmranlı, Turk. 62/F5
İmroz, Gre. 47/J2
Imshil, SKor. 73/D5
Imst, Aus. 57/G3
Imuris, Mex. 142/C2
Ina, Japan 75/E3
Ina, Japan 77/E2
Ina, Japan 77/D2
Ina (riv.), Pol. 38/F5
Inabe, Japan 77/L5
Inabu, Japan 77/M5
Inagawa, Japan 77/H6
Inagi, Japan 77/D2
Inajá, Braz. 154/C3
Inambari (riv.), Peru 156/D4
Inami, Japan 77/G6
Inaouene (riv.), Mor. 100/B2
Inapari, Peru 156/D3
Inarjärvi (lake), Fin. 37/H1
Inău (peak), Rom. 49/G2
Inawashiro (lake), Japan 75/F2
Inazawa, Japan 77/L5
Inca, Sp. 45/G3
Incekum (pt.), Turk. 91/C1
Incheville, Fr. 52/A3
Inchinnan, Sc, UK 36/B5
Inchkeith (isl.), Sc, UK 36/C4
Inchnadamph, Sc, UK 31/R7
Inch'ŏn, SKor. 73/F7
Inch'on-Gwangyŏksi (prov.), SKor. 73/D4
Incirliova, Turk. 90/A2
Incisa in Val d'Arno, It. 59/E5
Inconfidentes, Braz. 211/G7
Incudine, Mont l' (peak), Fr. 46/A2
Indaiá (riv.), Braz. 155/C1
Indaiatuba, Braz. 155/C2
Indalsälven (riv.), Swe. 37/E3
Indanan, Phil. 81/F2
Inde (riv.), Ger. 53/F2
Inden, Ger. 53/F2
Independence (mts.), Nv, US 126/E5
Independence, Ks, US 129/J3
Independence, Ca, US 128/C3
Independence, Mo, US 137/E5
Independence, Belz. 144/D2
Independence Nat'l Hist. Park, Pa, US 138/C4
Independência, Braz. 154/B2
Independencia, Peru 156/B4
Index, Wa, US 135/D2
India (ctry.) 67/G7
Indian (ocean) 23/N6
Indian Echo Caverns, Pa, US 138/B3
Indian Head, Sk, Can. 127/H3
Indian Hills, Co, US 137/B3
Indian Peaks Wilderness Area, Co, US 137/A2
Indiana, Pa, US 130/E3
Indiana (state), US 130/C3
Indianapolis (int'l arpt.), In, US 130/C4
Indianapolis (cap.), In, US 130/C4
Indianola, Ms, US 129/K4
Indianola, Wa, US 135/B2
Indiantown, Fl, US 133/H5
Indiaporã, Braz. 155/B1
Indigirka (riv.), Rus. 67/P3
Indija, Yugo. 48/E3
Indio, Ca, US 128/C4
Indira Gandhi (int'l arpt.), India 86/D5
Indochina (reg.), Laos 83/H4
Indonesia (ctry.) 81/E4
Indore, India 89/L4
Indragiri (riv.), Indo. 80/B4
Indramayu (cape), Indo. 80/C5
Indrāvati (riv.), India 70/D8
Indre (riv.), Fr. 42/D3
Indre Arna, Nor. 38/A1
Indrois (riv.), Fr. 42/D3
Induno Olona, It. 57/E6
Indus (riv.), Asia 67/G6
Industry, Ca, US 136/G7
Inebolu, Turk. 62/E4
Inece, Turk. 49/H5
İnecik, Turk. 49/H5
Inedbirenne (int'l arpt.), Alg. 99/H4
İnegöl, Turk. 62/D4
Iner (riv.), Ger. 54/C3
Ineu, Rom. 48/E2
Inezgane, Mor. 98/C3
Inezgane (Agadir) (int'l arpt.), Mor. 98/C3
Infanta (cape), SAfr. 106/C4
Infiernillo (res.), Mex. 140/A4
Infiernillo, Presa del (dam), Mex. 142/E5
Infiesto, Sp. 44/C1
Ingapirca (ruin), Ecu. 152/B5
Ingatestone, Eng, UK 30/E2
Ingelmunster, Belg. 52/C2
Ingeniero Jacobacci, Arg. 158/C4
Ingeniero Luiggi, Arg. 158/D2
Ingenio, Sp. 98/B4
Ingersheim, Fr. 56/D1
Ingettolgoy, Mong. 70/H2
Ingham, Austl. 114/B2
Ingleside, Md, US 138/C5
Inglewood, Austl. 115/B3
Inglewood, Austl. 114/C5
Inglewood, Ca, US 136/F8
Inglewood-Finn Hill, Wa, US 135/C2
Inglis, Fl, US 133/H4
Ingoda (riv.), Rus. 65/M4
Ingolstadt, Ger. 55/E5
Ingrid Christianson (coast), Ant. 160/F
Ingushetia (aut. rep.), Rus. 63/H4
Ingwavuma, SAfr. 107/E2
Ingwiller, Fr. 53/G6
Inhambane, Moz. 105/G5
Inhambupe, Braz. 154/C3
Inharrime, Moz. 105/G5
Inhuma, Braz. 154/B2
Inhumas, Braz. 151/J7
Iniesta, Sp. 44/E3
Inifel (well), Alg. 99/F3
Inini (riv.), FrG. 153/H4
Inírida (riv.), Col. 150/E3
Inishbofin (isl.), Ire. 30/N10
Inishowen (pen.), Ire. 34/A1
Inishowen (pt.), Ire. 34/B1
Inje, SKor. 73/E3
Injune, Austl. 114/C4
Inkster, Mi, US 135/F7
Inland (sea), Japan 74/C4
Inle (lake), Myan. 83/G3
Inn (riv.), Aus. 43/J3
Inn (riv.), Ger. 43/K2
Inn (riv.), Swi. 43/J3
Innbach (riv.), Aus. 55/H6
Innellan, Sc, UK 36/B5
Inner (chan.), Belz. 144/D2
Inner (sound), Sc, UK 31/R8
Inner Hebrides (isls.), Sc, UK 31/Q8
Inner Mongolia (reg.), China 67/L5
Innerdouny (hill), Sc, UK 36/C4
Innerleithen, Sc, UK 36/C5
Innerste (riv.), Ger. 51/G4
Innertkirchen, Swi. 57/E4
Innes NP, Austl. 113/H5
Innichen (San Candito), It. 43/K3
Innisfail, Ab, Can. 126/E2
Innisfail, Austl. 114/B2
Innoko (riv.), Ak, US 134/G3
Innoko NWR, US 134/G3
Innsbruck, Aus. 57/H3
Innviertel (reg.), Aus. 55/G6
Inny (riv.), Eng, UK 32/B5
Ino, Japan 74/C4
Inocência, Braz. 155/B1
Inongo, D.R. Congo 97/J8
İnönü, Turk. 62/D5
Inowrocław, Pol. 41/K2
Insch, Sc, UK 36/D2
Inscription (cape), Austl. 112/B3
Insein, Myan. 83/G4
Inside (passg.), BC, Can. 126/A2
Insjön, Swe. 38/F1
Inta, Rus. 61/N2
Intendente Alvear, Arg. 158/E2
İntepe, Turk. 47/K2
Intercourse, Pa, US 138/B3
Interior (plat.), BC, Can. 126/B2
Interlaken, Swi. 56/D4
Internacional (int'l arpt.), Braz. 156/D2
Internacional (int'l arpt.), Mex. 143/E5
International Peace Garden, ND, US 127/H3
Inthanon (peak), Thai. 83/G4
Întorsura Buzăului, Rom. 49/H3
Intracoastal Waterway, La, US 137/P17
Intragna, Swi. 57/E5
Introbio, It. 57/F6
Inubō-zaki (pt.), Japan 75/G3
Inukjuak, Qu, Can. 123/J3
Inutil (bay), Chile 159/C7
Inuvik, NW, Can. 134/M2
Inuyama, Japan 77/L5
Inver (bay), Sc, UK 36/C1
Inveraray, Sc, UK 36/A4
Inverbervie, Sc, UK 36/D3
Invercargill, NZ 117/R12
Inverclyde (pol. reg.), Sc, UK 36/B5
Inverell, Austl. 115/D1
Invergordon, Sc, UK 36/B1
Inverie, Sc, UK 31/R8
Inverigo, It. 58/B1
Inverkeithing, Sc, UK 36/C4
Inverloch, Austl. 115/C3
Invermay, Sk, Can. 127/H3
Inverness, Fl, US 133/H4
Inverness, Al, US 133/G3
Inverness, Sc, UK 36/B2
Inveruno, It. 58/B1
Inverurie, Sc, UK 36/D2
Investigator (str.), Austl. 109/C4
Invorio, It. 58/B1
Inwood, NY, US 139/L9
Inyanga, Zim. 105/F4
Inyangani (peak), Zim. 105/F4
Inymney (peak), Rus. 134/D2
Inyo (mts.), Ca, US 128/C3
Inza, Rus. 63/H1
Inzai, Japan 77/E2
Inzigkofen, Ger. 57/F1
Inzing, Aus. 57/H3
Io-shima (isl.), Japan 74/B5
Ioánnina (int'l arpt.), Gre. 47/G3
Ioánnina, Gre. 47/G3
Iolotan', Trkm. 89/H1
Iona (isl.), Sc, UK 31/Q8
Iona, PN da, Ang. 105/B4
Ione, Co, US 137/C2
Ionia, Mi, US 130/C3
Ionian (sea), Gre. 47/F3
Ionian (isls.), Gre. 27/F5
Íos (isl.), Gre. 47/J4
Iouîk (cape), Mrta. 102/A2
Iowa (riv.), Ia, US 127/K5
Iowa (state), US 129/J2
Iowa Falls, Ia, US 127/K5
Ipameri, Braz. 155/B1
Ipanema, Braz. 155/D1
Iparia, Peru 156/C3
Ipatinga, Braz. 155/D1
Ipel' (riv.), Slvk. 41/K4
Iphofen, Ger. 54/D3
Ipiales, Col. 152/B4
Ipiaú, Braz. 154/C4
Ipil, Phil. 79/D6
Ipirá, Braz. 154/C4
Ipiranga, Braz. 155/B3
Ipoh, Malay. 80/B3
Ipoly (riv.), Hun. 41/K4
Iporá, Braz. 151/H7
Ipsala, Turk. 47/K2
Ipsheim, Ger. 54/D3
Ipswich, SD, US 127/J4
Ipswich, Eng, UK 33/H2
Ipu, Braz. 154/B1
Ipuã, Braz. 155/B2
Ipubi, Braz. 154/B2
Ipueiras, Braz. 154/B2
Ipuiúna, Braz. 211/G7
Ipumba (hill), Tanz. 104/A4
Ipun, Isla (isl.), Chile 158/B5
Ipupiara, Braz. 154/B3
Iqaluit (cap.), Nun, Can. 123/K2
Iquique, Chile 150/D8
Iquitos, Peru 156/C1
Irago (chan.), Japan 77/L6
Irago-misaki (cape), Japan 77/M6
Iráklia, Gre. 47/H2
Iráklia (isl.), Gre. 47/J4
Iráklion, Gre. 47/J5
Iráklion (int'l arpt.), Gre. 47/J5
Iramaia, Braz. 154/B4
Iran (mts.), Indo.,Mal 80/D3
Iran (ctry.) 67/E6
Irapa, Ven. 153/F2
Irapuato, Mex. 143/E4
Iraq (ctry.) 88/D2
Irará, Braz. 154/C4
Irati, Braz. 155/B3
Irauçuba, Braz. 154/C1
Irbid (gov.), Jor. 91/D3
Irbid, Jor. 91/D3
Irbīl, Iraq 90/F2
Irecê, Braz. 154/B3
Ireland (ctry.) 31/P10
Ireland's Eye (isl.), Ire. 34/B5
Iremel' (peak), Rus. 61/N5
Iretama, Braz. 155/A3
Irfon (riv.), Wal, UK 32/C2
Irharhar, Oued (riv.), Alg. 99/G4
Irhazer Oua-n-Agadez (riv.), Niger 103/G2
Iri, SKor. 73/D5
Irian Jaya (reg.), Indo. 81/H4
Iricoume (mts.), Braz. 153/G4
Irig, Yugo. 48/D3
Irigui (phys. reg.), Mali 102/D2
Iriklinskiy (res.), Rus. 63/L2
Iringa (prov.), Tanz. 104/B5
Iringa, Tanz. 104/B4
Iriomote (isl.), Japan 79/D3
Iriri (riv.), Braz. 151/H4
Irish (sea), Ire.,UK 34/C4
Irlam, Eng, UK 35/F5
Irō-zaki (pt.), Japan 75/F3
Iroise (bay), Fr. 42/A2
Iron Baron, Austl. 113/H5
Iron Knob, Austl. 113/H5
Iron Mountain, Mi, US 127/L4
Irondale, Co, US 137/C3
Ironton, Oh, US 130/D4
Ironton, Ut, US 137/K13
Ironwood, Mi, US 127/L4
Irput' (riv.), Rus. 62/E1
Irrawaddy (Ayeyarwady) (riv.), Myan. 67/J7
Irrawaddy, Mouths of the (delta), Myan. 83/F4
Irsch, Ger. 53/F4
Irsen (riv.), Ger. 53/F3
Irsina, It. 46/E2
Irt (riv.), Eng, UK 35/E3
Irthing (riv.), Eng, UK 35/F1
Irthlingborough, Eng, UK 33/F2
Irtysh (riv.), Rus. 67/G4
Iruma, Japan 77/C2
Irumu, D.R. Congo 104/A2
Irún, Sp. 44/E1
Irvine, Ca, US 136/G8
Irvine, Sc, UK 36/B5
Irvine (bay), Sc, UK 36/B5
Irvine (riv.), Sc, UK 36/B5
Irving, Tx, US 132/D3
Irvington, NJ, US 139/J9
Irvington, NY, US 139/K7
Is (peak), Sudan 101/C4
Is-sur-Tille, Fr. 56/B2
Īsa Khel, Pak. 86/A3
Isaac (riv.), Austl. 109/D3
Isabela, Phil. 81/F2
Isabela, PR 141/M8
Isabela (isl.), Ecu. 156/E7
Isabelia (mts.), Nic. 144/E3
Isabella (bay), Nun., Can. 123/K2
Isaccea, Rom. 49/J3
Isachsen (cape), Nun., Can. 123/R7
Ísafjardhardjúp (inlet), Ice. 37/M6
Ísafjördhur, Ice. 37/M6
Isahaya, Japan 74/B4
Isalo, PN de l', Madg. 107/H8
Isalo Ruiniform (mass.), Madg. 107/H8
Isana (riv.), Col. 152/D4
Isandhlwana Battlesite, SAfr. 107/E3
Isangano NP, Zam. 104/A5
Isaouanne-n-Irarraren (des.), Alg. 99/G4
Isaouanne-n-Tifernine (des.), Alg. 99/G4
Isarco (riv.), It. 43/J3
Isarco (Eisack) (riv.), It. 57/H4
Isaszeg, Hun. 49/R9
Isawa, Japan 77/B2
Isbergues, Fr. 52/B2
Iscar, Sp. 44/C2
Ischgl, Aus. 57/G3
Ischia, It. 48/A5
Ise (bay), Japan 75/E3
Ise (riv.), Eng, UK 33/F2
Ise, Japan 77/L7
Ise-Shima NP, Japan 75/E3
Isehara, Japan 75/F3
Iselin, NJ, US 139/H9
Isen, Ger. 55/F6
Isen (riv.), Ger. 40/G4
Isenthal, Swi. 57/E4
Iseo (lake), It. 43/J4
Iseo, It. 58/D1
Iseo, Lago d' (lake), It. 58/C1
Isère (riv.), Fr. 42/F4
Isère (dept.), Fr. 56/B6
Iserlohn, Ger. 51/E6
Isernia, It. 46/D2
Isesaki, Japan 75/F2
Iset' (riv.), Rus. 87/D1
Iseyin, Nga. 103/F5
'Isfiyā, Isr. 91/G6

196

Jinch – Kapsa

Jinchuan, China 70/H5
Jinci Temple, China 72/C3
Jind, India 86/D5
Jindabyne (dam), Austl. 115/D3
Jindabyne, Austl. 115/D3
Jindřichuv Hradec, Czh. 41/H4
Jing Xian, China 71/L5
Jing Xian, China 83/J2
Jingbian, China 72/B3
Jingde, China 79/C1
Jingdezhen, China 79/C2
Jingdong, China 83/H3
Jinggangshan, China 83/K2
Jinghai, China 72/H7
Jinghe, China 70/D3
Jinghong, China 83/H3
Jingjiang, China 72/E4
Jingle, China 72/B3
Jingmen, China 72/C5
Jingshan, China 72/C5
Jingxi, China 83/J3
Jingyuan, China 70/H4
Jinhu, China 72/D4
Jinhua, China 79/C2
Jining, China 72/C2
Jining, China 72/D4
Jinja, Ugan. 104/B2
Jinkouhe, China 83/H2
Jinotega, Nic. 144/E3
Jinotepe, Nic. 144/E4
Jinping, China 83/J2
Jinsha, China 83/J2
Jinsha (riv.), China 67/J7
Jinshan, China 72/L9
Jinshi, China 83/K2
Jintan, China 72/D5
Jintotolo (chan.), Phil. 79/D5
Jintūr, India 89/L5
Jinxi, China 79/C2
Jinxi, China 72/E2
Jinxian, China 79/C2
Jinxiang, China 72/D4
Jinyun, China 79/D2
Jinzhai, China 72/C5
Jinzhou (bay), China 73/A3
Jinzhou, China 72/E2
Jiparana (riv.), Braz. 150/F5
Jipijapa, Ecu. 152/A5
Jiquilpan de Juárez, Mex. 142/E5
Jiquipilco, Mex. 143/Q9
Jiřkov, Czh. 55/G1
Jishan, China 72/B4
Jishou, China 83/J2
Jishui, China 79/C2
Jisr ash Shughūr, Syria 91/E2
Jiu (riv.), Rom. 62/B3
Jiujiang, China 79/C2
Jiujiang, China 79/C2
Jiulong, China 83/H2
Jiutai, China 71/N3
Jiutepec, Mex. 143/K8
Jiuwan (mts.), China 70/J6
Jixi, China 71/P2
Jixi, China 79/C1
Jiyang, China 72/D3
Jiyuan, China 72/C4
Jīzān, SAr. 88/D5
Jize, China 72/C3
Jizera (riv.), Czh. 41/H3
Jizō-zaki (pt.), Japan 74/C3
Jizzakh, Uzb. 87/E4
Jizzakh (pol. reg.), Uzb. 87/E4
Joaçaba, Braz. 155/B3
Joachín, Mex. 143/N8
Joaíma, Braz. 154/B5
João Câmara, Braz. 154/D2
João Lisboa, Braz. 154/A2
João Monlevade, Braz. 155/D1
João Pessoa, Braz. 154/D2
João Pinheiro, Braz. 154/A5
Joaquín V. González, Arg. 157/D2
Jobabo, Cuba 145/G1
Jockgrim, Ger. 54/B4
Jocón, Hon. 144/E3
Jódar, Sp. 44/D4
Jodhpur, India 89/K3
Jodoigne, Belg. 53/D2
Joensuu, Fin. 60/F3
Jōetsu, Japan 75/F2
Jogbani, India 85/F2
Johannesberg, Ger. 54/C2
Johannesburg, SAfr. 106/E2
Johanngeorgenstadt, Ger. 55/F2
Johilla (riv.), India 84/C4
John Day, Or, US 126/D4
John Day (riv.), Or, US 124/B2
John Day Fossil Beds Nat'l Mon., Or, US 126/C4
John Day, Middle Fork (riv.), Or, US 126/D4
John Day, North Fork (riv.), Or, US 126/D4
John F. Kennedy (int'l arpt.), NY, US 139/K9
John Forrest NP, Austl. 112/L6
John H. Kerr (res.), NC,Va, US 133/J2
John Martin (res.), Co, US 132/C2
John Wayne/Orange County (int'l arpt.), Ca, US 136/G8
Johnson (co.), Ks, US 137/D6
Johnson City, Tn, US 130/D4
Johnsonburg, NJ, US 138/D2
Johnsons Crossing, Yk, Can. 134/M3
Johnston (falls), Zam. 104/A5
Johnston (lake), Austl. 109/B4
Johnston Atoll (isl.), Pac., US 117/J3
Johnstone, Sc, UK 36/B5
Johnstown, Pa, US 130/E3
Johnstown, Co, US 137/C2
Johnsville, Md, US 138/A4
Johor Baharu, Malay. 80/B3
Jöhstadt, Ger. 55/G1
Joigny, Fr. 42/E3
Joinvile, Braz. 155/B3
Joinville, Fr. 56/B1
Jojutla, Mex. 143/K8
Jokioinen, Fin. 39/K1
Jokkmokk, Swe. 37/F2
Jökulsargljufur NP, Ice. 37/P6
Jolanda di Savoia, It. 59/E3
Joliette, Qu, Can. 130/F2
Jollyville, Tx, US 129/H5
Jolo (isl.), Phil. 81/F2
Jolo, Phil. 81/F2
Jomala, Fin. 39/H1
Jombang, Indo. 80/D5
Jomda, China 70/G5
Jomo Kenyatta (int'l arpt.), Kenya 104/C3
Jona, Swi. 57/E3
Jonacatepec, Mex. 143/L8
Jonava, Lith. 39/L4
Jonchery-sur-Vesle, Fr. 52/C5
Jones, Ok, US 137/N14
Jones (inlet), NY, US 139/L9
Jones (mtn.), Pa, US 138/A2
Jones (sound), Nun., Can. 123/S7
Jones Beach State Park, NY, US 139/L9
Jonesboro, Ar, US 129/K4
Jonesboro, La, US 129/J4
Jönköping (co.), Swe. 37/E4
Jönköping, Swe. 38/F3
Jonquière, Qu, Can. 131/G1
Jonuta, Mex. 140/C4
Joondalup (lake), Austl. 112/K6
Joplin, Mo, US 129/J3
Joppatowne (Joppa), Md, US 138/B5
Jora, India 84/A2
Jordan, Mt, US 126/G4
Jordan, On, Can. 131/R9
Jordan (riv.), Isr.,Jor. 91/D4
Jordan (ctry.) 88/C2
Jordan Valley, Or, US 126/D5
Jordânia, Braz. 154/B4
Jorge (cape), Chile 159/B6
Jorge Chavez (int'l arpt.), Peru 156/B4
Jork, Ger. 51/G1
Jornada del Muerto (valley), NM, US 132/B3
Jørpeland, Nor. 38/B2
Jos (plat.), Nga. 96/G6
Jos, Nga. 103/H4
Jose Abad Santos, Phil. 81/G2
José Batlle y Ordóñez, Uru. 159/G2
José Bonifácio, Braz. 155/B2
José Cardel, Mex. 143/N7
José de Freitas, Braz. 154/B2
José de San Martín, Arg. 157/B5
José Enrique Rodó, Uru. 159/K10
José María Morelos, Mex. 144/D2
Jose Marti (int'l arpt.), Cuba 145/F1
José Pedro Varela, Uru. 159/G2
José, South (dept.), Uru. 159/F2
Josefa Camejo (int'l arpt.), Ven. 152/D2
Joseph Bonaparte (gulf), Austl. 109/B2
Joshin-Etsu Kogen NP, Japan 75/F2
Joshua (pt.), Ct, US 139/F1
Joshua Tree NP, Ca, US 128/D4
Jossa (riv.), Ger. 54/C2
Jotunheimen NP, Nor. 38/C1
Jouanne (riv.), Fr. 42/C2
Jouarre, Fr. 30/M5
Joué-lès-Tours, Fr. 42/D3
Jœuf, Fr. 53/F5
Jourama Falls NP, Austl. 114/B2
Jourdanton, Tx, US 129/H5
Joure, Neth. 50/C3
Joutseno, Fin. 39/N1
Joux (lake), Swi. 56/C4
Jouy-en-Josas, Fr. 30/J5
Jouy-le-Châtel, Fr. 30/M6
Jouy-le-Moutier, Fr. 30/J4
Jouy-sur-Morin, Fr. 52/C6
Jovellanos, Cuba 145/F1
Joveyn (riv.), Iran 89/G1
Jowai, India 83/F2
Joy (mt.), Yk, Can. 134/M3
Jōyō, Japan 77/J6
Jozankei Spa, Japan 76/B2
Ju Xian, China 72/D4
Juan Aldama, Mex. 142/E3
Juan de Fuca (str.), BC, Can.,US 122/D4
Juan de Fuca, Strait of (str.), US,Can. 126/B3
Juan de Nova (isl.), Fr. 93/G6
Juan Fernández (isls.), Chile 147/A6
Juan Fernández, Arg. 158/F3
Juan José Paso, Arg. 158/E2
Juan L. Lacaze, Uru. 159/K11
Juan Santamaria (int'l arpt.), CR 145/E4
Juancheng, China 72/C4
Juangriego, Ven. 153/F2
Juanjuí, Peru 156/B2
Juárez, Arg. 158/F3
Juarez, Sierra de (mts.), Mex. 128/D4
Juatinga, Ponta de (pt.), Braz. 211/J8
Juazeirinho, Braz. 154/C2
Juazeiro, Braz. 154/B3
Juazeiro do Norte, Braz. 154/C2
Juba, Sudan 97/M7
Jubany, Arg., Ant. 160/W
Jubba (riv.), Som. 97/P7
Jübek, Ger. 40/E1
Jubones (riv.), Ecu. 156/B1
Juby (cape), Mor. 98/B4
Júcar (riv.), Sp. 44/D3
Jucás, Braz. 154/C2
Jüchen, Ger. 53/F1
Juchipila, Mex. 142/E4
Juchique de Ferrer, Mex. 143/N7
Juchitán de Zaragoza, Mex. 144/C2
Juchitepec, Mex. 143/R10
Jucurutu, Braz. 154/C2
Judaberg, Nor. 38/A2
Judenburg, Aus. 43/L3
Judith (riv.), Mt, US 126/F4
Juelsminde, Den. 38/D4
Juhaynah, Egypt 101/B3
Juigalpa, Nic. 144/E3
Juilly, Fr. 30/L4
Juine (riv.), Fr. 42/E2
Juist (isl.), Ger. 50/D1
Juist, Ger. 50/E1
Juiz de Fora, Braz. 211/K6
Jujurieux, Fr. 56/B5
Julbach, Ger. 55/F6
Julesburg, Co, US 127/H5
Juli, Peru 156/D5
Julia Creek, Austl. 114/A3
Juliaca, Peru 156/D4
Julian Alps (mts.), It. 43/K3
Juliana Top (peak), Sur. 151/G3
Jülich, Ger. 53/F2
Julio A. Mella, Cuba 145/H1
Juliustown, NJ, US 138/D3
Jullundur, India 86/C4
Julu, China 72/C3
Jumbilla, Peru 156/B2
Jumeauville, Fr. 30/H5
Jumilla, Sp. 44/E3
Juminda (pt.), Est. 39/L2
Jumla, Nepal 84/D1
Jümme (riv.), Ger. 51/E2
Jūmonji, Japan 76/B4
Jūnāgadh, India 89/K4
Junan, China 72/D4
Juncal (peak), Chile 158/N8
Junction, Ut, US 128/D3
Junction, Tx, US 129/H5
Junction City, Or, US 126/C4
Jundiaí, Braz. 211/G8
Jundu (mts.), China 72/H6
Juneda, Sp. 45/F2
Junee, Austl. 115/C2
Jungar Qi, China 72/B3
Jungfrau (peak), Swi. 56/D4
Jungfraujoch, Swi. 56/D4
Junglinster, Lux. 53/F4
Juniata (riv.), Pa, US 130/E3
Juniata (co.), Pa, US 138/A2
Junik, Yugo. 47/G1
Junín, Peru 156/B3
Junín (dept.), Peru 156/C3
Junín, Ecu. 152/A5
Junín, Arg. 158/D3
Junín, Arg. 158/E2
Junín de los Andes, Arg. 158/C3
Juniper Hills, Ca, US 136/C2
Junji (pass), China 72/C3
Juno Beach, Fl, US 133/H5
Junqueirópolis, Braz. 155/B2
Junsele, Swe. 37/F3
Juparanã, Lagoa (lake), Braz. 155/D1
Jupiter (riv.), Qu, Can. 131/J1
Jupiter, Fl, US 133/H5
Jupiter (mt.), Wa, US 125/A2
Juquiá, Braz. 155/C3
Juquitiba, Braz. 211/F8
Jur (riv.), Sudan 97/L6
Jur pri Bratislave, Slvk. 48/C1
Jura (mts.), Fr. 42/F3
Jura (dept.), Fr. 56/B4
Jura (pen.), Sc, UK 31/R8
Jura (isl.), Sc, UK 31/R8
Juradó, Col. 152/B3
Jurançon, Fr. 42/C5
Jurbise, Belg. 52/C2
Jurien, Austl. 112/B4
Jūrmala, Lat. 39/K3
Juruá (riv.), Braz. 147/C3
Juruena (riv.), Braz. 147/D4
Juruti, Braz. 151/G4
Jushiyama, Japan 77/L5
Juskatla, BC, Can. 134/M5
Jussey, Fr. 56/B2
Jussy, Swi. 56/C5
Jussy, Fr. 52/C4
Justo Daract, Arg. 158/D2
Jutaí, Braz. 150/E5
Jutaí (riv.), Braz. 150/E4
Jutiapa, Guat. 144/D3
Juticalpa, Hon. 144/E3
Jutland, NJ, US 138/D2
Jutland (pen.), Den. 37/D4
Juventud, La (isl.), Cuba 145/F1
Juye, China 72/D4
Juzhang (riv.), China 72/C5
Juziers, Fr. 30/H4
Južna Morava (riv.), Yugo. 48/E4
Juzur Qarqannah (isl.), Congo 99/H2
Jyderup, Den. 38/D4

K

Ka (riv.), Nga. 96/F5
Ka (isl.), NKor. 73/C3
Ka Lae (cape), Hi, US 124/U11
Kaaawa, Hi, US 124/W12
Kaabong, Ugan. 104/B2
Kaala (peak), Hi, US 124/V12
Kaalualu, Hi, US 124/U11
Kaap Plato (plat.), SAfr. 106/C3
Kaarina, Fin. 39/K1
Kaarst, Ger. 50/D6
Kaba, Hun. 48/E2
Kabadak (riv.), Bang. 85/G4
Kabaena (isl.), Indo. 116/B5
Kabah (ruin), Mex. 144/D1
Kabala, SLeo. 102/C4
Kabale, Ugan. 104/A3
Kabalega (falls), Ugan. 104/A2
Kabalega NP, Ugan. 97/M7
Kabalo, D.R. Congo 105/E2
Kabamba, Lac (lake), D.R. Congo 105/E2
Kabankalan, Phil. 81/F2
Kabardino-Balkaria (aut. rep.), Rus. 63/G4
Kabare, D.R. Congo 104/A3
Kaberamaido, Ugan. 104/B2
Kabinakagani (lake), On, Can. 130/C1
Kabinda, D.R. Congo 105/D2
Kabīr, Oued el (riv.), Alg. 100/H4
Kabīrwāla, Pak. 86/A4
Kabīyah, Sabkhat al (swamp), Tun. 46/A5
Kableshkovo, Bul. 49/H4
Kābol (Kabul) (cap.), Afg. 89/J2
Kabompo (riv.), Zam. 105/D3
Kabongo, D.R. Congo 105/E2
Kabrai, India 84/C3
Kābul (riv.), Afg. 89/J2
Kabul (Kābol) (cap.), Afg. 89/J2
Kaburuang (isl.), Indo. 81/G3
Kabwe, Zam. 105/E3
Kačanik, Yugo. 47/G1
Kachalola, Zam. 105/F3
Kachemak (bay) 134/H4
Kachemak, Ak, US 134/H4
Kachin (div), Myan. 70/G6
Kaçkar Dai (peak), Turk. 63/G4
Kadaianallur, India 82/C6
Kadam (peak), Ugan. 104/B2
Kadam (isl.), Myan. 83/G5
Kadan (isl.), Myan. 83/G5
Kadaň, Czh. 55/G2
Kadavu (isl.), Fiji 116/G6
Kadéï (riv.), CAfr.,Cam 96/J7
Kadina, Austl. 113/H5
Kadınhanı, Turk. 90/C2
Kadiogo (prov.), Burk. 103/E3
Kadiolo, Mali 102/D4
Kadiri, India 82/C5
Kadirli, Turk. 90/D2
Kadışehri, Turk. 62/E5
Kadoka, SD, US 127/H5
Kadoma, Zim. 105/E4
Kadoma, Japan 77/J6
Kaduna (state), Nga. 103/G4
Kaduna, Nga. 103/G4
Kaduna (riv.), Nga. 93/C4
Kāduqlī, Sudan 97/L5
Kaech'ŏn, NKor. 73/C3
Kaédi, Mrta. 102/B2
Kaélé, Camr. 96/H5
Kaena (pt.), Hi, US 124/V12
Kaeng Krachan NP, Thai. 78/B3
Kaesŏng, NKor. 73/D3
Kaesŏng-si (prov.), NKor. 73/D4
Kafar Jar Ghar (mts.), Afg. 89/J2
Kaffraria (reg.), SAfr. 106/D4
Kaffrine, Sen. 102/B3
Kafirévs (cape), Gre. 47/J3
Kafr Ash Shaykh (gov.), Egypt 101/B1
Kafr ash Shaykh, Egypt 91/B4
Kafr az Zayyāt, Egypt 91/B4
Kafr Kannā, Isr. 91/G6
Kafr Mandā, Isr. 91/G6
Kafr Qari', Isr. 91/G6
Kafr Qāsim, Isr. 91/F7
Kafu (riv.), Ugan. 104/A2
Kafue (riv.), Zam. 105/E4
Kafue, Zam. 105/E4
Kafue NP, Zam. 105/E3
Kaga, Japan 74/E2
Kaga Bandoro, CAfr. 97/J6
Kagan, Uzb. 87/D5
Kāgān (valley), Pak. 86/B2
Kagawa (pref.), Japan 74/D3
Kagera (riv.), Tanz. 104/A3
Kağızman, Turk. 63/G4
Kagoshima (int'l arpt.), Japan 74/B5
Kagoshima, Japan 74/B5
Kagoshima (bay), Japan 74/B5
Kagoshima (dept.), Japan 75/L5
Kahaluu, Hi, US 124/W13
Kahama, Tanz. 104/B3
Kahayan (riv.), Indo. 80/D4
Kahiu (pt.), Hi, US 124/T10
Kahl am Main, Ger. 54/C2
Kāhna, Pak. 86/C4
Kahoka, Mo, US 127/L5
Kahoolawe (isl.), Hi, US 124/T10
Kahperusvaara (peak), Fin. 37/G1
Kahraman Maraş (prov.), Turk. 90/D2
Kahramanmaraş, Turk. 90/D2
Kahror Pakka, Pak. 86/A5
Kāhta, Turk. 90/D2
Kahuku, Hi, US 124/W12
Kahuku (pt.), Hi, US 124/W12
Kahului, Hi, US 124/T10
Kahuzi-Biega, PN de, D.R. Congo 105/E1
Kai (isls.), Indo. 116/C5
Kai Besar (isl.), Indo. 81/H5
Kai Kecil (isl.), Indo. 81/H5
Kaiapoi, NZ 117/S11
Kaibab (plat.), Az, US 128/D3
Kaibara, Japan 77/H5
Kaieteur (falls), Guy. 153/G3
Kaieteur NP, Guy. 153/G3
Kaifeng, China 71/K5
Kaifeng, China 72/C4
Kaihua, China 79/C2
Kaikohe, NZ 117/S10
Kaikoura, NZ 117/S11
Kaili, China 83/J2
Kailu, China 72/E2
Kailua, Hi, US 124/U11
Kailua, Hi, US 124/W13
Kaimganj, India 84/B2
Kaimur (range), India 84/C3
Kainab (riv.), Namb. 106/B2
Kainach (riv.), Aus. 48/B2
Kainan, Japan 74/D3
Kainji (dam), Nga. 103/G4
Kainji (lake), Nga. 93/C3
Kainji Lake NP, Nga. 103/F4
Kainoúryion, Gre. 47/G3
Kaipara (har.), NZ 117/S10
Kairāna, India 86/D5
Kairi, Austl. 114/B2
Kaisei, Japan 77/C3
Kaiseregg (peak), Swi. 56/D4
Kaisersesch, Ger. 53/G3
Kaiserslautern, Ger. 53/G5
Kaisheim, Ger. 54/D5
Kaitaia, NZ 117/S10
Kaithal, India 86/D5
Kaiwi (chan.), Hi, US 124/T10
Kaiyang, China 83/J2
Kaiyuan, China 83/H3
Kaiyuan, China 72/F2
Kaizu, Japan 77/L5
Kaizuka, Japan 77/H7
Kajaani, Fin. 64/C3
Kaji-san (peak), SKor. 74/A3
Kajiado, Kenya 104/C3
Kajikazawa, Japan 77/A2
Kakamas, SAfr. 106/C3
Kakamega, Kenya 104/B2
Kakamigahara, Japan 77/L5
Kakanj, Bosn. 48/D3
Kake, Ak, US 134/M4
Kaketsa (mtn.), BC, Can. 134/M4
Kakhovka, Ukr. 49/L2
Kakhovs'ke Vodoskhovyshche (res.), Ukr. 62/E3
Kākināda, India 82/D4
Kakiri, Ugan. 104/B2
Kako (riv.), Japan 77/G6
Kakogawa, Japan 77/G6
Kākori, India 84/C2
Kakrāla, India 84/B2
Kakrima (riv.), Gui. 102/B4
Kaktovik, Ak, US 134/K1
Kakuda, Japan 75/G2
Kakunodate, Japan 76/B4
Kalaa Kebira, Tun. 46/B5
Kālābāgh, Pak. 86/A3
Kalabo, Zam. 105/D3
Kalach, Rus. 63/G2
Kalach-na-Donu, Rus. 63/G2
Kalachinsk, Rus. 87/F1
Kaladan (riv.), Myan. 83/F3
Kālāgarh, India 84/B1
Kalahari (des.), Namb. 93/D7
Kalahari-Gemsbok NP, SAfr. 105/C6
Kalaheo, Hi, US 124/S10
Kalaiya, Nepal 85/E2
Kalalé, Ben. 103/F4
Kalamákion, Gre. 47/N8
Kalamaloué, PN de, Camr. 96/H5
Kalamariá, Gre. 47/H2
Kalamáta, Gre. 47/H4
Kalamazoo, Mi, US 130/C3
Kalampáka, Gre. 47/G3
Kalandy, Madg. 107/J6
Kalaoa, Hi, US 124/U11
Kalasin, Thai. 78/C2
Kalaswāla, Pak. 86/C3
Kalāt, Pak. 89/J3
Kalaupapa, Hi, US 124/T10
Kalávrita, Gre. 47/H3
Kalbach, Ger. 54/B2
Kalbar, Austl. 114/D4
Kalbarri, Austl. 112/B3
Kalbarri NP, Austl. 112/B3
Kaldakvísl (riv.), Ice. 37/N7
Kale, Turk. 62/F4
Kale, Turk. 91/A1
Kalecik, Turk. 62/E4
Kalefeld, Ger. 51/H5
Kalemie (int'l arpt.), D.R. Congo 104/A4
Kalemie, D.R. Congo 104/A4
Kalemyo, Myan. 83/F3
Kalety, Pol. 41/K3
Kalewa, Myan. 83/F3
Kaleya, Zam. 105/E4
Kalgoorlie-Boulder, Austl. 112/D4
Kāli (riv.), India 84/B1
Kāli (riv.), India 84/B2
Kāli (riv.), Nepal 84/D2
Kalianda, Indo. 80/C5
Kalima, D.R. Congo 97/L8
Kalimantan (reg.), Indo. 80/D4
Kálimnos, Gre. 90/A2
Kálimnos (isl.), Gre. 90/A2
Kālimpong, India 85/G2
Kaliningrad, Rus. 61/W9
Kaliningrad, Rus. 39/J4
Kaliningradskaya (obl.), Rus. 60/D5
Kalininsk, Rus. 63/H2
Kalinkavichy, Bela. 62/D1
Kaliro, Ugan. 104/B2
Kalisizo, Ugan. 104/A3
Kalispell, Mt, US 126/E3
Kalisz, Pol. 41/K3
Kalix, Swe. 60/D2
Kalixälven (riv.), Swe. 37/G2
Kāliyāganj, India 85/G3
Kalkaska, Mi, US 130/C2
Kallham, Aus. 55/G6
Kallinge, Swe. 38/F3
Kallinge (int'l arpt.), Swe. 38/F3
Kallithéa, Gre. 47/N9
Kallsjön (lake), Swe. 37/E3
Kalmar (int'l arpt.), Swe. 38/G3
Kalmar, Swe. 38/G3
Kalmar (co.), Swe. 37/F4
Kalmarsund (sound), Swe. 38/G3
Kalmthout, Belg. 50/B6
Kalmykia (aut. rep.), Rus. 64/E5
Kālna, India 85/G4
Kalni (riv.), Bang. 85/H3
Kalocsa, Hun. 48/D2
Kalofer, Bul. 47/J1
Kaloli (chan.), Hi, US 124/T10
Kalokhórion, Gre. 47/H2
Kālol, India 89/K4
Kalomo, Zam. 105/E4
Kalongo, Ugan. 104/B2
Kālpi, India 84/B2
Kalpin, China 70/C3
Kalsdorf bei Graz, Aus. 43/L3
Kaltag, Ak, US 134/G3
Kaltbrunn, Swi. 57/E3
Kaltenleutgeben, Aus. 49/N7
Kaltennordheim, Ger. 54/D1
Kaltern (Caldaro), It. 43/J3
Kalu (riv.), SrL. 82/D6
Kaluga, Rus. 60/H5
Kalundborg, Den. 38/D4
Kalungu, Ugan. 104/A3
Kalungwishi (riv.), Zam. 104/A5
Kalūr Kot, Pak. 86/A3
Kalush, Ukr. 62/C2
Kalutara, SrL. 82/C6
Kaluzkskaya (obl.), Rus. 60/G5
Kalyān, India 89/K5
Kama, D.R. Congo 105/E1
Kama (res.), Rus. 61/M4
Kama (riv.), Rus. 27/K3
Kamagaya, Japan 77/E2
Kamaishi, Japan 76/B4
Kamakou (peak), Hi, US 124/T10
Kamakura, Japan 77/D3
Kamālia, Pak. 86/B4
Kamalo, Hi, US 124/T10
Kāman, India 84/A2
Kaman, Turk. 62/E5
Kamango (lake), Mali 102/E2
Kamanjab, Namb. 105/B4
Kamarang, Guy. 153/F3
Kāmāreddi, India 82/C4
Kāmārhāti, India 82/E3
Kamaria (falls), Guy. 153/G3
Kambalda, Austl. 112/D4
Kambar, Pak. 82/A2
Kambara, Japan 77/B3
Kambia, SLeo. 102/B4
Kambove, D.R. Congo 105/E3
Kambuno (peak), Indo. 81/F4
Kamchatka (pen.), Rus. 67/Q4
Kamchatskaya (obl.), Rus. 65/R4
Kamchiya (riv.), Bul. 62/C4
Kamen, Ger. 51/E5
Kamen'-na-Obi, Rus. 87/H2
Kamenka, Rus. 63/H1
Kameno, Bul. 49/H4
Kamensk-Shakhtinskiy, Rus. 62/G2
Kamensk-Ural'skiy, Rus. 61/P4
Kameoka, Japan 77/J5
Kameyama, Japan 77/K6
Kami, Japan 77/G5
Kami (isl.), Japan 77/M6
Kami-koshiki (isl.), Japan 74/A5
Kamiah, Id, US 126/D4
Kamień Pomorski, Pol. 38/F5
Kamieskroon, SAfr. 106/B3
Kamifukuoka, Japan 77/D2
Kamiisco, Japan 76/B3
Kamiishizu, Japan 77/K5
Kamiizumi, Japan 77/C1
Kamikawa, Japan 76/C2
Kamikuishiki, Japan 77/B2
Kamilo (pt.), Hi, US 124/U11
Kamina, D.R. Congo 105/E2
Kaminaka, Japan 77/J5
Kaminoho, Japan 77/M4
Kaminoyama, Japan 75/G1
Kamisato, Japan 77/C1
Kamishak (bay), Ak, US 134/H4
Kamiyahagi, Japan 77/M5
Kamiyaku, Japan 75/L5
Kamla (riv.), India 85/F3
Kamloops, BC, Can. 126/C3
Kammaki, Japan 77/J6
Kamnik, Slov. 43/L3
Kamo, Japan 75/F2
Kamo, Japan 77/J6
Kamo (riv.), Japan 77/J6
Kamogawa, Japan 75/G3
Kamojima, Japan 74/D3
Kāmoke, Pak. 86/C4
Kamp (riv.), Aus. 41/H4
Kamp-Bornhofen, Ger. 53/G3
Kamp-Lintfort, Ger. 50/D5
Kampala (cap.), Ugan. 104/B2
Kampar, Malay. 80/B3
Kampar (riv.), Indo. 80/B3
Kampen, Neth. 50/C3
Kampen, Ger. 38/C4
Kamphaeng Phet, Thai. 78/C5
Kamphaeng Phet (ruin), Thai. 78/B2
Kampinoski NP, Pol. 62/B1
Kamp'o, SKor. 73/E5
Kampong Kuala Besut, Malay. 80/B2
Kampong Saom (bay), Camb. 80/B1
Kampong Saom, Camb. 78/C4
Kampville, Mo, US 137/F8
Kamsack, Sk, Can. 127/H3
Kamsdorf, Ger. 55/E1
Kamuchawie (lake), Mb,Sk, Can. 127/H1
Kamui-misaki (cape), Japan 76/B2
Kámuk (mtn.), CR 145/F4
Kamuli, Ugan. 104/B2
Kam'yanets'-Podil's'kyy, Ukr. 62/C2
Kamyshin, Rus. 63/H2
Kanaaupscow (riv.), Qu, Can. 123/J3
Kanab, Ut, US 128/D3
Kanaga (isl.), Ak, US 134/C6
Kanairiktok (riv.), Nf, Can. 123/K3
Kanan, Japan 77/J7
Kananga, D.R. Congo 105/D2
Kanangra-Boyd NP, Austl. 115/D2
Kanash, Rus. 61/K5
Kanasin, Mex. 144/D1
Kanawake Ind. Res., Qu, Can. 131/N7
Kanawha (riv.), WV, US 133/H2
Kanazawa, Japan 75/E2
Kanchanaburi, Thai. 78/B3
Kānchenjunga (peak), Nepal 82/E2
Kānchīpuram, India 82/C5
Kandalaksha, Rus. 60/G2
Kandalaksha (gulf), Rus. 37/K2
Kándanos, Gre. 47/H5
Kandé, Togo 103/F4
Kandel (peak), Ger. 56/E1
Kandel, Ger. 54/B4
Kander (riv.), Swi. 56/D4
Kandern, Ger. 56/D2
Kandersteg, Swi. 56/D5
Kandhkot, Pak. 89/J3
Kāndhla, India 86/D5
Kandi (cape), Indo. 81/F3
Kandi, Ben. 103/F4
Kāndi, India 85/G4
Kandıra, Turk. 49/K5
Kandos, Austl. 115/D2
Kandukūr, India 82/C4
Kandy, SrL. 82/D6
Kane (basin), Grld. 123/T7
Kane (co.), Il, US 135/P16
Kanem (reg.), Chad 96/H5
Kaneohe, Hi, US 124/W13
Kaneohe (bay), Hi, US 124/W13
Kaneohe Marine Air Corps Station, Hi, US 124/W13
Kaneville, Il, US 135/N16
Kaneyama, Japan 76/B4
Kang, Bots. 105/D5
Kanga (riv.), Bang. 85/G5
Kangaba, Mali 102/C4
Kangal, Turk. 90/D2
Kangān, Iran 88/F3
Kangan Abor. Land, Austl. 112/C2
Kanganpur, Pak. 86/C4
Kangar, Malay. 78/C5
Kangaroo (isl.), Austl. 109/C4
Kangasala, Fin. 39/L1
Kangāvar, Iran 88/E2
Kangbao, China 71/K3
Kangding, China 70/H5
Kangean (isls.), Indo. 81/E5
Kanggye, NKor. 73/D2
Kanggyŏng, SKor. 73/D4
Kanghwa, SKor. 73/F6
Kangiqsualujjuaq, Qu, Can. 123/K3
Kangiqsujuaq, Qu, Can. 123/J2
Kangirsuk, Qu, Can. 123/J2
Kangjin, SKor. 73/D5
Kangmar, China 85/G1
Kangnam (mts.), NKor. 73/C2
Kangnŭng, SKor. 74/A2
Kangping, China 72/E2
Kāngra, India 86/D3
Kangrinboqê (peak), China 70/D5
Kangshan, Tai. 79/D3
Kangto (peak), China 83/F2
Kangwŏn-do (prov.), SKor. 74/A2
Kanha NP, India 84/C4
Kanhān (riv.), India 82/C3
Kani, Japan 77/M5
Kanie, Japan 77/L5
Kanin (pen.), Rus. 160/C
Kanin Nos (pt.), Rus. 64/E3
Kaniva, Austl. 115/B3
Kanjiža, Yugo. 48/E2
Kankakee (riv.), Il,In, US 130/C3
Kankan (pol. reg.), Gui. 102/C4
Kankan, Gui. 102/C4
Kanmuri-yama (peak), Japan 74/C3
Kannami, Japan 77/B3
Kannapolis, NC, US 133/H3
Kannauj, India 84/B2
Kannon-zaki (pt.), Japan 77/D3
Kannus, Fin. 60/D3
Kano, Nga. 103/H4
Kano (state), Nga. 103/H4
Kan'onji, Japan 74/C3
Kanouse (mtn.), NJ, US 139/H7
Kanoya, Japan 74/B5
Kanra, Japan 77/B1
Kansai (int'l arpt.), Japan 77/H7
Kansai (isl.), Japan 77/H7
Kansas (state), US 129/H3
Kansas (riv.), Ks, US 129/H3
Kansas City (int'l arpt.), Mo, US 129/J3
Kansas City, Ks, US 137/D5
Kansas City, Mo, US 137/D5
Kansasville, Wi, US 135/P14
Kansk, Rus. 64/K4
Kansŏng, SKor. 73/E3
Kantābānji, India 82/D3
Kānth, India 84/B1
Kantō (prov.), Japan 75/F2
Kantunilkin, Mex. 144/E1
Kanuku (mts.), Guy. 150/G3
Kanuma, Japan 75/F2
Kanuti NWR, Ak, US 134/H2
Kanye, Bots. 105/E5
Kaohsiung, Tai. 79/D3
Kaohsiung (int'l arpt.), Tai. 79/D3
Kaokoveld (mts.), Namb. 105/B4
Kaolack, Sen. 102/A3
Kaolack (pol. reg.), Sen. 102/B3
Kaolinovo, Bul. 49/H4
Kaoma, Zam. 105/D3
Kapaa, Hi, US 124/S9
Kapaahu, Hi, US 124/U11
Kapaau, Hi, US 124/U10
Kapalong, Phil. 79/E6
Kapan, Arm. 63/H5
Kapchorwa, Ugan. 104/B2
Kapellen, Belg. 50/B6
Kapenguria, Kenya 104/B2
Kapidaği (pen.), Turk. 49/H5
Kapingamarangi (isl.), Micr. 116/E4
Kapiri Mposhi, Zam. 105/E3
Kapiskau (riv.), On, Can. 123/H3
Kaplice, Czh. 55/H5
Kapos (riv.), Hun. 48/C2
Kaposvár, Hun. 48/C2
Kappl, Aus. 57/G3
Kapsan, NKor. 73/E2

197
Kapua – Khirp

Kapuas (riv.), Indo. 80/C4
Kapuas Hulu (mts.), Indo.,Mal 80/D3
Kapunda, Austl. 113/H5
Kapūrthala, India 86/C4
Kapuskasing, On, Can. 130/D1
Kapuskasing (riv.), On, Can. 130/D1
Kapuvár, Hun. 43/M3
Kapydzhik (peak), Azer. 63/H5
Kap'yŏng, SKor. 73/D4
Kara, Togo 103/F4
Kara (sea), Rus. 160/A
Kara (riv.), Rus. 61/Q1
Kara-saki (pt.), Japan 74/A3
Karaali, Turk. 62/E5
Karabiğa, Turk. 49/H5
Karabük, Turk. 62/E4
Karaburun, Turk. 49/J5
Karaca (peak), Turk. 90/D2
Karacabey, Turk. 62/D4
Karacaköy, Turk. 49/J5
Karaçal (peak), Turk. 91/C1
Karacaoğlan, Turk. 49/H5
Karachayevo-Cherkesiya (aut. rep.), Rus. 63/G4
Karachev, Rus. 62/E1
Karāchi, Pak. 89/J4
Karadere, Turk. 49/K5
Karaginskiy (isl.), Rus. 67/R4
Karaj, Iran 88/F1
Karakax (riv.), China 89/L1
Karakaya (dam), Turk. 90/D2
Karakelong (isl.), Indo. 81/G3
Karakhoto (ruin), China 70/H3
Karakol, Kyr. 87/G4
Karakoram (range), India 70/C4
Karakoram (pass), India 86/D2
Karakoro (riv.), Mali 102/C3
Karakorum (ruin), Mong. 70/H2
Karakorum (ruin), Mong. 87/G5
Karakorum (pass), China 89/L1
Karaköse, Turk. 63/G5
Karaköy, Turk. 90/E2
Karakul' (lake), Taj. 87/F5
Karakumy (des.), Trkm. 64/F5
Karakyon (peak), Trkm. 87/B4
Karakyr (peak), Trkm. 89/H1
Karam (riv.), Indo. 81/E4
Karaman (prov.), Turk. 90/C2
Karaman, Turk. 90/C2
Karamay, China 70/D2
Karamea Bight (bay), NZ 109/H7
Karamoja (prov.), Ugan. 104/B2
Karamürsel, Turk. 49/J5
Karangasem, Indo. 81/E5
Karanginskiy (isl.), Rus. 65/S4
Karanginskiy (bay), Rus. 65/S4
Kāranja, India 82/C3
Karanpur, India 86/B5
Karapınar, Turk. 90/C2
Karasabai, Guy. 153/G3
Karaşar, Turk. 49/L5
Karasburg, Namb. 106/B3
Karasjohka-Karasjok, Nor. 37/H1
Karasu, Turk. 49/K5
Karasu, Japan 77/L6
Karasuk, Rus. 87/G2
Karatá (lag.), Nic. 145/F3
Karataş, Turk. 91/D1
Karatoya (riv.), Bang. 85/G3
Karatsu, Japan 74/A4
Karauli, India 84/A2
Karaurgan, Turk. 63/G4
Karáva (peak), Gre. 47/G3
Karawang, Indo. 80/C5
Karayaka, Turk. 62/F4
Karayazı, Turk. 63/G5
Karazhal, Kaz. 87/F3
Karbalā' (gov.), Iraq 90/E3
Karbalā', Iraq 90/F3
Karben, Ger. 54/B2
Karcag, Hun. 48/E2
Kardhámila, Gre. 47/K3
Kardhítsa, Gre. 47/G3
Kardhitsomagoúla, Gre. 47/G3
Kareha (riv.), India 85/E3
Karelī, India 84/B4
Karelia (reg.), Rus. 37/J2
Karelia (aut. rep.), Rus. 64/D3
Karera, India 84/B3
Karesuando, Swe. 37/G1
Karēt (reg.), Mrta. 98/D4
Karf Ash Shaykh (gov.) 90/B4
Kargı, Turk. 62/E4
Kargil, India 86/D2
Karhal, India 84/B2
Karhijärvi (lake), Fin. 39/K1
Karhula, Fin. 39/M1
Kariá, Gre. 47/G3
Karia Ba Mohammed, Mor. 100/B2
Kariaí, Gre. 47/J2
Karianga, Madg. 107/H8
Kariba (dam), Zam. 105/E4
Kariba, Zim. 105/E4
Kariba (lake), Zim. 93/E6
Kariba-yama (peak), Japan 76/A2
Karibib, Namb. 105/C5
Karimama, Ben. 103/F3
Karimata (isl.), Indo. 80/D4
Karimata (str.), Indo. 80/C4
Karīmnagar, India 82/C4
Karimunjawa (isls.), Indo. 80/D5
Kariótissa, Gre. 47/H2
Karise, Den. 38/E4
Karisimbi (vol.), D.R. Congo 104/A3
Karisimbi (vol.), Rwa. 105/E1
Káristos, Gre. 47/J3
Kariya, Japan 77/L6
Karkaar (mts.), Som. 97/Q6
Kārkāl, India 82/B5
Karkar (isl.), PNG 116/D5
Karkinits'ka Zatoka (gulf), Ukr. 62/D3
Karkkila, Fin. 39/L1
Karkonski NP, Pol. 41/H3
Karla Marksa (peak), Taj. 89/K1
Karlholmsbruk, Swe. 38/G1
Karlino, Pol. 38/F4
Karlovac, Cro. 48/B3
Karlovo, Bul. 47/J1
Karlovy Vary, Czh. 55/F2
Karlsdorf-Neuthard, Ger. 54/B4
Karlsfeld, Ger. 55/E6
Karlshamn, Swe. 38/F3
Karlshuld, Ger. 54/E5
Karlskoga, Swe. 38/F2
Karlskron, Ger. 55/E5
Karlskrona, Swe. 38/F3
Karlsruhe, Ger. 54/B4
Karlstad, Swe. 38/E2
Karlstadt, Ger. 54/C3
Karlstein am Main, Ger. 54/C2
Karluk, Ak, US 134/H4
Karmāla, India 89/L5
Karnali (riv.), Nepal 70/D6
Karnali (zone), Nepal 84/C1
Karnaphuli (res.), Bang. 85/H4
Karnataka (state), India 82/C4
Karnes City, Tx, US 129/H5
Karnobat, Bul. 47/K1
Kärnten (prov.), Aus. 43/K3
Karonga, Malw. 104/B5
Karoo NP, SAfr. 106/D4
Karoo NP, SAfr. 106/C4
Karoonda, Austl. 115/A2
Karor, Pak. 86/A4
Karoso (cape), Indo. 81/E5
Kárpathos, Gre. 90/A3
Kárpathos (isl.), Gre. 90/A3
Karpatskiy NP, Ukr. 49/G1
Karpenísion, Gre. 47/G3
Karratha, Austl. 112/C2
Kars, Turk. 63/G4
Kars (prov.), Turk. 63/G4
Kars (riv.), Turk. 63/G4
Kärsämäki, Fin. 60/E3
Karsantı, Turk. 90/C2
Karshi (int'l arpt.), Uzb. 87/E5
Kartaly, Rus. 63/M1
Kartārpur, India 86/C4
Kartuzy, Pol. 38/H4
Karuah, Austl. 115/D2
Karuma (falls), Ugan. 104/B2
Karumba, Austl. 114/A2
Karūn (riv.), Iran 64/E6
Karup, Den. 38/C3
Karviná, Czh. 41/K4
Kaş, Turk. 91/A1
Kås, Den. 38/C3
Kasaan, Ak, US 134/M4
Kasabonika (lake), On, Can. 127/L2
Kasagi, Japan 77/J6
Kasahara, Japan 77/M5
Kāsai (riv.), India 85/F4
Kasai, Japan 74/D3
Kasai (riv.), D.R. Congo 93/D5
Kasama, Zam. 104/A5
Kasama, Japan 75/G2
Kasamatsu, Japan 77/L5
Kasane, Bots. 105/E4
Kasaoka, Japan 74/C3
Kasar (cape), Sudan 101/D5
Kāsaragod, India 82/C5
Kasartori-yama (peak), Japan 77/K6
Kasba (lake), NW,Nun., Can. 122/F2
Kasba Tadla, Mor. 98/D2
Kaseda, Japan 74/B5
Kasese, Ugan. 104/A2
Kashaf (riv.), Iran 89/H1
Kāshān, Iran 88/F2
Kashi, China 87/G5
Kashiba, Japan 77/J6
Kashihara, Japan 77/J6
Kashima, Japan 74/B4
Kashima, Japan 75/G3
Kashima (bay), Japan 77/F1
Kashin, Rus. 60/H4
Kāshīpur, India 84/B1
Kashiwa, Japan 77/D2
Kashiwara, Japan 77/J6
Kashiwazaki, Japan 75/F2
Kāshmar, Iran 89/G1
Kashmir (reg.), India,Pak 87/G5
Kashmūnd Ghar (range), Afg. 86/A2
Kasigau (peak), Kenya 104/C3
Kasigluk, Ak, US 134/F3
Kasilof, Ak, US 134/H3
Kasimov, Rus. 60/J5
Kasiruta (isl.), Indo. 81/G4
Kasiui (isl.), Indo. 81/H4
Kaskaskia (riv.), Il, US 129/K3
Kaslo, BC, Can. 126/D3
Kasongo, D.R. Congo 105/E1
Kásos (isl.), Gre. 90/A3
Kaspichan, Bul. 49/H4
Kaspiysk, Rus. 63/H4
Kassala, Sudan 88/C5
Kassándra (pen.), Gre. 62/B5
Kassándria, Gre. 47/H2
Kassel, Ger. 51/G6
Kassikaityu (riv.), Guy. 153/G4
Kassler, Co, US 137/B4
Kasson, Mn, US 127/K4
Kastamonu, Turk. 62/E4
Kastamonu (prov.), Turk. 62/E4
Kastanéai, Gre. 47/K2
Kaštel Stari, Cro. 48/C4
Kaštel Sućurac, Cro. 48/C4
Kastellaun, Ger. 53/G3
Kastéllion, Gre. 47/J5
Kasterlee, Belg. 50/B6
Kastl, Ger. 55/E4
Kastoría, Gre. 47/G2
Kastrakíou (lake), Gre. 47/G3
Kasuga, Japan 77/H5
Kasuga, Japan 77/K5
Kasugai, Japan 77/B2
Kasugai, Japan 77/L5
Kasukabe, Japan 75/F3
Kasumiga (lake), Japan 75/G2
Kasungu, Malw. 105/F3
Kasūr, Pak. 86/C4
Kat O Chau (isl.), China 71/V9
Katahdin (mt.), Me, US 131/G2
Katákolon, Gre. 47/G4
Katanga (reg.), D.R. Congo 105/D2
Katanga (pol. reg.), D.R. Congo 104/A5
Katangi, India 84/B4
Katanning, Austl. 112/C5
Katano, Japan 77/J6
Katastárion, Gre. 47/G4
Katavi NP, Tanz. 105/F2
Katchall (isl.), India 83/F6
Katerini, Gre. 47/H2
Kates Needle (peak), Ak, US 134/M4
Katete, Zam. 105/F3
Katghora, India 84/D4
Kāthgodām, India 84/B1
Kathiawar (pen.), India 89/K4
Kathleen (mt.), Austl. 113/G2
Kāthmāndu (cap.), Nepal 85/E2
Kathua, India 86/C3
Kati, Mali 102/C3
Katiola, C.d'Iv. 102/D4
Katlehong, SAfr. 106/E2
Katlenburg-Lindau, Ger. 51/H5
Katmai (vol.), Ak, US 134/H4
Katmai NP, Ak, US 134/G4
Káto Akhaïa, Gre. 47/G3
Katokhí, Gre. 47/G3
Katonah, NY, US 139/E1
Katonga (riv.), Ugan. 104/A2
Katoúna, Gre. 47/G3
Katowice, Pol. 41/K3
Katra, India 86/C3
Kātrās, India 85/F4
Katrine (lake), Sc, UK 36/B4
Katrineholm, Swe. 38/G2
Katsikás, Gre. 47/G3
Katsina (state), Nga. 103/G3
Katsina, Nga. 103/G3
Katsina Ala (riv.), Nga. 103/H5
Katsunuma, Japan 77/B2
Katsura (riv.), Japan 77/J5
Katsuragi, Japan 74/D3
Katsuragi-san (peak), Japan 77/H7
Katsuta, Japan 75/G2
Katsuura, Japan 75/G3
Katsuyama, Japan 74/E2
Katsuyama, Japan 77/B3
Kattakurgan, Uzb. 87/E5
Kattegat (str.), Den. 27/F3
Katumbi, Malw. 104/B5
Kātwa, India 85/G4
Katwe-Kabatooro, Ugan. 104/A3
Katwijk aan Zee, Neth. 50/B4
Katy, Tx, US 129/J5
Katzenbach (riv.), Ger. 54/B4
Katzenbuckel (peak), Ger. 54/C4
Katzenelnbogen, Ger. 53/G3
Katzhütte, Ger. 54/D1
Katzwinkel, Ger. 53/F3
Kau-ye (isl.), Myan. 78/B4
Kauai (chan.), Hi, US 124/S10
Kauai (isl.), HI, US 117/K2
Kaufbeuren, Ger. 57/G2
Kaufering, Ger. 57/G1
Kaufungen, Ger. 51/G6
Kauhava, Fin. 60/D3
Kauhola (pt.), Hi, US 124/U10
Kauiki (pt.), Hi, US 124/U10
Kaukaveld (uplands), Namb. 105/C5
Kaukura (isl.), FrPol. 117/L6
Kaulakahi (chan.), Hi, US 124/R9
Kaulsdorf, Ger. 55/E1
Kaumalapau, Hi, US 124/T10
Kauna (pt.), Hi, US 124/U11
Kaunakakai, Hi, US 124/T10
Kaunas (int'l arpt.), Lith. 39/K4
Kaunas (res.), Lith. 39/L4
Kaunas, Lith. 39/K4
Kaupanger, Nor. 38/B1
Kauttua, Fin. 39/K1
Kavadarci, FYROM 47/H2
Kavajë, Alb. 47/F2
Kavála, Gre. 47/J2
Kavalerovo, Rus. 71/Q3
Kāvali, India 82/C5
Kavangel (isls.), Indo. 116/C4
Kavaratti, India 82/B5
Kavarna, Bul. 49/J4
Kavgolovskoye (lake), Rus. 61/T6
Kavieng, PNG 116/E5
Kavīr-e Namak (dry lake), Iran 87/C6
Kävlinge, Swe. 38/E4
Kaw (lake), Ok, US 129/H3
Kawa (ruin), Sudan 101/B5
Kawabe, Japan 76/B4
Kawachi, Japan 77/E2
Kawachi-Nagano, Japan 77/J7
Kawage, Japan 77/L6
Kawagoe, Japan 75/F3
Kawagoe, Japan 77/L5
Kawaguchi, Japan 75/F3
Kawaguchiko, Japan 77/B3
Kawai, Japan 77/J6
Kawaihoa (pt.), Hi, US 124/R10
Kawaikini (peak), Hi, US 124/S9
Kawajima, Japan 77/C2
Kawakami, Japan 77/B2
Kawakami, Japan 77/J7
Kawamata, Japan 75/G2
Kawambwa, Zam. 104/A5
Kawamoto, Japan 77/C1
Kawanishi, Japan 77/H6
Kawanishi, Japan 77/J6
Kawardha, India 84/C4
Kawartha (lakes), On, Can. 130/E2
Kawasaki, Japan 75/F3
Kawasato, Japan 77/D1
Kawashima, Japan 77/C1
Kawaue, Japan 77/M4
Kawela (Kawela Bay), Hi, US 124/V12
Kawerau, NZ 117/T10
Kawlin, Myan. 83/G3
Kawthaung, Myan. 78/B4
Kax (riv.), China 64/J5
Kay (pt.), Yk, Can. 134/L2
Kaya, SKor. 73/E5
Kaya, Japan 77/H5
Kaya-san (peak), SKor. 73/D4
Kayadibi, Turk. 62/E5
Kayagangiri (peak), CAfr. 96/J6
Kayah (div.), Myan. 70/G8
Kayah (state), Myan. 83/G4
Kayan (riv.), Indo. 67/L9
Kayanga (riv.), Sen. 102/B3
Kaycee, Wy, US 126/G5
Kayenta, Az, US 128/E3
Kayes, Mali 102/C3
Kayes (pol. reg.), Mali 102/C3
Kayin (state), Myan. 83/G4
Kayl, Lux. 53/F5
Kaymaz, Turk. 49/K5
Kaynarca, Turk. 49/J5
Kaynaşlı, Turk. 49/K5
Kayoa (isl.), Indo. 81/G3
Kayser (mts.), Sur. 153/G4
Kayseri, Turk. 90/C2
Kayseri (prov.), Turk. 90/C2
Kaysersberg, Fr. 56/D1
Kaysville, Ut, US 137/K11
Kayuagung, Indo. 80/B4
Kazakhstan (ctry.) 64/G5
Kazan', Rus. 61/L5
Kazan (int'l arpt.), Rus. 61/L5
Kazan (riv.), Nun., Can. 122/F2
Kazancı, Turk. 91/C1
Kazanlı, Turk. 91/D1
Kazanlŭk, Bul. 47/J1
Kazbek (peak), Geo. 63/H4
Kāzerūn, Iran 88/F3
Kazgar (riv.), China 70/C4
Kazimierza Wielka, Pol. 41/L3
Kāzimkarabekir, Turk. 90/C2
Kazincbarcika, Hun. 41/L4
Kazo, Japan 77/D1
Kazuno, Japan 76/B3
Ke Ga (cape), Viet. 78/E3
Ké Macina, Mali 102/D3
Kéa (isl.), Gre. 47/J4
Kéa, Gre. 47/J4
Keaau, Hi, US 124/U11
Keady, NI, UK 34/B3
Keahole (pt.), Hi, US 124/T11
Keanapapa (pt.), Hi, US 124/T10
Keansburg, NJ, US 139/J10
Kearney, Ne, US 129/H2
Kearney, Mo, US 137/E5
Kearns, Ut, US 137/K12
Kearny, NJ, US 139/J8
Kearny (pt.), NI, UK 34/C3
Keawakapu, Hi, US 124/T10
Keawekaheka (pt.), Hi, US 124/U11
Keban (dam), Turk. 90/D2
Kebbi (state), Nga. 103/G4
Kébémer, Sen. 102/A3
Kebnekaise (peak), Swe. 37/F2
Kebumen, Indo. 80/C5
Kecel, Hun. 48/D2
Keçiborlu, Turk. 90/B2
Kecskemét, Hun. 48/D2
Kedah (state), Malay. 78/C5
Kėdainiai, Lith. 39/K4
Kediri, Indo. 80/D5
Kédougou, Sen. 102/B3
Kędzierzyn-Koźle, Pol. 41/K3
Keego Harbor, Mi, US 135/F6
Keele (riv.), NW, Can. 122/D2
Keele (peak), Yk, Can. 122/C2
Keelung, Tai. 79/D2
Keelung, Japan 75/G8
Keen (mt.), Sc, UK 36/D3
Keene, NH, US 131/F3
Keepit (dam), Austl. 115/D1
Keer-Weer (cape), Austl. 114/A1
Keetmanshoop, Namb. 106/B2
Kefallinía (isl.), Gre. 47/G3
Kefar Sava, Isr. 91/F7
Kefar Vitkin, Isr. 91/F7
Keflavík (int'l arpt.), Ice. 37/M7
Keflavík, Ice. 37/M7
Kehl, Ger. 56/D1
Kehrsatz, Swi. 56/D4
Keighley, Eng, UK 35/G4
Keihoku, Japan 77/J5
Keila, Est. 39/L2
Keimoes, SAfr. 106/C3
Kéita (riv.), Chad 97/J6
Keith, Austl. 115/B3
Keith, Sc, UK 36/D1
Kejimkujik NP, NS, Can. 131/H2
Kekaha, Hi, US 124/S10
Kékes (peak), Hun. 41/K5
Kelan, China 72/B3
Kelang (isl.), Indo. 81/G4
Kelang, Malay. 80/B3
Kelberg, Ger. 53/F3
Keles, Turk. 62/D5
Kelheim, Ger. 55/E5
Kelkheim, Ger. 54/B2
Kelkıt (riv.), Turk. 90/D1
Kelkit, Turk. 62/F4
Kell, Ger. 53/F4
Kellenhusen, Ger. 38/D4
Keller (peak), Ca, US 136/C2
Keller (lake), NW, Can. 122/D2
Kellerberrin, Austl. 112/C4
Kellogg, Id, US 126/D4
Kells, NI, UK 34/B2
Kélo, Chad 96/J6
Kelowna, BC, Can. 126/D3
Kelsey (pt.), Eng, UK 32/A6
Kelso, Wa, US 126/C4
Kelso, Sc, UK 36/D5
Kelsterbach, Ger. 54/B2
Keluang, Malay. 80/B3
Kelvington, Sk, Can. 127/H2
Kem', Rus. 64/D3
Kem', Rus. 60/G2
Kemah, Turk. 62/F5
Kemaliye, Turk. 90/D2
Kemalpaşa, Turk. 63/G4
Kemasik, Malay. 80/B3
Kematen an der Ybbs, Aus. 55/H6
Kematen in Tirol, Aus. 57/H3
Kembs, Fr. 56/D2
Kemecse, Hun. 41/L4
Kemena (riv.), Malay. 80/D3
Kemence, Hun. 41/K4
Kemer (dam), Turk. 90/B2
Kemer, Turk. 91/B1
Kemerhisar, Turk. 90/C2
Kemerovo, Rus. 64/J4
Kemi, Fin. 64/C3
Kemijärvi, Fin. 60/E2
Kemijoki (riv.), Fin. 37/H2
Kemmerer, Wy, US 126/F5
Kemnath, Ger. 55/E3
Kemnay, Sc, UK 36/D2
Kemp (lake), Tx, US 129/H4
Kempele, Fin. 60/E2
Kempen, Ger. 50/D6
Kempenich, Ger. 53/G3
Kempenland (phys. reg.), Belg. 50/C6
Kempisch Kanaal (canal), Belg. 53/E1
Kempsey, Austl. 115/E1
Kempston, Eng, UK 33/F2
Kempt (res.), Qu, Can. 130/F2
Kempten, Ger. 57/G2
Kempton, Austl. 115/C4
Kempton Park, SAfr. 106/Q13
Kemptown, Md, US 138/A5
Kemri, India 84/B1
Kemul (peak), Indo. 81/E3
Ken (riv.), India 84/C3
Ken (lake), Sc, UK 34/D1
Ken-zaki (pt.), Japan 77/D3
Kenadsa, Alg. 99/E3
Kenai, Ak, US 134/H3
Kenai Fjords NP, Ak, US 134/H4
Kenai NWR, Ak, US 134/H3
Kendal, Eng, UK 35/F3
Kendalia, Tx, US 137/T20
Kendall, Austl. 115/E1
Kendall, Fl, US 133/H5
Kendall (co.), Tx, US 137/T20
Kendall (co.), Il, US 135/P16
Kendall Park, NJ, US 138/D3
Kendallville, In, US 130/C3
Kendari, Indo. 81/F4
Kéndavros, Gre. 47/J2
Kendel (riv.), Ger. 50/D5
Kendrāpāra, India 82/E3
Kénédougou (prov.), Burk. 102/D4
Kenema, SLeo. 102/C5
Kenge, D.R. Congo 105/C1
Kenhardt, SAfr. 106/C3
Kenhorst, Pa, US 138/C3
Kenié-Baoulé, Réserve de, Mali 102/C3
Kenilworth, Eng, UK 33/E2
Kenilworth, NJ, US 139/H9
Kénitra (prov.), Mor. 100/A2
Kénitra, Mor. 100/A2
Kenli, China 72/D3
Kenmare, ND, US 127/H3
Kenmare, Ire. 31/P11
Kenmore, NY, US 131/S10
Kenmore, Wa, US 135/C2
Kenn (reef), Austl. 109/E3
Kenn, Ger. 53/F4
Kennebec (riv.), Me, US 131/G2
Kennebunk, Me, US 131/G3
Kennedy (chan.), Grld.,Nun., Can. 123/T6
Kennedy (range), Austl. 112/B3
Kennedy Entrance (chan.) 134/H4
Kennedyville, Md, US 138/C5
Kennelbach, Aus. 57/F3
Kennemerduinen, NP de, Neth. 50/B4
Kenner, La, US 137/P17
Kennet (riv.), Eng, UK 33/E4
Kennet and Avon (canal), Eng, UK 32/D4
Kenneth, Ks, US 137/D6
Kennett, Mo, US 129/K3
Kennett Square, Pa, US 138/C4
Kennewick, Wa, US 126/D4
Keno Hill, Yk, Can. 134/L3
Kenogami (riv.), On, Can. 123/H3
Kenora, On, Can. 127/K3
Kenosha (co.), Wi, US 135/P14
Kensico (res.), NY, US 139/K7
Kensington and Chelsea (bor.), Eng, UK 30/A1
Kent, Wa, US 126/C4
Kent, Oh, US 130/D3
Kent (pt.), Md, US 138/B6
Kent (pen.), Nun., Can. 122/F2
Kent (isl.), Md, US 138/B6
Kent (lake), Mi, US 135/E7
Kent (co.), On, Can. 135/G6
Kent (riv.), Eng, UK 35/F3
Kent County (int'l arpt.), Mi, US 130/C3
Kent Group (isls.), Austl. 115/C3
Kentaū, Kaz. 87/E4
Kenton, Oh, US 130/D3
Kenton, De, US 138/C5
Kentucky (riv.), Ky, US 130/C4
Kentucky (state), US 133/G2
Kentucky (lake), Ky, US 133/F2
Kentville, NS, Can. 131/H2
Kenya (ctry.) 104/C2
Kenzingen, Ger. 56/D1
Keonjhar, India 82/E3
Kep i Gjuhëzës (cape), Alb. 47/F2
Kep i Rodonit (cape), Alb. 47/F2
Kępno, Pol. 41/J3
Keppel Sands, Austl. 114/C3
Kerala (state), India 82/C5
Kéran, PN de la, Togo 103/F4
Kerang, Austl. 115/B2
Keratéa, Gre. 47/N9
Kerava, Fin. 39/L1
Kerch' (str.), Rus.,Ukr. 62/F3
Kerch, Ukr. 62/F3
Keremeos, BC, Can. 126/D3
Kerempe (pt.), Turk. 62/E4
Kerempe Burnu (cape), Turk. 90/C1
Keren, Erit. 88/C5
Kerepestarcsa, Hun. 49/R9
Keret' (lake), Rus. 37/K2
Kerguélen (isl.), Fr. 23/N8
Kericho, Kenya 104/B3
Kerikeri (cape), NZ 117/S9
Kerinci (peak), Indo. 80/B4
Kerio (riv.), Kenya 104/C2
Kerio Valley Nat'l Rsv., Kenya 104/B2
Kerkdriel, Neth. 50/C5
Kerken, Ger. 50/D6
Kerki, Trkm. 87/E5
Kerkínis (lake), Gre. 47/H2
Kérkira, Gre. 47/F3
Kerkrade, Neth. 53/F2
Kerkwijk, Neth. 50/C5
Kermadec (isls.), NZ 116/G8
Kermān, Iran 89/G2
Kern (riv.), Ca, US 128/C4
Kern, South Kern (riv.), Ca, US 128/C4
Kerns, Swi. 57/E4
Kéros (isl.), Gre. 47/J4
Kérou, Ben. 103/F4
Kerr (lake), Ok, US 129/J4
Kerr (res.), NC,Va, US 133/J2
Kerrobert, Sk, Can. 126/F3
Kerrville, Tx, US 129/H5
Kert (riv.), Mor. 100/C2
Kerulen (riv.), Mong. 67/L5
Kerzaz, Alg. 99/E3
Kerzenheim, Ger. 53/H4
Kerzers, Swi. 56/D4
Kesagami (riv.), On, Can. 130/D1
Keşan, Turk. 47/K2
Kesch (peak), Swi. 57/F4
Kesen'numa, Japan 76/B4
Keshan, China 71/N2
Keshod, India 82/B3
Keski-Suomi (prov.), Fin. 37/H3
Keskin, Turk. 62/E5
Kesselbach (riv.), Ger. 54/D5
Kestel, Turk. 62/D4
Kesteren, Neth. 50/C5
Keszthely, Hun. 48/C2
Ket' (riv.), Rus. 64/J4
Keta, Gha. 103/F5
Keta (riv.), Rus. 64/K3
Ketchikan, Ak, US 134/M4
Kete Krachi, Gha. 103/E5
Ketelmeer (lake), Neth. 50/C3
Kétou, Ben. 103/F5
Kętrzyn, Pol. 39/J4
Ketsch, Ger. 54/B4
Kettering, Eng, UK 33/F2
Kettle (riv.), Mn, US 126/D3
Kettle Moraine State Forest, Wi, US 135/P14
Ketzin, Ger. 40/P7
Keukenhof, Neth. 50/B4
Kevelaer, Ger. 50/D5
Kewaunee, Wi, US 130/C2
Keweenaw (pen.), Mi, US 127/L4
Keweenaw (pt.), Mi, US 127/M4
Keweenaw (bay), Mi, US 127/L4
Key Largo, Fl, US 133/H5
Key West, Fl, US 133/H5
Keymar, Md, US 138/A4
Keyport, NJ, US 139/J10
Keyport, Wa, US 135/B2
Keystone (lake), Ok, US 129/H3
Kežmarok, Slvk. 41/L4
Khaanziir (cape), Som. 97/Q5
Khabarovsk, Rus. 71/Q2
Khabarovskiy (kray), Rus. 65/P4
Khagaria, India 85/F3
Khair, India 84/A2
Khairābād, India 84/C2
Khairpur, Pak. 86/B5
Khairpur, Pak. 89/J3
Khairpur, Pak. 89/J3
Khakasiya (aut. rep.), Rus. 65/P6
Khalándrion, Gre. 47/N8
Khalīj al Hammāmāt (gulf), Tun. 46/B4
Khalīlābād, India 84/D2
Khalkhāl, Iran 88/E1
Khalkidhikhi (pen.), Gre. 47/H2
Khalkidhón, Gre. 47/H2
Khalkís, Gre. 47/H3
Khamar-Daban (mts.), Rus. 70/H1
Khambhāliya, India 89/J4
Khambhat, India 89/K4
Khamīs Mushayt, SAr. 88/D5
Khammam, India 82/D4
Khamr, Yem. 88/D5
Khān Yūnus, Gaza 91/D4
Khānābād, Afg. 89/J1
Khānaqīn, Iraq 90/F3
Khandwa, India 89/L4
Khanem (well), Alg. 99/F3
Khānewāl, Pak. 86/A4
Khāngāh Dogrān, Pak. 86/B4
Khāngarh, Pak. 86/A5
Khaniá, Gre. 47/J5
Khanka (lake), China,Rus 67/N5
Khanna, India 86/D4
Khānpur, Pak. 86/A5
Khanty-Mansiysk, Rus. 64/G3
Khanty-Mansiyskiy (aut. okrug), Rus. 64/G3
Khao Chamao-Khao Wong NP, Thai. 78/C3
Khao Khitchakut NP, Thai. 78/C3
Khao Laem (res.), Thai. 83/G4
Khao Sam Roi Yot NP, Thai. 78/B3
Khao Yai NP, Thai. 78/C3
Kharagpur, India 85/F4
Kharagpur, India 85/F3
Kharak, Pak. 86/A3
Khārān, Pak. 89/J3
Kharar, India 85/F4
Kharar, India 86/D4
Kharbatā, Isr. 91/G8
Khargon, India 89/L4
Khāriān, Pak. 86/B3
Kharkiv (int'l arpt.), Ukr. 62/F2
Kharkiv, Ukr. 62/F2
Kharkivs'ka (obl.), Ukr. 62/F2
Kharmanli, Bul. 47/J2
Kharovsk, Rus. 60/J4
Kharrour (riv.), Mor. 100/B2
Kharsia, India 84/D5
Khartoum (Kharṭūm) (cap.), Sudan 88/B5
Khasavyurt, Rus. 63/H4
Khāsh (riv.), Afg. 89/H2
Khashuri, Geo. 63/G4
Khasi (hills), India 85/H3
Khaskovo (pol. reg.), Bul. 47/J2
Khaskovo (prov.), Bul. 49/G5
Khatanga (riv.), Rus. 160/Z
Khatanga (gulf), Rus. 65/L2
Khatauli, India 86/D5
Khātegaon, India 84/A4
Khatīma, India 84/B1
Khatlon (obl.), Taj. 87/E5
Khatmia (pass), Egypt 91/C4
Khātra, India 85/F4
Khatt Atoui (riv.), Mrta. 96/B3
Khaur, Pak. 86/B3
Khaybar (pass), Afg. 86/A2
Khazzān Dūkān (res.), Iraq 90/F3
Khazzān Jabal Al Awliyā (dam), Sudan 97/M4
Khekra, India 86/D5
Khemis el Khechna, Alg. 100/G4
Khemis Miliana, Alg. 100/G4
Khémisset (prov.), Mor. 100/A3
Khémisset, Mor. 100/A3
Khenchela (prov.), Alg. 99/G2
Khenchela, Alg. 100/K7
Khénifra, Mor. 98/D2
Khepoyarvi (lake), Rus. 61/T6
Kheri, India 84/C1
Khersān (riv.), Iran 88/F2
Kherson, Ukr. 49/L2
Kherson (int'l arpt.), Ukr. 49/L2
Khersons'ka (obl.), Ukr. 62/E3
Khilok, Rus. 71/K1
Khimki, Rus. 61/W9
Khíos, Gre. 47/K3
Khíos (isl.), Gre. 47/K3
Khirpai, India 85/F4

Königsbrunn, Ger. 57/G1
Königsdorf, Ger. 57/H2
Königsfeld im Schwarzwald, Ger. 57/E1
Königslutter am Elm, Ger. 51/H4
Königstein im Taunus, Ger. 54/B2
Königswinter, Ger. 53/G2
Konin, Pol. 41/K2
Kónitsa, Gre. 47/G2
Köniz, Swi. 56/D4
Konjic, Bosn. 48/C4
Könkämäeno (riv.), Fin. 60/D1
Konkouré (riv.), Gui. 102/B4
Konnevesi, Fin. 60/E3
Konolfingen, Swi. 56/D4
Kōnosu, Japan 77/D1
Konotop, Ukr. 62/E2
Konqi (riv.), China 64/J5
Konsen (plat.), Japan 76/D2
Końskie, Pol. 41/L3
Konstancin-Jeziorna, Pol. 41/L2
Konstantynów Łódzki, Pol. 41/K3
Konstanz, Ger. 57/F2
Kontich, Belg. 53/D1
Kontiolahti, Fin. 60/F3
Konuralp, Turk. 49/K5
Kóny, Hun. 48/C2
Konya, Turk. 90/C2
Konya (prov.), Turk. 90/C2
Konz, Ger. 53/F4
Koondrook, Austl. 115/C2
Koorawatha, Austl. 115/D2
Koorda, Austl. 112/C4
Kootenai (riv.), Id, US 126/D3
Kootenay (lake), BC, Can. 122/E3
Kootenay NP, BC, Can. 126/D3
Kootingal, Austl. 115/D1
Kop-Geçdi (pass), Turk. 63/G4
Kopāganj, India 84/D2
Kopargaon, India 89/K5
Kópavogur, Ice. 37/N7
Kope (peak), C.d'Iv. 102/D5
Köpenick, Ger. 40/Q7
Koper, Slov. 43/K4
Kopervik, Nor. 38/A2
Kopeysk, Rus. 61/P5
Kopfing im Innkreis, Aus. 55/G6
Köping, Swe. 38/G2
Kopondei (cape), Indo. 81/F5
Koporskiy (bay), Rus. 39/N2
Koppang, Nor. 38/D1
Kopparberg (co.), Swe. 37/E3
Kopparberg, Swe. 38/F2
Koppies, SAfr. 106/D2
Koprivnica, Cro. 48/C2
Koprivshtitsa, Bul. 47/J1
Köprü (riv.), Turk. 91/B1
Köprülü, Turk. 91/C1
Köprülü Kanyon NP, Turk. 90/B2
Kor (riv.), Iran 88/F2
Kora, India 84/C2
Kōra, Japan 77/K5
Kora NP, Kenya 104/C3
Korab (peak), Alb. 47/G2
Koráb (peak), Czh. 55/G4
Korakuen Garden, Japan 74/C3
Koraluk (riv.), Nf, Can. 123/K3
Korana (riv.), Cro. 43/L4
Koraput, India 82/D4
Korba, India 84/D4
Korbach, Ger. 51/F6
Korçë, Alb. 47/G2
Korčula (isl.), Cro. 46/E1
Korčulanski Kanal (chan.), Cro. 46/E1
Kord Küy, Iran 88/F1
Kordel, Ger. 53/F4
Korea (bay), China,NKor. 65/N6
Korea (str.), Japan,SKor. 65/P6
Korean Folk Village, SKor. 73/G7
Korenovsk, Rus. 62/F3
Korhogo, C.d'Iv. 102/D4
Korinós, Gre. 47/H2
Kórinthos (Corinth), Gre. 47/H4
Kőris-hegy (peak), Hun. 48/C2
Kōriyama, Japan 75/G2
Korizo, Passe de (pass), Chad 96/J3
Korkodon (riv.), Rus. 65/R3
Korkuteli, Turk. 91/B1
Korla, China 70/E3
Kormakiti (cape), Cyp. 91/C2
Körmend, Hun. 43/M3
Kornat (isl.), Cro. 48/B4
Körner, Ger. 51/H6
Korneuburg, Aus. 49/N7
Korntal-Münchingen, Ger. 54/C5
Kornwestheim, Ger. 54/C5
Koro (sea), Fiji 116/G6
Köroğlu (peak), Turk. 49/K5
Korogwe, Tanz. 104/C4
Koroit, Austl. 115/B3
Koronadal, Phil. 81/F2
Korónia (lake), Gre. 47/H2
Koronowo, Pol. 41/J2
Koropíon, Gre. 47/N9
Koror (cap.), Palau 116/C4
Körös (riv.), Hun. 48/E2
Korosten', Ukr. 62/D2
Korostyshiv, Ukr. 62/D2
Korotaikha (riv.), Rus. 61/P1
Korovin (vol.), Ak, US 134/D5
Korpo (Korppoo), Fin. 39/J1
Korsakov, Rus. 71/R2
Korschenbroich, Ger. 50/D6
Korsør, Den. 38/D4
Korsze, Pol. 39/J4
Kortemark, Belg. 52/C1
Kortenaken, Belg. 53/E2
Kortenberg, Belg. 53/D2
Kortessem, Belg. 53/E2
Kortrijk, Belg. 52/C2
Korup, PN de, Camr. 103/H5
Koryak (range), Rus. 67/R3
Koryakskiy (aut. okrug), Rus. 65/S3
Koryazhma, Rus. 61/K3
Kōryō, Japan 77/J6
Koryŏng, SKor. 73/E5
Kós (isl.), Gre. 90/A2
Kós, Gre. 90/A2
Kosai, Japan 75/E3
Kosai, Japan 77/A2
Kösching, Ger. 55/E5
Kościan, Pol. 41/J2
Kościerzyna, Pol. 38/G4
Kosciusko (mt.), Austl. 115/D3
Kosciusko, Ms, US 133/F3
Kosciusko NP, Austl. 115/D3
Köse, Turk. 62/F4
Kosei, Japan 77/K6
Koshigaya, Japan 75/F3
Kōshim (riv.), Kaz. 87/B3
Koshiki (isls.), Japan 75/K5
Kosi, India 84/A2
Kosi (zone), Nepal 85/F2
Kosi (riv.), India 82/E2
Košice, Slvk. 41/L4
Koskinoú, Gre. 90/B2
Kosoba (peak), Kaz. 87/G3
Kosŏng, SKor. 73/E5
Kosŏng, NKor. 73/E3
Kosovo (reg.), Yugo. 47/G1
Kosovo (prov.), Yugo. 48/E4
Kosovo Polje, Yugo. 47/G1
Kosovska Kamenica, Yugo. 47/G1
Kosovska Mitrovica, Yugo. 47/G1
Kosový (riv.), Czh. 55/F3
Kosrae (isl.), Micr. 116/F4
Kossi (prov.), Burk. 102/D3
Kossou, Barrage de (dam), C.d'Iv. 102/D5
Kossou, Lac de (lake), C.d'Iv. 96/D6
Kosta, Swe. 38/F3
Kostelec nad Černými Lesy, Czh. 55/H3
Koster, SAfr. 106/D2
Kostinbrod, Bul. 47/H1
Kostopil', Ukr. 62/C2
Kostroma (riv.), Rus. 60/J4
Kostroma, Rus. 60/J4
Kostromskaya (obl.), Rus. 60/J4
Kostrzyn, Pol. 41/H2
Kostrzyn, Pol. 41/J2
Kostyantynivka, Ukr. 62/F2
Kosuge, Japan 77/B2
Kos'va (riv.), Rus. 61/N4
Kos'yu (riv.), Rus. 61/N2
Koszalin, Pol. 38/G4
Koszalin (prov.), Pol. 38/F5
Kőszeg, Hun. 43/M3
Kot Addu, Pak. 86/A4
Kot Kapūra, India 86/C4
Kot Mūmin, Pak. 86/B3
Kot Rādha Kishan, Pak. 86/C4
Kot Samāba, Pak. 86/A5
Kota, India 84/D4
Kota, India 89/L3
Kōta, Japan 77/M6
Kota Baharu, Malay. 83/H6
Kota Kinabalu, Malay. 81/E2
Kotaagung, Indo. 80/B5
Kotabaru, Indo. 81/E4
Kotabumi, Indo. 80/B4
Kotapād, India 82/D4
Kotdwāra, India 84/B1
Kotel, Bul. 47/K1
Kotel'nich, Rus. 61/L4
Kotel'nikovo, Rus. 63/G3
Kotel'nyy (isl.), Rus. 65/P2
Kothagūdem, India 82/D4
Köthen, Ger. 40/F3
Kotido, Ugan. 104/B2
Kotka, Fin. 39/M1
Kotlas, Rus. 61/K3
Kotli Lohārān, Pak. 86/C3
Kotlik, Ak, US 134/F3
Kotlin (isl.), Rus. 61/S7
Kotō, Japan 77/K5
Kotoka (int'l arpt.), Gha. 103/E5
Kotor, Yugo. 47/F1
Kotor Varoš, Bosn. 48/C3
Kotovo, Rus. 63/H2
Kotovsk, Rus. 63/G1
Kotri, Pak. 89/J3
Kottayam, India 82/C6
Kotto (riv.), CAfr. 97/K6
Kotuy (riv.), Rus. 67/K3
Kotzebue, Ak, US 134/F2
Kotzebue (sound), Ak, US 134/E2
Kötzting, Ger. 55/F4
Kouandé, Ben. 103/F4
Kouchibouguac NP, NB, Can. 131/H2
Koudougou, Burk. 103/E3
Koufonísion (isl.), Gre. 47/J5
Kougarok (mtn.), Ak, US 134/E2
Koukdjuak (riv.), Nun., Can. 123/J2
Koula-Moutou, Gabon 96/H8
Koulikoro, Mali 102/D3
Koulikoro (pol. reg.), Mali 102/C3
Koulountou (riv.), Sen. 102/B3
Koumbi Saleh (ruin), Mrta. 102/D3
Koumi, Japan 77/A1
Koumra, Chad 96/J6
Koundara, Gui. 102/B3
Kounradskiy, Kaz. 87/G3
Kountze, Tx, US 129/J5
Koupela, Burk. 103/E3
Kouritenga (prov.), Burk. 103/E3
Kourou, FrG. 151/H2
Koussi (peak), Chad 96/J4
Koutiala, Mali 102/D3
Kouvola, Fin. 39/M1
Kovačica, Yugo. 48/E3
Kovada Gölü NP, Turk. 90/B2
Kovashi (riv.), Rus. 61/S7
Kovdozero (lake), Rus. 37/J2
Kovel', Ukr. 62/C2
Kovilj, Yugo. 48/E3
Kovilpatti, India 82/C6
Kovrov, Rus. 60/J4
Kovūr, India 82/C5
Kovylkino, Rus. 63/G1
Kowanyama Aboriginal Community, Austl. 114/A1
Kowkcheh (riv.), Afg. 89/J1
Kowl-e Namaksār (lake), Afg. 87/D6
Kowloon, China 79/B3
Kowt-e 'Ashrow, Afg. 89/J2
Kōyaguchi, Japan 77/J7
Kōyama, Japan 74/B5
Koynare, Bul. 49/G4
Koyuk, Ak, US 134/F3
Koyukuk (riv.), Ak, US 134/H2
Koyukuk, Ak, US 134/G3
Koyukuk NWR, Ak, US 134/G2
Koyukuk, South Fork (riv.), Ak, US 134/H2
Kozakai, Japan 77/M6
Kōzaki, Japan 77/E2
Kozaklı, Turk. 62/E5
Kozan, Turk. 90/C2
Kozáni, Gre. 47/G2
Kozara NP, Aus. 48/C3
Kozhozero (lake), Rus. 60/H3
Kozhva (riv.), Rus. 61/M2
Kozienice, Pol. 41/L3
Kozloduy, Bul. 49/F4
Kozlu, Turk. 49/K5
Kozluk, Turk. 90/E2
Koźmin, Pol. 41/J3
Koznitsa (peak), Bul. 47/H1
Kōzu (isl.), Japan 75/F3
Kożuchów, Pol. 41/H3
Kozyatyn, Ukr. 62/D2
Kpalimé, Togo 103/F5
Kpandu, Gha. 103/F5
Kpémé, Togo 103/F5
Kra (isth.), Myan. 83/G6
Kraai (riv.), SAfr. 106/D3
Kraaifontein, SAfr. 106/L10
Krabi, Thai. 78/B4
Kragerø, Nor. 38/C2
Kragujevac, Yugo. 48/E3
Kraiburg am Inn, Ger. 55/F6
Kraichbach (riv.), Ger. 54/B4
Kraichgau (reg.), Ger. 43/H2
Krailling, Ger. 55/E6
Krakatau (vol.), Indo. 80/C5
Kraków, Pol. 41/K3
Kraków (prov.), Pol. 41/K3
Kralendijk, NAnt. 152/D1
Kraljevo, Yugo. 48/E4
Kralkızı (dam), Turk. 90/E2
Kralovice, Czh. 55/G3
Kralupy nad Vltavou, Czh. 55/H2
Kramators'k, Ukr. 62/F2
Kramfors, Swe. 37/F3
Krammer (chan.), Neth. 50/B5
Kranéa Elassónos, Gre. 47/G3
Kranebitten (int'l arpt.), Aus. 57/H3
Kranenburg, Ger. 50/D5
Kranídhion, Gre. 47/H4
Kranj, Slov. 43/L3
Kranskop, SAfr. 107/E3
Krapkowice, Pol. 41/J3
Kraslice, Czh. 55/F2
Kraśnik, Pol. 41/M3
Kraśnik Fabryczny, Pol. 41/M3
Krasnoarmeysk, Rus. 63/H2
Krasnodar, Rus. 62/F3
Krasnodar (int'l arpt.), Rus. 62/F3
Krasnodarskiy (kray), Rus. 64/D5
Krasnogorsk, Rus. 61/W9
Krasnohrad, Ukr. 62/E2
Krasnokamensk, Rus. 71/L1
Krasnokamsk, Rus. 61/M4
Krasnoslobodsk, Rus. 63/H2
Krasnotur'insk, Rus. 64/G4
Krasnoural'sk, Rus. 61/P4
Krasnowodsk (int'l arpt.), Trkm. 63/K4
Krasnowodsk (Tŕkmenbashi), Trkm. 63/K5
Krasnoyarsk, Rus. 64/K4
Krasnoyarskiy (kray), Rus. 64/J4
Krasnyy Kut, Rus. 63/H2
Krasnyy Luch, Ukr. 62/F2
Krasnyy Sulin, Rus. 62/G3
Kratovo, FYROM 47/H1
Krautheim, Ger. 54/C4
Kravanh (mts.), Camb. 83/H5
Kreb en Nâga (cliff), Mali 98/D5
Kreck (riv.), Ger. 54/D2
Krefeld, Ger. 50/D6
Kreiensen, Ger. 51/G5
Kremastón (lake), Gre. 47/G3
Křemelna (riv.), Czh. 55/G4
Kremenchuk, Ukr. 62/E2
Kremenchuts'ke Vodoskhovyshche (res.), Ukr. 62/E2
Kremlin, Rus. 61/W9
Kremmen, Ger. 40/Q6
Kremmling, Co, US 128/F2
Krempe, Ger. 51/G1
Krems an der Donau, Aus. 41/H4
Kremsmünster, Aus. 55/H6
Krenglbach, Aus. 55/G6
Kresgeville, Pa, US 138/C2
Kresna, Bul. 47/H2
Kressbronn am Bodensee, Ger. 57/F2
Kresta (gulf), Rus. 65/T3
Kréstena, Gre. 47/G4
Kretinga, Lith. 39/J4
Kreuzau, Ger. 53/F2
Kreuzberg (peak), Ger. 54/C2
Kreuzlingen, Swi. 57/F2
Kreuztal, Ger. 53/G2
Kreuzwertheim, Ger. 54/C3
Kría Vrísi, Gre. 47/H2
Kribi, Camr. 96/G7
Krieglach, Aus. 43/L3
Kriens, Swi. 57/E3
Kriftel, Ger. 54/B2
Kril'on (pen.), Rus. 76/B1
Kril'on (cape), Rus. 76/C1
Krimpen aan de IJssel, Neth. 50/B5
Krinídhes, Gre. 47/J2
Kriós (cape), Gre. 47/H5
Krishna (riv.), India 67/G8
Krishnagiri, India 82/C5
Krishnanagar, India 85/G4
Kristdala, Swe. 38/G3
Kristiansand, Nor. 38/B2
Kristianstad (co.), Swe. 37/E4
Kristianstad (int'l arpt.), Swe. 38/F4
Kristianstad, Swe. 38/F3
Kristiansund, Nor. 37/C3
Kristinehamn, Swe. 38/F2
Kriva Palanka, FYROM 47/H1
Krk (isl.), Cro. 48/B3
Krk, Cro. 48/B3
Krnov, Czh. 41/J3
Krokom, Swe. 37/E3
Krókos, Gre. 47/G2
Krolevets', Ukr. 62/E2
Krombach, Ger. 54/C2
Kroměříž, Czh. 41/J4
Kronach, Ger. 55/E2
Kronberg im Taunus, Ger. 54/B2
Kronoberg (co.), Swe. 37/E4
Kronshtadt, Rus. 61/S6
Kronstorf, Aus. 55/H6
Kroombit Tops NP, Austl. 114/C4
Kroonstad, SAfr. 106/D2
Kropotkin, Rus. 63/G3
Kropp, Ger. 38/C4
Krosno (prov.), Pol. 41/L4
Krosno, Pol. 41/L4
Krosno Odrzańskie, Pol. 41/H2
Krotoszyn, Pol. 41/J3
Krottenkopf (peak), Aus. 57/G3
Krousón, Gre. 47/J5
Kröv, Ger. 53/G4
Krško, Slov. 43/L4
Kruckau (riv.), Ger. 51/G1
Kruger NP, SAfr. 105/F5
Krugersdorp, SAfr. 106/P13
Kruglitsa (peak), Rus. 61/N5
Kruibeke, Belg. 50/B6
Kruisfontein, SAfr. 106/D4
Krujë, Alb. 47/F2
Krumbach, Ger. 57/G1
Krummenau, Swi. 57/F3
Krumovgrad, Bul. 47/J2
Krün, Ger. 57/H3
Krupina, Slvk. 48/D1
Kruså, Den. 38/C4
Krusenstern (cape), Ak, US 134/F2
Kruševac, Yugo. 48/E4
Kruševo, FYROM 47/G2
Krušné Hory (Erzgebirge) (mts.), Czh.,Ger. 43/K1
Kruszwica, Pol. 41/K2
Kruzof (isl.), Ak, US 134/L4
Krychaw, Bela. 62/D1
Krym (aut. rep.), Ukr. 62/E3
Krymsk, Rus. 62/F3
Krynica, Pol. 41/L4
Kryvyy Rih, Ukr. 49/L2
Krzna (riv.), Pol. 41/M3
Krzyż, Pol. 41/J2
Ksar el Kebir, Mor. 100/B2
Ksel (peak), Alg. 99/F2
Ktima, Cyp. 91/C2
Ku-Ring-Gai NP, Austl. 114/H8
Ku Sathan (peak), Thai. 78/C2
Kuah, Malay. 78/B5
Kuala Belait, Bru. 80/D3
Kuala Dungun, Malay. 80/B3
Kuala Kerai, Malay. 83/H6
Kuala Lipis, Malay. 80/B3
Kuala Lumpur (cap.), Malay. 80/B3
Kuala Pilah, Malay. 80/B3
Kuala Selangor, Malay. 80/B3
Kuala Terengganu, Malay. 83/H6
Kualapuu, Hi, US 124/T10
Kuancheng, China 72/D2
Kuandian, China 73/C2
Kuantan, Malay. 80/B3
Kuban' (riv.), Rus. 64/D5
Kubaysah, Iraq 90/E3
Kubenskoye (lake), Rus. 60/H4
Kubokawa, Japan 74/C4
Kubrat, Bul. 49/H4
Kučevo, Yugo. 48/E3
Kuchen (peak), Aus. 57/G3
Kuchen, Ger. 54/C5
Kuching, Malay. 80/D3
Kuchino (isl.), Japan 75/K6
Kuchinoerabu (isl.), Japan 74/A5
Kuchl, Aus. 43/K3
Küçükbahçe, Turk. 47/K3
Küçükkuyu, Turk. 47/K3
Kudamatsu, Japan 74/B3
Kudat, Malay. 81/E2
Kudus, Indo. 80/D5
Kudymkar, Rus. 61/M4
Kufrah (oasis), Libya 97/K3
Kufrinjah, Jor. 91/D3
Kufstein, Aus. 43/K3
Kugluktuk, Nun., Can. 122/E2
Kuhardt, Ger. 54/B4
Kühbach, Ger. 54/E6
Kuhmo, Fin. 60/F2
Kuhmoinen, Fin. 39/L1
Kuhn, Il, US 137/H8
Kūhpāyeh, Iran 88/F2
Kuinder of Tjonger (riv.), Neth. 50/C3
Kuito, Ang. 105/C3
Kuiu (isl.), Ak, US 122/C3
Kujawy (reg.), Pol. 41/K2
Kuji, Japan 76/B3
Kujū-san (peak), Japan 74/B4
Kujūkuri, Japan 77/E2
Kukalaya (riv.), Nic. 145/E3
Kuki, Japan 75/F2
Kukizaki, Japan 77/E2
Kukkia (lake), Fin. 39/L1
Kūl (riv.), Iran 88/C3
Kula, Yugo. 48/D3
Kula, Bul. 48/F4
Kula Kangri (peak), Bhu. 85/H1
Kulachi, Pak. 86/A4
Kulai, Malay. 80/B3
Kulal (mt.), Kenya 104/C2
Kulaly (isl.), Kaz. 63/J3
Kulandag (mts.), Kaz. 87/B4
Kuldīga, Lat. 39/J3
Kulebaki, Rus. 60/J5
Kulgām, India 86/C3
Kulin, Austl. 112/C5
Kullen (cape), Swe. 38/E3
Kullu, India 86/D4
Kulmbach, Ger. 55/E2
Kŭlob, Taj. 89/J1
Kuloy (riv.), Rus. 61/J2
Kulpahār, India 84/B3
Kulpmont, Pa, US 138/B2
Kulpsville, Pa, US 138/C3
Kul'sary, Kaz. 63/K3
Külsheim, Ger. 54/C3
Kulsi (riv.), India 85/H2
Kulti, India 85/F4
Kulunda (lake), Rus. 87/G2
Kulunda, Rus. 87/G2
Kŭm (riv.), SKor. 73/D4
Kuma (riv.), Rus. 64/E5
Kumagaya, Japan 75/F2
Kumaishi, Japan 76/A2
Kumamoto, Japan 74/B4
Kumamoto (int'l arpt.), Japan 74/B4
Kumamoto (pref.), Japan 74/B4
Kumano (riv.), Japan 74/D4
Kumano, Japan 74/E4
Kumanovo, FYROM 47/G1
Kumār (riv.), Bang. 85/G4
Kumasi, Gha. 103/E5
Kumatori, Japan 77/H7
Kumba, Camr. 96/G7
Kumbia, Austl. 114/C4
Kumbo, Camr. 96/H6
Kŭmch'on, SKor. 73/F6
Kumé (isl.), Japan 79/E2
Kumertau, Rus. 63/K1
Kumgang-san (peak), NKor. 73/E3
Kŭmho (riv.), SKor. 73/E5
Kumi, Ugan. 104/B2
Kumi, SKor. 73/E4
Kumihama, Japan 77/G4
Kumiyama, Japan 77/J6
Kumkale, Turk. 49/H6
Kumköy, Turk. 49/J5
Kumla, Swe. 38/F2
Kumluca, Turk. 91/B1
Kümmersbruck, Ger. 55/E4
Kumo, Nga. 96/H5
Kumon (range), Myan. 70/G6
Kŭmsan, SKor. 73/D4
Kumta, India 89/K6
Kunashiri (isl.), Rus. 65/Q5
Kūnch, India 84/B3
Kunda, India 84/C3
Kundapura (Coondapoor), India 89/K6
Kundarkhi, India 84/B1
Kundelungu, PN de, D.R. Congo 105/E3
Kundiān, Pak. 86/A3
Kundla, India 89/K4
Kungälv, Swe. 38/D3
Kungsangen (int'l arpt.), Swe. 38/G2
Kungsbacka, Swe. 38/E3
Kungshamn, Swe. 38/D2
Kungur, Rus. 61/N4
Kunhegyes, Hun. 48/E2
Kunimi-dake (peak), Japan 74/B4
Kuningan, Indo. 80/C5
Kunishiri (isl.), Rus. 67/P5
Kunitachi, Japan 77/C2
Kunjāh, Pak. 86/B3
Kunjirap (pass), China 89/L1
Kunkletown, Pa, US 138/C2
Kunlun (mts.), China 67/H6
Kunmadaras, Hun. 41/L5
Kunming, China 83/H2
Kunsan, SKor. 73/D5
Kunshan, China 72/L8
Kunszentmárton, Hun. 48/E2
Kunu (riv.), India 89/L3
Kunwāri (riv.), India 84/A2
Kunwi, SKor. 73/E4
Kunyu (mtn.), China 72/E3
Künzell, Ger. 54/C1
Kunžvartské (pass), Czh. 55/G5
Kuocang (peak), China 71/M6
Kuohijärvi (lake), Fin. 39/L1
Kuolimo (lake), Fin. 39/M1
Kuopio, Fin. 60/E3
Kuopio (prov.), Fin. 37/H3
Kupa (riv.), Cro. 48/B3
Kupang, Indo. 81/F6
Kupino, Rus. 87/G2
Kuppenheim, Ger. 54/B5
Kupreanof (isl.), Ak, US 122/C3
Kup'yans'k, Ukr. 62/F2
Kuqa, China 71/L3
Kür (riv.), Azer. 64/E6
Kūrālī, India 86/D4
Kurama-yama (peak), Japan 77/J5
Kurashiki, Japan 74/C3
Kurayoshi, Japan 74/C3
Kurdistan (reg.), Asia 64/E6
Kŭrdzhali, Bul. 47/J2
Kŭrdzhali (res.), Bul. 47/J2
Küre (mts.), Turk. 90/C1
Kure, Japan 74/C3
Küre, Turk. 62/E4
Kure (isl.), Hi, US 116/H2
Kuressaare, Est. 39/K2
Kureyka (riv.), Rus. 64/K3
Kurgan, Rus. 61/Q5
Kurganskaya (obl.), Rus. 87/D1
Kuri, SKor. 73/G6
Kuria (isl.), Kiri. 116/G4
Kuria Muria (isls.), Oman 67/F5
Kurīgrām, Bang. 85/G3
Kurihashi, Japan 77/D1
Kurikoma-yama (peak), Japan 76/B4
Kuril (isls.), Rus. 67/Q5
Kurimoto, Japan 77/F2
Kurinwas (riv.), Nic. 145/E3
Kurisawa, Japan 76/B2
Kuriyama, Japan 76/B2
Kürkçü, Turk. 91/C1
Kurla, India 82/B4
Kurnool, India 82/C4
Kuro-shima (isl.), Japan 74/A5
Kurodashō, Japan 77/G5
Kuroishi, Japan 76/B3
Kuroiso, Japan 75/G2
Kuroso-yama (peak), Japan 77/K6
Kurotaki, Japan 77/J7
Kurrajong, Austl. 114/G8
Kurram (riv.), Afg.,Pak. 89/K2
Kurrimine Beach, Austl. 114/B2
Kuršėnai, Lith. 39/K3
Kurseong, India 85/G2
Kursiu Nerija NP, Lith. 39/J4
Kursk, Rus. 62/F2
Kurskskaya (obl.), Rus. 62/E2
Kurskaya Spit (bar), Lith.,Rus. 39/J4
Kurskiy (lag.), Lith.,Rus. 39/J4
Kuršumlija, Yugo. 47/G1
Kurşunlu, Turk. 62/E4
Kurtalan, Turk. 90/E2
Kürten, Ger. 53/G1
Kuru (riv.), Sudan 97/L6
Kuruca (pass), Turk. 90/E2
Kuruçay, Turk. 62/F5
Kuruçay (riv.), Turk. 63/G4
Kuruktag (mts.), China 70/E3
Kuruman, SAfr. 106/C2
Kurumansrivier (riv.), SAfr. 106/C2
Kurume, Japan 74/B4
Kurunegala, SrL. 82/D6
Kurupukari, Guy. 153/G3
Kurur (peak), Sudan 101/B4
Kurwongbah (lake), Austl. 114/E6
Kurye, SKor. 73/D5
Kuryong (riv.), NKor. 73/C3
Kuş Cenneti NP, Turk. 62/D4
Kuşadası, Turk. 90/A2
Kusatsu, Japan 77/J5
Kusel, Ger. 53/G4
Kushālgarh, India 89/K4
Kushida (riv.), Japan 77/K7
Kushigata, Japan 77/A2
Kushihara, Japan 77/M5
Kushikino, Japan 74/B5
Kushima, Japan 74/B5
Kushimoto, Japan 74/D4
Kushiro, Japan 76/D2
Kushiro (riv.), Japan 76/D2
Kushiro-Shitsugen NP, Japan 76/D2
Kushtia (pol. reg.), Bang. 85/G4
Kushtia, Bang. 85/G4
Kusiyana (riv.), Bang. 85/H3
Kuskokwim (bay), Ak, US 134/F4
Kuskokwim (mts.), Ak, US 134/G3
Kuskokwim (riv.), Ak, US 134/F3
Kuskokwim, North Fork (riv.), Ak, US 134/H3
Kuskokwim, South Fork (riv.), Ak, US 134/H3
Küsnacht, Swi. 57/E3
Kusŏng, NKor. 73/C3
Kussharo (lake), Japan 76/C2
Küssnacht am Rigi, Swi. 57/E3
Küstenkanal (canal), Ger. 51/E3
Kusterdingen, Ger. 54/C5
Kūstī, Sudan 97/M5
Kusu, Japan 77/L6
Kut (isl.), Thai. 83/H5
Kütahya, Turk. 62/D5
K'ut'aisi (int'l arpt.), Geo. 63/G4
K'ut'aisi, Geo. 63/G4
Kutch (reg.), India 89/J4
Kutch, Gulf of (gulf), India 89/J4
Kutchan, Japan 76/B1
Kutcharo (lake), Japan 76/C1
Kutenholz, Ger. 51/G2
Kutná Hora, Czh. 41/H4
Kutno, Pol. 41/K2
Kutsuki, Japan 77/J5
Küttigen, Swi. 56/E3
Kutu, D.R. Congo 96/J8
Kutzenhausen, Ger. 54/D6
Kutztown, Pa, US 138/C2
Kuujjua (riv.), NW, Can. 122/E1
Kuujjuaq, Qu, Can. 123/K3
Kuusamo, Fin. 37/J2
Kuusankoski, Fin. 39/M1
Kuutse (hill), Est. 39/M2
Kuvandyk, Rus. 63/L2
Kuwait (cap.), Kuw. 88/E3
Kuwait (ctry.) 88/E3
Kuwānā (riv.), India 82/D2
Kuwana, Japan 77/L5
Kuybyshev (res.), Rus. 64/E4
Kuyto (lake), Rus. 37/J2
Kuytun, China 70/E3
Kuyuwini (riv.), Guy. 153/G4
Kuze, Japan 77/K4
Kuzitrin (riv.), Ak, US 134/E2
Kuznetsk, Rus. 63/H1
Kuzucubelen, Turk. 91/D1
Kuzumaki, Japan 76/B3
Kvaløy (isl.), Nor. 37/F1
Kværndrup, Den. 38/D4
Kvarner (gulf), Cro. 48/B3
Kvarnerić (chan.), Cro. 48/B3
Kvigtinden (peak), Nor. 37/E2
Kvinesdal, Nor. 38/B2
Kvinnherad, Nor. 38/B2
Kviteseid, Nor. 38/C2
Kwa (riv.), D.R. Congo 93/D5
Kwach'ŏn, SKor. 73/F7
Kwajalein (isl.), Mrsh. 116/F4
Kwale, Kenya 104/C4
KwaMashu, SAfr. 107/E3
Kwanak-san (peak), SKor. 73/F7
Kwangch'ŏn, SKor. 73/D4
Kwangju, SKor. 73/D5
Kwangju, SKor. 73/G7
Kwangju-Gwangyŏksi (prov.), SKor. 73/D5
Kwangmyŏng, SKor. 73/F7
Kwango (riv.), D.R. Congo 93/D5
Kwangyang, SKor. 73/D5
Kwania (lake), Ugan. 97/M7
Kwansan, SKor. 73/D5
Kwara (state), Nga. 103/G4
Kwaraha (peak), Tanz. 104/B4
Kwataboahegan (riv.), On, Can. 130/D1
Kwazulu Natal (prov.), SAfr. 107/E3
Kwekwe, Zim. 105/E4
Kwethluk, Ak, US 134/F3
Kwidzyn, Pol. 39/H5
Kwigillingok, Ak, US 134/F4
Kwili (riv.), D.R. Congo 105/C1
Kwilu (riv.), D.R. Congo 93/D5
Kwinana, Austl. 112/K7
Kyabé, Chad 97/J6
Kyabram, Austl. 115/C3
Kyaiktiyo Pagoda, Myan. 78/B2
Kyaikto, Myan. 83/G4
Kyakhta, Rus. 70/J1
Kyan-zaki (cape), Japan 75/J7
Kyangin, Myan. 83/G4
Kyaukpadaung, Myan. 83/G3
Kyaukpyu, Myan. 83/F4
Kyaukse, Myan. 83/G3
Kyenjojo, Ugan. 104/A2
Kyeryong-san NP, SKor. 73/D4
Kyjov, Czh. 41/J4
Kyle, Sk, Can. 126/F3
Kyle (reg.), Sc, UK 36/B5
Kyll (riv.), Ger. 40/D3
Kym (riv.), Eng, UK 33/F2
Kymi (prov.), Fin. 37/H3
Kymijoki (riv.), Fin. 39/M1
Kymore, India 84/B4
Kyneton, Austl. 115/C3
Kynšperk nad Ohří, Czh. 55/F2
Kyoga (lake), Ugan. 97/M7
Kyōga-misaki (cape), Japan 74/D3
Kyogle, Austl. 114/D5
Kyonan, Japan 75/F3
Kyŏngbok Palace, SKor. 73/F6
Kyŏnggi (bay), SKor. 73/C4
Kyŏnggi-do (prov.), SKor. 73/D4
Kyŏngju, SKor. 74/A3
Kyŏngju NP, SKor. 74/A3
Kyŏngsan, SKor. 74/A3
Kyŏngsang-bukto (prov.), SKor. 73/E4
Kyŏngsang-namdo (prov.), SKor. 73/E5
Kyōto (pref.), Japan 74/D3
Kyōto, Japan 77/J5
Kyōtō Imperial Palace, Japan 77/J6
Kyōwa, Japan 77/E1
Kyrenia (dist.), Cyp. 91/C2
Kyrenia, Cyp. 91/C2
Kyrgyzstan (ctry.) 87/F4
Kyritz, Ger. 40/G2
Kyrösjärvi (lake), Fin. 39/K1
Kythrea, Cyp. 91/C2
Kyūshū (isl.), Japan 67/M6
Kyūshū Highlands (uplands), Japan 74/B4
Kyustendil, Bul. 47/H1
Kywebwe, Myan. 83/F4
Kyyivs'ka (obl.), Ukr. 62/D2
Kyyivs'ke Vodoskhovyshche (res.), Ukr. 62/D2
Kyzyl, Rus. 70/F1

L

La Algaba, Sp. 44/B4
La Almunia de Doña Godina, Sp. 44/E2
La Amistad Int'l Park, CR 140/E6
La Araucanía (pol. reg.), Chile 158/B3
La Ascensión, Mex. 143/F3
La Asunción, Ven. 153/F2

La Aurora (int'l arpt.), Guat. 144/D3
La Babia, Mex. 132/C4
La Baie, Qu, Can. 131/G1
La Banda, Arg. 157/D2
La Bañeza, Sp. 44/C1
La Bassée, Fr. 52/B2
La Baule-Escoublac, Fr. 42/B3
La Belle, Fl, US 133/H5
La Birse (riv.), Swi. 56/D3
La Blanquilla (isl.), Ven. 153/E2
La Bocana, Mex. 142/B3
La Bresse, Fr. 56/C2
La Broque, Fr. 56/D1
La Calera, Chile 158/N8
La Campana, Sp. 44/C4
La Cañada (peak), Cuba 145/F1
La Canada-Flintridge, Ca, US 136/F7
La Capelle, Fr. 52/C4
La Carlota, Sp. 44/C4
La Carlota, Arg. 158/E2
La Carolina, Sp. 44/D3
La Catedral (peak), Mex. 143/Q9
La Ceiba, Hon. 144/E3
La Ceiba (int'l arpt.), Hon. 144/E3
La Celle-les-Bordes, Fr. 30/H6
La Celle-Saint-Cloud, Fr. 30/J5
La Celle-sur-Morin, Fr. 30/L5
La Chapelle-de-Guinchay, Fr. 56/A5
La Chapelle-Saint-Luc, Fr. 42/F2
La Chaux-de-Bonds, Swi. 56/C3
La Chinita (int'l arpt.), Ven. 152/D2
La Chorrera, Pan. 150/C2
La Cienega, NM, US 129/F4
La Ciotat, Fr. 42/F5
La Clusaz, Fr. 56/C6
La Concepcion, Ven. 152/D2
La Concepción, Nic. 144/E4
La Concepción, Pan. 145/F4
La Coronilla, Uru. 159/G2
La Coruña, Sp. 44/A1
La Couronne, Fr. 42/D4
La Crèche, Fr. 42/C3
La Crescenta-Montrose, Ca, US 136/F7
La Croix-en-Brie, Fr. 30/M6
La Croix, Lac (lake), On, Can. 127/L3
La Cruz, CR 144/E4
La Cruz, Col. 152/B4
La Cruz, Chile 158/N8
La Cruz, Mex. 142/D4
La Cruz, Uru. 159/K10
La Cumbre (vol.), Ecu. 156/E7
La Dôle (peak), Swi. 56/C5
La Dorada, Col. 150/D2
La Dormida, Arg. 158/D2
La Esperanza, Hon. 144/D3
La Estrada, Sp. 44/A1
La Estrella, Chile 158/N9
La Falda, Arg. 157/D3
La Fayette, Ga, US 133/G3
La Fère, Fr. 52/C4
La Ferté-Gaucher, Fr. 52/C6
La Ferté-Macé, Fr. 42/C2
La Ferté-Milon, Fr. 30/M7
La Ferté-Sous-Jouarre, Fr. 52/C6
La Flèche, Fr. 42/C3
La Fria, Ven. 152/C2
La Garamba NP, D.R. Congo 104/A2
La Garita (mts.), US 132/B2
La Garriga, Sp. 45/L6
La Gineta, Sp. 44/E3
La Gloria, Col. 152/C2
La Gran Sabana (plain), Ven. 150/F2
La Grande, Or, US 126/D4
La Grande (riv.), Qu, Can. 123/J3
La Grande Ruine (peak), Fr. 43/G4
La Grange, Ga, US 133/G3
La Grange, Tx, US 129/H5
La Grita, Ven. 145/J4
La Gruyère (lake), Swi. 56/D4
La Guajira (dept.), Col. 145/H4
La Guajira (pen.), Col. 145/H4
La Guardia, Sp. 44/A2
La Guardia (int'l arpt.), NY, US 139/K8
La Habana (Havana) (cap.), Cuba 140/E3
La Habra, Ca, US 136/G8
La Have (riv.), NS, Can. 131/H2
La Higuera, Chile 157/B2
La Honda, Ca, US 135/K12
La Houssaye-en-Brie, Fr. 30/L5
La Huaca, Peru 156/A2
La Huacana, Mex. 143/E5
La Huerta, Mex. 142/D5
La Isla, Mex. 143/Q10
La Jalca, Peru 156/B2
La Joya, Peru 156/D5
La Joya de los Sachas, Ecu. 152/B5
La Junta, Co, US 129/G3
La Junta, Mex. 142/D2
La Laguna, Sp. 98/A3
La Libertad (dept.), Peru 156/B3
La Libertad, Hon. 144/E3
La Libertad, Guat. 144/D2
La Libertad, Ecu. 152/A5
La Ligua, Chile 158/C2
La Línea de la Concepción, Sp. 44/C4
La Llagosta, Sp. 45/L6
La Loche, Sk, Can. 126/F1
La Loggia, It. 58/A3
La Louvière, Belg. 53/D3
La Luisiana, Sp. 44/C4
La Luz, NM, US 129/F4
La Machine, Fr. 42/E3
La Maddalena, It. 46/A2
La Madeleine, Fr. 52/C2
La Malbaie, Qu, Can. 131/G2
La Martre (lake), NW, Can. 122/E2
La Masica, Hon. 144/E3
La Mauricie NP, Qu, Can. 130/F2
La Mensura (peak), Col. 152/C4
La Merca, Sp. 44/B1
La Merced, Peru 156/C3
La Mesa, Ca, US 136/C5
La Mesa (int'l arpt.), Hon. 144/E3
La Mesa, Ven. 152/D2
La Mira, Mex. 142/E5
La Mirada, Ca, US 136/F8
La Moine (riv.), Il, US 130/B3
La Montaña (phys. reg.), Peru 147/B3
La Moure, ND, US 127/J4
La Neuveville, Swi. 56/D3
La Norville, Fr. 30/J6
La Orchila (isl.), Ven. 141/H5
La Orotava, Sp. 98/A3
La Oroya, Peru 156/C3
La Palma, Pan. 145/G4
La Palma (isl.), Sp. 93/A2
La Paloma, Uru. 159/G2
La Pampa (prov.), Arg. 158/D3
La Paz, Arg. 157/E3
La Paz (cap.), Bol. 150/E7
La Paz (dept.), Bol. 156/D4
La Paz (bay), Mex. 142/C3
La Paz, Mex. 142/C3
La Paz, Hon. 144/E3
La Paz, Col. 152/C2
La Paz, Col. 152/C3
La Paz, Arg. 158/D2
La Paz, Uru. 159/K11
La Pêche, Qu, Can. 130/F2
La Peña, Pan. 140/E6
La Perla, Mex. 132/B4
La Pérouse (str.), Japan,Rus 71/R2
La Perouse (str.), Japan,Rus. 67/P5
La Petite-Raon, Fr. 56/C1
La Piedad Cavadas, Mex. 142/E4
La Plata, Md, US 130/E4
La Plata, Col. 152/C4
La Plata, Arg. 159/K11
La Pobla de Lillet, Sp. 45/F1
La Pocatière, Qu, Can. 131/G2
La Pola de Gordón, Sp. 44/C1
La Ponge (lake), Sk, Can. 126/G2
La Porte, In, US 130/C3
La Prairie, Qu, Can. 131/P7
La Pryor, Tx, US 129/H5
La Puebla, Sp. 45/G3
La Puebla de Almoradiel, Sp. 44/D3
La Puebla de Cazalla, Sp. 44/C4
La Puebla de Montalbán, Sp. 44/C3
La Puente, Ca, US 136/G7
La Puntilla (pt.), Ecu. 152/A5
La Quebrada, Ven. 152/D2
La Queue-les-Yvelines, Fr. 52/A6
La Quiaca, Arg. 150/E8
La Rambla, Sp. 44/C4
La Reforma, Mex. 142/C3
La Rinconada, Sp. 44/C4
La Rioja, Arg. 157/C2
La Rioja (aut. comm.), Sp. 44/D1
La Rioja (prov.), Sp. 44/D1
La Robla, Sp. 44/C1
La Roche (lake), Sk, Can. 126/F1
La Roche, Swi. 56/D4
La Roche-en-Ardenne, Belg. 53/E3
La Roche-sur-Foron, Fr. 56/C5
La Roche-sur-Yon, Fr. 42/C3
La Rochelle, Fr. 42/C3
La Roda, Sp. 44/D3
La Romana, DRep. 141/H4
La Ronge, Sk, Can. 127/G2
La Rúa, Sp. 44/B1
La Salle, Co, US 137/C2
La Sarraz, Swi. 56/C4
La Sarre, Qu, Can. 130/E1
La Sauvette (peak), Fr. 43/G5
La Scie, Nf, Can. 131/L1
La Serena, Chile 157/B2
La Seu d'Urgell, Sp. 45/F1
La Seyne-sur-Mer, Fr. 42/F5
La Sierpe, Cuba 145/G1
La Sila (mts.), It. 46/E3
La Silueta (peak), Chile 159/B7
La Solana, Sp. 44/D3
La Souterraine, Fr. 42/D3
La Spezia (prov.), It. 58/C4
La Spezia, It. 58/C4
La Tabatière, Qu, Can. 131/K1
La Teste, Fr. 42/C4
La Tête à l'Ane (peak), Fr. 56/C6
La Tigra, PN, Hon. 144/E3
La Toma, Arg. 158/D2
La Tortue (isl.), Haiti 145/H1
La Tortuga (isl.), Ven. 153/E2
La Tortuga, Isla (isl.), Ven. 150/E1
La Tour-de-Peilz, Swi. 56/C5
La Tour-de-Trême, Swi. 56/D4
La Tremblade, Fr. 42/C4
La Trinitaria, Mex. 144/C2
La Troncal, Ecu. 152/B5
La Tuque, Qu, Can. 131/F2
La Turbie, Fr. 58/H8
La Unión, Peru 156/A2
La Unión, Peru 156/B3
La Unión, Mex. 143/E5
La Unión, Sp. 45/E4
La Unión, Chile 158/B4
La Unión, Col. 152/B4
La Unión, ESal. 144/E3
La Union, Ven. 152/E2
La Vecilla, Sp. 44/C1
La Verna, It. 59/E5
La Verne, Ca, US 136/C2
La Vernia, Tx, US 137/U21
La Verrière, Fr. 30/H5
La Víbora, Mex. 132/C5
La Victoria, Ven. 150/E1
La Victoria, Ven. 152/D2
La Wantzenau, Fr. 53/G6
Laa an der Thaya, Aus. 43/M2
Laaber, Ger. 55/E4
Laage, Ger. 38/E5
Laakirchen, Aus. 55/G7
Laarne, Belg. 52/C1
Laas Caanood, Som. 97/Q6
Laas Qoray, Som. 97/Q5
Laatzen, Ger. 51/G4
Laax, Swi. 57/F4
Labason, Phil. 79/D6
L'Abbaye, Swi. 56/C4
Labdah (Leptis Magna) (ruin), Libya 96/H1
Labé, Gui. 102/B4
Labé (pol. reg.), Gui. 102/B4
Labe (Elbe) (riv.), Czh. 43/L1
Laberweinting, Ger. 55/F5
Labian (cape), Malay. 81/E2
Labin, Cro. 48/B3
Labinsk, Rus. 63/G3
Labná (ruin), Mex. 144/D1
Laborde, Arg. 158/E2
Laborec (riv.), Slvk. 41/L4
Laboulaye, Arg. 158/E2
Labrador (reg.), Nf, Can. 123/K3
Labrador (sea), Can.,Grld. 119/M4
Labrador City, Nf, Can. 123/K3
Lábrea, Braz. 150/F5
Labruguière, Fr. 42/E5
Labry, Fr. 53/E5
Labuk (riv.), Malay. 81/E2
Labuk (bay), Malay. 81/E2
Labuništa, FYROM 47/G2
Labutta, Myan. 83/F4
Laç, Alb. 47/F2
Lac Afwein (riv.), Kenya 104/C2
Lac du Bonnet, Mb, Can. 127/J3
Lac La Biche, Ab, Can. 126/F2
Lac-Mégantic, Qu, Can. 131/G2
L'Acadie, Qu, Can. 131/P7
Lacantum (riv.), Mex. 144/D2
Lacaune, Fr. 42/E5
Laccadive (sea), India 82/B5
Lacchiarella, It. 58/C2
Lacepede (bay), Austl. 109/C4
Lach Dera (riv.), Som. 97/P7
Lacha (lake), Rus. 60/H3
Lachapelle-aux-Pots, Fr. 52/A5
Lachay (pt.), Peru 156/B3
Lachen, Swi. 57/E3
Lachenaie, Qu, Can. 131/N6
Lachendorf, Ger. 51/H3
Lāchi, Pak. 86/A3
L'Achigan (riv.), Qu, Can. 131/N6
Lachine, Qu, Can. 131/N7
Lachlan (riv.), Austl. 109/D4
Lachte (riv.), Ger. 51/H3
Lackawanna, NY, US 131/S10
Lackawanna (co.), Pa, US 138/C1
Läckö, Swe. 38/E2
Lacombe, Ab, Can. 126/E2
Lacombe, La, US 137/Q16
Laconia, NH, US 131/G3
Lacroix-Saint-Ouen, Fr. 52/B5
Ladainha, Braz. 154/B5
Ladakh (mts.), India 89/L2
Ladbergen, Ger. 51/E4
Ladder (hills), Sc, UK 36/C2
Lądek-Zdrój, Pol. 41/J3
Ladenburg, Ger. 54/B4
Ladera Heights, Ca, US 136/F8
Ladismith, SAfr. 106/C4
Ladispoli, It. 46/C2
Ladoga (lake), Rus. 160/D
Ladoix-Serrigny, Fr. 56/A3
Ladrillero (mtn.), Chile 159/B7
Ladue, Mo, US 137/G8
Lādwa, India 86/D5
Lady Isle (isl.), Sc, UK 36/B5
Ladybank, Sc, UK 36/C4
Ladybower (res.), Eng, UK 35/G5
Ladybrand, SAfr. 106/D3
Ladysmith, SAfr. 107/E3
Lae (isl.), Mrsh. 116/F4
Laer, Ger. 51/E4
Lafayette, In, US 130/C3
Lafayette, La, US 129/J5
Lafayette, Co, US 137/B3
Lafayette, NJ, US 138/D1
Lafayette, Ca, US 135/K11
Lafia, Nga. 103/H4
Lafitte, La, US 137/P17
Laflamme (riv.), Qu, Can. 130/E1
Lafnitz (riv.), Aus. 43/L3
Lafontaine, Qu, Can. 131/M6
Lafourche (parish), La, US 137/T17
Laga Balal (riv.), Kenya 104/C2
Laga Mado Gali (riv.), Kenya 104/C2
Laga Merille (riv.), Kenya 104/C2
Lagan, Swe. 38/E3
Lagan (riv.), Swe. 38/E3
Lagarto, Braz. 154/C3
Lagawe, Phil. 79/D4
Lagdo, Lac de (lake), Camr. 96/H6
Lage, Ger. 51/F5
Lage Vaart (canal), Neth. 50/C4
Lågen (riv.), Nor. 38/C1
Lages, Braz. 155/B3
Laggan (lake), Sc, UK 36/B3
Lagh Bogal (riv.), Kenya 104/C2
Lagh Bor (riv.), Kenya 97/N7
Lagh Kutulo (riv.), Kenya 104/D2
Laghouat (prov.), Alg. 99/F2
Laghouat, Alg. 99/F2
Lagnieu, Fr. 56/B6
Lagny-le-Sec, Fr. 30/L4
Lagny-sur-Marne, Fr. 30/L5
Lago da Pedra, Braz. 154/A2
Lago de Atitlán, PN, Guat. 144/D3
Lago Puelo, PN, Arg. 158/C4
Lago Verde, Chile 158/C5
Lagoa, Port. 44/A4
Lagoa da Prata, Braz. 155/C2
Lagoa Formosa, Braz. 155/C1
Lagoa Vermelha, Braz. 155/B4
Lagoda (lake), Rus. 37/J3
Lagonegro, It. 46/D2
Lagord, Fr. 42/C3
Lagos, Nga. 103/F5
Lagos (state), Nga. 103/F5
Lagos, Port. 44/A4
Lagos de Moreno, Mex. 142/E4
Lagosanto, It. 59/F3
Laguardia, Sp. 44/D1
Laguna, Braz. 155/B4
Laguna Beach, Ca, US 136/C3
Laguna Blanca, PN, Arg. 158/C3
Laguna de Duero, Sp. 44/C2
Laguna de la Restinga, PN, Ven. 153/E2
Laguna del Laja, PN, Chile 158/C3
Laguna del Rey, Mex. 142/E3
Laguna Hills, Ca, US 136/C3
Laguna San Rafael, PN, Chile 157/B6
Lagunas, Peru 156/C2
Lagunas, Peru 156/B2
Lagunas de Chacahua, PN, Mex. 144/B2
Lagunas de Montebello, PN, Mex. 140/C4
Lagunas de Zempoala, PN, Mex. 143/Q10
Lagunillas, Ven. 152/D2
Laguntara (lag.), Hon. 145/E3
Lahad Datu, Malay. 81/E2
Lahār, India 84/B2
Lāharpur, India 84/C2
Lahat, Indo. 80/B4
Lāhījān, Iran 88/F1
Lahn (riv.), Ger. 40/E3
Lahnstein, Ger. 53/G3
Laholm, Swe. 38/E3
Laholms (bay), Den. 38/F3
Lahore, Pak. 86/C4
Lahore (int'l arpt.), Pak. 86/C4
Lahr, Ger. 56/D1
Lahti, Fin. 39/L1
Laï, Chad 96/J6
Lai Chau, Viet. 78/C1
Lai'an, China 72/D4
Laibin, China 79/A3
Laichingen, Ger. 54/C5
Laidon (lake), Sc, UK 36/B3
Laie, Hi, US 124/W12
Laifeng Tujiazu Zizhixian, China 79/A2
L'Aigle, Fr. 42/D2
Laigueglia, It. 58/B5
Laihia, Fin. 37/G3
Lainate, It. 58/C1
Laingsburg, SAfr. 106/C4
Lainioälven (riv.), Swe. 37/G1
Laishui, China 72/G7
Laisvall, Swe. 37/F2
Laitila, Fin. 39/J1
Laives (Leifers), It. 57/H5
Laiwu, China 72/D3
Laixi, China 72/E3
Laiyuan, China 72/C3
Laizhou (bay), China 72/D3
Laja (lake), Chile 158/C3
Lajas, Peru 156/B2
Laje, Braz. 154/B3
Lajeado, Braz. 155/B4
Lajedo, Braz. 154/C3
Lajes, Braz. 154/C2
Lajes, Azor., Port. 45/S12
Lajes (int'l arpt.), Azor., Port. 45/S12
Lajing (pass), Nepal 85/E1
Lajinha, Braz. 155/D2
Lajosmizse, Hun. 48/D2
L'Akagera, PN de, Rwa. 104/A3
Lakato, Madg. 107/J7
Lake (co.), Il, US 135/P15
Lake Aluma, Ok, US 137/N14
Lake Amadeus Abor. Land, Austl. 113/F3
Lake Arrowhead, Ca, US 136/C2
Lake Barrington, Il, US 135/P15
Lake Beulah, Wi, US 135/P14
Lake Bluff, Il, US 135/Q15
Lake Boga, Austl. 115/B2
Lake Bogoria Nat'l Rsv., Kenya 104/C2
Lake Bolac, Austl. 115/B3
Lake Cargelligo, Austl. 115/C2
Lake Catherine, Il, US 135/P15
Lake Chany (lake), Rus. 87/G2
Lake Charles, La, US 129/J5
Lake Chelan Nat'l Rec. Area, Wa, US 126/C3
Lake City, Fl, US 133/H4
Lake Clark NP and Prsv., Ak, US 134/G3
Lake District NP, Eng, UK 35/E2
Lake Elsinore, Ca, US 136/C3
Lake Forest, Il, US 135/Q15
Lake Forest Park, Wa, US 135/C2
Lake Fork (res.), Tx, US 132/E3
Lake Grace, Austl. 112/C5
Lake Havasu City, Az, US 128/D4
Lake Hiwassee, Ok, US 137/N14
Lake in the Hills, Il, US 135/P15
Lake Jackson, Tx, US 129/J5
Lake Lotawana, Mo, US 137/E6
Lake Louise, Ab, Can. 126/D3
Lake Malawi NP, Malw. 105/F3
Lake Manyara NP, Tanz. 104/B3
Lake Mburo NP, Ugan. 104/A3
Lake Mead Nat'l Rec. Area, US 128/D4
Lake Meredith Nat'l Rec. Area, Tx, US 132/C3
Lake Minchumina, Ak, US 134/H3
Lake Mohawk, NJ, US 138/D1
Lake Nakuru NP, Kenya 104/C3
Lake of the Woods (lake), US,Can. 127/K3
Lake Orion, Mi, US 135/F6
Lake Point Junction, Ut, US 137/J12
Lake Providence, La, US 129/K4
Lake Ronkonkoma, NY, US 139/E2
Lake Shore, Md, US 138/B5
Lake Station, In, US 135/R16
Lake Success, NY, US 139/L8
Lake Villa, Il, US 135/P15
Lake Wales, Fl, US 133/H5
Lake Winnebago, Mo, US 137/E6
Lake Worth, Fl, US 133/H5
Lake Zurich, Il, US 135/P15
Lakehurst, NJ, US 138/D3
Lakehurst Naval Air Eng. Ctr., NJ, US 138/D3
Lakeland, Fl, US 133/H4
Lakeland Village, Ca, US 136/C3
Lakemoor, Il, US 135/P15
Lakeport, Ca, US 128/B3
Lakes Entrance, Austl. 115/D3
Lakes NP, The, Austl. 115/C3
Lakesfjorden (inlet), Nor. 37/H1
Lakeside, Ca, US 136/D5
Lakeview, Or, US 126/C5
Lakeview, Ut, US 137/K13
Lakeview, Ca, US 136/C3
Lakeville (lake), Mi, US 135/F6
Lakeway, Tx, US 129/H5
Lakewood, Wa, US 126/C3
Lakewood, Co, US 137/B3
Lakewood, NJ, US 138/D3
Lakewood, Ca, US 136/F8
Lakewood, Il, US 135/P15
Lakhemaa NP, Est. 39/L2
Lakhīmpur, India 84/C2
Lakhnādon, India 84/B4
Laki (vol.), Ice. 37/N7
Lakki, Pak. 86/A3
Lakkion, Gre. 90/A2
Lakonía (gulf), Gre. 47/H4
Lakshadweep (terr.), India 82/B6
Lakshadweep (isls.), India 67/F8
Lal Suhanra NP, Pak. 86/B5
Lāla Mūsa, Pak. 86/B3
Lalana (riv.), Madg. 107/H8
Lalang (riv.), Indo. 80/B4
Lālganj, India 85/E3
Lālgola, India 85/G3
Lāliān, Pak. 86/B4
Lalín, Sp. 44/A1
Lalinde, Fr. 42/D4
Lalitpur, India 84/B3
Lalitpur (Pāṭan), Nepal 85/E2
Lalla Rookh Abor. Land, Austl. 112/C2
Lamachan (peak), Sc, UK 34/D1
Lamadrid, Mex. 132/C5
Lamanai (ruin), Belz. 144/D2
Lamandau (riv.), Indo. 80/D4
Lamar, Co, US 129/G3
Lamarche, Fr. 56/B1
Lamarche-sur-Saône, Fr. 56/B3
Lamarque, Arg. 158/D3
Lamas, Peru 156/B2
Lambach, Aus. 55/G6
Lamballe, Fr. 42/B2
Lambaré, Par. 157/E2
Lambaréné, Gabon 96/H8
Lambari, Braz. 211/H6
Lambay (isl.), Ire. 31/Q10
Lambayeque (dept.), Peru 156/A2
Lambayeque, Peru 156/B2
Lambé Coba (riv.), Mali 102/C3
Lambert-St. Louis (int'l arpt.), Mo, US 129/K3
Lambert's Bay, SAfr. 106/B4
Lambertville, Mi, US 130/D3
Lambertville, NJ, US 138/D3
Lambesc, Fr. 42/F5
Lambeth (bor.), Eng, UK 30/C2
Lambrama, Peru 156/C4
Lambrecht, Ger. 54/B4
Lambro (riv.), It. 58/C2
Lambsheim, Ger. 54/B3
Lambton (co.), On, Can. 135/H6
Lambunao, Phil. 79/D5
Lamego, Port. 44/B2
Lamèque (isl.), NB, Can. 131/H2
Lameroo, Austl. 113/J5
Lamesa, Tx, US 129/G4
Lamía, Gre. 47/H3
Lamington (riv.), NJ, US 138/D2
Lamington NP, Austl. 114/D5
Lamitan, Phil. 81/F2
Lamlash, Sc, UK 36/A5
Lamma (isl.), China 71/U11
Lammermuir (hills), Sc, UK 36/D5
Lammhult, Swe. 38/F3
Lammi, Fin. 39/L1
Lamone (riv.), It. 43/J4
Lamont, Ca, US 128/C4
Lamorlaye, Fr. 30/K4
Lamotrek (isl.), Micr. 116/D4
Lampa, Peru 156/D4
Lampa, Chile 158/N8
Lampang, Thai. 78/B2
Lampasas, Tx, US 129/H5
Lampasas (riv.), Tx, US 143/F2
Lampazos de Naranjo, Mex. 132/C5
Lampedusa, It. 46/C5
Lampedusa (isl.), It. 27/F5
Lampertheim, Ger. 54/B3
Lampeter, Pa, US 138/B4
Lamphun, Thai. 78/B2
Lampman, Sk, Can. 127/H3
Lamporecchio, It. 59/D5
Lamstedt, Ger. 51/G1
Lamu, Kenya 104/D3
Lamud, Peru 156/B2
Lamwa (peak), Ugan. 104/B2
Lan Sang NP, Thai. 78/B2
Lana, It. 57/H4
Lana, Río de la (riv.), Mex. 144/C2
Lanai (isl.), Hi, US 117/K2
Lanaihale (peak), Hi, US 124/T10
Lanaken, Belg. 53/E2
Lanark, Sc, UK 36/C5
Lanbi (isl.), Myan. 83/G5
Lancang Lahuzu Zizhixian, China 83/G3
Lancashire (plain), Eng, UK 35/E4
Lancashire (co.), Eng, UK 35/F4
Lancaster, SC, US 133/H3
Lancaster, Ca, US 128/C4
Lancaster, NY, US 131/S10
Lancaster (sound), Nun., Can. 123/H1
Lancaster, Pa, US 138/B3
Lancaster (co.), Pa, US 138/B4
Lancaster, Eng, UK 35/F3
Lancelin, Austl. 112/B4
Lanciano, It. 46/D1
L'Ancienne-Lorette, Qu, Can. 131/G2
Lanco, Chile 158/B3
Łańcut, Pol. 41/M3
Lancy, Swi. 56/C5
Land Kehdingen (reg.), Ger. 51/G1
Landau an der Isar, Ger. 55/F5
Landau in der Pfalz, Ger. 54/B4
Landeck, Aus. 57/G3
Landen, Belg. 53/D2
Lander, Wy, US 126/F5
Landerneau, Fr. 42/A2
Landes (reg.), Fr. 42/C4
Landes de Lanvaux (mts.), Fr. 42/B3
Landesbergen, Ger. 51/G3
Landis, Sk, Can. 126/F2
Landis Valley Museum, Pa, US 138/B3
Landisburg, Pa, US 138/A3
Landivisiau, Fr. 42/A2
Landrecies, Fr. 52/C3
Landri Sales, Braz. 154/B2
Landriano, It. 58/C2
Land's End (pt.), Eng, UK 32/A6
Landsberg, Ger. 55/G6
Landser, Fr. 56/D2
Landshut, Ger. 55/F5
Landskrona, Swe. 38/E4
Landsmeer, Neth. 50/B4
Landstuhl, Ger. 53/G5
Landvetter (int'l arpt.), Swe. 38/E3
Lane End, Eng, UK 30/A2
Lanester, Fr. 42/B3
Lanett, Al, US 133/G3
Lang Craig (pt.), Sc, UK 36/D3
Lang Kha Tuk (peak), Thai. 78/B4
Lang Son, Viet. 83/J3
Lang Suan, Thai. 78/B4
Langadhás, Gre. 47/H2
Langdon, ND, US 127/J3
Langeac, Fr. 42/E4
Langebaanweg, SAfr. 106/L10
Langeberg (mts.), SAfr. 106/L10
Langeland (isl.), Ger. 38/D4
Langelsheim, Ger. 51/H5
Langen, Ger. 51/F1
Langen, Ger. 54/B3
Langenaltheim, Ger. 54/D5
Langenargen, Ger. 57/F2
Langenau, Ger. 54/D5
Langenbach, Ger. 55/E6
Langenberg, Ger. 51/E6
Langenburg, Sk, Can. 127/H3
Längenfeld, Aus. 57/G3
Langenfeld, Ger. 53/F1
Langenhagen, Ger. 51/G4
Langenhorn, Ger. 38/C4
Langenlois, Aus. 41/H4
Langenpreising, Ger. 55/E6
Langenselbold, Ger. 54/C2
Langenstein, Aus. 55/H6
Langenthal, Swi. 56/D3
Langenzenn, Ger. 54/D3
Langenzersdorf, Aus. 49/N7
Langeoog, Ger. 51/E1
Langeoog (isl.), Ger. 51/E1
Langerringen, Ger. 57/G1
Langeskov, Den. 38/D4
Langesund, Nor. 38/C2
Langeten (riv.), Swi. 56/D3
Langfang, China 72/H7
Langfurth, Ger. 54/D4
Langham, Sk, Can. 126/G2
Langhirano, It. 58/D3
Langholm, Sc, UK 35/F1
Langhorne, Pa, US 138/D3
Langjökull (glacier), Ice. 37/N7
Langkawi (isl.), Malay. 83/G6
Langley, Wa, US 135/C1
Langnau im Emmental, Swi. 56/D4
Langney (pt.), Eng, UK 33/G5
Langogne, Fr. 42/E4
Langon, Fr. 42/C4
Langøya (isl.), Nor. 37/E1
Langquaid, Ger. 55/F5
Langres, Fr. 56/B2
Langres, Plateau de (plat.), Fr. 42/F3
Langsa, Indo. 80/A3
Langshyttan, Swe. 38/G1
Langtang Lirung (peak), Nepal 85/E1
Langtang NP, Nepal 85/E1
Langtry, Tx, US 132/C4
Languedoc (reg.), Fr. 42/E5
Languedoc-Roussillon (pol. reg.), Fr. 42/E5
Langwedel, Ger. 51/G3
Langweid an Lech, Ger. 54/E6
Langwies, Swi. 57/F4
Langxi, China 72/D5
Lanham-Seabrook, Md, US 138/B6
Lanigan, Sk, Can. 127/G3
Laniloa (pt.), Hi, US 124/W12
Lanin (vol.), Arg. 158/C3
Lanín, PN, Arg. 157/B4
Länkäran, Azer. 63/J5
Lanlacuni Bajo, Peru 156/D4
Lannemezan (plat.), Fr. 42/D5
Lannion (bay), Fr. 42/B2
Lannion, Fr. 42/B2
Lansdale, Pa, US 138/C3
Lansdowne, India 84/B1
Lansdowne, Pa, US 138/C4
Lansdowne-Baltimore Highlands, Md, US 138/B5
Lansford, Pa, US 138/C2
Lanshan, China 83/K2
Lansing (cap.), Mi, US 130/C3
Lansing, Ks, US 137/D5
Lansing, Il, US 135/Q16
Lanta (isl.), Thai. 83/G6
Lantau (chan.), China 71/T11
Lantau (peak), China 71/T11
Lantau (isl.), China 71/T10
Lanterne (riv.), Fr. 56/C2
Lanús, Arg. 159/J11
Lanusei, It. 46/A3
Lanxi, China 79/C2
Lanzarote (int'l arpt.), Sp. 98/B3
Lanzarote (isl.), Canl., Sp. 93/A2
Lanžhot, Czh. 41/J4
Lanzhou, China 70/H4
Lao (mts.), China 73/D2
Lao (peak), China 72/E3
Lao Cai, Viet. 70/H7
Laoag, Phil. 79/D4
Laoang, Phil. 79/E5
Laohekou, China 72/B4
Laojun (mtn.), China 72/B4
Laon, Fr. 52/C4
Laos (ctry.) 78/C2
Laoshan, China 72/E3
Laotuding (peak), China 73/C2
Laou (riv.), Mor. 100/B2
Lapa, Braz. 155/B3
Lapeer, Mi, US 130/D3
Lapeer (co.), Mi, US 135/F6
Lapinlahti, Fin. 60/E3
Lapithos, Cyp. 91/C2
Lapland (reg.), Swe. 160/D
Laporte, Co, US 137/B1
Lappeenranta, Fin. 39/N1
Lappersdorf, Ger. 55/F4
Lappi (prov.), Fin. 37/H2
Laptev (sea), Rus. 67/M2
Lapua, Fin. 60/D3
Łapy, Pol. 41/M2
L'Aquila, It. 46/C1
Lār, Iran 89/F3
Lara, Austl. 115/C3
Lara (state), Ven. 152/D2
Laracha, Sp. 44/A1
Larache (prov.), Mor. 100/B2
Larache, Mor. 100/A2
Laragne-Montéglin, Fr. 42/F4
Laramie (riv.), Wy, US 127/G5
Laramie, Wy, US 127/G5
Laramie (mts.), Wy, US 124/E3
Laranjeiras do Sul, Braz. 155/A3
Larat (isl.), Indo. 81/H5
Larba, Alg. 100/G4
Larchmont, NY, US 139/K8
Lærdalsøyri, Nor. 38/B1
Laredo, Peru 156/B3

201
Lared – Lichu

Laredo (int'l arpt.), Tx, US 132/D5
Laredo, Tx, US 132/D5
Laredo, Sp. 44/D1
Laren, Neth. 50/C4
Lares, Peru 156/C4
Largo, Fl, US 133/H5
Largo, Md, US 138/B6
Largo (bay), Sc, UK 36/D4
Largo, Cayo (isl.), Cuba 145/F1
Largs, Sc, UK 36/B5
Largue (riv.), Fr. 56/D2
Lariang (riv.), Indo. 81/E4
Larino, It. 46/D2
Lárisa, Gre. 47/H3
Lark (riv.), Eng, UK 33/G2
Lārkāna, Pak. 89/J3
Larkhall, Sc, UK 36/C5
Larkspur, Ca, US 135/J11
Larmor-Plage, Fr. 42/B3
Larnaca (int'l arpt.), Cyp. 91/C2
Larnaca (dist.) 91/C2
Larnaca, Cyp. 91/C2
Larne, NI, UK 34/C2
Larne (dist.), NI, UK 34/C2
Larne Lough (inlet), NI, UK 34/C2
Larned, Ks, US 129/H3
Larochette, Lux. 53/F4
Laroque-d'Olmes, Fr. 42/D5
Larose, La, US 133/F4
Larreynaga, Nic. 144/E3
Larroque, Arg. 159/J10
Larsen Bay, Ak, US 134/H4
Larsen Ice Shelf, Ant. 160/V
Larsen Sound (bay), Nun., Can. 122/G1
L'Artois, Collines de (hills), Fr. 40/A3
Laruns, Fr. 42/C5
Larvik, Nor. 38/D2
Las Animas, Co, US 129/G3
Las Aves (isls.), Ven. 141/H5
Las Breñas, Arg. 157/D2
Las Cabezas de San Juan, Sp. 44/C4
Las Cabras, Chile 158/N9
Las Cruces, NM, US 128/F4
Las Cruces (int'l arpt.), NM, US 142/D1
Las Delicias, Ven. 152/C3
Las Eutimias, Mex. 132/C4
Las Flores, Arg. 158/F3
Las Guacamayas, Mex. 142/E5
Las Hermosas, PN, Col. 152/C4
Las Higueras, Arg. 158/D2
Las Lajas, Arg. 158/C3
Las Lajas (peak), Arg. 158/C3
Las Lomas, Peru 156/A2
Las Lomitas, Arg. 157/D1
Las Margaritas, Mex. 144/D2
Las Martinas, Cuba 145/E1
Las Mercedes, Ven. 153/E2
Las Minas (peak), Hon. 144/D3
Las Nieves, Mex. 142/D3
Las Orquídeas, PN, Col. 152/B3
Las Palmas, Pan. 145/F4
Las Palmas de Cocalán, PN, Chile 158/N9
Las Palmas de Gran Canaria, Sp. 98/B3
Las Pedroñeras, Sp. 44/D3
Las Perdices, Arg. 158/E2
Las Perlas (arch.), Pan. 145/G4
Las Piedras, Peru 156/D4
Las Piedras, Ven. 152/C2
Las Piedras, Uru. 159/K11
Las Pipinas, Arg. 159/F2
Las Rosas, Mex. 144/C2
Las Rozas de Madrid, Sp. 45/N9
Las Tablas, Pan. 152/A3
Las Varas, Mex. 142/D4
Las Varillas, Arg. 157/D3
Las Vegas, NM, US 129/F4
Las Vegas, Nv, US 128/D3
Lasalle, Qu, Can. 131/N7
Lasberg, Aus. 55/H6
Lascano, Uru. 159/G2
Lashio, Myan. 83/G3
Lashkar Gāh, Afg. 89/H2
Lasne-Chapelle-Saint-Lambert, Belg. 53/D2
Læsø (isl.), Den. 38/D3
Lasolo (riv.), Indo. 81/F4
Lassen (peak), Ca, US 126/C5
Lassen Volcanic NP, Ca, US 128/B2
L'Assomption (co.), Qu, Can. 131/N6
L'Assomption (riv.), Qu, Can. 131/P6
L'Assomption, Qu, Can. 131/P6
Last Mountain (lake), Sk, Can. 127/G3
Lastovo (isl.), Cro. 46/E1
Lastovski (chan.), Cro. 48/C4
Lastovski Kanal (chan.), Cro. 46/E1
Lastra a Signa, It. 59/E5
Lastrup, Ger. 51/E3
Lata, Sol. 116/F6
Latacunga, Ecu. 152/B5
Latady (isl.), Ant. 160/U
L'Atakora (prov.), Ben. 103/F4
Lātehār, India 85/E4
Latemar (peak), It. 57/H5
Laterza, It. 46/E2
Lathan (riv.), Fr. 42/C3
Lathrop, Ca, US 135/M11
Latina, It. 46/C2
Latisana, It. 59/G1
Latorica (riv.), Slvk.,Ukr. 41/M4
Latrobe (riv.), Austl. 115/C3
Latrobe (mt.), Austl. 115/C3
Latrobe, Austl. 115/C4
Lattes, Fr. 42/E5
Lattingtown, NY, US 139/L8
Lātūr, India 89/L5
Latvia (ctry.) 39/L3
Lau Group (isl.), Fiji 116/H6
Laubach, Ger. 54/B1
Lauca, PN, Chile 150/D7
Lauch (riv.), Fr. 43/G3
Lauchert (riv.), Ger. 54/C6
Lauchheim, Ger. 54/D5
Lauda-Königshofen, Ger. 54/C3
Lauder, Sc, UK 36/D5
Lauderdale (lakes), Wi, US 135/N14
Lauenbrück, Ger. 51/G2
Lauenburg, Ger. 51/H2
Lauenen, Swi. 56/D5
Lauenförde, Ger. 51/H5
Lauer (riv.), Ger. 54/D2
Lauf, Ger. 54/E3
Laufach, Ger. 54/C2
Laufen, Swi. 56/D3
Laufen, Ger. 55/F7
Laufenburg, Swi. 56/E2
Lauffen am Neckar, Ger. 54/C4
Laughlen (mt.), Austl. 113/G2
Lauhanvuoren NP, Fin. 60/D3
Lauingen, Ger. 54/D5
Launceston, Austl. 115/C4
Launette (riv.), Fr. 30/L4
Laupahoehoe, Hi, US 124/U11
Laupen, Swi. 56/D4
Lauperswil, Swi. 56/D4
Laupheim, Ger. 57/F1
Laura, Austl. 113/H5
Laureana di Borrello, It. 46/E3
Laurel, Mt, US 126/F4
Laurel, Ms, US 133/F4
Laurel, Md, US 138/B5
Laurel Springs, NJ, US 138/C4
Laureldale, Pa, US 138/C3
Laurelton, Pa, US 138/A2
Laurence Harbor, NJ, US 139/J10
Laurencekirk, Sc, UK 36/D3
Laurens, SC, US 133/H3
Laurentian (plat.), On, Can. 122/G3
Laurentides, Qu, Can. 131/N6
Laurinburg, NC, US 133/J3
Laurium, Mi, US 127/L4
Lausanne, Swi. 56/C4
Lauscha, Ger. 54/E2
Laut (isl.), Indo. 81/E4
Lautaro, Chile 158/B3
Lauter, Ger. 55/F1
Lauter (riv.), Ger. 40/E3
Lauterach (riv.), Ger. 55/E4
Lauterbach (riv.), Ger. 54/E2
Lauterbach, Ger. 54/C1
Lauterbourg, Fr. 54/B5
Lauterbrunnen, Swi. 56/D4
Lauterecken, Ger. 53/G4
Lauve, Nor. 38/D2
Lauwers (chan.), Neth. 50/D1
Lauwersmeer (lake), Neth. 50/D2
Lava Beds Nat'l Mon., Ca, US 126/C5
Lavagna (riv.), It. 58/C4
Lavagna, It. 58/C4
Laval, Fr. 42/C2
Laval, Qu, Can. 131/N6
Lavalleja (dept.), Uru. 159/G2
Lavallette, NJ, US 138/D4
Lavans-lès-Saint-Claude, Fr. 56/B5
Lavant (riv.), Aus. 43/L3
Lavapié (pt.), Chile 158/B3
Lavaur, Fr. 42/D5
Laveen, Az, US 137/R19
Lavelanet, Fr. 42/D5
Lavello, It. 46/D2
Laveno, It. 57/E6
Laverton, Austl. 112/D4
Lavey, Swi. 56/D5
Lavezzola, It. 59/E3
Lavino (riv.), It. 59/E4
Lavis, It. 57/H5
Lavos, Port. 44/A2
Lavras, Braz. 155/C2
Lavras da Mangabeira, Braz. 154/C2
Lávrion, Gre. 47/J4
Lawa (riv.), FrG. 153/H4
Lāwar Khās, India 84/A1
Lawarai (pass), Pak. 86/A2
Lawit (mtn.), Indo. 80/D3
Lawit (peak), Malay. 83/H6
Lawndale, Ca, US 136/F8
Lawnhill, BC, Can. 134/M5
Lawra, Gha. 102/E4
Lawrence, Ma, US 131/G3
Lawrence, Ks, US 129/J3
Lawrence, NY, US 139/L9
Lawrenceburg, In, US 130/C4
Lawrenceburg, Tn, US 133/G3
Lawrenceburg, Ky, US 133/G2
Lawrencetown, NI, UK 34/B3
Lawrenceville, Ga, US 133/H3
Lawrenceville, NJ, US 138/D3
Lawson, Mo, US 137/E5
Lawu (peak), Indo. 80/D5
Lawz, Jabal al (peak), SAr. 88/C3
Laxå, Swe. 38/F2
Laxey, IM, UK 34/D3
Laxou, Fr. 53/F6
Lay (riv.), Fr. 42/C3
Lay-Saint-Christophe, Fr. 53/F6
Laya (riv.), Rus. 61/N2
Layar (cape), Indo. 81/E4
Laylān, Iraq 90/F3
Layon (riv.), Fr. 42/C3
Laysan (isl.), HI, US 117/H2
Layton, Ut, US 137/K11
Layton, NJ, US 138/D1
Lazarevac, Yugo. 48/E3
Lázaro Cárdenas, Mex. 128/D5
Lázaro Cárdenas, Mex. 142/B2
Lázaro Cárdenas, Mex. 142/E5
Lazio (prov.), It. 43/J5
Llbriktepe, Turk. 47/K2
Le Ban-Saint-Martin, Fr. 53/F5
Le Blanc, Fr. 42/D3
Le Blanc-Mesnil, Fr. 30/K5
Le Breuil, Fr. 42/F3
Le Cannet, Fr. 43/G5
Le Cateau-Cambrésis, Fr. 52/C3
Le Chasseral (peak), Swi. 56/D3
Le Chasseron (peak), Swi. 56/C4
Le Chesnay, Fr. 30/J5
Le Chesne, Fr. 53/D4
Le Cheval Blanc (peak), Fr. 56/C5
Le Cheylard, Fr. 42/F4
Le Cornate (peak), It. 43/J5
Le Creusot, Fr. 42/F3
Le Crotoy, Fr. 52/A3
Le Gore, Md, US 138/A4
Le Grammont (peak), Swi. 56/C5
Le Grand (cape), Austl. 112/D5
Le Grand Ballon (peak), Fr. 56/D2
Le Grau-du-Roi, Fr. 42/F5
Le Grazie, It. 58/C4
Le Havre, Fr. 42/D2
Le Landeron, Swi. 56/D3
Le Lavandou, Fr. 43/G5
Le Locle, Swi. 56/C3
Le Luc, Fr. 43/G5
Le Mans, Fr. 42/D2
Le Mée-sur-Seine, Fr. 30/K6
Le Mesnil-Amelot, Fr. 30/K4
Le Mesnil-Aubry, Fr. 30/K4
Le Mesnil-Esnard, Fr. 52/A5
Le Mesnil-le-Roi, Fr. 30/J5
Le Mesnil-Saint-Denis, Fr. 30/H5
Le Mesnil-sur-Oger, Fr. 52/D6
Le Môle (peak), Fr. 56/C5
Le Morond (peak), Fr. 56/C4
Le Moure de la Gardille (peak), Fr. 42/E4
Le Murge (mts.), It. 46/E2
Le Noirmont (peak), Fr. 56/C4
Le Noirmont (peak), Swi. 56/C5
Le Noirmont, Swi. 56/C3
Le Nouvion-en-Thiérache, Fr. 52/C3
Le Palais, Fr. 42/B3
Le Palais-sur-Vienne, Fr. 42/D4
Le Passage, Fr. 42/D4
Le Perray-en-Yvelines, Fr. 30/H5
Le Petit Ballon (peak), Fr. 56/D2
Le Plessis-Belleville, Fr. 30/L4
Le Plessis-Feu-Aussoux, Fr. 30/M5
Le Plessis-Placy, Fr. 30/L4
Le Port, Reun. 107/S15
Le Portel, Fr. 52/A2
Le Puy-en-Velay, Fr. 42/E4
Le Quesnoy, Fr. 52/C3
Le Russey, Fr. 56/C3
Le Suchet (peak), Swi. 56/C4
Le Tampon, Reun. 107/S15
Le Teil, Fr. 42/F4
Le Tholy, Fr. 56/C1
Le Touquet-Paris-Plage, Fr. 52/A2
Le Tréport, Fr. 52/A3
Le Val-d'Ajol, Fr. 56/C2
Le Vésinet, Fr. 30/J5
Le Vigan, Fr. 42/E5
Lea (riv.), Eng, UK 33/F3
Leach (lake), Ca, US 127/K4
Leach (riv.), Eng, UK 33/E3
Leacock-Leola-Bareville, Pa, US 138/B3
Lead, SD, US 127/H4
Leader, Sk, Can. 126/F3
Leader Water (riv.), Sc, UK 36/D5
Leadon (riv.), Eng, UK 32/D3
Leadville, Co, US 132/B2
Leaf (riv.), Ms, US 133/F4
Leaghur (lake), Austl. 115/B2
League City, Tx, US 129/J5
Leakey, Tx, US 129/H5
Leam (riv.), Eng, UK 33/E2
Leamington, On, Can. 130/D3
Le'an, China 79/C2
Leander (pt.), Austl. 112/B4
Leaota (peak), Rom. 49/G3
Learmonth, Austl. 112/B2
Leatherhead, Eng, UK 30/C3
Leavenworth, Wa, US 126/C4
Leavenworth (co.), Ks, US 137/D5
Leavenworth, Ks, US 137/D5
Leawood, Ks, US 137/D6
Leba, Pol. 38/G4
Lebach, Ger. 53/F5
Lebak, Phil. 79/D6
Lebane, Yugo. 47/G1
Lebanon, Or, US 126/C4
Lebanon, In, US 130/C3
Lebanon, Tn, US 130/C4
Lebanon, Ky, US 130/C4
Lebanon, NH, US 131/F3
Lebanon, Mo, US 129/J3
Lebanon (mts.), Leb. 91/D3
Lebanon (ctry.) 91/D3
Lebanon, NJ, US 138/D2
Lebanon, Pa, US 138/B3
Lebbeke, Belg. 53/D2
Lebedyn, Ukr. 62/E2
Lebel-sur-Quévillon, Qu, Can. 130/E1
Lebene (riv.), Mor. 100/B2
Lébény, Hun. 48/C2
Lębork, Pol. 38/G4
Lebrija, Sp. 44/B4
Lebu, Chile 157/B4
Lebu, Chile 158/B3
Leça da Palmeira, Port. 44/A2
Lecce, It. 47/F2
Lecco, It. 43/H4
Lecco, Lago di (lake), It. 58/C1
Lech (riv.), Ger. 43/K2
Lech, Aus. 57/G3
Lechang, China 83/K2
Lechbruck, Ger. 57/G2
Leche (lake), Cuba 145/G1
Lechtaler Alps (mts.), Aus. 57/G3
Leck, Ger. 38/C4
Lectoure, Fr. 42/D5
Łęczna, Pol. 41/M3
Leda (riv.), Ger. 51/E2
Ledang (peak), Malay. 80/B3
Lede, Belg. 52/C2
Ledegem, Belg. 52/C2
Ledesma, Sp. 44/B2
Ledge Point, Austl. 112/B4
Ledong, China 83/J4
Ledro (lake), It. 57/G6
Ledu (peak), It. 57/F5
Leduc, Ab, Can. 126/E2
Lee (riv.), Ire. 31/P11
Lee (mtn.), Pa, US 138/B1
Leech (lake), Mn, US 125/H2
Leeds, Eng, UK 35/G4
Leeds and Bradford (int'l arpt.), Eng, UK 35/G4
Leeds and Liverpool (canal), Eng, UK 35/G4
Leeds Point, NJ, US 138/D5
Leegebruch, Ger. 40/Q6
Leek, Neth. 50/D2
Leek, Eng, UK 35/F5
Leeman, Austl. 112/B4
Leer, Ger. 51/E2
Leerdam, Neth. 50/C5
Leersum, Neth. 50/C4
Lees Summit, Mo, US 137/E6
Leesburg, Fl, US 133/H4
Leesburg, NJ, US 138/D5
Leese, Ger. 51/G3
Leesport, Pa, US 138/C3
Leesville, La, US 129/J5
Leeton, Austl. 115/C2
Leeu (riv.), SAfr. 106/L10
Leeudoringstad, SAfr. 106/D2
Leeuwarden, Neth. 50/C2
Leeuwin (cape), Austl. 112/B5
Leeuwin-Naturaliste NP, Austl. 112/B5
Leeward (isls.), NAm. 141/J4
Leff (riv.), Fr. 42/B2
Lefka, Cyp. 91/C2
Lefo (peak), Camr. 103/H5
Lefroy (lake), Austl. 112/D4
Legana, Austl. 115/C4
Leganés, Sp. 45/N9
Legaspi, Phil. 79/D5
Legau, Ger. 57/G2
Legazpia, Sp. 44/D1
Legges Tor (peak), Austl. 115/C4
Legionowo, Pol. 41/L2
Léglise, Belg. 53/E4
Legnago, It. 59/E2
Legnano, It. 43/H4
Legnaro, It. 59/E2
Legnica, Pol. 41/J3
Legnone (peak), It. 57/F5
Leh, India 86/D2
Leh Palace, India 86/D2
Lehi, Ut, US 137/K13
Lehigh (co.), Pa, US 138/C2
Lehigh Acres, Fl, US 133/H5
Lehighton, Pa, US 138/C2
Lehinch, Ire. 31/P10
Lehrberg, Ger. 54/D4
Lehrte, Ger. 51/G4
Lei (riv.), China 83/K2
Leiah, Pak. 86/A4
Leiblfing, Ger. 55/F5
Leibo, China 83/H2
Leicester, Eng, UK 33/E1
Leicester (co.), Eng, UK 33/E1
Leicestershire (co.), Eng, UK 35/H6
Leichhardt (riv.), Austl. 109/C2
Leichhardt (dam), Austl. 113/H2
Leichlingen, Ger. 53/G1
Leiden, Neth. 50/B4
Leiderdorp, Neth. 50/B4
Leidschendam, Neth. 50/B4
Leie (riv.), Belg. 42/E1
Leifers (Laives), It. 43/J3
Leigh, Eng, UK 35/F5
Leigh Creek, Austl. 113/H4
Leimebamba, Peru 156/B2
Leimen, Ger. 54/B4
Leimersheim, Ger. 54/B4
Leine (riv.), Ger. 40/D3
Leinefelde, Ger. 51/H6
Leinfelden-Echterdingen, Ger. 54/C5
Leinster (mt.), Ire. 31/Q10
Leinster, Austl. 112/D3
Leinster (reg.), Ire. 34/A5
Leipheim, Ger. 54/D6
Leipsic, De, US 138/C5
Leipsic (riv.), De, US 138/C5
Leipzig, Ger. 64/B4
Leira, Nor. 38/C1
Leiria, Port. 44/A3
Leiria (dist.), Port. 44/A3
Leisler (mt.), Austl. 113/F2
Leith (hill), Eng, UK 30/B3
Leitha (riv.), Aus. 41/J5
Leixlip, Ire. 34/B5
Leizhou (pen.), China 83/J3
Lek (riv.), Neth. 40/C3
Lekhainá, Gre. 47/G4
Lekkerkerk, Neth. 50/B5
Lekki (lag.), Nga. 103/G5
Leksands-Noret, Swe. 38/F1
Leksozero (lake), Rus. 37/J3
Lelai (cape), Indo. 81/G3
Leland, Ms, US 129/K4
Lelång (lake), Swe. 38/E2
Leling, China 72/D3
Lelystad, Neth. 50/C3
Lem, Den. 38/C3
Lema (peak), It. 57/E5
Léman (Geneva) (lake), Fr. 43/G3
Lemberg (peak), Ger. 57/E1
Lemberg, Ger. 53/G5
Lembu (peak), Indo. 80/A3
Leme, Braz. 155/C2
Lemenjoen NP, Fin. 37/H1
Lemgo, Ger. 51/F4
Lemland (isl.), Fin. 39/H2
Lemland, Fin. 39/J1
Lemmer, Neth. 50/C3
Lemmon, SD, US 127/H4
Lemon Grove, Ca, US 136/C5
Lempa (riv.), ESal. 144/D3
Lempäälä, Fin. 39/K1
Lempdes, Fr. 42/E4
Lemva (riv.), Rus. 61/P2
Lemvig, Den. 38/C3
Lemwerder, Ger. 51/F2
Lena (riv.), Rus. 67/M3
Lena, Nor. 38/D1
Lenape, Ks, US 137/D6
Lenape (lake), NJ, US 138/D5
Lençóis Maranhenses, PN dos, Braz. 151/K4
Lençóis Paulista, Braz. 155/B2
Lendinara, It. 59/E2
Lenexa, Ks, US 137/D6
Lengau, Aus. 55/G6
Lengdorf, Ger. 55/F6
Lengede, Ger. 51/H4
Lengenfeld, Ger. 55/F1
Lengerich, Ger. 51/E4
Lenggries, Ger. 57/H2
Lengnau, Swi. 56/D3
Lengshuitan, China 83/K2
Lengua de Vaca (pt.), Chile 157/B3
Lenhartsville, Pa, US 138/C2
Lenina (peak), Taj. 87/F5
Leninabad (int'l arpt.), Taj. 87/E4
Leningradskaya (obl.), Rus. 60/G3
Leninobod (obl.), Taj. 87/E5
Leninogorsk, Rus. 61/M5
Leninsk-Kuznetskiy, Rus. 64/J4
Leninváros, Hun. 41/L5
Lenk, Swi. 56/D5
Lenne (riv.), Ger. 53/G1
Lennestadt, Ger. 51/F6
Lenningen, Ger. 54/C5
Lennox (isl.), Chile 159/D7
Lennox, Ca, US 136/F8
Lennox (hills), Sc, UK 36/B5
Lennoxtown, Sc, UK 36/B5
Leno, It. 58/D2
Lenoir, NC, US 133/H3
Lenoir City, Tn, US 133/G3
Lens, Swi. 56/D5
Lens, Fr. 52/B3
Lens, Belg. 52/C2
Lensahn, Ger. 38/D4
Lensk, Rus. 65/M3
Lenting, Ger. 55/E5
Lentini, It. 46/D4
Lenvik, Nor. 37/F1
Leny, Pass of (pass), Sc, UK 36/B4
Lenzburg, Swi. 56/E3
Lenzing, Aus. 55/G7
Lenzkirch, Ger. 57/E2
Léo, Burk. 103/E4
Leoben, Aus. 43/L3
Leográ (riv.), It. 59/E1
Leola, SD, US 127/J4
Leon (riv.), Tx, US 140/B1
León, Mex. 143/E4
Leon (int'l arpt.), Mex. 142/C3
León, Sp. 44/C1
León, Nic. 144/E3
León, Étang de (lake), Fr. 42/C4
Leon-Guanajuato (int'l arpt.), Mex. 143/E4
Leon Springs, Tx, US 137/T20
Leon Valley, Tx, US 137/T21
Leona Valley, Ca, US 136/B1
Leonard, Tx, US 129/H4
Leonard, Mi, US 135/F6
Leonardo, NJ, US 139/J10
Leonardo da Vinci (int'l arpt.), It. 46/C2
Leonberg, Ger. 54/C5
Leonding, Aus. 55/H6
Leone (peak), It. 56/E5
Leones, Arg. 158/E2
Leonforte, It. 46/D4
Leongatha, Austl. 115/C3
Leonia, NJ, US 139/K8
Leonídhion, Gre. 47/H4
Leonora, Austl. 112/D4
Leopoldina, Braz. 211/L6
Leopoldkanaal (riv.), Belg. 52/C1
Leopoldsburg, Belg. 53/E1
Leopoldsdorf, Aus. 49/N7
Leopoldsdorf im Marchfelde, Aus. 49/P7
Leopoldshöhe, Ger. 51/F4
Leoville, Sk, Can. 126/G2
Lepaera, Hon. 144/D3
Lépanges-sur-Vologne, Fr. 56/C1
Lepe, Sp. 44/B4
Lepenoú, Gre. 47/G3
L'Épiphanie, Qu, Can. 131/P6
Lepontine Alps (mts.), Swi 43/H3
Leptokariá, Gre. 47/H2
Léraba (riv.), Burk. 102/D4
Lercara Friddi, It. 46/C4
Lerdo de Tejada, Mex. 144/C2
Leribe, Les. 106/E3
Lerici, It. 58/C4
Lerín, Sp. 44/E1
Lerma, Sp. 44/D1
Lerma, Mex. 143/Q10
Lerma (riv.), Mex. 143/K7
Lermoos, Aus. 57/G3
Lérouville, Fr. 53/E6
Lerum, Swe. 38/E3
Lerwick, Sc, UK 31/W13
Lery (lake), La, US 137/Q17
Léry, Qu, Can. 131/N7
Les Alluets-le-Roi, Fr. 30/H5
Les Bois, Swi. 56/C3
Les Breuleux, Swi. 56/D3
Les Bréviaires, Fr. 30/H5
Les Cayes, Haiti 145/H2
Les Cèdres, Qu, Can. 131/M7
Les Clayes-sous-Bois, Fr. 30/H5
Les Contamines-Montjoie, Fr. 56/C6
Les Diablerets (range), Swi. 56/D5
Les Essarts-le-Roi, Fr. 30/H5
Les Gets, Fr. 56/C5
Les Hautes-Rivières, Fr. 53/D4
Les Herbiers, Fr. 42/C3
Les Islettes, Fr. 53/E5
Les Mesnuls, Fr. 30/H5
Les Molières, Fr. 30/J6
Les Mureaux, Fr. 52/A6
Les Ponts-de-Martel, Swi. 56/C4
Les Rousses, Fr. 56/C5
Les Sables-d'Olonne, Fr. 42/C3
Les Salines (int'l arpt.), Alg. 100/K6
Les Ulis, Fr. 30/J5
Les Verrières, Swi. 56/C4
Lesa, It. 58/B1
Leshan, China 83/H2
Lésigny, Fr. 30/K5
Lesima (peak), It. 58/C3
Lesja, Nor. 37/D3
Lesjöfors, Swe. 38/F2
Lesko, Pol. 41/M4
Leskovac, Yugo. 47/G1
Leslie, Sc, UK 36/C4
Lesmahagow, Sc, UK 36/C5
Lesneven, Fr. 42/A2
Lešnica, Yugo. 48/D3
Lesotho (ctry.) 106/E6
Lesozavodsk, Rus. 71/P2
Lesparre-Médoc, Fr. 42/C4
Lesquin (int'l arpt.), Fr. 52/C2
Lesse (riv.), Belg. 40/C3
Lessebo, Swe. 38/F3
Lesser Antilles (isls.), NAm. 141/M8
Lesser Caucasus (mts.), Asia 63/G4
Lesser Slave (lake), Ab, Can. 122/E3
Lesser Sunda (isls.), Indo. 81/E5
Lessines, Belg. 52/C2
Lesung (peak), Indo. 80/D3
Lésvos (isl.), Gre. 62/C5
Leszno, Pol. 41/J3
Létavértes, Hun. 48/E2
Letchworth, Eng, UK 33/F3
Letham, Sc, UK 36/D3
Lethbridge, Ab, Can. 126/E3
Lethe (riv.), Ger. 51/F2
Lethem, Guy. 153/G4
Leti (isls.), Indo. 116/B5
Leticia, Col. 156/D2
Leting, China 72/D3
Letlhakane, Bots. 105/E5
Letlhakeng, Bots. 105/D5
Letnitsa, Bul. 49/G4
L'Étoile, Fr. 52/B3
Letpadan, Myan. 83/G4
Letschin, Ger. 41/H2
Letsôk-Aw (isl.), Myan. 80/A1
Letterkenny, Ire. 31/Q9
Leucate, Fr. 42/E5
Leuchars, Sc, UK 36/D4
Leuk, Swi. 56/D5
Leukerbad, Swi. 56/D5
Leun, Ger. 54/B1
Leusden-Zuid, Neth. 50/C4
Leuser (peak), Indo. 80/A3
Leuterhausen, Ger. 54/D4
Leutkirch im Allgäu, Ger. 57/G2
Leuze-en-Hainaut, Belg. 52/C2
Levádhia, Gre. 47/H3
Levallois-Perret, Fr. 30/J5
Levanger, Nor. 37/D3
Levante, Riviera di (coast), It. 58/C4
Levanto, It. 58/C4
Levasy, Mo, US 137/E5
Level (isl.), Chile 158/B5
Level, Md, US 138/B4
Levelland, Tx, US 129/G4
Levelock, Ak, US 134/G4
Leven (pt.), SAfr. 107/F2
Leven (lake), Sc, UK 36/A3
Leven, Sc, UK 36/D4
Leven (riv.), Sc, UK 36/C4
Leveque (cape), Austl. 109/B2
Leverburgh, Sc, UK 31/Q8
Leverkusen, Ger. 53/F1
Levice, Slvk. 48/D1
Levico Terme, It. 57/H5
Levier, Fr. 56/C4
Levin, NZ 117/T11
Lévis, Qu, Can. 131/G2
Lévis-Saint-Nom, Fr. 30/H5
Levittown, Pa, US 138/D3
Levittown, NY, US 139/L9
Levkás, Gre. 47/G3
Levkás (isl.), Gre. 47/G3
Levkímmi, Gre. 47/G3
Levoča, Slvk. 41/L4
Levrier (bay), Mrta. 98/A5
Levski, Bul. 49/G4
Lewes, Eng, UK 33/G5
Lewin Brzeski, Pol. 41/J3
Lewis (riv.), Wa, US 126/C4
Lewis (range), Mt, US 126/E3
Lewis (hills), Nf, Can. 131/K1
Lewis (pass), NZ 117/S11
Lewis (isl.), Sc, UK 31/Q7
Lewis and Clark (lake), Ne,SD, US 127/J5
Lewis Smith (lake), Al, US 133/G3
Lewisburg, Tn, US 133/G3
Lewisburg, WV, US 130/D4
Lewisburg, Pa, US 138/B2
Lewisham (bor.), Eng, UK 30/C2
Lewisporte, Nf, Can. 131/L1
Lewiston, Id, US 126/D4
Lewiston, Me, US 131/G2
Lewiston, NY, US 131/R9
Lewistown, Mt, US 126/F4
Lewistown, Pa, US 130/E3
Lewotobi (peak), Indo. 81/F5
Lexington, Ne, US 127/J5
Lexington, Tn, US 130/B5
Lexington, Ky, US 130/C4
Lexington, NC, US 133/H3
Lexington Park, Md, US 130/E4
Leyburn, Eng, UK 35/G3
Leyden, Co, US 137/B3
Leye, China 83/J3
Leyland, Eng, UK 35/F4
Leysin, Swi. 56/D5
Leyte (isl.), Phil. 67/M8
Leytron, Swi. 56/D5
Lez (riv.), Fr. 42/F4
Leżajsk, Pol. 41/M3
Lezhë, Alb. 47/F2
Lézignan-Corbières, Fr. 42/E5
Lezuza, Sp. 44/D3
L'gov, Rus. 62/E2
Lhanbyrd, Sc, UK 36/C1
Lhari, China 70/F5
Lhasa, China 82/F2
Lhazê, China 85/F1
L'Hongrin (lake), Swi. 56/D5
Lhorong, China 70/G5
L'Hospitalet de Llobregat, Sp. 45/L7
Lhozhag, China 85/H1
Lhünzê, China 83/G2
Li (riv.), China 79/B2
Li (riv.), China 83/K2
Li (mtn.), China 72/B4
Li Xian, China 79/B2
Lian (riv.), China 79/B3
Lian Xian, China 83/K3
Liancheng, China 79/C2
Liancourt, Fr. 52/B5
Liancourt Rocks (isl.), Asia 74/B2
Liangcheng, China 72/C2
Liangpran (peak), Indo. 80/D3
Liangzi (lake), China 72/C5
Lianhua, China 83/K2
Lianjiang, China 79/C2
Lianjiang, China 83/K3
Liannan Yaozu Zizhixian, China 79/B3
Lianshui, China 72/D4
Lianyuan, China 79/B2
Lianyungang, China 72/D4
Liao (riv.), China 67/M5
Liaocheng, China 72/C3
Liaodong (pen.), China 73/A3
Liaodong (isls.), China 72/E3
Liaodong, Gulf of (gulf), China 71/M3
Liaoning (prov.), China 71/M3
Liaoyang, China 73/B2
Liaoyuan, China 71/N3
Liaozhong, China 73/B2
Liāquatpur, Pak. 86/A5
Liard (riv.), NW, Can. 122/D2
Libby, Mt, US 126/E3
Liběchovka (riv.), Czh. 55/H2
Libenge, D.R. Congo 97/J7
Libercourt, Fr. 52/C3
Liberdade (riv.), Braz. 151/H6
Liberdade, Braz. 211/J7
Liberec, Czh. 41/H3
Liberia, CR 144/E4
Liberia (ctry.) 102/C5
Libertad, Belz. 144/D2
Libertad, Ven. 152/D2
Libertad, Uru. 159/K11
Libertador General San Martín, Arg. 157/D1
Liberty, Tx, US 129/J5
Liberty, Ky, US 130/C4
Liberty, Ms, US 129/K5
Liberty, Mo, US 137/E5
Liberty, Ut, US 137/K11
Liberty (res.), Md, US 138/B5
Liberty Grove, Md, US 138/B4
Libertyville, Il, US 135/P15
Libin, Belg. 53/E4
Libo, China 83/J2
Libobo (cape), Indo. 81/G4
Liboc (riv.), Czh. 41/G3
Libochovice, Czh. 55/H2
Libon, Phil. 79/D5
Librazhd, Alb. 47/G2
Libres, Mex. 143/M7
Libreville (cap.), Gabon 96/G7
Libya (ctry.) 97/J2
Libyan (plat.), Libya 97/K1
Libyan (des.), Egypt,Libya 97/K2
Licantén, Chile 158/B2
Licata, It. 46/C4
Lice, Turk. 90/E2
Lich, Ger. 54/B1
Licheng, China 72/C3
Licheng, China 72/D3
Lichfield, Eng, UK 33/E1
Lichinga, Moz. 105/G3
Lichtenau, Ger. 51/F5
Lichtenau, Ger. 54/D4
Lichtenau, Ger. 54/B5
Lichtenburg, SAfr. 106/D2
Lichtenfels, Ger. 54/D2
Lichtenrade, Ger. 40/Q7
Lichtensteig, Swi. 57/F3
Lichtenvoorde, Neth. 50/D5
Lichtervelde, Belg. 52/C1
Lichuan, China 79/A1

202

Licin – Los A

Licinio de Almeida, Braz. 154/B4
Lick Observatory, Ca, US 135/L12
Licking (riv.), Ky, US 130/C4
Licosa (cape), It. 46/D2
Licques, Fr. 52/A2
Lida, Bela. 39/L5
Liddell Water (riv.), Sc, UK 35/F1
Liddes, Swi. 56/D6
Liddon (gulf), NW, Can. 123/R7
Lidhorikion, Gre. 47/H3
Lidingö, Swe. 38/H2
Lidköping, Swe. 38/E2
Lido, It. 59/F2
Lido di Iesolo, It. 59/F1
Lido di Ostia, It. 46/C2
Lidzbark, Pol. 41/K2
Lidzbark Warmiński, Pol. 39/J4
Liebenau, Aus. 55/H5
Liebenbergsvlei (riv.), SAfr. 106/E2
Liebig (mt.), Austl. 113/F2
Liechtenstein (ctry.) 57/F3
Liedekerke, Belg. 53/D2
Liège, Belg. 53/E2
Liège (prov.), Belg. 53/E3
Lieksa, Fin. 60/F3
Lienden, Neth. 50/C5
Lienen, Ger. 51/E4
Lienz, Aus. 43/K3
Liepāja, Lat. 39/J3
Lier, Belg. 53/D1
Lierneux, Belg. 53/E3
Lieser (riv.), Ger. 53/F3
Liesjärven NP, Fin. 39/K1
Liesse-Notre-Dame, Fr. 52/C4
Liestal, Swi. 56/D3
Lieto, Fin. 39/K1
Liévin, Fr. 52/B3
Lièvre (riv.), Qu, Can. 130/F2
Liez (lake), Fr. 56/B2
Liezen, Aus. 43/L3
Liffey (riv.), Ire. 34/B5
Liffol-le-Grand, Fr. 56/B1
Lifford, Ire. 31/Q9
Ligao, Phil. 81/F1
Lightning Ridge, Austl. 115/C1
Lightwater, Eng, UK 30/B3
Lignano Sabbiadoro, It. 59/G1
Ligny-en-Barrois, Fr. 53/E6
Ligoncio (peak), It. 57/F5
Ligoúrion, Gre. 47/H4
Liguori, Mo, US 137/G9
Liguria (pol. reg.), It. 58/B4
Liguria (prov), It. 43/H4
Ligurian (sea), Fr.,It. 43/H5
Lihou (reefs), Austl. 109/E2
Lihue, Hi, US 124/S10
Lijiang Naxizu Zizhixian, China 83/H2
Lijin, China 72/D3
Likasi, D.R. Congo 105/E3
Likely, BC, Can. 126/C2
Likoma (isl.), Malw. 105/F3
Likouala (riv.), Congo 96/H7
Likova (riv.), Rus. 61/W9
L'Île-Perrot, Qu, Can. 131/N7
L'île-Rousse, Fr. 46/A1
Liliāni, Pak. 86/B3
Lilienthal, Ger. 51/F2
Liling, China 83/K2
Lilla Edet, Swe. 38/E2
Lille, Belg. 50/B6
Lille, Fr. 52/C2
Lille Bælt (chan.), Ger. 38/C4
Lillehammer, Nor. 38/D1
Lillers, Fr. 52/B2
Lillesand, Nor. 38/C2
Lillestrøm, Nor. 38/D2
Lilliwaup, Wa, US 135/A3
Lillo, Sp. 44/D3
Lillooet, BC, Can. 126/C3
Lillooet (riv.), BC, Can. 126/C3
Lilongwe (cap.), Malw. 105/F3
Liloy, Phil. 79/D6
Lim (riv.), Yugo. 47/F1
Lima (dept.), Peru 156/B3
Lima (cap.), Peru 156/B4
Lima, Oh, US 130/C3
Lima (riv.), It. 59/D4
Lima (riv.), Port. 45/A2
Lima, Arg. 159/J11
Lima Duarte, Braz. 211/K6
Limache, Chile 158/N8
Limanowa, Pol. 41/L4
Limassol, Cyp. 91/C2
Limassol (dist.), Cyp. 91/C2
Limavady (dist.), NI, UK 34/A2
Limavady, NI, UK 34/B1
Limay (riv.), Arg. 147/C7
Limbach, Ger. 54/C4
Limbani, Peru 156/D4
Limbara (peak), It. 46/A2
Limbdi, India 89/K4
Limbé, Haiti 145/H2
Limbiate, It. 58/C1
Limbourg, Belg. 53/E2
Limburg (prov.), Belg. 53/E1
Limburg an der Lahn, Ger. 54/B2
Limburgerhof, Ger. 54/B4
Lime Village, Ak, US 134/G3
Limedsforsen, Swe. 38/E1
Limeira, Braz. 155/C2
Limekilns, Sc, UK 36/C4
Limena, It. 59/E2
Limenária, Gre. 47/J2
Limerick, Ire. 31/P10
Limfjorden (chan.), Den. 38/C3
Limidario (peak), It. 57/E5
Limite, It. 59/D5
Limmat (riv.), Swi. 57/E3
Limmen Bight (bay), Austl. 109/C2
Límni, Gre. 47/H3
Límnos (isl.), Gre. 62/C5
Limoeiro, Braz. 154/D2
Limoeiro do Norte, Braz. 154/C2
Limoges, Fr. 42/D4
Limogne, Causse de (plat.), Fr. 42/D4
Limón, Hon. 144/E3
Limón, CR 145/F4
Limours, Fr. 30/J6
Limousin (mts.), Fr. 42/D4
Limousin (pol. reg.), Fr. 42/D4
Limoux, Fr. 42/E5
Limpopo (riv.), Moz. 93/F7
Lin Xian, China 72/C3
Lin'an, China 79/C1
Linapacan (isl.), Phil. 79/C5
Linard (peak), Swi. 57/G4
Linares, Mex. 143/F3
Linares, Sp. 44/D3
Linares, Chile 158/C2
Linariá, Gre. 47/J3
Linate (int'l arpt.), It. 58/C2
Lincang, China 83/H3
Lincheng, China 72/C3
Linchuan, China 79/C2
Lincoln, Il, US 127/L5
Lincoln (cap.), Ne, US 127/J5
Lincoln, Me, US 131/G2
Lincoln (co.), Ok, US 137/N14
Lincoln, On, Can. 131/R9
Lincoln, Arg. 158/E2
Lincoln (sea), Can.,Grld. 119/L1
Lincoln, Pa, US 138/B3
Lincoln, De, US 138/C6
Lincoln, Eng, UK 35/H5
Lincoln Beach, Or, US 126/B4
Lincoln City, Or, US 126/B4
Lincoln Heath (woodld.), Eng, UK 35/H5
Lincoln NP, Austl. 113/G5
Lincoln Park, NJ, US 139/H8
Lincoln Park, Mi, US 135/F7
Lincolnshire (co.), Eng, UK 35/H5
Lincolnshire Wolds (grsld.), Eng, UK 35/H4
Lincroft, NJ, US 138/D3
Lind, Den. 38/C3
Lind NP, Austl. 115/D3
Lindau, Ger. 57/F2
Lindau, Swi. 57/E3
Linde (riv.), Neth. 50/D3
Lindeman (chan.), Austl. 114/C3
Linden, Al, US 133/G3
Linden, Tx, US 129/J4
Linden, Guy. 153/G3
Linden, NJ, US 139/J9
Linden, Mi, US 135/E6
Linden, Ger. 54/B1
Linden Beach, On, Can. 135/G7
Lindenberg im Allgäu, Ger. 57/F2
Lindenfels, Ger. 54/B3
Lindenhurst, NY, US 139/E2
Lindenhurst, Il, US 135/P15
Lindenwold, NJ, US 138/D4
Lindern, Ger. 51/E3
Lindesberg, Swe. 38/F2
Lindesnes (cape), Nor. 38/B3
Lindewitt, Ger. 38/C4
Lindhorst, Ger. 51/E5
Líndhos (ruin), Gre. 90/B2
Lindi (pol. reg.), Tanz. 104/C5
Lindi, Tanz. 104/C5
Lindlar, Ger. 53/G1
Lindley, SAfr. 106/D2
Lindome, Swe. 38/E3
Lindon, Ut, US 137/K13
Lindre (lake), Fr. 53/F6
Lindsay, Ca, US 128/C3
Lindsay, On, Can. 130/E2
Lindsay (mt.), Austl. 112/C5
Lindsay (mt.), Austl. 113/F3
Lindsdal, Swe. 38/G3
Line (isls.), Kiri. 117/J4
Line Mountain (mtn.), Pa, US 138/B2
Líneas de Nazca, Peru 156/C4
Lineboro, Md, US 138/B4
Linfen, China 72/B3
Ling (riv.), Sc, UK 36/A2
Ling Xian, China 83/K2
Ling Xian, China 72/D3
Lingbao, China 72/B4
Lingbi, China 72/D4
Lingchuan, China 83/K2
Lingchuan, China 72/C4
Linge (riv.), Neth. 50/C5
Lingen, Ger. 51/E3
Lingfield, Eng, UK 30/C3
Lingga (isls.), Indo. 80/B3
Linglestown, Pa, US 138/B3
Lingolsheim, Fr. 56/D1
Lingqiu, China 72/C3
Lingshan, China 83/J3
Lingshan, China 72/C3
Lingshi, China 72/B3
Lingshui, China 83/K4
Linguère, Sen. 102/B3
Lingyin Si, China 72/L9
Lingyuan, China 72/D2
Lingyun, China 83/J3
Linhai, China 79/D2
Linhares, Braz. 155/D1
Linhe, China 70/J3
Linköping, Swe. 38/F2
Linli, China 79/B2
Linlithgow, Sc, UK 36/C5
Linliu (mtn.), China 72/C3
Linney (pt.), Wal, UK 32/A3
Linnhe (lake), Sc, UK 36/A3
Linnich, Ger. 53/F2
Linntown, Pa, US 138/B2
Linosa (isl.), It. 100/N7
Linqing, China 72/C3
Linqu, China 72/D3
Linquan, China 72/C4
Linru, China 72/C4
Lins, Braz. 155/B2
Linschoten, Neth. 50/B4
Linshu, China 72/D4
Linta (riv.), Madg. 107/H9
Linth (riv.), Swi. 57/F3
Linthal, Swi. 57/F4
Linton, ND, US 127/H4
Linwood, Eng, UK 35/H5
Linwu, China 83/K2
Linxi, China 72/C3
Linyi, China 72/B4
Linyi, China 72/D3
Linyi, China 72/D4
Linying, China 72/C4
Linz (int'l arpt.), Aus. 55/H6
Linz, Aus. 55/H6
Linz am Rhein, Ger. 53/G2
Linzhang, China 72/C3
Lion (gulf), Fr.,Sp. 45/G1
Lipa, Phil. 79/D5
Lipari (isl.), It. 46/D3
Lipari (isls.), It. 46/D3
Lipari, It. 46/D3
Liperi, Fin. 60/F3
Lipetsk, Rus. 62/F1
Lipetsk (int'l arpt.), Rus. 62/F1
Lipetskaya (obl.), Rus. 62/F1
Lipez (riv.), Bol. 150/E8
Lipez, Cordillera de (mts.), Bol. 150/E8
Liping, China 83/J2
Lipljan, Yugo. 47/G1
Lipno (res.), Czh. 55/H5
Lipno, Pol. 41/K2
Lipno, Údolní nádrž (lake), Czh. 43/L2
Lipova, Rom. 48/E2
Lippe (riv.), Ger. 40/D3
Lippstadt, Ger. 51/F5
Liptovský Svätý Mikuláš, Slvk. 41/K4
Liptrap (cape), Austl. 115/C3
Lira, Ugan. 104/B2
Lircay, Peru 156/C4
Liri (riv.), It. 46/C2
Liria, Sp. 45/E3
Liro (riv.), It. 57/F5
Lisboa (dist.), Port. 44/A3
Lisboa (int'l arpt.), Port. 45/P10
Lisboa (Lisbon) (cap.), Port. 45/P10
Lisbon, ND, US 127/J4
Lisbon, Me, US 131/G2
Lisbon, Md, US 138/A5
Lisburn, NI, UK 34/B2
Lisburn (dist.), NI, UK 34/B3
Lisburne (cape), Ak, US 134/E2
Lisdoonvarna, Ire. 31/P10
Liseleje, Den. 38/D3
Lisha (riv.), China 83/H2
Lishu, China 72/F2
Lishui, China 79/C2
Lisianski (isl.), HI, US 117/H2
Lisieux, Fr. 42/D2
Liski, Rus. 62/F2
Lisle, Il, US 135/P16
L'Isle-Adam, Fr. 30/J4
L'Isle-en-Dodon, Fr. 42/D5
L'Isle-sur-la-Sorgue, Fr. 42/F5
L'Isle-sur-le-Doubs, Fr. 56/C3
Lisle-sur-Tarn, Fr. 42/D5
Lismore, Austl. 115/E1
Lisnacree, NI, UK 34/B3
Lišov, Czh. 55/H4
Lispeszentadorján, Hun. 48/C2
Lisse, Neth. 50/B4
Lisses, Fr. 30/K6
List, Ger. 38/C4
Lister (riv.), Ger. 51/E6
Listowel, On, Can. 130/D3
Listowel, Ire. 31/P10
Lit. Scarcies (riv.), SLeo. 102/B4
Litang, China 70/H6
Litang (riv.), China 83/H2
Līṭānī (riv.), Leb. 91/D3
Litavka (riv.), Czh. 55/G3
Litchfield, Mn, US 127/K4
Litchfield, Il, US 129/K3
Litchfield Park, Az, US 137/R19
Lith, Neth. 50/C5
Litherland, Eng, UK 35/F5
Lithgow, Austl. 115/D2
Lithuania (ctry.) 39/K4
Litija, Slov. 43/L3
Lititz, Pa, US 138/B3
Litókhoron, Gre. 47/H2
Litoměřice, Czh. 55/H1
Litabella NP, Austl. 114/D4
Littau, Swi. 57/E3
Little (riv.), Ar, US 129/J4
Little (riv.), Ga, US 133/H4
Little (riv.), Tx, US 132/D4
Little (riv.), NC, US 133/J3
Little (riv.), Ok, US 137/N15
Little Abitibi (riv.), On, Can. 130/D1
Little Andaman (isl.), India 83/F5
Little Belt (mts.), Mt, US 126/F4
Little Bighorn Battlefield Nat'l Mon., Mt, US 126/G4
Little Bitter (lake), Egypt 91/C4
Little Blue (riv.), Ks,Ne, US 129/H2
Little Calumet (riv.), Il, US 135/Q16
Little Cayman (isl.), Cay. 141/E4
Little Colorado (riv.), Az, US 128/E4
Little Creek, De, US 138/C5
Little Cumbrae (isl.), Sc, UK 36/A5
Little Current (riv.), On, Can. 127/M3
Little Current, On, Can. 130/D2
Little Desert NP, Austl. 115/B3
Little Diomede (isl.), Ak, US 134/E2
Little Egg (har.), NJ, US 138/D4
Little Falls, Mn, US 127/K4
Little Falls, NJ, US 139/J8
Little Ferry, NJ, US 139/J8
Little Fork (riv.), Mn, US 127/K3
Little Inagua (isl.), Bahm. 141/G3
Little Karoo (valley), SAfr. 106/C4
Little Lehigh (riv.), Pa, US 138/C3
Little Minch (str.), Sc, UK 31/Q8
Little Missouri (riv.), Ar, US 129/J4
Little Neck (bay), NY, US 139/K8
Little Nicobar (isl.), India 83/F6
Little Para (res.), Austl. 113/M8
Little Para (riv.), Austl. 113/M8
Little Patuxent (riv.), Md, US 138/B5
Little Peconic (bay), NY, US 139/F2
Little Platte (riv.), Mo, US 137/D5
Little Prairie, Wi, US 135/N14
Little Red (riv.), Ar, US 129/J4
Little Rock (cap.), Ar, US 129/J4
Little Schuylkill (riv.), Pa, US 138/B2
Little Sioux (riv.), Ia, US 125/G3
Little Smoky (riv.), Ab, Can. 126/D2
Little Snake (riv.), Co, US 128/E2
Little Stour (riv.), Eng, UK 33/H4
Little Wabash (riv.), Il, US 129/K3
Little White (riv.), SD, US 129/G2
Little Wood (riv.), Id, US 126/E5
Little Zab (riv.), Iraq 90/E3
Littleborough, Eng, UK 35/F4
Littlefield, Tx, US 129/G4
Littlehampton, Eng, UK 33/F5
Littlerock, Ca, US 136/C1
Littlestown, Pa, US 138/A4
Littleton, NH, US 131/G2
Littleton, Co, US 137/B3
Litvínov, Czh. 55/G1
Liu (riv.), China 79/A3
Liu (riv.), China 65/N6
Liuba, China 70/J5
Liucheng, China 83/J3
Liulin, China 72/B3
Liuwa Plain NP, Zam. 105/D3
Liuyang, China 83/K2
Liuzhou, China 83/J3
Livádhion, Gre. 47/H2
Livanátai, Gre. 47/H3
Live Oak, Fl, US 133/H4
Live Oak, Tx, US 137/U20
Livengood, Ak, US 134/J2
Livenza (riv.), It. 59/F2
Liverdun, Fr. 53/F6
Liverdy-en-Brie, Fr. 30/L5
Livermore (mt.), Tx, US 129/F5
Liverpool, NS, Can. 131/H2
Liverpool (cape), Nun., Can. 123/J1
Liverpool (bay), NW, Can. 122/C1
Liverpool, Pa, US 138/B2
Liverpool, Eng, UK 35/F5
Liverpool (bay), Wal, UK 35/E5
Livigno, It. 57/G4
Livilliers, Fr. 30/J4
Livingston, Mt, US 126/F4
Livingston (lake), Tx, US 129/J5
Livingston, Tx, US 129/J5
Livingston, Guat. 144/D3
Livingston, NJ, US 139/H8
Livingston (co.), Mi, US 135/E6
Livingston, Sc, UK 36/C5
Livingstone, Zam. 105/E4
Livingstone (falls), Congo 105/B2
Livingstone (range), Ab, Can. 126/E3
Livno, Bosn. 48/C4
Livny, Rus. 62/F1
Livojoki (riv.), Fin. 37/H2
Livonia, Mi, US 130/D3
Livorno (prov.), It. 58/D6
Livorno, It. 58/D5
Livorno Ferraris, It. 58/B2
Livramento do Brumado, Braz. 154/B4
Livron-sur-Drôme, Fr. 42/F4
Livry-Gargan, Fr. 30/K5
Lixin, China 72/D4
Lixnaw, Ire. 31/P10
Lixoúrion, Gre. 47/G3
Lixus (ruin), Mor. 100/A2
Liyang, China 72/D5
Lizard (pt.), Eng, UK 32/A7
Lizard, The (pen.), Eng, UK 32/A6
Lizy-sur-Ourcq, Fr. 52/C5
Ljubic, Yugo. 48/E4
Ljubija, Bosn. 48/C3
Ljubinje, Bosn. 47/F1
Ljubljana (cap.), Slov. 43/L3
Ljubuški, Bosn. 47/E1
Ljungan (riv.), Swe. 37/F3
Ljungby, Swe. 38/E3
Ljungsbro, Swe. 38/F2
Ljungskile, Swe. 38/D2
Ljusnan (riv.), Swe. 37/E3
Ljusne, Swe. 38/G1
Ljusterø (isl.), Swe. 39/H2
Lkst (peak), Mor. 98/C3
Llabanere (int'l arpt.), Fr. 42/E5
Llaillay, Chile 158/N8
Llaima (vol.), Chile 158/C3
Llallagua, Bol. 150/E7
Llalli, Peru 156/D4
Llanberis, Pass of (pass), Wal, UK 34/D5
Llancañelo (lake), Arg. 158/C2
Llandovery, Wal, UK 32/C3
Llandrindod Wells, Wal, UK 32/C2
Llandudno, Wal, UK 34/E5
Llanes, Sp. 44/C1
Llanfairfechan, Wal, UK 34/E5
Llangollen, Wal, UK 35/E6
Llanidloes, Wal, UK 32/C2
Llano (riv.), Tx, US 129/H5
Llano, Tx, US 129/H5
Llano Estacado (plain), US 129/G4
Llanos (plain), Col.,Ven. 147/B2
Llanquihue (lake), Chile 158/B4
Llata, Peru 156/B3
Lleida, Sp. 45/F2
Llera de Canales, Mex. 143/F4
Llerena, Sp. 44/B3
Lleyn (pen.), Wal, UK 34/D6
Llivia, Sp. 45/F1
Llobregat (riv.), Sp. 45/F1
Llodio, Sp. 44/D1
Lloret de Mar, Sp. 45/G2
Llorona (pt.), CR 140/E6
Lloyd (pt.), NY, US 139/M8
Lloyd Harbor, NY, US 139/M8
Lloydminster, Sk, Can. 126/F2
Lloyds (riv.), Nf, Can. 131/K1
Lluchmayor, Sp. 45/G3
Llullaillaco (vol.), Arg.,Chil 157/C1
Llwchwr (riv.), Wal, UK 32/B3
Llynfi (riv.), Wal, UK 32/C3
Loa, Ut, US 128/E3
Loa (riv.), Chile 147/C5
Loanhead, Sc, UK 36/C5
Loano, It. 58/B4
Loaoya (canal), Sp. 45/N8
Lobbes, Belg. 53/D3
Lobería, Arg. 158/F3
Lobethal, Austl. 113/M8
Lobez, Pol. 41/H2
Lobito, Ang. 105/B3
Lobitos, Peru 156/A2
Lobo (riv.), C.d'Iv. 102/D5
Lobos, Arg. 159/J11
Lobos de Tierra, Isla (isl.), Peru 150/B5
Lobos, Punta de (pt.), Chile 158/M9
Locarno, Swi. 57/E5
Loch na Sealga (lake), Sc, UK 36/A1
Loch Raven (res.), Md, US 138/B5
Lochaber (reg.), Sc, UK 36/A3
Locharbriggs, Sc, UK 34/E1
Lochau, Aus. 57/F2
Lochboisdale, Sc, UK 31/Q8
Lochbuie, Co, US 137/C2
Lochem, Neth. 50/D4
Loches, Fr. 42/D3
Lochgelly, Sc, UK 36/C4
Lochgilphead, Sc, UK 36/A4
Lochindorb (lake), Sc, UK 36/C2
Lochmaben, Sc, UK 34/E1
Lochmaddy, Sc, UK 31/Q8
Lochów, Pol. 41/L2
Lochristi, Belg. 52/C1
Lochwinnoch, Sc, UK 36/B5
Lochy (lake), Sc, UK 36/B3
Lochy (riv.), Sc, UK 36/B3
Lock, Austl. 113/G5
Lock Haven, Pa, US 130/E3
Locke, Ca, US 135/L10
Lockerbie, Sc, UK 35/E1
Lockhart, Austl. 115/C2
Lockington, Austl. 115/C3
Locknitz (riv.), Ger. 40/F2
Lockport, NY, US 131/S9
Lockport, Il, US 135/P16
Lockwood (res.), Eng, UK 30/C2
Locon, Fr. 52/B2
Locri, It. 46/E3
Locumba, Peru 156/D5
Locust Fork (riv.), Al, US 133/G3
Lod, Isr. 91/F8
Loddon (riv.), Austl. 115/A1
Loddon (riv.), Eng, UK 33/E4
Lodenice (riv.), Czh. 55/H2
Lodève, Fr. 42/E5
Lodeynoye Pole, Rus. 60/G3
Lodhrān, Pak. 86/A5
Lodi, Ca, US 128/B3
Lodi, It. 58/C2
Lodi, NJ, US 139/J8
Lodi Vecchio, It. 58/C2
Lodja, D.R. Congo 105/D1
Lodosa, Sp. 44/D1
Lodrino, Swi. 57/E5
Łódź, Pol. 41/K3
Lodz (prov.), Pol. 41/K3
Loei, Thai. 78/C2
Loenen, Neth. 50/C4
Loeriesfontein, SAfr. 106/B3
Lofa (co.), Libr. 102/C5
Lofa (riv.), Libr. 102/C5
Löffingen, Ger. 57/E2
Lofoten (isle.), Nor. 37/D2
Lofty (range), Austl. 112/C3
Lofty (mt.), Austl. 113/M8
Logan (mt.), Yk, Can. 134/K3
Logan, Ut, US 126/F5
Logan, WV, US 130/D4
Logan, NM, US 132/C3
Logan, Oh, US 130/C4
Logan (co.), Ok, US 137/N14
Logansport, In, US 130/C3
Loganton, Pa, US 138/A1
Loganville, Pa, US 138/B4
Logatec, Slov. 43/L4
Logone (riv.), Chad 93/D3
Lograto, It. 58/D2
Logroño, Sp. 44/D1
Logrosán, Sp. 44/C3
Løgstør, Den. 38/C3
Løgten, Den. 38/D3
Lohals, Den. 38/D4
Lohārdaga, India 85/E4
Lohfelden, Ger. 51/G6
Lohja, Fin. 39/L1
Lohjanjärvi (lake), Fin. 39/K1
Lohmar, Ger. 53/G2
Löhnberg, Ger. 54/B1
Lohne, Ger. 51/F3
Löhne, Ger. 51/F4
Lohr, Ger. 54/C3
Loi-kaw, Myan. 83/G4
Loi Lun (range), China,Mya 70/G7
Loing (riv.), Fr. 40/B5
Loir (riv.), Fr. 42/D3
Loire (riv.), Fr. 27/E4
Loisin (riv.), Fr. 53/E5
Loita (hills), Kenya 97/N8
Loja (prov.), Ecu. 156/B2
Loja, Ecu. 156/B2
Loja, Sp. 44/C4
Løjt Kirkeby, Den. 38/C4
Lokeren, Belg. 52/D1
Lokitaung, Kenya 104/B1
Løkken, Den. 38/C3
Lokoja, Nga. 103/G5
Lokolo (riv.), D.R. Congo 97/K8
Lokomby, Madg. 107/H8
Lokoro (riv.), D.R. Congo 97/J8
Lökösháza, Hun. 48/E2
Lokossa, Ben. 103/F5
Loks (isl.), Nun., Can. 123/K2
Lol (riv.), Sudan 97/L6
Lolland (isl.), Den. 37/D5
Lollar, Ger. 54/B3
Lolo (peak), Mt, US 126/E4
Lolui (isl.), Ugan. 104/B3
Lom, Nor. 37/D3
Lom Sak, Thai. 78/C2
Loma (mts.), SLeo. 96/C6
Loma (pt.), Ca, US 136/C5
Loma Bonita, Mex. 144/C2
Loma Linda, Ca, US 136/C2
Loma Mansa (peak), SLeo. 102/C4
Loma Negra, Arg. 158/E3
Lomami (riv.), D.R. Congo 93/E5
Lomas de Zamora, Arg. 159/J11
Lomazzo, It. 58/C1
Lombard, Il, US 135/P16
Lombarda, Serra (mts.), Braz. 151/H3
Lombardia, Mex. 142/E5
Lombardia (pol. reg.), It. 43/H4
Lomblen (isl.), Indo. 81/F5
Lombok (isl.), Indo. 67/L10
Lomé (int'l arpt.), Togo 103/F5
Lomé (cap.), Togo 103/F5
Lomello, It. 58/B2
Lomita, Ca, US 136/F8
Lomma, Swe. 38/E4
Lomme, Fr. 52/B2
Lommel, Belg. 50/C6
Lomnice (riv.), Czh. 55/G4
Lomnice nad Lužnicí, Czh. 55/H4
Lomond (lake), Sc, UK 36/B4
Lomond (hills), Sc, UK 36/C4
Lomone (riv.), It. 59/E4
Lomonosov, Rus. 61/S7
Lompobatang (peak), Indo. 81/E5
Lompoc, Ca, US 128/B4
Łomża, Pol. 41/M2
Lonato, It. 58/D2
Lonāvale, India 89/K5
Loncoche, Chile 158/B3
Loncopué, Arg. 158/C3
Londerzeel, Belg. 53/D2
London, On, Can. 130/D3
London, Ky, US 130/C4
London (reef), Nic. 145/F3
London (cap.), UK 30/C2
London, City of (bor.), Eng, UK 30/A1
Londonderry (cape), Austl. 109/B2
Londonderry (isl.), Chile 159/C7
Londonderry (dist.), NI, UK 34/A2
Londonderry, NI, UK 34/A2
Londrina, Braz. 155/B2
Lone (riv.), Ger. 54/C5
Lone Grove, Ok, US 129/H4
Lone Jack, Mo, US 137/E6
Lone Pine Sanctuary, Austl. 114/E7
Lonesome NP, Austl. 114/C4
Long, Ak, US 134/G3
Long (lake), On, Can. 127/M3
Long (lake), Sc, UK 36/A2
Long (riv.), China 79/A3
Long (isl.), Bahm. 141/F3
Long (isl.), NY, US 131/F3
Long (mtn.), Wal, UK 32/C1
Long (str.), Rus. 65/T2
Long Beach, Wa, US 126/B4
Long Beach, On, Can. 131/R10
Long Beach (isl.), NJ, US 138/D4
Long Beach, Ca, US 136/F8
Long Beach, NY, US 139/L9
Long Branch, NJ, US 138/E3
Long Cay (isl.), India 145/H1
Long Crag (hill), Eng, UK 36/E6
Long Eaton, Eng, UK 35/G6
Long Grove, Il, US 135/P15
Long Hill, Ct, US 139/E1
Long, Loch (inlet), Sc, UK 36/B4
Long Mynd, The (hill), Eng, UK 32/D1
Long Neck (pt.), Ct, US 139/M7
Long Range (mts.), Nf, Can. 131/K2
Long Valley, NJ, US 138/D2
Long Xuyen, Viet. 78/D4
Longá (riv.), Braz. 154/B1
Longare, It. 59/E2
Longaví, Chile 158/C2
Longboat Key, Fl, US 133/H5
Longbranch, Wa, US 135/B3
Longchang, China 83/J2
Longchuan, China 79/C3
Longchuan, China 83/G3
Longde, China 70/J4
Longeau (riv.), Fr. 53/E5
Longeville-en-Barrois, Fr. 53/E6
Longeville-lès-Metz, Fr. 53/F5
Longeville-lès-Saint-Avold, Fr. 53/F5
Longfellow (mts.), Me, US 131/G2
Longfield, Eng, UK 30/D2
Longford, Austl. 115/C4
Longford, Ire. 31/Q10
Longhua, China 72/D2
Longhui, China 83/K2
Longjumeau, Fr. 30/J5
Longkou, China 72/E3
Longlac, On, Can. 127/M3
Longli, China 83/J2
Longmen, China 79/B3
Longmen Shiyao, China 72/C4
Longmont, Co, US 137/B2
Longnan, China 79/B3
Longniddry, Sc, UK 36/D5
Longonot (peak), Kenya 104/C3
Longperrier, Fr. 30/K4
Longpont-sur-Orge, Fr. 30/J6
Longport, NJ, US 138/D5
Longpré-les-Corps-Saints, Fr. 52/A3
Longquan, China 79/C2
Longreach, Austl. 114/B3
Longshan, China 79/A2
Longshou (mts.), China 70/H4
Longueau, Fr. 52/B4
Longueil-Annel, Fr. 52/B5
Longuenesse, Fr. 52/B2
Longuesse, Fr. 30/H4
Longueuil, Qu, Can. 131/P6
Longuyon, Fr. 53/E5
Longvic, Fr. 56/B3
Longview, Wa, US 126/C4
Longview, Tx, US 129/J4
Longwood Gardens, Pa, US 138/C4
Longwy, Fr. 53/E4
Longyan, China 79/C2
Longyearbyen, Nor. 64/B2
Longyou, China 79/C2
Longzhou, China 78/D1
Loni, India 86/D5
Lonigo, It. 59/E2
Löningen, Ger. 51/E3
Lonquimay, Arg. 158/E3
Lons, Fr. 42/C5
Lons-le-Saunier, Fr. 56/B4
Lönsboda, Swe. 38/F3
Lontzen, Belg. 53/F2
Lonza (riv.), Swi. 56/D5
Looe (isl.), Eng, UK 32/B6
Lookout (cape), NC, US 133/J3
Lookout (pt.), Austl. 114/B1
Loolmalasin (peak), Tanz. 104/B3
Loon Lake, Sk, Can. 126/F2
Loon op Zand, Neth. 50/C5
Loop Head (pt.), Ire. 30/P10
Loos, Fr. 52/C2
Lop Buri, Thai. 78/C3
Lopary, Madg. 107/H8
Lopez (cape), Gabon 96/G8
López Mateos, Mex. 143/Q9
Lopik, Neth. 50/B5
Lopori (riv.), D.R. Congo 97/K7
Lopphavet (bay), Nor. 37/G1
Loppi, Fin. 39/L1
Lora del Río, Sp. 44/C4
Lorain, Oh, US 130/D3
Loralai, Pak. 89/J2
Lorca, Sp. 44/E4
Lord Howe (isl.), Austl. 116/E8
Lordsburg, NM, US 128/E4
Lorelei, Ger. 53/G3
Lorena, Braz. 211/H7
Lorengau, PNG 116/D5
Lørenskog, Nor. 38/D2
Lorentz (riv.), Indo. 81/J5
Lorentzsluizen (dam), Neth. 50/C2
Loreo, It. 59/F2
Loreto, Braz. 154/A2
Loreto, It. 59/G6
Loreto, Mex. 142/C3
Loreto (int'l arpt.), Mex. 142/C3
Loreto, Mex. 142/E4
Loreto, Ecu. 152/B5
Loreto (state), Peru 152/C5
Lorette, Mb, Can. 127/J3
Lorgues, Fr. 43/G5
Lorian (swamp), Kenya 97/N7
Lorica, Col. 152/C2
Lorient, Fr. 42/B3
L'Oriental (pol. reg.), Mor. 99/E2
Lorillard (riv.), Nun., Can. 122/G2
Lorinci, Hun. 41/K5
Loring, Ks, US 137/D5
Loriol-sur-Drôme, Fr. 42/F4
Lorn, Firth of (inlet), Sc, UK 31/Q8
Lorne, Austl. 115/B3
Lorosuk (peak), Kenya 104/B2
Lorquin, Fr. 53/G6
Lörrach, Ger. 56/D2
Lorrain (plat.), Fr. 40/D4
Lorraine (pol. reg.), Fr. 42/G2
Lorraine (pol. reg.), Fr. 56/C1
Lorraine, Qu, Can. 131/N6
Lorraine (reg.), Fr. 53/E5
Lorsch, Ger. 54/B3
Lorup, Ger. 51/E3
Los Alamitos, Ca, US 136/F8
Los Alamos, NM, US 129/F4
Los Alerces, PN, Arg. 157/B5
Los Altos, Ca, US 135/K12
Los Amates, Guat. 144/D3
Los Andes, Col. 152/B4

203
Los A – Maghn

Los Andes, Chile 158/N8
Los Angeles (riv.), Ca, US 136/B2
Los Angeles (co.), Ca, US 136/B2
Los Ángeles, Chile 158/B3
Los Angeles, Ca, US 136/F7
Los Angeles (int'l arpt.), Ca, US 136/F8
Los Angeles Outer (har.), Ca, US 136/F8
Los Aquijes, Peru 156/C4
Los Aztecas, Mex. 143/F4
Los Banos, Ca, US 128/B3
Los Barrios, Sp. 44/C4
Los Canarreos (arch.), Cuba 145/F1
Los Cardales, Arg. 159/J11
Los Cerrillos, Uru. 159/K11
Los Chonos (arch.), Chile 147/B7
Los Corrales de Buelna, Sp. 44/C1
Los Glaciares, PN, Arg. 157/B6
Los Katios, PN, Col. 152/B3
Los Lagos, Chile 158/B3
Los Lagos (pol. reg.), Chile 158/B4
Los Llanos de Aridane, Sp. 98/A3
Los Lunas, NM, US 128/F4
Los Mármoles, PN, Mex. 144/B1
Los Menucos, Arg. 158/C4
Los Mochis, Mex. 142/C3
Los Mosquitos (gulf), Pan. 145/F4
Los Muermos, Chile 158/B4
Los Navalmorales, Sp. 44/C3
Los Navalucillos, Sp. 44/C3
Los Órganos, Peru 156/A2
Los Padres National Forest, Ca, US 136/A1
Los Palacios y Villafranca, Sp. 44/C4
Los Pingüinos, PN, Chile 159/C7
Los Planes, Mex. 142/C3
Los Reyes, Mex. 143/R10
Los Reyes de Salgado, Mex. 142/E5
Los Ríos (prov.), Ecu. 156/B1
Los Roques, Islas (isls.), Ven. 150/E1
Los Santos, Pan. 152/A3
Los Santos de Maimona, Sp. 44/B3
Los Sauces, Chile 158/B3
Los Taques, Ven. 152/D2
Los Teques, Ven. 150/E1
Los Testigos (isls.), Ven. 153/F2
Los Vilos, Chile 158/C1
Los Yébenes, Sp. 44/D3
Losai Nat'l Rsv., Kenya 104/C2
Losheim, Ger. 53/F4
Łosice, Pol. 41/M2
Lošinj (isl.), Cro. 48/B3
Losne, Fr. 56/B3
Losone, Swi. 57/E5
Losoya, Tx, US 137/U21
Lossburg, Ger. 57/E1
Losser, Neth. 50/E4
Lossie (riv.), Sc, UK 36/C1
Lössnitz, Ger. 55/F1
Lossoganeu (hill), Tanz. 104/C4
Lost River (range), Id, US 128/D1
Lost River Caverns, Pa, US 138/C2
Lostallo, Swi. 57/F5
Lot (riv.), Fr. 42/D4
Lota, Chile 158/B3
Lotawana (lake), Mo, US 137/E6
Løten, Nor. 38/D1
Lotte, Ger. 51/E4
Lotuke (peak), Sudan 104/B1
Lotung, Tai. 79/D3
Lou (riv.), China 72/B5
Louang Namtha, Laos 83/H3
Louangphrabang, Laos 83/H4
Loubomo, Congo 105/B1
Loudéac, Fr. 42/B2
Loudi, China 83/K2
Loudun, Fr. 42/D3
Loue (riv.), Fr. 42/F3
Loufan, China 72/B3
Louga (pol. reg.), Sen. 102/B3
Louga, Sen. 102/A3
Lough Foyle (lake), UK 34/A1
Loughborough, Eng, UK 33/E1
Loughbrickland, NI, UK 34/B3
Lougheed (isl.), Nun., Can. 123/R7
Loughgall, NI, UK 34/B3
Loughrea, Ire. 31/P10
Loughton, Eng, UK 30/D2
Louhans, Fr. 56/B4
Louis Botha (Durban) (int'l arpt.), SAfr. 107/E3
Louisiade (arch.), PNG 116/E6
Louisiana (state), US 132/E4
Louisville, Ms, US 133/F3
Louisville, Ky, US 130/C4
Louisville, Co, US 137/B3
Loukkos (riv.), Mor. 100/A2
Loulé, Port. 44/A4
Louny, Czh. 55/G2
Loup (riv.), Ne, US 127/J5
Loup, Middle (riv.), Ne, US 127/H5
Loup, North (riv.), Ne, US 127/H5
Loup, South (riv.), Ne, US 127/J5
Lourches, Fr. 52/C3
Lourdes, Fr. 42/C5
Lourdes/Tarbes (int'l arpt.), Fr. 42/D5
Loures, Port. 45/P10
Louriçal, Port. 44/A2
Lourinhã, Port. 44/A3
Lousã, Port. 44/A2
Lousa, Port. 45/Q10
Louth, Eng, UK 35/H5
Louth (co.), Ire. 34/B4
Louth, Ire. 34/B4
Loutrá Aidhipsoú, Gre. 47/H3
Loutrákion, Gre. 47/H4
Loútsa, Gre. 47/P9
Louvain (Leuven), Belg. 53/D2
Louveira, Braz. 211/G8
Louviers, Fr. 42/D2
Louviers, Co, US 137/B4
Louvigné-du-Désert, Fr. 42/C2
Louvres, Fr. 30/K4
Louvroil, Fr. 52/C3
Lovaart (riv.), Belg. 52/B1
Lovat' (riv.), Rus. 60/F4
Lovat' (riv.), Bela.,Rus. 39/P3
Lovćen NP, Yugo. 47/F1
Lovćenac, Yugo. 48/D3
Love Point, Md, US 138/B5
Lovech (prov.), Bul. 47/J1
Loveland, Co, US 137/B2
Loveland (lake), Co, US 137/B2
Lovell, Wy, US 126/F4
Lovelock, Nv, US 128/C2
Lovere, It. 58/D1
Loving, NM, US 129/F4
Lovington, NM, US 129/G4
Lovios, Sp. 44/A2
Lövő, Hun. 43/M3
Lovosice, Czh. 55/H1
Lovozero (lake), Rus. 60/G2
Low (cape), Nun., Can. 123/H2
Lowa (riv.), D.R. Congo 93/E5
Lowell, Ma, US 131/G3
Löwen (riv.), Namb. 106/B2
Löwenstein, Ger. 54/C4
Lower (bay), NJ, US 138/D2
Lower (dam), Wa, US 135/D3
Lower Arrow (lake), BC, Can. 126/D3
Lower Engadine (valley), Swi. 57/G4
Lower Ganges (canal), India 84/B2
Lower Glenelg NP, Austl. 115/B3
Lower Hutt, NZ 117/S11
Lower Kalskag, Ak, US 134/F3
Lower Latham (res.), Co, US 137/C2
Lower Otay (lake), Ca, US 136/D5
Lower Red (lake), Mn, US 127/K4
Lower Rhine (riv.), Neth. 50/C5
Lower Rouge (riv.), Mi, US 135/E7
Lower Trajan's Wall, Mol.,Ukr. 62/D3
Lower Tunguska (riv.), Rus. 67/J3
Lower Zambezi NP, Zam. 105/E4
Lowestoft, Eng, UK 33/H2
Lowi (riv.), D.R. Congo 105/E1
Łowicz, Pol. 41/K2
Lowther (hills), Sc, UK 36/C6
Loxstedt, Ger. 51/F1
Loxton, SAfr. 106/C3
Loxton, Austl. 113/J5
Loyalton, Pa, US 138/B2
Loyalty (isls.), NCal. 116/F7
Loyettes, Fr. 56/B6
Loyne (lake), Sc, UK 36/A2
Loysville, Pa, US 138/A3
Loznica, Yugo. 48/D3
Loznitsa, Bul. 49/H4
Lozova, Ukr. 62/F2
Lozovik, Yugo. 48/E3
Lu (mtn.), China 72/D3
Lu (riv.), China 72/C5
Lu Xian, China 83/J2
Lualaba (riv.), D.R. Congo 93/E5
Luan (riv.), China 65/M5
Lu'an, China 72/D5
Luan Xian, China 72/D3
Luanchuan, China 72/B4
Luanco, Sp. 44/C1
Luanda (cap.), Ang. 105/B2
Luang (peak), Thai. 78/B4
Luang Lagoon (lag.), Thai. 83/H6
Luangwa (riv.), Zam. 105/F2
Luangwe, Zam. 104/A5
Luanping, China 72/D2
Luanshya, Zam. 105/E3
Luapula (prov.), Zam. 104/A5
Luarca, Sp. 44/B1
Luba, EqG. 96/G7
Lubaantun (ruin), Belz. 144/D2
Lubaczów, Pol. 41/M3
Lubań, Pol. 41/H3
Lubango, Ang. 105/B3
Lubansenshi (riv.), Zam. 104/A5
Lubartów, Pol. 41/M3
Lubawa, Pol. 41/K2
Lübbecke, Ger. 51/F4
Lubbeek, Belg. 53/D2
Lubbock, Tx, US 129/G4
Lubelska (uplands), Pol. 41/M3
Lubero (riv.), D.R. Congo 104/A3
Lubień Kujawski, Pol. 41/K2
Lubin, Pol. 41/J3
Lublin (prov.), Pol. 41/M3
Lublin, Pol. 41/M3
Lubliniec, Pol. 41/K3
Lubmin, Ger. 38/E4
Lubnaig (lake), Sc, UK 36/B4
Lubny, Ukr. 62/E2
Luboń, Pol. 41/J2
Lubrín, Sp. 44/D4
Lubsko, Pol. 41/H3
Lubudi, D.R. Congo 105/E2
Lubukklinggau, Indo. 80/B4
Lubuksikaping, Indo. 80/B3
Lubumbashi, D.R. Congo 105/E3
Lucan, Ire. 34/B5
Lucania (mt.), Yk, Can. 134/K3
Lucas González, Arg. 159/J10
Lucca (prov.), It. 58/D5
Lucca, It. 58/D5
Lucciana, Fr. 46/A1
Luce (bay), Sc, UK 34/D2
Lucedale, Ms, US 133/F4
Lucélia, Braz. 155/B2
Lucena, Phil. 79/D5
Lucena, Sp. 44/C4
Lucena del Cid, Sp. 45/E2
Lučenec, Slvk. 41/K4
Lucens, Swi. 56/C4
Lucerne, Co, US 137/C2
Lucerne (lake), Swi. 43/H3
Lucerne (Vierwaldstättersee) (lake), Swi. 57/E3
Lucheng, China 72/C3
Lüchow, Ger. 40/F2
Lucindale, Austl. 115/B3
Luckeesarai, India 85/F3
Luckenwalde, Ger. 41/G2
Lucknow, India 84/C2
Lucky Lake, Sk, Can. 126/G3
Luco dei Marsi, It. 46/C2
Lucomagno, Passo del (pass), Swi. 57/E4
Lucrecia (cape), Cuba 145/H1
Lucrezia, It. 59/F5
Luda Kamchiya (riv.), Bul. 47/K1
Lüdenscheid, Ger. 51/E6
Lüderitz, Namb. 106/A2
Ludesch, Aus. 57/F3
Ludhiāna, India 86/C4
Ludian, China 83/H2
Ludinghausen, Ger. 51/E5
Ludington, Mi, US 130/C3
Ludogorie (reg.), Bul. 49/H4
Ludvika, Swe. 38/F1
Ludwigs (canal), Ger. 55/E4
Ludwigsburg, Ger. 54/C5
Ludwigsfelde, Ger. 40/Q7
Ludwigshafen, Ger. 57/F2
Ludwigshafen, Ger. 54/B4
Ludwigslust, Ger. 40/F2
Ludwigsstadt, Ger. 55/E2
Luebo, D.R. Congo 105/D2
Luena, Ang. 105/C3
Lufeng, China 79/C3
Lufkin, Tx, US 129/J5
Luga (bay), Rus. 39/N2
Luga, Rus. 39/N2
Luga (riv.), Rus. 39/N2
Lugagnano, It. 59/D2
Lugagnano Val d'Arda, It. 58/C3
Lugano, Swi. 57/E6
Lugano (lake), It. 57/E6
Luganville, Van. 116/F6
Lugards (falls), Kenya 104/C3
Lugavčina, Yugo. 48/E3
Lügde, Ger. 51/G5
Lugenda (riv.), Moz. 105/G3
Lugg (riv.), Eng, UK 32/D2
Lugg (riv.), Wal, UK 32/C2
Lugnaquillia (peak), Ire. 34/B6
Lugo, It. 59/E4
Lugo, Sp. 44/B1
Lugogo (riv.), Ugan. 104/B2
Lugoj, Rom. 48/E3
Lugrin, Fr. 56/C5
Lugunga (peak), Tanz. 104/C4
Luhan (int'l arpt.), Ukr. 62/F2
Luhans'k, Ukr. 62/F2
Luhans'ka (obl.), Ukr. 62/F2
Lühe (riv.), Ger. 51/H2
Luhe, China 72/D4
Luhe (riv.), Ger. 55/F3
Luhe-Wildenau, Ger. 55/F3
Luhombero (peak), Tanz. 104/C4
Luichart (lake), Sc, UK 36/B1
Luino, It. 57/E6
Luis B. Sánchez, Mex. 142/B1
Luís Correia, Braz. 154/B1
Luján, Arg. 159/J11
Lujiang, China 72/D5
Lukácsháza, Hun. 43/M3
Lukang, Tai. 79/D3
Lukavac, Bosn. 48/D3
Luke (mt.), Austl. 112/C3
Lukenie (riv.), D.R. Congo 105/C1
Lukovit, Bul. 47/J1
Łuków, Pol. 41/M3
Lukuga (riv.), D.R. Congo 104/A4
Lukulu, Zam. 105/D3
Lukulu (riv.), Zam. 104/A5
Lukunor (isl.), Micr. 116/E4
Luleå, Swe. 60/D2
Luleälven (riv.), Swe. 37/G2
Luliang, China 83/H2
Luling, La, US 137/P17
Luling (pass), China 72/B4
Lulong, China 72/D3
Lulonga (riv.), D.R. Congo 93/E4
Lulsgate (int'l arpt.), Eng, UK 32/D4
Lulua (riv.), D.R. Congo 93/E5
Lumangwe (falls), Zam. 104/A5
Lumberton, Tx, US 129/J5
Lumberton, NC, US 133/J3
Lumberton, NJ, US 138/D4
Lumbini (zone), Nepal 84/D2
Lumbo, Moz. 105/H4
Lumbrales, Sp. 44/B2
Lumbrein, Swi. 57/F4
Lumbres, Fr. 52/B2
Lumby, BC, Can. 126/D3
Lumding, India 83/F2
Lumigny-Nesles-Ormeaux, Fr. 30/L5
Luminárias, Braz. 211/J6
Lummen, Belg. 53/E2
Lumparland, Fin. 39/J1
Lumsden, Sk, Can. 127/G3
Lumsden, NZ 117/R12
Lumut, Malay. 80/B3
Luna (mtn.), Ca, US 136/C2
Lunahuaná, Peru 156/B4
Lund, Swe. 38/E4
Lundazi, Zam. 105/F3
Lundby, Den. 38/D4
Lundi (riv.), Zim. 105/F5
Lundy (isl.), Eng, UK 32/B4
Lune (riv.), Eng, UK 35/E3
Lüneburg, Ger. 51/H2
Lüneburger Heide (reg.), Ger. 40/F2
Lunel, Fr. 42/F5
Lünen, Ger. 51/E5
Lunenburg, NS, Can. 131/H2
Lunestedt, Ger. 51/F1
Lunéville, Fr. 43/G2
Lung Kwu Chau (isl.), China 71/T10
Lunga (riv.), Zam. 105/E3
Lungern, Swi. 56/E4
Lungi, SLeo. 102/B4
Lungi (Freetown) (int'l arpt.), SLeo. 102/B4
Lunglei, India 83/F3
Lungue-Bungo (riv.), Ang. 105/C3
Luni (riv.), India 89/K3
Lünne, Ger. 51/E4
Luocheng, China 83/J3
Luodian, China 83/J2
Luoding, China 83/K3
Luohe, China 72/C4
Luoma (lake), China 72/D4
Luongo (riv.), Zam. 104/A5
Luoning, China 72/B4
Luoshan, China 72/C4
Luoshuikan, China 79/A1
Luoyang, China 72/C4
Luoyuan, China 79/C2
Luozi, D.R. Congo 105/B1
Lupanshui, China 83/H2
Luqa (int'l arpt.), Malta 46/L7
Luqu, China 70/H5
Luquan, China 83/H3
Lūrah (riv.), Afg. 89/J2
Lure, Fr. 56/C2
Lurgan, NI, UK 34/B3
Luri, Fr. 43/H5
Lurín, Peru 156/B4
Lúrio, Moz. 105/H3
Lúrio (riv.), Moz. 93/F6
Lurnfeld, Aus. 43/K3
Lurøy, Nor. 37/E2
Lusaka (cap.), Zam. 105/E4
Lusambo, D.R. Congo 105/D1
Lusen (peak), Ger. 55/G5
Lusenga NP, Zam. 104/A5
Lushan, China 72/C4
Lushi, China 72/B4
Lushnjë, Alb. 47/F2
Lushoto, Tanz. 104/C4
Lushui, China 83/G2
Lusignan, Fr. 42/D3
Lusk, Wy, US 127/G5
Lusk, Ire. 34/B4
Lustenau, Aus. 57/F3
Lutanga (riv.), D.R. Congo 97/J7
Luther, Ok, US 137/N14
Lutherville, Md, US 138/B5
Lütjehorn (isl.), Ger. 50/D1
Lütjenburg, Ger. 38/D4
Luton, Eng, UK 33/F3
Luton (co.), Eng, UK 33/F3
Luton (int'l arpt.), Eng, UK 33/F3
Lutry, Swi. 56/C5
Lutsel'k'e, NW, Can. 122/E2
Luts'k, Ukr. 62/C2
Lutter (riv.), Ger. 51/F5
Lutterbach, Fr. 56/D2
Lutz (riv.), Aus. 57/F3
Lützow-Holm (bay), Ant. 160/C
Luumäki, Fin. 39/M1
Luverne, Mn, US 127/J5
Luvua (riv.), D.R. Congo 104/A4
Luwegu (riv.), Tanz. 105/G2
Luwero, Ugan. 104/B2
Luwingu, Zam. 104/A5
Lux, Fr. 56/A4
Luxembourg (prov.), Belg 53/E4
Luxembourg (ctry.) 53/E4
Luxembourg (cap.), Lux. 53/F4
Luxeuil-les-Bains, Fr. 56/C2
Luxi, China 83/H3
Luxi, China 83/K2
Luxi, China 83/G3
Luxor (int'l arpt.), Egypt 101/C3
Luyi, China 72/C4
Luz, Braz. 155/C1
Luz (coast), Port.,Sp. 44/B4
Luza (riv.), Rus. 61/L3
Luzarches, Fr. 30/K4
Luzein, Swi. 57/F4
Luzern (canton), Swi. 56/E3
Luzern, Swi. 57/E3
Luzerne (co.), Pa, US 138/B1
Luzhai, China 83/J3
Luzhi, China 83/J2
Luzhou, China 83/J2
Luziânia, Braz. 154/A5
Luzilândia, Braz. 154/B1
Lužnice (riv.), Czh. 41/H4
Luzon (isl.), Phil. 67/M8
Luzon (str.), Phil. 116/A3
Lužuice (riv.), Czh. 43/L2
Luzzara, It. 59/D3
Luzzi, It. 46/E3
L'viv, Ukr. 62/C2
L'vivs'ka (obl.), Ukr. 62/B2
L'vivs'ka (prov.), Ukr. 41/M4
Lwala (peak), Ugan. 104/B2
Lwi (riv.), Myan. 78/C1
Lyantonde, Ugan. 104/A3
Lyapin (riv.), Rus. 61/P2
Lycksele, Swe. 37/F2
Lycoming (co.), Pa, US 138/A1
Lyell Brown (mt.), Austl. 113/F2
Lykens, Pa, US 138/B2
Lyman, Wy, US 126/F5
Lyme (bay), Eng, UK 42/B1
Lymington, Eng, UK 33/E5
Lymm, Eng, UK 35/F5
Lyna (riv.), Pol. 41/L1
Lynas (pt.), Wal, UK 34/D5
Lynbrook, NY, US 139/L9
Lynch, Md, US 138/B5
Lynches (riv.), SC, US 133/H3
Lyndhurst, NJ, US 139/J8
Lyne (riv.), Eng, UK 35/F1
Lyngdal, Nor. 38/B2
Lyngen (inlet), Nor. 37/G1
Lynn, Ma, US 131/G3
Lynn Haven, Fl, US 133/G4
Lynn Lake, Mb, Can. 122/F3
Lynwood, Ca, US 136/F8
Lynx (lake), NW, Can. 122/F2
Lyon, Fr. 42/F4
Lyon (riv.), Sc, UK 36/B3
Lyon (lake), Sc, UK 36/B3
Lyon (Satolas) (int'l arpt.), Fr. 56/B6
Lyons, Ks, US 129/H3
Lyons, Co, US 137/B2
Lyons (riv.), Austl. 112/C3
Lyons, Wi, US 135/P14
Lype (hill), Eng, UK 32/C4
Lyra Reef (reef), PNG 116/E5
Lys (riv.), It. 58/A1
Lys (riv.), Fr. 42/E1
Lys-lez-Lannoy, Fr. 52/C2
Lysá (peak), Czh. 41/K4
Lysá nad Labem, Czh. 55/H2
Lysaker, Nor. 38/D2
Lysaya (hill), Bela. 39/M4
Lysekil, Swe. 38/D2
Łysica (peak), Pol. 41/L3
Lysina (peak), Czh. 55/F2
Lyss, Swi. 56/D3
Lystrup, Den. 38/D3
Lys'va, Rus. 61/N4
Lysychans'k, Ukr. 62/F2
Lytham Saint Anne's, Eng, UK 35/E4
Lytle, Tx, US 129/H5
Lytle Creek, Ca, US 136/C2
Lytton, BC, Can. 126/C3
Lyubertsy, Rus. 61/W9
Lyubotyn, Ukr. 62/E2
Lyudinovo, Rus. 62/E1
Lywd (riv.), Wal, UK 32/C3

M

M. Aleman (res.), Mex. 140/B4
Ma-Ubin, Myan. 83/G4
Ma'alot-Tarshiha, Isr. 91/D3
Ma'ān, Jor. 91/D4
Ma'an (gov.), Jor. 91/E4
Maanīt, Mong. 70/H2
Maanīt, Mong. 70/J2
Maanselkä (mts.), Fin. 37/H1
Ma'anshan, China 72/D5
Maarheeze, Neth. 50/C6
Maarianhamina (Mariehamn), Fin. 39/H1
Ma'arrat an Nu'mān, Syria 91/E2
Maarssen, Neth. 50/C4
Maartensdijk, Neth. 50/C4
Maas (riv.), Belg. 42/F1
Maasbracht, Neth. 53/E1
Maasbree, Neth. 50/D6
Maaseik, Belg. 53/E1
Maassluis, Neth. 50/B5
Maastricht, Neth. 53/E2
Maastricht (int'l arpt.), Neth. 53/E2
Mabalacat, Phil. 79/D4
Mabalane, Moz. 105/F5
Mabaruma, Guy. 153/G2
Mabechi (riv.), Japan 76/B3
Mabian, China 83/H2
Mabinay, Phil. 79/D6
Mabopane, SAfr. 106/Q12
Mabote, Moz. 105/F5
Mabule, Bots. 106/D2
Mac Robertson Land (phys. reg.), Ant. 160/D
Macá (peak), Chile 158/B5
Macachín, Arg. 158/E3
Macaé, Braz. 155/D2
Macael, Sp. 44/D4
Macaíba, Braz. 154/D2
Mação, Port. 44/A3
Macapá, Braz. 151/H3
Macará, Ecu. 156/B2
Macarani, Braz. 154/B4
Macaravita, Col. 152/C3
Macari, Peru 156/D4
Macarthur, Austl. 115/B3
Macas, Ecu. 152/B5
Macau, Braz. 154/C2
Macau, China 83/K3
Macau (dpcy.), China 67/L7
Macaúbas, Braz. 154/B4
Macauley (isl.), NZ 116/G7
Macaya (riv.), Col. 150/D3
Macaya, Pic de (peak), Haiti 145/H2
Maccagno, It. 57/E5
Macclenny, Fl, US 133/H4
Macclesfield (canal), Eng, UK 35/F5
Macclesfield, Eng, UK 35/F5
Macdhui (peak), SAfr. 106/D3
Macdona, Tx, US 137/T21
MacDonald (lake), Austl. 109/B3
Macdonnell (ranges), Austl. 109/C3
Macduff, Sc, UK 36/D1
Maceda, Sp. 44/B1
Macedonia (reg.), Gre. 47/G2
Macedonia (int'l arpt.), Gre. 47/H2
Macedonia (Former Yugoslav Republic of Macedonia) (ctry.) 47/G2
Maceió (pt.), Braz. 154/C2
Maceió, Braz. 154/D3
Macerata (prov.), It. 59/G6
Macerata, It. 43/K5
Macfarlane (lake), Austl. 113/H5
Machacalis, Braz. 154/B5
Machacamarca, Bol. 150/E7
Machache (peak), Les. 106/D3
Machachi, Ecu. 152/B5
Machado, Braz. 211/H6
Machado (swamp), Col. 145/H4
Machadodorp, SAfr. 107/E2
Machakos, Kenya 104/C3
Machala, Ecu. 156/B1
Machalí, Chile 158/N9
Machalilla, PN, Ecu. 152/A5
Machanga, Moz. 105/F5
Machaquilá (riv.), Guat. 144/D2
Machars, The (pen.), Sc, UK 34/D2
Machattie (lake), Austl. 113/H3
Machaze, Moz. 105/F5
Machecoul, Fr. 42/C3
Machemma (ruin), SAfr. 105/E5
Macheng, China 72/C5
Machens, Mo, US 137/G8
Machhlīshahr, India 84/D3
Machias, Me, US 131/H2
Machichaco (cape), Sp. 44/D1
Machida, Japan 77/C2
Machilipatnam, India 82/D4
Machiques, Ven. 152/C2
Machovo Jezero (lake), Czh. 55/H1
Machu Picchu (ruin), Peru 156/C4
Machupo (riv.), Bol. 150/F6
Machynlleth, Wal, UK 32/C1
Măcin, Rom. 49/J3
Macina (phys. reg.), Mali 96/E4
Macintyre (riv.), Austl. 109/E3
Mackay (lake), Austl. 109/B3
Mackay, Austl. 114/C3
Mackenzie, BC, Can. 126/C2
Mackenzie, Austl. 114/C3
Mackenzie (bay), NW,Yk, Can. 122/C2
Mackenzie (mts.), NW, Can. 122/C2
Mackenzie (riv.), NW, Can. 122/E2
Mackenzie King (isl.), NW, Can. 123/R7
Mackinac Island, Mi, US 130/C2
Mackinaw City, Mi, US 130/C2
Macklin, Sk, Can. 126/F2
Macknade, Austl. 114/B2
Macksville, Austl. 115/E1
Maclean, Austl. 115/E1
Maclear, SAfr. 106/E3
Macleay (isl.), Austl. 114/F7
Macleod (lake), Austl. 112/B3
Macmillan (riv.), Yk, Can. 134/L3
Macomb, Il, US 127/L5
Macomb, Ok, US 137/N15
Macomb (co.), Mi, US 135/G6
Macomer, It. 46/A2
Macon, Ga, US 133/H3
Macon, Mo, US 129/J3
Mâcon, Fr. 42/F3
Macondes, Planalto dos (plat.), Moz. 104/C5
Macosquin, NI, UK 34/B1
Macotera, Sp. 44/C2
Macoupin (co.), Il, US 137/G7
Macquarie (har.), Austl. 115/C4
Macquarie (riv.), Austl. 109/D4
Macquarie (isl.), Austl. 23/S8
Macroom, Ire. 31/P11
Macuelizo, Hon. 144/D3
Macuim (riv.), Braz. 150/F5
Macuira, PN, Col. 152/D1
Macuma (riv.), Ecu. 156/B1
Macumba (riv.), Austl. 109/C3
Macungie, Pa, US 138/C2
Macusani, Peru 156/D4
Macuspana, Mex. 144/C2
Macuzari, Presa (dam), Mex. 142/C3
Mādabā, Jor. 91/D4
Madagascar (ctry.) 107/H8
Madan, Bul. 47/J2
Madanapalle, India 82/C5
Madanīyīn, Tun. 96/H1
Madanīyīn (gov.), Tun. 99/H2
Madaoua, Niger 103/G3
Madaras, Hun. 48/D2
Madauk, Myan. 83/G4
Madawaska, Me, US 131/G2
Madawaska (riv.), On, Can. 130/E2
Madden (dam), Pan. 152/B2
Madeira (aut. reg.), Port. 45/U14
Madeira (riv.), Braz. 147/C3
Mädelegabel (peak), Ger. 57/G3
Madeleine, Îles de la (isls.), Qu, Can. 131/J2
Madeline (isl.), Wi, US 127/L4
Maden, Turk. 90/D2
Mäder, Aus. 57/F3
Madera, Mex. 142/C2
Maderas (vol.), Nic. 144/E4
Madgaon (Margao), India 89/K5
Madhipura, India 85/F3
Madhubani, India 85/F2
Madhumati (riv.), Bang. 85/G4
Madhupur, India 85/F3
Madhya Pradesh (state), India 70/D7
Madidi (riv.), Bol. 150/E6
Madīnat ath Thawrah, Syria 90/D3
Madirovalo, Madg. 107/H7
Madison, Ne, US 127/J5
Madison, SD, US 127/J4
Madison, Ms, US 133/F3
Madison, In, US 130/C4
Madison, Fl, US 133/H4
Madison, Al, US 133/G3
Madison, Il, US 137/G8
Madison (co.), Oh, US 137/G8
Madison (riv.), Mt, US 124/D2
Madison, Ct, US 139/F1
Madison, Ca, US 135/K9
Madison, NJ, US 139/H9
Madison Heights, Mi, US 135/F6
Madisonville, Tx, US 129/J5
Madisonville, Ky, US 130/C4
Madisonville, La, US 137/P16
Madiun, Indo. 80/D5
Mado Gashi, Kenya 104/C2
Madoi, China 70/G5
Madon (riv.), Fr. 40/D4
Madrakah, Ra's al (pt.), Oman 89/G5
Madre (lag.), Tx, US 140/B2
Madre de Deus de Minas, Braz. 211/J6
Madre de Dios (riv.), Bol. 150/E6
Madre de Dios (dept.), Peru 156/C4
Madre de Dios (isl.), Chile 159/A6
Madre del Sur, Sierra (mts.), Mex. 140/A4
Madre Occidental, Sierra (mts.), Mex. 142/D3
Madre Oriental, Sierra (mts.), Mex. 143/F4
Madrid (aut. comm.), Sp. 44/C2
Madrid (cap.), Sp. 45/N9
Madridejos, Sp. 44/D3
Madrigal, Peru 156/D4
Madrigal de las Altas Torres, Sp. 44/C2
Madrigalejo, Sp. 44/C3
Madrisahorn (peak), Swi. 57/F4
Madroñera, Sp. 44/C3
Madugula, India 82/D4
Madura (isl.), Indo. 67/L10
Madurai, India 82/C6
Mae Hong Son, Thai. 83/G4
Mae Ping NP, Thai. 78/B2
Mae Tho (peak), Thai. 78/B2
Mae Ya (mtn.), Thai. 78/B2
Maebashi, Japan 75/F2
Maella, Sp. 45/F2
Maep'o, SKor. 73/E4
Maerne, It. 59/F1
Maestra, Sierra (mts.), Cuba 145/G2
Maevatanana-Ambanivohitra, Madg. 107/H7
Maewo (isl.), Van. 116/F6
Mafeteng, Les. 106/D3
Maffra, Austl. 115/C3
Mafia (isl.), Tanz. 105/G2
Mafia (chan.), Tanz. 104/C5
Mafikeng, SAfr. 106/D2
Mafou (riv.), Gui. 102/C4
Mafra, Braz. 155/B3
Mafra, Port. 45/P10
Magadan, Rus. 65/R4
Magadino, Swi. 57/E5
Magalies Berg (mts.), SAfr. 106/P12
Magaliesburg, SAfr. 106/P12
Magallanes y Antártica Chilena (prov.), Chile 159/C7
Magangué, Col. 152/C2
Mağara, Turk. 91/C1
Magaria, Niger 103/H3
Magat (riv.), Phil. 79/D4
Magazine (mtn.), Ar, US 129/J4
Magdalena, Bol. 150/F6
Magdalena (peak), Malay. 81/E3
Magdalena (riv.), Col. 147/B2
Magdalena (dept.), Col. 145/H4
Magdalena, Arg. 159/K11
Magdalena de Kino, Mex. 142/C2
Magdeburg, Ger. 64/B4
Magdelaine Cays (isls.), Austl. 109/E2
Magé, Braz. 211/K7
Mage-shima (isl.), Japan 74/B5
Magee, Ms, US 133/F4
Magee (isl.), NI, UK 34/C2
Magelang, Indo. 80/D5
Magellan (str.), Arg.,Chile 147/B8
Magenta, It. 58/B2
Magenta (lake), Austl. 112/C5
Magerøya (isl.), Nor. 37/H1
Maggia, Swi. 57/E5
Maggia (riv.), Swi. 57/E5
Maggio (peak), It. 59/E6
Maggiorasca (peak), It. 58/C3
Maggiore (peak), It. 59/E5
Maggiore (lake), It. 43/H4
Maghāghah, Egypt 101/B2
Maghar, India 84/D2
Maghera, NI, UK 34/B2
Magherafelt (co.), NI, UK 34/B2
Magherafelt, NI, UK 34/B2
Maghīla (peak), Tun. 100/L7
Maghnia, Alg. 100/D2

204
Magil – Marat

Magilligan (pt.), NI, UK 34/B1
Maglaj, Bosn. 48/D3
Maglić (peak), Yugo. 47/F1
Maglie, It. 47/F2
Maglód, Hun. 49/R10
Magna, Ut, US 137/J12
Magnac-Laval, Fr. 42/D3
Magnetawan (riv.), On, Can. 130/D2
Magnetic Passage, Austl. 114/B2
Magnitogorsk, Rus. 61/N5
Magnitogorsk (int'l arpt.), Rus. 61/N5
Magnolia, Ar, US 129/J4
Magnolia, De, US 138/C5
Magny-en-Vexin, Fr. 52/A5
Magny-les-Hameaux, Fr. 30/J5
Mago NP, Eth. 97/N6
Mágoè, Moz. 105/F4
Magog, Qu, Can. 131/F2
Magpie (riv.), Qu, Can. 131/H1
Magpie (lake), Qu, Can. 131/H1
Magpie Ouest (riv.), Qu, Can. 131/H1
Magra (riv.), It. 58/C4
Magreta, It. 59/D3
Maguan, China 78/D1
Magude, Moz. 105/F6
Magugnano, It. 59/D1
Magway (div.), Myan. 70/F8
Magway (Magwe), Myan. 83/F3
Magwe (Magway), Myan. 83/F3
Maha Sarakham, Thai. 78/C2
Mahābād, Iran 88/E1
Mahabe, Madg. 107/H8
Mahābhārat (range), Nepal 84/C1
Mahabo, Madg. 107/H8
Mahaboboka, Madg. 107/H7
Mahād, India 89/K5
Mahadeo (range), India 84/A4
Mahaica, Guy. 153/G3
Mahaica-Berbice (pol. reg.), Guy. 153/G3
Mahaicony Village, Guy. 153/G3
Mahajamba (riv.), Madg. 107/H7
Mahajamba (bay), Madg. 107/H6
Mahajanga (prov.), Madg. 107/H6
Mahajanga, Madg. 107/H6
Mahajilo (riv.), Madg. 107/H7
Mahakali (zone), Nepal 84/C1
Mahakam (riv.), Indo. 81/E3
Mahalapye, Bots. 105/E5
Mahale Mountains NP, Tanz. 104/A4
Maḩallāt, Iran 88/F2
Maham, India 86/D5
Māhān (riv.), India 84/D4
Māhān, Iran 89/G2
Mahānadī (riv.), India 70/D7
Mahananda (riv.), India 85/F3
Mahandiabiani (riv.), C.d'Iv. 102/D4
Mahanoro, Madg. 107/J7
Mahanoy City, Pa, US 138/B2
Mahantango (mtn.), Pa, US 138/B2
Mahārājganj, India 85/E2
Mahārājganj, India 84/D2
Mahārajpur, India 82/C2
Mahārāshtra (state), India 82/B4
Mahāsamund, India 82/D3
Mahāshān (ruin), Bang. 85/G3
Mahasoabe, Madg. 107/H8
Mahavavy (riv.), Madg. 107/H7
Mahawa (riv.), India 84/B1
Mahazoarivo, Madg. 107/H8
Mahazoma, Madg. 107/H7
Mahbubnagar, India 82/C4
Mahdia, Guy. 153/G3
Mahébourg, Mrts. 107/T15
Mahendranagar, Nepal 84/C1
Mahesāna, India 89/K4
Mahgawān, India 84/B2
Mahia (pen.), NZ 109/H6
Mahilyow (int'l arpt.), Bela. 39/P5
Mahilyow, Bela. 39/P5
Mahilyowskaya (prov.), Bela. 60/F5
Mahīshādal, India 85/F4
Mahitsy, Madg. 107/H7
Mahlaing, Myan. 83/G3
Mahlberg, Ger. 56/D1
Mahleur (lake), Or, US 126/D5
Mahlow, Ger. 40/Q7
Mahmel (peak), Alg. 96/G1
Maḩmūd-e 'Erāqī, Afg. 89/J1
Mahmūdābād, India 84/C2
Mahón, Sp. 45/H3
Mahroni, India 84/B3
Mahukona, Hi, US 124/U10
Mahuva, India 89/K4
Mahwah, India 84/A2
Mahwah, NJ, US 139/J7
Mai-Ndombe (lake), D.R. Congo 96/J8
Maia, Port. 44/A2
Maiala NP, Austl. 114/E6
Maials, Sp. 45/F2
Maiana (isl.), Kiri. 116/G4
Maicao, Col. 152/C2
Maîche, Fr. 56/C3
Maicuru (riv.), Braz. 151/H3
Maidenhead, Eng, UK 33/F3
Maidens, Sc, UK 36/B6
Maidstone, Sk, Can. 126/F2
Maidstone, Eng, UK 33/G4
Maidstone, On, Can. 135/G7
Maiduguri, Nga. 96/H5
Maienfeld, Swi. 57/F4
Maigue (riv.), Ire. 31/P10
Maihar, India 84/C3
Maihara, Japan 77/K5
Maikala (range), India 84/C4
Maiko, PN de la, D.R. Congo 97/L8
Mailāni, India 84/C1
Maili, Hi, US 124/V13
Mailly-le-Camp, Fr. 53/D6
Mailsi, Pak. 86/B5
Main (riv.), NI, UK 34/B2
Main (riv.), Ger. 40/E4
Main-Donau (canal), Ger. 54/D3
Main Range NP, Austl. 114/C5
Maināguri, India 85/G2
Mainbernheim, Ger. 54/D3
Maincy, Fr. 30/L6
Maine (riv.), Ire. 31/P10
Maine (reg.), Fr. 42/C2
Maine (state), US 131/G2
Maine, Collines du (hills), Fr. 42/C2
Maine, Gulf of (gulf), Me, US 131/G3
Mainhardt, Ger. 54/C4
Mainhausen, Ger. 54/B2
Mainland (isl.), Sc, UK 31/V14
Mainling, China 83/F2
Mainpurī, India 84/B2
Mainstockheim, Ger. 54/D3
Maintirano, Madg. 107/H7
Mainz, Ger. 54/B3
Maio (isl.), CpV. 93/K10
Maipo (vol.), Chile 158/P9
Maipo (riv.), Chile 158/N8
Maipú, Arg. 158/F3
Maipú, Chile 158/N8
Maira (riv.), It. 43/G4
Maire (str.), Arg. 159/D7
Mairiporã, Braz. 211/G8
Mairwa, India 85/E2
Mais Gate (int'l arpt.), Haiti 145/H2
Maisach, Ger. 54/E6
Maisí (cape), Cuba 141/G3
Maisome (isl.), Tanz. 104/A3
Maison-Rouge, Fr. 30/M6
Maisons-Alfort, Fr. 30/K5
Maisons-Laffitte, Fr. 30/J5
Maithon (res.), India 85/F4
Maitland, Austl. 115/D2
Maitland (riv.), On, Can. 130/D3
Maitland, Austl. 113/H5
Maitri, India, Ant. 160/A
Maizhokunggar, China 83/F2
Maizières-lès-Metz, Fr. 53/F5
Maizuru, Japan 77/H5
Maizuru (bay), Japan 77/H4
Maja e Zezë (peak), Alb. 47/G2
Majadahonda, Sp. 45/N9
Majagual, Col. 152/C2
Majardah (mts.), Alg. 100/K6
Majāz Al Bāb, Tun. 100/L6
Majdanpek, Yugo. 48/E3
Majene, Indo. 81/E4
Majia (riv.), China 72/D3
Majiang, China 79/A2
Majorca (isl.), Sp. 45/G3
Majur, Yugo. 48/D3
Majuro (cap.), Mrsh. 116/G4
Makabe, Japan 77/E1
Makaha, Hi, US 124/V13
Makakilo City, Hi, US 124/V13
Makālu (peak), China 85/F2
Makālu (peak), Nepal 82/E2
Makarska, Cro. 47/E1
Makassar (str.), Indo. 67/L10
Makatea (isl.), FrPol. 117/L6
Makawao, Hi, US 124/T10
Makay (mass.), Madg. 107/H8
Makemo (isl.), FrPol. 117/L6
Makena, Hi, US 124/T10
Makeni, SLeo. 102/B4
Makgadikgadi (salt pans), Bots. 105/D5
Makhachkala, Rus. 63/H4
Makhdūmpur, Pak. 86/B4
Makhfar al Busayyah, Iraq 88/E2
Makhmūr, Iraq 90/E3
Makian (isl.), Indo. 81/G3
Makin (isl.), Kiri. 116/G4
Makino, Japan 77/K5
Makinsk, Kaz. 87/F2
Makioka, Japan 77/B2
Makiyivka, Ukr. 62/F2
Makkah, SAr. 88/C4
Makkovik, Nf, Can. 123/L3
Makó, Hun. 48/E2
Makokou, Gabon 96/H7
Makonde (plat.), Tanz. 104/C5
Maków Mazowiecki, Pol. 41/L2
Makrakómi, Gre. 47/H3
Makran (coast), Iran 89/G3
Makran (reg.), Iran 89/H3
Makrokhórion, Gre. 47/H2
Maksutlu, Turk. 47/K2
Makteir (reg.), Mrta. 98/C5
Makthar, Tun. 100/L7
Makurazaki, Japan 74/B5
Makurdi, Nga. 103/H5
Makushin (vol.), Ak, US 134/E5
Mal Abrigo, Uru. 159/K11
Mala, Peru 156/B4
Mala (pt.), CR 144/E4
Mala (pt.), Pan. 152/B3
Malabar (coast), India 82/B5
Malabata (pt.), Mor. 100/B2
Malabo (cap.), EqG. 96/G7
Malacacheta, Braz. 154/B5
Malacca (str.), Asia 67/J9
Malacky, Slvk. 41/J4
Maladers, Swi. 57/F4
Maladzyechna, Bela. 39/M4
Málaga (int'l arpt.), Sp. 44/C4
Málaga, Sp. 44/C4
Malaga, NJ, US 138/C4
Malaga Cove (bay), Ca, US 136/F8
Malagarasi (riv.), Tanz. 104/A4
Malagón, Sp. 44/D3
Malagueta (bay), Cuba 145/G1
Malahide, Ire. 34/B5
Malaimbandy, Madg. 107/H8
Malaita (isl.), Sol. 116/F5
Malakāl, Sudan 97/M6
Malakanagiri, India 82/D4
Malakwāl, Pak. 86/B3
Malambo, Col. 152/C2
Malang, Indo. 80/D5
Malangawa, Nepal 85/E2
Malanje, Ang. 105/C2
Malans, Swi. 57/F4
Malanville, Ben. 103/F4
Malargüe, Arg. 158/C2
Malartic, Qu, Can. 130/E1
Malasoro (pt.), Indo. 81/E5
Malatya (prov.), Turk. 90/D2
Malatya, Turk. 90/D2
Malaut, India 86/C4
Malawi (ctry.) 105/F3
Malawi (Nyasa) (lake), Malw. 104/B5
Malay (pen.), Thai. 83/G6
Malaya (reg.), Malay. 80/B3
Malaya Vishera, Rus. 39/Q2
Malaybalay, Phil. 79/E6
Malāyer, Iran 88/E2
Malaysia (ctry.) 80/C2
Malazemel'skaya (tundra), Rus. 61/L2
Malazgirt, Turk. 90/E2
Malbaie (riv.), Qu, Can. 131/G1
Malbork, Pol. 39/H4
Malcesine, It. 59/D1
Malchin, Ger. 38/E5
Malcontenta, It. 59/F2
Maldegem, Belg. 52/C1
Malden, Mo, US 129/K3
Malden (isl.), Kiri. 117/K5
Maldive (isls.), Mald. 82/B6
Maldives (ctry.) 67/G9
Maldon, Austl. 115/C3
Maldon, Eng, UK 33/G3
Maldonado, Uru. 159/G2
Maldonado (dept.), Uru. 159/G2
Male (cap.), Mald. 67/G9
Maléa (cape), Gre. 47/H4
Mālegaon, India 89/K4
Malekula (isl.), Van. 116/F6
Malemort-sur-Corrèze, Fr. 42/D4
Malente, Ger. 38/D4
Maleny, Austl. 114/D4
Maleo, It. 58/C2
Malesina, Gre. 47/H3
Malfa, It. 46/D3
Malgobek, Rus. 63/H4
Malgrat de Mar, Sp. 45/G2
Malgrate, It. 58/C1
Malheur (lake), Or, US 128/C2
Malheur (riv.), Or, US 126/D5
Malheureux (cape), Mrts. 107/T14
Mali (riv.), Myan. 83/G2
Mali (isl.), Myan. 78/B3
Mali (ctry.) 96/E4
Mali Lošinj, Cro. 48/B3
Mália, Gre. 47/J5
Malibu, Ca, US 136/B2
Malīhābād, India 84/C2
Mālilla, Swe. 38/F3
Malin Head (pt.), Ire. 31/Q9
Malinau, Indo. 81/E3
Malindang (mt.), Phil. 81/F2
Malindi, Kenya 104/D3
Maling (pass), China 72/C3
Malio (riv.), Madg. 107/H8
Malipo, China 78/D1
Malīr Cantonment, Pak. 89/J4
Malka Mari NP, Kenya 97/P7
Malkara, Turk. 49/H5
Malko Tŭrnovo, Bul. 49/H5
Mallacoota, Austl. 115/D3
Mallaig, Sc, UK 31/R8
Mallānwān, India 84/C2
Mallasvesi (lake), Fin. 39/K1
Mallee Cliffs NP, Austl. 115/B2
Mallén, Sp. 44/E2
Malleray, Swi. 56/D3
Mallero (riv.), It. 57/F5
Mallersdorf-Pfaffenberg, Ger. 55/F5
Malles (Mals), It. 57/G4
Malloa, Chile 158/N9
Mallow, Ire. 31/P10
Malmberget, Swe. 37/G2
Malmédy, Belg. 53/F3
Malmesbury, SAfr. 106/L10
Malmköping, Swe. 38/G2
Malmö, Swe. 38/E4
Malmöhus (co.), Swe. 37/E5
Malmslätt, Swe. 38/F2
Malnate, It. 58/B1
Malo, It. 59/E1
Maloelap (isl.), Mrsh. 116/G4
Malone, NY, US 130/F2
Malong, China 83/H2
Malonje (peak), Tanz. 104/A5
Malonno, It. 57/G5
Małopolska (uplands), Pol. 41/K3
Malpartida de Cáceres, Sp. 44/B3
Malpartida de Plasencia, Sp. 44/B3
Malpelo (isl.), Col. 147/A2
Malpensa (int'l arpt.), It. 58/B1
Malpica, Sp. 44/A1
Malsch (riv.), Aus. 55/H5
Malsch, Ger. 54/B5
Malše (riv.), Czh. 41/H4
Mälstek (peak), Czh. 55/G4
Malta, Mt, US 126/G3
Malta, Braz. 154/C2
Malta (chan.), Malta 46/C4
Malta (ctry.) 46/L7
Maltahöhe, Namb. 105/C5
Maltby, Eng, UK 35/G5
Malters, Swi. 56/E3
Maltorne (riv.), Fr. 30/G6
Malung, Swe. 38/E1
Malvaglia, Swi. 57/E5
Malvan, India 89/K5
Malveira, Port. 45/P10
Malvern, Pa, US 138/C3
Malverne, NY, US 139/L9
Malvinas (Falkland) (isls.), UK 160/W
Malyy Uzen' (riv.), Rus. 63/H2
Malyn, Ukr. 62/D2
Malyy Yenisey (riv.), Rus. 70/G1
Malzéville, Fr. 53/F6
Mamanguape, Braz. 154/D2
Mamaroneck, NY, US 139/L8
Mamba, Zam. 105/E4
Mamba, Japan 77/B1
Mambajao, Phil. 79/D6
Mambasa, D.R. Congo 104/A2
Mamberamo (riv.), Indo. 81/J4
Mambéré (riv.), CAfr. 96/J7
Mambij, Syria 90/D2
Mamburao, Phil. 81/F1
Mamer, Lux. 53/F4
Mamers, Fr. 42/D2
Mamfé, Camr. 103/H5
Mammendorf, Ger. 57/H1
Mamming, Ger. 55/F5
Mammoth, Az, US 128/E4
Mammoth Cave NP, Ky, US 133/G2
Mamoré (riv.), Braz. 150/E6
Mamou, La, US 129/J5
Mamoutzou, May. 107/H6
Mampikony, Madg. 107/H7
Mampong, Gha. 103/E5
Mamry (lake), Pol. 39/J4
Mamuju, Indo. 81/E4
Mamuri (riv.), Braz. 151/G4
Mamwera (peak), Tanz. 104/C4
Man, C.d'Iv. 102/D5
Man, Isle of (isl.), IM, UK 34/D3
Man Mia (peak), Thai. 78/B4
Mana (riv.), FrG. 153/H3
Manabí (prov.), Ecu. 152/A5
Manacapuru, Braz. 150/F4
Manacle (pt.), Eng, UK 32/A6
Manacor, Sp. 45/G3
Manado, Indo. 81/F3
Manage, Belg. 53/D3
Managua (lake), Nic. 140/D5
Managua (cap.), Nic. 144/E3
Manahawkin, NJ, US 138/D4
Manakambahiny, Madg. 107/J7
Manakara, Madg. 107/J8
Manalapan, NJ, US 138/D3
Manāli, India 86/D3
Manambaho (riv.), Madg. 107/H7
Manambolo (riv.), Madg. 107/H7
Mananantanana (riv.), Madg. 107/H8
Mananara, Madg. 107/J7
Mananara (riv.), Madg. 107/H8
Mananjary, Madg. 107/J8
Mananjary (riv.), Madg. 107/H8
Manara (pt.), It. 58/C4
Manaratsandry, Madg. 107/H7
Manas, China 70/E3
Manas (int'l arpt.), Kyr. 87/F4
Manas (peak), Kyr. 87/F4
Manās (riv.), India 85/H2
Manas (riv.), China 64/J5
Manāslu (peak), Nepal 85/E1
Manasquan, NJ, US 138/D3
Manasquan (riv.), NJ, US 138/D3
Manassa, Co, US 132/B2
Manastir Dečani, Yugo. 47/G1
Manastir Gračanica, Yugo. 47/G1
Manastir Sopoćani, Yugo. 47/G1
Manatsuru, Japan 77/C3
Manaus, Braz. 150/F4
Manawatu (riv.), NZ 117/T11
Mañazo, Peru 156/D4
Manazuru-misaki (cape), Japan 77/C3
Mance (riv.), Fr. 56/B2
Mancha Real, Sp. 44/D4
Mancheng, China 72/G7
Mancherāl, India 82/C4
Manchester, Ky, US 130/D4
Manchester, NH, US 131/G3
Manchester, Tn, US 133/G3
Manchester, Mo, US 137/F8
Manchester, Md, US 138/B4
Manchester, Pa, US 138/B3
Manchester (lake), Austl. 114/E7
Manchester, Wa, US 135/B2
Manchester, Eng, UK 35/F5
Manchester (Ringway) (int'l arpt.), Eng, UK 35/F5
Manchuria (reg.), China 65/N5
Mancieulles, Fr. 53/E5
Máncora, Peru 156/A2
Mand (riv.), Iran 89/F3
Manda, PN de, Chad 96/J6
Mandabe, Madg. 107/H8
Mandaguari, Braz. 155/B2
Mandal, India 82/B3
Mandal, Nor. 38/B2
Mandal-Ovoo, Mong. 70/H3
Mandala (peak), Indo. 81/K4
Mandalay (div.), Myan. 70/F7
Mandalay, Myan. 83/G3
Mandalgovĭ, Mong. 70/J2
Mandalī, Iraq 88/E2
Mandan, ND, US 127/H4
Mandasavu (peak), Indo. 81/F5
Mandaue, Phil. 79/D5
Mandeb (str.), Afr.,Asia 93/G3
Mandello del Lario, It. 57/F6
Mandera, Kenya 97/P7
Mandeure, Fr. 56/C3
Mandeville, La, US 137/P16
Mandeville, Jam. 145/G2
Mandi Bahāuddīn, Pak. 86/B3
Mandi Dabwāli, India 86/C5
Mandi Sādiqganj, Pak. 86/B4
Mandié, Moz. 105/F4
Mandiola (isl.), Indo. 81/G4
Mandira (res.), India 85/E4
Mandla, India 84/C4
Mandø (isl.), Den. 38/C4
Mándok, Hun. 41/M4
Mandoto, Madg. 107/H7
Mandoúdhion, Gre. 47/H3
Mándra, Gre. 47/N8
Mandrare (riv.), Madg. 107/H9
Mandritsara, Madg. 107/J6
Mandsaur, India 89/L4
Mandurah, Austl. 112/B5
Manduria, It. 47/E2
Māndvi, India 89/J4
Mandya, India 82/C5
Mane (pass), Nepal 84/D1
Manéngouba, Massif du (peak), Camr. 103/H5
Maner, India 85/E3
Manerbio, It. 58/D2
Manfalūt, Egypt 88/B3
Manfredonia, It. 46/D2
Manfredonia, Golfo di (gulf), It. 46/D2
Mang (riv.), China 72/B4
Manga, Braz. 154/B4
Manga, Burk. 103/E4
Mangabeiras, Chapada das (hills), Braz. 151/J6
Mangai, D.R. Congo 105/C1
Mangaia (isl.), Cookls. 117/K7
Mangaldai, India 83/F2
Mangaldan, Phil. 79/D4
Mangalia, Rom. 49/J4
Mangalisa (peak), Tanz. 104/C4
Mangalore, India 82/B5
Mangaratiba, Braz. 211/J7
Mangareva (isl.), FrPol. 117/M7
Manger, Nor. 38/A1
Mangghystaū (obl.), Kaz. 64/F5
Mangghystaū Tübegi (pen.), Kaz. 63/J3
Mangghystaū Üstirti (plat.), Kaz. 63/K4
Mangkalihat (cape), Indo. 81/E3
Mangla (dam), Pak. 86/B3
Mangla, Pak. 86/B3
Mangla (res.), Pak. 86/B3
Manglaralto, Ecu. 156/A1
Manglares (pt.), Col. 152/B4
Manglaur, India 84/A1
Mangles (bay), Austl. 112/K7
Mango, Togo 103/F4
Mangoche, Malw. 105/G3
Mangoky (riv.), Madg. 105/J11
Mangole (isl.), Indo. 81/G4
Mangoro (riv.), Madg. 107/J7
Mangotsfield, Eng, UK 32/D4
Māngrol, India 89/K4
Mangualde, Port. 44/B2
Mangueira (lake), Braz. 159/G2
Mangum, Ok, US 129/H4
Manhasset, NY, US 139/L8
Manhasset (bay), NY, US 139/L8
Manhattan, Mt, US 126/F4
Manhattan (isl.), NY, US 139/K9
Manhattan Beach, Ca, US 136/F8
Manhay, Belg. 53/E3
Manheim, Pa, US 138/B3
Manhiça, Moz. 105/F6
Manhuaçu, Braz. 155/D2
Manhumirim, Braz. 155/D2
Mania (riv.), Madg. 107/H7
Maniamba, Moz. 105/G3
Maniāri (riv.), India 84/C4
Manicoré (riv.), Braz. 150/F5
Manicoré, Braz. 150/F5
Manicouagan (riv.), Qu, Can. 123/K3
Manicouagan (res.), Qu, Can. 131/G1
Manifold (cape), Austl. 114/C3
Manigotagan, Mb, Can. 127/J3
Manihāri, India 85/F3
Manihi (isl.), FrPol. 117/L6
Manihiki (isl.), Cookls. 117/J6
Manikarchar, India 85/G3
Manila (cap.), Phil. 79/D5
Manilla, Austl. 115/D1
Maningory (riv.), Madg. 107/J7
Manipa (str.), Indo. 81/G4
Manipat (hills), India 84/D4
Manipur (state), India 70/F7
Manisa (prov.), Turk. 62/D5
Manistee (riv.), Mi, US 130/C2
Manistee, Mi, US 130/C2
Manistique, Mi, US 130/C2
Manitoba (prov.), Can. 122/G3
Manitoba (lake), Mb, Can. 127/J3
Manitou (riv.), Qu, Can. 131/H1
Manitou Springs, Co, US 129/F3
Manitoulin (isl.), On, Can. 130/D2
Manitowoc, Wi, US 127/M4
Maniwaki, Qu, Can. 130/F2
Manizales, Col. 150/C2
Manja, Madg. 107/H8
Manjakandriana, Madg. 107/J7
Manjimup, Austl. 112/C5
Mankono, C.d'Iv. 102/D4
Manley Hot Springs, Ak, US 134/H2
Manlleu, Sp. 44/D1
Manlyutka, Rus. 61/R4
Manmād, India 89/K4
Mannar, SrL. 82/C6
Mannar (gulf), SrL.,India 67/G9
Männedorf, Swi. 57/E3
Mannetjiesberg (peak), SAfr. 106/C4
Mannheim, Ger. 54/B4
Manning, SC, US 133/H3
Manning (cape), NW, Can. 123/Q7
Manning, Ab, Can. 122/E3
Mannington Meadow (lake), NJ, US 138/C4
Männlifluh (peak), Swi. 56/D4
Mannum, Austl. 113/H5
Mano (riv.), Libr. 96/C6
Manokotak, Ak, US 134/G4
Manolo Fortich, Phil. 79/D6
Manombo, Madg. 107/G8
Manono, D.R. Congo 105/E2
Manorville, NY, US 139/F2
Manosque, Fr. 42/F5
Manouane (riv.), Qu, Can. 131/G1
Manouane (lake), Qu, Can. 131/G1
Manp'o, NKor. 73/D2
Manra (Sydney) (isl.), Kiri. 117/H5
Manresa, Sp. 45/K6
Mansa, Zam. 104/A5
Mānsa, India 86/C5
Mansa Konko, Gam. 102/B3
Mansalay, Phil. 81/F1
Mānsehra, Pak. 86/B2
Mansel (isl.), Nun., Can. 123/H2
Mansfield, Austl. 115/C3
Mansfield, Oh, US 130/D3
Mansfield, La, US 129/J4
Mansfield, Eng, UK 35/G5
Mansfield Woodhouse, Eng, UK 35/G5
Mansilla de las Mulas, Sp. 44/C1
Manta, Ecu. 152/A5
Mantalingajan (mt.), Phil. 81/E2
Mantaro (riv.), Peru 150/C6
Manteca, Ca, US 128/B3
Mantecal, Ven. 152/D3
Manteigas, Port. 44/B2
Mantena, Braz. 155/D1
Manthani, India 82/C4
Manti, Ut, US 128/E3
Mantiqueira, Serra da (mts.), Braz. 151/K8
Mantorp, Swe. 38/F2
Mantova (prov.), It. 58/D2
Mantova, It. 59/D2
Mäntsälä, Fin. 39/L1
Mantua, Ut, US 137/K11
Mantua, Cuba 145/E1
Mantua, NJ, US 138/C4
Manturovo, Rus. 61/K4
Mäntyharju, Fin. 39/M1
Manu (riv.), India 150/D6
Manú, Peru 156/D4
Manú, PN, Peru 150/D6
Manua (isls.), ASam. 117/J6
Manuae Atoll (atoll), Cookls. 117/K6
Manuel Alves da Natividade (riv.), Braz. 151/J6
Manuel Benavides, Mex. 132/C4
Manuel J. Cobo, Arg. 159/K11
Manui (isl.), Indo. 81/F4
Manuk (riv.), Indo. 80/C5
Manukau, NZ 117/S10
Manumuskin (riv.), NJ, US 138/D5
Manuripe (riv.), Bol. 150/E6
Manuripe Heath Amazonica, Reserva Nacional, Bol. 156/D4
Manus (isl.), PNG 116/D5
Manville, NJ, US 138/D2
Many, La, US 129/J5
Many Farms, Az, US 128/E3
Manyara (lake), Tanz. 104/B3
Manych (riv.), Rus. 64/E5
Manych-Gudilo (lake), Rus. 63/G3
Manzanares, Sp. 44/D3
Manzanares (riv.), Sp. 45/N8
Manzanares el Real, Sp. 45/N8
Manzanillo, Mex. 142/D5
Manzanillo (int'l arpt.), Mex. 142/D5
Manzanillo, Cuba 145/G1
Manzano (mts.), NM, US 132/B3
Manzano, It. 59/G1
Manzhouli, China 71/L2
Manzil Bū Zalafah, Tun. 46/B4
Manzil Tamīn, Tun. 46/B4
Manzilah, Buḩayrat al (lake), Egypt 91/B4
Manzini, Swaz. 107/E2
Mao, Chad 96/J5
Maoke (mts.), Indo. 116/C5
Maoming, China 83/K3
Mapastepec, Mex. 144/C3
Mapi (riv.), Indo. 81/J5
Mapimí, Bolsón de (depr.), Mex. 142/D3
Mapire, Ven. 153/E3
Maple (riv.), ND, US 127/J4
Maple Creek, Sk, Can. 126/F3
Maple Grove, Qu, Can. 131/N7
Maple Park, Il, US 135/N16
Maple Shade, NJ, US 138/D4
Maple Valley, Wa, US 135/C3
Mapleton, Ut, US 137/K13
Maplewood, Mo, US 137/G8
Maplewood, NJ, US 139/H9
Maporal, Ven. 152/D3
Mapuera (riv.), Braz. 150/G3
Maputo (int'l arpt.), Moz. 107/F2
Maputo (cap.), Moz. 107/F2
Maqdam (cape), Sudan 101/D5
Maqên Gangri (peak), China 70/G5
Maquan (Damqog) (riv.), China 84/E1
Maquinchao, Arg. 158/C4
Maquoketa (riv.), Ia, US 129/K2
Mar (mts.), Braz. 147/E5
Mar (reg.), Sc, UK 36/D2
Mar Chiquita (lake), Arg. 157/D3
Mar de Ajó, Arg. 159/F3
Mar del Plata, Arg. 158/F3
Mar del Tuyú, Arg. 159/F3
Mara (pol. reg.), Tanz. 104/B3
Mara (riv.), Tanz. 104/B3
Marabá, Braz. 151/J5
Maracá, Ilha de (isl.), Braz. 151/H3
Maracaibo, Ven. 152/D2
Maracaibo (lake), Ven. 147/B2
Maracaju, Serra de (mts.), Braz. 151/G8
Maracás, Braz. 154/B4
Maracás, Chapada de (hills), Braz. 154/B4
Maracay, Ven. 150/E1
Maracena, Sp. 44/D4
Marādah, Libya 96/J2
Maradi, Niger 103/G3
Maradi (dept.), Niger 103/G3
Marāgheh, Iran 88/E1
Mārahra, India 84/B2
Marahuaca (peak), Ven. 153/E4
Marais de St-Gond (swamp), Fr. 52/C6
Marais des Cygnes (riv.), Ks,Mo, US 129/J3
Marajó (bay), Braz. 147/E3
Marajó, Ilha de (isl.), Braz. 147/D3
Maralal, Kenya 104/C2
Maralinga-Tjarutja Abor. Land, Austl. 113/F4
Maramag, Phil. 79/E6
Marambaia, Ilha (isl.), Braz. 211/K8
Maramureş (co.), Rom. 41/M5
Marana, Az, US 128/E4
Marano (lag.), Cro. 59/G1
Marand, Iran 63/H5
Marang, Malay. 80/B2
Marangani, Peru 156/D4
Maranguape, Braz. 154/C1
Maranhão (riv.), Braz. 151/J6
Maranhão (state), Braz. 154/A2
Marano Lagunare, It. 59/G1
Marano sul Panaro, It. 59/D4
Marano Vicentino, It. 59/E1
Maranoa (riv.), Austl. 109/D3
Marañón (riv.), Peru 147/B3
Marans, Fr. 42/C3
Maraoue, PN de la, C.d'Iv. 102/D5
Marapi (peak), Indo. 80/B4
Maras (peak), Indo. 80/C4
Mărăşeşti, Rom. 49/H3
Marathon, On, Can. 127/M3
Marathon, Fl, US 133/H5
Marathon, Tx, US 132/C4
Marathón, Gre. 47/N8

205
Marau – McNei

Marau, Braz. 155/A4
Marauliānwāla, Pak. 86/B3
Maravatío de Ocampo, Mex. 143/E5
Marawi, Phil. 81/F2
Marbach, Swi. 56/D4
Marbach am Neckar, Ger. 54/C5
Marbache, Fr. 53/F6
Marbella, Sp. 44/C4
Marble Bar, Austl. 112/C2
Marbleton, Wy, US 126/F5
Marburg, Ger. 43/H1
Marburg (lake), Pa, US 138/B4
Marca, Ponta da (pt.), Ang. 105/B4
Marcali, Hun. 48/C2
Marcallo, It. 58/B2
Marcapata, Peru 156/D4
March, Eng, UK 33/G1
Marche (prov.), It. 43/K5
Marche (mts.), Fr. 42/D3
Marche-en-Famenne, Belg. 53/E3
Marchémoret, Fr. 30/L4
Marchena, Sp. 44/C4
Marchena (isl.), Ecu. 156/E6
Marcheno, It. 58/D1
Marchiennes, Fr. 52/C3
Marchin, Belg. 53/E3
Marchtrenk, Aus. 55/H6
Marciana Marina, It. 46/B1
Marcilly, Fr. 30/L4
Marcilly-sur-Tille, Fr. 56/B2
Marck, Fr. 52/A2
Marckolsheim, Fr. 56/D1
Marco, Braz. 154/B1
Marco, Fl, US 133/H5
Marco Polo (int'l arpt.), It. 59/F2
Marcoing, Fr. 52/C3
Marcon, It. 59/F1
Marcona, Peru 156/C4
Marconi (mt.), BC, Can. 126/E3
Marcos Juárez, Arg. 158/E2
Marcoussis, Fr. 30/J6
Marcovia, Hon. 144/E3
Marcq-en-Barœul, Fr. 52/C2
Marcus Baker (mt.), Ak, US 134/J3
Marcy (mt.), NY, US 130/F2
Mardān, Pak. 86/B2
Marden, Eng, UK 30/E3
Mardeuil, Fr. 52/C5
Mardin (town), Turk. 90/E2
Marecchia (riv.), It. 59/F5
Maree (lake), Sc, UK 31/R8
Mareeba, Austl. 114/B2
Mareil-sur-Mauldre, Fr. 30/H5
Marengo, Il, US 135/N15
Marennes, Fr. 42/C4
Mareuil-sur-Ourcq, Fr. 30/M4
Marfa, Tx, US 129/F5
Margalla Hills NP, Pak. 86/B3
Marganets', Ukr. 62/E3
Margao (Madgaon), India 89/K5
Margaret (mt.), Austl. 112/C2
Margaret River, Austl. 112/B5
Margarita (peak), Ca, US 136/C4
Margarita, Isla de (isl.), Ven. 150/F1
Margarítion, Gre. 47/G3
Margate, SAfr. 107/E3
Margate, Eng, UK 33/H4
Margate City, NJ, US 138/D5
Margeride, Monts de la (mts.), Fr. 42/E4
Margherita (peak), Ugan. 104/A2
Marghilon, Uzb. 87/F4
Marghita, Rom. 48/F2
Margny-lès-Compiègne, Fr. 52/B5
Margos, Peru 156/B3
Margosatubig, Phil. 81/F2
Margraten, Neth. 53/E2
Mari, Braz. 154/D2
Mari-El (aut. rep.), Rus. 64/Q6
Maria (mt.), Austl. 115/D4
María Cleófas (isl.), Mex. 142/D4
Maria da Fé, Braz. 211/H7
Maria Island NP, Austl. 115/D4
María Madre (isl.), Mex. 142/D4
María Magdalena (isl.), Mex. 142/D4
Maria van Diemen (cape), NZ 117/S9
Mariāhū, India 84/D3
Marian, Austl. 114/C3
Marianao, Cuba 145/F1
Marianna, Fl, US 133/G4
Marianna, Ar, US 129/K4
Mariano Comense, It. 58/C1
Mariano Marcos, Phil. 79/D6
Mariánské Lázně, Czh. 55/F3
Marias (riv.), Mt, US 126/F3
Mariato (pt.), Pan. 152/A3
Maribo, Den. 38/D4
Maribor, Slov. 43/L3
Maricá, Braz. 211/L7
Maricopa (co.), Az, US 137/R18
Marié (riv.), Braz. 150/E4
Marie Byrd Land (phys. reg.), Ant. 160/S
Marie-Galante (isl.), Dom. 141/J4
Mariehamn (int'l arpt.), Fin. 39/H1
Mariel, Cuba 145/F1
Marienhafe, Ger. 51/E1
Marienheide, Ger. 53/G1
Mariental, Namb. 105/C5
Mariestad, Swe. 38/E2
Marietta, Ok, US 129/H4
Marietta, Ga, US 133/G3
Marietta, Pa, US 138/B3
Marignane, Fr. 42/F5
Marigot, Dom. 141/N9
Marijampolė, Lith. 39/K4
Marília, Braz. 155/B2
Marín, Sp. 44/A1
Marin (co.), Ca, US 135/J10
Marin-Epagnier, Swi. 56/D3
Marina, It. 46/D3
Marina del Rey, Ca, US 136/F8
Marina del Rey (har.), Ca, US 136/F8
Marina di Andora, It. 58/B5
Marina di Montemarciano, It. 59/G5
Marina di Ravenna, It. 59/F4
Marine Nat'l Rsv., Kenya 104/D3
Marine World Africa USA, Ca, US 135/K10
Marineland, Austl. 113/M8
Marines, Fr. 30/H4
Marinette, Wi, US 127/M4
Maringá, Braz. 155/B2
Marinha Grande, Port. 44/A3
Marinhas, Port. 44/A2
Marion, Ky, US 130/B4
Marion, Mi, US 130/C2
Marion, In, US 130/C3
Marion, Oh, US 130/D3
Marion (reef), Austl. 109/E2
Marion, Al, US 133/G3
Marion (lake), SC, US 125/K5
Maripa, Ven. 153/E3
Mariposa, Ca, US 128/C3
Mariscal Estigarribia, Par. 150/F8
Mariscal Sucre (int'l arpt.), Ecu. 152/B5
Maritime Alps (mts.), Fr. 43/G4
Maritsa (riv.), Bul. 62/C4
Mariupol' (int'l arpt.), Ukr. 62/F3
Mariupol', Ukr. 62/F3
Marj 'Uyūn, Leb. 91/D3
Mark (riv.), Belg. 50/B6
Mark Twain (lake), Mo, US 129/J3
Mark Twain NWR, Mo, US 137/G8
Mark Twain NWR, Il, US 137/F7
Marka (riv.), Ger. 51/E3
Marka (Merca), Som. 97/P7
Markam, China 83/G2
Markaryd, Swe. 38/E3
Markdorf, Ger. 57/F2
Markelsdorfer (pt.), Ger. 38/D4
Marken (isl.), Neth. 50/C4
Markerwaard (polder), Neth. 50/C3
Market Harborough, Eng, UK 33/F2
Markgroningen, Ger. 54/C5
Markham, On, Can. 131/R8
Markham (bay), Nun., Can. 123/J2
Marki, Pol. 41/L2
Markinch, Sc, UK 36/C4
Markit, China 87/G5
Markleeville, Ca, US 128/C3
Markneukirchen, Ger. 55/F2
Markópoulon, Gre. 47/N9
Markovac, Yugo. 48/E3
Marks, Rus. 63/H2
Marksville, La, US 129/J5
Markt Bibart, Ger. 54/D3
Markt Erlbach, Ger. 54/D4
Markt Indersdorf, Ger. 55/E6
Markt Rettenbach, Ger. 57/G2
Markt Sankt Florian, Aus. 55/H6
Markt Schwaben, Ger. 55/E6
Marktbreit, Ger. 54/D3
Marktheidenfeld, Ger. 54/C3
Marktl, Ger. 55/F6
Marktoberdorf, Ger. 57/G2
Marktredwitz, Ger. 55/F3
Marl, Ger. 51/E5
Marla, Austl. 113/G3
Marlboro, NJ, US 138/D3
Marlboro (Upper Marlboro), Md, US 138/B6
Marle, Fr. 52/C4
Marlengo (Marling), It. 57/H4
Marlenheim, Fr. 53/G6
Marles-en-Brie, Fr. 30/L5
Marles-les-Mines, Fr. 52/B3
Marlow, Eng, UK 33/F3
Marlow, Ger. 38/E4
Marlton, NJ, US 138/D4
Marly, Fr. 53/F5
Marly, Fr. 52/C3
Marly-la-Ville, Fr. 30/K4
Marly-le-Roi, Fr. 30/J5
Marmagão, India 89/K5
Marmande, Fr. 42/D4
Marmara, Turk. 49/H5
Marmara (isl.), Turk. 49/H5
Marmara (sea), Turk. 62/D4
Marmaraereğlisi, Turk. 49/H5
Marmaris, Turk. 90/B2
Marmelos (riv.), Braz. 150/F5
Marmion (lake), Austl. 109/A3
Marmirolo, It. 59/D2
Marmolada (peak), It. 43/J3
Marmolejo, Sp. 44/C3
Marmontana (peak), It. 57/F5
Marmora, NJ, US 138/D5
Marmoutier, Fr. 53/G6
Marnay, Fr. 56/B3
Marnaz, Fr. 56/C5
Marne (riv.), Fr. 42/F2
Marne, Ger. 38/C5
Marne (dept.), Fr. 52/C6
Marne au Rhin, Canal de la (canal), Fr. 53/D6
Maro Reef (reef), Hi, US 117/H2
Maroa, Ven. 153/E4
Maroantsetra, Madg. 107/J6
Marokau (isl.), FrPol. 117/L6
Marolambo, Madg. 107/J8
Maroldsweisach, Ger. 54/D2
Marolles-en-Brie, Fr. 30/M5
Marolles-en-Hurepoix, Fr. 30/J6
Maromokotro (peak), Madg. 107/J6
Marondera, Zim. 105/F4
Marone, It. 58/D1
Maroni (riv.), FrG.,Sur. 147/D2
Maroochydore-Mooloolaba, Austl. 114/D4
Maroon Town, Jam. 145/G2
Marostica, It. 59/E1
Marotandrano, Madg. 107/J7
Marotiri (Bass Is.) (isls.), FrPol. 117/L7
Marotta, It. 59/G5
Maroua, Camr. 96/H5
Marouini (riv.), FrG. 153/H4
Marovato, Madg. 107/J6
Marovoay, Madg. 107/H7
Marowijne (dist.), Sur. 153/H3
Marpingen, Ger. 53/G5
Marple, Eng, UK 35/F5
Marquan (riv.), China 82/E2
Marquard, SAfr. 106/D3
Marquarie (riv.), Austl. 116/D8
Marquesas (isls.), FrPol. 117/M5
Marquise, Fr. 52/A2
Marracuene, Moz. 107/F2
Marradi, It. 59/E4
Marrah (mts.), Sudan 97/K5
Marrah (peak), Sudan 97/K5
Marrakech, Mor. 98/D3
Marrero, La, US 137/P17
Marromeu, Moz. 105/G4
Marrupa, Moz. 105/G3
Mars (peak), It. 58/A1
Marsá al Burayqah, Libya 96/J1
Marsá Maṭrūḩ (cap.), Egypt 101/A2
Marsabit, Kenya 104/C2
Marsabit Nat'l Rsv., Kenya 104/C2
Marsala, It. 46/C4
Marsange (riv.), Fr. 30/L5
Marsannay, Fr. 56/A3
Marsberg, Ger. 51/F6
Marsciano, It. 43/K5
Marsdiep Texelstroom (chan.), Neth. 50/B3
Marseille, Fr. 42/F5
Marseille-en-Beauvaisis, Fr. 52/A4
Marsh (isl.), La, US 140/C2
Marshall, Sk, Can. 126/F2
Marshall, Mn, US 127/K4
Marshall, Tx, US 129/J4
Marshall, Mo, US 129/J3
Marshall, Co, US 137/B3
Marshall, Ut, US 137/J12
Marshall (riv.), Austl. 113/H2
Marshall Islands (ctry.) 116/G3
Marshallton, De, US 138/C4
Marshalltown, Ia, US 127/K5
Marshdale, Co, US 137/B3
Marshfield, Mo, US 129/J3
Märsta, Swe. 38/G2
Marston (lake), Co, US 137/B3
Marsyandi (riv.), Nepal 85/E1
Marta, It. 46/B1
Marta (mts.), Col. 145/H4
Martaban, Myan. 78/B2
Martaban (gulf), Myan. 78/B2
Martapura, Indo. 80/D4
Marte R. Gomez, Mex. 142/C3
Martelange, Belg. 53/E4
Martellago, It. 59/F1
Martensville, Sk, Can. 126/G2
Martfeld, Ger. 51/G3
Martha's Vineyard (isl.), Ma, US 131/G3
Martignacco, It. 59/G1
Martigny, Swi. 56/D5
Martigny-les-Bains, Fr. 56/B1
Martigues, Fr. 42/F5
Martil, Mor. 100/B2
Martin, Tn, US 130/B4
Martin (lake), Al, US 133/G3
Martin Vaz (isls.), Braz. 151/N8
Martina Franca, It. 47/E2
Martinengo, It. 58/C1
Martinez, Ga, US 133/H3
Martínez de la Torre, Mex. 143/M6
Martinho Campos, Braz. 155/C1
Martinique (isl.), Fr. 141/N9
Martinique Passage (chan.), Dom.,Mart. 141/J4
Martínon, Gre. 47/H3
Martinópole, Braz. 154/B1
Martinópolis, Braz. 155/B2
Martins, Braz. 154/C2
Martins Creek, Pa, US 138/C2
Martinsburg, WV, US 130/E4
Martinsville, Va, US 130/E4
Martorell, Sp. 45/K7
Martos, Sp. 44/D4
Martre (riv.), Qu, Can. 130/F1
Martres-Tolosane, Fr. 42/D5
Marty, SD, US 127/J5
Marugame, Japan 74/C3
Maruim, Braz. 154/C3
Maruko, Japan 75/F2
Marum, Neth. 50/D2
Maruoka, Japan 74/E2
Marutea (isl.), FrPol. 117/M7
Marv Dasht, Iran 88/F3
Marxheim, Ger. 54/D5
Mary, Trkm. 89/H1
Mary Anne Passage, Austl. 112/B2
Mary Esther, Fl, US 133/G4
Mary-sur-Marne, Fr. 30/M4
Maryborough, Austl. 115/B3
Maryborough, Austl. 114/D4
Marydale, SAfr. 106/C3
Marydel, Md, US 138/C5
Maryfield, Sk, Can. 127/H3
Maryland (co.), Libr. 102/C5
Maryland (state), US 130/E4
Maryland City, Md, US 138/B5
Maryland Heights, Mo, US 137/G8
Maryland Line, Md, US 138/B4
Marystown, Nf, Can. 131/L2
Marysville, Ks, US 129/H3
Marysville, Pa, US 138/B3
Maryville, Tn, US 133/H3
Maryville, Il, US 137/H8
Marzabotto, It. 59/E4
Marzano (peak), It. 46/D2
Marzo (pt.), Col. 152/B3
Marzūq, Libya 96/H2
Masada (ruin), Isr. 91/D4
Masai Mara Nat'l Rsv., Kenya 105/F1
Masai Steppe (grsld.), Tanz. 104/C4
Masaka, Ugan. 104/A3
Masākin, Tun. 46/B5
Masamagrell, Sp. 45/E3
Masamba, Indo. 81/F4
Masan, SKor. 73/E5
Masangwe (hill), Tanz. 104/A4
Masaya, Nic. 144/E4
Masbate (isl.), Phil. 116/B3
Mascara, Alg. 100/F5
Mascarene (isls.), Mrts 107/T15
Mascota, Mex. 142/D4
Mascouche, Qu, Can. 131/N6
Maselheim, Ger. 57/F1
Maserà di Padova, It. 59/E2
Maseru (cap.), Les. 106/D3
Masevaux, Fr. 56/D2
Masfjorden, Nor. 38/A1
Mashan, China 79/A3
Mashhad (int'l arpt.), Iran 87/C5
Mashike, Japan 76/B2
Māshkīd (riv.), Iran 89/H3
Mashtūl as Sūq, Egypt 91/B4
Mashū (lake), Japan 76/D2
Masiaca, Mex. 142/C3
Maside, Sp. 44/A1
Masim (peak), Rus. 63/L1
Masindi, Ugan. 104/A2
Maşīrah, Jazīrat (isl.), Oman 67/F5
Masisea, Peru 156/C3
Masjed-e Soleymān, Iran 88/E2
Mask (lake), Ire. 31/P10
Masker (peak), Mor. 98/D2
Masnou, Sp. 45/L7
Masoala (pen.), Madg. 105/L10
Masoala (cape), Madg. 107/J6
Masoarivo, Madg. 107/H7
Mason, Mi, US 130/C3
Mason, Tx, US 129/H5
Mason (lake), Wa, US 135/B3
Mason (co.), Wa, US 135/A3
Mason and Dixon Line, Pa, US 138/B4
Masone, It. 58/B4
Masonville, Co, US 137/B2
Masquefa, Sp. 45/K6
Massa, It. 58/D4
Massa-Carrara (prov.), It. 58/C4
Massa Finalese, It. 59/E3
Massa Fiscaglia, It. 59/F3
Massa Lombarda, It. 59/E4
Massa Marittima, It. 43/J5
Massa Martana, It. 43/K5
Massachusetts (bay), Ma, US 131/G3
Massachusetts (state), US 131/F3
Massaciuccoli, Lago di (lake), It. 58/D5
Massafra, It. 47/E2
Massangena, Moz. 105/F5
Massapê, Braz. 154/B1
Massapequa, NY, US 139/M9
Massapequa Park, NY, US 139/M9
Massarosa, It. 58/D5
Massbach, Ger. 54/D2
Massena, NY, US 131/F2
Masset, BC, Can. 134/M4
Massey (sound), Nun., Can. 123/S7
Massey, Md, US 138/C5
Massillon, Oh, US 130/D3
Massy, Fr. 30/J5
Masterton, NZ 117/T11
Mastgat (chan.), Neth. 50/B5
Mastic, NY, US 139/F2
Mastic Beach, NY, US 139/F2
Mastník (riv.), Czh. 55/H3
Mastūj (riv.), Pak. 86/A2
Mastung, Pak. 89/J3
Masuda, Japan 74/B3
Masuho, Japan 77/A2
Masurai (peak), Indo. 80/B4
Masvingo, Zim. 105/F5
Maswa Game Rsv., Tanz. 104/B3
Maşyāf, Syria 91/E2
Mat (riv.), Alb. 47/F2
Mata Grande, Braz. 154/C3
Mata Utu, Fr. 117/H6
Mātābhānga, India 85/G2
Matadi, D.R. Congo 105/B2
Matador, Tx, US 129/G4
Matagalpa, Nic. 144/E3
Matagami (lake), Qu, Can. 130/E1
Matagorda (bay), Tx, US 140/B2
Matagorda (isl.), Tx, US 140/B2
Matale, SrL. 82/D6
Matam, Sen. 102/B3
Matamoras, Pa, US 138/D1
Matamoros, Mex. 142/E3
Ma'ṭan as Sarra (well), Libya 97/K3
Matandu (riv.), Tanz. 104/C5
Matane (riv.), Qu, Can. 131/H1
Matane, Qu, Can. 131/H1
Matanga, Madg. 107/H8
Matanzas, Cuba 140/E3
Matão, Braz. 155/B2
Matape (riv.), Mex. 142/C2
Matapedia (riv.), Qu, Can. 131/H1
Mataquito (riv.), Chile 158/C2
Matara (ruin), Erit. 88/C6
Matara, SrL. 82/D6
Mataram, Indo. 81/E5
Mataránga, Gre. 47/G3
Mataró, Sp. 45/L6
Matatiele, SAfr. 106/E3
Mataura (riv.), NZ 117/R12
Matawan, NJ, US 139/J10
Matehuala, Mex. 143/E4
Matéri, Ben. 103/F4
Maternillos (pt.), Cuba 141/F3
Mátészalka, Hun. 41/M5
Mathay, Fr. 56/C3
Matheniko Game Rsv., Ugan. 104/B2
Mathew's (peak), Kenya 104/C2
Mathews (lake), Ca, US 136/C3
Mathis, Tx, US 132/D4
Mathoura, Austl. 115/C2
Mathurā, India 84/A2
Mati, Phil. 81/G2
Matias Barbosa, Braz. 211/K6
Matias Olímpio, Braz. 154/B1
Matías Romero, Mex. 144/C2
Matíguas, Nic. 144/E3
Matilija (dam), Ca, US 136/A2
Matinha, Braz. 154/A2
Matinhos, Braz. 155/B3
Matinicock (pt.), NY, US 139/L8
Mātir, Tun. 46/A4
Matiyuri (riv.), Ven. 152/D3
Mātla (riv.), India 85/G5
Matlock, Eng, UK 35/G5
Mato Grosso (plat.), Braz. 147/D4
Mato Grosso do Sul (state), Braz. 155/A1
Mato Grosso, Planalto do (plat.), Braz. 151/H6
Mato Verde, Braz. 154/B4
Matopos, Zim. 105/E5
Matosinhos, Port. 44/A2
Matoya (bay), Japan 77/L7
Maṭraḩ, Oman 89/G4
Matrei am Brenner, Aus. 57/H3
Matrei in Osttirol, Aus. 43/K3
Matriz de Camaragibe, Braz. 154/D3
Matroosberg (peak), SAfr. 106/L10
Matsalu (gulf), Est. 39/K2
Matsapa (Manzini) (int'l arpt.), Swaz. 107/E2
Matsiatra (riv.), Madg. 107/H8
Matsoandakana, Madg. 107/J6
Matsubara, Japan 77/J6
Matsubushi, Japan 77/D2
Matsuda, Japan 77/C3
Matsudo, Japan 77/D2
Matsue, Japan 74/C3
Matsuida, Japan 77/B1
Matsumae, Japan 76/B3
Matsumoto, Japan 75/E2
Matsuo, Japan 77/E2
Matsusaka, Japan 77/L6
Matsushima, Japan 76/B4
Matsutō, Japan 74/E2
Matsuyama, Japan 74/C4
Matt, Swi. 57/F4
Mattagami (riv.), On, Can. 130/D1
Mattarello, It. 57/H6
Mattawa, On, Can. 130/E2
Matterhorn (peak), It.,Swi. 56/D6
Mattertal (valley), Swi. 56/D5
Mattese, Mo, US 137/G9
Matthews (mtn.), Ak, US 134/H2
Mattig (riv.), Aus. 55/G6
Mattighofen, Aus. 55/G6
Mattituck, NY, US 139/F2
Mattmarksee (lake), Swi. 56/D5
Mattō, Japan 74/E2
Mattock (riv.), Ire. 34/B4
Mattsee, Aus. 55/G7
Matucana, Peru 156/B3
Maturín, Ven. 153/F2
Matusadona NP, Zim. 105/E4
Matutum (mt.), Phil. 81/G2
Matzen, Aus. 49/P7
Maú (riv.), Guy. 150/G3
Mau (peak), Kenya 104/B3
Mau Aimma, India 84/C3
Mau Rānīpur, India 84/B3
Mauá, Braz. 155/C2
Maubert-Fontaine, Fr. 53/D4
Maubeuge, Fr. 52/C3
Maubourguet, Fr. 42/D5
Mauchline, Sc, UK 36/B5
Maud (pt.), Austl. 112/B2
Maud, Sc, UK 36/D1
Maudaha, India 84/C3
Mauerbach, Aus. 49/N7
Mauerkirchen, Aus. 55/G6
Maués, Braz. 150/G2
Maués Açu (riv.), Braz. 150/G4
Maug (isls.), NMar. 116/D2
Mauganj, India 84/C3
Maughold, IM, UK 34/D3
Maughold (pt.), IM, UK 34/D3
Mauguio, Fr. 42/F5
Maui (isl.), Hi, US 117/K2
Mauke (isl.), CookIs. 117/K7
Maulbronn, Ger. 54/B5
Mauldre (riv.), Fr. 52/A6
Maule (pol. reg.), Chile 158/B2
Maule (riv.), Chile 158/C2
Maule, Fr. 30/H5
Mauléon, Fr. 42/C3
Maullín, Chile 158/B4
Maumee (riv.), In,Oh, US 130/C3
Maun, Bots. 105/D4
Mauna Kea (peak), Hi, US 124/U11
Mauna Loa (peak), Hi, US 124/U11
Maunath Bhanjan, India 84/D3
Maungdaw, Myan. 83/F3
Mauperthuis, Fr. 30/M5
Maupertus (int'l arpt.), Fr. 42/C2
Maupiti (isl.), FrPol. 117/K6
Maur, Swi. 57/E3
Maurāwān, India 84/C2
Maurecourt, Fr. 30/J5
Maurepas (lake), La, US 137/P16
Maurepas, Fr. 52/A6
Mauriac, Fr. 42/E4
Maurice (lake), Austl. 109/C3
Maurice (riv.), NJ, US 138/C5
Mauricetown, NJ, US 138/D5
Maurienne (valley), Fr. 43/G4
Maurilândia, Braz. 155/B1
Mauritania (ctry.) 96/C4
Mauriti, Braz. 154/C2
Mauritius (ctry.) 107/T15
Mauston, Wi, US 127/L5
Mauthausen, Aus. 55/H6
Mauvoisin, Barrage de (dam), Swi. 56/D6
Mavrommátion, Gre. 47/H3
Mavrovo NP, FYROM 47/G2
Maw Daung (pass), Thai. 78/B4
Mawāna, India 84/A1
Mawlaik, Myan. 83/F3
Mawlamyine (Moulmein), Myan. 78/B2
Mawson, Austl., Ant. 160/E
Maxaranguape, Braz. 154/D2
Maxcanú, Mex. 144/D1
Maxdorf, Ger. 54/B4
Maxéville, Fr. 53/F6
Maxhütte-Haidhof, Ger. 55/F4
May (cape), NJ, US 138/D5
May-en-Multien, Fr. 30/M4
May, Isle of (isl.), Sc, UK 36/D4
May Pen, Jam. 145/G2
Maya (isl.), Indo. 80/C4
Maya (riv.), Rus. 67/N4
Maya (mts.), Guat. 144/D2
Maya-san (peak), Japan 77/H6
Mayaguana (isl.), Bahm. 141/G3
Mayaguana Passage (chan.), Bahm. 145/H1
Mayagüez, PR 141/M8
Mayakovskogo (peak), Taj. 89/K1
Mayang, China 83/J2
Mayarí, Cuba 145/H1
Maybee, Mi, US 135/E8
Maybole, Sc, UK 36/B6
Maydān, Iraq 88/E2
Mayen, Ger. 53/G3
Mayenne, Fr. 42/C2
Mayenne (riv.), Fr. 42/C3
Mayerthorpe, Ab, Can. 126/E2
Mayfield, Ky, US 130/B4
Mayfield, Sc, UK 36/C5
Maykop, Rus. 62/G3
Maymyo, Myan. 83/G3
Maynooth, Ire. 31/Q10
Mayo (riv.), Arg. 157/B6
Mayo, Yk, Can. 134/L3
Mayo, Md, US 138/B6
Mayotte (isl.), May. 107/H6
Mays Landing, NJ, US 138/D5
Maysville, Ky, US 130/D4
Maythalūn, WBnk. 91/G7
Mayville, ND, US 127/J4
Maywood, NJ, US 139/J8
Maywood, Il, US 135/Q16
Maywood, Ca, US 136/F8
Mazabuka, Zam. 105/E4
Mazagão, Braz. 151/H4
Mazamet, Fr. 42/E5
Mazán, Peru 156/C1
Mazār-e Sharīf, Afg. 89/J1
Mazara del Vallo, It. 46/C4
Mazara, Val di (valley), It. 46/C4
Mazarrón, Sp. 44/E4
Mazaruni (riv.), Guy. 150/G2
Mazatán, Mex. 142/C2
Mazatenango, Guat. 144/D3
Mazatlán, Mex. 142/D4
Mažeikiai, Lith. 39/K3
Mazeppa NP, Austl. 114/B3
Mazgirt, Turk. 90/D2
Mazıkıran (pass), Turk. 90/D2
Mazingarbe, Fr. 52/B3
Mazocruz, Peru 156/D5
Mazong (peak), China 70/G3
Mazury (reg.), Pol. 41/L2
Mazyr, Bela. 62/D1
Mbabala (isl.), Zam. 104/A5
Mbabane (cap.), Swaz. 107/E2
Mbabo (peak), Camr. 96/H6
Mbacké, Sen. 102/B3
Mbaïki, CAfr. 96/J7
Mbakaou, Lac de (lake), Camr. 96/H6
Mbala, Zam. 104/A5
Mbale, Ugan. 104/B2
Mbalmayo, Camr. 96/H7
Mbandaka, D.R. Congo 97/J7
Mbarangandu (riv.), Tanz. 104/C5
Mbarara, Ugan. 104/A3
Mbata, CAfr. 97/J7
Mbeya (peak), Tanz. 104/B5
Mbeya (range), Tanz. 105/F2
Mbeya, Tanz. 104/B5
Mbeya (pol. reg.), Tanz. 104/B5
Mbini, EqG. 96/G7
Mbini (riv.), EqG.,Gabo 96/H7
Mbirizi, Ugan. 104/A3
Mbomou (riv.), CAfr. 97/L6
M'Bour, Sen. 102/A3
Mbuji-Mayi, D.R. Congo 105/D2
Mbwemburu (riv.), Tanz. 104/C5
McAdoo, Pa, US 138/C2
McAfee, NJ, US 138/D1
McAlester, Ok, US 129/J4
McAlisterville, Pa, US 138/A2
McAllen, Tx, US 132/D5
McBride, BC, Can. 126/C2
McCall, Id, US 126/D4
McCarran (int'l arpt.), Nv, US 128/D3
McCarthy, Ak, US 134/K3
McClain (co.), Ok, US 137/M15
McClure, Pa, US 138/A2
McClusky, ND, US 127/H4
McClusky, Il, US 137/G7
McComb, Ms, US 129/K5
McConaughy (lake), Ne, US 127/H5
McCook, Ne, US 129/G2
McCormick, SC, US 133/H3
McCreary, Mb, Can. 127/J3
McCullom Lake, Il, US 135/P15
McDaniel, Md, US 138/B6
McDermitt, Nv, US 126/D5
McDonald (mt.), Ak, US 134/F3
McDonald (isls.), Austl. 23/N8
McDonnell (mt.), Austl. 113/H5
McDougall (pass), NW,Yk, Can. 134/L2
McDowell (mts.), Az, US 137/S18
McElhattan, Pa, US 138/A1
McGhee Tyson (int'l arpt.), Tn, US 133/H3
McGrath, Ak, US 134/G3
McGregor (riv.), BC, Can. 126/C2
McGregor, On, Can. 135/G7
McHenry (co.), Il, US 135/N15
McKean (isl.), Kiri. 117/H5
McKeand (riv.), Nun., Can. 123/K2
McKee City, NJ, US 138/D5
McKeesport, Pa, US 130/E3
McKenzie, Tn, US 130/B4
McKinlay, Austl. 114/A3
McKinley (mt.), Ak, US 134/H3
McKinleyville, Ca, US 126/B5
McLaughlin, SD, US 127/H4
McLean, Va, US 138/A6
McLennan, Ab, Can. 126/D2
McLeod (riv.), BC, Can. 126/D2
McLeod (lake), Austl. 109/A3
McLeod (bay), NW, Can. 122/E2
McLeod Lake, BC, Can. 126/C2
M'Clintock (chan.), Nun., Can. 122/F1
McLoud, Ok, US 137/N15
M'Clure (str.), NW, Can. 123/Q7
McMinnville, Or, US 126/C4
McMinnville, Tn, US 130/C5
McMurdo, US, Ant. 160/M
McNeil (isl.), Wa, US 135/B3

207

Milev – Mont-R

Milevsko, Czh. 55/H4
Milford (lake), Ks, US 132/D2
Milford, Ut, US 128/D3
Milford, NJ, US 138/C2
Milford, Ct, US 139/E1
Milford, De, US 138/C6
Milford, Mi, US 135/E6
Milford Haven, Wal, UK 32/A3
Milford Haven (inlet), Wal., UK 32/A3
Milgis (riv.), Kenya 104/C2
Mili (isl.), Mrsh. 116/G4
Miliana, Alg. 100/G4
Milicz, Pol. 41/J3
Mililani Town, Hi, US 124/V13
Milk (hill), Eng, UK 33/E4
Milk (riv.), Can.,US 122/F4
Milk River, Ab, Can. 126/E3
Mill (isl.), Nun., Can. 123/J2
Mill (riv.), Ct, US 139/E1
Mill Neck, NY, US 139/L8
Millaa Millaa, Austl. 114/B2
Millau, Fr. 42/E4
Millbrae, Ca, US 135/K11
Millbrook (res.), Austl. 113/M8
Millburn, NJ, US 139/H9
Millcreek, Ut, US 137/K12
Mille Îles (riv.), Qu, Can. 131/N6
Mille Lacs (lake), Mn, US 125/H2
Milledgeville, Ga, US 133/H3
Miller, SD, US 127/J4
Miller (int'l arpt.), Tx, US 143/F3
Millerovo, Rus. 63/G2
Millers Ferry (dam), Al, US 133/G3
Millersburg, Pa, US 138/B2
Millerstown, Pa, US 138/A2
Millersville, Pa, US 138/B4
Millesimo, It. 58/B4
Milleur (pt.), Sc, UK 34/C1
Millevaches (plat.), Fr. 42/D4
Millgrove, On, Can. 131/Q9
Millicent, Austl. 115/B3
Milliken, Co, US 137/C2
Millingen aan de Rijn, Neth. 50/D5
Millington, Md, US 138/C5
Millinocket, Me, US 131/G2
Millisle, NI, UK 34/C2
Millmerran, Austl. 114/C4
Millmont, Pa, US 138/A2
Millport, Sc, UK 36/B5
Mills Junction, Ut, US 137/J12
Millstadt, Il, US 137/G9
Millstone (riv.), NJ, US 138/D3
Millstream-Chichester NP, Austl. 112/C2
Millthorpe, Austl. 115/D2
Milltown, NJ, US 139/H10
Milltown Malbay, Ire. 31/P10
Millville, Pa, US 138/B1
Millville, NJ, US 138/C5
Millwood (lake), Ar, US 132/E3
Milmay, NJ, US 138/D5
Milnathort, Wal, UK 35/E5
Milne (bay), PNG 116/E5
Milngavie, Sc, UK 36/B5
Milnrow, Eng, UK 35/F4
Milo, Me, US 131/G2
Milo (riv.), Gui. 102/C4
Miloli'i, Hi, US 124/U11
Milos (isl.), Gre. 47/J4
Mílos, Gre. 47/J4
Milseburg (peak), Ger. 54/C1
Miltenberg, Ger. 54/C3
Milton, Austl. 115/D2
Milton, Fl, US 133/G4
Milton, NH, US 131/G3
Milton, On, Can. 131/Q8
Milton, NZ 117/R12
Milton (res.), Co, US 137/C2
Milton, Ut, US 137/K11
Milton, Pa, US 138/B1
Milton, Wa, US 135/C3
Milton-Freewater, Or, US 126/D4
Milton Keynes, Eng, UK 33/F2
Milton Keynes (co.), Eng, UK 33/F2
Milton Ness (pt.), Sc, UK 36/D3
Milton of Campsie, Sc, UK 36/B5
Milwaukee, Wi, US 127/M5
Milwaukee (co.), Wi, US 135/P14
Milz (riv.), Ger. 54/D2
Mimi (riv.), Japan 74/B4
Mimizan, Fr. 42/C4
Mimmaya, Japan 76/B3
Min (riv.), China 70/H5
Min Xian, China 70/H5
Mīna (riv.), Alg. 100/F5
Mīnāb, Iran 89/G3
Minahasa (pen), Indo. 81/F3
Minakuchi, Japan 77/K6
Minamata, Japan 74/B4
Minami Alps NP, Japan 75/F3
Minami-tori-shima (isl.), Japan 116/E2
Minamiaiki, Japan 77/B1
Minamiashigara, Japan 77/C3
Minamichita, Japan 77/L6
Minamidaitō (isl.), Japan 75/L8
Minamiiō (isl.), Japan 116/D2
Minamikawara, Japan 77/C1
Minamimaki, Japan 77/A2
Minamiyamashiro, Japan 77/J6
Minano, Japan 77/C1
Minas (peak), Ecu. 152/B5
Minas, Cuba 145/G1
Minas, Uru. 159/G2
Minas de Matahambre, Cuba 145/F1
Minas de Ríotinto, Sp. 44/B4
Minas Gerais (state), Braz. 154/A5
Minas Novas, Braz. 154/B5
Minatitlán, Mex. 144/C2
Minbu, Myan. 83/F3
Minbya, Myan. 83/F3
Minch, The (North Minch) (str.), Sc, UK 31/Q8
Minchinābād, Pak. 86/B4
Minchinmávida (vol.), Chile 158/B4
Mincio (riv.), It. 59/D2
Mindanao (sea), Phil. 81/F2
Mindanao (isl.), Phil. 67/M9
Mindel (riv.), Ger. 40/F4
Mindelheim, Ger. 57/G1
Mindelo, CpV. 93/J10
Minden, La, US 129/J4
Minden, Ne, US 129/H2
Minden, Ger. 51/F4
Mindoro (str.), Phil. 79/C5
Mindoro (isl.), Phil. 67/L8
Mine (pt.), Ire. 31/Q10
Mineiros, Braz. 151/H7
Mineola, Tx, US 129/J4
Mineola, NY, US 139/L8
Mineral del Monte, Mex. 143/L6
Mineral Wells, Tx, US 129/H4
Mineral'nye Vody (int'l arpt.), Rus. 63/G3
Mineral'nye Vody, Rus. 63/G3
Minerbe, It. 59/E2
Minerbio, It. 59/E3
Minerbio (pt.), Fr. 43/H5
Minersville, Pa, US 138/B2
Minfeld, Ger. 54/B4
Minfeng, China 70/D4
Ming (riv.), China 83/J3
Mingäçevir, Azer. 63/H4
Mingäçevir Su Anbari (res.), Azer. 63/H4
Mingan (riv.), Qu, Can. 131/J1
Mingāora, Pak. 86/B2
Mingenew, Austl. 112/B4
Minglanilla, Sp. 44/E3
Mingshui, China 71/N2
Mingxi, China 79/C2
Minhe, China 70/H4
Minhla, Myan. 83/G4
Minho (riv.), Sp. 44/A1
Minigwal (lake), Austl. 112/D4
Minitonas, Mb, Can. 127/H2
Minlaton, Austl. 113/H5
Minle, China 70/H4
Minna, Nga. 103/G4
Minneapolis, Mn, US 127/K4
Minneapolis-St. Paul (Wold-Chamberlain) (int'l arpt.), Mn, US 127/K4
Minnedosa, Mb, Can. 127/J3
Minnesota (riv.), Mn, US 127/K4
Minnesota (state), US 127/K4
Minnigaff, Sc, UK 34/D2
Minnis (lake), On, Can. 130/B1
Minnitaki (lake), On, Can. 127/K3
Miño (riv.), Port.,Sp. 44/A1
Mino, Japan 77/L4
Minobu, Japan 75/F3
Minokamo, Japan 77/M5
Mino'o, Japan 77/H6
Mino'o (riv.), Japan 77/H6
Minori, Japan 77/E1
Minot, ND, US 127/H3
Minqin, China 70/H4
Minqing, China 79/C2
Minquan, China 72/C4
Minsener Oog (isl.), Ger. 51/E1
Minsk (cap.), Bela. 39/M5
Minsk (int'l arpt.), Bela. 39/M5
Mińsk Mazowiecki, Pol. 41/L2
Minskaya (prov.), Bela. 62/C1
Mintaka (pass), Pak. 87/F5
Mintaka (pass), China 89/K1
Mintlaw, Sc, UK 36/E1
Minto, Ak, US 134/J2
Minto, NB, Can. 131/H2
Minto (inlet), NW, Can. 122/E1
Minūf, Egypt 91/B4
Minusinsk, Rus. 64/K4
Minusio, Swi. 57/E5
Minyā al Qamḩ, Egypt 91/B4
Minyip, Austl. 115/B3
Miquan, China 70/E3
Mira, Port. 44/A2
Mira (riv.), Col. 152/B4
Mira Loma, Ca, US 136/C2
Mira Monte, Ca, US 136/A2
Mira Taglio, It. 59/F2
Mirabel (int'l arpt.), Qu, Can. 131/M6
Mirabel, Qu, Can. 131/M6
Mirabela, Braz. 154/A5
Mirabello, It. 59/E3
Miracema, Braz. 155/D2
Miracema do Norte, Braz. 151/J5
Miradolo Terme, It. 58/C2
Mirador, Braz. 154/A2
Mirador (pass), Chile 158/C4
Miraflores, Peru 156/B3
Miraflores, Mex. 142/C4
Miraflores, Col. 152/C4
Miraflores, Col. 152/C3
Miragoâne, Haiti 145/H2
Miraj, India 89/K5
Miramar, Ca, US 136/C5
Miramar, Arg. 158/F3
Miramar Naval Air Station, Ca, US 136/C5
Mirambéllou (gulf), Gre. 47/J5
Miramichi, NB, Can. 131/H2
Miramont-de-Guyenne, Fr. 42/D4
Miranda (riv.), Braz. 151/G8
Miranda de Ebro, Sp. 44/D1
Miranda do Corvo, Port. 44/A2
Miranda do Douro, Port. 44/B2
Mirande, Fr. 42/D5
Mirandela, Port. 44/B2
Mirandola, It. 43/J4
Mirandópolis, Braz. 155/B2
Mirano, It. 59/F2
Mīrānpur, India 84/A1
Mirante do Paranapanema, Braz. 155/B2
Mirassol, Braz. 155/B2
Miravalles (peak), Sp. 44/B1
Miravalles (vol.), CR 144/E4
Mirebalais, Haiti 145/H2
Mirebeau, Fr. 56/B3
Mirecourt, Fr. 56/C1
Mirfield, Eng, UK 35/G4
Miri, Malay. 80/D3
Miriam Vale, Austl. 114/C4
Mirim (lake), Braz. 157/F3
Mirimire, Ven. 152/D2
Mirina, Gre. 47/J3
Miritiparaná (riv.), Col. 152/D5
Mirna (riv.), Cro. 59/G2
Mirnyy, Rus. 65/M3
Mirnyy, Rus., Ant. 160/G
Mirond (lake), Sk, Can. 127/H2
Mirow, Ger. 40/G2
Mirror (lake), NJ, US 138/D4
Mirtóön (sea), Gre. 47/H4
Miryang, SKor. 74/A3
Mīrzāpur, India 84/D3
Misa (riv.), It. 59/G5
Misāha (well), Egypt 101/A4
Misaka, Japan 77/B2
Misaki, Japan 74/D3
Misaki, Japan 77/E3
Misano Adriatico, It. 59/F5
Misantla, Mex. 143/N7
Misato, Japan 77/C1
Misato, Japan 77/D2
Misato, Japan 77/K6
Misawa, Japan 76/B3
Mishan, China 71/P2
Mishawaka, In, US 130/C3
Misheguk (mtn.), Ak, US 134/F2
Mishima, Japan 75/F3
Misilmeri, It. 46/C3
Misiones, Sierra de (mts.), Arg. 157/E2
Miskitos, Cayos (isls.), Nic. 140/E5
Miskolc, Hun. 41/L4
Misono, Japan 77/L6
Misool (isl.), Indo. 116/B5
Misquah (hills), Mn, US 127/L4
Mişrātah (pt.), Libya 97/L1
Mişrātah, Libya 96/J1
Missinaibi (lake), On, Can. 130/D1
Missinaibi (riv.), On, Can. 123/H3
Mission, Tx, US 132/D5
Mission (bay), Ca, US 136/C5
Mission, Ks, US 137/D5
Mission Beach, Austl. 114/B2
Mission Hills, Ks, US 137/D5
Mission Ind. Res., Ca, US 136/C4
Mission San Buenaventura, Ca, US 136/A2
Mission San Jose, Ca, US 135/L12
Mission San Juan Capistrano, Ca, US 136/C3
Mission Viejo, Ca, US 136/C3
Missisa (lake), On, Can. 127/M2
Missisicabi (riv.), Qu, Can. 130/E1
Mississauga, On, Can. 131/Q8
Mississippi (pt.), Austl. 112/D5
Mississippi (riv.), US 125/H5
Mississippi (delta), la, US 133/F4
Mississippi (state), US 133/F3
Mississippi River Gulf Outlet (canal), La, US 137/Q17
Missoula, Mt, US 126/E4
Missouri (state), US 129/J3
Missouri (riv.), US 125/G3
Missouri City, Tx, US 129/J5
Missouri City, Mo, US 137/E5
Mistaken (pt.), Nf, Can. 131/L2
Mistassibi (riv.), Qu, Can. 131/F1
Mistassibi Nord-Est (riv.), Qu, Can. 131/G1
Mistassini, Qu, Can. 131/F1
Mistassini (riv.), Qu, Can. 131/F1
Mistassini (lake), Qu, Can. 123/J3
Mistelbach an der Zaya, Aus. 43/M2
Misti (vol.), Peru 156/D5
Mistissini, Qu, Can. 130/F1
Mistrás (ruin), Gre. 47/H4
Mistretta, It. 46/D4
Misty Fjords Nat'l Mon., US 134/M4
Misty Fjords Nat'l Mon., Ak, US 122/C3
Misugi, Japan 77/K6
Mita, Punta de (pt.), Mex. 142/D4
Mitaka, Japan 77/D2
Mitake, Japan 77/M5
Mitama, Japan 77/B2
Mitare, Ven. 152/D2
Mitchell, SD, US 127/J5
Mitchell (mt.), NC, US 133/H3
Mitchell (riv.), Austl. 109/D2
Mitchell, Il, US 137/G8
Mitchell, Austl. 114/B4
Mitchell River NP, Austl. 115/D2
Mitha Tiwāna, Pak. 86/B3
Mithankot, Pak. 86/A5
Mithi, Pak. 89/J4
Mithimna, Gre. 47/K3
Mitiaro (isl.), Cookls. 117/K6
Mitilíni, Gre. 47/K3
Mitla (pass), Egypt 91/C4
Mitla (ruin), Mex. 144/B2
Mito, Japan 75/G2
Mito, Japan 77/M6
Mitomi, Japan 77/B2
Mitra (peak), EqG. 96/G7
Mitre (pen.), Arg. 157/C7
Mitry-Mory, Fr. 30/K5
Mitsamiouli, Com. 107/G5
Mitsinjo, Madg. 107/H7
Mitsio, Nosy (isl.), Madg. 107/J6
Mits'iwa, Erit. 97/N4
Mitsue, Japan 77/K7
Mitsukaidō, Japan 75/F2
Mitsuke, Japan 75/F2
Mittagong, Austl. 115/D2
Mittagspitze (peak), Aus. 57/F3
Mittainville, Fr. 30/G5
Mittelberg, Aus. 57/G3
Mittelland (canal), Ger. 51/F4
Mittelradde (riv.), Ger. 51/E3
Mittenwald, Ger. 57/H3
Mittersill, Aus. 43/K3
Mitterteich, Ger. 55/F3
Mittlere-Isar (canal), Ger. 55/E6
Mittweida, Ger. 40/G3
Mitú, Col. 152/D4
Mitumba, Monts (mts.), D.R. Congo 105/E1
Mitwitz, Ger. 54/E2
Miura (pen.), Japan 77/D3
Miura, Japan 77/D3
Miwa, Japan 77/H5
Miwa, Japan 77/L5
Mixco Viejo (ruin), Guat. 144/D3
Mixquiahuala, Mex. 143/K6
Mixteco (riv.), Mex. 144/B2
Miya (riv.), Japan 77/K7
Miyagawa, Japan 77/K7
Miyagi (pref.), Japan 76/B4
Miyake (isl.), Japan 75/F3
Miyako (isl.), Japan 79/E3
Miyako, Japan 76/B4
Miyako (isls.), Japan 75/H8
Miyakonojō, Japan 74/B5
Miyama, Japan 77/J5
Miyama, Japan 77/L4
Miyanojō, Japan 74/B5
Miyashiro, Japan 77/D2
Miyazaki (pref.), Japan 74/B4
Miyazaki, Japan 74/B5
Miyazu, Japan 77/H4
Miyazu (bay), Japan 77/H4
Miyi, China 83/H2
Miyoshi, Japan 74/C3
Miyoshi, Japan 77/D2
Miyoshi, Japan 77/D3
Miyoshi, Japan 77/M5
Miyota, Japan 77/B1
Miyun (res.), China 72/H6
Miyun, China 72/H6
Mizen (pt.), Ire. 34/B6
Miziya, Bul. 49/F4
Mizoram (state), India 70/F7
Mizpah, NJ, US 138/D5
Miẕpe Ramon, Isr. 91/D4
Mizuho, Japan 77/C2
Mizuho, Japan 77/H5
Mizunami, Japan 77/M5
Mizusawa, Japan 76/B4
Mjölby, Swe. 38/F2
Mjøndalen, Nor. 38/D2
Mjörn (lake), Swe. 38/E3
Mjøsa (lake), Nor. 37/D3
Mkata (plain), Tanz. 104/C4
Mkokotoni, Tanz. 104/C4
Mkomazi Game Rsv., Tanz. 104/C4
Mkombo (riv.), Tanz. 104/A4
Mkondoa (riv.), Tanz. 104/C4
Mkorn (peak), Mor. 98/D3
Mkumbi (pt.), Tanz. 104/C4
Mkushi, Zam. 105/E3
Mkuze (riv.), SAfr. 107/F2
Mladá Boleslav, Czh. 55/H2
Mladá Vožice, Czh. 55/H3
Mladenovac, Yugo. 48/E3
Mlala (hills), Tanz. 104/A4
Mława, Pol. 41/L2
Mljet (isl.), Cro. 47/E1
Mljet NP, Cro. 47/E1
Mmabatho, SAfr. 106/D2
Mnyera (riv.), Tanz. 104/B5
Mo Duc, Viet. 78/E3
Moa (isl.), Indo. 81/G5
Moa (riv.), SLeo. 102/C5
Moa, Cuba 145/H1
Moab, Ut, US 128/E3
Moala Group (isl.), Fiji 116/G6
Moama, Austl. 115/C1
Moamba, Moz. 107/F2
Moaña, Sp. 44/A1
Moanda, Gabon 96/H8
Moate, Ire. 31/Q10
Mobara, Japan 77/E3
Mobaye, CAfr. 97/K7
Moberly, Mo, US 129/J3
Moberly Lake, BC, Can. 126/C2
Mobile, Al, US 133/F4
Mobridge, SD, US 127/H4
Moca (pass), Turk. 91/C1
Mocache, Ecu. 152/B5
Mocajuba, Braz. 151/J4
Moçambique, Moz. 105/H4
Mocanaqua, Pa, US 138/B1
Mocha (riv.), Rus. 61/W9
Moche (ruin), Peru 156/B3
Mochima, PN, Ven. 153/E2
Mochizuki, Japan 77/A1
Mochudi, Bots. 105/E5
Mochumí, Peru 156/B2
Mocímboa da Praia, Moz. 104/D5
Möckeln (lake), Swe. 38/E3
Mockfjärd, Swe. 38/F1
Möckmühl, Ger. 54/C4
Moclín, Sp. 44/D4
Mocoa, Col. 152/B4
Mococa, Braz. 211/F6
Mocorito, Mex. 142/D3
Moctezuma, Mex. 143/E4
Moctezuma, Mex. 142/C2
Mocuba, Moz. 105/G4
Modāsa, India 89/K4
Modderrivier (riv.), SAfr. 106/D3
Modena (prov.), It. 59/D3
Modena, It. 59/D3
Moder (riv.), Fr. 43/G2
Modesto, Ca, US 128/B3
Modica, It. 46/D4
Modigliana, It. 59/E4
Modjeska, Ca, US 136/C3
Modjigo (reg.), Niger 96/H4
Mödling, Aus. 49/N7
Modot, Mong. 71/J2
Modriča, Bosn. 48/D3
Modugno, It. 46/E2
Moe, Austl. 115/C3
Moeb (bay), Namb. 106/A2
Moel-y-Llyn (peak), Wal, UK 32/C2
Moëlan-sur-Mer, Fr. 42/B3
Moelfre (peak), Wal, UK 32/C1
Moen, Nor. 37/F1
Moenkopi (riv.), US 128/E3
Moerai (isl.), FrPol. 117/K7
Moerbeke, Belg. 52/C1
Moers, Ger. 50/D6
Moervaart (riv.), Belg. 52/C1
Moesa (riv.), Swi. 57/F5
Moffat, Sc, UK 36/C6
Moffett Field Naval Air Sta., Ca, US 135/K12
Moga, India 86/C4
Mogadouro, Port. 44/B2
Mogami (riv.), Japan 76/B4
Mogami, Japan 76/B4
Mogaung, Myan. 83/G2
Mogent (riv.), Sp. 45/E6
Mogglingen, Ger. 54/C5
Moghul Gardens, India 86/C3
Mogi das Cruzes, Braz. 211/G8
Mogi-Guaçu, Braz. 211/G7
Mogi-Guaçu (riv.), Braz. 211/G7
Mogi-Mirim, Braz. 211/G7
Mogilno, Pol. 41/J2
Moglia, It. 59/D3
Mogliano Veneto, It. 59/F1
Möglingen, Ger. 54/C5
Mogoro, It. 46/A3
Mogotes (pt.), Arg. 158/F3
Mogotón (peak), Nic. 144/E3
Moguer, Sp. 44/B4
Mohács, Hun. 48/D3
Mohaeli (isl.), Com. 107/G6
Mohales Hoek, Les. 106/D3
Mohall, ND, US 127/H3
Mohamed V (dam), Mor. 100/C2
Mohamed V, Barrage (res.), Mor. 100/C2
Mohamed V (Casablanca) (int'l arpt.), Mor. 98/D2
Mohammadia, Alg. 100/F5
Mohammadia-Znata (prov.), Mor. 100/A2
Mohammedia, Mor. 100/A3
Mohawk (lake), NJ, US 138/D1
Moheda, Swe. 38/F3
Mohembo, Bots. 105/D4
Mohican (cape), Ak, US 134/E3
Möhlin, Swi. 56/D2
Möhne (riv.), Ger. 51/F6
Möhnestausee (lake), Ger. 51/F5
Mohnton, Pa, US 138/C3
Moho, Peru 156/D4
Mohrsville, Pa, US 138/C3
Mohyliv-Podil's'kyy, Ukr. 49/H1
Moi (int'l arpt.), Kenya 104/C4
Moi, Nor. 38/B2
Moie, It. 59/G5
Moineşti, Rom. 49/H2
Moinkum (des.), Kaz. 64/H5
Moinsi (hills), Gha. 103/E5
Moira (riv.), On, Can. 130/E2
Moirans, Fr. 42/F4
Moirans-en-Montagne, Fr. 56/B5
Moisie (riv.), Qu, Can. 123/K3
Moislains, Fr. 52/B4
Moissac, Fr. 42/D4
Moisselles, Fr. 30/K4
Moisson, Fr. 30/G4
Moita, Port. 45/Q10
Moitaco, Ven. 153/E3
Mojácar, Sp. 44/E4
Mojave (riv.), Ca, US 128/C4
Mojave (des.), Ca, US 124/C5
Mojiang Hanizu Zizhixian, China 83/H3
Mojikit (lake), On, Can. 127/L3
Mojkovac, Yugo. 47/F1
Mojos, Llanos de (plain), Bol. 150/E6
Moju (riv.), Braz. 151/J4
Mōka, Japan 75/F2
Mokameh, India 85/E3
Mokapu (pt.), Hi, US 124/W13
Mokau (riv.), NZ 117/S10
Mokelumne (riv.), Ca, US 128/B3
Mokelumne (aqueduct), Ca, US 135/M11
Mokena, Il, US 135/Q16
Mokil (isl.), Micr. 116/E4
Mokochu (peak), Thai. 78/B3
Mokokchūng, India 83/F2
Mokolo, Camr. 96/H5
Mokp'o, SKor. 73/D5
Mokrin, Yugo. 48/E3
Moksha (riv.), Rus. 63/G1
Mokuleia, Hi, US 124/V12
Mol, Yugo. 48/E3
Mol, Belg. 50/C6
Moláoi, Gre. 47/H4
Molare, It. 58/B3
Molas, Punta (pt.), Mex. 144/E1
Molat (isl.), Cro. 48/B3
Molatón (peak), Sp. 44/E3
Molbergen, Ger. 51/E3
Mold, Wal, UK 35/E5
Moldavia (reg.), Rom. 49/H2
Moldavian Carpathians (range), Rom. 49/G2
Molde, Nor. 37/C3
Moldova (riv.), Rom. 49/G2
Moldova (ctry.) 49/H2
Moldova Nouă, Rom. 48/E3
Moldoveanu (peak), Rom. 49/G3
Mole (riv.), Eng, UK 32/C5
Mole NP, Gha. 103/E4
Môle Saint-Nicolas, Haiti 145/H2
Molepolole, Bots. 105/E5
Molina, Sp. 44/E2
Molina, Chile 158/C2
Molina de Segura, Sp. 44/E3
Moline, Il, US 127/L5
Molinella, It. 59/E3
Molinicos, Sp. 44/D3
Molino de Flores, PN, Mex. 143/R9
Molins de Rei, Sp. 45/L7
Molise (reg.), It. 46/D2
Molkom, Swe. 38/E2
Möll (riv.), Aus. 43/K3
Møllebjerg (peak), Den. 37/D5
Mollendo, Peru 156/C5
Mollendruz, Col du (pass), Swi. 56/C4
Mollerussa, Sp. 45/F2
Molles (pt.), Chile 158/C2
Molles, Uru. 159/K10
Mollet del Vallès, Sp. 45/L6
Mollis, Swi. 57/F3
Mölndal, Swe. 38/E3
Mölnlycke, Swe. 38/E3
Molodezhnaya, Rus., Ant. 160/D
Mologa (riv.), Rus. 60/G4
Molokai (isl.), HI, US 117/K2
Moloma (riv.), Rus. 61/L4
Molong, Austl. 115/D2
Molopo (riv.), Bots. 93/E7
Mólos, Gre. 47/H3
Molsheim, Fr. 56/D1
Molteno, SAfr. 106/D3
Molu (isl.), Indo. 81/H5
Molucca (isls.), Indo. 67/M10
Molucca (sea), Asia 67/M10
Moluccas (arch.), Indo. 81/G3
Molveno (lake), It. 57/G5
Molveno, It. 57/G5
Mombaça, Braz. 154/C2
Mombasa, Kenya 104/C4
Mombetsu, Japan 76/C1
Mombetsu, Japan 76/C2
Mömbris, Ger. 54/C2
Momchilgrad, Bul. 47/J2
Momfafa (cape), Indo. 81/H4
Momignies, Belg. 53/D3
Mömlingen, Ger. 54/C3
Momo, It. 58/B1
Momoishi, Japan 76/B3
Mompós, Col. 152/C2
Mon (state), Myan. 83/G4
Mon (riv.), Myan. 83/F3
Møn (isl.), Den. 37/E5
Mona (isl.), PR 141/M8
Mona (passg.), NAm. 141/L8
Monaco (ctry.) 58/J8
Monaco (cap.), Mona. 58/J8
Monaco, Port of (har.), Mona. 58/J8
Monadhliath (mts.), Sc, UK 36/B2
Monagas (state), Ven. 153/F2
Monaghan (co.), Ire. 34/A3
Monagrillo, Pan. 152/A3
Monagrillo (ruin), Pan. 152/A2
Monar (lake), Sc, UK 36/A2
Monashee (mts.), BC, Can. 126/D3
Moncada, Sp. 45/E3
Moncalieri, It. 43/G4
Moncalvo, It. 58/B2
Moncão, Braz. 154/A1
Moncayo, Sierra del (range), Sp. 44/E2
Mönch (peak), Swi. 56/D4
Monchegorsk, Rus. 60/G2
Mönchengladbach, Ger. 50/D6
Monchique, Serra de (mts.), Port. 44/A4
Monchique, Port. 44/A4
Moncks Corner, SC, US 133/H3
Monclova, Mex. 132/C5
Moncton, NB, Can. 131/H2
Mondego (cape), Port. 44/A2
Mondego (riv.), Port. 44/A2
Mondéjar, Sp. 44/D2
Mondolfo, It. 59/G5
Mondoñedo, Sp. 44/B1
Mondorf-les- Bains, Lux. 53/F4
Mondovì, It. 58/A4
Mondragón, Sp. 44/D1
Mondragone, It. 46/C2
Mondsee (lake), Aus. 55/G7
Mondsee, Aus. 55/G7
Moneglia, It. 58/C4
Monemvasía, Gre. 47/H4
Mones Cazón, Arg. 158/E3
Monesterio, Sp. 44/B3
Money (pt.), Sc, UK 34/C2
Moneyreagh, NI, UK 34/C2
Monferrato (reg.), It. 43/H4
Monforte, Sp. 44/B1
Monforte, Port. 44/B3
Mongaguá, Braz. 211/G9
Mongers (lake), Austl. 109/A3
Monghidoro, It. 59/E4
Mongo, Chad 97/J5
Mongo (riv.), Gui. 102/C4
Mongolia (ctry.) 70/G2
Mongu, Zam. 105/D4
Mönh Hayrhan (peak), Mong. 70/F2
Mönh Sarĭdag (peak), Mong. 70/H1
Monheim, Ger. 54/D5
Monheim, Ger. 53/F1
Monifieth, Sc, UK 36/D4
Moniquirá, Col. 152/C3
Monistrol de Montserrat, Sp. 45/K6
Monistrol-sur-Loire, Fr. 42/F4
Monitor (range), Nv, US 128/C3
Monkayo, Phil. 79/E6
Monkey (pt.), Nic. 145/F4
Monkey River Town, Belz. 144/D2
Mońki, Pol. 41/M2
Monks (isl.), Md, US 138/B5
Monmouth, Il, US 127/L5
Monmouth, Or, US 126/C4
Monmouth Beach, NJ, US 138/E3
Monmouth Junction, NJ, US 138/D3
Monmouth Mil. Res., NJ, US 138/D3
Monmouthshire (co.), Wal, UK 32/D3
Monmow (riv.), Eng, UK 32/C2
Monnickendam, Neth. 50/C4
Mono (riv.), Togo 96/F6
Mono (lake), Ca, US 128/C3
Mono (prov.), Ben. 103/F5
Monocacy (riv.), Md, US 138/A4
Monor, Hun. 48/D2
Monóvar, Sp. 45/E3
Monreal del Campo, Sp. 44/E2
Monreale, It. 46/C3
Monroe, Wi, US 127/L5
Monroe, Ut, US 128/D3
Monroe, Ga, US 133/H3
Monroe (lake), Fl, US 133/G2
Monroe, La, US 129/J4
Monroe, NC, US 133/H3
Monroe, Mi, US 130/D3
Monroe, Ct, US 139/E1
Monroe, NY, US 138/D1
Monroe, Wa, US 135/C2
Monroe City, Il, US 137/G9
Monroeville, Al, US 133/G4
Monroeville, NJ, US 138/C4
Monrovia (cap.), Libr. 102/C5
Monrovia, Ca, US 136/G7
Mons, Belg. 52/C3
Monsanto, Port. 44/B2
Monschau, Ger. 53/F2
Monsefú, Peru 156/B2
Monselice, It. 43/J4
Monsenhor Tabosa, Braz. 154/B2
Monsey, NY, US 139/J7
Monsheim, Ger. 54/B3
Monster, Neth. 50/B4
Mönsteras, Swe. 38/G3
Monsummano Terme, It. 59/D5
Mont-de-Marsan, Fr. 42/C5
Mont-Joli, Qu, Can. 131/G1
Mont-Laurier, Qu, Can. 130/F2
Mont Peko, PN du, C.d'Iv. 102/D5
Mont-Royal, Qu, Can. 131/N6

208

Mont-S – Mpulu

Mont-Saint-Martin, Fr. 53/E4
Mont-Saint-Michel, Qu, Can. 130/F2
Mont Sangbé, PN du, C.d'Iv. 102/D4
Mont-Sous-Vaudrey, Fr. 56/B4
Montà, It. 58/A3
Monta Fon (mts.), Aus. 57/F3
Montabaur, Ger. 53/G3
Montagnana, It. 59/E2
Montagne d'Ambre NP, Madg. 107/J6
Montagny-Sainte-Félicité, Fr. 30/L4
Montagu, SAfr. 106/M10
Montague (str.), Ak, US 134/J4
Montague, Tx, US 129/H4
Montague, PE, Can. 131/J2
Montague, NJ, US 138/D1
Montague (isl.), Ak, US 122/B2
Montaigu, Fr. 42/C3
Montaione, It. 59/D5
Montalbán, Sp. 45/E2
Montalbano Jonico, It. 46/E2
Montale, It. 59/E5
Montale, It. 59/D3
Montalieu-Vercieu, Fr. 56/B6
Montalvão, Port. 44/B3
Montalvo, Ca, US 136/A2
Montana (prov.), Bul. 47/H1
Montana, Bul. 49/F4
Montana, Swi. 56/D5
Montana (state), US 126/F4
Montanaro, It. 58/A2
Montanha, Braz. 154/B5
Montara, Ca, US 135/J11
Montargis, Fr. 42/E2
Montataire, Fr. 52/B5
Montauban, Fr. 42/D4
Montauk, NY, US 139/G1
Montauk (pt.), NY, US 139/G1
Montbard, Fr. 42/F3
Montbéliard, Fr. 56/C2
Montblanc, Sp. 45/F2
Montcada i Reixac, Sp. 45/L7
Montceau-les-Mines, Fr. 42/F3
Montclair, Ca, US 136/C2
Montclair, NJ, US 139/J8
Montcornet, Fr. 52/D4
Montdidier, Fr. 52/B4
Monte Albán (ruin), Mex. 144/B2
Monte Alegre, Braz. 151/H4
Monte Alegre de Goiás, Braz. 154/A4
Monte Alegre de Minas, Braz. 155/B1
Monte Alegre do Piauí, Braz. 154/A3
Monte Alto, Braz. 155/B2
Monte Azul, Braz. 154/B4
Monte Carmelo, Braz. 155/C1
Monte Carmelo, Ven. 152/D2
Monte Caseros, Arg. 157/E3
Monte Comán, Arg. 158/D2
Monte Escobedo, Mex. 142/E4
Monte Maíz, Arg. 158/E2
Monte Pascoal, PN de, Braz. 151/L7
Monte Pascoal, PN de, Braz. 154/C5
Monte Rosa (mts.), It. 56/D6
Monte San Savino, It. 59/E6
Montealegre, Sp. 44/E3
Montebello (isls.), Austl. 109/A3
Montebello, Ca, US 136/F7
Montebello Vicentino, It. 59/E2
Montebelluna, It. 59/F1
Montebruno, It. 58/C3
Montecarlo, Arg. 157/F2
Montecassiano, It. 59/G6
Montecatini Terme, It. 59/D5
Montecavolo, It. 58/D3
Montecchio, It. 59/F5
Montechiaro d'Asti, It. 58/B2
Montecito, Ca, US 136/A2
Montecristo (isl.), It. 46/B1
Montecristo, PN, ESal. 144/D3
Montefeltro (reg.), It. 59/F5
Monteforte d'Alpone, It. 59/E2
Montefrío, Sp. 44/C4
Montego Bay, Jam. 145/G2
Montegranaro, It. 43/K5
Montegrotto Terme, It. 59/E2
Montehermoso, Sp. 44/B2
Monteiro, Braz. 154/C2
Montelavar, Port. 45/P10
Montélimar, Fr. 42/F4
Montellano, Sp. 44/C4
Montello, Nv, US 126/E5
Montelupo Fiorentino, It. 59/E5
Montemagno, It. 58/B3
Montemarciano, It. 59/G5
Montemor-o-Novo, Port. 44/A3
Montemor-o-Velho, Port. 44/A2
Montemorelos, Mex. 143/F3
Montemuro (peak), Port. 44/A2
Montendre, Fr. 42/C4
Montenegro, Braz. 155/B4
Montenero di Bisaccia, It. 46/D2
Montepulciano, It. 43/J5
Montereau-Faut-Yonne, Fr. 42/E2
Montereau-sur-le-Jard, Fr. 30/L6
Monterey, Ca, US 128/B3
Monterey (bay), Ca, US 124/B4
Monterey Park, Ca, US 136/F7
Montería, Col. 152/C2
Montero, Bol. 150/F7
Monteros, Arg. 157/C2
Monterosso (peak), It. 57/G4
Monterosso al Mare, It. 58/C4
Monterotondo, It. 46/C1
Monterrey, Mex. 143/E3
Monterrey, Sp. 44/B2
Montes (pt.), Arg. 159/C6
Montes Altos, Braz. 154/A2
Montes Claros, Braz. 154/B5
Montescaglioso, It. 46/E2
Montese, It. 59/D4
Montespertoli, It. 59/E5
Montesson, Fr. 30/J5
Monteux, Fr. 42/F4
Montevarchi, It. 59/E5
Montevideo, Mn, US 127/K4
Montevideo (cap.), Uru. 159/K11
Montevideo (dept.), Uru. 159/K11
Montévrain, Fr. 30/L5
Montezuma (peak), Az, US 137/R19
Montezuma Castle Nat'l Mon., Az, US 128/E4
Montfermeil, Fr. 30/K5
Montferrand-le-Château, Fr. 56/B3
Montfoort, Neth. 50/B4
Montfort-L'Amaury, Fr. 52/A6
Montgeron, Fr. 30/K5
Montgomery, WV, US 130/D4
Montgomery (cap.), Al, US 133/G3
Montgomery, Wal, UK 32/C1
Montgomery, Pa, US 138/B1
Montgomery (co.), Md, US 138/A5
Montgomery, Il, US 135/P16
Montgomery Village, Md, US 138/A5
Montgomeryville, Pa, US 138/C3
Montgrand (peak), Fr. 42/E5
Monthermé, Fr. 53/D4
Monthey, Swi. 56/C5
Monthureux-sur-Saône, Fr. 56/B1
Monthyon, Fr. 30/L4
Monti Sabini (mts.), It. 46/C1
Monticelli d'Ongina, It. 58/C2
Monticelli Terme, It. 58/D3
Monticello, Mo, US 127/L5
Monticello, Ky, US 130/C4
Monticello, In, US 130/C3
Monticello, La, US 129/K4
Monticello, Fl, US 133/H4
Monticello, Va, US 133/J2
Monticello Conte Otto, It. 59/E1
Montichiari, It. 58/D2
Montier-en-Der, Fr. 56/A1
Montignies-le-Tilleul, Belg. 53/D3
Montigny-en-Gohelle, Fr. 52/B3
Montigny-le-Bretonneux, Fr. 30/J5
Montigny-le-Roi, Fr. 56/B2
Montijo, Sp. 44/B3
Montijo, Port. 45/Q10
Montilla, Sp. 44/C4
Montivilliers, Fr. 42/D2
Montlebon, Fr. 56/C3
Montlhéry, Fr. 30/J6
Montluçon, Fr. 42/E3
Montluel, Fr. 56/B6
Montmagny, Qu, Can. 131/G2
Montmédy, Fr. 53/E4
Montmerle-sur-Saône, Fr. 56/A5
Montmirail, Fr. 52/C6
Montmorency, Fr. 30/J5
Montmorillon, Fr. 42/D3
Montmorot, Fr. 56/B4
Monto, Austl. 114/C4
Montodine, It. 58/C2
Montoir-de-Bretagne, Fr. 42/B3
Montois-la-Montagne, Fr. 53/F5
Montone (riv.), It. 59/E4
Montopoli, It. 59/D5
Montorio Veronese, It. 59/E2
Montoro, Sp. 44/C3
Montour (ridge), Pa, US 138/B2
Montour, Pa, US 138/B1
Montoursville, Pa, US 138/B1
Montpelier (cap.), Vt, US 131/F2
Montpellier, Fr. 42/E5
Montreal (lake), Sk, Can. 127/G2
Montreal (riv.), On, Can. 130/C2
Montréal, Qu, Can. 131/N6
Montréal-Est, Qu, Can. 131/N6
Montréal-la-Cluse, Fr. 56/B5
Montréal-Nord, Qu, Can. 131/N6
Montréjeau, Fr. 42/D5
Montreuil, Fr. 30/K5
Montreuil, Fr. 52/A3
Montreuil-Bellay, Fr. 42/C3
Montreuil-sur-Epte, Fr. 30/G4
Montreux, Swi. 56/C5
Montreux-Château, Fr. 56/C2
Montrevel-en-Bresse, Fr. 56/B5
Montricher, Swi. 56/C4
Montrose, Co, US 128/F3
Montrose (basin), Sc, UK 36/D3
Montrose, Sc, UK 36/D3
Montrouge, Fr. 30/J5
Montry, Fr. 30/L5
Monts, Fr. 42/D3
Montseny, PN, Sp. 45/L6
Montserrado (co.), Libr. 102/C5
Montserrat (peak), Sp. 45/F2
Montserrat (dpcy.), UK 141/N8
Montsoult, Fr. 30/J4
Montvale, NJ, US 139/J7
Montville, NJ, US 139/H8
Monywa, Myan. 83/G3
Monza, It. 58/C1
Monze, Zam. 105/E4
Monzingen, Ger. 53/G4
Monzón, Peru 156/B3
Monzón, Sp. 45/F2
Mooirivier, SAfr. 107/E3
Mool (riv.), SAfr. 106/P13
Moonta, Austl. 113/H5
Moora, Austl. 112/C4
Moorcroft, Wy, US 127/G4
Moordrecht, Neth. 50/B5
Moore (lake), Austl. 109/A3
Moore, Ok, US 137/N15
Moore Haven, Fl, US 133/H5
Moore River NP, Austl. 112/B4
Moorea (isl.), FrPol. 117/K6
Moorenweis, Ger. 57/H1
Moorestown, NJ, US 138/D4
Mooresville, NC, US 133/H3
Mooretown, On, Can. 135/H6
Moorfoot (hills), Sc, UK 36/C5
Moorhead, Mn, US 127/J4
Moorook, Austl. 115/B2
Moorpark, Ca, US 136/B2
Moorreesburg, SAfr. 106/L10
Moorslede, Belg. 52/C2
Moosburg, Ger. 55/E6
Moose (mtn.), Sk, Can. 127/H3
Moose (riv.), On, Can. 130/D1
Moose Creek, Ak, US 134/J3
Moose Jaw, Sk, Can. 127/G3
Moose Pass, Ak, US 134/J3
Moosehead (lake), Me, US 125/N2
Mooseheart (mtn.), Ak, US 134/H3
Mooseheart, Il, US 135/P16
Moosinning, Ger. 55/E6
Moosomin, Sk, Can. 127/H3
Moosonee, On, Can. 130/D1
Moosseedorf, Swi. 56/D3
Moosthenning, Ger. 55/F5
Mopti (pol. reg.), Mali 102/E3
Mopti, Mali 102/D3
Moquegua (dept.), Peru 156/D5
Moquegua, Peru 156/D5
Moquehuá, Arg. 159/J11
Mor (riv.), India 85/F4
Mór, Hun. 48/D2
Mora, Camr. 96/H5
Mora (riv.), NM, US 129/F4
Mora, NM, US 129/F4
Mora, Sp. 44/D3
Mora, Port. 44/A3
Mora, Swe. 38/F1
Mora de Rubielos, Sp. 45/E2
Morača (riv.), Yugo. 47/F1
Morada Nova, Braz. 154/C2
Morada Nova de Minas, Braz. 155/C1
Morādābād, India 84/B1
Morado, PN, Chile 158/P8
Morafenobe, Madg. 107/H7
Morąg, Pol. 39/H5
Moraga, Ca, US 135/K11
Mórahalom, Hun. 48/D2
Morainvilliers, Fr. 30/H5
Moral de Calatrava, Sp. 44/D3
Moraleja, Sp. 44/B2
Morales, Guat. 144/D3
Moramanga, Madg. 107/J7
Moranbah, Austl. 114/C3
Morane (isl.), FrPol. 117/M7
Morangis, Fr. 30/K5
Morano Calabro, It. 46/E3
Morant Bay, Jam. 145/G2
Morar (lake), Sc, UK 31/R8
Morarano Chrome, Madg. 107/J7
Morat (lake), Swi. 56/D4
Morata de Tajuña, Sp. 45/N9
Moratalla, Sp. 44/E3
Moratuwa, SrL. 82/C6
Morava (riv.), Czh. 41/J4
Moravia (reg.), Czh. 41/J4
Moravská Třebová, Czh. 41/J4
Moravské Budějovice, Czh. 41/H4
Morawa, Austl. 112/C4
Morawhanna, Guy. 150/G2
Moray (pol. reg.), Sc, UK 36/E2
Moray Firth (inlet), Sc, UK 36/B1
Morbach, Ger. 53/G4
Morbegno, It. 57/F5
Morbier, Fr. 56/C4
Morbio Inferiore, Swi. 57/F6
Morbras (riv.), Fr. 30/K5
Mörbylånga, Swe. 38/G3
Morcenx, Fr. 42/C4
Morciano di Romagna, It. 59/F5
Morclan, Pic de (peak), Fr. 56/C5
Morden, Mb, Can. 127/J3
Mordoviya (aut. rep.), Rus. 64/Q6
Møre Og Romsdal (co.), Nor. 37/C3
Moreau (riv.), SD, US 127/H4
Morecambe (bay), Eng, UK 35/E3
Moree, Austl. 115/D1
Morehead, Ky, US 130/D4
Morehead City, NC, US 133/J3
Mörel, Swi. 56/E5
Morelia, Mex. 143/E5
Morella, Sp. 45/E2
Morelos (state), Mex. 140/A5
Morena, Sierra (range), Sp. 44/C4
Moreni, Rom. 49/G3
Moreno Valley, Ca, US 136/C3
Moresby (isl.), BC, Can. 122/C3
Moreton (isl.), Austl. 109/E3
Moreton (cape), Austl. 114/D4
Moreton (bay), Austl. 114/F6
Moreton Island NP, Austl. 114/D4
Moreuil, Fr. 52/B4
Moreyu (riv.), Rus. 61/P2
Morez, Fr. 56/C4
Morgan (co.), Ut, US 137/K11
Morgan, Ut, US 137/K11
Morgan, Austl. 113/H5
Morgan (pt.), Ct, US 139/F1
Morgan City, La, US 129/K5
Morganfield, Ky, US 130/C4
Morgantina (ruin), It. 46/D4
Morganton, NC, US 133/H3
Morgantown, Ky, US 130/C4
Morgantown, Pa, US 138/C3
Morge (riv.), Fr. 42/E3
Morgenzon, SAfr. 107/E2
Morges, Swi. 56/C4
Morgex, It. 56/D6
Morghāb (riv.), Afg. 64/G6
Morgongåva, Swe. 38/G2
Morguilla (pt.), Chile 158/B3
Morhange, Fr. 53/F6
Morhar (riv.), India 85/E3
Mori, It. 43/J4
Mori, Japan 76/B2
Mori Kazak Zizhixian, China 70/F3
Morialta Conservation Park, Austl. 113/M8
Moriarty, NM, US 129/F4
Morice (lake), BC, Can. 126/B2
Morie (lake), Sc, UK 36/B1
Moriguchi, Japan 77/J6
Morin Dawa Daurzu Zizhiqi, China 71/M2
Moringen, Ger. 51/G5
Morinville, Ab, Can. 126/E2
Morioka, Japan 76/B4
Morisset, Austl. 115/D2
Moriston (riv.), Sc, UK 36/B2
Moriya, Japan 77/D2
Moriyama, Japan 77/J5
Morlaix, Fr. 42/B2
Morlanwelz, Belg. 53/D3
Mörlenbach, Ger. 54/B3
Morley, Eng, UK 35/G4
Mormant, Fr. 30/L6
Mormond (hill), Sc, UK 36/D1
Mornington (isl.), Austl. 109/C2
Mörnsheim, Ger. 54/D5
Moro, Pak. 89/J3
Moro (gulf), Phil. 116/B4
Morocco (ctry.) 98/D2
Morocelí, Hon. 144/E3
Morococha, Peru 156/B3
Morogoro (pol. reg.), Tanz. 104/C4
Morogoro, Tanz. 104/C4
Morombe, Madg. 107/G8
Mörön, Mong. 70/H2
Morón, Ven. 152/D2
Morón, Cuba 145/G1
Morón, Arg. 159/J11
Morón de la Frontera, Sp. 44/C4
Morona (riv.), Peru 150/C4
Morona-Santiago (dept.), Ecu. 152/B5
Morondara (riv.), Madg. 107/H8
Morondava, Madg. 107/H8
Moroni (cap.), Com. 107/G5
Morotai (str.), Indo. 81/G3
Morotai (isl.), Indo. 67/M9
Moroto, Ugan. 104/B2
Moroto (mt.), Ugan. 104/B2
Moroyama, Japan 77/C2
Morpará, Braz. 154/B3
Morpeth, Eng, UK 35/G1
Morphou, Cyp. 91/C2
Morphou (bay), Cyp. 91/C2
Morra (lake), Neth. 50/C3
Morrinhos, Braz. 155/B1
Morris, Mb, Can. 127/J3
Morris, Mn, US 127/K4
Morris (res.), Ca, US 136/C2
Morris (mt.), Austl. 113/F3
Morris (co.), NJ, US 138/D2
Morris Jesup (cape), Grld 160/J
Morris Plains, NJ, US 139/H8
Morrison, Co, US 137/B3
Morristown, NJ, US 138/D2
Morristown NHP, NJ, US 138/D2
Morrisville, Pa, US 138/D3
Morro Bay, Ca, US 128/B4
Morro de Môco (peak), Ang. 105/C3
Morro de Puercos (pt.), Pan. 145/F5
Morro do Chapéu, Braz. 154/B3
Morro, Punta del (pt.), Mex. 143/N7
Morrocoy, PN, Ven. 152/D2
Mórrope, Peru 156/A2
Morropón, Peru 156/B2
Morros, Braz. 154/A1
Morrosquillo (gulf), Col. 145/G4
Mörrum, Swe. 38/F3
Mørs (isl.), Den. 38/C3
Morsang-sur-Orge, Fr. 30/K6
Morsbach, Ger. 53/G2
Morsbach, Fr. 53/F5
Morschwiller-le-Bas, Fr. 56/D2
Morse, Ks, US 137/D6
Morse Mill, Mo, US 137/F9
Morshansk, Rus. 63/G1
Morskoy (isl.), Kaz. 63/J3
Morsum, Ger. 51/G3
Mortagne (riv.), Fr. 56/C1
Mortagne-sur-Sèvre, Fr. 42/C3
Mortara, It. 58/B2
Mortcerf, Fr. 30/L5
Morte (pt.), Eng, UK 32/B4
Morte (riv.), Fr. 56/B3
Morteau, Fr. 56/C3
Mortefontaine, Fr. 30/K4
Mortegliano, It. 59/G1
Mortes, Rio das (riv.), Braz. 151/H6
Mortlake, Austl. 115/B3
Morton, Wa, US 126/C4
Morton, Il, US 129/K2
Morton Grove, Il, US 135/Q15
Morton NP, Austl. 115/D2
Morton NWR, NY, US 139/F2
Mortsel, Belg. 50/B6
Morungaba, Braz. 211/G7
Moruya, Austl. 115/D2
Morvan (plat.), Fr. 42/E3
Morven, Austl. 114/B4
Morven (peak), Sc, UK 36/C2
Morvi, India 89/K4
Morvillars, Fr. 56/C2
Morwell, Austl. 115/C3
Morzine, Fr. 56/C5
Mos, Sp. 44/A1
Mosbach, Ger. 54/C4
Mosby, Mo, US 137/E5
Moscavide, Port. 45/P10
Moscovskaya (obl.), Rus. 60/H5
Moscow, Id, US 126/D4
Moscow (upland), Rus. 60/F5
Moscow University Ice Shelf, Ant. 160/J
Moselle (riv.), Fr. 43/G2
Moselle (dept.), Fr. 53/F5
Moselotte (riv.), Fr. 56/C2
Moses Lake, Wa, US 126/D4
Mosfellsbær, Ice. 37/N7
Mosgiel, NZ 117/S12
Moshaweng (riv.), SAfr. 106/C2
Moshchnyy (isl.), Rus. 39/M2
Moshi, Tanz. 104/C3
Moshoeshoe (Maseru) (int'l arpt.), Les. 106/D3
Mosina, Pol. 41/J2
Moskva (riv.), Rus. 60/G5
Moskva (Moscow) (cap.), Rus. 62/F1
Mosonmagyaróvár, Hun. 48/C2
Mosquera, Col. 152/B4
Mosquero, NM, US 129/G4
Mosquitia (phys. reg.), Hon. 145/E3
Mosquito (pt.), Pan. 145/G4
Mosquitos, Golfo de los (gulf), Pan. 150/B2
Moss, Nor. 38/D2
Moss Beach, Ca, US 135/J11
Moss Bluff, La, US 129/J5
Moss Point, Ms, US 133/F4
Moss-Side, NI, UK 34/B1
Moss Vale, Austl. 115/D2
Mosselbaai, SAfr. 106/C4
Mosses, Col des (pass), Swi. 56/D5
Mossi Highlands (uplands), Burk. 102/E4
Mössingen, Ger. 54/C6
Mossman, Austl. 114/B2
Mossoró, Braz. 154/C2
Most, Czh. 55/G1
Mostaganem (prov.), Alg. 100/F4
Mostaganem, Alg. 100/F5
Mostar, Bosn. 47/E1
Mostardas, Braz. 155/B4
Móstoles, Sp. 45/N9
Mota del Cuervo, Sp. 44/D3
Motagua (riv.), Guat. 140/D4
Motala, Swe. 38/F2
Motherwell, Sc, UK 36/C5
Motian (mtn.), China 72/E2
Motīhāri, India 85/E2
Motilla del Palancar, Sp. 44/E3
Motobu, Japan 75/J7
Motomiya, Japan 75/G2
Motono, Japan 77/E2
Motosu (lake), Japan 77/B3
Motosu, Japan 77/L5
Motovskiy (gulf), Rus. 37/K1
Motoyoshi, Japan 76/B4
Motozintla de Mendoza, Mex. 144/C3
Motril, Sp. 44/D4
Motsuta-misaki (cape), Japan 76/A2
Mott, ND, US 127/H4
Motta di Livenza, It. 59/F1
Motta Visconti, It. 58/B2
Mottarone (peak), It. 58/B1
Motueka, NZ 117/S11
Motul de Carrillo Puerto, Mex. 144/D1
Motupe, Peru 156/B2
Motygino, Rus. 64/K4
Mouchard, Fr. 56/B4
Mouchoir Passage (chan.), UK 145/J1
Moúdhros, Gre. 47/J3
Moudon, Swi. 56/C4
Mougris (well), Mrta. 102/B2
Mouhoun (prov.), Burk. 102/E3
Mouila, Gabon 96/H8
Mouïna (well), Alg. 99/F3
Moul (well), Niger 96/H4
Moulamein (riv.), Austl. 115/C2
Moulamein, Austl. 115/C2
Moulay Idriss, Mor. 100/B2
Moulins, Fr. 42/E3
Moulouya (riv.), Mor. 100/C2
Moultrie, Ga, US 133/H4
Moultrie (lake), SC, US 133/J3
Moundou, Chad 96/J6
Moundsville, WV, US 130/D4
Mount Aberdeen NP, Austl. 114/B3
Mount Abu, India 89/K4
Mount Airy, NC, US 130/D4
Mount Airy, Md, US 138/A5
Mount Allan Abor. Land, Austl. 113/G2
Mount Aspiring NP, NZ 117/R11
Mount Baker-Snoqualmie, Wa, US 135/D1
Mount Baker-Snoqualmie Nat'l For., Wa, US 135/D3
Mount Baldy, Ca, US 136/C2
Mount Barker, Austl. 112/C5
Mount Barker, Austl. 113/M9
Mount Barkly Abor. Land, Austl. 113/G2
Mount Beauty, Austl. 115/C3
Mount Bold (res.), Austl. 113/M9
Mount Buffalo NP, Austl. 115/C3
Mount Carmel, Il, US 130/C4
Mount Carmel, Pa, US 138/B2
Mount Darwin, Zim. 105/F4
Mount Diablo State Park, Ca, US 135/L11
Mount Eccles NP, Austl. 115/B3
Mount Elgon NP, Ugan. 104/B2
Mount Elliot NP, Austl. 114/B2
Mount Everard, Guy. 153/G3
Mount Field NP, Austl. 115/C4
Mount Gambier, Austl. 115/B3
Mount Garnet, Austl. 114/B2
Mount Holly, NJ, US 138/D4
Mount Holly Springs, Pa, US 138/A3
Mount Imlay NP, Austl. 115/D3
Mount Isa, Austl. 113/H2
Mount Joy, Pa, US 138/B3
Mount Kaputar NP, Austl. 115/D1
Mount Kenya NP, Kenya 104/C3
Mount Kisco, NY, US 139/E1
Mount Larcom, Austl. 114/C3
Mount Laurel, NJ, US 138/D4
Mount Lofty (ranges), Austl. 109/C4
Mount Lofty (range), Austl. 113/M9
Mount Magnet, Austl. 112/C4
Mount Mistake NP, Austl. 114/D4
Mount Morgan, Austl. 114/C3
Mount Morris, Mi, US 130/D3
Mount Nebo, Austl. 114/E6
Mount Olive, NC, US 133/J3
Mount Pearl, Nf, Can. 131/L2
Mount Penn, Pa, US 138/C3
Mount Pleasant, Ia, US 127/L5
Mount Pleasant, Mi, US 130/C3
Mount Pleasant, Ut, US 128/E3
Mount Pleasant, De, US 138/C4
Mount Pleasant (int'l arpt.), UK 159/F6
Mount Pleasant, Austl. 113/N8
Mount Pocono, Pa, US 138/C1
Mount Prospect, Il, US 135/P15
Mount Rainier, Md, US 138/B6
Mount Rainier NP, Wa, US 126/C4
Mount Remarkable NP, Austl. 113/H5
Mount Revelstoke NP, BC, Can. 126/D3
Mount Richmond NP, Austl. 115/B3
Mount Rushmore Nat'l Mem., SD, US 129/G2
Mount Spec NP, Austl. 114/B2
Mount St. Helens Nat'l Volcanic Mon., Wa, US 126/C4
Mount Sterling, Ky, US 130/D4
Mount Torrens, Austl. 113/M8
Mount Vernon, Wa, US 126/C3
Mount Vernon, Il, US 129/K3
Mount Vernon, Tx, US 129/J4
Mount Vernon, Oh, US 130/D3
Mount Vernon, Va, US 138/A6
Mount Vernon, NY, US 139/K8
Mount Walsh NP, Austl. 114/C4
Mount Warning NP, Austl. 114/D5
Mount Welcome Abor. Land, Austl. 112/C2
Mount William NP, Austl. 115/D4
Mount Wolf, Pa, US 138/B3
Mountain (riv.), NW, Can. 122/D2
Mountain Ash, Wal, UK 32/C3
Mountain Green, Ut, US 137/K11
Mountain Grove, Mo, US 129/J3
Mountain Home, Id, US 126/E5
Mountain Lakes, NJ, US 139/H8
Mountain Point, Ak, US 134/M4
Mountain Top, Pa, US 138/C1
Mountain View, Ar, US 129/J4
Mountain View, Hi, US 124/U11
Mountain View, Ca, US 135/K12
Mountain Village, Ak, US 134/F3
Mountain Zebra NP, SAfr. 106/D4
Mountainhome, Pa, US 138/C1
Mountainside, NJ, US 139/H9
Mountlake Terrace, Wa, US 135/C2
Mountmellick, Ire. 31/Q10
Mountrath, Ire. 31/Q10
Mount's (bay), Eng, UK 32/A6
Mountville, Pa, US 138/B3
Moura, Port. 44/B3
Moura, Austl. 114/C4
Mourão, Port. 44/B3
Mourenx, Fr. 42/C5
Mourmelon-le-Grand, Fr. 53/D5
Mourmelon-le-Petit, Fr. 53/D5
Mourne (mts.), NI, UK 34/B3
Mourniaí, Gre. 47/J5
Mouroux, Fr. 30/M5
Mouscron, Belg. 52/C2
Mousseaux-sur-Seine, Fr. 30/G4
Moussoro, Chad 96/J5
Moussy-le-Neuf, Fr. 30/K4
Moussy-le-Vieux, Fr. 30/K4
Mouths of the Niger, Nga. 96/G6
Moutier, Swi. 56/D3
Mouvaux, Fr. 52/C2
Mouy, Fr. 52/B5
Mouydir (plat.), Alg. 99/G4
Mouzákion, Gre. 47/G3
Mouzon (riv.), Fr. 56/B1
Mouzon, Fr. 53/E4
Moville, Ire. 34/A1
Moxotó (riv.), Braz. 154/C3
Moy, NI, UK 34/B3
Moyamba, SLeo. 102/B4
Moye (isl.), China 73/B4
Moyen Atlas (mts.), Mor. 96/D1
Moyenmoutier, Fr. 56/C1
Moyeuvre-Grande, Fr. 53/F5
Moyle (dist.), NI, UK 34/B1
Moyo (isl.), Indo. 81/E5
Moyo, Ugan. 104/A2
Moyobamba, Peru 156/B2
Moyowosi (riv.), Tanz. 104/A3
Moyu, China 70/C4
Moyuta, Guat. 144/D3
Mozambique ([illegible]y.) 105/G4
Mozambique (chan.), Afr. 105/G5
Mozhaysk, Rus. 60/H5
Mozhga, Rus. 61/M4
Mozzanica, It. 58/C2
Mozzecane, It. 59/D2
Mpanda, Tanz. 104/A4
Mpigi, Ugan. 104/B2
Mpika, Zam. 104/A5
Mporokoso, Zam. 104/A5
Mpraeso, Gha. 103/E5
Mpulungu, Zam. 104/A5

Mpumalanga (prov.), SAfr. 107/E2
Mpwapwa, Tanz. 104/C4
Mrągowo, Pol. 39/J5
Mrkonjić Grad, Bosn. 48/C3
M'Sila (prov.), Alg. 99/F2
M'sila, Alg. 100/H5
M'sila (riv.), Alg. 100/H5
Msoun (riv.), Mor. 100/C2
Msta (riv.), Rus. 60/G4
Mszana Dolna, Pol. 41/L4
Mtorwi (peak), Tanz. 104/B5
Mtsensk, Rus. 62/F1
Mtubatuba, SAfr. 107/F3
Mtunzini, SAfr. 107/E3
Mtwara, Tanz. 104/D5
Mtwara (pol. reg.), Tanz. 104/C5
Mu-kawa (riv.), Japan 76/C2
Mu Ko Similan NP, Thai. 78/B4
Mu Ko Surin NP, Thai. 78/B4
Mualama, Moz. 105/G4
Muan, SKor. 73/D5
Muang Hinboun, Laos 78/D2
Muang Khammouan, Laos 78/D2
Muang Khong, Laos 78/D3
Muang Khongxedon, Laos 78/D3
Muang Pak-lay, Laos 78/C2
Muang Pakxan, Laos 78/C2
Muang Sing, Laos 83/H3
Muang Vangviang, Laos 78/C2
Muang Xaignabouri, Laos 78/C2
Muang Xay, Laos 83/H3
Muar, Malay. 80/B3
Muarabungo, Indo. 80/B4
Muāri (pt.), Pak. 89/J4
Mubārakpur, India 84/D2
Mubende, Ugan. 104/A2
Mucajaí (riv.), Braz. 150/F3
Much, Ger. 53/G2
Muchinga (mts.), Zam. 105/F3
Muck (isl.), Sc, UK 31/Q8
Muckleshoot Ind. Res., Wa, US 135/C3
Mucojo, Moz. 105/H3
Mucupina (mtn.), Hon. 144/E3
Mucur, Turk. 90/C2
Mucuri (riv.), Braz. 151/K7
Mud Mountain (dam), Wa, US 135/D3
Mud Mountain (lake), Wa, US 135/D3
Mudanjiang, China 71/N3
Mudanya, Turk. 49/J5
Mudau, Ger. 54/C3
Mudbach (riv.), Ger. 54/C3
Muddan (riv.), China 65/N5
Muddas NP, Swe. 37/G2
Muddy Run (res.), Pa, US 138/B4
Müden, Ger. 51/H3
Mudersbach, Ger. 53/G2
Mudgee, Austl. 115/D2
Mudjatik (riv.), Sk, Can. 122/F3
Mudon, Myan. 78/B2
Mudurnu, Turk. 49/K5
Muela (peak), Chile 159/B7
Muerte, Cerro de la (peak), CR 145/F4
Muff, Ire. 34/A1
Mufulira, Zam. 105/E3
Mugardos, Sp. 44/A1
Mugegawa, Japan 77/L4
Mughal Sarai, India 84/D3
Mugi, Japan 77/L4
Mugia, Sp. 44/A1
Muğla, Turk. 90/B2
Mugla (prov.), Turk. 90/B2
Muğla (prov.), Turk. 91/A1
Mughalzhar Taūy (mts.), Kaz. 87/C3
Muhamdi, India 84/C2
Muḩammad (pt.), Egypt 101/C3
Muhammadābad, India 84/D3
Muhavura (vol.), Rwa. 104/A3
Muhila, Monts (mts.), D.R. Congo 105/E3
Mühlacker, Ger. 54/B5
Mühlbach (riv.), Ger. 54/A2
Mühldorf, Ger. 55/F6
Mühleberg, Swi. 56/D4
Mühlenbeck, Ger. 40/Q6
Mühlhausen, Ger. 55/E4
Mühlheim am Main, Ger. 54/B2
Mühlheim an der Donau, Ger. 57/E1
Mühltroff, Ger. 55/E1
Mühlviertel (reg.), Aus. 41/G4
Muhos, Fin. 60/E2
Muhu (isl.), Est. 60/D4
Muiden, Neth. 50/C4
Muir of Ord, Sc, UK 36/B1
Muir Woods Nat'l Mon., Ca, US 128/B3
Muir Woods Nat'l Mon., Ca, US 135/J11
Muirkirk, Sc, UK 36/B5
Muizon, Fr. 52/C5
Muju, SKor. 73/D4
Mukacheve, Ukr. 41/M4
Mukawa, Japan 76/B2
Mukawwar (isl.), Sudan 101/D4
Mukden, Bol. 156/D3
Mukeriān, India 86/C4
Mukhayyam al Yarmūk, Syria 91/E3
Mukhmās, Isr. 91/G8
Mukinbudin, Austl. 112/C4
Mukō, Japan 77/J6
Mukono, Ugan. 104/B2
Mukoshima (isls.), Japan 116/D2
Muktsar, India 86/C4
Mukwonago, Wi, US 135/P14
Mula, Sp. 44/E3
Mulanje, Malw. 105/G4
Mulchatna (riv.), Ak, US 134/G4
Mulchén, Chile 158/B3
Mulde (riv.), Ger. 40/G3
Mulegé, Mex. 142/C3
Muleshoe, Tx, US 129/G4
Mulhacén, Cerro de (peak), Sp. 44/D4
Mülhausen, Ger. 51/H6
Mülheim an der Ruhr, Ger. 50/D6
Mulhouse, Fr. 56/D2
Muli (riv.), Indo. 81/J5
Muli Zangzu Zizhixian, China 83/H2
Muling (pass), China 72/D3
Mull (isl.), Sc, UK 31/R8
Mull of Galloway (pt.), Sc, UK 34/D2
Mull of Kintyre (pt.), Sc, UK 34/C1
Mull of Logan (pt.), Sc, UK 34/D2
Mullach Coire Mhic Fhearchair (peak), Sc, UK 36/A1
Mullaghcleevaun (peak), Ire. 34/B5
Mullaghmore (peak), NI, UK 34/B2
Mullaittivu, SrL. 82/D6
Mullardoch (lake), Sc, UK 36/A2
Muller (mts.), Indo. 80/D4
Mullewa, Austl. 112/B4
Müllheim, Ger. 56/D2
Müllheim, Swi. 57/F2
Mullica (riv.), NJ, US 138/D4
Mullica Hill, NJ, US 138/C4
Mullingar, Ire. 31/Q10
Mullins, SC, US 133/J3
Mullumbimby, Austl. 115/E1
Mulobezi, Zam. 105/E4
Multai, India 84/B5
Multān, Pak. 86/A4
Multnomah (falls), Or, US 126/C4
Mulu (peak), Malay. 80/D3
Mulwala, Austl. 115/C2
Mum Nauk (pt.), Thai. 78/B5
Mumbai (Bombay), India 89/K5
Mumbwa, Zam. 105/E3
Mümling (riv.), Ger. 54/B3
Mumoni (peak), Kenya 104/C3
Mun (riv.), Thai. 83/H4
Muna (isl.), Indo. 116/B5
Muna, Mex. 144/D1
Munamägi (hill), Est. 39/M3
Muñani, Peru 156/D4
Muncar, Indo. 80/D5
Münchberg, Ger. 55/E2
München (Munich), Ger. 55/E6
Münchenstein, Swi. 56/D2
Munchique (peak), Col. 152/B4
Munchique, PN, Col. 152/B4
Münchmünster, Ger. 55/E5
Muncie, In, US 130/C3
Muncy, Pa, US 138/B1
Mundaring, Austl. 112/L6
Munday, Tx, US 129/H4
Mundelein, Il, US 135/Q15
Mundemba, Camr. 103/H5
Münden, Ger. 51/G6
Munderfing, Aus. 55/G6
Munderkingen, Ger. 57/F1
Mundo Novo, Braz. 157/F1
Mundo Novo, Braz. 154/B3
Mundubbera, Austl. 114/C4
Munera, Sp. 44/D3
Mungaolī, India 84/B3
Mungeli, India 84/C4
Munger, India 85/F3
Mungo NP, Austl. 115/B2
Mun'gyŏng, SKor. 73/E4
Munising, Mi, US 127/M4
Munkebo, Den. 38/D4
Munkedal, Swe. 38/D2
Munkfors, Swe. 38/E2
Munku-Sardyk (peak), Rus. 70/H1
Münnerstadt, Ger. 54/D2
Muñoz Gamero (pen.), Chile 157/B7
Munsan, SKor. 73/F6
Münsingen, Swi. 56/D4
Münsingen, Ger. 54/C6
Munster (reg.), Ire. 31/P10
Münster, Ger. 51/E5
Münster, Ger. 51/H3
Munster, Fr. 56/D1
Münster, Swi. 57/E5
Munster, In, US 135/R16
Münster, Ger. 54/B3
Münster/Osnabrück (int'l arpt.), Ger. 51/E4
Münstereifel, Ger. 53/F2
Münsterhausen, Ger. 54/D6
Münsterland (reg.), Ger. 40/D2
Münstermaifeld, Ger. 53/G3
Muntele Mare (peak), Rom. 49/F2
Muntendam, Neth. 50/D2
Muntok, Indo. 80/C4
Müntschemier, Swi. 56/D4
Münzenberg, Ger. 54/B2
Münzkirchen, Aus. 55/G6
Munzur Vadisi NP, Turk. 62/F5
Muonio, Fin. 37/G2
Muonioälven (riv.), Swe. 37/G1
Muotathal, Swi. 57/E4
Mupa, PN da, Ang. 105/C4
Muping, China 72/E3
Muqdisho (Mogadishu) (cap.), Som. 97/Q7
Muqeibila, Isr. 91/G6
Mur (riv.), Aus. 43/L3
Mura (riv.), Slov.,Hun 48/C2
Muradiye, Turk. 90/E2
Murādnagar, India 86/D5
Murakami, Japan 75/F1
Murallón (peak), Chile 159/B6
Murano, It. 59/F2
Murat (peak), Turk. 62/D5
Muratlı, Turk. 90/E2
Muratlı, Turk. 49/H5
Murayama, Japan 76/B4
Murchison, Austl. 115/C3
Murchison (riv.), Austl. 109/A3
Murchison, NZ 117/S11
Murchison (mt.), Austl. 112/C3
Murcia, Sp. 45/E4
Murcia (aut. comm.), Sp. 44/E4
Murderkill (riv.), De, US 138/C6
Murdochville, Qu, Can. 131/H1
Murdock (pt.), Austl. 114/B1
Mürefte, Turk. 49/H5
Mureș (riv.), Rom. 62/B3
Mureș (prov.), Rom. 49/G2
Muret, Fr. 42/D5
Murfreesboro, Ar, US 129/J4
Murg (riv.), Ger. 53/H6
Murgab (riv.), Turk. 87/D5
Murgap (riv.), Trkm. 64/G6
Murgon, Austl. 114/C4
Muri, Swi. 57/E3
Muri bei Bern, Swi. 56/D4
Muria (peak), Indo. 80/D5
Muriaé, Braz. 155/D2
Murias de Paredes, Sp. 44/B1
Murici, Braz. 154/D3
Murīdke, Pak. 86/C4
Müritz (lake), Ger. 40/G2
Murlīganj, India 85/F3
Murmansk, Rus. 60/G1
Murmansk (int'l arpt.), Rus. 60/G1
Murmanskaya (obl.), Rus. 37/J1
Murnau, Ger. 57/H2
Muro, Sp. 45/G3
Muro, Japan 77/K6
Muro Lucano, It. 46/D2
Murom, Rus. 60/J5
Muroran, Japan 76/B2
Muros, Sp. 44/A1
Muroto, Japan 74/D4
Muroto-zaki (pt.), Japan 74/D4
Murowana Goślina, Pol. 41/J2
Murphy, NC, US 133/G3
Murphy, Mo, US 137/G9
Murr (riv.), Ger. 54/C5
Murra, Nic. 144/E3
Murramarang NP, Austl. 115/D2
Murray (lake), SC, US 133/H3
Murray (riv.), Austl. 109/D4
Murray, Ky, US 130/B4
Murray, Ut, US 137/K12
Murray Bridge, Austl. 113/H5
Murraysburg, SAfr. 106/C3
Murrayville, Austl. 115/B2
Murree, Pak. 86/B3
Murrieta, Ca, US 136/C3
Murrieta Hot Springs, Ca, US 136/C3
Murrumbidgee (riv.), Austl. 109/D4
Murrumburrah, Austl. 115/D2
Mururundi, Austl. 115/D1
Murshidābād, India 85/G3
Murtala Muhammed (int'l arpt.), Nga. 103/F5
Murtaröl (peak), Swi. 57/G4
Murten, Swi. 56/D4
Murtoa, Austl. 115/B3
Murud (peak), Malay. 80/E3
Murupara, NZ 117/T10
Mururoa (isl.), FrPol. 117/M7
Murwāra, India 84/C4
Murwillumbah, Austl. 114/D5
Mürz (riv.), Aus. 41/H5
Mürzzuschlag, Aus. 41/H5
Muş (prov.), Turk. 90/E2
Muş, Turk. 90/E2
Musabeyli, Turk. 91/E1
Musāfirkhāna, India 84/C2
Musala (peak), Bul. 47/H1
Musan, NKor. 73/E1
Musashino, Japan 77/D2
Musconetcong (riv.), NJ, US 138/C2
Muscoot (res.), NY, US 139/E1
Muscoy, Ca, US 136/C2
Musekwapoort (pass), SAfr. 105/E5
Museum of Flight, Wa, US 135/C2
Musgrave (ranges), Austl. 109/C3
Musgrave (range), Austl. 116/B7
Musgrave Harbour, Nf, Can. 131/L1
Mushābani, India 85/F4
Mushie, D.R. Congo 96/J8
Mushin, Nga. 103/F5
Musi (riv.), Indo. 80/B4
Musile di Piave, It. 59/F1
Musinga (peak), Col. 152/B3
Muskego, Wi, US 135/P14
Muskegon, Mi, US 130/C3
Muskegon (riv.), Mi, US 130/C3
Muskingum (riv.), Oh, US 130/D4
Muskoka (lake), On, Can. 130/E2
Musoma, Tanz. 104/B3
Musone (riv.), It. 59/G6
Musquaro (riv.), Qu, Can. 131/J1
Mussau (isl.), PNG 116/D5
Musselburgh, Sc, UK 36/C5
Musselshell (riv.), Mt, US 124/E2
Mussomeli, It. 46/C4
Musson, Belg. 53/E4
Mustafābād, Pak. 86/B4
Mustafakemalpaşa, Turk. 62/D4
Müstair, Swi. 57/G4
Mustang, Ok, US 137/M15
Musters (lake), Arg. 158/C5
Musu-dan (pt.), NKor. 73/E2
Musún (mtn.), Nic. 144/E3
Mušutište, Yugo. 47/G1
Muswellbrook, Austl. 115/D2
Mūt, Egypt 101/B3
Mut, Turk. 91/C1
Mutá, Ponta do (pt.), Braz. 154/C4
Mutare, Zim. 105/F4
Muthill, Sc, UK 36/C4
Mutis (peak), Indo. 81/F5
Mutsamudu, Com. 107/H6
Mutsu (bay), Japan 76/B3
Mutsu, Japan 76/B3
Mutsuzawa, Japan 77/E3
Muttekopf (peak), Aus. 57/G3
Muttenz, Swi. 56/D2
Mutters, Aus. 57/H3
Mutterstadt, Ger. 54/B4
Muttler (peak), Swi. 57/G4
Muttonville, Mi, US 135/G6
Mutum, Braz. 155/D1
Mutzig, Fr. 56/D1
Mŭynoq, Uzb. 63/L4
Muzaffargarh, Pak. 86/A4
Muzaffarnagar, India 86/D5
Muzaffarpur, India 85/E2
Muzambinho, Braz. 211/G6
Muzon (cape), Ak, US 134/M4
Muztag (peak), China 70/D4
Muztagata (peak), China 87/G5
Muzzana del Turgnano, It. 59/G1
Mwadui, Tanz. 104/B3
Mwana (cape), Kenya 104/D3
Mwanza (pol. reg.), Tanz. 104/B3
Mwanza, Tanz. 104/B3
Mweelrea (peak), Ire. 31/P10
Mweka, D.R. Congo 105/D1
Mwene-Ditu, D.R. Congo 105/D2
Mwense, Zam. 104/A5
Mweru (lake), D.R. Congo 93/E5
Mweru-Wantipa NP, Zam. 104/A5
Mwesi (mtn.), Tanz. 104/A4
Mwinilunga, Zam. 105/D3
My Son Temples (ruin), Viet. 78/E3
My Tho, Viet. 78/D4
Myall Lakes NP, Austl. 115/E2
Myanaung, Myan. 83/G4
Myanmar (Burma) (ctry.) 83/G3
Myebon, Myan. 83/F3
Myerstown, Pa, US 138/B3
Myggenäs, Swe. 38/D2
Myingyan, Myan. 83/G3
Myitkyinā, Myan. 83/G2
Myjava, Slvk. 41/J4
Mykolayiv, Ukr. 49/L2
Mykolayiv (int'l arpt.), Ukr. 49/L2
Mykolayivs'ka (obl.), Ukr. 62/D3
Mylau, Ger. 55/F1
Mymensingh (pol. reg.), Bang. 85/H3
Mynämäki, Fin. 39/J1
Mynydd Eppynt (mts.), Wal, UK 32/C2
Mynydd Pencarreg (peak), Wal, UK 32/B2
Mynydd Preseli (mtn.), Wal, UK 32/B3
Myōgi, Japan 77/B1
Myohaung, Myan. 83/F3
Myōkō-san (peak), Japan 75/F2
Myŏngch'ŏn, NKor. 73/E2
Myrhorod, Ukr. 62/E2
Myrtle Beach, SC, US 133/J3
Myrtle Creek, Or, US 126/C5
Myrtleford, Austl. 115/C3
Mysen, Nor. 38/D2
Myślenice, Pol. 41/K4
Myślibórz, Pol. 41/H2
Myslivna (peak), Czh. 55/H5
Mysore, India 82/C5
Mystery Bay Rec. Area, Wa, US 135/B1
Mystic Island, NJ, US 138/D4
Myszków, Pol. 41/K3
Mytishchi, Rus. 61/W9
Mže (riv.), Czh. 40/G4
Mzimba, Malw. 104/B5
Mzuzu, Malw. 104/B5

N

Na (riv.), Viet. 78/C1
Naab (riv.), Ger. 43/J2
Naaldwijk, Neth. 50/B4
Naalehu, Hi, US 124/U11
Naama, Alg. 99/E2
Naantali, Fin. 39/K1
Naarden, Neth. 50/C4
Naarn im Machlande, Aus. 55/H6
Naas, Ire. 31/Q10
Nababeep, SAfr. 106/B3
Nabari, Japan 77/K6
Nabari (riv.), Japan 77/K6
Nabberu (lake), Austl. 112/D3
Nabburg, Ger. 55/F4
Naberezhnye Chelny, Rus. 61/M5
Nābha, India 86/D4
Nabiac, Austl. 115/E2
Nabisipi (riv.), Qu, Can. 131/J1
Nabón, Ecu. 156/B1
Nabua, Phil. 79/D5
Nābul, Tun. 46/B4
Nābul (gov.), Tun. 46/B4
Nacala, Moz. 105/H3
Nacaome, Hon. 144/E3
Nachi-Katsuura, Japan 74/D4
Nachingwea, Tanz. 104/C5
Náchod, Czh. 41/J3
Nachrodt-Wiblingwerde, Ger. 51/E6
Nacimiento, Chile 158/B3
Naco, Mex. 128/E5
Nacogdoches, Tx, US 129/J5
Nácori Chico, Mex. 142/C2
Nacozari de García, Mex. 142/C2
Nādbai, India 84/A2
Nadder (riv.), Eng, UK 32/D4
Nadiād, India 89/K4
Nădlac, Rom. 48/E2
Nador (prov.), Mor. 100/C2
Nador, Mor. 100/C2
Nadur, Malta 46/L6
Naejang-san NP, SKor. 73/D5
Näfels, Swi. 57/F3
Nafūsah, Jabal (mts.), Libya 99/H3
Naga, Phil. 79/D5
Nagagami (riv.), On, Can. 130/C1
Nagahama, Japan 74/C4
Nagahama, Japan 77/K5
Nagai, Japan 75/G1
Nagaizumi, Japan 77/B3
Nagakute, Japan 77/M5
Nāgāland (state), India 70/F6
Nagambie, Austl. 115/C3
Nagano, Japan 75/F2
Nagano (pref.), Japan 75/E3
Naganuma, Japan 76/B2
Nagaoka, Japan 75/F2
Nagaokakyō, Japan 77/J6
Nagaon (Nowgong), India 83/F2
Nagar, India 84/A2
Nagara (riv.), Japan 75/E3
Nagara, Japan 77/E3
Nagareyama, Japan 77/D2
Nāgārjuna Sāgar (res.), India 82/C4
Nagarote, Nic. 140/D5
Nagarzê, China 85/H1
Nagas (pt.), BC, Can. 134/M5
Nagasaka, Japan 77/A2
Nagasaki, Japan 74/A4
Nagasaki (int'l arpt.), Japan 74/A4
Nagasaki (pref.), Japan 74/A4
Nagasaki Peace, Japan 74/A4
Nagashima, Japan 77/L5
Nagato, Japan 74/B3
Nagato, Japan 74/B3
Nagatoro, Japan 77/C1
Nāgaur, India 89/K2
Nāgda, India 89/L4
Nagercoil, India 82/C6
Nagīna, India 84/B1
Nago, Japan 75/J7
Nago-Torbole, It. 57/G6
Nāgod, India 84/C3
Nagold (riv.), Ger. 54/B5
Nagold, Ger. 54/B5
Nagorno-Karabakh (prov.), Azer. 63/H5
Nagoya, Japan 77/L5
Nagoya Castle, Japan 77/L5
Nagpula (pass), China 85/F1
Nāgpur, India 82/C3
Nags Head, NC, US 133/K3
Naguri, Japan 77/C2
Nagy-Milic (peak), Hun. 41/L4
Nagyatád, Hun. 48/C2
Nagyecsed, Hun. 41/M5
Nagyhalász, Hun. 48/E1
Nagykanizsa, Hun. 48/C2
Nagykáta, Hun. 48/D2
Nagykőrös, Hun. 48/D2
Naha, Japan 75/J7
NaḥLal Shillo (riv.), Isr.,WBnk 91/G7
Nāhan, India 86/D4
Nahanni NP, NW, Can. 122/D2
Nahariyya, Isr. 91/D3
Nahāvand, Iran 88/E2
Nahe (riv.), Ger. 43/G2
NaḥLel Soreq (riv.), Isr.,WBnk 91/F8
Nahouri (prov.), Burk. 103/E4
Nahr 'Atbarah (riv.), Sudan 97/M4
Nahr Mufjir (riv.), Isr.,WBnk 91/G7
Nahr Ouassel (riv.), Alg. 100/F5
Nahuel Huapi (lake), Arg. 147/B7
Nahuel Huapi, PN, Arg. 158/C4
Nahuelbuta, PN, Chile 158/B3
Naica, Mex. 142/D3
Naihāti, India 85/G4
Naila, Ger. 55/E2
Naiman Qi, China 72/E2
Nā'īn, Iran 88/F2
Nain, Nf, Can. 123/K3
Nainital, India 84/B1
Nainpur, India 84/C4
Naintré, Fr. 42/D3
Nairn (riv.), Sc, UK 36/B2
Nairn, Sc, UK 36/C1
Nairne, Austl. 113/M9
Nairobi (cap.), Kenya 104/C3
Nairobi NP, Kenya 104/C3
Naivasha, Kenya 104/C3
Naives-Rosières, Fr. 53/E6
Najafābād, Iran 88/F2
Nájera, Sp. 44/D1
Najin, NKor. 71/P3
Naju, SKor. 73/D5
Naka (riv.), Japan 74/D4
Naka, Japan 77/G5
Nakadōri (isl.), Japan 74/A4
Nakai, Japan 77/C3
Nakajō, Japan 75/F1
Nakalele (pt.), Hi, US 124/T10
Nakamichi, Japan 77/B2
Nakaminato, Japan 75/G2
Nakamura, Japan 74/C4
Nakano, Japan 75/F2
Nakano (lag.), Japan 74/C3
Nakasato, Japan 76/B3
Nakashibetsu, Japan 76/D2
Nakasongola, Ugan. 104/B2
Nakatane, Japan 75/L5
Nakatomi, Japan 77/A3
Nakatsu, Japan 74/B4
Nakatsugawa, Japan 75/E3
Nakazato, Japan 77/B1
Nakhodka, Rus. 71/P3
Nakhon Nayok, Thai. 78/C3
Nakhon Pathom, Thai. 78/C3
Nakhon Phanom, Thai. 78/D2
Nakhon Ratchasima, Thai. 78/C3
Nakhon Sawan, Thai. 78/C3
Nakhon Si Thammarat, Thai. 78/B4
Nakkila, Fin. 39/J1
Nakło nad Notecią, Pol. 41/J2
Naknek, Ak, US 134/G4
Nakodar, India 86/C4
Nakonde, Zam. 104/B5
Naksan-sa, SKor. 73/E3
Nakskov, Den. 38/D4
Naktong, SKor. 73/E4
Naktong (riv.), SKor. 74/A3
Nakūr, India 86/D5
Nakuru, Kenya 104/C3
Nakusp, BC, Can. 126/D3
Nāl (riv.), Pak. 89/J3
Nalayh, Mong. 70/J2
Nalbach, Ger. 53/F5
Nalbāri, India 85/H2
Nalbaugh NP, Austl. 115/D3
Nal'chik (int'l arpt.), Rus. 63/G4
Nal'chik, Rus. 63/G4
Nalgonda, India 82/C4
Nalhāti, India 85/F3
Naliya, India 89/J4
Nallıhan, Turk. 49/K5
Nalón (riv.), Sp. 44/B1
Nālūt, Libya 99/H3
Nam (riv.), NKor. 73/D3
Nam Dinh, Viet. 83/J3
Nam Nao NP, Thai. 78/C2
Nam Un (res.), Thai. 78/C2
Namakzār-e Shadād (salt pan), Iran 89/G2
Namangan (pol. reg.), Uzb. 87/F4
Namangan, Uzb. 87/F4
Namaqualand (reg.), SAfr. 106/B3
Namaripi (cape), Indo. 81/J4
Namasagali, Ugan. 104/B2
Namatanai, PNG 116/E5
Namborn, Ger. 53/G4
Nambour, Austl. 114/D4
Nambu, Japan 77/A3
Nambucca Heads, Austl. 115/E1
Nambung NP, Austl. 112/B4
Namdae (riv.), NKor. 73/E2
Namdalseid, Nor. 37/D2
Namegawa, Japan 77/C1
Namekagon (riv.), Wi, US 127/L4
Namentenga (prov.), Burk. 103/E3
Namerikawa, Japan 75/E2
Nametil, Moz. 105/G4
Namhae (isl.), SKor. 73/D5
Namhae, SKor. 73/D5
Namib (des.), Namb. 105/B5
Namibe, Ang. 105/B4
Namibia (ctry.) 105/C5
Namie, Japan 75/G2
Namioka, Japan 76/B3
Namja (pass), Nepal 82/D2
Namjagbarwa (peak), China 83/G2
Namling, China 82/E2
Namloser Wetterspitze (peak), Aus. 57/G3
Nammoku, Japan 77/B1
Namnoi (peak), Myan. 78/B4
Namoi (riv.), Austl. 109/D4
Namonuito (isl.), Micr. 116/D4
Namorik (isl.), Mrsh. 116/F4
Namp'o, NKor. 73/C3
Nampula, Moz. 105/G4
Namsê (pass), China 82/D2
Namsos, Nor. 37/D2
Namu (isl.), Mrsh. 116/F4
Namur (prov.), Belg. 53/D3
Namur, Belg. 53/D3
Namwŏn, SKor. 73/D5
Namysłów, Pol. 41/J3
Nan (riv.), Thai. 83/H4
Nan, Thai. 78/C2
Nanae, Japan 76/B3
Nanaimo, BC, Can. 126/C3
Nanakuli, Hi, US 124/V13
Nanam, NKor. 73/E2
Nanango, Austl. 114/D4
Nanao, Japan 75/E2
Nanauta, India 86/D5
Nanay (riv.), Peru 150/D4
Nancagua, Chile 158/C2
Nanchang, China 79/C2
Nanchang, China 79/C2
Nancheng, China 79/C2
Nanchong, China 70/J5
Nancy, Fr. 53/F6
Nanda Devi (peak), India 70/C5
Nandan, China 83/J3
Nānded, India 82/C4
Nanding (riv.), China 83/G3
Nandrin, Belg. 53/E3
Nandu (riv.), China 79/A4
Nandurbār, India 89/K4
Nandy, Fr. 30/K6
Nandyāl, India 82/C4
Nanfeng, China 79/C2
Nang Xian, China 83/F2
Nanga Parbat (peak), Pak. 86/C2
Nangapinoh, Indo. 80/D4
Nangis, Fr. 30/M6
Nangnim (mts.), NKor. 73/D2
Nangong, China 72/C3
Nangtud (mt.), Phil. 81/F1
Nangwarry, Austl. 115/B3
Nanhui, China 72/L8
Nanjian Yizu Zizhixian, China 83/H2
Nanjing, China 72/D4
Nankāna Sāhib, Pak. 86/B4
Nankang, China 79/B2
Nankoku, Japan 74/C4
Nanle, China 72/C3
Nanliu (riv.), China 83/J3
Nannestad, Nor. 38/D1
Nanning, China 83/J3
Nannō, Japan 77/L5
Nannup, Austl. 112/B5
Nanny (riv.), Ire. 34/B4
Nānpāra, India 84/C2
Nanpi, China 72/D3
Nanping, China 79/C2
Nansei, Japan 77/L7
Nansen (sound), Nun., Can. 123/S6
Nant (lake), Sc, UK 36/A4
Nantai-san (peak), Japan 75/F2
Nanterre, Fr. 30/J5
Nantes, Fr. 42/C3
Nanteuil-le-Haudouin, Fr. 30/L4
Nanteuil-lès-Meaux, Fr. 52/B6
Nanticoke, On, Can. 130/D3
Nanticoke, Pa, US 138/B1
Nanton, Ab, Can. 126/E3
Nantong, China 72/E4
Nantua, Fr. 56/B5
Nantucket (isl.), Ma, US 131/G3
Nantwich, Eng, UK 35/F5
Nanuet, NY, US 139/J7
Nanumanga (isl.), Tuv. 116/G5
Nanumea (isl.), Tuv. 116/G5
Nanuque, Braz. 154/B5
Nanwon (res.), China 72/C4
Nanxi, China 83/H2
Nanxiong, China 79/B2
Nanyang, China 72/C4
Nanyang, China 72/D4
Nanyuki, Kenya 104/C2
Nanzhang, China 72/B5
Nanzhao, China 72/C4
Nao, Cabo de la (cape), Sp. 45/F3
Naococane (lake), Qu, Can. 123/J3
Naogaon, Bang. 85/G3
Naokot, Pak. 82/A3
Naolinco, Mex. 143/N7
Naoua (falls), C.d'Iv. 102/D5
Náousa, Gre. 47/J4
Náousa, Gre. 47/H2
Napa, Ca, US 128/B3
Napa (riv.), Ca, US 135/K10
Napa (valley), Ca, US 135/K9
Napa (co.), Ca, US 135/K10
Napa Junction, Ca, US 135/K10
Napak (peak), Ugan. 104/B2
Napakiak, Ak, US 134/F3
Napanee, On, Can. 130/E2
Napaskiak, Ak, US 134/F3
Napata (ruin), Sudan 101/B5
Naperville, Il, US 130/B3
Napf (peak), Swi. 56/D4
Napier, NZ 117/T10
Napier, SAfr. 106/L11
Naples, Fl, US 133/H5
Naples (Napoli), It. 46/D2
Napo (riv.), Peru 152/C5
Napo (riv.), Ecu.,Peru 147/B3
Napo (prov.), Ecu. 152/B5
Napoleon, ND, US 127/J4
Napoleonville, La, US 129/K5
Napoli, Golfo di (gulf), It. 46/C2
Napuka (isl.), FrPol. 117/L6
Naqīl Sumārah (pass), Yem. 88/D6
Nara, Mali 102/D3
Nāra (riv.), Pak. 89/J4
Nara, Japan 77/J6
Naracoorte, Austl. 115/B3
Naraini, India 84/C3
Naranbulag, Mong. 70/F2
Naranjal, Ecu. 152/B5

210

Naran – Newto

Naranjito, Ecu. 156/B1
Naranjos, Mex. 144/B1
Narāq, Iran 88/F2
Narasannapeta, India 82/D4
Narashino, Japan 77/E2
Narathiwat, Thai. 78/C5
Nārāyanganj, Bang. 85/H4
Nārāyani (zone), Nepal 85/E2
Narayani (riv.), Nepal 85/E2
Nārāyanpet, India 82/C4
Narbonne, Fr. 42/E5
Narceo (riv.), Sp. 44/B1
Nardò, It. 47/F2
Nare (pt.), Eng, UK 32/B6
Narellan, Austl. 114/G9
Narembeen, Austl. 112/C5
Nares (str.), Can.,Grld. 123/T6
Narew (riv.), Pol. 60/D5
Narganá, Pan. 152/B2
Narinda (bay), Madg. 107/H6
Nariño (dept.), Col. 152/B4
Narita (int'l arpt.), Japan 75/G3
Narita, Japan 77/E2
Nariz (peak), Chile 159/C7
Narkatiāganj, India 85/E2
Narmada (riv.), India 67/G7
Narman, Turk. 63/G4
Narni, It. 46/C1
Narodnaya (peak), Rus. 61/P2
Narok, Kenya 104/B3
Narón, Sp. 44/A1
Narooma, Austl. 115/D3
Nārowāl, Pak. 86/C3
Nærøy, Nor. 37/D2
Narra, Phil. 81/E2
Narrabri, Austl. 115/D1
Narrandera, Austl. 115/C2
Narrogin, Austl. 112/C5
Narromine, Austl. 115/D2
Narrows (riv.), NY, US 139/J9
Narsimhapur, India 84/B4
Narsingarh, India 89/L4
Narsinghdi, Bang. 85/H4
Narusawa, Japan 77/B3
Naruto, Japan 74/D3
Narutō, Japan 77/E2
Narva (res.), Rus. 60/F4
Narva (riv.), Est.,Rus. 60/E4
Narva (bay), Est.,Rus. 39/M2
Narva, Est. 39/N2
Narvacan, Phil. 79/D4
Narvik, Nor. 37/F1
Narwāna, India 86/D5
Nar'yan-Mar, Rus. 61/M2
Naryn, Kyr. 87/G4
Naryn (obl.), Kyr. 87/G4
Naryn (riv.), Kyr. 64/H5
Naryn Qum (plain), Kaz. 63/J2
Narzole, It. 58/A3
Năsăud, Rom. 49/G2
Naschel, Arg. 158/D2
Nash (pt.), Wal, UK 32/C4
Nashua, NH, US 131/G3
Nashville (int'l arpt.), Tn, US 130/C4
Nashville (cap.), Tn, US 130/C4
Našice, Cro. 48/D3
Nasielsk, Pol. 41/L2
Nasijärvi (lake), Fin. 39/K1
Nāsik, India 89/K5
Nasīrābād, India 89/K3
Naso (pt.), Phil. 81/F1
Nāsriganj, India 85/E3
Nass (riv.), BC, Can. 134/N4
Nassach (riv.), Ger. 54/D2
Nassau (cap.), Bahm. 141/F2
Nassau (isl.), Cookls. 117/J6
Nassau (co.), NY, US 139/E2
Nassau, De, US 138/C6
Nassau (bay), Chile 159/D7
Nassau, Ger. 53/G3
Nasser (lake), Egypt 93/E2
Nassereith, Aus. 57/G3
Nässjö, Swe. 38/F3
Nassogne, Belg. 53/E3
Nastapoka (isls.), Qu, Can. 123/J3
Nastätten, Ger. 53/G3
Næstved, Den. 38/D4
Nasu-dake (peak), Japan 75/F2
Nat (peak), Myan. 83/G4
Nata, Bots. 105/E5
Natá, Pan. 152/A2
Natagaima, Col. 152/C4
Natal, Braz. 154/D2
Naṭanz, Iran 88/F2
Natashō, Japan 77/J5
Natashquan (riv.), Qu, Can. 123/K3
Natchez, Ms, US 129/K5
Natchez Trace Nat'l Parkway, US 130/C5
Natchitoches, La, US 129/J5
Naters, Swi. 56/D5
Nāthdwāra, India 89/K4
Natimuk, Austl. 115/B3
Nation (riv.), BC, Can. 126/B2
National Agriculture Research Center, Md, US 138/B6
National Aquarium, Md, US 138/B5
National Archaeological Museum, Gre. 47/N8
National City, Ca, US 136/C5
National Cowboy Hall of Fame and Western Heritage Center, Ok, US 137/N14
National Exhibition Centre, Eng, UK 33/E2
National Institutes of Health, Md, US 138/A6
National Museum, Mona. 58/J8
National Security Agency, Md, US 138/B5
Natitingou, Ben. 103/F4
Natl, Jor. 91/D4
Natron (lake), Tanz. 104/B3
Natternbach, Aus. 55/G6
Nattheim, Ger. 54/D5
Nättraby, Swe. 38/F3
Natuna (isls.), Indo. 67/K9
Natural Bridge Caverns, Tx, US 137/U20
Natural Bridges Nat'l Mon., Ut, US 128/E3
Naturaliste (cape), Austl. 115/D4
Naturaliste (chan.), Austl. 112/B3
Naturaliste (cape), Austl. 112/B5
Naturno (Naturns), It. 57/G4
Naturns (Naturno), It. 43/J3
Naucalpan, Mex. 143/Q10
Naucelle, Fr. 42/E4
Nauders, Aus. 57/G4
Naudesnek (pass), SAfr. 106/E3
Nauen, Ger. 40/P6
Naugachhia, India 85/F3
Naugaon Sādāt, India 84/B1
Nauhcampatépetl (vol.), Mex. 143/M7
Nauheim, Ger. 54/B4
Naujan, Phil. 79/D5
Naujoji-Akmenė, Lith. 39/K3
Naumburg, Ger. 51/G6
Naumburg, Ger. 40/F3
Nauort, Ger. 53/G3
Nā'ūr, Jor. 91/D4
Nauru (ctry.) 116/F5
Naushahra, India 86/C3
Naushahra Virkhan, Pak. 86/B4
Nauta, Peru 156/C2
Nautla, Mex. 143/N6
Nauvo (Nagu), Fin. 39/J1
Nava, Mex. 132/C4
Nava, Colle di (pass), It. 58/A4
Nava del Rey, Sp. 44/C2
Navajo (res.), NM, US 128/F3
Navajo Nat'l Mon., Az, US 128/E3
Navalcarnero, Sp. 45/M9
Navalmoral de la Mata, Sp. 44/C3
Navalvillar de Pela, Sp. 44/C3
Navapolatsk, Bela. 39/N4
Navarin (cape), Rus. 65/T3
Navarino (isl.), Chile 157/C8
Navarra (aut. comm.), Sp. 44/D1
Navarro, Arg. 159/J11
Navàs, Sp. 45/F2
Navas de San Juan, Sp. 44/D3
Navasota (riv.), Tx, US 143/F2
Navassa (isl.), Myan. 145/H2
Navax (pt.), Eng, UK 32/A6
Nave, It. 58/D1
Navenne, Fr. 56/C2
Navia, Sp. 44/B1
Navia (riv.), Sp. 44/B1
Navidad, Chile 158/N8
Navina, Ok, US 137/M14
Naviraí, Braz. 157/F1
Năvodari, Rom. 49/J3
Navojoa, Mex. 142/C3
Navolato, Mex. 142/D3
Návpaktos, Gre. 47/G3
Návplion, Gre. 47/H4
Navsāri, India 89/K4
Navy Board (inlet), Nun., Can. 123/H1
Navy Yard City, Wa, US 135/B2
Nawābganj, India 84/B1
Nawābganj, India 84/C2
Nawābganj, Bang. 85/G3
Nawābshāh, Pak. 89/J3
Nawāda, India 85/E3
Nawān Jandānwāla, Pak. 86/A3
Nawāshahr, India 86/D4
Nawāshahr, Pak. 86/B2
Nawoiy, Uzb. 87/E4
Nawoiy (pol. reg.), Uzb. 87/D4
Nawş, Ra's (pt.), Oman 89/G5
Naxçivan (aut. rep.), Azer. 90/F2
Naxçıvan, Azer. 63/H5
Naxçivan Aut. Rep., Azer. 63/H5
Naxi, China 83/J2
Náxos, Gre. 47/J4
Náxos (isl.), Gre. 47/J4
Nayarit (state), Mex. 142/D4
Nayong, China 83/J2
Nayoro, Japan 76/C1
Nayramadlïn (peak), Mong. 70/E2
Nayzatash (pass), Taj. 87/F5
Nazaré, Braz. 154/C4
Nazaré, Port. 44/A3
Nazaré do Piauí, Braz. 154/B2
Nazaré Paulista, Braz. 211/G8
Nazareth, Pa, US 138/C2
Nazareth, Belg. 52/C2
Nazas (riv.), Mex. 142/D3
Nazas, Mex. 142/D3
Nazca, Peru 156/C4
Naze, Japan 75/K6
Naze, The (pt.), Eng, UK 33/H3
Nazerat (Nazareth), Isr. 91/G6
Nazilli, Turk. 90/B2
Nazrēt, Eth. 97/N6
Nazyvayevsk, Rus. 87/F1
Nchelenge, Zam. 104/A5
Ncheu, Malw. 105/F3
Ndalatando, Ang. 105/B2
Ndali, Ben. 103/F4
Ndele, CAfr. 97/K6
Ndende (isl.), Sol. 116/F6
N'djamena (cap.), Chad 96/J5
Ndola, Zam. 105/E3
Ndrhamcha (lake), Mrta. 102/B2
Né (riv.), Fr. 42/C4
Néa Alikarnassós, Gre. 47/J5
Néa Ankhíalos, Gre. 47/H3
Néa Artáki, Gre. 47/H3
Néa Ionía, Gre. 47/H3
Néa Ionía, Gre. 47/N8
Néa Kallikrátia, Gre. 47/H2
Néa Kíos, Gre. 47/H4
Néa Mikhaniona, Gre. 47/H2
Néa Moudhaniá, Gre. 47/H2
Néa Potídhaia, Gre. 47/H2
Néa Triglia, Gre. 47/H2
Néa Zíkhni, Gre. 47/H2
Neagh (lake), NI, UK 34/B2
Neale (lake), Austl. 109/C3
Neales (riv.), Austl. 113/G3
Neamț (prov.), Rom. 49/H2
Neaophli-le-Château, Fr. 30/H5
Neápolis, Gre. 47/H4
Neápolis, Gre. 47/G2
Neápolis, Gre. 47/J5
Near (isls.), Ak, US 134/A5
Neath, Wal, UK 32/C3
Neath (riv.), Wal, UK 32/C3
Neath Port Talbot (co.), Wal, UK 32/C3
Neavitt, Md, US 138/B6
Nebbi, Ugan. 104/A2
Nebel-Horn (peak), Ger. 57/G3
Nebikon, Swi. 56/D3
Nebitdag, Trkm. 63/K5
Neblina (peak), Braz. 153/E4
Nebo (mt.), Austl. 114/E6
Nebraska (state), US 129/G2
Nebrodi (mts.), It. 46/C4
Nechako (riv.), BC, Can. 122/D3
Neches (riv.), Tx, US 125/G5
Nechisar NP, Eth. 97/N6
Nechranice (res.), Czh. 55/G2
Neckar (riv.), Ger. 40/D4
Neckarbischofsheim, Ger. 54/B4
Neckargemünd, Ger. 54/B4
Neckarsteinach, Ger. 54/B4
Neckarsulm, Ger. 54/C4
Necker (isl.), Hi, US 117/J2
Necochea, Arg. 158/F3
Necoclí, Col. 152/B2
Necropoli (ruin), It. 46/C1
Neda, Sp. 44/A1
Nedelino, Bul. 47/J2
Nedelišće, Cro. 43/M3
Nederland, Tx, US 129/J5
Nederland, Co, US 137/A3
Nederweert, Neth. 50/C6
Neede, Neth. 50/D4
Needles, Ca, US 128/D4
Needles, The, Eng, UK 33/E5
Needmore, Ok, US 137/N15
Neepawa, Mb, Can. 127/J3
Neerabup NP, Austl. 112/K6
Neerpelt, Belg. 50/C6
Neetze (riv.), Ger. 51/H2
Neetze, Ger. 51/H2
Neffelbach (riv.), Ger. 53/F2
Neftekamsk, Rus. 61/M4
Nefud (des.), SAr. 67/B7
Nefyn, Wal, UK 34/D6
Negēlē, Eth. 97/N6
Negev (reg.), Isr. 90/C4
Negoiu (peak), Rom. 49/G3
Negombo, SrL. 82/C6
Negotin, Yugo. 48/F3
Negotino, FYROM 47/H2
Negra (pt.), Peru 156/A2
Negra (range), Braz. 154/A3
Negra (pt.), Belz. 144/D2
Negrais (cape), Myan. 83/F4
Negrar, It. 59/D1
Negreira, Sp. 44/A1
Negrești, Rom. 49/H2
Negritos, Peru 156/A2
Negro (riv.), Uru. 157/E3
Negro (riv.), Arg. 157/D5
Negro (peak), Arg. 158/C3
Negros (isl.), Phil. 67/M9
Nehbandān, Iran 89/H2
Nei Monggol (aut. reg.), China 71/K3
Nei Monggol (plat.), China 71/K3
Neiafu, Tonga 117/H6
Neiba, DRep. 141/G4
Neiba (mts.), DRep. 145/J2
Neiderösterreich (prov.), Aus. 43/L2
Neige, Crêt de la (peak), Fr. 56/B5
Neihuang, China 72/C4
Neijiang, China 70/J6
Neilston, Sc, UK 36/B5
Neiqiu, China 72/C3
Neisse (riv.), Ger. 41/H3
Neiva, Col. 152/C4
Neixiang, China 72/B4
Nejanilini (lake), Mb, Can. 122/G3
Nejdek, Czh. 55/F2
Nejrab (int'l arpt.), Syria 91/E1
Nek'emtē, Eth. 97/N6
Neksø, Den. 38/F4
Nelas, Port. 44/B2
Nelidovo, Rus. 60/G4
Nellingen, Ger. 54/C5
Nellore, India 82/C5
Nelson (cape), Austl. 115/B3
Nelson (isl.), Ak, US 134/E3
Nelson (str.), Chile 157/A7
Nelson, BC, Can. 126/D3
Nelson, NZ 117/S11
Nelson (riv.), Mb, Can. 122/G3
Nelson, Eng, UK 35/F4
Nelson-Atkins Museum of Fine Art, Mo, US 137/D5
Nelson Bay, Austl. 115/E2
Nelson Lagoon, Ak, US 134/F4
Nelson Lakes NP, NZ 117/S11
Nelspruit, SAfr. 105/F6
Néma, Mrta. 102/D2
Néma, Dhar (cliff), Mrta. 102/D2
Neman (riv.), Rus. 41/M1
Nembro, It. 58/C1
Neméa, Gre. 47/H4
Nemingha, Austl. 115/D1
Nemira (peak), Rom. 49/H2
Nemours, Fr. 42/E2
Nemunas (riv.), Lith. 60/D5
Nemuro (pen.), Japan 76/D2
Nemuro, Japan 76/D2
Nen (riv.), China 67/M5
Nenagh, Ire. 31/P10
Nenana, Ak, US 134/J3
Nendaz, Swi. 56/D5
Nene (riv.), Eng, UK 35/J6
Nenetskiy (aut. okrug), Rus. 61/L2
Nenjiang, China 71/N2
Nentershausen, Ger. 51/G6
Nentershausen, Ger. 53/G3
Nenzing, Aus. 57/F3
Neo Volcanica, Cordillera (mts.), Mex. 143/Q10
Néon Petrítsion, Gre. 47/H2
Neoria Husainpur, India 84/B1
Néos Marmarás, Gre. 47/H2
Neosho (riv.), Ks,Ok, US 129/J3
Nepal (ctry.) 84/D1
Nepālganj, Nepal 84/C1
Nepanagar, India 89/L4
Nepean, On, Can. 130/F2
Nepean (riv.), Austl. 114/G8
Nepeña, Peru 156/B3
Nepessina (lake), Mi, US 135/F6
Nephi, Ut, US 128/E3
Nepisiguit (riv.), NB, Can. 131/H2
Nepomuk, Czh. 55/G4
Neptune City, NJ, US 138/D3
Nera (riv.), It. 43/K5
Nérac, Fr. 42/D4
Neratovice, Czh. 55/H2
Nerekhta, Rus. 60/J4
Neresheim, Ger. 54/D5
Neretva (riv.), Bosn. 48/D4
Neris (riv.), Lith. 60/E5
Nerja, Sp. 44/D4
Nermete (pt.), Peru 156/A2
Nerokoúros, Gre. 47/J5
Nerone (peak), It. 59/F5
Nerpio, Sp. 44/D3
Nersingen, Ger. 54/D6
Nerva, Sp. 44/B4
Nervesa della Battaglia, It. 59/F1
Nerviano, It. 58/B1
Nes, Neth. 50/C2
Nes, Nor. 38/D1
Nes Ẕiyyona, Isr. 91/F8
Nesbyen, Nor. 38/C1
Nesebŭr, Bul. 47/K1
Nesher, Isr. 91/G6
Neskaupstadhur, Ice. 37/Q6
Nesle, Fr. 52/B4
Nesles-la-Vallée, Fr. 30/J4
Nesquehoning, Pa, US 138/C2
Ness (riv.), Sc, UK 36/B2
Ness (lake), Sc, UK 36/B2
Nesselrode (mt.), Ak, US 134/M4
Nesselwang, Ger. 57/G2
Nesslau, Swi. 57/F3
Neston, Eng, UK 35/E5
Nestórion, Gre. 47/G2
Néstos (riv.), Gre. 49/G5
Netanya, Isr. 91/F7
Netarhāt, India 85/E4
Netcong, NJ, US 138/D2
Nethe (riv.), Ger. 51/G5
Netherlands (ctry.) 40/C3
Netherlands Antilles (dpcy.), Neth. 141/H5
Netolice, Czh. 55/H4
Netphen, Ger. 53/H2
Netstal, Swi. 57/F3
Nette (riv.), Ger. 50/D6
Nettebach (riv.), Ger. 53/G3
Nettersheim, Ger. 53/F3
Nettetal, Ger. 50/D6
Nettilling (lake), Nun., Can. 123/J2
Nettuno, It. 46/C2
Netzschkau, Ger. 55/F1
Neu Darchau, Ger. 51/H2
Neu-Isenburg, Ger. 54/B2
Neu-Ulm, Ger. 54/D6
Neu Zittau, Ger. 40/Q7
Neubiberg, Ger. 55/E6
Neubrandenburg, Ger. 41/G2
Neubulach, Ger. 54/B5
Neuburg, Ger. 54/B5
Neuburg an der Donau, Ger. 54/E5
Neuburg an der Kammel, Ger. 57/G1
Neuchâtel, Swi. 56/C4
Neuchâtel (canton), Swi. 56/C4
Neuchâtel, Lac de (lake), Swi. 43/G3
Neuenbürg, Ger. 54/B5
Neuenburg am Rhein, Ger. 56/D2
Neuendettelsau, Ger. 54/D4
Neuenhagen, Ger. 40/Q6
Neuenhaus, Ger. 50/D3
Neuenkirchen, Ger. 51/F3
Neuenkirchen, Ger. 51/F3
Neuenkirchen, Ger. 51/E4
Neuenrade, Ger. 51/E6
Neuenstadt am Kocher, Ger. 54/C4
Neuenstein, Ger. 54/C4
Neuerburg, Ger. 53/F3
Neuf-Brisach, Fr. 56/D1
Neufahrn bei Freising, Ger. 55/E6
Neufchâteau, Fr. 56/B1
Neufchâteau, Belg. 53/E4
Neufchâtel-en-Bray, Fr. 42/D2
Neufchâtel-Hardelot, Fr. 52/A2
Neufchelles, Fr. 30/M4
Neufmanil, Fr. 53/D4
Neufmoutiers-en-Brie, Fr. 30/L5
Neuhaus am Inn, Ger. 55/G6
Neuhaus am Rennweg, Ger. 54/E1
Neuhaus-Schierschnitz, Ger. 54/E2
Neuhäusel, Ger. 53/G3
Neuhausen am Rheinfall, Swi. 57/E2
Neuhof, Ger. 54/C2
Neuhof an der Zenn, Ger. 54/D4
Neuhofen, Ger. 54/B4
Neuhofen an der Krems, Aus. 55/H6
Neuilly-en-Thelle, Fr. 52/B5
Neuilly-L'Évêque, Fr. 56/B2
Neuilly-sur-Marne, Fr. 30/K5
Neuilly-sur-Seine, Fr. 30/J5
Neukirchen, Ger. 38/C4
Neukirchen an der Vöckla, Aus. 55/G6
Neukirchen vorm Wald, Ger. 55/G5
Neumarkt am Wallersee, Aus. 55/G7
Neumarkt (Enga), It. 57/H5
Neumarkt im Mühlkreis, Aus. 55/H6
Neumarkt in der Oberpfalz, Ger. 55/E4
Neumarkt-Sankt Veit, Ger. 55/F6
Neumünster, Ger. 38/C4
Neunkirch, Swi. 57/E2
Neunkirchen, Aus. 43/M3
Neunkirchen, Ger. 53/H2
Neunkirchen, Ger. 53/G5
Neunkirchen-Seelscheid, Ger. 53/G2
Neupotz, Ger. 54/B4
Neuquén (riv.), Arg. 157/C4
Neuquén (prov.), Arg. 158/C3
Neuquén, Arg. 158/C3
Neuruppin, Ger. 40/G2
Neusäss, Ger. 54/D6
Neuse (riv.), NC, US 133/J3
Neusiedl am See, Aus. 43/M3
Neusiedler (lake), Aus. 41/J5
Neusiedler See (lake), Aus. 48/C2
Neuss, Ger. 50/D6
Neustadt, Ger. 53/G2
Neustadt am Rübenberge, Ger. 51/G3
Neustadt an der Aisch, Ger. 54/D3
Neustadt an der Donau, Ger. 55/E5
Neustadt an der Waldnaab, Ger. 55/F3
Neustadt an der Weinstrasse, Ger. 54/B4
Neustadt bei Coburg, Ger. 54/E2
Neustadt in Holstein, Ger. 38/D4
Neustift im Stubaital, Aus. 57/H3
Neustrelitz, Ger. 40/G2
Neutraubling, Ger. 55/F5
Neuves-Maisons, Fr. 42/F2
Neuvic, Fr. 42/E4
Neuville-sur-Saône, Fr. 56/A6
Neuwied, Ger. 53/G3
Neuzelle, Ger. 41/H2
Neva (riv.), Rus. 39/P2
Nevada, Mo, US 129/J3
Nevada (mts.), Col. 145/H4
Nevada (state), US 128/C3
Nevada, Sierra (mts.), Sp. 44/D4
Nevado de Colima PN, Mex. 142/D5
Nevado de Toluca, PN, Mex. 143/K7
Nevado del Huila, PN, Col. 150/C3
Nevado, Sierra del (mts.), Arg. 158/C3
Nevel', Rus. 39/N3
Nevele, Belg. 52/C1
Nevel'sk, Rus. 71/R2
Nevers, Fr. 42/E3
Nevesinje, Bosn. 47/F1
Nevinnomyssk, Rus. 63/G3
Nevis (peak), StK. 141/N8
Nevis (isl.), UK 141/J4
Nevola (riv.), It. 59/G5
Nevsehir (prov.), Turk. 90/C2
Nevşehir, Turk. 90/C2
New (riv.), Guy. 150/G3
New (riv.), WV, US 130/D4
New Albany, In, US 130/C4
New Albany, Ms, US 133/F3
New Amsterdam, Guy. 153/G3
New Ancholme (riv.), Eng, UK 35/H4
New Athens, Il, US 137/H9
New Baltimore, Mi, US 135/G6
New Bataan, Phil. 79/E6
New Bedford, Ma, US 131/G3
New Berlin, Tx, US 137/U21
New Berlin, Pa, US 138/B2
New Berlin, Wi, US 135/P14
New Berlinville, Pa, US 138/C3
New Bern, NC, US 133/J3
New Braunfels, Tx, US 137/U20
New Britain, Ct, US 131/F3
New Britain (isl.), PNG 116/D5
New Britain, Pa, US 138/C3
New Brunswick (prov.), Can. 131/H2
New Brunswick, NJ, US 139/H10
New Buffalo, Pa, US 138/B3
New Buildings, NI, UK 34/A2
New Caledonia (isl.), NCal. 116/F7
New Caledonia (terr.), Fr. 116/F6
New Canaan, Ct, US 139/M7
New Castle, In, US 130/C4
New Castle, Pa, US 130/D3
New Castle, De, US 138/C4
New Castle (co.), De, US 138/C5
New Chicago, In, US 135/R16
New City, NY, US 139/K7
New Columbia, Pa, US 138/B1
New Columbus, Pa, US 138/B1
New Cumberland, Pa, US 138/B3
New Cumnock, Sc, UK 36/B6
New Delhi (cap.), India 86/D5
New Denver, BC, Can. 126/D3
New Egypt, NJ, US 138/D3
New England NP, Austl. 115/E1
New Freedom, Pa, US 138/B4
New Galloway, Sc, UK 34/D1
New Georgia (isls.), Sol. 116/E5
New Georgia (sound), Sol. 116/E5
New Glasgow, NS, Can. 131/J2
New Glasgow, Qu, Can. 131/N6
New Gretna, NJ, US 138/D4
New Guinea (isl.), Indo.,PNG 67/N10
New Hampshire (state), US 131/G3
New Hanover, SAfr. 107/E3
New Hanover, Il, US 137/G9
New Hanover (isl.), PNG 116/D5
New Haven, Ct, US 131/F3
New Haven, Mi, US 135/G6
New Hebrides (isls.), Van. 116/F6
New Holland, Pa, US 138/B3
New Hope, Pa, US 138/D3
New Hyde Park, NY, US 139/L9
New Iberia, La, US 129/K5
New Ireland (isl.), PNG 116/E5
New Jersey (state), US 138/D3
New Kensington, Pa, US 130/E3
New Kowloon, China 71/U10
New Lenox, Il, US 135/Q16
New Lisbon, NJ, US 138/D4
New Liskeard, On, Can. 130/E2
New London, Ct, US 131/F3
New Madrid, Mo, US 129/K3
New Market, Md, US 138/A5
New Meadows, Id, US 126/D4
New Mexico (state), US 128/G4
New Milford, NJ, US 139/J8
New Mills, Eng, UK 35/F5
New Norfolk, Austl. 115/C4
New Orleans, La, US 137/P17
New Orleans (Moisant Field), La, US 137/P17
New Oxford, Pa, US 138/A4
New Philadelphia, Oh, US 130/D3
New Philadelphia, Pa, US 138/B2
New Pitsligo, Sc, UK 36/D1
New Plymouth, NZ 117/S10
New Port Richey, Fl, US 133/H4
New Providence (isl.), Bahm. 141/F3
New Providence, NJ, US 139/H9
New Richmond, Qu, Can. 131/H1
New River (mts.), Az, US 137/R18
New River, Az, US 137/R18
New Rochelle, NY, US 139/K8
New Rockford, ND, US 127/J4
New Romney, Eng, UK 33/G5
New Ross, Ire. 31/Q10
New Rossington, Eng, UK 35/G5
New Sarpy, La, US 137/P17
New Schwabenland (phys. reg.), Ant. 160/Z
New Scone, Sc, UK 36/C4
New Siberian (isls.), Rus. 67/N2
New Smyrna Beach, Fl, US 133/H4
New South Wales, Austl. 115/D1
New South Wales (state), Austl. 109/D4
New Stuyahok, Ak, US 134/G4
New Town, ND, US 127/H4
New Tripoli, Pa, US 138/C2
New Ulm, Mn, US 127/K4
New Waterford, NS, Can. 131/J2
New Westminster, BC, Can. 126/C3
New Windsor, Md, US 138/A4
New York (state), US 130/G3
New York, NY, US 139/K9
New Zealand (ctry.) 117/R10
Newark, Oh, US 130/D3
Newark, De, US 138/C4
Newark (int'l arpt.), NJ, US 139/J9
Newark, NJ, US 139/J9
Newark, Ca, US 135/K11
Newark (bay), NJ, US 139/J9
Newark-on-Trent, Eng, UK 35/H5
Newbern, Il, US 137/G8
Newberry, SC, US 133/H3
Newberry, Mi, US 130/C2
Newberry Nat'l Volcanic Mon., Or, US 126/C5
Newburgh, Sc, UK 36/C4
Newburn, Eng, UK 35/G2
Newbury, Eng, UK 33/E4
Newcastle, Austl. 115/D2
Newcastle, Wy, US 127/G5
Newcastle, SAfr. 107/E2
Newcastle, Ire. 31/P10
Newcastle, Ok, US 137/M15
Newcastle, NI, UK 34/C3
Newcastle (int'l arpt.), Eng, UK 35/G1
Newcastle, Ire. 34/B5
Newcastle-under-Lyme, Eng, UK 35/F6
Newcastle upon Tyne, Eng, UK 35/G2
Newcastleton, Sc, UK 35/F1
Newe Yam, Isr. 91/F6
Newel, Ger. 53/F4
Newell, Austl. 114/B2
Newellton, La, US 129/K4
Newenham (cape), Ak, US 134/F4
Newfane, NY, US 131/S9
Newfield, NJ, US 138/C4
Newfoundland (isl.), Can. 131/L1
Newfoundland (prov.), Can. 123/K3
Newfoundland, NJ, US 139/H7
Newfoundland, Pa, US 138/C1
Newhalen, Ak, US 134/H4
Newham (bor.), Eng, UK 30/D2
Newhaven, Eng, UK 33/F5
Newington, Eng, UK 30/F3
Newkirk, Ok, US 129/H3
Newllano, La, US 129/J5
Newmains, Sc, UK 36/C5
Newman (mt.), Austl. 112/C2
Newman, Austl. 112/C2
Newmarket, On, Can. 130/E2
Newmarket, Eng, UK 33/G2
Newmill, Sc, UK 36/D1
Newnan, Ga, US 133/G3
Newport, Eng, UK 32/D1
Newport, Eng, UK 33/E5
Newport, Wal, UK 32/D3
Newport (co.), Wal, UK 32/C3
Newport, Ar, US 129/K4
Newport (bay), Ca, US 136/C3
Newport, De, US 138/C4
Newport, Ky, US 130/C4
Newport, NJ, US 138/C5
Newport, Or, US 126/B4
Newport, Pa, US 138/A3
Newport, RI, US 131/G3
Newport, Tn, US 130/D5
Newport, Vt, US 131/F2
Newport, Wa, US 126/D3
Newport Beach, Ca, US 136/G8
Newport Meadows (lake), NJ, US 138/C5
Newport-on-Tay, Sc, UK 36/D4
Newport Pagnell, Eng, UK 33/F2
Newquay, Eng, UK 32/A6
Newry, NI, UK 34/B3
Newry (dist.), NI, UK 34/B3
Newry (canal), NI, UK 34/B3
Newtok, Ak, US 134/F3
Newton, Tx, US 129/J5
Newton, Ma, US 131/G3
Newton, NJ, US 138/D1
Newton Abbot, Eng, UK 32/C5
Newton-le-Willows, Eng, UK 35/F5
Newton Mearns, Sc, UK 36/B5
Newton Stewart, Sc, UK 34/D2
Newton Tors (hill), Eng, UK 36/D5
Newtonmore, Sc, UK 36/B2
Newtonville, NJ, US 138/D4
Newtown, Austl. 115/B3
Newtown, Wal, UK 32/C1
Newtown, Pa, US 138/D3
Newtown Mount Kennedy, Ire. 34/B5
Newtown Saint Boswells, Sc, UK 36/D5
Newtown Square, Pa, US 138/C4
Newtownabbey, NI, UK 34/C2
Newtownards, NI, UK 34/C2
Newtownhamilton, NI, UK 34/B3
Newtownstewart, NI, UK 34/A2

Newtyle, Sc, UK 36/C3
Nextlalpan, Mex. 143/Q9
Neyagawa, Japan 77/J6
Neyrīz, Iran 89/F3
Neyshābūr, Iran 89/G1
Neyva (riv.), Rus. 61/P4
Neyveli, India 82/C5
Neyyāttinkara, India 82/C6
Nezahualcóyotl, Mex. 143/Q10
Neznayka (riv.), Rus. 61/W9
Nezperce, Id, US 126/D4
Ngabang, Indo. 80/C3
Ngabordamlu (cape), Indo. 81/H5
Ngabu, Malw. 105/H4
Ngai-Ndethya Nat'l Rsv., Kenya 104/C3
Ngamring, China 85/F1
Nganda (peak), Malw. 104/B5
Ngangerabeli (plain), Kenya 104/C3
Ngaoundéré, Camr. 96/H6
Ngarkat Conservation Park, Austl. 113/J5
Ngatik (isl.), Micr. 116/E4
Ngoan Muc (pass), Viet. 78/E4
Ngoc Linh (peak), Viet. 83/J4
Ngomeni (cape), Kenya 104/D3
Ngong, Kenya 104/C3
Ngonye (falls), Zam. 105/D4
Ngorongoro Consv. Area, Tanz. 104/B3
Ngounié (riv.), Gabon 96/H8
Nguigmi, Niger 96/H5
Ngulu (isl.), Micr. 116/C4
Ngumbe Sukani (pt.), Tanz. 104/C5
Nguru (mts.), Tanz. 104/C4
Ngwenya (peak), Swaz. 107/E2
Nha Trang, Viet. 78/E3
Nhamunda (riv.), Braz. 147/G3
Nhill, Austl. 115/B3
Nhlangano, Swaz. 107/E2
Niagara (riv.), Can.,US 131/R9
Niagara (falls), Can.,US 131/R9
Niagara (co.), On, Can. 131/R9
Niagara Falls, NY, US 131/R9
Niagara Falls, On, Can. 131/R9
Niagara-on-the-Lake, On, Can. 131/R9
Niamey (dept.), Niger 103/F3
Niamey (cap.), Niger 103/F3
Niamey (int'l arpt.), Niger 103/F3
Niamtougou, Togo 103/F4
Niandan (riv.), Afr. 103/G5
Niangara, D.R. Congo 97/L7
Niangay (lake), Mali 96/E4
Niangzi (pass), China 72/C3
Nias (isl.), Indo. 67/J9
Niassa (prov.), Moz. 104/B5
Nicaragua (lake), Nic. 145/E3
Nicaragua (ctry.) 145/E3
Nicastro-Sambiase, It. 46/E3
Nice, Fr. 43/G5
Niceville, Fl, US 133/G4
Nichinan, Japan 74/B5
Nichlaul, India 84/D2
Nicholas (chan.), Bang. 145/F1
Nichols Hills, Ok, US 137/M14
Nicholson (range), Austl. 112/C3
Nickerie (dist.), Sur. 153/G3
Nickerie (riv.), Sur. 153/G3
Nickol (bay), Austl. 112/C2
Nicobar (isls.), India 67/J9
Nicolás Bravo, Mex. 144/D2
Nicolás Romero, Mex. 143/Q9
Nicolet, Qu, Can. 131/F2
Nicolls (pt.), NY, US 139/E2
Nicoma Park, Ok, US 137/N15
Nicosia, It. 46/D4
Nicosia (cap.), Cyp. 91/C2
Nicosia (dist.), Cyp. 91/C2
Nicotera, It. 46/D3
Nicoya (gulf), CR 140/D6
Nicoya, CR 144/E4
Nicoya, Peninsula de (pen.), CR 150/A1
Nidau, Swi. 56/D3
Nidd (riv.), Eng, UK 35/G3
Nidda, Ger. 54/B2
Nidda (riv.), Ger. 40/E3
Nidder (riv.), Ger. 54/C2
Nideggen, Ger. 53/F2
Nidge (prov.), Turk. 90/C2
Nidwalden (canton), Swi. 57/E4
Nidzica, Pol. 41/L2

Niebüll, Ger. 38/C4
Nied (riv.), Fr. 43/G2
Niedenstein, Ger. 51/G6
Nieder-Olm, Ger. 53/H4
Niederanven, Lux. 53/F4
Niederbipp, Swi. 56/D3
Niederbronn-les-Bains, Fr. 53/G6
Niedere Tauern (mts.), Aus. 43/K3
Niederfischbach, Ger. 53/G2
Niederlausitz (reg.), Ger. 41/G3
Niederhausen, Ger. 54/B2
Niederösterreich (prov.), Aus. 48/B2
Niedersachsen (state), Ger. 38/C5
Niedersächsisches Wattenmeer NP, Ger. 51/E1
Niedersachswerfen, Ger. 51/H5
Niederstetten, Ger. 54/C4
Niederstotzingen, Ger. 54/D5
Niederurnen, Swi. 57/F3
Niederwerrn, Ger. 54/D2
Niederwinkling, Ger. 55/F5
Niederzier, Ger. 53/F2
Niederzissen, Ger. 53/G3
Niefern-Öschelbronn, Ger. 54/B5
Niegocin (lake), Pol. 39/J5
Nieheim, Ger. 51/G5
Niemodlin, Pol. 41/J3
Nienburg, Ger. 51/G3
Nienhagen, Ger. 51/H3
Niénokoué (peak), C.d'Iv. 102/D5
Nieppe, Fr. 52/B4
Niéri (riv.), Sen. 102/B3
Niers (riv.), Ger. 53/F1
Nierstein, Ger. 54/B3
Niet Ban Tinh Xa, Viet. 78/D4
Nieuw-Amsterdam, Sur. 151/G2
Nieuw-Bergen, Neth. 50/D5
Nieuw-Loosdrecht, Neth. 50/C4
Nieuw-Nickerie, Sur. 153/G3
Nieuw-Schoonebeek, Neth. 50/D3
Nieuw-Vossemeer, Neth. 50/B5
Nieuwe Pekela, Neth. 50/D2
Nieuwegein, Neth. 50/C4
Nieuwerkerk aan de IJssel, Neth. 50/B5
Nieuweschans, Neth. 51/E2
Nieuwkoop, Neth. 50/B4
Nieuwleusen, Neth. 50/D3
Nieuwoudtville, SAfr. 106/B3
Nieuwpoort, Belg. 52/B1
Nieves, Mex. 142/E3
Niğde, Turk. 90/C2
Nihoa (isl.), Hi, US 117/J2
Nihonmatsu, Japan 75/G2
Nihtaur, India 84/B1
Nii (isl.), Japan 75/F3
Niigata (int'l arpt.), Japan 75/F2
Niigata, Japan 75/F2
Niigata (pref.), Japan 76/A4
Niihama, Japan 77/E1
Niihari, Japan 77/E1
Niihau (isl.), Hi, US 117/J2
Niimi, Japan 74/C3
Niitsu, Japan 75/F2
Niiza, Japan 77/D2
Nijar, Sp. 44/D4
Nijkerk, Neth. 50/C4
Nijlen, Belg. 53/D1
Nijmegen, Neth. 50/C5
Nikaia, Gre. 47/H3
Nikel', Rus. 37/J1
Nikishka, Ak, US 134/H3
Nikisiani, Gre. 47/J2
Nikki, Ben. 103/F4
Nikkō NP, Japan 75/F2
Niklasdorf, Aus. 43/K3
Nikolai, Ak, US 134/H3
Nikolayevsk-na-Amure, Rus. 65/Q4
Nikol'sk, Rus. 63/H1
Nikolski, Ak, US 134/E5
Nikonga (riv.), Tanz. 104/A3
Nikopol', Ukr. 62/E3
Nikopol, Bul. 49/G4
Niksar, Turk. 89/H3
Nīkshahr, Iran 89/H3
Nikšić, Yugo. 47/F1
Nikumaroro (Gardner) (isl.), Kiri. 117/H5
Nikunau (isl.), Kiri. 116/G5
Nile (prov.), Ugan. 104/A2

Nile (delta), Egypt 88/B2
Nile (riv.), Afr. 93/F2
Niles, Mi, US 130/C3
Niles, Oh, US 130/D3
Niles, Il, US 135/Q15
Ni'līn, Isr. 91/G8
Nilópolis, Braz. 211/K7
Nilsiä, Fin. 60/F3
Nilvange, Fr. 53/F5
Nīmaj, India 82/B2
Nimba (co.), Libr. 102/C5
Nimba (peak), C.d'Iv. 102/C5
Nîmes, Fr. 42/F5
Nimmsbach (riv.), Ger. 53/F4
Nimule NP, Sudan 104/A2
Nin, Cro. 48/B3
Nīnawá (gov.), Iraq 90/E3
Nīnawá (Nineveh) (ruin), Iraq 90/E2
Ninepin Group (isls.), China 71/V11
Ninfas (pt.), Arg. 158/D4
Ning'an, China 71/N3
Ningbo, China 72/E5
Ningde, China 79/C2
Ningdu, China 79/C2
Ningguang, China 83/K2
Ninghua, China 79/C2
Ningjin, China 72/C3
Ningjin, China 72/D3
Ninglang Yizu Zizhixian, China 83/H2
Ningling, China 72/C3
Ningming, China 83/J3
Ningwu, China 72/C3
Ningxia Huizu (aut. reg.), China 70/J4
Ningxiang, China 79/B2
Nīnh Binh, Viet. 78/D1
Ninilchik, Ak, US 134/H3
Niningo (isls.), PNG 116/D5
Ninohe, Japan 76/B3
Ninomiya, Japan 77/C3
Ninove, Belg. 52/D2
Ninoy Aquino (int'l arpt.), Phil. 79/D5
Niobara (riv.), Ne, US 127/H4
Niobrara (riv.), Ne, US 127/H5
Niokolo-Koba, PN du, Sen. 102/B3
Niono, Mali 102/B3
Nioro-du-Rip, Sen. 102/B3
Nioro du Sahel, Mali 102/C3
Niort, Fr. 42/C3
Nipawin, Sk, Can. 127/H2
Nipe (bay), Cuba 145/H1
Nipigon, On, Can. 127/L3
Nipigon (lake), On, Can. 122/G3
Nipissing (lake), On, Can. 123/J4
Niquen, Chile 158/C3
Niquero, Cuba 145/G1
Nirasaki, Japan 75/F3
Nirayama, Japan 77/B3
Nirimba Army Afld., Austl. 114/G8
Nirmal, India 82/C4
Nirmāli, India 85/F2
Niš (int'l arpt.), Yugo. 47/G1
Niš, Yugo. 47/G1
Nišava (riv.), Yugo. 47/H1
Niscemi, It. 46/D4
Nishiazai, Japan 77/K5
Nishibiwajima, Japan 77/L5
Nishiharu, Japan 77/L5
Nishikatsura, Japan 77/B2
Nishiki, Japan 74/B3
Nishiki, Japan 77/H5
Nishinomiya, Japan 77/H6
Nishino'omote, Japan 74/A4
Nishio, Japan 77/M6
Nishiwaki, Japan 77/G6
Nisko, Pol. 41/M3
Nisqually (riv.), Wa, US 135/B3
Nisqually Ind. Res., Wa, US 135/B3
Nisqually Reach (str.), Wa, US 135/B3
Nissan (isl.), PNG 116/E5
Nisser (lake), Nor. 38/C2
Nisshin, Japan 77/M5
Nissum (bay), Den. 38/C3
Nisswa, Mn, US 127/K4
Nistru (riv.), Mol. 49/H1
Niterói, Braz. 211/K7
Nith (riv.), Sc, UK 34/E1
Nithsdale (valley), Sc, UK 34/E1
Nitra, Slvk. 48/D1
Nitra (riv.), Slvk. 48/D1
Nitsa (riv.), Rus. 61/P4
Nitta, Japan 77/C1
Nittedal, Nor. 38/D1
Nittel, Ger. 53/F4
Nittenau, Ger. 55/F4
Niuafo'ou (isl.), Tonga 117/H6
Niuatoputapu Group (isls.), Tonga 117/H5
Niue (terr.), NZ 117/H7
Niue (isl.), Niue 117/J6
Niulakita (isl.), Tuv. 116/G6

Niulan (riv.), China 83/H2
Niut (peak), Indo. 80/C3
Niutao (isl.), Tuv. 116/G5
Nivelles, Belg. 53/D2
Nivernais, Collines de (hills), Fr. 42/E3
Niverville, Mb, Can. 127/J3
Niwot, Co, US 137/B2
Niyazov (int'l arpt.), Trkm. 87/C5
Niyodo (riv.), Japan 74/C4
Nizāmābād, India 82/C4
Nizhegorodskaya (obl.), Rus. 63/G1
Nizhnekama (res.), Rus. 61/M4
Nizhnekamsk, Rus. 61/L5
Nizhneudinsk, Rus. 65/K4
Nizhnevartovsk, Rus. 64/H3
Nizhniy Lomov, Rus. 63/G1
Nizhniy Novgorod, Rus. 61/K4
Nizhniy Tagil, Rus. 61/N4
Nizhyn, Ukr. 62/D2
Nizip, Turk. 90/D2
Nīzke Tatry NP, Slvk. 62/A2
Nizza Monferrato, It. 58/B3
Njazzanim, Isr. 91/F8
Njardhvik, Ice. 37/M7
Njombe (riv.), Tanz. 104/B4
Nkandla, SAfr. 107/E3
Nkayi, Congo 96/H8
Nkhata Bay, Malw. 104/B5
N'kongsamba, Camr. 96/G7
Nkululu (riv.), Tanz. 104/B4
Nkusi (riv.), Ugan. 104/A2
Nmai (riv.), Myan. 83/G2
Noailles, Fr. 52/B5
Noākhāli (pol. reg.), Bang. 85/H4
Noale, It. 59/F1
Noāmundi, India 85/E4
Noank, Ct, US 139/F1
Noatak, Ak, US 134/F2
Noatak (riv.), Ak, US 134/F2
Noatak Nat'l Prsv., Ak, US 134/F2
Nobeoka, Japan 74/B4
Noble, Ok, US 137/N15
Noboa, Ecu. 152/A5
Noboribetsu, Japan 76/B2
Noce (riv.), It. 57/G5
Noceto, It. 58/D3
Noci, It. 47/E2
Nockamixon State Park, Pa, US 138/C3
Noda, Japan 77/D2
Nodagawa, Japan 77/H4
Noé (riv.), Alg. 100/D2
Nogales, Az, US 128/E5
Nogales, Mex. 143/M8
Nogara, It. 59/E2
Nogaro, Fr. 42/C5
Nogat (riv.), Pol. 39/H4
Nogata, Japan 74/B4
Nogent, Fr. 56/B1
Nogent-l'Artaud, Fr. 52/C6
Nogent-le-Rotrou, Fr. 42/D2
Nogent-sur-Oise, Fr. 52/B5
Nogent-sur-Seine, Fr. 42/E2
Nogi, Japan 77/D1
Noginsk, Rus. 61/X9
Nogoa (riv.), Austl. 114/B4
Nogodan-san (peak), SKor. 73/D5
Nogoonnuur, Mong. 70/F2
Nogoyá, Arg. 157/E3
Nógrád (co.), Hun. 41/K5
Nogwak-san (peak), SKor. 74/A2
Nohar, India 86/C5
Noheji, Japan 76/B3
Nohfelden, Ger. 53/G4
Nohkú (pt.), Mex. 144/E2
Noidans-lès-Vesoul, Fr. 56/C2
Noire (riv.), Qu, Can. 130/E2
Noires, Montagnes (mts.), Fr. 42/B2
Noirmoutier, Île de (isl.), Fr. 42/B3
Noisiel, Fr. 52/B6
Noisy-le-Grand, Fr. 30/K5
Noisy-le-Mec, Fr. 30/K5
Noisy-le-Roi, Fr. 30/J5
Nojima-zaki (pt.), Japan 75/F3
Nojiri, Japan 74/B5
Nokia, Fin. 39/K1
Nokilalaki (peak), Indo. 81/F4
Nola, CAfr. 96/J7
Noli, It. 58/B3
Noli, Capo di (cape), It. 58/B3
Nomadgi NP, Austl. 115/D2
Nombre de Dios, Mex. 142/D4
Nombre de Dios (mts.), Hon. 144/E3
Nome, Ak, US 134/E3
Nome (cape), Ak, US 134/E3
Noménjy, Fr. 53/F6
Nomexey, Fr. 56/C1
Nomo-misaki (cape), Japan 74/A4
Nomo-zaki (pt.), Japan 74/A4
Nonacho (lake), NW, Can. 122/F2
Nonantola, It. 59/E3
Nondalton, Ak, US 134/H4
None, It. 43/G4

Nonette (riv.), Fr. 52/B5
Nong Han (res.), Thai. 78/D2
Nong Khai, Thai. 78/C2
Nong'an, China 71/N3
Nongoma, SAfr. 107/E2
Nongstoin, India 85/H3
Nonnweiler, Ger. 53/F4
Nonoava, Mex. 142/D3
Nonouti (isl.), Kiri. 116/G5
Nonsan, SKor. 73/D4
Nontron, Fr. 42/D4
Noord-Brabant (prov.), Neth. 50/C5
Noord Holland (prov.), Neth. 50/B3
Noordbeveland (isl.), Neth. 50/A5
Noorderhaaks (isl.), Neth. 50/A5
Noordhollandsch Kanaal (riv.), Neth. 50/B3
Noordoostpolder (polder), Neth. 50/C3
Noordwijk aan Zee, Neth. 50/B4
Noordwijkerhout, Neth. 50/B4
Noordzeekanaal (canal), Neth. 50/B4
Noormarkku, Fin. 39/J1
Noorvik, Ak, US 134/F2
Nootka (isl.), BC, Can. 126/B3
Nora, Swe. 38/F2
Norala, Phil. 81/F2
Norberg, Swe. 38/F1
Norberto de la Riestra, Arg. 159/J11
Norchia (ruin), It. 46/B1
Norco, La, US 137/P16
Nord (canal), Fr. 52/B4
Nord (prov.), Fr. 52/C3
Nord-Kivu (pol. reg.), D.R. Congo 104/A3
Nord-Ostsee (Kiel) (canal), Ger. 51/G1
Nord-Ouest (prov.), Camr. 103/H5
Nord-Ouest (pol. reg.), Mor. 100/B2
Nord-Pas-de-Calais (pol. reg.), Fr. 42/D1
Nord-Radde (riv.), Ger. 51/E3
Nord-Sud Kanal (canal), Ger. 51/E3
Nord-Trøndelag (co.), Nor. 37/E2
Nordborg, Den. 38/C4
Nordby, Den. 38/D4
Norddeich, Ger. 51/E1
Nordela (int'l arpt.), Azor., Port. 45/T13
Norden, Ger. 51/E1
Nordenham, Ger. 51/F1
Nordenskjöld (arch.), Rus. 64/J2
Norderney, Ger. 51/E1
Norderney (isl.), Neth. 51/E1
Norderstedt, Ger. 51/G1
Nordhausen, Ger. 40/F3
Nordholz, Ger. 51/F1
Nordhorn, Ger. 51/E4
Nordhouse, Fr. 56/D1
Nordjylland (co.), Den. 38/C3
Nordkapp (cape), Nor. 37/H1
Nordkapp, Nor. 37/H1
Nordkinn (pt.), Nor. 37/H1
Nordkirchen, Ger. 51/E5
Nordland (co.), Nor. 37/E2
Nordmaling, Swe. 37/F3
Nordreisa, Nor. 37/G1
Nordrhein-Westfalen (state), Ger. 40/E2
Nords Wharf, Austl. 115/D2
Nordsiel, Ger. 51/E4
Nordwalde, Ger. 51/E4
Nore (riv.), Ire. 31/Q10
Noresund, Nor. 38/C1
Norfolk (mt.), Austl. 115/C4
Norfolk (lake), Ar,Mo, US 129/J3
Norfolk, Ne, US 127/J5
Norfolk, Va, US 130/H3
Norfolk (isl.) 116/F7
Norfolk Broads (swamp), Eng, UK 33/H1
Norheim, Nor. 38/B1
Norheimsund, Nor. 38/B1
Norikura-dake (peak), Japan 75/E2
Noril'sk, Rus. 64/J3
Normal, Il, US 127/L5
Norman, Ok, US 137/N15
Norman Manley (int'l arpt.), Jam. 145/G2
Norman Wells, NW, Can. 122/D2
Normanby (isl.), PNG 116/E6
Normandie, Collines de (hills), Fr. 42/C2
Normandy (reg.), Fr. 42/C2
Normandy Beach, NJ, US 138/D4

Normandy Park, Wa, US 135/C3
Normanton, Austl. 114/A2
Normanton South, Eng, UK 35/G4
Norotshama (peak), Namb. 106/B3
Norquay, Sk, Can. 127/H3
Norquinco, Arg. 158/C4
Norrbotten (co.), Swe. 37/F2
Norridge, Il, US 135/Q16
Norris (lake), Tn, US 133/G2
Norristown, Pa, US 138/C4
Norrköping, Swe. 38/G2
Norrland (reg.), Swe. 37/F2
Norrsundet, Swe. 38/G1
Norrtälje, Swe. 39/H2
Nors, Den. 38/C3
Norseman, Austl. 112/D5
Norsjö, Swe. 37/F2
Norte (pt.), Arg. 159/F3
Norte, Cabo do (cape), Braz. 151/J3
Norte de Santander (dept.), Col. 145/H4
Norte Los Rodeos (int'l arpt.), Sp. 98/A3
Norte, Serra do (mts.), Braz. 150/G6
Nortelândia, Braz. 151/G6
Nörten-Hardenberg, Ger. 51/G5
North (pt.), Austl. 115/C3
North (str.), Sc, UK 31/Q8
North (cape), PE, Can. 131/J2
North (cape), Mb, Can. 127/J2
North (cape), NZ 117/S9
North (isl.), NZ 116/G8
North (prov.), Md, US 138/B5
North (sound), Sc, UK 31/V14
North (sea), Eur. 36/D4
North (chan.), UK 34/C1
North Albanian Alps (mts.), Yugo. 47/F1
North America (cont.) 119
North Andaman (isl.), India 83/F5
North Arlington, NJ, US 139/J8
North Aulatsivik (isl.), Nf, Can. 123/K3
North Aurora, Il, US 135/P16
North Battleford, Sk, Can. 126/F2
North Bay, On, Can. 130/E2
North Bay, Wi, US 135/Q14
North Beach, Md, US 138/B6
North Beach Haven, NJ, US 138/D4
North Bellmore, NY, US 139/L9
North Bend, Or, US 126/B5
North Bend, Wa, US 135/D3
North Bergen, NJ, US 139/J8
North Berwick, Sc, UK 36/D4
North Branch, Mn, US 127/K4
North Branch (riv.), Md, US 138/B5
North Branford, Ct, US 139/F1
North Brunswick, NJ, US 138/D3
North Buganda (prov.), Ugan. 104/B2
North Caicos (isl.), UK 145/J1
North Caldwell, NJ, US 139/J8
North Canadian (riv.), Ok, US 129/H3
North Cape May, NJ, US 138/D6
North Caribou (lake), On, Can. 127/L2
North Carolina (state), US 133/H3
North Cascades NP, Wa, US 126/C3
North Central (plain), Tx, US 143/F1
North Charleston, SC, US 133/J3
North Cowichan, BC, Can. 126/C3
North Dakota (state), US 127/H4
North Dorset Downs (uplands), Eng, UK 32/D5
North Down (dist.), NI, UK 34/C2
North East, Pa, US 130/E3
North East (pt.), Austl. 114/C3
North East, Md, US 138/C4
North Eastern (prov.), Kenya 104/C3
North Esk (riv.), Sc, UK 36/C5

North Foreland (pt.), Eng, UK 33/H4
North Fork Crow (riv.), Mn, US 127/K4
North Fort Myers, Fl, US 133/H5
North French (riv.), On, Can. 130/D1
North Frisian (isls.), Ger. 40/D1
North Front (int'l arpt.), UK 98/D1
North Gauhāti, India 85/H2
North Haledon, NJ, US 139/J8
North Hero, Vt, US 130/F2
North Highlands, Ca, US 135/L9
North Kansas City, Mo, US 137/D5
North Kitui Nat'l Rsv., Kenya 104/C3
North Korea (ctry.) 73/D2
North Lakhimpur, India 83/F2
North Lanarkshire (pol. reg.), Sc, UK 36/C5
North Las Vegas, Nv, US 128/D3
North Lincolnshire (co.), Eng, UK 35/H4
North Lindenhurst, NY, US 139/M9
North Little Rock, Ar, US 129/J4
North Luangwa NP, Zam. 105/F3
North Magnetic Pole 123/R7
North Minch (The Minch) (str.), Sc, UK 31/Q8
North Moose (lake), Mb, Can. 127/J2
North Mountain (mtn.), Pa, US 138/B1
North Myrtle Beach, SC, US 133/J3
North Ogden, Ut, US 137/K11
North Ossetian Aut. Rep., Rus. 63/G4
North Pacific (ocean) 22/A4
North Pine (riv.), Austl. 114/E6
North Plainfield, NJ, US 139/H9
North Platte, Ne, US 127/H5
North Platte (riv.), Ne,Wy, US 129/G2
North Pole, Ak, US 134/J3
North Pole 160/G
North Potomac, Md, US 138/A5
North Prairie, Wi, US 135/P14
North Puyallup (str.), Can. 131/J2
North Raccoon (riv.), Ia, US 127/K5
North Ronaldsay (isl.), Sc, UK 31/V14
North Salt Lake, Ut, US 137/K12
North Saskatchewan (riv.), Ab,Sk, Can. 122/E3
North Shields, Eng, UK 35/G2
North Siberian Lowland (plain), Rus. 64/K2
North Skunk (riv.), Ia, US 129/J2
North Somerset (co.), Eng, UK 32/D4
North Stadbroke (isl.), Austl. 109/E3
North Taranaki Bight (bay), NZ 109/H6
North Thompson (riv.), BC, Can. 126/D3
North Tolsta, Sc, UK 31/Q7
North Tonawanda, NY, US 139/M7
North Tyne (riv.), Eng, UK 35/F1
North Uist (isl.), Sc, UK 31/Q8
North Umpqua (riv.), Or, US 128/B2
North Valley Stream, NY, US 139/L9
North Vancouver, BC, Can. 122/C4
North Wales, Eng, UK 38/C3
North Weald Bassett, Eng, UK 30/D1
North West (cape), Austl. 112/B2
North-West Frontier (co.), India 86/A3
North West Highlands (uplands), Sc, UK 31/R8
North Wildwood, NJ, US 138/D6
North Wilton, Ct, US 139/F1
North York, Can. 131/R9
North York Moors NP, Eng, UK 35/G3
North Yorkshire (co.), Eng, UK 35/G3
Northallerton, Eng, UK 35/G3
Northam, Austl. 112/C4
Northampton, Ma, US 131/F3

Northampton, Eng, UK 33/F2
Northampton, Austl. 112/B4
Northampton (co.), Pa, US 138/C2
Northampton, Pa, US 138/C2
Northampton Uplands (uplands), Eng, UK 33/E2
Northamptonshire (co.), Eng, UK 33/E2
Northbrook, Il, US 135/Q15
Northeast (cape), Ak, US 134/C3
Northeast (pt.), Bahm. 141/G3
Northeast (pt.), Jam. 145/G2
Northeast (pt.), Bahm. 145/H1
Northeast Land (isl.), Sval. 160/E
Northeast Lincolnshire (co.), Eng, UK 35/H4
Northeim, Ger. 51/G5
Northern (prov.), Ugan. 104/B2
Northern (pol. reg.), Malw. 104/B2
Northern (prov.), SLeo. 102/B4
Northern (pol. reg.), Isr. 91/G7
Northern (dist.), Isr. 91/G7
Northern Areas (terr.), Pak. 87/F5
Northern Cape (prov.), SAfr. 106/C3
Northern Cook (isls.), Cookls. 117/J6
Northern Dvina (riv.), Rus. 27/J2
Northern Light (lake), On, Can. 130/B1
Northern Mariana Islands (dpcy.), US 116/D3
Northern Province (prov.), SAfr. 106/C3
Northern Sporades (isls.), Gre. 47/J3
Northern Territory (terr.), Austl. 109/C2
Northern Ural (mts.), Rus. 61/N3
Northern Uvals (hills), Rus. 61/K4
Northfield, Mn, US 127/K4
Northfleet, Eng, UK 30/D2
Northglenn, Co, US 137/C3
Northport, Al, US 133/G3
Northport (Old Northport), NY, US 139/E2
Northumberland (str.), Can. 131/J2
Northumberland (co.), Eng, UK 35/F1
Northumberland NP, Eng, UK 36/C6
Northvale, NJ, US 139/K7
Northville, Mi, US 135/E7
Northway, Ak, US 134/K3
Northwest Gander (riv.), Nf, Can. 131/L1
Northwest Territories (terr.), Can. 122/D2
Northwich, Eng, UK 35/F5
Northwood, ND, US 127/J4
Norton (bay), Ak, US 134/F3
Norton (sound), Ak, US 134/E3
Norton Shores, Mi, US 130/C3
Nortorf, Ger. 38/C4
Norvegia (cape), Ant. 53/F2
Nörvenich, Ger. 53/F2
Norwalk, Oh, US 130/D3
Norwalk, Ca, US 136/F8
Norwalk, Ct, US 139/M7
Norwalk (riv.), Ct, US 139/M7
Norway (ctry.) 37/C3
Norwegian (bay), Nun., Can. 123/S7
Norwegian (sea), Eur. 27/D2
Norwich, NY, US 130/F3
Norwich, Eng, UK 33/H1
Norwich (int'l arpt.), Eng, UK 33/H1
Norwood, NJ, US 139/K8
Nos Emine (cape), Bul. 49/J4
Nos Kaliakra (pt.), Bul. 49/J4
Nos Maslen Nos (pt.), Bul. 49/J4
Nosappu-misaki (cape), Japan 76/D2
Nose, Japan 77/H6
Noshappu-misaki (cape), Japan 76/B1
Noshaq (peak), Afg. 89/K1
Noshiro, Japan 76/B3
Nosivka, Ukr. 62/D2
Nosong (cape), Malay. 81/E2
Nosratābād, Iran 89/G3
Noss Head (pt.), Sc, UK 31/S0
Nossa Senhora da Glória, Braz. 154/E2
Nossa Senhora das Dores, Braz. 154/C3
Nossebro, Swe. 38/E2

212

Nosy-V – Oliva

Nosy-Varika, Madg. 107/J8
Notch (cape), Chile 159/B6
Notec (riv.), Pol. 41/J2
Noto (pen.), Japan 75/E2
Noto, It. 46/D4
Noto Antica (ruin), It. 46/D4
Noto, Golfo di (gulf), It. 46/D4
Noto, Val di (valley), It. 46/D4
Notodden, Nor. 38/C2
Notogawa, Japan 77/K5
Notoro (lake), Japan 76/C1
Notre Dame (mts.), Qu, Can. 123/J4
Notre Dame (bay), Nf, Can. 123/L4
Notre Dame, Fr. 30/K5
Notre-Dame-de-l'Île-Perrot, Qu, Can. 131/N7
Notsé, Togo 103/F5
Nott (mt.), Austl. 113/G5
Nottaway (riv.), Qu, Can. 123/J3
Nøtterøy, Nor. 38/D2
Nottingham (isl.), Nun., Can. 123/H2
Nottingham, Eng, UK 35/G6
Nottingham (co.), Eng, UK 35/G6
Nottinghamshire (co.), Eng, UK 35/G5
Nottuln, Ger. 51/E5
Nouâdhibou, Mrta. 98/A5
Nouâdhibou (int'l arpt.), Mrta. 98/A5
Nouakchott (cap.), Mrta. 102/B2
Nouakchott (int'l arpt.), Mrta. 102/B2
Nouna, Burk. 102/E3
Noupoort, SAfr. 106/D3
Nouvion-sur-Meuse, Fr. 53/D4
Nœux-les-Mines, Fr. 52/B3
Nouzonville, Fr. 53/D4
Nova Andradina, Braz. 151/H8
Nova Cruz, Braz. 154/D2
Nová Dubnica, Slvk. 41/K4
Nova Friburgo, Braz. 211/L7
Nova Gorica, Slov. 59/G1
Nova Gradiška, Cro. 48/C3
Nova Iguaçu, Braz. 211/K7
Nova Kakhovka, Ukr. 49/L2
Nova Olinda, Braz. 154/C2
Nova Olinda do Norte, Braz. 150/G4
Nova Pazova, Yugo. 48/E3
Nova Prata, Braz. 155/B4
Nova Russas, Braz. 154/B2
Nova Scotia (prov.), Can. 131/J2
Nova Sintra, CpV. 93/J11
Nova Soure, Braz. 154/C3
Nova Varoš, Yugo. 48/D4
Nova Venécia, Braz. 155/D1
Nova Xavantina, Braz. 151/H6
Nova Zagora, Bul. 47/K1
Novaci, Rom. 49/F3
Novafeltria, It. 59/F5
Novara, It. 58/B2
Novate Mezzola, It. 57/F5
Novaya Sibir' (isl.), Rus. 65/R2
Novaya Zemlya (isl.), Rus. 160/C
Nove, It. 59/E1
Nové Hrady, Czh. 55/H5
Nové Město nad Váhom, Slvk. 41/J4
Nové Strašecí, Czh. 55/G2
Nové Zámky, Slvk. 48/D2
Novelda, Sp. 45/E3
Novellara, It. 59/D3
Noventa, It. 59/E2
Noventa di Piave, It. 59/F1
Noventa Vicentina, It. 59/E2
Novgorod, Rus. 39/P2
Novgorodskaya (obl.), Rus. 60/G4
Novi, Mi, US 135/E7
Novi Bečej, Yugo. 48/E3
Novi di Modena, It. 59/D3
Novi Iskŭr, Bul. 47/H1
Novi Ligure, It. 43/H4
Novi Pazar, Yugo. 47/G1
Novi Pazar, Bul. 49/H4
Novi Sad, Yugo. 48/D3
Novi Vinodolski, Cro. 48/B3
Novillars, Fr. 56/C3
Nóvita, Col. 152/B3
Novo (riv.), Braz. 211/K6
Novo Alexeyevka (int'l arpt.), Geo. 63/H4
Novo Aripuanã, Braz. 150/F5
Novo Hamburgo, Braz. 155/B4
Novo Horizonte, Braz. 155/B2
Novo Miloševo, Yugo. 48/E3
Novo Oriente, Braz. 154/B2
Novoanninskiy, Rus. 63/G2
Novocheboksarsk, Rus. 61/K4
Novocherkassk, Rus. 62/G3
Novogrudok, Bela. 39/L5
Novohrad-Volyns'kyy, Ukr. 62/C2
Novohradské Hory (mts.), Czh. 55/H5
Novokuybyshevsk, Rus. 63/J1
Novokuznetsk, Rus. 64/J4
Novolazarevskaya, Rus., Ant. 160/A
Novomoskovsk, Rus. 62/F1
Novorossiysk, Rus. 62/F3
Novoshakhtinsk, Rus. 62/F3
Novosibirsk (res.), Rus. 87/H2
Novosibirsk, Rus. 87/H1
Novosibirsk (Tolmachevo) (int'l arpt.), Rus. 87/H1
Novosibirskaya (obl.), Rus. 87/G1
Novotroitsk, Rus. 63/L2
Novoukrayinka, Ukr. 62/D2
Novovolyns'k, Ukr. 62/C2
Novovyatsk, Rus. 61/L4
Novozybkov, Rus. 62/D1
Novska, Cro. 48/C3
Nový Jičín, Czh. 41/K4
Nowa Dęba, Pol. 41/L3
Nowa Ruda, Pol. 41/J3
Nowa Sarzyna, Pol. 41/M3
Nowa Sól, Pol. 41/H3
Nowata, Ok, US 129/J3
Nowe, Pol. 41/K2
Nowe Miasto Lubawskie, Pol. 41/K2
Nowgong, India 84/B3
Nowitna (riv.), Ak, US 134/G3
Nowitna NWR, Ak, US 134/H3
Nowogard, Pol. 38/F5
Nowood (riv.), Wy, US 128/F1
Nowshāk (peak), Afg. 87/F5
Nowshera, Pak. 86/A2
Nowy Dwór Gdański, Pol. 39/H4
Nowy Sącz, Pol. 41/L4
Nowy Sącz (prov.), Pol. 41/L4
Nowy Staw, Pol. 39/H4
Nowy Targ, Pol. 41/L4
Nowy Tomyśl, Pol. 41/J2
Noya, Sp. 44/A1
Noye (riv.), Fr. 52/B4
Noyon, Fr. 52/C4
Nsanje, Malw. 105/G4
Nsawam, Gha. 103/E5
Nsumbu NP, Zam. 104/A5
Nsuta, Gha. 103/E5
Ntoroko, Ugan. 104/A2
Ntungamo, Ugan. 104/A3
Ntusi, Ugan. 104/A2
Nu, Crêt du (peak), Fr. 56/B5
Nuangola, Pa, US 138/C1
Nūbah, Jibāl an (mts.), Sudan 97/M5
Nubian (des.), Sudan 93/F2
Nucet, Rom. 48/F2
Nucla, Co, US 132/A2
Nucourt, Fr. 30/H4
Nüdlingen, Ger. 54/D2
Nueces (riv.), Tx, US 140/B2
Nueltin (lake), Mb,Nun., Can. 122/G2
Nuenen, Neth. 50/C6
Nueva Alejandría, Peru 156/C2
Nueva Concepción, Guat. 144/D3
Nueva Esparta (state), Ven. 153/E2
Nueva Florida, Ven. 152/D2
Nueva Gerona, Cuba 145/F1
Nueva Helvecia, Uru. 159/K11
Nueva Imperial, Chile 158/B3
Nueva Italia de Ruiz, Mex. 142/E5
Nueva Loja, Ecu. 152/B4
Nueva Ocotepéque, Hon. 144/D3
Nueva Palmira, Uru. 159/J10
Nueva Rosita, Mex. 132/C5
Nueva Villa de Padilla, Mex. 143/F3
Nueve de Julio, Arg. 158/E2
Nuevitas, Cuba 145/G1
Nuevo, Ca, US 136/C3
Nuevo Balsas, Mex. 143/F5
Nuevo Berlín, Uru. 159/J10
Nuevo Casas Grandes, Mex. 142/D2
Nuevo Chagres, Pan. 145/F4
Nuevo, Gulfo (gulf), Arg. 157/D5
Nuevo Ideal, Mex. 142/D3
Nuevo Ixcatlán, Mex. 144/C2
Nuevo Laredo, Mex. 132/D5
Nuevo Leon (state), Mex. 140/A2
Nuevo Rocafuerte, Ecu. 152/C5
Nufenen, Swi. 57/F4
Nufenenpass (pass), Swi. 57/E5
Nuguria (isls.), PNG 116/E5
Nuhne (riv.), Ger. 51/F6
Nui (isl.), Tuv. 116/G5
Nuiqsut, Ak, US 134/H1
Nuits-Saint-Georges, Fr. 56/A3
Nukata, Japan 77/M6
Nuklunek (mtn.), Ak, US 134/F4
Nuku'alofa (cap.), Tonga 117/H7
Nukufetau (isl.), Tuv. 116/G5
Nukulaelae (isl.), Tuv. 116/H5
Nukumanu (atoll), PNG 116/E5
Nukunonu (isl.), Tok. 117/H5
Nukuoro (isl.), Micr. 116/E4
Nukus (int'l arpt.), Uzb. 87/C4
Nukus, Uzb. 87/C4
Nukutavake (isl.), FrPol. 117/M6
Nulato, Ak, US 134/G3
Nules, Sp. 45/E3
Nullarbor (plain), Austl. 109/B4
Nullarbor NP, Austl. 113/F4
Numana, It. 59/G5
Numansdorp, Neth. 50/B5
Numata, Japan 75/F2
Numazu, Japan 75/F3
Nümbrecht, Ger. 53/G2
Numfoor (isl.), Indo. 81/H4
Nummi, Fin. 39/K1
Numurkah, Austl. 115/C3
Nunapitchuk, Ak, US 134/F3
Nunchia, Col. 152/C3
Nundle, Austl. 115/D1
Nuneaton, Eng, UK 33/E1
Nungarin, Austl. 112/C4
Nungatta NP, Austl. 115/D3
Nunivak (isl.), Ak, US 134/E4
Nunningen, Swi. 56/D3
Nuñoa, Peru 156/D4
Nunspeet, Neth. 50/C4
Nuon (riv.), Libr. 102/C5
Nuoro, It. 46/A2
Nuquí, Col. 152/B3
Nur (mts.), Turk. 91/E1
Nura (riv.), Kaz. 87/F2
Nürburgring, Ger. 53/F3
Nure (riv.), It. 58/C3
Nuremberg, Pa, US 138/B2
Nurhak, Turk. 90/D2
Nuri (ruin), Sudan 101/B5
Nuriootpa, Austl. 113/H5
Nurmijärvi, Fin. 39/L1
Nürnberg (int'l arpt.), Ger. 54/E3
Nürnberg, Ger. 54/E4
Nūrpur, Pak. 86/B3
Nurri (mt.), Austl. 115/C1
Nürtingen, Ger. 54/C5
Nushagak (riv.), Ak, US 134/G4
Nushki, Pak. 89/J3
Nutberry (hill), Sc, UK 36/C5
Nuth, Neth. 53/E2
Nuthe-Graben (riv.), Ger. 40/Q7
Nutley, NJ, US 139/J8
Nutwood, Il, US 137/F7
Nuuk (Godthåb), Grld. 119/M3
Nuvolento, It. 58/D1
Nuy (riv.), SAfr. 106/L10
Nüziders, Aus. 57/F3
Nxai Pan NP, Bots. 105/D4
Nyabisindu, Rwa. 104/A3
Nyack, NY, US 139/K7
Nyah, Austl. 115/B2
Nyah West, Austl. 115/B2
Nyainqêntanglha (peak), China 70/F5
Nyaki NP, Malw. 104/B5
Nyala, Sudan 97/K5
Nyalam, China 85/E1
Nyandoma, Rus. 60/J3
Nyanza (prov.), Kenya 104/B3
Nyasa (lake), Malw. 93/F6
Nybro, Swe. 38/F3
Nyêmo, China 85/H1
Nyeri, Kenya 104/C3
Nyima, China 70/E5
Nyírábrány, Hun. 48/F2
Nyíradony, Hun. 41/L5
Nyírbátor, Hun. 41/M5
Nyíregyháza, Hun. 41/L5
Nyírmada, Hun. 41/M4
Nyiru (mt.), Kenya 104/C2
Nykøbing, Den. 38/C3
Nykøbing, Den. 38/D4
Nyköping, Swe. 38/G2
Nylstroom, SAfr. 105/E5
Nynäshamn, Swe. 38/G2
Nyngan, Austl. 115/C1
Nyoman (riv.), Bela. 62/B1
Nyon, Swi. 56/C5
Nyons, Fr. 42/F4
Nýřany, Czh. 55/G3
Nýrsko, Czh. 55/G4
Nýrsko (res.), Czh. 55/G4
Nysa, Pol. 41/J3
Nyssa, Or, US 126/D5
Nysted, Den. 38/D4
Nyūdō-zaki (pt.), Japan 76/A4
Nyuk (lake), Rus. 60/F2
Nyúl, Hun. 48/C2
Nyunzu, D.R. Congo 105/E2
Nyūzen, Japan 75/E2
Nzega, Tanz. 104/B4
Nzérékoré (pol. reg.), Gui. 102/C4
Nzérékoré, Gui. 102/C5
Nzi (riv.), C.d'Iv. 96/E6

O

Ō-shima (isl.), Japan 76/A3
Oa, Mull of (pt.), Sc, UK 31/Q9
Oahe (dam), SD, US 127/H4
Oahe (lake), ND,SD, US 124/F2
Oahu (isl.), Hi, US 117/K2
Oak Forest, Il, US 135/Q16
Oak Grove, Mo, US 137/E6
Oak Hill, WV, US 130/D4
Oak Park, Il, US 135/Q16
Oak Park, Mi, US 135/F7
Oak Ridge, Tn, US 130/C4
Oak Ridge, NJ, US 138/D1
Oak View, Ca, US 136/A2
Oakbank, Mb, Can. 127/J3
Oakdale, La, US 129/J5
Oakes, ND, US 127/J4
Oakey, Austl. 114/C4
Oakham, Eng, UK 33/F1
Oakhurst, Ca, US 128/C3
Oakland, Ca, US 128/B3
Oakland, Md, US 138/B5
Oakland (lake), Mi, US 135/F6
Oakland, NJ, US 139/J7
Oakland (bay), Wa, US 135/A3
Oakland (co.), Mi, US 135/E6
Oaklands, Austl. 115/C2
Oakley, Ca, US 135/L10
Oakover (riv.), Austl. 109/B3
Oakridge, Or, US 126/C5
Oakville, La, US 137/P17
Oakville, Mo, US 137/G8
Oakville, On, Can. 131/Q9
Oakwood Hills, Il, US 135/P15
Oamaru, NZ 117/S12
Ōamishirasato, Japan 77/E2
Oat (mtn.), Ca, US 136/B2
Oatlands, Austl. 115/C4
Oaxaca (state), Mex. 140/B4
Oaxaca de Juárez, Mex. 144/B2
Ob' (gulf), Rus. 67/G3
Ob' (riv.), Rus. 67/F3
Ob Luang Gorge, Thai. 78/B2
Obama, Japan 77/J5
Obama (bay), Japan 77/J4
Oban (hills), Nga. 103/H5
Oban, Sc, UK 31/R8
Obanazawa, Japan 76/B4
Obara, Japan 77/M5
Obata, Japan 77/L7
Ober-Olm, Ger. 54/B3
Ober Ramstadt, Ger. 54/B3
Oberá, Arg. 157/E2
Oberalppass (pass), Swi. 57/E4
Oberalpstock (peak), Swi. 57/E4
Oberammergau, Ger. 57/H2
Oberasbach, Ger. 54/D4
Oberau, Ger. 57/H2
Oberburg, Swi. 56/D3
Oberderdingen, Ger. 54/B4
Oberdiessbach, Swi. 56/D4
Oberding, Ger. 55/E6
Oberdorf, Swi. 56/D3
Oberdorla, Ger. 51/H6
Oberelsbach, Ger. 54/D2
Oberentfelden, Swi. 56/E3
Oberglatt, Swi. 57/E3
Obergünzburg, Ger. 57/G2
Oberhaching, Ger. 55/E6
Oberhausen, Ger. 50/D6
Oberkirch, Ger. 56/E1
Oberkochen, Ger. 54/D5
Oberkotzau, Ger. 55/E2
Oberlausitz (reg.), Ger. 41/H3
Oberlin, Ks, US 129/G3
Obernai, Fr. 56/D1
Obernburg am Main, Ger. 54/C3
Oberndorf am Neckar, Ger. 57/E1
Oberndorf bei Salzburg, Aus. 55/F7
Oberneukirchen, Aus. 55/H6
Obernkirchen, Ger. 51/G4
Oberon, Austl. 115/D2
Oberösterreich (prov.), Aus. 41/G4
Oberpfälzer Wald (for.), Ger. 55/F3
Oberrieden, Swi. 57/E3
Oberriet, Swi. 57/F3
Obersaxen, Swi. 57/F4
Oberschleissheim, Ger. 55/E6
Oberschneiding, Ger. 55/F5
Obersiggenthal, Swi. 57/E2
Oberstammheim, Swi. 57/E2
Oberstaufen, Ger. 57/G2
Oberstdorf, Ger. 57/G3
Oberthal, Ger. 53/G4
Obertrum am See, Aus. 55/G7
Obertshausen, Ger. 54/B2
Oberursel, Ger. 54/B2
Oberuzwil, Swi. 57/F3
Oberviechtach, Ger. 55/F4
Oberwald, Swi. 57/E4
Oberwart, Aus. 48/C2
Oberwesel, Ger. 53/G3
Oberwil, Swi. 56/D4
Obfelden, Swi. 57/E3
Obi (str.), Indo. 81/G4
Obi (isls.), Indo. 81/G4
Obi (isl.), Indo. 116/B5
Óbidos, Braz. 151/G4
Óbidos, Port. 44/A3
Obihiro, Japan 76/C2
Obilić, Yugo. 47/G1
Obing, Ger. 55/F6
Obira, Japan 76/B1
Obitsu (riv.), Japan 77/D3
Obluch'ye, Rus. 71/P2
Obninsk, Rus. 60/H5
Obo, CAfr. 97/L6
Oborniki, Pol. 41/J2
Oborniki Śląskie, Pol. 41/J3
Obra (riv.), Pol. 41/J2
Obrenovac, Yugo. 48/E3
Obrež, Yugo. 48/E4
Obrigheim, Ger. 54/C4
Obrigheim, Ger. 54/B3
Observatory, Austl. 115/G5
Obtrumer (lake), Aus. 55/F7
Ōbu, Japan 77/L6
Obuasi, Gha. 103/E5
Obw. (canton), Swi. 57/E4
Obzor, Bul. 49/H4
Ocala, Fl, US 133/H4
Ocampo, Mex. 142/E3
Ocaña, Sp. 44/D3
Ocaña, Col. 152/C2
Occhieppo Inferiore, It. 58/B1
Occhieppo Superiore, It. 58/A1
Occhiobello, It. 59/E3
Occidental, Cordillera (mts.), Ecu. 150/C3
Occimiano, It. 58/B2
Ocean (cape), Ak, US 134/L3
Ocean (co.), NJ, US 138/D4
Ocean Beach, NY, US 139/E2
Ocean City, Md, US 130/F4
Ocean City, NJ, US 138/D5
Ocean Falls, BC, Can. 126/B2
Ocean Gate, NJ, US 138/D4
Ocean Grove, NJ, US 138/D3
Ocean View, NJ, US 138/D5
Oceanographic Museum, Mona. 58/J8
Oceanside, Ca, US 136/C4
Oceanside, NY, US 139/L9
Oceanville, NJ, US 138/D5
Och'amch'ire, Geo. 63/G4
Ocheltree, Ks, US 137/D6
Ochiishi-misaki (cape), Japan 76/D2
Ochil (hills), Sc, UK 36/C4
Ocho Rios, Jam. 145/G2
Ochsenfurt, Ger. 54/D3
Ochsenhausen, Ger. 57/F1
Ochsenkopf (peak), Aus. 57/F3
Ochtendung, Ger. 53/G3
Ochtrup, Ger. 51/E4
Ochtum (riv.), Ger. 51/F2
Ockelbo, Swe. 38/G1
Ockenheim, Ger. 53/G4
Ocmulgee (riv.), Ga, US 133/H3
Ocmulgee Nat'l Mon., Ga, US 133/H3
Ocna Mureș, Rom. 49/F2
Ocna Sibiului, Rom. 49/G3
Ocoña (riv.), Peru 150/D6
Ocoña, Peru 156/C5
Oconee (lake), Ga, US 133/H3
Oconee (riv.), Ga, US 133/H3
Oconto, Wi, US 127/M4
Ocosingo, Mex. 144/C2
Ocotal, Nic. 144/E3
Ocotlán, Mex. 142/E4
Ocotlán de Morelos, Mex. 144/B2
Ocoyoacac, Mex. 143/Q10
Ocozocoautla de Espinosa, Mex. 144/C2
Ocracoke, NC, US 133/K3
Ocros, Peru 156/B3
Octeville, Fr. 42/C2
October Revolution (isl.), Rus. 67/H2
Oda (peak), Sudan 101/D4
Oda, Japan 74/C3
Oda, Gha. 103/E5
Odaesan NP, SKor. 74/A2
Ōdai, Japan 77/K7
Ōdaigahara-san (peak), Japan 74/E3
Ōdate, Japan 76/B3
Odawara, Japan 75/F3
Odda, Nor. 38/B1
Odder, Den. 38/D4
Odeborn (riv.), Ger. 51/F6
Odelzhausen, Ger. 54/E6
Odemira, Port. 44/A4
Ödemiş, Turk. 90/A2
Odendaalsrus, SAfr. 106/D2
Odense, Den. 38/D4
Odense (int'l arpt.), Den. 38/D4
Odenthal, Ger. 53/G1
Odenton, Md, US 138/B5
Odenwald (reg.), Ger. 54/B3
Oder (Odra) (riv.), Ger.,Pol. 41/H2
Oder-Spree Kanal (canal), Ger. 40/Q7
Oderen, Fr. 56/C2
Oderhaff (lag.), Ger. 41/H2
Oderzo, It. 59/F1
Odesa, Turk. 90/B1
Odesa, Ukr. 49/K2
Odes'ka (obl.), Ukr. 62/D3
Odessa, Wa, US 126/D4
Odessa, Tx, US 129/G5
Odessa, De, US 138/C5
Odet (riv.), Fr. 42/B2
Odienné, C.d'Iv. 102/D4
Odintsovo, Rus. 61/W9
Odiongan, Phil. 79/D5
Odivelas, Port. 45/P10
Odobeşti, Rom. 49/H3
Odon (riv.), Fr. 42/C2
Odoorn, Neth. 50/D3
Odorheiu Secuiesc, Rom. 49/G2
Odžaci, Yugo. 48/D3
Odzala, PN d', Congo 96/J7
Ōe, Japan 77/H5
Ōe-yama (peak), Japan 77/H5
Oegstgeest, Neth. 50/B4
Oeiras, Braz. 154/B2
Oelde, Ger. 51/F5
Oelsnitz, Ger. 55/F2
Oeno (isl.), Pitc. 117/M7
Oensingen, Swi. 56/D3
Oer-Erkenschwick, Ger. 51/E5
Oesling (mts.), Lux. 53/E4
Oesterdam (dam), Neth. 50/B6
Oestrich-Winkel, Ger. 54/B3
Oeta NP, Gre. 47/H3
Oetz, Aus. 57/G3
Oey'ŏn (isl.), SKor. 73/D3
Of, Turk. 62/G4
O'Fallon, Mo, US 137/F8
O'Fallon, Il, US 137/H8
Ofanto (riv.), It. 46/D2
Ofaqim, Isr. 91/D4
Ofenhorn (peak), Swi. 57/E5
Offa, Nga. 103/G4
Offaly (co.), Ire. 34/A5
Offanengo, It. 58/C2
Offement, Fr. 56/C2
Offenbach, Ger. 54/B2
Offenbach an der Queich, Ger. 54/B4
Offenburg, Ger. 56/D1
Offingen, Ger. 54/D6
Offstein, Ger. 54/B3
Oftersheim, Ger. 54/B4
Oftringen, Swi. 56/D3
Ōfunato, Japan 76/B4
Oga, Japan 76/A4
Oga (pen.), Japan 76/A4
Ogachi, Japan 76/B4
Ogadēn (reg.), Eth. 97/P6
Ōgaki, Japan 77/L5
Ogano, Japan 77/C2
Ogasawara, Japan 116/D2
Ogatsu, Japan 76/B4
Ogawa, Japan 77/E1
Ogawa, Japan 77/C1
Ogawara (lake), Japan 76/B3
Ogbomosho, Nga. 103/G4
Ogden, Ut, US 137/K11
Ogden Bay (bay), Ut, US 137/J11
Ogden, South Fork (riv.), Ut, US 137/K11
Ogdensburg, NY, US 130/F2
Ogdensburg, NJ, US 138/D1
Ogeechee (riv.), Ga, US 133/H3
Oggiono, It. 58/C1
Ogi, Japan 75/F2
Ogidaki (mtn.), On, Can. 130/D2
Ogies, SAfr. 106/E2
Ogilvie (mts.), Yk, Can. 122/C2
Ogilvie (riv.), Yk, Can. 122/C2
Ogles, Il, US 137/G8
Oglesby, Tx, US 143/F2
Oglio (riv.), It. 43/J4
Ognon (riv.), Fr. 40/C5
Ogoamas (peak), Indo. 81/F3
Ogoki (lake), On, Can. 127/M3
Ogoki (res.), On, Can. 127/L3
Ogoki (riv.), On, Can. 127/M3
Ogooué (riv.), Gabon 93/C5
Ogose, Japan 77/C2
Ogosta (riv.), Bul. 49/F4
Ogre, Lat. 39/L3
Oguchi, Japan 77/L5
Ogulin, Cro. 48/B3
Ogun (riv.), Nga. 96/F6
Ogun (state), Nga. 103/F5
Ogurjaly (isl.), Trkm. 87/B5
Oğuz, Turk. 62/F5
Oh Me Edge (hill), Eng, UK 36/D6
Ōhara, Japan 77/E3
Oharu, Japan 77/L5
Ōhata, Japan 76/B3
Ohey, Belg. 53/E3
O'Higgins (pol. reg.), Chile 158/B1
O'Higgins (lake), Chile 159/B6
Ohio (riv.), US 130/B4
Ohio (state), US 130/D3
Ōhira, Japan 77/D1
Ohlsdorf, Aus. 55/G7
Ohlstadt, Ger. 57/H2
Ohm (riv.), Ger. 54/C1
Ōho, Japan 77/E1
Ohoopee (riv.), Ga, US 133/H3
Ohře (riv.), Czh. 40/H3
Ohre (riv.), Ger. 40/F2
Ohrid, FYROM 47/G2
Ohrid (lake), Alb., Mac 47/G2
Oi (riv.), China 83/G2
Ōi, Japan 77/J5
Ōi, Japan 77/C3
Ōi, Japan 77/D2
Oiapoque (riv.), Braz. 151/H3
Oiapoque, Braz. 151/H3
Oich (lake), Sc, UK 36/B2
Oieras, Port. 45/P10
Oignies, Fr. 52/B3
Oignin (riv.), Fr. 56/B5
Oil City, Pa, US 130/E3
Oinófita, Gre. 47/H3
Oinóï, Gre. 47/N8
Oirschot, Neth. 50/C5
Oise (dept.), Fr. 52/B5
Oise (riv.), Fr. 40/B4
Oise à l'Aisne, Canal de l' (canal), Fr. 52/C4
Oiseaux du Djoudj, PN des, Sen. 102/A2
Ōiso, Japan 77/C3
Oissery, Fr. 30/L4
Oisterwijk, Neth. 50/C5
Ōita (riv.), Japan 74/B4
Ōita (pref.), Japan 74/B4
Ōita, Japan 74/B4
Ōizumi, Japan 77/C1
Ōizumi, Japan 77/A2
Ojai, Ca, US 136/A2
Ojcowski NP, Pol. 41/K3
Öjebyn, Swe. 37/G2
Ōji, Japan 77/J6
Ojima, Japan 77/C1
Ojinaga, Mex. 129/F5
Ojiya, Japan 75/F2
Ojo de Agua, Mex. 143/Q9
Ojo de Liebre (lag.), Mex. 142/B3
Ojocaliente, Mex. 142/E4
Ojos del Salado (peak), Chile 157/C2
Ojos Negros, Sp. 44/E2
Ojuelos de Jalisco, Mex. 143/E4
Oka, Nga. 103/G5
Oka (riv.), Rus. 65/L4
Oka, Qu, Can. 131/M7
Okabe, Japan 77/C1
Okahandja, Namb. 105/C5
Okak (isl.), Nf, Can. 123/K3
Okanagan (lake), BC, Can. 122/D4
Okanagan Falls, BC, Can. 126/D3
Okanda, PN de l', Gabon 105/B1
Okanogan, Wa, US 126/D3
Okanogan (riv.), Wa, US 126/D3
Okāra, Pak. 86/B4
Okavango (delta), Bots. 105/D4
Ōkawa, Japan 74/B4
Okaya, Japan 75/F2
Okayama (pref.), Japan 74/C3
Okayama, Japan 74/C3
Okazaki, Japan 77/M6
Okch'ŏn, SKor. 73/D4
Okęcie (int'l arpt.), Pol. 41/L2
Okeechobee, Fl, US 133/H5
Okeechobee (lake), Fl, US 125/K6
Okegawa, Japan 77/D2
Okement (riv.), Eng, UK 32/B5
Okha, Rus. 65/Q4
Ókhi Óros (peak), Gre. 47/J3
Okhotsk (sea), Rus. 67/P4
Okhotsk, Sea of (sea), Japan,Rus 71/R2
Okhta (riv.), Rus. 61/T6
Okhtyrka, Ukr. 62/E2
Oki (isls.), Japan 65/P6
Okidaitō (isl.), Japan 75/L8
Okiep, SAfr. 106/B3
Okinawa (isl.), Japan 67/M7
Okinawa (pref.), Japan 75/J8
Okino-shima (isl.), Japan 74/C4
Okinoerabu (isl.), Japan 75/K7
Okitipupa, Nga. 103/G5
Okkan, Myan. 83/G4
Okku, SKor. 73/D5
Oklahoma (state), US 129/H4
Oklahoma City (cap.), Ok, US 137/M15
Okmulgee, Ok, US 129/J4
Oko, Nga. 103/G5
Okobaji (lakes), Ia, US 127/K5
Okok (riv.), Ugan. 104/B2
Okolona, Ms, US 133/F3
Okoppe, Japan 76/C1
Okotoks, Ab, Can. 126/E3
Okovango (riv.), Namb. 93/E6
Oksbøl, Den. 38/C4
Oksskolten (peak), Nor. 37/E2
Oktyabr'sk, Rus. 63/J1
Oktyabr'skiy, Rus. 61/M5
Ōkuchi, Japan 74/B4
Okulovka, Rus. 60/G4
Okushiri, Japan 76/A2
Okutama (lake), Japan 77/C2
Okutama, Japan 77/C2
Okwa (riv.), Bots. 105/D5
Ol Doinyo Sabuk NP, Kenya 104/C3
Ólafsfjördhur, Ice. 37/N6
Ólafsvík, Ice. 37/M7
Olalla, Wa, US 135/B3
Olan, Pic d' (peak), Fr. 43/G4
Olanchito, Hon. 144/E3
Öland (isl.), Swe. 37/F4
Ölands södra udde (pt.), Swe. 38/G3
Olathe, Ks, US 137/D6
Olavarría, Arg. 158/E3
Oława, Pol. 41/J3
Ölbach (riv.), Ger. 51/F5
Olberg, Az, US 137/S19
Olbia, It. 46/A2
Olching, Ger. 55/E6
Olcott, NY, US 131/S9
Old (riv.), Ca, US 135/L11
Old Bahama (chan.), Cuba 145/G1
Old Bar, Austl. 115/E1
Old Bedford (canal), Eng, UK 33/G2
Old Bethpage, NY, US 139/M9
Old Bridge, NJ, US 139/H10
Old City, Isr. 91/G8
Old Crow, Yk, Can. 134/L2
Old Faithful Geyser, Wy, US 126/F4
Old Field (pt.), NY, US 139/E2
Old Fort Niagara, NY, US 131/R9
Old Harbor, Ak, US 134/H4
Old Man of Hoy, Sc, UK 31/V14
Old Mill Creek, Il, US 135/Q15
Old Nene (riv.), Eng, UK 33/F2
Old Rhine (riv.), Neth. 50/B4
Old Saybrook, Ct, US 139/F1
Old Tappan, NJ, US 139/K8
Old Town, Me, US 131/G2
Old Windsor, Eng, UK 30/B2
Old Wives (lake), Sk, Can. 127/G3
Oldeani (peak), Tanz. 104/B3
Oldebroek, Neth. 50/C4
Oldemarkt, Neth. 50/C3
Oldenburg, Ger. 51/F2
Oldenburg, Ger. 38/D4
Oldenzaal, Neth. 50/D4
Oldham, Eng, UK 35/F4
Oldman (riv.), Ab, Can. 126/E3
Oldmeldrum, Sc, UK 36/D2
Oldoog (isl.), Ger. 51/E1
Olds, Ab, Can. 126/E3
Olduvai Gorge, Tanz. 104/B3
Oldwick, NJ, US 138/D2
Olean, NY, US 130/E3
Olecko, Pol. 39/K4
Oleggio, It. 58/B1
Oleiros, Port. 44/B3
Oleiros, Sp. 44/A1
Olekma (riv.), Rus. 65/N4
Oleksandriya, Ukr. 62/E2
Olele (pt.), Wa, US 135/B2
Olemari (riv.), Sur. 153/H4
Ølen, Nor. 38/A2
Olenegorsk, Rus. 60/G1
Olenëk (riv.), Rus. 65/L3
Olenek (bay), Rus. 65/M2
Oléron, île (isl.), Fr. 42/C4
Olesa de Montserrat, Sp. 45/K6
Oleśnica, Pol. 41/J3
Olesno, Pol. 41/K3
Oley, Pa, US 138/C3
Olfen, Ger. 51/E5
Olga (mt.), Austl. 113/F3
Olginate, It. 58/C1
Ölgiy, Mong. 70/E2
Ølgod, Den. 38/C4
Olhão, Port. 44/B4
Öli Qoltyq Sory (swamp), Kaz. 87/B3
Oliena, It. 46/A2
Olifantshoek, SAfr. 106/P12
Olifantsrivier (riv.), SAfr. 105/E5
Olimarao (isl.), Micr. 116/D4
Olimbía (Olympia) (ruin), Gre. 47/G4
Ólimbos, Gre. 90/A3
Ólimbos NP (Olympos NP), Gre. 47/H2
Olímpia, Braz. 155/B2
Olimpos Beydağları NP, Turk. 91/B1
Olinalá, Mex. 144/B2
Olinda, Braz. 154/D3
Olindina, Braz. 154/C3
Oliva, Sp. 45/E3
Oliva de la Frontera, Sp. 44/B3

Olivais, Port. 44/A3
Oliveira, Braz. 155/C2
Olivenza, Sp. 44/B3
Oliver, BC, Can. 126/D3
Olivet, Fr. 42/D3
Olivone, Swi. 57/E4
Olla, La, US 129/J5
Ollachea, Peru 156/D4
Ollagüe (vol.) 150/E8
Ollainville, Fr. 30/J6
Ollería, Sp. 45/E3
Olleros, Peru 156/B3
Ollon, Swi. 56/D5
Ollür, India 82/C5
Olmaliq, Uzb. 87/E4
Olmos (state), Nga. 103/G5
Olmos, Peru 156/B2
Olmos Park, Tx, US 137/U21
Olmstead, Ut, US 137/K13
Olmué, Chile 158/N8
Olney, Tx, US 129/H4
Olney, Md, US 138/A5
Olofström, Swe. 38/F3
Olomane (riv.), Qu, Can. 131/J1
Olomouc, Czh. 41/J4
Olongapo, Phil. 79/D5
Olonne-sur-Mer, Fr. 42/C3
Olorgasailie Nat'l Mon., Kenya 104/C3
Oloron-Sainte-Marie, Fr. 42/C5
Olot, Sp. 45/G1
Oloy (range), Rus. 65/S3
Olpe (riv.), Ger. 51/F6
Olpe, Ger. 53/G1
Olsberg, Ger. 51/F6
Olst, Neth. 50/D4
Olsztyn, Pol. 39/J5
Olsztyn (prov.), Pol. 41/L2
Olsztynek, Pol. 41/L2
Olt (riv.), Rom. 62/C3
Olt (prov.), Rom. 49/G3
Olte, Sierra de (hills), Arg. 158/C4
Olten, Swi. 56/D3
Oltenița, Rom. 49/H3
Oltet (riv.), Rom. 49/F3
Oltre il Colle, It. 57/F6
Oltu (riv.), Turk. 63/G4
Oltu, Turk. 63/G4
Olur, Turk. 63/G4
Olvera, Sp. 44/C4
Olympia (cap.), Wa, US 126/C4
Olympic (mts.), Wa, US 126/C4
Olympic Dam, Austl. 113/H4
Olympic Game Farm, Wa, US 135/A1
Olympic National Forest, Wa, US 135/A2
Olympic NP, Wa, US 126/B4
Olympic Park, SKor. 73/G6
Olympos (Mount Olympus) (peak), Gre. 47/H2
Olympus (mt.), Wa, US 126/C4
Olympus (peak), Cyp. 91/C2
Olyutorskiy (bay), Rus. 65/S3
Ōma, Japan 76/B3
Oma (riv.), Rus. 61/K2
Japan 76/B3
Ōmachi, Japan 75/E2
Omae-zaki (pt.), Japan 75/F3
Ōmagari, Japan 76/B4
Omagh (dist.), NI, UK 34/A2
Omagh, NI, UK 34/A2
Omak, Wa, US 126/D3
Oman (gulf), Asia 89/H4
Oman (ctry.) 89/G4
Omar Torrijos Herrera (int'l arpt.), Pan. 152/B2
Omaruru, Namb. 105/C5
Omas, Peru 156/B4
Omatako (riv.), Namb. 105/C4
Omate, Peru 156/D5
Ombai (str.), Indo. 81/F5
Ombrone (riv.), It. 43/J5
Ombúes de Lavalle, Uru. 159/K10
Ōme, Japan 77/C2
Omeath, Ire. 34/B3
Omegna, It. 43/H4
Omeo, Austl. 115/C3
Ōmerli, Turk. 90/E2
Ometepe (isl.), Nic. 144/E4
Ometepec, Mex. 144/B2
Ōmi, Japan 77/K5
Ōmihachiman, Japan 77/K5
Omiš, Cro. 46/E1
Omitlán (riv.), Mex. 144/B2
Ōmiya, Japan 75/G2
Ōmiya, Japan 77/K7
Ommaney (cape), Ak, US 134/M4
Ommen, Neth. 50/D3
Ömnögovi (prov.), Mong. 70/H3
Omo NP, Eth. 97/N6
Omo Wenz (riv.), Eth. 97/N6
Omodeo (lake), It. 46/A2
Omolon (riv.), Rus. 67/Q3
Omono (riv.), Japan 76/B4
Omsk, Rus. 87/F1
Omsk (int'l arpt.), Rus. 87/F1
Omskaya (obl.), Rus. 87/F1
Ōmu, Japan 76/C1
Omul (peak), Rom. 49/G3
Ōmura, Japan 74/A4

Omurtag, Bul. 49/H4
Ōmuta, Japan 74/B4
Omutninsk, Rus. 61/M4
Onagawa, Japan 76/B4
Onalaska, Tx, US 132/E4
Onaping (lake), On, Can. 130/D2
Oñate, Sp. 44/D1
Onaway, Mi, US 130/C2
Onchan, IM, UK 34/D3
Onda, Sp. 45/E3
Ondava (riv.), Slvk. 41/L4
Ondjiva, Ang. 105/C2
Ondo, Nga. 103/G5
Ondo (state), Nga. 103/G5
Öndörhaan, Mong. 71/K2
Onè, It. 59/E1
Onega (lake), Rus. 160/D
Onega (riv.), Rus. 64/D3
Onega (bay), Rus. 60/G2
Onega (pen.), Rus. 60/H2
Onega, Rus. 60/H3
Oneida, NY, US 130/F3
Oneida, Tx, US 129/J5
Oneida, Pa, US 138/B2
Oneonta, NY, US 130/F3
Onex, Swi. 56/C5
Ongjin, NKor. 73/C4
Ongole, India 82/D4
Ongtüstik Qazaqstan, Kaz. 64/G5
Onhaye, Belg. 53/D3
Onida, SD, US 127/H4
Onil, Sp. 45/E3
Onilahy (riv.), Madg. 107/G8
Onishi, Japan 77/C1
Onitsha, Nga. 103/G5
Onjuku, Japan 77/E3
Onkaparinga (riv.), Austl. 113/M8
Onnaing, Fr. 52/C3
Onny (riv.), Eng, UK 32/D2
Ōno, Japan 74/E3
Ono, Japan 77/L5
Onoda, Japan 74/B4
Onomichi, Japan 74/C3
Onon, Mong. 71/K2
Onon (riv.), Rus. 71/K1
Onoto, Ven. 153/E2
Onotoa (isl.), Kiri. 116/G5
Onrusrivier, SAfr. 106/L11
Onslow, Austl. 112/B2
Ontake-san (peak), Japan 75/D3
Ontario, Or, US 126/D4
Ontario, Ca, US 136/C2
Ontario (prov.), Can. 56/C1
Ontario (lake), Can,US 130/E3
Ontelaunee (lake), Pa, US 138/C3
Onteniente, Sp. 45/E3
Ontonagon, Mi, US 127/L4
Ontong Java (isl.), Sol. 116/E5
Onyang, SKor. 73/D4
Onzaga, Col. 152/C3
Oologah (lake), Ok, US 132/D2
Oona River, BC, Can. 134/M5
Oost-Vlaanderen (prov.), Belg. 52/C2
Oost-Vlieland, Neth. 50/C2
Oostburg, Neth. 52/C1
Oostelijk Flevoland (polder), Neth. 50/C3
Oostende (Ostend), Belg. 52/B1
Oosterhout, Neth. 50/B5
Oosterscheidedam (dam), Neth. 50/A5
Oosterschelde (riv.), Neth. 40/B3
Oosterwolde, Neth. 50/D2
Oosterzele, Belg. 52/C2
Oostkamp, Belg. 52/C1
Oostvaarderplassen (lake),Neth. 50/C3
Oostzaan, Neth. 50/B4
Ootmarsum, Neth. 50/E3
Opaka, Bul. 49/H4
Opalenica, Pol. 41/J2
Opasatika (riv.), On, Can. 130/D1
Opatija, Cro. 48/B3
Opatów, Pol. 41/L3
Opava, Czh. 41/J4
Opelika, Al, US 133/G3
Opelousas, La, US 129/J5
Opera, It. 58/C2
Öpfingen, Ger. 57/F1
Opglabbeek, Belg. 53/E1
Ophir, Ak, US 134/G3
Ophir, Ut, US 137/J13
Ophthalmia (range), Austl. 112/C2
Oploo, Neth. 50/C5
Opmeer, Neth. 50/B3
Opoczno, Pol. 41/L3
Opole, Pol. 41/J3
Opole Lubelskie, Pol. 41/L3
Opovo, Yugo. 48/E3
Opp, Al, US 133/G4
Oppeano, It. 59/E2
Oppenau, Ger. 56/E1
Oppenheim, Ger. 54/B3
Oppland (co.), Nor. 37/D3
Opportunity, Wa, US 126/D4
Opwijk, Belg. 53/D2
Oquirrh (mts.), Ut, US 137/J12

Or 'Aqiva, Isr. 91/F6
Or Yehuda, Isr. 91/F7
Or, Mont d' (peak), Fr. 56/C4
Ora (riv.), Mex. 142/D3
Ōra, Japan 77/C1
Oradell, NJ, US 139/J8
Oradell (res.), NJ, US 139/J8
Orahovac, Yugo. 47/G1
Orahovica, Cro. 48/C3
Orai, India 84/B3
Orain (riv.), Fr. 56/B4
Oral, Kaz. 63/J2
Oran, Alg. 100/E5
Orang (cape), Braz. 151/H3
Orange (lake), Rus. 160/D
Orange, Austl. 115/D2
Orange (riv.), SAfr.,Nam 105/C6
Orange (pen.), It. 59/G5
Orange Walk, Belz. 144/D2
Orangeburg, SC, US 133/H3
Orangeburg, NY, US 139/K7
Orangeville, On, Can. 130/D3
Orangeville, Pa, US 138/B1
Orango (isl.), GBis. 102/A4
Oranienburg, Ger. 40/Q6
Oranjekanaal (riv.), Neth. 50/D3
Oranjemund, Namb. 106/B3
Oranjestad, Aruba 152/D1
Oranmore, Ire. 31/P10
Orapa, Bots. 105/E5
Oras, Phil. 79/E5
Orăștie, Rom. 49/F3
Oravița, Rom. 48/E3
Orb (riv.), Fr. 42/E5
Orba (riv.), It. 58/B3
Orbe, Swi. 56/C4
Orbe (riv.), Swi. 56/C4
Orbetello, It. 46/D3
Örbigo (riv.), Sp. 44/C1
Orbost, Austl. 115/D3
Örbyhus, Swe. 38/G1
Orcemont, Fr. 30/H6
Orcera, Sp. 44/D3
Orchamps, Fr. 56/B3
Orchamps-Vennes, Fr. 56/C3
Orchard (lake), Mi, US 135/F6
Orchard City, Co, US 128/F3
Orchard Farm, Mo, US 137/G8
Orchard Homes, Mt, US 126/E4
Orchard Lake Village, Mi, US 135/F6
Orchid (isl.), Tai. 79/D3
Orchies, Fr. 52/C1
Orchy (riv.), Sc, UK 36/B4
Orciano di Pesaro, It. 59/F5
Orco (riv.), It. 43/G4
Orcopampa, Peru 156/C4
Orcotuna, Peru 156/B4
Ord, Ne, US 127/J5
Ordaz (int'l arpt.), Mex. 142/D4
Ordes, Sp. 44/A1
Ordesa y Monte Perdido, PN de, Sp. 45/F1
Ordos (Mu Us Shamo) (des.), China 70/J4
Ordos, China 70/J4
Ordu, Turk. 62/F4
Ordu (prov.), Turk. 62/F4
Ore, Nga. 103/G5
Orealla, Guy. 153/G3
Örebro, Swe. 38/F2
Örebro (prov.), Swe. 37/E4
Örebro (int'l arpt.), Swe. 38/F2
Öregrund, Swe. 38/H1
Orël, Rus. 62/F1
Orellana, Peru 156/C2
Orellana la Vieja, Sp. 44/C3
Orem, Ut, US 137/K13
Orenberg (int'l arpt.), Rus. 63/K2
Orenburg, Rus. 63/K2
Orenburgskaya (obl.), Rus. 63/K2
Orense, Sp. 44/B1
Orestiás, Gre. 47/K2
Øresund (sound), Swe. 38/E4
Oreti (riv.), NZ 117/R12
Orford, Austl. 115/C4
Orford, Eng, UK 33/H2
Organ Pipe Cactus Nat'l Mon., Az, US 142/B1

Órgãos, Serra dos (mts.), Braz. 211/K7
Orgaz, Sp. 44/D3
Orgelet, Fr. 56/B4
Orgeurs, Fr. 30/H5
Orgeval, Fr. 30/H5
Orgosolo, It. 46/A2
Orhaneli, Turk. 62/D5
Orhangazi, Turk. 49/J5
Orhei, Mol. 49/J2
Orhon (riv.), Mong. 70/J2
Orient (pt.), NY, US 139/F1
Oriental, Mex. 143/M7
Oriental, Cordillera (mts.), SAm. 150/C5
Orientale (prov.), D.R. Congo 104/A2
Oriente, Arg. 158/E3
Origny-Sainte-Benoîte, Fr. 52/C4
Orihuela, Sp. 45/E3
Orillia, On, Can. 130/E2
Orimattila, Fin. 39/L1
Orinda, Ca, US 135/K11
Orinoco (delta), Ven. 147/C2
Orinoco (riv.), Col.,Ven. 147/C2
Orio al Serio (int'l arpt.), It. 58/C1
Oriolo, It. 46/E2
Orion (lake), Mi, US 135/F6
Orissa (state), India 70/D7
Orissa Coast (canal), India 85/F5
Oristano, It. 46/A3
Oristano, Golfo di (gulf), It. 46/A3
Orivesi, Fin. 39/L1
Oriximiná, Braz. 151/G4
Orizaba, Mex. 143/M8
Orizona, Braz. 154/A5
Orjen (peak), Yugo. 47/F1
Orjiva, Sp. 44/D4
Orke (riv.), Ger. 51/F6
Orkelljunga, Swe. 38/E3
Orkhomenós, Gre. 47/H3
Orkney, SAfr. 106/D2
Orkney (isls.), UK 160/G
Orla, Tx, US 132/C4
Orland Park, Il, US 135/Q16
Orlândia, Braz. 155/C2
Orlando (int'l arpt.), Fl, US 133/H4
Orlando, Fl, US 133/H4
Orlando, Capo d' (cape), It. 46/D3
Orléanais (reg.), Fr. 42/D2
Orleans, Ca, US 126/C5
Orleans (parish), La, US 137/P16
Orleans, In, US 133/G1
Orlik (res.), Czh. 55/H3
Orlová, Czh. 41/K4
Orly (int'l arpt.), Fr. 30/K5
Orly, Fr. 30/K5
Ormanlı, Turk. 49/K5
Ōrma, Japan 76/B2
Ormea, It. 58/A4
Ormilia, Gre. 47/H2
Orminston, Sc, UK 36/D5
Ormoc, Phil. 81/F1
Ormond Beach, Fl, US 133/H4
Ormskirk, Eng, UK 35/F4
Ornain (riv.), Fr. 42/F2
Ornans, Fr. 56/C3
Ornavasso, It. 57/E6
Ōrne (riv.), Fr. 40/C4
Ørnes, Nor. 37/E2
Orneta, Pol. 39/J4
Örnsköldsvik, Swe. 37/F3
Oro (riv.), Mex. 154/C2
Oro Grande, Ca, US 136/C2
Oro, Monte d' (peak), Fr. 46/A1
Oro Valley, Az, US 128/E4
Orocó, Braz. 154/C3
Orocué, Col. 152/D3
Orodara, Burk. 102/D4
Orofino, Id, US 126/D4
Orolo (riv.), It. 59/E1
Oroluk (isl.), Micr. 116/E4
Oromocto, NB, Can. 131/H2
Oron-la-Ville, Swi. 56/C4
Orona (Hull) (isl.), Kiri. 117/H5
Orono, Me, US 131/G2
Orontes (riv.), Syria 90/D3
Oropesa, Sp. 44/C3
Oroqen Zizhiqi, China 71/M1
Orós, Braz. 154/C2
Orosei, Golfo di (gulf), It. 46/A2
Oroséja, Fr. 42/D5
Orosháza, Hun. 48/E2
Oroszlány, Hun. 48/D2
Orovada, Nv, US 130/D5
Oroville, Wa, US 126/D3
Oroville, Ca, US 128/B3
Orphin, Fr. 42/D3
Orpund, Swi. 56/D3
Orrefors, Swe. 38/F3
Orrell, Eng, UK 35/F4
Orrick, Mo, US 137/E5
Orrin (riv.), Sc, UK 36/B3
Orrin (res.), Sc, UK 36/B3
Orroli, It. 46/A3
Orroroo, Austl. 113/H5
Orsa, Swe. 38/F1
Orsago, It. 59/E1
Orsay, Fr. 30/H2

Orsett, Eng, UK 30/E2
Orsha, Bela. 39/P4
Orsk, Rus. 63/K2
Orsonnens, Swi. 56/D4
Orşova, Rom. 48/F3
Ørsta, Nor. 37/C3
Órtiz, Mex. 142/C2
Orta (lake), It. 43/H4
Orta, Turk. 62/E4
Orta Nova, It. 46/D2
Ortaca, Turk. 90/B2
Ortaköy, Turk. 90/C2
Ortaköy, Turk. 62/E4
Ortega, Col. 152/C4
Ortegal (cape), Sp. 44/B1
Ortenberg, Ger. 54/C2
Orth an der Donau, Aus. 49/P7
Orthez, Fr. 42/C5
Ortigara (peak), It. 57/H5
Ortigueira, Sp. 44/B1
Orting, Wa, US 135/C3
Ortiz, Mex. 142/C2
Ortles (mts.), It. 43/J3
Ortles (peak), It. 57/G4
Ortón (riv.), Bol. 156/D4
Ortona, It. 46/D1
Ortonville, Mn, US 127/J4
Ortonville, Mi, US 135/F6
Örtze (riv.), Ger. 51/H3
Orümīyeh, Iran 90/F2
Orurillo, Peru 156/D4
Oruro, Bol. 150/E7
Orrożeła, Pol. 41/L2
Orust (isl.), Swe. 38/D2
Orvieto, It. 43/K5
Orvilliers, Fr. 30/G5
Orwell (riv.), Eng, UK 33/H4
Orwigsburg, Pa, US 138/B2
Oryakhovo, Bul. 49/F4
Orzinuovi, It. 58/C2
Orzysz, Pol. 39/J5
Os, Nor. 38/A1
Osa, Rus. 61/M4
Osa, Peninsula de (pen.), CR 150/B2
Osage (riv.), Mo, US 129/J3
Osage Beach, Mo, US 129/J3
Osaka (pref.), Japan 74/D3
Osaka (int'l arpt.), Japan 77/H6
Ōsaka, Japan 77/H6
Ōsaka Castle, Japan 77/H6
Osasco, Braz. 211/G8
Ōsato, Japan 77/C1
Osborn (mt.), Ak, US 134/C1
Osceola, Ar, US 130/B5
Oschersleben, Ger. 40/P7
Oschiri, It. 46/A2
Oscura (mts.), NM, US 132/B3
Osh (obl.), Kyr. 87/F5
Osh, Kyr. 87/F4
Oshamambe, Japan 76/B2
Oshawa, On, Can. 131/S8
Oshika (pen.), Japan 76/B4
Oshima, Japan 77/B3
Oshkosh, Ne, US 127/H5
Oshnovīyeh, Iran 90/F2
Oshogbo, Nga. 103/G5
Osijek, Cro. 48/D3
Osio Sotto, It. 58/C1
Otero de Rey, Sp. 44/B1
Oteros (riv.), Mex. 142/C3
Osipaonca, Yugo. 48/E3
Oskarshamn, Swe. 38/F3
Oskarström, Swe. 38/E3
Oskol (riv.), Rus.,Ukr. 62/F2
Oslo (cap.), Nor. 38/D2
Osmānābād, India 89/L5
Osmancık, Turk. 62/E4
Osmaneli, Turk. 49/K5
Osmaniye, Turk. 90/E2
Osnabrück, Ger. 51/F4
Osnago, It. 58/C1
Osny, Fr. 30/J4
Osório, Braz. 155/B4
Osorno, Chile 158/B4
Osorno, Sp. 44/C1
Osoyoos, BC, Can. 126/D3
Ospaletti, It. 58/A5
Ospedaletto Euganeo, It. 59/E2
Osprey (reef), Austl. 109/D2
Oss, Neth. 50/C5
Ossa (mt.), Austl. 115/C4
Ossa, Sierra de (mts.), Port. 44/B3
Osse (riv.), Nga. 103/G5
Osséja, Fr. 42/D5
Osset, It. 46/A2
Ossining, NY, US 139/F5
Ossineke, Mi, US 130/D2
Ostashkov, Rus. 60/G4
Ostbevern, Ger. 51/F4
Ostellato, It. 59/G2
Osten, Ger. 51/G1
Österbybruk, Swe. 38/G1
Osterburg, Ger. 54/C4
Osterburken, Ger. 54/C2
Ostercappeln, Ger. 51/F4
Osterdalälven (riv.), Swe. 38/E1
Osterems (chan.), Ger. 51/F2
Östergötland (co.), Swe. 38/F2
Osterhofen, Ger. 55/G5

Osterholz-Scharmbeck, Ger. 51/F2
Osteria Grande, It. 59/E4
Ostermiething, Aus. 55/F6
Osterode am Harz, Ger. 51/H5
Östersund, Swe. 37/E3
Östervåla, Swe. 38/G1
Ostfildern, Ger. 54/C5
Östfold (co.), Nor. 37/D4
Ostfriesland (reg.), Ger. 51/E2
Ostheim vor der Rhön, Ger. 54/C2
Ostia Antica (ruin), It. 46/C2
Ostiglia, It. 59/E2
Ostional NWR, CR 144/E4
Ostra, It. 59/G5
Östra Silen (lake), Aus. 43/J3
Ostra Vetere, It. 59/G5
Ostrach (riv.), Ger. 54/C6
Ostrava, Czh. 41/K4
Ostricourt, Fr. 52/C3
Ostróda, Pol. 39/J5
Ostrogozhsk, Rus. 62/F2
Ostrołęka, Pol. 41/L2
Ostrov, Rus. 39/N3
Ostrov, Czh. 55/F2
Ostrów Mazowiecka, Pol. 41/L2
Ostrów Wielkopolski, Pol. 41/J3
Ostrowiec Świętokrzyski, Pol. 41/L3
Ostrzeszów, Pol. 41/J3
Ostseebad Binz, Ger. 38/E4
Ostseebad Göhren, Ger. 38/E4
Ostseebad Prerow, Ger. 38/E4
Oststeinbek, Ger. 51/H1
Ostuni, It. 47/E2
Ostwald, Fr. 54/A5
Osūm (riv.), Bul. 47/J1
Ōsumi (pen.), Japan 74/B5
Osun (state), Nga. 103/G5
Osun, SKor. 73/D4
Osuna, Sp. 44/C4
Osvaldo Cruz, Braz. 155/B2
Oswaldtwistle, Eng, UK 35/F4
Oswego, NY, US 130/E3
Oswego, Il, US 135/P16
Osburg, Ger. 53/F4
Oswestry, Eng, UK 35/E6
Oświęcim (Auschwitz), Pol. 41/K3
Óta (riv.), Japan 74/C3
Ōta, Japan 75/F2
Ōtake, Japan 74/C3
Ōtaki, Japan 75/G3
Ōtaki, Japan 77/B2
Ōtakine-yama (peak), Japan 75/G2
Otava (riv.), Czh. 43/K3
Otavalo, Ecu. 152/B4
Otavi, Namb. 105/C4
Ōtawara, Japan 75/G2
Otay, Ca, US 136/C5
Oțelu Roșu, Rom. 48/F3
Otero de Rey, Sp. 44/B1
Oteros (riv.), Mex. 142/C3
Otgon Tenger (peak), Mong. 70/G2
Othello, Wa, US 126/D4
Othis, Fr. 30/L4
Othonoí (isl.), Gre. 47/F3
Oti (riv.), Gha. 103/F4
Otjiwarongo, Namb. 105/C5
Otley, Eng, UK 35/G4
Otočac, Cro. 48/B3
Otofuke, Japan 76/C2
Otog Qi, China 70/J4
Otok, Cro. 48/D3
Otok (mt.), Ca, US 135/M12
Otopeni (int'l arpt.), Rom. 49/H3
Otoskwin (riv.), On, Can. 127/L3
Otra (riv.), Nor. 64/A4
Otradnyy, Rus. 63/J1
Otranto, Strait of (str.), It. 47/F2
Otrokovice, Czh. 41/J4
Otse, Bots. 106/D2
Ōtsu, Japan 77/J5
Otta (riv.), Nga. 103/G5
Ōtsuki, Japan 77/B2
Ottawa (cap.), On, Can. 130/E2
Ottawa, Oh, US 130/D3
Ottawa, Il, US 130/D3
Ottawa, Ks, US 129/J3
Ottawa (int'l arpt.), On, Can. 130/E2
Ottawa (isls.), Nun., Can. 123/H3
Ottenby, Swe. 38/G3
Ottensheim, Aus. 55/H6
Otter (riv.), Eng, UK 32/C5
Otterbach, Ger. 53/G4
Otterberg, Ger. 53/G4
Otterndorf, Ger. 51/F1
Ottersberg, Ger. 51/G2
Ottersweier, Ger. 54/B5
Otterville, Il, US 137/G8
Ottignies-Louvain-la-Neuve, Belg. 52/D2

Öttingen im Bayern, Ger. 54/D5
Ottmarsheim, Fr. 56/D2
Ottnang am Hausruck, Aus. 55/G6
Otto, Mo, US 137/F9
Ottobeuren, Ger. 57/G2
Ottobrunn, Ger. 55/E6
Ottone, It. 58/C3
Ottosdal, SAfr. 106/D2
Ottsville, Pa, US 138/C3
Ottumwa, Ia, US 127/K5
Ottweiler, Ger. 53/G5
Otumba de Gómez Farías, Mex. 143/L7
Otuzco, Peru 156/B2
Otway (cape), Austl. 115/B3
Otway (bay), Chile 159/C7
Otway NP, Austl. 115/B3
Otwock, Pol. 41/L2
Ouachita (mts.), Ar,La, US 125/D5
Ouachita (riv.), Ar,La, US 125/D5
Ouaddaï (reg.), Chad 97/K5
Ouadi Haddad (riv.), Chad 97/J4
Ouadi Rimé (riv.), Chad 96/J5
Ouagadougou (int'l arpt.), Burk. 103/E3
Ouagadougou (cap.), Burk. 103/E3
Ouahigouya, Burk. 103/E3
Ouaka (riv.), CAfr. 97/K6
Oualâta, Dhar (cliff), Mrta. 102/D2
Ouallam, Niger 103/F3
Ouanda Djalle, CAfr. 97/K6
Ouanne (riv.), Fr. 42/E3
Ouarane (pol. reg.), Mrta. 96/C3
Ouarane (reg.), Mrta. 98/C5
Ouargla (prov.), Alg. 99/G3
Ouargla, Alg. 99/G3
Ouarkziz, Jebel (mts.), Mor. 98/C3
Ouarzazate (int'l arpt.), Mor. 98/D3
Ouarzazate, Mor. 98/D3
Ouasiemsca (riv.), Qu, Can. 130/F1
Oubangui (riv.), CAfr. 96/J7
Oubritenga (prov.), Burk. 103/E3
Ouche (riv.), Fr. 56/B3
Oud-Beijerland, Neth. 50/B5
Oud-Turnhout, Belg. 50/B6
Ōuda, Japan 77/J7
Oudalan (prov.), Burk. 103/E3
Ouddorp, Neth. 50/A5
Oude IJssel (riv.), Neth. 50/D5
Oude Pekela, Neth. 50/E2
Oude Westereems (chan.), Neth. 50/D1
Oudenaarde, Belg. 52/C2
Oudenbosch, Neth. 50/B5
Oudenburg, Belg. 52/C1
Oudewater, Neth. 50/B4
Oudon (riv.), Fr. 42/C3
Oudtshoorn, SAfr. 106/C4
Oued el Hadjar (well), Mali 103/F?
Oued Moulouyadeu (riv.), Mor. 96/E1
Oued Sous (riv.), Mor. 96/D1
Oued Zem, Mor. 98/D2
Ouémé (riv.), Ben. 96/F6
Ouémé (prov.), Ben. 103/F5
Ouenza, Alg. 100/G3
Ouerrha (riv.), Mor. 100/G3
Ouessé, Ben. 103/F4
Ouesso, Congo 96/J7
Ouest (prov.), Camr. 103/H5
Ouest (prov.), Haiti 145/H1
Ouest (pt.), Haiti 145/H2
Ouezzane, Mor. 100/B2
Oughterard, Ire. 31/P10
Ouham (riv.), CAfr. 96/J6
Ouidah, Ben. 103/F5
Oujda, Mor. 100/D2
Oujda (prov.), Mor. 100/C2
Oujda (Angads), (int'l arpt.), Mor. 100/D2
Oulad Teïma, Mor. 98/C3
Oulangan NP, Fin. 60/F2
Ould Birni (well), Alg. 99/E4
Oulnina (peak), Austl. 113/H5
Oulu, Fin. 60/F2
Oulu (prov.), Fin. 37/M2
Oulujärvi (lake), Fin. 37/M2
Oum El Bouaghi, Alg. 100/K7
Oum er Rbia, Oued (riv.), Mor. 98/D2
Oum er Rhia, Oued (riv.), Mor. 96/D1
Ounasjoki (riv.), Fin. 37/M2
Oupeye, Belg. 53/E2
Our (riv.), Eur. 53/F3
Ource (riv.), Fr. 42/F3

Ourcq (riv.), Fr. 40/B4
Ourcq, Canal de l' (canal), Fr. 30/K5
Øure Anarjokka NP, Nor. 37/H1
Øure Dividal NP, Nor. 37/F1
Ouricuri, Braz. 154/B2
Ourinhos, Braz. 155/B2
Ourique, Port. 44/A4
Ouro Fino, Braz. 211/G7
Ouro, Ponta do (pt.), Moz. 107/F2
Ouro Preto, Braz. 155/D2
Ouroux-sur-Saône, Fr. 56/A4
Ourthe Occidentale (riv.), Belg. 53/E3
Ourthe Orientale (riv.), Belg. 53/E3
Ouse (riv.), Eng, UK 35/H4
Oust (riv.), Fr. 42/B3
Outaouais (riv.), Qu, Can. 130/E2
Outardes (riv.), Qu, Can. 131/G1
Outardes Quatre (lake), Qu, Can. 131/G1
Outeïd Arkas (well), Mali 102/D2
Outer Hebrides (isls.), Sc, UK 31/P8
Outes, Sp. 44/A1
Outjo, Namb. 105/C5
Outlook, Sk, Can. 126/G3
Outreau, Fr. 52/A2
Outremont, Qu, Can. 131/N6
Ouvéze (riv.), Fr. 42/F4
Ouyen, Austl. 115/B2
Ouzinkie, Ak, US 134/H4
Ovacık, Turk. 62/E5
Ovacık, Turk. 62/E4
Ovada, It. 58/B3
Ovalle, Chile 157/B3
Ovana (peak), Ven. 153/E3
Ovar, Port. 44/A2
Overath, Ger. 53/G2
Overflakkee (isl.), Neth. 50/B5
Overhalla, Nor. 37/D2
Overholser (lake), Ok, US 137/M14
Overijse, Belg. 53/D2
Overijssel (prov.), Neth. 50/D3
Overijssels (riv.), Neth. 50/D4
Överkalix, Swe. 37/G2
Overland, Mo, US 137/G8
Overland Park, Ks, US 137/D6
Overlea, Md, US 138/B5
Overo (peak), Arg. 158/C5
Overpelt, Belg. 50/C6
Overton, Nv, US 128/C3
Övertorneå, Swe. 60/D2
Överum, Swe. 38/G3
Oviedo, Sp. 44/C1
Ovoca, It. 34/B6
Övörhangay (prov.), Mong. 70/H2
Övre Fryken (lake), Swe. 38/E1
Øvre Pasvik NP, Nor. 37/J1
Ovriá, Gre. 47/G3
Owando, Congo 96/J8
Owani, Japan 76/B3
Owariasahi, Japan 77/M5
Owase, Japan 74/E3
Owassa (lake), NJ, US 138/D1
Owasso, Ok, US 129/J3
Owego, NY, US 130/E3
Owen (mt.), NZ 117/S11
Owen, Austl. 113/H5
Owen, Wi, US 134/C5
Owen Falls (dam), Ugan. 104/B2
Owen Roberts (int'l arpt.), UK 145/F2
Owen Sound, On, Can. 130/D2
Owenkillew (riv.), NI, UK 34/A2
Owens (riv.), Ca, US 128/C3
Owensboro, Ky, US 130/C4
Owerri, Nga. 103/G5
Owingen, Ger. 57/F2
Owings, Md, US 138/B6
Owings Mills, Md, US 138/B5
Owl Creek (mts.), Wy, US 126/F4
Owo, Nga. 103/G5
Owosso, Mi, US 130/C3
Owyhee, Nv, US 126/D5
Owyhee (lake), Or, US 128/D2
Owyhee (mts.), Id, US 128/D2
Owyhee, South Fork (riv.), Nv, US 126/D5
Oxapampa, Peru 156/C4
Oxbow, Sk, Can. 127/H3
Oxbow (lake), Mi, US 135/F6
Oxelösund, Swe. 38/G2
Oxford (lake), Mb, Can. 127/K2
Oxford, Ms, US 133/F3
Oxford (canal), Eng, UK 33/E3
Oxford, Eng, UK 33/E3
Oxford, Pa, US 138/C4

Pau Brasil, Braz. 154/C4
Pau dos Ferros, Braz. 154/C2
Paucarbamba, Peru 156/C4
Paucartambo, Peru 156/C3
Paucartambo, Peru 156/D4
Pauillac, Fr. 42/C4
Pauini (riv.), Braz. 150/E5
Paulaya (riv.), Hon. 144/E3
Paulínia, Braz. 211/F7
Paulins Kill (riv.), NJ, US 138/D2
Paulistana, Braz. 154/B3
Paullo, It. 58/C2
Paulo Afonso, Braz. 154/C3
Paulo Afonso, PN de, Braz. 154/C3
Paulo Ramos, Braz. 154/A2
Paulpietersburg, SAfr. 107/E2
Pauls Valley, Ok, US 129/H4
Paulsboro, NJ, US 138/C4
Pauma Valley, Ca, US 136/D4
Paungde, Myan. 83/G4
Pavão, Braz. 154/B5
Pavel Banya, Bul. 47/J1
Pavia (prov.), It. 58/C2
Pavia, It. 58/C2
Pavie, Fr. 42/D5
Pavlikeni, Bul. 49/G4
Pavlodar (obl.), Kaz. 87/G2
Pavlodar, Kaz. 87/G2
Pavlof (vol.), Ak, US 134/F4
Pavlohrad, Ukr. 62/E2
Pavlovo, Rus. 60/J5
Pavone Canavese, It. 58/A2
Pavone del Mella, It. 58/D2
Pavullo nel Frignano, It. 59/D4
Paw Paw, Mi, US 130/C3
Pawan (riv.), Indo. 80/D4
Pawāyan, India 84/C1
Pawhuska, Ok, US 129/H3
Pawnee (riv.), Ks, US 129/G3
Pawtucket, RI, US 131/G3
Paxoí (isl.), Gre. 47/F3
Paxson, Ak, US 134/J3
Paxton, Austl. 115/D2
Pay-Khoy (mts.), Rus. 64/G3
Payakumbuh, Indo. 80/B4
Payerne, Swi. 56/C4
Payette (riv.), Id, US 126/D5
Payne (lake), Qu, Can. 123/J3
Paynesville, Austl. 115/C3
Pays de Caux (reg.), Fr. 42/D2
Pays de France (reg.), Fr. 30/K4
Pays de la Loire (reg.), Fr. 42/C3
Paysandú, Uru. 159/J10
Payson, Ut, US 128/E2
Payson, Az, US 128/E4
Payún (peak), Arg. 158/C4
Paz (riv.), Guat. 144/D3
Paz de Ariporo, Col. 152/D3
Paz de Río, Col. 152/C3
Pazar, Turk. 90/D1
Pazar, Turk. 63/G4
Pazarcık, Turk. 90/D2
Pazardzhik, Bul. 47/J1
Pazaryeri, Turk. 62/D5
Pazin, Cro. 48/A3
Peabiru, Braz. 155/A2
Peace (riv.), BC, Can. 122/D3
Peace Memorial Park, Japan 74/C3
Peaceful Valley, Co, US 137/B2
Peachland, BC, Can. 126/D3
Peachtree City, Ga, US 133/G3
Peak Charles NP, Austl. 112/D5
Peak District NP, Eng, UK 35/G5
Peak Hill, Austl. 112/C3
Peal de Becerro, Sp. 44/D4
Peapack-Gladstone, NJ, US 138/D2
Pearblossom, Ca, US 136/C1
Pearl, Ms, US 133/F3
Pearl (har.), Hi, US 124/W13
Pearl (riv.), La,Ms, US 125/J5
Pearl and Hermes (reef), Hi, US 117/H2
Pearl Beach, Mi, US 135/G6
Pearl City, Hi, US 124/W13
Pearl River (estu.), China 79/B3
Pearl River, La, US 137/Q16
Pearl River, NY, US 139/J7
Pearland, Ca, US 136/B1
Pearsall, Tx, US 129/H5
Pearson (int'l arpt.), On, Can. 131/Q8
Pearston, SAfr. 106/D4
Peary (chan.), Nun., Can. 123/R7
Pease (riv.), Tx, US 129/G4
Pebane, Moz. 105/G4
Pebas, Peru 156/D1
Pebble (isl.), Mald. 159/E6
Peccia, Swi. 57/E5
Peccioli, It. 59/D5
Pécel, Hun. 49/R10
Pech de Guillaument (peak), Fr. 42/E5
Pechanga Ind. Res., Ca, US 136/C4
Pechora, Rus. 61/N2
Pechora (riv.), Rus. 67/C3
Pechora (bay), Rus. 61/M1
Peckham, Co, US 137/C2
Peconic (riv.), NY, US 139/F2
Pecos, Tx, US 132/C4
Pecos (riv.), Tx, US 132/C4
Pecq, Belg. 52/C2
Pecquencourt, Fr. 52/C3
Pécs, Hun. 48/D2
Peculiar, Mo, US 137/E6
Pecy, Fr. 30/M6
Pedasí, Pan. 152/A3
Pedder (lake), Austl. 109/D5
Pedemonte, It. 59/D2
Pedernales (riv.), Tx, US 143/F2
Pederneiras, Braz. 155/B2
Pedley, Ca, US 136/C3
Pedra Azul, Braz. 154/B5
Pedra Lume, CpV. 93/K10
Pedralva, Braz. 211/H7
Pedregal, Ven. 152/D2
Pedreguer, Sp. 45/F3
Pedreira, Braz. 211/G7
Pedreiras, Braz. 154/A2
Pedricktown, NJ, US 138/C4
Pedro (pt.), SrL. 82/D6
Pedro Avelino, Braz. 154/C2
Pedro Bay, Ak, US 134/H4
Pedro Betancourt, Cuba 145/F1
Pedro Carbo, Ecu. 152/A5
Pedro Cays (isl.), Jam. 141/F4
Pedro Ii, Braz. 154/B2
Pedro IV (isl.), Braz. 153/E4
Pedro Juan Caballero, Par. 157/E1
Pedro Leopoldo, Braz. 155/C1
Pedro Luro, Arg. 158/E3
Pedro Osório, Braz. 155/A4
Peebles, Sc, UK 36/C5
Peedamulla Abor. Land, Austl. 112/B2
Peekskill, NY, US 138/E1
Peel (inlet), Austl. 112/B5
Peel (isl.), Austl. 114/F6
Peel (co.), On, Can. 131/Q8
Peel (riv.), Yk, Can. 122/C2
Peel (sound), Nun., Can. 122/G1
Peel, IM, UK 34/D3
Peel Fell (peak), Eng, UK 36/D6
Peene (riv.), Ger. 38/E5
Peer, Belg. 53/E1
Pegasus (bay), NZ 117/S11
Pegnitz, Ger. 55/E3
Pegnitz (riv.), Ger. 40/F4
Pego, Sp. 45/E3
Pego do Altar, Barragem de (res.), Port. 44/A3
Pegognaga, It. 59/D3
Pegwell (bay), Eng, UK 33/H4
Pehlivanköy, Turk. 49/H5
Pehowa, India 86/D5
Pehuajó, Arg. 158/E2
Pehuenche (pass), Chile 158/C2
Pei Xian, China 72/D4
Peine, Ger. 51/H4
Peipus (lake), Est.,Rus. 64/C4
Peiting, Ger. 57/G2
Peixe (riv.), Braz. 155/B2
Peixoto, Reprêsa de (res.), Braz. 155/C2
Pekalongan, Indo. 80/C5
Pekan, Malay. 80/B3
Pekan Nanas, Malay. 80/B3
Pekhora (riv.), Rus. 61/W9
Pekin, Il, US 127/L5
Pelada, Pampa (plain), Arg. 158/C5
Pelado (vol.), Mex. 143/Q10
Pelagie (isls.), It. 46/C5
Peleaga (peak), Rom. 48/F3
Pelee (isl.), On, Can. 130/D3
Pelee (pt.), On, Can. 123/H4
Pelée (peak), Fr. 141/N9
Pelham, Al, US 133/G3
Pelham, On, Can. 131/R9
Pelham, NY, US 139/K8
Pelham Bay Park, NY, US 139/K8
Pelham Manor, NY, US 139/K8
Pelhřimov, Czh. 41/H4
Pelican (mts.), Ab, Can. 126/E2
Pelican (lake), Sk, Can. 127/H2
Pelican, Ak, US 134/L4
Pelican Narrows, Sk, Can. 127/H2
Pelindã, Ponta de (pt.), GBis. 102/A4
Pelister (peak), FYROM 47/G2
Pelister NP, FYROM 47/G2
Peljekaise NP, Swe. 37/F2
Pelješac (pen.), Cro. 47/E1
Pelješac (pen.), Cro. 48/C4
Pell Lake, Wi, US 135/P14
Pélla (ruin), Gre. 47/H2
Pélla, Gre. 47/H2
Pellegrini, Arg. 158/E3
Pellestrina, It. 59/F2
Pello, Fin. 60/E2
Pelly (riv.), Yk, Can. 122/C2
Pelly (bay), Nun., Can. 122/H2
Pelly Bay, Nun., Can. 122/H2
Peloponnesus (reg.), Gre. 47/G3
Peloritani, Monti (mts.), It. 46/D4
Pelotas (riv.), Braz. 157/F2
Pelotas, Braz. 155/A4
Pelplin, Pol. 39/H5
Pemali (cape), Indo. 81/F5
Pemali (cape), Indo. 81/F4
Pematangsiantar, Indo. 80/A3
Pemba, Moz. 105/H3
Pemba (isl.), Tanz. 105/G2
Pemba North (prov.), Tanz. 104/C4
Pemba South (prov.), Tanz. 104/C4
Pemberton, BC, Can. 126/C3
Pemberton, Austl. 112/C5
Pemberton, NJ, US 138/D4
Pembina (riv.), ND, US 126/E2
Pembina, ND, US 127/J3
Pembroke, On, Can. 130/E2
Pembroke, Wal, UK 32/B3
Pembrokeshire (co.), Wal, UK 32/A3
Pembrokeshire Coast NP, Wal, UK 32/A3
Pembury, Eng, UK 33/G4
Pemuco, Chile 158/B3
Pen Argyl, Pa, US 138/C2
Pen, The (lake), La, US 137/P17
Pen-y-Ghent (peak), Eng, UK 35/F3
Pen-y-Gogarth (pt.), Wal, UK 34/E5
Pen y Gurnos (peak), Wal, UK 32/C2
Peña Blanca (mtn.), Pan. 145/F4
Peña de Cerredo (mtn.), Sp. 44/C1
Peñafiel, Sp. 44/D2
Peñafiel, Port. 44/A2
Peñaflor, Chile 158/N8
Penalva, Braz. 154/A1
Penamacor, Port. 44/B2
Penápolis, Braz. 155/B2
Peñaranda de Bracamonte, Sp. 44/C2
Peñarroya (peak), Sp. 45/E2
Peñarroya-Pueblonuevo, Sp. 44/C3
Penarth, Wal, UK 32/C4
Peñas (cape), Sp. 44/C1
Peñas (cape), Arg. 159/D7
Penas, Golfo de (gulf), Chile 157/A6
Peñasco (riv.), NM, US 129/F4
Pench (riv.), India 84/B5
Penchard, Fr. 30/L5
Penco, Chile 158/B3
Pend Oreille (lake), Id, US 126/D4
Pendelikón (peak), Gre. 47/N8
Pendembu, SLeo. 102/C4
Pendências, Braz. 154/C2
Pendjar (riv.), Burk. 103/F4
Pendjari, PN de la, Ben. 96/F5
Pendle (hill), Eng, UK 35/F4
Pendleton, Or, US 126/D4
Peneda-Gerês NP, Port. 44/A2
Penedo, Braz. 154/C3
Penetanguishene, On, Can. 130/E2
Penghu (Pescadores) (isls.), Tai. 79/C3
Penglai, China 72/E3
Penguin, Austl. 115/C4
Penha, Braz. 155/B3
Penhold, Ab, Can. 126/E2
Penibético, Sistema (range), Sp. 44/C4
Penice (peak), It. 58/C3
Peniche, Port. 44/A3
Penicuik, Sc, UK 36/C5
Península de Paria, PN, Ven. 153/F2
Peñíscola, Sp. 45/F2
Penitente, Serra do (mts.), Braz. 151/J5
Penmaenmawr, Wal, UK 34/E5
Penmarch, Fr. 42/A3
Penmarc'h, Pointe de (pt.), Fr. 42/A3
Penn Forest (res.), Pa, US 138/C2
Penn Hills, Pa, US 130/E3
Penn Yan, NY, US 130/E3
Penna, Punta della (cape), It. 46/D1
Penne (pt.), It. 47/E2
Penne, It. 46/C1
Penner (riv.), India 82/C5
Pennine Alps (mts.), Swi. 43/G4
Pennine Chain (mts.), Eng, UK 35/F2
Pennington, NJ, US 138/D3
Pennino (peak), It. 43/K5
Penns Creek (mtn.), Pa, US 138/A2
Penns Grove, NJ, US 138/C4
Penns Park, Pa, US 138/D3
Pennsauken, NJ, US 138/C4
Pennsburg, Pa, US 138/C3
Pennsville, NJ, US 138/C4
Pennsylvania (state), US 130/E3
Penny (str.), Nun., Can. 123/S7
Penobscot (riv.), Me, US 131/G2
Penola, Austl. 115/B3
Peñón Blanco, Mex. 142/D3
Penon de Al Hoceima (isl.), Sp. 100/C2
Penonomé, Pan. 152/A2
Penrhyn Mawr (pt.), Wal, UK 34/D6
Penrhyn Mawr (pt.), IM, UK 34/D5
Penrith, Eng, UK 35/F2
Pensacola, Fl, US 133/G4
Pensacola (mts.), Ant. 160/X
Pense, Sk, Can. 127/G3
Penshurst, Austl. 115/B3
Pentagon Fed. Govt. Res., Va, US 138/A6
Pentecost (isl.), Van. 116/F6
Pentecoste, Braz. 154/C1
Penteleu (peak), Rom. 49/H3
Penthalaz, Swi. 56/C4
Penticton, BC, Can. 126/D3
Pentire (pt.), Eng, UK 32/B5
Pentland, Austl. 114/B3
Pentland (hills), Sc, UK 36/C5
Pentland Firth (inlet), Sc, UK 31/V14
Peñuelas, PN, Chile 158/N8
Penwith (pen.), Eng, UK 32/A6
Penza, Rus. 63/H1
Penzance, Eng, UK 32/A6
Penzberg, Ger. 57/H2
Penzenskaya (obl.), Rus. 63/G1
Penzhina (riv.), Rus. 65/S3
Penzhina (bay), Rus. 65/S3
Penzing, Ger. 57/G1
Penzlin, Ger. 40/G2
Peoria, Az, US 137/R18
Pepe (cape), Cuba 145/F1
Pepeekeo, Hi, US 124/U11
Pepeekeo (pt.), Hi, US 124/U11
Pepel, SLeo. 102/B4
Pepinster, Belg. 53/E2
Pequannock, NJ, US 139/H8
Pequeña Isla del Maíz (isl.), Nic. 145/F3
Pequest (riv.), NJ, US 138/D2
Perabumulih, Indo. 80/B4
Perales (riv.), Sp. 45/M9
Peralta, Sp. 44/E1
Pérama, Gre. 47/J5
Pérama, Gre. 47/N9
Percé, Qu, Can. 131/H1
Percée (peak), Fr. 56/C6
Perche, Collines du (hills), Fr. 42/D2
Perchtoldsdorf, Aus. 49/N7
Percival (lakes), Austl. 109/B3
Percy (isls.), Austl. 109/E3
Percy Isles (chan.), Austl. 114/C3
Perdekop, SAfr. 107/E2
Pérdhika, Gre. 47/G3
Perdida (riv.), Braz. 154/A3
Perdido (mtn.), Sp. 45/F1
Peregian Beach, Austl. 114/D4
Pereira, Col. 150/C3
Pereira Barreto, Braz. 155/B2
Pereiro, Braz. 154/C2
Perelló, Sp. 45/F2
Perenjori, Austl. 112/C4
Peretola (int'l arpt.), It. 59/E5
Perg, Aus. 55/H6
Pergamino, Arg. 158/E2
Pergamum (ruin), Turk. 62/C5
Pergine Valsugana, It. 57/H5
Pergola, It. 43/K5
Péribonca (riv.), Qu, Can. 131/G1
Perico, Cuba 145/F1
Pericos, Mex. 142/D3
Pericos, Mex. 142/D3
Périgueux, Fr. 42/D4
Perijá, Sierra de (mts.), Col. 150/D2
Peristéra (isl.), Gre. 47/H3
Peristéri, Gre. 47/N8
Perito Moreno, Arg. 158/C5
Perito Moreno, PN, Arg. 157/B6
Perkasie, Pa, US 138/C3
Perl, Ger. 53/F5
Perlas (lag.), Nic. 140/E5
Perlas (pt.), Nic. 145/F3
Perleberg, Ger. 40/F2
Perlez, Yugo. 48/E3
Perlis (state), Malay. 78/B5
Perm', Rus. 61/N4
Permskaya (obl.), Rus. 61/N4
Përmet, Alb. 47/G2
Pernambuco (state), Braz. 154/C3
Pernate, It. 58/B2
Pernes-les-Fontaines, Fr. 42/F4
Pernik, Bul. 47/H1
Perniö, Fin. 39/K1
Peron (pen.), Austl. 112/B3
Péronne, Fr. 52/B4
Perote, Mex. 143/M7
Pérouges, Fr. 56/B6
Perpignan, Fr. 42/E5
Perray (riv.), Fr. 30/H6
Perrigny, Fr. 56/B4
Perris (res.), Ca, US 136/C3
Perris, Ca, US 136/C3
Perris State Rec. Area, Ca, US 136/C3
Perros-Guirec, Fr. 42/B2
Perrot, Île (isl.), Qu, Can. 131/N7
Perry, Ga, US 133/H3
Perry, Ok, US 129/H3
Perry, Fl, US 133/H4
Perry, Ut, US 137/J11
Perry (co.), Pa, US 138/A3
Perry (riv.), Nun., Can. 122/F2
Perry Hall, Md, US 138/B5
Perryman, Md, US 138/B5
Perryton, Tx, US 129/G3
Perryville, Ak, US 134/G4
Perryville, Md, US 138/B4
Persan, Fr. 30/J4
Persian (gulf), Asia 67/D7
Perstorp, Swe. 38/E3
Perth, Austl. 115/C4
Perth, On, Can. 130/E2
Perth (int'l arpt.), Austl. 112/K6
Perth, Austl. 112/K6
Perth, Sc, UK 36/C4
Perth Amboy, NJ, US 139/H9
Perth nd Kinross (pol. reg.), Sc, UK 36/C4
Perth Zoo, Austl. 112/K6
Pertuis, Fr. 42/F5
Pertuis Breton (inlet), Fr. 42/C3
Pertusato (cape), Fr. 46/A2
Peru, Il, US 127/L5
Peru, In, US 130/C3
Peru (ctry.) 156/C3
Perućačko (lake), Bosn. 48/D4
Perugia, It. 43/K5
Peruíbe, Braz. 211/G9
Peruque, Mo, US 137/F8
Perushtitsa, Bul. 47/J1
Péruwelz, Belg. 52/C2
Pervari, Turk. 90/E2
Pervomays'k, Ukr. 49/K1
Pervomaysk, Rus. 61/J5
Pervoural'sk, Rus. 61/N4
Perwez, Belg. 53/D2
Péry, Swi. 56/D3
Pesa (riv.), It. 59/E5
Pesagi (peak), Indo. 80/B4
Pesaro, It. 59/F5
Pesaro e Urbino (prov.), It. 59/F5
Pescadores (Penghu) (isls.), China 79/C3
Pescantina, It. 58/D2
Pescara, It. 46/D1
Peschanyy (cape), Kaz. 63/J4
Pescia, It. 59/D5
Peseux, Swi. 56/C4
Pesha (riv.), Rus. 61/L2
Peshāwar, Pak. 86/A2
Peshawar (int'l arpt.), Pak. 86/A2
Peshtera, Bul. 47/J1
Peshtigo, Wi, US 127/M4
Peshtigo (riv.), Wi, US 130/B2
Pesmes, Fr. 56/B3
Peso da Régua, Port. 44/B2
Pesqueira, Braz. 154/C3
Pessac, Fr. 42/C4
Pest (prov.), Hun. 48/D2
Pestovkoye (lake), Rus. 61/W9
Pestovo, Rus. 60/G4
Petaḥ Tiqwa, Isr. 91/F7
Petal, Ms, US 133/F4
Petalioi (gulf), Gre. 47/J4
Petaluma (riv.), Ca, US 135/J10
Pétange, Lux. 53/E4
Petare, Ven. 150/E1
Pétas, Gre. 47/G3
Petatlán (riv.), Mex. 142/D3
Petatlán, Mex. 143/E5
Petauke, Zam. 105/F3
Petawawa (riv.), On, Can. 130/E2
Petawawa, On, Can. 130/E2
Peten Itzá (lake), Guat. 144/D2
Petenwell (lake), Wi, US 127/L4
Peter (isl.), Nor. 160/U
Peterborough, Austl. 113/H5
Peterborough, On, Can. 130/E2
Peterborough, Eng, UK 33/F1
Peterborough (co.), Eng, UK 33/F1
Peterhead, Sc, UK 36/E1
Peterlee, Eng, UK 35/G2
Petermann Abor. Land, Austl. 113/F3
Peteroa (vol.), Chile 158/C2
Petersaurach, Ger. 54/D4
Petersberg, Ger. 54/C1
Petersburg, Ak, US 134/M4
Petersfield, Eng, UK 33/F4
Petershagen, Ger. 51/F4
Petershagen, Ger. 40/Q6
Petershausen, Ger. 55/E6
Peterson, Ut, US 137/K11
Pétervására, Hun. 41/L4
Petilia Policastro, It. 46/E3
Pétionville, Haiti 145/H2
Petit Goâve, Haiti 145/H2
Petit Lac Manicouagan (lake), Qu, Can. 131/H1
Petit Loango, PN du, Gabon 105/A1
Petit-Noir, Fr. 56/B4
Petit Rosne (riv.), Fr. 30/J4
Petitcodiac, NB, Can. 131/H2
Petite Miquelon (isl.), StP. 131/K2
Petite Rivière de l'Artibonite, Haiti 145/H2
Petite Rivière Noire (peak), Mrts. 107/T15
Petite-Rosselle, Fr. 53/F5
Petit Morin (riv.), Fr. 42/E2
Petkeljärven NP, Fin. 60/F3
Petlād, India 89/K4
Petlalcingo, Mex. 144/B2
Peto, Mex. 144/D1
Petorca, Chile 158/C2
Petoskey, Mi, US 130/C2
Petra (isls.), Rus. 65/M2
Petrel, Sp. 45/E3
Petrella (peak), It. 46/C2
Petrich, Bul. 47/H2
Petrified Forest NP, Az, US 128/E4
Petrila, Rom. 49/F3
Petrodvorets, Rus. 61/S7
Petrokhanski Prokhod (pass), Bul. 47/H1
Petrokrepost' (bay), Rus. 61/U7
Petrolândia, Braz. 154/C3
Petrolina, Braz. 154/B3
Petropavl, Kaz. 87/E2
Petropavlovsk-Kamchatskiy, Rus. 65/R4
Petrópolis, Braz. 211/K7
Petrovaradin, Yugo. 48/D3
Petrovsk, Rus. 63/H1
Petrovsk-Zabaykal'skiy, Rus. 70/J1
Petrozavodsk, Rus. 60/G3
Petrus Steyn, SAfr. 106/E2
Petrusburg, SAfr. 106/D3
Petrusville, SAfr. 106/D3
Pettenbach, Aus. 55/H7
Petteril (riv.), Eng, UK 35/F2
Petzeck (peak), Aus. 43/K3
Peuerbach, Aus. 55/G6
Peulik (mt.), Ak, US 134/G4
Peumo, Chile 158/N9
Pevely, Mo, US 137/G9
Pewaukee (lake), Wi, US 135/X13
Pewaukee, Wi, US 135/P13
Peyrehorade, Fr. 42/C5
Peza (riv.), Rus. 61/K2
Pézenas, Fr. 42/E5
Pfaffenhausen, Ger. 57/G1
Pfaffenhofen an der Ilm, Ger. 54/D6
Pfaffenhofen an der Ilm, Ger. 55/E5
Pfaffenhoffen, Fr. 53/G6
Pfäffikon, Swi. 57/E3
Pfaffing, Ger. 55/F6
Pfaffnau, Swi. 56/D3
Pfahl (ridge), Ger. 55/F4
Pfälzer Wald (mts.), Ger. 53/G5
Pfälzerwald (mts.), Ger. 54/A4
Pfalzgrafenweiler, Ger. 54/B5
Pfarrhof Esternberg, Aus. 55/G5
Pfarrkirchen, Ger. 55/F6
Pfatter, Ger. 55/F5
Pfeffenhausen, Ger. 55/E5
Pfettrach (riv.), Ger. 55/E5
Pfieffe (riv.), Ger. 51/G6
Pfinztal, Ger. 54/B5
Pforzheim, Ger. 54/B5
Pfreimd, Ger. 55/F3
Pfreimd (riv.), Ger. 55/F3
Pfronstetten, Ger. 57/F1
Pfronten, Ger. 57/G2
Pfroslkopf (peak), Aus. 57/G4
Pfullendorf, Ger. 57/F2
Pfunds, Aus. 57/G4
Pfungstadt, Ger. 54/B3
Phagwāra, India 86/C4
Phalauda, India 86/D5
Phalempin, Fr. 52/C2
Phālia, Pak. 86/B3
Phalodi, India 89/K3
Phalsbourg, Fr. 53/G6
Phan Rang, Viet. 78/E4
Phan Thiet, Viet. 78/E4
Phanat Nikhom, Thai. 78/C3
Phang Hoei (range), Thai. 78/C3
Phangnga, Thai. 78/B4
Phanom Dongrak (mts.), Thai. 83/H5
Pharr, Tx, US 132/D5
Phatthalung, Thai. 78/C5
Phaya Fo (peak), Thai. 78/C2
Phayao, Thai. 78/B2
Phelan, Ca, US 136/C2
Phenix City, Al, US 133/G3
Phet Buri, Thai. 78/B3
Phetchabun, Thai. 78/C2
Phichit, Thai. 78/C2
Philadelphia, Ms, US 133/F3
Philadelphia, Pa, US 138/C4
Philadelphia (int'l arpt.), Pa, US 138/C4
Philip, SD, US 127/H4
Philip S.W. Goldson (int'l arpt.), Belz. 144/D2
Philippeville, Belg. 53/D3
Philippi, WV, US 130/D4
Philippine (sea), Asia 79/D4
Philippines (ctry.) 79/D5
Philippsburg, Ger. 54/B4
Philipsburg, Mt, US 126/E4
Philipsdam (dam), Neth. 50/B5
Philipstown, SAfr. 106/D3
Phillaur, India 86/C4
Phillipsburg, NJ, US 138/C2
Phimai (ruin), Thai. 78/C3
Phitsanulok, Thai. 78/C2
Phnom Penh (Phnum Pénh) (cap.), Camb. 78/D4
Phnum Penh (int'l arpt.), Camb. 78/D4
Pho (pt.), Thai. 78/C5
Phoenix (cap.), Az, US 137/R19
Phoenix, La, US 137/Q17
Phoenix (isls.), Kiri. 117/H5
Phoenix Park, Ire. 34/B5
Phoenix Sky Harbor (int'l arpt.), Az, US 137/S19
Phoenixville, Pa, US 138/C3
Phongsali, Laos 83/H3
Phou Bia (peak), Laos 78/C2
Phou Huatt (peak), Viet. 83/H4
Phou Loi (peak), Laos 83/H3
Phou Xai Lai Leng (peak), Laos 78/D2
Phra Nakhon Si Ayutthaya, Thai. 78/C3
Phra Thong (isl.), Thai. 78/B4
Phrae, Thai. 78/C2
Phu Hin Rong Kla NP, Thai. 78/C2
Phu Kradung NP, Thai. 78/C2
Phu Luong (peak), Viet. 83/H3
Phu Phan NP, Thai. 78/D2
Phu Quoc (isl.), Viet. 83/H5
Phu Rua NP, Thai. 78/C2
Phu Tho, Viet. 83/J3
Phuket (isl.), Thai. 83/G6
Phuket, Thai. 78/B5
Phularwan, Pak. 86/B3
Phūlpur, India 84/D3
Piaçabuçu, Braz. 154/C3
Piacenza (prov.), It. 58/C3
Piacenza, It. 58/C2
Piadena, It. 58/D2
Pian di Serra (peak), It. 59/F6
Pian-Upe Game Rsv., Ugan. 104/B2
Piancastagnaio, It. 46/B1
Piancó, Braz. 154/C2
Pianello val Tidone, It. 58/C3
Pianezza, It. 58/A2
Piangipane, It. 59/E4
Pianoro, It. 59/E4
Pianosa (isl.), It. 46/A1
Piarco (int'l arpt.), Trin. 153/F2
Piaseczno, Pol. 41/L2
Piatra Neamț, Rom. 49/H2
Piauí (riv.), Braz. 154/B3
Piauí (state), Braz. 154/B2
Piave (riv.), It. 43/K3
Piazza, It. 58/D1
Piazza, It. 58/D1
Piazza al Serchio, It. 58/D4
Piazza Armerina, It. 46/D4
Piazza Brembana, It. 57/F6
Piazzola sul Brenta, It. 59/E1
Pic (riv.), On, Can. 130/C1
Pic de Nore (peak), Fr. 42/E5
Pic d'Orhy (peak), Fr. 42/C5
Pic du Canigou (peak), Fr. 42/E5
Pica, Chile 150/E8
Picacho del Centinela (peak), Mex. 129/G5
Picachos, Cerro Dos (peak), Mex. 142/B2
Picardie (pol. reg.), Fr. 42/E2
Picardy (reg.), Fr. 52/B4
Picatinny Arsenal, NJ, US 138/D2
Picayune, Ms, US 133/F4
Piccolo (lag.), It. 47/E2
Pichacani, Peru 156/D5
Pichanal, Arg. 157/D1
Pichidegua, Chile 158/N9
Pichilemu, Chile 158/B2
Pichincha (dept.), Ecu. 152/B4
Pichincha, Ecu. 152/B5
Pichl bei Wels, Aus. 55/G6
Pichor, India 84/B3
Pichucalco, Mex. 144/C2
Pickens, Ms, US 129/K4
Pickering, On, Can. 131/R8
Pickering, Vale of (valley), Eng, UK 35/H3
Pickle Lake, On, Can. 127/L3
Picnic Bay, Austl. 114/B2
Pico (isl.), Azor., Port. 45/S12
Pico da Neblina, PN do, Braz. 150/F3
Pico de Orizaba, PN, Mex. 143/M7
Pico Rivera, Ca, US 136/F8
Pico Truncado, Arg. 158/D5
Picos, Braz. 154/B2
Picota, Peru 156/B2
Picsi, Peru 156/B2
Picton, On, Can. 130/E3
Pictou, NS, Can. 131/J2
Picture Rocks, Pa, US 138/B1
Pictured Rocks Nat'l Lakeshore, Mi, US 127/M4
Pictured Rocks Nat'l Lakeshore, Mi, US 130/C2
Picuí, Braz. 154/C2
Piddle (riv.), Eng, UK 32/D5
Pidurutagala (peak), SrL. 82/D6
Piedade, Port. 45/P10
Piedade do Rio Grande, Braz. 211/J6
Piedecuesta, Col. 152/C3
Piedimulera, It. 57/E5
Piedmont (upland), US 133/H3
Piedmont, Ok, US 137/M14
Piedmont, Ca, US 135/K11
Piedra Grande, Ven. 152/D2
Piedrabuena, Sp. 44/C3
Piedrahita, Sp. 44/C2
Piedras (pt.), Arg. 159/K11
Piedras Coloradas, Uru. 159/K10
Piedras Negras, Mex. 132/C4
Piedras Negras, Mex. 143/N8
Piedras, Río de las (riv.), Peru 150/D6
Piedritas, Arg. 158/E2
Piekary Śląskie, Pol. 41/K3
Piekenierskloof (pass), SAfr. 106/L10
Pieksämäki, Fin. 60/E3
Pielinen (lake), Fin. 37/J3
Piemonte (prov.), It. 43/G4
Pieniński NP, Pol. 41/L4
Piennes, Fr. 53/E5
Pieńsk, Pol. 41/H3
Piera, Sp. 45/K6
Pierce, Ne, US 127/J5
Pierce, Co, US 137/C1
Pierceland, Sk, Can. 126/F2
Pieris, It. 59/G1
Piermont, NY, US 139/K7
Pierowall, Sc, UK 31/V14
Pierre (cap.), SD, US 127/H4
Pierre-de-Bresse, Fr. 56/B4
Pierre-Levée, Fr. 30/M5
Pierrefitte-sur-Seine, Fr. 30/K5
Pierrefonds, Qu, Can. 131/N7
Pierrefontaine-les-Varans, Fr. 56/C3
Pierrelatte, Fr. 42/F4
Pierrelaye, Fr. 30/J4
Pierrevert, Fr. 42/F5
Pierry, Fr. 52/C5
Piešťany, Slvk. 41/J4
Piesting (riv.), Aus. 49/P7
Piet Retief, SAfr. 107/E2
Pieterlen, Swi. 56/D3
Pietermaritzburg, SAfr. 107/E3
Pietersburg, SAfr. 105/E5
Pietra Ligure, It. 58/B4
Pietralunga, It. 59/F6
Pietramelara, It. 46/D2
Pietravecchia (peak), It. 58/A5
Pietrosul (peak), Rom. 49/G2
Pietrosul (peak), Rom. 49/G2
Pieve del Cairo, It. 58/B2
Pieve di Cento, It. 59/E3
Pieve di Soligo, It. 59/F1
Pieve di Teco, It. 58/A4
Pieve Emanuele, It. 58/C2
Pieve Ligure, It. 58/C4
Pieve Porto Morone, It. 58/C2
Pieve Santo Stefano, It. 59/F5
Pieve Vergonte, It. 57/E6
Pievepelago, It. 58/D4
Pigeon (lake), Ab, Can. 126/E2
Pigeon (riv.), On, Can. 122/G4
Piggott, Ar, US 129/K3
Pigs (bay), Cuba 140/E3
Pigüé, Arg. 158/E3
Pigŭm (isl.), SKor. 73/C5
Pihāni, India 84/C2
Pijijiapan, Mex. 144/C3
Pijnacker, Neth. 50/B4
Pijol (peak), Hon. 144/E3
Pike (co.), Pa, US 138/C1
Pikelot (isl.), Micr. 116/D4
Pikes Creek (res.), Pa, US 138/B1
Pikesville, Md, US 138/B5
Piketberg, SAfr. 106/L10
Pikeville, Ky, US 130/D4
Pikit, Phil. 79/D6

216
Pila – Port C

Pila, Arg. 159/J12
Piła, Pol. 41/J2
Pilanesberg (range), SAfr. 106/P12
Pilani, India 86/C5
Pilão Arcado, Braz. 154/B3
Pilar, Phil. 81/F1
Pilar, Par. 157/E2
Pilar, Braz. 154/D3
Pilar, Arg. 158/E1
Pilatus (peak), Swi. 57/E4
Pilaya (riv.), Bol. 150/F8
Pilchuck (riv.), Wa, US 135/D1
Pilcomayo (riv.), SAm. 147/C5
Pili, Phil. 79/D5
Pīlībhīt, India 84/B1
Pilica (riv.), Pol. 62/B2
Pilion (peak), Gre. 47/H3
Pilis, Hun. 48/D2
Pilis (peak), Hun. 49/Q9
Pilis (mts.), Hun. 49/R9
Piliscsaba, Hun. 49/Q9
Pilisvörösvár, Hun. 49/Q9
Pilkhua, India 86/D5
Pillar (cape), Austl. 115/C4
Pillar (pt.), Ca, US 135/J12
Pillar (peak), Eng, UK 35/E3
Pilliga, Austl. 115/D1
Pillon, Col du (pass), Swi. 56/D5
Pillow, Pa, US 138/B2
Pilões, Serra dos (mtn.), Braz. 154/A5
Pilos, Gre. 47/G4
Pilot (mtn.), Tn, US 130/C4
Pilot Point, Ak, US 134/G4
Pilot Station, Ak, US 134/F3
Pilsting, Ger. 55/F5
Pima, Az, US 128/E4
Pimpri-Chinchwad, India 89/K5
Piña (pt.), Pan. 145/G5
Pináculo (peak), Arg. 159/B6
Pinal, Az, US 137/R19
Pinamar, Arg. 159/F3
Pinang (cape), Malay. 80/A2
Pinang (isl.), Malay. 80/A2
Pinar del Río, Cuba 145/F1
Pınarbaşı, Turk. 90/D2
Pınarhisar, Turk. 49/H5
Piñas, Ecu. 156/B1
Pinatubo (mt.), Phil. 79/D4
Pinawa, Mb, Can. 127/K3
Pincher Creek, Ab, Can. 126/E3
Pinconning, Mi, US 130/D3
Pîncota, Rom. 48/E2
Pincourt, Qu, Can. 131/N7
Pińczów, Pol. 41/L3
Pind Dādan Khān, Pak. 86/B3
Pindamonhangaba, Braz. 211/H7
Pindaré (riv.), Braz. 151/J4
Pindaré-Mirim, Braz. 154/A1
Píndhos NP, Gre. 47/G3
Pindi Bhattiān, Pak. 86/B4
Pindi Gheb, Pak. 86/B3
Pindobaçu, Braz. 154/B3
Pindus (mts.), Gre. 47/G2
Pindwāra, India 89/K4
Pine Barrens (phys. reg.), NJ, US 138/D4
Pine Bluff, Ar, US 129/J4
Pine Bluffs, Wy, US 127/G5
Pine Creek (pt.), Ct, US 139/E1
Pine Falls, Mb, Can. 127/J3
Pine Grove, Pa, US 138/B2
Pine Hill, NJ, US 138/D4
Pine Island, Mn, US 130/A2
Pine Island Bay (flat), Ant. 160/S
Pine Lawn, Mo, US 137/G8
Pine Point, NW, Can. 122/E2
Pine Ridge, SD, US 127/H5
Pine, South Branch (riv.), Mi, US 135/G6
Pine, The (hills), Mt, US 127/G4
Pinecliff (lake), NJ, US 139/H7
Pinecliffe, Co, US 137/B3
Pinedale, Wy, US 126/F5
Pinega (riv.), Rus. 64/E3
Pineimuta (riv.), On, Can. 127/L2
Pinelands, SAfr. 106/L10
Piñera, Uru. 159/K10
Pinerolo, It. 43/G4
Pinetown, SAfr. 107/E3
Pineuilh, Fr. 42/D4
Pineview (res.), Ut, US 137/K11
Pineville, La, US 129/J5
Pinewood Springs, Co, US 137/B2
Ping (riv.), Thai. 83/G4
Ping Chau (isl.), China 71/V9
Pingbian Miaozu Zizhixian, China 83/H3
Pingding, China 72/C3
Pingdingshan, China 72/C4
Pingdu, China 72/D3
Pingelap (isl.), Micr. 116/F4
Pingelly, Austl. 112/C5
Pinggu, China 72/H6
Pingguo, China 83/J3
Pinghe, China 79/C3
Pinghu, China 72/L9
Pingjiang, China 79/B2
Pingjing (pass), China 72/C5
Pingle, China 83/K3
Pinglu, China 72/B4
Pinglu, China 72/C3
Pingnan, China 79/B3
Pingquan, China 72/D2
Pingshan, China 72/C3
Pingshun, China 72/C3
Pingtan, China 79/C2
Pingtang, China 83/J2
P'ingtung, Tai. 79/D3
Pingxiang, China 83/K2
Pingxiang, China 83/J3
Pingxing Guan (pass), China 72/C3
Pingyao, China 72/C3
Pingyi, China 72/D4
Pingyin, China 72/D3
Pingyu, China 72/C4
Pingyuan, China 72/D3
Pinhal, Braz. 211/G7
Pinhal Novo, Port. 45/Q10
Pinhão, Braz. 155/B3
Pinheiro, Braz. 154/A1
Pinheiros, Braz. 154/B5
Pinhel, Port. 44/B2
Piniós (riv.), Gre. 47/G4
Pinjar (lake), Austl. 112/K6
Pinjarra, Austl. 112/B5
Pink, Ok, US 137/N15
Pinkafeld, Aus. 48/C2
Pinkawillinie Conservation Park, Austl. 113/G5
Pinkegat (chan.), Neth. 50/C2
Pinnacles Nat'l Mon., Ca, US 128/B3
Pinnaroo, Austl. 113/J5
Pinnau (riv.), Ger. 51/G1
Pinneberg, Ger. 51/G1
Pino Hachado (pass), Arg. 158/C3
Pino Torinese, It. 58/A2
Pinole, Ca, US 135/K10
Pinon Hills, Ca, US 136/C2
Pinos (mt.), Ca, US 128/C4
Pinos, Mex. 143/E4
Pinos, Isla de (Isla de la Juventud) (isl.), Cuba 140/E3
Pinos-Puente, Sp. 44/D4
Pinoso, Sp. 45/E3
Pins, Île des (isl.), NCal. 116/F7
Pinsdorf, Aus. 55/G7
Pinsk, Bela. 62/C1
Pinta, Isla (isl.), Ecu. 156/E6
Pinto, Sp. 45/N9
Pinto, Chile 158/C3
Pinzolo, It. 57/G5
Pio Ix, Braz. 154/B2
Pio Xii, Braz. 154/A1
Piobbico, It. 59/F5
Pioche, Nv, US 128/D3
Piombino, It. 43/J5
Piombino Dese, It. 59/F1
Pioneer World, Austl. 112/L7
Pioner (isl.), Rus. 64/J2
Pionki, Pol. 41/L3
Piorini (riv.), Braz. 150/F4
Piorini (lake), Braz. 153/F5
Piota (riv.), It. 58/B3
Piotrków Trybunalski, Pol. 41/K3
Piove di Sacco, It. 59/F2
Piovene-Rocchette, It. 59/E1
Pipariā, India 84/B4
Pipe Spring Nat'l Mon., Az, US 128/D3
Piper, Ks, US 137/D5
Pipersville, Pa, US 138/C3
Pipestone (riv.), On, Can. 122/G3
Piplān, Pak. 86/A3
Pipmuacan (res.), Qu, Can. 123/J4
Pipingarra Abor. Land, Austl. 112/C2
Pipra, India 84/D3
Pipraich, India 84/D2
Piqua, Oh, US 130/C3
Piquet Carneiro, Braz. 154/C2
Piquete, Braz. 211/H7
Piquiri (riv.), Braz. 151/H7
Pīr Mahal, Pak. 86/B4
Pir Panjal (range), India 86/C3
Piracanjuba, Braz. 155/B1
Piracicaba, Braz. 155/C2
Piracuruca, Braz. 154/B1
Pirae-bong (peak), NKor. 73/C2
Piraí, Braz. 211/K7
Piraí do Sul, Braz. 155/B3
Piraiévs, Gre. 47/N9
Piraju, Braz. 155/B2
Pirajuí, Braz. 155/B2
Pirámide (peak), Chile 159/B6
Piran, Slov. 59/G1
Pirané, Arg. 157/E2
Piranga (riv.), Braz. 155/D2
Piranhas (riv.), Braz. 151/L5
Piranji (riv.), Braz. 154/C2
Pirapemas, Braz. 154/A1
Pirapora, Braz. 154/A5
Pirapòzinho, Braz. 155/B2
Pirarajá, Uru. 159/G2
Pirássununga, Braz. 155/C2
Pires do Rio, Braz. 155/B1
Pírgos, Gre. 47/G4
Pírgos, Gre. 47/J5
Piriápolis, Uru. 159/G2
Pirin (mts.), Bul. 47/H2
Pirin (peak), Bul. 47/H2
Pirin NP, Bul. 47/H2
Piripiri, Braz. 154/B2
Piritiba, Braz. 154/B3
Píritu, Ven. 152/D2
Pirkkala, Fin. 39/K1
Pirmasens, Ger. 53/G5
Pirna, Ger. 41/G3
Piro, India 85/E3
Pirot, Yugo. 47/H1
Pirre (mtn.), Pan. 152/B3
Pirthīpur, India 84/B3
Piru (lake), Ca, US 136/B1
Piru, Ca, US 136/B2
Piryion, Gre. 47/J3
Pisa (prov.), It. 59/D6
Pisa, It. 58/D5
Pisac, Peru 156/D4
Pisanino (peak), It. 58/D4
Pisau (cape), Malay. 81/E2
Pisba, PN de, Col. 152/C3
Piscataway, Md, US 138/B6
Piscataway, NJ, US 138/D2
Pisco (riv.), Peru 150/C6
Pisco, Peru 156/B4
Piscobamba, Peru 156/B3
Písek (peak), Czh. 55/H3
Písek, Czh. 55/H4
Pishan, China 70/C4
Pishīn, Pak. 89/J2
Pīshīn, Iran 89/H3
Piskavica, Bosn. 48/C3
Pisoc (peak), Swi. 57/G4
Pisogne, It. 58/D1
Pissis (peak), Arg. 157/C2
Pistakee (lake), Il, US 135/P15
Pisticci, It. 46/E2
Pistoia (prov.), It. 59/D5
Pistoia, It. 59/D5
Pisuerga (riv.), Sp. 44/C1
Pisz, Pol. 41/L2
Pit (riv.), Ca, US 128/B2
Pitalito, Col. 152/B4
Pitanga, Braz. 155/B3
Pitcairn (isl.), Pitc. 117/N7
Pitcairn Islands (dpcy.), UK 117/N7
Piteå, Swe. 37/G2
Piteälven (riv.), Swe. 37/F2
Pitești, Rom. 49/G3
Píthion, Gre. 47/K2
Pithiviers, Fr. 42/E2
Pithoragarh, India 84/C1
Pitigliano, It. 46/B1
Pitiquito, Mex. 142/B2
Pitjantjatjara Abor. Lands, Austl. 113/F3
Pitkas Point, Ak, US 134/F3
Pitlochry, Sc, UK 36/C3
Pitman, NJ, US 138/C4
Pitmedden, Sc, UK 36/D2
Pitomača, Cro. 48/C3
Piton de la Fournaise (peak), Reun. 107/S15
Piton des Neiges (peak), Reun. 107/S15
Pitrufquén, Chile 158/B3
Pitt Water (bay), Austl. 114/H8
Pittenweem, Sc, UK 36/D4
Pittsburg, Ks, US 129/J3
Pittsburgh, Pa, US 130/E3
Pittsfield, Me, US 131/G2
Pittsfield, Ma, US 130/F3
Pittston, Pa, US 130/F3
Pittstown, NJ, US 138/D2
Pittsworth, Austl. 114/C4
Pitzbach (riv.), Aus. 57/G4
Piuí, Braz. 155/C2
Piumazzo, It. 59/E3
Piura, Peru 156/A2
Piura (dept.), Peru 156/A2
Pivdenny Buh (riv.), Ukr. 64/C5
Pivijay, Col. 152/C2
Pixoyal, Mex. 140/C4
Piz d'Err (peak), Swi. 57/F4
Pizacoma, Peru 156/D5
Pizarra, Sp. 44/C4
Pizhma (riv.), Rus. 61/K4
Pizol (peak), Swi. 57/F4
Pizzighettone, It. 58/C2
Pizzo, It. 46/E3
Pizzo dei Tre Signori (peak), It. 57/F6
Pizzo della Presolana (peak), It. 57/G6
Pizzo di Coca (peak), It. 57/G5
Pizzo di Vogorno (peak), Swi. 57/E5
Pizzuto (peak), It. 46/C1
Placentia, Nf, Can. 131/L2
Placentia (bay), Nf, Can. 131/L2
Placentia, Ca, US 136/G8
Placer, Phil. 79/E6
Placer (co.), Ca, US 135/M9
Placetas, Cuba 145/G1
Plachkovtsi, Bul. 47/J1
Plaffeien, Swi. 56/D4
Plai Mat (riv.), Thai. 78/C3
Plaidt, Ger. 53/G3
Plailly, Fr. 30/K4
Plain City, Ut, US 137/J11
Plain Dealing, La, US 129/J4
Plaine (riv.), Fr. 56/C1
Plainfield, NJ, US 139/H9
Plainfield, Il, US 135/P16
Plains, Tx, US 129/G4
Plains, Pa, US 138/C1
Plainsboro, NJ, US 138/D3
Plainview, Tx, US 129/G4
Plainview, Mn, US 130/A2
Plainview, NY, US 139/M8
Plaisir, Fr. 30/H5
Plan-les-Ouates, Swi. 56/C5
Planá, Czh. 55/F3
Plana Cays (isls.), Bahm. 145/H1
Planaltina, Braz. 154/A4
Plancher-Bas, Fr. 56/C2
Plancher-les-Mines, Fr. 56/C2
Plandište, Yugo. 48/E3
Planeta Rica, Col. 152/C2
Planken, Lcht. 57/F3
Plant City, Fl, US 133/H4
Plantation, Fl, US 133/H5
Plaquemines (parish), La, US 137/Q17
Plasencia, Sp. 44/B2
Plasy, Czh. 55/G3
Plata (riv.), Arg. 147/D6
Plata (estu.), Arg.,Uru. 159/K11
Platani (riv.), It. 46/C4
Plate Taile, Barrage de la (dam), Belg. 53/D3
Plateau (state), Nga. 103/H4
Platí, Gre. 47/H2
Platinum, Ak, US 134/F4
Plato, Col. 152/C2
Platón Sánchez, Mex. 144/B1
Platte (riv.), Ne, US 129/H2
Platte City, Mo, US 137/D5
Platte, North (riv.), Ne,Wy, US 124/E3
Platte, South (riv.), Co, US 124/F3
Platteville, Co, US 137/C2
Plattling, Ger. 55/F5
Plattsburgh, NY, US 130/F2
Plauen, Ger. 55/F1
Plav, Yugo. 47/F1
Plavna Dadaint (peak), Swi. 57/G4
Playa de los Muertos (ruin), Hon. 144/E3
Playa del Carmen, Mex. 144/E1
Playa Noriega (lake), Mex. 142/C2
Playa Vicente, Mex. 144/C2
Playas (lake), NM, US 128/E5
Playas, Ecu. 152/A5
Playgreen (lake), Mb, Can. 127/J2
Pleasant (lake), Az, US 137/R18
Pleasant Grove, Ut, US 137/K13
Pleasant Hill, Ca, US 135/K11
Pleasant Hill, Mo, US 137/E6
Pleasant Hills, Md, US 138/B5
Pleasant Valley, Mo, US 137/E5
Pleasant View, Ut, US 137/K11
Pleasant View, Co, US 137/B3
Pleasanton, Tx, US 129/H5
Pleasanton, Ca, US 135/L11
Pleasantville, NJ, US 138/D5
Pleasantville, NY, US 139/K7
Pleaux, Fr. 42/E4
Pleiku, Viet. 78/D3
Pleinfeld, Ger. 54/D4
Pleisse (riv.), Ger. 40/G3
Plenty (riv.), Austl. 115/G5
Plenty (bay), NZ 109/H6
Plentywood, Mt, US 127/G3
Plérin, Fr. 42/B2
Plesná (riv.), Czh. 55/F2
Pleso (int'l arpt.), Cro. 48/C3
Pleszew, Pol. 41/J3
Plétipi (lake), Qu, Can. 131/G1
Plettenberg, Ger. 51/E6
Pleurtuit (int'l arpt.), Fr. 42/B2
Pleven, Bul. 49/G4
Pliska, Bul. 49/H4
Plitvice Lakes NP, Cro. 48/B3
Pljevlja, Yugo. 47/F1
Plobsheim, Fr. 56/D1
Plöckenstein (peak), Ger. 55/G5
Ploče, Cro. 47/E1
Plochingen, Ger. 54/C5
Płock, Pol. 41/K2
Pločno (peak), Bosn. 48/C4
Ploemeur, Fr. 42/B3
Ploiești, Rom. 49/H3
Plomárion, Gre. 47/K3
Plombières, Belg. 53/E2
Plombières-lès-Dijon, Fr. 56/A3
Plön, Ger. 38/D4
Płońsk, Pol. 41/L2
Plouay, Fr. 42/B3
Ploučnice (riv.), Czh. 41/H3
Ploufragan, Fr. 42/B2
Plougastel-Daoulas, Fr. 42/A2
Plouguernével, Fr. 42/B2
Plouzané, Fr. 42/A2
Plovdiv (pol. reg.), Bul. 47/J2
Plover Cove (res.), China 71/U10
Pluguffan (int'l arpt.), Fr. 42/A3
Plum (isl.), NY, US 139/F1
Plumridge Lakes Nature Rsv., Austl. 112/E4
Plumsteadville, Pa, US 138/C3
Plungė, Lith. 39/J4
Plymouth, NC, US 133/J3
Plymouth, NH, US 131/G3
Plymouth, In, US 130/C3
Plymouth, Wi, US 130/C3
Plymouth (cap.), Monts. 141/N8
Plymouth, Eng, UK 32/B6
Plymouth (sound), Eng, UK 32/B6
Plymouth, Pa, US 138/C1
Plynlimon (peak), Wal, UK 32/C2
Plzeň, Czh. 55/G3
PNC Bank Arts Center, NJ, US 139/J10
Pniel, SAfr. 106/L10
Pniewy, Pol. 41/J2
Pô, Burk. 103/E4
Po (riv.), It. 27/F4
Po di Venezia (riv.), It. 59/F2
Po di Volano (riv.), It. 59/E3
Po Klong Garai Cham Towers, Viet. 78/E4
Po, Mouths of the (delta), It. 43/K4
Pô, PN de, Burk. 103/E4
Po Toi Group (isls.), China 71/V11
Po, Valle del (valley), It. 43/J4
Poá, Braz. 211/G8
Poa (riv.), Ven. 153/E2
Poag, Il, US 137/G8
Pobé, Ben. 103/F5
Pobedy (peak), Kyr. 70/D3
Pobiedziska, Pol. 41/J2
Pobla de Segur, Sp. 45/F1
Pocahontas, Ar, US 129/K3
Poção de Pedra, Braz. 154/A2
Pochep, Rus. 62/E1
P'och'ŏn, SKor. 73/G6
Pocinhos, Braz. 154/C2
Pöcking, Ger. 57/H2
Pöcking, Ger. 55/G6
Pocklington Reef (reef), PNG 116/E6
Poço Fundo, Braz. 211/H6
Poções, Braz. 154/B4
Pocola, Ok, US 129/J4
Poconé, Braz. 151/G7
Pocono (mts.), Pa, US 138/C1
Pocono (lake), Pa, US 138/C1
Pocono Lake, Pa, US 138/C1
Pocono Pines, Pa, US 138/C1
Poços de Caldas, Braz. 211/G6
Pocrí, Pan. 152/A2
Podbořany, Czh. 55/G2
Poddębice, Pol. 41/K3
Podenzano, It. 58/C3
Podgorica, Yugo. 47/F1
Podlasie (reg.), Bela.,Pol. 41/M3
Podol'sk, Rus. 61/W9
Podor, Sen. 102/B2
Podporozh'ye, Rus. 60/G3
Podravska Slatina, Cro. 48/C3
Podujevo, Yugo. 47/G1
Pofadder, SAfr. 106/B3
Poggibonsi, It. 59/E6
Poggio Renatico, It. 59/E3
Poggio Rusco, It. 59/E3
Poggiola, It. 59/E6
Pogromni (vol.), Ak, US 134/F5
P'ohang, SKor. 74/A2
Pohénégamook, Qu, Can. 131/G2
Pohja (Pojo), Fin. 39/K1
Pohjanmaa (reg.), Fin. 37/G3
Pohjois-Karjala (prov.), Fin. 60/F3
Pohnpei (isl.), Micr. 116/E4
Pohoiki, Hi, US 124/U11
Pohopoco Mtn. (mtn.), Pa, US 138/C2
Poigny-la-Forêt, Fr. 30/H5
Poing, Ger. 55/E6
Poinsett (cape), Ant. 160/H
Point (lake), NW, Can. 122/E2
Point au Fer (isl.), La, US 129/K5
Point Baker, Ak, US 134/M4
Point Fortin, Trin. 153/F2
Point Hope, Ak, US 134/E2
Point Lay, Ak, US 134/F2
Point Lookout (peak), Austl. 115/E1
Point Mugu Naval Air Sta., Ca, US 136/A2
Point Mugu State Park, Ca, US 136/A2
Point of Aire (pt.), Wal, UK 35/E5
Point of Ayre (pt.), IM, UK 34/D3
Point Pelee NP, On, Can. 130/D3
Point Pleasant, WV, US 130/D4
Point Pleasant, Pa, US 138/C3
Point Pleasant, NJ, US 138/D3
Point Pleasant Beach, NJ, US 138/D3
Point Salines (int'l arpt.), Gren. 153/F1
Point Salvation Abor. Rsv., Austl. 112/D4
Pointe-à-Pitre, Fr. 141/N8
Pointe à Raquette, Haiti 145/H2
Pointe-aux-Trembles, Qu, Can. 131/P6
Pointe-Calumet, Qu, Can. 131/N6
Pointe-Claire, Qu, Can. 131/N7
Pointe de Chassiron (pt.), Fr. 42/C3
Pointe de l'Arcouest (pt.), Fr. 42/B2
Pointe des Verres (peak), Fr. 56/C6
Pointe-du-Lac, Qu, Can. 131/F2
Pointe du Sablon (pt.), Fr. 42/F5
Pointe-Noire, Congo 105/B1
Poirino, It. 58/A3
Poissonier (pt.), Austl. 112/C1
Poissy, Fr. 30/J5
Poitiers, Fr. 42/D3
Poitou (reg.), Fr. 42/C3
Poitou-Charentes (reg.), Fr. 42/C3
Poix-de-Picardie, Fr. 52/A4
Poix-Terron, Fr. 53/D4
Pojuca, Braz. 154/C4
Pok Liu Chau (isl.), China 71/U11
Pokaran, India 89/K3
Pokharā, Nepal 84/D1
Pokhvistnevo, Rus. 63/K1
Pol-e Khomrī, Afg. 89/J1
Pola de Laviana, Sp. 44/C1
Pola de Lena, Sp. 44/C1
Pola de Siero, Sp. 44/C1
Polabská Nížina (phys. reg.), Czh. 43/L1
Pol'ana (peak), Slvk. 62/A2
Poland (ctry.) 41/K2
Połaniec, Pol. 41/L3
Polatlı, Turk. 62/E5
Polatsk, Bela. 39/N4
Polch, Ger. 53/G3
Połczyn-Zdrój, Pol. 38/G5
Pole of Inaccessibility, Ant. 160/E
Polesella, It. 59/E3
Polesine (reg.), It. 59/E3
Poleski NP, Pol. 41/M3
Polgár, Hun. 48/E2
Pŏlgyo, SKor. 73/D5
Políaigos (isl.), Gre. 47/J4
Policastro, Golfo di (gulf), It. 46/D3
Police, Pol. 38/F5
Policoro, It. 46/E2
Poligny, Fr. 56/B4
Polikastron, Gre. 47/H2
Políkhni, Gre. 47/H2
Polikhnitos, Gre. 47/K3
Polillo (isl.), Phil. 79/D4
Polis, Cyp. 91/C2
Polistena, It. 46/E3
Políyiros, Gre. 47/H2
Polje, Slov. 43/L3
Polkowice, Pol. 41/J3
Polla, It. 46/D2
Pollença, Sp. 45/G3
Polochic (riv.), Guat. 144/D3
Polomolok, Phil. 81/G2
Polonia (cape), Uru. 159/G2
Polonnaruwa, SrL. 82/D6
Polonne, Ukr. 62/C2
Polski Trŭmbesh, Bul. 49/G4
Polson, Mt, US 126/E4
Poltava, Ukr. 62/E2
Poltavs'ka (obl.), Ukr. 62/E2
Poluostrov Barsakel'mes (isl.), Kaz. 87/C3
Poluška (peak), Czh. 55/H5
Polvijärvi, Fin. 60/F3
Polyarnyy, Rus. 60/G1
Polynesia (reg.) 116/G6
Pomabamba, Peru 156/B3
Pomarance, It. 43/J5
Pomarico, It. 46/E2
Pomáz, Hun. 49/R9
Pomba (riv.), Som. 155/D2
Pombal, Braz. 154/C2
Pombal, Port. 44/A3
Pombas, CpV. 93/J9
Pomerania (reg.), Pol. 38/F4
Pomeranian (bay), Ger.,Pol. 38/F4
Pomerode, Braz. 155/B3
Pomeroon-Supenaam (pol. reg.), Guy. 153/G3
Pomeroy, Wa, US 126/D4
Pomeroy, NI, UK 34/B2
Pommersfelden, Ger. 54/D3
Pomona, Ca, US 136/C2
Pomona, NJ, US 138/D5
Pomona, Md, US 138/B5
Pomorie, Bul. 49/H4
Pomos (pt.), Cyp. 91/C2
Pompano Beach, Fl, US 133/H5
Pompei (ruin), It. 46/D2
Pompeu, Braz. 155/C1
Pompey, Fr. 53/F6
Pompiano, It. 58/C2
Pompton (riv.), NJ, US 139/H8
Pompton Lakes, NJ, US 139/H8
Poncarale, It. 58/D2
Ponce, PR 141/M8
Ponchatoula, La, US 137/P16
Poncheville (lake), Qu, Can. 130/E1
Pond, Mo, US 137/F8
Pond (inlet), Nun., Can. 123/J1
Pond (pt.), Ct, US 139/E1
Pond Inlet, Nun., Can. 123/J1
Pondicherry (terr.), India 70/D8
Pondicherry, India 82/C5
Ponente, Riviera di (coast), Fr. 58/B5
Ponferrada, Sp. 44/B1
Pongdong, SKor. 73/D5
Ponghwa, SKor. 74/A2
Pongolo (riv.), SAfr. 107/E2
Poni (prov.), Burk. 102/E4
Poniatowa, Pol. 41/M3
Ponnaiyar (riv.), India 82/C5
Ponoka, Ab, Can. 126/E2
Ponoy (riv.), Rus. 64/D3
Pons, Fr. 42/C4
Ponsacco, It. 58/D5
Pont-à-Celles, Belg. 53/D3
Pont-à-Marcq, Fr. 52/C2
Pont-D'Ain, Fr. 56/B5
Pont-de-Chéruy, Fr. 56/B6
Pont-de-Roide, Fr. 56/C3
Pont-de-Vaux, Fr. 56/A5
Pont-de-Veyle, Fr. 56/A5
Pont-du-Château, Fr. 42/E4
Pont-Remy, Fr. 52/A3
Pont-Saint-Esprit, Fr. 42/F4
Pont-Saint-Martin, It. 58/A1
Pont-Sainte-Maxence, Fr. 52/B5
Ponta Delgada, Azor., Port. 45/T13
Ponta do Pico (peak), Azor., Port. 45/S12
Ponta Grossa, Braz. 155/B3
Ponta Porã, Braz. 157/E1
Pontalina, Braz. 155/B1
Pontarlier, Fr. 56/C4
Pontarmé, Fr. 30/K4
Pontassieve, It. 59/E5
Pontault-Combault, Fr. 30/K5
Pontax (riv.), Qu, Can. 130/E1
Pontcarré, Fr. 30/L5
Pontchartrain (lake), La, US 125/H5
Pontchâteau, Fr. 42/B3
Ponte Alta do Bom Jesus, Braz. 154/A4
Ponte Alta do Tocantins, Braz. 154/A3
Ponte Buggianese, It. 59/D5
Ponte de Sor, Port. 44/A3
Ponte dell'Olio, It. 58/C3
Ponte di Legno, It. 57/G5
Ponte di Piave, It. 59/F1
Ponte do Lima, Port. 44/A2
Ponte Lambro, It. 58/C1
Ponte Nova, Braz. 155/D2
Ponte San Nicolò, It. 59/E2
Pontecagnano, It. 46/D2
Pontecorvo, It. 46/C2
Pontecurone, It. 58/B3
Pontedera, It. 58/D5
Pontefract, Eng, UK 35/G4
Ponteland, Eng, UK 35/G1
Pontelongo, It. 59/F2
Pontenure, It. 58/C3
Pontes e Lacerda, Braz. 150/G7
Pontestura, It. 58/B2
Pontevedra, Sp. 44/A1
Pontevico, It. 58/D2
Ponthévrard, Fr. 30/H6
Ponthieu (reg.), Fr. 52/A3
Pontiac, Il, US 127/L5
Pontiac, Mi, US 130/D3
Pontiac (lake), Mi, US 135/E6
Pontianak, Indo. 80/C4
Pontivy, Fr. 42/B2
Pontoise, Fr. 30/J4
Pontoon Beach, Il, US 137/G8
Pontotoc, Ms, US 133/F3
Pontpoint, Fr. 52/B5
Pontremoli, It. 58/C4
Pontresina, Swi. 57/F5
Pontypool, Wal, UK 32/C3
Ponza, It. 46/C2
Ponziane, Isole (isls.), It. 46/C2
Poole (bay), Eng, UK 33/E5
Poole, Eng, UK 32/E5
Poole (co.), Eng, UK 32/D5
Poolewe, Sc, UK 31/R8
Poona (Pune), India 89/K5
Poondarrie (peak), Austl. 112/C3
Poondinna (mt.), Austl. 113/F3
Poopó (lake), Bol. 147/C4
Poortugaal, Neth. 50/B5
Pöösapää (pt.), Est. 39/K2
Poosepatuck Ind. Res., NY, US 139/F2
Popayán, Col. 152/B4
Poperinge, Belg. 52/B2
Popigochic (riv.), Mex. 142/C2
Popilta (lake), Austl. 113/J5
Popio (lake), Austl. 115/B2
Poplar, Mt, US 127/G3
Poplar (riv.), Mb,On, Can. 122/G3
Poplar (isl.), Md, US 138/B6
Poplar Bluff, Mo, US 129/K3
Poplarville, Ms, US 133/F4
Popocatépetl (vol.), Mex. 143/L7
Popoli, It. 46/C1
Popovo, Bul. 49/H4
Poppberg (peak), Ger. 55/E4
Poppenhausen, Ger. 54/D2
Poppenhausen, Ger. 54/C2
Poppi, It. 59/E5
Poprad, Slvk. 41/L4
Poprad (riv.), Slvk. 41/L4
Poranga, Braz. 154/B2
Porangatu, Braz. 151/J6
Porbandar, India 89/J4
Porcari, It. 58/D5
Porce (riv.), Col. 152/C3
Porcheville, Fr. 30/H5
Porcia, It. 59/F1
Porcuna, Sp. 44/C4
Porcupine (riv.), Can.,US 134/K2
Porcupine Gorge NP, Austl. 114/B3
Porcupine Plain, Sk, Can. 127/H2
Pordenone (prov.), It. 59/F2
Pordenone, It. 59/F1
Pordim, Bul. 49/G4
Poreč, Cro. 59/G2
Poretta (int'l arpt.), Fr. 46/A1
Pori (int'l arpt.), Fin. 39/J1
Pori, Fin. 39/J1
Porirua, NZ 117/S11
Porlezza, It. 57/F5
Pornic, Fr. 42/B3
Porongurup NP, Austl. 112/C5
Póros, Gre. 47/H4
Porpoise (bay), Ant. 160/J
Porrentruy, Swi. 56/D3
Porretta Terme, It. 59/D4
Porriño, Sp. 44/A1
Porsangen (inlet), Nor. 37/H1
Porsgrunn, Nor. 38/C2
Porsuk (riv.), Turk. 62/D5
Port (isl.), Japan 77/H6
Port Alberni, BC, Can. 126/B3
Port Albert, Austl. 115/C3
Port Alexander, Ak, US 134/M4
Port Alfred, SAfr. 106/D4
Port Alice, BC, Can. 126/B3
Port Angeles, Wa, US 126/C3
Port Antonio, Jam. 145/G2
Port Appin, Sc, UK 36/A3
Port Arthur, Tx, US 129/J5
Port au Choix, Nf, Can. 131/K1
Port-au-Prince (cap.), Haiti 145/H2
Port Augusta, Austl. 113/H5
Port Bannatyne, Sc, UK 36/A5
Port Blair, India 83/F5
Port Blakely, Wa, US 135/C2
Port Bolivar, Tx, US 132/E4
Port-Bouët, C.d'Iv. 102/E5
Port Bouet (Abidgan) (int'l arpt.), C.d'Iv. 102/E5
Port Broughton, Austl. 113/H5
Port Canning, India 85/G4
Port Carbon, Pa, US 138/B2
Port Charlotte, Fl, US 133/H5
Port Chester, NY, US 139/L8
Port Clements, BC, Can. 134/M5
Port Clinton, Oh, US 130/D3
Port Clinton, Pa, US 138/B2
Port Colborne, On, Can. 131/R10
Port Columbus (int'l arpt.), Oh, US 130/D4

217

Port D – Punta

Port Davey (har.), Austl. 115/C4
Port-de-Paix, Haiti 145/H2
Port Deposit, Md, US 138/B4
Port Dickson, Malay. 80/B3
Port Discovery (bay), Wa, US 135/B1
Port Douglas, Austl. 114/B2
Port Edward, BC, Can. 134/M4
Port Elgin, On, Can. 130/D2
Port Elizabeth, SAfr. 106/D4
Port Elizabeth, NJ, US 138/D5
Port Ellen, Sc, UK 31/Q9
Port Elliot, Austl. 113/H5
Port Erin, IM, UK 34/D3
Port-Eynon (pt.), Wal, UK 32/B3
Port Fairy, Austl. 115/B3
Port Gamble, Wa, US 135/B2
Port Gamble Ind. Res., Wa, US 135/B2
Port-Gentil, Gabon 96/G8
Port Gibson, Ms, US 129/K5
Port Glasgow, Sc, UK 36/B5
Port Graham, Ak, US 134/H4
Port Harcourt (int'l arpt.), Nga. 103/G5
Port Harcourt, Nga. 103/G5
Port Hardy, BC, Can. 126/B3
Port Hawkesbury, NS, Can. 131/J2
Port Hedland, Austl. 112/C2
Port Hedland (int'l arpt.), Austl. 112/C2
Port Heiden, Ak, US 134/G4
Port Hueneme, Ca, US 136/A2
Port Huron, Mi, US 130/D3
Port Isaac (bay), Eng, UK 32/B5
Port Jefferson, NY, US 139/E2
Port-la-Nouvelle, Fr. 42/E5
Port Lambton, On, Can. 135/H6
Port Lavaca, Tx, US 129/H5
Port Lincoln, Austl. 113/G5
Port Lions, Ak, US 134/H4
Port Loko, SLeo. 102/B4
Port-Louis, Fr. 141/N8
Port Louis (cap.), Mrts. 107/T15
Port Macdonnell, Austl. 115/B3
Port Macquarie, Austl. 115/E1
Port Madison Ind. Res., Wa, US 135/B2
Port Maria, Jam. 145/G2
Port McNeill, BC, Can. 126/B3
Port-Menier, Qu, Can. 131/H1
Port Monmouth, NJ, US 139/J10
Port Nolloth, SAfr. 106/B3
Port Norris, NJ, US 138/C5
Port of Ness, Sc, UK 31/Q7
Port-of-Spain (cap.), Trin. 153/F2
Port Orange, Fl, US 133/H4
Port Penn, De, US 138/C4
Port Phillip (bay), Austl. 115/C3
Port Pirie, Austl. 113/H5
Port Reading, NJ, US 139/J9
Port Republic, NJ, US 138/D4
Port Royal, Pa, US 138/A2
Port Saint Joe, Fl, US 133/G4
Port-Saint-Louis-du-Rhône, Fr. 42/F5
Port Saint Lucie, Fl, US 133/H5
Port Saint Mary, IM, UK 34/D3
Port Shepstone, SAfr. 107/E3
Port Stevens (bay), Austl. 109/E4
Port-sur-Saône, Fr. 56/C2
Port Townsend, Wa, US 126/C3
Port-Vendres, Fr. 42/E5
Port Victoria, Austl. 113/H5
Port-Vila (cap.), Van. 116/F6
Port Wakefield, Austl. 113/H5
Port Washington, NY, US 139/L8
Port Weld, Malay. 80/B3
Porta Westfalica (pass), Ger. 51/F4
Porta Westfalica, Ger. 51/F4
Portachuelo, Bol. 150/F7
Portadown, NI, UK 34/B3
Portaferry, NI, UK 34/C3
Portage, Mi, US 130/C3
Portage Des Sioux, Mo, US 137/G8
Portage la Prairie, Mb, Can. 127/J3
Portalegre (dist.), Port. 44/B3
Portalegre, Port. 44/B3
Portales, NM, US 129/G4
Portarlington, Ire. 31/Q10
Portbou, Sp. 42/E5
Porteirinha, Braz. 154/B4
Portel, Braz. 151/H4
Porters (lake), Pa, US 138/C1
Porterville, Ca, US 128/C3
Porterville, Ut, US 137/K12
Porterville, SAfr. 106/L10
Portes-lès-Valence, Fr. 42/F4
Portet-sur-Garonne, Fr. 42/D5
Portete (bay), Col. 145/J3
Portglenone, NI, UK 34/B2
Portimão, Port. 44/A4
Portishead, Eng, UK 32/D4
Portknockie, Sc, UK 36/D1
Portland, Austl. 115/D2
Portland (cape), Austl. 115/C4
Portland, Austl. 115/B3
Portland (int'l arpt.), Or, US 126/C4
Portland, Or, US 126/C4
Portland, Tn, US 130/C4
Portland, In, US 130/C3
Portland, Me, US 131/G3
Portland (pt.), Jam. 145/G2
Portland Canal (inlet), BC, Can. 134/M4
Portland Jetport (int'l arpt.), Me, US 131/G3
Portlaoise, Ire. 31/Q10
Portlaw, Ire. 31/Q10
Portlethen, Sc, UK 36/D2
Portmarnock, Ire. 34/B5
Portmore, Jam. 145/G2
Portneuf (riv.), Qu, Can. 131/G1
Porto (dist.), Port. 44/A2
Porto (int'l arpt.), Port. 44/A2
Porto (gulf), Fr. 46/A1
Porto, Port. 44/A2
Porto Azzurro, It. 43/J5
Porto Belo, Braz. 155/B3
Porto Calvo, Braz. 154/D3
Porto Ceresio, It. 57/E6
Pôrto da Fôlha, Braz. 154/C3
Porto de Mós, Port. 44/A3
Porto Empedocle, It. 46/C4
Porto Ercole, It. 46/B1
Porto Ferreira, Braz. 155/C2
Porto Franco, Braz. 154/A2
Porto Garibaldi, It. 59/F3
Porto Inglês, CpV. 93/K10
Porto Nacional, Braz. 151/J6
Porto-Novo (cap.), Ben. 103/F5
Porto Potenza Picena, It. 59/G6
Porto Recanati, It. 59/G6
Porto Sant'Elpidio, It. 43/K5
Porto Santo (isl.), Port. 98/A2
Porto Santo Stefano, It. 46/B1
Porto Seguro, Braz. 154/C5
Porto Tolle, It. 59/F3
Porto Torres, It. 46/A2
Porto União, Braz. 155/B3
Porto Valtravaglia, It. 57/E6
Porto-Vecchio, Fr. 46/A2
Porto Velho, Braz. 150/F5
Portobelo, PN, Pan. 145/G4
Portocannone, It. 46/D2
Portocivitanova, It. 43/K5
Portoferraio, It. 43/J5
Portofino, It. 58/C4
Portogruaro, It. 59/F1
Portomaggiore, It. 59/E3
Portovenere, It. 58/C4
Portoviejo, Ecu. 152/A5
Portpatrick, Sc, UK 34/C2
Portree, Sc, UK 31/Q8
Portrush, NI, UK 34/B1
Portsea (isl.), Eng, UK 33/E5
Portslade-by-Sea, Eng, UK 33/F5
Portsmouth, Dom. 141/N9
Portsmouth, NH, US 131/G3
Portsmouth, Eng, UK 33/E5
Portsmouth (co.), Eng, UK 33/E5
Portsoy, Sc, UK 36/D1
Portstewart, NI, UK 34/B1
Portugal (ctry.) 44/A3
Portugalete, Sp. 44/D1
Portuguesa (riv.), Ven. 141/H6
Portuguesa (state), Ven. 152/D2
Portumna, Ire. 31/P10
Porvenir, Uru. 159/K10
Porvenir, Chile 159/C7
Porzuna, Sp. 44/C3
Posada, It. 46/A2
Posadas, Arg. 157/E2
Posadas, Sp. 44/C4
Posavina (valley), Bosn. 48/C3
Poschiavo, Swi. 57/G5
Posio, Fin. 60/F2
Poso (lake), Indo. 81/F4
Posof, Turk. 63/G4
Posŏng (riv.), SKor. 73/D5
Posŏng, SKor. 73/D5
Posorja, Ecu. 152/A5
Posse, Braz. 154/A4
Possession (pt.), Wa, US 135/C2
Possession (sound), Wa, US 135/C2
Post, Tx, US 129/G4
Post Falls, Id, US 126/D4
Poste Maurice Cortier (ruin), Alg. 99/F5
Postmasburg, SAfr. 106/C3
Postojna, Slov. 43/L4
Postolprty, Czh. 55/G2
Potam, Mex. 142/C3
Potamós, Gre. 47/H5
Potaro-Siparuni (pol. reg.), Guy. 153/G3
Potchefstroom, SAfr. 106/D2
Poteau, Ok, US 129/J4
Potenza (riv.), It. 46/C1
Potenza, It. 46/D2
Potenza Picena, It. 59/G6
Potes, Sp. 44/C1
Potholes (res.), Wa, US 126/D4
Poti (riv.), Braz. 151/K5
P'ot'i, Geo. 63/G4
Potiraguá, Braz. 154/C4
Potomac (riv.), US 130/E4
Potomac, Md, US 138/A5
Potosí, Bol. 150/E7
Potosi, Mo, US 129/K3
Potrerillos, Chile 157/C2
Potsdam, NY, US 130/F2
Potsdam, Ger. 40/Q7
Potta-Watomie (co.), Ok, US 137/N15
Pottendorf, Aus. 43/M3
Pottenstein, Ger. 55/E3
Potters Bar, Eng, UK 30/C1
Pöttmes, Ger. 54/E5
Pottstown, Pa, US 138/C3
Pottsville, Pa, US 138/B2
Pottuvil, SrL. 82/D6
Poudre d'Or, Mrts. 107/T15
Poughkeepsie, NY, US 130/F3
Pouilley-les-Vignes, Fr. 56/B3
Poulaphouca (res.), Ire. 34/B5
Poulter (riv.), Eng, UK 35/G5
Poulton-le-Fylde, Eng, UK 35/F4
Poŭn, SKor. 73/D4
Pourri (peak), Fr. 43/G4
Pouru-Saint-Remy, Fr. 53/E4
Pouso Alegre, Braz. 211/H7
Pouthisat (riv.), Camb. 83/H5
Pouzauges, Fr. 42/C3
Považská Bystrica, Slvk. 41/K4
Povegliano Veronese, It. 59/D2
Poverty Point Nat'l Mon., La, US 129/K4
Poviglio, It. 58/D3
Póvoa de Varzim, Port. 44/A2
Povoação, Azor., Port. 45/T13
Povorino, Rus. 63/G2
Povungnituk (riv.), Qu, Can. 123/J2
Povungnituk, Qu, Can. 123/J2
Poway, Ca, US 136/C5
Powder (riv.), Mt,Wy, US 124/E2
Powell, Wy, US 126/F4
Powell (lake), Az,Ut, US 128/E3
Powell River, BC, Can. 126/B3
Power (res.), NY, US 131/R9
Powers (lake), Wi, US 135/P14
Powys (co.), Wal, UK 35/E6
Powys, Vale of (valley), Wal, UK 32/C1
Poxoreo, Braz. 151/H7
Poyang (lake), China 79/C2
Poynton, Eng, UK 35/F5
Poyo, Sp. 44/A1
Poysdorf, Aus. 41/J4
Poza Rica, Mex. 143/M6
Požarevac, Yugo. 48/E3
Požega, Yugo. 48/E4
Poznań, Pol. 41/J2
Pozo Alcón, Sp. 44/D4
Pozoblanco, Sp. 44/C3
Pozohondo, Sp. 44/E3
Pozuelo de Alarcón, Sp. 45/N9
Pozuelos, Ven. 153/E2
Pozuzo, Peru 156/C3
Pozza, It. 59/D3
Pozzallo, It. 46/D4
Pozzolo Formigaro, It. 58/B3
Pozzonovo, It. 59/E2
Ppa. de Salamanca (plain), Arg. 158/F1
Prabuty, Pol. 39/H5
Pracham Hiang (pt.), Thai. 78/B4
Prachatice, Czh. 55/H4
Prachin Buri (riv.), Thai. 78/C3
Prachin Buri, Thai. 78/C3
Prachuap Khiri Khan, Thai. 78/B4
Praděd (peak), Czh. 41/J3
Pradera, Col. 152/B4
Prades, Fr. 42/E5
Prado, Braz. 154/C5
Prado del Rey, Sp. 44/C4
Prado Flood Control (basin), Ca, US 136/C3
Pragelpass (pass), Swi. 57/E4
Praha (pol. reg.), Czh. 41/H3
Praha (peak), Czh. 55/G3
Praha (Prague) (cap.), Czh. 55/H2
Prahova (prov.), Rom. 49/G3
Praia (cap.), CpV. 93/K11
Praia (int'l arpt.), CpV. 93/K11
Praia da Vitória, Azor., Port. 45/S12
Praia Grande, Braz. 211/G9
Prairie Dog Town Fk. (riv.), Tx, US 124/F4
Prairie du Chien, Wi, US 127/L5
Prairie Grove, Il, US 135/P15
Prairie View, Tx, US 129/J5
Prairie Village, Ks, US 137/D6
Prairies (riv.), Qu, Can. 131/N6
Prairietown, Il, US 137/H8
Pralboino, It. 58/D2
Pralungo, It. 58/B1
Pram (riv.), Aus. 55/G6
Prambachkirchen, Aus. 55/G6
Pran Buri (res.), Thai. 83/G5
Prangins, Swi. 56/C5
Prānhita (riv.), India 82/C4
Prapat, Indo. 80/A3
Præstø, Den. 38/E4
Praszka, Pol. 41/K3
Prat, Chile, Ant. 160/W
Prata (riv.), Braz. 154/A5
Prata, Braz. 155/B1
Prata di Pordenone, It. 59/F1
Prathersville, Mo, US 137/E5
Prätlgau (valley), Swi. 57/F4
Prato, It. 59/E5
Prato allo Stelvio (Prad am Stilfserjoch), It. 57/G4
Prato (Leventina), Swi. 57/E5
Pratola Peligna, It. 46/C1
Pratomagno (mts.), It. 59/E5
Pratovecchio, It. 59/E5
Pratt, Ks, US 129/H3
Pratt (isl.), Chile 159/B6
Pratteln, Swi. 56/D2
Prattville, Al, US 133/G3
Prauthoy, Fr. 56/B2
Pravets, Bul. 47/H1
Pravia, Sp. 44/B1
Prawle (pt.), Eng, UK 32/C6
Praxedis G. Guerrero, Mex. 129/F5
Praya, Indo. 81/E5
Pré-Saint-Didier, It. 56/C6
Preah Vihear (ruin), Camb. 78/D3
Précy-sur-Oise, Fr. 52/B5
Predappio, It. 59/E4
Predazzo, It. 43/J3
Predeal, Rom. 49/G3
Predosa, It. 58/B3
Preeceville, Sk, Can. 127/H3
Preetz, Ger. 38/D4
Preganziol, It. 59/F1
Pregarten, Aus. 55/H6
Pregolya (riv.), Pol. 39/J4
Pregolya (riv.), Rus. 41/L1
Pregonero, Ven. 152/D2
Preissac (lake), Qu, Can. 130/E1
Premana, It. 57/F5
Prémery, Fr. 42/E3
Premià de Mar, Sp. 45/L7
Prenzlau, Ger. 41/G2
Přerov, Czh. 41/J4
Presanella (peak), It. 57/G5
Prescot, Eng, UK 35/F5
Prescott, Az, US 128/D4
Prescott, On, Can. 130/F2
Preševo, Yugo. 47/G1
Presidencia Roque Sáenz Peña, Arg. 157/D2
Presidente Dutra, Braz. 154/A2
Presidente Epitácio, Braz. 155/A2
Presidente Olegário, Braz. 155/C1
Presidente Venceslau, Braz. 155/B2
Presidential Lake Estates, NJ, US 138/D4
Presidio, Tx, US 129/F5
Presidio (riv.), Mex. 142/D4
Preslav, Bul. 49/H4
Presles, Fr. 30/J4
Presles-en-Brie, Fr. 30/L5
Prešov, Slvk. 41/L4
Prespa (lake), Eur. 47/G2
Presque Isle, Me, US 131/G2
Pressath, Ger. 55/E3
Pressbaum, Aus. 49/N7
Prestatyn, Wal, UK 35/E5
Prestea, Gha. 103/E5
Prestfoss, Nor. 38/C1
Přeštice, Czh. 55/G3
Preston (cape), Austl. 112/C2
Preston, Md, US 138/C6
Preston, Wa, US 135/D2
Preston, Eng, UK 35/F4
Prestonpans, Sc, UK 36/D5
Prestonsburg, Ky, US 130/D4
Prestwich, Eng, UK 35/F4
Prestwick (int'l arpt.), Sc, UK 36/B5
Prestwick, Sc, UK 36/B6
Prêto (riv.), Braz. 151/J6
Pretoria (cap.), SAfr. 106/E2
Pretty Boy (res.), Md, US 138/B4
Preussisch Olendorf, Ger. 51/F4
Prevalje, Slov. 43/L3
Préveza, Gre. 47/G3
Prévost, Qu, Can. 131/M6
Prey Veng, Camb. 78/D4
Pribilof (isls.), Ak, US 134/D4
Priboj, Yugo. 48/D4
Příbram, Czh. 55/H3
Price (riv.), Ut, US 128/E3
Price, Ut, US 128/E3
Price, Md, US 138/C5
Prichard, Al, US 133/F4
Prichsenstadt, Ger. 54/D3
Priego, Sp. 44/D2
Priego de Córdoba, Sp. 44/C4
Prien am Chiemsee, Ger. 55/F7
Prieska, SAfr. 106/C3
Priest (lake), Id, US 126/D3
Priest River, Id, US 126/D3
Prieta (mtn.), Sp. 44/C1
Prievidza, Slvk. 41/K4
Prignitz (reg.), Ger. 40/F2
Prijedor, Bosn. 48/C3
Prijepolje, Yugo. 47/F1
Prikaspian (plain), Kaz.,Rus. 64/E5
Prikumsk, Rus. 63/H3
Prilep, FYROM 47/G2
Prilly, Swi. 56/C4
Prima Porta, It. 46/C1
Prima Tapia, Mex. 128/C4
Prime Hook NWR, De, US 138/C6
Primeira Cruz, Braz. 154/B1
Primero (cape), Chile 159/B6
Primorskiy (kray), Rus. 65/P5
Primorsko, Bul. 49/H4
Primorsko-Akhtarsk, Rus. 62/F3
Prims (riv.), Ger. 53/F4
Prince Albert, Sk, Can. 127/G2
Prince Albert (pen.), NW, Can. 122/E1
Prince Albert (sound), NW, Can. 122/E1
Prince Albert NP, Sk, Can. 122/F3
Prince Albert, SAfr. 106/C4
Prince Alfred (cape), NW, Can. 122/D1
Prince Charles (isl.), Nun., Can. 123/J2
Prince Edward (isl.), Can. 119/L5
Prince Edward Island (prov.), Can. 131/J2
Prince Edward Island NP, PE, Can. 131/J2
Prince Edward (isls.), SAfr. 23/L7
Prince George, BC, Can. 126/C2
Prince Georges (co.), Md, US 138/B6
Prince Gustav Adolf (sea), Nun., Can. 123/R7
Prince Leopold (isl.), Nun., Can. 122/G1
Prince of Wales (str.), NW, Can. 122/E1
Prince of Wales (isl.), Ak, US 122/C3
Prince Olav (coast), Ant. 160/D
Prince Patrick (isl.), NW, Can. 123/R7
Prince Regent (inlet), Nun., Can. 122/G1
Prince Rupert, BC, Can. 134/M4
Prince William (sound), Ak, US 122/B2
Princenhof (lake), Neth. 50/C2
Princes Risborough, Eng, UK 33/F3
Princes Town, Trin. 141/J5
Princesa Isabel, Braz. 154/C2
Princess Charlotte (bay), Austl. 109/D2
Princess Margaret (range), Nun., Can. 123/S6
Princess Royal (isl.), BC, Can. 122/C3
Princeton, Mn, US 127/K4
Princeton, BC, Can. 126/C3
Princeton, In, US 130/C4
Princeton, Ky, US 130/C4
Princeton, NJ, US 138/D3
Princeton Junction, NJ, US 138/D3
Princeville, Hi, US 124/S9
Príncipe (isl.), SaoT. 96/G7
Prindle (vol.), Ak, US 134/K3
Prineville, Or, US 126/C4
Pringsewu, Indo. 80/B5
Pringy, Fr. 56/C6
Prinsenbeek, Neth. 50/B5
Prinses Margriet (canal), Neth. 50/C3
Prinzapolka, Nic. 145/F3
Prinzapolka (riv.), Nic. 145/E3
Priolo di Gargallo, It. 46/D4
Prior (cape), Sp. 44/A1
Priore (peak), It. 43/K5
Priozersk, Rus. 39/P1
Pripet Marshes (swamp), Bela.,Ukr 62/C1
Prlpyat' (riv.), Ukr. 62/C2
Prisdorf, Ger. 51/G1
Priština, Yugo. 47/G1
Prittriching, Ger. 57/G1
Pritzwalk, Ger. 40/G2
Privas, Fr. 42/F4
Privolzhskiy, Rus. 63/H2
Priyutovo, Rus. 63/K1
Prizren, Yugo. 47/G1
Prnjavor, Yugo. 48/D3
Prnjavor, Bosn. 48/C3
Probištip, FYROM 47/H1
Probolinggo, Indo. 80/D5
Probstzella, Ger. 55/E1
Proctor (lake), Tx, US 132/D3
Proctor (pt.), La, US 137/Q17
Proddatūr, India 82/C5
Proença-a-Nova, Port. 44/B3
Profondeville, Belg. 53/D3
Progreso, Pan. 145/F4
Progreso, Mex. 144/D1
Progreso, Uru. 159/K11
Progreso, Mex. 143/K6
Progress, Rus. 71/N2
Progresso, It. 59/E3
Prokhladnyy, Rus. 63/G4
Prokuplje, Yugo. 47/G1
Promised Land (lake), Pa, US 138/C1
Promissão, Braz. 155/B2
Promissão, Represa (res.), Braz. 155/B2
Propriá, Braz. 154/C3
Propriano, Fr. 46/A2
Proserpine, Austl. 114/C3
Prosna (riv.), Pol. 41/J2
Prospect Park, NJ, US 139/J8
Prospector (mtn.), Yk, Can. 134/L3
Prosperidad, Phil. 79/E6
Prosperous, Ire. 31/Q10
Prostějov, Czh. 41/J4
Proston, Austl. 114/C4
Proszowice, Pol. 41/L3
Protivín, Czh. 55/H4
Provadiya, Bul. 49/H4
Provence (reg.), Fr. 42/F5
Provence (int'l arpt.), Fr. 42/F5
Provence-Alpes-Côte-d'Azur, Fr. 43/G4
Providence (cap.), RI, US 131/G3
Providencia, Isla de (isl.), Col. 140/E5
Providência, Serra de (mts.), Braz. 150/F6
Providenciales (isl.), Bahm. 145/H1
Provins, Fr. 42/E2
Provo (riv.), Ut, US 137/K13
Provo (peak), Ut, US 137/K13
Provo, Ut, US 137/K13
Provost, Ab, Can. 126/F2
Prozor, Bosn. 48/C4
Prudentópolis, Braz. 155/B3
Prudhoe (bay), Ak, US 134/J1
Prudhoe, Eng, UK 35/G2
Prudhoe Bay, Ak, US 134/J1
Prudnik, Pol. 41/J3
Prüm (riv.), Ger. 40/D4
Prüm, Ger. 53/F3
Prunay-en-Yvelines, Fr. 30/H6
Prunelli-di-Fiumorbo, Fr. 46/A1
Pruszcz Gdański, Pol. 38/H4
Pruszków, Pol. 41/L2
Prut (riv.), Eur. 64/C5
Prutz, Aus. 57/G3
Pryluky, Ukr. 62/E2
Pryor, Ok, US 129/J3
Prypyats' (riv.), Bela. 64/C4
Przasnysz, Pol. 41/L2
Przemków, Pol. 41/H3
Przemyś (prov.), Pol. 41/M4
Przemyśl, Pol. 41/M4
Przeworsk, Pol. 41/M3
Przylądek Rozewie (cape),Pol. 38/H4
Przysucha, Pol. 41/L3
Psakhná, Gre. 47/H3
Psará (isl.), Gre. 47/J3
Psárion, Gre. 47/G4
Psël (riv.), Rus.,Ukr. 62/E2
Pskov (lake), Rus. 60/E5
Pskov, Rus. 39/N3
Pskovskaya (obl.), Rus. 60/F4
Pšovka (riv.), Czh. 55/H2
Pszczyna, Pol. 41/K4
Ptolemaís, Gre. 47/G2
Ptuj, Slov. 43/L3
Pu Xian, China 72/B3
Puan, SKor. 73/D5
Pubei, China 79/A3
Pucacaca, Peru 156/B2
Pucallpa, Peru 156/C3
Pucará, Ecu. 156/B1
Pucará, Peru 156/B2
Pucará, Peru 156/D4
Pucarani, Bol. 156/D5
Pucaurco, Peru 152/D5
Puchenau, Aus. 55/H6
Pucheng, China 79/C2
Pucheng, China 72/B4
Puchheim, Ger. 55/E6
Puch'on, SKor. 73/F7
Puchuncaví, Chile 158/N8
Pucioasa, Rom. 49/G3
Puck, Pol. 38/H4
Pucking, Aus. 55/H6
Pucón, Chile 158/C3
Pucusana, Peru 156/B4
Pudasjärvi, Fin. 60/E2
Puderbach, Ger. 53/G2
Pudsey, Eng, UK 35/G4
Pudu (riv.), China 82/H2
Puebla (state), Mex. 140/B4
Puebla, Mex. 143/L7
Puebla de Alcocer, Sp. 44/C3
Puebla de Don Fadrique, Sp. 44/D4
Puebla de la Calzada, Sp. 44/B3
Puebla de Sanabria, Sp. 44/B1
Puebla de Trives, Sp. 44/B1
Puebla del Caramiñal, Sp. 44/A1
Pueblillo, Mex. 143/M6
Pueblito, Col. 152/C2
Pueblo, Co, US 129/F3
Pueblo Nuevo, Nic. 144/E3
Pueblo Nuevo, Ven. 152/D2
Pueblo Yaqui, Mex. 142/C3
Puente (hills), Ca, US 136/G8
Puente Alto, Chile 158/N8
Puente Caldelas, Sp. 44/A1
Puente-Ceso, Sp. 44/A1
Puente de Ixtla, Mex. 143/K8
Puente del Inca, Arg. 158/C2
Puente-Genil, Sp. 44/C4
Puente Nacional, Col. 152/C3
Puente Piedra, Peru 156/B3
Puenteareas, Sp. 44/A1
Puentedeume, Sp. 44/A1
Puentes de García Rodríguez, Sp. 44/B1
Pueo (pt.), Hi, US 124/R10
Puerco (riv.), NM, US 128/E4
Puerto Acosta, Bol. 156/D4
Puerto Aisén, Chile 158/B5
Puerto América, Peru 156/B2
Puerto Ángel, Mex. 144/B3
Puerto Armuelles, Pan. 145/F4
Puerto Asís, Col. 152/B4
Puerto Ayacucho, Ven. 153/E3
Puerto Ayora, Ecu. 156/E7
Puerto Baquerizo Moreno, Ecu. 156/F7
Puerto Barrios, Guat. 144/D3
Puerto Bermúdez, Peru 156/C3
Puerto Berrío, Col. 152/C3
Puerto Cabello, Ven. 152/D2
Puerto Cabezas, Nic. 145/F3
Puerto Carreño, Col. 153/E3
Puerto Cisnes, Chile 158/B5
Puerto Cortés, Mex. 142/B3
Puerto Cortés, Hon. 144/E3
Puerto Cumarebo, Ven. 152/D2
Puerto de la Cruz, Sp. 98/A3
Puerto de la Libertad, Mex. 142/B2
Puerto de Navacerrada (pass), Sp. 45/M8
Puerto del Rosario, Sp. 98/B3
Puerto del Son, Sp. 44/A1
Puerto Deseado, Arg. 159/D5
Puerto El Carmen, Ecu. 152/C4
Puerto Escondido, Col. 152/B2
Puerto Escondido, Mex. 144/B3
Puerto Heath, Bol. 156/D4
Puerto Iguazú, Arg. 157/F2
Puerto Inca, Peru 156/C3
Puerto Ingeniero Ibáñez, Chile 158/C5
Puerto Inírida, Col. 152/E4
Puerto La Cruz, Ven. 153/E2
Puerto Leguízamo, Col. 152/C5
Puerto Lempira, Hon. 145/F3
Puerto López, Col. 152/C3
Puerto Lumbreras, Sp. 44/E4
Puerto Madero, Mex. 144/C3
Puerto Madryn, Arg. 158/D4
Puerto Magdalena, Mex. 142/B3
Puerto Maldonado, Peru 156/D4
Puerto Montt, Chile 158/B4
Puerto Morazán, Nic. 144/E3
Puerto Morelos, Mex. 140/D3
Puerto Napo, Ecu. 152/B5
Puerto Natales, Chile 159/B6
Puerto Obaldía, Pan. 152/B2
Puerto Ocopa, Peru 156/C3
Puerto Padre, Cuba 145/G1
Puerto Páez, Ven. 153/E3
Puerto Peñasco, Mex. 128/D5
Puerto Píritu, Ven. 153/E2
Puerto Portillo, Peru 156/C3
Puerto Prado, Peru 156/C3
Puerto Princesa, Phil. 81/E2
Puerto Quellón, Chile 158/B4
Puerto Real, Sp. 44/B4
Puerto Rico, Col. 152/C4
Puerto Rico, Col. 152/C4
Puerto Rico (dpcy.), US 141/M8
Puerto Rondón, Col. 152/D3
Puerto San Carlos, Mex. 142/B3
Puerto San Julián, Arg. 159/D6
Puerto Santa Cruz, Arg. 159/C6
Puerto Serrano, Sp. 44/C4
Puerto Suárez, Bol. 150/G7
Puerto Supe, Peru 156/B3
Puerto Tejada, Col. 152/B4
Puerto Vallarta, Mex. 142/D4
Puerto Varas, Chile 158/B4
Puerto Viejo, CR 145/E4
Puerto Villamil, Ecu. 156/E7
Puerto Wilches, Col. 152/C3
Puerto Williams, Chile 159/D7
Puertollano, Sp. 44/C3
Pueyrredón (lake), Arg. 158/C5
Puffin (isl.), Wal, UK 34/D5
Pugachev, Rus. 63/J1
Puget (sound), Wa, US 124/B2
Puglia (pol. reg.), It. 46/E2
Puglia (prov.), It. 48/C5
Puigcerdà, Sp. 45/F1
Puiseux-en-France, Fr. 30/K4
Pujehun, SLeo. 102/C5
Pujiang, China 79/C2
Pujilí, Ecu. 152/B5
Pujŏn (lake), NKor. 73/D2
Pujut (cape), Indo. 80/C5
Pukalani, Hi, US 124/T10
Puk'an-san (peak), SKor. 73/F6
Puk'an-san NP, SKor. 73/D4
Pukapuka (isl.), CookIs. 117/J6
Pukarua (isl.), FrPol. 117/M6
Pukaskwa NP, On, Can. 130/C1
Pukch'ŏng, NKor. 73/E2
Pukdae (riv.), NKor. 73/E2
Pukhan (riv.), NKor.,SKor. 73/D3
Pukhrāyān, India 84/B2
Pukovac, Yugo. 47/G1
Pukp'ot'ae-san (peak), NKor. 73/E2
Pula, Cro. 48/A3
Pulacayo, Bol. 150/E8
Pulandian (bay), China 73/A3
Pulanduta (pt.), Phil. 81/F1
Pulap (isl.), Micr. 116/D4
Pulaski, Va, US 130/D4
Pulaski, Tn, US 133/G3
Pulau (riv.), Indo. 81/J5
Puławy, Pol. 41/L3
Pulguk-sa, SKor. 74/A3
Pulheim, Ger. 53/F2
Pulisan (cape), Indo. 81/G3
Pulkovo (int'l arpt.), Rus. 61/T7
Pullach im Isartal, Ger. 57/H1
Pullman, Wa, US 126/D4
Pully, Swi. 56/C5
Pulsnitz (riv.), Ger. 41/G3
Pułtusk, Pol. 41/L2
Pülümür, Turk. 62/F5
Puluwat (isl.), Micr. 116/D4
Pulversheim, Fr. 56/D2
Pum (riv.), China 85/F1
Puma (lake), China 85/H1
Pumu (pass), China 83/F2
Puna de Atacama (plat.), Arg. 157/C2
Puná, Isla (isl.), Ecu. 150/B4
Punākha, Bhu. 85/G2
Punata, Bol. 150/E7
Pūnch, India 86/C3
Pūnch (riv.), India 86/C3
Pūndri, India 86/D5
Pune (Poona), India 89/K5
Punggai (cape), Malay. 80/B3
P'unggi, SKor. 73/E4
P'ungsan, NKor. 73/E2
Pungwe (falls), Zim. 105/F4
Punjab (plain), Pak. 89/K2
Punjab (state), Pak. 82/B2
Puno, Peru 156/D4
Puno (dept.), Peru 156/D4
Pünpün (riv.), India 85/E3
Punta, Ca, US 136/A2
Punta Alta, Arg. 158/E3
Punta Arena (pt.), Mex. 142/C4
Punta Arenas, Chile 159/C7
Punta Banda (cape), Mex. 142/A2
Punta Cardón, Ven. 152/D2

218

Punta – Rauda

Punta Celarain (pt.), Mex. 144/E1
Punta Colnett (pt.), Mex. 142/A2
Punta Colonet, Mex. 142/A2
Punta de Bombón, Peru 156/D5
Punta de Mata, Ven. 153/F2
Punta del Este, Uru. 159/G2
Punta del Este (Capitán Curbelo) (int'l arpt.), Uru. 159/G2
Punta Gorda, Fl, US 133/H5
Punta Gorda (bay), Nic. 140/E5
Punta Gorda, Belz. 144/D2
Punta Marina, It. 59/F4
Punta Raisi (int'l arpt.), It. 46/C3
Punta Umbría, Sp. 44/B4
Puntarenas, CR 145/E4
Puolo (pt.), Hi, US 124/S10
Pupiales, Col. 152/B4
Pupuya (peak), Bol. 156/D4
Puquio, Peru 156/C4
Pur (riv.), Rus. 64/H3
Puracé (vol.), Col. 152/B4
Puracé, PN, Col. 150/C3
Pūranpur, India 84/C1
Purbeck (isl.), Eng, UK 32/D5
Purcell (mts.), BC, Can. 126/D3
Purcell, Ok, US 129/H4
Puré (riv.), Col. 152/D5
Purén, Chile 158/B3
Purgatoire (riv.), Co, US 129/G3
Pürgen, Ger. 57/G1
Purgstall an der Erlauf, Aus. 43/L2
Purī, India 82/D3
Purificación, Col. 152/C4
Purikari (pt.), Est. 39/L2
Purkersdorf, Aus. 49/N7
Purmerend, Neth. 50/B3
Pūrna, India 82/C4
Purnia, India 85/F3
Purranque, Chile 157/B5
Puruê (riv.), Braz. 152/D5
Purūlia, India 85/F4
Puruni (riv.), Guy. 153/G3
Purús (riv.), Braz. 147/C3
Purushottampur, India 82/D4
Pŭrvomay, Bul. 47/J1
Purwa, India 84/C2
Purwokerto, Indo. 80/C5
Pusad, India 82/C4
Pusan, SKor. 71/N4
Pusan-Gwangyŏksi (prov.), SKor. 74/A3
Pusat Gayo (mts.), Indo. 80/A3
Puschendorf, Ger. 54/D3
Pushkin, Rus. 61/T7
Püspökladány, Hun. 48/E2
Pusur (riv.), Bang. 85/G4
Putaendo, Chile 158/C2
Putian, China 79/C2
Putina, Peru 156/D4
Puting (cape), Indo. 80/D4
Putla de Guerrero, Mex. 144/B2
Putomayo (dept.), Col. 152/C4
Putorana (mts.), Rus. 64/K3
Putrachoique (peak), Arg. 158/C4
Putre, Chile 156/D5
Puttalam, SrL. 82/C6
Putte, Belg. 53/D1
Puttelange-aux-Lacs, Fr. 53/F5
Putten, Neth. 50/C4
Putten (isl.), Neth. 50/B5
Püttlach (riv.), Ger. 55/E3
Püttlingen, Ger. 53/F5
Putu (range), Libr. 102/C5
Putumayo (riv.), SAm. 152/C5
Putumayo (riv.), SAm. 147/B3
Putussibau, Indo. 80/D3
Puu Kukui (peak), Hi, US 124/T10
Puu Moaulanui (peak), Hi, US 124/T10
Puu o Mahuka Heiau State Mon., Hi, US 124/V12
Puuanahulu, Hi, US 124/U11
Puuiki, Hi, US 124/T10
Puula (lake), Fin. 39/M1
Puurs, Belg. 53/D1
Puuwai, Hi, US 124/R10
Puy de Sancy (peak), Fr. 42/E4
Puyallup, Wa, US 126/C4
Puyallup (riv.), Wa, US 135/C3
Puyallup Ind. Res., Wa, US 135/C3
Puyang, China 72/C4
Puyehué (lake), Chile 158/B4
Puyehue (vol.), Chile 158/B4
Puylaurens, Fr. 42/E5
Puymorens, Col de (pass), Fr. 42/D5
Puyŏ, SKor. 73/D4
Puyo, Ecu. 152/B5
Puzal, Sp. 45/E3
Pwani (pol. reg.), Tanz. 104/C4
Pwllheli, Wal, UK 34/D6
Pyandzh (riv.), Taj. 87/F5
Pyaozero (lake), Rus. 37/J2
Pyapon, Myan. 83/G4
Pyasina (riv.), Rus. 64/J2
Pyatigorsk, Rus. 63/G3
Pyfara (peak), Fr. 42/F4
Pyhä-Häkin NP, Fin. 60/E3
Pyhäjärvi, Fin. 60/E3
Pyhäjärvi (lake), Fin. 39/K1
Pyhäntä, Fin. 60/E2
Pyhätunturi (peak), Fin. 60/E2
Pyinmana, Myan. 83/G4
P'yŏngan-bukto (prov.), NKor. 73/C2
P'yŏngan-namdo (prov.), NKor. 73/C3
P'yŏngch'ang, SKor. 73/E4
P'yŏnggang, NKor. 73/D3
P'yŏnghae, SKor. 73/E4
P'yŏngsan, NKor. 73/D3
P'yŏngsong, NKor. 73/C3
Pyŏngt'aek, SKor. 73/D4
P'yŏngyang (int'l arpt.), NKor. 73/C3
P'yŏngyang (cap.), NKor. 73/C3
P'yŏngyang-si (prov.), NKor. 73/C3
Pyŏnsanbando NP, SKor. 73/D5
Pyramid (lake), Nv, US 128/B3
Pyramid (mtn.), BC, Can. 134/M4
Pyramids Of Jīzah, Egypt 91/B5
Pyrenees (mts.), Fr.,Sp. 27/D4
Pyrénées Occidental, PN des, Fr. 42/C5
Pyrjatyn, Ukr. 62/E2
Pyrzyce, Pol. 41/H2
Pyshma (riv.), Rus. 61/Q4
Pyu, Myan. 83/G4
Pyuthān, Nepal 84/D1

Q

Qā 'al Jafr (salt pan), Jor. 91/E4
Qabalān, WBnk. 91/G7
Qabātiyah, WBnk. 91/G7
Qābis, Tun. 96/H1
Qābis (gov.), Tun. 99/H2
Qadima, Isr. 91/F7
Qādirpur Rān, Pak. 86/A4
Qā'en, Iran 89/G2
Qafa e Malit (pass), Alb. 47/G1
Qaffīn, WBnk. 91/G7
Qafşah, Tun. 96/G1
Qafşah (gov.), Tun. 99/H2
Qahar Youyi Qianqi, China 72/C2
Qahar Youyi Zhongqi, China 72/C2
Qaidam (basin), China 70/F4
Qalansuwa, Isr. 91/F7
Qal'at Al Andalus, Tun. 46/B4
Qal'at Dizah, Iraq 90/F2
Qal'eh-ye Now, Afg. 87/D6
Qalqīlyah, WBnk. 91/F7
Qalyūb, Egypt 91/B4
Qamdo, China 70/G5
Qamīnis, Libya 96/K1
Qandahār, Afg. 89/J2
Qapshagay Bögeni (res.), Kaz. 87/G4
Qapshaghay, Kaz. 87/G4
Qaraghandy, Kaz. 87/F3
Qaraghandy (obl.), Kaz. 87/F3
Qarataū, Kaz. 87/F4
Qarataū Zhotasy (mts.), Kaz. 87/E4
Qareh Chāy (riv.), Iran 88/E2
Qareh Sū (riv.), Iran 63/H5
Qarqan (riv.), China 70/E4
Qarrit (pass), Alb. 47/G2
Qarshi, Uzb. 87/E5
Qārūn (lake), Egypt 101/B2
Qashqadaryo (pol. reg.), Uzb. 87/D5
Qaşr-e Qand, Iran 89/H3
Qaşr-e-Shīrīn, Iran 88/E2
Qaşr Hallāl, Tun. 46/B5
Qa'ṭabah, Yem. 88/D6
Qatar (ctry.) 88/F3
Qattara (depr.), Egypt 90/A4
Qaţţīnah, Buḩayrat (lake), Syria 91/E2
Qaydaq Sory (swamp), Kaz. 63/K3
Qayyārah, Iraq 90/E3
Qazaqtyng Usaqshoqylyghy (uplands), Kaz. 64/H5
Qāzi Ahmad, Pak. 82/A2
Qazvīn, Iran 88/F1
Qedma, Isr. 91/F8
Qendrevica (peak), Alb. 47/F2
Qezel Owzan (riv.), Iran 88/E1
Qi Xian, China 72/C4
Qian (mts.), China 73/B2
Qian (riv.), China 72/D5
Qian'an, China 71/M3
Qianxi, China 72/J6
Qianyang, China 79/B2
Qiaojia, China 83/H2
Qibyā, Isr. 91/G8
Qidong, China 83/K2
Qidong, China 72/L8
Qiemo, China 70/E4
Qihe, China 72/D3
Qijiang, China 79/A2
Qikiqtarjuaq, Nun., Can. 123/K2
Qila Dīdār Singh, Pak. 86/C3
Qila Sobha Singh, Pak. 86/C3
Qilian (peak), China 70/G4
Qilian (mts.), China 67/J6
Qimantag (mts.), China 70/F4
Qimen, China 79/C2
Qin (mts.), China 72/B4
Qinā (gov.), Egypt 101/C3
Qing (riv.), China 79/B1
Qing'an, China 71/N2
Qingdao, China 72/E3
Qingfeng, China 72/C4
Qinghai (mts.), China 70/G4
Qinghai (prov.), China 70/G4
Qinghe, China 72/C3
Qinglong, China 72/D2
Qingpu, China 72/L8
Qingshui (riv.), China 79/A2
Qingshuihe, China 72/B3
Qingyuan, China 83/K3
Qingyun, China 72/D3
Qingzhou, China 72/D3
Qinhuangdao, China 72/D3
Qinshui, China 72/C4
Qinyang, China 72/C4
Qinyuan, China 72/C3
Qinzhou, China 83/J3
Qionghai, China 83/K4
Qionglai (mts.), China 70/H5
Qiongshan, China 83/K4
Qiongzhong, China 78/E2
Qiqihar, China 71/M2
Qira, China 70/D4
Qiryat Ata, Isr. 91/G6
Qiryat Bialik, Isr. 91/G6
Qiryat Gat, Isr. 91/D4
Qiryat Mal'akhi, Isr. 91/F8
Qiryat Motzkin, Isr. 91/G6
Qiryat Shemona, Isr. 91/D3
Qiryat Tiv'on, Isr. 91/G6
Qiryat Yam, Isr. 91/G6
Qitai, China 70/E3
Qitaihe, China 71/P2
Qixia, China 72/E3
Qixing (riv.), China 65/P5
Qizilqum (des.), Kaz. 64/G5
Qogir (peak), China 89/L1
Qom (riv.), Iran 88/F2
Qom, Iran 88/F2
Qomsheh, Iran 88/F2
Qondūz (riv.), Afg. 89/J1
Qonggyai, China 85/H1
Qoraqalpoghiston Aut. Rep., Uzb. 63/L3
Qormi, Malta 46/L7
Qorveh, Iran 88/E1
Qostanay (obl.), Kaz. 87/D2
Qostanay (int'l arpt.), Kaz. 61/P5
Qostanay, Kaz. 61/P5
Qoţūr, Iran 90/F2
Qu (riv.), China 71/L6
Quabbin (res.), Ma, US 131/F3
Quairading, Austl. 112/C5
Quakenbrück, Ger. 51/E3
Quakertown, Pa, US 138/C3
Quambatook, Austl. 115/B2
Quanah, Tx, US 129/H4
Quanbao (mtn.), China 72/B4
Quang Ngai, Viet. 78/E3
Quang Tri, Viet. 78/D2
Quanjiao, China 72/D4
Quannan, China 79/B3
Quantocks, The (hills), Eng, UK 32/C4
Quanzhou, China 79/C3
Qu'appelle (dam), Sk, Can. 127/G3
Qu'appelle (riv.), Sk, Can. 127/G3
Qu'appelle, Sk, Can. 127/H3
Quaqtaq, Qu, Can. 123/K2
Quaregnon, Belg. 52/C3
Quarles (mts.), Indo. 81/E4
Quarona, It. 58/B1
Quarrata, It. 59/D5
Quarryville, Pa, US 138/B4
Quarto d'Altino, It. 59/F1
Quartu Sant'Elena, It. 46/A3
Quartz Hill, Ca, US 136/B1
Quatre Bornes, Mrts. 107/T15
Quattervals (peak), Swi. 57/G4
Quba, Azer. 63/J4
Qūchān, Iran 89/G1
Queanbeyan, Austl. 115/D2
Québec (int'l arpt.), Qu, Can. 131/G2
Québec (cap.), Qu, Can. 131/G2
Québec (prov.), Can. 123/J3
Quebra-Cangalha, Serra (mts.), Braz. 211/H8
Quecholac, Mex. 143/M8
Quechutenango, Mex. 143/F5
Quedal (pt.), Chile 158/B4
Queen Alia (int'l arpt.), Jor. 91/E4
Queen Anne, Md, US 138/C6
Queen Annes (co.), Md, US 138/C5
Queen Charlotte (str.), BC, Can. 126/B3
Queen Charlotte, BC, Can. 134/M5
Queen Charlotte (isls.), BC, Can. 122/C3
Queen Charlotte (sound), BC, Can. 122/C3
Queen City, Tx, US 129/J4
Queen Creek, Az, US 137/S19
Queen Elizabeth (isls.), NW,Nun., Can. 123/Q7
Queen Mary (coast), Ant. 160/G
Queen Mary (res.), Eng, UK 30/B2
Queen Mary, Ca, US 136/F8
Queen Maud (gulf), Nun., Can. 122/F2
Queen Maud (mts.), Ant. 160/P
Queen Maud Land (phys. reg.), Ant. 160/Z
Queen Victoria Spring Nature Reserve, Austl. 112/D4
Queens (chan.), Nun., Can. 123/S7
Queens (co.), NY, US 139/E2
Queensberry (peak), Sc, UK 36/C6
Queensferry, Sc, UK 36/C5
Queensland, Austl. 115/B1
Queensland (state), Austl. 109/C3
Queenstown, Austl. 115/C4
Queenstown, SAfr. 106/D3
Queenstown, NZ 117/R12
Queenstown, Md, US 138/B6
Queich (riv.), Ger. 53/H5
Queidersbach, Ger. 53/G5
Queilén, Chile 158/B4
Queimada, Ilha (isl.), Braz. 151/H4
Queimadas, Braz. 154/D2
Queimadas, Braz. 154/C3
Quelimane, Moz. 105/G4
Queluz, Port. 45/P10
Quemado, Punta del (pt.), Cuba 145/H1
Quemú Quemú, Arg. 158/E3
Quepos, CR 145/E4
Quequén, Arg. 158/F3
Quequén Grande (riv.), Arg. 158/F3
Querecotillo, Peru 156/A2
Querétaro, Mex. 143/E4
Querétaro de Arteaga (state), Mex. 140/A5
Querimbas, Arquipélago das (arch.), Moz. 105/H3
Quero, It. 59/E1
Querobabi, Mex. 142/C2
Quesada, Sp. 44/D4
Quesada, CR 145/E4
Queshan, China 72/C4
Quesnel, BC, Can. 126/C2
Quesnel (lake), BC, Can. 122/D3
Quesnoy-sur-Deûle, Fr. 52/C2
Questa, NM, US 129/F3
Questembert, Fr. 42/B3
Quetigny, Fr. 56/B3
Quetta, Pak. 89/J2
Queulat, PN, Chile 158/B5
Quevedo, Ecu. 150/C4
Quevedo (riv.), Ecu. 152/B5
Quezaltenango, Guat. 144/D3
Quezon, Phil. 81/E2
Quezon City, Phil. 79/D5
Qufu, China 72/D4
Qui Nhon, Viet. 78/E3
Quibdó, Col. 152/B3
Quiberon, Fr. 42/B3
Quiberon (bay), Fr. 42/B3
Quíbor, Ven. 152/D2
Quicacha, Peru 156/C4
Quiçama, PN da, Ang. 105/B2
Quickborn, Ger. 51/G1
Quiers, Fr. 30/L6
Quierschied, Ger. 53/G5
Quila, Mex. 142/D3
Quilán (cape), Chile 158/B4
Quilca, Peru 156/C5
Quilcene, Wa, US 135/B2
Quiliano, It. 58/B4
Quilicura, Chile 158/N8
Quill (lakes), Sk, Can. 127/G2
Quillabamba, Peru 156/C4
Quillacollo, Bol. 150/E7
Quillagua (pt.), Chile 158/B4
Quillan, Fr. 42/E5
Quilleco, Chile 158/C3
Quillota, Chile 158/N8
Quilmaná, Peru 156/B4
Quilon, India 82/C6
Quilpie, Austl. 114/B4
Quilpué, Chile 158/N8
Quimilí, Arg. 157/D2
Quimper, Fr. 42/A2
Quimperlé, Fr. 42/B3
Quincey, Fr. 56/C2
Quincy, Wa, US 126/D4
Quincy, Fl, US 133/G4
Quincy, Ma, US 131/G3
Quincy-sous-Sénart, Fr. 30/K5
Quincy-Voisins, Fr. 30/L5
Quindío (dept.), Col. 152/A4
Quinhagak, Ak, US 134/F4
Quinn (riv.), Nv, US 128/C2
Quinns Rocks, Austl. 112/K6
Quintana de la Serena, Sp. 44/C3
Quintana Roo (state), Mex. 140/D4
Quintanar de la Orden, Sp. 44/D3
Quintanar del Rey, Sp. 44/E3
Quintero, Chile 158/N8
Quinto, Sp. 45/E2
Quinto, Swi. 57/E4
Quinto (riv.), Arg. 158/D2
Quinto di Treviso, It. 59/F1
Quinto di Valpantena, It. 59/E2
Quinton, NJ, US 138/C4
Quinzano d'Oglio, It. 58/C2
Quionga, Moz. 104/D5
Quipapá, Braz. 154/C3
Quirihue, Chile 158/B3
Quirindi, Austl. 115/D1
Quirinópolis, Braz. 155/B1
Quiriquire, Ven. 153/F2
Quiroga, Mex. 143/E5
Quiroga, Sp. 44/B1
Quiruvilca, Peru 156/B3
Quisiro, Ven. 152/D2
Quispamsis, NB, Can. 131/H2
Quissico, Moz. 105/F5
Quistello, It. 59/D3
Quitilipi, Arg. 157/D2
Quitman, Ga, US 133/H4
Quitman, Ms, US 133/F3
Quito (cap.), Ecu. 152/B5
Quixeramobim, Braz. 154/C2
Qujing, China 83/K3
Qujing, China 83/H2
Qulaybīyah, Tun. 46/B4
Quogue, NY, US 139/F2
Quoich (riv.), Nun., Can. 122/G2
Quoich (lake), Sc, UK 36/A2
Quoile (riv.), NI, UK 34/C3
Quoin (pt.), SAfr. 106/L11
Quorn, Austl. 113/H5
Qūqon, Uzb. 87/F4
Quranbāliyah, Tun. 46/B4
Qurbah, Tun. 46/B4
Qūrghonteppa, Taj. 89/J1
Qurnat as Sawdā' (peak), Leb. 91/E2
Qūş, Egypt 101/C3
Qusmuryn Köli (lake), Kaz. 87/D2
Qusum, China 70/F6
Quşūr As Sāf, Tun. 46/B5
Quttinirpaaq NP, Nun., Can. 123/T6
Quwo, China 72/B4
Quwu (mts.), China 70/H4
Quyang, China 72/C3
Quzhou, China 79/C2
Quzhou, China 72/C3
Qyzylorda, Kaz. 87/D4
Qyzylorda (obl.), Kaz. 87/D4

R

Raab (riv.), Aus. 43/L3
Raab, Aus. 55/G6
Raabs an der Thaya, Aus. 41/H4
Raahe, Fin. 60/E2
Raalte, Neth. 50/D4
Raamsdonk, Neth. 50/B5
Ra'ananna, Isr. 91/F7
Raanes (pen.), Nun., Can. 123/S7
Rab (isl.), Cro. 48/B3
Rab, Cro. 48/B3
Rába (riv.), Hun. 48/C2
Rábahidvég, Hun. 43/M3
Rabat (cap.), Mor. 100/A2
Rabat, Malta 46/L7
Rabat (Sale) (int'l arpt.), Mor. 100/A2
Rabat (Victoria), Malta 46/L6
Rabbi (riv.), It. 43/K4
Rabgala (pass), China 85/F2
Rabil, CpV. 93/K10
Rabinal, Guat. 144/D3
Rabiusa (riv.), Swi. 57/F4
Rabka, Pol. 41/K4
Rabkavi-Banhatti, India 89/L5
Raby (pt.), On, Can. 131/S8
Racconigi, It. 43/G4
Raccoon (pt.), La, US 129/K5
Rach Gia (bay), Viet. 78/D4
Rach Gia, Viet. 78/D4
Racibórz, Pol. 41/K3
Racine, Wi, US 127/M5
Racine (peak), Swi. 56/C3
Racine (co.), Wi, US 135/P14
Rada Tilly, Arg. 158/D5
Radaur, India 86/D4
Rădăuţi, Rom. 49/G2
Radbuza (riv.), Czh. 40/G4
Radcliffe, Eng, UK 35/F4
Raddestorf, Ger. 51/F4
Rade de Caen (bay), Fr. 42/C2
Radeč (peak), Czh. 55/G3
Radevormwald, Ger. 51/E6
Radisson, Sk, Can. 126/G2
Radlett, Eng, UK 30/C2
Radnice, Czh. 55/G3
Radolfzell, Ger. 57/E2
Radom (prov.), Pol. 41/L3
Radom, Pol. 41/L3
Radomir, Bul. 47/H1
Radomsko, Pol. 41/K3
Radoviš, FYROM 47/H2
Radovljica, Slov. 43/L3
Radøy (isl.), Nor. 38/A1
Radstadt, Aus. 43/K3
Radviliškis, Lith. 39/K4
Radwá, Jabal (peak), SAr. 88/C4
Radziejów, Pol. 41/K2
Radzymin, Pol. 41/L2
Radzyń Podlaski, Pol. 41/M3
Rae (isth.), Nun., Can. 123/H2
Rae (riv.), Nun., Can. 122/E2
Rāe Bareli, India 84/C2
Rae-Edzo, NW, Can. 122/E2
Raeford, NC, US 133/J3
Raeren, Belg. 53/F2
Raesfeld, Ger. 50/D5
Raeside (lake), Austl. 112/D4
Rafael J. García, Mex. 143/M7
Rafael Núñez (int'l arpt.), Col. 152/C2
Rafaela, Arg. 157/D3
Rafaḩ, Gaza 91/D4
Rafai, CAfr. 97/K7
Rafīdīyah, WBnk. 91/G7
Rafiganj, India 85/E3
Rafína, Gre. 47/P8
Rafsanjān, Iran 89/G2
Raft (riv.), Id, US 126/E5
Rafz, Swi. 57/E2
Ragang (mt.), Phil. 81/F2
Ragged (mt.), Austl. 112/D5
Ragged (pt.), Chile 159/B7
Rāghugarh, India 84/A3
Raghunāthpur, India 85/F4
Rago NP, Nor. 37/E2
Ragstone (range), Eng, UK 30/D3
Ragusa, It. 46/D4
Rāhatgarh, India 84/B4
Rahden, Ger. 51/F4
Rahīmyār Khān, Pak. 86/A5
Rahole Nat'l Rsv., Kenya 104/C2
Råholt, Nor. 38/D1
Rāhuri, India 82/B4
Rahway, NJ, US 139/H9
Raiatea (isl.), FrPol. 117/K6
Raichūr, India 82/C4
Raiganj, India 85/F3
Raigarh, India 84/D5
Raikot, India 86/C4
Railroad, Pa, US 138/B4
Railroad Canyon (res.), Ca, US 136/C3
Rainbach im Mühlkreis, Aus. 55/H5
Rainbow, Austl. 115/B2
Rainbow (valley), Az, US 137/R19
Rainbow, Ca, US 136/C4
Rainbow Beach, Austl. 114/D4
Rainbow Bridge Nat'l Mon., Ut, US 128/E3
Rainier (mt.), Wa, US 126/C4
Rainsville, Al, US 133/G3
Rainy (lake), On, Can. 122/G4
Rainy Lake (riv.), US,Can. 127/K3
Rainy River, On, Can. 127/K3
Raipur, India 82/D3
Rairoa (atoll), FrPol. 117/L6
Raisdorf, Ger. 38/D4
Raisen, India 84/A4
Rāisinghnagar, India 86/B5
Raisio, Fin. 39/K1
Raismes, Fr. 52/C3
Raivavae (isl.), FrPol. 117/L7
Rāiwind, Pak. 86/C4
Raizeux, Fr. 30/H6
Rāj Gāngpur, India 85/E4
Raja (pt.), Indo. 80/A3
Raja Jang, Pak. 86/C4
Rājahmundry, India 82/D4
Rājampet, India 82/C5
Rajang (riv.), Malay. 80/D3
Rājanpur, Pak. 86/A5
Rājaori, India 86/C3
Rājapālaiyam, India 82/C6
Rājāpur, India 84/C3
Rājāpur, India 89/K5
Rājasthān (state), India 82/B2
Rājbirāj, Nepal 85/F2
Rājgarh, India 84/A2
Rājgarh, India 86/C5
Rājgarh, India 84/A4
Rājgīr, India 85/E3
Rajka, Hun. 48/C1
Rājkot, India 89/K4
Rājmahal (hills), India 85/F3
Rājmahal, India 85/F3
Rājpur, India 85/G4
Rājpura, India 86/D4
Rājshāhi (pol. reg.), Bang. 85/G3
Rājshāhi (pol. div.), Bang. 85/G3
Rājshāhi, Bang. 85/G3
Rājula, India 89/K4
Raka (riv.), China 85/F1
Rakahanga (isl.), Cookls. 117/J5
Rakamaz, Hun. 48/E1
Rakaposhi (peak), Pak. 86/C1
Rakhine (div.), Myan. 70/F8
Rakhine (state), Myan. 83/F4
Rakhshān (riv.), Pak. 89/H3
Rakkestad, Nor. 38/D2
Rakos-patak (riv.), Hun. 49/R9
Rakovnicky Potok (riv.), Czh. 55/G2
Rakovník, Czh. 55/G2
Rakovski, Bul. 47/J1
Rakushechnyy (cape), Kaz. 87/B4
Rakvere, Est. 39/M2
Raldon, It. 59/E2
Raleigh (cap.), NC, US 133/J3
Raleigh-Durham (int'l arpt.), NC, US 133/J3
Ralik Chain (isls.), Mrsh. 116/F4
Ralingen, Ger. 53/F4
Ralston, Ab, Can. 126/F3
Rām Allāh, Isr. 91/G8
Ramalho, Serra do (mts.), Braz. 151/K6
Ramapo (riv.), NJ, US 138/J7
Ramapo (mts.), NJ, US 139/H7
Ramat Gan, Isr. 91/F7
Ramat Hasharon, Isr. 91/F7
Rambervillers, Fr. 56/C1
Rame (pt.), Eng, UK 32/B6
Ramenskoye, Rus. 61/X9
Rāmeswaram, India 82/C6
Rāmgangā (riv.), India 84/B1
Rāmgarh, India 85/E4
Rāmhormoz, Iran 88/E2
Ramírez, Mex. 143/M7
Rāmjībanpur, India 85/F4
Ramla, Isr. 91/F8
Ramlu (peak), Erit. 88/D6
Ramme, Den. 38/C3
Rammūn, Isr. 91/G8
Rāmnagar, India 84/B1
Rāmnagar, India 84/D3
Rāmnagar, India 86/C3
Ramnäs, Swe. 38/G2
Ramonchamp, Fr. 56/C2
Ramor (lake), Ire. 34/A4
Ramos (riv.), Mex. 132/B5
Ramosch, Swi. 57/G4
Rampart, Ak, US 134/H2
Rampillon, Fr. 30/M6
Rāmpur, India 84/B1
Rāmpur, India 86/D4
Rāmpur Hāt, India 85/F3
Rāmpura Phūl, India 86/C4
Ramree (isl.), Myan. 83/F4
Rāmsanehīghāt, India 84/C2
Ramsbottom, Eng, UK 35/F4
Ramsden Heath, Eng, UK 30/E2
Ramsen, Swi. 57/E2
Ramsey (lake), On, Can. 130/D2
Ramsey (isl.), Wal, UK 32/A3
Ramsey, NJ, US 139/J7
Ramsey, IM, UK 34/D3
Ramsey (bay), IM, UK 34/D3
Ramsgate, Eng, UK 33/H4
Ramstein-Miesenbach, Ger. 53/G5
Ramu (riv.), PNG 116/D5
Rana, Nor. 37/E2
Rānāghāt, India 85/G4
Rancagua, Chile 158/N9
Rance (riv.), Fr. 42/C2
Rancharia, Braz. 155/B2
Rancheria (riv.), Col. 152/C2
Rānchī, India 85/E4
Rancho Palos Verdes, Ca, US 136/F8
Rancho Santa Fe, Ca, US 136/C4
Ranchos, Arg. 158/F2
Ranco (lake), Chile 158/B4
Rancocas, NJ, US 138/D4
Rancul, Arg. 158/D2
Randaberg, Nor. 38/A2
Randallstown, Md, US 138/B5
Randalstown, NI, UK 34/B2
Randazzo, It. 46/D4
Randburg, SAfr. 106/P13
Randers, Den. 38/D3
Randolph, NJ, US 138/D2
Randow (riv.), Ger. 41/H2
Randsfjorden (lake), Nor. 38/D1
Råneå, Swe. 60/D2
Rang (peak), Thai. 78/C2
Rang-du-Fliers, Fr. 52/A3
Rāngāmāti (pol. reg.), Bang. 85/H4
Rāngāmāti, Bang. 83/F3
Rangasa (cape), Indo. 81/E4
Rangely, Co, US 128/E2
Ranger, Tx, US 129/H4
Rangia, India 85/H2
Rangiora, NZ 117/S11
Rangiroa (isl.), FrPol. 117/L6
Rangoon (Yangon) (cap.), Myan. 83/G4
Rangpur, Bang. 85/G3
Rangpur (pol. reg.), Bang. 85/G3
Rangsdorf, Ger. 40/Q7
Rānībennur, India 89/L6
Rānīganj, India 85/F4
Rānīkhet, India 84/B1
Rānīpur, India 84/B3
Rankin, Tx, US 129/G5
Rankin Inlet, Nun., Can. 122/G2
Rankweil, Aus. 57/F3
Rannoch (lake), Sc, UK 36/B3
Ranohira, Madg. 107/H8
Ranomafana, Madg. 107/H8
Ranong, Thai. 78/B4
Ranotsara, Madg. 107/H8
Ransbach-Baumbach, Ger. 53/G3
Ransomville, NY, US 131/S9
Ranst, Belg. 50/B6
Ranstadt, Ger. 54/B2
Rantabe, Madg. 107/J6
Rantekombola (peak), Indo. 81/F4
Rantigny, Fr. 52/B5
Rantīs, WBnk. 91/G7
Rantoul, Il, US 127/L5
Rantsila, Fin. 60/E2
Ranzan, Japan 77/C1
Rao Co (peak), Laos 78/D2
Raon-l'Étape, Fr. 56/C1
Raoping, China 79/C3
Raoui, 'Erg er (des.), Alg. 98/E3
Raoul (isl.), NZ 116/H7
Raoyang (riv.), China 73/A2
Raoyang, China 72/C3
Rapa (isl.), FrPol. 117/L7
Rapallo, It. 58/C4
Rapel (lake), Chile 158/N9
Rapid City, SD, US 127/H4
Rappahannock (riv.), Va, US 130/E4
Rapper (cape), Chile 158/B5
Rāpti (zone), Nepal 84/D1
Rapti (riv.), India 82/D2
Rara NP, Nepal 84/D1
Raritan (bay), NJ, US 138/D3
Raritan (riv.), NJ, US 138/D2
Raritan, South Branch (riv.), NJ, US 138/D2
Raron, Swi. 56/D5
Rarotonga (isl.), Cookls. 117/J7
Ra's al 'Ayn, Syria 90/E2
Ra's al Basīt (pt.), Syria 91/D2
Ra's Al Jabal, Tun. 46/B4
Ra's al Khaymah, UAE 89/G3
Ra's al Unūf, Libya 97/J7
Ra's An Naqb, Jor. 91/D5
Ra's aţ Ţīb (Cape Bon) (cape), Tun. 46/B4
Ras Dashen (peak), Eth. 97/N5
Râs el Ma, Alg. 100/D2
Râs el Oued, Alg. 100/H5
Ras il-Qammieħ (pt.), Malta 46/L7
Ras San Dimitri (pt.), Malta 46/L6
Ra's Şawqirah (pt.), Oman 89/G5
Rasa (pt.), Arg. 158/E4
Raschau, Ger. 55/F1
Rashaant, Mong. 70/F2
Rasharkin, NI, UK 34/B2
Rāshayyā, Leb. 91/D3
Rashīd, Egypt 91/B4
Rasht, Iran 88/E1
Raška, Yugo. 47/G1
Rasmussen (basin), Nun., Can. 122/G2
Raso (cape), Port. 45/P10
Rason (lake), Austl. 109/B3
Rasrā, India 84/D3
Rassina, It. 59/E5
Rasskazovo, Rus. 63/G1
Rastatt, Ger. 54/B5
Rastede, Ger. 51/F2
Rasūlnagar, Pak. 86/B3
Rat (isls.), Ak, US 134/B6
Rat Buri, Thai. 78/B3
Rata (cape), Indo. 80/B5
Ratak Chain (isls.), Mrsh. 116/F3
Ratangarh, India 89/K3
Ratanpur, India 84/D4
Rāth, India 84/B3
Rathbun (lake), Ia, US 127/K5
Rathcoole, Ire. 34/B5
Rathdowney, Ire. 31/Q10
Rathdrum, Ire. 34/B6
Rathedaung, Myan. 83/F3
Rathenow, Ger. 40/G2
Rathfriland, NI, UK 34/B3
Rathkeale, Ire. 31/P10
Rathlin (isl.), NI, UK 34/B1
Rathlin (sound), NI, UK 34/B1
Rathluirc, Ire. 31/P10
Rathmore, Ire. 31/P10
Rathnew, Ire. 34/B6
Ratia, India 86/C5
Ratingen, Ger. 50/D6
Ratlām, India 89/L4
Ratnāgiri, India 89/K5
Ratnapura, SrL. 82/D6
Ratoath, Ire. 34/B4
Raton, NM, US 128/F3
Rattray (pt.), Sc, UK 36/E1
Rättvik, Swe. 38/F1
Raub, Malay. 80/B3
Rauch, Arg. 158/F3
Raudales Malpaso, Mex. 144/C2

219
Raudh – Rober

Raudhinúpur (pt.), Ice. 37/P6
Raufarhöfn, Ice. 37/P6
Raufoss, Nor. 38/D1
Rauhe Ebrach (riv.), Ger. 54/D3
Raul Soares, Braz. 155/D2
Rauma, Fin. 39/J1
Raunheim, Ger. 54/B2
Raurkela, India 85/E4
Rausu, Japan 76/D1
Rautjärvi, Fin. 39/N1
Ravanusa, It. 46/C4
Rāvar, Iran 89/G2
Ravarino, It. 59/E3
Ravels, Belg. 50/B6
Ravenna, It. 59/F4
Ravenna (prov.), It. 59/E4
Ravenna, Ca, US 136/B2
Ravensburg, Ger. 57/F2
Ravensdale, Wa, US 135/D3
Ravenshoe, Austl. 114/B2
Ravensthorpe, Austl. 112/D5
Ravenswood, WV, US 130/D4
Rāvi (riv.), Ind.,Pak. 89/K2
Ravne na Koroškem, Slov. 43/L3
Rawa Mazowiecka, Pol. 41/L3
Rāwah, Iraq 90/E3
Rawaki (Phoenix) (isl.), Kiri. 117/H5
Rāwalpindi, Pak. 86/B3
Rāwatsār, India 86/C5
Rawicz, Pol. 41/J3
Rawlins, Wy, US 126/G5
Rawlinson (mt.), Austl. 113/E3
Rawmarsh, Eng, UK 35/G5
Rawson, Arg. 158/D4
Rawtenstall, Eng, UK 35/F4
Raxaul Bazar, India 85/E2
Ray (cape), Nf, Can. 131/K2
Raya (peak), Indo. 80/D4
Rāyadrug, India 82/C5
Raychikhinsk, Rus. 71/N2
Rayleigh, Eng, UK 33/G3
Raymond, Ab, Can. 126/E3
Raymond, Wa, US 126/C4
Raymond, Co, US 137/B2
Raymond, Wi, US 135/P14
Raymondville, Tx, US 132/D5
Raymore, Sk, Can. 127/G3
Raymore, Mo, US 137/E6
Rayón, Mex. 143/F4
Rayón, Mex. 142/C2
Rayón, Mex. 143/Q10
Rayón, PN, Mex. 143/E5
Rayong, Thai. 78/C3
Raytown, Mo, US 137/E5
Rayville, La, US 129/K4
Raz, Pointe de (pt.),Fr. 42/A2
Razelm (lake), Rom. 49/J3
Razgrad, Bul. 49/H4
Razlog, Bul. 47/H2
Re di Castello (peak), It. 57/G5
Ré, Île de (isl.), Fr. 42/C3
Rea (riv.), Eng, UK 32/D1
Reading, Eng, UK 33/F4
Reading, Pa, US 138/C3
Realicó, Arg. 158/D2
Realp, Swi. 57/E4
Reamstown, Pa, US 138/B3
Reao (isl.), FrPol. 117/M6
Réau, Fr. 30/K6
Rebais, Fr. 52/C6
Rebecca (lake), Austl. 109/B4
Rębiechowo (int'l arpt.), Pol. 38/H4
Rebouças, Braz. 155/B3
Rebstein, Swi. 57/F3
Rebun, Japan 76/B1
Recanati, It. 59/G6
Recco, It. 58/C4
Recherche (arch.), Austl. 109/B4
Rechnitz, Aus. 43/M3
Rechthalten, Swi. 56/D4
Rechytsa, Bela. 62/D1
Recife (cape), SAfr. 106/D4
Recke, Ger. 51/E4
Reckingen, Swi. 57/E5
Recklinghausen, Ger. 51/E5
Recknitz (riv.), Ger. 40/G2
Réclère, Swi. 56/C3
Recoaro Terme, It. 59/E1
Reconquista, Arg. 157/E2
Reconvilier, Swi. 56/D3
Recuay, Peru 156/B3
Red (sea), Afr.,Asia 67/C7
Red (riv.), Mb, Can. 127/J3
Red (riv.), China,Vie 70/H7
Red (riv.), US 129/J5
Red (riv.), La, US 140/C1
Red (riv.), Mn, US 125/G2
Red (lakes), Mn, US 122/G4
Red (bay), NI, UK 34/B1
Red (riv.), Viet. 83/H3
Red Bank, NJ, US 138/D3
Red Bluff (lake), Tx, US 129/G5
Red Bluff, Ca, US 128/B2
Red Cliffs, Austl. 115/B2
Red Cloud, Ne, US 129/H2
Red Deer, Ab, Can. 126/E2
Red Deer (riv.), Sk, Can. 122/E3
Red Devil, Ak, US 134/G3
Red Hill (peak), Hi, US 124/T10
Red Hill, Pa, US 138/C3
Red Indian (lake), Nf, Can. 131/K1
Red Lake (riv.), Mn, US 127/K3
Red Lake, On, Can. 127/K3
Red Lion, De, US 138/C4
Red Lion, Pa, US 138/B4
Red Lodge, Mt, US 126/F4
Red, North Fork (riv.), US 129/G4
Red River of the North (riv.), US,Can. 127/J3
Red Rock (lake), Ia, US 127/K5
Red Rocks (pt.), Austl. 113/E5
Red Sea (hills), Sudan 93/F2
Red Volta (riv.), Burk. 103/E4
Red Wing, Mn, US 127/K4
Reda, Pol. 38/H4
Redange-sur-Attert, Lux. 53/E4
Redbridge (bor.), Eng, UK 30/D2
Redcar, Eng, UK 35/G2
Redcar and Cleveland (co.), Eng, UK 35/G2
Redcliff, Ab, Can. 126/F3
Redcliffe (mt.), Austl. 112/D4
Redden, De, US 138/C6
Reddersburg, SAfr. 106/D3
Redding, Ca, US 128/B2
Redding, Ct, US 139/E1
Redditch, Eng, UK 33/E2
Rede (riv.), Eng, UK 35/F1
Redenção do Gurguéia, Braz. 154/A3
Redfield, SD, US 127/J4
Redford, Mi, US 135/F7
Redhill, Eng, UK 30/C3
Rédics, Hun. 48/C2
Redland, Md, US 138/A5
Redlands, Ca, US 136/C2
Redmond, Or, US 126/C4
Rednitz (riv.), Ger. 54/D4
Redon, Fr. 42/B3
Redondela, Sp. 44/A1
Redondo, Port. 44/B3
Redondo, Wa, US 135/C3
Redondo Beach, Ca, US 136/F8
Redoubt (vol.), Ak, US 134/H3
Redstone (riv.), NW, Can. 122/D2
Redvers, Sk, Can. 127/H3
Redwater, Ab, Can. 126/E2
Redway, Ca, US 126/C5
Redwood Falls, Mn, US 127/K4
Redwood NP, Ca, US 128/A2
Ree, Lough (lake), Ire. 31/P10
Reed City, Mi, US 130/C3
Reeding, Ok, US 137/M14
Reedley, Ca, US 128/C3
Reeds (bay), NJ, US 138/D5
Reedsburg, Wi, US 127/L5
Reef (pt.), Belz. 143/J5
Reef (isls.), Sol. 116/F6
Reefton, NZ 117/S11
Rees, Ger. 50/D5
Reese (riv.), Nv, US 124/C4
Reessum, Ger. 51/G2
Reest (riv.), Neth. 50/D3
Reeuwijk, Neth. 50/B4
Refahiye, Turk. 90/D2
Reforma, Mex. 144/C2
Refugio, Tx, US 132/D4
Rega (riv.), Pol. 38/F5
Regen, Ger. 55/G5
Regen (riv.), Ger. 55/F4
Regência, Pontal da (pt.), Braz. 155/E1
Regeneração, Braz. 154/B2
Regensburg, Ger. 55/F4
Regensdorf, Swi. 57/E3
Regenstauf, Ger. 55/F4
Reggane, Alg. 99/F4
Regge (riv.), Neth. 50/D4
Reggello, It. 59/E5
Reggio, La, US 137/Q17
Reggio di Calabria (prov.), It. 46/D3
Reggio di Calabria, It. 46/D3
Reggio nell' Emilia (prov.), It. 58/D3
Reggio nell'Emilia, It. 58/D3
Reggiolo, It. 59/D3
Reghin, Rom. 49/G2
Regina (cap.), Sk, Can. 127/G3
Régina, FrG. 151/H3
Regina, NM, US 132/B2
Regina Beach, Sk, Can. 127/G3
Región Metropolitana (pol. reg.), Chile 158/B1
Registro, Braz. 155/C3
Regnitz (riv.), Ger. 43/J2
Regoledo, It. 57/F5
Reguengos de Monsaraz, Port. 44/B3
Rehau, Ger. 55/F2
Rehburg-Loccum, Ger. 51/G4
Rehfelde, Ger. 40/Q6
Rehlī, India 84/B4
Rehling, Ger. 54/D6
Rehlingen-Siersburg, Ger. 53/F5
Rehoboth, Namb. 105/C5
Réhon, Fr. 53/E4
Reḥovot, Isr. 91/F8
Rehrersburg, Pa, US 138/B3
Reichelsheim, Ger. 54/B2
Reichelsheim, Ger. 54/B3
Reichenbach, Ger. 55/F1
Reichenbach im Kandertal, Swi. 56/D4
Reichenbach-Steegen, Ger. 53/G4
Reichenberg, Ger. 54/C3
Reichertshausen, Ger. 55/E6
Reichshof, Ger. 53/G2
Reichshoffen, Fr. 53/G6
Reichstett, Fr. 53/G6
Reid (lake), Sk, Can. 126/F3
Reiden, Swi. 56/D3
Reigate, Eng, UK 30/C3
Reignier, Fr. 56/C5
Reims, Fr. 52/D5
Reina Adelaida (arch.), Chile 157/A7
Reina Beatrix (int'l arpt.), NAnt. 152/D1
Reinach, Swi. 56/D3
Reinach, Swi. 56/E3
Reinbek, Ger. 51/H1
Reindeer (isl.), Mb, Can. 127/J2
Reindeer (lake), Mb,Sk, Can. 122/F3
Reindeer (riv.), Sk, Can. 127/H1
Reinerton-Orwin-Muir, Pa, US 138/B2
Reinheim, Ger. 54/B3
Reinosa, Sp. 44/C1
Reinsfeld, Ger. 53/F4
Reischach, Ger. 55/F6
Reisdorf, Lux. 53/F4
Reisduoddarhal'di (peak), Nor. 37/G1
Reiskirchen, Ger. 54/B1
Reisterstown, Md, US 138/B5
Reitdiep (riv.), Neth. 50/D2
Reitz, SAfr. 106/E2
Rejón (int'l arpt.), Mex. 144/D1
Rekkam (plat.), Mor. 100/C2
Reliance, NW, Can. 122/F2
Relizane (prov.), Alg. 100/F5
Relizane, Alg. 100/F5
Rellingen, Ger. 51/G1
Remagen, Ger. 53/G2
Remanso, Braz. 154/B3
Remanzacco, It. 59/G1
Remarde (riv.), Fr. 30/H6
Remarkable (mt.), Austl. 113/H5
Rembang, Indo. 80/D5
Remchi, Alg. 100/D2
Remedios, Pan. 145/F4
Remich, Lux. 53/F4
Remicourt, Belg. 53/E2
Rémire, FrG. 151/H3
Remiremont, Fr. 56/C1
Remlingen, Ger. 51/H4
Rems (riv.), Ger. 43/H2
Remscheid, Ger. 51/E6
Remy, Fr. 52/B5
Rena, Nor. 38/D1
Renāla Khurd, Pak. 86/B4
Renan, Swi. 56/C3
Renarde (riv.), Fr. 30/J6
Renazzo, It. 59/E3
Renca, Chile 158/N8
Rench (riv.), Ger. 54/A5
Renchen, Ger. 56/E1
Rend (lake), Il, US 133/F2
Rendeux, Belg. 53/E3
Rendsburg, Ger. 38/C4
Renens, Swi. 56/C4
Renfrew, On, Can. 130/E2
Renfrew, Sc, UK 36/B5
Renfrewshire (pol. reg.), Sc, UK 36/B5
Rengam, Malay. 80/B3
Rengat, Indo. 80/B4
Rengo, Chile 158/N9
Rengsdorf, Ger. 53/G3
Renhua, China 83/K2
Reni, Ukr. 49/J3
Renish (pt.), Sc, UK 31/Q8
Renkum, Neth. 50/C5
Renmark, Austl. 113/J5
Rennell (isl.), Sol. 116/F6
Rennerod, Ger. 53/H2
Rennertshofen, Ger. 54/E5
Rennes, Fr. 42/C2
Renningen, Ger. 54/B5
Reno (riv.), It. 43/J4
Reno, Nv, US 128/C3
Renoster (riv.), SAfr. 106/C3
Renqiu, China 72/D3
Rensselaer, In, US 130/C3
Rentchler, Il, US 137/H9
Rentería, Sp. 44/E1
Renton, Wa, US 126/C4
Renton, Sc, UK 36/B5
Renwez, Fr. 53/D4
Réo, Burk. 103/E3
Reoti, India 85/E3
Répcelak, Hun. 43/M3
Repelón, Col. 145/H4
Repentigny, Qu, Can. 131/P6
Replonges, Fr. 56/A5
Republic, Wa, US 126/D3
Republican (riv.), Ks,Ne, US 125/G3
Repulse (bay), Austl. 109/D3
Repulse Bay (isl.), Austl. 114/C3
Repulse Bay, Nun., Can. 123/H2
Requena, Peru 156/C2
Requena, Sp. 45/E3
Requínoa, Chile 158/N9
Reriutaba, Braz. 154/B2
Reşadiye, Turk. 62/F4
Reschensee (Resia) (lake), It. 57/G4
Rescue (pt.), Chile 158/B5
Resegone (peak), It. 58/C1
Resen, FYROM 47/G2
Resende, Braz. 211/J7
Resende, Port. 44/B2
Reserve, NM, US 128/E4
Resia, Passo di (pass), It. 57/G4
Resia (Reschensee) (lake), It. 57/G4
Resistencia, Arg. 157/E2
Reşiţa, Rom. 48/E3
Resolution (isl.), Nun., Can. 123/K2
Respenda de la Peña, Sp. 44/C1
Resplendor, Braz. 155/D1
Restigouche (riv.), NB, Can. 131/H2
Reston, Mb, Can. 127/H3
Reston, Va, US 138/A6
Reszel, Pol. 39/J4
Retalhuleu, Guat. 144/D3
Rethel, Fr. 53/D4
Rethem, Ger. 51/G3
Réthimnon, Gre. 47/J5
Retie, Belg. 50/C6
Retezat NP, Rom. 62/B3
Rétság, Hun. 48/D2
Rettenberg, Ger. 57/G2
Retz, Aus. 41/H4
Réunion (dpcy.), Fr. 107/S15
Reus, Sp. 45/F2
Reusel, Neth. 50/C6
Reuss (riv.), Swi. 57/E3
Reuterstadt Stavenhagen, Ger. 38/E5
Reutlingen, Ger. 54/C6
Reutov, Rus. 61/W9
Reutte, Aus. 57/G3
Revadim, Isr. 91/F8
Réveillon (riv.), Fr. 30/K5
Revel, Fr. 42/D5
Revelstoke, BC, Can. 126/D3
Revere, It. 59/E2
Revfülöp, Hun. 48/C2
Revigny-sur-Ornain, Fr. 53/D6
Revillagigedo (isls.), Mex. 142/B5
Revin, Fr. 53/D4
Revolyutsii (peak), Taj. 87/F5
Revsbotn (inlet), Nor. 37/G1
Rewa, India 84/C3
Rewa (riv.), Guy. 153/G4
Rex (mtn.), Ak, US 134/J3
Rey (isl.), Pan. 141/F6
Rey, Isla del (isl.), Pan. 150/C2
Reyes, Bol. 150/E6
Reyes (pt.), Ca, US 128/B3
Reyhanlı, Turk. 91/E1
Reykjanestá (cape), Ice. 37/M7
Reykjavík (int'l arpt.), Ice. 37/N7
Reykjavík (cap.), Ice. 37/N7
Reynosa, Mex. 132/D5
Reyssouze (riv.), Fr. 56/B5
Rezé, Fr. 42/C3
Rēzekne, Lat. 39/M3
Rezzato, It. 58/D1
Rhaetian Alps (mts.), Swi., Aus 43/H3
Rhallamane (reg.), Mrta. 98/C5
Rhallamane (lake), Mrta. 98/C4
Rhart (peak), Mor. 98/D3
Rhat (peak), Mor. 98/D3
Rhätikon (mts.), Swi.,Aus. 57/F3
Rheda-Wiedenbrück, Ger. 51/F5
Rhede, Ger. 50/D5
Rhede, Ger. 51/E2
Rheden, Neth. 50/D4
Rheidol (riv.), Wal, UK 32/C2
Rheinau, Swi. 57/E2
Rheinbach, Ger. 53/F2
Rheinberg, Ger. 50/D5
Rheinbreitbach, Ger. 53/G2
Rheinbrohl, Ger. 53/G3
Rheine, Ger. 51/E4
Rheinfall, Swi. 57/E2
Rheinfelden, Ger. 56/D2
Rheinland-Pfalz (state), Ger. 54/A3
Rheinwaldhorn (peak), Swi. 57/F5
Rheinzabern, Ger. 54/B4
Rhemiles (well), Alg. 98/D3
Rhenen, Neth. 50/C5
Rheris, Oued (riv.), Mor. 98/D3
Rhinau, Fr. 56/D1
Rhine (riv.), Eur. 27/E4
Rhine-Herne (canal), Ger. 51/E5
Rhinns (pt.), Sc, UK 31/Q9
Rhinns, The (pt.), Sc, UK 34/C2
Rhino Camp, Ugan. 104/A2
Rhiou (riv.), Alg. 100/F5
Rhiou (riv.), Alg. 100/F5
Rhir (cape), Mor. 98/C3
Rhisnes, Belg. 53/D3
Rhiw (riv.), Wal, UK 32/C1
Rho, It. 58/C1
Rhode Island (state), US 125/M3
Rhodes (isl.), Gre. 27/G5
Rhön (mts.), Ger. 54/D1
Rhondda, Wal, UK 32/C3
Rhondda Cynon Taff (co.), Wal, UK 32/C3
Rhône (dept.), Fr. 56/A6
Rhône (glacier), Swi. 57/E4
Rhône (riv.), Fr. 27/E4
Rhône-Alpes (pol. reg.), Fr. 56/B5
Rhône au Rhin (canal), Fr. 56/B3
Rhonelle (riv.), Fr. 52/C3
Rhosllanerchrugog, Wal, UK 35/E6
Rhum (isl.), Sc, UK 31/Q8
Rhume (riv.), Ger. 51/H5
Rhumel, Oued el (riv.), Alg. 100/J4
Rhyddhywel (peak), Wal, UK 32/C2
Rhyl, Wal, UK 34/E5
Riachão, Braz. 154/A2
Riachão das Neves, Braz. 154/A3
Riachão do Jacuípe, Braz. 154/C3
Riacho de Santana, Braz. 154/B4
Riachuelo, Braz. 154/D2
Rialto, Ca, US 136/C2
Rianjo, Sp. 44/A1
Riaño, Sp. 44/C1
Riāsi, India 86/C3
Riau (isls.), Indo. 80/B3
Riaza, Sp. 44/D2
Ribadeo, Sp. 44/B1
Ribadesella, Sp. 44/C1
Riban'i Manamby (mts.), Madg. 107/H9
Ribble (riv.), Eng, UK 35/F4
Ribblesdale (valley), Eng, UK 35/F3
Ribe, Den. 38/C4
Ribe (co.), Den. 38/C4
Ribeauvillé, Fr. 56/D1
Ribécourt-Dreslincourt, Fr. 52/B4
Ribeira (riv.), Braz. 155/B3
Ribeira Brava, CpV. 93/J10
Ribeira de Pena, Port. 44/B2
Ribeira do Pombal, Braz. 154/C3
Ribeira Grande, Azor., Port. 45/T13
Ribeira Grande, CpV. 93/J9
Ribeirão, Braz. 154/D3
Ribeirão do Pinha, Braz. 155/B2
Ribeiro Gonçalves, Braz. 154/A2
Ribera, It. 46/C4
Riberalta, Bol. 150/E6
Ribniţa, Mol. 49/J2
Ribnitz-Damgarten, Ger. 38/E4
Říčany u Prahy, Czh. 55/H3
Ricaurte, Col. 152/B4
Riccia, It. 46/D2
Riccione, It. 59/F5
Ricco'del Golfo, It. 58/C4
Rice (lake), On, Can. 130/E2
Richard Toll, Sen. 102/B2
Richards (isl.), NW, Can. 122/C2
Richard's Bay, SAfr. 107/F3
Richardson (lakes), Me, US 131/G2
Richboro, Pa, US 138/C3
Riche (cape), Austl. 112/C5
Richebourg, Fr. 30/G5
Richel (isl.), Neth. 50/C2
Richelieu, Qu, Can. 131/P7
Richfield, Ut, US 128/D3
Richfield, Pa, US 138/A2
Richhill, NI, UK 34/B3
Richland, Wa, US 126/D4
Richland, Ok, US 137/M14
Richland, NJ, US 138/D5
Richland, Pa, US 138/B3
Richland Balsam (peak), NC, US 133/H3
Richland Center, Wi, US 127/L5
Richland Creek (res.), US 129/H5
Richlandtown, Pa, US 138/C3
Richmond, BC, Can. 126/C3
Richmond, Ky, US 130/C4
Richmond, Qu, Can. 131/F2
Richmond, SAfr. 107/E3
Richmond, SAfr. 106/C3
Richmond, Austl. 114/A3
Richmond (co.), NY, US 138/D2
Richmond, Il, US 135/P15
Richmond Beach-Innis Arden, Wa, US 135/B2
Richmond Heights, Mo, US 137/G8
Richmond Hill, On, Can. 131/R8
Richmond Park (bor.), Eng, UK 30/C2
Richmond Upon Thames (bor.), Eng, UK 30/B2
Richmond-Windsor, Austl. 114/G8
Richtersveld NP, SAfr. 106/B3
Richterswil, Swi. 57/E3
Richwiller, Fr. 56/D2
Rickenbach, Ger. 56/D2
Ricketts Glen State Park, Pa, US 138/B1
Rickmansworth, Eng, UK 30/B2
Ricla, Sp. 44/E2
Ricse, Hun. 41/L4
Ridā', Yem. 88/D6
Ridderkerk, Neth. 50/B5
Rideau (lake), On, Can. 130/E2
Ridgecrest, Ca, US 128/C4
Ridgefield, Ct, US 139/E1
Ridgefield, NJ, US 139/K8
Ridgefield Park, NJ, US 139/J8
Ridgeland, Ms, US 129/K4
Ridgely, Mo, US 137/D5
Ridgely, Md, US 138/C6
Ridgewood, NJ, US 139/J8
Ridgewood State Park, NJ, US 138/D2
Riding Mountain NP, Mb, Can. 127/H3
Ridlees Cairn (hill), Eng, UK 36/D6
Riecito (riv.), Col. 152/D3
Ried im Innkreis, Aus. 55/G6
Ried im Traunkreis, Aus. 55/H6
Riede, Ger. 51/F3
Riedenburg, Ger. 55/E5
Riedisheim, Fr. 56/D2
Riedlingen, Ger. 57/F1
Riegelsberg, Ger. 53/F5
Riegelsville, Pa, US 138/C2
Riegsee (lake), Ger. 57/H2
Riehen, Swi. 56/D2
Riemst, Belg. 53/E2
Rieneck, Ger. 54/C2
Riesa, Ger. 41/G3
Rieschweiler-Mühlbach, Ger. 53/G5
Riesco (isl.), Chile 157/B7
Riese Pio X, It. 59/E1
Riet (riv.), SAfr. 106/D3
Rietberg, Ger. 51/F5
Rietbron, SAfr. 106/C4
Rieti, It. 46/C1
Riffe (lake), Wa, US 126/C4
Rifle, Co, US 128/F3
Rifsnes (pt.), Ice. 37/N6
Rift Valley (prov.), Kenya 104/B2
Riga (gulf), Eur. 64/C4
Rīga (Riga) (cap.), Lat. 39/L3
Rigby, Id, US 126/F5
Rīgestan (pol. reg.), Afg. 89/H2
Riggins, Id, US 126/D4
Rigi (peak), Swi. 57/E3
Rignano sull'Arno, It. 59/E5
Rigolet, Nf, Can. 123/L3
Rihand (dam), India 84/D3
Rihand (riv.), India 84/D3
Rihand Sāgar (res.), India 82/D3
Riihimäki, Fin. 39/L1
Riiser-Larsen (pen.), Ant. 160/C
Riiser-Larsen Ice Shelf, Ant. 160/Y
Riisitunturin NP, Fin. 60/F2
Rijeka, Cro. 48/B3
Rijksmuseum Kröller Müller, Neth. 50/C4
Rijnsburg, Neth. 50/B4
Rijnsbergen, Neth. 50/B5
Rijssen, Neth. 50/D4
Rijswijk, Neth. 50/B4
Rikers (isl.), NY, US 139/K8
Rikitea, FrPol. 117/M7
Rikuchū-Kaigan NP, Japan 76/C4
Rikuzentakata, Japan 76/B4
Rila (mts.), Bul. 47/H1
Rila, Bul. 47/H1
Rillieux-la-Pape, Fr. 56/A6
Rilski Manastir, Bul. 47/H1
Rimatara (isl.), FrPol. 117/K7
Rimavská Sobota, Slvk. 41/L4
Rimbach, Ger. 54/B3
Rimbey, Ab, Can. 126/E2
Rimforsa, Swe. 38/F2
Rimini, It. 59/F4
Rîmnicu Sărat, Rom. 49/H3
Rîmnicu Vîlcea, Rom. 49/G3
Rimogne, Fr. 53/D4
Rimouski, Qu, Can. 131/G1
Rimpar, Ger. 54/C3
Rimpfischhorn (peak), Swi. 56/D5
Rinas (int'l arpt.), Alb. 47/F2
Rinbung, China 85/G1
Rinchnach, Ger. 55/G5
Rincón de la Vieja, PN, CR 140/D5
Rincón de Romos, Mex. 142/E4
Ringarooma, Austl. 115/C4
Ringboy (pt.), NI, UK 34/C3
Ringebu, Nor. 38/D1
Ringelspitz (peak), Swi. 57/F4
Ringgold, La, US 129/J4
Ringkøbing (fjord), Den. 38/B3
Ringkøbing (co.), Den. 38/B3
Ringkøbing, Den. 38/C3
Ringoes, NJ, US 138/D3
Ringsend, NI, UK 34/B1
Ringsted, Den. 38/D4
Ringtown, Pa, US 138/B2
Ringvaart (riv.), Neth. 50/B4
Ringvassøy (isl.),Nor. 37/F1
Ringwood, Eng, UK 33/E5
Ringwood, NJ, US 139/H7
Ringwood State Park, NJ, US 138/D1
Rinia (isl.), Gre. 47/J4
Rinteln, Ger. 51/G4
Rinxent, Fr. 52/A2
Río Abiseo, PN, Peru 150/C5
Rio Azul, Braz. 155/B3
Río Blanco, Mex. 143/M8
Rio Bonito, Braz. 211/L7
Rio Branco, Braz. 150/E5
Rio Branco do Sul, Braz. 155/B3
Río Bravo, Mex. 132/D5
Río Bueno, Chile 158/B4
Rio Casca, Braz. 155/D2
Río Cauto, Cuba 145/G1
Río Clarillo, PN, Chile 158/N8
Rio Claro, Braz. 211/J7
Rio Claro, Trin. 153/F2
Río Colorado, Arg. 158/D3
Río Cuarto, Arg. 158/D2
Rio de Janeiro (state), Braz. 155/D2
Rio de Janeiro (int'l arpt.), Braz. 211/K7
Rio Dell, Ca, US 126/B5
Río Gallegos, Arg. 159/C6
Rio Grande (riv.), US,Mex. 129/F5
Rio Grande, Braz. 155/A5
Rio Grande (plain), Tx, US 140/B2
Rio Grande, NJ, US 138/D5
Río Grande, Arg. 159/D7
Rio Grande City, Tx, US 132/D5
Rio Grande da Serra, Braz. 211/G8
Rio Grande Do Norte , (state) Braz. 154/C2
Rio Grande do Piauí, Braz. 154/B2
Rio Grande Valley (int'l arpt.), Tx, US 132/D5
Rio Jaú, PN do, Braz. 150/F4
Río Lagartos, Mex. 144/D1
Rio Largo, Braz. 154/D3
Rio Maior, Port. 44/A3
Río Mayo, Arg. 158/C5
Rio Negrinho, Braz. 155/B3
Rio Negro, Braz. 155/B3
Río Negro (prov.), Arg. 158/E3
Río Negro, Chile 158/B4
Río Negro, Embalse de (res.), Uru. 157/E3
Rio Paranaíba, Braz. 155/C1
Rio Pardo, Braz. 155/A4
Rio Pilcomayo, PN, Arg. 157/E2
Rio Prêto (range), Braz. 154/A5
Rio Rancho, NM, US 128/F4
Rio Real, Braz. 154/C3
Rio Saliceto, It. 59/D3
Río Simpson, PN, Chile 158/B5
Río Tala, Arg. 159/J10
Río Tercero, Arg. 157/D3
Río Tigre, Ecu. 152/B5
Rio Tinto, Braz. 154/D2
Rio Verde, Braz. 155/B1
Río Verde, Mex. 143/F4
Río Verde, Chile 159/C7
Rio Verde de Mato Grosso, Braz. 151/H7
Rio Vista, Ca, US 135/L10
Riobamba, Ecu. 152/B5
Riohacha, Col. 152/C2
Rioja, Peru 156/B2
Riolândia, Braz. 155/B1
Riolo Terme, It. 59/E4
Riom, Fr. 42/E4
Riom-ès-Montagne, Fr. 42/E4
Riomaggiore, It. 58/C4
Rion-des-Landes, Fr. 42/C5
Riondel, BC, Can. 126/D3
Rionegro, Col. 152/C3
Rionero in Vulture, It. 46/D2
Riorges, Fr. 42/F3
Ríos, Sp. 44/B2
Ríos (lake), Chile 158/B5
Riosucio, Col. 152/B3
Rioz, Fr. 56/C3
Ripalti, Punta dei (pt.), It. 46/B1
Ripanj, Yugo. 48/E3
Riparbella, It. 58/D6
Ripley, Ms, US 133/F3
Ripley, Eng, UK 35/G5
Ripoll, Sp. 45/G1
Ripoll (riv.), Sp. 45/L6
Ripollet, Sp. 45/L6
Ripon, Wi, US 127/L5
Ripon, Eng, UK 35/G3
Riposto, It. 46/D4
Ripponden, Eng, UK 35/G4
Rippowam (riv.), Ct, US 139/L7
Ris-Orangis, Fr. 30/K6
Risaralda (dept.), Col. 152/A4
Rishiri, Japan 76/B1
Rishiri-Rebun-Sarobetsu NP, Japan 76/B1
Rishon LeẔiyyon, Isr. 91/F8
Rising Sun, Md, US 138/B4
Rising Sun-Lebanon, De, US 138/C5
Risle (riv.), Fr. 42/D2
Risnjak (peak), Cro. 48/B3
Risnjak NP, Cro. 48/B3
Rîşnov, Rom. 49/G3
Rison, Ar, US 129/J4
Risør, Nor. 38/C2
Riss (riv.), Ger. 57/F1
Risse (riv.), Fr. 56/C5
Ristiina, Fin. 39/M1
Ritacuba (peak), Col. 152/C3
Ritaiō (isl.), Japan 116/D2
Ritoio (peak), It. 59/E5
Ritterhude, Ger. 51/F2
Rittō, Japan 77/J5
Ritzville, Wa, US 126/D4
Riva, It. 57/G6
Riva Ligure, It. 58/A5
Riva Presso Chieri, It. 58/A3
Riva San Vitale, Swi. 57/E6
Rivadavia, Arg. 157/C3
Rivadavia, Arg. 158/E2
Rivalta, It. 58/B2
Rivalta di Torino, It. 58/A2
Rivanazzano, It. 58/C3
Rivarolo Canavese, It. 58/A2
Rivarolo Mantovano, It. 58/D2
Rivas, Nic. 144/E4
Rive-de-Gier, Fr. 42/F4
River Cess, Libr. 102/C5
River Edge, NJ, US 139/J8
River Kwai Bridge, Thai. 78/B3
River Rouge, Mi, US 135/F7
River Vale, NJ, US 139/J8
Rivera, Uru. 157/E3
Rivera, Swi. 57/E5
Rivera (isl.), Chile 158/B5
Rivera, Arg. 158/E3
Riverdale, Ut, US 137/K11
Riverdale, NJ, US 139/H8
Rivergaro, It. 58/C3
Riverhead, NY, US 139/F2
Rivers (inlet), BC, Can. 126/B3
Rivers, Mb, Can. 127/H3
Rivers (state), Nga. 103/G5
Riversdale, SAfr. 106/C4
Riverside (co.), Ca, US 136/C3
Riverside, Ca, US 136/C3
Riverside, Mo, US 137/D5
Riverside, NJ, US 138/D3
Riverside, Pa, US 138/B2
Riverton, Mb, Can. 127/J3
Riverton, NZ 117/R12
Riverton, Ut, US 137/K12
Riverton, Austl. 113/H5
Riverview, NB, Can. 131/H2
Riverwoods, Il, US 135/Q15
Riviera Beach, Fl, US 133/H5
Riviera Beach, Md, US 138/B5
Rivière-du-Loup, Qu, Can. 131/G2
Riviersonderendreeks (mts.), SAfr. 106/L11
Rivignano, It. 59/G1
Rivne, Ukr. 62/C2
Rivnens'ka (obl.), Ukr. 62/C2
Rivoli, It. 43/G4
Rivolta d'Adda, It. 58/C2
Rixensart, Belg. 53/D2
Rixheim, Fr. 56/D2
Riyāq, Leb. 91/D3
Rize (prov.), Turk. 63/G4
Rize, Turk. 63/G4
Rizhao, China 72/D4
Rizokarpasso, Cyp. 91/D2
Rizzuto (cape), It. 47/E3
Rjukan, Nor. 38/C2
Rkîz (lake), Mrta. 102/B2
Roa, Sp. 44/D2
Roa, Nor. 38/D1
Road Town (cap.), BVI 141/M8
Roan (plat.), Co, US 128/E3
Roan Fell (hill), Sc, UK 35/F1
Roanne, Fr. 42/F3
Roanoke, Al, US 133/G3
Roanoke (riv.), Va, US 130/E4
Roanoke (pt.), NY, US 139/F2
Roatán (isl.), Hon. 140/D4
Roatán, Hon. 144/E2
Robāţ Karīm, Iran 88/F1
Robbiate, It. 58/C1
Robbins (isl.), Austl. 115/C4
Robbio, It. 58/B2
Robe, Austl. 115/A3
Robe (mt.), Austl. 115/B1
Robe (riv.), Ire. 31/P10
Robecchetto con Induno, It. 58/B1
Röbel, Ger. 38/E4
Robert (peak), Fr. 56/B5
Robert Lee, Tx, US 129/G5
Roberts (mtn.), Ak, US 134/E4
Roberts (Monrovia) (int'l arpt.), Libr. 102/C5
Robertsfors, Swe. 37/G2
Robertsganj, India 84/D3
Robertson, SAfr. 106/L10
Robertsport, Libr. 102/C5
Robertstown, Ire. 31/Q10
Roberval, Qu, Can. 131/F1

220
Robes – Sachs

Robesonia, Pa, US 138/B3
Robinson (range), Austl. 109/A3
Robinson Crusoe (isl.), Chile 147/B6
Robinson Gorge NP, Austl. 114/C4
Robinvale, Austl. 115/B2
Roblin, Mb, Can. 127/H3
Roboré, Bol. 150/G7
Robson (mt.), BC, Can. 126/D2
Robstown, Tx, US 132/D5
Roby, Tx, US 129/G4
Roc du Haut du Faite (peak), Fr. 56/D1
Roca, Cabo da (cape), Port. 45/P10
Roca Partida (isl.), Mex. 142/B5
Roca Partida, Punta (pt.), Mex. 144/C2
Rocafuerte, Ecu. 152/A5
Rocas (isl.), Braz. 151/M4
Rocca San Casciano, It. 59/E4
Roccabianca, It. 58/D2
Roccastrada, It. 43/J5
Rocciamelone (peak), It. 43/G4
Rocha (dept.), Uru. 159/G2
Rocha, Uru. 159/G2
Rochdale, Eng, UK 35/F4
Roche, Swi. 56/C5
Roche du Sapin Sec (peak), Fr. 56/C1
Roche-lez-Beaupré, Fr. 56/C3
Rochefort, Fr. 42/C4
Rochefort, Belg. 53/E3
Rochelle Park, NJ, US 139/J8
Rochers du Bourbet (peak), Fr. 56/C3
Rochester, Austl. 115/C3
Rochester, Mn, US 127/K4
Rochester, NY, US 130/E3
Rochester, In, US 130/C3
Rochester, NH, US 131/G3
Rochester, Eng, UK 33/G4
Rochester, Mi, US 135/F6
Rochester, Wi, US 135/P14
Rochford, Eng, UK 30/F2
Rock (riv.), Ia,Mo, US 129/H2
Rock (riv.), Il, US 125/J3
Rock Creek, Yk, Can. 134/L3
Rock Forest, Qu, Can. 131/G2
Rock Glen, Pa, US 138/B2
Rock Hall, Md, US 138/B5
Rock Hill, SC, US 133/H3
Rock Island, Il, US 127/L5
Rock Springs, Wy, US 126/F5
Rockall (isl.), UK 27/C3
Rockaway (riv.), NJ, US 138/D2
Rockaway, NJ, US 138/D2
Rockaway (pt.), NY, US 139/K9
Rockaway (inlet), NY, US 139/K9
Rockdale, Il, US 135/P17
Rockefeller (plat.), Ant. 160/R
Rockenhausen, Ger. 53/G4
Rockford, Il, US 127/L5
Rockglen, Sk, Can. 127/G3
Rockhampton, Austl. 114/C3
Rockingham, NC, US 133/J3
Rockingham, Austl. 112/K7
Rockland, Me, US 131/G2
Rockland, On, Can. 130/F2
Rockland (co.), NY, US 138/D1
Rockland Lake, NY, US 139/K7
Rocklands (res.), Austl. 109/D4
Rockledge, Fl, US 133/H4
Rockledge, Pa, US 138/C3
Rockport, Tx, US 132/D4
Rocks, Md, US 138/B4
Rocksprings, Tx, US 129/G5
Rockstone, Guy. 153/G3
Rockville, Md, US 130/E4
Rockville Centre, NY, US 139/L9
Rockwall, Tx, US 129/H4
Rockwood, Tn, US 133/G3
Rocky (mtn.), Ky, US 130/D4
Rocky (mts.), Can.,US 119/E4
Rocky (pt.), NY, US 139/F1
Rocky Cape NP, Austl. 115/C4
Rocky Harbour, Nf, Can. 131/K1
Rocky Island (lake), On, Can. 130/D2
Rocky Mount, NC, US 133/J3
Rocky Mountain House, Ab, Can. 126/E2
Rocky Mountain NP, Co, US 128/F2
Rocroi, Fr. 53/D4
Rodach (riv.), Ger. 55/E2
Rodach bei Coburg, Ger. 54/D2
Rodalben, Ger. 53/G5
Rødberg, Nor. 38/C1
Rødbyhavn, Den. 38/D4
Roddickton, Nf, Can. 131/L1
Rødding, Den. 38/C4
Roden (riv.), Eng, UK 35/F6
Rodenbach, Ger. 54/C2
Rodeo, Mex. 142/D3
Rodeo, Ca, US 135/K10
Rödermark, Ger. 54/B3
Rodewisch, Ger. 55/F1
Rodez, Fr. 42/E4
Rodholívos, Gre. 47/H2
Ródhos (ruin), Gre. 90/B2
Ródhos (Rhodes), Gre. 90/B2
Rodigo, It. 58/D2
Roding (riv.), Eng, UK 30/D2
Roding, Ger. 55/F4
Rodinga (mt.), Austl. 113/G3
Rödinghausen, Ger. 51/F4
Rodoč, Bosn. 47/E1
Rodolfo Sánchez Toboada, Mex. 142/A2
Rodríguez, Uru. 159/K11
Roe (riv.), NI, UK 34/B2
Roebourne, Austl. 112/C2
Roebuck (bay), Austl. 109/B2
Roeland Park, Ks, US 137/D5
Roen (peak), It. 57/H5
Roer (riv.), Neth. 50/D6
Roermond, Neth. 50/C6
Roes Welcome Sound (str.), Nun., Can. 123/H2
Roeselare, Belg. 52/C2
Roesiger (lake), Wa, US 135/D2
Rogachev, Bela. 62/D1
Rogaland (co.), Nor. 37/C4
Rogaška Slatina, Slov. 43/L3
Rogatica, Bosn. 48/D4
Rogers (mt.), Va, US 130/D4
Rogers, Ar, US 129/J3
Rogers City, Mi, US 130/D2
Rogersville, Tn, US 130/D4
Roggwil, Swi. 56/D3
Rogliano, Fr. 43/H5
Roglio (riv.), It. 59/D5
Rognon (riv.), Fr. 42/F2
Rogoźno, Pol. 41/J2
Rogue (riv.), Or, US 128/B2
Rohl (riv.), Sudan 97/L6
Rohr, Ger. 55/E5
Rohrbach bei Mattersburg, Aus. 43/M3
Rohrbach in Oberösterreich, Aus. 55/G5
Rohrbach-lès-Bitche, Fr. 53/G5
Rohri, Pak. 89/J3
Röhrmoos, Ger. 55/E6
Rohtak, India 86/D5
Roi Et, Thai. 78/C2
Roine (lake), Fin. 39/L1
Roissy, Fr. 30/K5
Roissy-en-France, Fr. 30/K4
Rojas, Arg. 158/E2
Rojo (cape), PR 141/M8
Rojo, Cabo (cape), Mex. 144/B1
Rokan (riv.), Indo. 80/B3
Rokeby Croll Creek NP, Austl. 114/A1
Rokel (riv.), SLeo. 102/C4
Rokkasho, Japan 76/B3
Rokkō-san (peak), Japan 77/H6
Rokugō, Japan 77/A3
Rokycany, Czh. 55/G3
Rokytka (riv.), Czh. 55/H2
Rolampont, Fr. 56/B2
Rolândia, Braz. 155/B2
Rolava (riv.), Czh. 55/F2
Rolde, Neth. 50/D3
Rolla, ND, US 127/J3
Rolla, BC, Can. 126/C2
Rolla, Mo, US 129/K3
Rolle, Swi. 56/C5
Rolling Fork, Ms, US 129/K4
Rolling Hills Estates, Ca, US 136/F8
Rolling Meadows, Il, US 135/P15
Rollingbay, Wa, US 135/B2
Rollinsville, Co, US 137/A3
Rolo, It. 59/D3
Rom (peak), Ugan. 104/B2
Roma, Austl. 114/C4
Roma, Swe. 38/H3
Roma (Rome) (cap.), It. 46/C2
Romagnano Sesia, It. 58/B1
Romagnat, Fr. 42/E4
Romain (cape), SC, US 133/J3
Romaine (riv.), Qu, Can. 123/K3
Roman, Bul. 47/H1
Roman, Rom. 49/H2
Romang (str.), Indo. 81/G5
Romang (isl.), Indo. 81/G5
Romania (ctry.) 49/F3
Romano Canavese, It. 58/A2
Romano, Cayo (isl.), Cuba 145/G1
Romano d'Ezzelino, It. 59/E1
Romano di Lombardia, It. 58/C1
Romans d'Isonzo, It. 59/G1
Romans-sur-Isère, Fr. 42/F4
Romanshorn, Swi. 57/F2
Romanzof (cape), Ak, US 134/E3
Rombas, Fr. 53/F5
Romblon, Phil. 81/F1
Rome, NY, US 130/F3
Rome, Ga, US 133/G3
Rome, Wi, US 135/N14
Romenay, Fr. 56/B4
Romeoville, Il, US 135/P16
Römhild, Ger. 54/D2
Romilly-sur-Seine, Fr. 42/E2
Rommani, Mor. 98/D2
Rommerskirchen, Ger. 53/F1
Romney Marsh (phys. reg.), Eng, UK 33/G4
Romny, Ukr. 62/E2
Rømø (isl.), Den. 40/E1
Romoland, Ca, US 136/C3
Romont, Swi. 56/C4
Romorantin-Lanthenay, Fr. 42/D3
Romsey, Eng, UK 33/E5
Rømskog, Nor. 38/D2
Ronald Reagan Washington National (int'l arpt.), DC, US 138/A6
Ronan, Mt, US 126/E4
Roncade, It. 59/F1
Roncador Cay (isl.), Col. 141/F5
Roncador, Serra do (mts.), Braz. 151/H6
Ronchamp, Fr. 56/C2
Ronchi dei Legionari (int'l arpt.), It. 59/G1
Ronchi dei Legionari, It. 59/G1
Ronciglione, It. 46/C1
Ronco (riv.), It. 59/F5
Ronco All'Adige, It. 59/E2
Ronco Scrivia, It. 58/B3
Roncoferraro, It. 59/D2
Roncq, Fr. 52/C2
Ronda, Sp. 44/C4
Rondane NP, Nor. 37/D3
Ronde, Tête (peak), Swi. 56/D5
Rondonópolis, Braz. 151/H7
Rong (riv.), China 83/J2
Rong Xian, China 83/K3
Rongcheng, China 73/B4
Rongcheng, China 72/G7
Ronge (lake), Sk, Can. 122/F3
Rongelap (isl.), Mrsh. 116/F3
Rongerik (isl.), Mrsh. 116/F3
Ronkonkoma, NY, US 139/E2
Rønne, Den. 38/F4
Ronne Ice Shelf, Ant. 160/W
Ronneby, Swe. 38/F3
Ronnenberg, Ger. 51/G4
Ronquerolles, Fr. 30/J4
Ronsard (cape), Austl. 112/B3
Ronsberg, Ger. 57/G2
Ronse, Belg. 52/C2
Ronuro (riv.), Braz. 151/H6
Roodeport, SAfr. 106/P13
Rooiberg (peak), Namb. 106/B2
Roorkee, India 82/C2
Roosendaal, Neth. 50/B5
Roosevelt, Ut, US 128/E2
Roosevelt (canal), Az, US 137/S19
Roosevelt (riv.), Braz. 147/C4
Roosevelt (mt.), BC, Can. 122/D3
Roosevelt, NJ, US 138/D3
Roosevelt (isl.), Ant. 160/N
Roosevelt, NY, US 139/L9
Root (riv.), Ak, US 134/L4
Root (riv.), Wi, US 135/P14
Root, West Branch (riv.), Wi, US 135/P14
Roque Pérez, Arg. 159/J11
Roquetas de Mar, Sp. 44/D4
Roraima (peak), Braz. 150/F2
Roraima (peak), Ven. 153/F3
Roraima (state), Braz. 153/F4
Rorke's Drift, SAfr. 107/E3
Rorke's Drift Battlesite, SAfr. 107/E3
Rorketon, Mb, Can. 127/J3
Røros, Nor. 37/D3
Rorschach, Swi. 57/F3
Rosa (cape), Alg. 100/L6
Rosà, It. 59/E1
Rosa (lake), Bahm. 145/H1
Rosa Punta (pt.), Mex. 142/C3
Rosa Zárate, Ecu. 152/B4
Rosablanche (peak), Swi. 56/D5
Rosal, Sp. 44/A2
Rosales, Mex. 132/B4
Rosamorada, Mex. 142/D4
Rosanna (riv.), Aus. 57/G3
Rosário, Braz. 154/A1
Rosario, Mex. 142/C3
Rosario, Mex. 142/D4
Rosario, Arg. 158/E2
Rosario, Uru. 159/K11
Rosario de la Frontera, Arg. 157/D2
Rosario del Tala, Arg. 159/J10
Rosário do Sul, Braz. 157/F3
Rosarito, Mex. 128/C4
Rosarno, It. 46/D3
Rosas, Col. 152/B4
Rosas, Golfo di (gulf), Sp. 45/G1
Rosate, It. 58/C2
Rosay, Fr. 30/G5
Rosbach vor der Höhe, Ger. 54/B2
Rosche, Ger. 51/H3
Roscoff, Fr. 42/B2
Roscommon, Ire. 31/P10
Roscrea, Ire. 31/Q10
Rosdorf, Ger. 51/G5
Rose (isl.), ASam. 117/J6
Rose (pt.), BC, Can. 134/M4
Rose Belle, Mrts. 107/T15
Roseau, Mn, US 127/K3
Roseau (riv.), Mn, US 127/J3
Roseau (cap.), Dom. 141/N9
Roseaux, Haiti 145/H2
Rosebery, Austl. 115/C4
Roseburg, Or, US 126/C5
Rosedale, Ms, US 129/K4
Rosedale, Il, US 137/F7
Rosedale, Md, US 138/B5
Rosehearty, Sc, UK 36/D1
Roseira, Braz. 211/H7
Roseland, NJ, US 139/H8
Roselette, Aiguille de (peak), Fr. 56/C6
Roselle, NJ, US 139/H9
Roselle, Il, US 135/P16
Roselle Park, NJ, US 139/H9
Rosemead, Ca, US 136/F7
Rosemère, Qu, Can. 131/N6
Rosenberg, Tx, US 129/J5
Rosenberg, Ger. 54/D4
Rosenfeld, Ger. 57/E1
Rosenhayn, NJ, US 138/C5
Rosenheim, Ger. 43/K3
Roses, Sp. 45/G1
Roseto, Pa, US 138/C2
Roseto degli Abruzzi, It. 43/L5
Rosetown, Sk, Can. 126/G3
Rosetta (riv.), Egypt 91/B4
Roseville, Mi, US 135/G6
Rosewood Heights, Il, US 137/G8
Rosh Ha'ayin, Isr. 91/F7
Rosh Hakarmel (pt.), Isr. 91/F6
Rosh Haniqra (pt.), Isr. 91/D3
Rosheim, Fr. 56/D1
Rosières-en-Santerre, Fr. 52/B4
Rosignano Marittimo, It. 58/D6
Roşiori de Vede, Rom. 49/G3
Roskilde, Den. 38/E4
Roskilde (co.), Den. 38/D4
Roslavl', Rus. 62/E1
Roslev, Den. 38/C3
Rosmalen, Neth. 50/C5
Rosmaninhal, Port. 44/B3
Rosneath, Sc, UK 36/B4
Rosny-sous-Bois, Fr. 30/K5
Rosolina, It. 59/F2
Rosolini, It. 46/D4
Rosporden, Fr. 42/B3
Rösrath, Ger. 53/G2
Ross (isl.), Ant. 160/M
Ross (sea), Ant. 160/P
Ross, Austl. 115/C4
Ross (isl.), Mb, Can. 127/J2
Ross (pt.), On, Can. 131/S8
Ross (dist.), Sc, UK 36/C1
Ross Ice Shelf, Ant. 160/N
Rossa (peak), It. 43/K3
Rossa, Swi. 57/F5
Rossall (pt.), Eng, UK 35/E4
Rossano Stazione, It. 46/E3
Rossano Veneto, It. 59/E1
Rossbach, Ger. 55/F5
Rossberg (peak), Fr. 56/D2
Rossdorf, Ger. 54/B3
Rossel (isl.), PNG 116/E6
Rosselange, Fr. 53/F5
Rosshaupten, Ger. 57/G2
Rossiglione, It. 58/B3
Rossignol (lake), NS, Can. 131/H2
Rosskeeragh (pt.), Ire. 31/P9
Rossland, BC, Can. 122/E5
Rosso, Mrta. 102/B2
Rossosh', Rus. 62/F2
Rossstock (peak), Swi. 57/E4
Rosstal, Ger. 54/D4
Rossville, Ok, US 137/N14
Røst, Nor. 37/E2
Rosthern, Sk, Can. 127/G2
Rostock, Ger. 38/E4
Rostov, Rus. 62/F3
Rostov (int'l arpt.), Rus. 62/F3
Rostov, Rus. 60/H4
Rostovskaya (obl.), Rus. 63/G2
Rostrenen, Fr. 42/B2
Rostrevor, NI, UK 34/B3
Roswell, NM, US 129/F4
Rot (riv.), Ger. 40/E4
Rota, Sp. 44/B4
Rota (isl.), NMar. 116/D3
Rote Wand (peak), Aus. 57/F3
Rotenburg, Ger. 51/G2
Rotenburg an der Fulda, Ger. 51/G7
Roter Main (riv.), Ger. 40/F3
Rötgen, Ger. 53/F2
Roth (riv.), Ger. 57/G1
Roth bei Nürnberg, Ger. 54/E4
Rothaargebirge (mts.), Ger. 51/F6
Rothau, Fr. 56/D1
Röthenbach an der Pegnitz, Ger. 54/E4
Rothenberg, Ger. 54/B3
Rothenburg, Swi. 57/E3
Rothenburg ob der Tauber, Ger. 54/D4
Rothera, UK, Ant. 160/V
Rotherham, Eng, UK 35/G5
Rothes, Sc, UK 36/C1
Rothesay, Sc, UK 36/A5
Rotheux-Rimière, Belg. 53/E2
Rothschild, Wi, US 127/L4
Rothwell, Eng, UK 33/F2
Rothwell, Eng, UK 35/G4
Roti (isl.), Indo. 81/F6
Rotorua, NZ 117/T10
Rotselaar, Belg. 53/D2
Rott (riv.), Ger. 40/G4
Rott am Inn, Ger. 55/F7
Rottach-Egern, Ger. 40/F5
Rotte (riv.), Fr. 53/F6
Rotten (riv.), Swi. 56/E5
Rottenacker, Ger. 57/F1
Röttenbach, Ger. 54/E4
Rottenberg, Ger. 54/C2
Rottenburg am Neckar, Ger. 54/B6
Rottenburg an der Laaber, Ger. 55/F5
Rotterdam (int'l arpt.), Neth. 50/B5
Rotterdam, Neth. 50/B5
Rotthalmünster, Ger. 55/G6
Röttingen, Ger. 54/C3
Rottne, Swe. 38/F3
Rottnest (isl.), Austl. 112/B5
Rottofreno, It. 58/C2
Rottum (riv.), Ger. 57/F1
Rottumeroog (isl.), Neth. 50/D1
Rottumerplaat (isl.), Neth. 50/D1
Rottweil, Ger. 57/E1
Rotuma (isl.), Fiji 116/G6
Rötz, Ger. 55/F4
Roubaix, Fr. 52/C2
Roubion (riv.), Fr. 42/F4
Roudnice nad Labem, Czh. 55/H2
Rouen, Fr. 42/D2
Rouffach, Fr. 56/D2
Rouge (riv.), Qu, Can. 123/J4
Rouge, Middle (riv.), Mi, US 135/F7
Rougemont, Fr. 56/C3
Rougemont-le-Château, Fr. 56/C2
Rough (riv.), Ky, US 133/G2
Roullet-Saint-Estèphe, Fr. 42/D4
Round (hill), Pa, US 138/B3
Round Hill (pt.), Austl. 114/C4
Round Lake, Il, US 135/P15
Round Lake Beach, Il, US 135/P15
Round Lake Park, Il, US 135/P15
Round Rock, Tx, US 129/H5
Round Valley (res.), NJ, US 138/D2
Roundup, Mt, US 126/F4
Roundway (hill), Eng, UK 32/E4
Rousay (isl.), Sc, UK 31/V14
Rousies, Fr. 52/D3
Rousinov, Czh. 41/J4
Roussillon, Fr. 42/F4
Rouvres, Fr. 30/M4
Rouvroy, Belg. 53/E4
Rouxville, SAfr. 106/D3
Rouyn-Noranda, Qu, Can. 130/E1
Rovaniemi, Fin. 60/E2
Rovaniemi (int'l arpt.), Fin. 60/E2
Rovasenda, It. 58/B1
Rovato, It. 58/C1
Roverbella, It. 59/D2
Rovereto, It. 59/D3
Rovereto, It. 57/H6
Rovigo (prov.), It. 59/E2
Rovigo, It. 59/E2
Rovinj, Cro. 59/G2
Rovuma (riv.), Moz. 104/B5
Rowley (isl.), Nun., Can. 123/J2
Rowley Shoals (isl.), Austl. 109/A2
Roxa (isl.), GBis. 102/B4
Roxana, Il, US 137/G8
Roxas, Phil. 81/E1
Roxas, Phil. 81/F1
Roxas, Phil. 79/D4
Roxboro, NC, US 130/E4
Roxen (lake), Swe. 38/F2
Roxo (cape), Sen. 102/A3
Roy, NM, US 132/B3
Roy, Ut, US 137/J11
Roy, Wa, US 135/B3
Roya (riv.), Fr. 43/G5
Royal (canal), Ire. 35/B3
Royal Botanical Garden, On, Can. 131/Q9
Royal Chitwan NP, Nepal 85/E2
Royal Lakes, Il, US 137/H7
Royal Natal NP, SAfr. 106/E3
Royal NP, Austl. 115/D2
Royal NP, The, Austl. 114/H9
Royal Oak, Mi, US 135/F7
Royal Paekje Tombs, SKor. 73/D4
Royal Tombs, Viet. 78/D2
Royal Tunbridge Wells, Eng, UK 33/G4
Royale, Isle (isl.), Mi, US 127/L4
Royalton, Pa, US 138/B3
Royan, Fr. 42/C4
Roye, Fr. 56/C2
Roye, Fr. 52/B4
Royersford, Pa, US 138/C3
Røyken, Nor. 38/D2
Royston, Eng, UK 33/F2
Royston, Eng, UK 35/G4
Royton, Eng, UK 35/F4
Rožaj, Yugo. 47/G1
Rozay-en-Brie, Fr. 52/B6
Rozenburg, Neth. 50/B5
Rozhava (riv.), Rus. 61/W9
Rožmberk (lake), Czh. 55/H4
Rožmitál pod Třemšínem, Czh. 55/G3
Rožňava, Slvk. 41/L4
Roztoczański NP, Pol. 62/B2
Roztoczański PN, Pol. 41/M3
Roztoky, Czh. 55/H2
Rozzano, It. 58/C2
Rrëshen, Alb. 47/F2
Rt Kamenjak (cape), Cro. 48/A3
Rt Ploča (pt.), Cro. 48/B4
Rtishchevo, Rus. 63/G1
Ruacana (falls), Ang. 105/B4
Ruaha NP, Tanz. 104/B4
Ruapehu (vol.), NZ 117/T10
Rub' al Khali (des.), SAr. 67/D7
Rubelles, Fr. 30/L6
Rubeshibe, Japan 76/C2
Rubí, Sp. 45/L7
Rubidoux, Ca, US 136/C3
Rubiera, It. 59/D3
Rubigen, Swi. 56/D4
Rubim, Braz. 154/B5
Rubizhne, Ukr. 62/F2
Rubondo NP, Tanz. 104/A3
Řubřina (riv.), Czh. 55/G4
Ruby, Ak, US 134/G3
Ruby (lake), Nv, US 128/D2
Ruby (mts.), Nv, US 128/D2
Rubyvale, Austl. 114/B3
Rucheng, China 79/B2
Rucphen, Neth. 50/B5
Ruda Woda (lake), Pol. 41/K2
Rudall River NP, Austl. 112/D2
Rūdarpur, India 84/D2
Ruduali, India 84/C2
Rüdersdorf, Ger. 40/Q7
Rüdesheim, Ger. 53/G4
Rudiano, It. 58/C2
Rudkøbing, Den. 38/D4
Rudnik, Pol. 41/M3
Rudnyy, Kaz. 61/P5
Rudolf (isl.), Rus. 64/F1
Rudolstadt, Ger. 43/J1
Rudong, China 72/E4
Rūdsar, Iran 88/F1
Rue, Swi. 56/C4
Rue (pt.), NI, UK 34/B1
Rue, Fr. 52/A3
Rueda, Sp. 44/C2
Rueil-Malmaison, Fr. 30/J5
Ruell (riv.), Sc, UK 36/A4
Ruelle-sur-Touvre, Fr. 42/D4
Ruen (peak), Bul. 48/F4
Ruetzbach (riv.), Aus. 57/H3
Ruffano, It. 47/F3
Ruffec, Fr. 42/D3
Rufiji (riv.), Tanz. 93/F5
Rufina, It. 59/E5
Rufino, Arg. 158/E2
Rufisque, Sen. 102/A3
Rugao, China 72/E4
Rugby, ND, US 127/J3
Rugby, Eng, UK 33/E2
Rugeley, Eng, UK 33/E1
Rügen (isl.), Ger. 38/E4
Ruggell, Lcht. 57/F3
Ruhmannsfelden, Ger. 55/F5
Ruhnu saar (isl.), Lat. 39/K3
Ruhr (riv.), Ger. 40/D3
Ruhr (reg.), Ger. 40/E3
Ruhrgebiet (phys. reg.), Ger. 50/D6
Ruhstorf an der Rott, Ger. 55/F5
Rui'an, China 79/D2
Ruicheng, China 72/B4
Ruidoso, NM, US 129/F4
Ruinen, Neth. 50/D3
Ruiselede, Belg. 52/C1
Ruiz, Mex. 142/D4
Rujen (peak), FYROM 47/H1
Ruki (riv.), D.R. Congo 93/D5
Rukwa (pol. reg.), Tanz. 104/B4
Rukwa (lake), Tanz. 93/F5
Rulles (riv.), Belg. 53/E4
Rülzheim, Ger. 53/H5
Rum, Aus. 57/H3
Rum Cay (isl.), Bahm. 141/G3
Ruma, Yugo. 48/D3
Ruma NP, Kenya 104/B3
Rumbek, Sudan 97/L6
Rumes, Belg. 52/C2
Rumford, Me, US 131/G2
Rumia, Pol. 38/H4
Rumilly, Fr. 56/B6
Rümlang, Swi. 57/E3
Rumoi, Japan 76/B2
Rumphi, Malw. 104/B5
Rumson, NJ, US 138/E3
Rumst, Belg. 53/D1
Rumuruti, Kenya 104/C2
Runabay (pt.), NI, UK 34/B1
Runan, China 72/C4
Runcorn, Eng, UK 35/F5
Runding, Ger. 55/F4
Rundu, Namb. 105/C4
Rungwa (riv.), Tanz. 104/B4
Rungwa Game Rsv., Tanz. 104/B4
Rungwe (peak), Tanz. 104/B5
Runkel, Ger. 54/B2
Runn (lake), Swe. 38/F1
Runnemede, NJ, US 138/C4
Running Springs, Ca, US 136/C2
Ruo (riv.), China 65/K5
Ruokolahti, Fin. 39/N1
Ruoqiang, China 70/E4
Rupat (isl.), Indo. 80/B3
Rupea, Rom. 49/G2
Rupel (riv.), Belg. 53/D1
Rupert (riv.), Qu, Can. 123/J3
Rūpnagar, India 86/D4
Ruppichteroth, Ger. 53/G2
Rupt-sur-Moselle, Fr. 56/C2
Rupununi (riv.), Guy. 153/G4
Rur (riv.), Ger. 40/D3
Rur-Strasse (lake), Ger. 53/F2
Rurrenabaque, Bol. 150/E6
Rurutu (isl.), FrPol. 117/K7
Rusape, Zim. 105/F4
Rüschegg, Swi. 56/D4
Rüschlikon, Swi. 57/E3
Ruscom (riv.), On, Can. 135/G7
Ruse (pol. reg.), Bul. 47/K1
Ruse, Bul. 49/G4
Rusera, India 85/F3
Rush (lake), Ut, US 137/J13
Rush, Ire. 34/B4
Rushan, China 72/E3
Rushden, Eng, UK 33/F2
Rushville, In, US 130/C4
Rusk, Tx, US 129/J5
Russ, Fr. 56/D1
Russ Lake Nat'l Rec. Area, Wa, US 126/C3
Russbach (riv.), Aus. 49/N7
Russell (isls.), Austl. 114/F7
Russell, Mb, Can. 127/H3
Russell (lake), Mb, Can. 127/H1
Russell (isl.), Nun., Can. 122/F1
Russell (lake), Ga,SC, US 133/H3
Russell Gulch, Co, US 137/A3
Russellville, Al, US 133/G3
Russellville, Ar, US 129/J4
Russellville, Ky, US 130/C4
Rüsselsheim, Ger. 54/B3
Russi, It. 59/F4
Russia (ctry.) 64/H3
Russian (riv.), Ca, US 128/B3
Russian Mission, Ak, US 134/F3
Russkaya, Rus., Ant. 160/Q
Rust'avi, Geo. 63/H4
Rustenburg, SAfr. 105/E6
Ruston, La, US 129/J4
Ruston, Wa, US 135/B3
Rute, Sp. 44/C4
Ruteng, Indo. 81/F5
Rüthen, Ger. 51/F6
Rutherford, NJ, US 139/J8
Rutherglen, Sc, UK 36/B5
Rüthi, Swi. 57/F3
Ruthin, Wal, UK 35/E5
Ruthven, On, Can. 135/G7
Rüti, Swi. 57/E3
Rüti, Swi. 57/F4
Rutland, Vt, US 130/F3
Rutland (co.), Eng, UK 33/F1
Rutland Water (res.), Eng, UK 33/F1
Rutog, China 70/C5
Rutshuru (riv.), D.R. Congo 104/A3
Ruukki, Fin. 60/E2
Ruurlo, Neth. 50/D4
Ruvo di Puglia, It. 46/E2
Ruvu (riv.), Tanz. 104/C4
Ruvubu (riv.), Buru. 104/A3
Ruvuma (pol. reg.), Tanz. 104/C5
Ruvuma (riv.), Moz.,Tanz 104/B5
Ruwāndūz, Iraq 90/F2
Ruwenzori (range), Ugan. 104/A2
Ruwenzori NP, Ugan. 104/A3
Ruy Barbosa, Braz. 154/B4
Ruyang, China 72/C4
Ruzayevka, Rus. 63/H1
Ruzizi (riv.), D.R. Congo 104/A3
Ružomberok, Slvk. 41/K4
Ruzyně (int'l arpt.), Czh. 55/H2
Rwanda (ctry.) 104/A3
Ryan (mt.), Austl. 115/D2
Ryan (mt.), Austl. 114/A1
Ryan (inlet), Sc, UK 34/C2
Ryazan', Rus. 63/G1
Ryazanskaya (obl.), Rus. 63/G1
Ryazhsk, Rus. 62/G1
Rybachiy (pen.), Rus. 37/K1
Rybinsk, Rus. 60/H4
Rybinsk (res.), Rus. 27/J2
Rybnik, Pol. 41/K3
Rycroft, Ab, Can. 126/D2
Ryd, Swe. 38/F3
Rydaholm, Swe. 38/F3
Ryde, Eng, UK 33/E5
Ryde, Ca, US 136/L9
Rydet, Swe. 38/D3
Rye (bay), Eng, UK 33/G5
Rye, Eng, UK 33/G5
Rye, NY, US 139/L8
Rye (riv.), Eng, UK 35/G3
Rye Brook, NY, US 139/L7
Rye Patch (res.), Nv, US 128/C2
Rygge, Nor. 38/D2
Ryki, Pol. 41/L3
Rylstone, Austl. 115/D2
Ryōkami, Japan 77/B2
Ryōtsu, Japan 75/F1
Ryōzen-yama (peak), Japan 77/K5
Rypin, Pol. 41/K2
Rysy (peak), Pol. 41/L4
Ryton, Eng, UK 35/G2
Rytterknægten (peak), Den. 38/F4
Ryūgasaki, Japan 75/G3
Ryukyu (isls.), Japan 67/M7
Ryūō, Japan 77/B2
Ryūō, Japan 77/K5
Rzeszów (prov.), Pol. 41/M3
Rzeszów, Pol. 41/M3
Rzhev, Rus. 60/G4

S

's-Graveland, Neth. 50/C4
's Gravendeel, Neth. 50/B5
's Heerenberg, Neth. 50/D5
's Hertogenbosch, Neth. 50/C5
Sa Dec, Viet. 78/D4
Saab (int'l arpt.), Swe. 38/F2
Sääksjärvi (lake), Fin. 39/K1
Saal an der Donau, Ger. 55/E5
Saalbach (riv.), Ger. 54/B4
Saaldorf, Ger. 55/E2
Saale (riv.), Ger. 40/F3
Saales, Col de (pass), Fr. 56/D1
Saalfeld, Ger. 43/J1
Saalfelden am Steinernen Meer, Aus. 43/K3
Saane (riv.), Swi. 56/D5
Saanen, Swi. 56/D5
Saanta (peak), Kenya 104/C2
Saar (riv.), Ger. 53/F5
Saarbrücken, Ger. 53/F5
Saarburg, Ger. 53/F4
Saaremaa (isl.), Est. 60/D4
Saarland (state), Ger. 43/G2
Saarlouis, Ger. 53/F5
Saas, Swi. 57/F4
Saas Fee, Swi. 56/D5
Saastal (valley), Swi. 56/D5
Sab (riv.), Camb. 78/D3
Saba (isl.), NAnt. 141/N8
Šabac, Yugo. 48/D3
Sabadell, Sp. 45/L6
Sabae, Japan 74/E3
Sabah (reg.), Malay. 67/L9
Sabalgarh, India 84/A2
Sabana (arch.), Bang. 145/F1
Sabana de Uchire, Ven. 153/E2
Sabanalarga, Col. 152/C3
Sabanalarga, Col. 152/C2
Sabancuy, Mex. 144/D2
Sabaneta, Ven. 152/D2
Sabang, Indo. 80/A2
Sabanita, Pan. 145/G4
Sabasṭīyah, WBnk. 91/G7
Sabat (riv.), Sudan 93/F4
Sabbio Chiese, It. 58/D1
Sabbioneta, It. 58/D3
Sabhā, Libya 96/H2
Sabie (riv.), Moz. 107/F2
Sabinal, Cayo (isl.), Cuba 145/G1
Sabiñánigo, Sp. 45/E1
Sabinas, Mex. 132/C5
Sabinas (riv.), Mex. 140/A2
Sabinas Hidalgo, Mex. 132/C5
Sabine (lake), La,Tx, US 129/J5
Sabine (riv.), La,Tx, US 129/J5
Sabinópolis, Braz. 155/D1
Sabkhat al Bardawīl (lag.), Egypt 91/C4
Sabkhat al Jabbūl (lake), Syria 90/D3
Sabkhat al Mūḩ (lake), Syria 90/D3
Sablayan, Phil. 81/F1
Sable (isl.), NS, Can. 131/K3
Sable (cape), NS, Can. 131/H3
Sablé-sur-Sarthe, Fr. 42/C3
Saboeiro, Braz. 154/C2
Sabor (riv.), Port. 44/B2
Sabra (cape), Indo. 81/H4
Sabrina (coast), Ant. 160/J
Sabugal, Port. 44/B2
Sabzevār, Iran 89/G1
Sacajawea (peak), Or, US 126/D4
Sácama, Col. 152/C3
Sacaton, Az, US 137/S19
Sacavém, Port. 45/P10
Saccarello (peak), It. 58/A4
Sacco (riv.), It. 46/C2
Sacedón, Sp. 44/D2
Săcele, Rom. 49/G3
Sachigo (lake), On, Can. 127/K2
Sachigo (riv.), On, Can. 122/G3
Sachs Harbour, NW, Can. 122/D1
Sachseln, Swi. 57/E4
Sachsen (state), Ger. 40/G3

221
Sachs – Salas

Sachsen-Anhalt (state), Ger. 40/F3
Sachsenbrunn, Ger. 54/D2
Sachsenhagen, Ger. 51/G4
Sacile, It. 59/F1
Säckingen, Ger. 56/D2
Sackville, NB, Can. 131/H2
Saclay, Fr. 30/J5
Saco, Me, US 131/G3
Sacramento (cap.), Ca, US 128/B3
Sacramento, Braz. 155/C1
Sacramento (valley), Ca, US 128/B3
Sacramento (riv.), Ca, US 124/B4
Sacramento (mts.), NM, US 124/E5
Sacramento (co.), Ca, US 135/M10
Sacramento, Pampa del (plain), Peru 156/C2
Sacramento River Deep Water Ship Canal, Ca, US 135/L10
Sacratif (cape), Sp. 44/D4
Sacred (falls), Hi, US 124/W12
Sacro (peak), It. 46/E2
Sacro Monte, It. 58/B1
Sada, SAfr. 106/D4
Sádaba, Sp. 44/E1
Sadābād, India 84/B2
Sa'dah, Yem. 88/D5
Saddam (int'l arpt.), Iraq 90/F3
Saddle (hills), Ab,BC, Can. 126/C2
Saddle (riv.), NJ, US 139/J8
Saddle Brook, NJ, US 139/J8
Saddle River, NJ, US 139/J7
Saddle Rock, NY, US 139/K8
Saddle, The (peak), Sc, UK 36/A2
Saddleworth, Austl. 113/H5
Sādhaura, India 86/D4
Sādiqābād, Pak. 89/K3
Sado (isl.), Japan 71/Q4
Sado (riv.), Port. 44/A3
Sadovo, Bul. 47/J1
Sadowara, Japan 74/B4
Sādri, India 89/K3
Sadripante (mt.), Phil. 81/F1
Sadulshahar, India 86/C5
Saerbeck, Ger. 51/E4
Saeul, Lux. 53/E4
Şafājah (well), Egypt 101/C3
Safāqis, Tun. 96/H1
Safāqis (gov.), Tun. 99/H2
Safed Koh (range), Pak. 86/A3
Saffānīyah, Ra's as (pt.), SAr. 88/E3
Saffig, Ger. 53/G3
Säffle, Swe. 38/E2
Safford, Az, US 128/E4
Saffron Walden, Eng, UK 33/G2
Safi (cape), Mor. 98/C2
Safi, Mor. 98/C2
Safīd (riv.), Afg. 89/J1
Safid Khers (mts.), Afg. 89/K1
Safid Kūh (mts.), Afg. 89/H2
Safidon, India 86/D5
Safien, Swi. 57/F4
Safīpur, India 84/C2
Şāfītā, Syria 91/E2
Safonovo, Rus. 60/G5
Safranbolu, Turk. 62/E4
Sag Harbor, NY, US 139/F2
Saga (pref.), Japan 74/A4
Saga, China 85/E1
Saga, Japan 74/B4
Sagae, Japan 76/B4
Sagaing (div.), Myan. 70/F7
Sagaing, Myan. 83/G3
Sagaing (state), Myan. 83/F3
Sagami (sea), Japan 75/F3
Sagami (riv.), Japan 77/C2
Sagami (lake), Japan 77/C2
Sagami (bay), Japan 77/C3
Sagamihara, Japan 75/F3
Sagamiko, Japan 77/C2
Sagamore Hill Nat'l Hist. Site, NY, US 139/M8
Sāgar, India 84/B4
Sagard, Ger. 38/E4
Sagarmatha (zone), Nepal 85/F2
Sagarmatha (Everest) (mtn.), China,Nepal 85/F2
Sagarmatha NP, Nepal 85/F2
Sagauli, India 85/E2
Sagavanirktok (riv.), Ak, US 134/J2
Sagay, Phil. 81/F1
Saggart, Ire. 34/B5
Saghyz (riv.), Kaz. 63/K2
Saginaw, Mi, US 130/D3
Saginaw (bay), Mi, US 130/D3
Saglek (bay), Nf, Can. 123/K3
Sagone, Golfe de (gulf), Fr. 46/A1
Sagter Ems (riv.), Ger. 51/E2
Sagua de Tánamo, Cuba 145/H1
Sagua la Grande, Cuba 145/F1
Saguaro NP, Az, US 128/E4
Saguenay (riv.), Qu, Can. 131/G1
Saguia el Hamra (riv.), WSah. 96/C2
Sagunto, Sp. 45/E3
Sagy, Fr. 30/H4
Sa'gya, China 85/G1
Saḩāb, Jor. 91/D4
Sahagún, Sp. 44/C1
Sahagún, Col. 152/C2
Sahagún, Mex. 143/L7
Saḩam, Jor. 91/D3
Sahand (mtn.), Iran 88/E1
Sahara (des.), Afr. 93/B2
Sahāranpur, India 86/D5
Saharsa, India 85/F3
Sahaspur, India 84/B1
Sahaswān, India 84/B1
Sahavato, Madg. 107/J8
Sahāwar, India 84/B2
Sahel (riv.), Alg. 100/H4
Sāhibganj, India 85/F3
Şahinli, Turk. 49/H5
Sāhīwāl, Pak. 86/B4
Sahiwal, Pak. 86/B4
Şaḩrā Marzūq (des.), Libya 96/H3
Şaḩrā' Rabyānah (des.), Libya 97/K3
Sahrho, Jebel (mts.), Mor. 98/D3
Sahuaripa, Mex. 142/C2
Sahuayo de Morelos, Mex. 142/E4
Šahy, Slvk. 41/K4
Sai (canal), India 82/D2
Sai Yok NP, Thai. 78/B3
Saïda, Alg. 100/F5
Saidpur, Bang. 85/G3
Saidpur, India 84/D3
Saignelégier, Swi. 56/D3
Saigō, Japan 74/C2
Saigon, Viet. 78/D4
Saijō, Japan 74/C4
Saikai NP, Japan 74/A4
Saiki, Japan 74/B4
Sailly, Fr. 30/H4
Sailly-sur-la-Lys, Fr. 52/B2
Sailu, India 89/L5
Saimaa (lake), Fin. 37/J3
Sain Alto, Mex. 142/E4
Sainghin-en-Weppes, Fr. 52/B2
Sains-du-Nord, Fr. 52/D3
Saint Abb's (pt.), Sc, UK 36/D5
Saint-Affrique, Fr. 42/E5
Saint Agnes (pt.), Eng, UK 32/A6
Saint Albans, WV, US 130/D4
Saint Alban's, Nf, Can. 131/L2
Saint Albans, Vt, US 130/F2
Saint Albans, Eng, UK 30/C1
Saint Albert, Ab, Can. 126/E2
Saint-Amable, Qu, Can. 131/P6
Saint-Amand-les-Eaux, Fr. 52/C3
Saint-Amand-Montrond, Fr. 42/E3
Saint-Amarin, Fr. 56/D2
Saint-Ambroise, Qu, Can. 131/G1
Saint-Amé, Fr. 56/C1
Saint-André, Reun. 107/S15
Saint-André, Fr. 52/C2
Saint-André-de-Cubzac, Fr. 42/C4
Saint-André-les-Vergers, Fr. 42/F2
Saint Andrew's (bay), Sc, UK 36/D4
Saint Andrews, Sc, UK 36/D4
Saint Ann (cape), SLeo. 102/B5
Saint Anns, On, Can. 131/Q9
Saint Ann's (pt.), Wal, UK 32/A3
Saint Ann's Bay, Jam. 141/F4
Saint Anthony, Nf, Can. 131/L1
Saint-Antoine, Qu, Can. 131/N6
Saint Arnaud, Austl. 115/B3
Saint-Arnoult-en-Yvelines, Fr. 30/H6
Saint Aubin, Chl, UK 42/B2
Saint-Aubin, Swi. 56/C4
Saint-Aubin, Fr. 56/B3
Saint-Augustin, Fr. 30/M5
Saint Augustine, Fl, US 133/H4
Saint Augustine Beach, Fl, US 133/H4
Saint Austell (bay), Eng, UK 32/B6
Saint Austell, Eng, UK 32/B6
Saint-Avé, Fr. 42/B3
Saint-Avold, Fr. 53/F5
Saint-Barthélemy (isl.), Fr. 141/N8
Saint-Barthélemy-d'Anjou, Fr. 42/C3
Saint-Barthélemy, Pic de (peak), Fr. 42/D5
Saint Bees (pt.), Eng, UK 34/E2
Saint-Benoît, Fr. 42/D3
Saint-Benoît, Reun. 107/S15
Saint-Benoît, Qu, Can. 131/M6
Saint Bernard, La, US 137/Q17
Saint Bernard (parish), La, US 137/Q17
Saint-Berthevin, Fr. 42/C2
Saint-Blaise, Swi. 56/C3
Saint-Blaise, Qu, Can. 131/P7
Saint Blaize (cape), SAfr. 106/C4
Saint Boswells, Sc, UK 36/D5
Saint-Brice-Courcelles, Fr. 52/C5
Saint-Brice-sous-Forêt, Fr. 30/K5
Saint Bride's (bay), Wal, UK 32/A3
Saint-Brieuc, Fr. 42/B2
Saint-Brieuc (bay), Fr. 42/B2
Saint-Bruno-de-Montarville, Qu, Can. 131/P6
Saint-Calais, Fr. 42/D3
Saint-Canut, Qu, Can. 131/M6
Saint Catharines, On, Can. 131/R9
Saint Catherine (mt.), Gren. 153/F1
Saint Catherine's (pt.), Eng, UK 33/E5
Saint Catherine's (hill), Eng, UK 33/E5
Saint-Céré, Fr. 42/D4
Saint-Cergue, Swi. 56/C5
Saint-Cergues, Fr. 56/C5
Saint-Chamond, Fr. 42/F4
Saint Charles, Md, US 130/E4
Saint Charles, Mo, US 137/G8
Saint Charles (parish), La, US 137/P17
Saint Charles (co.), Mo, US 137/F8
Saint Charles, Il, US 135/P16
Saint-Chély-d'Apcher, Fr. 42/E4
Saint-Chéron, Fr. 30/J6
Saint Christoffel (peak), NAnt. 152/D1
Saint Clair (lake), Can.,US 135/G7
Saint Clair (peak), Az, US 137/S18
Saint Clair (co.), Il, US 137/G9
Saint Clair (co.), Mi, US 135/G6
Saint Clair, Mi, US 130/D3
Saint Clair, Pa, US 138/B2
Saint Clair Beach, On, Can. 135/G7
Saint Clair Shores, Mi, US 135/G6
Saint-Claude, Fr. 56/B5
Saint Cloud, Mn, US 127/K4
Saint-Cloud, Fr. 30/J5
Saint-Constant, Qu, Can. 131/N7
Saint Croix (riv.), US 130/A2
Saint Croix (isl.), USVI 141/M8
Saint Cyr (mt.), Yk, Can. 134/M3
Saint-Cyr-l'École, Fr. 30/J5
Saint-Cyr-sous-Dourdan, Fr. 30/J6
Saint-Cyr-sur-Morin, Fr. 30/M5
Saint David's (pt.), Wal, UK 32/A3
Saint David's, Wal, UK 32/A3
Saint-Denis, Fr. 30/K5
Saint-Denis, Reun. 107/S15
Saint-Denis-en-Bugey, Fr. 56/B6
Saint-Dié, Fr. 56/C1
Saint-Dizier, Fr. 53/D6
Saint-Doulchard, Fr. 42/E3
Saint-Édouard, Qu, Can. 131/N7
Saint Eleanors, PE, Can. 131/J2
Saint Elias (mt.), Ak, US 134/K3
Saint Elias (cape), Ak, US 134/K4
Saint Elias (mts.), Ak, US 122/B2
Saint-Éloy-les-Mines, Fr. 42/E3
Saint-Esprit, Qu, Can. 131/N6
Saint-Estève, Fr. 42/E5
Saint-Étienne, Fr. 42/F4
Saint-Étienne-au-Mont, Fr. 52/A2
Saint-Étienne-de-Baïgorry, Fr. 42/C5
Saint-Étienne-de-Tinée, Fr. 43/G4
Saint-Étienne-du-Rouvray, Fr. 42/D2
Saint-Étienne-lès-Remiremont, Fr. 56/C1
Saint-Eustache, Qu, Can. 131/N6
Saint Eustatius (isl.), NAnt. 141/N8
Saint-Fargeau-Ponthierry, Fr. 30/K6
Saint-Félicien, Qu, Can. 131/F1
Saint-Félix, Fr. 56/B6
Saint-Florent-sur-Cher, Fr. 42/E3
Saint-Florentin Fr. 42/E2
Saint-Floris, PN de, CAfr. 97/K6
Saint-Four, Fr. 42/E4
Saint Francis (riv.), Ar, US 129/K4
Saint Francis (riv.), Mo, US 133/F2
Saint Francis, Ks, US 129/G3
Saint Francis (cape), SAfr. 106/D4
Saint Francis, Wi, US 135/Q14
Saint Francisville, La, US 129/K5
Saint Francois (mts.), US 133/F2
Saint Gallen (canton), Swi. 57/F3
Saint-Gaudens, Fr. 42/D5
Saint-Genis-Pouilly, Fr. 56/C5
Saint George, Austl. 114/C5
Saint George (isl.), Ak, US 134/E4
Saint George, Ak, US 134/E4
Saint George (pt.), Ca, US 126/B5
Saint George, SC, US 133/H3
Saint George, Ut, US 128/D3
Saint George, NB, Can. 131/H2
Saint George (cape), Nf, Can. 131/K1
Saint George's (bay), Nf, Can. 131/J2
Saint George's, Nf, Can. 131/K1
Saint-Georges, Qu, Can. 131/G2
Saint George's (cap.), Gren. 153/F1
Saint Georges, De, US 138/C4
Saint George's (chan.), Ire.,UK 31/Q11
Saint-Germain, Fr. 56/C2
Saint-Germain-de-la-Grange, Fr. 30/H5
Saint-Germain-du-Bois, Fr. 56/B4
Saint-Germain-du-Corbéis, Fr. 42/D2
Saint-Germain-du-Plain, Fr. 56/A4
Saint-Germain-en-Laye, Fr. 30/J5
Saint-Germain-lès-Corbeil, Fr. 30/K6
Saint-Germain-sous Doue, Fr. 30/M5
Saint-Germain-sur-Morin, Fr. 30/L5
Saint-Germer-de-Fly, Fr. 52/A5
Saint-Gervais, Fr. 30/H4
Saint-Gervais-les-Bains, Fr. 56/C6
Saint-Ghislain, Belg. 52/C3
Saint-Gilles, Fr. 42/F5
Saint-Gilles-Croix-de-Vie, Fr. 42/C3
Saint-Gingolph, Swi. 56/C5
Saint-Girons, Fr. 42/D5
Saint-Gobain, Fr. 52/C4
Saint Govan's (pt.), Wal, UK 32/B3
Saint-Gratien, Fr. 30/J5
Saint Hedwig, Tx, US 137/U21
Saint Helena (bay), SAfr. 105/C7
Saint Helena (isl.), Austl. 114/F6
Saint Helens, Austl. 115/D4
Saint Helens (pt.), Austl. 115/D4
Saint Helens (mt.), Wa, US 126/C4
Saint Helens, Or, US 126/C4
Saint Helens, Eng, UK 35/F5
Saint Helier (cap.), Chl, UK 42/B2
Saint-Herblain, Fr. 42/C3
Saint-Hilarion, Fr. 30/H6
Saint-Hippolyte, Fr. 56/C3
Saint-Honoré, Qu, Can. 131/G1
Saint-Hubert, Qu, Can. 131/P6
Saint-Hubert, Belg. 53/E3
Saint-Hyacinthe, Qu, Can. 130/F2
Saint Ignace (isl.), On, Can. 127/L3
Saint Ignace, Mi, US 130/C2
Saint-Imier, Swi. 56/D3
Saint-Isidore-de-Laprairie, Qu, Can. 131/N7
Saint Ives (bay), Eng, UK 32/A6
Saint Ives, Eng, UK 33/F2
Saint Ives, Eng, UK 32/A6
Saint Jacques (int'l arpt.), Fr. 42/C2
Saint-Jacques-le-Mineur, Qu, Can. 131/P7
Saint James, NY, US 139/E2
Saint James (cape), BC, Can. 122/C3
Saint-Jean (riv.), Qu, Can. 131/H1
Saint-Jean (lake), Qu, Can. 123/J4
Saint-Jean-d'Angély, Fr. 42/C4
Saint-Jean-de-la-Ruelle, Fr. 42/D3
Saint-Jean-de-Losne, Fr. 56/B3
Saint-Jean-Port-Joli, Qu, Can. 131/G2
Saint-Jean-sur-Richelieu, Qu, Can. 130/F2
Saint-Jeoire, Fr. 56/C5
Saint-Jérôme, Qu, Can. 131/N6
Saint Joe, La, US 137/Q16
Saint Joe (riv.), Id,Wa, US 124/C2
Saint John, NB, Can. 131/H2
Saint John (isl.), USVI 141/M8
Saint John (riv.), Me, US 123/K4
Saint John The Baptist (parish), La, US 137/P16
Saint Johns, Az, US 128/E4
Saint Johns (riv.), Fl, US 133/H4
Saint John's (cap.), Anti. 141/N8
Saint John's (pt.), NI, UK 34/C3
Saint Johnsbury, Vt, US 131/F2
Saint Jones (riv.), De, US 138/C5
Saint Joseph (riv.), US 130/C3
Saint Joseph (isl.), On, Can. 130/C2
Saint Joseph, La, US 129/K5
Saint Joseph, Mo, US 129/J3
Saint Joseph (lake), On, Can. 122/G3
Saint-Joseph, Reun. 107/S15
Saint-Juéry, Fr. 42/E5
Saint-Julien, Fr. 56/B3
Saint-Julien-en-Genevois, Fr. 56/C5
Saint-Julien-les-Villas, Fr. 42/F2
Saint-Junien, Fr. 42/D4
Saint-Just-en-Chaussée, Fr. 52/B4
Saint Kilda (isl.), UK 31/P8
Saint Kitts (isl.), StK. 141/J4
Saint Kitts and Nevis (ctry.) 141/N8
Saint-Lambert, Qu, Can. 131/P6
Saint Laurent, Mb, Can. 127/J3
Saint-Laurent (riv.), Qu, Can. 131/G1
Saint-Laurent, Qu, Can. 131/N6
Saint-Laurent-Blangy, Fr. 52/B3
Saint-Laurent-de-Cerdans, Fr. 42/E5
Saint-Laurent du Maroni, FrG. 151/H2
Saint-Laurent-en-Grandvaux, Fr. 56/B4
Saint-Laurent-sur-Saône, Fr. 56/A5
Saint Lawrence, Nf, Can. 131/L2
Saint Lawrence (riv.), US,Can. 130/F2
Saint Lawrence, Pa, US 138/C3
Saint Lawrence (isl.), Ak, US 134/D3
Saint Lawrence (gulf), Can. 131/J1
Saint Lawrence Islands NP, On, Can. 130/E2
Saint-Lazare, Qu, Can. 131/M7
Saint-Léger, Belg. 53/E4
Saint-Léger-en-Yvelines, Fr. 30/H5
Saint-Léger-lès-Domart, Fr. 52/B3
Saint Leonard (mt.), Austl. 115/G5
Saint-Léonard, Qu, Can. 131/N6
Saint-Léonard, Fr. 52/A2
Saint-Leu, Reun. 107/S15
Saint-Leu-d'Esserent, Fr. 52/B5
Saint-Leu-la-Forêt, Fr. 30/J4
Saint Llorenc del Munt, PN, Sp. 45/K6
Saint-Lô, Fr. 42/C2
Saint Louis, Sk, Can. 127/G2
Saint Louis (riv.), Mn, US 130/A2
Saint-Louis, Sen. 102/A2
Saint-Louis (pol. reg.), Sen. 102/B3
Saint Louis, Mo, US 137/G8
Saint Louis (co.), Mo, US 137/F8
Saint-Louis, Fr. 56/D2
Saint Louis (lake), Qu, Can. 131/N7
Saint-Louis, Reun. 107/S15
Saint-Louis-de-Gonzague, Qu, Can. 131/N7
Saint-Louis-de-Kent, NB, Can. 131/H2
Saint-Louis du Nord, Haiti 145/H2
Saint-Loup-sur-Semouse, Fr. 56/C2
Saint-Lubin-des-Joncherets, Fr. 42/D2
Saint-Luc, Qu, Can. 131/P7
Saint Lucia (lake), SAfr. 107/F3
Saint Lucia (cape), SAfr. 107/F3
Saint Lucia (chan.), Mart.,StL. 141/N9
Saint Lucia (ctry.) 141/N9
Saint Lucia Estuary, SAfr. 107/F3
Saint-Lucien, Fr. 30/G6
Saint Maarten (isl.), NAnt. 141/N8
Saint Magnus (bay), Sc, UK 31/W13
Saint-Maixent l'École, Fr. 42/C3
Saint Malo, Mb, Can. 127/J3
Saint-Malo, Fr. 42/B2
Saint-Malo, Golfe de (gulf), Fr. 42/B2
Saint-Mandrier-sur-Mer, Fr. 42/F5
Saint-Marc, Haiti 145/H2
Saint-Marc-sur-Richelieu, Qu, Can. 131/P6
Saint-Marcel, Fr. 56/A4
Saint-Mard, Fr. 30/L4
Saint Maries, Id, US 126/D4
Saint Martin (lake), Mb, Can. 127/J3
Saint-Martin (isl.), Fr. 141/J4
Saint-Martin, Swi. 56/D5
Saint-Martin-Boulogne, Fr. 52/A2
Saint-Martin-d'Ablois, Fr. 52/C6
Saint-Martin-d'Hères, Fr. 42/F4
Saint-Martin-du-Tertre, Fr. 30/K4
Saint-Martin-la-Garenne, Fr. 30/H4
Saint Martinville, La, US 129/K5
Saint Mary (cape), Gam. 102/A3
Saint Mary (peak), Austl. 113/H4
Saint Mary's, Ak, US 134/F3
Saint Marys, Austl. 115/D4
Saint Marys, Ga, US 133/H4
Saint Marys, Pa, US 130/E3
Saint Mary's, On, Can. 130/D3
Saint Mary's (riv.), NS, Can. 131/J2
Saint-Mathieu-de-Beloeil, Qu, Can. 131/N7
Saint Matthew (isl.), Ak, US 134/D3
Saint Matthews, SC, US 133/H3
Saint Matthias Group (isls.), PNG 116/E5
Saint-Maur-des-Fossés, Fr. 30/K5
Saint-Maurice, Swi. 56/D5
Saint-Maurice (riv.), Qu, Can. 123/J4
Saint-Max, Fr. 53/F6
Saint-Maximin-la-Sainte-Baume, Fr. 42/F5
Saint-Memmie, Fr. 53/D6
Saint-Méry, Fr. 30/L6
Saint Michael, Ak, US 134/F3
Saint Michaels, Md, US 138/B6
Saint-Michel (bay), Fr. 42/C2
Saint-Michel, Fr. 53/D4
Saint-Michel-sur-Meurthe, Fr. 56/C1
Saint-Michel-sur-Orge, Fr. 30/J6
Saint-Mihiel, Fr. 53/E6
Saint Monance, Sc, UK 36/D4
Saint-Nabord, Fr. 56/C1
Saint-Nazaire, Fr. 42/B3
Saint Neots, Eng, UK 33/F2
Saint-Nicolas, Belg. 53/E2
Saint-Nicolas-d'Aliermont, Fr. 42/D2
Saint Niklaus, Swi. 56/D5
Saint-Nom-la-Bretèche, Fr. 30/J5
Saint-Omer, Fr. 52/B2
Saint-Omer-en-Chaussée, Fr. 52/A4
Saint-Ouen, Fr. 52/B3
Saint-Ouen-en-Brie, Fr. 30/L6
Saint-Ouen-L'Aumône, Fr. 30/J4
Saint-Pamphile, Qu, Can. 131/G2
Saint-Pascal, Qu, Can. 131/G2
Saint-Pathus, Fr. 30/L4
Saint Paul, Ak, US 134/D4
Saint Paul (riv.), Libr. 96/C6
Saint Paul (isl.), Ak, US 134/W23
Saint Paul (cap.), Mn, US 127/K4
Saint Paul, Ab, Can. 126/F2
Saint Paul, Ks, US 132/E2
Saint Paul (cape), Gha. 103/F5
Saint Paul, Reun. 107/S15
Saint-Paul-lès-Dax, Fr. 42/C5
Saint Paul Rocks (isl.), Braz. 22/H5
Saint Paul's Church Nat'l Hist. Site, NY, US 139/K8
Saint-Pé-de-Bigorre, Fr. 42/C5
Saint Peter, Mn, US 127/K4
Saint Peter (isl.), Austl. 113/G5
Saint Peter Port (cap.), Chl, UK 42/B2
Saint Peters, Mo, US 137/F8
Saint Petersburg, Fl, US 133/H5
Saint Petersburg, Rus. 61/T7
Saint-Philippe-de-Laprairie, Qu, Can. 131/P7
Saint-Pierre (isl.), StP. 131/K2
Saint-Pierre, Fr. 131/K2
Saint-Pierre, Fr. 141/N9
Saint-Pierre, Reun. 107/S15
Saint Pierre and Miquelon (dpcy.), Fr. 131/K2
Saint-Pierre-des-Corps, Fr. 42/D3
Saint-Pierre-du-Mont, Fr. 42/C5
Saint-Pierre-du-Perray, Fr. 30/K6
Saint-Pierre-en-Faucigny, Fr. 56/C5
Saint Pierre-Jolys, Mb, Can. 127/J3
Saint-Pierre-sur-Dives, Fr. 42/C2
Saint-Point (lake), Fr. 56/C4
Saint-Pol-de-Léon, Fr. 42/B2
Saint-Pol-sur-Mer, Fr. 52/B1
Saint-Pol-sur-Ternoise, Fr. 52/B3
Saint-Pourçain-sur-Sioule, Fr. 42/E3
Saint-Prex, Swi. 56/C5
Saint-Prix, Fr. 30/J4
Saint-Quentin, Fr. 52/C4
Saint-Quentin, Canal de (canal), Fr. 52/C4
Saint-Rambert-en-Bugey, Fr. 56/B6
Saint-Raphaël, Fr. 43/G5
Saint-Rémi, Qu, Can. 131/N7
Saint-Rémy-de-Provence, Fr. 42/F5
Saint-Rémy-lès-Chevreuse, Fr. 30/J5
Saint-Rémy-l'Honoré, Fr. 30/H5
Saint-Roch-de-l'Achigan, Qu, Can. 131/N6
Saint Rose, La, US 137/P17
Saint Sampson's, Chl, UK 42/B2
Saint-Saulve, Fr. 52/C3
Saint-Sauveur, Fr. 56/C2
Saint-Sauveur-des-Monts, Qu, Can. 131/M6
Saint-Sever, Fr. 42/C5
Saint Simons (isl.), Ga, US 133/H4
Saint Simons Island, Ga, US 133/H4
Saint-Soupplets, Fr. 30/L4
Saint Stephen, NB, Can. 131/H2
Saint-Sulpice, Fr. 42/D5
Saint Tammany, La, US 137/Q16
Saint Tammany (parish), La, US 137/P16
Saint Thomas, On, Can. 130/D3
Saint Thomas (isl.), USVI 141/H4
Saint-Timothée, Qu, Can. 131/M7
Saint-Trivier-de-Courtes, Fr. 56/B5
Saint-Tropez, Fr. 43/G5
Saint-Urbain-Premier, Qu, Can. 131/N7
Saint-Ursanne, Swi. 56/D3
Saint-Valery-en-Caux, Fr. 42/D2
Saint-Valery-sur-Somme, Fr. 52/A3
Saint-Vallier, Fr. 42/F3
Saint-Vaury, Fr. 42/D3
Saint Vincent (pt.), Austl. 115/C4
Saint Vincent (isl.), StV. 141/N9
Saint Vincent, It. 58/A1
Saint Vincent and the Grenadines (ctry.) 141/N9
Saint-Vincent-de-Tyrosse, Fr. 42/C5
Saint Vincent Passage (chan.), StL.,StV. 141/N9
Saint-Vit, Fr. 56/B3
Saint-Vith, Belg. 53/F3
Saint-Vrain, Fr. 30/K6
Saint Walburg, Sk, Can. 126/F2
Saint-Witz, Fr. 30/K4
Saint-Yrieix-la-Perche, Fr. 42/D4
Sainte-Agathe-des-Monts, Qu, Can. 130/F2
Sainte-Anne-des-Monts, Qu, Can. 131/H1
Sainte-Anne-des-Plaines, Qu, Can. 131/N6
Sainte-Aulde, Fr. 30/M5
Sainte-Croix, Swi. 56/C4
Sainte-Croix-aux-Mines, Fr. 56/D1
Sainte-Foy, Qu, Can. 131/G2
Sainte-Geneviève-des-Bois, Fr. 30/K6
Sainte-Julie, Qu, Can. 131/P6
Sainte-Marie, Qu, Can. 131/G2
Sainte-Marie, Fr. 141/N9
Sainte-Marie-aux-Chênes, Fr. 53/F5
Sainte Marie, Nosy (isl.), Madg. 105/L10
Sainte-Martine, Qu, Can. 131/N7
Sainte-Maxime, Fr. 43/G5
Sainte-Mesme, Fr. 30/H6
Sainte Rose du Lac, Mb, Can. 127/J3
Sainte-Sigolène, Fr. 42/F4
Sainte-Thérèse, Qu, Can. 131/N6
Sainte-Tulle, Fr. 42/F5
Saintes, Fr. 42/C4
Sainthia, India 85/F4
Sāipal (peak), Nepal 82/D2
Saipan (isl.), NMar. 116/D3
Saitama (pref.), Japan 75/F2
Saito, Japan 74/B4
Saiwa Swamp NP, Kenya 104/B2
Sajama, Bol. 156/D5
Sajama, PN, Bol. 156/D5
Sajószentpéter, Hun. 41/L4
Sak (riv.), SAfr. 106/C3
Sakado, Japan 77/C2
Sakae, Japan 77/E2
Sakahogi, Japan 77/L5
Sakai, Japan 74/E2
Sakai, Japan 75/F2
Sakai (riv.), Japan 77/C3
Sakai, Japan 77/C1
Sakaide, Japan 74/C3
Sakaigawa, Japan 77/B2
Sakaiminato, Japan 74/C3
Sakakawea (lake), ND, US 127/H3
Sakami (lake), Qu, Can. 123/J3
Sakaraha, Madg. 107/H8
Sakarya (riv.), Turk. 62/D4
Sakarya (prov.), Turk. 62/D4
Sakauchi, Japan 77/K4
Sakawa, Japan 74/C4
Sakay (riv.), Madg. 107/H7
Sakçagöze, Turk. 90/D2
Sakeny (riv.), Madg. 107/H7
Sakété, Ben. 103/F5
Sakha (Yakutiya) (aut. rep.), Rus. 65/Q4
Sakhalin (gulf), Rus. 65/Q4
Sakhalin (isl.), Rus. 65/Q4
Sakhalinskaya (obl.), Rus. 65/Q4
Sakhnīn, Isr. 91/G6
Sakht Sar, Iran 88/F1
Şäki, Azer. 63/H4
Sakishima (isl.), Japan 67/M7
Sakmara (riv.), Rus. 87/C2
Sakon Nakhon, Thai. 78/D2
Sakrand, Pak. 89/J3
Sakti, India 84/D4
Saku, Japan 75/F2
Saku, Japan 77/A1
Sakura, Japan 77/E1
Sakura, Japan 77/E2
Sakuragawa, Japan 77/E2
Sakurai, Japan 77/J6
Saky, Ukr. 62/E3
Sakya Monastery, China 85/G1
Säkylä, Fin. 39/K1
Sal (riv.), Rus. 63/G3
Sal (pt.), Hon. 144/E3
Sal (isl.), CpV. 93/K10
Sal Rei, CpV. 93/K10
Šal'a, Slvk. 48/C1
Sala, Swe. 38/G2
Sala Baganza, It. 58/D3
Sala Consilina, It. 46/D2
Salada (lake), Mex. 142/B1
Saladas, Arg. 157/E2
Saladillo (riv.), Arg. 159/J11
Saladillo, Arg. 158/F2
Salado (riv.), Mex. 132/D5
Salado (riv.), Arg. 147/C6
Salado del Norte (riv.), Arg. 147/C5
Salaga, Gha. 103/E4
Şalaḩ Ad Din (gov.), Iraq 90/E3
Sălaj (co.), Rom. 41/M5
Sălaj (prov.), Rom. 49/F2
Salālah, Oman 88/F5
Salamá, Guat. 144/D3
Salamajärven NP, Fin. 60/E3
Salamanca, NY, US 130/E3
Salamanca, Mex. 143/E4
Salamanca, Sp. 44/C2
Salamat (riv.), Chad 96/J6
Salamatof, Ak, US 134/H3
Salamina, Col. 152/C2
Salamís, Gre. 47/H3
Salamís (isl.), Gre. 47/H3
Salamīyah, Syria 91/E2
Salangen, Nor. 37/F1
Salas, Peru 156/B2
Salas, Sp. 44/B1
Salas de los Infantes, Sp. 44/D1

222
Salav – San P

Salavat, Rus. 63/K1
Salaverry, Peru 156/B3
Salayar (isl.), Indo. 116/B5
Salbris, Fr. 42/E3
Salcantay (peak), Peru 156/C4
Saldaña, Sp. 44/C1
Saldanhabaai (bay), Safr. 106/K10
Saldus, Lat. 39/K3
Sale, Austl. 115/C3
Sale, It. 58/B3
Salé, Mor. 100/A2
Salé (prov.), Mor. 100/A3
Sale, Eng, UK 35/F5
Sale Marasino, It. 58/D1
Salebabu (isl.), Indo. 81/G3
Salekhard, Rus. 64/G3
Salem (cap.), Or, US 126/C4
Salem, NH, US 131/G3
Salem, In, US 130/C4
Salem, India 82/C5
Salem, Ger. 57/F2
Salem (co.), NJ, US 138/C4
Salem, NJ, US 138/C4
Salem, Mi, US 135/F7
Salemi, It. 46/C4
Salentina (pen.), It. 47/F2
Salerno, It. 46/D2
Salerno, Golfo di (gulf), It. 46/D2
Sales (pt.), Eng, UK 33/G3
Saleux, Fr. 52/B4
Salfit, WBnk. 91/G7
Salford, Eng, UK 35/F5
Salgado Filho (int'l arpt.), Braz. 155/B4
Salgar, Col. 152/C3
Salgesch, Swi. 56/D5
Salgótarján, Hun. 41/K4
Salgueiro, Braz. 154/C3
Salhus, Nor. 38/A1
Salies-de-Béarn, Fr. 42/C5
Salies-du-Salat, Fr. 42/D5
Şalif, Yem. 88/D5
Salihli, Turk. 62/D5
Salihorsk, Bela. 62/C1
Salima, Malw. 105/F3
Salīmah (oasis), Sudan 101/B4
Salina, Ut, US 128/E3
Salina (isl.), It. 46/D3
Salina (pt.), Bahm. 145/H1
Salina Cruz, Mex. 144/C2
Salinas (riv.), Ca, US 128/B3
Salinas, Braz. 154/B5
Salinas, Ca, US 128/B3
Salinas (cape), Sp. 45/G3
Salinas, Ecu. 152/A5
Salinas de Hidalgo, Mex. 143/E4
Salinas Pueblo Missions Nat'l Mon., NM, US 129/F4
Salinas Y Aguada Blanca, Reserva Nacional, Peru 156/D4
Saline (riv.), Ks, US 132/D2
Saline, It. 59/D6
Saline, Sc, UK 36/C4
Salinópolis, Braz. 151/J4
Salins-les-Bains, Fr. 56/B4
Salisbury, NC, US 133/H3
Salisbury (plain), Eng, UK 32/D4
Salisbury, Eng, UK 33/E4
Salisbury (isl.), Nun., Can. 123/J2
Salisbury, NY, US 139/L9
Salitre (riv.), Braz. 154/B3
Salitre, Ecu. 152/B5
Salla, Fin. 60/F2
Salladasburg, Pa, US 138/A1
Sallanches, Fr. 56/C6
Salland (phys. reg.), Neth. 50/D4
Sallatouk (pt.), Gui. 102/B4
Sallaumines, Fr. 52/B3
Sallent, Sp. 45/F2
Salliqueló, Arg. 158/E3
Sallisaw, Ok, US 129/J4
Sally (pass), Ire. 34/B5
Salm (riv.), Ger. 53/F3
Salmān Pāk, Iraq 90/F3
Salmās, Iran 90/F2
Salmon (riv.), BC, Can. 126/C2
Salmon, Id, US 126/E4
Salmon (riv.), Id, US 124/C2
Salmon Arm, BC, Can. 126/D3
Salmon Falls (riv.), Id,Nv, US 128/D2
Salmon River (mts.), Id, US 124/C2
Salmon, South Fork (riv.), US 128/C2
Salmtal, Ger. 53/F4
Salò, It. 58/D1
Salo, Fin. 39/K1
Salon, India 84/C2
Salon (riv.), Fr. 40/C5
Salon-de-Provence, Fr. 42/F5
Salonga, PN de la, D.R. Congo 97/K8
Salonta, Rom. 48/E2
Salouël, Fr. 52/B4
Salpausselkä (mts.), Fin. 39/M1
Salpo, Peru 156/B3
Salses-le-Château, Fr. 42/E5
Sal'sk, Rus. 63/G3
Salso (riv.), It. 46/C4
Salsomaggiore Terme, It. 58/C3
Salt (riv.), SAfr. 106/C4
Salt (riv.), Az, US 137/R19
Salt (range), Pak. 86/B3
Salt Cay (isl.), UK 145/J1
Salt Draw (riv.), Tx, US 142/D2
Salt Fork Arkansas (riv.), US 129/H3
Salt Fork Red (riv.), US 129/G4
Salt Lake (co.), Ut, US 137/J12
Salt Lake City (cap.), Ut, US 126/F5
Salt Lake City, Ut, US 137/K12
Salt Meadow NWR, Ct, US 139/F1
Salt, North Fork (riv.), Mo, US 129/J2
Salt River Ind. Res., Az, US 137/S18
Salta, Arg. 157/C1
Saltaire, NY, US 139/E2
Saltash, Eng, UK 32/B6
Saltcoats, Sc, UK 36/B5
Saltdal, Nor. 37/E2
Saltee (isls.), Ire. 31/Q10
Saltfjorden (inlet), Nor. 37/E2
Saltillo, Mex. 143/E3
Salto, Uru. 157/E3
Salto, Braz. 155/C2
Salto, Arg. 158/E2
Salto da Divisa, Braz. 154/C5
Salto del Guairá, Par. 157/F1
Salto Grande (res.), Arg. 157/E3
Salto Santiago, Represa de (res.), Braz. 155/A3
Salton Sea (lake), Ca, US 124/C5
Saltvik, Fin. 39/J1
Saluda (riv.), SC, US 133/H3
Salug, Phil. 79/D6
Saluggia, It. 58/B2
Salunga-Landisville, Pa, US 138/B3
Sālūr, India 82/D4
Salurn (Salorno), It. 57/H5
Salut, Îles du (isls.), FrG. 151/H2
Saluzzo, It. 43/G4
Salvación (bay), Chile 159/B6
Salvador (lake), La, US 137/P17
Salvaleón de Higüey, DRep. 141/H4
Salvaterra de Magos, Port. 44/A3
Salvatierra, Mex. 143/E4
Salvatierra de Miño, Sp. 44/A1
Salween (riv.), Asia 67/J8
Salyan, Azer. 63/J5
Salyersville, Ky, US 130/D4
Salza (riv.), Aus. 41/H5
Salzach (riv.), Ger. 40/G5
Salzano, It. 59/F1
Salzbergen, Ger. 51/E4
Salzburg, Aus. 43/K3
Salzburg (int'l arpt.), Aus. 43/K3
Salzburg (prov.), Aus. 41/G5
Salzgitter, Ger. 51/H4
Salzhausen, Ger. 51/H2
Salzhemmendorf, Ger. 51/G4
Salzkotten, Ger. 51/F5
Salzwedel, Ger. 40/F2
Sam Rayburn (res.), Tx, US 140/C1
Sam Sao (mts.), Laos,Viet. 78/C1
Sam Son, Viet. 78/D2
Sama, Sp. 44/C1
Samak (cape), Indo. 80/C4
Samales Group (isls.), Phil. 81/F2
Samālkha, India 86/D5
Sāmalkot, India 82/D4
Samāna, India 86/D4
Samaná (cape), DRep. 141/H4
Samana (isl.), Bahm. 145/H1
Samandağı, Turk. 91/D1
Samani, Japan 76/C2
Samaniego, Col. 152/B4
Samannūd, Egypt 91/B4
Samaqua (riv.), Qu, Can. 131/F1
Samar, Jor. 91/D3
Samar (isl.), Phil. 67/M8
Samara (riv.), Rus. 87/B2
Samara (int'l arpt.), Rus. 63/J1
Samara, Rus. 63/J1
Samarskaya (obl.), Rus. 87/A2
Samarai, PNG 116/E6
Samarate, It. 58/B1
Samaria (reg.), WBnk. 91/G7
Samarinda, Indo. 81/E4
Samarqand, Uzb. 87/E5
Samarqand (pol. reg.), Uzb. 87/E5
Sāmarrā', Iraq 90/E3
Samasata, Pak. 86/A5
Samastipur, India 85/E3
Şamaxi, Azer. 63/J4
Sāmba, India 86/C3
Sambalpur, India 82/D3
Sambao (riv.), Madg. 107/H7
Sambar (cape), Indo. 80/D4
Sambas, Indo. 80/C3
Sambava, Madg. 107/J6
Sambhal, India 84/B1
Sambir, Ukr. 41/M4
Sambor Prei Kuk (ruin), Camb. 78/D3
Samborobón (riv.), Arg. 159/K11
Samborombón (bay), Arg. 159/F2
Sambre (riv.), Fr. 40/C3
Sambre à l'Oise, Canal de (canal), Fr. 52/C4
Sambriāl, Pak. 86/C3
Sambu, Japan 77/E2
Samburu Nat'l Rsv., Kenya 104/C2
Samch'ŏk, SKor. 74/A2
Samch'ŏnp'o, SKor. 73/E5
Samedan, Swi. 57/F4
Samer, Fr. 52/A2
Samfya Mission, Zam. 104/A5
Sámi, Gre. 47/G3
Samiria (riv.), Peru 156/C2
Samit (cape), Camb. 78/C4
Samkos (peak), Camb. 78/C3
Sammamish (lake), Wa, US 135/C2
Sammeron, Fr. 30/M5
Samnangjin, SKor. 74/A3
Samnaun, Swi. 57/G4
Samoa (ctry.) 117/H6
Samobor, Cro. 48/B3
Samoëns, Fr. 56/C5
Samoggia (riv.), It. 59/E4
Samokov, Bul. 47/H1
Samora (riv.), Port. 45/Q10
Samora Correia, Port. 45/Q10
Sámos (isl.), Gre. 90/A2
Sámos, Gre. 90/A2
Samothráki, Gre. 47/J2
Sampacho, Arg. 158/D2
Samper de Calanda, Sp. 45/E2
Sampit (riv.), Indo. 80/D4
Sampit, Indo. 80/D4
Samsø (isl.), Den. 38/D4
Samsø Bælt (chan.), Den. 38/D4
Samson (mt.), Austl. 114/E6
Samsonvale (lake), Austl. 114/E6
Samsun, Turk. 62/F4
Samsun (prov.), Turk. 62/F4
Samthar, India 84/B3
Samugheo, It. 46/A3
Samui (isl.), Thai. 83/H6
Samukawa, Japan 77/C3
Samundri, Pak. 86/B4
Samur (riv.), Azer.,Rus. 64/E5
Samut Prakan, Thai. 78/C3
Samut Sakhon, Thai. 78/C3
Samut Songkhram, Thai. 78/B3
Samye Monastery, China 85/H1
San, Mali 102/D3
San (riv.), Pol. 62/B2
San (riv.), Camb. 78/D3
San Adrián, Cabo de (cape), Sp. 44/A1
San Agustin (cape), Phil. 81/G2
San Agustín, Col. 152/B4
San Agustin de Guadalix, Sp. 45/N8
San Agustín, Parque Arqeológico, Col. 152/B4
San Ambrosio (isl.), Chile 147/B5
San Andreas (lake), Ca, US 135/J11
San Andres (mts.), NM, US 128/F4
San Andrés (lake), Mex. 144/B1
San Andrés, Col. 152/C3
San Andrés, Col. 145/F3
San Andrés Cuexcontitlán, Mex. 143/Q10
San Andrés de Giles, Arg. 159/J11
San Andrés de Machaca, Bol. 156/D5
San Andrés del Rabanedo, Sp. 44/C1
San Andrés, Isla de (isl.), Col. 140/E5
San Andrés Tuxtla, Mex. 144/C2
San Angelo, Tx, US 132/C4
San Anselmo, Ca, US 135/J11
San Antonio, Peru 156/B4
San Antonio (int'l arpt.), Tx, US 129/H5
San Antonio, Mex. 142/C4
San Antonio (riv.), Tx, US 140/B2
San Antonio (mt.), Ca, US 136/C2
San Antonio, Ecu. 152/B4
San Antonio, Ven. 153/F2
San Antonio (cape), Arg. 159/F3
San Antonio, Uru. 159/K11
San Antonio, Chile 158/N8
San Antonio Abad, Sp. 45/F3
San Antonio de Areco, Arg. 159/J11
San Antonio de Caparo, Ven. 152/D3
San Antonio del Golfo, Ven. 153/F2
San Antonio del Táchira, Ven. 152/C3
San Antonio Oeste, Arg. 158/D4
San Antonio, Punta (pt.), Mex. 142/B2
San Augustine, Tx, US 132/E4
San Bartolo, Peru 156/B4
San Bartolomé de Tirajana, Canl. 45/X17
San Bartolome Tlaltelulco, Mex. 143/Q10
San Bartolomeo in Bosco, It. 59/E3
San Bartolomeo in Galdo, It. 46/D2
San Bautista, Uru. 159/L11
San Benedetto (range), It. 59/E5
San Benedetto del Tronto, It. 43/K5
San Benedetto in Alpe, It. 59/E5
San Benedetto Po, It. 59/D2
San Benedicto (isl.), Mex. 142/C5
San Bernardino (co.), Ca, US 136/C2
San Bernardino (mts.), Ca, US 136/C2
San Bernardino, Ca, US 136/C2
San Bernardino Nat'l Forest, Ca, US 136/C2
San Bernardo (pt.), Col. 152/C2
San Bernardo, Chile 158/N8
San Blas (cape), Fl, US 133/G4
San Blas, Mex. 142/D4
San Blas, Mex. 142/C3
San Bonifacio, It. 59/E2
San Borja, Bol. 150/E6
San Bruno, Mex. 142/B3
San Bruno, Ca, US 135/K11
San Buenaventura, Mex. 132/C5
San Buenaventura (Ventura), Ca, US 136/A2
San Candido (Innichen), It. 43/K3
San Carlos (lake), Az, US 128/E4
San Carlos, Mex. 129/G5
San Carlos, Phil. 79/D4
San Carlos, Mex. 143/F3
San Carlos, Pan. 152/B2
San Carlos, Ven. 152/D2
San Carlos, Nic. 145/E4
San Carlos, Chile 158/B3
San Carlos, Uru. 159/G2
San Carlos, Ca, US 135/K11
San Carlos de Bariloche, Arg. 158/C4
San Carlos de Bariloche (int'l arpt.), Arg. 158/C4
San Carlos de Río Negro, Ven. 153/E4
San Carlos del Zulia, Ven. 152/D2
San Casciano in Val di Pesa, It. 59/E5
San Cataldo, It. 47/F2
San Cayetano, Arg. 158/F3
San Cesario sul Panaro, It. 59/E3
San Ciro de Acosta, Mex. 143/F4
San Clemente (isl.), Ca, US 128/C4
San Clemente, Ca, US 136/C4
San Clemente, Sp. 44/D3
San Clemente, Chile 158/C2
San Clemente del Tuyú, Arg. 159/F3
San Colombano al Lambro, It. 58/C2
San Cristóbal, Arg. 157/D3
San Cristobal (isl.), Sol. 116/F6
San Cristóbal (vol.), Nic. 144/E3
San Cristóbal, Ven. 152/C3
San Cristóbal, Cuba 145/F1
San Cristóbal (isl.), Ecu. 156/F7
San Cristóbal de las Casas, Mex. 144/C2
San Cristobal Wash (riv.), Az, US 142/B1
San Damiano d'Asti, It. 58/B3
San Diego, Tx, US 132/D5
San Diego (aqueduct), Ca, US 136/C4
San Diego (bay), Ca, US 136/C5
San Diego, Ca, US 136/C5
San Diego (co.), Ca, US 136/C4
San Diego (cape), Arg. 159/D7
San Diego International-Lindbergh Field (int'l arpt.), Ca, US 136/C5
San Diego Naval Station, Ca, US 136/C5
San Diego Wild Animal Park, Ca, US 136/C4
San Diego Zoo, Ca, US 136/C5
San Diequito (riv.), Ca, US 136/C5
San Dimas, Ca, US 136/C2
San Donà di Piave, It. 59/F1
San Donnino, It. 59/E5
San Dorligo della Valle, It. 59/G1
San Esteban de Gormaz, Sp. 44/D2
San Felice Circeo, It. 46/C2
San Felice del Benaco, It. 58/D1
San Felice sul Panaro, It. 59/E3
San Felipe, Mex. 142/B2
San Felipe, Ven. 152/D2
San Felipe, Chile 158/N8
San Felipe de Puerto Plata, DRep. 141/G4
San Felipe de Vichayal, Peru 156/A2
San Felipe Jalapa de Díaz, Mex. 143/F5
San Felipe Torres Mochas, Mex. 143/E4
San Felix (isl.), Chile 147/A5
San Fernando (riv.), Mex. 132/D5
San Fernando, Phil. 79/D4
San Fernando, Phil. 79/D4
San Fernando (valley), Ca, US 136/B2
San Fernando, Sp. 44/B4
San Fernando, Trin. 153/F2
San Fernando, Chile 158/B3
San Fernando, Arg. 159/J11
San Fernando, Ca, US 136/F7
San Fernando de Apure, Ven. 153/E3
San Fernando de Atabapo, Ven. 152/E3
San Fernando de Henares, Sp. 45/N9
San Fernando de Presas, Mex. 143/F3
San Fior di Sopra, It. 59/F1
San Francesco al Campo, It. 58/A2
San Francisco, Arg. 157/D3
San Francisco (int'l arpt.), Ca, US 128/B3
San Francisco (riv.), US 128/E4
San Francisco, Ca, US 128/B3
San Francisco, Phil. 79/E6
San Francisco, Col. 152/B4
San Francisco, ESal. 144/D3
San Francisco, Ven. 152/D2
San Francisco (co.), Ca, US 135/K11
San Francisco Acuautla, Mex. 143/R10
San Francisco Bay NWR, Ca, US 135/K11
San Francisco, Cabo de (cape), Ecu. 152/A4
San Francisco Chimalpa, Mex. 143/Q10
San Francisco de la Paz, Hon. 144/E3
San Francisco de Macorís, DRep. 141/G4
San Francisco de Mostazal, Chile 158/N8
San Francisco del Mezquital, Mex. 142/D4
San Francisco del Monte de Oro, Arg. 158/D2
San Francisco del Oro, Mex. 142/D3
San Francisco del Rincón, Mex. 143/E4
San Francisco Telixtlahuaca, Mex. 140/B4
San Fratello, It. 46/D3
San Gabriel (riv.), Ca, US 136/C2
San Gabriel (pt.), Mex. 142/B2
San Gabriel (res.), Ca, US 136/C2
San Gabriel, Ecu. 152/B4
San Gabriel, Ca, US 136/F7
San Gavino Monreale, It. 46/A3
San Germán, Cuba 145/G1
San Germano Vercellese, It. 58/B2
San Gil, Col. 152/C3
San Gimignano, It. 59/E6
San Giorgio delle Pertiche, It. 59/E1
San Giorgio di Piano, It. 59/E3
San Giorgio Ionico, It. 47/E2
San Giorgio Piacentino, It. 58/C3
San Giovanni al Natisone, It. 59/G1
San Giovanni Bianco, It. 58/C1
San Giovanni Gemini, It. 46/C4
San Giovanni in Croce, It. 58/D2
San Giovanni in Fiore, It. 46/E3
San Giovanni in Marignano, It. 59/F5
San Giovanni in Persiceto, It. 59/E3
San Giovanni Lupatoto, It. 59/E2
San Giovanni Valdarno, It. 59/E5
San Giuliano, It. 58/B3
San Giuliano Terme, It. 58/D5
San Giustino, It. 59/F5
San Giusto Canavese, It. 58/A2
San Gorgonio (mtn.), Ca, US 128/C4
San Gottardo, Passo del (pass), Swi. 57/E4
San Gregorio, Arg. 158/E2
San Gregorio, Uru. 159/L10
San Gregorio, Ca, US 135/K12
San Guiliano Milanese, It. 58/C2
San Hipólito Punta (pt.), Mex. 142/B3
San Ignacio, Bol. 150/E6
San Ignacio, Peru 156/B2
San Ignacio, Bol. 150/F7
San Ignacio, Mex. 142/B3
San Ignacio, Mex. 142/D4
San Ignacio, Belz. 144/D2
San Ignacio, Chile 158/B3
San Ildefonso, Sp. 44/D2
San Isidro, Nic. 144/E3
San Isidro, CR 145/F4
San Jacinto, Col. 152/C2
San Jacinto, Uru. 159/L11
San Javier, Sp. 45/E4
San Javier, Chile 158/C2
San Javier, Uru. 159/J10
San Jerónimo, Mex. 142/E3
San Joaquín, Bol. 150/F6
San Joaquin (riv.), Ca, US 128/C3
San Joaquín, Col. 152/C3
San Joaquin (hills), Ca, US 136/G8
San Joaquin (co.), Ca, US 135/L11
San Joaquín (peak), Ecu. 156/F7
San Jorge (bay), Mex. 142/B2
San Jorge (riv.), Col. 145/H5
San Jorge (gulf), Arg. 147/C7
San Jorge (cape), Arg. 158/D5
San Jorge, Golfo di (gulf), Sp. 45/F2
San Jose, Phil. 81/F1
San José, Peru 156/D4
San José, Peru 156/B2
San Jose (int'l arpt.), Ca, US 128/B3
San Jose, Phil. 79/D4
San Jose, Phil. 79/D5
San Jose, Ca, US 128/B3
San José (isl.), Mex. 142/C3
San José, Sp. 45/F3
San José, Col. 152/B4
San José (cap.), CR 145/E4
San José (gulf), Arg. 158/D4
San Jose (hills), Ca, US 136/G7
San José (dept.), Uru. 159/K11
San Jose (riv.), Uru. 159/K10
San José de Chiquitos, Bol. 150/F7
San José de Guanipa, Ven. 153/E2
San José de Guaribe, Ven. 153/E2
San José de Jáchal, Arg. 157/C3
San José de la Esquina, Arg. 158/E2
San Jose de Los Molinos, Peru 156/C4
San José de los Remates, Nic. 144/E3
San José de Maipo, Chile 158/N8
San José de Mayo, Uru. 159/K11
San José de Raíces, Mex. 143/E3
San José de Seque, Ven. 152/D2
San José del Cabo, Mex. 142/C4
San José del Guaviare, Col. 152/C4
San José Iturbide, Mex. 143/E4
San José Viejo, Mex. 142/C4
San Juan, Arg. 157/C3
San Juan (riv.), Arg. 157/C3
San Juan, Peru 156/C4
San Juan (basin), NM, US 132/A2
San Juan (riv.), NM, US 132/B2
San Juan, Phil. 79/D5
San Juan, PR 141/M8
San Juan (riv.), Nic. 140/E5
San Juan (pt.), ESal. 144/D3
San Juan (mts.), Co, US 124/E4
San Juan (cape), Arg. 159/E7
San Juan Abajo, Mex. 142/D4
San Juan Bautista, Par. 157/E2
San Juan Bautista Coixtlahuaca, Mex. 144/B2
San Juan Bautista Tuxtepec, Mex. 144/B2
San Juan Bautista Valle Nacional, Mex. 144/B2
San Juan Capistrano, Ca, US 136/C3
San Juan de Alicante, Sp. 45/E3
San Juan de Aznalfarache, Sp. 44/B4
San Juan de la Costa, Mex. 142/C3
San Juan de Lima (pt.), Mex. 142/E5
San Juan de los Cayos, Ven. 152/D2
San Juan de los Lagos, Mex. 142/E4
San Juan de los Morros, Ven. 150/E2
San Juan del Norte, Nic. 145/F4
San Juan del Río, Mex. 143/F4
San Juan Guichicovi, Mex. 140/B4
San Juan Hot Springs, Ca, US 136/C3
San Juan Ixcaquixtla, Mex. 143/M8
San Juan Juquila Mixes, Mex. 144/C2
San Juan Nepomuceno, Col. 152/C2
San Juanico, Mex. 142/B3
San Juanico Punta (pt.), Mex. 142/B3
San Juanito, Mex. 142/D2
San Justo, Arg. 157/D3
San Lázaro (cape), Mex. 142/B3
San Lazzaro, It. 59/E4
San Leandro, Ca, US 135/K11
San Leandro (res.), Ca, US 135/K11
San Lorenzo (cape), Ecu. 150/B4
San Lorenzo, Bol. 150/E6
San Lorenzo, Peru 156/D3
San Lorenzo (riv.), Mex. 142/D3
San Lorenzo (cape), It. 46/A3
San Lorenzo, Nic. 144/E3
San Lorenzo, Hon. 144/E3
San Lorenzo, Ecu. 152/B4
San Lorenzo, Ca, US 135/K11
San Lorenzo (peak), Chile 159/B5
San Lorenzo al Mare, It. 58/A5
San Lorenzo de El Escorial, Sp. 45/M8
San Lorenzo in Campo, It. 59/F5
San Lucas, Nic. 144/E3
San Lucas, Cabo (cape), Mex. 142/C4
San Luis, Peru 156/B4
San Luis (valley), Co, US 132/B2
San Luis, Ven. 152/D2
San Luis, Guat. 144/D2
San Luis, Cuba 145/H1
San Luis, Arg. 158/D2
San Luis Acatlán, Mex. 144/B2
San Luis al Medio, Uru. 159/G2
San Luis de la Paz, Mex. 143/E4
San Luis Obispo, Ca, US 128/B4
San Luis Potosí (state), Mex. 140/A3
San Luis Potosí, Mex. 143/E4
San Luis Rey (riv.), Ca, US 136/C4
San Luis Rey, Ca, US 136/C4
San Luis Río Colorado, Mex. 128/D4
San Luis, Sierra de (mts.), Arg. 158/D2
San Manuel, Az, US 128/E4
San Marcello Pistoiese, It. 59/D4
San Marcos, Peru 156/B3
San Marcos, Peru 156/B2
San Marcos, Tx, US 129/H5
San Marcos, Ca, US 136/C4
San Marcos, Mex. 140/B4
San Marcos, Guat. 144/D3
San Marcos, CR 145/E4
San Marcos, Col. 152/C2
San Maria di Porto Novo, It. 59/G5
San Mariano, Phil. 79/D4
San Marino (cap.), SMar. 59/F5
San Marino (ctry.) 59/F5
San Marino, Ca, US 136/F7
San Martín (riv.), Bol. 150/F6
San Martín (dept.), Peru 156/B2
San Martín, Mex. 143/R9
San Martín, Col. 152/C4
San Martín (lake), Arg. 147/B7
San Martín, Arg. 158/C2
San Martin Cuautlalpan, Mex. 143/R10
San Martín de los Andes, Arg. 158/C4
San Martín de Valdeiglesias, Sp. 44/C2
San Martino Buon Albergo, It. 59/E2
San Martino-di-Lota, Fr. 46/A1
San Martino di Lupari, It. 59/E1
San Martino di Venezze, It. 59/E2
San Martino in Passiria (Sankt Martin in Passeier), It. 57/H4
San Martino in Rio, It. 59/D3
San Martino in Strada, It. 58/C2
San Martino Siccomario, It. 58/C2
San Mateo, Peru 156/B3
San Mateo (mts.), NM, US 132/B3
San Mateo, Ca, US 128/B3
San Mateo, Sp. 45/F2
San Mateo, Ven. 153/E2
San Mateo (co.), Ca, US 135/K12
San Mateo Atarasquillo, Mex. 143/Q10
San Mateo Xoloc, Mex. 143/Q9
San Matías, Bol. 150/G7
San Matías, Golfo (gulf), Arg. 147/C7
San Maurizio d'Opaglio, It. 58/B1
San Mauro Pascoli, It. 59/F4
San Mauro Torinese, It. 58/A2
San Michele al Tagliamento, It. 59/F1
San Miguel (riv.), Bol. 150/F6
San Miguel, Peru 156/B2
San Miguel, Peru 156/C4
San Miguel, Mex. 132/C4
San Miguel, ESal. 144/D3
San Miguel (gulf), Pan. 145/G4
San Miguel (riv.), Col. 152/B4
San Miguel Coatlincham, Mex. 143/R10
San Miguel de Allende, Mex. 143/E4
San Miguel de los Bancos, Ecu. 152/B4
San Miguel de Tucumán, Arg. 157/C2
San Miguel del Monte, Arg. 159/J11
San Miguel Tlaixpan, Mex. 143/R9
San Miguel Totolapan, Mex. 140/A4
San Miniato, It. 59/D5
San Nicolas (isl.), Ca, US 128/B4
San Nicolás de los Arroyos, Arg. 158/E2
San Nicolò, It. 58/C2
San Onofre (mtn.), Ca, US 136/C4
San Onofre, Ca, US 136/C4
San Onofre, Col. 152/C2
San Pablo, Peru 156/B2
San Pablo, Phil. 79/D5
San Pablo (int'l arpt.), Sp. 44/C4
San Pablo, Ven. 153/E2
San Pablo, Col. 152/B4
San Pablo, Chile 158/B4
San Pablo, Ca, US 135/K11
San Pablo (res.), Ca, US 135/K11
San Pablo Bay NWR, Ca, US 135/K10
San Pablo de las Salinas, Mex. 143/Q9
San Pablo Huixtepec, Mex. 144/B2
San Paolo, It. 58/D2
San Pawl il-Baħar, Malta 46/L7
San Pedro, Arg. 157/D1
San Pedro, Par. 157/E1
San Pedro (vol.), Chile 157/C1
San Pedro (riv.), Mex. 132/B5
San Pédro, C.d'Iv. 102/D5
San Pedro, Belz. 144/E2
San Pedro (riv.), Guat. 144/D2
San Pedro, Chile 158/N8
San Pedro, Arg. 159/J10
San Pedro Arriba, Mex. 143/Q10
San Pedro Carchá, Guat. 144/D3
San Pedro de Cajas, Peru 156/C3
San Pedro de la Cueva, Mex. 142/C2
San Pedro de las Colonias, Mex. 132/C5
San Pedro de Lloc, Peru 156/B2
San Pedro de Lóvago, Nic. 145/E3
San Pedro de Macorís, DRep. 141/H4
San Pedro del Pinatar, Sp. 45/E4
San Pedro Huamelula, Mex. 144/C2
San Pedro Pochutla, Mex. 144/B3
San Pedro, Sierra de (mts.), Sp. 44/B3
San Pedro Sula, Hon. 144/D3
San Pedro Tapanatepec, Mex. 144/C2
San Pedro Totoltepec, Mex. 143/Q10
San Pellegrino Terme, It. 58/C1
San Piero a Sieve, It. 59/E5
San Piero in Bagno, It. 59/E5

223
San P – São R

San Pietro (isl.), It. 46/A3
San Pietro in Casale, It. 59/E3
San Pietro in Gù, It. 59/E1
San Pietro in Vincoli, It. 59/F4
San Pietro in Volta, It. 59/F2
San Polo d'Enza, It. 58/D3
San Polo di Piave, It. 59/F1
San Possidonio, It. 59/D3
San Quentin, Ca, US 135/K11
San Quintín (cape), Mex. 142/B2
San Quintín, Mex. 142/B2
San Rafael (riv.), Ut, US 128/E3
San Rafael, Peru 156/B3
San Rafael, Peru 156/B2
San Rafael, Mex. 143/N6
San Rafael, Arg. 158/C2
San Rafael (hills), Ca, US 136/F7
San Rafael del Moján, Ven. 152/D2
San Ramón, Peru 156/C3
San Ramón, CR 145/E4
San Ramon, Ca, US 135/L11
San Ramón, Uru. 159/L11
San Ramón de la Nueva Orán, Arg. 157/D1
San Remo, It. 58/A5
San Rocco al Porto, It. 58/C2
San Romano, It. 59/D5
San Roque, Sp. 44/C4
San Rosendo, Chile 158/B3
San Saba (riv.), Tx, US 143/F2
San Salvador (cap.), ESal. 144/D3
San Salvador (riv.), Uru. 159/J10
San Salvador de Jujuy, Arg. 157/C1
San Salvador el Seco, Mex. 143/M7
San Salvador, Isla (isl.), Bahm. 141/G3
San Salvador (Watling) (isl.), Bahm. 141/G3
San Salvatore Monferrato, It. 58/B3
San Salvo, It. 46/D1
San Sebastián, Sp. 44/E1
San Sebastián de los Reyes, Sp. 45/N8
San Sebastián de Yalí, Nic. 144/E3
San Sebastiano, It. 58/D1
San Secondo Parmense, It. 58/D3
San Severo, It. 46/D2
San Telmo (pt.), Mex. 142/E5
San Timoteo, Ven. 152/D2
San Valentín (peak), Chile 158/B5
San Valentino, It. 59/G1
San Vicente (res.), Ca, US 136/D5
San Vicente, Mex. 142/A2
San Vicente, ESal. 144/D3
San Vicente, Chile 158/C2
San Vicente de Alcántara, Sp. 44/B3
San Vicente de Cañete, Peru 156/B4
San Vicente del Caguán, Col. 152/C4
San Vicente del Raspeig, Sp. 45/E3
San Vicino (peak), It. 43/K5
San Vincenzo, It. 43/J5
San Vito (cape), It. 46/C3
San Vito, CR 145/F4
San Vito al Tagliamento, It. 59/F1
San Ysidro, Ca, US 136/C5
Saña, Peru 156/B2
Sana (riv.), Bosn. 48/C3
Şan'ā' (Sanaa) (cap.), Yem. 88/D5
Sanae IV, SAfr., Ant. 160/Z
Sanaga (riv.), Camr. 93/C4
Sanak (isl.) 134/F5
Sanana (isl.), Indo. 81/G4
Sanandaj, Iran 88/E1
Sananduva, Braz. 155/B3
Sanaur, India 86/D4
Sānāwad, India 89/L4
Sanborn, NY, US 131/S9
Sanch'ŏng, SKor. 73/D5
Sancti Spíritu, Arg. 158/E2
Sancti Spíritus, Cuba 145/G1
Sand (riv.), Ab, Can. 126/F2
Sand (riv.), SAfr. 106/D3
Sand (pt.), Eng, UK 32/D4
Sand (hills), Ne, US 124/F3
Sand, Nor. 38/B2
Sand am Main, Ger. 54/D3
Sand Point, Ak, US 134/F4
Sanda, Japan 77/H6
Sanda (isl.), Sc, UK 34/C1
Sandakan, Malay. 81/E2
Sandane, Nor. 37/C3
Sandanski, Bul. 47/H2
Sandarne, Swe. 38/G1
Sanday (isl.), Sc, UK 31/V14
Sandbach, Eng, UK 35/F5
Sandberg, Ger. 54/C2
Sande, Ger. 51/F1
Sandefjord, Nor. 38/D2
Sandersville, Ga, US 133/H3
Sandhurst, Eng, UK 33/F4
Sandia, Peru 156/D4
Sandıklı, Turk. 90/B2
Sandīla, India 84/C2
Sandino, Cuba 140/E3
Sandnes, Nor. 38/A2
Sandomierz, Pol. 41/L3
Sandonà, Col. 152/B4
Sándorfalva, Hun. 48/E2
Sandougou (riv.), Sen. 102/B3
Sandover (riv.), Austl. 113/G2
Sandoway, Myan. 83/F4
Sandpoint, Id, US 126/D3
Sandrakatsy, Madg. 107/J7
Sandrigo, It. 59/E1
Sands (pt.), NY, US 139/L8
Sands Point, NY, US 139/L8
Sandspit, BC, Can. 134/M5
Sandstedt, Ger. 51/F2
Sandstone, Austl. 112/C3
Sandu Shuizu Zizhixian, China 83/J2
Sandusky, Mi, US 130/D3
Sandusky, Oh, US 130/D3
Sandvika, Nor. 38/D2
Sandviken, Swe. 38/G1
Sandweiler, Lux. 53/F4
Sandwich, Eng, UK 33/H4
Sandwich (cape), Austl. 114/B2
Sandwīp (isl.), Bang. 85/H4
Sandy, Ut, US 137/K12
Sandy (cape), Austl. 114/D4
Sandy (lake), On, Can. 122/G3
Sandy (pt.), RI, US 139/G1
Sandy Bay, Sk, Can. 127/H2
Sandy Hook (bay), NJ, US 138/D3
Sandy Hook (bar), NJ, US 139/J10
Sandy Hook Lighthouse, NJ, US 139/J10
Sandy Springs, Ga, US 133/G3
Sanem, Lux. 53/E4
Sånfjällets NP, Swe. 37/E3
Sanford (mt.), Ak, US 134/K3
Sanford, Me, US 131/G3
Sanford, NC, US 133/J3
Sanford, Fl, US 133/H4
Sangamner, India 89/K5
Sangamon (riv.), Il, US 129/K3
Sangān (mtn.), Afg. 89/H2
Sangaria, India 86/C5
Sangatte, Fr. 52/A2
Sangay (vol.), Ecu. 152/B5
Sangay, PN, Ecu. 150/C4
Sangenjo, Sp. 44/A1
Sanggan (riv.), China 72/C2
Sanggau, Indo. 80/D3
Sanggou (bay), China 73/B4
Sangha (riv.), CAfr. 96/J7
Sangihe (isl.), Indo. 81/G3
Sangihe (isl.), Phil. 67/M9
Sangju, SKor. 73/E4
Sangkulirang, Indo. 81/E3
Sāngla, Pak. 86/B4
Sāngli, India 89/K5
Sangmélima, Camr. 96/H7
Sangō, Japan 77/J6
Sangre de Cristo (mts.), US 129/F3
Sangre Grande, Trin. 153/F2
Sangri, China 85/J1
Sangro (riv.), It. 46/D2
Sangrūr, India 86/C4
Sangster (int'l arpt.), Jam. 145/G2
Sangue, Rio do (riv.), Braz. 150/G6
Sangüesa, Sp. 44/E1
Sanguie (prov.), Burk. 103/E4
Sanguinetto, It. 59/E2
Sangzhi, China 79/B2
Sanhe, China 72/H7
Sani (pass), Les. 106/E3
Sāni Bheri (riv.), Nepal 84/D1
San'in Kaigin NP, Japan 74/D3
Saniquellie, Libr. 102/C5
Sanjō, Japan 75/F2
Sankanbiriwa (peak), SLeo. 102/C4
Sankh (riv.), India 85/E4
Sankoroni (riv.), Gui. 102/C4
Sankosh (riv.), India 85/G2
Sankt Aegyd am Neuwalde, Aus. 43/L3
Sankt Agatha, Aus. 55/G6
Sankt Andrä, Aus. 43/L3
Sankt Andrä-Wördern, Aus. 49/N7
Sankt Andreasberg, Ger. 51/H5
Sankt Anton am Arlberg, Aus. 57/G3
Sankt Augustin, Ger. 53/G2
Sankt Blasien, Ger. 56/E2
Sankt Florian am Inn, Aus. 55/G6
Sankt Gallen, Swi. 57/F3
Sankt Gallenkirch, Aus. 57/F3
Sankt Georgen bei Salzburg, Aus. 55/F7
Sankt Georgen im Attergau, Aus. 55/G7
Sankt Georgen im Schwarzwald, Ger. 57/E1
Sankt Goar, Ger. 53/G3
Sankt Goarshausen, Ger. 53/G3
Sankt Ingbert, Ger. 53/G5
Sankt Johann im Pongau, Aus. 43/K3
Sankt Johann in Tirol, Aus. 43/K3
Sankt Leonhard im Pitztal, Aus. 57/G3
Sankt Leonhard in Passeier (San Leonardo in Passiria), It. 57/H4
Sankt Marien, Aus. 55/H6
Sankt Martin im Mühlkreis, Aus. 55/H6
Sankt Michael in Obersteiermark, Aus. 43/L3
Sankt Moritz, Swi. 57/F5
Sankt Oswald bei Freistadt, Aus. 55/H5
Sankt Pantaleon, Aus. 55/F6
Sankt Peter am Hart, Aus. 55/G6
Sankt Peter in der Au, Aus. 55/H6
Sankt Peter-Ording, Ger. 38/C4
Sankt Pölten, Aus. 41/H4
Sankt Stephan, Swi. 56/D4
Sankt Ulrich bei Steyr, Aus. 55/H6
Sankt Valentin, Aus. 55/H6
Sankt Veit, Aus. 48/B1
Sankt Veit an der Glan, Aus. 43/L3
Sankt Wendel, Ger. 53/G5
Sankt Wolfgang, Ger. 55/F6
Sanlúcar de Barrameda, Sp. 44/B4
Sanmatenga (prov.), Burk. 103/E3
Sanmen, China 79/D2
Sanmenxia, China 72/B4
Sanming, China 79/C2
Sannan, Japan 77/H5
Sannazzaro de'Burgondi, It. 58/B2
Sannicandro Garganico, It. 46/D2
Sannikova (str.), Rus. 65/P2
San'nohe, Japan 76/B3
Sannois, Fr. 30/J5
Sano, Japan 75/F2
Sanok, Pol. 41/M4
Sanquhar, Sc, UK 36/C6
Sanquianga, PN, Col. 150/C3
Sans Bois (mts.), Ok, US 132/E3
Sansepolcro, It. 59/F5
Sanshui, China 79/B3
Sant Adrià de Besòs, Sp. 45/L7
Sant Boi de Llobregat, Sp. 45/L7
Sant Carles de la Ràpita, Sp. 45/F2
Sant Celoni, Sp. 45/L6
Sant Cugat del Vallès, Sp. 45/L7
Sant Feliu de Guíxols, Sp. 45/G2
Sant Feliu de Llobregat, Sp. 45/L7
Sant Julia, And. 42/D5
Sant Pere de Ribes, Sp. 45/K7
Sant Sadurní d'Anoia, Sp. 45/K7
Sant Vicenç de Castellet, Sp. 45/K6
Sant Vicenç dels Horts, Sp. 45/L7
Santa (riv.), Peru 156/B3
Santa, Peru 156/B3
Santa Ana, Bol. 150/E6
Santa Ana (mts.), Ca, US 136/C3
Santa Ana (riv.), Ca, US 136/C3
Santa Ana, Mex. 142/C2
Santa Ana (vol.), ESal. 144/D3
Santa Ana, ESal. 144/D3
Santa Ana, Ecu. 152/A5
Santa Ana, Ven. 152/C3
Santa Ana, Ven. 152/D2
Santa Ana, Hon. 144/E3
Santa Ana, Ca, US 136/G8
Santa Ana del Alto Beni, Bol. 150/E7
Santa Anna, Tx, US 129/H5
Santa Bárbara, Braz. 155/D1
Santa Bárbara, Mex. 142/D3
Santa Barbara, Ca, US 136/A2
Santa Barbara (co.), Ca, US 136/A1
Santa Bárbara, Ven. 152/D3
Santa Bárbara, Chile 158/B3
Santa Bárbara, Ven. 152/D2
Santa Bárbara, Hon. 144/D3
Santa Bárbara d'Oeste, Braz. 155/C2
Santa Barbara Mountains Nat'l Rec. Area, Ca, US 136/E7
Santa Catalina, Phil. 79/D6
Santa Catalina, Ven. 152/D3
Santa Catalina, Pan. 145/F4
Santa Catalina (isl.), CA, US 124/B5
Santa Catalina, Gulf of (gulf), Ca, US 128/C4
Santa Catarina (state), Braz. 155/B3
Santa Catarina, Mex. 143/E3
Santa Catarina, Ilha de (isl.), Braz. 157/G2
Santa Cecilia, Braz. 155/B3
Santa Clara, Mex. 142/E3
Santa Clara, Ven. 153/E2
Santa Clara, Cuba 145/G1
Santa Clara (co.), Ca, US 135/L12
Santa Clara, Ca, US 135/L12
Santa Clara, Barragem de (res.), Port. 44/A4
Santa Clara de Olimar, Uru. 159/G2
Santa Clarita, Ca, US 136/B2
Santa Clotilde, Peru 152/C5
Santa Coloma de Farners, Sp. 45/G2
Santa Coloma de Gramanet, Sp. 45/L7
Santa Comba, Sp. 44/A1
Santa Croce di Magliano, It. 46/D2
Santa Croce sull'Arno, It. 59/D5
Santa Cruz (riv.), Az, US 129/E5
Santa Cruz, Braz. 154/C2
Santa Cruz, Peru 156/C2
Santa Cruz, Mex. 128/E5
Santa Cruz, Phil. 79/E6
Santa Cruz, Phil. 79/D5
Santa Cruz, Ca, US 128/B3
Santa Cruz, Phil. 79/D5
Santa Cruz (isls.), Sol. 116/F6
Santa Cruz (riv.), Arg. 147/B8
Santa Cruz (mts.), Guat. 144/D3
Santa Cruz, CR 144/E4
Santa Cruz, Chile 158/C2
Santa Cruz (prov.), Arg. 158/C5
Santa Cruz (isl.), Ecu. 156/E7
Santa Cruz da Graciosa, Azor., Port. 45/S12
Santa Cruz da Vitória, Braz. 154/C4
Santa Cruz das Flores, Azor., Port. 45/R12
Santa Cruz de Bucaral, Ven. 152/D2
Santa Cruz de El Seibo, DRep. 141/H4
Santa Cruz de la Palma, Sp. 98/A3
Santa Cruz de la Sierra, Bol. 150/F7
Santa Cruz de la Zarza, Sp. 44/D3
Santa Cruz de Mudela, Sp. 44/D3
Santa Cruz de Orinoco, Ven. 153/E2
Santa Cruz de Tenerife, Sp. 98/A3
Santa Cruz del Quiché, Guat. 144/D3
Santa Cruz del Sur, Cuba 145/G1
Santa Cruz do Capibaribe, Braz. 154/C2
Santa Cruz do Piauí, Braz. 154/B2
Santa Cruz do Rio Pardo, Braz. 155/B2
Santa Cruz do Sul, Braz. 155/A4
Santa Cruz Island (isl.), Ca, US 128/C4
Santa Elena, Peru 156/C2
Santa Elena (bay), CR 144/E4
Santa Elena, Hon. 144/E2
Santa Elena (cape), CR 144/E4
Santa Elena, Ecu. 152/A5
Santa Elena (peak), Arg. 158/D5
Santa Elena de Uairén, Ven. 153/F3
Santa Eugenia de Ribeira, Sp. 44/A1
Santa Eulalia del Río, Sp. 45/F3
Santa Fe, Arg. 157/D3
Santa Fe (cap.), NM, US 129/F4
Santa Fe (riv.), Fl, US 133/H4
Santa Fé, Sp. 44/D4
Santa Fe, Cuba 145/F1
Santa Fé do Sul, Braz. 155/B2
Santa Fe Springs, Ca, US 136/F8
Santa Felicia (dam), Ca, US 136/B2
Santa Filomena, Braz. 154/A3
Santa Giustina (lake), It. 57/H5
Santa Helena, Braz. 154/A1
Santa Helena de Goiás, Braz. 155/B1
Santa Inés (isl.), Chile 157/B7
Santa Inês, Braz. 154/C4
Santa Inês, Braz. 154/A1
Santa Isabel, Ecu. 156/B1
Santa Isabel, Braz. 211/G8
Santa Isabel (isl.), Sol. 116/E5
Santa Isabel (riv.), Guat. 144/D2
Santa Isabel, Arg. 158/D3
Santa Isabel, Arg. 158/E2
Santa Isabel de Sihuas, Peru 156/C5
Santa Isabel, Pico de (peak), EqG. 96/G7
Santa Juliana, Braz. 155/C1
Santa Lucía, Peru 156/D4
Santa Lucía, Canl. 45/X17
Santa Lucía, Ven. 152/D2
Santa Lucía, Ecu. 152/B5
Santa Lucía, Uru. 159/K11
Santa Lucia di Piave, It. 59/F1
Santa Luz, Braz. 154/C3
Santa Luzia, Braz. 154/A1
Santa Luzia, Braz. 155/D1
Santa Luzia, Braz. 154/C2
Santa Luzia (isl.), CpV. 93/J10
Santa Magdalena (isl.), Mex. 142/B3
Santa Magdalena, Arg. 158/E2
Santa Margarita (isl.), Mex. 142/B3
Santa Margarita (riv.), Ca, US 136/C4
Santa Margherita Ligure, It. 58/C4
Santa Maria, Braz. 157/F2
Santa Maria, Ca, US 128/B4
Santa María (riv.), Mex. 132/B4
Santa María (riv.), Mex. 142/D2
Santa Maria (bay), Mex. 142/C3
Santa María (cape), Port. 44/B4
Santa Maria (isl.), Azor., Port. 45/T13
Santa María (isl.), Chile 158/B3
Santa Maria, CpV. 93/K10
Santa María, Chile 158/N8
Santa María, Ecu. 156/E7
Santa María (isl.), Ecu. 156/E7
Santa Maria a Monte, It. 59/D5
Santa Maria, Cabo de (cape), Moz. 107/F2
Santa Maria Capua Vetere, It. 46/D2
Santa Maria, Chapadão de (hills), Braz. 154/A4
Santa Maria da Boa Vista, Braz. 154/C3
Santa Maria da Vitória, Braz. 154/A4
Santa María de Cayón, Sp. 44/D1
Santa María de Ipire, Ven. 153/E2
Santa María de Nanay, Peru 156/C1
Santa María del Oro, Mex. 142/D3
Santa Maria della Versa, It. 58/C3
Santa Maria di Leuca, Capo (cape), It. 47/F3
Santa Maria do Suaçuí, Braz. 154/B5
Santa Maria Maddalena, It. 59/E3
Santa Maria Maggiore, It. 57/E5
Santa Maria Nuova, It. 59/G6
Santa María Xadani, Mex. 140/B4
Santa Marta, Col. 152/C2
Santa Marta Grande (cape), Braz. 155/B4
Santa Marta, Sierra Nevada de (mts.), Col. 152/C2
Santa Monica (bay), Ca, US 136/B3
Santa Monica (mts.), Ca, US 136/B2
Santa Monica, Ca, US 136/F7
Santa Monica Mountains Nat'l Rec. Area, Ca, US 136/B2
Santa Olalla del Cala, Sp. 44/B4
Santa Paula (peak), Ca, US 136/A2
Santa Paula, Ca, US 136/A2
Santa Pola, Sp. 45/E3
Santa Pola, Cabo de (cape), Sp. 45/E3
Santa Quitéria, Braz. 154/B2
Santa Quitéria do Maranhão, Braz. 154/B1
Santa Rita, Braz. 154/A1
Santa Rita, Braz. 154/D2
Santa Rita, Ven. 152/D2
Santa Rita de Cássia, Braz. 154/A3
Santa Rita do Sapucaí, Braz. 211/H7
Santa Rosa, Arg. 157/C3
Santa Rosa, Braz. 157/F2
Santa Rosa, Peru 156/D4
Santa Rosa, Ecu. 156/B1
Santa Rosa, Arg. 150/F8
Santa Rosa (range), Nv, US 128/C2
Santa Rosa, NM, US 129/F4
Santa Rosa, Ca, US 128/B3
Santa Rosa, CR 144/E4
Santa Rosa, Ven. 152/D2
Santa Rosa, Arg. 158/D3
Santa Rosa (mts.), Nv, US 124/C3
Santa Rosa, Uru. 159/K11
Santa Rosa, Bajo de (plain), Arg. 158/D4
Santa Rosa de Aguán, Hon. 144/E3
Santa Rosa de Copán, Hon. 144/D3
Santa Rosa de Osos, Col. 152/C3
Santa Rosa de Viterbo, Braz. 155/C2
Santa Rosa Island (isl.), Ca, US 128/B4
Santa Rosalía (pt.), Mex. 142/B2
Santa Rosalía, Mex. 142/B3
Santa Rosalía, Ven. 152/D2
Santa Rosalía, Ven. 153/E3
Santa Sofia, It. 59/E5
Santa Susana (mts.), Ca, US 136/B2
Santa Teresa (riv.), Braz. 151/J6
Santa Teresa, Austl. 113/G3
Santa Teresa Abor. Land, Austl. 113/G2
Santa Teresa, PN, Uru. 159/G2
Santa Teresinha, Braz. 151/H6
Santa Teresita, Arg. 159/F3
Santa Vitória, Braz. 155/B1
Santa Vitória do Palmar, Braz. 159/G2
Santa Ynez (mts.), Ca, US 136/A2
SantAantioco (isl.), It. 46/A3
Santaella, Sp. 44/C4
Sant'Agata Bolognese, It. 59/E3
Sant'Agata di Militello, It. 46/D3
Sant'Agata Feltria, It. 59/F5
Sant'Agostino, It. 59/E3
Sant'Alberto, It. 59/F3
Santan (canal), Az, US 137/S19
Santana, Braz. 154/A4
Santana (isl.), Braz. 154/B1
Santana do Acaraú, Braz. 154/B1
Santana do Ipanema, Braz. 154/C3
Santana do Livramento, Braz. 157/E3
Santander, Sp. 44/D1
Santander (dept.), Col. 145/H5
Santander de Quilichao, Col. 152/B4
Santander Jiménez, Mex. 143/F3
Sant'Angelo in Vado, It. 59/F5
Sant'Angelo Lodigiano, It. 58/C2
Sant'Antioco, It. 46/A3
Sant'Antonio, It. 59/D2
Santañy, Sp. 45/G3
Sant'Apollinare in Classe, It. 59/F4
Santarcángelo, It. 59/F4
Santarém, Braz. 151/H4
Santarém (dist.), Port. 44/A3
Santarém, Port. 44/A3
Sant'arsenio, It. 46/D2
Santee (riv.), SC, US 133/J3
Santee, Ca, US 136/D5
Sant'Eufemia (gulf), It. 46/D3
Santena, It. 58/A3
Santerno (riv.), It. 43/J4
Santeuil, Fr. 30/H4
Santhia, It. 58/B2
Santiago, Braz. 157/F2
Santiago, Peru 156/C4
Santiago, Phil. 79/D4
Santiago (res.), Ca, US 136/C3
Santiago (peak), Ca, US 136/C3
Santiago (int'l arpt.), Sp. 44/A1
Santiago (riv.), Peru 152/B5
Santiago, Pan. 152/A2
Santiago (mtn.), Pan. 145/F4
Santiago (mts.), Tx, US 124/F5
Santiago (cap.), Chile 158/N8
Santiago (cape), Chile 159/B6
Santiago Cuautlalpan, Mex. 143/R10
Santiago Cuautlalpan, Mex. 143/Q9
Santiago de Cao, Peru 156/B2
Santiago de Chocorvos, Peru 156/C4
Santiago de Chuco, Peru 156/B3
Santiago de Compostela, Sp. 44/A1
Santiago de Cuba, Cuba 145/H1
Santiago de los Caballeros, DRep. 141/G4
Santiago de Machaca, Bol. 156/D5
Santiago del Estero, Arg. 157/D2
Santiago do Cacém, Port. 44/A3
Santiago Ixcuintla, Mex. 142/D4
Santiago Jamiltepec, Mex. 144/B2
Santiago Juxtlahuaca, Mex. 144/B2
Santiago Miahuatlán, Mex. 143/M8
Santiago Papasquiaro, Mex. 142/D3
Santiago Pinotepa Nacional, Mex. 144/B2
Santiago Tilapa, Mex. 143/Q10
Santiago Tolman, Mex. 143/R9
Santiago Vázquez, Uru. 159/K11
Santiago Zacatepec, Mex. 144/C2
Sant'Ilario d'Enza, It. 58/D3
Sāntipur, India 85/G4
Säntis (peak), Swi. 57/F3
Santisteban del Puerto, Sp. 44/D3
Santō, Japan 77/G5
Santō, Japan 77/K5
Santo Amaro, Braz. 154/C4
Santo Amaro, Ilha de (isl.), Braz. 211/G8
Santo Anastácio, Braz. 155/B2
Santo André, Braz. 211/G8
Santo Ângelo, Braz. 157/F2
Santo Antão (isl.), CpV. 93/J9
Santo António, SaoT. 96/G7
Santo Antônio de Jesus, Braz. 154/C4
Santo Antônio de Pádua, Braz. 155/D2
Santo Antônio do Içá, Braz. 152/E5
Santo Antônio do Jacinto, Braz. 154/B5
Santo Antônio dos Lopes, Braz. 154/A2
Santo Domingo (cap.), DRep. 141/H4
Santo Domingo, Mex. 143/E4
Santo Domingo (pt.), Mex. 142/B3
Santo Domingo, Cuba 145/F1
Santo Domingo, Chile 158/N8
Santo Domingo de la Calzada, Sp. 44/D1
Santo Domingo de los Colorados, Ecu. 152/B5
Santo Domingo Petapa, Mex. 144/C2
Santo Domingo Tehuantepec, Mex. 144/C2
Santo Domingo Zanatepec, Mex. 144/C2
Santo Estêvão, Braz. 154/C4
Santo Onofre (riv.), Braz. 154/B4
Santo Stefano Belbo, It. 58/B3
Santo Stefano d'Aveto, It. 58/C3
Santo Stefano di Magra, It. 58/C4
Santo Stino di Livenza, It. 59/F1
Santo Tomás, Peru 156/C4
Santo Tomás, Peru 156/B2
Santo Tomás, Mex. 142/A2
Santo Tomás (pt.), Mex. 142/A2
Santo Tomás (vol.), Ecu. 156/E7
Santo Tomé, Arg. 157/E2
Santo Tomé, Arg. 157/D3
Santoña, Sp. 44/D1
Santorso, It. 59/E1
Santos, Braz. 211/G8
Santos Dumont (int'l arpt.), Braz. 211/K7
Santos Dumont, Braz. 211/K6
Santos Reyes Nopala, Mex. 144/B2
Santuario di Crea, It. 58/B2
Santuario di Oropa, It. 58/A1
Šanūr, WBnk. 91/G7
Sanwa, Japan 77/D1
São Benedito, Braz. 154/B2
São Benedito do Rio Prêto, Braz. 154/B1
São Bento, Braz. 154/C2
São Bento, Braz. 154/A1
São Bento do Sapucaí, Braz. 211/H7
São Bento do Sul, Braz. 155/B3
São Bento do Una, Braz. 154/C3
São Bernardo do Campo, Braz. 211/G8
São Borja, Braz. 157/E2
São Carlos, Braz. 155/C2
São Cristóvão, Braz. 154/C3
São Desidério, Braz. 154/A4
São Domingos (riv.), Braz. 154/A4
São Domingos, Braz. 154/A4
São Domingos do Maranhão, Braz. 154/A2
São Félix do Xingu, Braz. 151/H5
São Fidélis, Braz. 155/D2
São Filipe, CpV. 93/J11
São Francisco, Braz. 154/A4
São Francisco (riv.), Braz. 147/F3
São Francisco do Sul, Braz. 155/B3
São Francisco, Ilha de (isl.), Braz. 157/G2
São Fransisco de Paula, Braz. 155/B4
São Gabriel, Braz. 157/F3
São Gabriel da Palha, Braz. 155/D1
São Gonçalo, Braz. 211/K7
São Gonçalo do Abaeté, Braz. 154/A5
São Gonçalo do Sapucaí, Braz. 211/H6
São Gotardo, Braz. 155/C1
São Joachim da Barra, Braz. 155/C2
São João Batista, Braz. 154/A1
São João Batista, Braz. 155/B3
São João da Aliança, Braz. 154/A4
São João da Barra, Braz. 155/D2
São João da Boa Vista, Braz. 211/G6
São João da Madeira, Port. 44/A2
São João da Pesqueira, Port. 44/B2
São João da Ponte, Braz. 154/A4
São João das Lampas, Port. 45/P10
São João de Meriti, Braz. 211/K7
São João del Rei, Braz. 155/C2
São João do Paraíso, Braz. 154/B4
São João do Piauí, Braz. 154/B3
São João dos Patos, Braz. 154/B2
São João Evangelista, Braz. 155/D1
São João, Ilhas de (isl.), Braz. 151/K4
São João Nepomuceno, Braz. 211/K6
São João, Serra de (mts.), Braz. 150/F5
São Joaquim, Braz. 155/B4
São Joaquim, PN de, Braz. 155/B4
São Jorge (isl.), Azor., Port. 45/S12
São José, Braz. 155/B3
São José da Laje, Braz. 154/C3
São José de Mipibu, Braz. 154/D2
São José de Piranhas, Braz. 154/C2
São José de Ribamar, Braz. 154/A1
São José do Belmonte, Braz. 154/C2
São José do Egito, Braz. 154/C2
São José do Norte, Braz. 155/A5
São José do Peixe, Braz. 154/B2
São José do Rio Pardo, Braz. 211/G6
São José do Rio Prêto, Braz. 155/B2
São José dos Campos, Braz. 211/H8
São José dos Pinhais, Braz. 155/B3
São Julião, Braz. 154/B2
São Leopoldo, Braz. 155/B4
São Lourenço (riv.), Braz. 151/G7
São Lourenço, Braz. 211/H7
São Lourenço, Port. 45/P11
São Lourenço do Sul, Braz. 155/B4
São Luís, Braz. 154/A1
São Luís do Curu, Braz. 154/C1
São Luís do Quitunde, Braz. 154/D3
São Manoel, Braz. 155/B2
São Marcos (riv.), Braz. 154/A5
São Marcos (bay), Braz. 147/E3
São Martinho do Porto, Port. 44/A3
São Mateus, Braz. 155/E1
São Mateus (riv.), Braz. 155/D1
São Mateus do Maranhão, Braz. 154/A2
São Mateus do Sul, Braz. 155/B3
São Miguel, Braz. 154/C2
São Miguel (isl.), Azor., Port. 45/T13
São Miguel Arcanjo, Braz. 155/C2
São Miguel do Tapuio, Braz. 154/B2
São Miguel dos Campos, Braz. 154/C3
São Nicolau (isl.), CpV. 93/J10
São Paulo (state), Braz. 155/B2
São Paulo, Braz. 211/G8
São Paulo de Olivença, Braz. 150/E4
São Paulo do Potengi, Braz. 154/D2
São Pedro da Aldeia, Braz. 155/D2
São Pedro do Piauí, Braz. 154/B2
São Pedro do Sul, Port. 44/A2
São Raimundo das Mangabeiras, Braz. 154/A2

São Raimundo Nonato, Braz. 154/B3
São Romão, Braz. 154/A5
São Roque, Cabo de (cape), Braz. 154/D2
São Roque do Pico, Azor., Port. 45/S12
São Sebastião (pt.), Moz. 105/G5
São Sebastião, Braz. 211/H8
São Sebastião do Paraíso, Braz. 155/C2
São Sebastião, Ilha de (isl.), Braz. 211/H8
São Simão, Barragem de (res.), Braz. 155/B1
São Teotónio, Port. 44/A4
São Tiago, Braz. 155/C2
São Tiago (isl.), CpV. 93/K10
São Tomé (cap.), SaoT. 96/G7
São Tomé (isl.), SaoT. 96/G7
São Tomé and Príncipe (ctry.) 96/F7
São Tomé, Cabo de (cape), Braz. 155/D2
São Vicente, Braz. 211/G8
São Vicente (cape), Port. 44/A4
São Vicente (isl.), CpV. 93/J10
Saône (riv.), Fr. 42/F3
Saône-et-Loire (dept.), Fr. 56/B4
Saori, Japan 77/L5
Saouru (riv.), Alg. 96/E1
Sápai, Gre. 47/J2
Sapallanga, Peru 156/C4
Sapanca, Turk. 49/K5
Sapatgrām, India 85/H2
Sapé, Braz. 154/D2
Sapelo, Ga, US 133/H4
Sapelo (isl.), Ga, US 133/H4
Saphane, Turk. 62/D5
Sapiéndza (isl.), Gre. 47/G4
Sapkyo, SKor. 73/D4
Sapo (mts.), Pan. 145/G5
Sapo NP, Libr. 102/C5
Saposoa, Peru 156/B2
Sappemeer, Neth. 50/D2
Sapphire, Austl. 114/B3
Sappington, Mo, US 137/G8
Sapporo, Japan 76/B2
Sapri, It. 46/D2
Sapsi (isl.), SKor. 73/D3
Sapt Kosi (riv.), Nepal 85/F2
Sapucaí (riv.), Braz. 211/H7
Sapucaia, Braz. 211/L6
Saqqez, Iran 88/E1
Saquena, Peru 156/C2
Saquisilí, Ecu. 152/B5
Šar (mts.), Yugo 47/G1
Sar Dasht, Iran 90/F2
Sar-e Pol, Afg. 87/E5
Sara Buri, Thai. 78/C3
Saráb, Iran 88/E1
Saraguro, Ecu. 156/B1
Saráī Alamgir, Pak. 86/B3
Saráī Sidhu, Pak. 86/A4
Sarajevo (cap.), Bosn. 48/D4
Saraland, Al, US 133/F4
Saramacca (dist.), Sur. 153/H3
Saran (peak), Indo. 80/D4
Saran', Kaz. 87/F3
Saranac Lake, NY, US 130/F2
Sarandapótamos (riv.), Gre. 47/N8
Sarandë, Alb. 47/G3
Sarandí de Navarro, Uru. 159/K10
Sarandí del Yi, Uru. 159/G2
Sarandí Grande, Uru. 159/N10
Sarangami (isls.), Phil. 81/G2
Sārangpur, India 89/L4
Saransk, Rus. 63/H1
Sarapul, Rus. 61/M4
Sarare (riv.), Ven. 152/D3
Sarasota, Fl, US 133/H5
Saratoga, Wy, US 126/G5
Saratoga, Ca, US 135/K12
Saratoga Springs, NY, US 130/F3
Saratov (res.), Rus. 63/J1
Saratov, Rus. 63/H2
Saratovskaya (obl.), Rus. 87/A2
Saravan, Laos 78/D3
Sarawak (reg.), Malay. 67/L9
Saray, Turk. 49/H5
Sarayacu, Ecu. 152/B5
Sarāyan (riv.), India 84/C2
Sarayköy, Turk. 90/B2
Sarayönü, Turk. 90/C2
Sárbogárd, Hun. 48/D2
Sarcelles, Fr. 30/K5
Sárda (riv.), India 84/C1
Sārda (canal), India 84/C1
Sárda (riv.), India 82/D2
Sardara, It. 46/A3
Sardhana, India 86/D5
Sardinata, Col. 152/C2
Sardinaux, Cap des (cape), Fr. 43/G5
Sardinia (isl.), It. 46/A2
Sardis (lake), Ms, US 129/K4
Sardis (lake), Ok, US 129/J4
Sareks NP, Swe. 37/F2

Sarektjåkko (peak), Swe. 37/F2
Sarempaka (peak), Indo. 81/E4
Sarentino, It. 57/H4
Sarezzo, It. 58/D1
Sargans, Swi. 57/F3
Sargodha, Pak. 86/B3
Sarh, Chad 96/J6
Sārī, Iran 88/F1
Sari-Solenzara, Fr. 46/A2
Sariaya, Phil. 79/D5
Saribi (cape), Indo. 81/J4
Sarigan (isl.), NMar. 116/D3
Sargöl, Turk. 90/B2
Sarkamış, Turk. 63/G4
Sarikaya (prov.), Turk. 62/E5
Sarikaya, Turk. 62/E5
Sarikei, Malay. 80/D3
Sarina, Austl. 114/C3
Sarine (riv.), Swi. 43/G3
Sariñena, Sp. 45/E2
Sarīr Kalanshiyū (des.), Libya 96/K2
Sarīr Tibasti (des.), Libya 96/J3
Sarita, Tx, US 132/D5
Sariwŏn, NKor. 73/C3
Sarju (riv.), India 84/C1
Sark (isl.), ChI, UK 42/B2
Sarkad, Hun. 48/F2
Sarkant, Kaz. 70/C2
Şarkikaraağaç, Turk. 90/B2
Sarkışla, It. 62/F5
Sarköy, Turk. 49/H5
Sarlat-la-Canéda, Fr. 42/D4
Sarleinsbach, Aus. 55/G5
Sarmato, It. 58/C2
Sarmeola, It. 59/E2
Sarmiento, Arg. 158/C5
Sarmiento (peak), Chile 159/C7
Särna, Swe. 38/E1
Sarnano, It. 43/K5
Sarnen, Swi. 57/E4
Sarnia, On, Can. 130/D3
Sarnico, It. 58/C1
Sarny, Ukr. 62/C2
Saroma (lake), Japan 76/C1
Saronic (gulf), Gre. 47/H4
Saronno, It. 58/C1
Saros (gulf), Turk. 62/C4
Sárospatak, Hun. 41/L4
Sarpsborg, Nor. 38/D2
Sarralbe, Fr. 53/G6
Sarre (riv.), Fr. 52/F6
Sarre-Union, Fr. 53/G6
Sarrebourg, Fr. 53/G6
Sarria, Sp. 44/B1
Sarroch, It. 46/A3
Sarry, Fr. 53/D6
Sarsāwa, India 86/D4
Sarsina, It. 59/F5
Sarstedt, Ger. 51/G4
Sarstún (riv.), Guat. 144/D3
Sartang (riv.), Rus. 65/P3
Sarteano, It. 46/B1
Sartène, Fr. 46/A2
Sarthe (riv.), Fr. 42/C3
Sartrouville, Fr. 30/J5
Sarufutsu, Japan 76/C1
Saruhanlı, Turk. 62/C5
Sárvár, Hun. 43/M3
Sárvíz (riv.), Hun. 48/D2
Saryesik Atgraü Qumy (des.), Kaz. 70/C2
Saryshaghan, Kaz. 87/F3
Sarysu (riv.), Kaz. 64/G5
Sarzana, It. 58/C2
Sas Van Gent, Neth. 52/C1
Sasaginnigack (lake), Mb, Can. 127/K3
Sasarām, India 85/E3
Sasayama, Japan 77/H5
Sasebo, Japan 74/A4
Sashima, Japan 77/D1
Saskatchewan (prov.), Can. 122/F3
Saskatchewan (riv.), Can. 122/F3
Saskatoon, Sk, Can. 126/G2
Saslaya (mtn.), Nic. 144/E3
Saslaya, PN, Nic. 144/E3
Sásni, India 84/B2
Sasolburg, SAfr. 106/D2
Sasovo, Rus. 63/G1
Saspamco, Tx, US 137/U21
Sassafras, Md, US 138/C5
Sassafras (riv.), C.d'Iv. 96/D6
Sassandra, C.d'Iv. 102/D5
Sassari, It. 46/A2
Sassenberg, Ger. 51/F4
Sassenheim, Neth. 50/B4
Sassnitz, Ger. 38/E4
Sasso Marconi, It. 59/E4
Sassocorvaro, It. 59/F6
Sassoferrato, It. 59/F6
Sassuolo, It. 59/D3
Sástago, Sp. 45/E2
Sasyk (lake), Ukr. 49/J3
Sáta-misaki (cape), Japan 74/B5
Sātāra, India 89/K15
Satawan (isl.), Micr. 116/E4

Säter, Swe. 38/F1
Saticoy, Ca, US 136/A2
Satilla (riv.), Ga, US 133/H4
Satipo, Peru 156/C3
Sätkhira, Bang. 85/G4
Sátoraljaújhely, Hun. 41/L4
Satpayev, Kaz. 87/E3
Satpura (range), India 89/K4
Satte, Japan 77/D1
Satteins, Aus. 57/F3
Satteldorf, Ger. 54/D4
Sattler, Tx, US 137/U20
Satu Mare (co.), Rom. 41/M5
Satu Mare, Rom. 41/M5
Satun, Thai. 78/C5
Sauce, Peru 156/B2
Sauce Grande (riv.), Arg. 158/E3
Saucillo, Mex. 132/B4
Sauda, Nor. 38/B2
Saúde, Braz. 154/B3
Saudhárkrókur, Ice. 37/N6
Saudi Arabia (ctry.) 88/D4
Sauer (riv.), Ger. 51/F5
Sauerlach, Ger. 57/H2
Sauerland (reg.), Ger. 40/D3
Sauêruiná (riv.), Braz. 150/D4
Saugatuck (riv.), Ct, US 139/E1
Saujon, Fr. 42/C4
Sauk (riv.), Mn, US 127/K4
Sauk Centre, Mn, US 127/K4
Sauk Rapids, Mn, US 127/K4
Saül, FrG. 151/H3
Sauldre (riv.), Fr. 42/D3
Saulgau, Ger. 57/F1
Saulheim, Ger. 54/B3
Saulieu, Fr. 42/F3
Sault-lès-Rethel, Fr. 53/D5
Sault Sainte Marie, On, Can. 130/C2
Sault Ste. Marie, Mi, US 130/C2
Saulx, Fr. 56/C2
Saulx (riv.), Fr. 40/C4
Saulxures-sur-Moselotte, Fr. 56/C2
Saumur, Fr. 42/C3
Saunders (peak), Austl. 112/E3
Saura (riv.), India 85/F3
Saurimo, Ang. 105/D2
Sausalito, Ca, US 135/J11
Sausseron (riv.), Fr. 30/J4
Sauteurs, Gren. 153/F1
Sava (riv.), It. 47/E2
Sava (riv.), Slov. 43/L3
Savá, Hon. 144/E3
Savage (dam), Ca, US 136/D5
Savage River, Austl. 115/C4
Savai'i (isl.), Sam. 117/H6
Savalou, Ben. 103/F5
Savane (riv.), Qu, Can. 131/G1
Savanna-la-Mar, Jam. 145/G2
Savannah, Ga, US 133/H4
Savannah, Tn, US 133/F3
Savannah (riv.), US 133/H3
Savannakhet, Laos 78/D2
Savant (lake), On, Can. 127/L3
Sāvantvādi, India 82/B4
Sävar, Swe. 37/G3
Savaştepe, Turk. 62/C5
Save (riv.), Moz. 93/F7
Sãveh, Iran 88/F1
Savena (riv.), It. 59/E4
Sãveni, Rom. 49/H2
Saverdun, Fr. 42/D5
Saverne, Fr. 53/G6
Savièse, Swi. 56/D5
Savigliano, It. 43/G4
Savignano sul Panaro, It. 59/E4
Savignano sul Rubicone, It. 59/F4
Savigny-le-Temple, Fr. 30/K6
Savigny-sur-Orge, Fr. 30/J6
Savio (riv.), It. 43/K5
Sävja, Swe. 38/G2
Savognin, Swi. 57/F4
Savoie (dept.), Fr. 56/C6
Savona, BC, Can. 126/C3
Savona (prov.), It. 58/B4
Savona, It. 58/B4
Savoonga, Ak, US 134/D3
Savoy (reg.), Fr. 42/F4
Savoy Alps (mts.), Fr. 56/C6
Savşat, Turk. 63/G4
Sävsjö, Swe. 38/E3
Savu (sea), Phil. 67/M10
Sawahlunto, Indo. 80/B4
Sawankhalok, Thai. 78/B2
Sawara, Japan 75/G3
Sawasaki-bana (pt.), Japan 75/F2
Sawatch (range), Co, US 128/F3
Sawdā', Jabal (peak), SAr. 88/D5
Saweba (cape), Indo. 81/H4
Sawel (mtn.), NI, UK 34/A2
Sawi, Thai. 78/B4
Sawtooth (range), Id, US 126/E4
Sawtooth Nat'l Rec. Area, Id, US 126/E5
Sawu (isls.), Indo. 81/F6

Sax, Sp. 45/E3
Saxman, Ak, US 134/M4
Saxon, Swi. 56/D5
Say, Niger 103/F3
Saya, Japan 77/L5
Sayama, Japan 75/F3
Sayama, Japan 77/J6
Sayán, Peru 156/B3
Şaydā, Leb. 91/D3
Sayil (ruin), Mex. 144/D1
Saynbach (riv.), Ger. 57/F3
Sayreville, NJ, US 139/H10
Sayula, Mex. 142/E5
Sayville, NY, US 139/E2
Saywün, Yem. 88/E5
Sazan (isl.), Alb. 47/F2
Sázava (riv.), Czh. 43/L2
Sbaa, Alg. 99/E3
Scafell Pikes (peak), Eng, UK 35/E3
Scalasaig, Sc, UK 31/Q8
Scald Law (peak), Sc, UK 31/V13
Scalea, It. 46/D3
Scalino (peak), It. 57/F5
Scalloway, Sc, UK 31/W13
Scammon Bay, Ak, US 134/E3
Scandia, Wa, US 135/B2
Scandiano, It. 59/D3
Scandicci, It. 59/E5
Scapa Flow (chan.), Sc, UK 31/V14
Scar Water (riv.), Sc, UK 34/E1
Scarborough, Can. 131/R8
Scarborough, Eng, UK 35/H3
Scarborough Shoal (isl.), Phil. 79/C4
Scardovari, It. 59/F3
Scarpe (riv.), Fr. 40/B3
Scarperia, It. 59/E5
Scarriff, Ire. 33/P10
Scarsdale, La, US 137/Q17
Scarsdale, NY, US 139/K7
Sceaux, Fr. 30/J5
Scenic Oaks, Tx, US 137/T20
Scey-sur-Saône-et-St-Albin, Fr. 56/B2
Schaefferstown, Pa, US 138/B3
Schaerbeek, Belg. 53/D2
Schaffhausen (canton), Swi. 57/E2
Schaffhausen, Swi. 57/E2
Schäftlarn, Ger. 57/H2
Schagen, Neth. 50/B3
Schaijk, Neth. 50/C5
Schalchen, Aus. 55/G6
Schalkau, Ger. 54/E2
Schalksmühle, Ger. 51/E6
Schanck (cape), Austl. 115/C3
Schangnau, Swi. 56/D4
Scharans, Swi. 57/F4
Schardenberg, Aus. 55/G5
Schärding, Aus. 55/G6
Scharfreiter (peak), Aus. 57/H3
Scharhorn (isl.), Ger. 51/F1
Scharnebeck, Ger. 51/H2
Scharnitz (pass), Ger. 57/H3
Scharnstein, Aus. 55/G7
Schashagen, Ger. 40/F1
Schattdorf, Swi. 57/E4
Schauenstein, Ger. 54/E2
Schaumburg, Il, US 135/P15
Scheemda, Neth. 50/D2
Scheer, Ger. 57/F1
Scheessel, Ger. 51/G2
Schefferville, Qu, Can. 123/K3
Scheibbs, Aus. 41/H4
Scheidegg, Ger. 57/F2
Scheinfeld, Ger. 54/D3
Schelde (riv.), Belg. 42/E1
Schelklingen, Ger. 54/C6
Schell Creek (range), Nv, US 128/D3
Schellerten, Ger. 51/H4
Schellville, Ca, US 135/K10
Schenectady, NY, US 130/F3
Schenefeld, Ger. 51/G1
Schermbeck, Ger. 54/C5
Scherpenzeel, Neth. 50/B6
Schertz, Tx, US 137/U20
Schesaplana (peak), Aus. 57/F3
Schesslitz, Ger. 54/E3
Scheyern, Ger. 55/E5
Schiedam, Neth. 50/B5
Schieder-Schwalenberg, Ger. 51/G5
Schiehallion (peak), Sc, UK 34/B1
Schier Monnikoog (isl.), Neth. 40/D2
Schierling, Ger. 55/F5
Schiermonnikoog (isl.), Neth. 50/D1
Schiermonnikoog, Neth. 50/D1
Schiers, Swi. 57/F4
Schifferstadt, Ger. 54/B4
Schiffweiler, Ger. 53/G5
Schijndel, Neth. 50/C5
Schilde, Belg. 50/B6
Schildmeer (lake), Neth. 50/D2
Schillighörn (cape), Ger. 51/F2
Schillingfürst, Ger. 54/D4
Schiltach, Ger. 57/E1

Schiltigheim, Fr. 56/D1
Schinnen, Neth. 53/E2
Schinznach-Dorf, Swi. 56/E3
Schio, It. 59/E1
Schipbeek (riv.), Neth. 50/D4
Schirmeck, Fr. 56/D1
Schkumbin (riv.), Alb. 47/G2
Schladen, Ger. 51/H4
Schladming, Aus. 43/K3
Schlanders (Silandro), It. 43/J3
Schlangen, Ger. 51/F5
Schlangenbad, Ger. 53/F5
Schleiden, Ger. 53/F2
Schleitheim, Swi. 57/E2
Schleiz, Ger. 55/E1
Schlema, Ger. 55/E1
Schleswig, Ger. 38/C4
Schleswig-Holstein (state), Ger. 38/B4
Schleswig-Holsteinisches Wattenmeer NP, Ger. 38/C4
Schleuse (riv.), Ger. 54/D2
Schleusingen, Ger. 54/D1
Schliengen, Ger. 56/D2
Schlierbach, Aus. 55/H7
Schlieren, Swi. 51/G3
Schloss Herrenchiemsee, Ger. 55/F7
Schloss Holte-Stukenbrock, Ger. 51/F5
Schloss Sansouci, Ger. 40/Q7
Schloss Wilhelmstein, Ger. 51/G4
Schlotheim, Ger. 51/H6
Schluchsee, Ger. 56/E2
Schlüchtern, Ger. 54/C2
Schlüsselfeld, Ger. 54/D3
Schlüsslberg, Aus. 55/G6
Schmalkalden, Ger. 43/J1
Schmallenberg, Ger. 51/F6
Schmeich (riv.), Ger. 54/C6
Schmelz, Ger. 53/F5
Schmiech (riv.), Ger. 57/F1
Schmitten, Swi. 56/D4
Schmutter (riv.), Ger. 54/D5
Schnaitsee, Ger. 55/F6
Schnaittach, Ger. 55/E3
Schnaittenbach, Ger. 55/F3
Schnarrtanne, Ger. 55/F1
Schnecksville, Pa, US 138/C2
Schneeberg (peak), Ger. 55/E2
Schneeberg, Ger. 55/F1
Schneeberg, Ger. 54/C3
Schneifel (upland), Ger. 40/D3
Schneverdingen, Ger. 51/G2
Schofield Barracks, Hi, US 124/V12
Schollene, Ger. 40/G2
Schöllkrippen, Ger. 54/C2
Schömberg, Ger. 57/E1
Schömberg, Ger. 54/B5
Schönaich, Ger. 54/C5
Schönau im Schwarzwald, Ger. 56/D2
Schönberg, Ger. 38/D2
Schönberg, Ger. 51/G1
Schönberg, Ger. 54/C3
Schönbrunn, It. 59/E2
Schondorf am Ammersee, Ger. 57/H1
Schondra (riv.), Ger. 54/C2
Schönebeck, Ger. 40/F2
Schöneck, Ger. 54/B2
Schöneck, Ger. 53/F3
Schönefeld (int'l arpt.), Ger. 40/Q7
Schongau, Ger. 57/G2
Schöningen, Ger. 40/F2
Schonungen, Ger. 54/D2
Schönwald, Ger. 55/E2
Schoonebeek, Neth. 50/D3
Schoonhoven, Neth. 50/B5
Schoorl, Neth. 50/B3
Schopfheim, Ger. 56/D2
Schopfloch, Ger. 54/D4
Schöppenstedt, Ger. 51/H4
Schörfling, Aus. 55/G7
Schorndorf, Ger. 54/C5
Schortens, Ger. 51/E1
Schoten, Belg. 50/B6
Schotten, Ger. 54/C1
Schouten (isls.), Austl. 115/D4
Schouten (isls.), Indo. 116/C5
Schouwen (isl.), Neth. 50/A5
Schramberg, Ger. 57/E1
Schrankogel (peak), Aus. 57/H3
Schreckhorn (peak), Swi. 56/E4
Schriesheim, Ger. 54/B4
Schrobenhausen, Ger. 54/E5
Schroffenstein (peak), Namb. 106/B2
Schrozberg, Ger. 54/D4
Schruns, Aus. 57/F3
Schübelbach, Swi. 57/F3
Schuby, Ger. 38/C4
Schulenburg, Tx, US 129/H5
Schulzendorf, Ger. 40/Q7
Schunter (riv.), Ger. 51/H4
Schüpfheim, Swi. 56/D4
Schussen (riv.), Ger. 57/F2
Schussenried, Ger. 57/F2
Schutter (riv.), Ger. 54/A6
Schütterwald, Ger. 56/D1
Schüttorf, Ger. 51/E4
Schuylkill (riv.), Pa, US 138/C3

Schuylkill Haven, Pa, US 138/B2
Schwabach, Ger. 55/E4
Schwabhausen bei Dachau, Ger. 55/E6
Schwäbisch Gmünd, Ger. 54/C5
Schwäbisch Hall, Ger. 54/C4
Schwäbische Alb (range), Ger. 40/E4
Schwabmünchen, Ger. 57/G1
Schwaig bei Nürnberg, Ger. 55/G1
Schwaigern, Ger. 54/C4
Schwalbach, Ger. 53/F5
Schwalbach am Taunus, Ger. 54/B2
Schwalm (riv.), Ger. 40/E3
Schwalmtal, Ger. 50/D6
Schwanden, Swi. 57/G2
Schwandorf im Bayern, Ger. 55/F4
Schwanebeck, Ger. 40/Q6
Schwanenstadt, Aus. 55/G6
Schwaner (mts.), Indo. 80/D4
Schwanewede, Ger. 51/F2
Schwanfeld, Ger. 54/D3
Schwangau, Ger. 57/G2
Schwarmstedt, Ger. 51/G3
Schwartz Elster (riv.), Ger. 41/G3
Schwarzerberg (peak), Namb. 106/B2
Schwarza (riv.), Ger. 54/E1
Schwarzach, Ger. 55/F5
Schwarzach im Pongau, Aus. 43/K3
Schwarze Laber (riv.), Ger. 55/E4
Schwarzenbach am Wald, Ger. 55/E2
Schwarzenbek, Ger. 51/H1
Schwarzenberg, Ger. 55/F1
Schwarzenbruck, Ger. 54/E4
Schwarzenburg, Swi. 56/D4
Schwarzenfeld, Ger. 55/F4
Schwarzer Mann (peak), Ger. 53/F3
Schwarzhorn, Ger. 54/B2
Schwarzwald (Black Forest) (for.), Ger. 54/B6
Schwaz, Aus. 43/J3
Schwebheim, Ger. 54/D3
Schwechat, Aus. 49/N7
Schwechat (int'l arpt.), Aus. 49/P7
Schwedt, Ger. 41/H2
Schwegenheim, Ger. 54/B4
Schweich, Ger. 53/F4
Schweifel (upland), Ger. 40/D3
Schweighouse-sur-Moder, Fr. 53/G6
Schweinfurt, Ger. 54/D2
Schweitenkirchen, Ger. 55/E5
Schweizer-Reneke, SAfr. 106/D2
Schwelm, Ger. 51/E6
Schwendi, Ger. 57/F1
Schwenksville, Pa, US 138/C3
Schwerin, Ger. 38/D5
Schweringen, Ger. 51/G3
Schwerte, Ger. 51/E6
Schwetzingen, Ger. 54/B4
Schwinge (riv.), Ger. 51/G1
Schwörstadt, Ger. 56/D2
Schwülme (riv.), Ger. 51/G5
Schwülper, Ger. 51/H4
Schwyz (canton), Swi. 57/E3
Schwyz, Swi. 57/E3
Sciacca, It. 46/C4
Scicli, It. 46/D4
Scilly (isls.), Eng, UK 31/Q11
Scinawa, Pol. 41/J3
Scionzier, Fr. 56/C5
Sciota, Pa, US 138/C2
Scioto (riv.), Oh, US 130/D4
Scobey, Mt, US 127/G3
Scolt (pt.), Eng, UK 33/G1
Scone, Austl. 115/D2
Scopello, It. 58/B2
Scordia, It. 46/D4
Scorzè, It. 59/F2
Scotch Corner, Eng, UK 35/G3
Scotch Plains, NJ, US 139/H9
Scotia (sea) 160/W
Scotland, UK 34/D1
Scott (cape), BC, Can. 122/D3
Scott (lake), NW,Sk, Can. 122/F2
Scott, NZ, Ant. 160/M
Scott NP, Austl. 112/B5
Scott City, Ks, US 129/G3
Scott Corner, Me, US 130/G2
Scott Reef (reef), Austl. 109/B2
Scottburgh, SAfr. 107/E3
Scotts (cr.), Austl. 113/M9
Scottsbluff Nat'l Mon., Ne, US 129/F2
Scottsbluff, Ne, US 129/F2
Scottsboro, Al, US 133/G3
Scottsburg, In, US 130/C4
Scottsdale, Austl. 115/C4
Scottsdale, Az, US 128/E4
Scottsville, Ky, US 130/C4
Scottville, Mi, US 130/C2
Scourie, Sc, UK 31/R7
Scranton, Pa, US 130/F3
Scribante, It. 58/B3
Scugog (lake), On, Can. 131/S7
Scunthorpe, Eng, UK 35/H4
Scuol, Swi. 57/G3
Scuppernong (riv.), Wi, US 135/N14

Scurdie Ness (pt.), Sc, UK 36/D3
Scutari (lake), Yugo. 47/F1
Sea Cliff, Ca, US 136/A2
Sea Cliff, NY, US 139/L8
Sea Isle City, NJ, US 138/D5
Sea Lake, Austl. 115/B2
Sea-Tac, Wa, US 135/B2
Seabeck, Wa, US 135/B2
Seabold, Wa, US 135/B2
Seabra, Braz. 154/B4
Seabrook, NJ, US 138/C5
Seaford, Eng, UK 33/G5
Seaford, NI, UK 34/C3
Seaforde, NI, UK 34/C3
Seaforth, Austl. 114/C3
Seagraves, Tx, US 129/G4
Seaham, Eng, UK 35/G2
Seahorse (isl.), Nun. Can. 123/J2
Seahurst, Wa, US 135/C3
Seal, Eng, UK 30/D3
Seal (riv.), MB, Can. 122/G3
Seal (pt.), Chile 158/B5
Seal (cape), SAfr. 106/C4
Seal Beach, Ca, US 136/C3
Seale, Eng, UK 30/A3
Seamer, Eng, UK 35/H3
Seano, It. 59/E6
Seascale, Eng, UK 34/E3
Seaside, Or, US 126/B4
Seaside Heights, NJ, US 138/D4
Seaside Park, NJ, US 138/D4
Seaton, Eng, UK 32/C5
Seaton (riv.), Eng, UK 32/B6
Seaton Carew, Eng, UK 35/G2
Seattle, Wa, US 126/C4
Sébaco, Nic. 144/E3
Sebago (riv.), Alg. 100/H4
Sebastian, Fl, US 133/H5
Sebastián Vizcaíno (bay), Mex. 142/B2
Sebastopol, Ca, US 135/J10
Sebatik (isl.), Indo. 81/E4
Sebauo (riv.), Alg. 100/H4
Sebderup, Den. 38/D4
Sebdou, Alg. 100/D2
Sebeş, Rom. 49/F3
Sebeş (riv.), Rom. 49/F3
Sebezh, Rus. 39/N3
Sebinkarahisar, Turk. 126/C4
Sebiş, Rom. 48/F2
Sebkhet al Kalī yah (drylake), Alg. 100/M7
Sebnitz, Ger. 41/H3
Seboruco, Ven. 152/C2
Sebou, Oued (riv.), Mor. 98/D2
Sebou (riv.), Mor. 100/B2
Sebring, Fl, US 133/H5
Sebuku (isl.), Indo. 81/E4
Secaucus, NJ, US 139/J8
Secchia (riv.), It. 43/J4
Sechura, Peru 156/A2
Sechura (bay), Peru 156/A2
Sechura, Desierto de (des.), Peru 156/A2
Seco (riv.), Mex.,US 142/C2
Seco (riv.), Arg. 159/D6
Seco (riv.), Mex. 143/C2
Second Mountain, Pa, US 138/B3
Second Watchung (mtn.), NJ, US 139/H9
Secunda, SAfr. 106/E2
Secure (riv.), Bol. 150/E7
Seda, Lith. 39/K3
Sedalia, Mo, US 129/J3
Sedan, Fr. 53/E5
Sedano, Sp. 44/D1
Sedauong (mtn.), Myan. 78/B3
Sedbergh, Eng, UK 35/F3
Seddülbahir, Turk. 47/K2
Sedeh, Iran 89/G2
Sederot, Isr. 91/D4
Sedgefield, Eng, UK 35/G2
Sedhiou, Sen. 102/B3
Sedlčany, Czh. 55/H3
Sedlo (peak), Czh. 55/H1
Sedna, Az, US 128/E4
Sedrata, Alg. 100/K6
Seduva, Lith. 39/K4
Sée (riv.), Fr. 42/C2
Seebeodn, Ger. 54/B4
Seeboden, Aus. 43/K3
Seefeld in Tirol, Aus. 57/H3
Seeg, Ger. 57/G2
Seehausen, Ger. 40/F2
Seeheim, Namb. 106/B2
Seeheim-Jugenheim, Ger. 54/B3
Seekirchen Markt, Aus. 55/G7
Seekooi (riv.), SAfr. 106/D3
Seelow, Ger. 41/H2
Seer Green, Eng, UK 30/B2
Seesen, Ger. 51/H5
Seeshaupt, Ger. 57/G2
Seeve (riv.), Ger. 51/G2
Seewalchen, Aus. 55/G7
Seewis im Prättigau, Swi. 57/F4

Segovia, Col. 152/C3
Segovia, Sp. 44/C2
Segozero (lake), Rus. 60/G3
Segrate, It. 58/C3
Segré, Fr. 42/C3
Segre (riv.), Sp. 45/F2
Seguam (isl.), Ak, US 134/C5
Séguéla, C.d'Iv. 102/D5
Séguédine, Niger 96/H3
Séguénega, Burk. 103/E3
Seguin, Tx, US 132/D4
Segura (riv.), Sp. 44/D3
Sehithwa, Bots. 105/D5
Sehnde, Ger. 51/G4
Sehonghong, Les. 106/D3
Sehore, India 82/C3
Sehwan, India 89/J3
Seibersbach, Ger. 53/G4
Seiersberg, Aus. 48/B2
Seika, Japan 77/J6
Seiling, Ok, US 129/H3
Seille (riv.), Fr. 40/C5
Seinäjoki, Fin. 60/D3
Seine (riv.), On, Can. 127/L3
Seine (bay), Fr. 42/C2
Seine-et-Marne (dept.), Fr. 52/B5
Seine-Maritime (dept.), Fr. 52/A4
Seine-st-Denis (dept.), Fr. 52/B5
Seitenstetten, Aus. 55/H6
Seiwa, Japan 77/K7
Seix, Fr. 42/D5
Seixal, Port. 45/P10
Sejerø (isl.), Den. 38/D4
Sejny, Pol. 39/K4
Sekayu, Indo. 80/B4
Seke, Tanz. 104/A2
Sekenke, Tanz. 104/A3
Seki (riv.), Turk. 91/A1
Seki, Japan 77/L5
Seki, Japan 77/K6
Sekigahara, Japan 77/K5
Sekijo, Japan 77/D1
Sekiyado, Japan 77/D1
Sekondi, Gha. 103/E5
Sekoma, Bots. 106/C2
Sekondi-Takoradi, Gha. 103/E5
Selah, Wa, US 126/C4
Selaphum, Thai. 78/D2
Selargius, It. 46/A3
Selaru (isl.), Indo. 81/H5
Selatan (cape), Indo. 80/D4
Selawik (lake), Ak, US 134/F2
Selayar (isl.), Indo. 81/F5
Selb, Ger. 55/F2
Selbitz, Ger. 55/E2
Selbitz (riv.), Ger. 55/E2
Selbu, Nor. 37/D3
Selby, SD, US 127/H4
Selby, Eng, UK 35/G4
Selby-on-the-Bay, Md, US 138/B6
Selçi, It. 59/F6
Selçuk, Turk. 90/A2
Selden, NY, US 139/E2
Sele (riv.), It. 46/D2
Selebi-Phikwe, Bots. 105/E5
Seleli (hill), Tanz. 104/B5
Selemdzha (riv.), Rus. 65/N4
Selenča, Yugo. 48/D3
Selenge (prov.), Mong. 70/J2
Selenge (riv.), Mong. 70/J2
Selenginsk, Rus. 65/L4
Seleničë, Alb. 47/F2
Selestat, Fr. 56/D1
Selety (riv.), Kaz. 87/F2
Seleucia, Turk. 90/A2
Selfoss, Ice. 37/N7
Selfselss, Ice. 37/N7
Seligenstadt, Ger. 54/B2
Seliger (lake), Rus. 60/G4
Selimiye, Turk. 90/A2
Selinsgrove, Pa, US 138/B3
Seljord, Nor. 38/C2
Selkan (tun.), Japan 76/B3
Selkirk, Sc, UK 36/D5
Selkirk, Mb, Can. 122/G3
Selkirk (mts.), BC, Can. 126/D3
Selleck, Wa, US 135/D3
Sellersville, Pa, US 138/C3
Sellières, Fr. 56/B4
Sells, Az, US 128/E5
Selly Oak, Eng, UK 24/E5
Sellye, Hun. 48/C3
Selma, Al, US 133/G3
Selmer, Tn, US 133/F3
Selongey, Fr. 56/B2
Selouma, Gui. 102/C4
Selous Game Reserve, Tanz. 104/B4
Selsey, Eng, UK 33/F5
Selsey Bill (pt.), Eng, UK 33/F5
Selsingen, Ger. 51/G2
Seltz, Fr. 54/B5
Selune (riv.), Fr. 42/C2
Selva (for.), Braz. 147/C3
Selvik, Nor. 37/R9
Selwyn, Austl. 114/A3
Selwyn (range), Austl. 114/A3
Selz (riv.), Ger. 54/B2
Segamat, Malay. 80/B3
Selz (riv.), Ger. 54/B2
Segarcea, Rom. 49/F3
Ségbana, Ben. 103/F4
Semarang, Indo. 80/D4
Ségélo-Koro, C.d'Iv. 102/D3
Semarsot, India 84/D4
Sembehun, SLeo. 102/B5
Seget, Indo. 81/H4
Sembera (riv.), Turk. 55/H2
Segezha, Rus. 60/G3
Semberong (riv.),
Segorbe, Sp. 45/E3
Semdinli, Turk. 90/F2
Ségou, Mali 102/D3
Ségou (pol. reg.), Mali 102/D3
Séméac, Fr. 42/D5

225

Semen – Sigüe

Semenivka, Ukr. 62/E1
Semenivka, Ukr. 62/E2
Semenov, Rus. 61/K4
Semeru (peak), Indo. 80/D5
Semey, Kaz. 87/H2
Semikarakorsk, Rus. 63/G3
Semilovo, Rus. 63/G1
Semiluki, Rus. 62/F2
Seminole (lake), Ga, US 133/G4
Seminole, Tx, US 132/C3
Seminoe (res.), Wy, US 128/F2
Semitau, Indo. 80/D4
Semliki (riv.), D.R. Congo 104/A2
Semnān, Iran 88/F1
Semnon (riv.), Fr. 42/C3
Semois (riv.), Belg. 42/F2
Semporna, Malay. 81/E3
Semsales, Swi. 56/C4
Semskefjellet (peak), Nor. 37/E2
Sen (riv.), Camb. 83/H5
Sen-san (peak), Japan 77/G7
Sena, Thai. 83/H5
Senador Pompeu, Braz. 154/C2
Senaja, Malay. 81/E2
Senaki, Geo. 63/G4
Senanga, Zam. 105/D4
Sénas, Fr. 90/B5
Senatobia, Ms, US 133/F3
Sence (riv.), Eng, UK 33/E1
Send, Eng, UK 30/B3
Sendai (riv.), Japan 74/D3
Sendai, Japan 75/G1
Sendai, Japan 74/B5
Sendai (int'l arpt.), Japan 75/G1
Sendai (bay), Japan 76/B4
Sendal (riv.), Japan 74/B5
Senden, Ger. 54/D6
Senden, Ger. 51/E5
Sendenhorst, Ger. 51/E5
Senec, Slvk. 41/J4
Seneca Creek State Park, Md, US 138/A5
Seneffe, Belg. 53/D2
Sénégal (riv.), Afr. 102/B2
Senegal (ctry.) 102/B3
Senekal, SAfr. 106/D3
Seney NWR, Mi, US 130/C2
Senezhskoye (lake), Rus. 61/W8
Senfi, Gha. 103/E5
Senftenberg, Ger. 41/H3
Sengenthal, Ger. 55/E4
Sengilev, Rus. 63/J1
Sengor, Bhu. 85/H2
Senguer (riv.), Arg. 158/D3
Senhor do Bonfim, Braz. 154/B3
Senica, Slvk. 41/J4
Senirkent, Turk. 90/B2
Senise, It. 46/E2
Senj, Cro. 43/L4
Senja (isl.), Nor. 37/F1
Senkaku-Shotō (isl.), Japan 75/G8
Şenkaya, Turk. 90/E1
Şenköy, Turk. 91/E1
Senlis, Fr. 52/B5
Senmonoron, Camb. 78/D3
Sennan, Japan 77/H7
Sennar (dam), Sudan 97/M5
Senne (riv.), Belg. 53/D2
Sennecy-le-Grand, Fr. 56/A4
Sennfeld, Ger. 54/D2
Senno, Bela. 39/N4
Sennoy, Rus. 63/G2
Sennoy, Rus. 63/H1
Sennwald, Swi. 57/F3
Sennybridge, Wal, UK 32/C3
Séno (prov.), Burk. 103/F3
Senones, Fr. 56/C1
Senorbì, It. 46/A3
Senou (Bamako) (int'l arpt.), Mali 102/D3
Senovo, Bul. 49/H4
Sens, Fr. 42/E2
Sensuntepeque, ESal. 144/D3
Senta, Yugo. 48/E3
Sentani, Indo. 81/K4
Sentery, D.R. Congo 105/E2
Senya Beraku, Gha. 103/E5
Senyavin (isls.), Micr. 116/E4
Senzig, Ger. 40/Q7
Seohārā, India 84/B1
Seon, Swi. 56/E3
Seondha, India 84/B2
Seoni, India 84/B4
Seonī Mālwā, India 84/A4
Seoul (Sŏul) (cap.), SKor. 73/D4
Seoul Grand Park, SKor. 73/G7
Seoul Jikhalsi (prov.), SKor. 73/D4
Sepetiba (bay), Braz. 155/J8
Sepik (riv.), PNG 116/D5
Sep'o, NKor. 73/D3
Sepo, Indo. 81/G3
Sępólno Krajeńskie, Pol. 41/J2
Sept-Îles, Qu, Can. 131/H2
Septemvri, Bul. 47/J1
Septeuil, Fr. 30/H5
Sepulveda (dam), Ca, US 136/F7
Sequeros, Sp. 44/B2
Sequoia NP, Ca, US 128/C3
Serafimovich, Rus. 63/G2
Seraincourt, Fr. 30/H4
Seraing, Belg. 53/E2
Serampore, India 85/G4
Sèran (riv.), Fr. 56/D3
Serasan (str.), Indo.,Malay. 80/C3
Serasan, Indo. 80/C3
Seravezza, It. 58/D6
Serbia (reg.), Yugo. 48/E4
Serchio (riv.), It. 58/D4
Serdobsk, Rus. 63/H1
Serebryansk, Kaz. 64/J5
Serednikovo, Rus. 60/H5
Seregno, It. 58/C2
Serein (riv.), Fr. 40/D4
Serémange-Erzange, Fr. 53/F5
Seremban, Malay. 80/B3
Serengeti NP, Tanz. 97/M8
Serenje, Zam. 105/F3
Serere, Ugan. 104/A1
Sergach, Rus. 61/K5
Sergeantsville, NJ, US 138/D3
Sergen, Turk. 49/H5
Sergeya Kirova (isls.), Rus. 64/J2
Sergeyevka, Kaz. 61/Q5
Sergipe (state), Braz. 154/C3
Sergiyev Posad, Rus. 60/H4
Sergnano, It. 58/C3
Seria, Bru. 80/D3
Seriate, It. 58/C2
Sérifontaine, Fr. 52/A5
Sérifos, Gre. 47/J4
Sérifos (isl.), Gre. 47/J4
Sérignan, Fr. 42/E5
Serik, Turk. 90/B2
Seringa, Serra da (mts.), Braz. 151/h5
Serio (riv.), It. 58/C2
Serkout (peak), Alg. 99/G5
Sermaize-les-Bains, Fr. 53/D6
Sermide, It. 59/E4
Sernovodsk, Rus. 63/J1
Sernur, Rus. 61/L4
Serón, Sp. 44/D4
Serós, Sp. 45/F2
Serottini (peak), It. 57/G5
Serov, Rus. 64/G4
Serowe, Bots. 105/E5
Serpa, Port. 44/B4
Serpeddi (peak), It. 46/A3
Serpent's Mouth (str.), Trin.,Ven. 153/F2
Serpentine (dam), Austl. 115/C4
Serpentine Lakes, Austl. 113/F4
Serpukhov, Rus. 60/H5
Serra (peak), It. 58/D6
Serra, Braz. 155/D2
Serra Branca, Braz. 154/C2
Serra da Bocaína, PN da, Braz. 155/C2
Serra da Canastra, PN da, Braz. 155/C2
Serra da Capivara, PN da, Braz. 154/B3
Serra da Estrela (peak), Port. 44/B2
Serra da Estrela (mts.), Port. 44/A3
Serra do Cipó, PN da, Braz. 155/D1
Serra dos Órgãos, PN da, Braz. 155/K7
Serra San Bruno, It. 46/E3
Serra San Quirico, It. 59/G7
Serra Talhada, Braz. 154/C2
Sérrai, Gre. 47/H2
Serralta di San Vito (peak), It. 46/E3
Serramanna, It. 46/A3
Serramazzoni, It. 59/D5
Serrana Bank (isl.), Col. 141/F5
Serranía de la Cerbatana (mts.), Ven. 153/E3
Serranía de la Neblina, PN, Ven. 153/E4
Serranías del Burro (mts.), Mex. 142/E2
Serranilla Bank (isl.), Col. 141/F4
Serrano, Arg. 158/E2
Serranópolis, Braz. 155/B1
Serrat (cape), Tun. 100/L6
Serravalle, It. 59/F4
Serravalle, SMar. 59/F6
Serravalle Scrivia, It. 58/B4
Serravalle Sesia, It. 58/B2
Serre (riv.), Fr. 40/B4
Serrenti, It. 46/A3
Serrinha, Braz. 154/C3
Serris, Fr. 30/L5
Sersale, It. 46/E3
Sertã, Port. 44/A3
Sertânia, Braz. 154/C3
Sertãozinho, Braz. 155/H2
Sertavul (pass), Turk. 90/C2
Serteng (mts.), China 70/F4
Serui, Indo. 81/J4
Seruyan (riv.), Indo. 80/D4
Servance, Fr. 56/C2
Servi, Turk. 90/E2
Sérvia, Gre. 47/G2
Serviceton, Austl. 115/B3
Sese (isls.), Ugan. 104/A3
Sesebi (ruin), Sudan 101/B4
Sesepe, Indo. 81/G4
Sesheke, Zam. 105/D4
Sesia (riv.), It. 43/H4
Sesimbra, Port. 44/A3
Sesimbra, Port. 45/P11
Seskar (isl.), Rus. 39/N1
Sespe, Ca, US 136/B2
Sespe (cr.), Ca, US 136/A1
Sespe Condor Sanctuary, Ca, US 136/C3
Sesslach, Ger. 54/D2
Sesto Calende, It. 58/B2
Sesto Fiorentino, It. 59/E6
Sesto San Giovanni, It. 58/C2
Sesto Ulteriano, It. 58/C3
Sestola, It. 59/D5
Sestra (riv.), Rus. 60/W9
Sestri Levante, It. 58/C5
Sestroretsk, Rus. 60/S6
Sestroretskiy (lake), Rus. 60/T6
Sestu, It. 46/A3
Sesvenna (peak), It. 57/G4
Sesvete, Cro. 48/C3
Šeta, Lith. 39/L4
Setana, Japan 76/A2
Sète, Fr. 42/E5
Sete Lagoas, Braz. 155/C1
Sethārja, Pak. 89/J3
Seti (riv.), Nepal 84/C1
Seti (zone), Nepal 84/C1
Sétif, Alg. 100/H4
Sétif (wilaya), Alg. 100/H4
Seto, Japan 77/M5
Seto-Naikai NP, Japan 74/C4
Setouchi, Japan 75/K6
Settat, Mor. 98/D2
Settepani (peak), It. 58/B5
Settimo Torinese, It. 58/A2
Settimo Vittone, It. 58/A1
Settle, Eng, UK 35/F3
Settsu, Japan 77/J6
Setúbal (dist.), Port. 44/A3
Setúbal (bay), Port. 44/A3
Setúbal, Port. 45/Q10
Seubersdorf, Ger. 55/E4
Seudre (riv.), Fr. 42/C4
Seugne (riv.), Fr. 42/C4
Seuil-d'Argonne, Fr. 53/E6
Seul (lake), On, Can. 122/G3
Seulimeum, Indo. 80/A2
Seurre, Fr. 56/B4
Seuzach, Swi. 57/E2
Sevan, Arm. 63/H4
Sevana (lake), Arm. 64/E5
Sevastopol', Ukr. 62/E3
Sevelen, Swi. 57/F3
Seven (riv.), Eng, UK 35/H3
Seven Heads (pt.), Ire. 31/P11
Seven Valleys, Pa, US 138/B4
Sevenoaks, Eng, UK 30/D3
Sevenoaks Weald, Eng, UK 30/D3
Severn (riv.), Wal, UK 35/F6
Severn (riv.), On, Can. 122/G3
Severn (riv.), Md, US 138/B5
Severn, Md, US 138/B5
Severna Park, Md, US 138/B5
Severnaya Osetiya-Alaniya (aut. rep.), Rus. 63/G4
Severnaya Sos'va (riv.), Rus. 61/N3
Severnaya Zemlya (isls.), Rus. 64/J2
Severnyy, Rus. 61/P2
Severo-Kuril'sk, Rus. 65/R4
Severo-Yeniseyskiy, Rus. 64/K3
Severobaykal'sk, Rus. 65/L4
Severočeský (pol. reg.), Czh. 43/L1
Severodvinsk, Rus. 60/H2
Severomoravsky (pol. reg.), Czh. 41/J4
Severomoravský (pol. reg.), Czh. 43/M1
Severomorsk, Rus. 60/G1
Severomuysk, Rus. 65/M4
Severoural'sk, Rus. 61/N3
Severskaya, Rus. 62/F3
Severukha, Rus. 61/P4
Seveso, It. 58/C2
Sevier (des.), Ut, US 128/D3
Sevierville, Tn, US 133/H3
Sevilla, Col. 152/C3
Seville, Sp. 44/C4
Seville, Austl. 115/G5
Sevlievo, Bul. 49/G4
Sevnica, Slov. 48/B2
Sevojno, Yugo. 48/D4
Sevran, Fr. 30/K5
Sevsk, Rus. 62/E1
Sewa (riv.), SLeo. 102/C5
Seward (pen.), Ak, US 134/E2
Seward, Ak, US 134/J3
Seward, Ne, US 129/H2
Sewaren, NJ, US 139/J9
Sewell, Chile 158/N9
Seyah Cheshmeh, Iran 63/H5
Seybaplaya, Mex. 144/D2
Seybouse, Oued (riv.), Alg. 100/K6
Seychelles (ctry.) 23/M6
Seydhisfjördhur, Ice. 37/Q6
Seydişehir, Turk. 90/B2
Seyhan (dam), Turk. 90/C2
Seyhan (riv.), Turk. 91/D1
Seyitgazi, Turk. 90/B2
Seym (riv.), Rus. 96/E2
Seymour, Austl. 115/C3
Seymour, Tx, US 129/H4
Seynod, Fr. 56/C6
Seyssel, Fr. 56/B6
Sežana, Slov. 43/K4
Sézanne, Fr. 52/C6
Sezimovo Ústí, Czh. 55/H4
Sezze, It. 46/C2
Sfintu Gheorghe, Rom. 49/J3
Sfintu Gheorghe, Rom. 49/G3
Sfintu Gheorghe Branch (riv.), Rom. 49/J3
Sfizef, Alg. 100/E5
Sgurr na Lapaich (peak), Sc, UK 36/A2
Sha (riv.), China 72/C4
Sha Tin, China 71/U10
Shaanxi (prov.), China 70/J5
Shaba Nat'l Rsv., Kenya 104/C2
Shābāzpur (riv.), Bang. 85/H4
Shabeelle (riv.), Som. 97/P7
Shabla, Bul. 49/J4
Shabqadar, Pak. 86/A2
Shabunda, D.R. Congo 97/L8
Shache, China 87/G5
Shade (mtn.), Pa, US 138/A2
Shadrinsk, Rus. 61/P4
Shafter, Tx, US 132/B4
Shagamu, Nga. 103/F5
Shagany (lake), Ukr. 49/J3
Shageluk, Ak, US 134/G3
Shah Alam, Malay. 80/B3
Shāh Kot, Pak. 86/B4
Shāhābād, India 84/B2
Shāhābād, India 84/B1
Shāhābād, India 86/D4
Shahdād, Iran 89/G2
Shāhdādkot, Pak. 89/J3
Shahdol, India 84/C4
Shāhganj, India 84/D2
Shaḩḩāt, Libya 97/K1
Shāhjahānpur, India 84/B2
Shāhpur, Pak. 86/B3
Shāhpur Chākar, Pak. 82/A2
Shāhpura, India 84/C4
Shahr-e Kord, Iran 88/F2
Shahr Sultān, Pak. 86/A5
Shāhrūd (Emāmshahr), Iran 89/F1
Shā'ib al Banāt (peak), Egypt 101/C3
Shaikhpura, India 85/E3
Shājāpur, India 89/L4
Shakargarh, Pak. 86/C3
Shakaskraal, SAfr. 107/E3
Shakawe, Bots. 105/D4
Shakhrisabz, Uzb. 87/E5
Shakhtinsk, Kaz. 87/F3
Shakhty, Rus. 62/G3
Shakhun'ya, Rus. 61/K4
Shaki, Nga. 103/F4
Shakotan (pen.), Japan 76/B2
Shaktoolik, Ak, US 134/F3
Shalbuzdag (peak), Rus. 63/H4
Shallow Reach (inlet), Austl. 113/M8
Shalqar, Kaz. 63/L3
Shaluli (mts.), China 70/G5
Shām, Jabal ash (peak), Oman 89/G4
Shama (riv.), Tanz. 105/F2
Shamattawa (riv.), On, Can. 123/H3
Shāmgarh, India 89/L4
Shamīl, Iran 89/G3
Shāmli, India 86/D5
Shammar, Jabal (mts.), SAr. 88/D3
Shamokin, Pa, US 138/B2
Shamokin Dam, Pa, US 138/B2
Shamrock (mtn.), Yk, Can. 134/L3
Shamrock, Tx, US 129/G4
Shamsābād, India 84/B2
Shamva, Zim. 105/F4
Shan (div.), Myan. 70/G7
Shan (plat.), Myan. 70/G7
Shan (state), Myan. 83/G3
Sha'nabī, Jabal ash (peak), Tun. 100/L7
Shandong (prov.), China 71/L4
Shandong (isl.), China 72/E3
Shangcai, China 72/C4
Shangcheng, China 72/C5
Shangdu, China 71/K3
Shanghai (prov.), China 71/M5
Shanghai, China 72/L8
Shanghang, China 79/C2
Shanghe, China 72/D3
Shangqiu, China 72/C4
Shangshui, China 72/C4
Shangyi, China 72/C2
Shangyou, China 79/B2
Shannon (riv.), Ire. 31/P10
Shanshan, China 70/F3
Shantar (isls.), Rus. 65/P4
Shantar (isl.), Rus. 67/N4
Shantou, China 79/C3
Shanxi (prov.), China 71/K4
Shanyin, China 72/C3
Shaoguan, China 83/K3
Shaowu, China 79/C2
Shaoxing, China 79/D2
Shaoyang, China 79/B2
Shaoyang, China 83/K2
Shapkina (riv.), Rus. 61/M2
Shaqlāwah, Iraq 90/F2
Sharafkhāneh, Iran 90/F2
Sharbatāt, Ra's ash (pt.), Oman 89/G5
Sharga, Mong. 70/G2
Shari, Japan 76/D2
Sharīngol, Mong. 70/J2
Shark (bay), Austl. 109/A3
Shark River (inlet), NJ, US 138/D3
Sharon, Pa, US 130/D3
Sharp (mtn.), Ut, US 137/K11
Sharpe (lake), SD, US 127/J4
Sharqpur, Pak. 86/C4
Shar'ya, Rus. 61/K4
Shashi, China 79/B1
Shasta (lake), Ca, US 126/C5
Shasta (mt.), Ca, US 126/C5
Shatskiy NP, Ukr. 41/M3
Shatt al Arab (riv.), Iraq 88/E2
Shaţţ al Jarīd (dry lake), Gabon 96/G1
Shattuck, Ok, US 129/H3
Shaunavon, Sk, Can. 126/F3
Shavano Park, Tx, US 137/T20
Shaw, Eng, UK 33/E4
Shawano, Wi, US 127/L4
Shawinigan, Qu, Can. 131/F2
Shawnee, Ok, US 129/H4
Shawnee (res.), Ok, US 137/N15
Shawnee, Ks, US 137/D5
Shay Gap, Austl. 112/D2
Shaykhān, Iraq 90/E2
Shchara (riv.), Bela. 62/C1
Shchekino, Rus. 62/F1
Shchelkovo, Rus. 61/W9
Shchigry, Rus. 62/F2
Shchūchīnsk, Kaz. 87/F2
She Xian, China 79/C2
Shea Stadium, NY, US 139/K9
Shebelē Wenz (riv.), Eth. 97/P6
Sheberghān, Afg. 89/J1
Sheboygan, Wi, US 127/M5
Shediac, NB, Can. 131/H2
Shee (riv.), Sc, UK 36/C3
Sheelin (lake), Ire. 34/A4
Sheep (mtn.), Ak, US 134/F2
Shefar'am, Isr. 91/G6
Shefayim, Isr. 91/F7
Sheffield, Austl. 115/C4
Sheffield, Al, US 133/G3
Sheffield (isl.), Ct, US 139/M7
Sheffield, Eng, UK 35/G5
Shehuén (riv.), Arg. 157/B6
Shek Uk (peak), China 71/V10
Shekak (riv.), On, Can. 130/C1
Shekhūpura, Pak. 86/B4
Shelagskiy (cape), Rus. 65/S2
Shelburne, NS, Can. 131/H3
Shelby, Mt, US 126/F3
Shelby, Ms, US 129/K4
Shelby, Mi, US 130/C3
Shelby, NC, US 133/H3
Shelbyville (lake), Il, US 133/F2
Shelbyville, Tn, US 133/G3
Shelbyville, In, US 130/C4
Sheldon Point, Ak, US 134/F3
Shelekhov (gulf), Rus. 67/Q3
Shelikof (str.), Ak, US 134/H4
Shell (pt.), Eng, UK 33/G4
Shell Lake, Wi, US 127/L4
Shell Rock (riv.), Ia, US 127/K5
Shellbrook, Sk, Can. 127/G2
Shelley (isl.), Pa, US 138/B3
Shelter (isl.), NY, US 139/F1
Shelter Island (sound), NY, US 139/F1
Shelton, Wa, US 126/C4
Shelton, Ct, US 139/E1
Shen Xian, China 72/C3
Shenandoah, Pa, US 138/B2
Shenandoah NP, Va, US 130/E4
Shenchi, China 72/C3
Sheng Xian, China 79/D2
Shenge (pt.), SLeo. 102/B5
Shengena (peak), Tanz. 104/C4
Shennongjia, China 72/B5
Shenqiu, China 72/C4
Shenyang, China 73/B2
Shenzhen, China 83/K3
Shepetivka, Ukr. 62/C2
Shepherd (isls.), Van. 116/F6
Sheppey, Isle of (isl.), Eng, UK 33/G4
Shepshed, Eng, UK 33/E1
Sheqi, China 72/C4
Sherbro (isl.), SLeo. 102/B5
Sherbrooke, Qu, Can. 131/G2
Shere (hill), Nga. 103/H4
Sheremetyevo (int'l arpt.), Rus. 61/W9
Sherghāti, India 85/E3
Sheridan, Wy, US 126/G4
Sheridan, Co, US 137/B3
Sherman, Tx, US 129/H4
Sherpur, Bang. 85/H3
Sherwood (pt.), Ct, US 139/E1
Shetland (isls.), UK 160/G
Sheung Shui-Fanling, China 71/U10
Shevchenko (int'l arpt.), Kaz. 63/J4
Sheyang (riv.), China 72/D4
Sheyang, China 72/E4
Sheyenne (riv.), ND, US 127/J4
Shi (riv.), China 72/C4
Shi San Ling, China 72/H6
Shibakawa, Japan 77/B3
Shibata, Japan 75/F2
Shibayama, Japan 77/E2
Shibecha, Japan 76/D2
Shibetsu, Japan 76/C1
Shibetsu, Japan 76/D2
Shibīn al Kaum, Egypt 91/B4
Shibīn al Qanāţir, Egypt 91/B4
Shibogama (lake), On, Can. 127/L2
Shibotsu (isl.), Rus. 76/E2
Shibushi (bay), Japan 74/B5
Shicheng, China 79/C2
Shicheng (isl.), China 73/B3
Shickshinny, Pa, US 138/B1
Shiderty (riv.), Kaz. 87/F2
Shido, Japan 74/D3
Shiga, Japan 77/J5
Shigaraki, Japan 77/K6
Shihezi, China 70/E3
Shijak, Alb. 47/F2
Shijiazhuang, China 72/C3
Shijōnawate, Japan 77/J6
Shikabe, Japan 76/B2
Shikārpur, India 84/B1
Shikārpur, Pak. 89/J3
Shikata, Japan 77/G6
Shikatsu, Japan 77/L5
Shikishima, Japan 77/B2
Shikohābād, India 84/B2
Shikoku (mts.), Japan 74/C4
Shikoku (isl.), Japan 67/N6
Shikotsu (lake), Japan 76/B2
Shikotsu-Tōya NP, Japan 76/B2
Shildon, Eng, UK 35/G2
Shilka (riv.), Rus. 67/L4
Shilla (peak), India 89/L2
Shillington, Pa, US 138/C3
Shillong, India 83/F2
Shiloh, Il, US 137/H8
Shiloh, NJ, US 138/C5
Shilou, China 72/B3
Shimabara, Japan 74/B4
Shimagahara, Japan 77/K6
Shimamoto, Japan 77/J6
Shimane (pref.), Japan 74/C3
Shimasahi, Japan 77/K5
Shimba Hills Nat'l Rsv., Kenya 104/C4
Shimbara (bay), Japan 74/B4
Shimber Berris (peak), Som. 97/Q5
Shimizu, Japan 76/C2
Shimizu, Japan 77/B3
Shimo-Koshiki (isl.), Japan 74/A5
Shimobe, Japan 77/A3
Shimoda, Japan 75/F3
Shimodate, Japan 75/F2
Shimofusa, Japan 77/E2
Shimoichi, Japan 77/J7
Shimokita (pen.), Japan 76/B3
Shimonita, Japan 77/B1
Shimonoseki, Japan 74/B4
Shimotsuma, Japan 77/D1
Shimoyama, Japan 77/M5
Shimukappu, Japan 76/C2
Shin, Japan 77/C1
Shin (lake), Sc, UK 31/R7
Shindo, SKor. 73/F6
Shingū, Japan 74/D4
Shinhyŏn, SKor. 74/A3
Shinji (lake), Japan 74/C3
Shinjō, Japan 76/B4
Shinjō, Japan 77/J7
Shinkawa, Japan 77/L5
Shinminato, Japan 75/E2
Shinnecock (bay), NY, US 139/F2
Shinnecock Ind. Res., NY, US 139/F2
Shinsei, Japan 77/L5
Shintoku, Japan 76/C2
Shintone, Japan 77/E2
Shinyanga, Tanz. 104/B3
Shinyanga (pol. reg.), Tanz. 104/B3
Shio-no-misaki (cape), Japan 74/D4
Shiogama, Japan 75/G1
Shioya-saki (pt.), Japan 75/G2
Ship Bottom, NJ, US 138/D4
Shipley, Eng, UK 35/G4
Shippan (pt.), Ct, US 139/L7
Shippegan, NB, Can. 131/H2
Shippo, Japan 77/L5
Shiprock, NM, US 128/E3
Shīr (mtn.), Iran 88/F2
Shirakami-misaki (cape), Japan 76/B3
Shirakawa, Japan 75/G2
Shirakawa, Japan 77/M4
Shirakawa-tōge (pass), Japan 74/E3
Shirako, Japan 77/E3
Shirane, Japan 77/A2
Shirane-san (peak), Japan 75/F3
Shirane-san (peak), Japan 75/F2
Shiranuka, Japan 76/D2
Shiraoi, Japan 76/B2
Shiraoka, Japan 77/D1
Shīrāz, Iran 88/F3
Shirbīn, Egypt 91/B4
Shiretoko-misaki (cape), Japan 76/D1
Shiretoko NP, Japan 76/D1
Shiriya-zaki (pt.), Japan 76/B3
Shirjiu (lake), China 72/D5
Shirley, NY, US 139/F2
Shiroi, Japan 77/E2
Shiroishi, Japan 75/G1
Shirone, Japan 75/F2
Shiroyama, Japan 77/C2
Shīrvān, Iran 89/G1
Shishaldin (vol.), Ak, US 134/F5
Shīshgarh, India 84/B1
Shishi, China 79/C3
Shishmaref, Ak, US 134/E2
Shishou, China 79/B2
Shisui, Japan 77/E2
Shithātha, Iraq 90/E3
Shivpurī, India 84/A3
Shivpuri NP, India 84/A3
Shixing, China 83/K3
Shiyan, China 72/B4
Shizhu, China 79/A2
Shizugawa, Japan 76/B4
Shizuishan, China 70/J4
Shizukuishi, Japan 76/B4
Shizunai, Japan 76/C2
Shizuoka (pref.), Japan 75/E3
Shkumbin (riv.), Alb. 48/E5
Shmidta (cape), Rus. 134/C2
Shoal (pt.), Austl. 112/B4
Shoal Lake, Mb, Can. 127/H3
Shoalhaven (riv.), Austl. 115/D2
Shōbara, Japan 74/C3
Shōbu, Japan 77/D1
Shōdo (isl.), Japan 74/D3
Shoemakersville, Pa, US 138/C3
Shokanbetsu-dake (peak), Japan 76/B2
Sholāpur, India 89/L5
Sholl (peak), Arg. 159/D6
Shomron (ruin), WBnk. 91/G7
Shōnan, Japan 77/E2
Shorāpur, India 82/C4
Shoreham-by-Sea, Eng, UK 33/F5
Shorewood, Wi, US 135/Q13
Shorewood, Il, US 135/P16
Shorkot, Pak. 86/B4
Short (mtn.), Tn, US 133/G3
Shortland (isls.), Sol. 116/E5
Shoshone (riv.), Wy, US 126/F4
Shoshone (mts.), Nv, US 128/C3
Shoshoni, Wy, US 126/F5
Shostka, Ukr. 62/E2
Shotts, Sc, UK 36/C5
Shou Xian, China 72/D4
Shouguang, China 72/D3
Shouyang, China 72/C3
Show Low, Az, US 128/E4
Shōwa, Japan 77/B2
Shōwa, Japan 77/D2
Shpanberga (chan.), Rus. 76/E2
Shpola, Ukr. 62/D2
Shreveport, La, US 129/J4
Shrewsbury, Mo, US 137/G8
Shrewsbury, Eng, UK 32/D1
Shrewsbury, Pa, US 138/B4
Shriner (mtn.), Pa, US 138/A2
Shropshire (co.), Eng, UK 35/E6
Shropshire Union (canal), Eng, UK 35/F6
Shū (riv.), Kaz. 65/H5
Shu (riv.), China 72/D5
Shuangbai, China 83/H3
Shuangcheng, China 71/N2
Shuangliao, China 72/E2
Shuangpai, China 83/K2
Shuangyashan, China 71/P2
Shu'ayb, Jabal an (peak), Yem. 88/D5
Shubrā al Khaymah, Egypt 91/B4
Shubrā Khīt, Egypt 91/B4
Shucheng, China 72/D5
Shu'fāţ, Isr. 91/G8
Shufu, China 87/G5
Shuiyang (riv.), China 72/D5
Shujāābād, Pak. 86/A5
Shulan, China 71/N3
Shule, China 87/G5
Shule (riv.), China 64/K6
Shumagin (isls.), Ak, US 134/G4
Shumen, Bul. 49/H4
Shumerlya, Rus. 61/K5
Shuna (isl.), Sc, UK 36/A3
Shunak (peak), Kaz. 87/F3
Shungnak, Ak, US 134/G2
Shunyi, China 72/H6
Shuo Xian, China 72/C3
Shupīyan, India 86/C3
Shūr (riv.), Iran 89/G2
Shurugwi, Zim. 105/E4
Shūshtar, Iran 88/E2
Shuswap (lake), BC, Can. 126/D3
Shuwaykah, WBnk. 91/G7
Shuya, Rus. 60/J4
Shuyang, China 72/D4
Shwebo, Myan. 83/G3
Shwegyin, Myan. 83/G4
Shyghys Qazaqstan (obl.), Kaz. 64/J5
Shymkent, Kaz. 87/E4
Shyok (riv.), India 89/L2
Si Satchanalai (ruin), Thai. 78/B2
Si Xian, China 72/D4
Siāh Kūh (mts.), Afg. 89/H2
Siak (riv.), Indo. 80/B3
Siālkot, Pak. 86/C3
Sianów, Pol. 38/G4
Siapa (riv.), Ven. 153/E4
Siargao (isl.), Phil. 79/E6
Siasi, Phil. 81/F2
Siaton (pt.), Phil. 81/F2
Siaton, Phil. 79/D6
Siau (isl.), Indo. 81/G3
Šiauliai, Lith. 39/K4
Sibalom, Phil. 79/D5
Sibay, Rus. 63/L1
Sibbo (Sipoo), Fin. 39/L1
Šibenik, Cro. 48/B4
Siberia (reg.), Rus. 67/H3
Siberut (isl.), Indo. 67/J10
Sibi, Pak. 89/J3
Sibiloi NP, Kenya 97/N7
Sibiti, Congo 105/B1
Sibiu (prov.), Rom. 49/G2
Sibiu, Rom. 49/G3
Sibley, Mo, US 137/E5
Sibolga, Indo. 80/A3
Sibu, Malay. 80/D3
Sibuco, Phil. 81/F2
Sibut, CAfr. 97/J6
Sibuyan (sea), Phil. 81/F1
Sibuyan (isl.), Phil. 81/F1
Sicamous, BC, Can. 126/D3
Sichuan (prov.), China 70/H5
Sicilia (pol. reg.), It. 46/C4
Sicily (isl.), It. 27/F5
Sicily, Strait of (str.), It. 46/B3
Sico (riv.), Hon. 140/D4
Sicuani, Peru 156/D4
Šid, Yugo. 48/D3
Siddipet, India 82/C4
Siderno Marina, It. 46/E3
Sideŕopolis, Braz. 155/B4
Sidewinder (mtn.), Ca, US 136/C1
Sidhaulī, India 84/C2
Sidhi, India 84/C3
Sidhirókastron, Gre. 47/H2
Sidhpur, India 89/K4
Sidi Aïssa, Alg. 100/G5
Sīdī Barrānī, Egypt 101/A2
Sidi Bel-Abbes, Alg. 100/E5
Sidi Bennour, Mor. 98/C2
Sīdī Bū Zayd, Tun. 96/G1
Sīdī Bū Zayd (gov.), Tun. 46/A5
Sidi Ifni, Mor. 98/C3
Sidi Kacem, Mor. 100/B2
Sidi Kacem (prov.), Mor. 100/B2
Sīdī Sālim, Egypt 91/B4
Sidi Slimane, Mor. 100/B2
Sidi Yahya du Rharb, Mor. 100/A2
Sidlaw (hills), Sc, UK 36/C3
Sidmouth, Eng, UK 32/C5
Sidney, BC, Can. 126/C3
Sidney, Mt, US 127/G4
Sidney, Oh, US 130/C3
Sidney Lanier (lake), Ga, US 133/H3
Sidra (gulf), Libya 93/D1
Sieci, It. 59/E5
Siedlce, Pol. 41/M2
Siedlce (prov.), Pol. 41/L2
Sieg (riv.), Ger. 43/G1
Siegburg, Ger. 53/G2
Siegen, Ger. 53/H2
Siegenburg, Ger. 55/E5
Siegendorf im Burgenland, Aus. 43/M3
Siemianówka (lake), Pol. 41/M2
Siemiatycze, Pol. 41/M2
Siemreab, Camb. 78/C3
Siena (prov.), It. 59/E6
Siena, It. 43/J5
Sienne (riv.), Fr. 42/C2
Sieradz, Pol. 41/K3
Sieradz (prov.), Pol. 41/K3
Sieraków, Pol. 41/J2
Sierning, Aus. 55/H6
Sierpc, Pol. 41/K2
Sierra (peak), Ca, US 136/C3
Sierra Blanca, Tx, US 129/F5
Sierra de la Macarena, PN, Col. 150/D3
Sierra de San Pedro Mártir, Mex. 142/B2
Sierra Estrella (mts.), Az, US 137/R19
Sierra Grande, Arg. 158/D4
Sierra Leone (cape), SLeo. 102/B4
Sierra Leone (ctry.) 102/B4
Sierra Madre, Ca, US 136/F7
Sierra Mojada, Mex. 132/C5
Sierra Nevada (mts.), US 128/B3
Sierra Nevada de Santa Marta, PN, Col. 152/C2
Sierra Nevada, PN, Ven. 152/D2
Sierra Vieja (mts.), US, Mex. 132/B4
Sierras Bayas, Arg. 158/E3
Sierre, Swi. 56/D5
Siete Picos (peak), Sp. 45/M8
Siete Tazas, PN, Chile 158/C2
Sieve (riv.), It. 59/E5
Sif Fatima, Alg. 99/H3
Sifnos (isl.), Gre. 47/J4
Sig, Alg. 100/E5
Siga Hills (hills), Tanz. 104/B3
Sigean, Fr. 42/E5
Siġġiewi, Malta 46/L7
Sighetu Marmaţiei, Rom. 49/F2
Sighişoara, Rom. 49/G2
Sighty Crag (hill), Eng, UK 35/F1
Sigillo, It. 59/F6
Sigli, Indo. 80/A2
Sigli (cape), Alg. 100/H4
Siglufjördhur, Ice. 37/N6
Sigmaringen, Ger. 57/F1
Sigmarszell, Ger. 57/F2
Signa, It. 59/E5
Signal de la Mère Boitier (peak), Fr. 42/F3
Signal de Toussaines (peak), Fr. 42/B2
Signal d'Écouves (peak), Fr. 42/D2
Signal Hill, Ca, US 136/F8
Signau, Swi. 56/D4
Signy-L'Abbaye, Fr. 53/D4
Signy-le-Petit, Fr. 53/D4
Signy-Signets, Fr. 30/M5
Sigriswil, Swi. 56/D4
Sigtuna, Swe. 38/G2
Siguatepeque, Hon. 144/E3
Sigüenza, Sp. 44/D2

226

Sihl – Somot

Sihl (riv.), Swi. 57/E3
Sihlsee (lake), Swi. 57/E3
Sihochac, Mex. 144/D2
Sihong, China 72/D4
Sihorā, India 84/C4
Sihuas, Peru 156/B3
Siilinjärvi, Fin. 60/E3
Siirt (prov.), Turk. 90/E2
Siirt, Turk. 90/E2
Sikandarābād, India 84/A1
Sikandarpur, India 85/E2
Sikandra Rao, India 84/B2
Sikanni Chief (riv.), BC, Can. 122/D3
Sīkar, India 89/L3
Sikasso, Mali 102/D4
Sikasso (pol. reg.), Mali 102/D4
Sikeston, Mo, US 129/K3
Sikhote-Alin' (mts.), Rus. 65/P5
Síkinos, Gre. 47/J4
Síkinos (isl.), Gre. 47/J4
Sikkim (state), India 70/E6
Siklós, Hun. 48/D3
Sikoúrion, Gre. 47/H3
Sil (riv.), Sp. 44/B1
Silai (riv.), India 85/F4
Silandro (Schlanders), It. 57/G4
Silao, India 85/E3
Silao, Mex. 143/E4
Sīlat Az Zahr, WBnk. 91/G7
Silay, Phil. 81/F1
Silchar, India 83/F3
Şile, Turk. 49/J5
Silea, It. 59/F1
Silenen, Swi. 57/E4
Silesia (reg.), Pol. 41/H3
Siletitengiz (lake), Kaz. 87/F2
Silgadhī, Nepal 84/C1
Silifke, Turk. 91/C1
Silīguri, India 85/G2
Silistra, Bul. 49/H3
Silivri, Turk. 49/J5
Siljan (lake), Swe. 38/F1
Siljansnäs, Swe. 38/F1
Silkeborg, Den. 38/C3
Sill (riv.), Aus. 57/H3
Silla, Sp. 45/E3
Silla Tombs, SKor. 74/A3
Sillamäe, Est. 39/M2
Sillānwāli, Pak. 86/B4
Sillaro (riv.), It. 59/E4
Silleda, Sp. 44/A1
Sillian, Aus. 43/K3
Sillustani (ruin), Peru 156/D4
Silly-le-Long, Fr. 30/L4
Siloam Springs, Ar, US 129/J3
Silopi, Turk. 90/E2
Silsbee, Tx, US 129/J5
Silsden, Eng, UK 35/G4
Silsersee (lake), Swi. 57/F5
Siltou (well), Chad 96/J4
Šilutė, Lith. 39/J4
Silvan (dam), Turk. 90/E2
Silvaplana, Swi. 57/F5
Silvassa, India 82/B3
Silver (lake), Or, US 128/B2
Silver (riv.), Or, US 128/C2
Silver (mtn.), Ca, US 136/C1
Silver Bay, Mn, US 127/L4
Silver City, NM, US 128/E4
Silver Lake, Wi, US 135/P14
Silver Lake-Fircrest, Wa, US 135/C2
Silver Meadow (lake), NJ, US 138/C5
Silver Run, Md, US 138/A4
Silver Spring, Md, US 138/A6
Silverado, Ca, US 136/C3
Silverton, Or, US 126/C4
Silverton, Co, US 128/F3
Silverton, NJ, US 138/D3
Silverwood (lake), Ca, US 136/C2
Silves, Port. 44/A4
Silvi, It. 46/D1
Silvia, Col. 152/B4
Silvies (riv.), Or, US 128/C2
Silvretta (mts.), Aus. 57/G4
Silyānah (gov.), Tun. 46/A4
Silyānah, Tun. 100/L6
Silz, Aus. 57/G3
Sim (cape), Mor. 98/C3
Simão Dias, Braz. 154/C3
Simard (lake), Qu, Can. 130/E2
Simav, Turk. 62/D5
Simbach am Inn, Ger. 55/G6
Simcoe, On, Can. 130/D3
Simcoe (lake), Qu, Can. 123/J4
Simdega, India 85/E4
Simēn (mts.), Eth. 97/N5
Simeria, Rom. 48/F3
Simeulue (isl.), Indo. 67/J9
Simferopol', Ukr. 62/E3
Simi (hills), Ca, US 136/B2
Simi Valley, Ca, US 136/B2
Similaun (peak), It. 43/J3
Similaun (peak), Aus.,It. 57/G4
Simití, Col. 152/C3
Simitli, Bul. 47/H2
Simiyu (riv.), Tanz. 104/B3
Simla, India 86/D4
Simleu Silvaniei, Rom. 49/F2
Simme (riv.), Swi. 43/G3
Simmelsdorf, Ger. 55/E3
Simmerath, Ger. 53/F2
Simmerbach (riv.), Ger. 53/G4
Simmern, Ger. 53/G4
Simmertal, Ger. 53/G4
Simmszand (isl.), Neth. 50/D2
Simni (isl.), NKor. 73/C3
Simo, Fin. 60/E2
Simões, Braz. 154/B2
Simões Filho, Braz. 154/C4
Simojovel de Allende, Mex. 144/C2
Simón Bolívar (int'l arpt.), Ecu. 152/B5
Simoncello (peak), It. 59/F5
Simonstown, SAfr. 106/L11
Simpang-Kiri (riv.), Indo. 80/A3
Simpelveld, Neth. 53/E2
Simplício Mendes, Braz. 154/B2
Simplon, Swi. 56/E5
Simplonpass (pass), Swi. 56/E5
Simpson (des.), Austl. 109/C3
Simpson (pen.), Nun., Can. 122/G2
Simpson (riv.), Nun., Can. 122/G2
Simpson Desert Conservation Park, Austl. 113/H3
Simpson Desert NP, Austl. 113/H3
Simpsons Gap NP, Austl. 113/G2
Simrishamn, Swe. 38/F4
Simunul, Phil. 81/E3
Sin-le-Noble, Fr. 52/C3
Sinai (pen.), Egypt 97/M1
Sinaia, Rom. 49/G3
Sinaloa (state), Mex. 142/D3
Sinaloa de Leyva, Mex. 142/C3
Sinalunga, It. 43/J5
Sinan, China 79/A2
Sīnāwin, Libya 99/H3
Sincé, Col. 152/C2
Sincelejo, Col. 152/C2
Sinceny, Fr. 52/C4
Sinch'ŏn, NKor. 73/C3
Sinclair, Wy, US 126/G5
Sinclair (lake), Ga, US 133/H3
Sinclair (pt.), Austl. 113/G5
Sincorá, Serra do (range), Braz. 154/B4
Sind (riv.), India 82/C2
Sindal, Den. 38/D3
Sindañgan, Phil. 79/D6
Sindangbarang, Indo. 80/C5
Sindelfingen, Ger. 54/C5
Sindh (prov.), Pak. 82/A2
Sindhulimādi, Nepal 85/E2
Sındırgı, Turk. 62/D5
Sinekçi, Turk. 49/H5
Sinendé, Ben. 103/F4
Sines, Port. 44/A4
Sines (cape), Port. 44/A4
Sinfra, C.d'Iv. 102/D5
Sing Buri, Thai. 78/C3
Singapore (cap.), Sing. 80/B3
Singapore (ctry.) 80/B3
Singen, Ger. 57/E2
Sîngeorz-Băi, Rom. 49/G2
Singida (pol. reg.), Tanz. 104/B4
Singida, Tanz. 104/B4
Singitic (gulf), Gre. 47/H2
Singkawang, Indo. 80/C3
Singkep (isl.), Indo. 80/B4
Singleton, Austl. 115/D2
Singleton (mt.), Austl. 112/C4
Singleton (mt.), Austl. 113/F2
Singou, Réserve Totale de Faune du, Burk. 103/F4
Sinincay, Ecu. 152/B5
Siniscola, It. 46/A2
Sinjār, Iraq 90/E2
Sinjil, WBnk. 91/G7
Sinn (riv.), Ger. 40/E3
Sinnam-dok-san (peak), NKor. 73/D2
Sinnamary, FrG. 151/H2
Sinnard, Co, US 137/C1
Sînnicolau Mare, Rom. 48/E2
Sinnūris, Egypt 91/B5
Sinnyŏng, SKor. 73/E4
Sino (co.), Libr. 102/C5
Sinoe (lake), Rom. 49/J3
Sinop, Braz. 151/G6
Sinop (prov.), Turk. 62/E4
Sinop (pt.), Turk. 62/E4
Sinop, Turk. 62/E4
Sinp'o, NKor. 73/E2
Sint-Genesius-Rode, Belg. 53/D2
Sint-Gillis-Waas, Belg. 50/B6
Sint-Katelijne-Waver, Belg. 53/D1
Sint-Laureins, Belg. 52/C1
Sint-Martens-Voeren, Belg. 53/E2
Sint-Michielsgestel, Neth. 50/C5
Sint-Niklaas, Belg. 50/B6
Sint-Oedenrode, Neth. 50/C5
Sint-Pieters-Leeuw, Belg. 53/D2
Sint-Truiden, Belg. 53/E2
Sint'aein, SKor. 73/D5
Sintang, Indo. 80/D3
Sinton, Tx, US 132/D4
Sintra, Port. 45/P10
Sintra (range), Port. 45/P10
Sinú (riv.), Col. 150/C2
Sinŭiju, NKor. 73/C2
Sinzheim, Ger. 54/B5
Sinzig, Ger. 53/G2
Sió (riv.), Hun. 48/D2
Siocon, Phil. 81/F2
Siófok, Hun. 48/D2
Sioma Ngwezi NP, Zam. 105/D4
Sion, Swi. 56/D5
Sion Mills, NI, UK 31/Q9
Sioule (riv.), Fr. 42/E4
Sioux City, Ia, US 127/J5
Sioux Lookout, On, Can. 127/L3
Sipalay, Phil. 79/D6
Sipaliwini (dist.), Sur. 153/H4
Sipaliwini (riv.), Sur. 153/G4
Sipanok (chan.), Mb,Sk, Can. 127/H2
Siparia, Trin. 153/F2
Sipí, Col. 152/B3
Siping, China 72/F2
Sipiwesk (lake), Mb, Can. 122/G3
Siple (isl.), Ant. 160/R
Siponto (ruin), It. 46/D2
Sipsey (riv.), Al, US 133/G3
Sipura (isl.), Indo. 80/A4
Siqueira Campos, Braz. 155/B2
Siquia (riv.), Nic. 140/E5
Siquisique, Ven. 152/D2
Sir Alexander (mt.), BC, Can. 126/C2
Sir Edward Pellew Group (isls.), Austl. 109/C2
Sir James Macbrien (mt.), NW, Can. 122/D2
Sir James Mitchell NP, Austl. 112/C5
Sir John (cape), Austl. 115/D4
Sir Seewoosagur Ramgoolam (int'l arpt.), Mrts. 107/T15
Sir Thomas (mt.), Austl. 113/F3
Sira (riv.), Nor. 37/C4
Siracusa (Syracuse), It. 46/D4
Sirājganj, Bang. 85/G3
Şiran, Turk. 62/F4
Sirdaryo (pol. reg.), Uzb. 87/E4
Siret, Rom. 49/H2
Siret (riv.), Rom. 62/C3
Sirha, Nepal 85/F2
Sirhind, India 86/D4
Sirik (cape), Malay. 80/D3
Sīrīk, Iran 89/G3
Sirikit (res.), Thai. 83/H4
Sirinhaém, Braz. 154/D3
Sīrīs, WBnk. 91/G7
Sirius (pt.), Ak, US 134/B5
Sirmilik Nat'l Park, Nun., Can. 123/J1
Sirmione, It. 58/D2
Sirnach, Swi. 57/F3
Şırnak, Turk. 90/E2
Sirolo, It. 59/G5
Sironj, India 84/A3
Siros (isl.), Gre. 47/J4
Siroua (peak), Mor. 98/D3
Sirsa, India 86/C5
Sirsāganj, India 84/B2
Sirsi, India 84/B1
Sirsi, India 89/K6
Sisak, Cro. 48/C3
Sisaket, Thai. 78/D3
Sishui, China 72/D4
Sisikon, Swi. 57/E4
Sisipuk (lake), Mb,Sk, Can. 127/H2
Sissach, Swi. 56/D3
Sisseton, SD, US 127/J4
Sissili (prov.), Burk. 103/E4
Sissonne, Fr. 52/C4
Sissonville, WV, US 130/D4
Sisterdale, Tx, US 137/T20
Sisteron, Fr. 42/F4
Siswā Bāzār, India 84/D2
Sitacocha, Peru 156/B2
Sītākunda, Bang. 83/F3
Sītāmarhi, India 85/E2
Sītāpur, India 84/C2
Sitārganj, India 84/B1
Siteki, Swaz. 107/E2
Sitges, Sp. 45/K7
Sithoniá (pen.), Gre. 62/C5
Sitía, Gre. 47/K5
Sitidgi (lake), NW, Can. 134/M2
Sítio Novo do Grajaú, Braz. 154/A2
Sitka, Ak, US 134/L4
Sitno (peak), Slvk. 48/D1
Sittard, Neth. 53/E2
Sittensen, Ger. 51/G2
Sitter (riv.), Swi. 57/F3
Sittingbourne, Eng, UK 33/G4
Sitton (peak), Ca, US 136/C3
Sittwe (Akyab), Myan. 83/F3
Sivac, Yugo. 48/D3
Sivakāsi, India 82/C6
Sīvand, Iran 88/F2
Sivas (prov.), Turk. 62/F5
Sivas, Turk. 62/F5
Siverek, Turk. 90/D2
Siviriez, Swi. 56/C4
Sivrihisar, Turk. 62/D5
Sivry-Courtry, Fr. 30/L6
Siwa Oasis (oasis), Egypt 101/A2
Sīwah, Egypt 97/L2
Siwalik (range), Nepal 70/C5
Siwān, India 85/E2
Siwāni, India 86/C5
Six Flags Great Adventure, NJ, US 138/D3
Six Flags Great America, Il, US 135/Q15
Six Flags Magic Mountain, Ca, US 136/B2
Sixmilecross, NI, UK 34/A2
Sixth (falls), Sudan 97/M4
Siyabuswa, SAfr. 105/E6
Siyāna, India 84/B1
Siyang, China 72/D4
Siziano, It. 58/C2
Siziwang, China 71/K3
Sjælland (isl.), Den. 37/D5
Sjenica, Yugo. 47/G1
Sjöbo, Swe. 38/E4
Sjónfridh (peak), Ice. 37/M6
Sjuntorp, Swe. 38/E2
Skaftafell NP, Ice. 37/P7
Skagen, Den. 38/D3
Skagens (The Skaw) (cape), Den. 38/D3
Skagern (lake), Swe. 38/F2
Skagerrak (str.), Nor.,Den. 27/E3
Skaget (peak), Nor. 38/C1
Skagway, Ak, US 134/L3
Skála, Gre. 47/H4
Skälderviken (bay), Swe. 38/E3
Skálfandafljót (riv.), Ice. 37/P7
Skalica, Slvk. 41/J4
Skalice (riv.), Czh. 43/K2
Skalka (res.), Czh. 55/F2
Skælskør, Den. 38/D4
Skanderborg, Den. 38/C3
Skåne (reg.), Swe. 38/E4
Skanes (int'l arpt.), Tun. 46/B5
Skånland, Nor. 37/F1
Skänninge, Swe. 38/F2
Skanör, Swe. 38/E4
Skantzoura (isl.), Gre. 47/J3
Skara, Swe. 38/E2
Skaraborg (co.), Swe. 37/E4
Skärblacka, Swe. 38/F2
Skåre, Swe. 38/E2
Skarszewy, Pol. 38/H4
Skarżysko-Kamienna, Pol. 41/L3
Skateraw, Sc, UK 36/D5
Skattkärr, Swe. 38/E2
Skawina, Pol. 41/K4
Skeena (riv.), BC, Can. 122/D3
Skeena (mts.), BC, Can. 122/D3
Skegness, Eng, UK 35/J5
Skellefteå, Swe. 37/G2
Skellefteälven (riv.), Swe. 37/F2
Skelleftehamn, Swe. 37/G2
Skelmersdale, Eng, UK 35/F4
Skelmorlie, Sc, UK 36/B5
Skerne (riv.), Eng, UK 35/G2
Skerries, Ire. 34/B4
Skhimatárion, Gre. 47/H3
Skhirat, Mor. 100/A3
Skhirat Temara (prov.), Mor. 100/A3
Skhiza (isl.), Gre. 47/G4
Skhodnya (riv.), Rus. 61/W9
Ski, Nor. 38/D2
Skíathos, Gre. 47/H3
Skiatook, Ok, US 129/H3
Skibbereen, Ire. 31/P11
Skidegate, BC, Can. 134/M5
Skídhra, Gre. 47/H2
Skien, Nor. 38/C2
Skierniewice (prov.), Pol. 41/K3
Skierniewice, Pol. 41/L3
Skikda, Alg. 100/K6
Skinári (cape), Gre. 47/G4
Skinnskatteberg, Swe. 38/F2
Skipton, Eng, UK 35/F4
Skirfare (riv.), Eng, UK 35/F3
Skíros, Gre. 47/J3
Skive, Den. 38/C3
Skjærhollen, Nor. 38/D2
Skjeberg, Nor. 38/D2
Skjelåtinden (peak), Nor. 37/E2
Skjern, Den. 38/C4
Skjern (riv.), Den. 38/C4
Škofja Loka, Slov. 43/L3
Skoghall, Swe. 38/E2
Skogstorp, Swe. 38/G2
Skokholm (isl.), Wal, UK 32/A3
Skokie (riv.), Il, US 135/Q15
Skokloster, Swe. 38/G2
Sköllersta, Swe. 38/F2
Skolniki Park, Rus. 61/W9
Skomer (isl.), Wal, UK 32/A3
Skópelos (isl.), Gre. 47/H3
Skópelos, Gre. 47/H3
Skopin, Rus. 62/F1
Skopje (cap.), FYROM 47/G1
Skopje (int'l arpt.), FYROM 48/E5
Skotterud, Nor. 38/E2
Skoútari, Gre. 47/H2
Skövde, Swe. 38/E2
Skowhegan, Me, US 131/G2
Skukum (mt.), Yk, Can. 134/L3
Skull, Ire. 31/P11
Skultorp, Swe. 38/E2
Skultuna, Swe. 38/G2
Skunk (riv.), Ia, US 130/A3
Skurup, Swe. 41/G1
Skutskär, Swe. 38/G1
Skwentna, Ak, US 134/H3
Skwierzyna, Pol. 41/H2
Skye (isl.), Sc, UK 31/Q8
Skyring (sound), Chile 159/B7
Skytop, Pa, US 138/C1
Slagelse, Den. 38/D4
Slakovský Les (for.), Czh. 55/F2
Slamannan, Sc, UK 36/C5
Slana, Ak, US 134/K3
Slaná (riv.), Slvk. 41/L4
Slane, Ire. 34/B4
Slaney (riv.), Ire. 31/Q10
Slănic, Rom. 49/G3
Slănic-Moldova, Rom. 49/H2
Slantsy, Rus. 39/N2
Slaný, Czh. 55/H2
Slapy (res.), Czh. 55/H3
Slatedale, Pa, US 138/C2
Slatina, Rom. 49/G3
Slatington, Pa, US 138/C2
Slaton, Tx, US 129/G4
Slattum, Nor. 38/D1
Slaughter Beach, De, US 138/C6
Slaughterville, Ok, US 137/N15
Slave (coast), Afr. 103/F5
Slave (riv.), NW, Can. 122/E2
Slave Lake, Ab, Can. 126/E2
Slavgorod, Rus. 87/G2
Slavkov u Brna, Czh. 43/M2
Slavonia (reg.), Cro. 48/C3
Slavonska Požega, Cro. 48/C3
Slavonski Brod, Cro. 48/D3
Slavuta, Ukr. 62/C2
Slavyanovo, Bul. 49/G4
Slavyansk-na-Kubani, Rus. 62/F3
Sławno, Pol. 38/G4
Sleen, Neth. 50/D3
Sleeper (isls.), On, Can. 123/H3
Sleeping Bear Dunes Nat'l Lakeshore, US 130/C2
Sleepy Hollow, NY, US 139/K7
Sleepy Hollow, Il, US 135/P15
Sleetmute, Ak, US 134/G3
Slidell, La, US 137/Q16
Sliedrecht, Neth. 50/B5
Sliema, Malta 46/M7
Slieve Binnian (peak), NI, UK 34/C3
Slieve Croob (peak), NI, UK 34/C3
Slieve Donard (peak), NI, UK 34/C3
Slieve Gullion (peak), NI, UK 34/B3
Slieve Snaght (peak), Ire. 34/A1
Slioch (peak), Sc, UK 36/A1
Slite, Swe. 39/H3
Sliven, Bul. 47/K1
Slivnitsa, Bul. 47/H1
Sloan, NY, US 131/S10
Sloatsburg, NY, US 139/J7
Slobodskoy, Rus. 61/L4
Slobozia, Rom. 49/H3
Slochteren, Neth. 50/D2
Slonim, Bela. 62/C1
Sloten, Neth. 50/C3
Slotermeer (lake), Neth. 50/C3
Slough, Eng, UK 30/B2
Slovakia (ctry.) 41/K4
Slovenia (ctry.) 48/B3
Slovenj Gradec, Slov. 43/L3
Slovenska Bistrica, Slov. 43/L3
Slovenska L'upča, Slvk. 41/K4
Slovenske Konjice, Slov. 43/L3
Slovenské Rudohorie (mts.), Slvk. 41/L4
Slov'yans'k, Ukr. 62/F2
Słowiński PN, Pol. 38/G4
Słubice, Pol. 41/H2
Sluch' (riv.), Ukr. 62/C2
Sluderno (Schluderns), It. 57/G4
Sluis, Neth. 52/C1
Słupca, Pol. 41/J2
Słupia (riv.), Pol. 38/G4
Słupsk, Pol. 38/G4
Słupsk (prov.), Pol. 38/G4
Slutsk, Bela. 62/C1
Slyne Head (pt.), Ire. 30/F10
Smålandsstenar, Swe. 38/E3
Smallwood (res.), Nf, Can. 123/K3
Smeaton, Sk, Can. 127/G2
Smederevo, Yugo. 48/E3
Smederevska Palanka, Yugo. 48/E3
Smedjebacken, Swe. 38/F1
Smendou (riv.), Alg. 100/J4
Śmigiel, Pol. 41/J2
Smila, Ukr. 62/D2
Smilde, Neth. 50/D3
Smith (riv.), Mt, US 126/F4
Smith (inlet), BC, Can. 126/B3
Smith (isl.), Qu, Can. 123/J2
Smith Mountain (lake), Va, US 130/E4
Smith Village, Ok, US 137/N15
Smithburg, NJ, US 138/D3
Smithers, BC, Can. 126/B2
Smithfield, Ut, US 126/F5
Smithfield, NC, US 133/J3
Smiths Creek, Mi, US 135/G6
Smiths Falls, On, Can. 130/E2
Smithton, Austl. 115/C4
Smithton, Il, US 137/H9
Smithtown (bay), NY, US 139/E2
Smithtown, NY, US 139/E2
Smithville, Ok, US 132/E3
Smithville (lake), Mo, US 137/D5
Smithville, Mo, US 137/D5
Smoky (cape), Austl. 115/E1
Smoky (hills), Ks, US 129/H3
Smoky (riv.), Ab, Can. 122/E3
Smoky Hill (riv.), Ks, US 124/F4
Smoky Lake, Ab, Can. 126/E2
Smøla (isl.), Nor. 37/C3
Smolensk, Rus. 60/G5
Smolenskaya (obl.), Rus. 60/F5
Smólikas (peak), Gre. 47/G2
Smolyan, Bul. 47/J2
Smooth Rock Falls, On, Can. 130/D1
Smrčina (peak), Czh. 55/G5
Smutná (riv.), Czh. 55/H4
Smyadovo, Bul. 49/H4
Smyrna, Ga, US 133/G3
Smyrna (riv.), De, US 138/C5
Smyrna, De, US 138/C5
Snaefell (peak), IM, UK 34/D3
Snake (riv.), US 126/D4
Snake River (plain), Id, US 126/E5
Snares (isls.), NZ 117/R12
Snåsa, Nor. 37/E2
Snedsted, Den. 38/C3
Sneek, Neth. 50/C2
Sneekermeer (lake), Neth. 50/C2
Sneeuberg (peak), SAfr. 106/B4
Sneeuberg (mts.), SAfr. 106/D3
Sneeuwkop (peak), SAfr. 106/L11
Snejbjerg, Den. 38/C3
Sněžka (peak), Czh. 41/H3
Snežnik (peak), Slov. 43/L4
Sni Mills, Mo, US 137/E6
Śniardwy (lake), Pol. 41/L2
Snodland, Eng, UK 33/G4
Snøhetta (peak), Nor. 37/D3
Snohomish, Wa, US 135/C2
Snohomish (co.), Wa, US 135/C2
Snohomish (riv.), Wa, US 135/C2
Snoqualmie (riv.), Wa, US 135/D2
Snoqualmie (falls), Wa, US 135/D2
Snoqualmie, Wa, US 135/D2
Snoqualmie Falls, Wa, US 135/D2
Snoqualmie, Middle Fk. (riv.), Wa, US 135/D2
Snoqualmie, North Fork (riv.), Wa, US 135/D2
Snoqualmie, South Fork (riv.), Wa, US 135/D3
Snøtind (peak), Nor. 37/E2
Snowdon (peak), IM, UK 34/D5
Snowdonia NP, Wal, UK 34/D6
Snowflake, Az, US 128/E4
Snowtown, Austl. 113/H5
Snowy (peak), Ak, US 134/K2
Snowy (riv.), Austl. 115/D3
Snowy River NP, Austl. 115/D3
Snyder (co.), Pa, US 138/A2
Snydertown, Pa, US 138/B2
Snyderville, Ut, US 137/K12
Soalala, Madg. 107/H7
Soanierana-Ivongo, Madg. 107/J7
Soanindrariny, Madg. 107/H7
Soar (riv.), Eng, UK 35/G6
Soavina, Madg. 107/H8
Soavina, Madg. 107/J8
Soavinandriana, Madg. 107/H7
Sobaek (mts.), SKor. 73/D5
Soběslav, Czh. 55/H4
Sobger (riv.), Indo. 81/K4
Sobhādero, Pak. 89/J3
Sobradinho, Represa (res.), Braz. 147/E3
Sobral, Braz. 154/B1
Sobretta (peak), It. 57/G5
Sobue, Japan 77/L5
Soc Trang, Viet. 78/D4
Soča (riv.), Slov. 43/K3
Socabaya, Peru 156/D5
Sochaczew, Pol. 41/L2
Sochi, Rus. 62/F4
Sŏch'ŏn, SKor. 73/D4
Söchtenau, Ger. 55/F7
Soci, It. 59/E5
Society (isls.), FrPol. 117/K6
Socorro, Tx, US 129/F5
Socorro, NM, US 128/F4
Socorro, Braz. 211/G7
Socorro (isl.), NM, Mex. 142/C5
Socorro, Col. 152/C3
Socota, Peru 156/B2
Socotá, Col. 152/C3
Socotra (isl.), Yem. 67/E8
Socuéllamos, Sp. 44/D3
Soda Springs, Id, US 126/F5
Sodankylä, Fin. 60/E2
Sodegaura, Japan 77/D3
Söderbärke, Swe. 38/F1
Söderhamn, Swe. 38/G1
Söderköping, Swe. 38/G2
Södermanland (co.), Swe. 37/E4
Södertälje, Swe. 38/G2
Sodo, Eth. 97/N6
Sŏdu (riv.), NKor. 73/E2
Sodwana Bay NP, SAfr. 107/F2
Soest, Ger. 51/F5
Soest, Neth. 50/C4
Soeste (riv.), Ger. 40/D2
Sofádhes, Gre. 47/H3
Sofia (int'l arpt.), Bul. 47/H1
Sofia (riv.), Madg. 107/J6
Sofia (Sofiya) (cap.), Bul. 47/H1
Sofiya (prov.), Bul. 47/H1
Sogamoso (riv.), Col. 152/C3
Sogamoso, Col. 152/C3
Sögel, Ger. 51/E3
Sogn Og Fjordane (co.), Nor. 37/C3
Sognafjorden (inlet), Nor. 37/C3
Sogndal, Nor. 38/B1
Søgne, Nor. 38/B2
Sogollé (well), Chad 96/J4
Soğuksu NP, Turk. 62/E4
Söğüt, Turk. 62/D5
Söğütlü, Turk. 49/K5
Sogwass (peak), Ugan. 104/B2
Sohāgpur, India 84/B4
Sohren, Ger. 53/G4
Sŏhŭng, NKor. 73/D3
Soignies, Belg. 53/D2
Soignolles-en-Brie, Fr. 30/L6
Soissons, Fr. 52/C5
Sōja, Japan 74/C3
Sojat, India 89/K3
Sojosŏn (bay), NKor. 73/C3
Sok (riv.), Rus. 63/J1
Sok (pt.), Thai. 78/C3
Sōka, Japan 77/D2
Sokch'o, SKor. 73/E3
Söke, Turk. 90/A2
Sokhós, Gre. 47/H2
Sokhumi, Geo. 63/G4
Sokna, Nor. 38/C1
Soko (isls.), China 71/T11
Soko Banja, Yugo. 48/E4
Sokodé, Togo 103/F4
Sokol, Rus. 60/J4
Sokol (peak), Czh. 55/G4
Sokółka, Pol. 41/M2
Sokolov, Czh. 55/F2
Sokołów Podlaski, Pol. 41/M2
Sokoto (plain), Nga. 96/F5
Sokoto (riv.), Nga. 96/F5
Sokoto, Nga. 103/G3
Sokoto (state), Nga. 103/G3
Sol, Costa del (coast), Sp. 44/C4
Sol'-Iletsk, Rus. 63/K2
Sola, Nor. 38/A2
Sola (int'l arpt.), Nor. 38/A2
Solana, Phil. 79/D4
Solana Beach, Ca, US 136/C5
Solânea, Braz. 154/D3
Solano, Phil. 79/D4
Solano (pt.), Col. 152/B3
Solano (co.), Ca, US 135/L10
Solarolo, It. 59/E4
Solca, Rom. 49/G2
Sölden, Aus. 57/H4
Soldier (riv.), Ia, US 129/J2
Soldotna, Ak, US 134/H3
Soledad, Col. 152/C2
Soledad, Ven. 153/F2
Soledad Canyon (canyon), Ca, US 136/B2
Soledad de Doblado, Mex. 143/N7
Soledad de Graciano, Mex. 143/E4
Soledade, Braz. 155/A4
Solent, The (chan.), Eng, UK 33/E5
Solesino, It. 59/E2
Solesmes, Fr. 52/C3
Soleuvre (peak), Lux. 53/E4
Solferino, It. 58/D2
Solhan, Turk. 90/E2
Soliera, It. 59/D3
Soligo, It. 59/F1
Solihull, Eng, UK 33/E2
Solimões (riv.), Braz. 153/E5
Solingen, Ger. 50/E6
Sollefteå, Swe. 37/F3
Sollentuna, Swe. 38/G2
Sóller, Sp. 45/G3
Sollerön, Swe. 38/F1
Solling (mts.), Ger. 40/E3
Solmsbach (riv.), Ger. 54/B2
Søln (peak), Nor. 37/D3
Solnan (riv.), Fr. 42/F3
Solntsevo, Rus. 61/W9
Solo (riv.), Indo. 80/D5
Solok, Indo. 80/B4
Sololá, Guat. 144/D3
Solomon, Ak, US 134/F3
Solomon (riv.), Ks, US 129/H3
Solomon (sea), PNG,Sol. 116/D5
Solomon Islands (ctry.) 116/E6
Solomon, North Fork (riv.), Ks, US 129/G3
Solonchak Goklenkui (swamp), Trkm. 87/C4
Solonópole, Braz. 154/C2
Solothurn, Swi. 56/D3
Solothurn (canton), Swi. 56/D3
Solovetskiy (isls.), Rus. 60/G2
Solre-le-Château, Fr. 53/D3
Solsona, Sp. 45/F2
Solt, Hun. 48/D2
Šolta (isl.), Cro. 46/E1
Soltau, Ger. 51/G3
Soltustik Qazaqstan (obl.), Kaz. 64/G4
Soltvadkert, Hun. 48/D2
Solunska (peak), FYROM 47/G2
Solva (riv.), Wal, UK 32/A3
Solvang, Ca, US 128/B4
Sölvesborg, Swe. 38/F3
Solway Firth (inlet), Eng.,Sc, UK 34/E2
Solwezi, Zam. 105/E3
Solymár, Hun. 49/Q9
Sōma, Japan 75/G2
Soma, Turk. 62/C5
Somain, Fr. 52/C3
Somalia (ctry.) 97/Q6
Sombor, Yugo. 48/D3
Sombra, On, Can. 135/H6
Sombreffe, Belg. 53/D2
Sombrerete, Mex. 142/E4
Sombrio, Braz. 155/B4
Someren, Neth. 50/C6
Somero, Fin. 39/K1
Somers, Mt, US 126/E3
Somers, Wi, US 135/Q14
Somers Point, NJ, US 138/D5
Somerset, Ky, US 130/C4
Somerset, NY, US 131/S9
Somerset, Tx, US 137/T21
Somerset (co.), Eng, UK 32/D4
Somerset, NJ, US 138/D3
Somerset (isl.), Nun., Can. 122/G1
Somerset East, SAfr. 106/D4
Somerset West, SAfr. 106/L11
Somersworth, NH, US 131/G3
Somerton, Az, US 128/D4
Somerville (lake), Tx, US 129/H5
Somerville, NJ, US 138/D2
Someş (riv.), Rom. 62/B3
Someşul Mare (riv.), Yugo. 49/G2
Someswar (range), India 85/E2
Somis, Ca, US 136/B2
Sŏmjin (riv.), SKor. 73/D5
Somma Lombardo, It. 58/B1
Sommacampagna, It. 59/D2
Sommam (riv.), Alg. 100/H4
Sommariva del Bosco, It. 58/A3
Somme (bay), Fr. 42/D1
Somme (dept.), Fr. 52/B4
Somme (riv.), F 40/B3
Somme, Canal de la (canal), Fr. 52/B4
Somme-Leuze, Belg. 53/E3
Somme-Soude (riv.), Fr. 53/D6
Sommedieue, Fr. 53/E5
Sommen (lake), Swe. 38/F2
Sommet de Finiels (peak), Fr. 42/E4
Sommevoire, Fr. 56/A1
Somogy (prov.), Hun. 48/C2
Somoto, Nic. 144/E3

227
Son – Stirl

Son (riv.), India 70/D7
Son Servera, Sp. 45/G3
Sona, It. 59/D2
Sonāmukhi, India 85/F4
Sonāmura, India 85/H4
Sonār (riv.), India 84/B4
Sonchamp, Fr. 30/H6
Sŏnch'ŏn, NKor. 73/C3
Soncino, It. 58/C2
Sondalo, It. 57/G5
Sønder Nissum, Den. 38/C3
Sønderborg (int'l arpt.), Den. 38/C4
Sønderborg, Den. 38/C4
Sonderend (riv.), SAfr. 106/L11
Sønderjylland (co.), Den. 38/C4
Sondica (int'l arpt.), Sp. 44/D1
Sondrio, It. 57/F5
Sondrio (dept.), It. 57/F5
Sonepur, India 82/D3
Song (peak), China 72/C4
Song Xian, China 72/C4
Songea, Tanz. 104/B5
Songeons, Fr. 52/A4
Songhua (riv.), China 67/M5
Sŏnghwan, SKor. 73/D4
Songi (isl.), SKor. 73/C5
Songino, Mong. 70/G2
Songjiang, China 72/L8
Sŏngju, SKor. 73/E5
Songkhla, Thai. 78/C5
Songkhram (riv.), Thai. 83/H4
Songling, China 71/M2
Songming, China 83/H2
Sŏngnam, SKor. 73/G7
Songnim, NKor. 73/C3
Songololo, D.R. Congo 105/B2
Songt'an, SKor. 73/D4
Songtao Miaozu Zizhixian, China 79/A2
Songxi, China 79/C2
Songzi, China 79/B1
Songzi (pass), China 72/C5
Soni, Japan 77/K6
Sonid Youqi, China 71/K3
Sonid Zuoqi, China 71/K3
Sonīpat, India 86/D5
Sonneberg, Ger. 54/E2
Sonnefeld, Ger. 54/E2
Sonnjoch (peak), Aus. 57/H3
Sonntagshorn (peak), Ger. 43/K3
Sonobe, Japan 77/H5
Sonoma (mts.), Ca, US 135/J10
Sonoma (co.), Ca, US 135/J10
Sonora, Ca, US 128/B3
Sonora, Tx, US 129/G5
Sonora (state), Mex. 142/C2
Sonoyta, Mex. 128/D5
Sonoyta (riv.), Mex. 142/B2
Sonpur, India 85/E3
Sonqor, Iran 88/E2
Sŏnsan, SKor. 73/E4
Sonsbeck, Ger. 50/D5
Sonseca, Sp. 44/D3
Sonsonate, ESal. 144/D3
Sonsorol (isls.), Palau 116/C4
Sonta, Yugo. 48/D3
Sontheim, Ger. 57/G2
Sontheim an der Brenz, Ger. 54/D5
Sonthofen, Ger. 57/G2
Sontra, Ger. 51/G6
Sonvico, Swi. 57/E5
Sopetrán, Col. 152/C3
Sopi (cape), Indo. 81/G3
Sopor, India 86/C2
Sopot, Bul. 47/J1
Sopot, Pol. 38/H4
Sopron, Hun. 43/M3
Sör (riv.), Wal, UK 32/D3
Sor Karatuley (salt pan), Kaz. 87/C4
S'ør-Trøndelag (co.), Nor. 37/D3
Sør-Varanger, Nor. 37/J1
Sora, It. 46/C2
Soragna, It. 58/D3
Sŏrak-san (peak), SKor. 73/E3
Sŏraksan NP, SKor. 73/E3
Sorata, Bol. 150/E7
Sorbas, Sp. 44/D4
Sorbolo, It. 58/D3
Sorcy-Saint-Martin, Fr. 53/E6
Sorel, Qu, Can. 130/F2
Sorell-Midway Point, Austl. 115/C4
Soresina, It. 58/C2
Sörforsa, Swe. 38/G1
Sorgues, Fr. 42/F5
Sorgun, Turk. 62/E5
Sori, It. 58/C4
Soria, Sp. 44/D2
Soriano (dept.), Uru. 158/G3
Soriano, Uru. 159/J10
Sorikmerapi (peak), Indo. 80/A3
Soritor, Peru 156/B2
Sormonne (riv.), Fr. 53/D4
Sorø, Den. 38/D4
Soro, Rio do (riv.), Braz. 151/J5
Soroca, Mol. 49/J1
Sorocaba, Braz. 155/C2
Sorochinsk, Rus. 63/K1
Sorol (isl.), Micr. 116/D4
Soron, India 84/B2
Sorong, Indo. 81/H4
Soroti, Ugan. 104/B2
Sørøya (isl.), Nor. 37/G1
Sørøysundet (chan.), Nor. 37/G1
Sorpestausee (lake), Ger. 51/E6
Sorraia (riv.), Port. 44/A3
Sorrento, It. 46/D2
Sorsele, Swe. 37/F2
Sorso, It. 46/A2
Sorsogon, Phil. 79/D5
Sort, Sp. 45/F1
Sörve (pt.), Est. 39/K3
Sos del Rey Católico, Sp. 44/E1
Sŏsan, SKor. 73/D4
Sŏsan Haean NP, SKor. 73/C4
Sösdala, Swe. 38/E3
Söse (riv.), Ger. 51/H5
Soshanguve, SAfr. 105/E6
Sosna (riv.), Rus. 62/F1
Sosneado (peak), Arg. 158/C2
Sosnogorsk, Rus. 61/M3
Sosnovka, Rus. 61/L4
Sosnowiec, Pol. 41/K3
Sospiro, It. 58/D2
Sosúa, DRep. 141/G4
Sos'va (riv.), Rus. 64/G3
Sot (riv.), India 84/B1
Soto del Real, Sp. 45/N8
Soto la Marina, Mex. 143/F4
Sotouboua, Togo 103/F4
Sottrum, Ger. 51/G2
Sotuta, Mex. 144/D1
Soude (riv.), Fr. 53/D6
Souderton, Pa, US 138/C3
Soúdha, Gre. 47/J5
Souffelweyersheim, Fr. 53/G6
Soufflenheim, Fr. 53/G6
Souflíon, Gre. 47/K2
Soufrière (peak), StV. 141/N9
Soufrière (peak), Guad. 141/N8
Souillac, Fr. 42/D4
Souillac, Mrts. 107/T15
Souk Ahras, Alg. 100/K6
Souk Ahras (prov.), Alg. 100/K6
Souk el Arba du Rharb, Mor. 100/A2
Sŏul (Seoul) (cap.), SKor. 71/N4
Soultz-Haut-Rhin, Fr. 56/D2
Soultz-sous-Forêts, Fr. 54/A5
Soum (prov.), Burk. 103/E3
Soumagne, Belg. 53/E2
Sound, The (chan.), Den. 37/E5
Souppes-sur-Loing, Fr. 42/E2
Sour El Ghozlane, Alg. 100/G4
Sources, Mont aux (peak), Les. 106/E3
Soure, Braz. 151/J4
Soure, Port. 44/A2
Souris, Mb, Can. 127/H3
Souris, PE, Can. 131/J2
Souris (riv.), Can.,US 127/H3
Sourou (prov.), Burk. 102/E3
Sous le Vent, Îles (isls.), FrPol. 117/K6
Sousa, Braz. 154/C2
Sout (riv.), SAfr. 106/C3
South (mts.), NS, Can. 131/H2
South (bay), Nun., Can. 123/H2
South (mtn.), Pa, US 138/A3
South (cape), NZ 117/R12
South (isl.), NZ 109/H7
South Africa (ctry.) 105/D6
South Amboy, NJ, US 139/H10
South America (cont.) 147
South Andaman (isl.), India 83/F5
South Anna (riv.), Va, US 133/J2
South Augusta, Ga, US 133/H3
South Aulatsivik (isl.), Nf, Can. 123/K3
South Australia (state), Austl. 109/C3
South Ayrshire (pol. reg.), Sc, UK 36/B6
South Bend, Wa, US 126/C4
South Bend, In, US 130/C3
South Benfleet, Eng, UK 33/G3
South Buganda (prov.), Ugan. 104/A3
South Burlington, Vt, US 130/F2
South Caicos (isl.), UK 145/J1
South Carolina (state), US 125/K5
South China (sea), Asia 67/L8
South Colby, Wa, US 135/B2
South Dakota (state), US 127/H4
South Dorset Downs (uplands), Eng, UK 32/D5
South Downs (hills), Eng, UK 33/F5
South Dum Dum, India 85/G4
South East (pt.), Austl. 115/C3
South East (cape), Austl. 109/D5
South Elgin, Il, US 135/P16
South Esk (riv.), Austl. 115/C4
South Esk (riv.), Sc, UK 36/C3
South Farmingdale, NY, US 139/M9
South Fork, Co, US 132/B2
South Fulton, Tn, US 130/B4
South Gate, Md, US 138/B5
South Gate, Ca, US 136/F8
South Georgia (isl.), UK 22/H8
South Gloucestershire (co.), Eng, UK 32/D3
South Hams (plain), Eng, UK 32/C6
South Holland, Il, US 135/Q16
South Island NP, Kenya 104/C2
South Jordan, Ut, US 137/K12
South Koel (riv.), India 85/E4
South Korea (ctry.) 73/D4
South Lake Tahoe, Ca, US 128/C3
South Lanarkshire (pol. reg.), Sc, UK 36/E5
South Loup (riv.), Ne, US 127/J5
South Luangwa NP, Zam. 105/F3
South Lyon, Mi, US 135/E7
South Magnetic Pole, Ant. 160/K
South Moose (lake), Mb, Can. 127/J2
South Moresby NP and Prsv., BC, Can. 134/M5
South Naknek, Ak, US 134/G4
South Normanton, Eng, UK 35/G5
South Nyack, NY, US 139/K7
South Ockendon, Eng, UK 30/D2
South Ogden, Ut, US 137/K11
South Orange, NJ, US 139/H9
South Orkney (isls.), UK 160/X
South Ossetia (reg.), Geo. 63/G4
South Oxhey, Eng, UK 30/B2
South Oyster (bay), NY, US 139/M9
South Pacific (ocean) 22/B7
South Para (res.), Austl. 113/M8
South Pasadena, Ca, US 136/F7
South Pine (riv.), Austl. 114/E6
South Plainfield, NJ, US 139/H9
South Platte (riv.), Co, US 137/C2
South Polar (plat.), Ant. 160/Y
South Pole, Ant. 160/A
South Prairie, Wa, US 135/C3
South River, NJ, US 139/H10
South Rockwood, Mi, US 135/F7
South Ronaldsay (isl.), Sc, UK 31/V14
South Roxana, Il, US 137/G8
South Salt Lake, Ut, US 137/K12
South San Francisco, Ca, US 135/K11
South Sandwich (isls.), UK 22/H8
South Saskatchewan (riv.), Sk, Can. 122/E3
South Seaville, NJ, US 138/D5
South Shetland (isls.), UK 160/W
South Shields, Eng, UK 35/G2
South Sioux City, Ne, US 127/J5
South Skunk (riv.), Ia, US 129/J2
South Taranaki Bight (bay), NZ 117/S10
South Turkana Nat'l Rsv., Kenya 104/B2
South Tyne (riv.), Eng, UK 35/F2
South Ubian, Phil. 81/F2
South Uist (isl.), Sc, UK 31/Q8
South Umpqua (riv.), Or, US 128/B2
South Valley Stream, NY, US 139/L9
South Weber, Ut, US 137/K11
South West (cape), Austl. 115/C4
South West NP, Austl. 115/C4
South West Rocks, Austl. 115/E1
South Whittier, Ca, US 136/F8
South Williamsport, Pa, US 138/B1
South Woodham Ferrers, Eng, UK 30/E2
South Yorkshire (co.), Eng, UK 35/G5
Southampton (cape), Nun., Can. 123/H2
Southampton (isl.), Nun., Can. 123/H2
Southampton, On, Can. 130/D2
Southampton, Eng, UK 33/E5
Southampton (co.), Eng, UK 33/E5
Southampton, NY, US 139/F2
Southampton Water (inlet), Eng, UK 33/E5
Southaven, Ms, US 129/K4
Southeast (cape), Ak, US 134/E3
Southeast (pt.), Bahm. 145/H1
Southeast (pt.), Jam. 145/G2
Southend (int'l arpt.), Eng, UK 33/G3
Southend-on-Sea, Eng, UK 33/G3
Southern (prov.), Ugan. 104/A3
Southern (dist.), Isr. 91/D4
Southern (mts.), NZ 109/G7
Southern (riv.), Austl. 112/K7
Southern Cook (isls.), CookIs. 117/J6
Southern Cross, Austl. 112/C4
Southern Indian (lake), Mb, Can. 122/G3
Southern NP, Sudan 97/L6
Southern Pines, NC, US 133/J3
Southern Uplands (hills), Sc, UK 35/D1
Southern Ural (mts.), Rus. 61/N5
Southesk Tablelands (plat.), Austl. 109/B2
Southold, NY, US 139/F1
Southport, NC, US 133/J3
Southport, Eng, UK 35/E4
Southton, Tx, US 137/U21
Southwark (bor.), Eng, UK 30/A1
Southwood NP, Austl. 114/C4
Southworth, Wa, US 135/C3
Sovata, Rom. 49/G2
Soverato Marina, It. 46/E3
Sovere, It. 58/D1
Sovetsk, Rus. 39/J4
Sōwa, Japan 77/D1
Sowerby Bridge, Eng, UK 35/G4
Soweto, SAfr. 106/D2
Sōya-misaki (cape), Japan 76/B1
Soyana (riv.), Rus. 60/J2
Soyang (lake), SKor. 74/A2
Soyaux, Fr. 42/D4
Soyen, Ger. 55/F6
Soyhières, Swi. 56/D3
Sozh (riv.), Bela. 62/D1
Sozopol, Bul. 49/H4
Spa, Belg. 53/E3
Spada (lake), Wa, US 135/D2
Spain (ctry.) 44/C2
Spalding, Austl. 113/H5
Spalding, Eng, UK 35/H6
Spalt, Ger. 54/D4
Spanish Lake, Mo, US 137/G8
Spanish Town, Jam. 145/G2
Spannort (peak), Swi. 57/E4
Sparanise, It. 46/D2
Sparks, Nv, US 128/C3
Sparlingville, Mi, US 135/G6
Sparreholm, Swe. 38/G2
Sparta, Wi, US 127/L5
Sparta, Tn, US 130/C5
Sparta, NC, US 130/D4
Sparta, NJ, US 138/D1
Spartanburg, SC, US 133/H3
Spartel (cape), Mor. 100/B2
Spárti (Sparta), Gre. 47/H4
Spartivento (cape), It. 46/E4
Sparwood, BC, Can. 126/E3
Spassk-Dal'niy, Rus. 71/P3
Spáta, Gre. 47/N9
Spátha (cape), Gre. 47/H5
Spean (riv.), Sc, UK 36/B3
Speer (peak), Swi. 57/F3
Speer Canal (canal), Co, US 137/C2
Speicher, Swi. 57/F3
Speicher, Ger. 53/F4
Speichersdorf, Ger. 55/E3
Speke (gulf), Tanz. 104/B3
Speke (int'l arpt.), Eng, UK 35/F5
Spelle, Ger. 51/E4
Spence Bay, Nun., Can. 122/G2
Spencer (pt.), Ak, US 134/E2
Spencer, Ia, US 127/K5
Spencer (gulf), Austl. 109/C4
Spencer, Ok, US 137/N14
Spencer (cape), Austl. 113/H5
Spenge, Ger. 51/F4
Spennymoor, Eng, UK 35/G2
Spentrup, Den. 38/D3
Sperkhiás, Gre. 47/H3
Sperkhíos (riv.), Gre. 47/H3
Sperrin (mts.), NI, UK 34/A2
Spessart (range), Ger. 54/C3
Spétsai, Gre. 47/H4
Spey (riv.), Sc, UK 36/B2
Spey (bay), Sc, UK 36/C1
Speyer, Ger. 54/B4
Speyerbsch (riv.), Ger. 54/B4
Spezzano Albanese, It. 46/E3
Špičák (peak), Czh. 55/F2
Spicer (isls.), Nun., Can. 123/H2
Spiekeroog (isl.), Ger. 51/E1
Spiez, Swi. 56/D4
Spigno Monferrato, It. 58/B3
Spijkenisse, Neth. 50/B5
Spike (mtn.), Ak, US 134/K2
Spilamberto, It. 59/E3
Spílion, Gre. 47/J5
Spilve (int'l arpt.), Lat. 39/L3
Spina (peak), It. 46/A2
Spinetta Marengo, It. 58/B3
Spino d'Adda, It. 58/C2
Spirano, It. 58/C1
Spirit River, Ab, Can. 126/D2
Spiritwood, Sk, Can. 126/G2
Spišská Nová Ves, Slvk. 41/L4
Spiti (riv.), India 86/D3
Spitsbergen (isl.), Sval. 160/E
Split, Cro. 48/C4
Split (int'l arpt.), Cro. 48/C4
Split (lake), Mb, Can. 122/G3
Splitrock (res.), NJ, US 139/H8
Spluga, Passo dello (pass), Swi. 57/F5
Splügen, Swi. 57/F4
Spokane, Wa, US 126/D4
Spokane (riv.), Wa, US 126/D4
Spöl (riv.), It. 57/G5
Spoleto, It. 43/K5
Spoon (riv.), Il, US 130/B3
Spooner, Wi, US 127/L4
Spotorno, It. 58/B4
Spotswood, NJ, US 139/H10
Sprague, Mb, Can. 127/K3
Sprang, Neth. 50/C5
Spratly (isls.) 80/D2
Spree (riv.), Ger. 41/H2
Sprendlingen, Ger. 53/G4
Spresiano, It. 59/F1
Sprimont, Belg. 53/E3
Spring, Tx, US 129/J5
Spring City, Pa, US 138/C3
Spring Grove, Pa, US 138/B4
Spring Grove, Il, US 135/P15
Spring Hill, Ks, US 137/D6
Spring Lake, NJ, US 138/D3
Spring Valley, Ca, US 136/D5
Spring Valley, NY, US 139/J7
Springbok, SAfr. 106/B3
Springdale, Nf, Can. 131/K1
Springdale, Ar, US 129/J3
Springe, Ger. 51/G4
Springer, NM, US 129/F3
Springerville, Az, US 128/E4
Springfield, Or, US 126/C4
Springfield, Tn, US 130/C4
Springfield, Vt, US 131/F3
Springfield, Ma, US 131/F3
Springfield, Mo, US 129/J3
Springfield, Va, US 138/A6
Springfield, NJ, US 139/H9
Springfontein, SAfr. 106/D3
Springhill, La, US 129/J4
Springhill, NS, Can. 131/H2
Springs, SAfr. 106/E2
Springs, NY, US 139/F1
Springside, Sk, Can. 127/H3
Springsure, Austl. 114/C4
Springville, Ut, US 137/K13
Sprockhövel, Ger. 51/E6
Spruce (peak), WV, US 130/E4
Spruce Run (res.), NJ, US 138/C2
Spui (riv.), Neth. 50/B5
Spurn (pt.), Eng, UK 35/J4
Squamish, BC, Can. 126/C3
Squaw Harbor, Ak, US 134/F4
Squaxin Island Ind. Res., Wa, US 135/A3
Squillace, Golfo di (gulf), It. 46/E3
Squinzano, It. 47/F2
Squires (mt.), Austl. 113/E3
Srbobran, Yugo. 48/D3
Srebrenica, Bosn. 48/D3
Sredna (mts.), Bul. 47/J1
Srednogorie, Bul. 47/J1
Śrem, Pol. 41/J2
Sremčica, Yugo. 48/E3
Sremska Mitrovica, Yugo. 48/D3
Sreng (riv.), Camb. 78/C3
Srepok (riv.), Camb. 78/D3
Sri Dungargarh, India 89/K3
Sri Gangānagar, India 86/B5
Sri Jayawardanapura (Kotte), SrL. 82/C6
Sri Lanka (ctry.) 82/D6
Srikākulam, India 82/D4
Srīnagar, India 86/C2
Srīvardhan, India 89/K5
Środa Śląska, Pol. 41/J3
Środa Wielkopolska, Pol. 41/J2
St. Albans, Vale of (valley), Eng, UK 30/B1
St. John's (cap.), Nf, Can. 131/L2
Stabbursdalen NP, Nor. 37/H1
Staberhuk (pt.), Ger. 38/D4
Stabroek, Belg. 50/B6
Stade, Ger. 51/G1
Staden, Belg. 52/C2
Stadl-Paura, Aus. 55/G6
Stadskanaal, Neth. 50/D3
Stadtbergen, Ger. 54/D6
Stadthagen, Ger. 51/G4
Stadtlauringen, Ger. 54/D2
Stadtlohn, Ger. 50/D5
Stadtoldendorf, Ger. 51/G5
Stadtsteinach, Ger. 55/E2
Stäfa, Swi. 57/E3
Staffanstorp, Swe. 38/E4
Staffelberg (peak), Ger. 54/E2
Staffelegg (pass), Swi. 56/E3
Staffelsee (lake), Ger. 57/H2
Staffhorst, Ger. 51/F3
Staffora (riv.), It. 58/C3
Stafford, Eng, UK 35/F6
Stagno, It. 58/D5
Stagnone Isole Della (isl.), It. 46/B4
Stahnsdorf, Ger. 40/Q7
Staines, Eng, UK 30/B2
Stains, Fr. 30/K5
Stakes (mt.), Ca, US 135/M12
Stakhanov, Ukr. 62/F2
Stalden, Swi. 56/D5
Stalingrad (Volgograd), Rus. 63/H2
Stallings, Il, US 137/G8
Stallworthy (cape), Nun., Can. 123/S6
Stalowa Wola, Pol. 41/M3
Stalybridge, Eng, UK 35/F5
Stamboliyski, Bul. 47/J1
Stamford, Tx, US 129/H4
Stamford, Eng, UK 33/F1
Stamford, Ct, US 139/L7
Stampa, Swi. 57/F5
Stampriet, Namb. 105/C5
Stamullen, Ire. 34/B4
Standerton, SAfr. 106/E2
Standish-with-Langtree, Eng, UK 35/F4
Standley (lake), Co, US 137/B3
Stanford-le-Hope, Eng, UK 33/G3
Stange, Nor. 38/D1
Stanger, SAfr. 107/E3
Stanghella, It. 59/E2
Stanhope, NJ, US 138/D2
Stanišić, Yugo. 48/D3
Stanislaus (riv.), Ca, US 128/B3
Stanislaus (co.), Ca, US 135/M12
Stanley, Austl. 115/C4
Stanley (mt.), Austl. 115/C4
Stanley (falls), D.R. Congo 97/L8
Stanley, ND, US 127/H3
Stanley, NB, Can. 131/H2
Stanley, Ks, US 137/D6
Stanley (res.), India 82/C5
Stanley (mt.), Austl. 113/F2
Stanley (cap.), Falk. 159/F6
Stanley, Sc, UK 36/C4
Stanley, Eng, UK 35/G2
Stanley Draper (lake), Ok, US 137/N15
Stanovo, Yugo. 48/E4
Stanovoy (range), Rus. 67/M4
Stans, Swi. 57/E4
Stansted (int'l arpt.), Eng, UK 33/G3
Stanthorpe, Austl. 114/C5
Stanton, Ky, US 130/D4
Stanton, Tx, US 129/G4
Stanton, De, US 138/C4
Stanton, NJ, US 138/D2
Stanton, Ca, US 136/G8
Staphorst, Neth. 50/D3
Staplehurst, Eng, UK 33/G4
Staples, On, Can. 135/G7
Staporków, Pol. 41/L3
Stara Pazova, Yugo. 48/E3
Stara Planina (mts.), Yugo. 48/F3
Stara Zagora, Bul. 47/J1
Starachowice, Pol. 41/L3
Staranzano, It. 59/G1
Staraya Russa, Rus. 39/P2
Starbuck (isl.), Kiri. 117/K5
Starcke NP, Austl. 114/B1
Stargard Szczeciński, Pol. 38/F5
Starke, Fl, US 133/H4
Starkville, Ms, US 133/F3
Starnbergersee (lake), Ger. 57/H2
Starodub, Rus. 62/E1
Starogard Gdański, Pol. 38/H5
Start (bay), Eng, UK 32/C6
Start (pt.), Eng, UK 32/C6
Start (pt.), Sc, UK 31/V14
Startup, Wa, US 135/D2
Staryy Oskol', Rus. 62/F2
Staszów, Pol. 41/L3
State College, Pa, US 130/E3
State Fairgrounds, De, US 138/C6
State Park Place, Il, US 137/G8
Staten (isl.), NY, US 138/D2
States (int'l arpt.), Chl, UK 42/B2
Statesboro, Ga, US 133/H3
Statesville, NC, US 133/H3
Statue of Liberty Nat'l Mon., NY, US 139/J9
Staufen im Breisgau, Ger. 56/D2
Staufenberg, Ger. 40/E3
Stavanger, Nor. 38/A2
Staveley, Eng, UK 35/G5
Stavelot, Belg. 53/E3
Staveren, Neth. 50/C3
Stavern, Nor. 38/D2
Stavropol', Rus. 63/G3
Stavropol'skiy (kray), Rus. 64/E5
Stavrós, Gre. 47/H2
Stawell, Austl. 115/B3
Stayton, Or, US 126/C4
Ste-Marguerite (riv.), Qu, Can. 131/H1
Steamboat Slough (riv.), Ca, US 135/L10
Steamboat Springs, Co, US 128/F2
Stebbins, Ak, US 134/F3
Steckborn, Swi. 57/E2
Stederau (riv.), Ger. 51/H3
Steeg, Aus. 57/G3
Steele, ND, US 127/J4
Steele's Knowe (hill), Sc, UK 36/C4
Steelpoortrivier (riv.), SAfr. 107/E2
Steelton, Pa, US 138/B3
Steenbergen, Neth. 50/B5
Steens (mtn.), Or, US 128/C2
Steensby (inlet), Nun., Can. 123/J1
Steenvoorde, Fr. 52/B2
Steenwijk, Neth. 50/D3
Steep (pt.), Austl. 112/B3
Steep Holm (isl.), Eng, UK 32/C4
Steephill (lake), Sk, Can. 127/G1
Steeping (riv.), Eng, UK 35/J5
Steese Nat'l Conservation Area, Ak, US 134/J2
Stefansson (isl.), Nun., Can. 122/F1
Steffen (peak), Chile 158/C5
Steffisburg, Swi. 56/D4
Steg, Swi. 56/D5
Stege, Den. 38/E4
Steiermark (prov.), Aus. 41/H5
Steigerwald (for.), Ger. 43/J2
Steilacoom, Wa, US 135/B3
Steimbke, Ger. 51/G3
Stein, Neth. 53/E2
Stein am Rhein, Swi. 57/E2
Stein bei Nünnberg, Ger. 54/E4
Steina (riv.), Ger. 57/E2
Steinach, Ger. 55/F5
Steinach (riv.), Ger. 54/E2
Steinach am Brenner, Aus. 57/H3
Steinbach, Mb, Can. 127/J3
Steinbach an der Steyr, Aus. 55/H7
Steinbourg, Fr. 53/G6
Steinen, Ger. 56/D2
Steinerkirchen an der Traun, Aus. 55/G6
Steinfeld, Ger. 51/F3
Steinfeld, Ger. 54/B4
Steinfeld, Ger. 54/C3
Steinfort, Lux. 53/E4
Steingaden, Ger. 57/G2
Steinhagen, Ger. 51/F4
Steinhausen, Swi. 57/E3
Steinhausen an der Rottum, Ger. 57/F1
Steinheim, Ger. 51/G5
Steinheim am Albuch, Ger. 54/D5
Steinheim an der Murr, Ger. 54/C5
Steinhorst, Ger. 51/H3
Steinhuder (lake), Ger. 51/G4
Steinkjer, Nor. 37/D2
Steinsland, Nor. 38/A1
Steinweiler, Ger. 54/B4
Stekene, Belg. 50/B6
Stella, SAfr. 106/D2
Stella (peak), It. 57/F5
Stellarton, NS, Can. 131/J2
Stelle, Ger. 51/H2
Stellenbosch, SAfr. 106/L10
Stello (peak), Fr. 43/H5
Stelvio, Passo di (pass), It. 57/G4
Stelvio, PN Dello, It. 43/J3
Stenay, Fr. 53/E5
Stendal, Ger. 40/F2
Steneto NP, Bul. 47/J1
Stenhousemuir, Sc, UK 36/C4
Stenungsund, Swe. 38/D2
Stephansposching, Ger. 55/F5
Stephenville, Nf, Can. 131/K1
Stephenville, Tx, US 129/H4
Sterkstroom, SAfr. 106/D3
Sterling, Ak, US 134/H3
Sterling, Co, US 129/G2
Sterlitamak, Rus. 63/K1
Sternstein (peak), Aus. 55/H5
Sterzing (Vipiteno), It. 57/H4
Stęszew, Pol. 41/J2
Štěti, Czh. 55/H2
Stettler, Ab, Can. 126/E2
Steubenville, Oh, US 130/D3
Stevenage, Eng, UK 33/F3
Stevens Village, Ak, US 134/J2
Stevenson (lake), Mb, Can. 127/J2
Stevenson Entrance (str.), Ak, US 134/H4
Stevenston, Sc, UK 36/B5
Stevensville, Mt, US 126/E4
Stevensville, Md, US 138/B6
Stevinsluizen (dam), Neth. 50/C3
Stevzing (Vipiteno), It. 43/J3
Stewart, BC, Can. 134/N4
Stewart (riv.), Yk, Can. 122/C2
Stewart (isl.), NZ 109/G7
Stewart Crossing, Yk, Can. 134/L3
Stewarton, Sc, UK 36/B5
Stewartstown, Pa, US 138/B4
Stewartstown, NI, UK 34/B2
Stewartville, Mn, US 127/K5
Steynrus, SAfr. 106/D2
Steynsburg, SAfr. 106/D3
Steyr, Aus. 55/H6
Steyr (riv.), Aus. 41/H5
Steyregg, Aus. 55/H6
Steytlerville, SAfr. 106/D4
Stia, It. 59/E5
Stiava, It. 58/D5
Stickney (mt.), Wa, US 135/D2
Stiens, Neth. 50/C2
Stigler, Ok, US 129/J4
Stigtomta, Swe. 38/G2
Stikine (riv.), Can.,US 134/M4
Stilbaai, SAfr. 106/C4
Stilfontein, SAfr. 106/D2
Stilis, Gre. 47/H3
Still Creek (res.), Pa, US 138/C2
Still Pond, Md, US 138/B5
Stilling, Den. 38/D3
Stillings, Mo, US 137/D5
Stillwater (range), Nv, US 128/C3
Stillwater, Ok, US 129/H3
Stillwater, Pa, US 138/B1
Stillwater (lake), Pa, US 138/C1
Stilo (cape), It. 46/E3
Stilwell, Ok, US 129/J4
Stilwell, Ks, US 137/D6
Štimlje, Yugo. 47/G1
Stimpfach, Ger. 54/D4
Stinchar (riv.), Sc, UK 34/D1
Stinnett, Tx, US 129/G4
Štip, FYROM 47/H2
Stiring-Wendel, Fr. 53/F5
Stírka (peak), Czh. 55/G4
Stirling (mt.), Austl. 112/C4
Stirling, Sc, UK 36/C4
Stirling (pol. reg.), Sc, UK 36/B4

228

Stirl – Tabir

Stirling Range NP, Austl. 112/C5
Stirone (riv.), It. 58/C3
Stjørdal, Nor. 37/D3
Stob a' Choin (peak), Sc, UK 36/B4
Stob Choire Claurigh (peak), Sc, UK 36/B3
Stochov, Czh. 55/G2
Stock, Eng, UK 30/E2
Stock (lake), Fr. 53/F6
Stockach, Ger. 57/F2
Stockerau, Aus. 49/N7
Stockertown, Pa, US 138/C2
Stockholm (co.), Swe. 38/G2
Stockholm (cap.), Swe. 37/F4
Stockhorn (peak), Swi. 56/D4
Stockport, Eng, UK 35/F5
Stocks (res.), Eng, UK 35/F4
Stocksbridge, Eng, UK 35/G5
Stockstadt am Rhein, Ger. 54/B3
Stockton (lake), Mo, US 129/J3
Stockton, Ca, US 128/B3
Stockton (plat.), Tx, US 142/E2
Stockton, Ut, US 137/J13
Stockton, NJ, US 138/D3
Stockton-on-Tees, Eng, UK 35/G2
Stockton-on-Tees (co.), Eng, UK 35/G2
Stod, Czh. 55/G3
Stoddard, Ut, US 137/K11
Stoke (pt.), Eng, UK 32/B6
Stoke-on-Trent, Eng, UK 35/F5
Stoke-on-Trent (co.), Eng, UK 35/F5
Stoke Poges, Eng, UK 30/B2
Stokenchurch, Eng, UK 30/A2
Stokes (pt.), Austl. 115/B4
Stokes NP, Austl. 112/D5
Stolac, Bosn. 47/E1
Stolberg, Ger. 53/F2
Stolbovoy (isl.), Rus. 65/P2
Stöllet, Swe. 38/E1
Stolzenau, Ger. 51/G3
Stompneuspunt (pt.), SAfr. 106/K10
Ston, Cro. 47/E1
Stone, Eng, UK 35/F6
Stone Harbor, NJ, US 138/D5
Stonehaven, Sc, UK 36/D3
Stonehenge (ruin), Eng, UK 33/E4
Stonehouse, Sc, UK 36/C5
Stonewall, Mb, Can. 127/J3
Stoney Creek, On, Can. 131/Q9
Stoney Point, On, Can. 135/G7
Stoneyburn, Sc, UK 36/C5
Stonington, Ct, US 139/G1
Stony (pt.), Mb, Can. 127/J2
Stony Brook, NY, US 139/E2
Stony Creek (lake), Mi, US 135/E7
Stony Mountain, Mb, Can. 127/J3
Stony Point, NY, US 138/E1
Stony River, Ak, US 134/G3
Stony Tunguska (riv.), Rus. 67/J3
Stonybrook-Wilshire, Pa, US 138/B4
Stooping (riv.), Co, US 130/D1
Stor (isl.), Nun., Can. 123/S7
Stör (riv.), Ger. 51/G1
Stor-Elvdal, Nor. 38/D1
Storå, Swe. 38/F2
Stora Le (lake), Swe. 38/D2
Stora Sjöfallets NP, Swe. 37/F2
Storavan (lake), Swe. 37/F2
Stord (isl.), Nor. 38/A2
Store Bælt (chan.), Den. 38/D4
Storebø, Nor. 38/A1
Støren, Nor. 37/D3
Storfors, Swe. 38/F2
Storm (bay), Austl. 109/D5
Stormberg (mtn.), SAfr. 106/D3
Stormont, NI, UK 34/C2
Stornoway, Sc, UK 31/Q7
Storo, It. 58/D1
Storr, The (peak), Sc, UK 31/Q8
Storsjön (lake), Swe. 37/E3
Storsteinsfjellet (peak), Nor. 37/F1
Storstrøm (co.), Den. 38/D4
Storvik, Swe. 38/G1
Storvreta, Swe. 38/G2
Story, Wy, US 126/G4
Stosch (isl.), Chile 159/A6
Stötten am Auerberg, Ger. 57/G2
Stoughton, Sk, Can. 127/H3
Stoumont, Belg. 53/E3
Stour (riv.), Eng, UK 32/D5
Stourbridge, Eng, UK 32/D2
Stourport-on-Severn, Eng, UK 32/D2
Stovring, Den. 38/C3
Stowe, Pa, US 138/C3
Stowmarket, Eng, UK 33/G2
Stra, It. 59/F2
Strabane (dist.), NI 34/A2
Strabane, NI, UK 31/Q9
Stradella, It. 58/C2
Straelen, Ger. 50/D6
Strahan, Austl. 115/C4
Strakonice, Czh. 55/G4
Straldzha, Bul. 47/K1
Stralsund, Ger. 38/E4
Strambino, It. 58/A2
Strand, SAfr. 106/L11
Strangford, NI, UK 34/C3
Strangford (lake), NI, UK 34/C3
Strängnäs, Swe. 38/G2
Strangways (mt.), Austl. 113/G2
Stranocum, NI, UK 34/B1
Stranraer, Sc, UK 34/C2
Strasbourg, Fr. 56/D1
Strasbourg (Entzheim) (int'l arpt.), Fr. 56/D1
Strasburg, Mo, US 137/E6
Strasburg, Pa, US 138/B4
Strassen, Lux. 53/F4
Strasshof an der Nordbahn, Aus. 49/P7
Strasswalchen, Aus. 55/G7
Stratford, Tx, US 129/G3
Stratford, On, Can. 130/D3
Stratford, NZ 117/S10
Stratford, Ct, US 139/E1
Stratford, NJ, US 138/C4
Stratford (pt.), Ct, US 139/E1
Stratford (har.), Ct, US 139/L8
Stratford and Worcester (canal), Eng, UK 32/D2
Stratford-upon-Avon, Eng, UK 33/E2
Strathalbyn, Austl. 113/H5
Strathaven, Sc, UK 36/B5
Strathbeg (bay), Sc, UK 36/E1
Strathblane, Sc, UK 36/B5
Strathearn (valley), Sc, UK 36/C4
Strathmore, Ab, Can. 126/E3
Strathmore (valley), Sc, UK 36/C3
Strathpeffer, Sc, UK 36/B1
Strathspey (valley), Sc, UK 36/C2
Straubing, Ger. 55/F5
Straumnes Horn (pt.), Ice. 37/M6
Strausberg, Ger. 40/Q6
Strausstown, Pa, US 138/B3
Strawberry (peak), Ca, US 136/B2
Strazhitsa, Bul. 49/G4
Streaky (bay), Austl. 109/C4
Streaky Bay, Austl. 113/G5
Streamwood, Il, US 135/P15
Streator, Il, US 127/L5
Středočeská Žulová Vrchovina (mts.), Czh. 41/H4
Středočeský (pol. reg.), Czh. 43/L2
Středoslovenský (pol. reg.), Czh. 41/H3
Street, Md, US 138/B4
Strehaia, Rom. 49/F3
Streich (peak), Austl. 112/D4
Střela (riv.), Czh. 41/G3
Strelley Abor. Land, Austl. 112/C2
Strel'na (riv.), Rus. 60/H2
Strengberg, Aus. 55/H6
Strengelbach, Swi. 56/D3
Strengen, Aus. 57/G3
Stresa, It. 58/B1
Stretford, Eng, UK 35/F5
Strettoia, It. 58/D5
Streu (riv.), Ger. 54/D2
Strib, Den. 38/C4
Stříbro, Czh. 55/G3
Strichen, Sc, UK 36/D1
Strigno, It. 57/H5
Strijen, Neth. 50/B5
Strimón (gulf), Gre. 62/C4
Strimónas (riv.), Gre. 47/H2
Striven (lake), Sc, UK 36/A5
Strobel (lake), Arg. 159/C6
Stroeder, Arg. 158/E4
Strofádhes (isl.), Gre. 47/G4
Strom Thurmond (lake), Ga,SC, US 133/H3
Stromberg, Ger. 53/G4
Stromboli (isl.), It. 46/D3
Strømmen, Nor. 38/D2
Stromness, Sc, UK 31/V14
Strömstad, Swe. 38/D2
Strömsund, Swe. 37/E3
Strona (riv.), It. 57/E6
Strongoli, It. 47/E3
Stronie Śląskie, Pol. 41/J3
Stronsay (isl.), Sc, UK 31/V14
Stronsay Firth (inlet), Sc, UK 31/V14
Strood, Eng, UK 30/E2
Stropnice (riv.), Czh. 55/H5
Stroppiana, It. 58/B2
Stroud, Eng, UK 32/D3
Stroudsburg, Pa, US 138/C2
Struan, Sc, UK 31/Q8
Struer, Den. 38/C3
Struga, FYROM 47/G2
Struisbaai (bay), SAfr. 106/C4
Strule (riv.), NI, UK 34/A2
Struma (riv.), Bul. 62/B4
Strumble (pt.), Wal, UK 32/A2
Strumica, FYROM 47/H2
Strydenburg, SAfr. 106/C3
Stryn, Nor. 37/C3
Strzegom, Pol. 41/J3
Strzelce Krajeńskie, Pol. 41/H2
Strzelce Opolskie, Pol. 62/A2
Strzelecki (mt.), Austl. 115/D4
Strzelecki (mt.), Austl. 113/G2
Strzelin, Pol. 41/J3
Strzelno, Pol. 41/K2
Strzyżów, Pol. 41/L4
Stuart (lake), BC, Can. 126/B2
Stuart (riv.), BC, Can. 126/B2
Stuart, Fl, US 133/H5
Stuarts Draft, Va, US 130/E4
Stubbekøbing, Den. 38/E4
Stubbenkammer (pt.), Ger. 38/E4
Stühlingen, Ger. 57/E2
Stupava, Slvk. 43/M2
Stupino, Rus. 60/H5
Stura di Lanzo (riv.), It. 58/A2
Sturgeon (lake), On, Can. 127/L3
Sturgeon (bay), Mb, Can. 127/J3
Sturgeon (riv.), On, Can. 130/D2
Sturgeon Falls, On, Can. 130/E2
Sturgis, Mi, US 130/C3
Štúrovo, Slvk. 41/K5
Sturt (des.), Austl. 109/D3
Sturt (mt.), Austl. 113/J4
Sturt (riv.), Austl. 113/M8
Sturt NP, Austl. 115/B1
Sturup (int'l arpt.), Swe. 38/E4
Stutterheim, SAfr. 106/D4
Stuttgart, Ger. 54/C5
Stykkishólmur, Ice. 37/M6
Styr (riv.), Ukr. 62/C2
Suaçui Grande (riv.), Braz. 155/D1
Suakin (arch.), Sudan 97/N4
Suam (riv.), Kenya 104/B2
Suaqui Grande, Mex. 142/C2
Suār, India 84/B1
Suárez (riv.), Col. 152/C3
Subang, Indo. 80/C5
Subarnarekhā (riv.), India 85/E4
Sūbāṭ (riv.), Sudan 97/M6
Subayṭilah, Tun. 100/L7
Subei Monggolzu Zizhixian, China 70/F4
Subi (isl.), Indo. 80/C3
Subotica, Yugo. 48/D2
Succasunna-Kenvil, NJ, US 138/D2
Succiso, Alpe di (peak), It. 58/D4
Suceava, Rom. 49/H2
Suceava (prov.), Rom. 49/G2
Suchedniów, Pol. 41/L3
Suches, Bol. 156/D4
Suck (riv.), Ire. 31/P10
Sucre (cap.), Bol. 150/E7
Sucre, Ecu. 152/A5
Sucre (state), Ven. 153/F2
Sucre (dept.), Col. 145/H4
Sucúa, Ecu. 152/B5
Sucumbíos (prov.), Ecu. 152/B4
Sucunduri (riv.), Braz. 150/G5
Sucupira do Norte, Braz. 154/A2
Sucuriú (riv.), Braz. 151/H7
Sucy-en-Brie, Fr. 30/K5
Sud (pol. reg.), Mor. 98/C3
Sud-Ouest (prov.), Camr. 103/H5
Suda (riv.), Rus. 60/H4
Sudama, Japan 77/A2
Sudan (ctry.) 97/L5
Sudbury, On, Can. 130/D2
Sudbury, Eng, UK 33/G2
Suddie, Guy. 153/G3
Sude (riv.), Ger. 40/F2
Süderbrarup, Ger. 38/C4
Sudeten (mts.), Czh.,Pol. 41/H3
Sudlersville, Md, US 138/C5
Südlohn, Ger. 50/D5
Sue (riv.), Sudan 93/E4
Sueca, Sp. 45/E3
Sŭedinenie, Bul. 47/J1
Suez (gulf), Egypt 97/M2
Suez (canal), Egypt 93/D1
Sūf, Jor. 91/D3
Sufers, Swi. 57/F4
Suffern, NY, US 139/J7
Suffolk (co.), NY, US 139/F2
Suga (isl.), Japan 77/L7
Sugar Creek, Mo, US 137/E5
Sugar Grove, Il, US 135/P16
Sugar Land, Tx, US 132/E4
Sugar Loaf (peak), Wal, UK 32/C3
Sugar Notch, Pa, US 138/C1
Sugenheim, Ger. 54/D3
Sugito, Japan 77/D1
Suğla (lake), Turk. 90/C2
Suhāj (gov.), Egypt 101/B3
Suhāj, Egypt 101/B3
Sühbaatar (prov.), Mong. 71/K2
Suhl, Ger. 54/D1
Suhlendorf, Ger. 51/H3
Şuhut, Turk. 90/B2
Sui (riv.), China 79/B3
Sui (pt.), Thai. 78/B4
Sui Xian, China 72/C4
Suia-Missu (riv.), Braz. 151/H6
Suichang, China 79/C2
Suichuan, China 83/K2
Suifenhe, China 71/P3
Suihua, China 71/N2
Suijiang, China 83/H2
Suileng, China 71/N2
Suining, China 72/D4
Suipacha, Arg. 159/J11
Suiping, China 72/C4
Suippe (riv.), Fr. 40/C4
Suippes, Fr. 53/D5
Suir (riv.), Ire. 31/Q10
Suis (well), Libya 99/H4
Suishō (isl.), Rus. 76/D2
Suita, Japan 77/J6
Suitland-Silver Hill, Md, US 138/B6
Suixi, China 83/K3
Suixi, China 72/D4
Suiyang, China 79/A2
Suize (riv.), Fr. 56/B2
Suizhong, China 72/E2
Suizhou, China 71/K5
Sūjāngarh, India 89/K3
Sukabumi, Indo. 80/C5
Sukadana (bay), Indo. 80/C4
Sukadana, Indo. 80/C4
Sukagawa, Japan 75/G2
Sukheke, Pak. 86/B4
Sukhindol, Bul. 47/J1
Sukhinichi, Rus. 62/E1
Sukhodol'skoye (lake), Rus. 39/N1
Sukhona (riv.), Rus. 64/E4
Sukhothai (ruin), Thai. 78/B2
Sukhothai, Thai. 78/B2
Sukkur, Pak. 89/J3
Sükösd, Hun. 48/D2
Sukumo, Japan 74/C4
Sula (isls.), Phil. 67/M10
Sula (riv.), Rus. 61/L2
Sulaimān (range), Pak. 89/J3
Sulakyurt, Turk. 62/E4
Sulawesi (Celebes) (isl.), Indo. 81/E4
Sulb Temple (ruin), Sudan 101/B4
Sulby (riv.), IM, UK 34/D3
Sulechów, Pol. 41/H2
Sulęcin, Pol. 41/H2
Sulejów, Pol. 41/K3
Sulejówek, Pol. 41/L2
Sulina, Rom. 49/J3
Sulina Branch (riv.), Rom. 49/J3
Sulingen, Ger. 51/F3
Sulitjelma (peak), Nor. 37/F2
Sullana, Peru 156/A2
Sullivan (lake), Ab, Can. 126/F3
Sullivan, Qu, Can. 130/E1
Sullivan, Wi, US 135/N13
Sully-sur-Loire, Fr. 42/E3
Sulmona, It. 46/C1
Sulphur (riv.), Tx, US 129/J4
Sulphur, Ok, US 129/H4
Sulphur Springs, Tx, US 129/J4
Sulphur Springs, Ca, US 136/A2
Sultan, Wa, US 135/D2
Sultan (riv.), Wa, US 135/D2
Sultan Kudarat, Phil. 79/D6
Sultānpur, India 84/D2
Sulu (arch.), Phil. 67/L9
Sulu (sea), Asia 67/M9
Sülüklü, Turk. 90/C2
Suluova, Turk. 62/E4
Sulūq, Libya 97/K1
Sülysáp, Hun. 49/R10
Sulz, Swi. 56/E2
Sulz (riv.), Ger. 55/E4
Sülz (riv.), Ger. 53/G2
Sulz am Neckar, Ger. 54/B6
Sulzach (riv.), Ger. 54/D4
Sulzbach, Ger. 53/G5
Sulzbach (riv.), Ger. 55/F6
Sulzbach am Main, Ger. 54/C3
Sulzbach-Rosenberg, Ger. 55/E3
Sulzberg, Ger. 57/G2
Sulzberger (bay), Ant. 160/Q
Sulzburg, Ger. 56/D2
Sulzfluh (peak), Aus. 57/F3
Sulzheim, Ger. 54/D3
Šumadija (reg.), Yugo. 48/E3
Sumapaz, PN, Col. 152/C4
Sumatra (isl.), Indo. 67/J9
Sumba (str.), Indo. 81/E5
Sumba (isl.), Indo. 67/L11
Sumbar (riv.), Trkm. 87/C5
Sumbawa (isl.), Indo. 67/L10
Sumbawa Besar, Indo. 81/E5
Sumbawanga, Tanz. 104/A4
Sumbe, Ang. 105/B3
Sumburgh Head (pt.), Sc, UK 31/W14
Sumdum (mt.), Ak, US 134/M4
Sümeg, Hun. 48/C2
Sumenep, Indo. 80/D5
Sumiswald, Swi. 56/D3
Summerland, BC, Can. 126/D3
Summerland, Ca, US 136/A2
Summerside, PE, Can. 131/J2
Summerville, SC, US 133/H3
Summerville, Ga, US 133/G3
Summit (co.), Ut, US 137/K12
Summit, NJ, US 139/H9
Summit Bridge, De, US 138/C4
Summit Hill, Pa, US 138/C2
Sumner, Wa, US 135/C3
Sumoto, Japan 74/D3
Šumperk, Czh. 41/J4
Sumqayıt, Azer. 63/J4
Sums'ka (obl.), Ukr. 62/E2
Sumter, SC, US 133/H3
Sumy, Ukr. 62/E2
Sun (riv.), Mt, US 126/E4
Sun City, Az, US 137/R18
Sun City, Ca, US 136/C3
Sun City West, Az, US 137/R18
Sun Kosi (riv.), Nepal 85/F2
Sun Lakes, Az, US 137/S19
Sunagawa, Japan 76/B2
Sunām, India 86/C4
Sunami, Japan 77/L5
Sunbury, Pa, US 138/B2
Sunbury, Austl. 115/F5
Sunbury-on-Thames, Eng, UK 30/B2
Sunch'ang, SKor. 73/D5
Sunch'ŏn, NKor. 73/C3
Sunch'ŏn, SKor. 73/D5
Suncook, NH, US 131/G3
Sunda (isls.), Indo. 67/J10
Sunda (str.), Indo. 67/K10
Sundance, Wy, US 127/G4
Sundarbans (phys. reg.), India 85/G5
Sundargarh, India 85/E4
Sundarnagar, India 86/D4
Sundays (riv.), SAfr. 106/D4
Sunderland, Eng, UK 35/G2
Sundern, Ger. 51/F6
Sundhouse, Fr. 56/D1
Sundown, Tx, US 129/G4
Sundown NP, Austl. 115/D1
Sundre, Ab, Can. 126/E3
Sunds, Den. 38/C3
Sungai Petani, Malay. 83/H6
Sungaipenuh, Indo. 80/B4
Sŭngju, SKor. 73/D5
Sungurlare, Bul. 47/K1
Sungurlu, Turk. 62/E4
Suning, China 72/C3
Sunndal, Nor. 37/D3
Sunne, Swe. 38/E2
Sunningdale, Eng, UK 33/F4
Sunnyside, Ca, US 136/C5
Sunnyside, Il, US 135/P15
Sunnyvale, Ca, US 128/B3
Sunol, Ca, US 135/L11
Sunomata, Japan 77/L5
Sunrise (mtn.), NJ, US 138/D1
Sunset, Ut, US 137/J11
Sunset Beach, Hi, US 124/V12
Sunset Beach, Ca, US 136/F8
Sunset Country (reg.), Austl. 115/B2
Sunset Crater Volcano Nat'l Mon., Az, US 128/E4
Suntar-Khayata (mts.), Rus. 65/P3
Süntel (mts.), Ger. 51/G4
Sunwi (isl.), NKor. 73/C4
Sunwu, China 71/N2
Sunyani, Gha. 103/E5
Sunzu (peak), Zam. 104/A5
Suo (sea), Japan 74/B4
Suomenlinna, Fin. 39/L1
Suomenselkä (reg.), Fin. 37/H3
Supaul, India 85/F2
Supawna Meadows NWR, NJ, US 138/C4
Supe, Peru 156/B3
Superior, Mt, US 126/E4
Superior, Az, US 128/E4
Superior (upland), Wi, US 130/B2
Superior, Co, US 137/B3
Superior (lake), Can.,US 130/B2
Suphan Buri, Thai. 78/C3
Supiori (isl.), Indo. 81/J4
Sup'ung (res.), China 73/C2
Sup'ung (dam), NKor. 73/C2
Sūq ash Shuyūkh, Iraq 88/E2
Şuqaylabīyah, Syria 91/E2
Suqian, China 72/D4
Suquamish, Wa, US 135/B2
Şūr, Leb. 91/D3
Sur (pt.), Arg. 159/F3
Sur Reina Sofia (int'l arpt.), Sp. 98/A3
Sura (riv.), Rus. 61/K5
Surabaya, Indo. 80/D5
Surada, India 82/D4
Surahammar, Swe. 38/G2
Sūrajgarh, India 86/C5
Surak-san (peak), SKor. 73/G6
Surakarta, Indo. 80/D5
Surallah, Phil. 81/F2
Suran (riv.), Fr. 56/B5
Šurany, Slvk. 48/D1
Surat, India 89/K4
Surat, Austl. 114/C4
Surat Thani, Thai. 78/B4
Suratgarh, India 86/B5
Surčin, Yugo. 48/E3
Surdulica, Yugo. 47/H1
Sure (riv.), Kenya 104/D2
Sûre (riv.), Lux. 40/C4
Surendranagar, India 89/K4
Surf City, NJ, US 138/D4
Surgères, Fr. 42/C3
Surgut, Rus. 64/H3
Sūri, India 85/F4
Súria, Sp. 45/F2
Surigao, Phil. 81/G2
Surin, Thai. 78/C3
Suriname (ctry.) 153/G3
Surma (riv.), Bang. 85/H3
Surprise, Az, US 137/R18
Surrey, BC, Can. 126/C3
Surrey (co.), Eng, UK 33/F4
Sursee, Swi. 56/E3
Surt, Libya 96/J1
Surte, Swe. 38/E3
Surtsey (isl.), Ice. 37/N7
Surubim, Braz. 154/D2
Sürüç, Turk. 90/D2
Suruga (bay), Japan 75/F3
Surumu (riv.), Braz. 153/F4
Surveyor General's Corner, Austl. 113/F3
Survilliers, Fr. 30/K4
Surwakwima (falls), Guy. 153/F3
Surwold, Ger. 51/E3
Sūsah, Tun. 46/B5
Sūsah (gov.), Tun. 46/B5
Susaki, Japan 74/C4
Susanville, Ca, US 126/C5
Susegana, It. 59/F1
Suşehri, Turk. 62/F4
Sushan (isl.), China 73/B4
Sušice, Czh. 55/G4
Susitna (riv.), Ak, US 122/A2
Susono, Japan 75/F3
Susquehanna (riv.), Md,Pa, US 130/E3
Susquehanna NWR, Md, US 138/B5
Sussex, NB, Can. 131/H2
Sussex (co.), De, US 138/C6
Sussex, NJ, US 138/D1
Sussex Inlet, Austl. 115/D2
Sussex, Vale of (valley), Eng, UK 33/F4
Sustenhorn (peak), Swi. 57/E4
Sustenpass (pass), Swi. 57/E4
Susteren, Neth. 53/E1
Susuman, Rus. 65/Q3
Susurluk, Turk. 62/D5
Sütçüler, Turk. 90/B2
Sutherland, SAfr. 106/C4
Sutherland Springs, Tx, US 137/U21
Sutherlin, Or, US 126/C5
Sutjeska NP, Bosn. 47/F1
Sutlej (riv.), India 70/C5
Sütlücc, Turk. 47/K2
Sutter (co.), Ca, US 135/L9
Sutton, Ak, US 134/J3
Sutton (bor.), Eng, UK 30/C2
Sutton Coldfield, Eng, UK 33/E1
Sutton in Ashfield, Eng, UK 35/G5
Suttsu, Japan 76/B2
Suur (str.), Est. 39/K2
Suurberge (mts.), SAfr. 106/D4
Suurbraak, SAfr. 106/C4
Suvorovo, Bul. 49/H4
Suwa, Japan 75/F2
Suwałki (prov.), Pol. 39/K5
Suwałki, Pol. 39/K4
Suwannee (riv.), Fl, US 140/E1
Suwanose (isl.), Japan 75/K6
Suwarrow (isl.), CookIs. 117/J6
Şuwaylih, Jor. 91/D3
Suwŏn, SKor. 73/G7
Suyo, Peru 156/B2
Suze (riv.), Swi. 56/D3
Suzhou, China 72/D4
Suzhou, China 72/L8
Suzi (riv.), China 73/C2
Suzu, Japan 75/E2
Suzu-misaki (cape), Japan 75/E2
Suzuka, Japan 77/L6
Suzuka (riv.), Japan 77/L6
Suzuka (range), Japan 77/K6
Suzzara, It. 59/D3
Svalbard (isls.), Nor. 160/E
Svaneke, Den. 38/F4
Svängsta, Swe. 38/F3
Svanstein, Swe. 60/D2
Svatava (riv.), Czh. 55/F2
Svealand (reg.), Swe. 37/E4
Svedala, Swe. 38/E4
Sveio, Nor. 38/A2
Svelvik, Nor. 38/D2
Svendborg, Den. 38/D4
Svendsen (pen.), Nun., Can. 123/S7
Svenljunga, Swe. 38/E3
Svenstrup, Den. 38/C3
Sverdlovskaya (obl.), Rus. 64/G4
Sverdrup (chan.), Nun., Can. 123/S7
Sverdrup (isls.), Nun., Can. 123/R7
Sverdrup (isl.), Rus. 64/H2
Svetlogorsk, Bela. 62/D1
Svetlograd, Rus. 63/G3
Svetlyy, Rus. 63/M2
Svetozarevo, Yugo. 48/E4
Svíahnúkar (peak), Ice. 37/P7
Svilajnac, Yugo. 48/E3
Svilengrad, Bul. 47/K2
Svishtov, Bul. 49/G4
Svitavy, Czh. 41/J4
Svobodnyy, Rus. 71/N1
Svoge, Bul. 47/H1
Svratka (riv.), Czh. 43/M2
Svrljig, Yugo. 48/F4
Svyatyy Nos (cape), Rus. 65/Q2
Swābi, Pak. 86/B2
Swadlincote, Eng, UK 33/E1
Swain (reefs), Austl. 109/E3
Swains (isl.), ASam. 117/H6
Swainsboro, Ga, US 133/H3
Swakopmund, Namb. 105/B5
Swale, The (riv.), Eng, Ire. 33/G4
Swalmen, Neth. 50/D6
Swan (riv.), Austl. 112/C4
Swan (riv.), Mb,Sk, Can. 127/H3
Swan (isls.), Hon. 140/E4
Swan (mt.), Austl. 113/G2
Swan (hills), Ab, Can. 122/E3
Swan Hill, Austl. 115/B2
Swan Hills, Ab, Can. 126/E2
Swan Reach, Austl. 113/H5
Swan River, Mb, Can. 127/H2
Swanscombe, Eng, UK 30/D2
Swansea, Austl. 115/D4
Swansea, Il, US 137/H8
Swansea (bay), Eng, UK 32/C3
Swansea, Wal, UK 32/C3
Swansea (co.), Wal, UK 32/B3
Swart Kei (riv.), SAfr. 106/D3
Swarthmore, Pa, US 138/C4
Swartswood (lake), NJ, US 138/D1
Swarzędz, Pol. 41/J2
Swarzenbach an der Sächsischen Saale, Ger. 55/E2
Swarzrand (mts.), Namb. 106/B2
Swāt (riv.), Pak. 86/B2
Swatragh, NI, UK 34/B2
Swayambhunath, Nepal 85/E2
Swaziland (ctry.) 107/E2
Sweden (ctry.) 37/E3
Swedesboro, NJ, US 138/C4
Sweet Home, Or, US 126/C4
Sweetwater (riv.), Wy, US 126/F5
Sweetwater, Tx, US 129/G4
Sweetwater (res.), Ca, US 136/D5
Swellendam, SAfr. 106/C4
Świdnica, Pol. 41/J3
Świdnik, Pol. 41/M3
Świdwin, Pol. 38/F5
Świebodzice, Pol. 41/J3
Świebozin, Pol. 41/H2
Świecie, Pol. 41/K2
Świętokrzysky NP, Pol. 41/L3
Swift Current, Sk, Can. 126/G3
Swifts Creek, Austl. 115/C3
Swilly, Lough (inlet), Ire. 31/Q9
Swimming River (res.), NJ, US 138/D3
Swindon, Eng, UK 33/E3
Swindon (co.), Eng, UK 33/E3
Świnoujście, Pol. 38/F5
Swinton, Eng, UK 35/G5
Swist Bach (riv.), Ger. 53/F2
Switzerland (ctry.) 59/D4
Swords, Ire. 34/B5
Swoyersville, Pa, US 138/C1
Syamozero (lake), Rus. 60/G3
Sych, Moel (peak), Wal, UK 35/E6
Syców, Pol. 41/J3
Sydney, NS, Can. 131/J2
Sydney, Austl. 114/H8
Sydney-Kingsford Smith (int'l arpt.), Austl. 114/H8
Syeverodonets'k, Ukr. 62/F2
Syke, Ger. 51/F3
Sykesville, Md, US 138/B5
Sykkylven, Nor. 37/C3
Syktyvkar, Rus. 61/L3
Sylacauga, Al, US 133/G3
Sylarna (peak), Swe. 37/E3
Sylhet (pol. reg.), Bang. 85/H3
Sylva (riv.), Rus. 61/N4
Sylvan Lake, Mi, US 135/F6
Sylvania, Oh, US 130/D3
Sylvenstein-Stausee (lake), Ger. 57/H2
Sými, Gre. 90/A2
Syntagma, Gre. 47/N8
Syosset, NY, US 139/L8
Syowa, Japan, Ant. 160/C
Syracuse, NY, US 130/E3
Syracuse, Ut, US 137/J11
Syracuse Hancock (int'l arpt.), NY, US 130/E3
Syrdarīya (riv.), Kaz. 67/F5
Syria (ctry.) 90/D3
Syriam, Myan. 83/G4
Syrian (des.), Jor. 88/C2
Sysmä, Fin. 39/L1
Sysola (riv.), Rus. 61/L3
Syzran', Rus. 63/J1
Szabolcs-Szatmár-Bereg (co.), Hun. 41/L4
Szamotuły, Pol. 41/J2
Szarvas, Hun. 48/E2
Százhalombatta, Hun. 49/Q10
Szczebrzeszyn, Pol. 41/M3
Szczecin, Pol. 38/F5
Szczecin (prov.), Pol. 38/F5
Szczecinek, Pol. 38/G5
Szczytna, Pol. 41/J3
Szczytno, Pol. 41/L2
Szeged, Hun. 48/E2
Szeghalom, Hun. 48/E2
Székesfehérvár, Hun. 48/D2
Szekszárd, Hun. 48/D2
Szendro, Hun. 48/E1
Szent László-Vize (riv.), Hun. 49/Q10
Szentendre, Hun. 49/R9
Szentes, Hun. 48/E2
Szentlorinc, Hun. 48/C2
Szerencs, Hun. 41/L4
Szeskie (peak), Pol. 39/K4
Sziget-Szentmiklós, Hun. 49/R10
Szigetvár, Hun. 48/C2
Szirák, Hun. 41/K5
Szolnok, Hun. 48/E2
Szombathely, Hun. 43/M3
Szprotawa, Pol. 41/H3
Sztum, Pol. 39/H5
Szubin, Pol. 41/J2
Szydłowiec, Pol. 41/L3

T

Ta Khmau, Camb. 78/D4
Taabo, Barrage de (dam), C.d'Iv. 102/D5
Tabaco, Phil. 79/D5
Tabaquite, Trin. 153/F2
Ţabarqah, Tun. 100/L6
Ţabas, Iran 89/G2
Tabasará (mts.), Pan. 145/F4
Tabasco (state), Mex. 140/C4
Tabatinga, Serra da (mts.), Braz. 151/K6
Tabayama, Japan 77/B2
Tabelbala, Alg. 98/E3
Tabelbalet (well), Alg. 99/G4
Ta'benghisa, Ponta (pt.), Malta 46/L7
Taber, Ab, Can. 126/E3
Tabernes de Valldigna, Sp. 45/E3
Tabiang, Kiri. 116/F5
Tabira, Braz. 154/C2

229
Tabit – Teifi

Tabiteuea (isl.), Kiri. 116/G5
Tablas (isl.), Phil. 81/F1
Tablas de Daimiel NP, Sp. 44/D3
Table (bay), SAfr. 106/B4
Table (mtn.), SAfr. 106/L10
Table Rock (lake), Mo, US 129/J3
Tabligbo, Togo 103/F5
Tábor, Czh. 55/H4
Tabora (pol. reg.), Tanz. 104/B4
Tabora, Tanz. 104/B4
Tabou, C.d'Iv. 102/D5
Tabuk, Phil. 79/D4
Tabūk, SAr. 88/C3
Tabuleiro do Norte, Braz. 154/C2
Ţaburbah, Tun. 46/A4
Tabwemasana (peak), Van. 116/F6
Tacabamba, Peru 156/B2
Tacámbaro de Codallos, Mex. 143/E5
Tacaná (vol.), Mex. 144/C3
Tacarcuna (mtn.), Pan. 152/B2
Tacheng, China 70/D2
Tachibana (bay), Japan 74/A4
Tachikawa, Japan 75/F3
Tachinger (lake), Ger. 55/F7
Tachira (state), Ven. 145/H5
Tachov, Czh. 55/F3
Tacloban, Phil. 79/E5
Tacna, Peru 156/D5
Tacna (dept.), Peru 156/D5
Tacoma, Wa, US 126/C4
Tacora (vol.), Chile 156/D5
Tacotalpa, Mex. 144/C2
Tacuarembó, Uru. 157/E3
Tacuarembó (dept.), Uru. 159/G2
Tacutu (riv.), Braz. 153/F4
Tadaoka, Japan 77/H7
Ta'Delimara (pt.), Malta 46/M7
Tademaït, Plateau du (plat.), Alg. 96/F2
Tādepallegūdem, India 82/D4
Tadley, Eng, UK 33/E4
Tadmur, Syria 90/D3
Tadó, Col. 152/B3
Tado, Japan 77/L5
Tadohae Hasang NP, SKor. 73/C5
Tadotsu, Japan 74/C3
Tādpatri, India 82/C5
Tadrart (mts.), Alg.,Libya 96/H2
Tadworth, Eng, UK 30/C3
T'aean, SKor. 73/D4
T'aebaek, SKor. 73/E4
Taebudo (isl.), SKor. 73/F7
Taech'ŏn, SKor. 73/D4
Taech'ŏng (isl.), SKor. 73/C4
Taedŏk, SKor. 73/D5
Taedong (riv.), NKor. 73/D3
Taegang-got (pt.), NKor. 73/D3
Taegu, SKor. 73/E5
Taegu Gwangyŏksi (prov.), SKor. 74/A3
Taehŭksan (isl.), SKor. 73/C5
Taehwa (isl.), NKor. 73/C3
T'aein, SKor. 73/D5
Taejŏn, SKor. 73/D4
Taejŏn Gwangyŏksi (prov.), SKor. 73/D4
Taeryŏng (riv.), NKor. 73/C2
Tafalla, Sp. 44/E1
Tafassasset, Oued (riv.), Alg. 99/H4
Taff (riv.), Wal, UK 32/C3
Tafi Viejo, Arg. 157/C2
Tafraout, Mor. 98/C3
Taft, La, US 137/P17
Taft, Iran 88/F2
Taftān (mtn.), Iran 89/H3
Taga, Japan 77/K5
Taganrog, Rus. 62/F3
Tagant (pol. reg.), Mrta. 102/C2
Tagarav (peak), Trkm. 63/L5
Tagawa, Japan 74/B4
Taggia, It. 58/A5
Taghit, Alg. 99/E3
Tagish, Yk, Can. 134/M3
Tagliamento (riv.), It. 43/K3
Taglio di Po, It. 59/F3
Tagolo (pt.), Phil. 81/F2
Taguasco, Cuba 145/G1
Taguatinga, Braz. 151/J7
Tagula (isl.), PNG 116/E6
Tagum, Phil. 81/G2
Tagun (riv.), Rus. 61/P4
Tagus (riv.), Sp. 27/D5
Tagus Rio Tejo (lake), Port. 45/P10
Tagus (Tajo) (riv.), Sp. 44/C3
Tahan (peak), Malay. 80/B3
Tahanea (isl.), FrPol. 117/L6
Tahanroz'ka Zatoka (gulf), Rus.,Ukr. 62/F3
Tahara, Japan 77/M6
Tahat (peak), Alg. 99/G5
Tahat, Oued et (riv.), Alg. 100/F5
Tahe, China 71/M1
Tahilt, Mong. 70/G2
Tahir (pass), Turk. 63/G5
Tahiti (isl.), FrPol. 117/L6
Tahkuna (pt.), Est. 39/K2
Tahlequah, Ok, US 129/J4
Tahmoor, Austl. 115/D2
Tahneta (pass), Ak, US 134/J3
Tahoe (lake), Ca,Nv, US 122/D5
Tahoka, Tx, US 129/G4
Tahoua (dept.), Niger 103/G3
Tahoua, Niger 103/G3
Tahsis, BC, Can. 126/B3
Tahuamanu (riv.), Peru 156/D3
Tahuamanú, Peru 156/D3
Tahuata (isl.), FrPol. 117/L6
Tahulandang (isl.), Indo. 81/G3
Tahuya, Wa, US 135/A3
Tahuya (riv.), Wa, US 135/B3
Tai Long Wan (bay), China 71/V10
Tai Mo Shan (peak), China 71/U10
Taï, PN de, C.d'Iv. 96/D6
Tai Po, China 71/U10
Tai Xian, China 72/E4
Tai'an, China 73/B2
Tai'an, China 72/D3
Taiaret (well), Mor. 98/B5
Taibus, China 71/L3
Taicang, China 72/L8
T'aichung, Tai. 79/D3
Taiei, Japan 77/E2
Taieri (riv.), NZ 117/S12
Taigu, China 72/C3
Taihang (mts.), China 72/C3
Taihe, China 79/B2
Taihe, China 72/C4
Taikang, China 72/C4
Taiki, Japan 76/C2
Tailem Bend, Austl. 113/H5
Taima, Japan 77/J6
Tain, Sc, UK 36/B1
T'ainan, Tai. 79/D3
Tainaron (cape), Gre. 47/H4
Taingainony, Madg. 107/H8
Taino, It. 58/B1
Taiobeiras, Braz. 154/B4
T'aipei (cap.), Tai. 79/D2
Taiping, Malay. 80/B3
Taiping, China 79/C1
Taisha, Japan 74/C3
Taishan, China 79/B3
Taishi, Japan 77/J6
Taishun, China 79/C2
Taiskirchen im Innkreis, Aus. 55/G6
Taissy, Fr. 53/D5
Taitao (pen.), Chile 147/B7
Taiti (peak), Kenya 104/B2
T'aitung, Tai. 79/D3
Taiwan (ctry.) 79/D3
Taiwan (str.), China,Tai 116/A2
Taixing, China 72/E4
Taiyetos (mts.), Gre. 47/H4
Taiyuan, China 72/C3
Taizhou, China 72/D4
Taizi (riv.), China 72/F2
Ta'izz, Yem. 88/D6
Tāj Mahal, India 84/B2
Tajikistan (ctry.) 87/E5
Tajima, Japan 75/F2
Tajimi, Japan 77/M5
Tajiri, Japan 77/H7
Tājpur, India 84/B1
Tajrīsh, Iran 88/F1
Tajumulco (vol.), Guat. 144/D3
Tajuña (riv.), Sp. 44/D2
Tak, Thai. 78/B2
Takahagi, Japan 75/G2
Takahama, Japan 77/J5
Takahama, Japan 77/L6
Takahashi (riv.), Japan 74/C3
Takahashi, Japan 74/C3
Takahata, Japan 75/G1
Takaishi, Japan 77/H6
Takamatsu, Japan 74/D3
Takami-yama (peak), Japan 77/K7
Takanabe, Japan 74/B4
Takane, Japan 77/A2
Takanosu, Japan 76/B3
Takanosu-yama (peak), Japan 77/C2
Takaoka, Japan 75/E2
Takapuna, NZ 117/S10
Takarazuka, Japan 77/H6
Takaroa (isl.), FrPol. 117/L6
Takasaki, Japan 75/F2
Takashima, Japan 77/K5
Takatomi, Japan 77/L5
Takatsuki, Japan 77/J7
Takatsuki, Japan 77/K5
Takatsuki, Japan 77/J6
Takayama, Japan 75/E2
Takefu, Japan 74/E3
Takehara, Japan 74/C3
Tākestān, Iran 88/E1
Taketa, Japan 74/B4
Taketoyo, Japan 77/L6
Takhatgarh, India 82/B2
Takhatpur, India 84/C4
Takht-e Jamshīd (ruin), Iran 88/F3
Takht-i-Bhāi, Pak. 86/A2
Taki, Japan 77/L7
Takijuq (lake), Nun., Can. 122/E2
Takikawa, Japan 76/B2
Takino, Japan 77/G6
Takla (lake), BC, Can. 126/B2
Takla Makan (des.), China 67/H6
Tako, Japan 77/E2
Takoradi, Gha. 103/E5
Takouch (cape), Alg. 100/K6
Taksony, Hun. 49/R10
Tala, Mex. 142/E4
Talā, Egypt 91/B4
Tala, Uru. 159/L11
Talagang, Pak. 86/B3
Talagante, Chile 158/N8
Talāja, India 89/K4
Talak (phys. reg.), Niger 96/G4
Talamanca (mts.), CR 145/F4
Talamba, Pak. 86/B4
Talamona, It. 57/F5
Talang (peak), Indo. 80/B4
Talanga, Hon. 144/E3
Talange, Fr. 53/F5
Talant, Fr. 56/A3
Talara, Peru 156/A2
Talas (obl.), Kyr. 87/F4
Talas, Turk. 90/C2
Talas, Kyr. 87/F4
Talas (riv.), Kaz. 87/F4
Talaud (isl.), Phil. 67/M9
Talavera de la Reina, Sp. 44/C3
Talawakele, SrL. 82/D6
Talayuela, Sp. 44/C3
Talbingo, Austl. 115/D2
Talbot (mt.), Austl. 112/E3
Talbot (co.), Md, US 138/B6
Talca, Chile 158/C2
Talcahuano, Chile 158/B3
Tālcher, India 82/E3
Taldyqorghan (obl.), Kaz. 87/G3
Taldyqorghan, Kaz. 87/G3
Talence, Fr. 42/C4
Talent (riv.), Swi. 56/C4
Talfer (Talvera) (riv.), It. 57/H4
Talgar, Kaz. 87/G4
Taliabu (isl.), Indo. 81/F4
Taliouine, Mor. 98/D3
Talkeetna, Ak, US 134/H3
Ţalkhā, Egypt 91/B4
Tall 'Afar, Iraq 90/E2
Tall al Muqayyar (ruin), Iraq 88/E2
Tall 'Āsūr (peak), Isr. 91/G8
Tall Kayf, Iraq 90/E2
Talladega, Al, US 133/G3
Tallahassee (cap.), Fl, US 133/G4
Tallahatchie (riv.), Ms, US 129/K4
Tallangatta, Austl. 115/C3
Tallanstown, Ire. 34/B4
Tallering (peak), Austl. 112/B4
Talleyville, De, US 138/C4
Tallinn (cap.), Est. 39/L2
Tallman Mountain State Park, NY, US 139/K7
Talloires, Fr. 56/C6
Tallow, Ire. 31/Q10
Tallulah, La, US 129/K4
Tallulah (falls), Ga, US 133/H3
Talmassons, It. 59/G1
Talo (peak), Eth. 97/N5
Taloda, India 89/K4
Tāloqān, Afg. 89/J1
Talpa de Allende, Mex. 142/D4
Talsperre Pöhl (res.), Ger. 55/F1
Taltal, Chile 157/B2
Taltson (riv.), NW, Can. 122/E2
Talumphuk (pt.), Thai. 78/C4
Talvera (Talfer) (riv.), It. 57/H4
Talwāra, India 86/C4
Tam Ky, Viet. 78/E3
Tama, Japan 77/C2
Tama (riv.), Japan 77/C2
Tamagawa, Japan 77/C2
Tamaho, Japan 77/B2
Tamaki, Japan 77/L7
Tamalameque, Col. 152/C2
Tamale, Gha. 103/E4
Tamamura, Japan 77/C1
Taman, Indo. 80/D5
Taman-Rasset, Oued (riv.), Alg. 99/F5
Tamaná (peak), Col. 152/B3
Tamana (isl.), Kiri. 116/G5
Tamanar, Mor. 98/C3
Tamanghasset (prov.), Alg. 103/F1
Tamanghasset, Oued (riv.), Alg. 99/F5
Tamanrasset, Alg. 99/G5
Tamanrasset (prov.), Alg. 99/F4
Tamaqua, Pa, US 138/C2
Tamar (riv.), Eng, UK 32/B5
Tamara (isl.), Japan 75/H8
Tamari, Japan 77/E1
Tamarindo NWR, CR 144/E4
Tamarite de Litera, Sp. 45/F2
Tamaro (peak), Swi. 57/E5
Tamási, Hun. 48/D2
Tamatsukuri, Japan 77/E1
Tamaulipas (state), Mex. 140/B3
Tamazula de Gordiano, Mex. 142/E5
Tamazunchale, Mex. 144/B1
Tamba, Japan 77/H5
Tamba (uplands), Japan 77/H5
Tambacounda (pol. reg.), Sen. 102/B3
Tambacounda, Sen. 102/B3
Tambaoura, Falaise de (cliff), Mali 102/C3
Tambelan (isls.), Indo. 80/C3
Tambellup, Austl. 112/C5
Tambo (riv.), Peru 156/C3
Tambo (peak), Swi. 57/F5
Tambo, Austl. 114/B4
Tambo Colorado (ruin), Peru 156/C4
Tambo de Mora, Peru 156/B4
Tambo Grande, Peru 156/A2
Tambobamba, Peru 156/C4
Tambohorano, Madg. 107/G7
Tambopata (riv.), Peru 156/D4
Tambora (peak), Indo. 81/E5
Tamboril, Braz. 154/B2
Tamboritha (mt.), Austl. 115/C3
Tambov, Rus. 63/G1
Tambovskaya (obl.), Rus. 63/G1
Tambre (riv.), Sp. 44/A1
Tame (riv.), Eng, UK 33/E1
Tame, Col. 152/D3
Tâmega (riv.), Port. 44/B2
Tamentit, Alg. 99/E4
Tamgak (peak), Niger 103/H2
Tamgue (mass.), Gui. 102/B3
Tamiahua, Mex. 144/B1
Tamiahua (lag.), Mex. 144/B1
Tamil Nādu (state), India 82/C5
Taminango, Col. 152/B4
Ţāmīyah, Egypt 91/B5
Tamlūk, India 85/F4
Tammany (mt.), NJ, US 138/C2
Tammela, Fin. 39/K1
Ţammūn, WBnk. 91/D3
Tampa, Fl, US 133/H5
Tampa (int'l arpt.), Fl, US 133/H5
Tampere, Fin. 39/K1
Tampere-Pirkkala (int'l arpt.), Fin. 39/K1
Tampico, Mex. 144/B1
Tampoc (riv.), FrG. 153/H4
Tampon Ambohitra (peak),Madg. 107/J6
Tampulonanjing (peak), Indo. 80/A3
Tamra, Isr. 91/G6
Tamshiyacu, Peru 156/C2
Tamuín (riv.), Mex. 144/B1
Tamuín, Mex. 144/B1
Tamur (riv.), Nepal 85/F2
Tamworth, Austl. 115/D1
Tamworth, Eng, UK 33/E1
Tamyang, SKor. 73/D5
Tan (riv.), China 83/K3
Tan An, Viet. 78/D4
Tan-Tan, Mor. 98/C3
Tana (riv.), Kenya 93/G5
Tana (lake), Eth. 93/F3
Tana River Primate Nat'l Rsv., Kenya 104/D3
Tanabe, Japan 74/D4
Tanabe, Japan 77/J6
Tanabi, Braz. 155/B2
Tanacross, Ak, US 134/K3
Tanafjorden (estu.), Nor. 37/J1
Tanaga (vol.), Ak, US 134/C6
Tanaga (isl.), Ak, US 65/U4
Tanagura, Japan 75/G2
Tanah Merah, Malay. 83/H6
Tanahbala (isl.), Indo. 80/A4
Tanakpur, India 84/C1
Tanambe, Madg. 107/J7
Tanami (des.), Austl. 109/C2
Tanana, Ak, US 134/H2
Tanana (riv.), Ak, US 134/J3
Tanandava, Madg. 107/G8
Tanaro (riv.), It. 43/G4
Tancheng, China 72/D4
Tanch'ŏn, NKor. 73/E2
Tancítaro, Pico de (peak), Mex. 142/E5
Tancitaro, PN de, Mex. 140/A4
Tanda (lake), Mali 102/D3
Tānda, India 84/D2
Tānda, India 84/B1
Tandag, Phil. 81/G2
Ţăndărei, Rom. 49/H3
Tandil, Arg. 158/F3
Tāndliānwāla, Pak. 86/B4
Tando Ādam, Pak. 89/J3
Tando Allāhyār, Pak. 89/J3
Tando Muhammad Khān, Pak. 89/J3
Tandou (lake), Austl. 109/D4
Tandragee, NI, UK 34/B3
Tanem Taunggyi (range), Thai. 83/G4
Tanezrouft (des.), Alg. 93/B2
Tanezrouft-n-Ahenet (des), Alg. 99/F5
Tang (riv.), China 72/C4
Tanga (pol. reg.), Tanz. 104/C4
Tanga, Tanz. 104/C4
Tangail, Bang. 85/G3
Tangail (pol. reg.), Bang. 85/G3
Tanganyika (lake), D.R. Congo 93/F5
Tangará da Serra, Braz. 150/G6
Tangent (pt.), Ak, US 134/G1
Tanger, Mor. 100/B2
Tanger (prov.), Mor. 100/A2
Tangerhütte, Ger. 40/F2
Tangermünde, Ger. 40/F2
Tanggula (mts.), China 70/E5
Tanghe, China 72/C4
Tangi, Pak. 86/A2
Tangipahoa (riv.), La, US 137/P16
Tangipahoa (parish), La, US 137/P16
Tangjin, SKor. 73/D4
Tanglewilde-Thompson Place, Wa, US 135/B3
Tangshan, China 72/J7
Tangub, Phil. 79/D6
Tangyin, China 72/C4
Tangyuan, China 71/N2
Tanhaçu, Braz. 154/B4
Tanigumi, Japan 77/L4
Tanimbar (isl.), Indo. 67/N10
Taninges, Fr. 56/C5
Tanintharyi (state), Myan. 83/G5
Tanjay, Phil. 79/D6
Tanjungbalai, Indo. 80/A3
Tanjungkarang-Telukbetung, Indo. 80/C5
Tanjungpandan, Indo. 80/C4
Tanjungpinang, Indo. 80/B3
Tanjungpura, Indo. 80/A3
Tānk, Pak. 86/A3
Tankwa Karoo NP, SAfr. 106/B4
Tann, Ger. 55/F6
Tanna (isl.), Van. 116/F6
Tannan, Japan 77/H5
Tannersville, Pa, US 138/C1
Tannheim, Aus. 57/G3
Tannu-Ola (mts.) 70/F1
Tano (riv.), Gha. 96/E6
Tânout, Niger 103/H3
Tanquián de Escobedo, Mex. 144/B1
Tansen, Nepal 84/D2
Ţanţā, Egypt 91/B4
Tantallon, Md, US 138/A6
Tantō, Japan 77/G5
Tantoyuca, Mex. 144/B1
Tanuku, India 82/D4
Tanumshede, Swe. 38/D2
Tanunda, Austl. 115/A2
Tanyang, SKor. 73/E4
Tanzania (ctry.) 104/B4
Tanzawa-yama (peak), Japan 77/C3
Tao (isl.), Myan. 78/B3
Taolañaro, Madg. 107/H9
Taormina, It. 46/D4
Tāoru, India 86/D5
Taos, NM, US 129/F3
Taounate (town), Mor. 100/B2
Taounate, Mor. 100/B2
Taourirt, Alg. 99/F4
Taourirt, Mor. 100/C2
T'aoyüan, Tai. 79/D2
Taoyuan, China 83/K2
Tap Mun Chau (isl.), China 71/V10
Tap O'Noth (hill), Sc, UK 36/D2
Tapa, Est. 39/L2
Tapachula, Mex. 144/C3
Tapajós (riv.), Braz. 147/D3
Tapanahoni (riv.), Sur. 151/G3
Tapanti Nat'l Wild. Ref., CR 145/F4
Tapauá (riv.), Braz. 150/E5
Tapauá, Braz. 150/F5
Tapaz, Phil. 79/D5
Tapejara, Braz. 155/A4
Tapes, Braz. 155/B4
Tapeta, Libr. 102/C5
Tapia de Casariego, Sp. 44/B1
Tápiche (riv.), Peru 156/C2
Tapilula, Mex. 144/C2
Tapis (peak), Malay. 80/B3
Tapo, Peru 156/C3
Tapoa (prov.), Burk. 103/F3
Tapolca, Hun. 48/C2
Tappahannock, Va, US 130/E4
Tappan, NY, US 139/K7
Tappan Zee (lake), NY, US 139/E1
Tappan Zee (riv.), NY, US 139/K7
Tappi-zaki (pt.), Japan 76/B3
Tapps (lake), Wa, US 135/C3
Tāpti (riv.), India 89/J4
Ţāq Kisrā (Ctesiphon) (ruin), Iraq 90/F3
Taquara, Braz. 155/B4
Taquari (riv.), Braz. 151/G7
Taquari, Braz. 155/B4
Taquaritinga, Braz. 155/B2
Taquarituba, Braz. 155/B2
Taquil, Ecu. 156/B1
Tar (riv.), Kyr. 87/F4
Tara, Rus. 87/F1
Tara (riv.), Yugo. 48/D4
Tara, Austl. 114/C4
Taraba (state), Nga. 103/H5
Taraba (riv.), Nga. 103/H4
Ţarābulus, Leb. 91/D2
Ţarābulus (Tripoli) (cap.), Libya 96/H1
Tarakan, Indo. 81/E3
Taraklı, Turk. 49/K5
Taraku (isl.), Rus. 76/E2
Taralga, Austl. 115/D2
Taranagar, India 86/C5
Tarancón, Sp. 44/D2
Tarangire NP, Tanz. 105/G1
Taranto, It. 47/E2
Taranto, Golfo di (gulf), It. 46/E2
Tarapoto, Peru 156/B2
Tarare, Fr. 42/F4
Tarariras, Uru. 159/K11
Tarascon, Fr. 42/F5
Tarascon-sur-Ariège, Fr. 42/D5
Tarata, Peru 156/D5
Tarauacá, Braz. 156/D3
Tarauacá (riv.), Braz. 156/D2
Taravai (isl.), FrPol. 117/M7
Tarawa (cap.), Kiri. 116/G4
Tarawa (isl.), Kiri. 116/G4
Tarazona, Sp. 44/E3
Tarazona, Sp. 44/E2
Tarbagatay (mts.), Kaz. 70/D2
Tarbat Ness (pt.), Sc, UK 36/C1
Tarbela (dam), Pak. 86/B2
Tarbela (res.), Pak. 86/B2
Tarbes, Fr. 42/D5
Tarbolton, Sc, UK 36/B5
Tarboro, NC, US 133/J3
Tarcento, It. 43/K3
Tarcutta, Austl. 115/C2
Tardes (riv.), Fr. 42/E3
Tardienta, Sp. 45/E2
Tardoire (riv.), Fr. 42/D4
Taree, Austl. 115/E1
Tarf Water (riv.), Sc, UK 34/D2
Tarfâwi (well), Egypt 101/B4
Tarfaya, Mor. 98/B4
Target Rock NWR, NY, US 139/M8
Targuist, Mor. 100/B2
Tarhūnah, Libya 96/H1
Tarifa, Ecu. 156/B1
Tarifa, Sp. 44/C4
Tarija, Bol. 150/F8
Tariku (riv.), Indo. 81/J4
Tariku-Taritatu (plain), Indo. 81/J4
Tarim (basin), China 64/J6
Tarim (riv.), China 64/J5
Tarin (riv.), Afg. 89/J2
Tarin (Torino), It. 43/G4
Taritatu (riv.), Indo. 81/J4
Tarkastad, SAfr. 106/D4
Tarkhankut (cape), Ukr. 49/L3
Tarkwa, Gha. 103/E5
Tarlac, Phil. 79/D4
Tarma, Peru 156/C3
Tarmstedt, Ger. 51/G2
Tarn (riv.), Fr. 42/D5
Tarn Tāran, India 86/C4
Tarnak (riv.), Afg. 89/J2
Tarnobrzeg, Pol. 41/L3
Tarnobrzeg (prov.), Pol. 41/M3
Tarnów, Pol. 41/L3
Tärnsjö, Swe. 38/G1
Taro (riv.), It. 43/J4
Tarō, Japan 76/B3
Ţārom, Iran 89/G3
Taroom, Austl. 114/C4
Tarouca, Port. 44/B2
Taroudannt, Mor. 98/C3
Tarp, Ger. 38/C4
Tarpa, Hun. 48/F1
Tarpon Springs, Fl, US 133/H4
Tarquinia, It. 46/B1
Tarqūmiyah, WBnk. 91/D4
Tarrafal, CpV. 93/K10
Tarragona, Sp. 45/F2
Tarraleah, Austl. 115/C4
Tàrrega, Sp. 45/F2
Tarrenz, Aus. 57/G3
Tarrytown, NY, US 139/K7
Tarsney Lakes, Mo, US 137/E6
Tarsus, Turk. 91/D1
Tarsus (riv.), Turk. 91/D1
Tartagal, Arg. 157/D1
Tartaro (riv.), It. 59/E2
Tartas, Fr. 42/C5
Tartu, Est. 39/M2
Ţarţūs (prov.), Syria 90/C3
Ţarţūs, Syria 91/D2
Tarui, Japan 77/L5
Tarumizu, Japan 74/B5
Tarutao NP, Thai. 78/B5
Tarvagatay (mts.), Mong. 70/G2
Taşağıl, Turk. 91/B1
Täsch, Swi. 56/D5
Taşçı, Turk. 90/C2
Tashkent (cap.), Uzb. 87/E4
Tashkent (int'l arpt.), Uzb. 87/E4
Tasikmalaya, Indo. 80/C5
Taşkent, Turk. 91/C1
Taşköprü, Turk. 62/E4
Taşlıçay, Turk. 63/G5
Tasman (pen.), Austl. 109/D5
Tasman (sea), Austl.,NZ 116/E8
Tasman (bay), NZ 109/H7
Tasman Head (cape), Austl. 115/C4
Tasmania, Austl. 115/C3
Tasmania (state), Austl. 109/D5
Tăşnad, Rom. 48/F2
Taşova, Turk. 62/F4
Tasquillo, Mex. 143/K6
Tassili-n-Ajjer (mts.), Alg. 99/G4
Tassili Oua-n Ahaggar (mts.), Alg. 99/G5
Tasu, BC, Can. 134/M5
Taşucu, Turk. 91/C1
Tata, Mor. 98/D3
Tata, Hun. 48/D2
Tatabánya, Hun. 48/D2
Tatachikapika (riv.), On, Can. 130/D2
Tatakoto (isl.), FrPol. 117/L6
Tatamy, Pa, US 138/C2
Tatar (str.), Rus. 67/P5
Tatarlar, Turk. 47/K2
Tatarsk, Rus. 87/G1
Tatarstan (aut. rep.), Rus. 64/Q6
Taţāwīn, Tun. 96/H1
Taţāwīn (gov.), Tun. 99/H2
Tate-yama (peak), Japan 75/E2
Tatebayashi, Japan 77/D1
Tateshina, Japan 77/A1
Tateyama, Japan 75/F3
Tathlina (lake), NW, Can. 122/E2
Tathra, Austl. 115/D3
Tatilt (well), Mrta. 102/B2
Tatitlek, Ak, US 134/J3
Tatnam (cape), Mb, Can. 122/G3
Tatomi, Japan 77/B2
Tatranský NP, Slvk. 41/K4
Tatsuno, Japan 75/E3
Tatsuta, Japan 77/L5
Tatura, Austl. 115/C3
Tatvan, Turk. 90/E2
Tauá, Braz. 154/B2
Taubaté, Braz. 211/H8
Tauber (riv.), Ger. 40/E4
Tauberbischofsheim, Ger. 54/C3
Tauca, Peru 156/B3
Taufkirchen, Ger. 55/F6
Taufkirchen an der Pram, Aus. 55/G6
Taufstein (peak), Ger. 54/C1
Taulihawa, Nepal 84/D2
Taung, SAfr. 106/D2
Taungdwingyi, Myan. 83/G3
Taunggyi, Myan. 83/G3
Taungup, Myan. 83/F4
Taunsa, Pak. 86/A4
Taunton, Ma, US 131/G3
Taunton, Eng, UK 32/C4
Taunus (range), Ger. 54/A2
Taunusstein, Ger. 54/B2
Taupo, NZ 117/T10
Taupo (lake), NZ 109/H6
Tauragė, Lith. 39/K4
Tauranga, NZ 117/T10
Taurion (riv.), Fr. 42/D3
Taurisano, It. 47/F3
Taurus (mts.), Turk. 90/C2
Tauste, Sp. 44/E2
Taute (riv.), Fr. 42/C2
Tauu (isls.), PNG 116/E5
Tavanbulag, Mong. 70/H2
Tavannes, Swi. 56/D3
Tavaputs (plat.), Ut, US 128/E3
Tavarnelle, It. 59/E5
Tavarnuzze, It. 59/E5
Tavas, Turk. 90/B2
Tavaux, Fr. 56/B4
Tavazzano, It. 58/C2
Tavda (riv.), Rus. 64/G4
Tavernerio, It. 58/C1
Taverny, Fr. 30/J4
Taviano, It. 47/F3
Tavira, Port. 44/B4
Tavoy (pt.), Myan. 78/B3
Tavoy (Dawei), Myan. 78/B3
Tavşanlı, Turk. 62/D5
Tavy (riv.), Eng, UK 32/B6
Taw (riv.), Eng, UK 32/C5
Tawaramoto, Japan 77/J6
Tawas City, Mi, US 130/D2
Tawau, Malay. 81/E3
Tawe (riv.), Wal, UK 32/C3
Tawern, Ger. 53/F4
Tāwī (riv.), India 86/C3
Tawi-Tawi (isl.), Phil. 79/C6
Ţāwūq, Iraq 90/F3
Tawzar, Tun. 96/G1
Tawzar (gov.), Tun. 99/G2
Taxco, Mex. 143/K8
Taxila (ruin), Pak. 86/B3
Taxila, Pak. 86/B3
Taxkorgan Tajik Zizhixian, China 89/L1
Tay (lake), Sc, UK 36/B3
Tay (riv.), Sc, UK 36/C3
Tay, Firth of (inlet), Sc, UK 36/C4
Tay Ninh, Viet. 78/D4
Tayabamba, Peru 156/B3
Taylor, Mi, US 135/F7
Taylorsville-Bennion, Ut, US 137/K12
Taymyr (riv.), Rus. 64/K2
Taymyr (isl.), Rus. 65/L2
Taymyr (pen.), Rus. 67/H2
Taymyrskiy (aut. okrug), Rus. 67/H2
Tayoltita, Mex. 142/D3
Tayport, Sc, UK 36/D4
Tayrona, PN, Col. 152/C2
Tayshet, Rus. 65/K4
Taytay, Phil. 81/E1
Taz (riv.), Rus. 67/H3
Taza (prov.), Mor. 100/C2
Taza, Mor. 100/B2
Tazawako, Japan 76/B4
Tazekka (peak), Mor. 100/B2
Tazenakht, Mor. 98/D3
Tazewell, Tn, US 130/D4
Tāzirbū (oasis), Libya 97/K2
Tazumal (ruin), ESal. 144/D3
T'bilisi (cap.), Geo. 63/H4
T'boli, Phil. 79/D6
Tchamba, Togo 103/F4
Tchaourou, Ben. 103/F4
Tchefuncta (riv.), La, US 137/P16
Tchibanga, Gabon 96/H8
Tcholliré, Camr. 96/H6
Tczew, Pol. 39/H4
Te Anau, NZ 117/R12
Te Araroa, NZ 117/T10
Te Aroha, NZ 117/T10
Te Awamutu, NZ 117/T10
Te Kao, NZ 117/S9
Te Kuiti, NZ 117/T10
Tea (riv.), Braz. 150/E4
Teacapán, Mex. 142/D4
Teague, Tx, US 129/H5
Teaneck, NJ, US 139/J8
Teano, It. 46/D2
Teapa, Mex. 144/C2
Tearce, FYROM 47/G1
Tebak (peak), Indo. 80/B4
Tébessa (prov.), Alg. 99/G2
Tébessa (mts.), Alg. 100/L7
Tébessa, Alg. 100/L7
Tebesselamane (well), Mali 103/F2
Tebicuary (riv.), Par. 157/E2
Tebingtinggi, Indo. 80/A3
Tebulos-mta (peak), Rus. 63/H4
Tecalitlán, Mex. 142/E5
Tecamac, Mex. 143/R9
Tecamachalco, Mex. 143/M8
Tecate, Mex. 128/C4
Tech (riv.), Fr. 42/E5
Techirghiol, Rom. 49/J3
Tecirli, Turk. 90/D2
Tecka, Arg. 158/C4
Tecka (riv.), Arg. 158/C4
Tecklenberg, Ger. 51/E4
Tecolutla, Mex. 143/M6
Tecomán, Mex. 142/E5
Tecozautla, Mex. 143/K6
Tecpan de Galeana, Mex. 143/E5
Tecuala, Mex. 142/D4
Tecuci, Rom. 49/H3
Tecumseh, Mi, US 130/D3
Tecumseh, Ne, US 129/H2
Tecumseh, On, Can. 135/G7
Tedjert (well), Alg. 99/H1
Tedzhen (riv.), Trkm. 64/G6
Tees (bay), Eng, Uk 35/G2
Tees (riv.), Eng, UK 35/G3
Teesside (int'l arpt.), Eng, UK 35/G3
Tefé (riv.), Braz. 150/E4
Tefé, Braz. 150/E4
Teferič, Yugo. 48/E4
Tega (lake), Japan 77/E2
Tegal, Indo. 80/C5
Tegel (int'l arpt.), Ger. 40/Q6
Tegelen, Neth. 50/D6
Tegeler (lake), Ger. 40/Q6
Tegheri (well), Libya 99/H4
Teghra, India 85/E3
Tegid, Llyn (lake), Wal, UK 34/E6
Teglio, It. 57/G5
Tégouma (riv.), Niger 103/H3
Tegsh, Mong. 70/G2
Tegucigalpa (cap.), Hon. 144/E3
Tehek (lake), Nun., Can. 122/G2
Tehrān (cap.), Iran 88/F1
Tehuacán, Mex. 143/M8
Tehuantepec (isth.), Mex. 143/G5
Tehuantepec (riv.), Mex. 144/C2
Tehuantepec (gulf), Mex. 144/C3
Teide, Pico de (peak), Sp. 98/A3
Teifi (riv.), Wal, UK 32/B2

Teifi – Tizay

Teifiside (valley), Wal, UK 32/B2
Teiga (plat.), Sudan 97/L4
Teign (riv.), Eng, UK 32/C5
Teignmouth, Eng, UK 32/C5
Teisendorf, Ger. 55/F7
Teith (riv.), Sc, UK 36/B4
Tejen, Trkm. 89/H1
Tejn, Den. 38/F4
Tejupilco de Hidalgo, Mex. 143/E5
Tekamah, Ne, US 127/J5
Tekāri, India 85/E3
Tekax de Álvaro Obregón, Mex. 144/D1
Teke, Turk. 49/J5
Tekeli, Kaz. 87/G4
Tekes (riv.), China 64/J5
Tekezē Wenz (riv.), Eth. 97/N5
Tekiliktag (peak), China 70/D4
Tekirdağ, Turk. 49/H5
Tekirdag (prov.), Turk. 62/C4
Tekirdağ (prov.), Turk. 49/H5
Tekit, Mex. 144/D1
Tekkali, India 82/D4
Tekke, Turk. 90/D1
Tekkeköy, Turk. 62/F4
Tekman, Turk. 63/G5
Tel Aviv (dist.), Isr. 91/D3
Tel Aviv-Yafo, Isr. 91/F7
Tel Megiddo (ruin), Isr. 91/G6
Tela, Hon. 144/E3
Télagh, Alg. 100/D2
T'elavi, Geo. 63/H4
Telde, Sp. 98/B3
Télé (lake), Mali 102/D2
Telêmaco Borba, Braz. 155/B3
Telemark (co.), Nor. 37/D4
Telen (riv.), Indo. 81/E3
Teleorman (prov.), Rom. 49/G4
Telertheba (peak), Alg. 99/G4
Teles Pires (riv.), Braz. 147/D3
Telford, Pa, US 138/C3
Telford and Wrekin (co.), Eng, UK 35/F6
Telford Dawley, Eng, UK 32/D1
Telfs, Aus. 57/H3
Telgate, It. 58/C1
Telgte, Ger. 51/E5
Telica, Nic. 144/E3
Télig (well), Mali 98/E5
Télimélé, Gui. 102/B4
Telkwa, BC, Can. 126/B2
Tell City, In, US 130/C4
Teller, Ak, US 134/E2
Telli (lake), Mrta. 98/C4
Tellicherry, India 82/C5
Tellin, Belg. 53/E3
Telluride, Co, US 128/F3
Telok Anson, Malay. 80/B3
Teloloapan, Mex. 143/F5
Telšiai, Lith. 39/K4
Teltow, Ger. 40/Q7
Teltow (reg.), Ger. 41/G2
Tema, Gha. 103/E5
Temagami (lake), On, Can. 130/D2
Temax, Mex. 144/D1
Tembilahan, Indo. 80/B4
Tembisa, SAfr. 106/E2
Temblador, Ven. 153/F2
Teme (riv.), Eng, UK 32/C2
Temecula, Ca, US 136/C4
Temelkovo, Bul. 47/H1
Temerin, Yugo. 48/D3
Temerloh, Malay. 80/B3
Temirtau, Kaz. 87/F2
Témiscamie (riv.), Qu, Can. 131/F1
Témiscaming, Qu, Can. 130/E2
Temoaya, Mex. 143/Q10
Temoe (isl.), FrPol. 117/M7
Temora, Austl. 115/C2
Tempe, Az, US 137/S19
Tempio Pausania, It. 46/A2
Temple, Pa, US 138/C3
Temple City, Ca, US 136/F7
Temple of Lady Chua Xu, Viet. 78/D4
Templemore, Ire. 31/Q10
Templepatrick, NI, UK 34/B2
Templeuve, Fr. 52/C2
Templeville, Md, US 138/C5
Templin, Ger. 41/G2
Templiner (lake), Ger. 40/Q7
Tempoal de Sánchez, Mex. 144/B1
Temryuk, Rus. 62/F3
Temse, Belg. 53/D1
Temuco, Chile 158/B3
Temuka, NZ 117/S11
Ten Boer, Neth. 50/D2
Tena, Ecu. 152/B5
Tena Kourou (peak), Mali 96/D5
Tenabo, Mex. 144/D1
Tenafly, NJ, US 139/K8
Tenakee Springs, Ak, US 134/L4
Tenancingo, Mex. 143/K8
Tenango, Mex. 143/R10
Tenango de Arista, Mex. 143/Q10
Tenasserim (range), Myan. 78/B3
Tenasserim, Myan. 78/B3
Tenay, Fr. 56/B6
Tenby, Wal, UK 32/B3
Tende, Fr. 43/G4
Tende, Col de (pass), Fr. 58/A4
Tenderovsk (bay), Ukr. 49/K2
Tenderovsk Spit (isl.), Ukr. 49/K2
Tendō, Japan 76/B4
Tendre (peak), Swi. 56/C4
Ténenkou, Mali 102/D3
Ténéré (des.), Niger 96/G4
Ténéré du Tafassasset (des.), Niger 96/G3
Tenerife, Col. 152/C2
Tenerife (isl.), Sp. 93/A2
Ténès, Alg. 100/F4
Tenes (riv.), Sp. 45/L6
Teng (riv.), Myan. 83/G3
Teng Xian, China 72/D4
Tenggarong, Indo. 81/E4
Tengger (des.), China 70/H4
Tengiz Köli (lake), Kaz. 64/G4
Tenguel, Ecu. 152/B5
Tenibres (peak), It. 43/G4
Teniente Enciso, PN, Par. 157/D1
Teningen, Ger. 56/D1
Tenja, Cro. 48/D3
Tenkodogo, Burk. 103/E4
Tenmile (riv.), Az, US 128/D4
Tennessee (state), US 133/G3
Tennessee (riv.), US 133/F3
Tenneville, Belg. 53/E3
Tennuaca (well), Mor. 98/B5
Teno, Chile 158/C2
Tenojoki (riv.), Fin. 37/H1
Tenosique de Pino Suárez, Mex. 144/D2
Tenri, Japan 77/J6
Tenryū, Japan 75/E3
Tenryū (riv.), Japan 75/E3
Tensift (pol. reg.), Mor. 98/C3
Tensift, Oued (riv.), Mor. 98/C3
Tenterfield, Austl. 115/E1
Tentolomatinan (peak), Indo. 81/F3
Tenus (peak), Kenya 104/B2
Teo, Sp. 44/A1
Teocaltiche, Mex. 140/A3
Teocelo, Mex. 143/N7
Teodelina, Arg. 158/E2
Teodoro Sampaio, Braz. 155/A2
Teófilo Otoni, Braz. 154/B5
Teopisca, Mex. 144/C2
Teotihuacán (ruin), Mex. 143/R9
Teotihuacán, Mex. 143/R9
Teotitlán del Camino, Mex. 144/B2
Tepache, Mex. 142/C2
Tepalcatepec, Mex. 142/E5
Tepalcingo, Mex. 143/L8
Tepatitlán de Morelos, Mex. 140/A3
Tepatlaxco, Mex. 143/M7
Tepeapulco, Mex. 143/L7
Tepebaşı, Turk. 91/C1
Tepehuaje, Mex. 143/F4
Tepehuanes, Mex. 142/D3
Tepeji del Río de Ocampo, Mex. 143/K7
Tepelenë, Alb. 47/G2
Tepelská Plošina (mts.), Czh. 55/F2
Tepetlaoxtoc, Mex. 143/R9
Tepexi, Mex. 143/M8
Tepexpan, Mex. 143/R9
Tepic, Mex. 142/D4
Teplá (riv.), Czh. 40/G3
Teplá Vltava (riv.), Czh. 55/G5
Teplice, Czh. 41/G3
Tepoca (cape), Mex. 142/B2
Tepoca, Cabo (cape), Mex. 142/B2
Tepoto (isl.), FrPol. 117/L6
Tepotzotlán, Mex. 143/Q9
Tepoztlán, Mex. 143/K8
Tequila, Mex. 142/E4
Tequisquiapan, Mex. 143/F4
Tequixquiac, Mex. 143/K7
Ter (riv.), Sp. 45/G1
Ter Aar, Neth. 50/B4
Téra, Niger 103/F3
Tera (riv.), Sp. 44/B1
Teraina (Washington) (isl.), Kiri. 117/J4
Teramo, It. 43/K5
Terang, Austl. 115/B3
Tercan, Turk. 62/G5
Terceira (isl.), Azor., Port. 45/S12
Terek (riv.), Rus. 63/H4
Terepaima, PN, Ven. 152/D2
Teresina, Braz. 154/B2
Teresópolis, Braz. 211/L7
Terespol, Pol. 41/M2
Tergnier, Fr. 52/C4
Tergun Daba (mts.), China 70/F4
Terheijden, Neth. 50/B5
Teriberskiy (pt.), Rus. 60/G1
Terkaplesterpoelen (lake), Neth. 50/C2
Terlan (Terlano), It. 57/H4
Termas de Río Hondo, Arg. 157/D2
Termini Imerese, It. 46/C4
Términos (lag.), Mex. 144/D2
Termiz, Uzb. 89/J1
Termo, Ca, US 126/C5
Termoli, It. 46/D1
Termonfeckin, Ire. 34/B4
Termunten, Neth. 50/E2
Ternate, Indo. 81/G3
Ternberg, Aus. 55/H7
Terneuzen, Neth. 50/A6
Terni, It. 46/C1
Ternin (riv.), Fr. 42/F3
Ternoise (riv.), Fr. 52/B3
Ternopil', Ukr. 62/C2
Ternopil's'ka (obl.), Ukr. 62/C2
Terpeniya (bay), Rus. 65/Q5
Terpní, Gre. 47/H2
Terra Nova, Braz. 154/B4
Terra Nova, Braz. 154/C3
Terra Nova NP, Nf, Can. 131/L1
Terrace, BC, Can. 126/A2
Terrace Bay, On, Can. 127/M3
Terracina, It. 46/C2
Terråk, Nor. 37/E2
Terralba, It. 46/A3
Terranuova Bracciolini, It. 59/E5
Terrassa, Sp. 45/L6
Terrasson-la-Villedieu, Fr. 42/D4
Terre Hill, Pa, US 138/B3
Terrebonne, Qu, Can. 131/N6
Terrell Hills, Tx, US 137/U21
Terri (peak), Swi. 57/F4
Terry, Mt, US 127/G4
Terry (lake), Co, US 137/B2
Terrytown, La, US 137/P17
Terschelling (isl.), Neth. 50/C2
Tertenia, It. 46/A3
Teruel, Sp. 45/E2
Terutao (isl.), Thai. 83/G6
Tervel, Bul. 49/H4
Terza Grande (peak), It. 43/K3
Terzo d'Aquileia, It. 59/G1
Tešanj, Bosn. 48/C3
Tescou (riv.), Fr. 42/D5
Tesero, It. 57/H5
Teshekpuk (lake), Ak, US 134/G1
Teshikaga, Japan 76/D2
Teshio (riv.), Japan 76/C1
Teshio, Japan 76/B1
Teshio-dake (peak), Japan 76/C2
Teslić, Bosn. 48/C3
Teslin (riv.), Yk, Can. 122/C2
Teslin (lake), BC, Can. 122/C3
Tessaoua, Niger 103/G3
Tessenderlo, Belg. 53/E1
Tessenie (Teseney), Erit. 88/C5
Test (riv.), Eng, UK 33/E4
Testa del Gargano (pt.), It. 46/E2
Tét, Hun. 48/C2
Tete, Moz. 105/F4
Tête de l'Estrop (peak), Fr. 43/G4
Tetela, Mex. 143/M7
Teterow, Ger. 38/E5
Teteven, Bul. 47/J1
Tetiaroa (isl.), FrPol. 117/L6
Tetlin, Ak, US 134/K3
Tetlin NWR, Ak, US 134/K3
Teton (riv.), Mt, US 126/F4
Tétouan (prov.), Mor. 100/B2
Tétouan, Mor. 100/B2
Tetovo, FYROM 47/G1
Tettnang, Ger. 57/F2
Tetulia (riv.), Bang. 85/H4
Teublitz, Ger. 55/F4
Teuco (riv.), Arg. 157/D1
Teufen, Swi. 57/F3
Teúl de González Ortega, Mex. 142/E4
Teulada (cape), It. 46/A3
Teulon, Mb, Can. 127/J3
Teupasenti, Hon. 144/E3
Teuri (isl.), Japan 76/B1
Teuschnitz, Ger. 55/E2
Teutoburger Wald (for.), Ger. 51/F4
Tevere (Tiber) (riv.), It. 43/K5
Teverya, Isr. 91/D3
Teviot (riv.), Sc, UK 36/D6
Teviotdale (valley), Sc, UK 36/D6
Tewantin-Noosa, Austl. 114/D4
Tewkesbury, Eng, UK 32/D3
Texarkana, Tx, US 129/J4
Texas, Austl. 115/D1
Texas (state), US 132/C4
Texas City, Tx, US 129/J5
Texcoco, Mex. 143/R9
Texel (isl.), Neth. 40/C2
Texhoma, Ok, US 132/C2
Texmelucan, Mex. 143/L7
Texoma (lake), Ok, US 125/G5
Teyateyaneng, Les. 106/D3
Teykovo, Rus. 60/J4
Tezio (peak), It. 43/K5
Teziutlán, Mex. 143/M7
Tezonapa, Mex. 143/N8
Tezontepec, Mex. 143/L7
Tezontepec de Aldama, Mex. 143/K6
Tezoyuca, Mex. 143/R9
Tezpur, India 70/F6
Tezu, India 83/G2
Tezze, It. 59/E1
Tha-Anne (riv.), Nun., Can. 122/G2
Tha Chin (riv.), Thai. 78/B3
Thabana-Ntlenyana (peak), Les. 106/E3
Thabankulu (peak), SAfr. 107/E2
Thaen (pt.), Thai. 78/B4
Thai Binh, Viet. 83/J3
Thai Nguyen, Viet. 83/J3
Thailand (gulf), Asia 78/C4
Thailand (ctry.) 78/C3
Thākurdwāra, India 84/B1
Thal, Pak. 86/A3
Thal (des.), Pak. 86/A4
Thaleban NP, Thai. 78/C5
Thaleischweiler-Fröschen, Ger. 53/G5
Thalerhof (int'l arpt.), Aus. 43/L3
Thalgau, Aus. 55/G7
Thalheim bei Wels, Aus. 55/H6
Thalmässing, Ger. 54/E4
Thalwil, Swi. 57/E3
Thamar, Jabal (peak), Yem. 88/E6
Thame (riv.), Eng, UK 33/F3
Thames (riv.), On, Can. 130/D3
Thames, NZ 117/T10
Thames (riv), Eng., UK 33/G4
Thames Barrier, Eng, UK 30/D2
Thāna, India 89/K5
Thāna Bhawan, India 86/D5
Thānesar, India 86/D5
Thangool, Austl. 114/C4
Thanh Hoa, Viet. 83/J4
Thanjavur, India 82/C5
Thann, Fr. 56/D2
Thannhausen, Ger. 57/G1
Thaon-les-Vosges, Fr. 56/C1
Thar (des.), Pak. 86/A5
Tharād, India 89/K4
Thargomindah, Austl. 114/A5
Tharrawaddy, Myan. 83/G4
Thásos, Gre. 47/J2
Thásos (isl.), Gre. 62/C4
Thatcham, Eng, UK 33/E4
Thatcher, Az, US 128/E4
Thaton, Myan. 78/B2
Thaur, Aus. 57/H3
Thayetmyo, Myan. 83/G4
Thayngen, Swi. 57/E2
Thazi, Myan. 83/G3
The Alamo, Tx, US 137/U21
The Dalles, Or, US 126/C4
The Hague ('s-Gravenhage) (cap.), Neth. 50/B4
The Oaks, Ca, US 136/B1
The Pas, Mb, Can. 127/H2
The Rock, Austl. 115/C2
The Valley (cap.), Angu. 141/N8
The Village, Ok, US 137/M14
The Woodlands, Tx, US 129/J5
Thebes (ruin), Egypt 101/C3
Theilheim, Ger. 54/D3
Thelma, Tx, US 137/T21
Thelon (riv.), NW,Nun., Can. 122/F2
Thémericourt, Fr. 30/H4
Theo (mt.), Austl. 113/F2
Theodore, Sk, Can. 127/H3
Theodore, Austl. 114/C4
Theodore Roosevelt (lake), Az, US 128/E4
Theodore Roosevelt NP, ND, US 127/G4
Thérain (riv.), Fr. 42/D2
Thermaic (gulf), Gre. 62/B4
Thérmi, Gre. 47/H2
Thermopílai (Thermopylae) (pass), Gre. 47/H3
Thermopolis, Wy, US 126/F5
Thérouanne (riv.), Fr. 30/L4
Thesprotikón, Gre. 47/G3
Thessalon, On, Can. 130/D2
Thessaloníki, Gre. 47/H2
Thessaly (reg.), Gre. 47/H3
Thet (riv.), Eng, UK 33/G2
Thetford, Eng, UK 33/G2
Thetford Mines, Qu, Can. 131/G2
Theunissen, SAfr. 106/D3
Theux, Belg. 53/E2
Thève (riv.), Fr. 30/K4
Theydon Bois, Eng, UK 30/D2
Thiais, Fr. 30/K5
Thíamis (riv.), Gre. 47/G3
Thiant, Fr. 52/C3
Thiaucourt-Regniéville, Fr. 53/E6
Thief River Falls, Mn, US 127/J3
Thielle (riv.), Swi. 56/C4
Thielsen (mt.), Or, US 126/C5
Thiene, It. 59/E1
Thiérache (reg.), Fr. 52/C4
Thierhaupten, Ger. 54/D5
Thiers, Fr. 42/E4
Thiers-sur-Thève, Fr. 30/K4
Thierville-sur-Meuse, Fr . 53/E5
Thiès (pol. reg.), Sen. 102/A3
Thiès, Sen. 102/A3
Thika, Kenya 104/C3
Thingvellir NP, Ice. 37/N7
Thionville, Fr. 53/F5
Thíra, Gre. 47/J4
Thíra (isl.), Gre. 47/J4
Third Cataract (falls), Sudan 101/B5
Third Lake, Il, US 135/Q15
Thirlmere (lake), Eng, UK 35/E2
Thirsty (mt.), Austl. 112/D5
Thirtymile (pt.), NY, US 131/V9
Thise, Fr. 56/C3
Thisted, Den. 38/C3
Thistilfjördhur (estu.), Ice. 37/P6
Thistle (isl.), Austl. 113/H5
Thistle (mtn.), Yk, Can. 134/L3
Thitu (isl.) 79/B5
Thívai, Gre. 47/H3
Thiverval-Grignon, Fr. 30/H5
Thjórsá (riv.), Ice. 37/N7
Thlewiaza (riv.), Nun., Can. 122/G2
Thoiry, Fr. 30/H5
Tholen (isl.), Neth. 50/B5
Tholen, Neth. 50/B5
Tholey, Ger. 53/G5
Thomaston, Ga, US 133/G3
Thomastown, Ire. 31/Q10
Thomasville, Al, US 133/G4
Thomasville, NC, US 133/H3
Thomasville, Ga, US 133/H4
Thomasville, Pa, US 138/B4
Thompson, Mb, Can. 127/J2
Thompson (riv.), BC, Can. 126/C3
Thompson (lake), Austl. 112/K7
Thompson Falls, Mt, US 126/E4
Thomsen (riv.), NW, Can. 122/E1
Thomson (riv.), Austl. 109/D3
Thomson, Ga, US 133/H3
Thongwa, Myan. 78/B2
Thonnance-lès-Joinville, Fr . 56/B1
Thonon-les-Bains, Fr. 56/C5
Thoreau, NM, US 128/E4
Thorens-Glières, Fr. 56/C6
Thorhild, Ab, Can. 126/E2
Thorigny-sur-Marne, Fr. 30/L5
Thorlákshöfn, Ice. 37/N7
Thornaby-on-Tees, Eng, UK 35/G2
Thornbury, Eng, UK 32/D3
Thorndale, Pa, US 138/C4
Thorne, Eng, UK 35/H4
Thorne Bay, Ak, US 134/M4
Thornhill, Sc, UK 36/B4
Thornhill, Sc, UK 34/E1
Thornhurst, Pa, US 138/C1
Thornton, Co, US 137/C3
Thornton, Ca, US 135/M10
Thornton Cleveleys, Eng, UK 35/E4
Thorold, On, Can. 131/R9
Thórshöfn, Ice. 37/P6
Thouars, Fr. 42/C3
Thouet (riv.), Fr. 42/C3
Thourotte, Fr. 52/B5
Thousand Oaks, Ca, US 136/B2
Thowa (riv.), Kenya 104/C3
Thrace (reg.), Gre.,Turk 62/C4
Thracian (sea), Gre. 62/C4
Thredbo Village, Austl. 115/D3
Three Bridges, NJ, US 138/D2
Three Forks, Mt, US 126/F4
Three Guardsmen (mtn.), BC, Can. 134/L4
Three Hills, Ab, Can. 126/E3
Three Hummock (isl.), Austl. 115/C4
Three Kings (isls.), NZ 116/G8
Three Mile (isl.), Pa, US 138/B3
Three Pagodas (pass), Myan. 78/B3
Three Points (cape), Gha. 103/E5
Three Rivers, Mi, US 130/C3
Three Rivers, Austl. 112/C3
Three Springs, Austl. 112/B4
Throssell (lake), Austl. 109/B3
Thrushel (riv.), Eng, UK 32/B5
Thu Dau Mot, Viet. 78/D4
Thuin, Belg. 53/D3
Thuir, Fr. 42/E5
Thulba (riv.), Ger. 54/C2
Thule Air Base, Den. 123/T7
Thun, Swi. 56/D4
Thunderbird (lake), Ok, US 137/N15
Thuner See (lake), Swi. 43/G3
Thung Salaeng Luang NP, Thai. 78/C2
Thüngersheim, Ger. 54/C3
Thur (riv.), Swi. 43/H3
Thurgau (canton), Swi. 57/E2
Thüringen (state), Ger. 43/J1
Thüringen, Aus. 57/F3
Thüringer Schiefergebirge (mts.), Ger. 54/E2
Thüringer Wald (for.), Ger. 43/J1
Thurles, Ire. 31/Q10
Thurnau, Ger. 55/E2
Thurø By, Den. 38/D4
Thurso, Sc, UK 31/V14
Thurston (isl.), Ant. 160/T
Thurston (co.), Wa, US 135/A3
Thury-en-Valois, Fr. 30/M4
Thusis, Swi. 57/F4
Thyez, Fr. 56/C5
Thyolo, Malw. 105/G4
Ti-m-Merhsoï (riv.), Niger 103/G2
Ti-n-Jedane, Oued (riv.), Alg. 99/G4
Ti-n-Zaouâten, Alg. 96/F4
Ti-Tree Abor. Land, Austl. 113/G2
Tiahuanco (ruin), Bol. 156/D5
Tian (pt.), BC, Can. 134/M5
Tian Shan (mts.), China 67/H5
Tianchang, China 72/D4
Tianguá, Braz. 154/B1
Tianguistenco, Mex. 143/Q10
Tianjin (mun.), China 71/L4
Tianjin, China 72/H7
Tianlin, China 83/J3
Tianmen, China 79/B1
Tianmu (mts.), China 72/K9
Tianshui, China 70/J5
Tianyang, China 79/A3
Tianzhen, China 72/C2
Tianzhu, China 83/J2
Tiaret, Alg. 100/F5
Tibagi, Braz. 155/B3
Tibaji (riv.), Braz. 155/B3
Tibaná, Col. 152/C3
Tibati, Camr. 96/H6
Tibba, Pak. 86/A5
Tibé, Pic de (peak), Gui. 102/C4
Tiber (Tevere) (riv.), It. 43/J5
Tiberias (lake), Isr. 91/D3
Tibesti (mts.), Chad 93/D3
Tibet (reg.), China 67/H6
Tibet (Xizang) (aut. reg.), China 70/D5
Tibro, Swe. 38/F2
Tiburon (cape), Haiti 141/G4
Tiburon, Ca, US 135/K11
Tiburón, Isla (isl.), Mex. 142/B2
Ticaco, Peru 156/D5
Tichigan (lake), Wi, US 135/P14
Tichît, Dhar (cliff), Mrta. 102/C2
Ticino (canton), Swi. 57/E5
Ţicleni, Rom. 49/F3
Ticllos, Peru 156/B3
Ticonderoga, NY, US 130/F3
Ticul, Mex. 144/D1
Tidaholm, Swe. 38/E2
Tidikelt (plain), Alg. 96/F2
Tidjikdja, Mrta. 102/C2
Tidone (riv.), It. 58/C3
Tidore (isl.), Indo. 81/G3
Tidra, Île (isl.), Mrta. 102/A2
Tidsit (lake), WSah. 98/B5
Tiede, PN del, Sp. 98/A3
Tiefencastel, Swi. 57/F4
Tiel, Neth. 50/C5
Tieling, China 72/E2
Tielt, Belg. 52/C2
Tielt-Winge, Belg. 53/D2
Tiemba (riv.), C.d'Iv. 102/D4
Tienen, Belg. 53/D2
Tieri, Austl. 114/C3
Tieroko (peak), Chad 96/J3
Tierp, Swe. 38/G1
Tierra Amarilla, NM, US 128/F3
Tierra Blanca, Mex. 143/N8
Tierra Colorada, Mex. 143/F5
Tierra del Fuego (isl.), Arg. 147/C8
Tierra del Fuego, Antártida e Islas del Atlántico Sur, Arg. 159/C7
Tierra del Fuego, PN, Arg. 157/C7
Tierradentro, Col. 152/B4
Tierranueva, Mex. 143/E4
Tiétar (riv.), Sp. 44/C2
Tietê (riv.), Braz. 147/D5
Tiffin, Oh, US 130/D3
Tiflet, Mor. 100/A3
Tifton, Ga, US 133/H4
Tigeaux, Fr. 30/L5
Tighina (Bendery), Mol. 49/J2
Tighvein (hill), Sc, UK 36/A6
Tignère, Camr. 96/H6
Tignieu-Jameyzieu, Fr. 56/B6
Tigre (riv.), Ven. 150/C4
Tigre (riv.), Ven. 153/F2
Tigre, Arg. 159/J11
Tigris (riv.), Iraq 67/C6
Tigui (well), Chad 96/J4
Tiguidit, Falaise de (cliff), Niger 103/G2
Tigzirt, Alg. 100/H4
Tihosuco, Mex. 144/D1
Tihuatlán, Mex. 144/B1
Tiilikkajärven NP, Fin. 60/F3
Tijāra, India 84/A2
Tijuana, Mex. 136/C5
Tijuca, PN da, Braz. 211/K7
Tijucas, Braz. 155/B3
Tijuco (riv.), Braz. 155/B1
Tikal (ruin), Guat. 144/D2
Tikamgarh, India 84/B3
Tikchik (lakes), Ak, US 134/G3
Tikehau (isl.), FrPol. 117/L6
Tikhoretsk, Rus. 62/G3
Tikhvin, Rus. 60/G4
Tikrīt, Iraq 90/E3
Tikveš (lake), FYROM 47/H2
Tila, Mex. 144/C2
Tilburg, Neth. 50/C5
Tilbury, Eng, UK 30/E2
Tilden, Tx, US 132/D4
Tilghman, Md, US 138/B6
Tilghman (isl.), Md, US 138/B6
Tilhar, India 84/B2
Tilin, Myan. 83/F3
Tilisarao, Arg. 158/D2
Till (riv.), Eng, UK 36/F6
Tillabéri (dept .), Niger 103/F3
Tillabéry, Niger 103/F3
Tillamook, Or, US 126/C4
Tille (riv.), Fr. 40/C5
Tillicoultry, Sc, UK 36/C4
Tilst, Den. 38/D3
Tilt (riv.), Sc, UK 36/C3
Tiltil, Chile 158/N8
Tim, Den. 38/C3
Timan (ridge), Rus. 64/F3
Timaná, Col. 152/C4
Timanfaya, PN de, Sp. 98/B3
Timaru, NZ 117/S11
Timashevsk, Rus. 62/F3
Timbákion, Gre. 47/J5
Timbaúba, Braz. 154/D2
Timbédra, Mrta. 102/C2
Timber Lake, SD, US 127/H4
Timberlane, La, US 137/Q17
Timberwood Park, Tx, US 137/U20
Timbiquí, Col. 152/B4
Timbiras, Braz. 154/B2
Timbó, Braz. 155/B3
Timboon, Austl. 115/B3
Timehri (int'l arpt.), Guy. 153/G3
Timelkam, Aus. 55/G6
Timfristós (peak), Gre. 47/G3
Timimoun, Alg. 99/F3
Timiris (cape), Mrta. 102/A2
Timiş (prov.), Rom. 48/E3
Timiş (riv.), Rom. 62/B3
Timişoara (int'l arpt.), Rom. 48/E3
Timişoara, Rom. 48/E3
Timmins, On, Can. 130/D1
Timms (hill), Wi, US 127/L4
Timnath, Co, US 137/C1
Timon, Braz. 154/B2
Timonium, Md, US 138/B5
Timor (sea), Asia,Austl 67/M11
Timor (isl.), Indo. 67/M10
Timóteo, Braz. 155/D1
Timpanogos Cave Nat'l Mon., Ut, US 128/E2
Timpanogos Nat'l Mon., Ut, US 137/K13
Timpson, Tx, US 129/J5
Timpton (riv.), Rus. 65/N4
Tims Ford (lake), Tn, US 133/G3
Timurnī, India 84/A3
Tin Can Bay, Austl. 114/D4
Tin Shui Wai, China 71/T10
Tina (riv.), SAfr. 106/B1
Tinaca (pt.), Phil. 81/G2
Tinaco, Ven. 152/D2
Tindivanam, India 82/C5
Tindouf, Alg. 98/C4
Tindouf (prov.), Alg. 98/D3
Tineo, Sp. 44/B1
Tingalpa (res.), Austl. 114/F7
Tingaringy NP, Austl. 115/D3
Tingha, Austl. 115/D1
Tingi (mts.), SLeo. 102/C4
Tingmerkpuk (mtn.), Ak, US 134/F2
Tingo María, Peru 156/C3
Tingsryd, Swe. 38/F3
Tinguiririca (vol.), Chile 158/C2
Tinharé, Ilha de (isl.), Braz. 151/L6
Tinian (isl.), NMar. 116/D3
Tinicum Nat'l Consv. Area, Pa, US 138/C4
Tinkisso (riv.), Gui. 102/C4
Tinley Park, Il, US 135/Q16
Tinogasta, Arg. 157/C2
Tínos, Gre. 47/J4
Tínos (isl.), Gre. 47/J4
Tinqueux, Fr. 52/C5
Tinrhir, Mor. 98/D3
Tinta, Peru 156/D4
Tintagel (pt.), Eng, UK 32/B5
Tintern Abbey, Eng, UK 32/D3
Tintigny, Belg. 53/E4
Tintinara, Austl. 115/B2
Tinto (riv.), Sp. 44/B4
Tinto (peak), Sc, UK 36/C5
Tinton Falls (New Shrewsbury), NJ, US 138/D3
Tinyahuarco, Peru 156/B3
Tioga, ND, US 127/H3
Tioman (isl.), Malay. 80/B3
Tione di Trento, It. 57/G5
Tipasa (prov.), Alg. 100/F4
Tipasa, Alg. 100/G4
Tipperary, Ire. 31/P10
Tiptūr, India 82/C5
Tir Rhiwiog (peak), Wal, UK 32/C1
Tiracambu, Serra do (mts.), Braz. 151/J4
Tiran (str.), Egypt, SA 101/C3
Tiran (isl.), Egypt,SAr 101/C3
Tirān (isl.), Egypt 97/M2
Tirano, It. 57/G5
Tirari (des.), Austl. 113/H4
Tiraspol, Mol. 49/J2
Tirat Karmel, Isr. 91/F6
Tire, Turk. 90/A2
Tirebolu, Turk. 62/F4
Tiree (isl.), Sc, UK 31/Q8
Tirest (well), Mali 103/F1
Tîrgovişte, Rom. 49/G3
Tîrgu Bujor, Rom. 49/H3
Tîrgu Cărbuneşti, Rom. 49/F3
Tîrgu Frumos, Rom. 49/H2
Tîrgu Jiu, Rom. 49/F3
Tîrgu Lăpuş, Rom. 49/F2
Tîrgu Mureş, Rom. 49/G2
Tîrgu Neamţ, Rom. 49/H2
Tîrgu Ocna, Rom. 49/H2
Tîrgu Secuiesc, Rom. 49/H2
Tirich Mīr (peak), Pak. 89/K1
Tiris (reg.), WSah. 98/B5
Tiris Zemmour (pol. reg.), Mrta. 98/C4
Tîrnava Mare (riv.), Rom. 49/G2
Tîrnava Mică (riv.), Rom. 49/F2
Tîrnăveni, Rom. 49/G2
Tírnavos, Gre. 47/H3
Tiros, Braz. 155/C1
Tirschenreuth, Ger. 55/F3
Tirstrup (int'l arpt.), Den. 38/D3
Tiruchchirāppalli, India 82/C5
Tiruchendūr, India 82/C6
Tiruchengodu, India 82/C5
Tirunelveli, India 82/C6
Tiruntán, Peru 156/C2
Tirupati, India 82/C5
Tiruppattūr, India 82/C5
Tiruppūr, India 82/C5
Tiruvannāmalai, India 82/C5
Tisa (riv.), Ukr. 49/G1
Tisdale, Sk, Can. 127/G2
Tishomingo, Ok, US 129/H4
Tissa, Mor. 100/B2
Tissemsilt (prov.), Alg. 100/F5
Tissemsilt, Alg. 100/F5
Tista (riv.), Bang. 85/G2
Tisza (riv.), Hun. 62/B3
Tiszaföldvár, Hun. 48/E2
Tiszafüred, Hun. 48/E2
Tiszakécske, Hun. 48/E2
Tiszalök, Hun. 48/E1
Tiszavasvári, Hun. 41/L5
Titano (peak), SMar. 59/F5
Titel, Yugo. 48/E3
Titicaca (lake), Bol.,Peru 147/B4
Titisee-Neustadt, Ger. 56/E2
Titlagarh, India 82/D3
Titlis (peak), Swi. 57/E4
Tito, It. 46/D2
Titov Veles, FYROM 47/G2
Titov vrh (peak), FYROM 47/G2
Titting, Ger. 55/E4
Tittmoning, Ger. 55/F6
Titu, Rom. 49/G3
Titusville, Fl, US 133/H4
Titusville, NJ, US 138/D3
Tiva (riv.), Kenya 104/C3
Tivaouane, Sen. 102/A3
Tivat, Yugo. 47/F1
Tiverton, Eng, UK 32/C5
Tiwanacu, Bol. 156/D5
Tixán, Ecu. 156/B1
Tixtla de Guerrero, Mex. 143/F5
Tizayuca, Mex. 143/L7

231

Tizi O – Trona

Tizi Ouzou (prov.), Alg. 100/H4
Tizi Ouzou, Alg. 100/H4
Tizimín, Mex. 144/D1
Tiznap (riv.), China 89/L1
Tiznit, Mor. 98/C3
Tjæreborg, Den. 38/C4
Tjeldstø, Nor. 38/A1
Tjeukemeer (lake), Neth. 50/C3
Tjøme, Nor. 38/D2
Tjorn (isl.), Den. 38/D3
Tlachichuca, Mex. 143/M7
Tlacolula de Matamoros, Mex. 144/B2
Tlacotalpan, Mex. 143/P8
Tlacotepec, Mex. 143/F5
Tlahualilo de Zaragoza, Mex. 132/C5
Tlalixcoyan, Mex. 143/N8
Tlalmanalco, Mex. 143/Q10
Tlalnepantla, Mex. 143/Q9
Tláloc (vol.), Mex. 143/Q10
Tlaltenango de Sánchez Román, Mex. 142/E4
Tlaltizapan, Mex. 143/K8
Tlapa de Comonfort, Mex. 144/B2
Tlapacoya (ruin), Mex. 143/Q10
Tlapacoyan, Mex. 143/M7
Tlapehuala, Mex. 143/E5
Tlaquepaque, Mex. 142/E4
Tlaquiltenango, Mex. 143/K8
Tlatlauquitepec, Mex. 143/M7
Tlaxcala (state), Mex. 140/A5
Tlaxcala, Mex. 143/L7
Tlaxco, Mex. 143/L7
Tlaxcoapan, Mex. 143/K6
Tlell, BC, Can. 134/M5
Tlemcen, Alg. 100/D2
Toabré, Pan. 152/A2
Toaca (peak), Rom. 49/G2
Toachi (riv.), Ecu. 152/B4
Toamasina, Madg. 107/J7
Toamasina (prov.), Madg. 107/J7
Toandos (pen.), Wa, US 135/B2
Toau (isl.), FrPol. 117/L6
Toay, Arg. 158/D3
Toba (lake), Indo. 80/A3
Toba (inlet), BC, Can. 126/B3
Toba, China 70/G5
Toba, Japan 77/L7
Toba Kākar (range), Pak. 89/J2
Toba Tek Singh, Pak. 86/B4
Tobago (isl.), Trin. 150/F1
Tobarra, Sp. 44/E3
Tobbio (peak), It. 58/B3
Tobermore, NI, UK 34/B2
Tōbetsu, Japan 76/B2
Tobias Barreto, Braz. 154/C3
Tobin (lake), Austl. 109/B3
Tobique (riv.), NB, Can. 131/H2
Tobishima, Japan 77/L5
Tobol (riv.), Rus. 61/Q5
Tobu, Japan 77/A1
Tobyhanna (lake), Pa, US 138/C1
Tobyhanna (riv.), Pa, US 138/C1
Tobyhanna, Pa, US 138/C1
Tobyhanna St. Park, Pa, US 138/C1
Tobyl (riv.), Kaz. 63/M1
Tobysh (riv.), Rus. 61/L2
Tocache, Peru 156/B3
Tocantinópolis, Braz. 154/A2
Tocantins (state), Braz. 154/A3
Tocantins (riv.), Braz. 147/E4
Toccoa, Ga, US 133/H3
Toce (riv.), It. 43/H3
Tochigi (pref.), Japan 75/F2
Tochigi, Japan 75/F2
Tochimilco, Mex. 143/L8
Tochio, Japan 75/F2
Tocina, Sp. 44/C4
Töcksfors, Swe. 38/D2
Toco, Trin. 153/F2
Tocopilla, Chile 157/B1
Tocumen, Pan. 152/B2
Tocumwal, Austl. 115/C2
Tocuyito, Ven. 152/D2
Tocuyo (riv.), Ven. 150/E1
Toda, Japan 77/D2
Toda Bhīm, India 82/C2
Todi, It. 46/C1
Tödi (peak), Swi. 57/E4
Todmorden, Eng, UK 35/F4
Todos os Santos, Baía de (bay), Braz. 154/C4
Todos Santos, Mex. 142/C4
Todtmoos, Ger. 56/E2
Todtnau, Ger. 56/D2
Toffal (hill), Mrta. 98/C5
Toffo, Ben. 103/F5
Tofield, Ab, Can. 126/E2
Tofua (isl.), Tonga 117/H6
Tōgane, Japan 77/E2
Togba (well), Mrta. 102/C2
Toggenburg (valley), Swi. 57/F3
Togher, Ire. 34/B5
Togiak, Ak, US 134/F4
Togiak NWR, Ak, US 134/F4
Togo (ctry.) 103/F4
Tōgō, Japan 77/M5
Tögrög, Mong. 70/F2
Togtoh, China 72/B2
Tŏgyu-san NP, SKor. 73/D5
Tohāna, India 86/C5
Tohatchi, NM, US 132/A3
Tōhoku (prov.), Japan 75/F1
Toi, Japan 75/F3
Tōin, Japan 77/L5
Toiyabe (range), Nv, US 128/C3
Tojō, Japan 74/C3
Tōjō, Japan 77/H6
Tok, Ak, US 134/K3
Tokachi (riv.), Japan 76/C2
Tōkai, Japan 77/L5
Tokaj, Hun. 41/L4
Tōkamachi, Japan 75/F2
Tokar Nat'l Rsv., Sudan 101/B4
Tokara (isls.), Japan 116/B1
Tokat (prov.), Turk. 62/F4
Tokat, Turk. 62/F4
Tŏkchŏk (isl.), NKor. 73/C4
Tŏkchŏk (arch.), NKor. 73/C4
Tokeen, Ak, US 134/M4
Tokelau (terr.), NZ 117/H5
Toki, Japan 77/M5
Toki (riv.), Japan 77/M5
Tokigawa, Japan 77/C2
Tokoname, Japan 77/L6
Tokoro (riv.), Japan 76/C2
Tokoro, Japan 76/D1
Tokoroa, NZ 117/T10
Tokorozawa, Japan 75/F3
Toksook Bay, Ak, US 134/E3
Toksun, China 70/E3
Tokuno (isl.), Japan 75/K7
Tokunoshima, Japan 75/K7
Tokushima (pref.), Japan 74/C4
Tokushima, Japan 74/D3
Tokuyama, Japan 74/B3
Tōkyō (cap.), Japan 75/F3
Tōkyō (pref.), Japan 75/F3
Tōkyō (bay), Japan 77/D2
Tōkyō Disneyland, Japan 77/D2
Tola, Nic. 144/E4
Tolbo, Mong. 70/F2
Toledo, Braz. 157/F1
Toledo, Phil. 79/D5
Toledo, Oh, US 130/D3
Toledo, Sp. 44/C3
Toledo, Col. 152/C3
Toledo, Uru. 159/K11
Toledo Bend (dam), La,Tx, US 129/J5
Toledo Bend (res.), La,Tx, US 129/J5
Toledo, Montes de (mts.), Sp. 44/C3
Tolentino, It. 43/K5
Tolfa, It. 46/B1
Tolhuaca, PN, Chile 158/C3
Toli, China 70/D2
Toliara (prov.), Madg. 107/H8
Toliara, Madg. 107/G8
Tolima (dept.), Col. 152/C4
Tolitoli, Indo. 81/F3
Tolka (riv.), Ire. 34/B5
Tolleson, Az, US 137/R19
Tolmezzo, It. 43/K3
Tolna (prov.), Hun. 48/D2
Tolna, Hun. 48/D2
Tolo (chan.), China 71/U10
Tolo, Gulf of (gulf), Indo. 81/F4
Tolosa, Sp. 44/D1
Tolsan (isl.), SKor. 73/D5
Tolt (riv.), Wa, US 135/D2
Tolt (res.), Wa, US 135/D2
Tolt, North Fork (riv.), Wa, US 135/D2
Tolt, South Fork (riv.), Wa, US 135/D2
Toltén, Chile 158/B3
Toltén (riv.), Chile 158/B3
Tolú, Col. 152/C2
Toluca, Mex. 143/Q10
Tolúviejo, Col. 152/C2
Tol'yatti, Rus. 63/J1
Tom' (riv.), Rus. 64/J4
Tom Price, Austl. 112/C2
Tom White (mt.), Ak, US 134/K3
Tomakomai, Japan 76/B2
Tomamae, Japan 76/B1
Tomar, Port. 44/A3
Tómaros (peak), Gre. 47/G3
Tomarza, Turk. 90/C2
Tomás, Peru 156/C4
Tomás de Berlanga, Ecu. 156/E7
Tomaszów Lubelski, Pol. 41/M3
Tomaszów Mazowiecki, Pol. 41/L3
Tomatlán, Mex. 142/D5
Tomb of Qinshihuang, China 72/B4
Tombador, Serra do (mts.), Braz. 150/G6
Tombigbee (riv.), Al,Ms, US 125/J5
Tombolo, It. 59/E1
Tombouctou, Mali 102/E2
Tombouctou (pol. reg.), Mali 98/D5
Tombstone, Az, US 128/E5
Tombua, Ang. 105/B4
Tomé, Chile 158/B3
Tomé, Île (isl.), Fr. 42/B2
Tomelilla, Swe. 38/E4
Tomelloso, Sp. 44/D3
Tomika, Japan 77/L5
Tomini (gulf), Indo. 67/M10
Tomiño, Sp. 44/A2
Tomioka, Japan 77/B1
Tomisato, Japan 77/E2
Tomiura, Japan 77/D3
Tomiyama, Japan 75/F3
Tomizawa, Japan 77/A3
Tommot, Rus. 65/N4
Tomo (riv.), Col. 150/E2
Tompa, Hun. 48/D2
Tompkinsville, Ky, US 130/C4
Toms (riv.), NJ, US 138/D3
Toms River, NJ, US 138/D4
Tomsk, Rus. 64/J4
Tömük, Turk. 91/D1
Tonalá, Mex. 144/C2
Tonale, Passo del (pass), It. 57/G5
Tonasket, Wa, US 126/D3
Tonawanda, NY, US 131/S9
Tonawanda Ind. Res., US 131/S9
Tonbridge, Eng, UK 30/D3
Toncontín (int'l arpt.), Hon. 144/E3
Tondabayashi, Japan 77/J7
Tondano, Indo. 81/F3
Tondou, Massif du (plat.), CAfr.,Sud 97/K6
Tondu (peak), Fr. 56/C6
Tone (riv.), Japan 75/G3
Tone, Japan 77/E2
Tonekābon, Iran 88/F1
Tonelagee (peak), Ire. 34/B5
Tonga (ctry.) 117/H7
Tongaat, SAfr. 107/E3
Tongareva (Penrhyn) (isl.), CookIs. 117/J5
Tongariro NP, NZ 117/T10
Tongatapu (isl.), Tonga 117/H7
Tongbai, China 72/C4
Tongbu, SKor. 73/G6
Tongcheng, China 79/B2
Tongcheng, China 72/D5
T'ongch'ŏn, NKor. 73/D3
Tongchuan, China 72/B4
Tongdao Dongzu Zizhixian, China 83/J2
Tongduch'ŏn, SKor. 73/G6
Tongeren, Belg. 53/E2
Tonggu (peak), China 71/L7
Tongguan, China 83/K2
Tonghae, SKor. 73/E4
Tonghua, China 73/C2
Tonghua, China 73/C2
Tongliao, China 72/E2
Tongling, China 71/L5
Tongno (riv.), NKor. 73/D2
Tongo (peak), Indo. 81/E5
Tongobory, Madg. 107/H8
Tongren, China 83/J2
Tongsa (riv.), Bhu. 85/H2
Tongsa Dzong, Bhu. 85/H2
Tongshan, China 79/B2
Tongue (riv.), Mt, US 124/E2
Tongue, Sc, UK 31/R7
Tongxu, China 72/C4
Tongyu, China 71/M3
Tongzi, China 79/A2
Tonino-Anivskiy (pen.), Rus. 76/C1
Tönisvorst, Ger. 50/D6
Tonk, India 89/L3
Tonkawa, Ok, US 129/H3
Tonkin (gulf), China,Viet 67/K7
Tonkin, Gulf of (gulf), China,Vie 70/J7
Tonkoui (peak), C.d'Iv. 102/D5
Tonle Sap (lake), Camb. 83/H5
Tonneins, Fr. 42/D4
Tonnerre, Fr. 42/E3
Tönning, Ger. 38/C4
Tōno, Japan 76/B4
Tonopah, Nv, US 128/C3
Tonoshō, Japan 74/D3
Tonosí, Pan. 152/A3
Tonota, Bots. 105/E5
Tons (riv.), India 84/C3
Tønsberg, Nor. 38/D2
Tonsina, Ak, US 134/J3
Tonstad, Nor. 38/B2
Tonto Nat'l For., Az, US 137/S18
Tonto Nat'l Mon., Az, US 128/E4
Tonya, Turk. 62/F4
Ton-y-Pandy, Wal, UK 32/C3
Toodyay, Austl. 112/C4
Tooele, Ut, US 137/J12
Tooele (co.), Ut, US 137/J13
Tooradin, Austl. 115/C3
Toowoomba, Austl. 114/C4
Top (mt.), Austl. 113/G2
Topanaga State Park, Ca, US 136/B2
Topanga, Ca, US 136/B2
Topanga Beach, Ca, US 136/E7
Tope de Coroa (mtn.), CpV. 93/J10
Topia, Mex. 142/D3
Topley, BC, Can. 126/B2
Toplița, Rom. 49/G2
Topoľčany, Slvk. 41/K4
Topolobampo, Mex. 142/C3
Topoloveni, Rom. 49/G3
Topolovgrad, Bul. 47/K1
Topozero (lake), Rus. 37/J2
Toppenish, Wa, US 126/C4
Toprakkale, Turk. 91/E1
Topton, Pa, US 138/C3
Tor (bay), Eng, UK 32/C6
Torahime, Japan 77/K5
Torata, Peru 156/D5
Torawitan (cape), Indo. 81/G3
Torbalı, Turk. 90/A2
Torbat-e Ḩeydarīyeh, Iran 89/G1
Torbat-e Jām, Iran 87/D5
Torbay, Nf, Can. 131/L2
Torbeck, Haiti 145/H2
Torbert (mt.), Ak, US 134/H3
Torcy, Fr. 30/K5
Tordera (riv.), Sp. 45/L6
Tordesillas, Sp. 44/C2
Töreboda, Swe. 38/F2
Torelló, Sp. 45/G1
Torfaen (co.), Wal, UK 32/C3
Torgelow, Ger. 38/E5
Torghay, Kaz. 87/D3
Torghay (riv.), Kaz. 87/D3
Torghay Üstirti (plat.), Kaz. 87/D2
Torhamnsudde (pt.), Swe. 38/F3
Torhout, Belg. 52/C1
Tori-shima (isl.), Japan 116/D1
Toride, Japan 77/E2
Torigni-sur-Vire, Fr. 42/C2
Torii-tōge (pass), Japan 75/E3
Toriñana (cape), Sp. 44/A1
Torino (prov.), It. 58/A2
Torino (Turin), It. 43/G4
Torkestān (mts.), Afg. 89/H1
Tormes (riv.), Sp. 44/C2
Torndirrup NP, Austl. 112/C5
Torne (riv.), Eng, UK 35/H4
Torneälven (riv.), Swe. 60/D2
Tornesch, Ger. 51/G1
Tornik (peak), Yugo. 48/D4
Tornio, Fin. 37/H2
Tornionjoki (riv.), Fin. 37/G2
Toro, Sp. 44/C2
Toro, Cerro del (peak), Arg.,Chil 157/C2
Toro Nat'l Rsv., Ugan. 104/A2
Toro, PN, Ven. 152/D2
Törökbálint, Hun. 49/Q10
Törökszentmiklós, Hun. 48/E2
Toronaic (gulf), Gre. 47/H2
Torondoy, Ven. 152/D2
Toronto (cap.), On, Can. 131/R8
Toronto (isl.), On, Can. 131/R8
Toropets, Rus. 39/P3
Tororo, Ugan. 104/B2
Torote (riv.), Sp. 45/N8
Torp (int'l arpt.), Nor. 38/D2
Torpa, Swe. 38/E3
Torquay, Austl. 115/C3
Torquay, Eng, UK 32/C6
Torquemada, Sp. 44/C1
Torr (pt.), NI, UK 34/B1
Torrance, Ca, US 136/F8
Torraz, Tête du (peak), Fr. 56/C6
Torrazza Piemonte, It. 58/A2
Torre de Moncorvo, Port. 44/B2
Torre dè Passeri, It. 46/C1
Torre del Campo, Sp. 44/D4
Torre del Greco, It. 46/D2
Torre del Lago Puccini, It. 58/D5
Torre-Pacheco, Sp. 45/E4
Torrebelvicino, It. 59/E1
Torreblanca, Sp. 45/F2
Torredonjimeno, Sp. 44/D4
Torreglia, It. 59/E2
Torrejón de Ardoz, Sp. 45/N9
Torrejoncillo, Sp. 44/B3
Torrelaguna, Sp. 44/D2
Torrelavega, Sp. 44/C1
Torrelodones, Sp. 45/N8
Torremaggiore, It. 46/D2
Torremolinos, Sp. 44/C4
Torrens (lake), Austl. 109/C4
Torrens (riv.), Austl. 113/M8
Torrens (isl.), Austl. 113/M8
Torrente, Sp. 45/E3
Torreón, Mex. 142/E3
Torreperogil, Sp. 44/D3
Tôrres, Braz. 155/B4
Torres (str.), Austl.,PNG 116/D6
Torres (isls.), Van. 116/F6
Torres del Paine, PN, Chile 159/B6
Torres Novas, Port. 44/A3
Torres Vedras, Port. 44/A3
Torrevieja, Sp. 45/E4
Torri di Quartesolo, It. 59/E1
Torridge (riv.), Eng, UK 32/B5
Torrijos, Sp. 44/C3
Torrington, Wy, US 127/G5
Torrita di Siena, It. 43/J5
Torroella de Montgrí, Sp. 45/G1
Torrone Alto (peak), Swi. 57/F5
Torrox, Sp. 44/D4
Torsa (riv.), Bhu. 85/G2
Torsås, Swe. 38/F3
Torsby, Swe. 38/E1
Tórshavn, Den. 160/G
Tortola (isl.), UK 141/J4
Tortoli, It. 46/A3
Tortona, It. 58/B3
Tortosa (cape), Sp. 45/F2
Tortosa, Sp. 45/F2
Tortuga (isl.), Haiti 141/H5
Tortuguero, PN, CR 145/F4
Tortum, Turk. 63/G4
Torūd, Iran 89/F1
Torugart (pass), Kyr. 87/G4
Torul, Turk. 62/F4
Toruń, Pol. 41/K2
Torup, Swe. 38/E3
Tory (isl.), Ire. 31/P9
Torysa (riv.), Slvk. 41/L4
Torzhok, Rus. 60/G4
Tosa, Japan 74/C4
Tosagua, Ecu. 152/A5
Tosashimizu, Japan 74/C4
Toscana (reg.), It. 58/C4
Toscana (prov.), It. 43/J5
Toscanella, It. 59/E4
Toscolano-Maderno, It. 58/D1
Toshi (isl.), Japan 77/L6
Toshibetsu (riv.), Japan 76/A2
Toshkent (pol. reg.), Uzb. 87/E4
Tosna (riv.), Rus. 61/T7
Tosno, Rus. 39/P2
Tosontsengel, Mong. 70/G2
Töss (riv.), Swi. 43/H3
Tosson (hill), Eng, UK 36/E6
Tostado, Arg. 157/D2
Tostedt, Ger. 51/G2
Tosu, Japan 74/B4
Tosya, Turk. 62/E4
Totana, Sp. 44/E4
Totness, Sur. 153/G3
Totowa, NJ, US 139/J8
Totten (inlet), Wa, US 135/A3
Tottenham, Austl. 115/C2
Tottington, Eng, UK 35/F4
Tottori, Japan 74/D3
Tottori (pref.), Japan 74/C3
Totutla, Mex. 143/N7
Touat (reg.), Alg. 99/E4
Touba, C.d'Iv. 102/D4
Toubkal (peak), Mor. 98/D3
Toubkal, PN du, Mor. 98/D3
Touchwood (hills), Sk, Can. 127/G3
Toucy, Fr. 42/E3
Toudao (riv.), China 73/D1
Tougan, Burk. 102/E3
Touggourt, Alg. 99/G2
Toughkenamon, Pa, US 138/C4
Touiel (riv.), Alg. 100/G5
Toul, Fr. 53/E6
Toulnustouc (riv.), Qu, Can. 131/H1
Toulon, Fr. 42/F5
Toulouse, Fr. 42/D5
Toumo (well), Niger 96/H3
Toumodi, C.d'Iv. 102/D5
Toungoo, Myan. 83/G4
Touquin, Fr. 30/M5
Toura, Monts du (mts.), C.d'Iv. 102/D5
Tourcoing, Fr. 52/C2
Tourfourine (well), Mali 98/D4
Tourlaville, Fr. 42/C2
Tournai, Belg. 52/C2
Tournan-en-Brie, Fr. 30/L5
Tournus, Fr. 56/A4
Touros, Braz. 154/D2
Tours, Fr. 42/D3
Tous, Embalse de (res.), Sp. 45/E3
Toussidé (peak), Chad 96/J3
Toussoro (peak), CAfr. 97/K6
Touws (riv.), SAfr. 106/C4
Touwsrivier, SAfr. 106/M10
Toužim, Czh. 55/G2
Töv (prov.), Mong. 70/J2
Tovar, Ven. 152/D2
Tove (riv.), Eng, UK 33/E2
Towaco, NJ, US 139/H8
Towada, Japan 75/G2
Towada (lake), Japan 76/B3
Towada-Hachimantai NP, Japan 76/B3
Tower City, Pa, US 138/B2
Tower Hamlets (bor.), Eng, UK 30/A1
Tower of London, Eng, UK 30/C2
Towner, ND, US 127/H3
Townsend, Mt, US 126/F4
Townsend, De, US 138/C5
Townsend (mt.), Wa, US 135/A2
Townsends (inlet), NJ, US 138/D5
Townshend (cape), Austl. 114/C3
Townsville, Austl. 114/B2
Towson, Md, US 138/B5
Towuti (lake), Indo. 81/F4
Toya (lake), Japan 76/B2
Toyah, Tx, US 132/C4
Toyahvale, Tx, US 132/C4
Toyama, Japan 75/E2
Toyama (pref.), Japan 75/E2
Toyang, SKor. 73/D5
Toyoake, Japan 77/M5
Toyohashi, Japan 75/E3
Toyokawa, Japan 75/E3
Toyonaka, Japan 77/H6
Toyono, Japan 77/H6
Toyo'oka, Japan 74/D3
Toyosato, Japan 77/E1
Toyosato, Japan 77/K5
Toyoshina, Japan 75/E2
Toyota, Japan 77/M5
Toyotomi, Japan 77/B2
Toyoyama, Japan 77/L5
Tozi (mt.), Ak, US 134/H2
Tra Vinh, Viet. 78/D4
Traben-Trarbach, Ger. 53/G4
Trabuco Canyon, Ca, US 136/C3
Trabzon, Turk. 62/F4
Trabzon (prov.), Turk. 62/F4
Tracadie, NB, Can. 131/H2
Trachselwald, Swi. 56/D3
Tracy, Qu, Can. 130/F2
Tracy, Mo, US 137/D5
Tracyton, Wa, US 135/B2
Tradate, It. 58/B1
Trafalgar (cape), Sp. 44/B4
Tragwein, Aus. 55/H6
Traiguén, Chile 158/B3
Trail, BC, Can. 126/D3
Traipu, Braz. 154/C3
Trairi, Braz. 154/C1
Traisen (riv.), Aus. 41/H5
Traiskirchen, Aus. 49/N7
Traismauer, Aus. 41/H4
Trakai NP, Lith. 39/L4
Traki, Lith. 39/L4
Tralee, Ire. 31/P10
Tramandaí, Braz. 155/B4
Tramelan, Swi. 56/D3
Tramin (Termeno), It. 57/H5
Tranås, Swe. 38/F2
Tranbjerg, Den. 38/D3
Trancoso, Port. 44/B2
Tranebjerg, Den. 38/D4
Tranemo, Swe. 38/E3
Tranent, Sc, UK 36/D5
Tranet (peak), Fr. 53/D4
Trang, Thai. 78/B5
Trangan (isl.), Indo. 81/H5
Trangie, Austl. 115/C2
Trängsletsjön (lake), Swe. 38/E1
Trani, It. 46/E2
Tranoroa, Madg. 107/H9
Transantarctic (mts.), Ant. 160/W
Transylvania (reg.), Rom. 48/F2
Transylvanian Alps (mts.), Rom. 62/B3
Trapani, It. 46/C3
Trapper (peak), Mt, US 126/E4
Trappes, Fr. 30/J5
Traralgon, Austl. 115/C3
Trarza (pol. reg.), Mrta. 96/B4
Trasacco, It. 46/C2
Trasimeno (lake), It. 43/K5
Träslövsläge, Swe. 38/E3
Trat, Thai. 78/C3
Traun (riv.), Aus. 40/H4
Traun, Aus. 55/H6
Traunreut, Ger. 55/F7
Traunsee (lake), Aus. 43/K3
Traunstein, Ger. 55/F7
Trautmannsdorf an der Leitha, Aus. 49/P7
Travagliato, It. 58/D1
Trave (riv.), Ger. 40/F2
Travedona Monate, It. 58/B1
Travellers (lake), Austl. 109/D4
Travemünde, Ger. 40/F2
Traverse (peak), Ak, US 134/G2
Traverse (lake), Mn, SD, US 127/J4
Traverse City, Mi, US 130/C2
Traversetolo, It. 58/D3
Travis (lake), Tx, US 132/D4
Travis AFB, Ca, US 135/L10
Travnik, Bosn. 48/C3
Trawsalt (peak), Wal, UK 32/C2
Trawsfynydd, Llyn (lake), Wal, UK 34/D6
Trbovlje, Slov. 43/L3
Tré-la-Tête (peak), Fr. 56/C6
Treachery (mt.), Austl. 113/G2
Trebaseleghe, It. 59/F1
Trebbia (riv.), It. 43/H4
Trebel (riv.), Ger. 40/G1
Třebíč, Czh. 41/H4
Trebinje, Bosn. 47/F1
Trebisacce, It. 46/E3
Třeboň, Czh. 55/H4
Trebonne, Austl. 114/B2
Trebujena, Sp. 44/B4
Trebur, Ger. 54/B3
Trecate, It. 58/B2
Tregnago, It. 59/E1
Treia, Ger. 38/C4
Treig (lake), Sc, UK 36/B3
Treinta de Agosto, Arg. 158/E3
Treinta y Tres (dept.), Uru. 159/G2
Treinta y Tres, Uru. 159/G2
Trélazé, Fr. 42/C3
Trelew, Arg. 158/D4
Trélissac, Fr. 42/D4
Trelleborg, Swe. 38/E4
Tremadoc (bay), Wal, UK 34/D6
Tremblestown (riv.), Ire. 34/B4
Trembleur (lake), BC, Can. 126/B2
Tremelo, Belg. 53/D2
Tremiti (isl.), It. 46/D1
Tremont, Pa, US 138/B2
Třemošná (riv.), Czh. 55/G3
Tremp, Sp. 45/F1
Třemšín (peak), Czh. 55/G3
Trenche (riv.), Qu, Can. 130/F1
Trenčín, Slvk. 41/K4
Trenel, Arg. 158/D2
Trenque Lauquen, Arg. 158/E2
Trent (riv.), Eng, UK 35/F6
Trent and Mersey (canal), Eng, UK 35/F6
Trentino-Alto Adige (pol. reg.), It. 43/J3
Trento, It. 57/H5
Trento (prov.), It. 57/G5
Trenton, On, Can. 130/E2
Trenton, Ga, US 133/G3
Trenton, Fl, US 133/H4
Trenton, Tn, US 130/B5
Trenton, Mo, US 129/J2
Trenton (cap.), NJ, US 138/D3
Trenzano, It. 58/D2
Trepuzzi, It. 47/F2
Tres Algarrobos, Arg. 158/E2
Tres Arroyos, Arg. 158/E3
Três Corações, Braz. 211/H6
Três Irmãos, Represa (res.), Braz. 155/B2
Tres Isletas, Arg. 157/D2
Três Lagoas, Braz. 155/B2
Tres Lomas, Arg. 158/E3
Tres Marias, Braz. 154/A5
Tres Marías (isls.), Mex. 142/D4
Tres Marías, Mex. 143/Q10
Três Marias, Represa (res.), Braz. 151/J7
Tres Montes (cape), Chile 159/B5
Tres Morros, Alto de (peak), Col. 152/B3
Tres Picos, Mex. 144/C3
Tres Picos (peak), Arg. 158/C4
Tres Picos (peak), Arg. 158/E3
Três Pontas, Braz. 211/H6
Tres Puntas (cape), Arg. 158/D5
Três Rios, Braz. 211/K7
Tres Valles, Mex. 144/B2
Tresa (riv.), Swi. 57/E5
Tresckow, Pa, US 138/C2
Trescore Balneario, It. 58/C1
Trescore Cremasco, It. 58/C2
Tresigallo, It. 59/E3
Tresinaro (riv.), It. 58/D4
Trestina, It. 59/F6
Trets, Fr. 42/F5
Treuchtlingen, Ger. 54/D5
Treuen, Ger. 55/F1
Treuenbrietzen, Ger. 40/G2
Treungen, Nor. 38/C2
Trevelín, Arg. 158/C4
Treviglio, It. 58/C1
Trevignano, It. 59/F1
Treviso (int'l arpt.), It. 59/F1
Treviso (prov.), It. 59/F2
Treviso, It. 59/F1
Trevorton, Pa, US 138/B2
Trevose (pt.), Eng, UK 32/A5
Trezzano sul Naviglio, It. 58/C2
Trezzo sull'Adda, It. 58/C1
Trhové Sviny, Czh. 55/H5
Triabunna, Austl. 115/C4
Triadelphia (res.), Md, US 138/A5
Triángulos (reef), Mex. 144/C1
Tribbey, Ok, US 137/N15
Triberg, Ger. 57/E1
Tribhuvan (int'l arpt.), Nepal 85/E2
Tribugá (bay), Col. 152/B3
Tribulation (cape), Austl. 114/B2
Tribulaun (peak), Aus. 57/H4
Tricase, It. 47/F3
Trichūr, India 82/C5
Tricora (peak), Indo. 81/J4
Tricot, Fr. 52/B4
Trie-Château, Fr. 52/A5
Trier, Ger. 53/F4
Trierweiler, Ger. 53/F4
Triesen, Lcht. 57/F3
Trieste, It. 59/G1
Trieste (prov.), It. 59/G1
Trieste, It. 43/K4
Trieux, Fr. 53/E5
Triftern, Ger. 55/G6
Triggiano, It. 48/C5
Trigla NP, Slov. 43/K3
Triglav (peak), Slov. 43/K3
Trigolo, It. 58/C2
Tríkala, Gre. 47/G3
Trikhonís (lake), Gre. 47/G3
Trilport, Fr. 52/B6
Trimbach, Swi. 56/D3
Trimble, Mo, US 137/D5
Trimmis, Swi. 57/F4
Trin, Swi. 57/F4
Trincomalee, SrL. 82/D6
Trindade, Braz. 151/J7
Trindade, Ilha da (isl.), Braz. 151/N8
Třinec, Czh. 41/K4
Tring, Eng, UK 33/F3
Trinidad (isl.), Arg. 157/D4
Trinidad (isl.), Trin. 150/F2
Trinidad, Bol. 150/F6
Trinidad, Co, US 129/F3
Trinidad, Col. 152/D3
Trinidad (chan.), Chile 159/B6
Trinidad, Uru. 159/K10
Trinidad (gulf), Chile 159/A6
Trinidad and Tobago (ctry.) 141/N10
Trinity (isls.), Ak, US 134/H4
Trinity (range), Nv, US 128/C2
Trinity (riv.), Ca, US 126/C5
Trinity (bay), Nf, Can. 131/L2
Trinity (riv.), Tx, US 140/B1
Trinity, West Fork (riv.), Tx, US 129/H4
Trino, It. 58/B2
Triolet, Mrts. 107/T15
Trípolis, Gre. 47/H4
Tripolitania (reg.), Libya 96/H1
Trippstadt, Ger. 53/G5
Tripunittura, India 82/C6
Tripura (state), India 70/F7
Trisanna (riv.), Aus. 57/G4
Trissino, It. 59/E1
Tristan da Cunha (isl.), StH. 22/J7
Triste (peak), Arg. 158/D4
Trisuli (riv.), Nepal 85/E2
Trittau, Ger. 51/H1
Trivandrum, India 82/C6
Trivero, It. 58/B1
Trnava, Slvk. 48/C1
Trobriand (isls.), PNG 116/E5
Trochtelfingen, Ger. 57/F1
Troesne (riv.), Fr. 52/A5
Trofaiach, Aus. 43/L3
Trofarello, It. 58/A3
Trøgstad, Nor. 38/D2
Troia, It. 46/D2
Trois Fourches, Cap des (cape), Mor. 100/C2
Trois-Pistoles, Qu, Can. 131/G1
Trois-Ponts, Belg. 53/E3
Trois-Rivières, Qu, Can. 131/F2
Troisdorf, Ger. 53/G2
Troistorrents, Swi. 56/C5
Troisvierges, Lux. 53/F3
Troitsk, Rus. 61/P5
Trollhättan, Swe. 38/E2
Trombetas (riv.), Braz. 151/G3
Tromello, It. 58/B2
Tromie (riv.), Sc, UK 36/B3
Troms (co.), Nor. 37/F1
Tromsø, Nor. 37/F1
Tronador (peak), Arg. 158/C4

232

Trondh – Upper

Trondheim, Nor. 37/D3
Trondheims-Fjorden (estu.), Nor. 37/D3
Tronville-en-Barrios, Fr. 53/E6
Tronzano Vercellese, It. 58/B2
Troodos (mts.), Cyp. 91/C2
Trool (lake), Sc, UK 34/D1
Troon, Sc, UK 36/B5
Trooper, Pa, US 138/C3
Tropea, It. 46/D3
Trosa, Swe. 38/G2
Trosly-Breuil, Fr. 52/B5
Trossingen, Ger. 57/E1
Trostan (peak), NI, UK 34/B1
Trostberg an der Alz, Ger. 55/F6
Trou du Nord, Haiti 145/H2
Troup (pt.), Sc, UK 36/D1
Trout (lake), NW, Can. 122/D2
Trout Lake, Ab, Can. 126/E1
Trowbridge, Eng, UK 32/D4
Troxelville, Pa, US 138/A2
Troy, Al, US 133/G4
Troy, Mi, US 130/D3
Troy, NY, US 130/F3
Troy, Oh, US 133/G1
Troy, Il, US 137/H8
Troy Center, Wi, US 135/N14
Troyan, Bul. 47/J1
Troyanski Prokhod (pass), Bul. 47/J1
Troyes, Fr. 42/F2
Trstenik, Yugo. 48/E4
Trub, Swi. 56/D4
Truitt (peak), Yk, Can. 134/M3
Trujillo, Peru 156/B3
Trujillo, Sp. 44/C3
Trujillo, Ven. 152/D2
Trujillo (state), Ven. 152/D2
Trujillo, Hon. 144/E3
Truk (isls.), Micr. 116/E4
Trulben, Ger. 53/G5
Truman Library and Museum, Mo, US 137/E5
Trumau, Aus. 49/N8
Trumbauersville, Pa, US 138/C3
Trumbull, Ct, US 139/E1
Trümmelbachfälle (falls), Swi. 56/D4
Trün, Bul. 47/H1
Trundle, Austl. 115/C2
Truro, NS, Can. 131/J2
Truro, Eng, UK 32/A6
Truskmore (peak), Ire. 31/P9
Trüstenik, Bul. 49/G4
Truth or Consequences, NM, US 128/F4
Trutnov, Czh. 41/H3
Truyère (riv.), Fr. 42/E4
Trwyn Cilan (pt.), Wal, UK 34/D6
Tryavna, Bul. 47/J1
Trysil, Nor. 38/E1
Trysilelva (riv.), Nor. 38/D1
Trzcianka, Pol. 41/J2
Trzebiatów, Pol. 38/F4
Trzebnica, Pol. 41/J3
Trzemeszno, Pol. 41/J2
Tsabong, Bots. 106/C2
Tsagaan Bogd (peak), Mong. 70/G3
Tsakane, SAfr. 106/Q13
Tsalgar, Mong. 70/F2
Tsant, Mong. 70/J2
Tsao, Bots. 105/D5
Tsarahonenana, Madg. 107/J6
Tsaramandroso, Madg. 107/H7
Tsaratanana, Madg. 107/H7
Tsaratanana (mass.), Madg. 107/J6
Tsast (peak), Mong. 70/F2
Tsatsana (peak), Les. 106/E3
Tsavo East NP, Kenya 105/G1
Tsavo West NP, Kenya 105/G1
Tschagguns, Aus. 57/F3
Tschierv, Swi. 57/G4
Tschlin, Swi. 57/G4
Tselfat (peak), Mor. 100/B2
Tsetserleg, Mong. 70/F2
Tsetserleg, Mong. 70/H2
Tseung Kwan O, China 71/U10
Tsévié, Togo 103/F5
Tshane, Bots. 105/D5
Tshela, D.R. Congo 105/B1
Tshikapa, D.R. Congo 105/D2
Tshuapa (riv.), D.R. Congo 93/E5
Tsiafajavona (peak), Madg. 107/H7
Tsil'ma (riv.), Rus. 61/L2
Tsimlyansk (res.), Rus. 64/E5
Tsing Yi (isl.), China 71/U10
Tsiombe, Madg. 107/H9
Tsiribihina (riv.), Madg. 107/H7
Tsiroanomandidy, Madg. 107/H7
Tsitsikamma Forest and Coastal NP, SAfr. 106/C4
Tsivory, Madg. 107/H9
Ts'khinvali, Geo. 63/G4
Tsna (riv.), Rus. 60/G4
Tsomo (riv.), SAfr. 106/D3
Tsomog, Mong. 71/J2
Tsu (isl.), Japan 65/N6
Tsu, Japan 77/L6
Tsubame, Japan 75/F2
Tsubata, Japan 75/E2
Tsuchiura, Japan 75/G2
Tsuchiyama, Japan 77/K6
Tsuen Wan, China 71/U10
Tsugaru (pen.), Japan 76/B3
Tsuge, Japan 77/J6
Tsukidate, Japan 76/B4
Tsukigase, Japan 77/K6
Tsukuba, Japan 77/E1
Tsukude, Japan 77/M6
Tsukui, Japan 77/C2
Tsukumi, Japan 74/B4
Tsumeb, Namb. 105/C4
Tsuna, Japan 77/G7
Tsuru, Japan 75/F3
Tsuruga, Japan 74/E3
Tsurugashima, Japan 77/C2
Tsurugi, Japan 74/E2
Tsurugi-san (peak), Japan 74/D4
Tsuruoka, Japan 76/A4
Tsushima, Japan 77/L5
Tsuyama, Japan 74/D3
Tua (cape), Indo. 80/C5
Tua (riv.), Port.,Sp. 44/B2
Tuam, Ire. 31/P10
Tuamapu (chan.), Chile 158/B4
Tuamotu (arch.), FrPol. 117/L6
Tuan (pt.), Indo. 80/A3
Tuan (riv.), China 72/B4
Tuangku (isl.), Indo. 80/A3
Tuao, Phil. 79/D4
Tuapse, Rus. 62/F3
Tuba City, Az, US 128/E3
Tuban, Indo. 80/D5
Tuban (riv.), Yem. 88/D6
Tubarão, Braz. 155/B4
Tubbergen, Neth. 50/D4
Tübingen, Ger. 54/C5
Tubize, Belg. 53/D2
Tubmanburg, Libr. 102/C5
Ţubruq (Tobruk), Libya 97/K1
Tubuaï (isl.), FrPol. 117/K7
Tubualá, Pan. 152/B2
Tucacas, Ven. 152/D2
Tucano, Braz. 154/C3
Tuchola, Pol. 41/J2
Tuchów, Pol. 41/L4
Tuckahoe, NJ, US 138/D5
Tuckahoe (riv.), NJ, US 138/D5
Tuckahoe, NY, US 139/K8
Tuckerton, NJ, US 138/D4
Tucquegnieux, Fr. 53/E5
Tucson, Az, US 128/E4
Tucson (int'l arpt.), Az, US 142/C1
Tucumcari, NM, US 129/G4
Tucupido, Ven. 153/E2
Tucupita, Ven. 153/F2
Tucuruí, Braz. 151/J4
Tucuruí (res.), Braz. 147/E3
Tudela, Sp. 44/E1
Tudela de Duero, Sp. 44/C2
Tuen Mun, China 71/T10
Tuenno, It. 57/H5
Tufanbeyli, Turk. 90/D2
Tug Fork (riv.), Ky,WV, US 133/H2
Tugela (riv.), SAfr. 107/E3
Tugela, SAfr. 107/E3
Tugela (falls), SAfr. 106/E3
Tughlakabad (ruin), India 86/D5
Tuguegarao, Phil. 79/D4
Tukangbesi (isls.), Indo. 81/F5
Ţūkh, Egypt 91/B4
Tuktoyaktuk, NW, Can. 134/M2
Tukums, Lat. 39/K3
Tukung (peak), Indo. 80/D4
Tukuyu, Tanz. 104/B5
Tukwila, Wa, US 135/C3
Tula (riv.), Kenya 104/C3
Tula, Mex. 143/F4
Tula, Rus. 62/F1
Tula (riv.), Mex. 143/K6
Tula, Mex. 143/K6
Tula, PN, Mex. 143/K6
Tulancingo, Mex. 143/L6
Tulare, Ca, US 128/C3
Tularosa (valley), NM, US 129/F4
Tularosa, NM, US 129/F4
Tulcán, Ecu. 152/B4
Tulcea, Rom. 49/J3
Tulcea (prov.), Rom. 49/J3
Tule (canal), Ca, US 135/L9
Tüledi (isls.), Rus. 87/B3
Tulia, Tx, US 129/G4
Tulik (vol.), Ak, US 134/E5
Tulin (isls.), PNG 116/E5
Tulita, NW, Can. 122/D2
Ţūlkarm, WBnk. 91/G7
Tulla (lake), Sc, UK 36/B3
Tullahoma, Tn, US 133/G3
Tullamarine (int'l arpt.), Austl. 115/F5
Tullamore, Austl. 115/C2
Tullamore, Ire. 31/Q10
Tulle, Fr. 42/D4
Tullibody, Sc, UK 36/C4
Tullnerbach, Aus. 49/N7
Tullow, Ire. 31/Q10
Tully, Austl. 114/B2
Tullytown, Pa, US 138/D3
Tuloma (riv.), Rus. 64/D3
Tulsa, Ok, US 129/J3
Tulsipur, Nepal 84/D1
Tulsīpur, India 84/D2
Tul'skaya (obl.), Rus. 62/F1
Tultitlán, Mex. 143/Q9
Tuluá, Col. 152/B3
Tuluksak, Ak, US 134/F3
Tulum, Mex. 144/E1
Tulum, PN, Mex. 144/E1
Tulun, Rus. 65/L4
Tumacacori Nat'l Hist. Park, Az, US 128/E5
Tumaco, Col. 152/B4
Tumatumari, Guy. 153/G3
Tumauini, Phil. 79/D4
Tumba (lake), D.R. Congo 96/J8
Tumba, Swe. 38/G2
Tumbarumba, Austl. 115/D2
Tumbes (dept.), Peru 156/A1
Tumbes, Peru 156/A1
Tumbot (peak), Camb. 78/C3
Tumby Bay, Austl. 113/H5
Tumd Youqi, China 72/B2
Tumd Zuoqi, China 72/B2
Tumen, China 71/N3
Tumen (riv.), China 73/E1
Tumeremo, Ven. 153/F3
Tumereng, Guy. 153/F3
Tumkūr, India 82/C5
Tummel (riv.), Sc, UK 36/C3
Tumpat, Malay. 83/H6
Tumpu (peak), Indo. 81/F4
Tumu, Gha. 103/E4
Tumuc-Humac (mts.), Braz. 151/G3
Tumut, Austl. 115/D2
Tunadal, Swe. 60/C3
Tunceli (prov.), Turk. 90/D2
Tunceli, Turk. 90/D2
Tunchang, China 83/K4
Tundla, India 84/B2
Tundyk (riv.), Kaz. 87/G2
Tundzha (riv.), Bul. 47/K1
Tung Chung, China 71/T10
Tung Lung (riv.), China 71/V11
Tungabhadra (res.), India 82/C4
Tungabhadra (riv.), India 82/C4
Tungamah, Austl. 115/C3
Tüngsan-got (pt.), NKor. 73/C4
Tungsten, NW, Can. 122/D2
Tungurahua (prov.), Ecu. 152/B5
Tünhel, Mong. 70/J2
Tūnis (gov.), Tun. 46/B4
Tūnis (cap.), Tun. 46/B4
Tunis, Gulf of (gulf), Tun. 46/B4
Tunisia (ctry.) 99/H2
Tunjá, Col. 152/C3
Tunliu, China 72/C3
Tunnels of Vinh Moc, Viet. 78/D2
Tuntum, Braz. 154/A2
Tuntutuliak, Ak, US 134/F3
Tunungayualuk (isl.), Nf, Can. 123/K3
Tunuyán (riv.), Arg. 158/C2
Tunuyán, Arg. 158/C2
Tuolumne (riv.), Ca, US 128/B3
Tuoniang (riv.), China 83/J3
Tupã, Braz. 155/B2
Tupaciguara, Braz. 155/B2
Tupai (isl.), FrPol. 117/K6
Tupambaé, Uru. 159/G2
Tuparro (riv.), Col. 152/D3
Tupelo, Ms, US 133/F3
Tupi Paulista, Braz. 155/B2
Tupiza, Bol. 150/E8
Tupper Lake, NY, US 130/F2
Tupungato, Arg. 158/C2
Tupungato (peak), Arg. 158/P8
Tura, India 85/H3
Tura (riv.), Rus. 64/G4
Tura, Rus. 65/L3
Turaiçu (riv.), Braz. 154/A1
Turan Lowland (plain), Uzb. 64/G5
Turangi, NZ 117/T10
Turbaco, Col. 152/C2
Turbat, Pak. 89/H3
Turbenthal, Swi. 57/E3
Turbo, Col. 152/B2
Turbotville, Pa, US 138/B1
Turčiansky Svätý Martin, Slvk. 62/A2
Turckheim, Fr. 56/D1
Turda, Rom. 49/F2
Tureia (isl.), FrPol. 117/M7
Turek, Pol. 41/K2
Turgeon (riv.), Qu, Can. 130/E1
Türgovishte, Bul. 49/H4
Turgutlu, Turk. 62/C5
Turhal, Turk. 62/F4
Turia (riv.), Sp. 45/E3
Turiaçu, Braz. 151/J4
Turkana (Rudolf) (lake), Kenya 93/F4
Türkeli, Turk. 62/E4
Túrkeve, Hun. 48/E2
Turkey (riv.), Ia, US 129/K2
Turkey (ctry.) 90/C2
Türkheim, Ger. 57/G1
Türkistan, Kaz. 87/E4
Türkmenbashi (Krasnowodsk), Trkm. 63/K5
Turkmenistan (ctry.) 87/C5
Türkoğlu, Turk. 90/D2
Turks (isls.), Haiti 141/G3
Turks and Caicos (isls.), UK 141/G3
Turks Island Passage (chan.), UK 145/J1
Turku (int'l arpt.), Fin. 39/K1
Turku Ja Pori (prov.), Fin. 37/G3
Turkwel (riv.), Kenya 104/B2
Turlock, Ca, US 128/B3
Turmalina, Braz. 154/B5
Turneffe (isls.), Belz. 140/D4
Turner (mt.), Austl. 112/C2
Turnersville, NJ, US 138/C4
Turnhouse (int'l arpt.), Sc, UK 36/C5
Turnhout, Belg. 50/B6
Turnor Lake, Sk, Can. 126/F1
Turnov, Czh. 41/H3
Turnu Măgurele, Rom. 49/G4
Tuross Head, Austl. 115/D3
Tuross Head, Austl. 115/D3
Turpan, China 70/E3
Turpan (depr.), China 70/E3
Turquino (peak), Cuba 145/G2
Turriaco, It. 59/G1
Turriff, Sc, UK 36/D1
Turt, Mong. 70/H1
Turtle (isls.), SLeo. 102/B5
Turtleford, Sk, Can. 126/F2
Turugart (pass), China 87/G4
Turukhansk, Rus. 64/J3
Tuscaloosa, Al, US 133/G3
Tuscano (arch.), It. 46/B1
Tuscarora, Nv, US 126/D5
Tuscarora (mtn.), Pa, US 138/A3
Tuscarora Ind. Res., US 131/S9
Tuskegee, Al, US 133/G3
Tustin, Ca, US 136/G8
Tuszyn, Pol. 41/K3
Tutak, Turk. 63/G5
Tutayev, Rus. 60/G4
Tuticorin, India 82/C6
Tutin, Yugo. 47/G1
Tutóia, Braz. 154/B1
Tutong, Bru. 80/D3
Tutrakan, Bul. 49/H3
Tuttle Creek (lake), Ks, US 129/H3
Tuttlingen, Ger. 57/E2
Tutuila (isl.), ASam. 117/H6
Tutupaca (vol.), Peru 156/D5
Tutuilak (mtn.), Ak, US 134/F2
Tutzing, Ger. 57/H2
Tuusula, Fin. 39/L1
Tuvalu (ctry.) 116/G5
Ţuwayq, Jabal (mts.), SAr. 88/E3
Tuxpan, Mex. 142/E5
Tuxpan, Mex. 142/D4
Tuxpan de Rodríguez Cano, Mex. 144/B1
Tuxtla Gutiérrez, Mex. 144/C2
Túy, Sp. 44/A1
Tuy Hoa, Viet. 78/E3
Tuyen Quang, Viet. 78/D1
Tuymazy, Rus. 61/M5
Tūysarkān, Iran 88/E2
Tuz (lake), It. 90/C2
Ţūz Khurmātū, Iraq 90/F3
Tuzigoot Nat'l Mon., Az, US 128/D4
Tuzla, Bosn. 48/D3
Tuzla, Turk. 91/D1
Tuzluca, Turk. 63/G4
Tuzlukçu, Turk. 90/B2
Tvååker, Swe. 38/E3
Tvedestrand, Nor. 38/C2
Tver', Rus. 60/G4
Tverskaya (obl.), Rus. 39/P3
Tvertsa (riv.), Rus. 60/G4
Tvürditsa, Bul. 47/J1
Twardogóra, Pol. 41/J3
Tweed (riv.), Sc, UK 36/C5
Tweed Heads, Austl. 114/D5
Twello, Neth. 50/D4
Twente (canal), Neth. 50/D4
Twente (pol. reg.), Neth. 50/D4
Twin Buttes (res.), Tx, US 129/G5
Twin Hills, Ak, US 134/F4
Twin Lakes, Wi, US 135/P14
Twin Rivers, NJ, US 138/D3
Twiste (riv.), Ger. 51/G6
Twistringen, Ger. 51/F3
Twizel, NZ 117/S11
Two Hills, Ab, Can. 126/F2
Two Rivers, Wi, US 127/M4
Twofold (bay), Austl. 115/D3
Twyford, Eng, UK 33/F4
Twymyn (riv.), Wal, UK 32/C1
Tyatya (vol.), Rus. 76/E1
Tychy, Pol. 41/K3
Tyendinaga, On, Can. 130/E2
Tyger (riv.), SC, US 133/H3
Tyldesley, Eng, UK 35/F4
Tylersville, Pa, US 138/A2
Týn, Czh. 41/H4
Tyne (riv.), Sc, UK 36/D5
Tyne and Wear (co.), Eng, UK 35/G2
Tynemouth, Eng, UK 35/G1
Tynset, Nor. 37/D3
Tyonek, Ak, US 134/H3
Tyrifjorden (lake), Nor. 38/C1
Tyringe, Swe. 38/E3
Tyrnyauz, Rus. 63/G4
Tyrrell (lake), Austl. 115/B2
Tyrrhenian (sea), It. 27/F4
Tysnes, Nor. 38/A1
Tysnesøy (isl.), Nor. 38/A2
Tysons Corner, Va, US 138/A6
Tysse, Nor. 38/A1
Tystberga, Swe. 38/G2
Tyub-Karagan (pt.), Kaz. 63/J3
Tyuleniy (isl.), Rus. 63/H3
Tyumen (int'l arpt.), Rus. 61/Q4
Tyumen', Rus. 61/Q4
Tyumenskaya (obl.), Rus. 87/E1
Tyva (aut. rep.), Rus. 64/K4
Tywi (riv.), Wal, UK 32/B3
Tzaneen, SAfr. 105/F5
Tzucacab, Mex. 144/D1

U

U.C.-Irvine, Ca, US 136/G8
U.K. Sovereign Base Area (gov.), Cyp. 91/C2
U.S. Naval Weapons Station, Ca, US 136/F8
U.S.S. Arizona Nat'l Mem., Hi, US 124/W13
Uad Assag (riv.), WSah. 98/B4
Uad Atui (riv.), WSah. 98/B5
Uad el Jat (riv.), WSah. 98/B4
Uad Tenuaiur (riv.), WSah. 98/A5
Uamh Bheag (peak), Sc, UK 36/B4
Uatumã (riv.), Braz. 150/G4
Uauá, Braz. 154/C3
Uaupés (riv.), Braz. 150/E3
Uaxactún (ruin), Guat. 144/D2
Ub, Yugo. 48/E3
Ubá, Braz. 155/D2
Übach-Palenberg, Ger. 53/F2
Ubagan (riv.), Kaz. 61/Q5
Ubaira, Braz. 154/C4
Ubaitaba, Braz. 154/C4
Ubajara, Braz. 154/B1
Ubajara, PN de, Braz. 154/B1
Ubangi (riv.), D.R. Congo 93/D4
Ubatã, Braz. 154/C4
Ubatuba, Braz. 211/H8
Ubay, Phil. 79/D5
Ubaye (riv.), Fr. 43/G4
Ubbergen, Neth. 50/C5
Ube, Japan 74/B4
Úbeda, Sp. 44/D3
Uberaba (lake), Braz. 150/G7
Uberaba, Braz. 155/C1
Überherrn, Ger. 53/F5
Uberlândia, Braz. 155/B1
Überlingen, Ger. 57/F2
Überlingersee (lake), Ger. 57/F2
Ubia (peak), Indo. 81/J4
Ubinas, Peru 156/D5
Ubombo, SAfr. 107/F2
Ubon Ratchathani, Thai. 78/D3
Ubrique, Sp. 44/C4
Ubundu, D.R. Congo 97/L8
Ucayali (dept.), Peru 156/C3
Ucayali (riv.), Peru 147/B3
Uccle, Belg. 53/D2
Ucha (riv.), Rus. 61/W9
Uchaly, Rus. 61/N5
Uchāna, India 86/D5
Uchinskoye (res.), Rus. 61/W9
Uchiza, Peru 156/B3
Uchte, Ger. 51/F3
Uchte (riv.), Ger. 40/F2
Uchumarca, Peru 156/B2
Uchumayo, Peru 156/D5
Uchur (riv.), Rus. 65/P4
Ücker (riv.), Ger. 38/E5
Uckermark (reg.), Ger. 41/G2
Uckfield, Eng, UK 33/G5
Ucluelet, BC, Can. 126/B3
Uda (riv.), Rus. 65/M4
Udagamandalam, India 82/C5
Udaipur, India 89/K4
Udaipura, India 84/B4
Uddevalla, Swe. 38/D2
Uddingston, Sc, UK 36/B5
Uddjaure (lake), Swe. 37/F2
Üdem, Ger. 50/D5
Uden, Neth. 50/C5
Udenhout, Neth. 50/C5
Udgīr, India 82/C4
Udhampur, India 86/C3
Udine (prov.), It. 59/G1
Udine, It. 43/K3
Udipi, India 82/B5
Udmurtia (aut. rep.), Rus. 64/Q6
Udon Thani, Thai. 78/C2
Ueckermünde, Ger. 38/F5
Ueda, Japan 75/F2
Uele (riv.), D.R. Congo 93/E4
Uelsen, Ger. 50/D3
Uelzen, Ger. 51/H3
Ueno, Japan 77/B1
Ueno, Japan 77/K6
Uenohara, Japan 77/F3
Uetendorf, Swi. 56/D4
Uetersen, Ger. 51/G1
Uetze, Ger. 51/H4
Ufa (riv.), Rus. 87/C1
Ufa, Rus. 61/M5
Uffenheim, Ger. 54/D3
Uffing, Ger. 57/H2
Ugalla (riv.), Tanz. 104/A4
Ugalla River Game Rsv., Tanz. 104/A4
Uganda (ctry.) 104/B2
Ugento, It. 47/F3
Ugie (riv.), Sc, UK 36/E1
Ugine, Fr. 56/C6
Uglich, Rus. 60/H4
Ugod, Hun. 48/C2
Ugra (riv.), Rus. 60/G5
Ugürchin, Bul. 47/J1
Uherské Hradiště, Czh. 41/J4
Uhingen, Ger. 54/C5
Úhlava (riv.), Czh. 41/G4
Úhlavka (riv.), Czh. 55/F3
Uibaí, Braz. 154/B3
Uíge, Ang. 105/C2
Ŭihŭng, SKor. 73/E4
Ŭijŏngbu, SKor. 73/D6
Ŭiju, NKor. 73/C2
Uilkraal (riv.), SAfr. 106/L11
Uilpata (peak), Rus. 63/G4
Uinta (mts.), Ut, US 128/E2
Uintah, Ut, US 137/K11
Uiraúna, Braz. 154/C2
Ŭiryŏng, SKor. 73/E5
Ŭisŏng, SKor. 74/A2
Uitenhage, SAfr. 106/D4
Uitgeest, Neth. 50/B3
Uithoorn, Neth. 50/B4
Uithuizen, Neth. 50/D2
Ujae (isl.), Mrsh. 116/F4
Ujelang (isl.), Mrsh. 116/F4
Ujfehértó, Hun. 41/L5
Ujhāni, India 84/B1
Uji (riv.), Japan 74/D3
Uji, Japan 77/J6
Ujitawara, Japan 77/J6
Ujjain, India 89/L4
Ujung Pandang, Indo. 81/E5
Ukara (isl.), Tanz. 104/B3
Ukerewe (isl.), Tanz. 104/B3
Ukhta, Rus. 61/M3
Ukiah, Ca, US 128/B3
Uklāna, India 86/C5
Ukmergė, Lith. 39/L4
Ukraine (ctry.) 62/D2
Ulaanbaatar (cap.), Mong. 70/J2
Ulaangom, Mong. 70/F2
Ulaanjirem, Mong. 70/J2
Ulanhot, China 71/M2
Ulchin, SKor. 73/E4
Ulcumayo, Peru 156/C3
Ulefoss, Nor. 38/C2
Ulemiste (int'l arpt.), Est. 39/L2
Ulhāsnagar, India 89/K5
Uliastay, Mong. 70/G2
Ulindi (riv.), D.R. Congo 97/L8
Ulithi (isl.), Micr. 116/C3
Uljma, Yugo. 48/E3
Ülken Borsyq Qumy (des.), Kaz. 87/C3
Ülken-Qobda (riv.), Kaz. 63/K2
Ulla (riv.), Sp. 44/A1
Ulla Ulla, Bol. 156/D4
Ulla Ulla, Reserva Nacional, Bol. 156/D4
Ulladulla, Austl. 115/D2
Ullapool, Sc, UK 31/R8
Ullared, Swe. 38/E3
Ulldecona, Sp. 45/F2
Ullensvang, Nor. 38/B1
Ulló, Hun. 49/R10
Ullsfjorden (estu.), Nor. 37/F1
Ullswater (lake), Eng, UK 35/F2
Ulm, Ger. 54/C6
Ulmarra, Austl. 115/E1
Ulmen, Ger. 53/F3
Ulricehamn, Swe. 38/E3
Ulrichen, Swi. 57/E5
Ulrichsberg, Aus. 55/G5
Ulrichstein, Ger. 54/C1
Ulrum, Neth. 50/D2
Ulsan, SKor. 74/A3
Ulstein, Nor. 37/C3
Ulster (reg.), Ire. 34/A3
Ulster (riv.), Ger. 54/C1
Ulster American Folk Park, NI, UK 34/A2
Ulúa (riv.), Hon. 140/D4
Ulua (riv.), Hon. 144/E3
Uluçınar, Turk. 91/D1
Uludağ (peak), Turk. 62/D4
Uludoruk (peak), Turk. 88/D1
Uluguru (mts.), Tanz. 104/C4
Ulukışla, Turk. 90/C2
Ulundi, SAfr. 107/E3
Uluru NP, Austl. 113/F3
Ulverston, Eng, UK 35/E3
Ulverstone, Austl. 115/C4
Ulvik, Nor. 38/B1
Ulvila, Fin. 39/J1
Ul'yanovka, Rus. 39/P2
Ul'yanovsk, Rus. 61/L5
Ul'yanovskaya (obl.), Rus. 63/H1
Ulytaū (mts.),Kaz. 87/E3
Ulytau (peak), Kaz. 87/E3
Umag, Cro. 48/A3
Uman', Ukr. 62/D2
Umán, Mex. 144/D1
Umarizal, Braz. 154/C2
Umarkot, India 82/D4
Umāsi La (pass), India 86/D3
Umbertide, It. 43/K5
Umbogintwini, SAfr. 107/E3
Umboi (isl.), PNG 116/D5
Umbrail (peak), Swi. 57/G4
Umbrailpass (pass), Swi. 57/G4
Umbria (prov.), It. 43/K5
Ume (riv.), Swe. 64/B3
Umeå, Swe. 37/G3
Umeälven (riv.), Swe. 37/F2
Umfolozi (riv.), SAfr. 107/E3
Umgeni (riv.), SAfr. 107/E3
Umhausen, Aus. 57/G3
Umiat, Ak, US 134/H2
Umkirch, Ger. 56/D1
Umkomaas, SAfr. 107/E3
Umm Durmān, Sudan 88/B5
Umm el Faḥm, Isr. 91/G6
Umm Hibal (well), Egypt 101/C4
Ummendorf, Ger. 57/F1
Umnak (isl.), Ak, US 65/V4
Umnak Pass (chan.) 134/E5
Umpqua (riv.), Or, US 124/B3
Umraniye, Turk. 62/C4
Ŭmsŏng, SKor. 73/D4
Umtata, SAfr. 106/E3
Umuahia, Nga. 103/G5
Umuarama, Braz. 157/F1
Umurbey, Turk. 47/K2
Umzimvubu (riv.), SAfr. 106/E3
Umzinto, SAfr. 107/E3
Una, Braz. 154/C4
Una, India 86/D4
Una (mt.), NZ 117/S11
Una (riv.), Bosn.,Cro 43/L4
Unaí, Braz. 154/A5
Unalakleet, Ak, US 134/F3
Unalaska, Ak, US 134/E5
Unalaska (isl.), Ak, US 65/V4
Uncastillo, Sp. 45/E1
Unchahra, India 84/C3
Uncompahgre (plat.), Co, US 128/E3
Unden (lake), Swe. 38/F2
Undenheim, Ger. 54/B3
Underberg, SAfr. 106/E3
Underbool, Austl. 115/B2
Underwood, ND, US 127/H4
Unecha, Rus. 62/E1
Unga (isl.), Ak, US 134/F4
Ungama (bay), Kenya 105/H1
Ungarie, Austl. 115/C2
Ungava (pen.), Qu, Can. 123/J2
Ungava (bay), Qu, Can. 123/K3
Ungheni, Mol. 49/H2
Unhošť, Czh. 55/H2
União, Braz. 154/B2
União da Vitória, Braz. 155/B3
União dos Palmares, Braz. 154/C3
Unimak (isl.), Ak, US 65/V4
Unimak Pass (str.), Ak, US 134/E5
Unini (riv.), Braz. 150/F4
Union, Or, US 126/D4
Union, Mo, US 129/K3
Union, SC, US 133/H3
Union (lake), NJ, US 138/C5
Unión, Arg. 158/D2
Union, NJ, US 139/H9
Union (canal), Sc, UK 36/C5
Union Beach, NJ, US 139/J10
Union Bridge, Md, US 138/A4
Union City, Tn, US 130/B4
Union City, Ca, US 135/K11
Union City, NJ, US 139/J8
Unión de Reyes, Cuba 145/F1
Unión de Tula, Mex. 142/D5
Unión Hidalgo, Mex. 144/C2
Union Mills, Md, US 138/A4
Union Springs, Al, US 133/G3
Uniondale, SAfr. 106/C4
Uniondale, NY, US 139/L9
Uniontown, Pa, US 130/E4
Uniontown, Md, US 138/A4
Unionville, Mo, US 127/K5
United Arab Emirates (ctry.) 88/F4
United Kingdom (ctry.) 31/R9
United Nations, NY, US 139/K9
United Nations Mem. Cemetery, SKor. 74/A3
United States (range), Nun., Can. 123/T6
United States (ctry.) 124
United States Coast Guard Receiving Center, NJ, US 138/D6
United States Department of Energy, Md, US 138/A5
United States Naval Academy, Md, US 138/B6
United States Naval Reservation Mil. Res., PR 141/M8
Unity, Sk, Can. 126/F2
University City, Mo, US 137/G8
University Place, Wa, US 135/B3
Unjha, India 89/K4
Unkel, Ger. 53/G2
Unna, Ger. 51/E5
Unnāo, India 84/C2
Ŭnsan-ŭp, NKor. 73/D3
Unst (isl.), Sc, UK 31/W13
Unter Pleichfeld, Ger. 54/D3
Unterägeri, Swi. 57/E3
Unterargen (riv.), Ger. 57/F2
Untergriesbach, Ger. 55/G5
Unterhaching, Ger. 55/E6
Unteriberg, Swi. 57/E3
Unterkulm, Swi. 56/E3
Unterlüss, Ger. 51/H3
Unterschleissheim, Ger. 55/E6
Untersee (lake), Swi. 57/E2
Unterseen, Swi. 56/D4
Untersiggenthal, Swi. 57/E3
Unterthingau, Ger. 57/G2
Untervaz, Swi. 57/F4
Unterweissenbach, Aus. 55/H6
Ünye, Turk. 62/F4
Unzen-Amakusa NP, Japan 74/A4
Unzen-dake (peak), Japan 74/B4
Unzha (riv.), Rus. 64/E4
Uozu, Japan 75/E2
Upala, CR 145/E4
Upanema, Braz. 154/C2
Upata, Ven. 153/F2
Upemba, Lac (lake), D.R. Congo 105/E2
Upemba, PN de l', D.R. Congo 105/E2
Uphall, Sc, UK 36/C5
Upington, SAfr. 106/C3
Upland, Pa, US 138/C4
Upleta, India 89/K4
Upolu (pt.), Hi, US 124/U10
Upolu (isl.), Sam. 117/H6
Upper (lake), Ca, US 128/B2
Upper (bay), NY, US 138/D2
Upper (pen.), Mi, US 125/J2
Upper Arrow (lake), BC, Can. 126/D3
Upper Darby, Pa, US 138/C4
Upper Demerara-Berbice (pol. reg.), Guy. 153/G3
Upper East (pol. reg.), Gha. 103/E4
Upper Engadine (valley), Swi. 57/F5
Upper Falls, Md, US 138/B5
Upper Ganges (canal), India 84/A1
Upper Hutt, NZ 117/T11
Upper Iowa (riv.), Ia, US 129/J2
Upper Klamath (lake), Or, US 126/C5
Upper Lough Erne (lake), NI, UK 31/Q9
Upper Peoria (lake), Il, US 127/L5
Upper Red (lake), Mn, US 127/K3
Upper Rouge (riv.), Mi, US 135/F7
Upper Saddle River, NJ, US 139/J7
Upper Takutu-Upper Essequibo (pol. reg.), Guy. 153/G4
Upper Thames (valley), Eng, UK 33/E3
Upper Trajan's Wall, Mol. 62/D3
Upper West (pol. reg.), Gha. 103/E4

233

Upper – Verya

Upperlands, NI, UK 34/B2
Upplands-Väsby, Swe. 38/G2
Uppsala, Swe. 38/G2
Uppsala (co.), Swe. 37/F3
Upright (cape), Ak, US 134/D3
Upstart (cape), Austl. 114/B2
Upton, Wy, US 127/G4
Urabá (gulf), Col. 145/G4
Uracoa, Ven. 153/F2
Urad Qianqi, China 72/B2
Uraga (chan.), Japan 77/D3
Urahoro, Japan 76/C2
Uraim (riv.), Braz. 154/A1
Urakawa, Japan 76/C2
Ural (mts.), Rus. 27/L2
Uralla, Austl. 115/D1
Urana, Austl. 115/C2
Urandi, Braz. 154/B4
Uraricoera (riv.), Braz. 150/F3
Urasoe, Japan 75/J7
Urawa, Japan 75/F3
Uray, Rus. 64/G3
Urayasu, Japan 77/D2
Urbach, Ger. 54/C5
Urbana, Md, US 138/A5
Urbania, It. 59/F5
Urbano Santos, Braz. 154/B1
Urbenville, Austl. 114/D5
Urbino, It. 59/F5
Urcos, Peru 156/D4
Urda, Sp. 44/D3
Urdinarrain, Arg. 159/J10
Urdorf, Swi. 57/E3
Ure (riv.), Eng, UK 35/G3
Ures, Mex. 142/C2
Ureshino, Japan 77/K6
Urewera NP, NZ 117/T10
Urfa (prov.), Turk. 90/D2
Urfa, Turk. 90/D2
Urft (riv.), Ger. 51/G6
Urft (lake), Ger. 53/F2
Urganch, Uzb. 87/D4
Urgnano, It. 58/C1
Urho Kekkosen NP, Fin. 37/H1
Uri, India 86/C2
Uri-Rotstock (peak), Swi. 57/E4
Uriangato, Mex. 143/E4
Uribante (riv.), Ven. 152/D3
Uribia, Col. 152/C2
Urie (riv.), Sc, UK 36/D2
Uriménil, Fr. 56/C1
Urique (riv.), Mex. 142/D3
Urjala, Fin. 39/K1
Urk, Neth. 50/C3
Urla, Turk. 62/C5
Urlaţi, Rom. 49/H3
Urmar, India 86/C4
Urmia (lake), Iran 90/F2
Urmitz, Ger. 53/G3
Urmston, Eng, UK 35/F5
Urnäsch, Swi. 57/F3
Urnersee (lake), Swi. 57/E4
Uroševac, Yugo. 47/G1
Urr Water (riv.), Sc, UK 34/E1
Ursensollen, Ger. 55/E4
Ursulo Galván, Mex. 143/N7
Uruaçu, Braz. 151/J6
Uruapan, Mex. 142/E5
Urubamba (riv.), Peru 150/D6
Urubamba, Peru 156/C4
Urubu (riv.), Braz. 150/G4
Uruburetama, Braz. 154/C1
Uruçuca, Braz. 154/C4
Uruçui, Braz. 154/A2
Uruçui Preto (riv.), Braz. 154/A3
Uruçui, Serra do (mts.), Braz. 151/K5
Urucuia (riv.), Braz. 151/J7
Uruguaiana, Braz. 157/E2
Uruguay (ctry.) 157/E3
Uruguay (riv.), SAm. 157/E2
Urumaco, Ven. 152/D2
Ürümqi, China 70/E3
Urunga, Austl. 115/E1
Uruoca, Braz. 154/B1
Urup (isl.), Rus. 67/Q5
Ururi, It. 46/D2
Urussanga, Braz. 155/B4
Uryupinsk, Rus. 63/G2
Urziceni, Rom. 49/H3
Us, Fr. 30/H4
Usa, Japan 74/B4
Usa (riv.), Rus. 64/F3
Uşak (prov.), Turk. 90/B2
Uşak, Turk. 62/D5
Usakos, Namb. 105/C5
Usborne (mt.), UK 159/F6
Uscio, It. 58/C4
Usedom (isl.), Ger. 38/E4
Useldange, Lux. 53/E4
Useless Loop, Austl. 112/B3
Ushibori, Japan 77/F2
Ushibuka, Japan 74/B4
Ushiku, Japan 77/E2
Ushtobe, Kaz. 87/G3
Ushuaia, Arg. 159/C7
Usibelli, Ak, US 134/J3
Usicayos, Peru 156/D4
Usilampatti, India 82/C6
Usingen, Ger. 54/B2
Üsküp, Turk. 49/H5
Uslar, Ger. 51/G5
Usman', Rus. 62/F1
Uspallata, Arg. 158/C2
Uspallata, Paso de (pass), Chile 158/N8
Usquil, Peru 156/B2
Ussel, Fr. 42/E4
Ussel (riv.), Ger. 54/D5
Usses (riv.), Fr. 56/C5
Ussuri (riv.), China,Rus. 65/P5
Ussuriysk, Rus. 71/P3
Ussy-sur-Marne, Fr. 30/M5
Ust'-Ilimsk, Rus. 65/L4
Ust'-Kamchatsk, Rus. 65/S4
Ust'-Kut, Rus. 65/L4
Ust'-Ordynskiy Buryatskiy (aut. okrug), Rus. 65/Q7
Uštěk, Czh. 55/H1
Uster, Swi. 57/E3
Ústí nad Labem, Czh. 43/L1
Ustica (isl.), It. 46/C3
Ustica, It. 46/C3
Ustka, Pol. 38/G4
Ustrzyki Dolne, Pol. 41/M4
Ust'ya (riv.), Rus. 61/K3
Ustyurt (plat.), Kaz. 67/D5
Usu, China 70/D3
Usuda, Japan 77/A1
Usuki, Japan 74/B4
Usulután, ESal. 144/D3
Usumacinta (riv.), Mex. 140/C4
Utah (lake), Ut, US 128/D2
Utah (co.), Ut, US 137/K13
Utah (state), US 128/E3
Utangan (riv.), India 84/A2
Utano, Japan 77/J7
Utashinai, Japan 76/C2
Utena, Lith. 39/L4
Uterský (riv.), Czh. 55/G3
Uthai Thani, Thai. 78/C3
Utica, NY, US 130/F3
Utica, Mi, US 135/F6
Utiel, Sp. 44/E3
Utik (lake), Mb, Can. 127/J2
Utila (isl.), Hon. 144/E2
Utinga, Braz. 154/B4
Utirik (isl.), Mrsh. 116/G3
Utiroa, Kiri. 116/G5
Utmānzai, Pak. 86/A2
Utopia Abor. Land, Austl. 113/G2
Utraulā, India 84/D2
Utrecht, SAfr. 107/E2
Utrecht, Neth. 50/C4
Utrecht (prov.), Neth. 50/C4
Utrera, Sp. 44/C4
Utsunomiya, Japan 75/F2
Uttar Pradesh (state), India 70/C6
Uttaradit, Thai. 78/C2
Uttenweiler, Ger. 57/F1
Uttoxeter, Eng, UK 35/G6
Utuado, PR 141/M8
Utupua (isl.), Sol. 116/F6
Uturoa, FrPol. 117/K6
Utzenstorf, Swi. 56/D3
Uusikaupunki, Fin. 39/J1
Uusimaa (prov.), Fin. 37/H3
Uva (riv.), Col. 150/E3
Uvalde, Tx, US 129/H5
Uvarovo, Rus. 63/G2
Uverito, Ven. 153/E2
Uvira, D.R. Congo 104/A3
Uvongo, SAfr. 107/E3
Uvs (prov.), Mong. 70/F2
Uwajima, Japan 74/C4
Uwimmerah (riv.), Indo. 81/K5
Uxin Qi, China 72/B3
Uxmal (ruin), Mex. 144/D1
Üydzin, Mong. 70/J3
Uyo, Nga. 103/G5
Uyönch, Mong. 70/F2
Uyuni, Bol. 150/E8
Uzbekistan (ctry.) 87/D4
Uzbekistan Nat'l Park, Uzb. 87/E5
Uzein (int'l arpt.), Fr. 42/C5
Uzerche, Fr. 42/D4
Uzès, Fr. 42/F4
Uzhhorod, Ukr. 41/M4
Uzhok (pass), Ukr. 41/M4
Užice, Yugo. 48/D4
Uzlovaya, Rus. 62/F1
Uznach, Swi. 57/E3
Üzümlü, Turk. 62/F5
Uzunköprü, Turk. 47/K2
Uzwil, Swi. 57/F3

V

V.P. Rosales, PN, Chile 158/B4
Vaal (riv.), SAfr. 93/E7
Vaala, Fin. 37/H2
Vaalbos NP, SAfr. 106/D3
Vaaldam (res.), SAfr. 106/D2
Vaals, Neth. 53/F2
Vaalserberg (hill), Neth. 53/E2
Vaasa (prov.), Fin. 37/G3
Vaasa (int'l arpt.), Fin. 37/G3
Vaasa (Vasa), Fin. 37/G3
Vaassen, Neth. 50/C4
Vác, Hun. 48/D2
Vaca (mts.), Ca, US 135/K10
Vaca (mt.), Ca, US 135/K10
Vacaria, Braz. 155/B4
Vacaville, Ca, US 128/B3
Vachon (riv.), Qu, Can. 123/J2
Vada, It. 58/D6
Vado Ligure, It. 58/B4
Vadret (peak), Swi. 57/F4
Vadsø, Nor. 37/J1
Vadstena, Swe. 38/F2
Vaduz (cap.), Lcht. 57/F3
Vaernes (int'l arpt.), Nor. 37/D3
Vaga (riv.), Rus. 60/J3
Vågå, Nor. 37/D3
Vågan, Nor. 37/E1
Vaganski vrh (peak), Cro. 48/B3
Vagay (riv.), Rus. 61/R4
Vaggeryd, Swe. 38/F3
Vagney, Fr. 56/C1
Vagos, Port. 44/A2
Vågsøy, Nor. 37/C3
Vah (riv.), Slvk. 41/J4
Vahitahi (isl.), FrPol. 117/M6
Vaiano, It. 59/E5
Vaiano Cremasco, It. 58/C2
Vaich (lake), Sc, UK 36/B1
Vaihingen an der Enz, Ger. 54/B5
Vaijāpur, India 89/K5
Vail, Co, US 129/F3
Vailate, It. 58/C2
Vair (riv.), Fr. 56/B1
Vaisali (riv.), India 84/B2
Vaitupu (isl.), Tuv. 116/G5
Vaivre-et-Montoille, Fr. 56/C2
Vakfıkebir, Turk. 62/F4
Vakh (riv.), Rus. 64/J3
Vākhān (mts.), Afg. 89/K1
Vakhsh (riv.), Taj. 89/J1
Vál, Hun. 48/D2
Val-de-Marne (dept.), Fr. 52/B6
Val-d'Or, Qu, Can. 130/E1
Val Lagarina (valley), It. 59/D1
Val Marie, Sk, Can. 126/G3
Val Venosta (valley), It. 57/G4
Val Verda, Ut, US 137/K12
Val Verde, Ca, US 136/B2
Valais (canton), Swi. 56/D5
Valbo, Swe. 38/G1
Valburg, Neth. 50/C5
Valcheta, Arg. 158/D4
Valdagno, It. 59/E1
Valdahon, Fr. 56/C3
Valdai (hills), Rus. 60/G4
Valdarno (valley), It. 59/E5
Valdecañas, Embalse de (res.), Sp. 44/C3
Valdemarsvik, Swe. 38/G2
Valdemorillo, Sp. 45/M8
Valdense, Uru. 159/K11
Valdepeñas, Sp. 44/D3
Valderaduey (riv.), Sp. 44/C1
Valderrobres, Sp. 45/F2
Valdés (pen.), Arg. 147/C7
Valdeverdeja, Sp. 44/C3
Valdez, Ak, US 134/J3
Valdez, Ecu. 152/B4
Valdivia, Col. 152/C3
Valdivia, Chile 158/B3
Valdobbiadene, It. 59/F1
Valdoie, Fr. 56/C2
Valdosta, Ga, US 133/H4
Valdoviño, Sp. 44/A1
Vale, Or, US 126/D5
Vale of Glamorgan (co.), Wal, UK 32/C4
Valeggio sul Mincio, It. 59/D2
Valemount, BC, Can. 126/D2
Valença, Braz. 154/C4
Valença, Braz. 211/K7
Valença, Port. 44/A1
Valença do Piauí, Braz. 154/B2
Valence, Fr. 42/D4
Valence, Fr. 42/F4
Valence-sur-Baïse, Fr. 42/D5
Valencia, Ven. 150/E1
Valencia (int'l arpt.), Sp. 45/E3
Valencia, Sp. 45/E3
Valencia (aut. comm.), Sp. 44/E2
Valencia, Ecu. 152/B5
Valencia (isl.), Ire. 30/P11
Valencia de Alcántara, Sp. 44/B3
Valencia de Don Juan, Sp. 44/C1
Valencia, Golfo de (gulf), Sp. 45/F3
Valenciennes, Fr. 52/C3
Valendas, Swi. 57/E4
Vălenii de Munte, Rom. 49/H3
Valente, Braz. 154/C3
Valentigney, Fr. 56/C3
Valentim (range), Braz. 154/B2
Valentine, Tx, US 132/B4
Valentines, Uru. 159/G2
Valenton, Fr. 30/K5
Valenza, It. 58/B2
Våler, Nor. 38/D1
Våler, Nor. 38/D2
Valera, Ven. 152/D2
Valff, Fr. 56/D1
Valga, Est. 39/M3
Valhalla, NY, US 139/K7
Valinco, Golfe de (gulf), Fr. 46/A2
Valinhos, Braz. 211/F7
Valjevo, Yugo. 48/D3
Valkeakoski, Fin. 39/K1
Valkeala, Fin. 39/M1
Valkenburg, Neth. 53/E2
Valkenswaard, Neth. 50/C6
Vall de Uxó, Sp. 45/E3
Valladolid, Sp. 44/C2
Valladolid (int'l arpt.), Sp. 44/C2
Valladolid, Mex. 144/D1
Vallangoujard, Fr. 30/J4
Valle, Ecu. 152/B5
Valle, Nor. 38/B2
Valle d'Aosta (pol. reg.), It. 43/G4
Valle de Bravo, Mex. 143/E5
Valle de Cauca (dept.), Col. 152/B4
Valle de Guanape, Ven. 153/E2
Valle de La Pascua, Ven. 150/E2
Valle de Santiago, Mex. 143/E4
Valle de Zaragoza, Mex. 132/B5
Valle Hermoso, Mex. 143/F3
Valle Lomellina, It. 58/B2
Valle Mosso, It. 58/B1
Vallecitos de Zaragoza, Mex. 143/E5
Vallecrosia, It. 43/G5
Valledupar, Col. 152/C2
Valleé de l'Azaouak (riv.), Mali 103/G2
Vallée du Ferlo (riv.), Sen. 102/B3
Valleé du Mboune (riv.), Sen. 102/B3
Valleé du Saloum (riv.), Sen. 102/B3
Valleé du Serpent (riv.), Mali 102/C3
Vallegrande, Bol. 150/F7
Vallehermoso, Sp. 98/A3
Vallejo, Ca, US 128/B3
Vallenar, Chile 157/B2
Vallendar, Ger. 53/G3
Valleroy, Fr. 53/E5
Valletta (cap.), Malta 46/M7
Valley Brook, Ok, US 137/N15
Valley Center, Ca, US 136/C4
Valley City, ND, US 127/J4
Valley Cottage, NY, US 139/K7
Valley East, On, Can. 130/D2
Valley Forge Nat'l Hist. Park, Pa, US 138/C3
Valley of Desolation, SAfr. 106/D4
Valley of the Kings, Egypt 101/C3
Valley Park, Mo, US 137/G8
Valley Spring, Tx, US 129/H5
Valley Stream, NY, US 139/L9
Vallière (riv.), Fr. 56/B4
Vallorbe, Swi. 56/C4
Valls, Sp. 45/F2
Valluga (peak), Aus. 57/G3
Valmayor (res.), Sp. 45/M8
Valme (riv.), Ger. 51/F6
Valmeyer, Il, US 137/G9
Valmiera, Lat. 39/L3
Valmondois, Fr. 30/J4
Valognes, Fr. 42/C2
Valois (reg.), Fr. 52/B5
Valona, Bay of (bay), Alb. 47/F2
Valpaços, Port. 44/B2
Vālpārai, India 82/C5
Valparaiso, Fl, US 133/G4
Valparaiso, In, US 130/C3
Valparaíso, Mex. 142/E4
Valparaíso (pol. reg.), Chile 158/C2
Valparaíso, Chile 158/N8
Valpovo, Cro. 48/D3
Valréas, Fr. 42/F4
Vals (riv.), SAfr. 106/D2
Vals, Swi. 57/F4
Vals-les-Bains, Fr. 42/F4
Valsād, India 89/K4
Valsaquillo (res.), Mex. 143/L8
Valsbaai (bay), SAfr. 105/C7
Valserine (riv.), Fr. 56/B5
Valserrhein (riv.), Swi. 57/F4
Valsura (riv.), It. 57/G4
Valtellina (valley), It. 57/F5
Valtice, Czh. 43/M2
Valuyki, Rus. 62/F2
Valverde, Sp. 98/A4
Valverde del Camino, Sp. 44/B4
Valyermo, Ca, US 136/C2
Vâmhus, Swe. 38/F1
Vammala, Fin. 39/K1
Vámos, Gre. 47/J5
Vámosmikola, Hun. 48/D2
Vámospércs, Hun. 48/E2
Van, Turk. 90/E2
Van (lake), Turk. 64/E6
Van Buren, Me, US 131/H2
Van Buren, Ar, US 129/J4
Van Cortlandt Park, NY, US 139/K8
Van Diemen (cape), Austl. 109/C2
Van Diemen (gulf), Austl. 109/C2
Van Harinxmakanaal (riv.), Neth. 50/C2
Van Horn, Tx, US 129/F5
Van Norman Lakes, Ca, US 136/B2
Van Rees (mts.), Indo. 81/J4
Van Wert, Oh, US 130/C3
Vana-Javesi (lake), Fin. 39/K1
Vanadzor, Arm. 63/H4
Vanavaro (isl.), FrPol. 117/L7
Vancouver (mt.), Yk, Can. 134/L3
Vancouver, Wa, US 126/C4
Vancouver, BC, Can. 126/C3
Vancouver (int'l arpt.), BC, Can. 126/C3
Vancouver (cape), Austl. 112/C5
Vancouver (isl.), BC, Can. 122/D4
Vandalia, Mo, US 129/K3
Vandans, Aus. 57/F3
Vanderbijlpark, SAfr. 106/D2
Vanderbilt Museum, NY, US 139/E2
Vanderhoof, BC, Can. 126/B2
Vandœuvre-lès-Nancy, Fr. 53/F6
Vanegas, Mex. 143/E4
Vänern (lake), Swe. 64/B4
Vänersborg, Swe. 38/E2
Vangaindrano, Madg. 107/H8
Vanier (isl.), Nun., Can. 123/R7
Vanikolo (isl.), Sol. 116/F6
Vanil Noir (peak), Swi. 56/D4
Vanimo, PNG 116/D5
Vännäs, Swe. 37/F3
Vanne (riv.), Fr. 42/E2
Vannes, Fr. 42/B3
Vanoise, PN de la, Fr. 43/G4
Vanreenenpas (pass), SAfr. 106/E3
Vanrhynsdorp, SAfr. 106/B3
Vansbro, Swe. 38/F1
Vanse, Nor. 38/B2
Vansittart (isl.), Nun., Can. 123/H2
Vantaa, Fin. 39/L1
Vanua Levu (isl.), Fiji 116/G6
Vanuatu (ctry.) 116/F6
Vanwyksvlei, SAfr. 106/C3
Var (riv.), Fr. 43/G5
Vara (riv.), It. 58/C4
Vara, Swe. 38/E2
Varadero, Cuba 145/F1
Varaita (riv.), It. 58/A3
Varallo, It. 58/B1
Varāmīn, Iran 88/F1
Vārānasi, India 84/D3
Varanger-Halvøya (pen.), Nor. 37/J1
Varangerfjorden (estu.), Nor. 37/J1
Varangéville, Fr. 53/F6
Varano (lake), It. 46/D2
Varano Borghi, It. 58/B1
Varaždin, Cro. 43/M3
Varazze, It. 58/B4
Varberg, Swe. 38/E3
Vardar (riv.), FYROM 47/G2
Varde, Den. 38/C4
Várdha, Gre. 47/G3
Vardø, Nor. 37/J1
Varel, Ger. 51/F2
Varenne (riv.), Fr. 42/C2
Varennes, Qu, Can. 131/P6
Varennes-Jarcy, Fr. 30/K5
Varennes-Vauzelles, Fr. 42/E3
Vareš, Bosn. 48/D3
Varese, It. 58/B1
Varese (prov.), It. 57/E6
Varese Ligure, It. 58/C4
Vårgårda, Swe. 38/E2
Vargem Grande, Braz. 154/B1
Vargem Grande do Sul, Braz. 211/G6
Varginha, Braz. 211/H6
Vári, Gre. 47/H4
Varilhes, Fr. 42/D5
Värmeln (lake), Swe. 38/E2
Värmland (co.), Swe. 37/E3
Varna (pol. reg.), Bul. 47/K1
Varna, Bul. 49/H4
Värnamo, Swe. 38/F3
Varois-et-Chaignot, Fr. 56/B3
Varoška Rijeka, Bosn. 48/C3
Várpalota, Hun. 48/D2
Varraddes, Fr. 30/L5
Varsi, It. 58/C3
Vârsta, Swe. 38/G2
Vartholomión, Gre. 47/G4
Varto, Turk. 90/E2
Vartry (res.), Ire. 34/B5
Vartry (riv.), Ire. 34/B5
Várzea Alegre, Braz. 154/C2
Várzea da Palma, Braz. 154/A5
Várzea Grande, Braz. 154/B2
Várzea Grande, Braz. 151/G7
Varzelândia, Braz. 154/A4
Varzi, It. 58/C3
Varzo, It. 57/E5
Varzuga (riv.), Rus. 60/H2
Vas (prov.), Hun. 48/C2
Vasa Barris (riv.), Braz. 151/L5
Vásárosnamény, Hun. 41/M4
Vaşcău, Rom. 48/F2
Vashka (riv.), Rus. 61/K2
Vashon, Wa, US 135/C3
Vashon (isl.), Wa, US 135/C3
Vasiliká, Gre. 47/H2
Vasil'yevskiy (isl.), Rus. 61/S7
Vaslui (prov.), Rom. 49/H2
Vaslui, Rom. 49/H2
Vassar, Mi, US 130/D3
Vassdalsegga (peak), Nor. 38/B2
Vassouras, Braz. 211/K7
Västerås, Swe. 38/G2
Västerbotten (co.), Swe. 37/F2
Västerdalälven (riv.), Swe. 38/E1
Västernorrland (co.), Swe. 37/F3
Västervik, Swe. 38/G3
Västmanland (co.), Swe. 37/E3
Vasto, It. 46/D1
Västra Silen (lake), Swe. 38/E2
Vasvár, Hun. 48/C2
Vasyl'kiv, Ukr. 62/D2
Vaterstetten, Ger. 55/E6
Vatican City (ctry.) 46/C2
Vatnajökull (glacier), Ice. 37/P7
Vatomandry, Madg. 107/J7
Vatra Dornei, Rom. 49/G2
Vättern (lake), Swe. 37/E4
Vaucouleurs (riv.), Fr. 30/H5
Vaud (canton), Swi. 56/C4
Vaudoy-en-Brie, Fr. 30/M5
Vaudreuil-Dorion, Qu, Can. 131/M7
Vaughan, On, Can. 131/Q8
Vaughn, NM, US 129/F4
Vaughn, Wa, US 135/B3
Vaulruz, Swi. 56/C4
Vaulx-en-Velin, Fr. 56/A6
Vaupés (dept.), Col. 152/D4
Vaupés (riv.), Col. 147/B2
Vauréal, Fr. 30/J4
Vauvert, Fr. 42/F5
Vauvillers, Fr. 56/C2
Vaux (riv.), Fr. 40/C4
Vaux-sur-Seine, Fr. 30/H4
Vaux-sur-Sûre, Belg. 53/E4
Vauxhall, Ab, Can. 126/E3
Vavatenina, Madg. 107/J7
Vava'u Group (isls.), Tonga 117/H6
Vavuniya, SrL. 82/D6
Vawkavysk, Bela. 41/N2
Vaxjo (int'l arpt.), Swe. 38/F3
Växjö, Swe. 38/F3
Vaygach (isl.), Rus. 160/B
Vazante, Braz. 154/A5
Vázea Paulista, Braz. 211/G8
Vazuza (res.), Rus. 60/G5
Vazzola, It. 59/F1
Vecchiano, It. 58/D5
Vechigen, Swi. 56/D4
Vecht (riv.), Neth. 50/D3
Vechta, Ger. 51/F3
Vechte (riv.), Ger. 50/D3
Vecsés, Hun. 48/D2
Vedano Olona, It. 58/B1
Veddige, Swe. 38/E3
Vedea (riv.), Rom. 49/G3
Vedelago, It. 59/F1
Vedia, Arg. 158/E2
Vedra, Sp. 44/A1
Veendam, Neth. 50/D2
Veenendaal, Neth. 50/C4
Veere, Neth. 50/A5
Veerse Meer (res.), Neth. 50/A5
Vefsn, Nor. 37/E2
Vega, Tx, US 129/G4
Vega (pt.), Ak, US 134/B6
Vega (isl.), Nor. 37/D2
Vega de Alatorre, Mex. 143/N6
Vegafjorden (estu.), Nor. 37/D2
Veghel, Neth. 50/C5
Vègreville, Ab, Can. 126/E2
Véguela, Peru 156/B3
Vehkalahti, Fin. 39/M1
Vehne (riv.), Ger. 51/F2
Veigné, Fr. 42/D3
Veinticinco de Mayo, Arg. 158/E2
Veinticinco de Mayo, Arg. 158/D3
Veinticinco de Mayo, Uru. 159/K11
Veintiocho de Mayo, Ecu. 156/B1
Veintiocho de Noviembre, Arg. 159/B6
Veitsch, Aus. 48/B2
Veitshöchheim, Ger. 54/C3
Vejen, Den. 38/C4
Vejer de la Frontera, Sp. 44/C4
Vejle, Den. 38/C4
Vejle (co.), Den. 38/C4
Vejprty, Czh. 55/G2
Vela, Cabo de la (pt.), Col. 152/C1
Vela Luka, Cro. 46/E1
Velaines, Fr. 53/E6
Vélan (peak), Swi. 56/D6
Velardeña, Mex. 142/E3
Velas, Azor., Port. 45/S12
Velasco Ibarra, Ecu. 152/B5
Velázquez, Uru. 159/G2
Velbert, Ger. 50/E6
Velburg, Ger. 55/E4
Velddrif, SAfr. 106/L10
Velden, Ger. 55/F6
Velden am Wörthersee, Aus. 43/L3
Veldhoven, Neth. 50/C6
Velen, Ger. 50/D5
Velešta, FYROM 47/G2
Velestínon, Gre. 47/H3
Vélez, Col. 152/C3
Vélez-Blanco, Sp. 44/D4
Vélez-Málaga, Sp. 44/C4
Vélez-Rubio, Sp. 44/D4
Velhas, Rio das (riv.), Braz. 151/K7
Velika Gorica, Cro. 48/C3
Velika Kladuša, Bosn. 43/L4
Velika Plana, Yugo. 48/E3
Velikaya (riv.), Rus. 60/F4
Velikiy Ustyug, Rus. 61/K3
Velikiye Luki, Rus. 39/P3
Veliko Tŭrnovo, Bul. 47/J1
Velille, Peru 156/D4
Vélingara, Sen. 102/B3
Vélizy-Villacoublay, Fr. 30/J5
Vel'ké Kapušany, Slvk. 48/F1
Vel'ký Krtíš, Slvk. 41/K4
Velký Zvon (peak), Czh. 55/F3
Vellberg, Ger. 54/C4
Velletri, It. 46/C2
Vellinge, Swe. 38/E4
Vellmar, Ger. 51/G6
Vellón (res.), Sp. 45/N8
Vellore, India 82/C5
Vélon, Gre. 47/H4
Vel'sk, Rus. 60/J3
Veluwe (phys. reg.), Neth. 50/C4
Veluwemeer (lake), Neth. 50/C4
Veluwezoom, NP, Neth. 50/C4
Velva, ND, US 127/H3
Velvary, Czh. 55/H2
Velvendós, Gre. 47/H2
Vémars, Fr. 30/K4
Vemb, Den. 38/C3
Véménd, Hun. 48/D2
Venachar (lake), Sc, UK 36/B4
Venado Tuerto, Arg. 158/E2
Venafro, It. 46/D2
Venamo (peak), Ven. 153/F3
Venâncio Aires, Braz. 155/A4
Venaria, It. 43/G4
Vence, Fr. 43/G5
Venceslau Brás, Braz. 155/B2
Vendas Novas, Port. 44/A3
Vendôme, Fr. 42/D3
Vendrell, Sp. 45/F2
Vendrest, Fr. 30/M4
Veneta, Laguna (lake), It. 59/F2
Venetie, Ak, US 134/J2
Veneto (pol. reg.), It. 43/J4
Venezia (prov.), It. 59/F1
Venezia, Golfo di (gulf), Eur. 59/F2
Venezia (Venice), It. 59/F2
Venezuela (gulf), Col.,Ven. 153/D2
Venezuela (ctry.) 153/E3
Vengurla, India 89/K5
Veniaminof (vol.), Ak, US 134/G4
Venice, Fl, US 133/H5
Venice, Il, US 137/G8
Venice (Venezia), It. 43/K4
Vénissieux, Fr. 42/F4
Venjan, Swe. 38/E1
Venjansjön (lake), Swe. 38/E1
Venkatagiri, India 82/C5
Venlo, Neth. 50/D6
Vennesla, Nor. 38/B2
Veno (bay), Den. 38/C3
Venoge (riv.), Swi. 56/C4
Venosa, It. 46/D2
Venray, Neth. 50/C5
Vent, Îles du (isls.), FrPol. 117/L6
Venta (riv.), Lat. 60/D4
Venta de Baños, Sp. 44/C2
Ventauri (riv.), Ven. 150/E3
Ventersburg, SAfr. 106/D3
Ventersdorp, SAfr. 106/D2
Venterstad, SAfr. 106/D3
Ventiseri, Fr. 46/A2
Ventnor, Eng, UK 33/E5
Ventnor City, NJ, US 138/D5
Ventspils, Lat. 39/J3
Ventuari (riv.), Ven. 153/E3
Ventura (riv.), Ca, US 136/A2
Ventura (co.), Ca, US 136/A2
Venturina, It. 43/J5
Venturosa, Braz. 154/C3
Venustiano Carranza, Mex. 140/C4
Venustiano Carranza (res.), Mex. 143/E3
Vép, Hun. 43/M3
Ver-sur-Launette, Fr. 30/L4
Vera, Arg. 157/D2
Vera, Sp. 44/E4
Vera Cruz, Pan. 152/B2
Veracruz, Mex. 143/N7
Veracruz-Llave (state), Mex. 140/B3
Veranópolis, Braz. 155/B4
Verāval, India 89/K4
Verbania, It. 57/E6
Verberie, Fr. 52/B5
Verbicaro, It. 46/D3
Vercelli, It. 58/B2
Vercelli (prov.), It. 56/E6
Verdal, Nor. 37/D3
Verde (riv.), Par. 157/D1
Verde (cape), Sen. 96/B5
Verde (riv.), Braz. 151/G6
Verde (riv.), Mex. 143/F4
Verde (coast), Sp. 44/B1
Verde (cape), It. 58/A5
Verde (bay), Arg. 158/E3
Verde Grande (riv.), Braz. 151/K7
Verden, Ger. 51/G3
Verdhikoússa, Gre. 47/G3
Verdigris (riv.), Ks, US 129/J3
Verdinho (riv.), Braz. 155/B1
Verdon (riv.), Fr. 42/F5
Verdugo (mts.), Ca, US 136/F7
Verdun, Qu, Can. 131/N7
Vereeniging, SAfr. 106/D2
Verena (peak), It. 57/H6
Vereshchagino, Rus. 61/M4
Veretskiy (pass), Ukr. 41/M4
Verga (cape), Gui. 102/B4
Vergara, Uru. 159/G2
Vergato, It. 59/E4
Vergennes, Vt, US 130/F2
Vergiate, It. 58/B1
Vergina (ruin), Gre. 47/H2
Verigenstadt, Ger. 57/F1
Verín, Sp. 44/B2
Veríssimo, Braz. 155/B1
Verkhnetulomskiy (res.), Rus. 60/F1
Verkhoyansk (range), Rus. 67/M2
Verkhoyansk, Rus. 65/P3
Verl, Ger. 51/F5
Vermenagna (riv.), It. 58/A4
Vermilion (range), Mn, US 127/K4
Vermilion, Ab, Can. 126/F2
Vermilion (riv.), Ab, Can. 126/F2
Vermillion, SD, US 127/J5
Vermont (state), US 131/F2
Vernal, Ut, US 128/E2
Vernayaz, Swi. 56/D5
Vernazza, It. 58/C4
Verneuil-sur-Avre, Fr. 42/D2
Verneuil-sur-Seine, Fr. 30/H5
Verneukpan (salt pan), SAfr. 106/C3
Vernier, Swi. 56/C5
Vernon, BC, Can. 126/D3
Vernon, Fr. 42/D2
Vernon Hills, Il, US 135/Q15
Vernon Valley, NJ, US 138/D1
Vernouillet, Fr. 30/H5
Vero Beach, Fl, US 133/H5
Véroia, Gre. 47/H2
Verolanuova, It. 58/D2
Verolavecchia, It. 58/D2
Verolengo, It. 58/A2
Verona (prov.), It. 59/D1
Verona (int'l arpt.), It. 59/D2
Verona, It. 59/D2
Verona, NJ, US 139/J8
Verónica, Arg. 159/K11
Verrès, It. 58/A1
Verret, La, US 137/Q17
Verrières-le-Buisson, Fr. 30/J5
Versa (riv.), It. 58/B3
Versailles, Ky, US 130/C4
Versailles, Fr. 30/J5
Versigny, Fr. 30/L4
Verskla (riv.), Ukr.,Rus. 64/D4
Versmold, Ger. 51/F4
Versoix, Swi. 56/C5
Vert-le-Grand, Fr. 30/K6
Vert-le-Petit, Fr. 30/K6
Vert-Saint-Denis, Fr. 30/K6
Vertana (peak), It. 57/G4
Verte (peak), Fr. 56/C6
Vertemate, It. 58/C1
Vertientes, Cuba 145/G1
Vertou, Fr. 42/C4
Vertova, It. 58/C1
Vertus, Fr. 52/D6
Verviers, Belg. 53/E2
Vervins, Fr. 52/C4
Verwoerdburg, SAfr. 106/Q12
Veryan (bay), Eng, UK 32/B6

W du Niger, PN du, Ben. 96/F5
W du Niger, PN du, Niger 103/F3
W. J. van Blommestein (lake), Sur. 151/G2
Wa, Gha. 103/E4
Waal, Ger. 57/G2
Waal (riv.), Neth. 50/C5
Waalre, Neth. 50/C6
Waalwijk, Neth. 50/C5
Waarschoot, Belg. 52/C1
Wabasca, Ab, Can. 126/E2
Wabasca (riv.), Ab, Can. 122/E3
Wabash, In, US 130/C3
Wabash (riv.), Il,In, US 125/J4
Wabē Shebelē Wenz (riv.), Eth. 93/G4
Wabern, Ger. 51/G6
Wabigoon (lake), On, Can. 127/K3
Wabowden, Mb, Can. 127/J2
Wąbrzeźno, Pol. 41/K2
Wabu (lake), China 72/D4
Wabu, SKor. 73/G6
Wachenheim an der Weinstrasse, Ger. 54/B4
Wachi, Japan 77/H5
Wachtebeke, Belg. 52/C1
Wachtendonk, Ger. 50/D6
Wächtersbach, Ger. 54/C2
Wackernheim, Ger. 54/B3
Wackersdorf, Ger. 55/F4
Waco, Tx, US 129/H5
Waconda (lake), Ks, US 129/H3
Waconia, Mn, US 127/K4
Wad Medanī, Sudan 88/B6
Wada, Japan 77/E3
Wadayama, Japan 77/G5
Wadbilliga NP, Austl. 115/D3
Waddān, Libya 96/J2
Waddell, Az, US 137/R18
Waddell (dam), Az, US 137/R18
Waddenzee (sound), Neth. 40/C2
Waddington (mt.), BC, Can. 126/B3
Waddinxveen, Neth. 50/B4
Waddy (pt.), Austl. 114/D4
Wadena, Sk, Can. 127/H3
Wadena, Mn, US 127/K4
Wädenswil, Swi. 57/E3
Wadern, Ger. 53/F4
Wadersloh, Ger. 51/F5
Wadgassen, Ger. 53/F5
Wādī al Layl, Tun. 100/M6
Wādī As Sīr, Jor. 91/D4
Wādī Majardah (riv.), Tun. 46/A4
Wādī Mūsá, Jor. 91/D4
Wading (riv.), NJ, US 138/D4
Wading River, NY, US 139/F2
Wadowice, Pol. 41/K4
Wadsworth, Il, US 135/Q15
Waegwan, SKor. 73/E5
Wafangdian, China 73/A3
Wagenfeld-Hasslingen, Ger. 51/F3
Wageningen, Neth. 50/C5
Wager (bay), NW, Can. 122/G2
Wagga Wagga, Austl. 115/C2
Waggaman, La, US 137/P17
Waghäusel, Ger. 54/B4
Wagin, Austl. 112/C5
Waging am See, Ger. 55/F7
Waginger (lake), Ger. 55/F7
Wägitaler-see (lake), Swi. 57/E3
Wagna, Aus. 43/L3
Wagner, Braz. 154/B4
Wągrowiec, Pol. 41/J2
Wagstaff, Ks, US 137/D6
Wāh, Pak. 86/B3
Wah Wah (range), Ut, US 128/D3
Wahiawa, Hi, US 124/V12
Wahlern, Swi. 56/D4
Wahpeton, ND, US 127/J4
Wahrenholz, Ger. 51/H3
Wai, India 82/B4
Waialee, Hi, US 124/V12
Waialua, Hi, US 124/V12
Waianae, Hi, US 124/V13
Waiau (riv.), NZ 117/S11
Waibamiao, China 72/D2
Waiblingen, Ger. 54/C5
Waidhaus, Ger. 55/F3
Waidhofen an der Thaya, Aus. 43/L2
Waidhofen an der Ybbs, Aus. 55/H7
Waigeo (isl.), Indo. 116/C4
Waigolshausen, Ger. 54/D3
Waihou (riv.), NZ 117/T10
Waikane, Hi, US 124/W12
Waikari, NZ 117/S11
Waikato (riv.), NZ 109/H6
Waikerie, Austl. 113/H5
Waikiki, Hi, US 124/W13
Waikoloa Village, Hi, US 124/U11
Wailuku, Hi, US 124/T10
Waimanalo, Hi, US 124/W13
Waimanalo Beach, Hi, US 124/W13
Waimate, NZ 117/S11
Waimea, Hi, US 124/S10
Waimea (falls), Hi, US 124/V12
Waimes, Belg. 53/F3
Wainfleet, On, Can. 131/R10
Waingangā (riv.), India 82/C3
Waini (riv.), Guy. 153/G2
Wainwright, Ak, US 134/F1
Wainwright, Ab, Can. 126/F2
Waipahu, Hi, US 124/V13
Waipio, Hi, US 124/U10
Waipio Acres, Hi, US 124/V13
Waipukurau, NZ 117/T10
Wairau (riv.), NZ 117/S11
Wairoa, NZ 117/T10
Waischenfeld, Ger. 55/E3
Waitaki (riv.), NZ 117/S11
Waitara, NZ 117/S10
Waizenkirchen, Aus. 55/G6
Wajima, Japan 75/E2
Waka (cape), Indo. 81/G4
Wakakusa, Japan 77/A2
Wakasa, Japan 74/D3
Wakasa (bay), Japan 77/H4
Wakaw, Sk, Can. 127/G2
Wakayama, Japan 74/D3
Wakayama (pref.), Japan 74/D4
Wake (isl.), Pac., US 116/F3
Wakefield, Mi, US 130/B2
Wakefield, Eng, UK 35/G4
Wakema, Myan. 83/G4
Waki, Japan 74/D3
Wakkanai, Japan 76/B1
Wakool, Austl. 115/C2
Wakuya, Japan 76/B4
Wakwayowkastic (riv.), On, Can. 130/D1
Wala (riv.), Tanz. 104/B4
Walachia (reg.), Rom. 49/G3
Walagunya Abor. Land, Austl. 112/D2
Wałbrzych, Pol. 41/J3
Wałbrzych (prov.), Pol. 41/J3
Walbury (hill), Eng, UK 33/E4
Walcha, Austl. 115/D1
Walcheren (isl.), Neth. 50/A5
Walcourt, Belg. 53/D3
Wałcz, Pol. 41/J2
Wald, Swi. 57/E3
Wald, Ger. 55/F4
Waldbillig, Lux. 53/F4
Waldbreitbach, Ger. 53/G2
Waldbröl, Ger. 53/G2
Waldbronn, Ger. 54/B5
Waldbrunn, Ger. 54/C3
Waldburg, Ger. 57/F2
Walden, Co, US 129/F2
Waldenbuch, Ger. 54/C5
Waldenburg, Swi. 56/D3
Waldenburg, Ger. 54/C4
Waldershof, Ger. 55/F3
Waldesch, Ger. 53/G3
Waldheim, Sk, Can. 126/G2
Waldighofen, Fr. 56/D2
Walding, Aus. 55/H6
Waldkirch, Ger. 56/D1
Waldmünchen, Ger. 55/F4
Waldnaab (riv.), Ger. 55/F3
Waldrach, Ger. 53/F4
Waldron, Mo, US 137/D5
Waldsassen, Ger. 55/F3
Waldshut-Tiengen, Ger. 57/E2
Waldstetten, Ger. 54/C5
Waldviertel (reg.), Aus. 41/H4
Waldwick, NJ, US 139/J8
Walea (str.), Indo. 81/F4
Waleabahi (isl.), Indo. 81/F4
Walensee (lake), Swi. 57/F3
Walenstadt, Swi. 57/F3
Wales, Ak, US 134/E2
Wales, UK 32/B3
Wales (isl.), Nun., Can. 123/H2
Wales, Wi, US 135/P14
Walferdange, Lux. 53/F4
Walgett, Austl. 115/D1
Walhalla, ND, US 127/J3
Walhalla, SC, US 133/H3
Walhalla, Ger. 55/F4
Walker (riv.), Nv, US 128/C3
Walker (lake), Nv, US 128/C3
Walker (bay), SAfr. 106/L11
Walkerston, Austl. 114/C3
Walkerton, On, Can. 130/D2
Walkill (riv.), NY, US 138/D1
Walla Walla, Austl. 115/C2
Walla Walla, Wa, US 126/D4
Wallace, Id, US 126/E4
Wallaceburg, On, Can. 130/D3
Wallaroo, Austl. 113/H5
Wallasey, Eng, UK 35/E5
Walldorf, Ger. 54/B4
Walldürn, Ger. 54/C3
Walled (lake), Mi, US 135/F6
Walled City Hist. Site, SKor. 73/G7
Walled Lake, Mi, US 135/F6
Wallenhorst, Ger. 51/F4
Wallern im Burgenland, Aus. 43/M3
Wallers, Fr. 52/C3
Wallersee (lake), Aus. 55/G7
Wallerstein, Ger. 54/D5
Wallington, NJ, US 139/J8
Wallis (isls.), Wall. 117/H6
Wallis and Futuna (dpcy.), Fr. 116/G6
Wallisellen, Swi. 57/E3
Walloon Brabant (prov.), Belg. 53/D2
Wallowa (mts.), Or, US 126/D4
Wallsend, Eng, UK 35/G2
Wallumbilla, Austl. 114/C4
Walney, Isle of (isl.), Eng, UK 35/E3
Walnut, Ca, US 136/G7
Walnut Canyon Nat'l Mon., Az, US 128/E4
Walnut Creek, Ca, US 135/K11
Walnut Grove, Ca, US 135/L10
Walnut Park, Ca, US 136/F8
Walnut Ridge, Ar, US 129/K3
Walnutport, Pa, US 138/C2
Walpole, Austl. 112/C5
Walpole-Nornalup NP, Austl. 112/C5
Walrus (isls.), Ak, US 134/F4
Walsall, Eng, UK 32/E1
Walsenburg, Co, US 129/F3
Walsingham (cape), Nun., Can. 123/K2
Walsrode, Ger. 51/G3
Waltenhofen, Ger. 57/G2
Walter F. George (res.), US 133/G4
Walterboro, SC, US 133/H3
Walter's Ash, Eng, UK 30/A2
Waltham Abbey, Eng, UK 30/D1
Waltham Forest (bor.), Eng, UK 30/A1
Walton-on-Thames, Eng, UK 30/B2
Waltrop, Ger. 51/E5
Walvis Bay, Namb. 105/B5
Walworth, Wi, US 135/N14
Walworth (co.), Wi, US 135/N14
Walyahmoning (peak), Austl. 112/C4
Walyunga NP, Austl. 112/L6
Walzenhausen, Swi. 57/F3
Wamba, Kenya 104/C2
Wamba, D.R. Congo 97/L7
Wamel, Neth. 50/C5
Wami (riv.), Tanz. 104/C4
Wampool (riv.), Eng, UK 35/E2
Wamsutter, Wy, US 126/G5
Wanaka, NZ 117/R11
Wanamassa, NJ, US 138/D3
Wanaque (res.), NJ, US 138/D1
Wanaque, NJ, US 139/H7
Wanda (mts.), China 71/P2
Wanda, Il, US 137/G8
Wandering, Austl. 112/C5
Wanding, China 83/G3
Wando, SKor. 73/D5
Wandoan, Austl. 114/C4
Wandsworth (bor.), Eng, UK 30/C2
Wanfried, Ger. 51/H6
Wang (riv.), Thai. 83/G4
Wang Hip (peak), Thai. 78/B4
Wanganui, NZ 117/T10
Wangaratta, Austl. 115/C3
Wangdu, China 72/C3
Wangen, Ger. 57/F2
Wangen an der Aare, Swi. 56/D3
Wangen bei Olten, Swi. 56/D3
Wangerooge (isl.), Ger. 51/E1
Wanggamet (peak), Indo. 81/F6
Wanghai Shan (peak), China 73/A2
Wängi, Swi. 57/E3
Wangjiang, China 79/C1
Wangpan (bay), China 72/E5
Wani (peak), Indo. 81/F4
Wanica (dist.), Sur. 153/H3
Wank (peak), Ger. 57/H2
Wanning, China 83/K4
Wanouchi, Japan 77/L5
Wanquan, China 72/C2
Wanrong, China 72/B4
Wansbeck (riv.), Eng, UK 35/G1
Wantagh, NY, US 139/M9
Wanxian, China 70/J5
Wanze, Belg. 53/E2
Wapakoneta, Oh, US 130/C3
Wapawekka (lake), Sk, Can. 127/G2
Wapiti (riv.), Ab,BC, Can. 126/D2
Wapoga (riv.), Indo. 81/J4
Wappapello (lake), Mo, US 129/K3
Wapsipinicon (riv.), Ia, US 127/K5
Wapwallopen, Pa, US 138/B1
Warabi, Japan 77/D2
Warangal, India 82/C4
Waratah, Austl. 115/C4
Warburg, Ger. 51/G6
Warburton, Pak. 86/B4
Warburton, Austl. 112/E3
Warburton Range Abor. Rsv., Austl. 112/E3
Warche (riv.), Belg. 53/F3
Ward, Co, US 137/A2
Ward, NZ 117/S11
Ward Cove, Ak, US 134/M4
Warden, SAfr. 106/E2
Warden (pt.), Eng, UK 33/G4
Wardenburg, Ger. 51/F2
Wardha, India 82/C3
Ward's Stone (peak), Eng, UK 35/F3
Ware, Eng, UK 33/F3
Waregem, Belg. 52/C2
Waremme, Belg. 53/E2
Waren, Ger. 38/E5
Warendorf, Ger. 51/E5
Waretown, NJ, US 138/D4
Warffum, Neth. 50/D2
Wargrave, Eng, UK 33/F4
Warialda, Austl. 115/D1
Warin Chamrap, Thai. 78/D3
Waringstown, NI, UK 34/B3
Warka, Pol. 41/L3
Warkworth, NZ 117/S10
Warlingham, Eng, UK 30/C3
Warmbad, Namb. 106/B3
Warme Bode (riv.), Ger. 51/H5
Warmebach (riv.), Ger. 51/G6
Warmenhuizen, Neth. 50/B3
Warmeriville, Fr. 53/D5
Warmia (reg.), Pol. 41/K1
Warminster, Eng, UK 32/D4
Warminster, Pa, US 138/C3
Warner (mts.), Ca, US 126/C5
Warner Robins, Ga, US 133/H3
Warnow (riv.), Ger. 38/D5
Warnsveld, Neth. 50/D4
Waroona, Austl. 112/B5
Warr Acres, Ok, US 137/M14
Warrabri, Austl. 113/G2
Warrandirinna (lake), Austl. 113/H3
Warrego (range), Austl. 109/D3
Warrego (riv.), Austl. 109/D3
Warren (pt.), NW, Can. 134/M2
Warren, Austl. 115/C1
Warren, Mn, US 127/J3
Warren, Oh, US 130/D3
Warren, Pa, US 130/E3
Warren, Ar, US 129/J4
Warren, Mi, US 130/D3
Warren, Ut, US 137/J11
Warren (riv.), Austl. 112/C5
Warren, NJ, US 138/D2
Warren (co.), NJ, US 138/C2
Warrenpoint, NI, UK 34/B3
Warrensburg, Mo, US 129/J3
Warrenton, SAfr. 106/D3
Warrenville, Il, US 135/P16
Warri, Nga. 103/G5
Warrington, Fl, US 133/G4
Warrington, Eng, UK 35/F5
Warrnambool, Austl. 115/B3
Warroad, Mn, US 127/K3
Warrumbungle NP, Austl. 115/D1
Warsaw, In, US 130/C3
Warsaw (Warszawa) (cap.), Pol. 41/L2
Warscheneck (peak), Aus. 48/B2
Warsop, Eng, UK 35/G5
Warstein, Ger. 51/F6
Warszawa (prov.), Pol. 41/L2
Warta (riv.), Pol. 62/A1
Wartberg an der Krems, Aus. 55/H7
Wartberg ob der Aist, Aus. 55/H6
Wartburg, Il, US 137/G9
Warwick, RI, US 131/G3
Warwick, Ok, US 137/N14
Warwick, Eng, UK 33/E2
Warwick, Austl. 114/D5
Warwick, NY, US 138/D1
Warwick, Md, US 138/C5
Warwickshire (co.), Eng, UK 33/E2
Wasatch (co.), Ut, US 137/K12
Wasatch (range), Ut, US 124/D4
Wasbank, SAfr. 107/E3
Wasburn (riv.), Eng, UK 35/G4
Wasco, Ca, US 128/C4
Waseca, Mn, US 127/K4
Wash, The (bay), Eng, UK 35/J6
Washburn (lake), Nun., Can. 122/F1
Washimiya, Japan 77/D1
Washington, Il, US 127/L5
Washington (isl.), Wi, US 127/M4
Washington, NC, US 133/J3
Washington, Pa, US 130/D3
Washington (mt.), NH, US 131/G2
Washington, NJ, US 138/D2
Washington (state), US 126/C4
Washington (cap.), US 138/A6
Washington (lake), Wa, US 135/C2
Washington, Eng, UK 35/G2
Washington Dulles (int'l arpt.), Va, US 130/E4
Washington Park, Il, US 137/G8
Washington Terrace, Ut, US 137/K11
Washingtonville, Pa, US 138/B1
Washita (riv.), Ok, US 129/H4
Washtenaw (co.), Mi, US 135/E7
Wasilków, Pol. 41/M2
Wasilla, Ak, US 134/J3
Waskaganish (Rupert House), Qu, Can. 130/E1
Waskasa (bay), Japan 74/D3
Waskey (mt.), Ak, US 134/G4
Waspán, Nic. 145/F3
Wasselonne, Fr. 53/G6
Wassen, Swi. 57/E4
Wassenaar, Neth. 50/B4
Wassenberg, Ger. 53/F1
Wasserbillig, Lux. 53/F4
Wasserburg, Ger. 54/D6
Wasserburg am Inn, Ger. 55/F6
Wasserkuppe (peak), Ger. 54/C2
Wassuk (range), Nv, US 124/C4
Wassy, Fr. 56/A1
Wast Water (lake), Eng, UK 35/E3
Wasur-Rawa Biru NP, Indo. 81/K5
Waswanipi (lake), Qu, Can. 130/E1
Wat Phu, Laos 78/D3
Watampone, Indo. 81/F4
Watarai, Japan 77/L7
Watarase (riv.), Japan 75/F2
Watari, Japan 75/G1
Watch Hill (pt.), RI, US 139/G1
Watchung, NJ, US 139/H9
Watchung (mts.), NJ, US 139/H9
Water of Ae (riv.), Sc, UK 34/E1
Water of Girvan (riv.), Sc, UK 36/B6
Water of Ken (riv.), Sc, UK 34/D1
Waterbury, Ct, US 130/F3
Wateree (lake), SC, US 133/H3
Wateree (riv.), SC, US 133/H3
Waterford, Mi, US 130/D3
Waterford, Ire. 31/Q10
Waterford, Ct, US 139/F1
Waterford Works, NJ, US 138/D4
Watergate (bay), Eng, UK 32/A6
Waterhen (riv.), Sk, Can. 126/F2
Waterhen (lake), Mb, Can. 127/J2
Waterloo, On, Can. 130/D3
Waterloo, Il, US 137/G9
Waterloo, Ok, US 137/N14
Waterloo, Belg. 53/D2
Waterloo Battlesite, Belg. 53/D2
Waterloo Village, NJ, US 138/D2
Watermael-Boitsfort, Belg. 52/D2
Waterton Lakes Nat'l Pk., Ab, Can. 126/E3
Watertown, SD, US 127/J4
Watertown, NY, US 130/F3
Waterville, Wa, US 126/C4
Waterville, Me, US 131/G2
Waterville, Ire. 30/N11
Waterway, La, US 137/P17
Watford, Eng, UK 30/B1
Watford City, ND, US 127/H4
Wath-upon-Dearne, Eng, UK 35/G4
Watheroo NP, Austl. 112/B4
Watkins, Co, US 137/C3
Watonwan (riv.), Mn, US 129/J1
Watowato (peak), Indo. 81/G3
Watrous, Sk, Can. 127/G3
Watsa, D.R. Congo 104/A2
Watseka, Il, US 130/C3
Watson Lake, Yk, Can. 122/D2
Watsontown, Pa, US 138/B1
Watsonville, Ca, US 128/B3
Watten, Fr. 52/B2
Wattenberg, Co, US 137/C2
Wattenheim, Ger. 54/B3
Wattens, Aus. 57/H3
Wattignies, Fr. 52/C2
Wattrelos, Fr. 52/C2
Wattwil, Swi. 57/F3
Wauchope, Austl. 115/E1
Wauchula, Fl, US 133/H5
Wauconda, Il, US 135/P15
Waukarlycarly (lake), Austl. 109/B3
Waukesha, Wi, US 129/K2
Waukesha (co.), Wi, US 135/P14
Waun Fâch (peak), Wal, UK 32/C3
Waun-Oer (peak), Wal, UK 32/C1
Wauna, Wa, US 135/B3
Waupun, Wi, US 127/L5
Waurika, Ok, US 129/H4
Wauseon, Oh, US 130/C3
Waveney (riv.), Eng, UK 33/H2
Waver (riv.), Eng, UK 35/E2
Wavre, Belg. 53/D2
Wavrin, Fr. 52/B2
Wāw, Sudan 97/L6
Wawa (riv.), Nic. 145/E3
Wawagosic (riv.), Qu, Can. 130/E1
Wawasang (peak), Nic. 145/E3
Wawayanda State Park, NJ, US 138/D1
Waxahachie, Tx, US 129/H4
Waycross, Ga, US 133/H4
Wayne, Ne, US 127/J5
Wayne (co.), Pa, US 138/C3
Wayne, Pa, US 138/C3
Wayne, NJ, US 139/J8
Wayne, Mi, US 135/F7
Wayne, Il, US 135/P16
Waynesboro, Pa, US 130/E4
Waynesboro, Ms, US 133/F4
Waynesboro, Ga, US 133/H3
Waynesville, NC, US 133/H3
Waynesville, Mo, US 129/J3
Waziers, Fr. 52/C3
Wazīrābād, Pak. 86/C3
Wazuka, Japan 77/J6
Wda (riv.), Pol. 41/K2
Weald, The (grsld.), Eng, UK 33/F4
Wear (riv.), Eng, UK 35/F2
Weatherby Lake, Mo, US 137/D5
Weatherford, Tx, US 132/D3
Weatherly, Pa, US 138/C2
Weaver (riv.), Eng, UK 35/F5
Weaverville, Ca, US 128/B2
Weber (co.), Ut, US 137/J11
Weber (riv.), Ut, US 137/J11
Weber Hill, Mo, US 137/F9
Webi Jubba (riv.), Som. 93/G4
Webster, SD, US 127/J4
Webster City, Ia, US 127/K5
Webster Groves, Mo, US 137/G8
Weddell (isl.), Mald. 159/E6
Weddell (sea) 160/X
Wedderburn, Austl. 115/B3
Weddin Mountains NP, Austl. 115/C2
Wedel, Ger. 51/G1
Wedemark, Ger. 51/G3
Wee Waa, Austl. 115/D1
Weed, Ca, US 128/B2
Weehawken, NJ, US 139/J8
Weekapaug, RI, US 139/G1
Weenen, SAfr. 107/E3
Weerselo, Neth. 50/D4
Weert, Neth. 50/C6
Weesen, Swi. 57/F3
Weesp, Neth. 50/C4
Wegberg, Ger. 53/F1
Weggis, Swi. 57/E3
Węgorzewo, Pol. 39/J4
Węgrów, Pol. 41/M2
Wegscheid, Ger. 55/G5
Wehingen, Ger. 57/E1
Wehr, Ger. 56/D2
Wehra (riv.), Ger. 56/D2
Wehre (riv.), Ger. 51/G6
Wehrheim, Ger. 54/B2
Wei Xian, China 72/C3
Wei Xian, China 72/C3
Weibersbrunn, Ger. 54/C3
Weichang, China 71/L3
Weida, Ger. 43/K1
Weiden, Ger. 55/F3
Weidenthal, Ger. 54/A4
Weifang, China 72/D3
Weihai, China 73/B4
Weihenzell, Ger. 54/D4
Weikersheim, Ger. 54/C4
Weil (riv.), Ger. 54/B2
Weil der Stadt, Ger. 54/B5
Weilburg, Ger. 54/B2
Weiler-Simmerberg, Ger. 57/F2
Weilerswist, Ger. 53/F2
Weilheim, Ger. 57/H2
Weilheim an der Teck, Ger. 54/C5
Weilmünster, Ger. 54/B2
Weimar, Ger. 40/F3
Weinan, China 72/B4
Weinfelden, Swi. 57/F2
Weingarten, Ger. 57/F2
Weingarten, Ger. 54/B4
Weinheim, Ger. 54/B3
Weinsberg, Ger. 54/C4
Weinstadt, Ger. 54/C5
Weinviertel (reg.), Aus. 43/M2
Weirton, WV, US 130/D3
Weisendorf, Ger. 54/D3
Weisenheim am Berg, Ger. 54/B3
Weiser (riv.), Id, US 126/D4
Weishan, China 72/D4
Weishi, China 72/C4
Weiskirchen, Ger. 53/F4
Weismain, Ger. 54/E2
Weiss (lake), Al, US 133/G3
Weissach, Ger. 54/B5
Weisse Elster (riv.), Ger. 40/G3
Weisse Laber (riv.), Ger. 55/E4
Weissenbach am Lech, Aus. 57/G3
Weissenburg im Bayern, Ger. 54/D4
Weissenfels, Ger. 40/F3
Weissenhorn, Ger. 57/G1
Weissenstadt, Ger. 55/E2
Weissenthurm, Ger. 53/G3
Weisser (peak), Ger. 53/F3
Weisser Main (riv.), Ger. 55/E2
Weisshorn (peak), Swi. 56/D5
Weissmies (peak), Swi. 56/D5
Weisswasser, Ger. 41/H3
Weistrach, Aus. 55/H6
Weitefeld, Ger. 53/G2
Weiterstadt, Ger. 54/B3
Weitra, Aus. 41/H4
Weixi, China 83/G2
Weiyuan, China 70/H4
Weiz, Aus. 43/L3
Weizhou (isl.), China 83/J3
Wejherowo, Pol. 38/H4
Welby, Co, US 137/C3
Welch, WV, US 130/D4
Welch (hill), Pa, US 138/A3
Weld (co.), Co, US 137/C2
Welden, Ger. 54/D6
Weldiya, Eth. 97/N5
Weldon Spring, Mo, US 137/F8
Welel (peak), Eth. 97/M6
Weligama, SrL. 82/D6
Welkenraedt, Belg. 53/E2
Welkom, SAfr. 106/D3
Welland (canal), On, Can. 131/R10
Welland, On, Can. 131/R10
Welland (riv.), Eng, UK 35/H6
Wellandport, On, Can. 131/R9
Wellen, Belg. 53/E2
Wellesley (isls.), Austl. 109/C2
Wellin, Belg. 53/E3
Wellingborough, Eng, UK 33/F2
Wellington (lake), Austl. 115/C3
Wellington, Austl. 115/D2
Wellington, Tx, US 129/G4
Wellington (int'l arpt.), NZ 117/S11
Wellington (cap.), NZ 117/S11
Wellington, Eng, UK 32/C5
Wellington (chan.), Nun., Can. 123/S7
Wellington (isl.), Chile 147/B7
Wellington, SAfr. 106/L10
Wells, BC, Can. 126/C2
Wells, Nv, US 126/E5
Wells (lake), Austl. 109/B3
Wells, Eng, UK 32/D4
Wellston, Oh, US 130/D4
Wellston, Ok, US 137/N14
Wellsville, Pa, US 138/B3
Wellton, Az, US 128/D4
Wels, Aus. 55/H6
Welschbillig, Ger. 53/F4
Welshnofen (Nova Levante), It. 57/H5
Welshpool, Wal, UK 32/C1
Welty, Co, US 137/B2
Welver, Ger. 51/E5
Welzheim, Ger. 54/C5
Wembere (riv.), Tanz. 105/F1
Wembley, Ab, Can. 126/D2
Wembley Stadium, Eng, UK 30/C2
Wemding, Ger. 54/D5
Wemmel, Belg. 53/D2
Wemyss Bay, Sc, UK 36/B5
Wen Xian, China 72/C4
Wenatchee, Wa, US 126/C4
Wenchang, China 83/K4
Wencheng, China 79/D2
Wenchi, Gha. 103/E5
Wendeburg, Ger. 51/H4
Wenden, Ger. 53/G2
Wendeng, China 73/B4
Wendover, Nv, US 126/E5
Wendover, Eng, UK 33/F3
Wengyuan, China 83/K3
Wenling, China 79/D2
Wenlock Edge (ridge), Eng, UK 32/D2
Wenne (riv.), Ger. 51/F6
Wennigsen, Ger. 51/G4
Wenonah, NJ, US 138/C4
Wenshan, China 83/H3
Wenshang, China 72/D4
Wenshui, China 72/C3
Wensleydale (valley), Eng, UK 35/F3
Went (riv.), Eng, UK 35/G4
Wentworth, Austl. 115/B2
Wenxi, China 72/B4
Wenzhou, China 79/D2
Wepener, SAfr. 106/D3
Wer, India 84/A2
Werdau, Ger. 43/K1
Werdohl, Ger. 51/E6
Werkendam, Neth. 50/B5
Werl, Ger. 51/E5
Werlte, Ger. 51/E3
Wermelskirchen, Ger. 53/G1
Wern (riv.), Ger. 54/C3
Wernberg-Köblitz, Ger. 55/F3
Werne an der Lippe, Ger. 51/E5
Werneck, Ger. 54/D3
Wernigerode, Ger. 51/H5
Werong (mt.), Austl. 115/D2
Werra (riv.), Ger. 40/E3
Werre (riv.), Ger. 40/E2
Werrikimbe NP, Austl. 115/E1
Werris Creek, Austl. 115/D1
Werse (riv.), Ger. 51/E5
Wertach (riv.), Ger. 54/D6
Wertheim, Ger. 54/C3
Wertheim NWR, NY, US 139/F2
Werther, Ger. 51/F4
Wertingen, Ger. 54/D5
Wervershoof, Neth. 50/C3
Wervik, Belg. 52/C2
Weschnitz (riv.), Ger. 54/B3
Wesefgebirge (mts.), Ger. 51/F4
Wesel, Ger. 50/D5
Wesel-Datteln (canal), Ger. 51/E5
Weser (riv.), Ger. 40/E2
Weslaco, Tx, US 132/D5
Wesley Hills, NY, US 139/J7
Wessel (isls.), Austl. 109/C2
Wesselburen, Ger. 38/C4
Wesselsbron, SAfr. 106/D2
Wessex (reg.), Eng, UK 32/D4
Wessington Springs, SD, US 127/J4
West (pt.), Austl. 115/C4
West, Tx, US 129/H5
West (cape), NZ 117/R12
West (pt.), Wa, US 135/C2
West Allis, Wi, US 129/K2
West Alton, Mo, US 137/G8
West Babylon, NY, US 139/E2
West Bank (occ. zone), Isr. 91/D3
West Bend, Wi, US 127/L5
West Bengal (state), India 70/E7
West Bountiful, Ut, US 137/K12

236
West B – Wonth

West Branch, Mi, US 130/C2
West Bridgford, Eng, UK 35/G6
West Bromwich, Eng, UK 32/E1
West Caicos (isl.), UK 145/H1
West Calder, Sc, UK 36/C5
West Caldwell, NJ, US 139/H8
West Cap Howe NP, Austl. 112/C5
West Chester, Pa, US 138/C4
West Chicago, Il, US 135/P16
West Chyulu Game Consv. Area, Kenya 104/C3
West Coast NP, SAfr. 106/L10
West Columbia, SC, US 133/H3
West Covina, Ca, US 136/G7
West Creek, NJ, US 138/D4
West Dunbartonshire (pol. reg.), Sc, UK 36/B5
West Elk (mts.), Co, US 132/B2
West End, Eng, UK 30/B3
West Falkland (isl.), Falk. 157/D7
West Fargo, ND, US 127/J4
West Fayu (isl.), Micr. 116/D4
West Frisian (isls.), Neth. 40/C2
West Glen (riv.), Eng, UK 35/H6
West Grove, Pa, US 138/C4
West Haven, Ct, US 139/F1
West Haverstraw, NY, US 138/E1
West Helena, Ar, US 129/K4
West Hempstead, NY, US 139/L9
West Hills, NY, US 139/M8
West Hollywood, Ca, US 136/F7
West Humber (riv.), On, Can. 131/Q8
West Ice Shelf, Ant. 160/F
West Indies (isls.), NAm. 145/F2
West Islet (isl.), Austl. 109/E3
West Islip, NY, US 139/E2
West Jordan, Ut, US 137/K12
West Kilbride, Sc, UK 36/B5
West Kingsdown, Eng, UK 30/D3
West Knock (peak), Sc, UK 36/D3
West Lamma (chan.), China 71/U11
West Lincoln, Ne, US 129/H2
West Lothian (pol. reg.), Sc, UK 129/H2
West Lunga NP, Zam. 105/D3
West Memphis, Ar, US 129/K4
West Midlands (co.), Eng, UK 33/E1
West Milford, NJ, US 139/H7
West Milton, Pa, US 138/B1
West Monroe, La, US 129/J4
West New York, NJ, US 139/J8
West Nyack, NY, US 139/K7
West Orange, NJ, US 139/J8
West Palm Beach, Fl, US 133/H5
West Paterson, NJ, US 139/J8
West Pensacola, Fl, US 133/G4
West Plains, Mo, US 129/K3
West Point, Ne, US 127/J5
West Point (lake), US 133/G3
West Point, Ms, US 133/F3
West Point, Ut, US 137/J11
West Reading, Pa, US 138/C3
West Redding, Ct, US 139/E1
West Road (riv.), BC, Can. 126/B2
West Sacramento, Ca, US 135/L9
West Sayville, NY, US 139/E2
West Seneca, NY, US 131/S10
West Siberian (plain), Rus. 64/H3
West Sussex (co.), Eng, UK 33/F4
West-Terschelling, Neth. 50/C2
West Valley City, Ut, US 137/K12
West Vancouver, BC, Can. 126/C3
West Virginia (state), US 125/K4
West Warren, Ut, US 137/J11
West Water (riv.), Sc, UK 36/D3
West Weber, Ut, US 137/J11
West Wyalong, Austl. 115/C2
West York, Pa, US 138/B4
West Yorkshire (co.), Eng, UK 35/G4
Westall (pt.), Austl. 113/G5
Westbrook, Ct, US 139/F1
Westbury, NY, US 139/L9
Westchester (co.), NY, US 139/E1
Westcott, Eng, UK 30/B3
Westerbork, Neth. 50/D3
Westerburg, Ger. 53/G2
Westerham, Eng, UK 30/D3
Westerheim, Ger. 57/G1
Westerholt, Ger. 51/E1
Westerkappeln, Ger. 51/E4
Westerland, Ger. 38/C4
Westerlo, Belg. 53/D1
Western (prov.), Kenya 104/B2
Western (des.), Egypt 97/L2
Western (prov.), Ugan. 104/A2
Western (pol. reg.), Gha. 103/E5
Western (chan.), SKor. 74/A3
Western Area (prov.), SLeo. 102/B4
Western Australia (state), Austl. 109/B3
Western Cape (prov.), SAfr. 106/C4
Western Ghats (mts.), India 89/K5
Western Run (riv.), Md, US 138/B4
Western Sahara 93/A2
Western Sayans (mts.), Rus. 64/J4
Westerschelde (chan.), Belg. 50/A6
Westerstede, Ger. 51/E2
Westerville, Oh, US 130/D3
Westervoort, Neth. 50/C5
Westerwald (mts.), Ger. 40/D3
Westfield, NJ, US 139/H9
Westgat (chan.), Neth. 50/D2
Westhampton, NY, US 139/F2
Westhampton Beach, NY, US 139/F2
Westhausen, Ger. 54/D5
Westheim, Ger. 54/B4
Westhill, Sc, UK 36/D2
Westhofen, Ger. 54/B3
Westhoughton, Eng, UK 35/F4
Westkapelle, Neth. 50/A5
Westlake Village, Ca, US 136/B2
Westland, Mi, US 135/F7
Westland NP, NZ 117/R11
Westminster, Co, US 137/B3
Westminster, Md, US 138/B4
Westminster, Ca, US 136/F8
Westminster, City of (bor.), Eng, UK 30/A1
Westmont, Il, US 135/P16
Westmont (Haddon), NJ, US 138/C4
Westmorland (reg.), Eng, UK 35/F3
Westmount, Qu, Can. 131/N7
Weston, Mo, US 137/D5
Weston, Ct, US 139/E1
Weston-super-Mare, Eng, UK 32/D4
Westonaria, SAfr. 106/P13
Westport, Ire. 31/P10
Westport, NZ 117/S11
Westport, Ct, US 139/E1
Westray (isl.), Sc, UK 31/V14
Westview, Il, US 137/G8
Westwego, La, US 137/P17
Westwood, Ks, US 137/D5
Westwood, NJ, US 139/J8
Wet (mts.), Co, US 132/B2
Wetar (str.), Indo. 81/G5
Wetar (isl.), Indo. 67/M10
Wetaskiwin, Ab, Can. 126/E2
Wete, Tanz. 104/C4
Wétetnagami (riv.), Qu, Can. 130/E1
Wetherell (lake), Austl. 115/B2
Wetter, Ger. 51/E6
Wetter (riv.), Ger. 54/B2
Wetterau (reg.), Ger. 54/C2
Wetteren, Belg. 52/C2
Wetterhorn (peak), Swi. 56/E4
Wettingen, Swi. 57/E3
Wettringen, Ger. 51/E4
Wetzikon, Swi. 57/E3
Wetzlar, Ger. 54/B1
Wetzstein (peak), Ger. 55/E2
Wevelgem, Belg. 52/C2
Wewak, PNG 116/D5
Wewoka, Ok, US 129/H4
Wexford, Ire. 31/Q10
Wey (riv.), Eng, UK 30/A3
Weybridge, Eng, UK 30/B2
Weyburn, Sk, Can. 127/H3
Weygand (ruin), Alg. 99/F4
Weyhausen, Ger. 51/H4
Weyland (pt.), Austl. 113/G5
Weymouth, Eng, UK 32/D5
Weymouth (bay), Eng, UK 32/D5
Wha Ti, NW, Can. 122/E2
Whakatane, NZ 117/T10
Whale Cove, Nun., Can. 122/G2
Whalsey (isl.), Sc, UK 31/W13
Whangarei, NZ 117/S10
Wharfe (riv.), Eng, UK 35/G3
Wheat Ridge, Co, US 137/B3
Wheatland, Wy, US 127/G5
Wheaton, Il, US 130/B3
Wheaton-Glenmont, Md, US 138/A5
Wheaton Village, NJ, US 138/C5
Wheeler (peak), Nv, US 128/D3
Wheeler (peak), NM, US 129/F3
Wheeler (lake), Al, US 133/G3
Wheeler Springs, Ca, US 136/A1
Wheeling, WV, US 130/D3
Wheeling, Il, US 135/Q15
Wheelwright, Arg. 158/E2
Whernside (peak), Eng, UK 35/F3
Whickham, Eng, UK 35/G2
Whidbey (pt.), Austl. 113/G5
Whinham (mt.), Austl. 113/F3
Whitburn, Sc, UK 36/C5
Whitby, On, Can. 131/S8
Whitby, Eng, UK 35/H3
White (lake), La, US 129/J5
White (riv.), Ar, US 129/J4
White (riv.), SD, US 127/H5
White (riv.), Tx, US 129/K2
White (lake), Austl. 109/B3
White (lake), On, Can. 130/C1
White (riv.), In, US 130/C4
White (pass), Ak, US 134/L3
White (sea), Rus. 60/H2
White (bay), Nf, Can. 123/L3
White Bear (riv.), Nf, Can. 131/K1
White City, Sk, Can. 127/G3
White Cliffs, Austl. 115/B1
White Coomb (peak), Sc, UK 36/C6
White Esk (riv.), Sc, UK 36/C6
White Fox, Sk, Can. 127/G2
White Hall, Md, US 138/B4
White Haven, Pa, US 138/C1
White Marsh, Md, US 138/B5
White Mountain, Ak, US 134/F3
White Mountains Nat'l Rec. Area, Ak, US 134/J2
White Nile (riv.), Sudan 93/F4
White Oak, Md, US 138/B5
White Otter (lake), On, Can. 127/K3
White Plains, NY, US 139/K7
White River, On, Can. 130/C1
White Rock, NM, US 132/B3
White Sands, NM, US 128/F4
White Sands Nat'l Mon., NM, US 128/F4
White Sulphur Springs, Mt, US 126/F4
White Volta (riv.), Gha. 93/B4
White, West Fork (riv.), In, US 130/C4
Whiteadder Water (riv.), Sc, UK 36/D5
Whitecourt, Ab, Can. 126/E2
Whiteface (riv.), Mn, US 127/K4
Whitefield, Eng, UK 35/F4
Whitefish, Mt, US 126/E3
Whitefish (bay), US,Can. 130/C2
Whiteford (pt.), Wal, UK 32/B3
Whiteford, Md, US 138/B4
Whitehall, Mt, US 126/E4
Whitehall, Mi, US 130/C3
Whitehaven, Eng, UK 34/E2
Whitehead, NI, UK 34/C2
Whitehills, Sc, UK 36/D1
Whitehorse (cap.), Yk, Can. 134/L3
Whitehorse (hill), Eng, UK 33/E3
Whitehouse, Tx, US 129/J4
Whitemouth (riv.), Mb, Can. 127/K3
Whiteriver, Az, US 128/E4
Whiteside (chan.), Chile 159/C7
Whitesville, NJ, US 138/D3
Whiteville, NC, US 133/J3
Whitewater (lake), On, Can. 127/L3
Whitewood, Sk, Can. 127/H3
Whithorn, Sc, UK 34/D2
Whiting, In, US 135/R16
Whitley Bay, Eng, UK 35/G1
Whitmore Village, Hi, US 124/V12
Whitney (lake), Tx, US 129/H4
Whitney, Tx, US 129/H5
Whitsand (bay), Eng, UK 32/B6
Whitstable, Eng, UK 33/H4
Whitsunday (isl.), Austl. 109/D3
Whittaker, Mi, US 135/E7
Whittier, Ak, US 134/J3
Whittier, Ca, US 136/F8
Whittlesea, Austl. 115/G5
Whitton, Austl. 115/C2
Whitworth, Eng, UK 35/F4
Wholdaia (lake), NW, Can. 122/F2
Whyalla, Austl. 113/H5
Wi (isl.), SKor. 73/D5
Wiang Kosai NP, Thai. 78/B2
Wiarton, On, Can. 130/D2
Wiawso, Gha. 103/E5
Wichabai, Guy. 153/G4
Wichelen, Belg. 52/C2
Wichita (riv.), Tx, US 129/H4
Wichita (mts.), Ok, US 129/H4
Wichita Falls, Tx, US 129/H4
Wick, Sc, UK 31/S7
Wickenburg, Az, US 128/D4
Wickepin, Austl. 112/C5
Wickford, Eng, UK 30/E2
Wickham, Austl. 112/C2
Wicklow (mts.), Ire. 31/Q10
Wicklow (pass), Ire. 34/B5
Wicklow, Ire. 34/B6
Wicklow (pt.), Ire. 34/B6
Wickriede (riv.), Ger. 51/F4
Wid (riv.), Eng, UK 30/E2
Widnau, Swi. 57/F3
Widnes, Eng, UK 35/F5
Więcbork, Pol. 41/J2
Wied (riv.), Ger. 43/G1
Wiedau (riv.), Ger. 51/G2
Wiefelstede, Ger. 51/F2
Wiehengebirge (ridge), Ger. 51/F4
Wiehl, Ger. 53/G2
Wielenbach, Ger. 57/H2
Wieliczka, Pol. 41/L4
Wielkopolski NP, Pol. 41/J2
Wielsbeke, Belg. 52/C2
Wieluń, Pol. 41/K3
Wien (riv.), Aus. 49/N7
Wien (prov.), Aus. 41/J4
Wien (Vienna) (cap.), Aus. 49/N7
Wiener Neudorf, Aus. 49/N7
Wiener Neustadt, Aus. 43/M3
Wienerwald (reg.), Aus. 49/N7
Wienwald (reg.), Aus. 43/L2
Wieprz (riv.), Pol. 62/B2
Wierden, Neth. 50/D4
Wieringermeerpolder (polder), Neth. 50/B3
Wieringerwerf, Neth. 50/C3
Wieruszów, Pol. 41/K3
Wiesbaden, Ger. 54/B2
Wiese (riv.), Ger. 43/G3
Wiese (isl.), Rus. 160/A
Wieseck (riv.), Ger. 54/B1
Wiesendangen, Swi. 57/E2
Wiesensteig, Ger. 54/C5
Wiesent (riv.), Ger. 54/E4
Wiesentheid, Ger. 54/D3
Wiesloch, Ger. 54/B4
Wiesmoor, Ger. 51/E2
Wietmarschen, Ger. 51/D4
Wietze, Ger. 51/G3
Wietze (riv.), Ger. 51/G3
Wietzendorf, Ger. 51/G3
Wiezyca (peak), Pol. 38/H4
Wigan, Eng, UK 35/F4
Wiggins, Ms, US 133/F4
Wight (isl.), UK 42/C1
Wigierski NP, Pol. 41/M1
Wignehies, Fr. 52/D3
Wigry (lake), Pol. 39/K5
Wigston, Eng, UK 33/E1
Wigtown, Sc, UK 34/D2
Wigtown (bay), Sc, UK 34/D2
Wijchen, Neth. 50/C5
Wijhe, Neth. 50/D4
Wijk bij Duurstede, Neth. 50/C5
Wil, Swi. 57/F3
Wilber, Ne, US 129/H2
Wilberforce, Austl. 114/G8
Wilbur, Wa, US 126/D4
Wilburton, Ok, US 129/J4
Wilcannia, Austl. 115/B1
Wilchingen, Swi. 57/E2
Wilczek (isl.), Rus. 64/G1
Wild (coast), SAfr. 106/E4
Wild Creek (res.), Pa, US 138/C2
Wild Rice (riv.), Mn, US 127/J4
Wild World, Md, US 138/B6
Wildau, Ger. 40/Q7
Wildbad im Schwarzwald, Ger. 54/B5
Wildberg, Ger. 54/B5
Wilder, Ks, US 137/D5
Wilderswil, Swi. 56/D4
Wildeshausen, Ger. 51/F3
Wildflecken, Ger. 54/C2
Wildgrat (peak), Aus. 57/G3
Wildhaus, Swi. 57/F3
Wildhorn (peak), Swi. 56/D5
Wildomar, Ca, US 136/C3
Wildspitze (peak), Aus. 57/G4
Wildstrubel (peak), Swi. 56/D5
Wildwood, NJ, US 138/D6
Wildwood Crest, NJ, US 138/D6
Wilge (riv.), SAfr. 106/E2
Wilhelm II (coast), Ant. 160/F
Wilhelmina (mts.), Sur. 150/G3
Wilhelminakanaal (canal), Neth. 50/C5
Wilhelmshaven, Ger. 51/F1
Wilhering, Aus. 55/H6
Wilkes-Barre, Pa, US 138/C1
Wilkes Land (phys. reg.), Ant. 160/J
Wilkesboro, NC, US 130/D4
Wilkeson, Wa, US 135/C3
Wilkie, Sk, Can. 126/F2
Wilkins (sound), Ant. 160/U
Will (mt.), BC, Can. 134/N4
Will (co.), Il, US 135/P16
Willamette (riv.), Or, US 126/C4
Willandra NP, Austl. 115/C2
Willapa (bay), Wa, US 126/B4
Willard (bay), Ut, US 137/J11
Willard (res.), Ut, US 137/J11
Willard, Ut, US 137/J11
Willaura, Austl. 115/B3
Willcox, Az, US 128/E4
Willebadessen, Ger. 51/G5
Willebroek, Belg. 53/D1
Willemstad, Neth. 50/B5
Willemstad (cap.), NAnt. 152/D1
William (mt.), Austl. 115/B3
William B. Hartsfield Atlanta (int'l arpt.), Ga, US 133/G3
William Bay NP, Austl. 112/C5
Williams, Az, US 128/D4
Williams, Austl. 112/C5
Williams Lake, BC, Can. 126/C2
Williamsburg, Ky, US 130/C4
Williamsport, Pa, US 138/A1
Williamston, NC, US 133/J3
Williamstown, Pa, US 138/B2
Williamstown, NJ, US 138/D4
Williamsville, NY, US 131/S10
Willich, Ger. 50/D6
Willingboro, NJ, US 138/D3
Willingen, Ger. 51/F6
Willis, Tx, US 129/J5
Willis Islets (isls.), Austl. 109/E2
Willisau, Swi. 56/D3
Williston, ND, US 127/H3
Williston, Fl, US 133/H4
Williston, SAfr. 106/C3
Williston (lake), BC, Can. 122/D3
Williston Park, NY, US 139/L9
Willits, Ca, US 128/B3
Willmar, Mn, US 127/K4
Willow, Ak, US 134/H3
Willow (riv.), BC, Can. 126/C2
Willow Bunch, Sk, Can. 127/G3
Willow Grove, Pa, US 138/C3
Willow Grove, De, US 138/C4
Willow Grove Naval Air Sta., Pa, US 138/C3
Willow River, BC, Can. 126/C2
Willow Street, Pa, US 138/B4
Willow Tree, Austl. 115/D1
Willowbrook, Ca, US 136/F8
Willowbrook, Il, US 135/P16
Willowmore, SAfr. 106/C4
Willows, Ca, US 128/B3
Wills (lake), Austl. 109/B3
Wills Point, La, US 137/Q17
Willstätt, Ger. 56/D1
Willunga, Austl. 113/H5
Wilmette, Il, US 135/Q15
Wilmington, NC, US 133/J3
Wilmington, Austl. 113/H5
Wilmington, De, US 138/C4
Wilmington Island, Ga, US 133/H4
Wilmslow, Eng, UK 35/F5
Wilnsdorf, Ger. 53/H2
Wilrijk, Belg. 50/B6
Wilseder (peak), Ger. 51/G2
Wilson, NC, US 133/J3
Wilson (co.), Tx, US 137/U21
Wilson, NY, US 131/S9
Wilson (mt.), Ca, US 136/B2
Wilson, Pa, US 138/C2
Wilson (cape), Nun., Can. 123/H2
Wilsons Promontory (pen.), Austl. 109/D4
Wilsons Promontory NP, Austl. 115/C3
Wilsonville, Il, US 137/H7
Wilstedt, Ger. 51/G2
Wilster, Ger. 51/G1
Wilsum, Ger. 50/D3
Wilton, Eng, UK 33/E4
Wilton, Ct, US 139/E1
Wiltshire (co.), Eng, UK 33/E4
Wiltz, Lux. 53/E4
Wiltz (riv.), Lux. 53/E4
Wiluna, Austl. 112/D3
Wimborne Minster, Eng, UK 32/E5
Wimereux, Fr. 52/A2
Wimmis, Swi. 56/D4
Winam (gulf), Kenya 104/B3
Winburg, SAfr. 106/D3
Winchester, Ky, US 130/C4
Winchester, Tn, US 133/G3
Winchester, Ca, US 136/C3
Winchester, Eng, UK 33/E4
Winchester Mystery House, Ca, US 135/L12
Wind (riv.), Wy, US 126/F5
Wind (lake), Wi, US 135/P14
Wind Cave NP, SD, US 129/G2
Wind Gap, Pa, US 138/C2
Wind Lake, Wi, US 135/P14
Wind Point, Wi, US 135/Q14
Wind River (range), Wy, US 128/E2
Windach (riv.), Ger. 57/G2
Windach, Ger. 54/E6
Winder, Ga, US 133/H3
Windermere (lake), Eng, UK 35/F3
Windermere, Eng, UK 35/F3
Windesheim, Ger. 53/G4
Windhoek (cap.), Namb. 105/C5
Windlesham, Eng, UK 30/B2
Window Rock, Az, US 128/E4
Windrush (riv.), Eng, UK 33/E3
Windsbach, Ger. 54/D4
Windsor, Nf, Can. 131/L1
Windsor, NS, Can. 131/H2
Windsor, Qu, Can. 131/G2
Windsor, On, Can. 130/D3
Windsor, Co, US 137/C2
Windsor (res.), Co, US 137/C1
Windsor, Eng, UK 33/F4
Windsor, Pa, US 138/B4
Windward (isls.), StV. 141/J5
Windward Passage (passg.), Cuba,Haiti 145/H2
Winfield, BC, Can. 126/D3
Winfield, Ks, US 129/H3
Winfield, Pa, US 138/B2
Winfield, Md, US 138/A5
Wingene, Belg. 52/C1
Winger, On, Can. 131/R10
Wingham, Austl. 115/E1
Winifred (lake), Austl. 112/D2
Winifreda, Arg. 158/D3
Winisk (riv.), On, Can. 123/H3
Winkler, Mb, Can. 127/J3
Winneba, Gha. 103/E5
Winnebago (lake), Wi, US 127/L5
Winnenden, Ger. 54/C5
Winner, SD, US 127/J5
Winnetka, Il, US 135/Q15
Winnett, Mt, US 126/F4
Winnfield, La, US 129/J5
Winningen, Ger. 53/G3
Winnipeg (cap.), Mb, Can. 127/J3
Winnipeg (int'l arpt.), Mb, Can. 127/J3
Winnipeg (riv.), Mb,On, Can. 127/K3
Winnipeg (lake), Mb, Can. 127/J3
Winnipeg Beach, Mb, Can. 127/J3
Winnipegosis, Mb, Can. 127/J3
Winnipegosis (lake), Mb, Can. 127/H2
Winnsboro, La, US 129/K4
Winnsboro, SC, US 133/H3
Winnweiler, Ger. 53/G4
Winschoten, Neth. 50/E2
Winsford, Eng, UK 35/F5
Winslow, Az, US 128/E4
Winslow, NJ, US 138/D4
Winslow, Wa, US 135/B2
Winston-Salem, NC, US 133/H2
Winsum, Neth. 50/D2
Winter Haven, Fl, US 133/H4
Winter Park, Fl, US 133/H4
Winterberg, Ger. 51/F6
Winterberge (mts.), SAfr. 106/D4
Winterlingen, Ger. 57/F1
Winters, Tx, US 129/H5
Winters, Ca, US 135/K9
Winters Run (riv.), Md, US 138/B4
Winterstaude (peak), Aus. 57/F3
Winterswijk, Neth. 50/D5
Winterthur, Swi. 57/E3
Winterthur Museum and Gardens, De, US 138/C4
Winthrop, Me, US 131/G2
Winton, Austl. 114/A3
Wintzenheim, Fr. 56/D1
Wipper (riv.), Ger. 40/F3
Wipperau (riv.), Ger. 51/H2
Wipperfürth, Ger. 53/G1
Wirges, Ger. 53/G3
Wirrabara, Austl. 113/H5
Wirral (pen.), Eng, UK 35/E5
Wisbech, Eng, UK 33/G1
Wisch, Neth. 50/D5
Wischhafen, Ger. 51/G1
Wisconsin (riv.), Wi, US 127/L5
Wisconsin (state), US 127/L4
Wiseman, Ak, US 134/H2
Wisenta (riv.), Ger. 55/E1
Wishaw, Sc, UK 36/C5
Wishek, ND, US 127/J4
Wisła, Pol. 41/K4
Wiślany (lag.), Pol. 39/H4
Wisłoka (riv.), Pol. 41/L4
Wismar, Ger. 38/D5
Wisner, La, US 129/K5
Wissant, Fr. 52/A2
Wissembourg, Fr. 53/G5
Wissen, Ger. 53/G2
Wissey (riv.), Eng, UK 33/G1
Wit Kei (riv.), SAfr. 106/D3
Witbank, SAfr. 106/E2
Witham, Eng, UK 33/G3
Witham (riv.), Eng, UK 35/H5
Witherspoon (mt.), Ak, US 134/J3
Withlacoochee (riv.), US 133/H4
Withnell, Eng, UK 35/F4
Witjira NP, Austl. 113/G3
Witkowo, Pol. 41/J2
Witney, Eng, UK 33/E3
Witnica, Pol. 41/H2
Witry-lès-Reims, Fr. 53/D5
Wittelsheim, Fr. 56/D2
Wittem, Neth. 53/E2
Witten, Ger. 51/E6
Wittenbach, Swi. 57/F3
Wittenberg, Ger. 40/G3
Wittenberge, Ger. 40/F2
Wittenburg, Ger. 38/D5
Wittenheim, Fr. 56/D2
Wittenoom, Austl. 112/C2
Wittingen, Ger. 51/H3
Wittislingen, Ger. 54/D5
Wittlich, Ger. 53/F4
Wittman, Md, US 138/B6
Wittmund, Ger. 51/E1
Wittmunder (riv.), Ger. 51/E1
Witton (pen.), Ger. 41/G1
Wittstock, Ger. 40/G2
Witu, Kenya 104/D3
Witwatersrand (reg.), SAfr. 106/P12
Witzenhausen, Ger. 51/G6
Wivenhoe (lake), Austl. 109/E3
Wixom, Mi, US 135/E6
Wkra (riv.), Pol. 60/D5
Władysławowo, Pol. 38/H4
Włocławek, Pol. 41/K2
Włocławek (prov.), Pol. 41/K2
Włocławskie (lake), Pol. 41/K2
Włodawa, Pol. 41/M3
Włoszczowa, Pol. 41/K3
Wobulenzi, Ugan. 104/B2
Wodonga, Austl. 115/C3
Wodzisław Śląski, Pol. 41/K4
Woensdrecht, Neth. 50/B6
Woerden, Neth. 50/B4
Wognum, Neth. 50/C3
Wohlen, Swi. 57/E3
Wohlen bei Bern, Swi. 56/D4
Wohlford (lake), Ca, US 136/C4
Woippy, Fr. 53/F5
Wokam (isl.), Indo. 81/H5
Woking, Eng, UK 30/B3
Wokingham, Eng, UK 33/F4
Wŏlch'ul-san NP, SKor. 73/D5
Wolcott, Ks, US 137/D5
Wolcottsville, NY, US 131/S9
Wołczyn, Pol. 41/K3
Woleai (isl.), Micr. 116/D4
Wolf (mtn.), Ak, US 134/H2
Wolf (riv.), Wi, US 130/B2
Wolf (vol.), Ecu. 156/E7
Wolf (isl.), Ecu. 156/E6
Wolf (lake), In, US 135/Q16
Wolf Creek (mtn.), Ak, US 134/F3
Wolf Creek, Mt, US 126/E4
Wolf Point, Mt, US 127/G3
Wolfach, Ger. 57/E1
Wolfach (riv.), Ger. 54/B6
Wolfegg, Ger. 57/F2
Wolfen, Ger. 40/G3
Wolfenbüttel, Ger. 51/H4
Wolfern, Aus. 55/H6
Wolfersheim, Ger. 54/B2
Wolfhagen, Ger. 51/G6
Wolframs-Eschenbach, Ger. 54/D4
Wolfsburg, Ger. 51/H4
Wolfsegg am Hausruck, Aus. 55/G6
Wolfurt, Aus. 57/F3
Wolgast, Ger. 38/E4
Wolhusen, Swi. 56/E3
Wolin, Pol. 38/F5
Woliński PN, Pol. 41/H2
Wolkersdorf, Aus. 49/P7
Wollaston (isl.), Chile 157/C8
Wollaston (lake), Sk, Can. 122/F3
Wollaston (pen.), NW,Nun., Can. 122/E2
Wollemi NP, Austl. 115/D2
Wollerau, Swi. 57/E3
Wollongong, Austl. 115/D2
Wöllstadt, Ger. 54/B2
Wöllstein, Ger. 53/G4
Wolmaransstad, SAfr. 106/D2
Wolnzach, Ger. 55/E5
Wologizi (range), Libr. 96/C6
Wołomin, Pol. 41/L2
Wołów, Pol. 41/J3
Wolseley, SAfr. 106/L10
Wolsztyn, Pol. 41/J2
Woluwé-Saint-Lambert, Belg. 53/D2
Wolvega, Neth. 50/D3
Wolverhampton, Eng, UK 32/D1
Wolverine Lake, Mi, US 135/F6
Wolziger (lake), Ger. 40/Q7
Woman (riv.), On, Can. 130/D2
Wombourne, Eng, UK 32/D1
Wombwell, Eng, UK 35/G4
Womelsdorf, Pa, US 138/B3
Wondai, Austl. 114/C4
Wonder (lake), Il, US 135/P16
Wondervu, Co, US 137/B3
Wondreb (riv.), Ger. 55/F3
Wong Chu (riv.), Bhu. 85/G2
Wongan Hills, Austl. 112/C4
Wŏnju, SKor. 73/D4
Wonnangatta-Moroka NP, Austl. 115/C3
Wŏnsan, NKor. 73/D3
Wonthaggi, Austl. 115/C3

237
Wonyu – Yongq

Wonyulgunna (peak), Austl. 112/C3
Wood (mt.), Yk, Can. 134/K3
Wood (riv.), Sk, Can. 127/H2
Wood (mtn.), Sk, Can. 126/G3
Wood (riv.), Il, US 137/G8
Wood Buffalo NP, NW,Ab, Can. 122/E2
Wood Dale, Il, US 135/P16
Wood-Ridge, NJ, US 139/J8
Wood River, Il, US 137/G8
Woodbine, NJ, US 138/D5
Woodbine, Md, US 138/A5
Woodbridge, Ct, US 139/E1
Woodbridge, Ca, US 135/M10
Woodbridge, NJ, US 139/H9
Woodburn, Austl. 115/E1
Woodburn, Or, US 126/C4
Woodburn, Il, US 137/G7
Woodburn, On, Can. 131/Q9
Woodbury, NJ, US 138/C4
Woodcliff Lake, NJ, US 139/J7
Woodenbong, Austl. 115/E1
Woodenbridge, Ire. 34/B6
Woodend, Austl. 115/C3
Woodgate, Austl. 114/D4
Woodgate NP, Austl. 114/D4
Woodinville, Wa, US 135/C2
Woodland, Ca, US 128/B3
Woodlark (isl.), Sol. 116/E5
Woodlawn, Md, US 138/B5
Woodlawn Park, Ok, US 137/M14
Woodmere, NY, US 139/L9
Woodmont, Ct, US 139/F1
Woodridge, Il, US 135/P16
Woodroffe (mt.), Austl. 113/F3
Woods, Ok, US 137/N15
Woods (lake), On, Can. 122/G4
Woods Cross, Ut, US 137/K12
Woods Heights, Mo, US 137/E5
Woodsboro, Md, US 138/A4
Woodside, De, US 138/C5
Woodside, Austl. 113/M8
Woodside, Ca, US 135/K12
Woodside-Drifton, Pa, US 138/C2
Woodstock, Austl. 115/D2
Woodstock, NB, Can. 131/H2
Woodstock, Il, US 129/K2
Woodstock, Eng, UK 33/E3
Woodstock, Md, US 138/B5
Woodstown, NJ, US 138/C4
Woodville, Ms, US 129/K5
Woodway, Wa, US 135/C2
Woolgoolga, Austl. 115/E1
Wooli, Austl. 115/E1
Woolrich, Pa, US 138/A1
Woomera, Austl. 113/H4
Woomera Prohibited Area, Austl. 113/G4
Woonsocket, SD, US 129/H1
Woorabinda Aboriginal Community, Austl. 114/C4
Woramel (riv.), Austl. 112/B3
Wooster, Oh, US 130/D3
Worb, Swi. 56/D4
Worcester, Ma, US 131/G3
Worcester, Eng, UK 32/D2
Worcester, SAfr. 106/L10
Worcester and Birmingham (canal), Eng, UK 32/D2
Worden, Il, US 137/H8
Wörgl, Aus. 43/K3
Workington, Eng, UK 34/E2
Worksop, Eng, UK 35/G5
Workum, Neth. 50/C3
Worland, Wy, US 126/G4
World 22
World Trade Center, NY, US 139/J9
Wormer, Neth. 50/B3
Wormhoudt, Fr. 52/B2
Worms (pt.), Wal, UK 32/B3
Worms, Ger. 54/B3
Wörnitz (riv.), Ger. 43/J2
Worpswede, Ger. 51/F2
Wörrstadt, Ger. 54/B3
Wörsbach (riv.), Ger. 54/B2
Worsbrough, Eng, UK 35/G4
Worth, Il, US 135/Q16
Wörth am Rhein, Ger. 54/B4
Wörth an der Donau, Ger. 55/F4
Wörth an der Isar, Ger. 55/F5
Wortham, Tx, US 129/H5
Worthing, Eng, UK 33/F5
Wörthsee (lake), Ger. 54/E6
Worton, Md, US 138/B5
Wotho (isl.), Mrsh. 116/F3
Wotje (isl.), Mrsh. 116/G4
Woudenberg, Neth. 50/C4
Woudrichem, Neth. 50/B5
Wounta (lake), Nic. 145/F3
Wouw, Neth. 50/B5
Wowoni (isl.), Indo. 81/F4
Wrangel (isl.), Rus. 160/U
Wrangell, Ak, US 134/M4
Wrangell (mts.), Ak, US 122/B2
Wrangell-St. Elias NP and Prsv., Ak, US 134/K3
Wrath (cape), Sc, UK 31/R7
Wray, Co, US 129/G2
Wraysbury, Eng, UK 30/B2
Wraysbury (res.), Eng, UK 30/B2
Wreck (reef), Austl. 109/E3
Wreck (pt.), SAfr. 106/B3
Wrekin, The (hill), Eng, UK 32/D1
Wremen, Ger. 51/E2
Wrexham, Wal, UK 35/F5
Wrexham (co.), Wal, UK 35/E5
Wright, Wy, US 127/G5
Wrightstown, NJ, US 138/D3
Wrightwood, Ca, US 136/C2
Wrigley, NW, Can. 122/D2
Writtle, Eng, UK 33/G3
Wrocław, Pol. 41/J3
Wrocław (prov.), Pol. 41/J3
Września, Pol. 41/J2
Wschowa, Pol. 41/J3
Wu (riv.), China 79/A2
Wu'an, China 72/C3
Wuchang, China 71/N3
Wuchang (lake), China 72/D5
Wucheng, China 72/D3
Wuchuan, China 79/A2
Wuchuan, China 79/B3
Wuchuan, China 72/B2
Wudang (mtn.), China 72/B4
Wudi, China 72/D3
Wuding (riv.), China 72/B3
Wudinna, Austl. 113/G5
Wufeng, China 79/B1
Wugang, China 79/B2
Wuhai, China 70/J4
Wuhan, China 79/B1
Wuhe, China 72/D4
Wuhle (riv.), Ger. 40/Q6
Wuhu, China 72/D5
Wuhu, China 72/D5
Wuhua, China 79/C3
Wujal Wujal Aboriginal Community, Austl. 114/B1
Wujiang, China 72/L8
Wular (lake), India 86/C2
Wülfrath, Ger. 50/E6
Wulften, Ger. 51/H5
Wulian, China 72/D4
Wuling (mts.), China 79/B2
Wulong, China 79/A2
Wum, Camr. 103/H5
Wumang (isl.), China 73/B3
Wümme (riv.), Ger. 51/F2
Wün, India 82/C3
Wungong (res.), Austl. 112/L7
Wuning, China 79/C2
Wünnenberg, Ger. 51/F5
Wünnewil, Swi. 56/D4
Wunsiedel, Ger. 55/F2
Wunstorf, Ger. 51/G4
Wupatki Nat'l Mon., Az, US 128/E4
Wuppertal, Ger. 51/E6
Wuqi, China 72/B3
Wuqia, China 87/G5
Wuqiang, China 72/C3
Wuqiao, China 72/D3
Würm (riv.), Ger. 53/H6
Würm K. (canal), Ger. 57/H1
Würselen, Ger. 53/F2
Würzburg, Ger. 54/C3
Wusheng (pass), China 72/C5
Wushi, China 70/C3
Wüstegarten (peak), Ger. 51/G6
Wüstenrot, Ger. 54/C4
Wusuli (riv.), China 71/P2
Wutach (riv.), Ger. 57/E2
Wutai (peak), China 72/C3
Wutai, China 72/C3
Wuteve (mt.), Libr. 102/C4
Wutha-Farnroda, Ger. 54/D1
Wutöschingen, Ger. 57/E2
Wuustwezel, Belg. 50/B6
Wuwei, China 70/H4
Wuwei, China 72/D5
Wuxi, China 72/L8
Wuxiang, China 72/C3
Wuyang, China 72/C4
Wuyi (mts.), China 79/C2
Wuyi, China 72/C3
Wuyuan, China 70/J3
Wuyuan, China 79/C2
Wuzhai, China 72/B3
Wuzhi (peak), China 83/J4
Wuzhi, China 72/C4
Wuzhi (peak), China 72/J6
Wuzhou, China 83/K3
Wyalkatchem, Austl. 112/C4
Wyandanch, NY, US 139/M8
Wyandotte (co.), Ks, US 137/D5
Wyandotte County (lake), Ks, US 137/D5
Wyandotte NWR, Mi, US 135/F7
Wyangala (dam), Austl. 115/D2
Wycheproof, Austl. 115/B3
Wyckoff, NJ, US 139/J8
Wye (riv.), Eng, UK 32/C2
Wye Mills, Md, US 138/B6
Wyee, Austl. 115/D2
Wyk, Ger. 38/C4
Wynigen, Swi. 56/D3
Wynne, Ar, US 129/K4
Wynyard, Austl. 115/C4
Wynyard, Sk, Can. 127/G3
Wyoming (range), Wy, US 128/E2
Wyoming, Mi, US 130/C3
Wyoming (state), US 126/F5
Wyoming, De, US 138/C5
Wyoming, Pa, US 138/C1
Wyomissing, Pa, US 138/C3
Wyperfeld NP, Austl. 115/B2
Wyralinu (peak), Austl. 112/D5
Wyre (riv.), Eng, UK 35/F4
Wyrzysk, Pol. 41/J2
Wysokie Mazowieckie, Pol. 41/M2
Wyszków, Pol. 41/L2

X

X-Can, Mex. 144/E1
Xa Binh Long, Viet. 78/D4
Xaçmaz, Azer. 63/J4
Xagħra, Malta 46/L6
Xai-Xai, Moz. 105/F6
Xainza, China 70/E5
Xaitongmoin, China 85/G1
Xaltianguis, Mex. 143/F5
Xan (riv.), Viet. 79/A5
Xankändi, Azer. 63/H5
Xanten, Ger. 50/D5
Xánthi, Gre. 47/J2
Xanxerê, Braz. 155/A3
Xar Moron (riv.), China 65/M5
Xarba (pass), China 85/E1
Xavantes, Represa de (res.), Braz. 155/B2
Xavantes, Serra dos (mts.), Braz. 151/J6
Xayar, China 70/D3
Xel-há (ruin), Mex. 144/E1
Xenia, Oh, US 130/D4
Xerta, Sp. 45/F2
Xertigny, Fr. 56/C1
Xi (riv.), China 67/L7
Xi (lake), China 72/E2
Xiaguan, China 83/H2
Xiajin, China 72/C3
Xiamen, China 79/C3
Xiamen (int'l arpt.), China 79/C3
Xi'an, China 72/B4
Xiang (riv.), China 71/K6
Xiangcheng, China 83/G2
Xiangcheng, China 72/C4
Xiangcheng, China 72/C4
Xiangfan, China 72/C4
Xiangfen, China 72/B4
Xianghe, China 72/H7
Xiangkhoang, Laos 78/C2
Xiangkhoang (plat.), Laos 78/C2
Xiangning, China 72/B4
Xiangshan, China 79/D2
Xiangshui, China 72/D4
Xiangtan, China 83/K2
Xiangxiang, China 79/B2
Xiangyuan, China 72/C3
Xiangyun, China 83/H2
Xianju, China 79/D2
Xianning, China 79/B2
Xiantao, China 79/B1
Xianyang, China 70/J5
Xiao Hinggan (mts.), China 71/N2
Xiao Xian, China 72/D4
Xiaogan, China 71/K5
Xiaoqing (riv.), China 72/D3
Xiaoshan, China 72/L9
Xiaowutai (peak), China 72/C3
Xiaoyi, China 72/B3
Xiapu, China 79/D2
Xiayi, China 72/D4
Xichang, China 83/H2
Xichou, China 83/H3
Xico, Mex. 143/N7
Xicohténcatl, Mex. 143/F4
Xicotepec, Mex. 143/M6
Xifei (riv.), China 72/D4
Xifeng, China 70/J4
Xifeng, China 83/J2
Xifeng, China 72/F2
Xigazê, China 85/G1
Xihua, China 72/C4
Xilin, China 83/J3
Xilitla, Mex. 144/B1
Xilókastron, Gre. 47/H3
Ximeng Vazu Zizhixian, China 83/G3
Xin (riv.), China 79/C2
Xin Barag Zuoqi, China 71/L2
Xin'an, China 72/C4
Xin'an (riv.), China 72/D5
Xin'anjiang (res.), China 79/C2
Xin'anjiang (res.), China 72/D5
Xinbin, China 73/C2
Xincai, China 72/C4
Xinchang, China 79/D2
Xincheng, China 79/A3
Xincheng, China 72/G7
Xinfeng, China 79/B2
Xinfeng, China 83/K3
Xinfengjiang (res.), China 79/B3
Xing'an, China 79/B2
Xingcheng, China 72/E2
Xinghua, China 72/D4
Xinglong, China 72/H6
Xingshan, China 72/B5
Xingtai, China 72/C3
Xingu (riv.), Braz. 147/D3
Xingu, PN do, Braz. 151/H6
Xingyang, China 72/C4
Xingzi, China 79/C2
Xinhe, China 70/D3
Xinhe, China 72/C3
Xinhua, China 79/B2
Xinhuang Dongzu Zizhixian, China 79/A2
Xining, China 70/H4
Xinji, China 72/C3
Xinjiang, China 72/B4
Xinjiang Uygur (reg.), China 67/H5
Xinjin, China 73/A3
Xinle, China 72/C3
Xinmin, China 73/B1
Xintai, China 72/D4
Xinxiang, China 72/C4
Xinyang, China 71/K5
Xinyang, China 72/C4
Xinye, China 72/C4
Xinyi, China 83/K3
Xinyi, China 72/D4
Xinyu, China 79/B2
Xinzhou, China 70/D3
Xinzheng, China 72/C4
Xinzo de Limia, Sp. 44/B1
Xiong Xian, China 72/H7
Xiping, China 72/C4
Xiqing (mts.), China 70/H5
Xique-Xique, Braz. 154/B3
Xitang, China 72/L9
Xitiao (riv.), China 72/K9
Xiu (riv.), China 79/B2
Xiuning, China 79/C2
Xiuwen, China 83/J2
Xiuwu, China 72/C4
Xiuyan, China 73/B2
Xixabangma (peak), China 85/E1
Xixia, China 72/B4
Xiyang (riv.), China 83/J3
Xizang (Tibet) (aut. reg.), China 70/D5
Xochicalco (ruin), Mex. 143/K8
Xonacatlán, Mex. 143/Q10
Xpujil, Mex. 144/D2
Xu (riv.), China 79/C2
Xuan'en, China 79/A2
Xuanhua, China 72/G6
Xuchang, China 72/C4
Xun (riv.), China 79/B3
Xun Xian, China 72/C4
Xunke, China 71/N2
Xunwu, China 79/C3
Xunyang, China 72/B4
Xupu, China 72/C4
Xuwen, China 83/K3
Xuyi, China 72/D4
Xuzhou, China 72/D4

Y

Y Llethr (peak), Wal, UK 34/E6
Ya'an, China 70/H6
Ya'bad, Isr. 91/G7
Yabassi, Camr. 96/G7
Yablanitsa, Bul. 47/J1
Yablonovyy (range), Rus. 67/L4
Yabrūd, Isr. 91/G8
Yabucoa, PR 141/M8
Yabuki, Japan 75/G2
Yabuzukahon, Japan 77/C1
Yachi (riv.), China 79/A2
Yachiho, Japan 77/A1
Yachimata, Japan 77/E2
Yachiyo, Japan 77/D1
Yachiyo, Japan 77/G5
Yachiyo, Japan 77/E2
Yacimiento Río Turbio, Arg. 159/B6
Yacuiba, Bol. 150/F8
Yacuma (riv.), Bol. 150/E6
Yacumbu, PN, Ven. 152/D2
Yādgīr, India 82/C4
Yadkin (riv.), NC, US 133/H2
Yaeyama (isls.), Japan 75/G8
Yāfā, Isr. 91/G6
Yağcılar, Turk. 62/D5
Yagi, Japan 77/F2
Yagorlytsk (gulf), Ukr. 49/K2
Yagoua, Camr. 96/J5
Yagradagzê (peak), China 70/G4
Yaguale (riv.), Hon. 144/E3
Yaguarón (riv.), Uru. 159/G2
Yaguas (riv.), Peru 152/D5
Yague del Sur (riv.), DRep. 145/J2
Yagur, Isr. 91/G6
Yahagi (riv.), Japan 77/M6
Yahualica de Gonzalez Gallo, Mex. 142/E4
Yahyalı, Turk. 90/C2
Yáios (Paxoi), Gre. 47/G3
Yaita, Japan 75/F2
Yaizu, Japan 75/F3
Yajalón, Mex. 144/C2
Yakacık, Turk. 91/E1
Yakapınar, Turk. 91/D1
Yakima (riv.), Wa, US 126/C4
Yakima, Wa, US 126/C4
Yakishiri (isl.), Japan 76/B1
Yako, Burk. 103/E3
Yakoruda, Bul. 47/H1
Yakumo, Japan 76/B2
Yakuno, Japan 77/G5
Yakutat (bay), Ak, US 122/B3
Yakutsk, Rus. 65/N3
Yala, Thai. 78/C5
Yalahua (lag.), Mex. 144/E1
Yalangoz, Turk. 91/E1
Yalata Abor. Land, Austl. 113/F4
Yalbac (hills), Belz. 144/D2
Yalgoo, Austl. 112/C4
Yalgorup NP, Austl. 112/B5
Yalnızçam, Turk. 63/G4
Yaloké, CAfr. 96/J6
Yalong (riv.), China 67/K6
Yalova, Turk. 49/J5
Yalova, Turk. 49/H5
Yalpuh (lake), Ukr. 49/J3
Yalta, Ukr. 62/E3
Yalu (riv.), China,NKor. 65/N5
Yalutorovsk, Rus. 87/E1
Yalvaç, Turk. 90/B2
Yamada, Japan 76/B4
Yamaga, Japan 74/B4
Yamagata, Japan 71/Q4
Yamagata, Japan 75/G1
Yamagata (pref.), Japan 76/A4
Yamaguchi (pref.), Japan 74/B3
Yamaguchi, Japan 74/B3
Yamakita, Japan 77/C3
Yamal (pen.), Rus. 67/F2
Yamalo-Nenetskiy (aut. okrug), Rus. 64/H3
Yamanaka (lake), Japan 77/B3
Yamanashi, Japan 77/B2
Yamanie (falls), Austl. 114/B2
Yamanie Falls NP, Austl. 114/B2
Yamantau (peak), Rus. 61/N5
Yamaoka, Japan 77/M5
Yamarna Abor. Rsv., Austl. 112/D4
Yamashiro, Japan 77/J6
Yamato, Japan 77/J6
Yamato, Japan 77/E1
Yamato, Japan 77/C3
Yamato (riv.), Japan 77/J6
Yamato-Kōriyama, Japan 77/J6
Yamatotakada, Japan 77/J6
Yamazoe, Japan 77/K6
Yamba, Austl. 115/E1
Yambio, Sudan 97/L7
Yambol, Bul. 47/K1
Yambrasbamba, Peru 156/B2
Yamdena (isl.), Indo. 81/H5
Yamethin, Myan. 83/G3
Yamin (peak), Indo. 81/K4
Yamma Yamma (lake), Austl. 109/D3
Yamoto, Japan 76/B4
Yamoussoukro (cap.), C.d'Iv. 102/D5
Yampa (riv.), Co, US 128/F2
Yamuna (riv.), India 70/C6
Yamunānagar, India 86/D4
Yamzho Yumco (lake), China 83/F2
Yan (riv.), SrL. 82/D6
Yan Yean (res.), Austl. 115/G5
Yana (riv.), Rus. 67/N3
Yanagawa, Japan 74/B4
Yanahuanca, Peru 156/B3
Yanai, Japan 74/C4
Yanaizu, Japan 75/F2
Yan'an, China 72/B3
Yanaoca, Peru 156/D4
Yanaul, Rus. 61/M4
Yanbian, China 83/H2
Yancheng, China 72/C4
Yancheng, China 72/E4
Yanchep NP, Austl. 112/B4
Yanco, Austl. 115/C2
Yandeearra Abor. Rsv., Austl. 112/C2
Yandoon, Myan. 83/G4
Yanfolila, Mali 102/C4
Yangambi, D.R. Congo 97/K7
Yangbi (riv.), China 83/G2
Yangcheng, China 72/C4
Yangcheng (lake), China 72/L8
Yangchun, China 79/B3
Yangdang (mts.), China 79/C2
Yangdŏk, NKor. 73/D3
Yanggang-do (prov.), NKor. 73/D2
Yanggao, China 72/C2
Yanggu, SKor. 73/D3
Yanggu, China 72/C3
Yangiyul', Uzb. 87/E4
Yangjiang, China 83/K3
Yangma (isl.), China 73/A4
Yangon (state), Myan. 83/G4
Yangp'yŏng, SKor. 73/D4
Yangqu, China 72/C3
Yangquan, China 72/C3
Yangsan, SKor. 73/E5
Yangshan, China 83/K3
Yangtze (Chang) (riv.), China 79/C1
Yangudi Rassa NP, Eth. 97/P5
Yangxin, China 79/C2
Yangxin, China 72/D3
Yangyang, SKor. 73/E3
Yangyuan, China 72/C2
Yangzhong, China 72/D4
Yangzhou, China 72/D4
Yanhe, China 79/A2
Yanji, China 71/N3
Yanjin, China 83/H2
Yanjin, China 72/C4
Yankari Game Reserve, Nga. 97/H6
Yankee Stadium, NY, US 139/K8
Yanling, China 72/C4
Yanmen (pass), China 72/C3
Yanshan, China 79/C2
Yanshan, China 83/H3
Yanshan, China 72/D3
Yanshi, China 72/C4
Yanshou, China 71/N2
Yantai, China 72/E3
Yanyuan, China 83/H2
Yanzhou, China 72/D4
Yao, Japan 77/J6
Yao'an, China 83/H2
Yaotsu, Japan 77/M5
Yaoundé (cap.), Camr. 96/H7
Yap (isls.), Micr. 116/C4
Yapacana, PN, Ven. 150/E3
Yapei, Gha. 103/E4
Yapen (isl.), Indo. 116/C5
Yapen (str.), Indo. 81/J4
Yapraklı, Turk. 62/E4
Yaqui (riv.), Mex. 142/C2
Yara, Cuba 145/G1
Yaracuy (state), Ven. 152/D2
Yaralıgöz (peak), Turk. 62/E4
Yaransk, Rus. 61/K4
Yardımcı (pt.), Turk. 91/B1
Yardley, Pa, US 138/D3
Yardville-Groveville, NJ, US 138/D3
Yare (riv.), Eng, UK 33/H1
Yarí (riv.), Col. 150/D3
Yari-ga-take (peak), Japan 75/E2
Yarımca, Turk. 49/J5
Yaritagua, Ven. 152/D2
Yarkant (riv.), China 64/H6
Yarloop, Austl. 112/B5
Yarlung Zangbo (Brahmaputra) (riv.), China 85/G1
Yarmouth, NS, Can. 131/H3
Yaroslavl', Rus. 60/H4
Yaroslavskaya (obl.), Rus. 60/H4
Yarpuz, Turk. 91/E1
Yarra (riv.), Austl. 115/G5
Yarra Glen, Austl. 115/G5
Yarram, Austl. 115/C3
Yarraman, Austl. 114/D4
Yarrawonga, Austl. 115/C3
Yarrow Point, Wa, US 135/C2
Yartsevo, Rus. 64/K3
Yarumal, Col. 152/C3
Yasato, Japan 77/E1
Yasawa Group (isls.), Fiji 116/G6
Yasel'da (riv.), Bela. 62/C1
Yashima, Japan 76/B4
Yashio, Japan 77/D2
Yashiro, Japan 77/G6
Yasnyy, Rus. 63/L2
Yasothon, Thai. 78/D3
Yass, Austl. 115/D2
Yasu (riv.), Japan 77/K6
Yasu, Japan 77/K5
Yasugi, Japan 74/C3
Yāsūj, Iran 88/F2
Yasun Burnu (pt.), Turk. 62/F4
Yasuni, PN, Ecu. 150/C4
Yatabe, Japan 75/G2
Yatağan, Turk. 90/B2
Yateley, Eng, UK 33/F4
Yatenga (prov.), Burk. 103/E3
Yathkyed (lake), Nun., Can. 122/G2
Yatomi, Japan 77/L5
Yatsu-ga-take (peak), Japan 77/A2
Yatsuo, Japan 75/E2
Yatsushiro, Japan 74/B4
Yatsushiro, Japan 77/B2
Yaṭṭah, WBnk. 91/G8
Yauca (riv.), Peru 156/C4
Yauca, Peru 156/C4
Yauco, PR 141/M8
Yauli, Peru 156/B3
Yaupi, Ecu. 152/B5
Yaután, Peru 156/B3
Yauyos, Peru 156/C4
Yauza (riv.), Rus. 61/W9
Yavarí (riv.), Braz.,Peru 147/B3
Yavarí Mirim (riv.), Peru 156/C2
Yavaros, Mex. 142/C3
Yavay (pen.), Rus. 64/H2
Yaviza, Pan. 152/B2
Yavne, Isr. 91/F8
Yavuzeli, Turk. 90/D2
Yawahara, Japan 77/E2
Yawata, Japan 77/J6
Yawatahama, Japan 74/C4
Yaxchilán (ruin), Guat. 144/D2
Yaygın, Turk. 90/E2
Yayladaği, Turk. 91/E2
Yayladere, Turk. 90/E2
Yazd, Iran 89/F2
Yazmān, Pak. 86/A5
Yazoo (riv.), Ms, US 129/K4
Yazoo City, Ms, US 129/K4
Ybbs (riv.), Aus. 41/H4
Ybbsitz, Aus. 43/L3
Yding Skovhøj (peak), Den. 38/C3
Ye, Myan. 78/B3
Ye Xian, China 72/D3
Yeay Sen (cape), Camb. 78/C4
Yecheng, China 87/G5
Yech'ŏn, SKor. 73/E4
Yecla, Sp. 45/E3
Yécora, Mex. 142/C2
Yecuatla, Mex. 143/N7
Yedigöller Nat'l Park, Turk. 49/K5
Yeditepe, Turk. 91/E2
Yéfira, Gre. 47/H2
Yefremov, Rus. 62/F1
Yegizkara (peak), Kaz. 87/D3
Yegorlak (riv.), Rus. 63/G3
Yehualtepec, Mex. 143/M8
Yehud, Isr. 91/F7
Yejmiadzin, Arm. 63/H4
Yekaterinburg (Sverdlovsk), Rus. 61/P4
Yekateriny (chan.), Rus. 76/E1
Yelabuga, Rus. 61/M5
Yelan', Rus. 63/G2
Yelarbon, Austl. 114/C5
Yelets, Rus. 62/F1
Yélimané, Mali 102/C3
Yelizovo, Rus. 65/R4
Yell (isl.), Sc, UK 31/W13
Yellel, Alg. 100/F5
Yellow (riv.), Fl, US 133/G4
Yellow (sea), Asia 67/M6
Yellow Grass, Sk, Can. 127/G3
Yellowknife (riv.), NW, Can. 122/E2
Yellowknife (cap.), NW, Can. 122/E2
Yellowstone (lake), Wy, US 126/F4
Yellowstone (riv.), Mt, US 127/G4
Yellowstone NP, US 128/E1
Yellville, Ar, US 129/J3
Yemen (ctry.) 88/E5
Yenakiyeve, Ukr. 62/F2
Yenangyaung, Myan. 83/F3
Yenda, Austl. 115/C2
Yendi, Gha. 103/E4
Yengisar, China 87/G5
Yeniçağa, Turk. 49/L5
Yenice, Turk. 91/D1
Yenice, Turk. 49/L5
Yenice (riv.), Turk. 62/E4
Yenice, Turk. 49/H6
Yeniceoba, Turk. 90/C2
Yeniköy, Turk. 49/H5
Yenişehir, Turk. 49/J5
Yenisey (riv.), Rus. 67/H3
Yeniseysk, Rus. 64/K4
Yeo (lake), Austl. 109/B3
Yeo Lake Nature Rsv., Austl. 112/E3
Yeoval, Austl. 115/D2
Yeovil, Eng, UK 32/D5
Yeppoon, Austl. 114/C3
Yeraifia (well), WSah. 98/B4
Yerakovoúni (peak), Gre. 47/H3
Yères (riv.), Fr. 52/A4
Yerevan (cap.), Arm. 63/H4
Yerevan (int'l arpt.), Arm. 63/H4
Yerington, Nv, US 128/C3
Yerköy, Turk. 62/E5
Yerlisu, Turk. 47/K2
Yermak, Kaz. 87/G2
Yeroḩam, Isr. 91/D4
Yerolimín, Gre. 47/H4
Yerre (riv.), Fr. 42/D2
Yerres, Fr. 30/K5
Yerupaja (peak), Peru 156/B3
Yesagyo, Myan. 83/G3
Yesan, SKor. 73/D4
Yeşilhisar, Turk. 90/C2
Yeşilırmak (riv.), Turk. 62/F4
Yeşilkent, Turk. 91/E1
Yeşilova, Turk. 90/B2
Yesodot, Isr. 91/F8
Yesŏng (riv.), NKor. 73/D3
Yessentuki, Rus. 63/G3
Yeste, Sp. 44/D3
Yetti (reg.), Mrta. 98/D4
Yeu, Ile d' (isl.), Fr. 42/B3
Yevla, India 82/B3
Yevlax, Azer. 63/H4
Yevpatoriya, Ukr. 62/E3
Yèvre (riv.), Fr. 53/D5
Yeya (riv.), Rus. 62/G3
Yeysk, Rus. 62/F3
Ygos-Saint-Saturnin, Fr. 42/C5
Yi (riv.), Uru. 159/F2
Yialousa, Cyp. 91/D2
Yiannitsá, Gre. 47/H2
Yiánnouli, Gre. 47/H3
Yiaros (isl.), Gre. 47/J4
Yibin, China 70/H6
Yichang, China 71/K5
Yicheng, China 72/C5
Yicheng, China 72/B4
Yichuan, China 72/C4
Yichun, China 71/N2
Yichun, China 83/K2
Yifeng, China 83/K2
Yığılca, Turk. 49/K5
Yihuang, China 79/C2
Yıldız (peak), Turk. 90/D1
Yıldızeli, Turk. 62/F5
Yilehuli (mts.), China 71/M1
Yiliang, China 83/H2
Yima, China 72/B4
Yimen, China 83/H3
Yin (mts.), China 65/L5
Yinan, China 72/D4
Yinchuan, China 70/J4
Yindarlgooda (lake), Austl. 109/B4
Yingcheng, China 71/K5
Yingde, China 79/B3
Yingkou, China 73/B2
Yingshan, China 72/C5
Yingshang, China 72/D4
Yingtan, China 79/C2
Yining, China 70/D3
Yishan, China 79/A3
Yishui, China 72/D4
Yíthion, Gre. 47/H4
Yitong (riv.), SKor. 72/C5
Yiwu, China 70/F3
Yixing, China 72/K8
Yiyang, China 83/K2
Yiyang, China 72/C4
Yiyuan, China 72/D3
Yizhang, China 83/K2
Yizheng, China 72/D4
Ylöjärvi, Fin. 39/K1
Ÿnder (lake), Kaz. 63/K2
Yngaren (lake), Swe. 38/G2
Yobe (state), Nga. 103/H3
Yŏch'ŏn, SKor. 73/D5
Yodo (riv.), Japan 77/J6
Yoduma (riv.), Rus. 65/P4
Yoff (Dakar) (int'l arpt.), Sen. 102/A3
Yogo, Japan 77/K4
Yogoum (well), Chad 97/J4
Yoğuntaş, Turk. 49/H5
Yogyakarta, Indo. 80/D5
Yoho NP, BC, Can. 126/D3
Yoichi, Japan 76/B2
Yojoa (lake), Hon. 144/D3
Yŏju, SKor. 73/D4
Yokadouma, Camr. 96/J7
Yōkaichi, Japan 77/K5
Yokawa, Japan 77/H6
Yokkaichi, Japan 77/L6
Yokohama, Japan 75/F3
Yokoshiba, Japan 77/E2
Yokosuka, Japan 75/F3
Yokote, Japan 76/B4
Yokoze, Japan 77/C2
Yola, Nga. 96/H6
Yolaina (mts.), Nic. 145/E4
Yolboyu, Turk. 90/D2
Yolo, Ca, US 135/L9
Yolo (co.), Ca, US 135/L9
Yom (riv.), Thai. 83/H4
Yon (riv.), China 79/A3
Yon (riv.), Fr. 42/C3
Yonago, Japan 74/C3
Yonaguni (isl.), Japan 75/G8
Yonaha-dake (peak), Japan 75/K7
Yoneshiro (riv.), Japan 76/B3
Yonezawa, Japan 75/G2
Yŏng-yang, SKor. 73/E4
Yŏngam, SKor. 73/D5
Yongamp'o, NKor. 73/C3
Yong'an, China 79/C2
Yongchang, China 70/H4
Yongcheng, China 72/D4
Yŏngch'ŏn, SKor. 74/A3
Yongchun, China 79/C2
Yongde, China 83/G3
Yongding, China 79/C3
Yongding (riv.), China 65/M6
Yŏngdŏk, SKor. 74/A2
Yŏngdong, SKor. 73/D4
Yŏnggwang, SKor. 73/D5
Yŏnghae, SKor. 73/E4
Yonghe, China 72/B3
Yŏnghŭng (riv.), NKor. 73/D3
Yŏnghŭng, NKor. 73/D3
Yongji, China 72/B4
Yŏngjong (isl.), SKor. 73/F6
Yŏngju, SKor. 74/A2
Yongkang, China 79/D2
Yongmun-san (peak), SKor. 73/D4
Yongnian, China 72/C3
Yongqing, China 72/H7

238

Yongr – Żywie

Yongren, China 83/H2
Yŏngsan (riv.), SKor. 73/D5
Yongsheng, China 83/H2
Yongshun, China 83/J2
Yongtai, China 79/C2
Yŏngwŏl, SKor. 74/A2
Yongxing, China 79/B2
Yongxiu, China 79/C2
Yonkers, NY, US 139/K8
Yonne (riv.), Fr. 40/B5
Yono, Japan 77/D2
Yopal, Col. 152/C3
Yopurga, China 87/G5
Yoqne'am 'Illit, Isr. 91/G6
Yorba Linda, Ca, US 136/G8
Yorii, Japan 77/C1
York, Austl. 112/C4
York (cape), Austl. 109/D2
York (sound), Austl. 109/B2
York (riv.), Qu, Can. 131/H1
York, Eng, UK 35/G4
York (co.), Eng, UK 35/G4
York, Al, US 133/F3
York, Ne, US 127/J5
York, Pa, US 138/B4
York (co.), Pa, US 138/B4
York, SC, US 133/H3
York (riv.), Va, US 130/E4
York Haven, Pa, US 138/B3
York Landing, Mb, Can. 127/J1
York Minster, Eng, UK 35/G4
York Springs, Pa, US 138/A4
York, Vale of (valley), Eng, UK 35/G3
Yorke (pen.), Austl. 109/C4
Yorketown, Austl. 113/H5
Yorkshire Dales NP, Eng, UK 35/F3
Yorkshire Wolds (hills), Eng, UK 35/H3
Yorkton, Sk, Can. 127/H3
Yorktown, Tx, US 129/H5
Yorktown Heights, NY, US 139/E1
Yoro, Hon. 144/E3
Yŏrō (riv.), Japan 77/E3
Yorō, Japan 77/L5
Yoroi-zaki (pt.), Japan 77/L7
Yoron (isl.), Japan 75/K7
Yorosso, Mali 102/D3
Yorubaland (plat.), Nga. 96/F6
Yos Sudarso (isl.), Indo. 81/J5
Yosemite NP, Ca, US 128/C3
Yoshida, Japan 74/C4
Yoshida, Japan 77/C1
Yoshii (riv.), Japan 74/D3
Yoshii, Japan 77/B1
Yoshikawa, Japan 77/D2
Yoshima (riv.), Japan 74/D3
Yoshimi, Japan 77/C1
Yoshino (riv.), Japan 74/C4
Yoshino, Japan 77/J7
Yoshino-Kumano NP, Japan 77/J7
Yoshkar-Ola, Rus. 61/L4
Yŏsu, SKor. 73/D5
Yōtei-san (peak), Japan 76/B2
Yotsukaidō, Japan 77/E2
You (riv.), China 79/A3
Young, Austl. 115/D2
Young, Uru. 159/K10
Youngs (lake), Wa, US 135/C3
Youngstown, Oh, US 130/D3
Youngstown, NY, US 131/R9
Youngtown, Az, US 137/R18
Yountville, Ca, US 135/K10
Youssoufia, Mor. 98/C2
Youyang, China 83/J2
Yoví (peak), Ven. 153/E3
Yozgat, Turk. 62/E5
Ypsilanti, Mi, US 135/E7
Yr Eifl (peak), Wal, UK 34/D6
Yreka, Ca, US 128/B2
Yser (riv.), Fr. 40/B3
Ysieux (riv.), Fr. 30/K4
Ystad, Swe. 38/E4
Ysyk-Köl (lake), Kyr. 70/C3
Ysyk-Köl (obl.), Kyr. 87/G4
Ythan (riv.), Sc, UK 36/D2
Ytrac, Fr. 42/E4
Ytre Sula (isl.), Nor. 38/A1
Ytterby, Swe. 38/D3
Ytterbyn, Swe. 37/G2
Yü (peak), Tai. 79/D3
Yu (riv.), China 83/J3
Yu Xian, China 72/C3
Yu Xian, China 72/C4
Yuan (riv.), China 71/K6
Yuan (lake), China 72/C5
Yuan'an, China 72/B5
Yüanlin, Tai. 79/D3
Yuanping, China 72/C3
Yuanqu, China 72/B4
Yuanshi, China 72/C3
Yuanyang, China 72/C4
Yuba City, Ca, US 128/B3
Yūbari, Japan 76/B2
Yūbetsu, Japan 76/C1
Yūbetsu (riv.), Japan 76/C2
Yucaipa, Ca, US 136/C2
Yucatán (state), Mex. 144/D1
Yucatan (pen.), Mex. 144/D2
Yucatan (chan.), NAm. 144/E1
Yucca House Nat'l Mon., Co, US 128/E3
Yucheng, China 72/D3
Yucheng, China 72/C4
Yuci, China 72/C3
Yuen Long, China 71/U10
Yuendumu, Austl. 113/F2
Yuendumu Abor. Land, Austl. 113/F2
Yueqing, China 79/D2
Yueyang, China 79/B2
Yug (riv.), Rus. 64/E4
Yugan, China 79/C2
Yugawara, Japan 77/C3
Yugorskiy (pen.), Rus. 61/P1
Yugoslavia (ctry.) 48/D3
Yuhang, China 72/L9
Yuhuan, China 79/D2
Yui, Japan 77/B3
Yujiang, China 79/C2
Yūki, Japan 75/F2
Yukon, Ok, US 137/M14
Yukon (riv.), Can.,US 134/L3
Yukon-Charley Rivers Nat'l Prsv., Ak, US 134/K2
Yukon Delta NWR, Ak, US 134/F3
Yukon Flats NWR, Ak, US 134/J2
Yukon Territory (terr.), Can. 134/L2
Yüksekova, Turk. 90/F2
Yukuhashi, Japan 74/B4
Yulara, Austl. 113/F3
Yuleba, Austl. 114/C4
Yulin, China 83/K3
Yulin, China 83/J4
Yulin, China 72/B3
Yuma, Az, US 128/D4
Yuma, Co, US 129/G2
Yuma, Az, US 124/D5
Yumbarra Consv. Park, Austl. 113/G4
Yumbel, Chile 158/B3
Yumbo, Col. 152/B4
Yumen, China 70/G4
Yumin, China 70/D2
Yumurtalık, Turk. 91/D1
Yun (riv.), China 72/C5
Yun Xian, China 83/H3
Yun Xian, China 72/B4
Yunak, Turk. 90/B2
Yuncheng, China 72/C4
Yuncheng, China 72/B4
Yundum (Banjul) (int'l arpt.), Gam. 102/A3
Yungang Caves, China 72/C2
Yungas (phys. reg.), Bol. 150/E7
Yungay, Chile 158/B3
Yungk'ang, Tai. 79/D3
Yunguyo, Peru 156/D5
Yunkanjini Abor. Land, Austl. 113/F2
Yunlong, China 83/G2
Yunnan (prov.), China 70/H7
Yuntai (peak), China 72/D4
Yunxi, China 72/B4
Yunxiao, China 79/C3
Yunyan (riv.), China 72/D4
Yunzhong (mtn.), China 72/C3
Yuping, China 83/J2
Yupukarri, Guy. 153/G4
Yuqiao (res.), China 72/H7
Yuracyacu, Peru 156/B2
Yurga, Rus. 64/J4
Yuri (isl.), Rus. 76/E2
Yurimaguas, Peru 156/B2
Yuruari (riv.), Ven. 153/F3
Yürük, Turk. 49/H5
Yur'yevets, Rus. 60/J4
Yuryuzan' (riv.), Rus. 61/N5
Yuscarán, Hon. 144/E3
Yushan, China 79/C2
Yushe, China 72/C3
Yushu, China 71/N3
Yusŏng, SKor. 73/D4
Yusufeli, Turk. 63/G4
Yutai, China 72/D4
Yutian, China 70/D4
Yutian, China 72/H7
Yutz, Fr. 53/F5
Yuza, Japan 76/A4
Yuzawa, Japan 76/B4
Yuzhno-Sakhalinsk, Rus. 71/R2
Yverdon, Swi. 56/C4
Yvette (riv.), Fr. 52/B6
Yvoir, Belg. 53/D3
Yvonand, Swi. 56/C4
Yvron (riv.), Fr. 30/L6
Yzeure, Fr. 42/E3

Z

Za (riv.), Mor. 100/C2
Zaachila, Mex. 144/B2
Zaandam, Neth. 40/C2
Zaanstad, Neth. 50/B4
Żabbar, Malta 46/M7
Zaber (riv.), Ger. 54/C4
Ząbki, Pol. 41/L2
Ząbkowice Śląskie, Pol. 41/J3
Žabljak, Yugo. 47/F1
Zábřeh, Czh. 41/J4
Zabrze, Pol. 41/K3
Zacapa, Guat. 144/D3
Zacapoaxtla, Mex. 143/M7
Zacapu, Mex. 143/E5
Zacatecas (state), Mex. 140/A3
Zacatecas, Mex. 142/E4
Zacatecoluca, ESal. 144/D3
Zacatelco, Mex. 143/L7
Zacatepec, Mex. 143/K8
Zacatlán, Mex. 143/M7
Zachary, La, US 133/F4
Zacoalco de Torres, Mex. 142/E4
Zacualtipán, Mex. 144/B1
Zadar, Cro. 43/L4
Zadetkyi (isl.), Myan. 80/A2
Zafarwāl, Pak. 86/C3
Zafra, Sp. 44/B3
Żagań, Pol. 41/H3
Zaghwān (gov.), Tun. 46/A4
Zaghwān, Tun. 100/M6
Zagora, Mor. 98/D3
Zagorá, Gre. 47/H3
Zagorje ob Savi, Slov. 43/L3
Zagreb (cap.), Cro. 48/B3
Zagros (mts.), Iran 64/F6
Zāhedān, Iran 89/H3
Zahīrābād, India 82/C4
Zaḩlah, Leb. 91/D3
Záhony, Hun. 41/M4
Zahrez Chergui (dry lake), Alg. 100/G5
Zaidín, Sp. 45/F2
Zaidpur, India 84/C2
Zaïo, Mor. 100/C2
Zaire (see Congo, Democratic Republic of the)
Zakamensk, Rus. 70/H1
Zakarpats'ka (obl.), Ukr. 62/B2
Zakháro, Gre. 47/G4
Zakhodnyaya Dzvina (riv.), Bela. 60/E5
Zākhū, Iraq 90/E2
Zákinthos (isl.), Gre. 47/G4
Zákinthos, Gre. 47/G4
Zakopane, Pol. 41/K4
Zakouma, PN de, Chad 97/J5
Zala (riv.), Hun. 48/C2
Zala (prov.), Hun. 48/C2
Zalaapáti, Hun. 48/C2
Zalaegerszeg, Hun. 48/C2
Zalamea de la Serena, Sp. 44/C3
Zalamea la Real, Sp. 44/B4
Zalaszentgrót, Hun. 48/C2
Zalău, Rom. 49/F2
Žalec, Slov. 43/L3
Zalţan (well), Libya 96/J2
Zaltbommel, Neth. 50/C5
Zalun, Myan. 83/G4
Zama, Japan 77/C3
Zamānia, India 84/D3
Zambezi, Zam. 105/D3
Zambezi (riv.), Moz. 93/E6
Zambia (ctry.) 105/E3
Zamboanga, Phil. 81/F2
Zambrów, Pol. 41/M2
Zamfora (riv.), Nga. 103/G3
Zami (riv.), Myan. 78/B3
Zamora (riv.), Ecu. 150/C4
Zamora, Ecu. 156/B2
Zamora, Sp. 44/C2
Zamora-Chinchipe (prov.), Ecu. 156/B2
Zamora de Hidalgo, Mex. 142/E5
Zamość (prov.), Pol. 41/M3
Zamość, Pol. 41/M3
Zams, Aus. 57/G3
Záncara (riv.), Sp. 44/D3
Zanda, China 70/C5
Zandkreekdam (dam), Neth. 50/A5
Zandvoort, Neth. 50/B4
Zanè, It. 59/E1
Zanhuang, China 72/C3
Zanjān, Iran 88/E1
Zanjón (riv.), Mex. 128/E5
Zánka, Hun. 48/C2
Zanzibar, Tanz. 104/C4
Zanzibar (isl.), Tanz. 93/F5
Zanzibar (Kisauni) (int'l arpt.), Tanz. 104/C4
Zanzibar Central/South (pol. reg.),Tanz. 104/C4
Zanzibar North (prov.), Tanz. 104/C4
Zanzibar Urban/West (pol. reg.), Tanz. 104/C4
Zanzuzi (hill), Tanz. 104/B3
Zaō-san (peak), Japan 75/G1
Zaoqiang, China 72/C3
Zaouiet Kounta, Alg. 99/E4
Zaoyang, China 72/C4
Zaozhuang, China 72/D4
Západočeský (pol. reg.), Czh. 43/K2
Zapadocesky (pol. reg.), Czh. 40/G4
Zapadoslovensky (pol. reg.), Slvk. 41/J4
Zapala, Arg. 158/C3
Zapaleri (peak), SA 157/C1
Zapallar, Chile 158/C2
Zapata, Tx, US 132/D5
Zapata (pen.), Cuba 145/F1
Zapatoca, Col. 152/C3
Zapatosa (swamp), Col. 145/H4
Zapatosa (lake), Col. 152/C2
Záplatský Rybník (lake), Czh. 55/H4
Zapolyarnyy, Rus. 60/F1
Zapopan, Mex. 142/E4
Zaporizhzhya, Ukr. 62/E3
Zaporizhzhya (int'l arpt.), Ukr. 62/E3
Zaporiz'ka (obl.), Ukr. 62/E3
Zapotal, Ecu. 152/B5
Zapotillo, Ecu. 156/A2
Zapponeta, It. 46/D2
Zaprešić, Cro. 48/B3
Zara, Turk. 62/F5
Zaragoza, Mex. 132/C4
Zaragoza (int'l arpt.), Sp. 45/E2
Zaragoza, Mex. 143/M7
Zaragoza, Col. 152/C3
Zaragoza (Saragossa), Sp. 45/E2
Zarah, Ks, US 137/D6
Zarand, Iran 89/G2
Zaranda (hill), Nga. 103/H4
Zárate, Arg. 159/J11
Zarauz, Sp. 44/D1
Zaraza, Ven. 153/E2
Zard (mtn.), Iran 88/F2
Zareh Sharan, Afg. 89/J2
Zargān, Iran 88/F3
Zaria, Nga. 103/G4
Zarmast (pass), Afg. 89/H2
Zărneşti, Rom. 49/G3
Žarnovica, Slvk. 48/D1
Zarós, Gre. 47/J5
Záruby (peak), Slvk. 48/C1
Zaruma, Ecu. 156/B1
Zarumilla, Peru 156/A1
Żary, Pol. 41/H3
Zarza la Mayor, Sp. 44/B3
Zarzal, Col. 152/B3
Zāskār (range), India 70/C5
Zāskār (riv.), India 86/D3
Zastron, SAfr. 106/D3
Žatec, Czh. 55/G2
Zauche (reg.), Ger. 40/P7
Zavalla, Arg. 158/E2
Zavdi'el, Isr. 91/F8
Zaventem, Belg. 53/D2
Zavet, Bul. 49/H4
Zavidovići, Bosn. 48/D3
Zavitinsk, Rus. 71/N1
Zawadzkie, Pol. 41/K3
Zawiercie, Pol. 41/K3
Zaysan, Kaz. 70/D2
Zaysan (lake), Kaz. 67/H5
Zayü (riv.), China 83/G2
Zaza (riv.), Cuba 145/G1
Zazárida, Ven. 152/D2
Zbąszyń, Pol. 41/H2
Žďár nad Sázavou, Czh. 41/H4
Zdice, Czh. 55/G3
Zduńska Wola, Pol. 41/K3
Zeballos (peak), Arg. 159/C5
Żebbuġ, Malta 46/L7
Zeddine (riv.), Alg. 100/F5
Zedelgem, Belg. 52/C1
Zeehan, Austl. 115/C4
Zeeland, Mi, US 130/C3
Zeeland (prov.), Neth. 50/A5
Zeeland, Neth. 50/C5
Zeerust, SAfr. 105/E6
Zeewolde, Neth. 50/C4
Ẓefat, Isr. 91/D3
Zegrzyńskie (res.), Pol. 41/L2
Zehdenick, Ger. 41/G2
Zeil (mt.), Austl. 113/G2
Zeil, Ger. 54/D2
Zeiselmauer, Aus. 49/N7
Zeist, Neth. 50/C4
Zeitz, Ger. 40/G3
Żejtun, Malta 46/M7
Zekharya, Isr. 91/F8
Zele, Belg. 52/D1
Zelenodol'sk, Rus. 61/L5
Zelenogorsk, Rus. 61/S6
Zelenokumsk, Rus. 63/G3
Zelhem, Neth. 50/D4
Zell, Swi. 57/E3
Zell, Swi. 56/D3
Zell, Ger. 53/G3
Zell am Harmersbach, Ger. 56/E1
Zell am Main, Ger. 54/C3
Zell am Moos, Aus. 55/G7
Zell am See, Aus. 43/K3
Zell an der Pram, Aus. 55/G6
Zell in Wiesental, Ger. 56/D2
Zellersee (lake), Aus. 54/G7
Zellingen, Ger. 54/C3
Zelów, Pol. 41/K3
Zeltingen-Rachtig, Ger. 53/G4
Zeltweg, Aus. 43/L3
Zelzate, Belg. 52/C1
Zemaitija NP, Lith. 39/J3
Zembra (isls.), Tun. 46/B4
Zemen, Bul. 47/H1
Zemio, CAfr. 97/L6
Zemmer, Ger. 53/F4
Zemmora, Alg. 100/F5
Zempoala, Mex. 143/N7
Zempoala (peak), Mex. 143/Q10
Zempoaltepec, Cerro (peak), Mex. 144/C2
Zemst, Belg. 53/D2
Zenica, Bosn. 48/C3
Zenith, Wa, US 135/C3
Zenn (riv.), Ger. 43/J2
Zenne (riv.), Belg. 53/D1
Zenon Park, Sk, Can. 127/H2
Zentsūji, Japan 74/C3
Žepče, Bosn. 48/D3
Zepu, China 87/G5
Zeralda, Alg. 100/G4
Zeravshan (riv.), Taj.,Uzb. 87/E5
Zermatt, Swi. 56/D5
Zernez, Swi. 57/G4
Zernien, Ger. 51/H2
Zernograd, Rus. 62/G3
Zero Branco, It. 59/F1
Zeta (lake), Nun., Can. 122/F1
Zetel, Ger. 51/E2
Zeuthen, Ger. 40/Q7
Zeven, Ger. 51/G2
Zevenaar, Neth. 50/D5
Zevenbergen, Neth. 50/B5
Zevgolatión, Gre. 47/H4
Zevio, It. 59/E2
Zeya (res.), Rus. 67/M4
Zeya (riv.), Rus. 65/N4
Zeya-Bureya (plain), Rus. 65/N4
Zeytindağ, Turk. 62/C5
Zêzere (riv.), Port. 44/A3
Zghartā, Leb. 91/D2
Zgierz, Pol. 41/K3
Zgorzelec, Pol. 41/H3
Zhambyl (obl.), Kaz. 87/F4
Zhambyl, Kaz. 87/F4
Zhangaözen, Kaz. 63/K4
Zhangaqazaly, Kaz. 87/D3
Zhangatas, Kaz. 87/E4
Zhanghei, China 72/C2
Zhangjiakou, China 72/C2
Zhangping, China 79/C2
Zhangpu, China 79/C3
Zhangqiu, China 72/D3
Zhangshu, China 79/C2
Zhangwei (riv.), China 72/D3
Zhangye, China 70/H4
Zhangzhou, China 79/C3
Zhangzi (isl.), China 73/B3
Zhangzi, China 72/C3
Zhanhua, China 72/D3
Zhanjiang, China 83/K3
Zhao Xian, China 72/C3
Zhao'an, China 79/C3
Zhaojue, China 83/H2
Zhaoqing, China 83/K3
Zhaotong, China 83/H2
Zhaoyuan, China 72/E3
Zhaozhou, China 71/N2
Zhāyya (Ural) (riv.), Kaz.,Rus. 64/F5
Zhayyq (riv.), Kaz. 67/E5
Zhecheng, China 72/C4
Zhejiang (prov.), China 71/L6
Zhelaniya (cape), Rus. 64/G2
Zheleznodorozhnyy, Rus. 61/L3
Zheleznogorsk, Rus. 62/E1
Zheleznogorsk-Ilimskiy, Rus. 65/L4
Zhenfeng Bouyeizu Miaozu Zizhixian, China 83/J2
Zhengding, China 72/C3
Zhenglan, China 71/L3
Zhengning, China 72/B4
Zhengyang, China 72/C4
Zhengzhou, China 72/C4
Zhenhai, China 79/D2
Zhenjiang, China 72/D4
Zhenkang, China 83/G3
Zhenning Bouyeizu Miaozu Zizhixian, China 83/J2
Zhenping, China 72/C4
Zhentou (riv.), China 72/C4
Zhenwu (mtn.), China 72/B3
Zhenxiong, China 83/H2
Zhenyuan, China 79/A2
Zhenyuan, China 83/H3
Zhetiqara, Kaz. 63/M1
Zhezqazghan, Kaz. 87/E3
Zhezqazghan (obl.), Kaz. 87/E3
Zhicheng, China 79/B1
Zhigulevsk, Rus. 63/J1
Zhijiang, China 79/B1
Zhijin, China 83/J2
Zhiloy (isl.), Azer. 63/J4
Zhlobin, Bela. 62/D1
Zhmerynka, Ukr. 62/D2
Zhob, Pak. 89/J2
Zhob (riv.), Pak. 89/J2
Zhodino, Bela. 39/N4
Zhokhov (isl.), Rus. 65/R2
Zhongba, China 79/C3
Zhongshan, China 83/K3
Zhongxiang, China 72/C5
Zhongyang, China 72/B3
Zhoukou, China 72/C4
Zhoushan (isls.), China 79/D2
Zhouzhou, China 72/G7
Zhovtneve, Ukr. 49/L2
Zhuanghe, China 73/B3
Zhucheng, China 72/D4
Zhuhai, China 83/K3
Zhuji, China 79/D2
Zhujiang Kou (bay), China 71/T10
Zhukovka, Rus. 62/E1
Zhukovskiy, Rus. 61/X9
Zhumadian, China 72/C4
Zhuolu, China 72/G6
Zhuozi, China 72/C2
Zhushan, China 72/B4
Zhuxi, China 72/B4
Zhuzhou, China 83/K2
Zhuzhou, China 83/K3
Zhytomyr, Ukr. 62/D2
Zhytomyrs'ka (obl.), Ukr. 62/C2
Zi (riv.), China 79/B2
Zia (int'l arpt.), Bang. 85/H4
Zibo, China 72/D3
Ziębice, Pol. 41/J3
Zielona Góra, Pol. 41/H3
Zierenberg, Ger. 51/G6
Zierikzee, Neth. 50/A5
Ziftá, Egypt 91/B4
Zigong, China 83/H2
Zigui, China 72/B5
Ziguinchor (int'l arpt.), Sen. 102/A3
Ziguinchor, Sen. 102/A3
Ziguinchor (pol. reg.), Sen. 102/A3
Zihuatanejo, Mex. 143/E5
Zijing (mtn.), China 72/B3
Zikhron Ya'aqov, Isr. 91/F6
Zile, Turk. 62/E4
Žilina, Slvk. 41/K4
Zillah, Libya 96/J2
Ziller (riv.), Aus. 43/J3
Zillisheim, Fr. 56/D2
Zimapán, Mex. 143/F4
Zimatlán de Álvarez, Mex. 144/B2
Zimba, Zam. 105/E4
Zimbabwe (ctry.) 105/E4
Zimla (well), Alg. 99/E3
Zimnicea, Rom. 49/G4
Zinapécuaro de Figueroa, Mex. 143/E5
Zinave, PN de, Moz. 105/F5
Zinder, Niger 103/H3
Zinder (dept.), Niger 103/H3
Ziniaré, Burk. 103/E3
Zinjin, China 79/C3
Zion, Md, US 138/C4
Zion NP, Ut, US 128/D3
Zippori, Isr. 91/G6
Zirc, Hun. 48/C2
Žirje (isl.), Cro. 48/B4
Zirl, Aus. 57/H3
Ziro, India 83/F2
Zitácuaro, Mex. 143/E5
Žitava (riv.), Slvk. 41/K5
Zittau, Ger. 41/H3
Živinice, Bosn. 48/D3
Ziwa Magharibi (pol. reg.), Tanz. 104/A3
Zixi, China 79/C2
Zixing, China 83/K2
Ziya (riv.), China 72/D3
Ziyyon, Isr. 91/G8
Ziz, Oued (riv.), Mor. 98/D2
Zlatna, Rom. 49/F2
Zlatograd, Bul. 47/J2
Zlatorsko (lake), Yugo. 47/F1
Zlatoust, Rus. 61/N5
Zlín, Czh. 41/J4
Zliv, Czh. 55/H4
Złocieniec, Pol. 41/J2
Zlot, Yugo. 48/E3
Złotoryja, Pol. 41/H3
Złotów, Pol. 41/J2
Žlutice, Czh. 55/G2
Żmigród, Pol. 41/J3
Znam'yanka, Ukr. 62/E2
Żnin, Pol. 41/J2
Znojmo, Czh. 41/J4
Zocca, It. 59/D4
Zoersel, Belg. 50/B6
Zoetermeer, Neth. 50/B4
Zoeterwoude, Neth. 50/B4
Zofingen, Swi. 56/D3
Zogang, China 83/G2
Zogno, It. 58/C1
Zográfos, Gre. 47/N9
Zohreh (riv.), Iran 88/F2
Zola, It. 59/E4
Zollikon, Swi. 57/E3
Zolotonosha, Ukr. 62/E2
Zomba, Malw. 105/G4
Zone (pt.), Eng, UK 32/A6
Zongolica, Mex. 143/N8
Zonguldak (prov.), Turk. 62/E4
Zonguldak, Turk. 49/K5
Zonhoven, Belg. 53/E2
Zonnebeke, Belg. 52/B2
Zonza, Fr. 46/A2
Zorge (riv.), Ger. 51/H5
Zorgo, Burk. 103/E3
Zorn (riv.), Fr. 40/D4
Zorneding, Ger. 55/E6
Zornheim, Ger. 54/B3
Zorritos, Peru 156/A1
Zossen, Ger. 40/Q7
Zottegem, Belg. 52/C2
Zou (prov.), Ben. 103/F5
Zou Xian, China 72/D4
Zouérat, Mrta. 98/B5
Zound-Wéogo (prov.), Burk. 103/E4
Zouping, China 72/D3
Zousfana, Oued (riv.), Alg. 99/E3
Zrenjanin, Yugo. 48/E3
Zschopau (riv.), Ger. 55/F1
Zuata, Ven. 153/E2
Zubia, Sp. 44/D4
Zubūbā, Isr. 91/G6
Zucchero (peak), Swi. 57/E5
Zuckerhütl (peak), Aus. 57/H4
Zuehl, Tx, US 137/U21
Zug, Swi. 57/E3
Zugdidi, Geo. 63/G4
Zugersee (lake), Swi. 43/H3
Zughrār (well), Libya 99/H3
Zugspitze (peak), Ger. 57/G3
Zuid Holland (prov.), Neth. 50/A5
Zuid-Willemsvaart (canal), Belg.,Neth 50/C6
Zuidbeveland (isl.), Neth. 50/A6
Zuidelijk Flevoland (polder), Neth. 50/C4
Zuidhorn, Neth. 50/D2
Zuidlaardermeer (lake), Neth. 50/D2
Zuidlaren, Neth. 50/D2
Zuidwolde, Neth. 50/D3
Zuienkerke, Belg. 52/C1
Zújar (riv.), Sp. 44/C3
Zújar, Sp. 44/D4
Zújar, Embalse (res.), Sp. 44/C3
Zulia (riv.), Ven. 150/D2
Zulia (state), Ven. 145/H4
Zülpich, Ger. 53/F2
Zulte, Belg. 52/C2
Zululand (reg.), SAfr. 107/E2
Zumárraga, Sp. 44/D1
Zumba, Ecu. 156/B2
Zumbo, Moz. 105/F4
Zumpango de Ocampo, Mex. 143/K7
Zumpango del Río, Mex. 143/F5
Zundert, Neth. 50/B6
Zunhua, China 72/H6
Zuni (riv.), Az,NM, US 128/E4
Zuni, NM, US 128/E4
Zuni (mts.), NM, US 132/A3
Zunyi, China 83/J2
Zuo (riv.), China 79/A3
Zuo Jiang (riv.), China 78/D1
Zuoquan, China 72/C3
Zuoyun, China 72/C3
Zuoz, Swi. 57/F4
Županja, Cro. 48/D3
Žur, Yugo. 47/G1
Zurbāṭīyah, Iraq 88/E2
Zürich (canton), Swi. 57/E2
Zürich (int'l arpt.), Swi. 57/E3
Zürich, Swi. 57/E3
Zurichsee (lake), Swi. 43/H3
Żurrieq, Malta 46/L7
Zurzach, Swi. 57/E2
Zusam (riv.), Ger. 43/J2
Zushi, Japan 77/D3
Zusmarshausen, Ger. 54/D6
Zutiua (riv.), Braz. 154/A2
Zutphen, Neth. 50/D4
Zuurberg NP, SAfr. 106/D4
Zuwārah, Libya 96/H1
Zuyevka, Rus. 61/L4
Zvijesda NP, Bosn. 48/D4
Zvishavane, Zim. 105/F5
Zvolen, Slvk. 62/A2
Zvorničko (lake), Bosn. 48/D3
Zvornik, Bosn. 48/D3
Zwarte Meer (lake), Neth. 50/C3
Zwartsluis, Neth. 50/D3
Zwedru, Libr. 102/C5
Zweibrücken, Ger. 53/G5
Zweisimmen, Swi. 56/D5
Zwesten, Ger. 51/G6
Zwevelgem, Belg. 52/C2
Zwickau, Ger. 43/K1
Zwickauer Mulde (riv.), Ger. 40/G3
Zwijndrecht, Belg. 53/D1
Zwischenahner Meer (lake), Ger. 51/F2
Zwischenwasser, Aus. 57/F3
Zwoleń, Pol. 41/L3
Żychlin, Pol. 41/K2
Żyrardów, Pol. 41/L2
Żywiec, Pol. 41/K4

Acknowledgements

COMPUTERIZED CARTOGRAPHIC ADVISORY BOARD

Mitchell J. Feigenbaum, Ph.D
Chief Technical Consultant
Toyota Professor, The Rockefeller University
Wolf Prize in Physics, 1986
Member, The National Academy of Sciences

Judson G. Rosebush, Ph.D
Computer Graphics Animation
Producer, Director and Author

Gary Martin Andrew, Ph.D
Consultant in Operations Research,
Planning and Management

Warren E. Schmidt, B.A.
Former U.S.Geological Survey,
Chief of the Branch of Geographic
and Cartographic Research,
U.S. Geological Survey

HAMMOND PUBLICATIONS ADVISORY BOARD

John P. Augelli
Professor and Chairman,
Department of Geography-Meteorology,
University of Kansas

Roger S. Boraas
Former Professor of Religion,
Upsala College

Alice C. Hudson
Chief, Map Division,
The New York Public Library

P. P. Karan
Professor, Department of Geography,
University of Kentucky

Vincent H. Malmstrom
Professor, Department of Geography,
Dartmouth College

Tom L. McKnight
Professor, Department of Geography,
University of California, Los Angeles

Christopher L. Salter
Professor and Chairman,
Department of Geography,
University of Missouri

Whitney Smith
Executive Director,
The Flag Research Center,
Winchester, Massachusetts

Norman J. W. Thrower
Professor, Department of Geography,
University of California, Los Angeles

SPECIAL ADVISORS

TECHNOLOGY
Michael E. Agishtein, Ph.D
Shou-Wen Chen
Nadejda Naiman

DATA RESEARCH
Population Research Center
University of Texas
Austin, Texas

Office of Population Research
Princeton University
Princeton, New Jersey

HAMMOND WORLD ATLAS CORPORATION

CORPORATE EXECUTIVES

Andreas Langenscheidt
Chairman

Stuart Dolgins
President

Vera Benson
Director of Cartography

HAMMOND STAFF

Sales Administration
Charles L. Koch

Database Resources and Cartography
Theophrastos E. Giouvanos

John A. DiGiorgio
Sudha Govindaraju
Walter H. Jones, Jr.
Sharon Lightner
Harry E. Morin
Andrew Murphy
James Padykula
Ben Pogue
Thomas J. Scheffer
Denise Stankowitz

Media & Production Services
Susan Miskewitz

Technology
Andrey Rogalsky

Victor Bashmakov
Barry A. Moraller

Cover Design
Yang Zhao

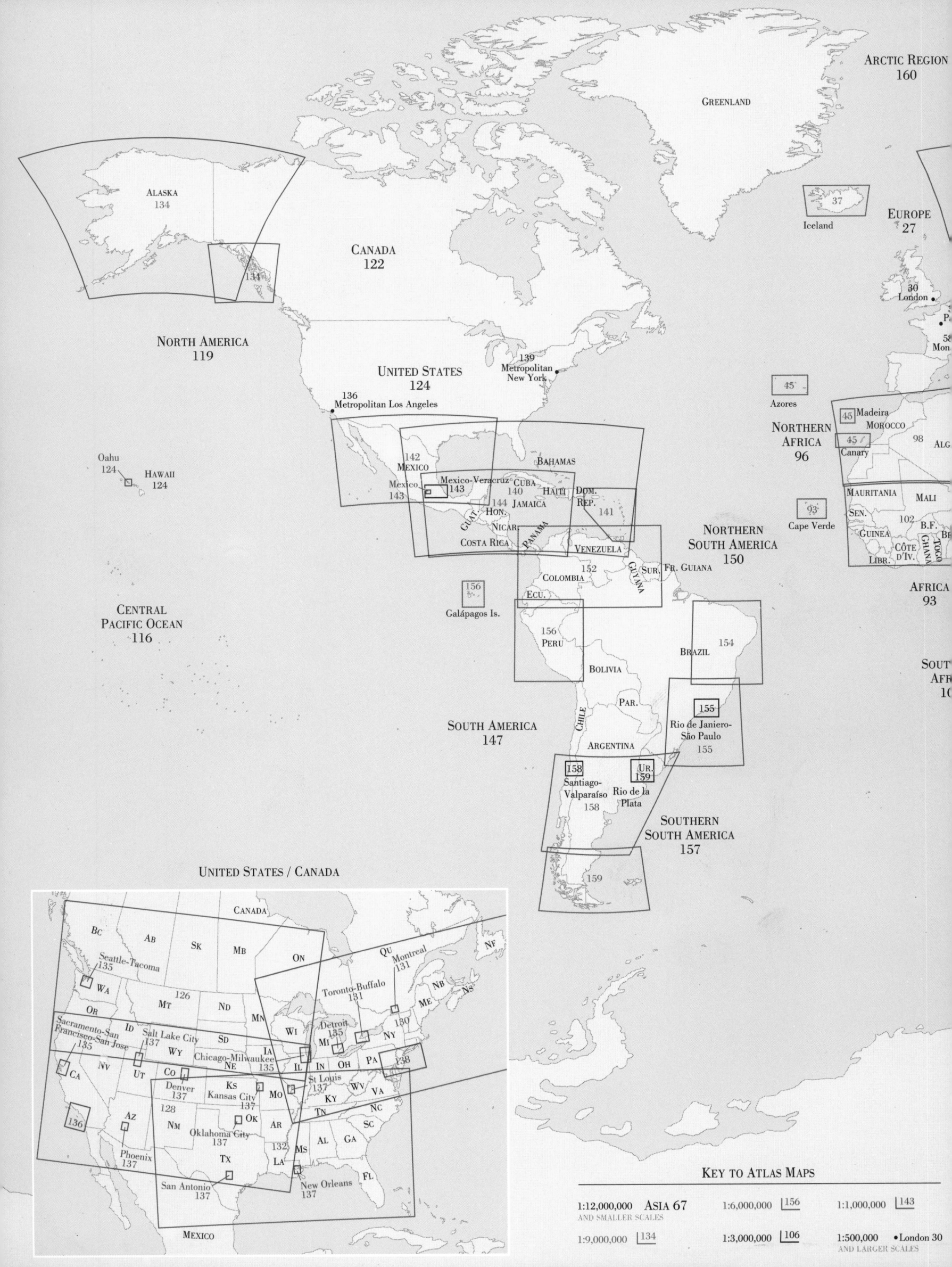